THE NEW INTERNATIONAL COMMENTARY
ON THE
NEW TESTAMENT

General Editors

NED B. STONEHOUSE
(1946–1962)

F. F. BRUCE
(1962–1990)

GORDON D. FEE
(1990–   )

The Gospel of
MATTHEW

R. T. FRANCE

WILLIAM B. EERDMANS PUBLISHING COMPANY
GRAND RAPIDS, MICHIGAN / CAMBRIDGE, U.K.

Published 2007 by

Wm. B. Eerdmans Publishing Co.

2140 Oak Industrial Drive N.E., Grand Rapids, Michigan 49505 /

P.O. Box 163, Cambridge CB3 9PU U.K.

Printed in the United States of America

12 11   7 6 5 4

Library of Congress Cataloging-in-Publication Data

France, R. T.

The Gospel of Matthew / R.T. France.

p.   cm.   — (The new international commentary on the New Testament)

Includes bibliographical references and index.

ISBN 978-0-8028-2501-8 (cloth: alk. paper)

1. Bible. N.T. Matthew — Commentaries.   I. Title.

BS2575.53.F77   2007

226.2′077 — dc22

2007013488

www.eerdmans.com

To Curly
my fellow student and inspiration
for more than forty years
gyda chariad

CONTENTS

CONTENTS

CONTENTS

INDEXES

EDITOR'S PREFACE

It is a special threefold pleasure to introduce R. T. (Dick) France's commentary on Matthew to the pastoral and scholarly community, who should find it a truly exceptional — and helpful — volume. As the first matter, and as promised in my preface to Phil Towner's commentary on Timothy and Titus a couple of years ago, this is the first of the final two volumes that will complete the original NICNT series (we await now only 2 Peter and Jude). But more importantly, second, this volume, by a scholar who has devoted much of his academic life to the Synoptic Gospels, and especially to the Gospel of Matthew, makes a very significant contribution to Matthean studies. Thus we have here the mature reflections on Matthew of one who made such study an important part of his academic life.

The third reason for delight is a personal one. Although Dr. France and I had known each other for a number of years, we were brought together in a special way in 1990 as members of the Committee on Bible Translation (CBT), the committee responsible for the New International Version (NIV) of the Scriptures. The committee was being convened to do a thorough review of the NIV, and some new faces were around the table, including mine and Dick's — he as a member of the British committee. So for sixteen years we have worked closely with the biblical text on a committee that has met annually and finally produced Today's New International Version (TNIV). So it was in a kind of moment of desperation, after having an NICNT Matthew commentary contract returned to me by a second (very capable) younger scholar, that I one day turned personally to Dick, who was about to enter retirement, and asked him if he would like to write this commentary. Much to my surprise, but great joy, he accepted. And now four years later the entire church and academy are the beneficiaries.

Dr. France hardly needs an introduction to those who are familiar with Matthean studies, which he has been able to pursue in a fruitful way over many years, even though he and Curly have had fully busy lives in ministry as well: as missionaries in Nigeria; as principal of Wycliffe Hall, Oxford; and as a parish pastor in a rural Anglican Church in England. They are now enjoying retirement in North Wales; and the church and the academy are the beneficiaries of that retirement.

Here is a commentary that was a sheer delight to read (my editorial input was especially minimal!). Dr. France never lets us lose sight of Matthew and what Matthew was about in presenting his story of Jesus, while at the same time, of course, one learns a great deal about Jesus himself. I am therefore pleased to commend this volume to the church and the academy for their learning and listening to what the Spirit would say to the churches of the twenty-first century.

GORDON D. FEE

AUTHOR'S PREFACE

This is designed to be an exegetical commentary. Its primary aim is to provide information and comment which will help the reader of the Gospel of Matthew to understand and appreciate that text. If in the process I can share something of my own deep appreciation of the insight and skill of its author, as well as of the importance and fascination of its subject matter, I shall be pleased.

It has been one of my major concerns to locate the individual parts of the gospel within the overall narrative flow of the whole — to look at the woods before focusing in on the trees. In the Introduction (pp. 2-5) I have set out my understanding of the structure of the gospel, which has determined the sections into which I have divided it for the purpose of commenting on it. Each section, large and small, is discussed as a whole before turning to the individual pericopae (a convenient scholarly term for "units" or paragraphs perceived in the text) into which I have subdivided it. It should be emphasized that these subdivisions, and indeed the overall structure I have discerned in the narrative, represent my own reading of the text, and do not claim to follow a pattern disclosed by the author. I am too well aware of the differences of opinion on even the most basic structural issues to assume that any such "author's design" is there to be read off from the surface of the text. Quite often I shall draw attention to competing views of the appropriate way of subdividing the text and explain my own decision. But it remains just that, *my* decision, representing only how one sympathetic reader has responded to the dynamics of the text.

Each of the pericopae into which I have divided the text is also discussed as a whole before any attempt is made to comment on the individual verses or groups of verses within it. This will often mean that the most fundamental issues for the meaning of the text will not emerge in my comments on a specific verse, as the long tradition of verse-by-verse commentary has conditioned many of us to expect. I have therefore dared to presume that the reader, even if seeking guidance on a particular phrase or sentence, will be prepared to read the comments on the pericope as a whole.

This last point applies also to the English translation of the text, which I have given at the beginning of each pericope. The translations are my own, and the footnotes to them often explain my renderings of specific words and phrases, which will then be presupposed in the commentary. The translations are designed to provide the basis for the commentary rather than for use on their own. They attempt to use contemporary idiom, and, where necessary, give priority to clarity over literary elegance. The notes to these translations also draw attention to some textual variations which are likely to be of exegetical interest; for this purpose I have generally been guided by the selection of variants made by the editors of *The Greek New Testament* (4th edn., Deutsche Bibelgesellschaft / United Bible Societies, 1998), though I have not always agreed with their textual judgment.

Some readers may be interested to know how I have set about writing a commentary on a gospel on which I already published a shorter commentary twenty years earlier (*The Gospel according to Matthew: An Introduction and Commentary.* Tyndale New Testament Commentaries. Leicester: Inter-Varsity Press, 1985). This is not a revision or expansion of that commentary, but a new work. I made it my practice to write the first draft of the present commentary on each pericope before looking at what I wrote twenty years ago (and indeed before looking at any other commentaries as well). I hope thus to ensure that priority is given to what I now understand to be the significant issues. The agenda is set by my interaction with the text rather than by my response to someone else's view of it, even my own twenty years ago. Often I found that I agreed substantially with what I wrote earlier, though now expressing myself in a different way in the light both of my own development and of my awareness of more recent discussion. But sometimes I discovered that I had changed my mind (indeed, sometimes I was quite surprised to see what I had said before!); where the change seems significant, I have drawn attention to it. As for other commentaries and exegetical discussions, I tried to take those available to me into account, largely in the footnotes, but my intention has always been to make this a commentary on Matthew, not a commentary on other commentaries. It makes no pretense to interact with all of the vast range of current scholarship on this fascinating gospel.

It is a particular regret that the long-awaited commentary on Matthew by my friend John Nolland (New International Greek Testament Commentary. Grand Rapids: Eerdmans, 2005) did not appear in time for me to take it into account: my commentary was finished late in 2005, just before John's was published.

R. T. FRANCE

ABBREVIATIONS

I. GENERAL PUBLICATIONS

AB	Anchor Bible
ABD	*Anchor Bible Dictionary*
AnBib	Analecta Biblica
ASTI	*Annual of the Swedish Theological Institute*
AUSS	*Andrews University Seminary Studies*
BBR	*Bulletin for Biblical Research*
BDAG	W. Bauer, *A Greek-English Lexicon of the New Testament and Other Early Christian Literature,* rev. and ed. F. W. Danker. Chicago: University of Chicago Press, 2000
BDF	F. Blass and A. Debrunner, *A Greek Grammar of the New Testament and Other Early Christian Literature,* rev. R. W. Funk. Chicago: University of Chicago Press, 1961
BETL	Bibliotheca Ephemeridum Theologicarum Lovaniensium
Bib	*Biblica*
BA	*Biblical Archaeologist*
BJRL	*Bulletin of the John Rylands Library*
BK	*Bibel und Kirche*
BT	*The Bible Translator*
BTB	*Biblical Theology Bulletin*
BZ	*Biblische Zeitschrift*
BZNW	Beihefte zur Zeitschrift für die neutestamentliche Wissenschaft
CBQ	*Catholic Biblical Quarterly*
CBQM	Catholic Biblical Quarterly Monographs
CNT	Commentaire du Nouveau Testament
EKKNT	Evangelisch-katholischer Kommentar zum Neuen Testament
EQ	*Evangelical Quarterly*

ET	English translation
E. V. Rieu	E. V. Rieu, *The Four Gospels: A New Translation from the Greek.* Harmondsworth: Penguin, 1952
EVV	English versions
ExpT	*Expository Times*
FRLANT	Forschungen zur Religion und Literatur des Alten und Neuen Testaments
FS	Festschrift for
GNB	Good News Bible
GP	R. T. France, D. Wenham, and C. L. Blomberg (eds.), *Gospel Perspectives,* vols. 1-6. Sheffield: JSOT, 1980-86
Hennecke	E. Hennecke, *New Testament Apocrypha,* ed. W. Schneemelcher. ET, 2 vols. London: SCM, 1963, 1965
HeyJ	*Heythrop Journal*
HTKNT	Herders theologischer Kommentar zum Neuen Testament
HTR	*Harvard Theological Review*
HUCA	*Hebrew Union College Annual*
ICC	International Critical Commentary
IEJ	*Israel Exploration Journal*
ISBE	*International Standard Bible Encyclopedia*
JB	Jerusalem Bible
JBL	*Journal of Biblical Literature*
JETS	*Journal of the Evangelical Theological Society*
JJS	*Journal of Jewish Studies*
JQR	*Jewish Quarterly Review*
JSNT	*Journal for the Study of the New Testament*
JSNTS	Journal for the Study of the New Testament Supplements
JSOTS	Journal for the Study of the Old Testament Supplements
JTS	*Journal of Theological Studies*
KJV	King James Version
LSJ	H. G. Liddell and R. Scott, *A Greek-English Lexicon,* rev. H. S. Jones. Oxford: Oxford University Press, 1996
LXX	Septuagint
MM	J. H. Moulton and G. Milligan, *The Vocabulary of the Greek Testament Illustrated from the Papyri and Other Non-Literary Sources.* London: Hodder & Stoughton, 1930
MS(S)	manuscript(s)
MT	Masoretic Text
NAC	New American Commentary
NCB	New Century Bible
NEB	New English Bible
Neot	*Neotestamentica*

NICNT	New International Commentary on the New Testament
NIDNTT	*New International Dictionary of New Testament Theology*
NIGTC	New International Greek Testament Commentary
NIV	New International Version
NJB	New Jerusalem Bible
NovT	*Novum Testamentum*
NRSV	New Revised Standard Version
NTD	Das Neue Testament Deutsch
NTS	*New Testament Studies*
OED	*Oxford English Dictionary*
OL	Old Latin
PNTC	Pillar New Testament Commentary
RB	*Revue Biblique*
REB	Revised English Bible
RevExp	*Review and Expositor*
RSV	Revised Standard Version
SBLDS	Society of Biblical Literature Dissertation Series
SBLM	Society of Biblical Literature Monographs
SBLSP	*Society of Biblical Literature Seminar Papers*
SBT	Studies in Biblical Theology
Schürer	E. Schürer, *The History of the Jewish People in the Age of Jesus Christ (175 B.C.–A.D. 135);* rev. Eng. edn. by G. Vermes, F. Millar, and M. Black. Edinburgh: T&T Clark, 1973-87
SE	*Studia Evangelica*
SJLA	Studies in Judaism in Late Antiquity
SJT	*Scottish Journal of Theology*
SNT	Supplements to Novum Testamentum
SNTSM	Society for New Testament Studies Monographs
ST	*Studia Theologica*
Str-B	H. L. Strack and P. Billerbeck, *Kommentar zum Neuen Testament aus Talmud und Midrasch.* Vols. 1-4, München: Beck, 1922-28; vols. 5-6 (by J. Jeremias and K. Adolph), München: Beck, 1956, 1961.
TDNT	*Theological Dictionary of the New Testament*
Thdt	Theodotion
THKNT	Theologischer Handkommentar zum Neuen Testament
TNIV	Today's New International Version
TNTC	Tyndale New Testament Commentary
TS	*Theological Studies*
TynBul	*Tyndale Bulletin*
TZ	*Theologische Zeitschrift*

WBC	Word Biblical Commentary
WTJ	*Westminster Theological Journal*
WUNT	Wissenschaftliche Untersuchungen zum Neuen Testament
ZAW	*Zeitschrift für die alttestamentliche Wissenschaft*
ZNW	*Zeitschrift für die neutestamentliche Wissenschaft*

II. OLD TESTAMENT APOCRYPHA

Tob	Tobit
Jdt	Judith
Wis	Wisdom of Solomon
Sir	Wisdom of Sirach (Ecclesiasticus)
Bar	Baruch
Sus	Susanna
1 Macc	1 Maccabees
2 Macc	2 Maccabees
1 Esdr	1 Esdras
3 Macc	3 Maccabees
4 Macc	4 Maccabees

III. OLD TESTAMENT PSEUDEPIGRAPHA

Apoc. Abr.	*Apocalypse of Abraham*
2 Bar.	*Syriac Apocalypse of Baruch*
3 Bar.	*Greek Apocalypse of Baruch*
1 En.	*Ethiopic Enoch*
2 En.	*Slavonic Enoch*
Jub.	*Letter of Jubilees*
Let. Aris.	*Letter of Aristeas*
Liv. Pro.	*Lives of the Prophets*
Odes Sol.	*Odes of Solomon*
Pss. Sol.	*Psalms of Solomon*
Sib. Or.	*Sibylline Oracles*
T. Benj.	*Testament of Benjamin*
T. Dan	*Testament of Dan*
T. Iss.	*Testament of Issachar*
T. Jos.	*Testament of Joseph*
T. Jud.	*Testament of Judah*

T. Levi	Testament of Levi
T. Naph.	Testament of Naphtali
T. Reu.	Testament of Reuben
T. Adam	Testament of Adam
T. Jac.	Testament of Jacob
T. Job	Testament of Job
T. Mos.	Testament of Moses
T. Sol.	Testament of Solomon

IV. QUMRAN LITERATURE

CD	Damascus Document
1QapGen	Genesis Apocryphon
1QH	Thanksgiving Hymns
1QIsaᵃ	First Isaiah Scroll from Cave 1
1QM	War Scroll
1QS	Rule of the Community
1QSa	Rule of the Congregation
1QSb	Rule of Benediction
1Q27	Mysteries
4Q174	Florilegium
4Q175	Testimonia
4Q246	Aramaic Apocalypse
4Q251	Messianic Apocalypse
4Q394-99 (MMT)	Halakhic Letter
4Q525	Beatitudes
11Q19 (Temple)	Temple Scroll

V. MISHNAIC AND RELATED LITERATURE

ʿArak.	ʿArakin
B. Bat.	Baba Batra
Bek.	Bekorot
Ber.	Berakot
B. Meṣ.	Baba Meṣiʿa
B. Qam.	Baba Qamma
Dem.	Demai
ʿEd.	ʿEduyyot

'Erub.	'Erubin
Giṭ.	Giṭṭin
Ḥag.	Ḥagigah
Ker.	Keritot
Ketub.	Ketubbot
Kil.	Kil'ayim
Ma'aś.	Ma'aśerot
Ma'aś. Š	Ma'aśer Šeni
Mak.	Makkot
Meg.	Megillah
Menaḥ.	Menaḥot
Mid.	Middot
Ned.	Nedarim
'Ohal.	'Ohalot
Pesaḥ.	Pesaḥim
Qidd.	Qiddušin
Sanh.	Sanhedrin
Šabb.	Šabbat
Šebu.	Šebu'ot
Šeqal.	Šeqalim
Suk.	Sukkah
Ta'an.	Ta'anit
Ṭehar.	Ṭeharot
Ter.	Terumot
'Uq.	'Uqṣin
Yad.	Yadayim
Yebam.	Yebamot
Zebaḥ.	Zebaḥim

The above titles of tractates are preceded by:

m.	Mishnah
t.	Tosefta
b.	Babylonian Talmud
j.	Jerusalem Talmud

VI. OTHER RABBINIC LITERATURE

Cant. Rab.	Canticles Rabbah
Der. Er. Rab.	Derek Ereṣ Rabbah
Eccl. Rab.	Ecclesiastes Rabbah

Exod. Rab.	*Exodus Rabbah*
Gen. Rab.	*Genesis Rabbah*
Mek.	*Mekilta*
Pesiq. Rab Kah.	*Pesiqta Rab Kahana*
Sifre Deut.	*Sifre Deuteronomy*
Sop.	*Soperim*

VII. TARGUMIC LITERATURE

Tg. Cant.	*Targum of Canticles*
Tg. Ps.-J.	*Targum Pseudo-Jonathan*

VIII. CLASSICAL AND HELLENISTIC LITERATURE

Dio Chrysostom
    Orat.   *Orationes*
Epictetus
    Diss.   *Dissertationes*
Herodotus
    Hist.   *History*
Isocrates
    Nic.   *Nicocles*
Josephus
    Ant.   *Antiquities of the Jews*
    C. Ap.   *Contra Apionem*
    Life   *Life of Flavius Josephus*
    War   *Jewish War*
Juvenal
    Sat.   *Satirae*
Lucian
    Philops.   *Philopseudes*
    Tox.   *Toxaris*
Philo
    Abr.   *De Abrahamo*
    Decal.   *De Decalogo*
    Flacc.   *In Flaccum*
    Legat.   *Legatio ad Gaium*
    Spec. leg.   *De specialibus legibus*

Philostratus
  Vit. Apoll.   *Vita Apollonii*
Plato
  Rep.   *De republica*
Pliny the Younger
  Ep.   *Epistulae*
Pliny the Elder
  Hist. nat.   *Historia naturalis*
Plutarch
  Apoph. Lac.   *Apophthegmata Laconica*
Seneca
  Ben.   *De beneficiis*
  Ep. mor.   *Epistulae morales*
Sophocles
  Oed Tyr.   *Oedipus Tyrannus*
Tacitus
  Ann.   *Annales*
  Hist.   *Historia*
Virgil
  Aen.   *Aeneid*

IX. EARLY CHRISTIAN LITERATURE

Barn.   *Barnabas*
Did.   *Didache*
Epiphanius
  Pan.   *Panarion*
Eusebius
  Hist. eccl.   *Historia ecclesiastica*
  Vit. Const.   *Vita Constantini*
Gos. Pet.   *Gospel of Peter*
Gos. Thom.   *Gospel of Thomas*
Hermas
  Mand.   *Mandates*
  Sim.   *Similitudes*
  Vis.   *Visions*
Ignatius
  Eph.   *Letter to the Ephesians*
Inf. Gos. Thom.   *Infancy Gospel of Thomas*

Irenaeus
  Haer.   *Adversus haereses*
Jerome
  Comm. Matt.   *In Mattheum Commentarium*
  Pelag.   *Adversus Pelagianos dialogi III*
Justin
  1 Apol.   *First Apology*
  Dial.   *Dialogue with Trypho*
Origen
  Cels.   *Contra Celsum*
Prot. Jas.   *Protevangelium of James*
Sextus
  Sent.   *Sententiae*
Tertullian
  Marc.   *Adversus Marcionem*

BIBLIOGRAPHY
of Works Cited in This Volume

COMMENTARIES ON MATTHEW

I will refer to these commentaries by author name only. Because of the large number of references to some of them, I will not list references to these commentaries in the Index of Modern Authors.

W. F. Albright and C. S. Mann, *Matthew: Introduction, Translation and Notes* (AB 26). New York: Doubleday. 1971.

W. C. Allen, *A Critical and Exegetical Commentary on the Gospel according to S. Matthew* (ICC). Edinburgh: T&T Clark, 3rd edn. 1912.

F. W. Beare, *The Gospel according to Matthew: A Commentary.* Oxford: Blackwell, 1981.

C. L. Blomberg, *Matthew* (NAC 22). Nashville: Broadman, 1992.

P. Bonnard. *L'Évangile selon Saint Matthieu* (CNT 1). Neuchâtel: Delachaux & Niestlé, 2nd edn. 1970.

D. A. Carson, "Matthew," in F. E. Gaebelein (ed.), *The Expositor's Bible Commentary,* vol. 8 (Matthew, Mark, Luke). Grand Rapids: Zondervan, 1984.

W. Carter, *Matthew and the Margins: A Socio-political and Religious Reading* (JSNTS 204). Sheffield: Sheffield Academic Press, 2000.

W. D. Davies and D. C. Allison, *A Critical and Exegetical Commentary on the Gospel according to Saint Matthew* (ICC). 3 vols. Edinburgh: T&T Clark, 1988, 1991, 1997.

R. T. France, *The Gospel according to Matthew: An Introduction and Commentary* (TNTC 1). Leicester: Inter-Varsity Press, 1985.

D. E. Garland, *Reading Matthew: A Literary and Theological Commentary on the First Gospel.* New York: Crossroad, 1993.

W. Grundmann, *Das Evangelium nach Matthäus* (THKNT). Berlin: Evangelische Verlagsanstalt, 1968.

R. H. Gundry, *Matthew: A Commentary on His Literary and Theological Art.*

Grand Rapids: Eerdmans, 1982 (2nd edn. entitled *Matthew: A Commentary on His Handbook for a Mixed Church under Persecution.* Grand Rapids: Eerdmans, 1994 [pagination unchanged, but additional preface and end notes].)

D. A. Hagner, *Matthew* (WBC 33A and 33B). 2 vols. Dallas: Word, 1993.

D. Hill, *The Gospel of Matthew* (NCB). London: Marshall, Morgan & Scott, 1972.

C. S. Keener. *A Commentary on the Gospel of Matthew.* Grand Rapids: Eerdmans, 1999.

U. Luz, *Das Evangelium nach Matthäus* (EKKNT 1). 4 vols. Zürich: Benzinger, 1985ff. English versions (to which reference is made here) are as follows: *Matthew 1–7: A Commentary.* Minneapolis: Augsburg/Fortress, 1989; *Matthew 8–20: A Commentary* (Hermeneia). Minneapolis: Fortress, 2001.

A. H. McNeile, *The Gospel according to Matthew: The Greek Text with Introduction, Notes, and Indices.* London: Macmillan, 1915.

L. Morris, *The Gospel according to Matthew* (PNTC). Grand Rapids: Eerdmans and Leicester: Inter-Varsity Press, 1992.

E. Schweizer, *The Good News according to Matthew.* ET, London: SPCK, 1976 (German original: *Das Evangelium nach Matthäus* [NTD 2]. Göttingen: Vandenhoeck & Ruprecht, 1973).

R. V. G. Tasker, *The Gospel according to St Matthew: An Introduction and Commentary* (TNTC). London: Tyndale, 1961.

M. J. Wilkins, *Matthew* (NIV Application Commentary). Grand Rapids: Zondervan, 2004.

BOOKS

K. and B. Aland, *The Text of the New Testament: An Introduction to the Critical Editions and to the Theory and Practice of Modern Textual Criticism.* ET, Grand Rapids: Eerdmans, 1987.

L. C. Allen, *Psalms 101–150* (WBC). Waco, TX: Word, 1983.

D. C. Allison, *The End of the Ages Has Come: An Early Interpretation of the Passion and Resurrection of Jesus.* Edinburgh: T&T Clark, 1987.

————, *The New Moses: A Matthean Typology.* Edinburgh: T&T Clark, 1993.

A. M. Ambrozic, *The Hidden Kingdom: A Redaction-Critical Study of the References to the Kingdom of God in Mark's Gospel.* Washington: Catholic Biblical Association, 1972.

D. E. Aune, *Prophecy in Early Christianity and the Ancient Mediterranean World.* Grand Rapids: Eerdmans, 1983.

R. D. Aus, *Water into Wine and the Beheading of John the Baptist: Early Jewish-Christian Interpretation of Esther 1 in John 2:1-11 and Mark 6:17-29.* Atlanta: Scholars Press, 1988.

M. Avi-Yonah (ed.), *Encyclopedia of Archeological Excavations in the Holy Land.* Oxford: Oxford University Press, 1976.

B. W. Bacon, *Studies in Matthew.* London: Constable, 1930.

K. E. Bailey, *Poet and Peasant.* Grand Rapids: Eerdmans, 1976.

————, *Through Peasant Eyes.* Grand Rapids: Eerdmans, 1980.

E. Bammel (ed.), *The Trial of Jesus: Cambridge Studies in Honour of C. F. D. Moule* (SBT 13). London: SCM, 1970.

———— and C. F. D. Moule (ed.), *Jesus and the Politics of His Day.* Cambridge: Cambridge University Press, 1984.

R. J. Banks, *Jesus and the Law in the Synoptic Tradition* (SNTSM 28). Cambridge: Cambridge University Press, 1975.

G. Barth. See G. Bornkamm.

M. Barth, *Ephesians 1–3* (AB 34). New York: Doubleday, 1974.

S. C. Barton, *Discipleship and Family Ties in Mark and Matthew* (SNTSM 80). Cambridge: Cambridge University Press, 1994.

R. J. Bauckham, *Jude and the Relatives of Jesus in the Early Church.* Edinburgh: T&T Clark, 1990.

D. R. Bauer, *The Structure of Matthew's Gospel: A Study in Literary Design* (JSNTS 31). Sheffield: Almond, 1988.

———— and M. A. Powell (ed.), *Treasures New and Old: Recent Contributions to Matthean Studies.* Atlanta: Scholars Press, 1996.

G. R. Beasley-Murray, *Jesus and the Kingdom of God.* Grand Rapids: Eerdmans, 1986.

————, *Jesus and the Last Days.* Peabody, MA: Hendrickson, 1993 (a revised and updated conflation of his earlier works *Jesus and the Future* [London: Macmillan, 1954] and *A Commentary on Mark* 13 [London: Macmillan, 1962]).

R. Beaton, *Isaiah's Christ in Matthew's Gospel* (SNTSM 123). Cambridge: Cambridge University Press, 2002.

M. A. Beavis, *Mark's Audience: The Literary and Social Setting of Mark 4.11-12* (JSNTS 33). Sheffield: Sheffield Academic Press, 1989.

F. Bclo, *A Materialist Reading of the Gospel of Mark.* ET, Maryknoll, NY: Orbis, 1981.

K. Berger, *Die Amen-Worte Jesu* (BZNW 39). Berlin: de Gruyter, 1970.

J. H. Bernard, *The Gospel according to St John* (ICC). 2 vols., Edinburgh: T&T Clark, 1928.

H. D. Betz, *Essays on the Sermon on the Mount.* Philadelphia: Fortress, 1985.

————, *The Sermon on the Mount: A Commentary on the Sermon on the Mount, including the Sermon on the Plain (Matthew 5:3–7:27 and Luke 6:20-49)* (Hermeneia). Minneapolis: Augsburg/Fortress, 1995.

J. Blinzler, *The Trial of Jesus: The Jewish and Roman Proceedings against Jesus Christ Described and Assessed from the Oldest Accounts.* ET, Cork: Mercier, 1959.

C. L. Blomberg, *Contagious Holiness: Jesus' Meals with Sinners.* Downers Grove: InterVarsity Press, 2005.

——, *Interpreting the Parables.* Downers Grove: InterVarsity Press, 1990.

D. L. Bock, *Blasphemy and Exaltation in Judaism and the Final Examination of Jesus: A Philological-Historical Study of the Key Jewish Themes Impacting Mark 14:61-64* (WUNT 106). Tübingen: Mohr Siebeck, 1998.

E. L. Bode, *The First Easter Morning: The Gospel Accounts of the Women's Visit to the Tomb of Jesus* (AnBib 45). Rome: Biblical Institute Press, 1970.

P. G. Bolt, *Jesus' Defeat of Death: Persuading Mark's Early Readers* (SNTSM 125). Cambridge: Cambridge University Press, 2003.

H. K. Bond, *Pontius Pilate in History and Interpretation* (SNTSM 100). Cambridge: Cambridge University Press, 1998.

R. P. Booth, *Jesus and the Laws of Purity: Tradition History and Legal History in Mark 7* (JSNTS 13). Sheffield: JSOT, 1986.

G. Bornkamm, G. Barth and H. J. Held, *Tradition and Interpretation in Matthew.* ET, London: SCM, 1963.

J. W. Bowker, *The Targums and Rabbinic Literature.* Cambridge: Cambridge University Press, 1969.

S. G. F. Brandon, *Jesus and the Zealots.* Manchester: Manchester University Press, 1967.

S. H. Brooks, *Matthew's Community: The Evidence of His Special Sayings Material* (JSNTS 16). Sheffield: Sheffield Academic Press, 1987.

R. Brow, *"Go Make Learners": A New Model for Discipleship in the Church.* Wheaton: Harold Shaw, 1981.

R. E. Brown, *The Birth of the Messiah: A Commentary on the Infancy Narratives in Matthew and Luke.* Rev. edn., New York: Doubleday, 1993.

——, *The Death of the Messiah: From Gethsemane to the Grave. A Commentary on the Passion Narratives in the Four Gospels.* New York: Doubleday, 1994.

——, *New Testament Essays.* London: Geoffrey Chapman, 1965.

——, *The Virginal Conception and Bodily Resurrection of Jesus.* New York: Paulist, 1973.

F. F. Bruce, *Jesus and Christian Origins outside the New Testament.* London: Hodder & Stoughton, 1974.

——, *New Testament History.* 3rd edn., London: Oliphants, 1980.

——, *This Is That: The New Testament Development of Some Old Testament Themes.* Exeter: Paternoster, 1968.

C. Bryan, *A Preface to Mark: Notes on the Gospel in Its Literary and Cultural Settings*. Oxford: Oxford University Press, 1993.

R. Bultmann, *The History of the Synoptic Tradition*. ET, Oxford: Blackwell, 1963.

S. Byrskog, *Jesus the Only Teacher: Didactic Authority and Transmission in Ancient Israel, Ancient Judaism and the Matthean Community*. Stockholm: Almqvist & Wiksell, 1994.

G. B. Caird, *The Language and Imagery of the Bible*. London: Duckworth, 1980.

P. S. Cameron, *Violence and the Kingdom: The Interpretation of Matthew 11:12*. Frankfurt: P. Lang, 1984.

G. S. Cansdale, *Animals of Bible Lands*. Exeter: Paternoster, 1970.

C. C. Caragounis, *Peter and the Rock* (BZNW 58). Berlin: de Gruyter, 1990.

W. Carter, *Households and Discipleship: A Study of Matthew 19–20* (JSNTS 103). Sheffield: JSOT, 1994.

M. Casey, *Aramaic Sources of Mark's Gospel* (SNTSM 102). Cambridge: Cambridge University Press, 1998.

———, *Son of Man: The Interpretation and Influence of Daniel 7*. London: SPCK, 1979.

D. R. Catchpole, *The Trial of Jesus: A Study in the Gospels and Jewish Historiography from 1770 to the Present Day* (Studia Post-Biblica 22). Leiden: Brill, 1971.

H. C. C. Cavallin, *Life after Death, Part 1: An Enquiry into the Jewish Background*. Lund: Gleerup, 1974.

B. Charette, *The Theme of Recompense in Matthew's Gospel* (JSNTS 79). Sheffield: Sheffield Academic Press, 1992.

B. D. Chilton, *A Galilean Rabbi and His Bible: Jesus' Own Interpretation of Isaiah*. London: SPCK, 1984.

———, *God in Strength: Jesus' Announcement of the Kingdom*. Sheffield: JSOT, 1987.

W. K. L. Clarke, *Divine Humanity*. London: SPCK, 1936.

O. L. Cope, *Matthew, A Scribe Trained for the Kingdom of Heaven* (CBQM 5). Washington: Catholic Biblical Association, 1976.

W. L. Craig, *Assessing the New Testament Evidence for the Historicity of the Resurrection of Jesus*. Lewiston: Edwin Mellen, 1989.

C. E. B. Cranfield, *The Gospel according to Saint Mark: An Introduction and Commentary*. Cambridge: Cambridge University Press, 1959.

G. Dalman, *Arbeite und Sitte in Palästina VI*. Gütersloh: Bertelsmann, 1939.

D. Daube, *The New Testament and Rabbinic Judaism*. London: Athlone, 1956.

W. D. Davies, *Christian Origins and Judaism*. London: Darton, Longman & Todd, 1962.

———, *The Gospel and the Land*. Berkeley: University of California Press, 1974.

————, *The Setting of the Sermon on the Mount.* Cambridge: Cambridge University Press, 1963.

J. D. M. Derrett, *Jesus' Audience.* London: Darton, Longman & Todd, 1973.

————, *Law in the New Testament.* London: Darton, Longman & Todd, 1970.

C. M. Deutsch, *Hidden Wisdom and the Easy Yoke: Wisdom, Torah and Discipleship in Matthew 11:25-30* (JSNTS 18). Sheffield: Sheffield Academic Press, 1987.

————, *Lady Wisdom, Jesus and the Sages: Metaphor and Social Context in Matthew's Gospel.* Valley Forge, PA: Trinity Press International, 1996.

M. Didier (ed.), *L'Évangile selon Matthieu: Rédaction et théologie* (BETL 29). Gembloux: Duculot, 1972.

A. Dihle, *Die goldene Regel.* Göttingen: Vandenhoeck & Ruprecht, 1962.

C. H. Dodd, *The Founder of Christianity.* New York: Macmillan, 1970.

————, *Historical Tradition in the Fourth Gospel.* Cambridge: Cambridge University Press, 1963.

T. L. Donaldson, *Jesus on the Mountain: A Study in Matthean Theology* (JSNTS 8). Sheffield: JSOT, 1985.

S. E. Dowd, *Prayer, Power and the Problem of Suffering: Mark 11:22-25 in the Context of Markan Theology* (SBLDS 105). Atlanta: Scholars Press, 1988.

J. D. G. Dunn, *Christology in the Making: A New Testament Inquiry into the Origins of the Doctrine of the Incarnation.* London: SCM, 1980.

————, *Jesus and the Spirit: A Study of the Religious and Charismatic Experience of Jesus and the First Christians as Reflected in the New Testament.* London: SCM, 1975.

————, *Jesus, Paul and the Law: Studies in Mark and Galatians.* London: SPCK, 1990.

J. K. Elliott, *The Apocryphal New Testament: A Collection of Apocryphal Christian Literature in an English Translation.* Oxford: Clarendon, 1993.

C. A. Evans, *Ancient Texts for New Testament Studies: A Guide to the Background Literature.* Peabody, MA: Hendrickson, 2005.

————, *Jesus and His Contemporaries: Comparative Studies.* Koln: Brill, 1995.

————, *To See and Not Perceive: Isaiah 6:9-10 in Early Jewish and Christian Interpretation* (JSOTS 64). Sheffield: Sheffield Academic Press, 1989.

K. Ferrari d'Occhieppo, *Der Stern der Weisen: Geschichte oder Legende?* 2nd edn., Wien / München: Herold, 1977.

J. Finegan, *The Archeology of the New Testament.* Princeton: Princeton University Press, 1969.

————, *Handbook of Biblical Chronology.* Princeton: Princeton University Press, 1964.

J. A. Fitzmyer, *To Advance the Gospel.* New York: Crossroad, 1981.

P. Foster, *Community, Law and Mission in Matthew's Gospel* (WUNT 177). Tübingen: Mohr Siebeck, 2004.

R. T. France, *Divine Government: The Kingship of God in the Gospel of Mark.* London: SPCK, 1990.

—————, *The Evidence for Jesus.* London: Hodder & Stoughton, 1986.

—————, *The Gospel of Mark: A Commentary on the Greek Text* (NIGTC). Grand Rapids: Eerdmans, 2002.

—————, *Jesus and the Old Testament: His Application of Old Testament Passages to Himself and His Mission.* London: Tyndale, 1971; repr. Carlisle, U.K.: Paternoster, 2007.

—————, *Matthew: Evangelist and Teacher.* Exeter: Paternoster, 1989.

H. Frankemölle, *Jahwe-Bund und Kirche Christi: Studien zur Form- und Traditionsgeschichte des 'Evangeliums' nach Matthäus.* 2nd edn., Münster: Aschendorff, 1974.

S. Freyne, *Galilee from Alexander the Great to Hadrian, 323 B.C.E. to 135 C.E.: A Study of Second Temple Judaism.* Wilmington: Glazier, 1980.

—————, *Galilee, Jesus and the Gospels: Literary Approaches and Historical Investigations.* Dublin: Gill & Macmillan, 1988.

D. E. Garland, *The Intention of Matthew 23* (SNT 52). Leiden: Brill, 1979.

A. J. P. Garrow, *The Gospel of Matthew's Dependence on the Didache* (JSNTS 254). London: T&T Clark International, 2004.

—————, *Revelation* (New Testament Readings). London: Routledge, 1997.

L. Gaston, *No Stone on Another: Studies in the Significance of the Fall of Jerusalem in the Synoptic Gospels* (SNT 23). Leiden: Brill, 1970.

T. J. Geddert, *Watchwords: Mark 13 in Markan Eschatology* (JSNTS 26). Sheffield: Sheffield Academic Press, 1989.

B. Gerhardsson, *The Mighty Acts of Jesus according to Matthew.* Lund: Gleerup, 1979.

—————, *The Testing of God's Son (Matt 4:1-11 and par.).* Lund: Gleerup, 1966.

J. A. Gibbs, *Jerusalem and Parousia: Jesus' Eschatological Discourse in Matthew's Gospel.* St. Louis: Concordia Academic Press, 2000.

M. D. Goulder, *Midrash and Lection in Matthew.* London: SPCK, 1974.

S. W. Gray, *The Least of My Brothers: Matthew 25.31-46: A History of Interpretation* (SBLDS 114). Atlanta: Scholars Press, 1989.

R. A. Guelich, *The Sermon on the Mount: A Foundation for Understanding.* Waco, TX: Word, 1982.

R. H. Gundry, *Mark: A Commentary on His Apology for the Cross.* Grand Rapids: Eerdmans, 1993.

—————, *Sōma in Biblical Theology: With Emphasis on Pauline Anthropology* (SNTSM 29). Cambridge: Cambridge University Press, 1976.

—————, *The Use of the Old Testament in St. Matthew's Gospel with Special Reference to the Messianic Hope* (SNT 18). Leiden: Brill, 1967.

D. R. A. Hare, *The Theme of Jewish Persecution of Christians in the Gospel according to St. Matthew* (SNTSM 6). Cambridge: Cambridge University Press, 1967.

A. E. Harvey, *Jesus and the Constraints of History.* London: Duckworth, 1982.

————, *Strenuous Commands: The Ethic of Jesus.* London: SCM, 1990.

V. Hasler, *Amen: Redaktionsgeschichtliche Untersuchung zur Einführungsformel der Herrenworte "Wahrlich ich sage euch."* Zürich: Theologischer Verlag, 1969.

D. M. Hay, *Glory at the Right Hand: Psalm 110 in Early Christianity* (SBLM 18). Nashville: Abingdon, 1973.

J. P. Heil, *Jesus Walking on the Sea* (AnBib 87). Rome: Biblical Institute Press, 1981.

H. J. Held. *See* G. Bornkamm.

B. W. Henaut, *Oral Tradition and the Gospels: The Problem of Mark 4* (JSNTS 82). Sheffield: Sheffield Academic Press, 1993.

M. Hengel, *The Charismatic Leader and His Followers.* ET, Edinburgh: T&T Clark, 1981.

————, *Crucifixion in the Ancient World and the Folly of the Message of the Cross.* ET, London: SCM, 1977.

————, *Property and Riches in the Early Church: Aspects of a Social History of Early Christianity.* ET, London: SCM, 1974.

————, *The Son of God: The Origin of Christology and the History of Jewish-Hellenistic Religion.* ET, London: SCM, 1976.

————, *Studies in the Gospel of Mark.* ET, London: SCM, 1985.

W. A. Heth and G. J. Wenham, *Jesus and Divorce: The Problem with the Evangelical Consensus.* Nashville: Nelson, 1984.

D. Hill, *Greek Words and Hebrew Meanings: Studies in the Semantics of Soteriological Terms* (SNTSM 5). Cambridge: Cambridge University Press, 1967.

H. W. Hoehner, *Herod Antipas* (SNTSM 17). Cambridge: Cambridge University Press, 1972.

J. W. Holleran, *The Synoptic Gethsemane: A Critical Study.* Rome: Universita Gregoriana Editrice, 1973.

R. A. Horsley, *Archaeology, History and Society in Galilee: The Social Context of Jesus and the Rabbis.* Valley Forge, PA: Trinity Press International, 1996.

————, *Galilee: History, Politics, People.* Valley Forge, PA: Trinity Press International, 1995.

————, *The Liberation of Christmas: The Infancy Narratives in Social Context.* New York: Continuum, 1993.

M. Hubaut, *La parabole des vignerons homicides.* Paris: Gabalda, 1976.

B. J. Hubbard, *The Matthean Redaction of a Primitive Apostolic Commis-*

sioning: An Exegesis of Matthew 28:16-20 (SBLDS 19). Missoula: Scholars Press, 1974.

J. M. Hull, *Hellenistic Magic and the Synoptic Tradition* (SBT 28). London: SCM, 1974.

————, *In the Beginning There Was Darkness: A Blind Person's Conversations with the Bible.* London: SCM, 2001.

D. Instone-Brewer, *Divorce and Remarriage in the Bible: The Social and Literary Context.* Grand Rapids: Eerdmans, 2002.

————, *Traditions of the Rabbis from the Era of the New Testament,* vol. 1: *Prayer and Agriculture.* Grand Rapids: Eerdmans, 2004.

J. Jeremias, *The Eucharistic Words of Jesus.* ET, London: SCM, 1966.

————, *Heiligengräber in Jesu Umwelt.* Göttingen: Vandenhoeck & Ruprecht, 1958.

————, *Infant Baptism in the First Four Centuries.* ET, London: SCM, 1960.

————, *Jerusalem in the Time of Jesus: An Investigation into Economic and Social Conditions during the New Testament Period.* ET, London: SCM, 1969.

————, *Jesus' Promise to the Nations.* ET, London: SCM, 1958.

————, *New Testament Theology,* vol. 1: *The Proclamation of Jesus.* ET, London: SCM, 1971.

————, *The Parables of Jesus.* ET, rev. edn., London: SCM, 1963.

————, *The Prayers of Jesus* (SBT 6). ET, London: SCM, 1967.

M. D. Johnson, *The Purpose of the Biblical Genealogies with Special Reference to the Setting of the Genealogies of Jesus* (SNTSM 8). Cambridge: Cambridge University Press, 1969.

I. H. Jones, *The Matthean Parables: A Literary and Historical Commentary* (SNT 80). Leiden: Brill, 1995.

D. Juel, *Messiah and Temple: The Trial of Jesus in the Gospel of Mark* (SBLDS 31). Missoula: Scholars Press, 1977.

————, *Messianic Exegesis: Christological Interpretation of the Old Testament in Early Christianity.* Philadelphia: Fortress, 1988.

H. C. Kee, *Medicine, Miracle and Magic in New Testament Times* (SNTSM 55). Cambridge: Cambridge University Press, 1986.

F. Kermode, *The Genesis of Secrecy: On the Interpretation of Narrative.* Cambridge, MA: Harvard University Press, 1979.

G. D. Kilpatrick, *The Origins of the Gospel according to Saint Matthew.* Oxford: Clarendon, 1946.

J. D. Kingsbury, *Matthew: Structure, Christology, Kingdom.* London: SPCK, 1975.

B. Kinman, *Jesus' Entry to Jerusalem.* Leiden: Brill, 1995.

E. F. Kirschner, "The Place of the Exorcism Motif in Mark's Christology with special reference to Mark 3.22-30." Unpublished Ph.D. diss., London: CNAA, 1988.

W. S. Kissinger, *The Sermon on the Mount: A History of Interpretation and Bibliography.* Metuchen: Scarecrow and ATLA, 1975.

W. Klassen, *Judas: Betrayer or Friend of Jesus?* London: SCM, 1996.

M. Knowles, *Jeremiah in Matthew's Gospel: The Rejected-Prophet Motif in Matthean Redaction* (JSNTS 68). Sheffield: Sheffield Academic Press, 1993.

R. Kraft, *Septuagintal Lexicography.* Missoula: Society of Biblical Literature, 1972.

D. D. Kupp, *Matthew's Emmanuel: Divine Presence and God's People in the First Gospel* (SNTSM 90). Cambridge: Cambridge University Press, 1996.

S. T. Lachs, *A Rabbinic Commentary on the New Testament: The Gospels of Matthew, Mark, and Luke.* Hoboken: KTAV, 1987.

W. L. Lane, *The Gospel of Mark* (NICNT). Grand Rapids: Eerdmans, 1974.

L. I. Levine, *The Ancient Synagogue.* New Haven: Yale University Press, 2000.

R. H. Lightfoot, *Locality and Doctrine in the Gospels.* London: Hodder & Stoughton, 1938.

B. Lindars, *New Testament Apologetic: The Doctrinal Significance of the Old Testament Quotations.* London: SCM, 1961.

E. Lohmeyer, *Galiläa und Jerusalem.* Göttingen: Vandenhoeck & Ruprecht, 1936.

R. N. Longenecker (ed.), *The Challenge of Jesus' Parables.* Grand Rapids: Eerdmans, 2000.

P. Luomanen, *Entering the Kingdom of Heaven: A Study on the Structure of Matthew's View of Salvation* (WUNT 101). Tübingen: Mohr Siebeck, 1998.

J. Lust, E. Eynikel, and K. Hauspie, *Greek-English Lexicon of the Septuagint.* Rev. edn., Stuttgart: Deutsche Bibelgesellschaft, 2003.

U. Luz, *The Theology of the Gospel of Matthew.* Cambridge: Cambridge University Press, 1995.

H. K. McArthur, *Understanding the Sermon on the Mount.* London: Epworth, 1961.

S. McKnight, *A Light among the Gentiles: Jewish Missionary Activity in the Second Temple Period.* Minneapolis: Fortress, 1991.

J. Marcus, *The Way of the Lord: Christological Exegesis of the Old Testament in the Gospel of Mark.* Edinburgh: T&T Clark, 1992.

I. H. Marshall, *The Gospel of Luke: A Commentary on the Greek Text* (NIGTC). Exeter: Paternoster, 1978.

———, *Last Supper and Lord's Supper.* Exeter: Paternoster, 1980.

E. L. Martin, *Secrets of Golgotha.* Alhambra, CA: ASK, 1988.

U. Mauser, *Christ in the Wilderness* (SBT 39). London: SCM, 1963.

J. P. Meier, *Law and History in Matthew's Gospel: A Redactional Study of Mt 5:17-48* (AnBib 71). Rome: Biblical Institute Press, 1976.

———, *A Marginal Jew: Rethinking the Historical Jesus.* 3 vols., New York: Doubleday, 1991-2001.

M. J. J. Menken, *Matthew's Bible: The Old Testament Text of the Evangelist* (BETL 173). Leuven: Leuven University Press, 2004.

R. E. Menninger, *Israel and the Church in the Gospel of Matthew.* New York: Peter Lang, 1994.

B. M. Metzger, *A Textual Commentary on the Greek New Testament.* London / New York: United Bible Societies, 1971.

B. F. Meyer, *The Aims of Jesus.* London: SCM, 1979.

E. M. Meyers and J. F. Strange, *Archaeology, the Rabbis and Early Christianity.* London: SCM Press, 1981.

R. Mohrlang, *Matthew and Paul: A Comparison of Ethical Perspectives* (SNTSM 48). Cambridge: Cambridge University Press, 1984.

D. J. Moo, *The Old Testament in the Gospel Passion Narratives.* Sheffield: Almond, 1983.

G. F. Moore, *Judaism.* Cambridge, MA: Harvard University Press, 1927.

L. Morris, *Studies in the Fourth Gospel.* Grand Rapids: Eerdmans and Exeter: Paternoster, 1969.

C. F. D. Moule, *Essays in New Testament Interpretation.* Cambridge: Cambridge University Press, 1982.

———, *The Origin of Christology.* Cambridge: Cambridge University Press, 1977.

K. G. C. Newport, *The Sources and* Sitz im Leben *of Matthew 23* (JSNTS 117). Sheffield: Sheffield Academic Press, 1995.

J. H. Neyrey, *Honor and Shame in the Gospel of Matthew.* Louisville: Westminster John Knox, 1998.

G. W. E. Nickelsburg, *Resurrection, Immortality and Eternal Life in Intertestamental Judaism.* Cambridge MA: Harvard University Press, 1972.

J. Nolland, *Luke 1–9:20* (WBC 35A). Dallas: Word, 1989.

L. Novakovic, *Messiah, the Healer of the Sick* (WUNT 170). Tübingen: Mohr Siebeck, 2003.

G. Ogg, *The Chronology of the Public Ministry of Jesus.* Cambridge: Cambridge University Press, 1940.

D. E. Orton, *The Understanding Scribe: Matthew and the Apocalyptic Ideal* (JSNTS 25). Sheffield: Sheffield Academic Press, 1989.

J. A. Overman, *Matthew's Gospel and Formative Judaism: The Social World of the Matthean Community.* Minneapolis: Fortress, 1990.

E. C. Park, *The Mission Discourse in Matthew's Interpretation* (WUNT 81). Tübingen: Mohr Siebeck, 1995.

N. Perrin, *Jesus and the Language of the Kingdom: Symbol and Metaphor in New Testament Interpretation.* Philadelphia: Fortress, 1976.

J. J. Petuchowski and M. Brocke (eds.), *The Lord's Prayer and Jewish Liturgy.* New York: Seabury, 1978.

J. Piper, *"Love Your Enemies": Jesus' Love Command in the Synoptic Gospels and the Early Christian Paraenesis. A History of the Tradition and Interpretation of Its Uses* (SNTSM 38). Cambridge: Cambridge University Press, 1979.

B. Przybylski, *Righteousness in Matthew and His World of Thought* (SNTSM 41). Cambridge: Cambridge University Press, 1980.

H. Riesenfeld, *Jésus transfiguré.* Copenhagen: Munksgaard, 1947.

J. A. T. Robinson, *The Priority of John.* London: SCM, 1985.

————, *Redating the New Testament.* London: SCM, 1976.

W. Rothfuchs, *Die Erfüllungszitate des Matthäus-Evangeliums.* Stuttgart: Kohlhammer, 1969.

A. J. Saldarini, *Matthew's Christian-Jewish Community.* Chicago: University of Chicago Press, 1994.

E. P. Sanders, *Jesus and Judaism.* London: SCM, 1985.

————, *Paul and Palestinian Judaism: A Comparison of Patterns of Religion.* London: SCM, 1977.

————, *The Tendencies of the Synoptic Tradition* (SNTSM 9). Cambridge: Cambridge University Press, 1969.

———— and M. Davies, *Studying the Synoptic Gospels.* London: SCM, 1989.

J. Schaberg, *The Father, the Son and the Holy Spirit: The Triadic Phrase in Matthew 28:19b* (SBLDS 61). Chico: Scholars Press, 1982.

A. Schalit, *König Herodes: Der Mann und sein Werk* (Studia Judaica 4). Berlin: de Gruyter, 1969.

T. E. Schmidt. *Hostility to Wealth in the Synoptic Gospels* (JSNTS 15). Sheffield: Sheffield Academic Press, 1987.

E. Schürer, *The History of the Jewish People in the Age of Jesus Christ (175 B.C. — A.D. 135).* Rev. Eng. edn. G. Vermes, F. Millar, and M. Black. Edinburgh: T&T Clark, 1973-87.

H. Schürmann, *Das Lukasevangelium 1: Kommentar zu Kap. 1,1-9,50* (HTKNT 3/1). Freiburg: Herder. 1969.

A. Schweitzer, *The Quest of the Historical Jesus: A Critical Study of Its Progress from Reimarus to Wrede.* ET, 2nd edn., London: A & C Black, 1911.

C. H. H. Scobie, *John the Baptist: A New Quest of the Historical John.* London: SCM, 1964.

D. P. Senior, *The Passion Narrative according to Matthew* (BETL 39). Leuven: Leuven University Press, 1975.

A. N. Sherwin-White, *Roman Society and Roman Law in the New Testament.* Oxford: Clarendon, 1963.

D. C. Sim, *Apocalyptic Eschatology in the Gospel of Matthew* (SNTSM 88). Cambridge: Cambridge University Press, 1996.

————, *The Gospel of Matthew and Christian Judaism: The History and Social Setting of the Matthean Community.* Edinburgh: T&T Clark, 1998.

E. M. Smallwood, *The Jews under Roman Rule: From Pompey to Diocletian* (SJLA 20). Leiden: Brill, 1976.

K. R. Snodgrass, *The Parable of the Wicked Tenants* (WUNT 27). Tübingen: Mohr, 1983.

G. M. Soares Prabhu, *The Formula-Quotations in the Infancy Narrative of Matthew: An Enquiry into the Tradition-History of Mt 1–2* (AnBib 63). Rome: Biblical Institute Press, 1976.

G. N. Stanton, *A Gospel for a New People: Studies in Matthew.* Edinburgh: T&T Clark, 1992.

———— (ed.), *The Interpretation of Matthew.* 2nd edn., Edinburgh: T&T Clark, 1995.

E. Stauffer, *Jesus and His Story.* ET, London: SCM, 1960.

R. H. Stein, *An Introduction to the Parables of Jesus.* Philadelphia: Westminster. 1981.

K. Stendahl, *The School of St. Matthew and Its Use of the Old Testament.* 2nd edn., Philadelphia: Fortress, 1968.

N. B. Stonehouse, *The Witness of Matthew and Mark to Christ.* London: Tyndale, 1944.

J. R. W. Stott, *The Message of the Sermon on the Mount* (original title, *Christian Counter-Culture*). Leicester: Inter-Varsity Press, 1978.

G. Strecker, *The Sermon on the Mount: An Exegetical Commentary.* ET, Nashville: Abingdon, 1988.

————, *Der Weg der Gerechtigkeit: Untersuchung zur Theologie des Matthäus* (FRLANT 82). 3rd edn., Göttingen: Vandenhoeck & Ruprecht, 1962.

B. H. Streeter, *The Four Gospels: A Study of Origins.* London: Macmillan, 1924.

M. J. Suggs, *Wisdom, Christology and Law in Matthew's Gospel.* Cambridge, MA: Harvard University Press, 1970.

J. E. Taylor, *John the Baptist within Second Temple Judaism.* London: SPCK, 1997.

W. R. Telford, *The Barren Temple and the Withered Tree: A Redaction-Critical Analysis of the Cursing of the Fig-Tree Pericope in Mark's Gospel and Its Relation to the Cleansing of the Temple Tradition* (JSNTS 1). Sheffield: JSOT, 1980.

G. Theissen, *The Gospels in Context: Social and Political History in the Synoptic Tradition.* ET, Minneapolis: Fortress, 1991.

————, *The Miracle Stories of the Early Christian Tradition.* ET, Edinburgh: T&T Clark, 1983.

W. G. Thompson, *Matthew's Advice to a Divided Community: Mt 17,22–18,35* (AnBib 44). Rome: Biblical Institute Press, 1970.

W. Trilling, *Das wahre Israel: Studien zur Theologie des Matthäus-Evangeliums.* 3rd edn., München: Kösel, 1964.

N. Turner, *A Grammar of New Testament Greek* (J. H. Moulton), vol. 3: *Syntax.* Edinburgh: T&T Clark, 1963.

G. Vermes, *Jesus the Jew: A Historian's Reading of the Gospels.* London: Collins, 1973.

——, *Scripture and Tradition in Judaism.* Leiden: Brill, 1961.

D. J. Verseput, *The Rejection of the Humble, Messianic King: A Study of the Composition of Matthew 11–12.* Frankfurt: P. Lang, 1986.

D. O. Via, *The Parables: Their Literary and Existential Dimension.* Philadelphia: Fortress, 1967.

——, *Self-Deception and Wholeness in Paul and Matthew.* Minneapolis: Fortress, 1990.

G. von Rad, *The Problem of the Hexateuch and Other Essays.* ET, New York: McGraw-Hill, 1966.

H. C. Waetjen, *A Reordering of Power: A Socio-Political Reading of Mark's Gospel.* Minneapolis: Fortress, 1989.

R. E. Watts, *Isaiah's New Exodus and Mark* (WUNT 88). Tübingen: Mohr Siebeck, 1997.

D. J. Weaver, *Matthew's Missionary Discourse: A Literary-Critical Analysis* (JSNTS 38). Sheffield: Sheffield Academic Press, 1990.

R. L. Webb, *John the Baptizer and Prophet: A Socio-Historical Study* (JSNTS 62). Sheffield: Sheffield Academic Press, 1991.

D. Wenham, *The Parables of Jesus: Pictures of Revolution.* London: Hodder & Stoughton, 1989.

——, *Paul: Follower of Jesus or Founder of Christianity?* Grand Rapids: Eerdmans, 1995.

J. W. Wenham, *Christ and the Bible.* London: Tyndale, 1972.

M. J. Wilkins, *The Concept of Disciple in Matthew's Gospel as Reflected in the Use of the Term Μαθητής* (SNT 59). Leiden: Brill, 1988.

J. Wilkinson, *Jerusalem as Jesus Knew It: Archaeology as Evidence.* London: Thames & Hudson, 1978.

S. K. Williams, *Jesus' Death as Saving Event: The Background and Origin of a Concept.* Missoula: Scholars Press, 1975.

A. I. Wilson, *When Will These Things Happen? A Study of Jesus as Judge in Matthew 21–25.* Carlisle: Paternoster, 2004.

N. T. Wright, *Jesus and the Victory of God* (*Christian Origins and the Question of God,* vol. 2). London: SPCK, 1996.

——, *The Resurrection of the Son of God* (*Christian Origins and the Question of God,* vol. 3). London: SPCK, 2003.

W. H. Wuellner, *The Meaning of "Fishers of Men."* Philadelphia: Westminster, 1967.

Y.-E. Yang, *Jesus and the Sabbath in Matthew's Gospel* (JSNTS 139). Sheffield: Sheffield Academic Press, 1997.

J. Zumstein, *La Condition du Croyant dans l'Évangile selon Matthieu.* Fribourg: Editions Universitaires / Göttingen: Vandenhoeck & Ruprecht, 1977.

ARTICLES

P. J. Achtemeier, "Miracles and the Historical Jesus: A Study of Mark 9:14-29," *CBQ* 37 (1975) 471-91.

E. Adams, "The Coming of the Son of Man in Mark's Gospel," *TynBul* 56 (2005) 39-61.

B. Ahern, "Staff or No Staff," *CBQ* 5 (1943) 332-37.

D. C. Allison, "Anticipating the Passion: The Literary Reach of Matthew 26:47–27:56," *CBQ* 56 (1994) 701-14.

———, "Divorce, Celibacy and Joseph (Matthew 1.18-25 and 19.1-12)," *JSNT* 49 (1993) 3-10.

———, "Elijah Must Come First," *JBL* 103 (1984) 256-58.

———, "The Eye Is the Lamp of the Body (Matt. 6.22-23 = Luke 11.34-36)," *NTS* 33 (1987) 61-87.

———, "The Hairs of Your Head Are All Numbered," *ExpT* 101 (1990) 334-36.

———, "Matt. 23:39 = Luke 13:35b as a Conditional Prophecy," *JSNT* 18 (1983) 75-84.

———, "Two Notes on a Key Text: Matthew 11:25-30," *JTS* 39 (1988) 477-85.

A. W. Argyle, "The Meaning of καθ' ἡμέραν in Mark 14.49," *ExpT* 63 (1952) 354.

———, "Wedding Customs at the Time of Jesus," *ExpT* 86 (1974/5) 214-15.

A. G. Arnott, "'The First Day of Unleavened . . .': Mt 26.17, Mk 14.12, Lk 22.7," *BT* 35 (1984) 235-38.

K. Atkinson, "On Further Defining the First-Century CE Synagogue: Fact or Fiction? A Rejoinder to H. C. Kee," *NTS* 43 (1997) 491-502.

N. Avigad, "A Depository of Inscribed Ossuaries in the Kidron Valley," *IEJ* 12 (1962) 1-12.

T. Baarda, "Gadarenes, Gerasenes, Gergesenes and the 'Diatessaron' Tradition," in E. E. Ellis and M. Wilcox (eds.), *Neotestamentica et Semitica* (FS M. Black. Edinburgh: T&T Clark, 1969) 181-97.

S. Bacchiocchi, "Matthew 11:28-30: Jesus' Rest and the Sabbath," *AUSS* 22 (1984) 289-316.

G. J. Bahr, "The Seder of Passover and the Eucharistic Words," *NovT* 12 (1970) 181-202.

K. E. Bailey, "The Manger and the Inn — The Cultural Background of Luke 2.7," *Near East School of Theology Review* 2 (1979) 33-44; reprinted in *Evangelical Review of Theology* 4 (1980) 201-17.

H. Baltensweiler, "Die Ehebruchsklauseln bei Matthäus," *TZ* 15 (1959) 340-56.

E. Bammel, "Crucifixion as a Punishment in Palestine," in E. Bammel (eds.), *Trial,* 162-65.

———, "The Feeding of the Multitude," in E. Bammel and C. F. D. Moule (eds.), *Jesus,* 211-40.

———, "The *Titulus,*" in E. Bammel and C. F. D. Moule (eds.), *Jesus,* 353-64.

———, "The Trial before Pilate," in E. Bammel and C. F. D. Moule (eds.), *Jesus,* 415-51.

T. D. Barnes, "The Date of Herod's Death," *JTS* 19 (1968) 204-9.

P. W. Barnett, "The Jewish Sign Prophets — A.D. 40-70: Their Intentions and Origin," *NTS* 27 (1981) 679-97.

C. K. Barrett, "The House of Prayer and the Den of Thieves," in E. E. Ellis and E. Grässer (eds.), *Jesus und Paulus* (FS W. G. Kümmel. Göttingen: Vandenhoeck & Ruprecht, 1975), 13-20.

R. A. Batey, "Is Not This the Carpenter?" *NTS* 30 (1984) 249-58.

R. J. Bauckham, "The Coin in the Fish's Mouth," in D. Wenham and C. Blomberg (eds.), *GP* 6 (Sheffield: JSOT, 1986), 219-52.

———, "Jesus' Demonstration in the Temple," in B. Lindars (ed.), *Law and Religion* (Cambridge: Clarke, 1988), 72-89.

———, "The Parable of the Royal Wedding Feast (Matthew 22:1-14) and the Parable of the Lame Man and the Blind Man (*Apocryphon of Ezekiel*)," *JBL* 115 (1996) 471-88.

———, "Salome the Sister of Jesus, Salome the Disciple of Jesus, and the Secret Gospel of Mark," *NovT* 33 (1991) 245-75.

———, "Tamar's Ancestry and Rahab's Marriage: Two Problems in the Matthean Genealogy," *NovT* 37 (1995) 313-29.

D. A. Bauer, "The Kingship of Jesus in the Matthean Infancy Narrative: A Literary Analysis," *CBQ* 57 (1995) 306-23.

———, "The Literary and Theological Function of the Genealogy in Matthew's Gospel," in D. A. Bauer and M. A. Powell (eds.), *Treasures,* 129-59.

R. Beaton, "Messiah and Justice: A Key to Matthew's Use of Isaiah 42:1-47?" *JSNT* 75 (1999) 5-23.

M. A. Beavis, "Ancient Slavery as an Interpretive Context for the New Testament Servant Parables with Special Reference to the Unjust Steward (Luke 16:1-8)," *JBL* 111 (1992) 37-54.

T. J. Bennett, "Matthew 7:6 — A New Interpretation," *WTJ* 49 (1987) 371-86.

K. Berger, "Jesus als Nasoräer/Nasiräer," *NovT* 38 (1996) 323-35.

————, "Zur Geschichte der Einleitungsformel 'Amen, ich sage euch,'" *ZNW* 63 (1972) 45-75.

H. D. Betz, "Matthew vi.22f and Ancient Greek Theories of Vision," in E. Best and A. McL. Wilson (eds.), *Text and Interpretation* (FS M. Black. Cambridge: Cambridge University Press, 1979), 43-56.

D. A. Black, "Jesus on Anger: The Text of Matthew 5:22a Revisited," *NovT* 30 (1988) 1-8.

M. Black, "'Not Peace but a Sword': Matt 10:34ff; Luke 12:51ff," in E. Bammel and C. F. D. Moule (eds.), *Jesus,* 289-94.

J. Blinzler, "Εἰσὶν εὐνοῦχοι," *ZNW* 48 (1957) 254-70.

M. Bockmuehl, "'Let the Dead Bury Their Dead' (Matt. 8:22/Luke 9:60): Jesus and the Halakah," *JTS* 49 (1998) 553-81.

————, "Matthew 5.32; 19.9 in the Light of Pre-rabbinic Halakhah," *NTS* 35 (1989) 291-95.

————, "Why Did Jesus Predict the Destruction of the Temple?" *Crux* 25/3 (1989) 11-18.

G. Bornkamm, "Der Aufbau der Bergpredigt," *NTS* 24 (1977/8) 419-32.

————, "The Risen Lord and the Earthly Jesus: Mt 28,16-20," in J. M. Robinson (ed.), *The Future of Our Religious Past* (FS R. Bultmann. London: SCM, 1971), 203-29.

L. C. Boughton, "'Being Shed for You/Many': Time-sense and Consequences in the Synoptic Cup Quotations," *TynBul* 48 (1997) 249-70.

M. M. Bourke, "The Literary Genus of Matthew 1–2," *CBQ* 22 (1960) 160-75.

D. Boyarin, "'After the Sabbath' (Matt. 28:1) — Once More into the Crux," *JTS* 52 (2001) 678-88.

D. Brady, "The Alarm to Peter in Mark's Gospel," *JSNT* 4 (1979) 42-57.

J. A. Brant, "Infelicitous Oaths in the Gospel of Matthew," *JSNT* 63 (1996) 3-20.

R. G. Bratcher, "A Note on Mark XI,3," *ExpT* 64 (1952/3) 93.

————, "A Study of Isaiah 7:14," *BT* 9 (1958) 97-126.

P. G. Bretscher, "Exodus 4:22-23 and the Voice from Heaven," *JBL* 87 (1968) 301-11.

O. S. Brooks, "Matthew xxviii 16-20 and the Design of the First Gospel," *JSNT* 10 (1981) 2-18.

C. Brown, "The Gates of Hell and the Church," in J. E. Bradley and R. A. Muller (eds.), *Church, Word and Spirit* (FS G. W. Bromiley. Grand Rapids: Eerdmans, 1987), 15-43.

R. E. Brown, "The Burial of Jesus (Mark 15:42-47)," *CBQ* 50 (1988) 233-45.

————, "*Rachab* in Mt 1,5 Probably Is Rahab of Jericho," *Bib* 63 (1982) 79-80.

S. Brown, "The Matthean Apocalypse," *JSNT* 4 (1979) 2-27.

S. G. Browne, "Leprosy: The Christian Attitude," *ExpT* 73 (1961/2) 242-45.

F. F. Bruce, "Render to Caesar," in E. Bammel and C. F. D. Moule (eds.), *Jesus,* 249-63.

J. E. Bruns, "The Magi Episode in Matthew 2," *CBQ* 23 (1961) 51-54.

F. W. Burnett, "Παλιγγενεσία in Matt. 19:28: A Window on the Matthean Community?" *JSNT* 17 (1983) 60-72.

G. B. Caird, "Expounding the Parables: 1. The Defendant (Matthew 5.25f; Luke 12.58f," *ExpT* 77 (1965/6) 36-39.

K. M. Campbell, "The New Jerusalem in Matthew 5:14," *SJT* 31 (1978) 335-63.

L. Cantwell, "The Parentage of Jesus," *NovT* 24 (1982) 304-15.

T. B. Cargal, "'His Blood Be upon Us and upon Our Children': A Matthean Double Entendre?" *NTS* 37 (1991) 101-12.

D. B. Carmichael, "David Daube on the Eucharist and the Passover Seder," *JSNT* 42 (1991) 45-67.

D. A. Carson, "The ὅμοιος Word-Group as Introduction to Some Matthean Parables," *NTS* 31 (1985) 277-82.

————, "Redaction Criticism: On the Legitimacy and Illegitimacy of a Literary Tool," in D. A. Carson and J. D. Woodbridge (eds.), *Scripture and Truth* (Grand Rapids: Zondervan, 1983), 119-42.

E. J. Carter, "Toll and Tribute: A Political Reading of Matthew 17.24-27," *JSNT* 25 (2003) 413-31.

W. Carter, "Are There Imperial Texts in the Class? Intertextual Eagles and Matthean Eschatology as 'Lights Out' Time for Imperial Rome (Matthew 24:27-31)," *JBL* 122 (2003) 467-87.

————, "Evoking Isaiah: Matthean Soteriology and an Intertextual Reading of Isaiah 7–9 and Matthew 1:23 and 4:15-16," *JBL* 119 (2000) 503-20.

————, "Jesus' 'I have come' Statements in Matthew's Gospel," *CBQ* 60 (1998) 44-62.

————, "Paying the Tax to Rome as Subversive Praxis: Matthew 17:24-27," *JSNT* 76 (1999) 3-31.

————, "'Solomon in All His Glory': Intertextuality and Matthew 6:29," *JSNT* 65 (1997) 3-25.

————, "'To See the Tomb': A Note on Matthew's Women at the Tomb (Matt 28.1)," *ExpT* 107 (1996) 201-5.

M. Casey, "Culture and Historicity: The Plucking of the Grain (Mark 2.23-28)," *NTS* 34 (1988) 1-23.

————, "The Date of the Passover Sacrifices and Mark 14:12," *TynBul* 48 (1997) 245-47.

————, "The Jackals and the Son of Man (Matt. 8.20 // Luke 9.58)," *JSNT* 23 (1985) 3-22.

R. J. Cassidy, "Matthew 17:24-27: A Word on Civil Taxes," *CBQ* 41 (1979) 571-80.

D. R. Catchpole, "The Answer of Jesus to Caiaphas," *NTS* 17 (1970/1) 213-26.

————, "The Poor on Earth and the Son of Man in Heaven: A Reappraisal of Matthew XXV.31-46," *BJRL* 61 (1979) 355-97.

———, "The Problem of the Historicity of the Sanhedrin Trial," in E. Bammel (ed.), *Trial*, 47-65.

———, "The 'Triumphal' Entry," in E. Bammel and C. F. D. Moule (eds.), *Jesus*, 319-34.

C. P. Ceroke, "Is Mark 2:10 a Saying of Jesus?" *CBQ* 22 (1960) 369-90.

B. Charette, "A Harvest for the People? An Interpretation of Matthew 9:37f.," *JSNT* 38 (1990) 29-35.

———, "'To Proclaim Liberty to the Captives': Matthew 11:28-30 in the Light of Old Testament Prophetic Expectation," *NTS* 38 (1992) 290-97.

B. Chenoweth, "Identifying the Talents: Contextual Clues for the Interpretation of the Parable of the Talents (Matthew 25:14-30)," *TynBul* 56 (2005) 61-72.

B. D. Chilton, "Jesus *ben David;* Reflections on the *Davidssohnfrage*," *JSNT* 14 (1982) 88-112.

———, "Targumic Transmission and Dominical Tradition," in R. T. France and D. Wenham (eds.), *GP* 1 (Sheffield: JSOT, 1980), 21-45.

D. H. Clark et al., "The Star of Bethlehem," *Quarterly Journal of the Royal Astronomical Society* 18 (1977) 443-49.

K. W. Clark, "The Meaning of [κατα]κυριεύειν," in J. K. Elliott (ed.), *Studies in New Testament Language and Text* (FS G. D. Kilpatrick; SNT 44. Leiden: Brill, 1976), 100-105.

D. M. Cohn-Sherbok, "An Analysis of Jesus' Arguments concerning the Plucking of Grain on the Sabbath," *JSNT* 2 (1979) 31-41.

———, "Jesus' Defence of the Resurrection of the Dead," *JSNT* 11 (1981) 64-73.

E. C. Colwell, "Has *Raka* a Parallel in the Papyri?" *JBL* 53 (1934) 351-54.

J. G. Cook, "The Sparrow's Fall in Mt 10,29b," *ZNW* 79 (1988) 138-44.

O. L. Cope, "The Death of John the Baptist in the Gospel of Matthew," *CBQ* 38 (1976) 515-19.

W. J. Cotter, "The Parable of the Children in the Marketplace, Q(Lk) 7.31-35," *NovT* 29 (1987) 289-304.

B. Couroyer, "'De la mesure dont vous mesurez il vous sera mesuré,'" *RB* 77 (1970) 366-70.

J. M. Court, "Right and Left: The Implications for Matthew 25.31-46," *NTS* 31 (1985) 223-33.

J. R. C. Cousland, "The Feeding of the Four Thousand *Gentiles* in Matthew? Matthew 15:29-39 as a Test Case," *NovT* 41 (1999) 1-23.

W. L. Craig, "The Guard at the Tomb," *NTS* 30 (1984) 273-81.

J. D. Crossan, "Hidden Treasure Parables in Late Antiquity," *SBLSP 1976*, 359-79.

———, "The Parable of the Wicked Husbandmen," *JBL* 90 (1971) 451-65.

S. D. Currie, "Matthew 5,39f. — Resistance or Protest?" *HTR* 57 (1964) 140-45.

D. Daube, "Responsibilities of Masters and Disciples in the Gospels," *NTS* 19 (1972/3) 1-15.

———, "Three Notes Having to Do with Johanan ben Zakkai," *JTS* 11 (1960) 59-62.

P. R. Davies and B. D. Chilton, "The Aqedah: A Revised Tradition History," *CBQ* 40 (1978) 514-46.

E. P. Deatrick, "Salt, Soil, Savour," *BA* 25 (1962) 41-48.

M. C. de Boer, "Ten Thousand Talents? Matthew's Interpretation and Redaction of the Parable of the Unforgiving Servant (Matt. 18:23-35)," *CBQ* 50 (1988) 214-32.

M. de Jonge, "Jewish Expectations about the 'Messiah' according to the Fourth Gospel," *NTS* 19 (1972/3) 246-70.

———, "Matthew 27:51 in Early Christian Exegesis," *HTR* 79 (1986) 67-79.

J. D. M. Derrett, "Allegory and the Wicked Vinedressers," *JTS* 25 (1974) 426-32.

———, "Binding and Loosing (Matthew 16:19; 18:18 and John 20:23)," *JBL* 102 (1983) 112-17.

———, "Christ and Reproof (Matthew 7.1-5/Luke 6.37-42)," *NTS* 34 (1988) 271-81.

———, "Contributions to the Study of the Gerasene Demoniac," *JSNT* 3 (1979) 2-17.

———, "Law in the New Testament: The Palm Sunday Colt," *NovT* 23 (1981) 241-58.

———, "Mark's Technique: The Haemorrhaging Woman and Jairus' Daughter," *Bib* 63 (1982) 474-505.

———, "The Merits of the Narrow Gate," *JSNT* 15 (1982) 20-29.

———, "Palingenesia (Matthew 19:28)," *JSNT* 20 (1984) 51-58.

———, "The Parable of the Two Sons," *ST* 25 (1971) 109-16.

———, "Receptacles and Tombs (Mt 23,24-30)," *ZNW* 77 (1986) 255-66.

———, "The Stone That the Builders Rejected," *SE* 4 (1968) 180-86.

———, "'Where Two or Three Are Convened in My Name . . .': A Sad Misunderstanding," *ExpT* 91 (1979/80) 83-86.

———, "Why and How Jesus Walked on the Sea," *NovT* 23 (1981) 330-48.

———, "Workers in the Vineyard: A Parable of Jesus," *JJS* 25 (1974) 64-91.

C. Deutsch, "Wisdom in Matthew: Transformation of a Symbol," *NovT* 32 (1990) 13-47.

J. R. Donahue, "Tax Collectors and Sinners: An Attempt at Identification," *CBQ* 33 (1971) 39-61.

T. L. Donaldson, "The Law That Hangs (Matthew 22:40): Rabbinic Formulation and Matthean Social World," *CBQ* 57 (1995) 689-709.

———, "The Mockers and the Son of God (Matthew 27:37-44): Two Characters in Matthew's Story of Jesus," *JSNT* 41 (1991) 3-18.

J. A. Draper, "The Development of 'the Sign of the Son of Man' in the Jesus Tradition," *NTS* 39 (1993) 1-21.

———, "The Genesis and Narrative Thrust of the Paraenesis in the Sermon on the Mount," *JSNT* 75 (1999) 25-48.

J. Drury, "The Sower, the Vineyard, and the Place of Allegory in the Interpretation of Mark's Parables," *JTS* 24 (1973) 367-79.

P. B. Duff, "The March of the Divine Warrior and the Advent of the Greco-Roman King: Mark's Account of Jesus' Entry into Jerusalem," *JBL* 111 (1992) 55-71.

I. Duguid, "Messianic Themes in Zechariah 9–14," in P. E. Satterthwaite et al. (eds.), *The Lord's Anointed: Interpretation of Old Testament Messianic Texts* (Carlisle: Paternoster, 1995), 265-80.

D. C. Duling, "Solomon, Exorcism and the Son of David," *HTR* 68 (1975) 235-52.

W. J. Dumbrell, "The Logic of the Role of the Law in Matthew V 1-20," *NovT* 23 (1981) 1-21.

J. H. Elliott, "Matthew 20:1-15: A Parable of Invidious Comparison and Evil Eye Accusation," *BTB* 22 (1992) 52-65.

E. E. Ellis, "Deity Christology in Mark 14:58," in J. B. Green and M. Turner (eds.), *Jesus of Nazareth, Lord and Christ: Essays on the Historical Jesus and NT Christology* (FS I. H. Marshall. Grand Rapids: Eerdmans, 1994), 192-203.

B. Englezakis, "*Thomas*, Logion 30," *NTS* 25 (1978/9) 262-72.

V. Eppstein, "The Historicity of the Gospel Account of the Cleansing of the Temple," *ZNW* 55 (1964) 42-58.

R. J. Erickson, "Divine Injustice? Matthew's Narrative Strategy and the Slaughter of the Innocents (Matthew 2:13-23)," *JSNT* 64 (1996) 5-27.

C. A. Evans, "Jesus' Action in the Temple: Cleansing or Portent of Destruction?" *CBQ* 51 (1989) 237-70.

———, "On the Isaianic Background of the Sower Parable," *CBQ* 47 (1985) 464-68.

———, "On the Vineyard Parables of Isaiah 5 and Mark 12," *BZ* 28 (1984) 82-86.

M. M. Faierstein, "Why Do the Scribes Say That Elijah Must Come First?" *JBL* 100 (1981) 75-86.

Z. W. Falk, "Binding and Loosing," *JJS* 25 (1974) 92-100.

F. C. Fensham, "The Good and Evil Eye in the Sermon on the Mount," *Neot* 1 (1967) 51-58.

J. Fenton, "Eating People," *Theology* 94 (1991) 414-23.

K. Ferrari d'Occhieppo, "The Star of the Magi and Babylonian Astronomy," in J. Vardaman and E. M. Yamauchi (eds.), *Chronos, Kairos, Christos* (FS J. Finegan. Winona Lake: Eisenbrauns, 1989) 41-53.

L. R. Fisher, "'Can This Be the Son of David?'" in F. T. Trotter (ed.), *Jesus and the Historian* (FS E. C. Colwell. Philadelphia: Westminster, 1968), 82-97.

J. A. Fitzmyer, "Anti-Semitism and the Cry of 'All the People' (Mt. 27:25)," *TS* 26 (1965) 667-71.

———, "Aramaic Evidence Affecting the Interpretation of Hosanna in the New Testament," in G. F. Hawthorne and O. Betz (eds.), *Tradition and Interpretation in the New Testament* (FS E. E. Ellis. Grand Rapids: Eerdmans, 1987), 110-18.

———, "Aramaic Kepha' and Peter's Name in the New Testament," in E. Best and R. McL. Wilson (eds.), *Text and Interpretation* (FS M. Black. Cambridge: Cambridge University Press, 1979), 121-32.

———, "The Aramaic Qorban Inscription from Jebel Hallet et-Turi and Mk 7:11 /Mt 15:5," *JBL* 78 (1959) 60-65.

———, "Crucifixion in Ancient Palestine, Qumran Literature and the New Testament," *CBQ* 40 (1978) 493-513.

C. H. T. Fletcher-Louis, "The Destruction of the Temple and the Relativization of the Old Covenant: Mark 13:31 and Matthew 5:18," in K. E. Brower and M. W. Elliott (eds.), *"The Reader Must Understand": Eschatology in Bible and Theology* (Leicester: Apollos, 1997), 145-69.

———, "'Leave the Dead to Bury Their Own Dead': Q 9.60 and the Redefinition of the People of God," *JSNT* 26 (2003) 39-68.

D. Flusser, "Blessed Are the Poor in Spirit," *IEJ* 10 (1960) 1-13.

P. Foster, "A Tale of Two Sons: But Which One Did the Far, Far Better Thing? A Study of Matt 21.28-32," *NTS* 47 (2001) 26-37.

———, "Why Did Matthew Get the *Shema* Wrong? A Study of Matthew 22:37," *JBL* 122 (2003) 309-33.

R. Foster, "Why on Earth Use 'Kingdom of Heaven'? Matthew's Terminology Revisited," *NTS* 48 (2002) 487-99.

R. T. France, "Chronological Aspects of 'Gospel Harmony,'" *Vox Evangelica* 16 (1986) 33-59.

———, "The Church and the Kingdom of God: Some Hermeneutical Issues," in D. A. Carson (ed.), *Biblical Interpretation and the Church: Text and Context* (Exeter: Paternoster, 1984), 30-44.

———, "Exegesis in Practice: Two Samples," in I. H. Marshall (ed.), *New Testament Interpretation* (Exeter: Paternoster, 1977), 252-81.

———, "The Formula-Quotations of Matthew 2 and the Problem of Communication," *NTS* 27 (1980/81) 236-37; reprinted in G. K. Beale (ed.) *The Right Doctrine from the Wrong Texts? Essays on the Use of the Old Testament in the New* (Grand Rapids: Baker, 1994), 114-34.

———, "God and Mammon," *EQ* 51 (1979) 3-21.

———, "Herod and the Children of Bethlehem," *NovT* 21 (1979) 98-120.

————, "Jesus the Baptist?" in J. B. Green and M. M. B. Turner (eds.), *Jesus of Nazareth: Lord and Christ* (FS I. H. Marshall. Carlisle: Paternoster, 1994), 94-111.

————, "Jewish Historiography, Midrash and the Gospels," in R. T. France and D. Wenham (eds.), *GP* 3 (Sheffield: JSOT Press, 1983) 99-127.

————, "Mark and the Teaching of Jesus," in R. T. France and D. Wenham (eds.), *GP* 1 (Sheffield: JSOT, 1980) 101-36.

————, "Scripture, Tradition and History in the Infancy Narratives of Matthew," in R. T. France and D. Wenham (eds.), *GP* 2 (Sheffield: JSOT, 1981) 239-66.

————, "The Servant of the Lord in the Teaching of Jesus," *TynBul* 19 (1968) 26-52.

E. O. Freed, "The Women in Matthew's Genealogy," *JSNT* 29 (1987) 3-19.

P. H. Furfey, "Christ as *Tekton*," *CBQ* 17 (1955) 204-15.

D. E. Garland, "Matthew's Understanding of the Temple Tax," in D. R. Bauer and M. A. Powell (eds.), *Treasures,* 69-98.

L. Gaston, "Beelzebul," *TZ* 18 (1962) 247-55.

S. Gathercole, "The Justification of Wisdom (Matt 11.19b/Luke 7.35)," *NTS* 49 (2003) 476-88.

C. Gempf, "The Imagery of Birth Pangs in the New Testament," *TynBul* 45 (1994) 119-35.

B. Gerhardsson, "Confession and Denial before Men," *JSNT* 13 (1981) 46-66.

————, "The Parable of the Sower and Its Interpretation," *NTS* 14 (1967/8) 165-93.

J. A. Gibbs, "Israel Standing with Israel: The Baptism of Jesus in Matthew's Gospel (Matt 3:13-17)," *CBQ* 64 (2002) 511-26.

J. M. Gibbs, "Purpose and Pattern in Matthew's Use of the Title 'Son of God,'" *NTS* 10 (1963/4) 446-64.

C. H. Giblin, "A Note on Doubt and Reassurance in Mt 28:16-20," *CBQ* 37 (1975) 68-75.

————, "Structural and Thematic Correlations in the Matthean Burial-Resurrection Narrative (Matt. xxvii.57–xxviii.20)," *NTS* 21 (1974/5) 406-20.

————, "'The Things of God' in the Question concerning Tribute to Caesar," *CBQ* 33 (1971) 510-27.

J. Gibson, "Jesus' Refusal to Produce a 'Sign,'" *JSNT* 38 (1990) 37-66.

————, "*Hoi telonai kai hai pornai,*" *JTS* 32 (1981) 429-33.

J. A. Glancy, "Slaves and Slavery in the Matthean Parables," *JBL* 119 (2000) 67-90.

T. F. Glasson, "Davidic Links with the Betrayal of Jesus," *ExpT* 85 (1973/4) 118-19.

————, "The Ensign of the Son of Man (Matt. xxiv.30)," *JTS* 15 (1964) 299-300.

A. M. Goldberg, "Sitzend zur Rechten der Kraft," *BZ* 8 (1964) 284-93.

D. Good, "The Verb ἀναχωρέω in Matthew's Gospel," *NovT* 32 (1990) 1-12.

M. D. Goulder, "Mark xvi.1-8 and Parallels," *NTS* 24 (1977/8) 235-40.

————, "Two Significant Minor Agreements (Mat. 4:13 Par.; Mat. 26:67-68 Par.)," *NovT* 45 (2003) 365-73.

K. Grayston, "The Translation of Matthew 28:17," *JSNT* 21 (1984) 105-9.

J. H. Greenlee, "'For Her Memorial': *Eis mnemosynon autes,* Mt 26.13, Mk 14,9," *ExpT* 71 (1959/60) 245.

J. Grindel, "Matthew 12.18-21," *CBQ* 29 (1967) 110-15.

J. J. Gunther, "The Fate of the Jerusalem Church: The Flight to Pella," *TZ* 29 (1973) 81-84.

D. M. Gurtner, "The *Velum Scissum:* Matthew's Exposition of the Death of Jesus" (summary of Ph.D. diss., St. Andrews, 2005), *TynBul* 56 (2005) 147-50.

K. Haacker, "Der Rechtssatz Jesu zum Thema Ehebruch (Mt 5,28)," *BZ* 21 (1977) 113-16.

S. Haber, "A Woman's Touch: Feminist Encounters with the Hemorrhaging Woman in Mark 5.24-34," *JSNT* 26 (2003) 171-92.

A. C. Hagedorn and J. H. Neyrey, "'It Was out of Envy That They Handed Jesus Over' (Mark 15:10): The Anatomy of Envy and the Gospel of Mark," *JSNT* 69 (1998) 15-56.

D. A Hagner, "Righteousness in Matthew's Theology," in M. J. Wilkins and T. Paige, *Worship, Theology and Ministry in the Early Church* (FS R. P. Martin; JSNTS 87. Sheffield: Sheffield Academic Press, 1992), 101-20.

N. Q. Hamilton, "Temple Cleansing and Temple Bank," *JBL* 83 (1964) 365-72.

D. R. A. Hare and D. J. Harrington, "Make Disciples of All the Gentiles (Matthew 28:19)," *CBQ* 37 (1975) 359-69.

H. StJ. Hart, "The Coin of 'Render unto Caesar . . .' (A Note on Some Aspects of Mark 12:13-17; Matt. 22:15-22; Luke 20:20-26)," in E. Bammel and C. F. D. Moule (eds.), *Jesus* 241-48.

————, "The Crown of Thorns in John 19:2-5," *JTS* 3 (1952) 66-75.

L. Hartman, "'Into the Name of Jesus': A Suggestion concerning the Earliest Meaning of the Phrase," *NTS* 20 (1974) 432-40.

————, "Scriptural Exegesis in the Gospel of Matthew and the Problem of Communication," in M. Didier (ed.), *Matthieu,* 131-52.

T. Hatina, "The Focus of Mark 13:24-27: The Parousia, or the Destruction of the Temple?" *BBR* 6 (1996) 43-66.

J. H. Hellerman, "Challenging the Authority of Jesus: Mark 11:27-33 and Mediterranean Notions of Honor and Shame," *JETS* 43 (2000) 213-28.

C. J. Hemer, "ἐπιούσιος," *JSNT* 22 (1984) 81-94.

M. Hengel and H. Merkel, "Die Magier aus dem Osten und die Flucht nach Ägypten (Mt 2) im Rahmen der antiken Religionsgeschichte und der Theologie des Matthäus," in P. Hoffmann (ed.), *Orientierung an Jesus: zur Theologie der Synoptiker* (FS J. Schmid. Freiburg: Herder, 1973), 139-69.

J. Héring, "Zwei exegetische Probleme in der Perikope von Jesus in Gethsemane (Markus XIV 32-42; Matthäus XXVI 36-46; Lukas XXII 40-46)," in W. C. Van Unnik (ed.), *Neotestamentica et Patristica* (SNT 6; FS O. Cullmann. Leiden: Brill, 1962), 64-69.

J. D. Hester, "Socio-rhetorical Criticism and the Parable of the Tenants," *JSNT* 45 (1992) 27-57.

R. H. Hiers, "'Binding and Loosing': The Matthean Authorizations," *JBL* 104 (1985) 233-50.

D. Hill, "DIKAIOI as a Quasi-technical Term," *NTS* 11 (1964/5) 296-302.

———, "False Prophets and Charismatics: Structure and Interpretation in Matthew 7,15-23," *Bib* 57 (1976) 327-48.

———, "On the Use and Meaning of Hosea vi.6 in Matthew's Gospel," *NTS* 24 (1977/8) 107-19.

———, "Son and Servant: An Essay in Matthean Christology," *JSNT* 6 (1980) 2-16.

T. Hirunuma, "Matthew 16,2b-3," in E. J. Epp and G. D. Fee (eds.), *New Testament Textual Criticism: Its Significance for Exegesis* (FS B. M. Metzger. Oxford: Clarendon, 1981), 35-45.

M. W. Holmes, "The Text of Matthew 5.11," *NTS* 32 (1986) 283-86.

W. Horbury, "The Temple Tax," in E. Bammel and C. F. D. Moule (eds.), *Jesus,* 265-86.

———, "The Twelve and the Phylarchs," *NTS* 32 (1986) 503-27.

E. H. Horne, "The Parable of the Tenants as Indictment," *JSNT* 71 (1998) 111-16.

C. B. Houk, "ΠΕΙΡΑΣΜΟΣ: The Lord's Prayer and the Massah Tradition (Ex. 12:1-7)," *SJT* 46 (1963) 216-25.

S. Hre Kio, "Understanding and Translating 'Nations' in Mt 28.19," *BT* 41 (1990) 230-38.

C. J. Humphreys, "The Star of Bethlehem, a Comet in 5 B.C., and the Date of Christ's Birth," *TynBul* 143 (1992) 31-56.

——— and W. G. Waddington, "The Jewish Calendar, a Lunar Eclipse, and the Date of Christ's Crucifixion," *TynBul* 43 (1992) 331-51.

T. Ilan, "Notes on the Distribution of Jewish Women's Names in Palestine in the Second Temple and Mishnaic Periods," *JJS* 40 (1989) 186-200.

D. Instone-Brewer, "Review Article: The Use of Rabbinic Sources in Gospel Studies," *TynBul* 50 (1999) 281-98.

liii

H. M. Jackson, "The Death of Jesus in Mark and the Miracle from the Cross," *NTS* 33 (1987) 16-37.

D. Janzen, "The Meaning of *Porneia* in Matthew 5:32 and 19:9: An Approach from the Study of Ancient Near Eastern Culture," *JSNT* 80 (2000) 66-80.

J. G. Janzen, "Resurrection and Hermeneutics: On Exodus 3.6 in Mark 12.26," *JSNT* 23 (1985) 43-58.

J. Jeremias, "Lampades in Matthew 25:1-13," in J. M. Richards (ed.), *Soli Deo Gloria* (FS W. C. Robinson. Richmond: John Knox, 1968), 83-87.

———, "Palästinakundliches zum Gleichnis vom Sämann," *NTS* 13 (1966/7) 48-53.

———, "Zum nichtresponsorischen Amen," *ZNW* 64 (1973) 122-23.

E. S. Johnson, "Is Mark 15.39 the Key to Mark's Christology?" *JSNT* 31 (1987) 3-22.

———, "Mark 15:39 and the So-Called Confession of the Roman Centurion," *Bib* 81 (2000) 406-13.

L. T. Johnson, "The New Testament's Anti-Jewish Slander and Conventions of Ancient Polemic," *JBL* 108 (1989) 419-41.

E. A. Judge, "The Regional *kanon* for Requisitioned Transport," in G. H. R. Horsley (ed.), *New Documents Illustrating Early Christianity,* vol. 1 (Macquarie University, 1981), 36-45.

L. E. Keck, "The Spirit and the Dove," *NTS* 17 (1970/1) 41-67.

H. C. Kee, "Defining the First-Century-CE Synagogue: Problems and Progress," *NTS* 41 (1995) 481-500.

A. J. Kerr, "Matthew 13:25. Sowing *Zizania* among Another's Wheat: Realistic or Artificial?" *JTS* 48 (1997) 108-9.

P. Ketter, "Zum Lokalisierung der Blindenheilung bei Jericho," *Bib* 15 (1934) 411-18.

G. D. Kilpatrick, "Jesus, His Family and His Disciples," *JSNT* 15 (1982) 3-19.

T. H. Kim, "The Anarthrous υἱὸς θεοῦ in Mark 15,39 and the Roman Imperial Cult," *Bib* 79 (1998) 221-41.

J. D. Kingsbury, "The Developing Conflict between Jesus and the Jewish Leaders in Matthew's Gospel: A Literary-Critical Study," in G. N. Stanton (ed.), *Interpretation,* 179-97 (originally published in *CBQ* 49 [1987] 57-83).

———, "The Title 'Son of David' in Matthew's Gospel," *JBL* 95 (1976) 591-602.

B. Kinman, "Jesus' 'Triumphal Entry' in the Light of Pilate's," *NTS* 40 (1994) 442-48.

W. Klassen, "The Sacred Kiss in the New Testament: An Example of Social Boundary Lines," *NTS* 39 (1993) 122-35.

J. S. Kloppenborg, "Self-Help or *Deus ex Machina* in Mark 12.9?" *NTS* 50 (2004) 494-518.

J. Knackstedt, "Die beiden Brotvermehrungen im Evangelium," *NTS* 10 (1963/4) 309-35.

C. Koester, "The Origin and Significance of the Flight to Pella Tradition," *CBQ* 51 (1989) 90-106.

H. Kosmala, "The Conclusion of Matthew," *ASTI* 4 (1965) 132-47.

———, "His Blood on Us and Our Children (The Background of Matt. 27,24-25)," *ASTI* 7 (1968/9) 94-126.

———, "Matthew 26.52 — A Quotation from the Targum," *NovT* 4 (1960/1) 3-5.

———, "The Time of the Cock-Crow," *ASTI* 2 (1963) 118-20; 6 (1968) 132-34.

D. Krause, "Narrated Prophecy in Mark 11:12-21," in C. A. Evans and W. R. Stegner (eds.), *The Gospels and the Scriptures of Israel* (JSNTS 104. Sheffield: Sheffield Academic Press, 1994), 235-48.

E. Krentz, "The Extent of Matthew's Prologue," *JBL* 83 (1964) 409-14.

S. T. Lachs, "On Matthew 23:27-28," *HTR* 68 (1975) 385-88.

———, "Some Textual Observations on the Sermon on the Mount," *JQR* 69 (1978) 98-111.

G. E. Ladd, "The Parable of the Sheep and the Goats in Recent Interpretation," in R. N. Longenecker and M. C. Tenney (eds.), *New Dimensions in New Testament Study* (Grand Rapids: Zondervan, 1974), 191-99.

G. W. H. Lampe, "AD 70 in Christian Reflection," in E. Bammel and C. F. D. Moule (eds.), *Jesus,* 153-71.

———, "St. Peter's Denial," *BJRL* 55 (1972/3) 346-68.

———, "The Two Swords (Luke 22:35-38)," in E. Bammel and C. F. D. Moule (eds.), *Jesus,* 335-51.

G. M. Landes, "Matthew 12:40 as an Interpretation of 'The Sign of Jonah' against Its Biblical Background," in C. L. Meyers and M. O'Connor (eds.), *The Word of the Lord Shall Go Forth* (Winona Lake: Eisenbraun, 1983), 665-84.

W. E. Langley, "The Parable of the Two Sons (Matthew 21:28-32) against Its Semitic and Rabbinic Backdrop," *CBQ* 58 (1996) 228-43.

S. C. Layton, "Leaves from an Onomastician's Notebook," *ZAW* 108 (1996) 608-20.

E. E. Lemcio, "External Evidence for the Structure and Function of Mark iv.1-20, vii.14-23 and viii.14-21," *JTS* 29 (1978) 323-38.

A.-J. Levine, "Discharging Responsibility: Matthean Jesus, Biblical Law, and Hemorrhaging Woman," in D. A. Bauer and M. A Powell (eds.), *Treasures,* 379-97.

E. Levine, "The Sabbath Controversy according to Matthew," *NTS* 22 (1975/6) 480-83.

L. I. Levine, "The Nature and Origin of the Palestinian Synagogue Reconsidered," *JBL* 115 (1996) 425-48.

W. L. Liefeld, "Theological Motifs in the Transfiguration Narrative," in R. N.

Longenecker and M. C. Tenney (eds.), *New Dimensions in New Testament Study* (Grand Rapids: Zondervan, 1974), 162-79.

O. Linton, "The Demand for a Sign from Heaven," *ST* 19 (1965) 112-29.

W. R. G. Loader, "Son of David, Blindness, Possession, and Duality in Matthew," *CBQ* 44 (1982) 570-85.

T. R. W. Longstaff, "The Women at the Tomb: Matthew 28:1 Reexamined," *NTS* 27 (1981) 277-82.

E. Lövestam, "The ἡ γενεὰ αὕτη Eschatology in Mk 13,30 parr.," in J. Lambrecht (ed.), *L'Apocalypse johannique et l'Apocalyptique dans le Nouveau Testament* (BETL 53. Leuven: Leuven University Press, 1980), 403-13.

P. Luomanen, "*Corpus Mixtum* — An Appropriate Description of Matthew's Community?" *JBL* 117 (1998) 469-80.

U. Luz, "The Final Judgment (Matt 25:31-46): An Exercise in 'History of Influence' Exegesis," in D. R. Bauer and M. A Powell (eds.), *Treasures,* 271-310.

B. R. McCane, "'Let the Dead Bury Their Own Dead': Secondary Burial and Matt. 8:21-22," *HTR* 83 (1990) 31-43.

H. Maccoby, "The Washing of Cups," *JSNT* 14 (1982) 3-15.

C. C. McCown, "ὁ τέκτων," in S. J. Case (ed.), *Studies in Early Christianity* (Chicago: University of Chicago Press, 1928), 173-89.

J. M. McDermott, "Mt 10:23 in Context," *BZ* 28 (1984) 230-40.

N. J. McEleney, "Does the Trumpet Sound or Resound? An Interpretation of Matthew 6,2," *ZNW* 76 (1985) 43-46.

———, "The Principles of the Sermon on the Mount," *CBQ* 41 (1979) 552-70.

B. C. McGing, "Pontius Pilate and the Sources," *CBQ* 53 (1991) 416-38.

A. McIver, "One Hundred-Fold Yield — Miraculous or Mundane? Matthew 13:8,23; Mark 4:8,20; Luke 8:8," *NTS* 40 (1994) 606-8.

———, "The Parable of the Weeds among the Wheat (Matt 13.24-30, 36-43) and the Relationship between the Kingdom and the Church as Portrayed in the Gospel of Matthew," *JBL* 114 (1995) 643-59.

K. L. McKay, "The Use of *hoi de* in Matthew 28.17: A Response to K. Grayston," *JSNT* 24 (1985) 71-72.

S. Mandell, "Who Paid the Temple Tax When the Jews Were under Roman Rule?" *HTR* 77 (1984) 223-42.

T. W. Manson, "The Cleansing of the Temple," *BJRL* 33 (1950/1) 271-82.

J. Marcus, "Entering the Kingly Power of God," *JBL* 107 (1988) 663-75.

———, "The Gates of Hades and the Keys of the Kingdom," *CBQ* 50 (1988) 443-55.

———, "Mark 14.61," *NovT* 31 (1989) 125-41.

I. H. Marshall, "Son of God or Servant of Yahweh? — A Reconsideration of Mark 1:11," *NTS* 15 (1968/9) 326-36.

A. J. Mattill, "The Way of Tribulation," *JBL* 98 (1979) 531-46.

A. H. Maynard, "ΤΙ ΕΜΟΙ ΚΑΙ ΣΟΙ," *NTS* 31 (1985) 582-86.

A. H. Mead, "The βασιλικός in John 4.46-53," *JSNT* 23 (1985) 69-72.

J. P. Meier, "The Historical Jesus and the Historical Herodians," *JBL* 119 (2000) 740-46.

———, "Nations or Gentiles in Matthew 28:19?" *CBQ* 39 (1977) 94-102.

———, "Two Disputed Questions in Matt 28:16-20," *JBL* 96 (1977) 407-24.

H. Merkel, "Peter's Curse," in E. Bammel (ed.), *Trial,* 66-71.

E. H. Merrill, "The Sign of Jonah," *JETS* 23 (1980) 23-30.

R. L. Merritt, "Jesus Barabbas and the Paschal Pardon," *JBL* 104 (1985) 57-68.

B. M. Metzger, "The Nazareth Inscription Once Again," in E. E. Ellis and E. Grässer (eds.), *Jesus und Paulus* (FS W. G. Kümmel. Göttingen: Vandenhoeck & Ruprecht, 1975), 221-38.

B. F. Meyer, "Jesus and the Remnant of Israel," *JBL* 84 (1965) 123-30.

———, "Many (= All) Are Called but Few (= Not All) Are Chosen," *NTS* 36 (1990) 89-97.

C. Mézange, "Simon le Zélote était-il un révolutionnaire?" *Bib* 81 (2000) 489-506.

J. R. Michaels, "Apostolic Hardships and Righteous Gentiles: A Study of Matthew 25.31-46," *JBL* 84 (1965) 27-37.

O. Michel, "The Conclusion of Matthew's Gospel: A Contribution to the History of the Easter Message," in G. N. Stanton (ed.), *Interpretation,* 39-51.

D. L. Miller, "ΕΜΠΑΙΖΕΙΝ: Playing the Mock Game (Luke 22:63-64)," *JBL* 90 (1971) 309-13.

J. V. Miller, "The Time of the Crucifixion," *JETS* 26 (1983) 157-66.

C. L. Mitton, "Leaven," *ExpT* 84 (1972/3) 339-43.

F. J. Moloney, "Matthew 19,3-12 and Celibacy: A Redactional and Form-Critical Study," *JSNT* 2 (1979) 42-60.

H. W. Montefiore, "Josephus and the New Testament," *NovT* 4 (1960) 139-60.

D. J. Moo, "Jesus and the Authority of the Mosaic Law," *JSNT* 20 (1984) 3-49.

———, "Tradition and Old Testament in Matt. 27:3-10," in R. T. France and D. Wenham (eds.), *GP* 3 (Sheffield: JSOT, 1983), 157-75.

W. E. Moore, "ΒΙΑΖΩ, ΑΡΠΑΖΩ and Cognates in Josephus," *NTS* 21 (1974/5) 519-43.

M. J. Moreton, "The Genealogy of Jesus," *SE* 2 (1964) 219-24.

W. G. Morrice, "The Parable of the Dragnet and the Gospel of Thomas," *ExpT* 95 (1984) 269-73.

S. Motyer, "The Rending of the Veil: A Markan Pentecost?" *NTS* 33 (1987) 155-57.

W. J. Moulder, "The Old Testament Background and the Interpretation of Mark x.45," *NTS* 24 (1977) 120-27.

C. F. D. Moule, "Fulfilment Words in the New Testament: Use and Abuse," *NTS* 14 (1967/8) 293-320.

————, "Mark 4:1-20 Yet Once More," in E. E. Ellis and M. Wilcox (eds.), *Neotestamentica et Semitica* (FS M. Black. Edinburgh: T&T Clark, 1969), 95-113.

R. L. Mowery, "Son of God in Roman Imperial Titles and Matthew," *Bib* 83 (2002) 100-110.

H. Must, "A Diatessaric Reading in Luke 2.7," *NTS* 32 (1986) 136-43.

A. Negoita and C. Daniel, "L'Énigme du Levain," *NovT* 9 (1967) 306-14.

J. Neusner, "'First Cleanse the Inside': The 'Halakhic' Background of a Controversy-Saying," *NTS* 22 (1975/6) 486-95.

————, "Money-Changers in the Temple: The Mishnah's Explanation," *NTS* 35 (1989) 287-90.

J. E. and R. R. Newell, "The Parable of the Wicked Tenants," *NovT* 14 (1972) 226-37.

J. H. Neyrey, "The Thematic Use of Isaiah 42.1-4 in Matthew 12," *Bib* 63 (1982) 457-73.

M. Nijman and K. A. Worp, "'ΕΠΙΟΥΣΙΟΣ' in a Documentary Papyrus?" *NovT* 41 (1999) 231-34.

J. Nolland, "The Four (Five) Women and Other Annotations in Matthew's Genealogy," *NTS* 43 (1997) 527-39.

————, "No Son-of-God Christology in Matthew 1:18-25," *JSNT* 62 (1996) 3-12.

————, "A Text-Critical Discussion of Matthew 1:16," *CBQ* 58 (1996) 665-73.

————, "What Kind of Genesis Do We Have in Matt 1.1?" *NTS* 42 (1996) 463-71.

L. Nortjé, "Matthew's Motive for the Composition of the Story of Judas' Suicide in Matthew 27:3-10," *Neot* 28 (1994) 41-51.

G. Ogg, "The Chronology of the Last Supper," in D. E. Nineham et al., *History and Chronology in the New Testament* (London: SPCK, 1965), 75-96.

M. Öhler, "The Expectation of Elijah and the Presence of the Kingdom of God," *JBL* 118 (1999) 461-76.

D. T. Owen-Ball, "Rabbinic Rhetoric and the Tribute Passage," *NovT* 35 (1993) 1-14.

S. H. T. Page, "The Authenticity of the Ransom Logion (Mark 10:45b)," in R. T. France and D. Wenham (eds.), *GP* 1 (Sheffield: JSOT, 1980), 137-61.

L. G. Parkhurst, "Matthew 28.16-20 Reconsidered," *ExpT* 90 (1978/9) 179-80.

P. B. Payne, "The Authenticity of the Parable of the Sower and Its Interpretation," in R. T. France and D. Wenham (eds.), *GP* 1 (Sheffield: JSOT, 1980), 163-207.

————, "The Order of Sowing and Ploughing in the Parable of the Sower," *NTS* 25 (1978/9) 123-29.

S. Pennells, "The Spear Thrust (Mt. 27.49b, *v.l.;* Jn 19.34)," *JSNT* 19 (1983) 99-115.

R. Pesch, "Der Gottessohn im matthäischen Evangelienprolog (Mt 1-2): Beobachtungen zu den Zitationsformeln der Reflexionszitate," *Bib* 48 (1967) 395-420.

W. L. Petersen, "The Parable of the Lost Sheep in the Gospel of Thomas and the Synoptics," *NovT* 23 (1981) 128-47.

J. Pobee, "The Cry of the Centurion — A Cry of Defeat," in E. Bammel (ed.), *Trial,* 91-102.

M. A. Powell, "Do and Keep What Moses Says (Matthew 23:2-7)," *JBL* 114 (1995) 419-35.

———, "The Magi as Kings: An Adventure in Reader-Response Criticism," *CBQ* 62 (2000) 459-80.

———, "The Magi as Wise Men: Re-examining a Basic Supposition," *NTS* 46 (2000) 1-20.

———, "Matthew's Beatitudes: Reversals and Rewards of the Kingdom," *CBQ* 58 (1996) 459-79.

R. Pregeant, "Wisdom Passages in Matthew," in D. R. Bauer and M. A. Powell (eds.), *Treasures,* 197-232.

J. W. Pryor, "John 3.3,5: A Study in the Relation of John's Gospel to the Synoptic Tradition," *JSNT* 41 (1991) 71-95.

E. Puech, "4Q525 et les Péricopes des Béatitudes en Ben Sira et Matthieu," *RB* 98 (1991) 80-106.

L. Y. Rahmani, "Stone Synagogue Chairs: Their Identification, Use and Significance," *IEJ* 40 (1990) 192-214.

M. Rastoin, "Pierre 'fils de la colombe' en Mt 16,17?" *Bib* 83 (2002) 549-55.

B. Reicke, "Synoptic Prophecies on the Destruction of Jerusalem," in D. E. Aune (ed.), *Studies in New Testament and Early Christian Literature* (FS A. P. Wigren. Leiden: Brill, 1972), 121-34.

B. A. Reid, "Violent Endings in Matthew's Parables and Christian Nonviolence," *CBQ* 66 (2004) 237-55.

M. Reiser, "Love of Enemies in the Context of Antiquity," *NTS* 47 (2001) 411-27.

K. H. Rengstorf, "Die Stadt der Mörder (Mt 22.7)," in W. Eltester (ed.), *Judentum, Urchristentum, Kirche* (FS J. Jeremias. Berlin: Töpelmann, 1960), 106-29.

P. Richardson, "Why Turn the Tables? Jesus' Protest in the Temple Precincts," *SBLSP 1992,* 507-23.

R. Riesner, "Das Prätorium des Pilatus," *BK* 41 (1986) 34-37.

B. P. Robinson, "Peter and His Successors: Tradition and Redaction in Matthew 16:17-19," *JSNT* 21 (1984) 85-104.

R. A. Rosenberg, "The 'Star of the Messiah' Reconsidered," *Bib* 53 (1972) 105-9.

J. M. Ross, "Epileptic or Moonstruck?" *BT* 29 (1978) 126-28.

R. Routledge, "Passover and Last Supper," *TynBul* 53 (2002) 203-21.

H. H. Rowley, "Jewish Proselyte Baptism and the Baptism of John," *HUCA* 15 (1940) 313-34; reprinted in his *From Moses to Qumran* (London: Lutterworth, 1963), 211-35.

H. P. Rüger, "'Mit welchem Mass ihr messt, wird euch gemessen werden,'" *ZNW* 60 (1969) 174-82.

M. Sabin, "Reading Mark 4 as Midrash," *JSNT* 45 (1992) 3-26.

E. P. Sanders, "Jesus and the Sinners," *JSNT* 19 (1983) 5-36.

———, "The Overlaps of Mark and Q and the Synoptic Problem," *NTS* 19 (1972/3) 453-65.

J. A. Sanders, "Ναζωραῖος in Matt. 2:23," *JBL* 84 (1965) 169-72.

B. Saunderson, "Gethsemane," *Bib* 70 (1989) 224-33.

L. Schiavo, "The Temptation of Jesus: The Eschatological Battle and the New Ethic of the First Followers of Jesus in Q," *JSNT* 25 (2002) 141-64.

T. E. Schmidt, "Mark 10:29-30; Matthew 19:29: 'Leaves Houses . . . and Region'?" *NTS* 38 (1992) 617-20.

———, "The Penetration of Barriers and the Revelation of Christ in the Gospels," *NovT* 34 (1992) 229-46.

K. Schubert, "Biblical Criticism Criticised: With Reference to the Markan Report of Jesus' Examination before the Sanhedrin," in E. Bammel and C. F. D. Moule (eds.), *Jesus,* 385-402.

G. Schwarz, "Ἰῶτα ἓν ἢ μία κεραία (Matthäus 5.18)," *ZNW* 66 (1975) 268-69.

———, "ΣΥΡΟΦΟΙΝΙΚΙΣΣΑ — ΧΑΝΑΝΑΙΑ (Markus 7.26/Matthäus 15.22)," *NTS* 30 (1984) 626-28.

E. Schweizer, "Matthew's Church," ET in G. N. Stanton (ed.), *Interpretation,* 149-77.

J. M. C. Scott, "Matthew 15.21-28: A Test-Case for Jesus' Manners," *JSNT* 63 (1996) 21-44.

D. Seeley, "Rulership and Service in Mark 10:41-45," *NovT* 35 (1993) 234-50.

P. Seidelin, "Das Jonaszeichen," *ST* 5 (1951) 119-31.

O. F. J. Seitz, "The Future Coming of the Son of Man: Three Midrashic Formulations in the Gospel of Mark," *SE* 6 (1973) 478-94.

M. J. Selvidge, "Mark 5.25-34 and Leviticus 15.19-20," *JBL* 103 (1984) 619-23.

D. Senior, "Between Two Worlds: Gentiles and Jewish Christians in Matthew's Gospel," *CBQ* 61 (1999) 1-23.

D. C. Sim, "The 'Confession' of the Soldiers in Matthew 27:54," *HeyJ* 34 (1993) 401-24.

———, "The Gospel of Matthew and the Gentiles," *JSNT* 57 (1995) 19-48.

———, "Matthew 22.13a and 1 Enoch 10,4a: A Case of Literary Dependence?" *JSNT* 47 (1992) 3-19.

———, "The Meaning of παλιγγενεσία in Matthew 19.28," *JSNT* 50 (1993) 3-12.

H. D. Slingerland, "The Transjordanian Origin of St. Matthew's Gospel," *JSNT* 3 (1979) 18-28.

B. D. Smith, "The More Original Form of the Words of Institution," *ZNW* 83 (1992) 166-86.

C. W. F. Smith, "Fishers of Men: Footnotes on a Gospel Figure," *HTR* 52 (1959) 187-203.

K. R. Snodgrass, "The Parable of the Wicked Husbandmen: Is the Gospel of Thomas Version the Original?" *NTS* 21 (1974/5) 142-44.

S. Sowers, "The Circumstances and Recollection of the Pella Flight," *TZ* 26 (1970) 305-20.

C. D. Stanley, "Who's Afraid of a Thief in the Night?" *NTS* 48 (2002) 468-86.

G. N. Stanton, "5 Ezra and Matthean Christianity," *JTS* 28 (1977) 67-83.

G. H. Stassen, "The Fourteen Triads of the Sermon on the Mount (Matthew 5:21–7:12)," *JBL* 122 (2003) 267-308.

K. Stendahl, "Quis et Unde: An Analysis of Matthew 1–2," in W. Eltester (ed.), *Judentum, Urchristentum, Kirche* (FS J. Jeremias. Berlin: Töpelmann, 1960), 94-105; reprinted in G. N. Stanton, *Interpretation,* 69-80.

W. B. Tatum, "Jesus' So-called Triumphal Entry: On Making an Ass of the Romans," *Forum* 1 (1998) 129-43.

————, "Matthew 2:23 — Wordplay and Misleading Translations," *BT* 27 (1976) 135-38.

J. Taylor, "'The Love of Many Will Grow Cold': Matt. 24:9-13 and the Neronian Persecution," *RB* 96 (1989) 352-57.

J. E. Taylor, "Golgotha: A Reconsideration of the Evidence for the Sites of Jesus' Crucifixion and Burial," *NTS* 44 (1998) 180-203.

B. E. Thiering, "Are the 'Violent Men' False Teachers?" *NovT* 21 (1979) 293-97.

M. E. Thrall, "Elijah and Moses in Mark's Account of the Transfiguration," *NTS* 16 (1969/70) 305-17.

C. C. Torrey, "The Foundry of the Second Temple at Jerusalem," *JBL* 55 (1936) 247-60.

A. Tosato, "Joseph, Being a Just Man (Matt 1:19)," *CBQ* 41 (1979) 547-51.

R. L. Troxel, "Matt 27.51-54 Reconsidered: Its Role in the Passion Narrative, Meaning and Origin," *NTS* 48 (2002) 30-47.

G. H. Twelftree, "Jesus in Jewish Traditions," in D. Wenham (ed.), *GP* 5 (Sheffield: JSOT, 1984), 289-341.

J. Van Bruggen, "The Year of the Death of Herod the Great," in T. Baarda et al. (eds.), *Miscellanea Neotestamentica,* vol. 2 (SNT 48. Leiden: Brill, 1978), 1-15.

P. W. Van der Horst, "Once More: The Translation of *hoi de* in Matthew 28.17," *JSNT* 27 (1986) 27-30.

B. Van Iersel, "The Sun, Moon and Stars of Mark 13,24-25 in a Greco-Roman Reading," *Bib* 77 (1996) 84-92.

B. Vawter, "Divorce and the New Testament," *CBQ* 39 (1977) 528-48.

———, "The Divorce Clauses in Mt 5.32 and 19.9," *CBQ* 16 (1954) 155-67.

D. J. Verseput, "The Role and Meaning of the 'Son of God' Title in Matthew's Gospel," *NTS* 33 (1987) 532-56.

B. T. Viviano, "The High Priest's Servant's Ear," *RB* 96 (1989) 71-80.

———, "The Least in the Kingdom: Matthew 11:11, Its Parallel in Luke 7:28 (Q), and Daniel 4:14," *CBQ* 62 (2000) 41-54.

———, "Social World and Community Leadership: The Case of Matthew 23.1-12, 34," *JSNT* 39 (1990) 3-21.

A. Vögtle, "Das christologische und ekklesiologische Anliegen von Mt 28,18-20," *SE* 2 (1964) 266-94.

———, "Die matthäische Kindheitsgeschichte," in M. Didier (ed.), *Matthieu,* 153-83.

U. C. Von Wahlde, "The Relationships between Pharisees and Chief Priests: Some Observations on the Texts in Matthew, John and Josephus," *NTS* 42 (1996) 506-22.

H. C. Waetjen, "The Genealogy as the Key to the Gospel according to Matthew," *JBL* 95 (1976) 205-30.

R. W. Wall, "Peter, 'Son' of Jonah: The Conversion of Cornelius in the Context of Canon," *JSNT* 29 (1987) 79-90.

K. L. Waters, "Matthew 27:52-53 as Apocalyptic Apostrophe: Temporal-Spatial Collapse in the Gospel of Matthew," *JBL* 122 (2003) 489-515.

D. J. Weaver, "Power and Powerlessness: Matthew's Use of Irony in the Portrayal of Political Leaders," in D. R. Bauer and M. A. Powell (eds.), *Treasures,* 179-96.

K. Weber, "The Image of Sheep and Goats in Matthew 25:31-46," *CBQ* 59 (1997) 657-78.

E. K. Wefald, "The Separate Gentile Mission in Mark: A Narrative Explanation of Markan Geography, the Two Feeding Accounts and Exorcisms," *JSNT* 60 (1995) 3-26.

D. Wenham, "A Note on Matthew 24:10-12," *TynBul* 31 (1980) 155-62.

———, "Paul's Use of the Jesus Tradition: Three Samples," in D. Wenham (ed.), *GP* 5 (Sheffield: JSOT, 1984), 7-37.

———, "The Resurrection Narratives in Matthew's Gospel," *TynBul* 24 (1973) 21-54.

———, "The Structure of Matthew XIII," *NTS* 25 (1978/9) 516-22.

———, "'This Generation Will Not Pass . . .': A Study of Jesus' Future Expectation in Mark 13," in H. H. Rowdon (ed.), *Christ the Lord* (FS D. Guthrie. Leicester: Inter-Varsity Press, 1982), 127-50.

G. J. Wenham, "Marriage and Divorce: An Old Crux Revisited," *JSNT* 22 (1984) 95-107.

———, "The Syntax of Matthew 19.9," *JSNT* 28 (1986) 17-23.

J. W. Wenham, "When Were the Saints Raised? A Note on the Punctuation of Matthew xxvii.51-53," *JTS* 32 (1981) 150-52.

W. J. C. Weren, "The Five Women in Matthew's Genealogy," *CBQ* 59 (1997) 288-305.

————, " 'His Disciples Stole Him Away' (Mt 28,13): A Rival Interpretation of Jesus' Resurrection," in R. Bieringer, V. Koperski, and B. Lataire (eds.), *Resurrection in the New Testament* (FS J. Lambrecht; BETL 165. Leuven: Leuven University Press, 2002), 147-63.

————, "The Use of Isaiah 5,1-7 in the Parable of the Tenants (Mark 12,1-12; Matthew 21,33-46)," *Bib* 79 (1998) 1-26.

K. D. White, "The Parable of the Sower," *JTS* 15 (1964) 300-307.

J. Wilkinson, "The Case of the Epileptic Boy," *ExpT* 79 (1967/8) 39-42.

————, "Leprosy and Leviticus: A Problem of Semantics and Translation," *SJT* 31 (1978) 153-66.

S. M. B. Wilmshurst, "The Historic Present in Matthew's Gospel: A Survey and Analysis Focused on Matthew 13:44," *JSNT* 25 (2003) 269-87.

J. M. Winger, "When Did the Women Visit the Tomb? Sources for Some Temporal Clauses in the Synoptic Gospels," *NTS* 40 (1994) 284-88.

W. Wink, "Beyond Just War and Pacifism: Jesus' Nonviolent Way," *RevExp* 89 (1992) 197-214.

R. E. Winkle, "The Jeremiah Model for Jesus in the Temple," *AUSS* 24 (1986) 155-72.

B. W. Winter, "The Messiah as Tutor: The Meaning of καθηγητής in Matthew 23:10," *TynBul* 42 (1991) 152-57.

B. Witherington, "Matt. 5.32 and 19.9 — Exception or Exceptional Situation?" *NTS* 31 (1985) 571-76.

E. K.-C. Wong, "The Matthaean Understanding of the Sabbath: A Response to G. N. Stanton," *JSNT* 44 (1991) 3-18.

E. M. Yamauchi, "The 'Daily Bread' Motif in Antiquity," *WTJ* 28 (1966) 145-56.

————, "The Episode of the Magi," in J. Vardaman and E. M. Yamauchi (eds.), *Chronos, Kairos, Christos* (FS J. Finegan. Winona Lake: Eisenbrauns, 1989) 15-39.

————, "Magic or Miracle? Diseases, Demons and Exorcisms," in D. Wenham and C. Blomberg (eds.), *GP* 6 (Sheffield: JSOT, 1986), 89-183.

J. Zias and J. H. Charlesworth, "Crucifixion: Archaeology, Jesus and the Dead Sea Scrolls," in J. H. Charlesworth (ed.), *Jesus and the Dead Sea Scrolls* (New York: Doubleday, 1992), 273-89.

J. A. Ziesler, "The Vow of Abstinence: A Note on Mark 14:25 and Parallels," *Colloquium* 5/1 (1972) 12-14.

————, "The Vow of Abstinence Again," *Colloquium* 6/1 (1973) 49-50.

R. Zimmermann, "Das Hochzeitsritual im Jungfrauengleichnis: Sozialgeschichtliche Hintergründe zu Mt 25,1-13," *NTS* 48 (2002) 48-70.

BIBLIOGRAPHY

T. Zöckler, "Light within the Human Person: A Comparison of Matthew 6:22-23 and *Gospel of Thomas* 24," *JBL* 120 (2001) 487-99.

E. Zolli, "Nazarenus Vocabitur," *ZNW* 49 (1958) 135-36.

INTRODUCTION

I have noticed that reviews of biblical commentaries often focus on the introduction rather than undertaking the more demanding task of reading and responding to the commentary itself. Potential reviewers of this commentary who hope to use that convenient shortcut will, I fear, be disappointed. If as a result this book receives only very short or superficial reviews, so be it. Let me explain.

Sixteen years ago I published a wide-ranging study of issues relating to the Gospel of Matthew under the title *Matthew: Evangelist and Teacher.* It covered most of the areas traditionally found in the introduction to a commentary, though at greater length than most commentary series would allow. Scholarship has moved on since then, and new approaches have emerged, but the issues on which today's debates are focused are not significantly different from those I dealt with then. Nor have my views on those issues changed to any significant degree. Those who are so inclined will be able to find places in the present commentary where I do not now express myself quite as I did in 1989. But these are not at a fundamental level, and I am loath to reinvent the wheel by attempting another full introduction in which I would be simply repeating myself. Nor does the present commentary series allow me to expand on such general issues at the sort of length I was able to indulge in a free-standing volume.

I hope, therefore, that a reader who wishes to find a fuller expression of my views set out in terms of general introduction rather than in the exegesis of specific passages will be willing to consult that earlier volume (repr. Carlisle, U.K.: Paternoster, 2007). I will from time to time draw attention to appropriate sections in it. But I hope also that such consultation will seldom be necessary for the purposes of this volume. This is intended to be an exegetical commentary which proceeds from the text outward rather than one which seeks confirmation in the text for a separately formulated position. It is intended for the use of those who are seeking help in understanding and appreciating the text rather than in locating my position within a constantly moving academic debate.

1

The remainder of this introduction therefore does not attempt to cover all the traditional issues normally included, and already discussed in my 1989 book. In particular it attempts no general summary of Matthew's theological perspective; this will emerge as issues arise in specific pericopae.[1] My only purpose here is to draw attention to a small number of broader issues which affect a number of passages and are therefore better introduced by a general summary here, so that I can use notes in the commentary to refer back to these overviews rather than have to repeat the discussion at each relevant point. But in no way are the following paragraphs intended to provide a comprehensive guide to Matthean issues and scholarship.

I. THE STRUCTURE OF MATTHEW

The text of the Gospel of Matthew is not provided with markers to draw attention to a comprehensive outline of sections within which the author intended it to be read. Any proposed outline of the gospel is thus imposed by the interpreter, not dictated by the author, and is therefore open to discussion as to whether it truly represents the intended shape of the narrative. It is not surprising, therefore, that this gospel, like most other NT books, has been analyzed in several different and sometimes contradictory ways. The debate up to the 1980s is well surveyed by D. R. Bauer.[2]

Recent discussion has often focused on the search for formulae which may be taken to mark structural divisions.[3] By far the most prominent is the slightly varying formula which concludes Matthew's five main collections of Jesus' teaching (see below): "And then, when Jesus had come to the end of these sayings . . ." (7:28; 11:1; 13:53; 19:1; 26:1). In each case this formula marks the end of a discourse and the beginning of a new phase of the narrative, but the proposal of B. W. Bacon[4] to use this formula as the basis for dividing the whole gospel into five "books" (which Bacon understood to be

---

1. Most of the second half of my *Matthew: Evangelist* was devoted to themes in Matthean theology, as may be seen from the chapter headings: "Fulfilment" (166-205), "Matthew and Israel" (206-41), "Matthew's Gospel and the Church" (242-78), and "Matthew's Portrait of Jesus" (279-317).

2. D. R. Bauer, *Structure* (1988). See also, more briefly, my *Matthew: Evangelist,* 141-53.

3. The following summary covers only the more widely noted proposals for the structure of the gospel. For other proposals, including those which postulate a "chiastic" structure for the gospel as a whole, see my *Matthew: Evangelist,* 145-49.

4. B. W. Bacon, "The Five Books of Matthew against the Jews," *The Expositor* 15 (1918) 56-66; more fully developed in his *Studies* (1930).

Matthew's deliberately polemical counterpart to the five books of Moses) has not been widely accepted, though it still appears in some more popular accounts of the gospel. The obvious fact that this formula marks the conclusion of the five discourses does not entail that the discourses are themselves the central structural principle of the gospel.

More recent structural schemes have sometimes been based on a different "formula": "From that time Jesus began to . . ." (4:17; 16:21). These words, like the discourse conclusion formula noted above, clearly mark the beginning of a new stage in the story, but a phrase which occurs only twice in the gospel seems a slender basis on which to construct a total framework for the narrative. This is, however, what has been proposed by J. D. Kingsbury and his pupil D. R. Bauer, among others.[5] They thus divide the gospel into three main sections dealing with Jesus' person (1:1–4:16), Jesus' proclamation (4:17–16:20), and Jesus' passion (16:21–28:20). The first two sections do in fact correspond closely to what I shall be proposing below, and the "formula" of 4:17 and 16:21 appropriately marks these two turning points in the narrative. But the long section following 16:21 seems to me to include a number of distinct phases of the story, and contains within it two or possibly three major turning points which Matthew has not marked by the same formula, but which represent significant new stages in the narrative development.

My own approach to the structure of Matthew derives from noting how closely Matthew has adhered in broad terms to the overall narrative pattern of Mark, which, after a brief prologue set in the wilderness (1:1-13), presents Jesus' public ministry in three phases set successively in Galilee, on the journey from Galilee to Judea, and in Jerusalem. In my commentary on Mark[6] I have argued that this represents a conscious structuring of the story within a geographical framework which owes more to Mark's systematization than to the actual movements of Jesus throughout the period after his baptism. The impression Mark gives is that Jesus did not visit Jerusalem at all until the final week of his life, but this conflicts with the far more historically plausible account of John, who has Jesus, like any other religiously observant Galilean, making regular trips between Galilee and Judea, particularly in connection with the major festivals. Moreover, there are elements in Mark's story of Jesus' week in Jerusalem which make it clear that Jesus has in fact been there before.[7] The simplified structure of a single progress from north to south is thus best understood as one devised by Mark for its dramatic

5. J. D. Kingsbury, *Matthew: Structure;* D. R. Bauer, *Structure.* For some others who have noted this formula see my *Matthew: Evangelist,* 151-52. See also below on 4:17.

6. R. T. France, *Mark,* 11-15. See also C. Bryan, *Preface,* 85-125.

7. See p. 767, n. 1.

effect in drawing attention to the hostile reception of the Galilean prophet when he ventures into the "foreign" territory of Judea (see further the next section on Galilee and Jerusalem).

Matthew tells the story in the same way (as indeed does Luke, though with a vastly expanded "travel narrative" from 9:51 to 19:28). Matthew's prologue is more extensive, providing richer material for scripturally based meditation on the origin and nature of the Messiah, but from 4:17 onward Jesus' ministry in Matthew, as in Mark, is set entirely in and around Galilee until Jesus announces his intention to travel south to Jerusalem in 16:21. Like Mark, Matthew offers a substantial body of material, particularly concerned with the reorientation and training of the disciples, on the journey between Galilee and Jerusalem. And Jesus' eventual arrival outside the walls of Jerusalem in 21:1-9 is his first narrated approach to the city within this gospel, even though Matthew, like Mark, will drop a number of hints that Jesus has in fact been there before (see, e.g., on 23:37; 27:57, and the fact that Jesus can apparently depend on already established local supporters in 21:2-3, 17; 26:6, 18). The story from that point to Jesus' resurrection is, as in Mark, entirely set in Jerusalem, though Matthew's expansion of Jesus' teaching in this part of the story has led me to treat the passion narrative which begins at 26:1 as a separate section, even though it is still set in the same location.[8] The one major departure of Matthew from Mark's geographical outline is that at the end of the Jerusalem phase of the story there will be a dramatic return to Galilee (28:16-20), so that the messianic mission is triumphantly relaunched in the place where it had originally begun before the debacle in Jerusalem. Yet even this "innovation" by Matthew only makes explicit what Mark had twice signaled, that the reunion of the disciples with their risen Lord was to take place back in Galilee (Mark 14:28; 16:7).[9]

This geographical outline of the story seems to me a more satisfying basis for discerning its narrative structure than the search for verbal division markers (even though in fact the "formula" of 4:17 and 16:21 fits snugly into it). I have therefore divided the text for commentary purposes into six major divisions. The outline found in the Table of Contents shows those major sections together with the more significant subsections, which in turn are subdivided into shorter pericopae for comment. Among these subsections are the five major discourses, or collections of Jesus' teaching, which are marked out by the concluding formula noted above. I shall say more about the nature and function of these "discourses" later in this introduction.

To read the Gospel of Matthew as a continous narrative, structured

---

8. See below, pp. 767-68, for my reasons for making this division.

9. See below, p. 1097, n. 17, for the suggestion that Mark originally planned, and even perhaps wrote, such an ending to his gospel too.

around the geographical progress of the Messiah from his Galilean homeland to his rejection in Jerusalem, with its final triumphant scene back home in Galilee, is to begin to appreciate its power as a work of literature, not simply as a source for theological or historical data. We should not forget, however, that the term "literature" may be anachronistic, since only a minority of those for whom it was first written would have been able to read: the majority would encounter the gospel as an oral presentation. It is now widely recognized that the Gospel of Mark would have been presented orally, probably at a single session, and its quality as a piece of arresting storytelling is increasingly applauded. Matthew is a much longer and more complex work, including long sections of quite concentrated teaching, and it is less easy to envisage an eager audience drinking in the whole gospel at a single sitting. It may be that sections of the gospel (most obviously the discourses) were designed for separate presentation in an oral context. It is possible, too, that the different phases of the story might lend themselves to presentation as a series of episodes of the one story, in the manner of a modern television serial.[10] But even so, I believe that an attentive audience would have been able to discern the continuity and force of the plot as I have outlined it, and to appreciate the buildup of dramatic tension and of theological challenge which becomes increasingly powerful as the story nears its remarkable end.

II. GALILEE AND JERUSALEM

Modern readers of the NT often know little about the geopolitical world of first-century Palestine. It is commonly assumed that "the Jews" were an undifferentiated community living amicably in the part of the world we now call "the Holy Land," united in their resentment of the political imposition of Roman rule to which all were equally subject. One of the more significant gains of recent NT studies has been the increasing recognition that this is a gross distortion of the historical and cultural reality.[11] In particular it is now widely recognized that Galilee was in the first century, as indeed it had been ever since the death of Solomon, a distinct province with a history, political

10. A. J. P. Garrow, *Revelation,* especially 35-53, has attempted to demonstrate that the (significantly shorter) book of Revelation was designed for oral presentation in six gripping installments. Perhaps something similar might have been attempted (and even intended) for the Gospel of Matthew?

11. The distinctiveness of Galilee was drawn to the attention of readers of the gospels especially by G. Vermes, *Jesus,* 42-57. For a more in-depth presentation see S. Freyne, *Galilee from Alexander to Hadrian;* idem, *Galilee, Jesus and the Gospels;* R. A. Horsley, *Archaeology.*

status, and culture which set it decisively apart from the southern province of Judea, despite the fact that the latter contained the holy city of Jerusalem to which all Jews felt a natural allegiance as the focus of the worship of the God of Israel.

The situation in the time of Jesus may be drastically oversimplified as follows. *Racially* the area of the former Northern Kingdom of Israel had had, ever since the Assyrian conquest in the eighth century B.C., a more mixed population, within which more conservative Jewish areas (like Nazareth and Capernaum) stood in close proximity to largely pagan cities, of which in the first century the new Hellenistic centers of Tiberias and Sepphoris were the chief examples. *Geographically* Galilee was separated from Judea by the non-Jewish territory of Samaria, and from Perea in the southeast by the Hellenistic settlements of Decapolis. *Politically* Galilee had been under separate administration from Judea during almost all its history since the tenth century B.C. (apart from a period of "reunification" under the Maccabees), and in the time of Jesus it was under a (supposedly) native Herodian prince, while Judea and Samaria had since A.D. 6 been under the direct rule of a Roman prefect. *Economically* Galilee offered better agricultural and fishing resources than the more mountainous territory of Judea, making the wealth of some Galileans the envy of their southern neighbors. *Culturally* Judeans despised their northern neighbors as country cousins, their lack of Jewish sophistication being compounded by their greater openness to Hellenistic influence. *Linguistically* Galileans spoke a distinctive form of Aramaic whose slovenly consonants (they dropped their aitches!) were the butt of Judean humor. *Religiously* the Judean opinion was that Galileans were lax in their observance of proper ritual, and the problem was exacerbated by the distance of Galilee from the temple and the theological leadership, which was focused in Jerusalem.

If, as I hope, this is not a complete caricature, it means that even an impeccably Jewish Galilean in first-century Jerusalem was not among his own people; he was as much a foreigner as an Irishman in London or a Texan in New York. His accent would immediately mark him out as "not one of us," and all the communal prejudice of the supposedly superior culture of the capital city would stand against his claim to be heard even as a prophet, let alone as the "Messiah," a title which, as everyone knew, belonged to Judea (cf. John 7:40-42).

To recognize the realities of the situation is to gain new insight into the obstacles facing Jesus *of Nazareth* in gaining acceptance as a credible "Messiah" in the southern province, despite (or even perhaps because of) the enthusiasm he had excited in his own province. We shall note this element in the narrative especially of Jesus' first arrival outside the walls of Jerusalem in 21:1-11, and it will be a constantly underlying element in the subsequent confrontation between the Galilean prophet and the Jerusalem establishment.

It has long been recognized that the geographical framework of Mark's gospel accentuates this north-south divide, and many have argued that there is an ideological, not merely a historical, basis for Mark's decision to tell the story in this way.[12] In Mark Jesus' ministry in Galilee is in general a success story, with enthusiastic crowds, copious miracles, and the open proclamation of the good news; the only mentions of Jerusalem in this part of the story are as the source of opposition and misunderstanding (Mark 3:22; 7:1). But from the moment Jesus, in the far northern area of Caesarea Philippi, turns toward Jerusalem the shadow of the cross falls across the story, and nothing but disaster is expected in Jerusalem. And so it transpires: the southern capital rejects and kills the northern prophet; hope for the future is found not in Jerusalem but in the declaration that the risen Jesus will be restored to his scattered flock back home in Galilee (Mark 14:28; 16:7).

Matthew has not only endorsed this ideological divide by his adoption of Mark's outline for his narrative (see the previous section), but he has also considerably enhanced it. His ch. 2 focuses on the link between the Messiah's birth in Judea and his eventual domicile in Galilee, and the final prophetic motif that "he should be *called* a Nazarene" (2:23) reflects the dismissive tone of a superior Judean observer. Jesus' decision to settle in Capernaum leads Matthew to insert a substantial formula-quotation from Isaiah which identifies "Galilee of the nations" as the place where the true light is to shine (4:13-16). When Jesus arrives at Jerusalem, it is only Matthew who comments on the reaction not only of the accompanying crowds but also of the people of the city (21:10-11), and the two rival "teams" of Galileans and Judeans are seen as starkly opposed in their attitudes to the northern prophet. When Peter, as distinctive a northerner as his master, is unmasked in the high priest's courtyard, it is, Matthew tells us, as a companion of "Jesus *the Galilean*" (26:69). Above all, whereas Mark's story (as we have it) merely looks forward to a new start back in Galilee, Matthew gives flesh to that hope in his magnificent Galilean climax in 28:16-20, and the juxtaposition of the last two pericopae of the gospel forms a poignant contrast between the desperate cover-up maneuvers of the defeated priests in Jerusalem and the triumphant launch of the messianic mission in Galilee. In these ways, distinctive to Matthew's telling of the story, the Marcan Galilee/Jerusalem schema is underlined. To read Matthew in blissful ignorance of first-century Palestinian sociopolitics is to miss his point. This is the story of Jesus *of Nazareth.*

---

12. This was classically argued by E. Lohmeyer, *Galiläa*; R. H. Lightfoot, *Locality*. See also my *Mark,* 11-15, 33-35 and the commentary passim.

III. THE MATTHEAN DISCOURSES

We noted above the prominently repeated formula "And then, when Jesus had come to the end of these sayings . . ." (7:28; 11:1; 13:53; 19:1; 26:1), and in the outline of the structure of the gospel given in the Contents I have marked out the five sections which lead up to this formula as the five "discourses" which are widely recognized as a distinctive feature of Matthew's gospel. Other gospels have substantial sections of teaching and/or dialogue (the latter particularly in the Gospel of John), as indeed Matthew has outside the five marked "discourses" (see, e.g., 11:1-19; 21:28–22:14; ch. 23), but only Matthew draws attention to a group of such collections with a formula which suggests that for him these are the main places to look for the concentrated teaching of Jesus. Moreover, it is relatively easy to discern in each of these sections a coherence of theme which suggests deliberate composition around a particular aspect of Jesus' teaching.

Each discourse is presented as what Jesus said at a particular time in the course of his ministry, and in each case the surrounding narrative portrays a situation to which that particular aspect of teaching is relevant. Those who think of the gospels as chronicles of the events and sayings of Jesus in the order in which they occurred therefore prefer to regard these "discourses" as actual sermons given at one time and place by Jesus in substantially the form in which Matthew has recorded them. But careful study of the gospels (particularly in comparison with each other) soon reveals that simple chronology is not the only or the main basis of their composition, and that the evangelists are authors capable of marshaling their material to form a coherent literary composition rather than simply chronicling events in the order in which they happened. If that is true of the narrative elements of the gospels, it is not unreasonable to expect the same method to be followed in the presentation of Jesus' sayings, and the study of Matthew's five discourses gives good grounds for concluding that they are not so much transcripts of actual sermons as anthologies of the remembered sayings of Jesus organized around some of the central themes of his ministry. This conclusion is strengthened by noting that where the content of these discourses is paralleled in the other Synoptic Gospels, the parallels are widely scattered.[13] As there is no obvious reason for Mark and (especially) Luke to deliberately dismember existing sermons and distribute their contents in other contexts, the natural conclusion is that it is Matthew who has collected related material together from his traditions in order to blend it into coherent discourses.

This conclusion becomes the more probable when it is noted that each

---

13. See, e.g., below, pp. 154-55 for chs. 5–7, p. 370 for ch. 10, and my *Matthew: Evangelist,* 159, 161 for tabulation of the parallels to those two discourses.

of the five discourses has a shorter "parallel" in either Mark or Luke, which forms the basis of the compilation but is expanded by varying amounts of related material found elsewhere. These basic units are as follows:

for Matthew 5–7 (107 verses)   Luke 6:20-49 (30 verses)
    Matthew 10 (38 verses)   Mark 6:7-13 (7 verses)
                                    [and Luke 9:1-6/10:1-12]
    Matthew 13 (50 verses)   Mark 4:3-34 (32 verses)
    Matthew 18 (33 verses)   Mark 9:35-48 (14 verses)
    Matthew 24–25 (94 verses)   Mark 13:5-37 (33 verses)

Each of these shorter units in Mark or Luke has a distinctive theme, and in each case the additional material introduced by Matthew belongs to the same subject area (and in the case of ch. 13 the same literary genre: parables). The longer Matthean discourses are thus apparently the work of a responsible anthologizer who had a wide range of traditional sayings of Jesus at his disposal, and, starting from the basic units of tradition he had received, integrated other related sayings into powerful thematic collections which would then serve as resources for his church as they explored and communicated the key aspects of Jesus' teaching. The generally didactic character of Matthew's gospel prompts the suggestion that "Matthew" was himself an experienced teacher, and that these discourses arise in part from his own way of presenting Jesus' teaching thematically, perhaps to groups of inquirers or catechumens in his local church.

The discourses differ in length and character, depending on the nature of the basic traditional unit around which they are compiled. The longest and most elaborate (chs. 5–7) expands on an existing sermon outline which is found in Luke 6:20-49 in roughly the same sequence and with the same opening and closing motifs, but Matthew's inclusion of three major sections not found as such in the Luke parallel (on fulfilling the law, 5:17-48; on religious observance, 6:1-18; and on material concerns, 6:19-34) produces a different and more systematic structure, though a satisfying outline of the Sermon on the Mount as a whole continues to elude commentators. In ch. 10 the basic element of the mission charge, with its varied form in the Synoptic parallels, is then superseded by more general reflections on the experience of Jesus' disciples in a hostile world. The parable discourse in ch. 13 corresponds to a similar collection in Mark 4, but Matthew has drastically reshaped it by omitting one parable and including six others, and has given to the whole a quasi-symmetrical structure (see below, pp. 500-501) which aids both the teacher and the learner in remembering its contents. Unlike the Sermon on the Mount and the mission discourse, the "discourse" of ch. 13 is modeled on that of Mark 4 in that it does not flow as a single speech but is punctuated by

a number of narrative introductions designating the intended audience, introducing new parables, and commenting on Jesus' parabolic method. The
Marcan basis for the discourse of ch. 18 is itself a collection of apparently independent sayings partly linked by catchwords (Mark 9:35-48). Thereafter,
as in the second and third discourses, Matthew, having started with Mark,
sets off into new territory with a series of separate sayings about the mutual
relationship of disciples. Here too, as in ch. 13, a brief narrative interruption
at v. 21 divides the discourse into two sections, each answering a specific
question asked by the disciples. The final discourse is also in two sections
dealing with different questions, though in this case the two questions are
asked together at the beginning (24:3), so that there is no interruption to the
discourse once begun. For most of ch. 24 Matthew stays fairly close to the
pattern of the Marcan discourse, but with the three parables and the concluding tableau which take up 24:45–25:46 he has massively expanded the account of the "unknown day and hour" which is tackled with tantalizing brevity in Mark 13:32-37.

These general observations will be filled out in the commentary
which follows. What they indicate is not that Matthew set out to create five
parallel discourses with a consistent pattern, but that where the traditional
material he had received provided a suitable basis for collecting other comparable sayings of Jesus he compiled his material in a manner appropriate to
the received unit of teaching and in the light of the narrative setting into
which he had placed it. The concluding formula then marks the end of such a
thematic anthology and returns the reader to the next phase of the narrative
with a deeper understanding of the theological and pastoral issues which will
underlie it.

IV. FULFILLMENT —
THE "FORMULA-QUOTATIONS"

I have argued elsewhere[14] that the central theme of Matthew's gospel is "fulfillment." The opening genealogy is designed to portray the coming of the
Messiah as the climax of the history of God's people, and the remainder of
chs. 1–2 directs the reader's attention to a wide variety of aspects of God's
revelation in the OT which find their fulfillment in the coming of Jesus. The
opening of the book thus sets the tone for Matthew's whole gospel. The UBS
Greek New Testament lists fifty-four direct citations of the OT in Matthew
and a further 262 "allusions and verbal parallels," and that is a conservative

14. R. T. France, *Matthew: Evangelist,* 166-205.

figure based only on the most widely recognized allusions. While not all of these are explicitly concerned with the theme of fulfillment, many are. In addition, we shall note in the commentary many places where Matthew's presentation of the story of Jesus, even without direct verbal allusion, is designed to bring to mind OT people, events, or institutions which may serve as models for understanding the continuity of God's purpose as now supremely focused in the coming of Jesus. This "typological" understanding of OT scripture, which is widely deployed in the NT (notably in the Letter to the Hebrews) finds one of its most enthusiastic exponents in the author of the first gospel.[15] It is thus for Matthew not only the explicitly predictive portions of the OT that can be seen to be "fulfilled" in Jesus, but also its historical characters, its narratives, and its cultic patterns, even the law itself (5:17; 11:13).

Copious quotation of and allusion to the OT is not of course peculiar to Matthew; it is found throughout the NT, some books of which would match and even exceed the statistics given above. But among the gospels Matthew stands out for his sustained and creative presentation of this theme of fulfillment in Jesus. And it comes to its most characteristic expression in the series of so-called "formula-quotations"[16] which are a distinctive feature of this gospel.[17] The introductory "formula" varies slightly, but the first is typical: "All this happened to fulfill what had been declared by the Lord through the prophet, who said . . ." (1:22).[18] Sometimes the prophet is named (but only where it is Isaiah or Jeremiah), and the agency of "the Lord" is more often left to be understood. In one case the formula is conspicuously varied by referring to "the prophets" in the plural and without the concluding "who said" (2:23; see comments there for the reasons for this different formula). But with these variations the formula occurs ten times (1:22; 2:15, 17, 23; 4:14; 8:17; 12:17; 13:35; 21:4; 27:9), and most commentators agree in including an eleventh member in the list at 2:5, where the editorial intention appears to be the same even though the insertion of the quotation into the direct speech of the priests and scribes leads to a modification of the formula (see p. 71). There are other specific quotations, such as 3:3; 11:10; 13:14-15;

15. Examples of Matthew's typological use of OT themes occur throughout the gospel. For some prominent examples see below on 2:1-12, 15; 4:1-11; 12:3-6, 40-42.

16. See my *Matthew: Evangelist,* 171-85, and references there to other scholarship on the subject.

17. The nearest parallel is the formula "that the scripture might be fulfilled," found six times (with variations) in the Gospel of John, though only three of these are, like Matthew's formula-quotations, presented as editorial comments (John 12:38; 19:24, 36), the others being integrated into Jesus' speeches (John 13:18; 15:25; 17:12).

18. For the solemn, formal character of the words used in this formula see on 1:22.

15:7-9; 21:42, which convey the same message of fulfillment, but because this is expressed by means of different introductory formulae they have not traditionally been included in accounts of Matthew's distinctive "formula-quotations"; they are, however, an equally important part of his project to trace in the story of Jesus the fulfillment of what was written in the OT, as are the statements, without reference to specific OT passages, of the necessity for the scriptures to be fulfilled (26:54, 56).

These formula-quotations (with the exception of 2:5-6; see above) are presented as editorial comments on the events being narrated. Some of them draw on what were probably well-known prophetic texts, whose fulfillment in the coming of Jesus would have been widely recognized among Christians (Mic 5:2; Isa 9:1-2; 42:1-4; 53:4; Zech 9:9), but others would not have been on anyone's list of "obvious" messianic proof-texts. One focuses specifically on events in the eighth century B.C. (Isa 7:14); one is simply a reminiscence of the exodus (Hos 11:1); one reflects on the trauma of the Babylonian exile (Jer 31:15); one is not even from the prophets at all but expresses the psalmist's agenda (Ps 78:2); one is an obscure prophecy of Zechariah, drastically reworked and attributed to Jeremiah (Zech 11:13); and one is so elusive that scholars are still debating what text (if any) Matthew is referring to (Matt 2:23). There is obviously something more subtle going on here than the simple claim that messianic predictions have been fulfilled.

We shall consider the bearing of each quotation as we come to it in the commentary. Some depend on apparently superficial points of correspondence, some on a more far-reaching typology. In many cases it is possible to suggest several different levels of significance depending on the degree of scriptural erudition and of shared interpretive assumptions the reader is able to bring to the quotation.[19] "Fulfillment" for Matthew seems to operate at many levels, embracing much more of the pattern of OT history and language than merely its prophetic predictions. It is a matter of tracing lines of correspondence and continuity in God's dealings with his people, discerned in the incidental details of the biblical text as well as in its grand design. Those who have studied the interpretation of Scripture among other Jews at the time, particularly at Qumran and among the rabbis, recognize that they are on familiar ground in Matthew, sometimes in the actual interpretive methods he employs, but also more widely in the creative ways he goes about discovering patterns of fulfillment, ways which modern exegetical scholarship often finds surprising and unpersuasive. But Matthew was not writing for modern exegetical scholars, and we may safely assume that at least some of his intended readers/hearers would have shared his delight in searching for pat-

19. I explored this theme in my article "The Formula-Quotations of Matthew 2 and the Problem of Communication," *NTS* 27 (1980/1) 233-51. See also below, pp. 44-45.

terns of fulfillment not necessarily in what the original authors of the OT texts had in mind but in what can be perceived in their writings with Christian hindsight.

One feature of the formula-quotations (and, to a much lesser extent, of some of Matthew's other scriptural quotations and allusions) that has been the subject of much scholarly interest has been the actual form of text which Matthew cites. Often it does not correspond to the LXX text which is the basis of most of his (and the other NT writers') quotations. Sometimes it looks like an independent rendering of the Hebrew, but often it does not correspond closely to any version of the text now available to us. While it is always possible to postulate variant Greek OT texts available to Matthew but since lost,[20] the prevalence of this textual "freedom" especially in the formula-quotations suggests that Matthew was sometimes willing to modify the wording of the text in order to draw out more clearly for his readers the sense in which he perceived it to have been fulfilled in Jesus. One particular way in which the text was modified was by the combination of two or more related OT texts into a single "quotation," as, for instance, in 2:6; 21:5 and most elaborately in the Zechariah/Jeremiah quotation in 27:9-10. For details of these and other textual variations see the commentary on the individual quotations.

The distinctive features of these formula-quotations have led some scholars to suggest that they came to Matthew as an already collected group, perhaps from some sort of book of "testimonies," OT proof-texts for Christian apologetic. But while some of them would find an appropriate place in such a collection, others, such as Rachel weeping for her children or the elusive prophetic motif that "he should be called a Nazorean" (2:18, 23), could hardly have done so. Such "texts" owe their presence in Matthew's gospel not to any "messianic" significance they possessed in their own right but to his imaginative perception of OT "pre-echoes" of details in the stories of Jesus. They are editorial comments, arising from Matthew's own creative biblical interpretation, on the story he is telling, inviting readers to join the author in his eager search for underlying patterns of fulfillment.

Five of the eleven generally recognized formula-quotations occur within the short section 1:18–2:23, where, together with the genealogy of 1:1-17, they form a concentrated "manifesto" setting out how Jesus the

---

20. Reference will be made in the commentary to the attempt by M. J. J. Menken, *Matthew's Bible,* to attribute all the textual variations to Matthew's use of a "revised LXX" more closely assimilated to the Hebrew. Such a thesis involving a hypothetical lost version cannot be simply proved or falsified, but most interpreters find such a blanket solution unnecessary, and are more prepared to attribute textual variation to Matthew's creative interpretation.

Messiah fulfills the hopes of OT Israel. Indeed, I shall argue that the whole narrative structure of 1:18–2:23 is designed to provide the basis for this scriptural argument, each successive scene of the story building up to the quotation of the text which it "fulfills" and its wording designed to highlight that fulfillment. Yet in several cases (notably Hos 11:1 and Jer 31:15) the text would have no reason to be brought into connection with the story of Jesus apart from the specific content of the incident to which it relates. There is thus a mutual interaction between story and text, the latter being chosen because of its relevance to the event being narrated, but the story being told in terms which draw attention to the correspondence. The same interaction between text and story may be seen especially in 27:3-10 (see below, p. 1039). So it seems that far from being a preexisting set of proof-texts, the OT passages cited in the formula-quotations have been brought freshly to Matthew's mind by the traditions he has received, and that he has then worded those traditional stories in such a way as to help the hearer/reader to see the connection. The formula-quotations are thus not themselves part of Matthew's tradition, but his own editorial gloss on the story of Jesus; their subtle and elusive quality is testimony to the ingenuity of his pervasive midrashic agenda, of which these eleven quotations are but the most prominent and distinctive outcrops.

V. WHO? WHERE? WHEN? HOW?
SOME BROAD PROPOSALS ON THE PROVENANCE
OF THE "GOSPEL OF MATTHEW"

As I explained above, I do not intend to argue again here the traditional issues of authorship, provenance, date, and sources which would normally be found in a commentary Introduction. This final section of the Introduction simply sets out quite baldly the conclusions to which I have come and for which I have argued in detail elsewhere.[21] The reader has a right to be informed of my views on these issues, since at some points they are likely to affect my exegetical choices, but I shall not seek here to persuade anyone to agree with them; those who wish may find my reasons in my earlier book.[22]

---

21. Hence the apparently immodest preponderance of references to my own work in the footnotes to the following section! The views of other scholars are extensively cited and responded to in that fuller study.

22. *Matthew: Evangelist,* chs. 1–3, particularly pp. 50-80 (authorship), 91-122 (place of origin and social and religious setting), 82-91 (date), and 24-49 (sources and composition).

A. AUTHOR

I think that much modern scholarship has too hastily assumed that the gospels circulated for a generation or more without attribution and that the names of proposed authors were rather arbitrarily attached to them some time in the second century.[23] Attribution of this gospel to Matthew the apostle goes back to our earliest surviving patristic testimonies, and there is no evidence that any other author was ever proposed. As far back as we can trace it, and from the earliest manuscript attributions that have survived, it is always the Gospel *kata Matthaion*. It often seems to be assumed that whatever the early church said about the origins of the NT books must be treated with suspicion unless it can be independently proved, but I do not share that assumption.[24] Of course authorship cannot now be proved, and for practical purposes of exegesis it does not matter very much, but the contents and tone of the gospel (including its "love-hate relationship" with Judaism; see below) seem to me to make someone like the apostle Matthew as likely a candidate as any, once it is accepted that the gospel is likely to have been written well within his lifetime (see below).

B. PROVENANCE AND SETTING

The actual geographical location in which the gospel was written remains a matter of debate. I am happy to accept the general consensus that it was somewhere in Syria or Palestine (the latter being generally assumed in patristic accounts), but am less convinced by the confident assertion of some that the specific location was Antioch.[25] Nor does it seem to me important to be able to locate it more precisely.

More important than the precise location is the nature of the community within which and for which the author was writing. Here, too, debate continues vigorously. Most scholars would now[26] agree that the gospel derives from a largely Jewish-Christian community, but there are differing

---

23. Against this assumption see especially M. Hengel, *Studies*, 64-84, and with special reference to Matthew my *Matthew: Evangelist* 50-52.

24. On the complications introduced by Papias's apparent linking of Matthew's authorship of the gospel with the equally strong patristic tradition that it was originally composed in Aramaic (which hardly fits the literary character of the text as we have it), see my *Matthew: Evangelist*, 53-66.

25. This specific suggestion is discussed in my *Matthew: Evangelist*, 92-93.

26. The suggestion that its author was non-Jewish enjoyed quite a vogue during the third quarter of the twentieth century (see my *Matthew: Evangelist*, 102-8), but is now not widely supported.

views both as to (a) how that community was related to non-Christian Judaism, and (b) its aims and expectations with regard to its own mission among Jews and Gentiles.

The former debate has, to my mind, been hindered by the historically dubious assumption that there was a relatively clear point in the latter first century at which the nascent Christian community parted company with non-Christian Judaism; scholars have thus debated whether the Matthean community was still operating (however uneasily) within the structures of Judaism or whether the decisive break had already taken place (the terms *intra muros* and *extra muros* have become traditional). This debate has usually been linked to the supposition that the *Birkat ha-Minim,* the denunciation of "Nazarenes (Christians) and *minim* (heretics)" which was introduced into the regular synagogue liturgy toward the end of the first century, came into use at roughly the same time throughout the Jewish world and at a date which can be fairly precisely determined (usually given as about A.D. 85), so that there is a cut-off point before which Christians were "inside" the synagogue and after which they were "outside." I believe that this scenario is far too simple: evidence for the introduction of the *Birkat ha-Minim* is sketchy, and it is improbable that it could have been universally imposed by some central authority at one time. It is more probable that the separation of Jewish Christians from the synagogue was a gradual process, prompted as much by Christian hostility toward non-Christian Judaism as by any official action on behalf of the synagogue to exclude them, and that the process developed at different rates in different communities. Thus at any time during the middle and latter part of the first century there might be Jewish-Christian groups in more and less amicable relations with their local synagogues. The specific point of "expulsion" in relation to which the situation of the Matthean community has commonly been assessed seems to me more a modern scholarly simplification than a realistic account of the likely pattern of relations between Jews and Christians in the first century.[27]

The debate on the missionary ideology and expectations of Matthew and his church in relation to Jews and Gentiles has gained new strength since my earlier book was written. At that time it was widely agreed that Matthew's church already contained a significant Gentile element and that the continuation of the mission to Gentiles was a clear priority for it. Indeed, D. R. A. Hare had argued[28] that the mission to Jews had already ceased, and that Matthew and his church had turned its back on non-Christian Judaism, so that the "great commission" of 28:19 should be understood as relating to

27. This argument is developed in my *Matthew: Evangelist,* 98-102 (and cf. also ibid., 85-86).

28. D. R. A. Hare, *Theme* (1967); cf. further below on 28:19.

16

"all the *Gentiles*" to the exclusion of Jews (this specific proposal was, how-ever, not widely shared). More recently, however, the significance of the Gentile mission for Matthew's church has been called in question by a num-ber of interpreters[29] who give greater weight to the handful of "anti-Gentile" comments in the gospel (5:46-47; 6:7-8, 31-32; 18:17) than to the expecta-tion of the extension of God's purpose outside Israel which most readers have taken to represent Matthew's essential perspective. They have thus un-derstood Matthew's church to be not only still comfortably within the bounds of Judaism but also content to stay there and to regard the adherence of Gentiles as at best a peripheral option. This recent trend, which of course co-heres well with the currently fashionable attempt to reclaim the historical Je-sus for Judaism and to play down the extent of his challenge to scribal tradi-tion, seems to me to be no less one-sided in its reading of the evidence than the curiously opposite position earlier advocated by Hare. I suspect that a commentary written in twenty years' time would not feel obliged to give it so much attention. I shall take up the issue exegetically at several points in the gospel, especially in relation to the thoroughgoing presentation of this read-ing of Matthew by David Sim.[30]

My own understanding of the situation of Matthew and his commu-nity locates the gospel in a period of uncomfortable tension, which may have been experienced at any point during the middle and latter parts of the first century depending on the way relations with the synagogue had developed in their particular local community. Interpreters regularly comment on the ap-parently incompatible elements within this one gospel of a deeply rooted Jewishness and pride in their OT heritage alongside a sharp antipathy to the Jewish establishment and a conviction that the future of the kingdom of heaven lies not in the institutions of Judaism but in a newly constituted peo-ple of God focused not on national origin but on allegiance to Jesus the Mes-siah. Elements of continuity and of discontinuity are equally prominent in Matthew's theology of "fulfillment." Such a gospel seems to me to be better explained not by a theory of incompetent editing of conflicting sources but by the existential situation of the author and his Jewish-Christian community. They have come to recognize in Jesus the true Messiah of Israel, and enthusi-astically search the OT scriptures for indications of how God's purposes for his people have come to their culmination in the prophet of Nazareth. But they have also recognized that the new covenant he has established is no lon-ger limited to the descendants of Abraham, and most probably already in-

29. Notably J. A. Overman, *Gospel* (1990); A. J. Saldarini, *Community* (1994); D. C. Sim, *Gospel* (1998).

30. See, e.g., p. 467, n. 5, p. 694, n. 16, p. 816, n. 38, p. 908, n. 43, p. 114, n. 30, p. 1119, n. 47.

clude Gentiles within their membership. They are thus inevitably becoming an increasingly distinct community from that of the synagogue, which has not recognized Jesus as Messiah. As Jewish Christians (who might today be referred to as "messianic Jews") they are both "inside" and "outside" that community, and that ambivalent relationship seems to me closely reflected in the love-hate relationship with "Judaism" which we find in this gospel. If it seems to speak with two voices, that is because its situation and its ideology contain these two apparently competing strands. But I believe that the "contradictions" of Matthew's gospel arise primarily in the minds of interpreters who do not appreciate the distinction he makes between, on the one hand, the values and ideals which derive from OT Israel and its scriptures and, on the other hand, the (in his view failing and obsolete) institutions of the current Jewish community with its scribal establishment and its ideological focus on the temple and its rituals. Matthew portrays a new community which is both faithful to its scriptural heritage and open to the new directions demanded by Jesus' proclamation of the kingdom of heaven, and therefore necessarily expanding beyond the bounds of the Jewish people. His contribution to an integrated Christian theology of salvation and of the people of God is thus similar to that of the Letter to the Hebrews, but with the added dimension of an explicit recognition that, as Paul puts it in Rom 4, Abraham is now the father of many nations.[31]

C. DATE

The current majority view that Matthew's gospel was written in the fourth quarter of the first century depends mainly on three arguments: (a) that its setting reflects the period of final separation between the church and the synagogue, probably around A.D. 85, (b) that it is written in the light of the experience of the Roman capture of Jerusalem and destruction of the temple in A.D. 70, and (c) that it is dependent on the gospel of Mark, which some scholars also date after A.D. 70, others shortly before.

I have expressed my scepticism on the first point in the previous section. The second depends on the assumption that neither Jesus nor Matthew would have foreseen the events of the Roman war, so that the destruction of the temple could be mentioned only after the event — though the substantial body of scholars who date Mark before A.D. 70 have clearly found this argument unpersuasive, and Matthew's language about the fate of the temple is not significantly more precise than that of Mark (see also below on 22:7 for

---

31. For Matthew's theology of Israel and the people of God see further my *Matthew: Evangelist*, ch. 6, especially 223-41.

the burning of the city, and p. 913 on the difficulty of identifying Matthew's "devastating pollution" in the light of known historical events). Moreover, there are a number of passages in the gospel which presuppose that the temple is still standing (see below on 5:23-24; 17:24-27; 23:16-22), and while it is of course possible that Matthew has preserved such sayings even after they have ceased to be applicable, in at least one case this would have been to risk significant misunderstanding by post-70 readers (see below p. 668, n. 15).

Probably the most influential reason for dating Matthew toward the end of the century is not a specific argument from the text of Matthew itself but a presumed order of composition of the gospels combined with a relative dating scheme which is widely adopted in current scholarship, but which has few if any fixed points. I shall comment briefly on the literary relations of the Synoptic Gospels in the next section. As for the wider dating scheme, I believe there are sound reasons for questioning the consensus, and for exploring an alternative scheme which takes its cue from the lack of reference in the book of Acts to any events later than A.D. 62, even though the Neronian persecution in Rome in A.D. 64/5 had such major implications for the church in Rome and was the probable cause of the death of both Peter and Paul, the two key figures of the book. In my commentary on Mark[32] I have noted the patristic tradition that Mark's gospel was written while Peter was still alive, that is, not later than the early sixties. While there is probably an element of guesswork in such traditions, such a dating would tie in with the proposal[33] that the main period of the writing of the Synoptic Gospels was in the sixties (a period when, incidentally, it is more likely that the apostle Matthew would still be active than in the fourth quarter of the century). A pre-70 date for Matthew remains a minority view, but one which has been strongly supported,[34] and which is usually dismissed not so much by specific arguments as on the basis of a preferred overall dating scheme. The issue is not of great exegetical importance for most of the gospel, but it does clearly affect one's assessment of the anti-temple theme which is such a prominent emphasis in Matthew. In the commentary that follows I shall favor the possibility that the gospel was, as Irenaeus declared, written in the sixties, while the temple was still standing.

32. R. T. France, *Mark,* 36-39.

33. See, e.g., J. A. T. Robinson, *Redating,* 86-117, developing the much earlier argument of A. von Harnack, *The Date of Acts and the Synoptic Gospels* (ET 1911).

34. Gundry, 599-609, has assembled an impressive range of arguments to this effect. While some of them depend on specific points of exegesis which are questionable, I am not aware that the argument as a whole has been seriously answered. John Nolland tells me that his new commentary will cautiously incline to this view, though I have not yet seen his arguments. For some other supporters of a pre-70 date see my *Matthew: Evangelist,* 82-91.

D. RELATION TO MARK AND LUKE

The literary relationship between the first three gospels which has come to be known as the "Synoptic Problem" is much more complex even than the questions of authorship, provenance, and date, and the intensification of the debate since the 1970s means that it would be foolish to attempt even an overview here. The most striking feature of the debate for our purposes has been the revival on the part of a vocal minority of scholars of the view held almost without exception by the church until the middle of the nineteenth century, that Matthew was the earliest gospel to be written. For more than a century after that it became the almost unquestioned scholarly consensus that Mark came first and that Matthew and Luke drew on Mark and on other shared tradition conveniently labeled "Q" and often supposed to have been a single lost document to which they both had access. But now everything seems, in the view of some scholars, to be up for grabs again. All I can do here is to state baldly my own approach to explaining the complicated literary relationship,[35] and to give some indication of how it may have affected my presentation of exegetical issues within the commentary.

Recent debate has to my mind made it impossible to claim that the simple "two-document hypothesis" is a total solution to the problem. The data have proved to be too complex and multifaceted for that. On the other hand, I am unable to explain how the Gospel of Mark could be written by someone who had the much fuller Gospel of Matthew in front of him; he would have had to omit, for instance, the whole of the Sermon on the Mount and yet find space for considerable and rather inconsequential expansion of the narrative detail in many of the stories of Jesus' ministry. To suggest that Mark was uninterested in what Jesus had to teach is simply untrue.[36] The remarkable "omissions" in his gospel, therefore, make much better sense if he did not have Matthew (and Luke), or the materials they used, in front of him. In other words, I continue to believe in the priority of Mark. But to conclude that Mark did not use Matthew does not necessarily lead to the view that Matthew "used" Mark, in the sense that he sat with a copy of Mark's gospel in front of him and consciously "edited" it by alteration, addition, and omission. The simple x-copied-y approach to the Synoptic Problem which has characterized many of the proposed "solutions" seems to me more appropriate to a modern scholar's study than to the real world of first-century church

---

35. See my *Matthew: Evangelist,* 24-46, for both a survey of the discussion up to the mid-eighties and a more nuanced presentation of my own view with arguments in its favor.

36. I have argued this in an article entitled "Mark and the Teaching of Jesus," *GP* 1:101-36.

tradition. I incline to the view promoted by E. P. Sanders[37] and developed by J. A. T. Robinson,[38] that neat theories of literary dependence (even complex ones like that of Boismard)[39] are unlikely to do justice to the varied data of the Synoptic texts, and that we should think rather of a more fluid process of mutual influence between the various centers of Christian gospel writing as people traveled around the empire and visited and consulted with one another. In such a scenario the Synoptic Gospels may better be seen as at least partially parallel developments of the common traditions, rather than placed in a simple line of "dependence." (This possibility would also cohere well with the proposal noted above that all three Synoptic Gospels reached their final form within a relatively short period — the sixties — rather than over some twenty years or more, as has been more commonly proposed.)

Within such a flexible process I would regard Mark as the earliest of the surviving compilations, but this does not necessarily mean that at every point Mark's version of a saying or event must be the "original" from which the others are "deviations." The most obvious point at which Mark has, on this view, provided a formative influence is in the overall narrative structure of his gospel, which, as we have noted above, is taken up and expanded by Matthew, and, rather less closely, by Luke. If, as I believe,[40] Mark's narrative structure with a single journey of Jesus from north to south is an artificial construction rather than a reflection of the likely geographical pattern of Jesus' total ministry (as perhaps more faithfully reflected in the Gospel of John), it is improbable that two or three writers independently made the same literary decision. To that extent Mark must be understood to be the foundation gospel among the three, but that is far from demanding that we assume that in the detailed contents of the gospel Matthew is always simply copying and/or editing Mark's text in the final form in which we know it. And as for a unitary document "Q," I am among the growing number of scholars who find it an improbably simple hypothesis; I am happy to talk about "Q tradition"

---

37. E.g., E. P. Sanders, *Tendencies,* 278-79; *NTS* 19 (1972/3) 464-65. For these and other indications of Sanders's view see my *Matthew: Evangelist,* 42-45. Note also the account of the Synoptic Problem given in E. P. Sanders and M. Davies, *Studying,* 51-119, especially the section entitled "In Favour of Complicated Solutions" (97-100).

38. J. A. T. Robinson, *Redating,* 92-117.

39. See P. Benoit and M. Boismard, *Synopse des quatres évangiles en français,* Tome II (Paris: Le Cerf, 1972). The diagram setting out Boismard's theory consists of a first row containing four (hypothetical) documents, A, B, C, Q, a second row containing intermediate editions of each of the four gospels, and a third row containing the final texts of the four gospels; arrows indicating dependence crisscross the diagram, so that each gospel depends on two or more of the intermediate gospels, and each intermediate gospel on at least two of the sources (two of them also on other intermediate gospels).

40. See above, pp. 3-4, and my *Mark,* 11-15.

(which may have been oral or written, and not necessarily all gathered into a single source), but not about Matthew "editing Q" if by that is meant making alterations to a supposedly fixed text (which is in any case not available to us). And I am afraid that the even more esoteric and hypothetical debates about "the Q community" or "recensions of Q" leave me cold.

Given this understanding of the Synoptic Problem, I am more reluctant than many other interpreters to speak simply of how Matthew has "redacted" Mark's material or to attempt in Q material to discern how Matthew has "adapted" the common tradition. I regard the Marcan and Lucan parallels as other witnesses to the traditions Matthew had available, but not necessarily as his direct sources. Where he differs from them, it may be because he is deliberately altering the tradition as they have recorded it, but it may also be because he has received the tradition in a rather different form. This commentary will therefore call attention to differences between the Synoptic accounts where they help to highlight the distinctive contribution of Matthew, but without always assuming direct dependence and therefore deliberate alteration of an already formulated tradition. The results may in many cases be quite similar to what would have been reached by a more rigid x-copied-y approach, but they are likely to be more cautiously expressed.

The Gospel of
MATTHEW

Text, Exposition, and Notes

I. INTRODUCING THE MESSIAH (1:1–4:11)

The prominent repetition of the title "Messiah" (or, in many English versions, "Christ") in 1:1, 16, 17, 18; 2:4, together with the other related titles which recur in these opening paragraphs of the gospel ("Son of David," 1:1, 20; "King of the Jews," 2:2), make it clear that Matthew is aiming to present an account not just of a historical figure (Jesus of Nazareth) but of the long-awaited deliverer of God's people Israel. He will begin to tell the story of the Messiah's revelation to Israel, and of the way people responded to his coming, in 4:17, where Jesus' public proclamation in Galilee begins. That public appearance, together with Matthew's introductory comment on why it must be in Galilee that the light dawns (4:12-16), will thus introduce the first main phase of the story, which will run right through to the end of the Galilean ministry in ch. 16.

But before we reach that point, Matthew will devote a lengthy preamble to introducing this Messiah. Using a number of different but related approaches, he will weave in 1:1–4:11 a rich tapestry of scenes and reflections which together help the reader to appreciate how in the coming of Jesus of Nazareth all God's purposes for his people, declared and illustrated throughout the writings of the OT and the history of Israel, are coming to their destined fulfillment. While these chapters will contain a variety of narrative elements about the events preceding and following Jesus' birth and about his personal preparation for his mission, they are presented not simply as biographical information, but as pointers, in the light of Scripture, to the theological significance of the story which Matthew is about to relate.

Sometimes the appeal to Scripture is overt, as in the five quotations which form the structural basis of 1:18–2:23 and in the biblically derived list of names which precedes those opening scenes. More often, however, the testimony of Scripture is woven into the way the stories are told, so that their significance depends on the ability of the reader to recognize allusions to biblical events and persons and to draw the appropriate conclusions. In the commentary that follows I shall try to explain this allusive material and to draw attention to the biblical passages which underlie the telling of the story. Clearly the author of this gospel knew the OT scriptures very well indeed, in their more obscure details as well as in their more prominent features, and felt that he could assume at least a reasonable scriptural background in his readers, though we may wonder whether the majority of them would have been able to pick up every detailed nuance without assistance. Most of those who heard Matthew's stories would have been illiterate, and even those who could read would not have had ready access to scrolls of the individual OT books. Even in our day, when printed texts of the whole OT are readily available, it may be doubted whether most readers of Matthew know the texts well enough to follow all the subtleties of his arguments from Scripture. But "to those who have, more will be given," and perhaps in Matthew's day his text was not simply left to do its work alone, but would have been the basis for theological instruction within the church, as teachers and taught delighted to trace the scriptural background to what may appear on the surface to be deceptively simple accounts of the family background and early experiences of Jesus of Nazareth. It will be the aim of this commentary to facilitate something of the same biblical exploration as we work through Matthew's introductory chapters.

The headings of the sections into which I have divided these chapters (see Contents, pp. vii-viii) indicate my understanding of how the various parts of this introduction relate to one another and together build up to a rounded portrayal of the Messiah as not only Son of David but also Son of God (an issue which will be raised again explicitly in 22:41-46). Further comment on the special contribution which each section makes to our understanding of Jesus of Nazareth as Israel's Messiah will be given in the introduction to each division of the text.

A. THE "BOOK OF ORIGIN" OF THE MESSIAH (1:1-17)

1 *The book of origin[1] of Jesus the Messiah, the son of David, the son of Abraham.*

1. Βίβλος γενέσεως occurs in LXX Gen 2:4 for the "account of the origin" of the heavens and the earth and in LXX Gen 5:1 for the "list of the descendants" of Adam. The phrase occurs nowhere else in the LXX. Its use here deliberately echoes the opening chapters of Genesis.

26

2 *Abraham[2] was the father of[3] Isaac, and Isaac was the father of Jacob, and Jacob was the father of Judah and his brothers, 3 and Judah was the father of Perez and Zerah by Tamar, and Perez was the father of Hezron, and Hezron was the father of Ram, 4 and Ram was the father of Amminadab, and Amminadab was the father of Nahshon, and Nahshon was the father of Salmon, 5 and Salmon was the father of Boaz by Rahab, and Boaz was the father of Obed by Ruth, and Obed was the father of Jesse, 6 and Jesse was the father of King David.*

David was the father of Solomon by the wife of Uriah, 7 and Solomon was the father of Rehoboam, and Rehoboam was the father of Abijah, and Abijah was the father of Asaph, 8 and Asaph[4] was the father of Jehoshaphat, and Jehoshaphat was the father of Joram, and Joram was the father of Uzziah, 9 and Uzziah was the father of Jotham, and Jotham was the father of Ahaz, and Ahaz was the father of Hezekiah, 10 and Hezekiah was the father of Manasseh, and Manasseh was the father of Amos, and Amos[5] was the father of Josiah, 11 and Josiah was the father of Jeconiah[6] and his brothers at the time of the exile to Babylon.

2. Matthew's list normally uses the LXX form of the OT names (though these vary among LXX manuscripts); the more familiar English forms, reflecting the Hebrew, are used in this translation for those names (down to Zerubbabel) which are known to us from the OT, except for Asa and Amon (see following notes).

3. Matthew's verb, γεννάω (which echoes the terminology of several OT genealogies, such as Ruth 4:18-22), is properly used of the male role in procreation, though in a formal genealogy its repetition apparently allows a less immediate relationship, including a gap of three generations in v. 8. See further the discussion below of how far this is meant to be a record of biological descent, and how far of official (royal) status.

4. The textual evidence strongly indicates that Matthew used the form Ἀσάφ in both vv. 7 and 8. While there is no historical reason to associate Asaph the psalmist with King Asa, Matthew (or his source) may have found the similarity of name suggestive.

5. As with Ἀσάφ in vv. 7-8, the textual evidence indicates that Matthew used the form Ἀμώς here, thus recalling the name of the prophet rather than Manasseh's undistinguished son Amon, even though of course there is no historical link. Several LXX MSS use the form Ἀμώς for the king, but this is likely to be due to the influence of Matthew.

6. Matthew follows the LXX in giving the name Ἰεχονίας, which sometimes occurs in the OT (Jer 24:1 etc.; also in the abbreviated form Coniah, Jer 22:24 etc.) as an alternative name for Jehoiachin, son of Jehoiakim; it was probably his given name, Jehoiachin being a throne name. The form Jeconiah occurs in both the Hebrew and LXX of the genealogy in 1 Chr 3:16-17, which was probably Matthew's source. The LXX fails to distinguish between Jehoiakim (whom Matthew omits from his list) and Jehoiachin, using Ἰωακιμ for both; Ἰεχονίας is thus the only distinguishable LXX name for this king. Some later MSS and versions (Θ Σ f[1] etc.) have added Jehoiakim's name between Josiah and Jeconiah.

12 *After the exile to Babylon Jeconiah was the father of Shealtiel, and Shealtiel was the father of Zerubbabel, 13 and Zerubbabel was the father of Abiud, and Abiud was the father of Eliakim, and Eliakim was the father of Azor, 14 and Azor was the father of Zadok, and Zadok was the father of Achim, and Achim was the father of Eliud, 15 and Eliud was the father of Eleazar, and Eleazar was the father of Matthan, and Matthan was the father of Jacob, 16 and Jacob was the father of Joseph the husband of Mary who was the mother of[7] Jesus who is called the Messiah.*

17 *So there were fourteen generations in all from Abraham until David, and fourteen generations from David until the exile to Babylon, and fourteen generations from the exile to Babylon until the Messiah.*

The first two words of Matthew's gospel are literally "book of genesis" (see n. 1 above).[8] The effect on a Jewish reader is comparable to that of John's opening phrase, "In the beginning. . . ." The theme of the fulfillment of Scripture is signaled from the very start, and these opening words suggest that a new creation is now taking place. That particular concept of fulfillment is not clearly developed elsewhere in the gospel, which is concerned rather with how Jesus brings the history of God's people to its climax, but this passing echo of the beginning of the world's history adds a further allusive dimension for those who wish to think it through, perhaps particularly in the light of the creative act of God which will result in Jesus' birth.[9]

---

7. This translation aims to preserve Matthew's careful distinction between the male relationship expressed in each of the preceding generations and Jesus' birth from Mary, *not* from Joseph. The feminine pronoun, ἐξ ἧς, makes the point more directly than the ungendered English relative would convey, and the passive form of γεννάω, conspicuously breaking the pattern of the list so far, indicates a different type of "generation"; the ἐκ picks up the formula used for the four mothers mentioned in vv. 3-6. All MSS and versions agree in making it explicit that Joseph was not Jesus' father, with the one exception of sy^s, which reads "Joseph, to whom was betrothed Mary the virgin, begot Jesus." The fact that this version mentions Mary as "betrothed" to Joseph and as "virgin" shows that the translator/scribe was aware of the story that follows, and his use of the verb "beget" for Joseph is therefore more likely due to unthinking repetition of the set formula than to a deliberate desire to assert Joseph's physical fatherhood; see B. M. Metzger, *Textual Commentary*, 2-7. The Greek text is not in doubt, the most significant variation being the reading of some OL and a few Greek MSS, ᾧ μνηστευθεῖσα παρθένος Μαριὰμ ἐγέννησεν Ἰησοῦν . . . , a patent attempt to underline further the supernatural conception of Jesus. This variant is close to the wording of sy^s, and may have been its source. See further J. Nolland, *CBQ* 58 (1996) 665-73.

8. See Davies & Allison, 1:151, for evidence that by the first century A.D. the Greek title Γένεσις was already in use for the first book of Moses.

9. W. D. Davies, *Setting*, 67-73, finds the theme of a new creation hinted at not

Matthew's "book of origin" is in effect a survey of the history of the people of God from its very beginning with Abraham, the ancestor of Israel, to the coming of the Messiah, the "son of David." He emphasizes the completeness of this history by setting it out in three balancing periods of fourteen generations each,[10] and the fact that it is only with difficulty that the actual history can be made to fit into this pattern indicates that for the author this is not so much a statistical observation as a theological reflection on the working out of God's purpose for his people. It shows that the period of preparation is now complete, and that the stage is set for the dawning of the time of fulfillment in the coming of the promised Messiah.

That Matthew's three fourteens are not simply a matter of historical observation is indicated by the imbalance between the three periods in terms of the actual historical time-scale involved. While there is debate about the possible date of Abraham, he is likely to have been at least seven or eight hundred years before David, which, even given the reported longevity of the patriarchs, is a lot to cover in fourteen generations. From David to the exile is about four hundred years, and, as we shall see, even that relatively modest period has been fitted into fourteen generations only by the omission of four members of the dynastic succession. From the exile to the birth of Jesus is a further six hundred years, so that Matthew's thirteen names for that whole period (compared with Luke's twenty-two for the same period) again give improbably long "generations." It seems then that Matthew's list, like some other biblical genealogies, is selective, and that the scheme of three fourteens is doing something other than recording statistical data.

The effect of the division into three sets of fourteen generations is to highlight the two turning points in the time of David and the exile. The specific mention that David was "King" (v. 6) indicates the significance of these divisions, as the central section of the list runs from the foundation of the united monarchy of Israel under David to the final dissolution of the monarchy of Judah at the time of the Babylonian exile. David and Jehoiachin thus represent the first and last kings of the dynasty of Judah (Zedekiah, Jehoiachin's uncle, 2 Kgs 24:17, being treated as an irrelevant appendix while the true king was in exile in Babylon), whose historical throne succession makes up the central section of the genealogical list. Matthew thus signals that this is a royal list, with the probable implication

---

only in the opening phrase but throughout ch. 1. J. Nolland, *NTS* 42 (1996) 463-71, is more sceptical, and finds the relevance of Matthew's use of γένεσις in 1:1, 18 in the genealogy which the two uses frame (as in the immediate sense of the term in Gen 5:1) rather than in any allusion to the book of Genesis or to a new creation.

10. Cf. the observation in *m. 'Abot* 5:2 that there were ten generations from Adam to Noah and ten generations from Noah to Abraham. For Matthew's fondness for balancing structures, and particularly for groups of three, see my *Matthew: Evangelist,* 130-32.

that the throne succession has continued while the actual monarchy has been in eclipse, until it reaches the destined "son of David" in the birth of the Messiah from this royal line. We shall see how this focus is maintained in v. 20 below.

In order to keep the number of generations between David and Jehoiachin to fourteen, Matthew has had to omit five of the actual kings recorded in the OT history: he goes straight from Joram to Uzziah, omitting the three generations of Ahaziah, Joash, and Amaziah (together with the usurping queen-mother Athaliah), and the brothers Jehoahaz and Jehoiakim are omitted between Josiah and Jehoiachin. It is possible to explain the former omission as an error resulting from the fact that the names of Ahaziah and Azariah (Uzziah) might be confused in Greek,[11] and the latter also by the similarity of the names of Jehoiakim and Jehoiachin (which LXX does not differentiate; see n. 6 above), while Jehoahaz as Jehoiakim's brother who reigned only three months does not represent a separate "generation." But to explain the number "fourteen" in the middle section as therefore the result of two happy accidents[12] also ignores the fact that even so the three groups are not equally balanced: the first group has fourteen names if both Abraham and David are included, the second has fourteen if David is not included again, but after Jehoiachin there are only twelve names down to Joseph, so that even with the addition of Mary's son there are only thirteen generations in the third group unless Jehoiachin, unlike David, is counted twice.[13]

If therefore Matthew's observation in v. 17 is not based on simple

11. Ὀζίας, the name used by Matthew after that of Joram, is the LXX version of the Hebrew name Uzziah, while the same king's alternative name Azariah is represented by Ἀζαρια. The name of Joram's actual son Ahaziah appears in the LXX as Οχοζια, which might be misread as Ὀζίας, and does in fact appear as such in some LXX MSS. M. D. Johnson, *Genealogies,* 181-82, argues from the LXX textual confusion that the omission of the three kings was originally accidental, but that then "the accident was turned into virtue" and Matthew's scheme of fourteens was the result.

12. The suggestion that Matthew omitted certain kings for ideological reasons, such as their being bad kings (so, e.g., M. D. Goulder, *Midrash,* 229), hardly fits the fact that Joash is excluded even though his reign began with a religious purge (2 Kgs 11:17-18) and was marked by a significant refurbishment of the temple (2 Kgs 12:4-16), while the notorious Manasseh has retained his place in the list. Even less probable is the view that the omission was motivated by the curse on the house of Ahab (1 Kgs 21:20-22), which was believed to have affected also the royal house of Judah via Athaliah, daughter of Ahab and mother of Ahaziah, to the fourth generation.

13. H. C. Waetjen, *JBL* 95 (1976) 209-15, suggests that "Jesus the Christ . . . represents both the thirteenth and the fourteenth generations in the third section of the genealogy" (214). This suggestion, deriving from K. Stendahl, is discussed by M. D. Johnson, *Genealogies,* 221-23.

mathematics, is there some special significance which he sees in the number "fourteen" which has made it worth his while to adjust the generations to fit into this symmetrical structure?[14]

It is often suggested that this is an example of *gematria,* the Jewish interpretive technique which depended on the numerical value of Hebrew letters: the name "David" (the fourteenth name in the list) consists of three Hebrew consonants, DWD, the numerical value of which are respectively four, six, and four, giving a total of fourteen; fourteen is thus the symbolic number of David. For a reader of Matthew's Greek gospel to recognize any such numerical symbolism would have to depend on quite a sophisticated awareness of Hebrew numerology. There is certainly evidence for *gematria* in Jewish and early Christian writings, sometimes involving Hebrew letters, sometimes Greek,[15] but usually it is signaled by an explicit link drawn between the letters and their numerical value. Matthew has made no such explicit connection, and it can be at best a matter of conjecture whether he intended or would have recognized it.[16]

If there is deliberate symbolism in the choice of fourteen, it is perhaps better perceived in the fact that fourteen is twice seven,[17] and seven is well known in the Bible as a significant number, deriving from the seven days of creation and occurring especially in connection with predetermined historical periods (e.g., Gen 41:2-7, 26-30; Dan 9:24-27), notably in the organization of history into several (though probably not seven, *pace* some commentators!) series of seven events in Revelation. Three fourteens is six sevens, and a sequence of six sevens points to the coming of the seventh seven, the

---

14. For a survey of suggestions see M. D. Johnson, *Genealogies,* 189-208.

15. The clearest NT example is the number "666" in Rev 13:18, one favored interpretation of which is that it represents the sum of the numerical value of the letters of the Greek name *Neron Caesar* when written in Hebrew letters. *Barn.* 9:8 finds a reference to Jesus and the cross in the three Greek letters which represent the 318 soldiers of Abraham (Gen 14:14). For some early Jewish examples see, e.g., *m. 'Uq.* 3:12; *Sib. Or.* 5:12-42 (the latter identifying the successive Roman emperors by the Greek numerical value of their initial letters). The practice became more widespread in later Jewish literature.

16. For an unusually positive account of this theory see Davies and Allison, 1:163-65.

17. The use of forty-two months (fourteen times three) for a determined period in the apocalyptic scheme in Rev 13:5 testifies to the symbolic attraction of multiples of seven, but is not easy to relate thematically to Matthew's scheme (M. J. Moreton, *SE* 2 [1964] 224). Even less promising is the vision of the dark and light waters in *2 Bar.* 53–74, which does indeed present an apocalyptic scheme in fourteen stages, but the numeral which is explicitly emphasized is not fourteen but the *twelve* (53:6, 11; 69:1) contrasting periods which are enumerated in chs. 56–68 before the (unnumbered) final phase. H. J. Waetjen, *JBL* 95 (1976) 210-13, favors the *Baruch* scheme as a background to Matthew's interest in fourteen.

climax of history when the ongoing purpose of God for his people from the time of Abraham reaches its culmination.[18]

But again, if this is what Matthew meant he has not said it explicitly, and the fact that he divides Israel's history into three fourteens rather than six sevens makes any such inference doubtful. Perhaps it is more likely that his focus on the number "fourteen" derives from his observation that there were in fact fourteen names in the genealogical list from Abraham to David as recorded in the OT, and his realization that a little adjustment of the king list would allow him to produce a symmetrical pattern with the period of the monarchy highlighted as its central phase. In that case the theological focus of Matthew's "book of origin" is not so much on the number "fourteen" itself as on the royal dimension which his symmetrical structure has brought to light by tracing the line of succession which finds its culmination in the coming of Jesus, the "son of David," and thus potentially in the restoration of the monarchy.[19]

To recognize Matthew's genealogy as essentially a dynastic document may give some clue as to why it differs so radically from the one provided by Luke 3:23-38. Quite apart from the structural differences that Luke goes in the reverse direction, has no subdivision into sections, and goes all the way back to "Adam, son of God," the actual names recorded coincide only from Abraham to David, with minor variations; between David and Joseph the only coincidence is of the two names Shealtiel and Zerubbabel, and Luke contains substantially more names. Both lists are presented explicitly as the genealogy of Joseph, even though his father's name differs between them, so that the popular explanation[20] that Luke's is in fact the genealogy of Mary (and thus the real biological genealogy of Jesus) runs aground on Luke's explicit wording (cf. also Luke 1:27) as well as on the fact that ancient Jewish genealogies were not traced through the mother — as opposed to the occasional mention of mothers within a patrilineal genealogy (see below on vv. 3-6). It is of course often argued that the explanation is simply that either Matthew or Luke (or more probably both) has simply invented names, with Zerubbabel son of Shealtiel coincidentally coming to both their minds as a well-known figure of the postexilic resettlement (Ezra 3:2ff.; Hag 1:1ff., etc.). But genealogy was too valued a pursuit in the Jewish world to make such a cavalier attitude plausible, and there is good evidence that genealogies

18. Cf. the "seventy weeks" of Dan 9:24-27 within which sixty-two weeks precede the coming of the "anointed one" to bring in the final week; also the seven "weeks" of *1 En.* 93:3-10.

19. Davies and Allison, 1:166, draw attention to *m. 'Abot* 5:1-6 as a parallel "manipulation of numbers for edifying ends," producing in that case nine sequences of ten.

20. This suggestion seems to have originated with Annius of Viterbo, c. A.D. 1500.

were carefully preserved and available for consultation (see below on vv. 12-16). Is it possible, then, that Matthew and Luke have offered two different types of "genealogy"? Matthew's, as we have seen, is focused on the royal line; Luke's is traced not through Solomon, David's royal successor, but through another son, Nathan. Might Luke then be giving us an actual (or at least claimed) "family tree" of biological parentage, while Matthew traces the throne succession of the actual and, after the exile, putative kings of Judah? Such a suggestion at least has the merit of taking seriously the perceived focus of Matthew's list, but it is of course totally incapable of proof. It must face the question how a biological and a dynastic line could run separately through different sons of David and yet converge briefly at Shealtiel, diverge again after Zerubbabel, and reconverge on Joseph the (actual) son of Eli and (dynastic) son of Jacob. Again, this is not inherently impossible, as royal lines can sometimes differ from strict parental succession where, for instance, a royal figure is childless or the eldest son proves unsuitable so that succession passes to a brother or nephew or some less immediately related member of the wider family.[21] But while such indirect successions do occur,[22] this can never be more than speculation in a given instance where all we have available is two unadorned lists of names.

The "book of orgin" thus holds many puzzles, both as to its intended scope and as to how Matthew has arrived at his list of names and its pattern. But its main aim is clear enough: to locate Jesus within the story of God's people, as its intended climax, and to do it with a special focus on the Davidic monarchy as the proper context for a theological understanding of the role of the person to whom Matthew, more than the other gospel writers, will delight to refer not only as "Messiah" but also more specifically as "Son of David."[23]

1   The opening verse is concerned with the "origin" (genesis) of the

---

21. A further factor in the Jewish context is the possibility of levirate marriage. Eusebius, *Hist. eccl.* 1.7, quotes at length a letter of Julius Africanus (early third century) explaining the discrepancy between the two genealogies on this basis, making Jacob and Eli stepbrothers; when Eli died childless, Jacob fathered Joseph as his (Eli's) legal son. Africanus claims to base his information on the carefully preserved genealogical traditions of "the human relatives of the Savior."

22. The OT provides ample illustration of this: even in Matthew's own list Solomon was not the "obvious" choice, and the succession after Josiah was not direct; see also below on v. 12, concerning the parentage of Zerubbabel.

23. For the purpose and methods of Jewish genealogies in general see the comprehensive survey in M. D. Johnson, *Genealogies*. His summary of the purpose of the OT genealogies, pp. 77-82, shows how they served especially "apologetic purposes, both nationalistic and theological. As such, a kind of midrashic exegesis could be utilized to construct genealogies that communicated the convictions of the author" (81). His book goes on to show how Matthew's genealogy fits this pattern.

Messiah, and thus serves primarily to introduce the pedigree which follows in vv. 2-17 (as will be indicated by the repetition of its key terms, Jesus, Messiah, David, and Abraham, in the concluding v. 17). The same word "genesis" will be repeated in v. 18, where Matthew will explain (in vv. 18-25) how the family line of Joseph, "son of David," is relevant to Jesus, who was not in fact Joseph's biological son, as Matthew will already have made plain at the end of the genealogy itself in v. 16. There is therefore a sense in which v. 1 introduces not only 1:1-17 but also at least the immediately following section concerning the "son of David" (vv. 18-25), and perhaps more fully the whole account of Jesus' family background which will make up 1:18–2:23. Some commentators go further and see it as the heading for the whole introductory section (1:1–4:11)[24] or even for the whole gospel, but this is to put too much weight on the term "book" rather than on the combined phrase "book of origin" which in LXX Gen 5:1 introduces the list of Adam's descendants. It is true that in LXX Gen 2:4 the same phrase sums up[25] not a list of names but the account of the origins of the earth, but there too it denotes only the immediately contiguous paragraphs, not the whole book which is to follow.[26]

The name "Jesus" will be explained theologically in v. 21. As the Greek form of the OT name Joshua it was among the commonest Jewish names in the first century,[27] so that a distinguishing title such as "of Nazareth" was needed. Here, however, Matthew uses a title which describes not the human background of this Jesus, but his theological status, "Messiah."[28] While some NT usage suggests the beginning of the tendency for "Christ" to become a sort of "surname" for Jesus of Nazareth, as it is in most modern usage, for Matthew it was clearly much more, as its repetition in vv. 16, 17, 18; 2:4 makes clear, and as is indicated here immediately by the addition of "son of David, son of Abraham." The colorless translation "Jesus Christ" here and in v. 18 in many English versions does not do justice to the excitement in

24. So D. R. Bauer, in D. R. Bauer and M. A. Powell (eds.), *Treasures,* 138-39. Bauer surveys other proposals for the function of 1:1 (ibid., 133-37).

25. Or introduces, depending on whether Gen 2:4a is construed as the closure to Gen 1:1–2:3 or as the introduction to 2:4b-25.

26. R. E. Brown, *Birth,* 583-85, surveys various views on the extent of the "book."

27. The NT mentions four other Jesuses in addition to the OT Joshua (Matt 27:16-17; Luke 3:29; Acts 13:6; Col 4:11). Four of the twelve high priests during the first century A.D. were called Jesus. Of the named characters who appear in the narrative of Josephus's *Life* (allowing for some uncertainty over whether in some cases he refers to the same or a different person) the commonest names are Jesus (4-6), Simon (3-5), Levi (4), Jonathan (3), and Herod (3). In Josephus as a whole A. E. Harvey, *Jesus,* 80, finds 21 Jesuses (sixteen of them in the first century A.D.), as compared with eighteen Josephs and eleven Johns.

28. Matthew's use of Χριστός, and its importance for his theology, is helpfully surveyed by R. E. Menninger, *Israel,* 82-85.

Matthew's introduction of Jesus under the powerfully evocative title "Messiah," the long-awaited deliverer of God's people, in whom their history has now come to its climax. In v. 16 he will draw attention to the titular force of *Christos* by using the phrase "Jesus *who is called* the Messiah."

David will play a central role in the genealogy (see vv. 6, 17, and comments above on the fourteen generations), and "Son of David" will recur several times in the gospel as a title indicating Jesus' messianic role (9:27; 12:23; 15:22; 20:30-31; 21:9, 15; 22:41-45). While the earliest use of the actual phrase in this sense in surviving literature is in *Pss. Sol.* 17:21, there is no reason to doubt its popular use by the time of Jesus in the way Matthew indicates, reflecting the abundant OT testimony to a Davidic hope based on the promise of 2 Sam 7:12-16. "Son of Abraham" locates David and his successor within the fuller history of the chosen people, but it is possible that in including this title Matthew also has in mind that Abraham was not merely the ancestor of Israel but also the ancestor of "a multitude of nations" (Gen 17:4-5) and the one through whom "all the families of the earth" were to be blessed (Gen 12:3; see comments on vv. 2-6).[29]

2-6a   These verses cover the first period from Abraham to David. While much of the data could have been derived from Genesis and the subsequent historical accounts, the names after Jacob are conveniently brought together in 1 Chr 2:1-15 and Ruth 4:18-22, and Matthew has followed that summary tradition. It is likely that those lists, like some other biblical genealogies, are deliberately selective, since the number of generations listed is hardly enough to cover seven or eight hundred years; if Gen 49:12 is compared with Num 1:7, it appears that Hezron, Ram, and Amminadab between them cover the whole period from the patriarchal arrival in Egypt to the exodus, which the OT records put at some four hundred years.

A few additions are made to the simple pattern "x was the father of y."[30] The mention of Judah's brothers in v. 2 reflects a natural Jewish interest in the twelve patriarchs from whom the Israelite tribes were named, even though inevitably only one of them can have a place in the genealogy.[31] Perez's twin brother Zerah is included because of the well-known story of the

29. B. Charette, *Recompense,* 66-72, explores more fully the significance of "son of Abraham" in Matthew as a whole, with special reference to 3:7-10 and 8:11-12.

30. J. Nolland, *NTS* 43 (1997) 527-39, draws attention to several "annotations" in Matthew's genealogy, and argues that the inclusion of the four mothers (see below), often treated as a subject on its own, should be understood as part of this larger pattern of annotations which are designed to "evoke the highs and lows" (533) of the story of God's dealings with his people which the genealogy encompasses. He is thus more sceptical than most of a single common feature uniting the four women.

31. M. D. Johnson, *Genealogies,* 151-52, suggests that the aim is to recall the unity of the twelve tribes, "the wholeness of Israel."

circumstances of their birth (Gen 38) and because they are also mentioned together in 1 Chr 2:4. That same record also mentions their mother, since it was not through the legitimate sons of Judah's wife, the daughter of Shua (who are listed first in 1 Chr 2:3), that the royal line would be derived, but from his irregular liaison with his daughter-in-law, Tamar. Tamar's contribution to the royal line is also specially mentioned in Ruth 4:12.

Tamar is the first of four mothers included in vv. 3-6. To mention a mother in the course of a biblical genealogy was not unprecedented: fourteen mothers are mentioned in 1 Chr 2 alone. As we have seen, Tamar comes to Matthew already in the 1 Chronicles genealogy, and one of Matthew's other women, the unnamed mother of Solomon, also appears in her due place in the OT list in 1 Chr 3:5.[32] Tamar and the wife of Uriah therefore came to Matthew already included in the 1 Chronicles lists, and the genealogy at the end of the book of Ruth is placed there to record how her role contributed to the growth of the royal house. Thus only Rahab, as the mother of Boaz, does not derive directly from Matthew's OT sources. But even so, the fact that Matthew includes four mothers in this first part of the list and none thereafter may suggest that he had a special reason to do so.

The only other person called Rahab in the OT is the prostitute of Jericho (Josh 2:1-21), but her date at the time of the Israelite conquest places her at least a century too early to be the wife of David's great-grandfather unless the genealogy is incomplete at that point, nor is there anything in the OT to connect her with the family of Boaz, whose story presupposes a family well settled in Canaan, not a new arrival. However, Matthew's mention of her without further identification suggests that he expected her name to be familiar to his readers, and so it is generally assumed (and it can be no more than an assumption)[33] that despite the chronological problem he had Rahab of Jericho in mind.

In that case, the four mothers included in the list certainly make a strikingly unconventional group to find within the pedigree of the Messiah of

32. Intriguingly, but perhaps coincidentally, she has in Hebrew (not LXX) the same name as Judah's wife, Bath-shua, daughter of Shua, rather than her more familiar name Bathsheba (2 Sam 11:3 etc.).

33. R. E. Brown, *Bib* 63 (1982) 79-80, argues for Rahab of Jericho on the grounds that Matthew is unlikely to have included a biblically unknown person; there must then be a gap in the genealogy, presumably between Salmon and Boaz, in order to cover the long period between the original conquest when Rahab lived and David's immediate ancestors. So also R. J. Bauckham, *NovT* 37 (1995) 322. For the possibility that rabbinic tradition connected Rahab with the tribe of Judah (which she joined as a proselyte) see M. D. Johnson, *Genealogies,* 162-65. R. J. Bauckham, *NovT* 37 (1995) 322-29, provides a midrashic explanation of her marriage to Salmon based on the recurrence of the name Salma in 1 Chr 2:11, 51, 54.

Israel, in that probably all four of them were non-Israelite (Tamar and Rahab were Canaanites,[34] Ruth a Moabite, and Bathsheba the wife of a Hittite). Moreover, their stories do not fit comfortably into traditional patterns of sexual morality. Tamar's seduction of her father-in-law, Rahab's prostitution, and Bathsheba's adultery are all explicit in the OT (and Matthew's phrase "the wife of Uriah" rather than giving Bathsheba's name makes the point rather obviously), and while Ruth 3–4 records without moral censure how her marriage to Boaz was arranged, the euphemistic language recounting the events at the threshing floor leaves many modern interpreters uneasy. It is therefore customarily asserted that in including these four "embarrassing" mothers Matthew may have intended to prepare his readers for the Messiah's "disreputable" origin in a pregnancy before marriage (1:18-25),[35] though the force of this suggestion is weakened by the fact that embarrassment over their sexual activities is primarily a modern phenomenon: in Jewish tradition Tamar, Rahab, and Ruth were regarded as heroines, and it is David rather than Bathsheba who is stigmatized for their adultery.[36] More appropriate to Matthew's own context is the view that the four "foreign" women prepare the reader for the coming of non-Israelites to follow Israel's Messiah[37] which will be foreshadowed in the homage of the magi in 2:1-12 and will be a recurrent and increasing theme throughout the gospel until it reaches its climax in the mission to all nations in 28:19 (and which was appropriate to the story of a son of Abraham; see on the previous verse). But if this was Matthew's

---

34. R. J. Bauckham, *NovT* 37 (1995) 314-20, rightly points out that, despite the assumptions of most commentators, Tamar is not actually said in Gen 38 to be a Canaanite; he shows that *Jub.* 41:1 and *T. Jud.* 10:1 provide her with an ancestry from Terah's son Nahor, but traces other Jewish speculations about her ancestry which conflict with this, especially Philo's view that she was a proselyte, which was perhaps more prevalent in Matthew's time. Cf. J. Nolland, *NTS* 43 (1997) 535, n. 26.

35. See especially E. D. Freed, *JSNT* 29 (1987) 3-19. There are already in the NT hints that Jesus faced accusations of illegitimate birth (John 8:41), and this became a feature of anti-Christian polemic in rabbinic Judaism as recorded by Origen, *Cels.* 1.32; for the rabbinic traditions of Jesus as "ben Pantera" and related names see, e.g., G. H. Twelftree, *GP* 5:318-19. See further R. E. Brown, *Birth,* 534-42.

36. For the generally positive treatment of these four women in Jewish tradition see M. D. Johnson, *Genealogies,* 159-75. He notes, however (pp. 176-79), that there were countercurrents, and argues that there was already controversy within Judaism concerning the purity of David's ancestry, with the Pharisees defending the reputation of these four women; Matthew is, then, deliberately supporting the Pharisaic view in order to legitimate Jesus' ancestry in the eyes of the now dominant strand of Judaism.

37. This implication is most clearly appropriate to Ruth, a foreigner who deliberately opted to follow Israel's God (Ruth 1:16-17), and whose integration into not only the people of Israel but into what was to become its royal house is the main point of her story as told in Scripture.

intention, he gives us no overt indication of it, so that, as with the significance of "fourteen," we cannot go beyond conjecture.[38]

6b-11   For this second period of the OT history Matthew is on very familiar ground, as he follows the royal dynasty of Judah from David to the exile. The historical data are set out in detail in the two books of Kings, and the throne succession is conveniently summarized in 1 Chr 3:10-17 (including the specific identification of Jeconiah as "the captive," which may have triggered Matthew's mention here of the exile). We have commented above on the omission of three kings between Joram and Uzziah. In v. 11 the addition of "and his brothers" alerts us not, as in v. 2, to a famous group who belong together in Israel's historical consciousness, but rather to the abbreviated nature of Matthew's account at this point, in that the succession from Josiah to Jehoiachin and on to Shealtiel simplifies a more complex story of succession involving, according to 2 Kgs 23:30–24:20, three brothers (Jehoahaz, Jehoiakim, and Zedekiah) who all ruled for a time but are omitted from Matthew's list. Only one of the three, Jehoiakim, strictly belongs in a father-to-son dynastic list, and we have commented on his omission above. According to 2 Kings the three omitted rulers were not Jehoiachin's brothers, but his father and uncles, but 2 Chr 36:10 (cf. also 1 Chr 3:16) says that Zedekiah was Jehoiachin's "brother" (though LXX has "father's brother"), while LXX 4 Kgdms 24:17 makes him the "son" of the exiled king, whom it calls by the same name as his father, "Ioakim"; see p. 27, n. 6, for the confusion of the names Jehoiakim and Jehoiachin. Matthew may, of course, have in mind here not "brothers" in the strict sense but a wider range of the relatives of Jehoiachin who would be among the seven thousand "men of valor" taken with him to Babylon.[39]

12-16   In the third section of his genealogy Matthew traces the throne succession after the exile. But whereas the OT has provided all the names in the preceding sections of the list, he now has no biblical source for most of the names he records. Jer 22:30 speaks of Jehoiachin as "childless," but this is

---

38. D. R. Bauer, in D. R. Bauer and M. A. Powell (eds.), *Treasures,* 149-50, suggests that the link between Mary and the four women lies not so much in sexual irregularity as in that "they were all relatively powerless, marginalized and in need of help." W. J. C. Weren, *CBQ* 59 (1997) 288-305, offers the more positive proposal that the OT stories of these women reveal that "Israel's history would have been cut short prematurely had these women not seen it as their task to map out alternative pathways to the future" (290). M. D. Johnson, *Genealogies,* 152-79, discusses at length the various views as to why Matthew included the four women.

39. D. R. Bauer, in D. R. Bauer and M. A. Powell (eds.), *Treasures,* 144-46, argues that the two references to "brothers" in vv. 2 and 11 are designed to make the reader think of the whole people of Israel in its original potential and its historical failure which led to the exile.

with reference to anyone who will "sit on the throne of David"; that it is not literal is indicated by the mention of Jehoiachin's "offspring" in Jer 22:28. Matthew follows 1 Chr 3:17 in giving Shealtiel as Jehoiachin's son, but according to the same source Zerubbabel was Shealtiel's nephew, not his son (though LXX has him as his son). See above for the possibility of a royal line going through a nephew rather than a son; in all other OT references Zerubbabel is described as the son of Shealtiel. His importance as the focus of the hopes of the returned exiles (note especially Hag 2:20-23) testifies to his quasi-royal status, even though the monarchy was not in fact restored.

After Zerubbabel Matthew does not trace the royal line through any of the seven sons of Zerubbabel listed in 1 Chr 3:19-20, and we have no information on his source for any of the subsequent names. Given the Jewish interest in genealogy in general and in the family of David in particular,[40] it is likely that the tradition of a throne succession would be preserved; Julius Africanus reported that Herod had destroyed Jewish family archives (including those of the [Davidic] family of Ruth) to prevent challenges to his own mixed pedigree (Eusebius, *Hist. eccl.* 1.7.13). Patristic writers assume that Matthew had access to such a source (Eusebius, *Hist. eccl.* 1.7.11, 14), but we cannot now trace it.[41] While most of the names between Zerubbabel and Joseph conform to familiar Jewish types of name, there is no reason to link any of the individuals listed with anyone who is known to us from other sources.

Joseph as the name of Jesus' human father is firmly established in the Christian tradition (Luke 1:27; 2:4, 16; 3:23; 4:22; John 1:45; 6:42), even though he plays no part in any of the gospel stories beyond the infancy narratives. In Luke he is a minor figure, but in Matthew's account it will be Joseph, as the legal father, who is the lead player in the stories of 1:18–2:23. By introducing him here as the "husband of Mary" rather than the father of Jesus Matthew prepares for the explanation of Jesus' actual parentage in 1:18-25. Mary will be named again in 1:18, 20; 2:11; 13:55, while in 2:13, 14, 20, 21;

---

40. For Roman persecution directed specifically against descendants of David (which presupposes that there were records of their genealogies) as "the royal house of the Jews," see Eusebius, *Hist. eccl.* 3.12.1; 3.19.1; 3.20.1-5; 3.32.3-4.

41. For the possibility of such records being kept see R. E. Brown, *Birth,* 87-88. Josephus can confidently refer those who question his own pedigree to the public records (*Life* 6; cf. *C. Ap.* 1.31 for publicly available archives containing priestly genealogies, part of a fuller account of Jewish genealogical concern, *C. Ap.* 1.28-36). Cf. *m. Qidd.* 4:4. For full discussion see J. Jeremias, *Jerusalem,* 275-90. Jeremias emphasizes that lay as well as priestly families kept written genealogical records; he applies his results to the NT genealogies (ibid., 290-97). M. D. Johnson, *Genealogies,* 99-108, discusses Jeremias's arguments, and is less convinced of the existence of comprehensive written records, though he suggests that genealogical traditions might be transmitted orally for several generations.

12:46 she will appear simply as Jesus' mother. No indication of her family background is given, nor is her experience related for its own sake as in Luke 1:26-56; 21:19, 33-35, 51. Her significance in Matthew's story is purely as Jesus' mother.

The genealogy reaches its intended goal with the mention of the birth of "Jesus who is called Messiah." In some contexts *legomenos* may suggest doubt ("so-called"), as when Pilate uses it in 27:17,[42] but it is also used without a pejorative sense for the title given to a person with a common name in order to distinguish him from namesakes (10:2; Col 4:11). For the significance of the title Matthew has chosen see above on v. 1.

17 For the significance of Matthew's balanced division of Israel's history, and for some suggestions as to why he singles out the number "fourteen" for emphasis, see the discussion above of 1:1-17 as a whole.

B. A DEMONSTRATION THAT JESUS OF NAZARETH IS THE MESSIAH: FIVE SCRIPTURAL PROOFS (1:18–2:23)

These thirty-one verses are one of Matthew's most distinctive contributions to the Christian story. Their narrative content is largely unparalleled in the other gospels (see below for the limited area of overlap with Luke), and in any case narrative is not their main focus, but rather a series of quite creative and sophisticated arguments to show how in the coming of Jesus a wide range of scriptural material finds its destined fulfillment. If the "formula-quotations" are one of the most distinctive features of this gospel (see above, pp. 11-14), then it is surely significant that five of them (nearly half of the total) occur in these thirty-one verses alone. Their function here is not merely that of incidental editorial comment; rather, these quotations form one of the key structural principles of the whole section. Each of the five scenes into which the narrative divides focuses on one of the formula-quotations, in such a way that it seems that the incident is narrated for the purpose of demonstrating the fulfillment of Scripture. In other words, Matthew's gospel contains different stories concerning the infancy of Jesus not only or mainly because Matthew had access to different traditions, but rather because he was mounting a carefully constructed argument from Scripture, and it is these particular incidents which enable him to present it.

Moreover, we shall see that the argument from Scripture which comes so clearly to the surface in these five quotations also runs much more deeply through this part of the gospel, as narrative echoes of other biblical scenes and language are woven together into a complex web of scriptural foreshad-

42. Cf. Josephus's use of the same phrase to describe Jesus in *Ant.* 20.200.

owing which has all found its fulfillment in the coming of the Messiah. Thus, in addition to the themes explicit in the five formula-quotations, we shall be invited to consider Jesus as the new Moses, the new Israel, the new Solomon (son of David), the "star out of Jacob," and perhaps other typological[1] and prophetic themes, while the remarkable concentration in these verses of angelic revelations and of guidance through dreams will alert us to the way God is directing events toward the fulfillment of his purpose.

That purpose, as 1:1-17 has already informed us, is the coming of Israel's Messiah, the son of David. It is Matthew's task in these verses to explain how that Messiah may be recognized in the person of Jesus of Nazareth. It is a necessary and potentially a difficult task, since on the face of it "Jesus of Nazareth" is a most unlikely candidate for the role of Messiah. There is, first, the problem that "the carpenter's son" from an obscure Galilean village who is known by the name of his mother Mary (13:55) does not look like a "son of David." The "book of origin" has provided a foundation for answering this objection, but has left us tantalizingly short of a full answer by pointing out that Jesus was not in fact the son (in the natural sense) of Joseph, the heir to the Davidic dynasty; this issue will be tackled first in 1:18-25.

But then there is also the problem of his geographical origins. Everyone knew that the Messiah, son of David, must come from Bethlehem, the city of David, as the prophets had foretold, but Jesus came from Nazareth, not only an obscure village with no royal connections, but also located in Galilee, which, as John 8:41-52 reminds us, was no place for a Messiah to come from.[2] This will be the apologetic problem which Matthew will tackle in ch. 2, as he traces the geographical movements of the newborn Jesus, who was indeed born in Bethlehem, but was not brought up there because his father Joseph, under the combined influence of royal hostility and divine guidance, took him first to Egypt, then back to Judea, only to find that that was no place to bring up his child, so that he moved north to Galilee and eventually settled in Nazareth. Each stage of this geographical progress is directed by dreams and angelic visions, and each is marked by a quotation from Scripture which includes a place name and is designed to show how each successive movement has been foretold in the OT. The argument thus reaches its climax in the triumphant conclusion that it was not an apologetic embarrassment but rather a prophetic requirement "that he should be called a Nazarene," and that God has successfully steered the whole course of events to that destined conclusion.

These thirty-one verses are therefore essentially an exercise in

1. For the nature of "typology" in the gospels, see my *Jesus and the OT,* 38-43.
2. See above, pp. 5-7, for the significance in Matthew of the contrast between Judea and Galilee.

apologetics.[3] Their aim is to enable Matthew's readers to recognize in the unlikely person of Jesus of Nazareth the Messiah, son of David. 1:18-25 (together with the "book of origin" which is its basis) deals with the issue of parentage, and ch. 2 with that of place of origin. This observation was made in a celebrated article in 1960 by Krister Stendahl under the title "Quis et Unde?" (who and from where?). Stendahl therefore divides chs. 1–2 into two sections answering two apologetic questions, "Quis?" in ch. 1 and "Unde?" in ch. 2. My subdivision of these chapters is made rather on the basis of the different literary character of 1:1-17 from the "five scenes" with their formula- quotations which make up the rest of chs. 1–2, but this in no way invalidates Stendahl's perception of the issues involved; there is a clear change of focus in the argument from the beginning of ch. 2, just as there is a clear continuity between 1:1-17 and 1:18-25.

The fact that Matthew has so clear an apologetic agenda leads many interpreters to question how much historical value may be attributed to these chapters. This question is raised for several different reasons: (1) the contrast with the corresponding chapters in Luke; (2) the lack of independent historical verification for the events involving Herod; (3) the central role of the scriptural quotations, which leads some to conclude that the stories have been created out of the cited texts; (4) the more obtrusively supernatural element in these chapters with their angels and dreams and the guiding star, and of course the physiological and genetic "impossibility" of a virginal conception.[4] I devoted an article to exploring these issues some years ago,[5] and hope that readers looking for a fuller discussion may be willing to consult that article. The following comments are therefore brief.

1. Matthew agrees with Luke on the basic elements: a betrothed couple called Mary and Joseph, the latter of Davidic descent; conception through the Holy Spirit without human intercourse; angelic revelation of the name Jesus;

3. J. H. Neyrey, *Honor,* 94-99, examines chs. 1–2 from the point of view of the rhetoric of encomium, and shows how Matthew aims here to establish the "honor" of Jesus by an account of his origins, both geographical and familial.

4. A full discussion of the historicity of the virginal conception of Jesus would go beyond the scope of a commentary on Matthew. The reader is referred to a brief and sensitive discussion with a primary focus on the gospel accounts in R. E. Brown, *Birth,* 517-33 (including bibliography), based on his fuller study in *The Virginal Conception and Bodily Resurrection of Jesus.* In the second edition of *Birth,* 697-712, Brown responds to critical assessments of his earlier study, particularly within Catholic scholarship. More recently Keener, 83-86, provides a helpful summary of the discussion. From the point of view of NT exegesis one must at least conclude that the tradition of a virginal conception came independently to both Matthew and Luke; wherever it may have originated, it was not simply in Matthew's imagination.

5. "Scripture, Tradition and History in the Infancy Narratives of Matthew," *GP* 2:239-66.

birth in Bethlehem in the reign of Herod; upbringing in Nazareth. Beyond this essential story line the accounts simply do not overlap, Luke focusing on the experiences of Mary, and Matthew (except in 2:1-12) on those of Joseph. Within the area of overlap, however, there is a discrepancy in that while Luke's story begins in Nazareth, with the birth in Bethlehem taking place on a census visit, Matthew's account of the move to Nazareth (2:22-23) betrays no awareness that this was previously the family home. The events of Matt 2:1-21 (including the events in Bethlehem, the escape to Egypt and return, and Herod's death) clearly cannot be fitted into the period between Jesus' birth and the account in Luke 2:22, 39 of the family's return to Nazareth after the presentation in the temple (when Jesus would be forty days old). Each writer is apparently unaware of the other's data, and their accounts can be harmonized chronologically only by assuming that Luke presents a simplified version of a more complex series of events, of which he was presumably unaware.

2. It is not clear why we should expect the events of Matt 2 to be the subject of an independent historical record; after all, virtually nothing in the gospel stories as a whole is specifically mentioned in a non-Christian record, however well they fit in general terms into our knowledge of the history of the period.[6] Our knowledge of the history of Judea in this period is very partial, and the events recorded in Matt 2 are not of such a character as to demand the attention of Josephus, our only significant source. See my comments on 2:16 on the likely scale of the "massacre" in Bethlehem. We will note in the commentary that the nature of the events (Herod's ruthless and paranoid defense of his throne and the attraction of Egypt as a place of political asylum) fits well with what we know of the period.[7]

3. While the scriptural citations clearly played an important role in the formulation of these stories, this does not mean that the stories were created out of the texts.[8] Three points seem important. First of all, the texts chosen in

6. I have discussed this issue in my *Evidence,* 19-58.

7. In addition to the more general article in *GP* 2 mentioned above, I have discussed the historical status of Herod's killing of the children at more length in *NovT* 21 (1979) 98-120.

8. The fashion of proposing this view on the basis of the term "midrash" is fortunately now waning. "Midrash," which means simply "interpretation," has often been misused as a term for purportedly historical material which is in fact fictional, being the result of creative interpretation of Scripture. While it is true that much Jewish midrash did embellish biblical accounts with apparently fictional features, that is not what "midrash" means, so that the deployment of that word alone does not resolve issues of historicity. I have discussed both the meaning of the term and the extent of historical embellishment in Jewish midrashic writings in my article, "Jewish Historiography, Midrash and the Gospels," *GP* 3:99-127, and with special reference to Matt 1–2 in the article in *GP* 2 mentioned above, pp. 243-55.

several cases (notably "Out of Egypt I have called my son" and "Rachel weeping for her children") are such that it is hard to understand why they should have come to mind at all in connection with Jesus' origins unless there was a narrative tradition already there to trigger the association; and in the case of the final quotation in 2:23 there simply is no existing text in the OT which could have prompted Matthew's reference to Nazareth — the text has been provided to support the settlement in Nazareth, not vice versa. Secondly, the textual form in which some of these quotations are presented differs from known OT texts, and in such a way as to highlight the argument from fulfillment. If these texts were the source of the stories in which they are set, no such adaptation (or, in the case of 2:23, apparent *creation* of a text) would be needed; it is the character of the existing narrative tradition which has required the adaptation of the texts. Thirdly, it is an odd sort of apologetics which could create a story out of a text and then parade this (fictional) story as proof that Scripture has in fact been fulfilled. I have argued elsewhere rather for a dialectic between narrative tradition and text in which each has affected the wording of the other, but the narrative tradition is necessarily prior.[9]

4. While angels and dreams are not a common feature of Matthew's gospel,[10] they are no more out of the ordinary than the healings, exorcisms, and nature miracles which occur throughout the story, and a virginal conception is hardly more miraculous than a physical resurrection. A philosophy which rules out such happenings will have equally great problems with the whole of the gospel tradition (and, one might add, with the essence of Christian faith), and it is not obvious why these chapters should be singled out for suspicion on this ground.

So while there is no doubt that Matthew is in these chapters doing a lot more than simply telling stories of what actually happened, and that his primary interest is not so much in the events for their own sake as in the contribution they make to his argument from Scripture, there is nothing in his presentation or in the nature of the events he outlines to suggest that he was doing other than recording and reflecting on traditions which he had received (apparently from a source related to Joseph, except perhaps for 2:1-12) of the actual events which led up to and followed from the birth of Jesus the Messiah.[11]

In an article published in 1981 I explored Matthew's argument from

9. *NovT* 21 (1979) 108-13; *NTS* 27 (1980/81) 236-37; *GP* 2:250-55.
10. The angels of 4:11 and 28:2 and the dream of 27:19 are the only other narrative instances.
11. Luz, 1:143, while he does not regard the narrative of 2:13-23 as historical (145), comments rather paradoxically on the economical way in which both 1:18-25 and 2:13-23 are narrated: "There is not a word too many; the evangelist forgoes any legendary or novelistic embellishment."

Scripture with special reference to the four formula-quotations of ch. 2.[12] It is often suggested that Matthew was quite cavalier in the uses to which he put OT texts, uses which would never have occurred to their original authors, and that his apparently arbitrary interpretations can have little to convey to modern readers who are used to a more "principled" handling of Scripture. If I was right in arguing above for an apologetic aim in these chapters, Matthew must have thought that at least some of his readers would be able to follow his scriptural allusions and find them convincing, and my article aimed to explore what the putative readers might be expected to get out of these particular formula-quotations. I concluded that we must allow in Matthew, as indeed in a great deal of other literature, ancient and modern, for different classes of readers who might be expected to engage at different levels with Matthew's argument, from the relatively superficial level of direct promise and fulfillment to a much more nuanced and allusive appreciation of themes and strands of OT prophecy and type, and that Matthew deliberately provided "bonus" meanings accessible only to the more "sharp-eyed" or better instructed among his readers since "it is a poor author who aims to communicate only with the lowest common denominator of his potential readership" (p. 241). I shall suggest some of those "bonus meanings" in the comments below on each of the quotations, but would like to record here my conclusion that while Matthew's way of interpreting OT texts is not the same as ours, and sometimes leaves us puzzled because we do not share his cultural background, it is very far from haphazard or unprincipled. These chapters show a remarkably detailed knowledge of the OT text and a subtlety of thought which perceives and exploits verbal and thematic connections. And the author seems to assume that at least some of the original readers of the book would have been able to follow such sophisticated patterns of thought, and would delight as much as he did in tracing the fulfillment of God's purpose through the details as well as in the essential events of the Messiah's coming. What we have in these chapters, in other words, is not a random gathering of embarrassingly inappropriate texts, but the product of a sophisticated and probably lengthy engagement with Scripture in a way which goes beyond our concepts of "scientific exegesis" precisely because it believes in God's purposeful control of both the words and the events of the OT, so that it is only in the light of their ultimate fulfillment in the Messiah that their significance can be appreciated by Christian hindsight.

---

12. "The Formula-Quotations of Matthew 2 and the Problem of Communication," *NTS* 27 (1980/1) 233-51; reprinted in G. K. Beale (ed.), *The Right Doctrine from the Wrong Texts? Essays on the Use of the Old Testament in the New* (Grand Rapids: Baker, 1994), 114-34.

1. Joseph, Son of David, Accepts Jesus as His Son (1:18-25)

18 *The Messiah's[13] origin[14] was like this. His mother Mary was engaged[15] to Joseph, but before they came together, she was found to be pregnant through[16] the Holy Spirit.* 19 *Joseph her husband, because he was a righteous man and yet[17] did not want to expose her to scandal, came to the conclusion that he should break the engagement[18] privately.* 20 *But when he had decided on this, suddenly[19] an angel of*

13. I have followed the reading Τοῦ δὲ Χριστοῦ, supported by all the early Latin and Syriac versions (which were translated before our earliest Greek MSS were written), against the reading Τοῦ δὲ Ἰησοῦ Χριστοῦ, found in all Greek MSS (except B, which has Τοῦ δὲ Χριστοῦ Ἰησοῦ; the different order suggests an original reading Τοῦ δὲ Χριστοῦ, with Ἰησοῦ in this case inserted in a different position) and in the later Syriac and Coptic versions. The definite article with the combination Ἰησοῦς Χριστός reads awkwardly, and occurs nowhere else in the NT, whereas it is normal with Χριστός alone. It is much more likely that the familiar form Ἰησοῦς Χριστός would be introduced in place of an original Χριστός than that the early Latin and Syriac tradition would consistently remove the name "Jesus." It is also more likely that Matthew, having used the form τοῦ Χριστοῦ in v. 17 (itself prepared for by the clearly titular use of ὁ λεγόμενος Χριστός in v. 16), would repeat it in this resumptive verse. He keeps the actual name "Jesus" back until it is formally introduced in vv. 21 and 25.

14. This is the same word γένεσις which was used in 1:1, and the same English translation is needed to preserve the link. "Birth" would properly be γέννησις (a common patristic term for the nativity) rather than γένεσις (γένεσις is occasionally used for birth, as in LXX Hos 2:5, but usually where the focus is on the time or place of origin rather than the birth itself, and sometimes with γέννησις as a variant reading, as also in Luke 1:14). The pericope that follows is not about the birth of Jesus, which is never narrated by Matthew but mentioned only in a subordinate clause in v. 25 (picked up by a past participle in 2:1), but about how the genealogical "origin" for the Messiah which has been spelled out in vv. 1-17 was enabled to become reality. The reading γέννησις in some later MSS testifies to the desire of some early readers to turn Matthew's account of "origin" into a story of the nativity like that in Luke's gospel, as most modern English versions have also done by using "birth" here.

15. The modern translator has the problem here and in v. 19 that while "engagement" now has far less force than μνηστεύω conveyed in first-century Judaism (see commentary), no other English term does justice to the cultural context; "betrothed," even if it were current English, does not differ in meaning from "engaged."

16. The preposition is ἐκ, as in v. 20 where I have translated more literally "from." The difference here is due only to the sentence construction: "pregnant from" would be unnatural English idiom, while "pregnant by" is too specifically used of natural male generation.

17. For the justification for adding "yet" see the comments below.

18. See note 15 above. The verb ἀπολύω is regularly used for "divorce" after marriage, but English usage hardly permits "divorce" in a premarriage context.

19. Matthew frequently uses ἰδού to alert the reader to an unexpected turn in the story. While it can often be left untranslated (since English usage no longer allows "Behold!"), "suddenly" here attempts to maintain the vividness of Matthew's narrative. (The

the Lord appeared to him in a dream and said, "Joseph, son of David,
do not be afraid to accept[20] Mary as your wife; for the child she has
conceived is from the Holy Spirit. 21 *She will give birth to a son, and*
you are to give him the name Jesus, because it is he who will save his
people from their sins."

22 *All this happened to fulfill what had been declared by the Lord*
through the prophet, who said,[21]

23 *"Look, the virgin will become pregnant and will give birth to a*
son, and they will give him the name Immanuel"[22] — which is
translated[23] "God with us."

24 *When Joseph got up from sleep, he did just as the angel of the*
Lord had directed him: he accepted his wife, 25 *and he did not have in-*
tercourse with her until she had given birth to a son;[24] and he gave
him the name Jesus.

The "book of origin" has left us with an unresolved problem. Joseph has been
shown to be the "son of David," the heir to the royal dynasty of Judah, but in
v. 16 Matthew has abandoned his regular formula to indicate that Jesus, the
son of Joseph's wife Mary, was not in fact Joseph's son (and Matthew carefully avoids ever referring to Joseph as Jesus' "father"). What then is the relevance of this dynastic list to the story of Jesus, son of Mary? These verses
will explain, therefore, how Jesus came to be formally adopted and named by
Joseph, despite his own natural inclinations, and thus to become officially
"son of David"; the angel's address to Joseph as "son of David" in v. 20 will
highlight the issue.[25]

---

translation of ἰδού by "Look" in the Isaiah quotation in v. 23 seems required by the dramatic nature of the pronouncement.)

20. παραλαμβάνω here and in v. 24 refers of course to the completion of the marriage formalities by taking Mary to his home, but the compound verb also conveys the
sense of welcome, not just dutiful compliance (cf John 1:11), which would also result in
the recognition of Jesus as his son.

21. While the availability of quotation marks makes a verb of saying not strictly
necessary in a modern translation, I have explicitly translated the quotation marker
λέγοντος which is a distinctive feature of all but one of the introductions to Matthew's
formula-quotations, because in the one case where it is absent (2:23) I shall wish to argue
that its absence is exegetically significant.

22. As with the names in 1:2-16, I have used the familiar English transliteration of
the Hebrew name rather than the LXX Ἐμμανουήλ which Matthew cites.

23. This is the only time Matthew uses the verb μεθερμηνεύω to indicate that he is
giving not just an interpretation but a literal Greek translation of a Hebrew word.

24. Many later MSS and versions read "her firstborn son," clearly an assimilation
to Luke 2:7.

25. Cf. L. Novakovic, *Messiah,* 43-45: "The crucial point is the continuity of the

Joseph's decision is directed by God, through an angelic revelation in a dream. Specific emphasis is placed both in the angel's message and in the subsequent narrative on Joseph's role in naming Jesus,[26] which was the responsibility of the legal father and which ensured the official status of the son and heir (cf. Isa 43:1: "I have called you by name; you are mine"). So not only is the name "Jesus" in itself theologically significant, but also the fact that it is given to him under divine direction, and by whom it is given. It is through this act of Joseph that Jesus also becomes "son of David."

Joseph is persuaded to take this bold step by the assurance that Mary's pregnancy is not the result of infidelity but is of divine origin. The tradition of Jesus' virgin conception, already hinted at in the formulation of v. 16, is thus central to these verses, and is underlined by Matthew's statement that Joseph had no intercourse with Mary until after Jesus' birth. Here is the most impressive agreement between the opening chapters of Matthew and those of Luke, despite their almost complete independence in terms of narrative content (on which see above). What Luke achieves by his story of the angelic annunciation to Mary (Luke 1:26-38) Matthew conveys by the angelic announcement to Joseph. Mary's incredulity in Luke 1:34 is matched here by Joseph's initial natural assumption as to the source of the pregnancy, and each needs explicit angelic explanation to overcome it. Both evangelists specifically attribute the pregnancy to the power of the Holy Spirit (Luke 1:35; Matt 1:18, 21), and both explicitly refer to Mary as "virgin" (Luke 1:34; Matt 1:23 with 1:25).[27]

It is this aspect of the story which prompts Matthew's first formula-quotation. The passage of Scripture which undergirds this first of the five narrative cameos in 1:18–2:23 is Isa 7:14, with its explicit mention (in Greek) of a virgin becoming pregnant and giving birth. While Matthew presents the quotation as his own editorial comment rather than as part of the angel's message to Joseph, he expects his readers to incorporate this scriptural authentication for Mary's unique experience into their understanding of why Joseph changed his mind. The Isaiah quotation underlines the assurance that this is from God.

But Matthew has noticed that Isaiah's words also include the naming of the child, which is just what Joseph is now being called on to do. Unlike most of Matthew's formula-quotations, this one sticks closely to the LXX

Davidic line. The adoption of Jesus by Joseph made him a legal descendant of David, the king."

26. Note the repeated phrase καλέω τὸ ὄνομα αὐτοῦ, "give him the name," in vv. 21, 23, 25; the Semitic rather than Greek character of the phrase draws attention to its scriptural origin.

27. See p. 42, n. 4, on the question of the historicity of the virginal conception and the significance of the independent accounts of it presented by Matthew and Luke.

text, but it diverges at one significant point. Whereas the Hebrew probably says "she" (the mother) will give the child his name, and the LXX probably[28] says "you" (singular, referring to Ahaz to whom the prophecy is addressed) will do so, Matthew has a generalizing "they," which leaves the way open for Jesus to be given his name not by Mary but by Joseph. The name given in Isaiah is not of course the name "Jesus," but far from being embarrassed by the problem of two different names, Matthew also draws the name "Immanuel" into his presentation of the theological significance of the coming of the Messiah by adding a literal translation of it as "God with us."[29] Probably Matthew expected his readers to reflect that the "salvation" which is the explicit meaning of the name "Jesus" in v. 21 was to be accomplished by the coming of God among his people, but he has not made any such linking of the meanings of the two names explicit.

The phrase "God with us" which thus marks the beginning of Matthew's presentation of Jesus will have its arresting counterpart at the end of the gospel, where Jesus himself declares, "I am with you always," with reference not to a continuing life on earth but to a spiritual presence (28:20). Cf. also the remarkable words of 18:20, "Where two or three have come together in my name, I am there among them."[30] At this point it would be possible to read "Immanuel" only in its probable OT sense as a statement of God's concern for his people, "God *is* with us," but the name as applied to one who has just been declared to owe his origin to the direct work of the Holy Spirit was probably in Matthew's mind a more direct statement of the presence of God *in Jesus himself,* so that Jesus' declaration in 28:20 is only drawing out what has already been true from the time of his birth, that God is present in the person of Jesus. Matthew's overt interpretation of "Immanuel" thus takes him close to an explicit doctrine of the incarnation such as is expressed in John 1:14.

Thus, while these verses do not use the title "Son of God," Matthew could hardly have recorded both the supernatural conception of Jesus and the scriptural title "God with us" without reflecting on the fact that the Messiah is much more than only a "son of David," as will later be made explicit in

28. There are textual variants for the verb form in both the Hebrew and LXX traditions (see p. 58, n. 67, for the Hebrew), but Matthew's third-person plural is not part of either tradition except in late LXX MSS which are presumably influenced by Matthew.

29. Matthew's rendering reproduces exactly the wording of LXX Isa 8:8, where the title Immanuel recurs.

30. This point has been developed at length by H. Frankemölle, *Jahwe-Bund,* 7-83, who finds in the theme of "being with" (which he reads as essentially covenant language) the key to both Matthew's christology and his ecclesiology. Cf. more briefly D. R. Bauer, *Structure,* 124-27, and at full monograph length D. D. Kupp, *Emmanuel.* Kupp aims to show that the theme of "divine presence" plays a much more fundamental role in Matthew than merely in the key texts 1:23; 18:20, and 28:20.

22:41-45. When we are invited to reflect on God's calling his "son" out of Egypt in 2:15, and still more when Jesus is explicitly declared to be God's Son in 3:17, the ground will have been well prepared.[31]

18 The order of the opening words, which is less natural in Greek than in my translation, draws attention again to the title "Messiah" by putting it first.[32] Verse 1 has promised to reveal the "origin" of the Messiah, and the repetition of that word here (see p. 46, n. 14) shows that that promise is still being fulfilled.[33] The list of names now requires to be supplemented by a narrative account in order to explain how the identity of Jesus of Nazareth as Messiah can be recognized despite the unusual and potentially self-defeating way the "book of origin" ended in v. 16.

The difference between our modern concept of "engagement" and that of first-century Jews is indicated by the description of Joseph already in v. 19 as Mary's husband[34] and by the use of the normal word for divorce to describe the ending of the engagement. Though the couple were not yet living together, it was a binding contract entered into before witnesses which could be terminated only by death (which would leave the woman a "widow") or by divorce as if for a full marriage (*m. Ketub.* 4:2); sexual infidelity during the engagement would be a basis for such divorce. About a year after the engagement (*m. Ketub.* 5:2; *Ned.* 10:5) the woman (then normally about thirteen or fourteen) would leave her father's home and go to live with the husband in a public ceremony (such as is described in 25:1-12), which is here referred to as "coming together" and will be recorded in v. 24.[35]

The role of the Holy Spirit in Jesus' conception (which will be explained in v. 20; as yet Joseph knows nothing of it) reflects the OT concept of the Spirit of God active in the original creation (Gen 1:2; Ps 33:6) and in the

31. J. Nolland, *JSNT* 62 (1996) 3-12, is of course right to stress that there is no explicit "Son of God" christology in this pericope (contrast Luke 1:35), but he also recognizes that there are pointers here to what will become explicit as Matthew's story unfolds.

32. See p. 46, n. 13, for the textual question, though even if the name "Jesus" was in the original text, the build-up in vv. 1-17 and especially the repeated title in vv. 16 and 17 ensures that it would be on the title "Messiah" that the emphasis would fall.

33. H. C. Waetjen, *JBL* 95 (1976) 205-30, presents a good argument for the continuity between 1:1-17 and 1:18-25, and argues in particular (217) that the repetition of the term γένεσις in vv. 1 and 18 is intended to underline this continuity. L. Cantwell, *NovT* 24 (1982) 304-5, suggests that γένεσις should be understood here more specifically of the "parentage" of Jesus.

34. The Greek ἀνήρ can of course mean simply "man" as well as "husband," but to refer to a woman's ἀνήρ in a context which is about marriage makes its reference more specific.

35. J. Jeremias, *Jerusalem,* 364-68, sets out the pattern of Jewish betrothal and marriage.

giving of life (Ps 104:30; Isa 32:15; Ezek 37:1-14); cf. the possibility considered above that v. 1 is intended to suggest a new creation. The Spirit is also thought of in the OT as having an eschatological role in connection with the coming of the Messiah (Isa 11:2; 42:1; 61:1, etc.), and this theme will be taken up in 3:16-17, but the mention here links the Spirit not just with Jesus' adult ministry but with his whole earthly life. The delicate way in which both Matthew and Luke express the process of Jesus' conception[36] contrasts sharply with Greek and Roman stories of gods (often having assumed the form of a male human or even animal) having intercourse with human women, resulting in the birth of demigod heroes like Heracles.

19 That Joseph was "righteous" is sometimes thought to explain his avoidance of a public scandal because he was "merciful" or "considerate," but the more basic sense of the word is of one who is careful to keep the law.[37] The law as then understood required the termination of the engagement in the case of "adultery";[38] in OT times the penalty for adultery was stoning. Deut 22:13-21 deals specifically with the case of a woman found not to be a virgin at the time of marriage, and 22:23-24 with that of consenting "adultery" on the part of an engaged woman.[39] But by the first century (when Roman rule had abolished Jewish death penalties)[40] divorce was the normal course. John 8:5-7, if historical, would then be describing a deliberately extreme response. As a law-abiding man Joseph would be expected to repudiate his errant fiancée publicly in a trial for adultery; for the force of *deigmatizō* cf. Col 2:15 where Jesus "makes a public example" of the principalities and powers, and for the public humiliation of an adulteress see *m. Soṭah* 1:4-6. If "righteous" is understood in that sense, therefore, it stands in contrast with rather than as an explanation of his desire to spare her; hence my inclusion of "yet" in the translation above. The resultant dilemma suggests to him the course, still legally correct but also more compassionate, of a "private" annulment of the contract, avoiding a public accusation of adultery and the resultant trial; the Mishnah allows for the divorce of a suspected adulteress before just two witnesses (*m. Soṭah* 1:1; for the necessity of witnesses to a

---

36. R. E. Brown, *Birth,* 124, points out that the Holy Spirit "is not male," and continues, "the manner of begetting is implicitly creative rather than sexual."

37. See D. Hill, *Greek Words,* 124; B. Przybylski, *Righteousness,* 101-2; R. E. Brown, *Birth,* 125-28, 605.

38. For mandatory divorce when adultery was proved cf. *m. Yebam.* 2:8; *Soṭah* 5:1. See Keener, 91, for further evidence of the strictness of this requirement in Greek and Roman as well as Jewish law.

39. Deut 22:25-27 rules, however, that if the woman was an unwilling partner she is not to be harmed, but only the man must be executed.

40. See below, pp. 1018-19, for the competence of the Sanhedrin in capital cases, and for the apparent exceptions in the cases of Stephen and of James the Just.

divorce cf., e.g., *m. Giṭ.* 9:4, 8),[41] though it is hard to see how this could long be kept secret from a society aware of the original engagement.[42]

20-21 My translations "came to the conclusion" (v. 19) and "when he had decided on this" reflect Matthew's aorist tenses, which suggest that before the divine intervention Joseph's mind was made up. Four times in these chapters we are told of divine communications to Joseph in dreams (cf. 2:13, 19, 22), in all but the last case with an angel[43] as the messenger. It is fanciful to explain this by Matthew's memory of the famous dreams of another Joseph in Gen 37:5-11, 19-20: the OT Joseph did not receive divine directions (or see angels) in his dreams, and Matthew makes no attempt to connect the two Josephs; moreover, he attributes comparable dreams to the magi (2:12) and to Pilate's wife (27:19). Divine guidance both by dreams[44] and by the appearance of angels is of course a regular feature of OT spirituality, and would need no explanation. The point of their concentration in these chapters is to emphasize the initiative of God in guiding Joseph's actions through this crucial period.[45]

41. Gundry, 21-22, argues that Joseph intended to do without witnesses altogether, but his argument depends on the dubious assumption that Matthew knew of the Lucan story of the annunciation and so assumed that Joseph was already aware of the source of the pregnancy (so that the angel announced to Joseph in v. 20 what he already knew from Mary). Matthew gives us no indication of how and when Mary learned the source of her pregnancy.

42. Keener, 90-94, provides a detailed and graphic account of the nature of Joseph's situation and decision in the light of the social and legal realities of first-century Palestine. See also A. Tosato, *CBQ* 41 (1979) 547-51.

43. The lack of the definite article in all Matthew's narrative introductions of an angel (cf. 2:13, 19; 28:2) indicates that he is not thinking of the "angel of the LORD" who appears sometimes in the OT as virtually a visible manifestation of God himself, or of a specific angel such as Luke's Gabriel (Luke 1:26), but simply of "an" angel, a supernatural divine messenger. There is no indication here of what visible form this angel took (though see 28:3).

44. Keener, 95-96, gives extensive documentation of the importance of dreams as divine communications in the ancient world. See also G. M. Soares Prabhu, *Formula-Quotations,* 222-27, for the OT background to Joseph's dreams (with special reference to 2:13-15).

45. There may be a further dimension to Joseph's dream in that Matthew and his readers may have been aware of the developing Jewish tradition concerning the birth of Moses, which included a specific revelation to Amram in a dream that his son was to be the deliverer of Israel (Josephus, *Ant.* 2.210-16; in Pseudo-Philo 9.10 a similar dream is given to Moses' sister Miriam), and even, in *Exodus Rabbah,* a rather confused tradition to the effect that Amram divorced Jochebed after she became pregnant, only to remarry her. For full discussion see D. C. Allison, *Moses,* 140-65 (pp. 148-49 for the divorce tradition). We shall have more to say on the relevance of the Moses traditions in ch. 2 (see below, pp. 63-64).

The angel's address to Joseph as "son of David" reminds us what is at stake in the decision Joseph has just reached: the loss of Jesus' royal pedigree if he is not officially recognized as Joseph's son. So, despite his previous decision, he is called to take two decisive actions, first to accept Mary as his wife rather than repudiating her and secondly to give her son a name, which will confirm his legal recognition of Jesus as his own son and hence as also a "son of David."

The second part of the angel's message (v. 21) corresponds quite closely to the wording of the quotation from Isa 7:14 which will follow in v. 23, though of course with Jesus' actual name rather than the symbolic name "Immanuel." The interpretations given to the two names ("he will save his people from their sins" and "God with us") invite the reader to reflect on the nature of the Messiah's mission. On the name "Jesus" see above on v. 1. The Hebrew *Yᵉhôšua'* is normally taken to mean "Yahweh is salvation," so that the interpretation in terms of saving from sin derives from the popular Hebrew understanding of the name; the similarity to the Hebrew verb *yôšîa'* ("he will save") may have helped with Matthew's formulation of the meaning of the name in a future verb, "he will save." But whereas the OT name spoke of *God* as the savior, Mary's son is himself to be the agent of salvation; here is scope for profound christological reflection on the part of any of Matthew's readers who can see behind the common Greek name to its Hebrew origin.[46] "His people" in relation to the mission of a "son of David" must in the first place denote Israel,[47] but even if at this stage Matthew's readers have not yet recognized the universalistic implications of the title "son of Abraham" and of the non-Israelite women in the genealogy, they will not have to read far into the book before they become aware that the scope of salvation is being spread more widely. Indeed, one of the key issues which will dominate the final confrontation in Jerusalem, and will be brought to its climax in 28:18-20, will be who are to constitute the continuing people of God and the role of Jesus in bringing into being what he will significantly describe in 16:18 as "my *ekklēsia*."[48]

---

46. This implication is strengthened if Gundry, *Use,* 127-28, is right in seeing the angel's words as a deliberate echo of Ps 130:8, where it is God who "will redeem Israel from all its iniquities." See further L. Novakovic, *Messiah,* 64-66; she argues that Matthew has used ὁ λαὸς αὐτοῦ in place of the LXX "Israel" in order to "refer to Jesus' church composed of both Jews and Gentiles" (66).

47. Matthew's use of λαός, the special term for Israel as the chosen people of God, ensures that this primary meaning is noticed. Cf the use of λαός in the quotation of Mic 5:2 / 2 Sam 5:2 at 2:6, and the comments below on 27:25.

48. See D. D. Kupp, *Emmanuel,* 60-62, for the tension set up in ch. 2 when those the reader naturally takes to be "his people" turn out to be his enemies; the tension, he argues, is not resolved until the end of the gospel, especially in 27:25; 28:16-20.

53

This universal scope of the Messiah's mission is not as yet on the surface, but there is a clear break from popular Jewish expectation in the statement that the salvation Jesus will achieve will be "from their sins." Several OT eschatological passages speak of the need for sins to be atoned for and forgiven, for example, Isa 53:4-12; Jer 31:31-34; Ezek 36:25-31. But while the spiritual condition of God's people was still the concern of at least some contemporary messianic expectation (notably the Pharisaic hope expressed in *Pss. Sol.* 17:21-46, though there it is intertwined with political restoration), there seems little doubt that the dominant concern in first-century Jewish hope was with their political subjection, with the restoration of the kingdom of David as the messianic goal. The angel's words thus signal at the start that any political euphoria which may have been evoked by the Davidic and royal theme of the "book of origin" is wide of the mark of what Jesus' actual mission is to be. His ministry will begin in the context of a call to repentance from sin (3:2, 6; 4:17), and while the focus of that ministry will be on teaching, healing, and exorcism, he will also assert his "authority on earth to forgive sins" (9:6). His mission will culminate in his death "as a ransom for many" (20:28), "for the forgiveness of sins" (26:28). This son of David will not conform to the priorities of popular messianic expectation.[49]

22 Matthew now introduces the first of his "formula-quotations" (see above, pp. 11-14), which typically take the form of editorial comment on the incident being narrated. Formally, this quotation interrupts the narrative,[50] but its role is in fact central to the pericope, which has been framed so as to demonstrate the fulfillment of the prophecy (note that phrases from Isa 7:14 are echoed in the narrative of vv. 18, 21, 25).[51] The introductory formula in these quotations varies, the common factor (except in 2:5 and 23; see comments there) being the phrase "to fulfill (or "then was fulfilled") what had been declared through the prophet [sometimes named],[52] who said." There are two expansions of the basic formula here. "What had been declared" is

---

49. See, however, the argument of L. Novakovic, *Messiah*, 73-75, that "salvation from sins" should not be understood only or even mainly as forgiveness so much as the undoing of the *consequences* of sin; as illness was understood to be a consequence of sin, she argues that the salvation envisaged here includes messianic healing.

50. *Pace* Carson, 76-77, who unusually argues that vv. 22-23 should be read as part of the angel's message.

51. Ἐν γαστρὶ ἔχω appears in v. 18; τέξεται υἱόν in v. 21; ἔτεκεν υἱόν in v. 25; καλέσουσιν τὸ ὄνομα αὐτοῦ in vv. 21, 25.

52. The name Ἡσαΐου appears here in D and in a number of later MSS and versions, but it is evidently an addition to conform to Matthew's practice in all his other formal quotations from Isaiah (3:3; 4:14; 8:17; 12:17; 13:14; 15:7). See below on 2:17 for the surprising omission of Isaiah's name here.

here (and in 2:15) explained by adding "by the Lord."[53] The verb-form translated "declared"[54] has a solemn, formulaic ring, and is used in the NT only by Matthew: in addition to its repetition ten times in this formula, his other three uses of it are all to introduce a biblical quotation or allusion (3:3; 22:31; 24:15); "by the Lord" therefore makes explicit what the verb form already implies, the authoritative declaration of God in Scripture. The other expansion is the opening phrase "All this happened" (cf. 21:4, "This happened"; in 26:56 the same wording as here introduces a general statement of scriptural fulfillment rather than a specific quotation), and again the language is slightly artificial in that Matthew uses the perfect of *ginomai* rather than the aorist which he normally uses in narrative.[55] The effect of this addition is to ensure that the reader looks for the fulfillment of Isa 7:14 not only in the virginal conception of Jesus but in the whole complex of events which "have come to pass," including conception, birth, and especially the naming of the child.

23 A reader familiar with modern study of Isaiah will notice two problems about Matthew's first formula-quotation. In the first place, while the LXX, which Matthew follows (except for one word), unambiguously refers to "the virgin," English versions of Isaiah generally translate the Hebrew as "the young woman." The definite article suggests that a particular woman is in view, but the context does not identify her; interpreters have suggested Ahaz's wife (note that the prophecy is addressed to the "house of David" v. 13), or Isaiah's (in view of the similar symbolic use made of the birth of Isaiah's son in 8:1-4). But if this is what he meant, it is remarkable that Isaiah did not use the normal Hebrew word for a "woman" or "wife," *'iššâ*, which

---

53. R. Pesch, *Bib* 48 (1967) 395-420, suggests that it is significant that the two introductory formulae which include this phrase are those where the following quotation mentions a "son," thus emphasizing that Jesus is *God's* son. But while Matthew emphasizes Jesus' birth "through the Holy Spirit," he does not link this directly with the title "Son of God" (contrast Luke 1:35), and Isa 7:14 makes no such claim; it is the virgin's "son" who is mentioned, not God's.

54. The aorist passive participle of ἐρῶ, occurring always in the form τὸ ῥηθέν except in 3:3 where the context requires the masculine form. The usage suggests a more solemn sense than merely "spoken," hence my translation "declared." The indicative form ἐρρέθη will be similarly used six times for the pronouncements of the law in 5:21 and parallels (cf. Rom 9:12, 26; Gal 3:16). Luke uses the perfect passive for biblical references: Luke 2:24; 4:12; Acts 2:16; 13:40 (cf. Rom 4:18). Nowhere in the NT are the aorist or perfect passive forms of the verb used except for divine or scriptural pronouncements. They thus have "the same sort of connotations as a deliberate archaism in English like 'Thus saith the Lord'" (my *Matthew: Evangelist,* 172). Cf. J. P. Meier, *Law,* 131-32.

55. He uses the perfect here and in 21:4; 26:56; cf. its use in 19:8 and 24:21 in tracing what "has come about" since the world was created. Only in 25:6 does it occur where a narrative ἐγένετο might have been expected.

would be expected of a childbirth within marriage. The word that is actually used is *'almâ,* which occurs very rarely in the OT.[56] While it is clear from some of those OT contexts that the *'almâ* is sexually mature,[57] the word is not used elsewhere of a married woman; the person referred to as *'almâ* in Gen 24:43 has been specifically described as a virgin in v. 16.[58] Isaiah's choice of this unusual word in connection with childbirth therefore draws attention; it does not explicitly mean "virgin" (the Hebrew for which is *bᵉtûlâ*), but it suggests something other than a normal childbirth within marriage. It was presumably on this basis that LXX translated it by *parthenos* ("virgin").[59] Matthew is following the LXX, but the Hebrew underlying it is sufficiently unusual to suggest that it was not an arbitrary translation.[60]

The second problem is that Isaiah's prophecy, uttered to Ahaz in about the year 735 B.C., is not about an event in the distant future. Its point is to specify the time of the imminent devastation of both Judah's enemies and Judah herself through the Assyrian invasion: it will be before the son called Immanuel, soon to be born,[61] has grown up (Isa 7:15-17). This raises an issue which we will note several times in Matthew's use of OT prophecy, that

56. Only here and at Gen 24:43; Exod 2:8; Ps 68:25; Prov 30:19; Song 1:3; 6:8. The plural *'ᵃlāmôt* also occurs as a musical direction in the title to Ps 46 and in 1 Chr 15:20, but this offers no help with the meaning of *'almâ* in narrative and poetic contexts.

57. A detailed study by R. G. Bratcher, *BT* 9 (1958) 98-105, concluded that "the word refers to a sexually mature young woman, capable of having sexual intercourse, without specifying whether or not she has had it."

58. This is, significantly, the one other place where LXX uses παρθένος for *'almâ.*

59. Like the English "maiden," παρθένος is sometimes found (especially in earlier Greek) with the meaning simply "girl," without reference to her sexual condition, but by the Hellenistic period this usage is rarely attested, and in almost all its LXX uses the meaning "virgin" is clear (Gen 34:3, often cited as an exception, ironically uses παρθένος of a girl whose virginity has just been violated); see R. G. Bratcher, *BT* 9 (1958) 112-16. The later Greek versions of the OT (Aquila, Symmachus, Theodotion), produced after the Christian use of this text had become known, use νεᾶνις ("young woman") in place of παρθένος in Isa 7:14, probably because the more specific meaning of παρθένος had become an apologetic embarrassment in Jewish-Christian polemics.

60. Such a "supernatural" understanding of Isa 7:14 is also supported by the fact that its language is closely similar to Gen 17:19, which foretells the miraculous birth of Isaac to the barren and aged Sarah. A probable allusion to Isa 7:14 in Luke 1:31 as part of the angelic announcement of the virginal conception indicates that Luke understood it in the same way. The LXX wording in itself does not *demand* a supernatural conception, as it *could* be understood to mean that one who is now a virgin will soon conceive (in the normal way), but if that is what the LXX translator intended he has certainly not made himself clear, and Matthew's understanding is the more natural sense of the words.

61. The pregnancy, which is expressed as future in LXX, is already a fact in the Hebrew text (*pace* NIV/TNIV, which was presumably influenced by the LXX as quoted by Matthew).

whereas we prefer to think of a single specific fulfillment of a prophet's prediction, Matthew's typological interest leads him rather to find patterns which will recur repeatedly throughout God's dealings with his people.[62] In this case, he has good warrant for taking the prophecy concerning "Immanuel" as having a relevance beyond its undoubted immediate aim, for the name "Immanuel" will occur again in Isa 8:8 as that of the one to whom the land of Judah belongs, and its meaning will be developed in 8:10, "for God is with us." Moreover, the prophecy in 7:14 of the birth to the "house of David" (Isa 7:13) of a child with so extraordinary an honorific title prepares us for the even more remarkable description in 9:6-7 of a child who is to be born "for us," and whose multiple and still more extravagant title marks him out not only as the Messiah of the line of David but also as "Mighty God, Everlasting Father." The theme will be taken up again in 11:1-5 with the prophecy of the spiritually endowed "shoot from the stump of Jesse." These last two passages would have been recognized then, as they still are today, as messianic prophecies, and it seems likely that Isaiah's thought has moved progressively from the virgin's child, "God with us," to whom the land of Judah belongs, to these fuller expressions of the Davidic hope. If then Isa 7:14 is taken as the opening of what will be the developing theme of a wonder child throughout Isa 7–11, it can with good reason be suggested that it points beyond the immediate political crisis of the eighth century B.C., not only in Matthew's typological scheme but also in Isaiah's intention.[63]

To focus on these issues raised by modern scholarship is, however, to be distracted from the purpose of Matthew in including this quotation.[64] Three elements in this Isaiah text would have attracted Matthew's attention, two with regard to his immediate narrative context (a child born to a virgin mother, and the naming of the child) and one in relation to his underlying christology, the title "God with us." His one deviation from the LXX[65] is in

---

62. See, e.g., comments below on his use of Hos 11:1 to speak of a *future* exodus (2:15), or of Daniel's description of Antiochus Epiphanes' "abomination of desolation" to refer to an event still future (24:15), and most remarkably his quite varied application of the vision of Dan 7:13-14 to refer to situations both far distant (19:28; 25:31-34) and imminent (10:23; 16:27-28; 26:64), and even in one case already present (28:18).

63. R. Beaton, *Isaiah's Christ,* 95-97, makes an interesting case that Matthew's use of this text "betrays an acquaintance with the original context and suggests a closer reading of this section of Isaiah than he has sometimes been given credit for in the past." W. Carter, *JBL* 119 (2000) 508-13, also argues that Matthew is "evoking" Isa 7–9 as a whole, but finds the relevance of the passage not simply in its messianic potential but in its exposé of the threat which imperial power poses to the purpose of God, so that the readers are led to ask how Jesus can "save his people" in the context of Roman imperial power.

64. So, rightly, D. D. Kupp, *Emmanuel,* 157-58.

65. There is, however, a textual variant within the LXX tradition with regard to the first verb: Matthew agrees with the A and א text ἕξει against the B text λήμψεται.

the plural subject of the verb, "*they* will call." In his immediate narrative context it will be Joseph who will give the child his name (which neither the Hebrew text's "she will call" nor the LXX's "you will call" would have allowed), but that name will be Jesus, not Immanuel. Matthew's plural may therefore be looking ahead to what "people" (especially those whom he will "save from their sins," v. 21)[66] will eventually learn to say about Jesus, that in him God is with us. We have no indication that Matthew's plural verb came from any source other than his own creative interpretation of the text.[67] For the theological significance of the title "Immanuel" see the introductory comments above.

24-25 Matthew's editorial comment in vv. 22-23 has interrupted the flow of the narrative which now resumes from the end of v. 21. Joseph's obedient response to the angel's words is indicated by the repetition of the same words to describe the first and third of his actions, accepting his wife and giving his son the name "Jesus." But between these two actions, which together completed the legal "adoption"[68] of Jesus as Joseph's son, Matthew mentions a third which was not explicit in the angel's instructions: "he did not have intercourse with her until she had given birth." For Joseph to "accept" his wife required the public completion of the marriage by taking Mary to his own house (the "coming together" of v. 18), which would normally have been the point at which sexual relations began. Matthew does not explain Joseph's abstinence,[69] but it is not hard to understand it in the light of the assurance that Mary was pregnant "through the Holy Spirit." If Matthew has an apologetic

66. D. D. Kupp, *Emmanuel,* 58, sees this as the implied reader's natural choice of subject for the plural verb. By calling him "Immanuel" they recognize that "Jesus himself, as the ultimately personal mode of YHWH's presence, is the means of his people's rescue."

67. On the Hebrew text see M. J. J. Menken, *Matthew's Bible,* 121. R. H. Gundry, *Use,* 90, suggests that the 1QIsaᵃ reading *qr'* (without the *t*) could be read either as "it shall be called" or "one shall call," which would then be "equivalent to Matthew's impersonal plural"; it remains, however, singular in form. There is certainly some fluidity in the text form of both Hebrew and LXX, but Matthew's plural version seems to be his own; the later LXX MSS which have καλέσουσιν were probably influenced by Matthew. (In his commentary, 25, Gundry appears to have accepted this.) At this point the attempt of Menken (ibid., 117-31) to derive Matthew's formula-quotations from a hypothetical "revised LXX" rather than from Matthew's creativity, while never capable of disproof (or indeed of proof), seems particularly inappropriate.

68. The recognition of his wife's son as his own is not of course "adoption" in the sense of bringing someone in from a different family, but the legal effect is the same.

69. Keener, 89-90, argues that Matthew intends to present Joseph and Mary as a model of sexual restraint for others to imitate, but the wording of the passage does not readily suggest this; the exceptional nature of their situation does not indicate a universalizable pattern.

reason for inserting this statement, it is presumably to take away any doubt as to the supernatural origin of Mary's child. Nothing in his text suggests that he subscribed to the later idea of Mary's "perpetual virginity," and indeed the "until" most naturally indicates that after Jesus was born normal marital relations began (as indeed the straightforward sense of Jesus having "brothers and sisters" requires, 13:55-56; cf. Luke 2:7, "her firstborn son").[70]

The pericope concludes triumphantly with the naming of Jesus. Verse 21 has explained the theological significance of the name, and the whole chapter so far has set up the problem of legal parentage to which this is the essential answer. Jesus of Nazareth is now securely adopted as the "son of David."[71]

2. The King of the Jews Born in the City of David (2:1-12)

1 *Now after Jesus was born in Bethlehem in Judea, in the days of King Herod, one day[1] some magi from the East arrived in Jerusalem, 2 inquiring, "Where is the child who has been born as King of the Jews? We saw his star when it rose,[2] and we have come to pay homage[3] to him." 3 When King Herod heard this he was thoroughly alarmed, and all Jerusalem with him. 4 He summoned all the chief priests and scribes of the people, and questioned them about the Mes-*

---

70. The clause οὐκ ἐγίνωσκεν αὐτὴν ἕως οὗ is omitted by the Old Latin Codex Bobbiensis and the Sinaitic Syriac, probably to avoid this implication that Mary did not remain virgin.

71. For the importance of the father's declaration, see the comment in *m. B. Bat.* 8:6, in the course of a discussion of inheritance rights, "If a man said, 'This is my son,' he may be believed."

1. An attempt to represent the narrative function of ἰδού as introducing a new and remarkable phase of the story.

2. The singular of ἀνατολή is used here and in v. 9 for the "rising" of a celestial body, as distinct from the plural in v. 1 and in 8:11; 24:27 for the "[place of] rising [of the sun]," the East. The singular can be used for the East, as in Rev 21:13, but not normally with the article (BDF 253[5]; see, however, Hermas, *Vis.* 1.4.1, 3); it is in any case most unlikely that Matthew would use singular and plural so close together in the same sense. If Num 24:17 underlies Matthew's account (see commentary), the use of ἀνατέλλω in the LXX there requires the meaning "rising" here.

3. While later Christian interpretation can appropriately find in Matthew's use of προσκυνέω the sense of "worship" of a divine being, neither the word itself nor its narrative context here requires this specialized sense. It is a normal term for social homage to one recognized as being in a position of superiority or authority (cf. 18:26). See, however, H. Greeven, *TDNT* 6:763-64, for the view that in Matthew the word always implies divinity; C. F. D. Moule, *Origin,* 175-76, gives a more nuanced account. See also D. D. Kupp, *Emmanuel,* 225-28.

59

siah's birthplace.[4] 5 *They told him, "In Bethlehem in Judea, because that is what has been written through the prophet:*

6 *'And you, Bethlehem, land of Judah,*[5]
  are certainly not the least important among the rulers[6] *of Judah;*
for from you there will emerge a leader
who will be the shepherd of my people Israel.' "

7 *Then Herod called the magi to a private meeting and got them to tell him the exact time when the star had appeared.* 8 *Then he sent them off to Bethlehem, and said, "Go and make detailed inquiries about the child, and when you have found him, come back and tell me, so that I too can come and pay homage to him."*

9 *When the magi had listened to the king, they set off, and there was the star which they had seen when it rose now going ahead of*[7] *them, until it came to rest*[8] *above the place where the child was.* 10 *When they saw the star, they were absolutely delighted,*[9] 11 *and they went into the house and saw the child with his mother Mary; then they prostrated themselves and paid homage to him, and opening their treasure chests, they offered him gifts of gold, frankincense,*[10] *and myrrh.*

4. Literally, "where the Messiah was being born," the present tense of the indirect question indicating a standing truth of prophecy; Herod was asking not for news of a recent event but for a theological ruling.

5. I have translated this phrase literally so as to draw attention to Matthew's rather awkward change of wording (see commentary); as it stands, γῆ Ἰούδα must be a vocative in apposition to Βηθλέεμ, though its function is in fact to define the territory within which Bethlehem lies. R. H. Gundry, *Use*, 91, points out a parallel usage in most MSS of LXX 3 Kgdms 19:3.

6. See the commentary for Matthew's distinctive wording as compared with Hebrew and LXX. ἡγεμών is a ruler or dignitary, used especially in the NT as the title for Roman provincial governors, while ἡγούμενος in the next line is a more general term for anyone who holds a position of leadership.

7. Etymologically προάγω can be understood to mean "leading on," and that sense may well be intended here (see comments below); but Matthew normally uses the verb to mean "go in front" without a necessary sense of "leading" (see 14:22; 21:9, 31; 26:32; 28:7).

8. Literally, "coming it stood." Matthew seems to intend us to envisage that, at least from the point of view of the magi, the star was first in motion and then stationary over a specific place. Even if in fact they would have had to work out their destination from the position at a given time of a continuously "moving" star, Matthew's language is that of the observer.

9. It is difficult to find an English idiom sufficiently extravagant to capture Matthew's ἐχάρησαν χαρὰν μεγάλην σφόδρα, "they rejoiced with an exceedingly great joy." More colloquially, "they were thrilled to bits."

10. λίβανος designates specifically frankincense, the resin of trees of the *Bos-*

> 12 *Then, being warned in a dream not to go back to Herod, they went away to their own country by a different route.*

The first point Matthew needs to establish in his "geographical apologetic" for the origins of the Messiah (see above, pp. 41-42) is that Jesus "of Nazareth" was in fact born where the Messiah must be born, in the Davidic town of Bethlehem. Central to this first infancy story therefore is the combined quotation of Mic 5:2 and 2 Sam 5:2, which identifies the Messiah's birthplace specifically as Bethlehem in Judah, and the surrounding narrative explains how this was in fact the birthplace of Jesus, even though subsequent events (equally attested to both by scriptural quotation and by divine guidance in dreams) were to dictate his relocation to Nazareth in Galilee.

But there is more to being born in Bethlehem than a correct geographical origin. If Bethlehem is the town of David, a "son of David" born there is born to be "King of the Jews" (as the "book of origin" in 1:1-17 with its royal dynastic focus has already indicated). This title will not reappear in Matthew's narrative until ch. 27, when it will sum up the political charge against Jesus. There, as here, it will be used only by non-Jews; Jews themselves will use the more theologically loaded equivalents "king of Israel," "Messiah," and "Son of David." But whereas in the circumstances of ch. 27, with Jesus a prisoner on trial and going to execution, there is a sharp irony about the title "King of the Jews," here in v. 2 it has no such connotation. It is the Gentile way of saying what a Jew would mean by "Messiah" (the term which Herod, who could hardly refer to someone else as "king of the Jews," substitutes in v. 4).

This royal note runs through the story as a whole. Several strands of scriptural fulfillment are woven into the story,[11] quite apart from the overt Davidic quotation in v. 6, all of them contributing to the reader's reflection on Jesus' specific role as "King of the Jews."[12]

Most obviously,[13] the visit of foreign dignitaries to Jerusalem to see

---

wellia family, rather than "incense" in general, which could contain a variety of aromatic ingredients.

11. See G. M. Soares Prabhu, *Formula-Quotations,* 277-81, 288-92.

12. See D. J. Weaver, in D. R. Bauer and M. A. Powell (eds.), *Treasures,* 182-87, for an interesting discussion of the irony involved in Matthew's use of royal language in relation to Herod as compared with Jesus. The significance of the motif of "kingship" for the infancy narratives as a whole is well explored by D. R. Bauer, *CBQ* 57 (1995) 306-23; he, too, notes the contrast between the two "kings" Jesus and Herod, and also between the magi and Herod in terms of response to true kingship.

13. Davies and Allison, 1:251, having set out effectively the evidence for this background (250-51), surprisingly refer to it only as "rather tempting"! For a more enthusiastic estimate see J. E. Bruns, *CBQ* 23 (1961) 51-54.

the son of David recalls the story of the Queen of Sheba (1 Kgs 10:1-10), and Matthew's specific mention of the presentation of gold, frankincense, and myrrh echoes her royal gift to Solomon of "gold and a great quantity of spices" (1 Kgs 10:10), as well as other OT passages which take her visit and gifts as a model for the future glory of the Messiah (Ps 72:10-11,15: "tribute," "gifts," "gold of Sheba"; Isa 60:5-6: "the wealth of the nations," "gold and frankincense," also with specific mention of Sheba). The "kings" who are the donors in Ps 72:10-11; Isa 60:3[14] are the source of the later Christian tradition which by the early third century had turned Matthew's "magi" into kings.[15] Matthew thus prepares the way for Jesus' later declaration that "something greater than Solomon is here" (12:42).

Secondly, the star which plays such a prominent role in the story invites reflection on Balaam's prophecy in Num 24:17-19 of the rise (LXX *anatelei*, echoed in Matthew's *anatolē*, vv. 2, 9) of a "star out of Jacob and a scepter out of Israel," which is then interpreted as a ruler who will destroy Israel's enemies and take possession of the lands of Moab and Edom, a prophecy which was understood to point forward to the conquests of King David, and which thus also foreshadows the victory of the "son of David."[16]

Thirdly, the likely influence of Balaam's prophecy suggests that perhaps Balaam himself, the man who "saw" the messianic star rise (Num 24:15-17), may also be in mind as a model for the magi. He, like them, was a non-Israelite "holy man" and visionary[17] from the East: Num 22:5 locates his home on the Euphrates, while LXX Num 23:7 speaks of his being summoned from Mesopotamia and uses the same phrase *ap' anatolōn* ("from the East") which Matthew uses in 2:1. He, like the magi, was pressurized by a king (Balak) intent on destroying the true people of God, but refused to cooperate and instead took the side of God's people.[18]

---

14. A further echo of Isa 60:3 may be detected in the "rising" of the star, reflecting the coming of nations and kings "to the brightness of your rising," though the LXX word is not the same.

15. This development is traced in an interesting article by M. A. Powell, *CBQ* 62 (2000) 459-80, in which he shows that historically magi were servants of kings rather than kings themselves, as Matthew and his readers would have known, but that early interpreters (he finds Tertullian and Augustine particularly significant) made this connection on the basis of the OT texts, a conclusion which "the first evangelist probably would have found appalling" (473).

16. For the continuing appeal of "star" as a messianic term, based on Balaam's prophecy, cf. CD 7:18; *T. Levi* 18:3; *T. Jud.* 24:1. When R. Akiba recognized the guerilla leader Simon ben Kosiba as the Messiah, he coined for him the title Bar-Kokhba, "son of the star" (Schürer 1:543-44). See further R. H. Gundry, *Use,* 128-29.

17. Philo's lengthy account of Balaam (*Moses* 1.264-99) normally refers to him as a μάντις, but once uses the term μάγος (*Moses* 1.276).

18. R. E. Brown, *Birth,* 188, speaks of Balaam as "the main candidate in the pro-

Fourthly, the prominent role of Herod in the story prepares the way for his infanticide in v. 16. The story of Herod's fear for his throne and his ruthless political massacre could hardly fail to remind a Jewish reader of the Pharaoh at the time of Moses' birth whose infanticide threatened to destroy Israel's future deliverer, while Jesus' providential escape to Egypt and subsequent return will echo the story of Moses' escape from slaughter and of his subsequent exile and return when "those who were seeking your life are dead" (Exod 4:19, echoed here in 2:20). Herod's place in the story thus ensures not only a reflection on who is the true "king of the Jews" and on the contrast between Herod's ruthlessly protected political power and Jesus' different way of being "king," but also sets up the typological model for the newborn Messiah to play the role of the new Moses, who will also deliver his people (cf. 1:21) and through whose ministry a new people of God will be constituted just as Israel became God's chosen people through the exodus and the covenant at Sinai under the leadership of Moses. We shall note frequent and quite varied pointers to this New Moses and New Exodus typology as we work through Matthew's story, but its foundation has been firmly laid at the outset as the reader is invited to recognize in Herod and Jesus a counterpart to Pharaoh and Moses.

This Moses typology suggests itself even by comparison with the basic story as recorded in Exodus. But as we have already noted (see above on 1:21), Jewish traditions about the birth of Moses had by the first century developed well beyond the Exodus story, and for those who know those fuller traditions there is further rich material for typological comparison.[19] According to this developing tradition, not only was Moses' father Amram informed in a dream of his son's future role (Josephus, *Ant.* 2.210-16; see above, p. 52, n. 45), but Pharaoh too, who according to the Exodus account was simply aiming at a genocidal reduction of the Israelite population, was, according to Josephus (*Ant.* 2.205,209), specifically warned of the birth of one child who was destined to humble Egypt and exalt Israel, as a result of which both Pharaoh and the Egyptians were alarmed (*Ant.* 2.206, 215; cf. Matt 2:3) and decided on the policy of infanticide. The warning was delivered, according to Josephus, by an Egyptian "sacred scribe" *(hierogrammateus),* but other sources attribute it more specifically to "astrologers" *(Exod. Rab.* 1:18; *b. Sanh.* 101b), which would correspond to Matthew's *magoi.* According to *Tg. Ps.-J.* Exod. 1:15, Pharaoh himself had a dream which was interpreted to

---

posals for OT background," and goes on to argue the case at length, pp. 190-96. Cf. J. M. Hull, *Magic,* 124-26.

19. For a full analysis of the traditions and their echoes in Matt 1–2 see D. C. Allison, *Moses,* 140-60. More briefly Davies and Allison, 1:192-93; M. M. Bourke, *CBQ* 22 (1960) 161-66; G. M. Soares Prabhu, *Formula-Quotations,* 288-92.

similar effect by his magicians, Jannes and Jambres. The element of a specific targeting of the destined deliverer which is missing from the Exodus account is thus supplied to make Matthew's typological parallel still more compelling for those in the know.[20]

The story of the homage of the magi is thus not only a demonstration of the fulfillment of the messianic prophecy of Mic 5:2 but also a multilayered study of the fulfillment of scriptural models in the coming of Jesus, with royal, messianic motifs at the heart of those models. It is, of course, also an infancy story (though not, like the rest of 1:18–2:23, one narrated from the point of view of Joseph), and the magi have appropriately taken their place in traditional nativity scenes alongside Luke's shepherds and angels, even though neither evangelist betrays any awareness of the other's narrative elements. The only internal clue to how much time Matthew may have thought to elapse between the birth of Jesus and this visit is Herod's targeting of children "up to two years old," but that need not reflect a precise interval. If the initial appearance of the star was understood to mark the time of the Messiah's birth (as Herod apparently thought, v. 7), the visit must be sufficiently long after that to allow the magi to reach Jerusalem from their unspecified country of origin (see on v. 1); the contiguous arrival at the manger of Luke's shepherds and Matthew's magi thus owes more to theatrical convenience than to historical probability!

But were there really any magi? As for most of the narratives in the gospels, there is of course no independent confirmation for this account (which appears to be from a different source from the rest of Matthew's infancy narratives; see on v. 11). A parallel is sometimes found in the famous visit by eastern magi to Rome to pay homage to Nero in A.D. 66,[21] but the parallels are not very close (Rome is not Jerusalem, and the political advantages of such a visit to the reigning emperor are hardly comparable to the motivation of Matthew's magi), and the visit took place after what I regard as the most likely date of Matthew's gospel. At the most it demonstrates that high-ranking eastern magi were willing and able to travel west for diplomatic reasons. There is evidence that astrologers in Babylonia were interested in events in "the Westland" (Palestine).[22] The alarm of Herod at the hint of a royal rival, and his subsequent violent response, ring true to what we know of

20. For less convincing parallels in Jewish tradition relating to threats to the lives of Abraham and Jacob see my article in *NovT* 21 (1979) 106-7.

21. Dio Cassius 63.1-7; Suetonius, *Nero* 13. The visitors were King Tiridates of Armenia and three local Parthian princes, and their homage to the emperor was motivated by their reading of the stars; Pliny, *Hist. nat.* 30.6.16-17 calls them magi. For a fuller account see R. A. Horsley, *Liberation,* 56-57.

22. W. C. Allen, *The Gospel according to S. Matthew* (ICC; Edinburgh: T&T Clark, [3]1912), 11, cites relevant passages from Mesopotamian astrological texts.

the later years of his reign (see below on v. 16). So the basic story line is not out of keeping with our knowledge of the period, but independent confirmation is in the nature of the case most improbable.[23]

The element in the story which most obviously invites scepticism is the guiding star with its apparently purposeful movement and stopping to indicate a specific location (see on v. 9). See below on v. 2 for some attempts to explain it in astronomical terms. But again, this is not a hopeful quest: the information Matthew provides is very limited, and in any case a story teller's account from the point of view of even astronomically alert observers in a prescientific culture (presumably after being relayed by a number of less sophisticated intermediary sources) is not a promising basis for scientific reconstruction. Nor is such reconstruction necessary to appreciate Matthew's story. That a group of astrologers believed that the star had "guided" them to the right place is quite credible, but what it was about the phenomenon which led them to this conclusion we cannot now hope to know.

See below for the dubious reputation of magi in Jewish and Christian circles. If there were no historical basis for this narrative, it is unlikely that a church which repudiated astrology and magic would have embarrassed itself by inventing such undesirable witnesses to the Messiah.[24]

1 Matthew has given us no information on where Joseph and Mary lived, or on how they came to be in Bethlehem. The natural assumption is that it was their home, to which they naturally tried to return after their asylum in Egypt (vv. 21-22); only Luke's independent narrative indicates otherwise. Matthew's "geographical apologetic" for a Galilean Messiah prompts him both here and in v. 5 to specify that Bethlehem is "in Judea" (and cf. the double mention of Judah in the quotation in v. 6) in contrast with Jesus' later domicile.[25]

---

23. A well-documented study of the history of magi and of the influence of astrology in the ancient world by E. M. Yamauchi, in J. Vardaman and E. M. Yamauchi (eds.), *Chronos, Kairos, Christos*, 23-39, concludes "that we can best understand the story of the Magi in Matthew not as a literary creation but as based on a historical episode."

24. Some of the church fathers (e.g., Ignatius, *Eph.* 19:2-3) saw the magi not as positive witnesses but as opponents of true religion who are here depicted as bowing in (reluctant) submission to the conquering Messiah. This view was most notably expressed in modern times by W. K. L. Clarke in a memorably titled article, "The Rout of the Magi," printed in his collection *Divine Humanity* (London: SPCK, 1936), 41-51; Clarke's article included the suggestion that the "gifts" of the magi were in fact "the instruments of their trade" now surrendered to the Messiah. In response see J. M. Hull, *Magic*, 123-28. W. D. Davies, *Setting*, 78-80, considers with some favor the view that Matthew represents Christ's victory over the magi as a parallel to Moses' conquest of the magicians of Egypt, but in Davies and Allison, 1:228-29, the suggestion is set aside.

25. A Bethlehem in Galilee is mentioned in Josh 19:15 and was perhaps the home of the minor judge Ibzan (Judg 12:8-10), but Matthew's specification would hardly be needed to differentiate the well-known city of David from this obscure place.

The proximity of Bethlehem to Jerusalem facilitates the final stage of the magi's quest and Herod's subsequent raid on the village. The date of Jesus' birth "in the days of King Herod" must be long enough before Herod's death, which is normally dated in the spring of 4 B.C.,[26] to allow for the journey of the magi and Herod's subsequent action before that date. Luke 1:5 also dates the conception of John the Baptist (and therefore presumably also the conception of Jesus six months later, Luke 1:36) during Herod's reign. There is no agreement on a more precise dating of Jesus' birth (but see below on the star, v. 2).

Magos,[27] originally the title of a Persian priestly caste who played an important role in advising the king, was applied more widely to learned men and priests who specialized in astrology and the interpretation of dreams, and in some cases magical arts.[28] It is the term used sometimes in LXX and more often in Theodotion for the Babylonian court "magicians" of Dan 1:20; 2:2, 10, 27, etc. who were expected to interpret dreams. I have used Matthew's term "magi"[29] in the translation because *magos* is not necessarily as specific as our term "astrologer," though the fact that these men were guided by a star indicates that this was at least part of their area of interest. Magi were found all over the Roman world but were specially associated with Babylonia, and that is the most likely meaning of the term "the East" when written from the point of view of Palestine. The gifts they brought are particularly associated with Arabia (see on v. 11), but even if that was their source, it is not necessary to suppose that the magi themselves came from there.[30]

Many uses of *magos,* especially in a Jewish or Christian context,[31] are

26. Schürer 1:326-28 (n. 165); T. D. Barnes, *JTS* 19 (1968) 204-9; J. Van Bruggen in T. Baarda et al. (eds.), *Miscellanea Neotestamentica,* 2:1-15. A more recent volume, J. Vardaman and E. M. Yamauchi (eds.), *Chronos, Kairos, Christos,* contains articles which present the arguments for, respectively, 1 B.C. (E. L. Martin, 85-92)) and 4 B.C. (H. W. Hoehner, 101-11). The latter is the majority view. See also the comments of R. E. Brown, *Birth,* 607-8.

27. For magi and astrology in the ancient world see the valuable survey by E. M. Yamauchi in the article cited at n. 23 above.

28. G. Delling, *TDNT* 4:356-59. See H. C. Kee, *Medicine,* 99-101, for the place of magic in the role of magi in Persia and beyond.

29. I have avoided the traditional English rendering "wise men" since it implies an evaluation which Matthew's technical term does not convey. M. A. Powell, *NTS* 46 (2000) 1-20, argues that the term μάγοι would predispose Matthew's readers to a negative evaluation, and that Matthew expects them to regard these visitors "not as wise men but as fools" (5-8). The fact that God chooses such men to receive his revelation is a sign not of their wisdom but of their foolishness and ignorance, on the principle set out in 11:25 (8-13).

30. See R. E. Brown, *Birth,* 168-70, for attempts to define their origin more precisely.

31. In pagan Greek, too, μάγος was sometimes used to mean a "charlatan"; e.g., Sophocles, *Oed. Tyr.* 387; Plato, *Rep.* 572E. For a Jewish parallel cf. Josephus, *Ant.* 20.142.

clearly pejorative,[32] notably of the "false prophet" Bar-Jesus in Acts 13:6, 8.[33] Not every mention of magi necessarily refers to what we would now call "magic," but it was a grey area from which Jews and Christians preferred to keep their distance.[34] It is therefore remarkable to find Matthew introducing magi into his story without any sign of disapproval. However widely respected the magi may have been in Mesopotamia and more widely in the Greek and Roman world, their title was not one which a careful Christian would willingly introduce without warrant into his account of the origins of his faith. The most satisfactory explanation for their presence in Matthew's narrative is that this was an element which he had received in his tradition and (probably because the role of the star required them to be identified as such) did not feel at liberty to disguise.[35]

Whatever the social and religious unsuitability of magi, the fact that they were not Jews[36] fitted more congenially with Matthew's universalist agenda. To have the "King of the Jews" recognized and honored first not by his own people but by representatives of the "many" who were later to come from the east and the west to take their place in the kingdom of heaven (8:11) appropriately set the scene for the ministry of the Israelite Messiah who would both be rejected by his own people (here foreshadowed by the stance of Herod and "all Jerusalem"; see on v. 3) and send out his disciples to recruit from all nations (28:19).

As foreigners Matthew's magi naturally began their inquiries in Jerusalem, the capital, and the place where a potential "king" might be expected

32. The expanded version of the Decalogue in *Did.* 2:2 includes the command οὐ μαγεύσεις. Cf. also Ignatius, *Eph.* 19:3, and the inclusion of μαγεία in the vice lists of *Did.* 5:1; *Barn.* 20:1.

33. Cf. also the cognate words μαγεύω and μαγεία used in Acts 8:9, 11 for Simon, who became famous in later Christian tradition as "Simon Magus" the arch-heretic.

34. See, however, Albright and Mann, 14, for the continuing fascination of astrology within Judaism, and more fully P. S. Alexander, in Schürer 3:342-79, on Jewish magic, including numerous examples of astrological interest.

35. See p. 65, n. 24, for the patristic notion that this encounter signified the Messiah's conquest over astrology and magical arts as Moses triumphed over the magicians of Egypt. Matthew's language does not support this view: the magi are presented in a positive light, and apparently return home to continue as magi.

36. Albright and Mann, 12, 16, dispute this, but only on the negative grounds that "there is no indication in the story that we were meant to identify the magi as Gentiles." For most interpreters their eastern origin (referred to in v. 12 as "their own country"), their ignorance of Jewish messianic tradition, their use of "King of the Jews," and not least the title μάγος itself are more than enough indication. Moreover, the OT passages which underlie Matthew's story provide non-Jewish models for the magi (Queen of Sheba, Balaam) and speak specifically of homage from foreign nations (Ps 72:10-11; Isa 60:5-6).

to be found. It was only through local information that they could discover the "correct" birthplace of the son of David.

2 Their astrological deductions from the "rising" of a star had convinced the magi of a royal birth in the "westland" (Palestine), hence the title "King of the Jews."[37] The idea that a special star heralded the birth of famous people (and other significant events) was widespread in the ancient world.[38] The magi were presumably aware of Herod's royal position, and perhaps assuming that a birth had taken place within his family, they had come to find out more.

Both astronomers and biblical historians continue to try to identify the nature of the rising of the star and its subsequent movements on the basis of Matthew's brief description and of astronomical data, but with little consensus.[39] Three recurrent suggestions[40] perhaps deserve a mention.

1. A comet. Comets have long been held to herald the arrival of important figures on the world stage, and a comet visible in the western sky might well explain the journey of the magi, but unfortunately astronomers have not been able to identify a comet which would have been visible at about the right historical date. Halley's comet appeared in 12-11 B.C., too early to fit the chronological data of the gospels.

2. A planetary conjunction (rather than a single star, as Matthew describes it). The favorite candidate here is a conjunction of Jupiter and Saturn in the constellation of Pisces, which would have taken place in 7 B.C., and which could have been interpreted to mean the birth of a king (Jupiter, the royal planet) in Palestine (Saturn was thought to be the planet representing the "westland"), while the constellation of Pisces represented the last days. This unusual conjunction thus indicated, "There will appear in Palestine in this year the ruler of the last days."[41]

37. See on 27:11 for the meaning of Ἰουδαῖοι in this phrase (and cf. comments on 28:15). The magi are unlikely to have seen the different areas of Herod's kingdom as significantly distinct, and at this time, unlike at the time of Jesus' trial, both Galilee and Judea came under the same political administration. Herod was "king of the Jews," not just king of Judea (see 65, n. 24 below).

38. See R. E. Brown, *Birth,* 170-71, 610; Davies and Allison, 233-34, for numerous examples. See also M. Hengel and H. Merkel in P. Hoffmann (ed.), *Orientierung an Jesus,* 147-50. See also J. H. Neyrey, *Honor,* 99-101, more generally for "dreams, celestial phenomena, prophecies of greatness" as regular features of ancient accounts of the birth of important people.

39. The various theories are set out by J. Finegan, *Chronology,* 238-48; R. E. Brown, *Birth,* 171-73, 610-13.

40. H. W. Montefiore, *NovT* 4 (1960) 140-46, imaginatively combines elements of all three, together with Josephus's account, *War* 6.289, of a star which stood over Jerusalem and a comet which appeared there for a year before its destruction by the Romans.

41. E. Stauffer, *Jesus,* 36-38 (quotation from p. 37); R. A. Rosenberg, *Bib* 53

3. A nova (or perhaps a supernova). This is the result of a stellar explosion and produces an extremely bright phenomenon which usually lasts for a number of months. This was the preferred theory of Johannes Kepler, even though he also noted the planetary conjunction of 7 B.C. Chinese astronomers recorded a nova which was visible for seventy days in 5/4 B.C., which would fit a date shortly before the death of Herod.[42]

While proponents of at least the second and third of the above theories are convinced that their astronomical results sufficiently match Matthew's description, those of us who are not astronomers may find it hard to envisage either of these phenomena first "rising," then "leading on" the magi, and eventually "coming to rest" in such a way as to indicate a specific location, even when due allowance is made for the phenomenal viewpoint of the storyteller's language. Despite the fascination of astronomical explanations, it may in the end be more appropriate to interpret Matt 2:9 as describing not a regular astronomical occurrence but the miraculous provision of what appeared to be a star which uniquely moved and then stopped (or at least which appeared to observers on the ground to do so), though of course there is no improbability in a natural astronomical phenomenon being the basis on which the magi made their initial deductions and set off on their journey.

The nature of the "homage" of the magi (the verb recurs in vv. 8 and 11) is not clearly spelled out, except for the offering of expensive gifts, such as might befit a royal birth. Their "prostration" (v. 11; literally, "falling") was a familiar act of homage in Eastern society, a recognition of social superiority. Neither term requires the attribution of divinity to the one so honored, and Matthew's narrative does not indicate that the magi had any such notion (they came looking for a "king," not a "god"), though he might expect his Christian readers with hindsight to read more into the "worship" of the magi.

3 Herod's alarm at the mention of a new "king of the Jews"[43] is

---

(1972) 105-9. The movements of Jupiter at this time are reconstructed in great detail, with "photographs" of the night sky at a series of relevant dates, by the astronomer Konradin Ferrari d'Occhieppo, *Stern;* he concludes that Jupiter and Saturn "stood still" and pointed to Bethlehem on 12 November, 7 B.C. He has published a summary of his views in English in J. Vardaman and E. M. Yamauchi (eds.), *Chronos, Kairos, Christos,* 41-53.

42. J. Finegan, *Chronology,* 246-48. The Chinese records were mentioned in this connection as early as F. Münter, *Der Stern der Weisen* (Copenhagen, 1827), 29. The idea was developed further by D. H. Clark and two colleagues (apparently unaware of Münter's work) in the *Quarterly Journal of the Royal Astronomical Society* 18 (1977) 443-49. C. J. Humphreys, *TynBul* 43 (1992) 31-56, argues, however, that what the Chinese astronomers saw was in fact a comet.

43. Josephus, *Ant.* 16.311, uses the same title for Herod (ὁ τῶν Ἰουδαίων βασιλεύς) which the magi have used here. In *Ant.* 15.373 he records how when Herod was a boy, an Essene prophet greeted him as (future) βασιλεὺς Ἰουδαίων.

hardly surprising, and reflects the extraordinary paranoia of his defense of his throne in his latter years (see below on v. 16). He was particularly vulnerable to one "born as king,"that is, of the traditional royal house, whereas Herod himself, son of an Idumean adventurer,[44] had no such ancestral right to the throne. The sharing of his alarm by "all Jerusalem" is more ambiguous. There seems to have been little love lost between the Idumean Herod and his Jewish subjects[45] by this time, and one might have expected them to welcome rather than fear the prospect of a new king, particularly one who truly represented the house of David (though it is interesting that the Davidic note is less pronounced in this pericope, coming to the surface only in the priests' ruling in vv. 5-6). Perhaps their fear was not so much of the toppling of Herod as of the violent reprisals which such a threat might be expected to evoke; an angry and threatened Herod was a danger to all around him. But probably Matthew has a more ideological motive in the way he has phrased this verse, in that throughout his gospel Jerusalem will be portrayed as the place of opposition and rejection for the true Messiah (see above, p. 7), so that it is appropriate that, just as "all the city" will be "stirred up" by Jesus' arrival as the royal son of David in 21:10 (long after Herod is off the scene), so "all Jerusalem" is already perturbed at the prospect of a dynastic revolution. It will be there in Jerusalem that eventually "all the people" will accept responsibility for the death of their Messiah (27:24-25).

4 Herod's concern over a potential rival leads him to consult the experts. The "chief priests and scribes of the people,"[46] together with the lay "el-

---

44. Herod was the son of Antipater, an Idumean (in OT terms Edomite; see Mal 1:4 for the implications of this) from a family which had accepted the Jewish religion; his mother was from Arabia (Josephus, *War* 1.181). From the Roman point of view Herod was in effect a Jew, but the Jews never accepted him as one of their own. Josephus, *Ant.* 14.403, records an objection to Herod's being made king on the ground that, as an Idumean, he was only a "half-Jew."

45. R. A. Horsley, *Liberation,* 49-52, points out, however, that Jerusalem was the power base of the high-priestly families who owed their position to Herod, so that if "all Jerusalem" here refers to "official Jerusalem" rather than the populace as a whole, the hostility to a new king of the Jews is historically plausible.

46. The addition of τοῦ λαοῦ may simply be Matthew's way of specifying that this was a group of representative Israelite leaders, but U. Luz, *Theology,* 27, may be right in seeing here as well as in the alarm of "all Jerusalem" in the previous verse a hint already of Matthew's interest in tracing the rejection of the Messiah by his people which will reach its terrible climax in 27:25. Here Luz sees the priests and scribes as "accomplices" in Herod's hostile plan, putting them with Herod and the people of Jerusalem "on the opposite side" to "the pagan elite who now stand on the side of Jesus." J. D. Kingsbury, in G. N. Stanton (ed.), *Interpretation,* 186-88, argues that "the Jewish leaders" are deliberately introduced here as those who, as the story develops, will take over from Herod the role of opposition to the Messiah.

ders," made up the Sanhedrin, the central Jewish authority under the Roman-appointed Herod. The introductory "all" makes this sound like a formal consultation,[47] but relations between Herod and the Sanhedrin were not cordial, and it may be that Matthew has exaggerated the formal nature of an ad hoc consultation with selected experts who were prepared to advise on a matter of Jewish tradition on which Herod, a politician with only limited Jewish background (see n. 44 above), may have felt ill informed. Matthew's interest is specifically in the birthplace of the Messiah, which was also the subject of the magi's question, but we may reasonably assume that Herod would wish to be forearmed with a full account of current messianic expectation.

5   For "in Judea" see on v. 1. The ruling of the experts, which would have been expected at the time (cf. John 7:41-42), is based not on history (since it would be more natural for a "son of David" to be born in Jerusalem, David's capital, as Solomon had been) but specifically on prophecy, thus providing Matthew with the first of the four "geographical quotations" which form the apologetic framework of this chapter (see above, pp. 40-42). The formula which introduces this quotation differs from the normal form (see on 1:22) because the quotation is presented not as an editorial comment but as part of the priests' and scribes' reply. So in place of an explicit statement that events had occurred "to fulfill [or "then was fulfilled"] what had been declared," we find here "because that is what has been written," a form which suits the role of the quotation within direct speech as providing the scriptural grounding for the ruling just given; the quotation formula *legontos*, "saying," is also omitted after a verb of writing rather than of speaking, even though a specific prophetic oracle is being cited (in 2:23 it will be omitted for a different reason). But while the formula has been adapted to the narrative context, most interpreters agree that the following quotation is of the same character as the other "formula-quotations," and thus forms the second of the five such quotations around which 1:18–2:23 is structured.[48]

6   The text cited is the recognized messianic prophecy of Mic 5:2 (Hebrew and LXX 5:1), which is the more appropriate to Matthew's context

---

47. The πάντας may also be intended to signal the complicity of the whole Jewish establishment in the eventual rejection of Jesus (see previous note); cf. πᾶς ὁ λαός in 27:25. Readers who knew of the later role of the Jerusalem authorities would perhaps recognize in their cooperation with Herod the beginnings of their opposition to Jesus, but Matthew does not place emphasis on their role at this point; they are merely a source of information. Still less does he indicate that their failure to profit from their theological knowledge by joining the magi in seeking the Messiah should be read as "challenging what he regards as spiritual complacency" (Keener, 103-4).

48. G. M. Soares Prabhu, *Formula-Quotations,* 36-40, concludes that it is "a formula quotation by adoption." See contra, however, M. J. J. Menken, *Matthew's Bible,* 255-56.

because it is immediately followed in Mic 5:3 by a specific mention of the time when "she who is in labor has brought forth." But the last eight words of Matthew's quotation, while reflecting the sense of the Micah passage, are in fact a more direct echo of 2 Sam 5:2: "a leader" *(hēgoumenon)* is the LXX term in 2 Sam 5:2 for David's role, as against "ruler" in Mic 5:2, and "who will be the shepherd of my people Israel" directly echoes God's call to David in 2 Sam 5:2 (alluding to David's shepherding background). The latter phrase reflects (but not so closely) the language of Mic 5:4, "he shall feed his flock in the strength of the LORD," and defines the caring rather than despotic role of this ideal king in contrast with Herod's reign.[49] The two OT passages are closely related, 2 Sam 5:2 giving God's original call to David, and Mic 5:2 taking up its language to describe the future role of the coming Davidic king in fulfillment of his great ancestor's achievements. Matthew's combined quotation of these two passages draws out the integral connection between them more effectively than a more pedantic exegetical commentary. For similar "combined quotations" see on 11:10 and 21:4-5, and for a much more elaborate and creative example see on 27:9-10.

But that is not the only alteration Matthew has made to the wording of Mic 5:2. For the familar but perhaps rather archaic title "Bethlehem Ephrathah" he has substituted the more specific geographical identification "Bethlehem, land of Judah" (see p. 60, n. 5). The change is not required to distinguish this Bethlehem from the other in Galilee (see p. 65, n. 25), since "Ephrathah," a well-attested alternative name for the Judean Bethlehem or its immediate neighborhood (Gen 35:19; 48:7; Ruth 4:11), would have achieved that; rather, it is to emphasize Jesus' Judean origins, as Matthew has already done in vv. 1 and 5 and as the next line of the prophecy will further underline. For Matthew's apologetic purpose this southern origin is essential. As the name Judah now appears twice in Matthew's amended quotation, the reader is also invited to remember that the "book of origin" traced the dynastic line through Judah the patriarch; only a member of the tribe of Judah could qualify for the throne of David.

Of the two changes which follow one may merely reflect a variant reading: the Hebrew *ʾalāphîm* is notoriously uncertain in meaning, and while LXX has opted for the frequent meaning "thousands," most English versions take the Hebrew here to mean "families" or "clans," while a slight revocalization would produce "chieftains," the probable source of Matthew's "rulers." There is no significant advantage in this change from the point of view of Matthew's argument. But the other change is blatantly to Matthew's advan-

---

49. For Jesus as shepherd cf. 9:36; 25:32-33; 26:31, and for the theme of sheep and shepherd in Matthew see R. E. Menninger, *Israel,* 142-48, who finds in it a significant pointer to a "remnant" theology in this gospel.

tage. Where Micah described Bethlehem as "small (insignificant)[50] to be among the clans of Judah" and LXX went further and made it "smallest," for Matthew it is "certainly not the least important." There is poor support for an original reading in Micah with the negative,[51] and Matthew's negative is emphatic; it derives not from the text of Micah but from Matthew's own reading of the text in the light of its fulfillment. The whole point of Micah's mentioning Bethlehem's insignificance was by way of contrast to the glory it was to achieve as the birthplace of the Messiah; now Matthew can claim that that glory has come to Bethlehem, so that it is no longer the least (and the addition of "for" to introduce the next clause underlines the point). Rather than add a footnote, Matthew has incorporated the fulfillment into the wording of the text.[52] For those who are familiar with the original text the alteration will stand out as a challenge to think through how Matthew's story relates to the prophetic tradition.

In a number of ways, therefore, Matthew has adapted Micah's words to suit what he can now see to be their fulfillment, and to advance his argument for the scriptural justification of the Messiah's origins. This relatively free and creative handling of the text (not unlike that found in contemporary Aramaic targums) differs little from the practice of many modern preachers who, if not reading directly out of the Bible, will often (probably quite unconsciously) quote a text in an adapted form which helps the audience to see how the text relates to the argument. No one is misled, and the hermeneutical procedure is well understood. Micah's words have been applied appropriately, even if not with the literalistic precision which the age of the printed Bible makes possible.[53]

7-8 Herod was probably interested in the *time* of the star's first ap-

---

50. The force of the Hebrew adjective *ṣāʿîr* is illustrated by the folk etymology of the name of the town Zoar in Gen 19:20: "Is it not a little one?"

51. R. H. Gundry, *Use,* 92, n. 3, attempts to find such support, but apart from the Arabic version (a late, secondary version not dependent on the Hebrew) and the Lucianic revision of the LXX (which here as often is best explained by the influence of the NT text) his grounds are speculative. The emphatic form of Matthew's negative renders improbable the suggestion (e.g., by G. M. Soares Prabhu, *Formula-Quotations,* 264: "a plausible variant") that the Hebrew *lihyôt,* "to be," has been misread as *lôʾheyît,* "you are not," which would produce a Greek οὐκ rather than οὐδαμῶς. I do not understand Soares Prabhu's bald assertion that a Matthean insertion of οὐδαμῶς is unlikely because "it does not really contribute . . . to the christological interpretation of the text." Quite the contrary!

52. G. M. Soares Prabhu, *Formula-Quotations,* 263-64, claims a tendency in this direction already in the LXX (which he reads [why?] as a rhetorical question) and the targum (with an added *kᵉ,* "as it were").

53. K. Stendahl, *School,* 101, n. 1, quotes Jerome's suggestion that Matthew has deliberately misquoted Micah in order "to show how carelessly the scribes handled the holy Scriptures." He could hardly have been further from the truth!

pearance because he assumed that the baby was born at the time it appeared; the response to his question thus becomes in v. 16 the basis for his killing of babies in Bethlehem up to two years old. It is often suggested that the real Herod would not have been so incompetent as to rely on the good faith of the magi rather than sending an escort with them to ensure a correct report back or even to carry out the intended assassination there and then. But Herod had a liking for the use of undercover agents,[54] and he had no reason to doubt their compliance, while an armed escort might well have jeopardized a successful search for the family concerned. Moreover, the impression one gets at least from Josephus's account of Herod's latter years is hardly that of a rational planner.[55] We may well suppose that the magi, even before their dream in v. 12, would have had their suspicions aroused by the desire of the reigning king to pay homage to a supposed "heir to the throne" whose whereabouts he did not know and of whose very existence he had hitherto been ignorant.

9-10 The question of the magi (v. 2) has been answered, and now they can complete their journey. But whereas hitherto Matthew has described them as traveling to Jerusalem because they saw the rising of the star, not as actually led by it, his words here indicate that the star now first moved ahead of the magi[56] and then stopped (literally, "having come took its stand," aorist tense) in a position which indicated the location of the child. What sort of phenomenon gave this impression to expert observers as they traveled south from Jerusalem must be a matter of conjecture.[57] They already knew from Herod that Bethlehem (a mere five or six miles from Jerusalem) was their destination, so that they did not need the star to tell them that; their extravagantly expressed joy (see p. 60, n. 9) is hard to explain unless the star somehow indicated the actual house rather than just the village as a whole.[58] It seems, then, that the star's movement gave them the final supernatural direction they needed to the specific house "where the child was."[59]

11 The mention of a "house" is often supposed either to contradict Luke's account of Jesus' birth in a stable or to indicate a sufficient time-lapse

54. Cf. Josephus, *Ant.* 15.366-67; 16.236.

55. A. Schalit, *König Herodes,* 648-49, describes Herod in his last years as "no longer in full possession of his faculties and right on the edge of insanity."

56. It "was going ahead of them," imperfect tense; the verb could mean "was leading them forward"; see p. 60, n. 7).

57. See on v. 2 for theories about what the "star" was.

58. D. C. Allison, *Moses,* 152-53, offers some interesting thoughts on how our scientific concept of stars may differ from ancient understanding, and suggests that the latter may have found it much easier to envisage a star coming down to and even entering a house.

59. For a pagan parallel to the idea of specific guidance by a moving star see Virgil, *Aen.* 2.692-98.

to allow the family to relocate to better quarters in Bethlehem. It is, however, becoming increasingly recognized that the "stable" owes more to Western misunderstanding than to Luke, who speaks only of a "manger." In a normal Palestinian home of the period the mangers would be found not in a separate building but on the edge of the raised family living area where the animals, who were brought into the lower section of the one-room house at night, could conveniently reach them.[60] The point of Luke's mention of the manger is not therefore that Jesus' birth took place outside a normal house, but that in that particular house the "guest room"[61] was already occupied (by other census visitors?) so that the baby was placed in the most comfortable remaining area, a manger on the living-room floor. There is therefore no reason why they should not be in the same "house" when Matthew's magi arrive.

In view of the prominence of Joseph throughout the rest of Matthew's infancy stories, it is remarkable that here only Mary is mentioned as being with the child — indeed, Joseph is not mentioned in the story of the magi at all. This suggests that this pericope does not come from the same source as 1:18-25 and 2:13-23, all of which is told as Joseph's story, but from an independent tradition, even though it provides the essential basis for the family's flight and Herod's infanticide in the following pericopes. Note that the phrase "the child and his mother" will recur in 2:13, 14, 20, 21, in each case with the child mentioned first, as here, but in all those other cases they are the object of Joseph's action, not mentioned independently of him as here.

We do not know what social position these magi held, but it was sufficient for them to have felt it appropriate to go to visit a newborn king, and to have been given an audience with the king in Jerusalem. For these foreign dignitaries to prostrate themselves in homage before a child in an ordinary house in Bethlehem is a remarkable illustration of the reversal of the world's values which will become such a prominent feature of the Messiah's proclamation of the kingdom of heaven (18:1-5; 20:25-28, etc.). Their gifts are those of the affluent: gold, then as now the symbol of ultimate value, and exotic spices, which would not normally come within the budget of an ordinary Jewish family. Frankincense (which came from Southern Arabia and Somalia) was an expensive perfume, and was burned not only in worship but at important social occasions; for its nonreligious use (with myrrh) see Song 3:6; 4:6, 14; cf. Sir 24:15. Despite the symbolism traditionally discerned in the

---

60. For a full presentation of this exegesis see K. E. Bailey, *Near East School of Theology Review* 2 (1979) 33-44, reprinted in *Evangelical Review of Theology* 4 (1980) 201-17. Also H. Must, *NTS* 32 (1986) 136-43; J. Nolland, *Luke 1–9:20*, 105-6.

61. κατάλυμα regularly means a lodging place or guest room, probably on an upper floor, as in Luke 22:11. The traditional Western translation "inn" owes nothing to Luke's wording, which is unambiguous; when Luke wants to refer to an inn (πανδοχεῖον) he is quite capable of doing so (Luke 10:34).

gifts of the magi since the time of Irenaeus (gold for royalty, frankincense for divinity, and myrrh for death and burial — the latter based on John 19:39), myrrh, too, was primarily used as a luxurious cosmetic fragrance (Esth 2:12; Ps 45:8; Prov 7:17; Song 1:13; 5:1, 5). These are luxury gifts, fit for a king. The reader who knows the OT stories cannot fail to be reminded of the visit of the Queen of Sheba with her gifts of "gold and a great quantity of spices" to the son of David in Jerusalem (1 Kgs 10:1-10), and of the imagery which that visit provided for subsequent depictions of the homage of the nations to the Jewish Messiah (Ps 72:10-11, 15; Isa 60:5-6).[62]

12 The role of the magi in Matthew's story is now complete, and they set off for home. But their route home, no less than their arrival, is supernaturally directed. This dream is not said to include an angelic messenger, but instead (as also in 2:22, where again an angel is not mentioned) the verb translated "warned" indicates the divine origin of the message; *chrēmatizō* is used especially for divine communications; cf. Luke 2:26; Acts 10:22; Heb 8:5; 11:7; 12:25. Dreams, like stars, were for magi an expected form of divine revelation, and God communicates with them in the terms they would understand. But the route he now prescribes is to have serious consequences (v. 16).

3. God's Son Brought out of Egypt (2:13-15)

13 *When they had gone away, suddenly*[1] *an angel of the Lord appeared to Joseph in a dream and said, "Get up, and take the child and his mother with you, and run away to Egypt, and stay there until I tell you; Herod is intending to search for the child so that he can destroy him."* 14 *So Joseph got up, and took the child and his mother with him that same night, and escaped*[2] *to Egypt,* 15 *and stayed there until Herod had died. This was to fulfill what had been declared by the Lord through the prophet, who said,*

"Out of Egypt I called my son."

62. For the royal honors implied by the gifts see J. H. Neyrey, *Honor,* 59-60.

1. See above, p. 46, n. 19; the wording here is very similar to that of 1:20 (and of 2:19).

2. While not every use of ἀναχωρέω in Matthew carries a necessary connotation of escaping from a place of danger (e.g., in vv. 12 and 13 it is used for the magi "going away," though there too the background is the menace of Herod), that sense is clear here and in v. 22, as it will be also in 4:12; 12:15; 14:13; 15:21, in each case following a threatening event or report. The verb here is not the same as in the angel's warning to "run away" (φεύγω), but this is clearly Joseph's obedient response to that warning. For a useful study of ἀναχωρέω in Matthew see D. Good, *NovT* 32 (1990) 1-12; she finds a consistent motif of "withdrawal" which she interprets as part of "a three-fold pattern of hostility / withdrawal / prophetic fulfilment."

The first relocation which Matthew narrates in this "geographical" chapter is one which is mentioned nowhere else in the NT tradition. While later Christian tradition has added imaginary elements to the story of the journey to Egypt,[3] Matthew's account is extremely brief and basic. He tells us nothing of the journey (except that it began at night) or of where the family lived in Egypt, nor of how that time was spent. Apart from explaining how the Messiah avoided Herod's infanticide, Matthew's purpose in mentioning the Egyptian visit seems to be to provide the basis for the second of his geographical formula-quotations, with its specific mention of Egypt as the place from which God's son has been called.

The tradition of a time spent in Egypt has perhaps left its mark in the rabbinic allegation that Jesus learned in Egypt the magical arts which enabled him to "lead Israel astray." This motif is found as early as R. Eliezer ben Hyrcanus at the end of the first century A.D.,[4] and became a recurrent feature in anti-Christian polemic,[5] reflected, for instance, in Origen, *Cels.* 1.29. This allegation may derive from a garbled awareness of the tradition as narrated by Matthew, but since in Jewish tradition Egypt was a center of magic, once Jesus came to be viewed as a sorcerer, an Egyptian connection could have been developed without any historical foundation. It certainly cannot carry the weight of an independent testimony to Matthew's narrative, which concerns Jesus' infancy rather than the age at which he might have learned magic.

The inclusion of Egypt in Jesus' infant itinerary has for Matthew two scriptural resonances which do not fit neatly together. On the one hand, Jesus is the new Moses, and it was in Egypt that Moses escaped the infanticide of Pharaoh, and from Egypt that as an adult he fled to escape Pharaoh's anger (Exod 2:11-15), returning eventually to Egypt when "those who sought your life are dead" (Exod 4:19, echoed by Matthew in 2:20; see comments there).

---

3. Traditions both of the journey and of the time in Egypt are quoted by R. E. Brown, *Birth,* 203-4. See especially the lengthy account from the *Gospel of Pseudo-Matthew* (8th century?, but drawing on earlier tradition), quoted in Hennecke, 1.410-13.

4. *B. Šabb.* 104b, taking Ben Stada as a rabbinic pseudonym for Jesus; see my *Evidence,* 37-38, and more fully D. R. Catchpole, *Trial,* 35, 44-47, 61-64. G. H. Twelftree, *GP* 5:316-18, is less convinced that it refers to Jesus. The identification depends partly on sections later censored from the talmudic texts.

5. An early association of Jesus with Egypt and magic (though without specifically deriving the latter from the former) is also found in the strange account (in a censored baraita in *b. Sanh.* 107b) of R. Joshua ben Perahiah's disagreement with Jesus the Nazarene; the setting is as they were returning together from a period of asylum in Egypt "when King Jannaeus [Alexander Jannaeus, 103-76 B.C.] was killing our rabbis." The story poses major problems of chronology as well as of intelligibility, but testifies to an association of Jesus with Egypt in a context of political asylum. For the baraita see my *Evidence,* 35-36.

But, on the other hand, Jesus is also the new Israel, God's "son," as the quotation from Hos 11:1 will presuppose; as patriarchal Israel went down to Egypt and came back to the promised land, so now does Jesus, the new Israel. If it is supposed that typology must depend on exact correspondences, Matthew's typology here is decidedly loose, not only in that Jesus is seen both as the deliverer and the delivered, but also in that whereas Moses escaped from Egypt and returned to it, Jesus (like Israel) does the opposite. But typology depends on meaningful associations rather than exact correspondences, and in each of these quite different ways the mention of Egypt is sufficient to provide food for thought on the relation between the events God directed in Egypt more than a millennium ago and what the same God is now accomplishing through the new deliverer, who is identified by the prophetic text as his Son.

A further effect of including Egypt in the story of Jesus' infancy is to add an important extra dimension to the geographical area which is involved in preparing for the coming of the Messiah. Not only is he the Galilean Messiah born in Judea, but he is honored by magi from "the East" (Mesopotamia?), who bring gifts particularly associated with Arabia (and with biblical echoes of Sheba), and part of his childhood is spent in safety in Egypt. Thus all the main elements of Israel's surrounding world as we know them from the OT are involved in welcoming God's Messiah, who, as the story unfolds, will prove to be much more than only the deliverer of Israel.[6]

13 The very similar wording to that in 1:20 indicates the next phase in God's careful direction of events by supernatural revelations to Joseph; v. 19 will repeat the same formula for the following phase, which will then be completed by a further dream in v. 22.[7] Meanwhile, the parallel revelation in a dream to the magi (v. 12) has secured time for the family's escape. The angel's message begins with exactly the same words as in 2:20, "Get up, and take the child and his mother with you, and . . . ," and in each case a following clause explains the reason for the change of location. The mention of "the child" before "his mother" becomes a fixed formula in this section (cf. vv. 14, 20, 21).[8] Here where Joseph is being addressed, the formula is more natural than in v. 11 where he was not mentioned (see note there), but the prior fo-

6. This theme is developed in my article in *NTS* 27 (1980/81) 237-40.

7. See above on 1:20 for the significance of Joseph's dreams in chs. 1–2.

8. The occurrence of the formula παράλαβε (παρέλαβεν) τὸ παιδίον καὶ τὴν μητέρα αὐτοῦ four times in vv. 13-21 suggests to some that here, too, there is an echo of the story of Moses: in Exod 4:20 Moses took τὴν γυναίκα καὶ τὰ παιδία back to Egypt on a donkey. But the echo is not close, and the prominence of the donkey in later Christian depictions of the flight has no NT basis. See D. C. Allison, *Moses,* 161-62, for the possible influence of this parallel on Christian art. But since there is no donkey in Matthew's account at all, there is no need to suggest a reason for Matthew's "omission of the donkey from 2:19-21" (ibid., 250, n. 277)!

cus on the child continues to concentrate the reader's attention on the primary significance of the events in which Joseph, as head of the family, necessarily takes the lead.

Egypt, the southwestern neighbor of Judea and now a Roman province with a large Jewish population especially in Alexandria,[9] was a natural place for Jews to seek asylum when in political danger at home;[10] a substitute for the Jerusalem temple had even been set up by Jewish exiles in Egypt (Josephus, *Ant.* 13.62-73). The angel's explanation spells out explicitly what readers should by now have been able to infer from Herod's alarm (v. 3), his careful questioning about the star (v. 7), his unconvincing declaration of intent (v. 8), and the diversion of the magi (v. 12), even if they had not yet drawn the obvious conclusion from the the Pharaoh/Herod parallel involved in the "new Moses" typology.[11]

14   As in 1:24-25, Joseph's action exactly matches the angelic instruction, while his setting off at night underlines the urgency of the situation (traveling by night was exceptional and potentially more dangerous) and demonstrates Joseph's exemplary obedience, which did not allow him even to delay until daylight.[12] While Roman Egypt controlled territory nearly as far north as Gaza, even the nearest parts of Egypt proper (Pelusium and the eastern branches of the Nile delta) would be at least 150 miles from Bethlehem, so more than a week's journey is indicated.

15   The statement that Joseph kept the family in Egypt until Herod died, which is apparently redundant (since the information will be repeated in vv. 19-21), is nevertheless needed here to justify Matthew's quotation of Hos 11:1, since this refers not to the escape to Egypt but to the (as yet future) return. The point of mentioning the Egyptian visit at all, from the point of view of the fulfillment of Scripture, has been to prepare for Jesus' coming "out of Egypt," and so the quotation is introduced at this point, while the geographical focus on Egypt dominates the narrative, rather than at the more logical point after v. 21 when that focus might have been forgotten and when in

---

9. Roughly one-third of the population was Jewish in the first century A.D.; Philo says there were a million Jews in and around Alexandria.

10. For examples see Josephus, *Ant.* 12.387-88; 14.21; 15.45-46; *War* 7.409-10, 416; 2 Macc 5:8, and in OT times 1 Kgs 11:17, 40; 2 Kgs 25:26; Jer 26:21; 42:13–44:30. R. A. Horsley, *Liberation*, 72-74, while not wishing to endorse the historicity of Matthew's narrative, argues that it "reflects the historical situation" of dispossessed peasants in "Jewish Palestine under Roman and Herodian rule."

11. There is a further possible verbal allusion here and in v. 14 to the Moses story, since in LXX Exod 2:15 Pharaoh ἐξήτει ἀνελεῖν Μωυσῆν, ἀνεχώρησεν δὲ Μωυσῆς (see p. 76, n. 2, for Matthew's use of ἀναχωρέω in v. 14).

12. D. C. Allison, *Moses*, 156, suggests that Matthew may also have had in mind that at the exodus the Israelites fled from Egypt at night.

any case Matthew's interest (and supporting quotation) will not be in the point of departure but in the new destination of Nazareth.[13]

The quotation-formula is exactly the same as in 1:22 except that the structure of the narrative here does not require a resumptive "All this happened." The phrase "by the Lord" is included here in order to make it clear that the "I" who has called is God himself; while all Scripture is, in a sense, spoken by God,[14] here the prophet has God speaking directly about "my son."[15] The quotation is in a form which fairly translates the Hebrew text but differs from the LXX in using the simple *kaleō,* "call," for *metakaleō,* "call to oneself, summon," and more importantly in that Matthew has not followed LXX in interpreting "my son" as "his [Israel's] children." This LXX rendering identifies the intended reference of the Hebrew text, but abandons its wording, and it is that wording which gives Matthew his specific point of entry to this instance of scriptural "fulfillment."[16]

Hos 11:1 introduces a section of Hosea's prophecy (11:1-11) in which God reflects on his experiences in trying to bring up his wayward child Israel/Ephraim. The focus is on the time of the original formation of the nation through the exodus and the wilderness period, and the calling of the "son" out of Egypt is clearly a reference to the historical event of the exodus.[17] It is a statement about the past, not a prediction of the future. It is therefore sometimes argued that Matthew's use of the text here is quite illegitimate, transferring to the future and to a different and individual "son" what God said about his "son" Israel in the past.

But of course that is the essence of typology, which depends not on predictions but on transferable "models" from the OT story. The exodus,

13. R. H. Gundry, *Use,* 93-94, argues rather improbably that the quotation does in fact refer to the time of "preservation of Jesus in Egypt" rather than to the subsequent return, and so wants to translate ἐξ Ἀιγύπτου as "'Since Egypt' (i.e., from the time he dwelt there)."

14. As τὸ ῥηθέν in the formula implies; see above, p. 55, n. 54.

15. See above, p. 55, n. 53, for the less probable suggestion that it is the presence of the word "son" in the quotation which has triggered the addition of ὑπὸ κυρίου here and in 1:22.

16. The clear relevance of this "retranslation" to Matthew's use of the text makes this an unpromising case for the thesis of M. J. J. Menken, *Matthew's Bible,* 133-42, that Matthew's formula-quotations are derived from a hypothetical "revised LXX" rather than from Matthew's own approximation to the wording of the Hebrew. Menken therefore asserts (135) that it is "virtually impossible to decide" the issue in this case, so that he can only "extrapolate the theory" from his other proposals.

17. In view of the possible allusions to the Balaam story in 2:1-12 (see above, p. 62) it may be worth noting that Balaam's oracles twice speak of Israel as "brought out of Egypt" by God (Num 23:22; 24:8), but there is no specific allusion to those texts here, even though Hosea's prophecy reflects that background.

leading as it did to the formation of a new people of God, was a potent symbol even within the OT of the even greater work of deliverance which God was yet to accomplish (e.g., Isa 43:16-21; 51:9-11; Jer 16:14-15; 31:31-34; Hos 2:14-15), and Matthew has taken up that prophetic typology and applied it to the "new exodus" which has now come about through Jesus. Later in this gospel we shall find the language of a new covenant (26:28) and we shall hear Jesus speaking to and about his disciples in terms which belong to the new people of God constituted at Sinai (see below, e.g., on 5:5, 48; 8:11-12); as Jesus sets up "his *ekklēsia*" (16:18) with its twelve leaders "judging the twelve tribes of Israel" (19:28), the message will be reinforced that the events which constituted Israel as the special people of God under Moses are now finding their counterpart in the even more fundamental and eschatological role of the "new Moses."

Not only is Jesus in Matthew's view the founder of a new community of the people of God, but he also himself embodies it as not only Israel's leader but himself the true Israel. Some of the most potent OT models for Jesus' mission in this gospel are drawn from passages which in their original context spoke, at least in part, about Israel as a corporate entity under the figure of an individual representative: see on 8:17 for the Servant of Yahweh and on 10:23 for the Son of Man. More directly parallel to the present typology is that which undergirds the story of Jesus' testing in the wilderness, when the nature of Jesus' status as "Son of God" is explored in relation to Israel's filial testing in the wilderness period which followed the first exodus (see on 4:1-11). Thus, far from Matthew's having seized on a convenient use of the word "son" (which, in any case, is not there in the LXX version of Hos 11:1) in relation to Egypt and illegitimately transferred it to a quite different kind of situation involving a different kind of son, this quotation in fact expresses in the most economical form a wide-ranging theology of the new exodus and of Jesus as the true Israel which will play a significant role throughout Matthew's gospel.[18] As usual, Matthew's christological interpretation consists not of exegesis of what the text quoted meant in its original context, but of a far-reaching theological argument which takes the OT text and locates it within an overarching scheme of fulfillment which finds in Jesus the end point of numerous prophetic trajectories. When Jesus "came out of Egypt," that was to be the signal for a new exodus in which Jesus would fill the role not only of the God-sent deliverer but also of God's "son" Israel himself.[19]

---

18. For a stimulating study of the importance of "New Exodus" typology in the Gospel of Mark see R. E. Watts, *Exodus.* A great deal of Watts's material applies *mutatis mutandis* also to Matthew.

19. D. C. Allison, *Moses,* 140-42, discusses Matthew's typological approach here with special reference to the "untidiness" of seeing Jesus as both Moses and Israel.

4. The King Tries to Thwart God's Purpose (2:16-18)

16 *When Herod realized that he had been tricked by the magi, he was absolutely furious, and sent men to kill[1] all the boys[2] in Bethlehem and in all its district who were up to two years old,[3] according to the time he had carefully discovered from the magi.* 17 *Then was fulfilled what had been declared through Jeremiah the prophet, who said,*

18   *"A voice was heard in Ramah,*
        weeping[4] and bitter lamentation:
    Rachel weeping for her children,
        and she would not be comforted,
    because they are no more."

God's direction to the magi in v. 12 has bought time for the family's escape, but it has only added frustrated rage to Herod's ruthless resolve, and his failure to secure a specific identification of the child leads instead to the indiscriminate killing of all male[5] infants in the area. As a result, Herod's action more closely resembles the indiscriminate infanticide of Pharaoh, as the "new Moses" motifs surrounding the birth of the Messiah continue to develop.[6]

This detail in Matthew's story is perhaps the aspect of his infancy narratives most often rejected as legendary. The lack of any independent evi-

---

1. ἀποστείλας ἀνεῖλεν, literally "sending he killed." The "sending" makes it clear that the singular verb covers the use of agents; Herod did not literally kill the children himself. The choice of ἀναιρέω (which Matthew does not use elsewhere) may be influenced by the occurrence of the same verb in LXX Exod 2:15 for Pharaoh's attempt to kill Moses.

2. τοὺς παῖδας does not in itself determine the sex of those killed; I am assuming that the masculine form is here gender-specific rather than inclusive because (a) Herod in eliminating a "king" had no need to kill girls, and (b) the underlying analogy with Pharaoh suggests a specific targeting of males (Exod 1:16, 22).

3. ἀπὸ διετοῦς (masculine singular adjective) καὶ κατωτέρω (adverb), literally "from a two-year-old and lower," a rather awkward but entirely clear way of saying that two years old was the upper limit.

4. Many MSS include a third noun, θρῆνος, before κλαυθμός, but this is probably due to assimilation with the LXX of Jer 31:15 (LXX 38:15), which has θρήνου καὶ κλαυθμοῦ καὶ ὀδυρμοῦ, rather woodenly reflecting the three nouns of the Hebrew instead of representing the construct state by an adjective.

5. See n. 2 above.

6. *Prot. Jas.* 22–23 has developed the theme further and has Herod seeking John the Baptist also (indeed, the emphasis falls primarily on John's escape); John's mother escapes with him and is miraculously hidden in the hills, but his father is martyred for refusing to reveal his whereabouts to Herod.

dence for so traumatic an event is usually mentioned, and the story is attributed either to the folklore motif of the newborn child threatened by the wicked king (and more specifically to the influence of Exod 1–2 and a deliberate assimilation of Herod to Pharaoh), or to an imaginative creation out of the Jeremiah text which Matthew goes on to quote. I have discussed the issue at length in an article in *NovT* 21 (1979) 98-120, and offer here only a brief summary of the main points.

The lack of independent evidence[7] is no more of a problem for this than for virtually every other incident recorded in the gospels, unless it is argued that this event was of such a character and magnitude that Josephus (our only significant source for Jewish history of the period) would be bound to have mentioned it. In the comments on v. 16 below I shall suggest that its magnitude should not be exaggerated; on the scale of atrocities known to have been perpetrated by Herod during his later years this would register very low. Nor should we assume that Josephus had a full record of all the events in the reign of a king who died forty years before he was born.

Stories of the rescue of newborn kings from jealous rivals include both Gentile[8] and Jewish[9] examples, but the only one of these which finds any clear echo in Matthew's story is, as we have already seen in other connections, Pharaoh's unsuccessful attempt to destroy Moses. It is clear that this scriptural model has been important in Matthew's telling of the story of Jesus, but not so clear that it would have given rise to this narrative without historical basis. In particular, the precise specification that children "up to two years old" were killed has no basis in the Moses story, which concerns the killing of babies at the time of birth.[10]

There is even less to be said for Jer 31:15 as the basis of the story, since nothing in the OT passage provides any basis for linking it with the story of Jesus unless there was already some tradition of the killing of children to draw attention to it in the first place. We shall note below the difficul-

---

7. In *NovT* 21 (1979) 116-18, I discuss some suggested non-Christian references to the incident, including the statement by Macrobius (c. A.D. 400) that Augustus's famous pun that he would rather be Herod's pig (ὗς) than his son (υἱός) was uttered "when he heard that among the boys up to two years old whom Herod king of the Jews ordered to be killed in Syria Herod's own son also was killed." Macrobius's comment probably reflects a garbled knowledge of Christian tradition rather than independent information.

8. See the details in my article, *NovT* 21 (1979) 98-99; notable examples are Sargon of Akkad, Gilgamesh, Romulus and Remus, Cyrus, Perseus, Oedipus, even Zeus himself; cf. more recently Snow White. Luz 1:152-55 sets out in tabular form the details of fourteen examples of "the story of the persecuted and rescued royal child" and adds a further twenty-two "more remote parallels."

9. Abraham, Jacob?, Moses; details *NovT* 21 (1979) 105-7.

10. See ibid., 108-13.

ties interpreters have in discovering messianic significance in this particular text beyond the mere coincidence of the motif of loss of children. The wording of the Jeremiah passage is not reflected at all in v. 16, which draws its terminology rather from the previous account of Herod and the magi, and the killing of the children, far from being simply a product of this OT text, is integrated into the whole narrative flow of the chapter, being planned in vv. 3-8, predicted in v. 13, and referred back to in v. 20. Like Matthew's other formula-quotations, vv. 17-18 function as an editorial comment on a traditional story, not as its source.[11]

On these grounds I find it more satisfactory to interpret v. 16 as recording a tradition which Matthew has received of what he himself at least believed to be an actual event, and one which was sadly not atypical of the later years of the Herod we know from Josephus (see comments below). But of course here, as throughout 1:18–2:23, Matthew's purpose in including this particular story is to develop further his presentation of Jesus as the fulfillment of Scripture. That argument is advanced in this little pericope first by further underlining the "new Moses" typology by depicting Herod in the role of the infanticide Pharaoh, and secondly by discovering in an obscure verse of Jeremiah a further typological model for the events surrounding the coming of the Messiah. Just how that model is meant to work will be our concern in the comments below on v. 18.

16 Herod's later years, as Josephus records them, were dominated by his obsessive defense of his throne, with the royal family of the Hasmoneans as the most immediate threat. Earlier in his reign his predecessors Antigonus (*Ant.* 15.8-10) and Hyrcanus (*Ant.* 15.173-78) were eliminated, together with large numbers of their supporters (*Ant.* 15.6) and eventually all remaining members of the Hasmonean family (*Ant.* 15.260-66); even those Hasmoneans directly related to Herod by marriage, his brother-in-law (*Ant.* 15.53-55), mother-in-law (*Ant.* 15.247-51), and even his favorite wife Mariamne (*Ant.* 15.222-36) were killed. In his final years his three eldest sons were also killed on suspicion of plotting to seize their father's throne, Alexander and Aristobulus as Mariamne's sons (and therefore part Hasmonean; *Ant.* 16.392-94) and Antipater because he had married a Hasmonean princess (*Ant.* 17.182-87). Outside the Hasmonean family we hear more generally of Herod's ruthless suppression of political suspects, relying on espionage (*Ant.* 15.366-69). On one occasion earlier in his reign he faced an assassination attempt, and the ten conspirators were executed together with their families (*Ant.* 15.280-90); such conspiracies and disloyalty, real or imagined, became a more frequent feature of his later years between 7 and 4 B.C. (*Ant.* 16.387-94; 17.41-44; 17.167; cf. *War* 1.654-55). Less directly re-

11. See ibid., 102-5.

lated to a threat to his throne, but a further testimony to Herod's remembered character, is his alleged plan (fortunately not carried out) to have all the Jewish nobility slaughtered at the time of his own death to ensure that mourning was genuine (*Ant.* 17.174-78). Several of these incidents involved the execution of large numbers of prominent citizens, and in some cases their families and supporters were included. In such a setting the murder of a few infants in a small village in order to eliminate a suspected dynastic rival is quite in character.[12]

Christian tradition has, of course, inflated the number of babies involved in the "massacre" into several thousands.[13] Estimates of the total population of Bethlehem in the first century are generally under a thousand, which would mean that the number of male[14] children up to two years old at any one time could hardly be more than twenty, even allowing for "all its district." Terrible as such a slaughter would be for the local community, it is not on a scale to match the more spectacular assassinations recorded by Josephus.

Matthew's narrative does not necessarily mean that a full two years[15] (or nearly three if the star was thought to mark the time of conception) had elapsed since the original sighting of the star by the magi. Herod's specification of age need be no more than a rough rule of thumb to make sure his soldiers did not miss any potential rival.

17   The tragic events in Bethlehem give rise to one of Matthew's most puzzling formula-quotations. But this time the fulfillment formula is varied in that in place of the purposive clause "in order to fulfill" we have the simple statement "Then was fulfilled." The same change will occur in 27:9. The different wording in these two cases may be designed to avoid directly attributing evil actions (infanticide and betrayal) to God's declared intention,[16] though the difference is not very great when what is being claimed is the fulfillment of God's words[17] in Scripture. Here for the first time the for-

---

12. For a fuller account of the nature of Herod's reign see R. A. Horsley, *Liberation,* 39-49. Horsley's concern is not to defend the historicity of Matthew's account, but he rightly concludes that "the story in Matthew 2 comes to life vividly against the background of Herodian exploitation and tyranny."

13. For examples see R. E. Brown, *Birth,* 204-5, to which add the slightly more sober but still wildly exaggerated number of three thousand in the *Martyrdom of Matthew* (sixth century A.D.).

14. See p. 82, n. 2.

15. Gundry, 35, asserts that "an infant would have been considered two years old immediately on entering his second year." If this is true (Gundry does not support it), the time would be reduced.

16. This common view is adopted by M. Knowles, *Jeremiah,* 34-35, listing many of its proponents. See also D. P. Senior, *Passion,* 364-66.

17. For this implication of the phrase τὸ ῥηθέν, see above, p. 55, n. 54.

mula includes the prophet's name (cf. 4:14; 8:17; 12:17; 27:9; also 3:3; 13:14; 15:7). Only the "major" prophets Isaiah and Jeremiah (who each had an OT book under their name) are so identified; those who occur in the Book of the Twelve (Micah, 2:6; Hosea, 2:15; Zechariah, 21:4) and those who are not identifiable as prophets at all (2:23; 13:35) remain anonymous, while in 27:9 Zechariah, the primary source of the quotation, is subsumed under the major prophet Jeremiah. The only exception to this pattern is 1:22, where there is no obvious reason for not identifying Isaiah.

18 Matthew's wording of the quotation from Jer 31:15 agrees with LXX in its first four and last three words. The intervening lines echo the sense and some of the words of the LXX, but not its actual phrasing; there is no significant difference in meaning, though it is surprising that Matthew uses "children" for LXX's "sons," where the latter would have fitted more exactly his account of the killing of male children.[18] Both Matthew and LXX fairly represent the Hebrew text apart from its repetition of "for her children."[19]

The superficial point of Matthew's quotation is that there is a scriptural precedent for the loss of children. By linking the two events in the context of scriptural fulfillment he invites his readers to find reassurance in the thought that even human tragedy can be interpreted within the overall purpose of God. But the situations are very different, in that Jeremiah depicts the grief of Rachel not during her life and for her own children, but in her grave as she watches her "children" (her later descendants, the exiles from the kingdom of Judah) being "lost" not through death but by being deported to Babylon. So why does Matthew feel that this text is appropriate here? The following suggestions seem to me possible, though other interpreters have offered quite different approaches.[20]

18. M. Knowles, *Jeremiah,* 37, suggests that Matthew intends to prepare for the disaster which is to come on Israel's "children" as a result of how they will treat Jesus (27:25; cf. 23:37).

19. For details of the textual data see G. M. Soares Prabhu, *Formula-Quotations,* 253-57; M. J. J. Menken, *Matthew's Bible,* 148-55. Soares Prabhu represents the general view when he describes Matthew's version as "a targumic translation from the Hebrew, with perhaps some reminiscence of the LXX." Menken here as elsewhere proposes that Matthew is using a hypothetical "revised LXX" closer to the Hebrew.

20. See, e.g., L. Hartman in M. Didier (ed.), *Matthieu,* 140-41, who links Jer 31:15 with Mic 5:2 since "Ramah was situated near to Bethlehem" and with Hos 11:1 because Jer 31:20 refers to Ephraim as God's son; he further sees Rachel as personifying "the future Zion." An even more imaginative approach is that of A. Vögtle in M. Didier (ed.), *Matthieu,* 173-74 (following W. Rothfuchs, *Erfüllungszitate,* 64-65), who on the basis of v. 3 reads Herod's infanticide as representing Israel as a whole rejecting its Messiah; Rachel is then understood to be weeping over Israel's consequent loss of its status as the people of God.

Jeremiah 31 is a chapter of hope and restoration, in which the grief of v. 15 strikes the only discordant note precisely because that grief is no longer appropriate. So the prophecy goes on (vv. 16-17) to call on Rachel to stop lamenting because the exiles will return. Is Matthew then inviting the reflection that, radically different as the situations are, there is again hope beyond the tragedy?[21] If so, it seems an oblique argument from context rather than from direct similarity in the text cited, since the restoration this time is not to be of those who were "lost" but of others through the agency of the one who escaped the slaughter; there is to be no "return" for the babies of Bethlehem.[22] And by quoting only the pessimistic v. 15 and not its reassuring sequel he has left a lot to the imagination and contextual awareness of his readers. If such a "bonus point" (see above, p. 45) was intended, would most of his readers have been able to grasp it? Perhaps some of them would, for the following reasons.

In this chapter in which geographical locations figure prominently, the name "Ramah" in the quotation draws attention.[23] Readers with a good knowledge of the OT might remember that it was specifically at Ramah that the exiles were gathered for the march to Babylon in 586 B.C. (Jer 40:1), Jeremiah himself being among them.[24] This then might be a trigger to thoughts of exile and (in the context of Jer 31, though not of Jer 40) return, of hope beyond the disaster. Moreover, Jeremiah was himself released at Ramah, and did not go to Babylon with the other exiles, but stayed in Judah to try (unsuccessfully) to influence those who remained (Jer 40:1-6). Is there a hint here of the role of the future Jeremiah (as Jesus will be described in 16:14; see comments there) who was to escape the fate of the "children" and go on to appeal (equally unsuccessfully) to the leaders of God's people in Judea? Might Matthew also have had in mind that it was to Egypt that Jeremiah, like Jesus, ultimately escaped (though unwillingly)?

21. This perspective on Jer 31 as a whole is well presented by Davies and Allison, 1.267-68; M. Knowles, *Jeremiah,* 38-43, is more sceptical.

22. R. J. Erickson, *JSNT* 64 (1996) 5-27, offers a wide-ranging and imaginative study of this pericope, which focuses on a perceived parallel between vv. 13-15 and 19-23. Erickson argues on this basis that the return of the Messiah from Egypt supplies the missing element, in that he represents the murdered children, and his eventual redemption reverses their fate as he in turn will die for his people, thus resolving the "divine injustice" perceived in the event when taken by itself.

23. Its retention by Matthew in his text, when he could have eliminated it either by omission or by a translation such as LXX A ἐν τῇ ὑψηλῇ (similarly Aquila, Targum, and Peshitta), suggests that he found it relevant to his purpose.

24. The targum on Jer 31:15 has noted this connection: it interprets Rachel's weeping as "the house of Israel weeping and sighing after the prophet Jeremiah when Nebuzaradan the chief slaughterer sent him from Ramah."

But there may be more to the name "Ramah" than that. Rachel's weeping is located there because it is in the territory of Benjamin which, unlike Judah, was one of the "Rachel" tribes and in which, according to one OT tradition, her grave was located (1 Sam 10:2). Later tradition, however, based on Gen 35:16-20; 48:7, located Rachel's tomb where it is still shown today, just outside Bethlehem (in Judah, twelve miles south of Ramah) — though what the Genesis texts actually say is that she died and was buried "on the way to Ephrath (Bethlehem)" and "still some distance from Ephrath." So the ambiguity[25] over the place of Rachel's burial (and therefore of her weeping) may have contributed to Matthew's feeling that this text about Ramah was in fact also relevant to the fate of Bethlehem's children, and that therefore Jeremiah's message of hope for the exiles from Ramah could also be applied *mutatis mutandis* to the tragedy at Bethlehem.

This is one of Matthew's most elusive OT quotations, and few claim with any confidence to have fathomed just what he intended, but the creativity which he displays in many of his formula-quotations perhaps encourages us to believe that in giving so prominent a place to Jer 31:15 he had more in mind than simply to point out that there was a precedent for sorrow arising out of the loss of children, even if we now lack the key to unlock the fuller meaning that some of his readers may have been able to draw from the quotation.[26]

5. A Galilean Messiah (2:19-23)

19 *After Herod had died, suddenly an angel of the Lord appeared in a dream to Joseph in Egypt* 20 *and said, "Get up, and take the child and his mother with you, and go to the land of Israel; for those who were seeking the child's life have died."* 21 *So he got up, and took the child and his mother with him, and came into the land of Israel.* 22 *But when he heard that Archelaus was now king of Judea in place of his father Herod, he was afraid to go there, and being warned in a dream,[1] he got safely away[2] to the region of Galilee.* 23 *On arrival there he made his home in a town called Nazareth, to fulfill what had*

---

25. The discrepancy of the two sites was noted and debated by rabbis in the third century (*Gen. Rab.* 82:10). See further J. Jeremias, *Heiligengräber,* 75-76.

26. M. Knowles, *Jeremiah,* 45-52, provides a good survey of the interpretive possibilities, which supports and develops some of the suggestions outlined above.

1. The phrase is the same as that used for the magi in v. 12, with the verb χρηματίζω indicating that the warning derives from God, even though here, as there, no angelic intermediary is mentioned (see comments on v. 12).

2. See p. 76, n. 2 for the meaning of ἀναχωρέω, which here clearly carries its normal Matthean sense of getting away from a place of danger or confrontation.

been declared through the prophets, that[3] he should be called a Nazorean.[4]

As Moses escaped from Egypt to Midian for a period when his life was in danger, so Joseph and his family have escaped *to* Egypt. Now the danger is over, and just as Moses in Midian received a divine call to return to Egypt, so now does Joseph in Egypt, using the same words as God had used to Moses in Exod 4:19. The "new Moses" can now return to the place in which his work of deliverance will be launched.

But that place is not Bethlehem. Judea has become an unsafe place for the new Moses, even after the death of the "Pharaoh" whose murderous jealousy initially caused his exile. As the story unfolds, we shall be reminded repeatedly that the Jerusalem which shared Herod's alarm in v. 3 will remain hostile territory for the new king of the Jews, and Bethlehem is too close to Jerusalem for comfort. Political wisdom thus dictates Joseph's relocation to the now independent state of Galilee to the north, but his move is directed not simply by prudence but also by divine guidance (another dream, v. 22), which will ensure that the Davidic Messiah born in Bethlehem will start his public career not as a Judean but as "Jesus of (Galilean) Nazareth." A lengthy quotation from Isaiah will in due course be deployed to authenticate his Galilean origin (4:12-16), but here in ch. 2 the focus is more specific. Not just Galilee in general but even little Nazareth itself has been chosen by God as the home of the Messiah, and the prophets have duly spoken of the one who "would be called a Nazorean." Just how Matthew has reached this triumphant prophetic climax to his geographical argument from the OT is one of the most intractable puzzles posed by Matthew's creative interpretation of Scripture, and will be discussed in the comments on v. 23. But whatever the origin of this elusive "quotation," its function is clear, to provide the QED toward which the whole argument of ch. 2 has been directed: Jesus of Nazareth *is* the Messiah from Bethlehem.

---

3. I have not used quotation marks here as in the other formula-quotations because in this case there is no participle λέγοντος introducing a direct quotation, but rather ὅτι, thus indicating something other than a simple quotation (see comments on this verse below). The future tense of κληθήσεται is thus appropriately rendered in English by the "would" of an indirect statement about the future where the main verb is in the past.

4. The term regularly used by Matthew and John and normally in Luke/Acts to designate Jesus as an inhabitant of Nazareth (and in Acts 24:5 for his followers) is Ναζωραῖος. The more familiar English form is "Nazarene," which derives from the Marcan term Ναζαρηνός, but here, where the form of the word is important for the exegesis of the text (see comments below), it seemed necessary to give a closer English approximation to Matthew's form. On the issues of translation raised in this and the previous note see further W. B. Tatum, *BT* 27 (1976) 135-38.

19-21 For the date of Herod's death see on v. 1. Apart from the addition of "in Egypt," the account of the dream is identical to that of v. 13 up to the point where a new specific direction is given, this time to make the same journey in reverse, and as in 1:24-25 and 2:14 Joseph's obedient response is narrated in v. 21 in exactly the terms used by the angel. Also as in v. 13 the angel gives a reason for the new move, in v. 13 Herod's death threat, and now his own death which has removed that threat. At this point the geographical direction is quite general, simply "the land of Israel,"[5] a term broad enough to cover both Judea and Galilee, though Joseph would presumably take it to mean a return to Bethlehem from which they had set out; it will not be until they get there, more than a week later, that they will discover more of the political situation and be given more specific guidance.

It is only Herod who has died, but the angel speaks in the plural, "those who were seeking." Of course Herod did not act alone, but it is apparently only he, not his agents, who has died. The plural therefore stands out as inappropriate, and invites the reader to look beyond the immediate context for an explanation. After so much Moses language in this chapter the reason is clear enough: the plural is supplied by the OT text which is here being closely echoed, God's words to Moses in Midian, "Go back to Egypt, for all those who were seeking your life have died" (Exod 4:19).[6] Here the Moses typology of this chapter comes most visibly to the surface of the narrative, even though the parallel is being drawn now not with Moses' escape in his infancy but with his adult life.[7]

22 Joseph has brought the family back to where their journey began in v. 14, but that is not to be the end of their travels. On Herod's death his kingdom was divided between three of his sons, with Judea/Samaria coming under the control of Archelaus, while Galilee (and Perea, east of the Jordan) was to be ruled by Antipas (the "Herod" whom we shall meet in 14:1-12 when the adult Jesus is active in Galilee); the third son, Philip, will appear in 14:3. Like their father they were local client rulers appointed by Rome, and none of them (unlike their father) was officially given the title "king" (Archelaus was "ethnarch," Antipas and Philip "tetrarchs"). But both Archelaus and Antipas lobbied hard to be granted the royal title, and local usage (reflected by Matthew both here and in 14:9) prudently presupposed it. Archelaus inherited his father's unpopularity without his political skill, and

---

5. K. Stendahl, *School*, 136, suggests that the term γῆ Ἰσραήλ (which appears nowhere else in the NT) is used to "point to the exodus at the time of Moses."

6. LXX τεθνήκασιν γὰρ πάντες οἱ ζητοῦντές σου τὴν ψυχήν, reproduced exactly by Matthew except for the omission of πάντες and the necessary change from σου to τοῦ παιδίου.

7. See further D. C. Allison, *Moses*, 142-44, on the appropriateness of this extension of the typology.

his rule was resented by most of his subjects; eventually he was deposed in A.D. 6 when a delegation to Rome from both Judea and Samaria denounced his "cruelty and tyranny" (Josephus, *Ant.* 17.342), and direct Roman rule was imposed on Judea/Samaria under a prefect who at the time of Jesus' public ministry was Pontius Pilatus (A.D. 26-36), while Galilee continued under the Herodian client-ruler Antipas.

Josephus's record (*Ant.* 17.200-344) of Archelaus's brief and unstable rule alone supplies an adequate basis for Joseph's conclusion that Judea would be no safer under him than under his father; Josephus says that he had begun his reign by massacring some three thousand Passover celebrants (*Ant.* 17.213-18). But Joseph was not left to work it out for himself, and another dream (this time only briefly alluded to without details of the messenger or the message) now prompts the final stage in his divinely guided migration which brings him to Galilee and thus eventually to Nazareth, some seventy miles north of Bethlehem.

23   "Town" *(polis)* in the NT does not necessarily indicate a large settlement, being used both for Jerusalem and for quite small local communities. Nazareth was a village probably smaller than Bethlehem and without its historical connections; it probably came into existence late in the OT period. Archeological evidence suggests that its population was "a maximum of about 480 at the beginning of the 1st century A.D." (J. F. Strange, *ABD* 4:1050).[8] It was an obscure Jewish village in the Galilean hills, rapidly being overshadowed by the growing Hellenistic city of Sepphoris only four miles away which Antipas rebuilt as the capital of Galilee. Matthew gives no hint that he was aware of Luke's tradition that Joseph and Mary had previously lived in Nazareth (see above, p. 43), and gives no reason for the choice of Nazareth except that it was to fulfill what the prophets had declared.

The quotation-formula differs from all Matthew's other formulae in two respects: instead of a single prophet (named or anonymous) he speaks here of "the prophets," and the participle *legontos* ("who said") which leads into all the other quotations is here missing; in its place is *hoti* ("that"), which sometimes functions as the equivalent of our quotation marks, but can also indicate not so much a direct quotation as a paraphrase or summary of what was said. These two distinctive features together suggest strongly that what Matthew is here providing is not a quotation of a specific passage but rather a theme of prophecy (as in 26:56, where again plural "prophets" are mentioned and no particular passage is cited).[9]

---

8. For a range of other estimates (from a hundred to two thousand) see Keener, 113.

9. See, however, M. J. J. Menken, *Matthew's Bible,* 162-64, for the suggestion

This conclusion is the more appropriate in view of the fact that "He shall be called a Nazorean" does not in fact occur anywhere in the OT, nor, as far as we know, in any other contemporary literature. As a matter of fact, Nazareth, as a rather newly founded settlement, is never mentioned in the OT, or indeed in any other non-Christian Jewish writing before it appears in an inscription listing priestly courses in the third or fourth century A.D. The search for a specific OT source for "He shall be called a Nazorean" is therefore likely to be futile.

It has, however, been attempted, despite the altered quotation-formula, by suggesting a wordplay on the name "Nazareth." Probably the most popular suggestion[10] is that Matthew has in mind the Hebrew word *nēṣer,* which in Isa 11:1 designates the "branch" from the stump of Jesse, a recognized messianic figure.[11] He would then be expecting his readers to perceive behind his Greek word *Nazōraios* the consonants of the Hebrew word *nēṣer* (which are the basic consonants of the Hebrew name represented by the Greek *Nazaret*) and to draw messianic conclusions, despite the OT use of a different term for the messianic "Branch." Others have suggested a wordplay rather on the Hebrew verb *nṣr,* "to watch, guard, preserve," and draw on passages such as Isa 42:6 (the servant who is "preserved"), Isa 49:6 (the "preserved" of Israel), or Jer 31:6 (the "watchmen" in the hills of Ephraim).[12] Apart from the fact that such theories "explain" only the word *Nazōraios* and not the preceding "He shall be called," they also suffer from the rather obvious embarrassment that such a wordplay is totally invisible in Greek, the language in which Matthew is writing. A suggestion which avoids this problem is to postulate an OT source in the Greek word *naziraios,* "nazirite," only one letter different from Matthew's word, even though its second consonant represents a different Hebrew consonant and the Hebrew word *nāzîr* has nothing to do with Nazareth. *Naziraios* occurs in the LXX only with reference to Samson in Judg 13:5, 7; 16:17,[13] and the phrase "he will be a *naziraios*" in

---

that the ὅτι is not introductory but is itself part of the quotation: "For he will be called a Nazorean."

10. Mentioned in most commentaries, and promoted, e.g., by K. Stendahl, *School,* 103-4, 198-99; R. H. Gundry, *Use,* 103-4.

11. The Isaiah Targum explicitly interprets the *nēṣer* as the Messiah. See above on 1:23 for the continuity in Isaiah's prophecy between the Immanuel of 7:14 and the "branch" of 11:1. It should be noted, however, that other OT passages which use "Branch" as a personal title for the Messiah use not *nēṣer* but *ṣemaḥ* (Jer 23:5; Zech 3:8; 6:12; possibly also Isa 4:2, though the personal application is not clear there).

12. The Jeremiah derivation was suggested by E. Zolli, *ZNW* 49 (1958) 135-36. Albright and Mann, 21-22, regard it as "essential."

13. Elsewhere in the LXX *nāzîr* is translated as "the one under a vow" or "the one consecrated."

Judg 13:5, 7 has been claimed as a source for Matthew's phrase "He will be called a *Nazōraios*."[14] It is not an exact echo, but at least it might be easier to detect in Greek than the alleged reference to Isa 11:1.[15] But if this was the passage Matthew had in mind, it is not obvious why he should have obscured the supposed allusion by altering "he will be" to "he will be called."[16] Moreover, while Samson was a miraculously born savior-figure, his notoriously amoral lifestyle is not an attractive option as a type of the Messiah. And the supposed echo would backfire rather badly when the reader reaches 11:18-19 where Jesus is set in deliberate contrast with the nazirite lifestyle of John the Baptist, and is labeled rather a "glutton and wine drinker." Jesus was no nazirite, and it does not seem that anyone "called" him that.

The problems faced by these various suggestions,[17] and the lack of agreement on them, suggest that we should rather take note of the distinctive wording of the introductory formula and look not for a specific passage but rather for a more general theme of prophetic expectation which pointed to a Messiah who would be "called a Nazorean."[18] But if *Nazōraios* is understood to mean "of Nazareth," as both the context here and other NT

14. "Almost certainly," according to Davies and Allison, 1:276; "the only one possible" (if Matthew "himself discovered the quotation"), according to Luz, 1:149. So also G. M. Soares Prabhu, *Formula-Quotations*, 205-7; M. J. J. Menken, *Matthew's Bible*, 170-72; K. Berger, *NovT* 38 (1996) 323-35. J. A. Sanders, *JBL* 84 (1965) 169-72, supports this derivation with the suggestion that Matthew may have understood Judg 13:2-7 to indicate a supernatural conception parallel to that of Jesus; this is not what the text says, however, and there is no parallel between the barrenness of Manoah's wife and Mary's virginity.

15. The Judges account of Samson is not what we would call a prophetic passage, but the fact that Judges falls within the "former prophets" of the Hebrew canon *might* be thought to justify referring to such an allusion as "what had been declared through the prophets" (so M. J. J. Menken, *Matthew's Bible*, 176-77). All Matthew's other references to "prophets" are, however, to the latter prophets.

16. R. E. Brown, *Birth*, 223-25 (followed by Davies and Allison, 1:276-77), attempts to resolve this problem by also bringing in Isa 4:3 ("will be called holy") on the grounds that LXX ἅγιος, which in that verse represents Hebrew *qādôš*, is elsewhere used to translate *nāzîr*. When he pronounces this alleged style of exegesis "complicated," he is understating the case! M. J. J. Menken, *Matthew's Bible*, 172-75, offers a similar proposal based not on Isa 4:3 but on Isa 7:14.

17. For a fuller account of these and other suggestions see R. H. Gundry, *Use*, 98-104. R. E. Brown, *Birth*, 210-13, 218-19, combines the suggested specific allusions as complementary aspects of what he terms "the allusive wealth" of the term Ναζωραῖος.

18. W. Rothfuchs, *Erfüllungszitate*, 66-67, avoids the problem of finding a suitable OT source for this "quotation" by suggesting that the "prophets" referred to in the introductory formula are those cited in vv. 6, 15, and 18, the settlement in Nazareth being the end-product of the itinerary established through these prophecies rather than having specific scriptural authentication of its own.

usage demand,[19] such a theme is not going to be easy to discern in the absence of any mention of Nazareth in the OT. Whatever Matthew is doing with this "quotation," it is not going to be at the level of simple prediction and fulfillment.

The most promising approach[20] paradoxically takes its cue from the very nonexistence of Nazareth in the OT — it is a scriptural nonentity. For someone to be "called a Nazorean," especially in connection with a messianic claim, was therefore to invite ridicule: the name is in itself a term of dismissal if not of actual abuse. We see precisely this reaction in Nathanael's response to Philip's suggestion of a Messiah from Nazareth, "Can anything good come out of Nazareth?" (John 1:46; cf. John 7:41-42, 52 for Judean scorn for the idea of a Messiah from Galilee). If Nathanael, a native of Cana only a few miles from Nazareth, reacted like that, what must have been the response in Judea, where most people had probably never heard of Nazareth? On this understanding it is not only the word *Nazōraios* which conveys Matthew's message, but also more specifically the verb "He shall be called": this is about derogatory name-calling. In 26:71 (the only other occurrence of *Nazōraios* in Matthew) we shall see the term used in just this way by a speaker in Jerusalem.

But where in the prophets could such an idea of the Messiah be found? Alongside the (probably dominant) royal strand of prophecy which Matthew has already tapped in 2:5-6 and which was the source of his apologetic problem in claiming a Messiah from Galilee not from Bethlehem, there is a less prominent but nonetheless significant expectation of a Messiah who would be unrecognized and who would not be taken seriously by his people. The series of messianic portraits which appear in Zech 9–14[21] begin (9:9-10) with a royal figure who is also unexpectedly humble and is described as "vindicated and saved," but then go on to speak of the shepherd whose authority is not accepted by his sheep (11:4-14) and of one who is pierced by the people of Jerusalem (12:10) and struck down by the sword of God (13:7). A similar impression would be gained from some of the psalms of the "righteous sufferer" (especially Pss 22, 69) insofar as these were understood to have messianic implications. The theme of nonrecognition and disdain is most clearly developed in the account of God's "servant" in Isa 52:13–53:12, most prominently in 53:1-3, which speaks of the unimpressive appearance of the

19. For the possible origin of Ναζωραῖος see G. M. Soares Prabhu, *Formula-Quotations,* 193-201. There is little agreement on how this surprising form came into use, but all agree that, whatever its origin, for Matthew, Luke, and John (and therefore presumably also for their readers) it meant "a person from Nazareth."
20. This line of interpretation goes back at least to Jerome in the fourth century.
21. See my *Jesus and the OT,* 103-10, 205-10, for messianic themes in Zech 9–14 and their use in the NT. Also B. Lindars, *Apologetic,* 110-34.

servant and the incredulity of the people, leading to his being "despised and rejected" and "held of no account" (cf. also Isa 49:7, "one deeply despised"). The imagery of the servant "springing up like a shoot out of dry ground" underlines the unexpectedness of the servant's origins. In John 7:27 there is an intriguing hint that this prophetic motif was still alive in the first century, when some people in Jerusalem assume (in contrast with the more traditional view expressed in 7:42) that "When the Messiah comes, no one knows where he is from."[22]

On this view, then, the words "He shall be called a Nazorean" represent the prophetic expectation that the Messiah would appear from nowhere and would as a result meet with incomprehension and rejection. Of course the prophets could not speak specifically of Nazareth, which did not even exist when they wrote. But the connotations of the derogatory term "Nazorean" as applied in the first century to the messianic pretender Jesus captured just what some of the prophets had predicted — a Messiah who came from the wrong place, who did not conform to the expectations of Jewish tradition, and who as a result would not be accepted by his people. Even the embarrassment of an origin in Nazareth is thus turned to advantage as part of the scriptural model which Matthew has worked so hard to construct in this introductory section of his account of the Messiah, Jesus of Nazareth.

No solution to the exegetical problem posed by 2:23 is straightforward, and it is surprising that Matthew has chosen to cap his apologetic argument with such an elusive "quotation," even given the problem that he could not appeal to any actual mention of Nazareth in the OT. Perhaps his readers shared some more clearly agreed understanding of the meaning of the word *Nazōraios* and of what aspect of "the prophets" Matthew was here appealing to, but if so it is not now available to us.[23]

22. R. H. Gundry, *Use,* 103-4, while discerning a primary reference to Isa 11:1, also argues that the messianic "branch" passages were understood at Qumran and in rabbinic literature "as meaning the Messiah will come out of obscurity and a low estate" and that at Qumran in particular *nēṣer* carried "thoughts of lowliness, despisedness, and suffering."

23. A further nuance may be perceived in the fact that by the middle of the first century Ναζωραῖος was becoming a recognized, and probably uncomplimentary, term for Christians (Acts 24:5; cf. Tertullian, *Marc.* 4.8; *nāṣrāyâ* became the standard term for Christians in Syriac), so that Matthew's readers would more readily grasp and sympathize with the connotations of the term as applied to Jesus.

C. THE MESSIAH'S HERALD (3:1-12)

1 *In those days John the Baptist appeared[1] in the Judean wilderness,[2] proclaiming 2 this message, "Repent, for the kingdom of heaven has arrived."[3] 3 He is the person who was announced[4] through Isaiah the prophet when he said,*

> *"A voice of someone shouting in the wilderness,*
> *'Prepare the way for the Lord;*
> *make straight his paths.'"*

4 *This John[5] wore a garment made of camel hair, with a leather belt round his waist, and his food was locusts and wild honey. 5 And people from Jerusalem and all Judea and all the region around the Jordan went out to him. 6 And confessing their sins, they were baptized by him in the River Jordan.*

7 *But when John saw that many of the Pharisees and Sadducees were coming to his baptism,[6] he said to them, "You brood of vipers, who warned you to escape from the coming judgment? 8 So produce fruit which fits repentance, 9 and don't think smugly to yourselves,[7] 'We have Abraham as our father.' I tell you, God is able to raise up*

---

1. In 2:1 I translated παραγίνομαι by "arrived." Matthew uses this verb only in these two places and in 3:13, in each case to introduce a new actor onto the scene. "Arrived" suitably conveyed the sense of visitors to a crowded city, but here in an uninhabited area the beginning of a dramatic new mission is better represented by "appeared."

2. The reference is to the uninhabited area down by the Jordan (see on v. 1 below), to which people from the inhabited areas "go out" (v. 5). It is not all "desert" in the sense of infertility. "Wilderness," though a little old-fashioned in English, appropriately conveys its remoteness as well as preserving its important OT connotations; see the comments below.

3. ἤγγικεν, literally "has come near." See the comments below on the significance of the tense and the appropriateness of the translation "has arrived."

4. The participial form is the same as in the formula of 1:22; 2:15, 17, 23, etc. (see p. 55, n. 54), except that here the masculine ῥηθείς is used for the person described. The translation "declared" which I have used in the standard formula is not, however, appropriate with a person as the object.

5. Literally, "John himself," but the function of the phrase is to take the reader from the indefinite "voice" of Isaiah's prophecy to the specific person in whom that prophecy has been fulfilled, the man who has already been named in v. 1 and whose introduction is resumed by this phrase.

6. ἐπὶ τὸ βάπτισμα αὐτοῦ leaves open the question whether they had come intending to be baptized or merely to see what was going on, perhaps carrying out a critical surveillance; see the comments below.

7. Literally, "Don't think to say to yourselves." δοκέω has the sense of supposing, in this case perhaps of wishful thinking: "Don't imagine you can say to yourselves." Following the threatening language of vv. 7-8, the implication is of a false reassurance.

children for Abraham from these stones. 10 *But the ax has already been placed against the root of the trees; so every tree which does not produce good fruit is chopped down and thrown into the fire.* 11 *My own role is to*[8] *baptize you in water with a view to repentance,*[9] *but the person who follows me*[10] *is stronger than I: I am not fit to take off*[11] *his sandals. He is the one who will baptize you in the Holy Spirit and fire.* 12 *He has his winnowing shovel in his hand, to clear his threshing floor; he will gather the grain into his granary, but the chaff he will burn up in a fire that cannot be put out."*

The next stage of Matthew's introduction of the Messiah involves a leap of some decades (see on v. 1 for the chronology) from Jesus' childhood to events preceding the beginning of his adult ministry. Jesus himself will not appear in the narrative until v. 13, but the account of John the Baptist is designed to prepare the reader for the coming of the "stronger one" (v. 11). John himself is presented only as the one who prepares the way and announces the Messiah's coming. As such he both fulfills prophecy (v. 3, and the echo of the prophetic lifestyle in v. 4) and (in his role as the last and greatest of the prophets, 11:9-15) utters a more immediate prediction of Jesus' messianic role (vv. 11-12). And his call for repentance in the light of imminent judgment sets the context in which Jesus' work of both judgment and salvation will be carried out. Whenever John the Baptist appears in the rest of this gospel (and indeed in the other gospels), this same perspective will be maintained: while Jesus will be seen as John's successor, he will always be the focus of attention to whom John acts as herald and authenticator. John's role is one of great honor and importance, but it is only that of the precursor.

All this is in contrast to the picture of John the Baptist we would have derived from Josephus's account (*Ant.* 18.116-19) without reference to the Christian tradition. While Josephus's account is brief (though not so brief as

8. The emphatic ἐγὼ μέν contrasts John's preliminary and symbolic action with the real "baptism," which will be performed by someone else (ὁ δὲ . . . αὐτός . . .).

9. Schweizer, 51, translates εἰς μετάνοιαν as "to show that you have repented" (and several commentators argue for a similar meaning), but this rendering seems to owe more to a Protestant theology of baptism than to the natural sense of εἰς. Rather than look for a different sense of εἰς, it may be more appropriate to suggest that μετάνοια here includes not only the initial "conversion" but also the changed lifestyle which results and should follow baptism.

10. This rendering attempts to maintain the ambiguity of ὀπίσω ἔρχομαι, to "come after (in time)" and to "be the disciple of" (cf. 4:19; 10:38; 16:24); see the comments below.

11. βαστάζω, "carry," often means "take away," and hence in this context "remove," as in 8:17; see MM 106b.

the questionably authentic account of Jesus in *Ant.* 18.63-64), it describes a significant prophetic figure who acquired a large and enthusiastic following (with no suggestion that this was later absorbed into the Christian movement) and who proved to be sufficiently influential to pose a more serious threat to Herod Antipas than apparently Jesus ever did.[12] The two accounts, both of which present John in a prophetic light, are not formally incompatible, and we shall see in 14:3-11 that there is basic agreement between Matthew (and Mark) and Josephus with regard to how John met his end, but the difference of perspective is marked. It has resulted in a tendency among Christians to undervalue John as no more than a "warm-up act" for Jesus rather than as a unique and distinctive representative of the Jewish prophetic tradition who deserves a prominent place in any account of the religious history of Palestine in the first century. While Matthew presents Jesus as going far beyond John's relatively limited "revival" ministry, he portrays Jesus as speaking with appreciation and respect of John's role (11:7-19) and taking it for granted that there is an essential continuity between John's ministry and his own (21:23-32).

The continuity between John and Jesus which was obvious to outsiders (14:1-2; 16:14) is further underlined in Matthew's account by the close links which he forges between John's preaching as he presents it here in vv. 2, 7-12 and that of Jesus later in the gospel. Only in Matthew is John's preaching summed up in exactly the same formula as that of Jesus (3:2; 4:17; cf. also the preaching of Jesus' disciples, 10:7). For parallels in Jesus' preaching to that of John in vv. 7-12 see

> 3:7 ("brood of vipers," escaping judgment) with 23:33; cf. also 12:34
> 3:8 (repentance) with 11:20-21; 12:41;
> 3:8, 10 (producing good fruit) with 7:16-20; 12:33; 21:41, 43;
> 3:9 (children of Abraham) with 8:11-12;
> 3:10b (fruitless tree cut down and burned) exactly repeated in 7:19;
> 3:11-12 (judgment by fire) with 5:22; 13:40-42, 50; 18:8-9; 25:41;
> 3:12 (grain gathered into the granary) with 13:30.

The continuity between John and Jesus is further underlined by Jesus' later comments on their relationship (11:16-19; 17:12; 21:23-27, and cf. the implications of 21:32). Their careers run parallel in significant ways: both are popularly regarded as prophets, opposed by the Jerusalem authorities, eventually rejected and executed, but given burial by their disciples.

So Jesus will take up where John leaves off, and this is just what John has said must happen. John's own distinctive ministry of water baptism will

---

12. For detailed recent studies of John as a figure in first-century Judaism (not merely in his NT role as a foil to Jesus) see R. L. Webb, *John;* J. E. Taylor, *John.*

give way to a baptism "in the Holy Spirit and fire." This pregnant phrase (see below on v. 11) points to a more searching and spiritual reality of both judgment and salvation for which water baptism was merely an outward and preliminary symbol. The repentance symbolized in John's baptism (a symbolism on which Josephus also agrees, *Ant.* 18.117) was an essential basis for Jesus' future ministry, but could not by itself bring the "salvation from sin" (1:21) which was to be Jesus' unique role.

As for the act of baptism itself, while John 3:22-23; 4:1-2 speaks of a parallel baptizing ministry by Jesus and his disciples at least at first, Matthew gives no hint of *Christian* baptism taking place until it suddenly emerges fully formed and taken for granted in 28:19. The only mention of baptism in this gospel between the end of ch. 3 and 28:19 is a single reference back to John's baptism in 21:25; Matthew even omits any mention of Jesus' metaphorical use of "baptism" for his own suffering, as in Mark 10:38-39; Luke 12:50. If it were not for 28:19, then, we might well assume that Matthew saw baptism as something pre-Christian and now left behind, but the climactic position of 28:19 shows the danger of such an argument from silence. Matthew clearly did know and expect Christian baptism, and felt that it mattered. His silence on baptism as a part of Jesus' own ministry might be taken to indicate that as long as the "baptizer with the Holy Spirit and fire" was around, water baptism had no place, but it is equally possible that he simply saw no need to mention what the church in his day took for granted, that both water baptism and baptism "in the Holy Spirit and fire" had their proper place within the Jesus movement, and that 28:19 brings to the surface what had been happening unmentioned during Jesus' ministry as well as in the post-Easter period as we know it from Acts.[13]

1 The vague phrase "in those days"[14] links the next phase of Matthew's introduction with the fulfillment theme of ch. 2 in principle, but leaves the chronology quite open. The narrative content will tell us that we have moved from Jesus' childhood to his adulthood, and in due course the appearance of Pontius Pilatus as prefect of Judea will make it clear that Jesus' public ministry comes to its end between A.D. 26 and 36, but Matthew makes no attempt to indicate Jesus' age at the time of his public ministry (contrast Luke 3:23) nor the length of that ministry. Nor does he suggest that Jesus was related to John the Baptist or of a similar age (Luke 1:36). John simply "appears" (see p. 96, n. 1) on the stage as suddenly and mysteriously as Elijah

---

13. I have argued for this understanding of baptism as a part of Jesus' movement from the beginning in J. B. Green and M. M. B. Turner (eds.), *Jesus of Nazareth: Lord and Christ,* 94-111.

14. Used only here by Matthew as a narrative connector; he uses "on that day" in 13:1 and 22:23, where he wants to make a closer connection.

(1 Kgs 17:1), on whom Matthew's account of his prophetic ministry will be modeled. His specific location within the broad area of "the Judean wilderness" (see p. 96, n. 2) is indicated only by the fact that he was beside the Jordan (v. 6) and therefore north of the Dead Sea rather than in the more extensive desert area south of Jericho. His later contretemps with Antipas the ruler of Perea (14:3-4) suggests (as the Fourth Gospel also states, John 1:28; 10:40) that he operated on the east side of the river, presumably near the fords where those coming from the Judean hills could cross; in that case Matthew is using the term "Judea" rather loosely, as he apparently does also in 19:1.[15]

But the term "wilderness" is much more than simply a geographical identifier. The voice "in the wilderness" in Isa 40:3 to which Matthew will refer in v. 3 is an example of a recurrent prophetic theme. It was in the wilderness after the escape from Egypt that Israel began its existence as the people of God, and it will be some of those wilderness experiences which will be brought back to our attention in 4:1-11 as Jesus goes through his own wilderness testing. The hope of a new exodus then led the prophets to speak of the wilderness as a place of new beginnings (Jer 2:2-3; Hos 2:14-15; cf. Ezek 20:35-38); the blossoming of the wilderness is one of the great themes of Deutero-Isaiah (Isa 41:18-19; 43:19-21; 44:3-4, etc.). The voice in the wilderness (Isa 40:3) was the inspiration for the Qumran community to take its place down near the Dead Sea to wait for God's eschatological intervention (1QS 8:12-14; 9:19-20), and it was on the area of the wilderness and the Jordan valley that several of the "prophetic" or "messianic" figures of the first century focused their appeal.[16] Particularly similar to John the Baptist was the ascetic prophet Bannus, who some years later also gathered disciples in the wilderness, practicing "frequent ablutions in cold water" (Josephus, *Life* 11–12).[17]

15. If John's location was east of the Jordan, his being "in the wilderness" does not place him particularly close to Qumran. The earlier enthusiasm for tracing links between John's teaching and practice and that of the Qumran community has now mellowed, and while, as we shall see, Qumran practices of ablution may help us to understand some aspects of current Jewish thought about purity, the contrasts between John's practice and that of Qumran outweigh any similarities. For a recent study concluding "that John should not be associated with the Essenes" see J. E. Taylor, *John,* 15-48. Taylor goes on to suggest that John was most closely associated with the Pharisees.

16. See Josephus, *Ant.* 20.97-98, 169-72; *War* 7.438, for specific examples, and *Ant.* 20.167-68 for the general pattern.

17. For a fuller account of the significance of the wilderness in the OT and in subsequent Jewish thought see U. Mauser, *Christ,* 15-61; J. Marcus, *Way,* 22-29. Mauser argues (ibid., 144-46) that Matthew "has reduced to mere topographical remarks what to Mark was a powerful theological concept," but this scarcely does justice to the focus on Israel's wilderness experience which underlies Matthew's quotations from Deuteronomy in 4:1-11 (see comments there).

Matthew will duly note the baptizing ministry after which John was named, but he mentions first what is for him John's most important role as a prophet, his proclamation. He will use this verb *kēryssō* (cf. *kēryx*, "herald") of Jesus' own ministry (4:17, 23; 9:35; 11:1) and that of his disciples (10:7, 27) as well as more generally of the subsequent spreading of the Christian message (24:14; 26:13), but as the one whose voice prepares the way of the Lord and who announces the coming of the "stronger one," John is in a special sense the herald of the coming salvation.

2 John's message of "repentance" is that of many of the OT prophets, calling on God's people to "return" to their true allegiance; its meaning is not far from what we mean by "conversion."[18] The verb *metanoeō* is not frequent in Matthew, but its use in this initial summary of the message of both John and Jesus (4:17) indicates its importance. It will be for their failure to "repent" that Jesus will declare judgment on his contemporaries (11:20-21; 12:41). But by comparison with the OT prophets there is now a new note of urgency, of a "now or never" opportunity — "the kingdom of heaven has arrived."

Matthew's phrase "the kingdom of the heavens" (literally) is functionally the same as "the kingdom of God" in Mark and Luke, and frequently occurs in direct parallel to it. There is general agreement that the form Jesus himself used was "the kingdom of God." On a few occasions Matthew retains "the kingdom of God" (6:33;[19] 12:28; 19:24; 21:31, 43), and I shall discuss at those points why he may have chosen to vary his normal form there. His general preference for "heaven" instead of "God" is conventionally explained as a typically Jewish reverential paraphrase to avoid pronouncing the name of God, but since Matthew seems to have no inhibitions about speaking of God by name elsewhere, this is hardly an adequate explanation.[20] He may have been influenced by the usage of Dan 4:26, "Heaven rules" (parallel to "the Most High rules" in the preceding verse), though most Jewish writers do not seem to find difficulty in speaking of God reigning (Pss 93:1; 95:3; 97:1; 99:1, etc.). "The kingdom of heaven" may be simply a stylistic preference which, as such, requires no explanation.[21]

---

18. Keener, 120, gives a useful survey of the usage of the word, especially in rabbinic writings.

19. The text is disputed in this case; see p. 264, n. 8.

20. Luz, 1:167, may be right in tracing it not so much to Matthew's own preference as to that of his Jewish-Christian community, perhaps influenced by synagogue and rabbinic usage, though evidence for the latter comes only from a later date.

21. See, however, R. Foster, *NTS* 48 (2002) 487-99, for a stimulating attempt. Foster notes the prevalence of another distinctively Matthean phrase, "your Father in heaven," and argues that "heaven" language is Matthew's way of reinforcing his readers' identity as the true people of God. It also serves to differentiate Jesus' "heavenly" messianic mission from more "earthly" ideas of the role of the Davidic Messiah.

The importance and meaning of "the kingdom of God/heaven" as a central element in Jesus' teaching according to the Synoptic Gospels has been voluminously discussed, and I have contributed to that discussion.[22] While no statement would command universal assent, there is general agreement that, rather than denoting a specific time, place, or situation called "the kingdom" — a misleading abbreviation which is as conspicuously absent from the Synoptic tradition as it is dominant in modern discussion[23] — the phrase "the kingdom of God" in both its Hebrew and Greek forms denotes the dynamic concept of "God ruling." It represents, in other words, a sentence of which the subject is not "kingdom" but "God." This dynamic sense is now better conveyed by an abstract noun such as "kingship" or "sovereignty" rather than by "kingdom," which has become in general usage a concrete noun.[24] Matthew's summary of John's (and Jesus') declaration, "The kingdom of heaven has arrived," might thus be paraphrased as "God's promised reign is beginning" or "God is now taking control."

Underlying this declaration is the prophetic hope of what G. R. Beasley-Murray suggestively refers to as "the coming of God."[25] While the actual phrase "the kingship of God" does not occur frequently in either the OT or later Jewish writings, the concept of God's rule or sovereignty is fundamental to both. The confident and repeated declaration by the psalmists that "Yahweh reigns" embodies the universal Hebrew conviction, expressed in a rich variety of ways from Genesis to Malachi, that God, as the creator of this world, is in control of it and of all who are in it. But alongside this un-

---

22. R. T. France, *Divine Government*. The first chapter, which in part draws on an earlier study in D. A. Carson (ed.), *Biblical Interpretation and the Church: Text and Context*, 30-44, focuses more generally on the background and significance of the phrase in the Synoptic tradition.

23. See below on 4:23 for the one exception to this in Matthew's compound phrases "the gospel/word/sons of the kingdom."

24. Our traditional English phrase derives from the KJV (following William Tyndale), which was translated at a time when "kingdom" in English still carried this dynamic sense of "kingship," a sense now rightly described by the OED as "obsolete." The concrete sense of "kingdom" in current English (as a place or group of people under a common rule) now inevitably distorts the more dynamic connotations of ἡ βασιλεία τοῦ θεοῦ when "the kingdom of God" continues to be used in Bible versions despite the changed meaning of the word. Translators have still to catch up with the scholarly preference for such phrases as "the rule of God" (or even B. D. Chilton's bold suggestion "God in strength," which is the title of his important study; Sheffield: JSOT, 1987). For a valuable discussion of the linguistic function of the phrase ἡ βασιλεία τοῦ θεοῦ/τῶν οὐρανῶν as a "tensive symbol" rather than a concrete noun to denote a specific time, place, or situation, cf. N. Perrin, *Jesus*, 16-32.

25. This is the phrase under which he discusses the eschatological hopes of the OT and of early Judaism, on pp. 3-62 of his book *Jesus and the Kingdom of God*.

questioned datum of the eternal sovereignty of God there developed a sense that all was not as God would have it in his world, and with this the hope of a time to come when God's rule would be more fully and openly implemented and acknowledged among the people of earth: "The LORD will become king over all the earth; on that day the LORD will be one, and his name one" (Zech 14:9). This expectation of the ultimate triumph of God appears in many different ways in the OT prophets, but reaches its most definitive expression in the book of Daniel, which explores the conflict between the kingdoms of this world and the ultimate sovereignty of the Most High God to whom they must all in the end submit. Subsequent Jewish writings, especially those of the apocalyptists, frequently returned to this theme, and in popular Jewish hope by the first century A.D. Jesus' choice of the phrase "the kingship of God" to sum up his message would have evoked a deep-rooted longing for this ultimate assertion of God's sovereignty over all who opposed his will. The regular synagogue liturgy at the time of Jesus concluded with the words of the Kaddish prayer: "May God let his kingship rule in your lifetime and in your days and in the whole lifetime of the house of Israel, speedily and soon."[26] Mark's description of Joseph of Arimathea as one who was "waiting expectantly for the kingship of God" (Mark 15:43) is probably typical of mainstream Jewish piety at the time.

But John (and Jesus) do not simply echo this hope of God's rule coming *soon*. It has already arrived; literally, it "has come near." There has been extensive debate over the significance of the choice of the verb *engizō*, and especially of its perfect tense. The present tense, *engizei*, would have conveyed the standard eschatological hope, it "is coming near," but the perfect *ēngiken* suggests something more actual. That which has completed the process of "coming near" is already present, not simply still on the way. There is a suggestive parallel use of the perfect tense of the same verb in 26:45-46, where Jesus' declaration that "the time has come near" is paralleled with the statement that the Son of Man *is being* betrayed (present tense), while the following declaration that the betrayer "has come near" leads into the statement that "while he was still speaking" Judas arrived. This is not the language of an event still in the future but of one now in the process of happening. In Mark 1:15 the same phrase summarizing Jesus' proclamation is balanced by the declaration (also in the perfect tense) that "the time has been fulfilled," which surely makes the sense of present reality unmistakable.[27] But even without that supplement Matthew's phrase is clear enough, and is further supported by the language of v. 10: the ax is *already* placed at the root

---

26. See J. Jeremias, *Theology,* 198-99; for some related "kingdom of God" texts from the period see D. C. Allison, *End,* 103.

27. See R. H. Gundry, *Mark,* 64-65, for arguments for this sense in Mark 1:15.

of the trees. The time of God's effective sovereignty has arrived, and now is the time for decisive action in response.[28]

3 We shall hear more of John's proclamation in vv. 7-12 (and by implication in v. 6), but first Matthew pauses to introduce him more fully, and especially to do for John as he has for Jesus in 1:18–2:23, to explain his significance in terms of a scriptural model.[29] That John is himself the subject of a prophetic oracle, not just the harbinger of the one predicted, further underlines his importance in Matthew's scheme of fulfillment. The verse quoted, Isa 40:3, is used in the same way in Mark 1:3, but whereas Mark there precedes it with a combined quotation of Mal 3:1 and Exod 23:20, Matthew will introduce that combined quotation separately in 11:10.[30]

This verse is not usually reckoned among Matthew's formula-quotations as such, though the formula which introduces it is similar. It differs in not using the verb "fulfill"[31] and in using the masculine participle "who was spoken about" rather than the regular neuter "was declared" (though the verb is the same; see p. 96, n. 4). It thus identifies John himself in terms of a prophetic model rather than tracing the fulfillment of Scripture in the course of events relating to Jesus' origins and ministry. But the difference is not great: even though the word "fulfill" is reserved for Jesus (though indirectly in 2:17), John also comes as predicted in Scripture.

Whereas in most of Matthew's formula-quotations the text quoted differs significantly from the LXX, here he follows it exactly except that he abbreviates by putting "his" for "of our God" at the end.[32] The LXX of Isa 40:3

---

28. For further arguments, both lexical and contextual, for the sense "has arrived" see J. A. Gibbs, *Jerusalem,* 35-38.

29. Morris, 53, unusually takes v. 3 as still part of John's words, so that it is John himself who is quoted. Morris does not explain why he has come to this conclusion, nor why in context one should take οὗτος as referring to Jesus, who will not feature in John's teaching until v. 11. This exegesis, which requires οὗτος to refer not to the "voice" but to the κύριος of whom the voice speaks, seems unnecessarily tortuous, especially as the quotation so naturally fits into Matthew's normal editorial style as a scriptural comment on the person being described in the narrative.

30. For the significance of Isa 40:3 in contemporary Jewish thought see J. E. Taylor, *John,* 25-29 (with special reference to its use at Qumran); R. E. Watts, *Exodus,* 82-84 (and cf. Watts's discussion of the text in its own canonical setting, ibid., 76-82).

31. "Fulfill" was absent also in 2:5, but there its absence was dictated by the narrative setting whereas this verse is an editorial comment like the other formula-quotations.

32. The citation of the same text in 1QS 8:14 is preceded by "to prepare the way of him" where there has been no antecedent to indicate that "he" is God, while in the quotation itself the name "Yahweh" is suppressed in the first line, though "for our God" remains in the second. Matthew's alteration of the LXX is sometimes attributed to similar sensitivity concerning writing the name of God, but it need be no more than simple abbreviation.

differs from the normal understanding of the Hebrew in three ways:
(1) where the Hebrew has simply "a voice calling," LXX personalizes it with
"the voice of someone shouting"; (2) LXX takes "in the wilderness" not as
part of the first line of the proclamation but as giving the location of the
speaker;[33] and (3) LXX omits the phrase "in the desert" in the second line,
which balances "in the wilderness" in the first. The resultant text better suits
Matthew's purpose to provide a scriptural warrant for John's personal role
and for his location "in the wilderness" (v. 1), and the words of the "voice" in
its LXX form avoid locating God's predicted coming directly "in the wilderness," thus leaving open the question of when and where John's preparatory
proclamation was to find its fulfillment.

Taken in the wider setting of the wilderness theme in Deutero-Isaiah,
the text in its original context announces God's coming to lead his people in
their "new exodus" through the wilderness from Babylon back to Palestine. It
is God himself who is to come and will use the processional way. There is no
hint of any other person (a Messiah) intermediate between the "voice" and
God himself. Christian interpretation has for so long taken it for granted that
John's role was to prepare the way for the Messiah that it is easy to miss the
radical significance of Matthew's choice of text: the coming one in Isa 40:3 is
not the Messiah, but God himself. The same is true of the forerunner texts in
Malachi (3:1 and 4:5-6), which will be cited in 11:10, 14 (see comments
there). We shall return to this theme at v. 11. Matthew's use of the LXX text
with its regular use of "the Lord" *(kyrios)* for Yahweh, together with his own
abbreviation of the quotation so that the more specific identification of this
"Lord" as "our God" is omitted, does of course make it easier for a Christian
reader to see in these words a preparation for the coming of *Jesus,* whom
Christians had gotten used to calling "the Lord" by the time Matthew wrote
(though not of course at the time of the events recorded). But even so, there is
a remarkable christological claim involved in applying Isaiah's depiction of
God's forerunner to the man who prepared the way for the coming of *Jesus.*[34]

4 John's appearance and lifestyle suit the ruggedness of his proclamation. His clothing was both appropriate to his rough lifestyle out in the
wilderness[35] and, probably, symbolic of his prophetic role; see Zech 13:4 for

---

33. R. H. Gundry, *Use,* 10, argues that it is the LXX (supported by the targum,
Peshitta, Vulgate, and rabbinic interpreters) rather than the MT which preserves the in-
tended sense of the Hebrew. The quotation in 1QS 8:14 seems, however, to require the
Masoretic reading.

34. M. Öhler, *JBL* 118 (1999) 468-73, argues cogently that both John and his disciples understood John's role as that of Elijah, preparing for the coming of *God.* It was
subsequent Christian reinterpretation that made him the forerunner of the Messiah.

35. Cf. the ascetic Bannus, who later lived in the same region wearing "garments
made from trees" (Josephus, *Life* 11); the suggestion of J. E. Taylor, *John,* 35, that this re-

the "hairy mantle" which identified a prophet in the sixth century B.C. and more specifically the description of Elijah in 2 Kgs 1:8 as "a hairy man" or "a man in a hair cloak"[36] with "a leather belt around his waist."[37] Elijah was also a man of the wilderness (1 Kgs 17:3-7; 19:3-8; 2 Kgs 2:6-12, the latter set in just this same area by the Jordan). Jesus will later explicitly identify John as (the returning) Elijah (see on 11:14; 17:11-13), but Matthew is already preparing his readers for this identification. In view of the considerable Jewish interest in the eschatological role of Elijah (see on 11:14 and 17:10-11) it is likely that John's clothing was deliberately adopted to promote this image.[38]

Locusts are the only type of insect permitted as food in the Mosaic law (Lev 11:20-23; cf. CD 12:14-15; 11QTemple 48:3-5 for their use as food at Qumran, roasted or boiled); they are still eaten by those in whose lands they flourish. Bonnard, 34, speaks with remarkable authority on the subject: "This insect was highly prized as nourishment, either in water and salt like our prawns, or dried in the sun and preserved in honey and vinegar, or powdered and mixed with wheat flour into a pancake."[39] For honey found in the wild cf. Judg 14:8-9; 1 Sam 14:25-26, and the OT description of Palestine as "a land flowing with milk and honey." John's diet represents the attempt to

fers to camel hair brushed off on the bushes and used by Bannus to make clothes would make the parallel between John and Bannus even closer.

36. LXX δασύς, "hairy," apparently describes John's personal appearance rather than his clothing, but the Hebrew term is literally "a man possessed of hair," which many commentators take to refer to a hair cloak such as Zech 13:4 presupposes. It is after all unlikely that a leather belt was Elijah's only or most conspicuous item of clothing, and Elijah's cloak is mentioned elsewhere as a notable feature of his equipment (1 Kgs 19:13, 19; 2 Kgs 2:8-14). It is also interesting that the term used for Elijah's cloak, 'adderet, occurs also in the description of Esau's hairy body as "like a cloak of hair" (Gen 25:25). See further M. Hengel, Leader, 36, n. 71. J. E. Taylor, John, 35-38, however, thinks that John's camel-hair clothing was simply sackcloth worn as a symbol of humility and repentance, not meant to imply a prophetic role.

37. ζώνην δερματίνην περὶ τὴν ὀσφὺν αὐτοῦ is virtually an exact quotation from LXX 4 Kgdms 1:8.

38. J. E. Taylor, John, 213-14, also suggests that the location of John's ministry just across the Jordan from Jericho had special significance as the place where Elijah had ascended to heaven (2 Kgs 2:4-12), and therefore perhaps the place where he was expected to appear again.

39. For the nutritional value and wide use of locusts for food see G. S. Cansdale, Animals, 242-44. D. Instone-Brewer, Traditions, 1:295-96, points out in the light of mishnaic regulations that John's food "was not noteworthy for being unusual but for being unprocessed." There is no basis in Greek usage for the strange notion, still sometimes encountered, that ἀκρίδες refers here not to locusts but to the carob or "locust" bean (so called because its pods resemble locusts), which thus came to be known as "St. John's bread." This idea derives from Western squeamishness rather than from the realities of Middle Eastern diet. John was an ascetic, but not a vegetarian!

live, like Bannus (see n. 35 above), on "food which grew by itself."[40] His diet is compatible with that of a Nazirite.

Insofar as John's clothing was meant to evoke a prophetic image, it corresponds to the way he was popularly perceived, as a prophet (11:9; 16:14; 21:26). It is sometimes stated that first-century Jews believed that prophecy had ceased with Malachi, whose book concludes with the promise of the eschatological return of Elijah, so that to identify John (and later Jesus) as a prophet was to make a quite stupendous claim. But it is more probable that the idea of the cessation of prophecy was confined to only one strand of rabbinic thinking,[41] and that in popular thought the title "prophet" would not have been so unthinkable; Josephus's accounts of popular leaders who claimed to be prophets at this period indicate as much.[42]

5 John's location near the Jordan, while it was uninhabited "wilderness," was only about twenty miles from Jerusalem. His reputation spread through the southern part of Palestine, including the region of Perea across the Jordan, and Matthew's hyperbolic language presumably indicates that a large number of people made the journey out from their towns and villages to hear him and to be baptized. Compare Josephus's mention of people flocking around John, so excited by his teaching that Antipas (the ruler of Perea, not of Judea) concluded that there was a real prospect of a popular uprising (*Ant.* 18.118). Matthew does not mention any Galileans in the crowd, but the fact that Jesus at least was there suggests that the geographical list is not exhaustive; cf. the Galileans who were there according to John 1:35-51.

6 So far Matthew has spoken of John only as a preacher of repentance, though his familiar title "the Baptist" has already indicated a more specific role. He does not speak directly of a "baptism of repentance" (as Mark 1:4 does), perhaps because he feels that Jesus, who will receive John's baptism, has no need of repentance.[43] But whatever may be the case for Jesus, John's followers as a whole confessed their sins when they were baptized, the proper response to John's call for repentance (v. 2). Josephus (*Ant.* 18.117) carefully explains that John's baptism was not itself a means to the forgiveness of sins, but rather a symbol of "a soul already purified by righteousness." Matthew does not enter into such a "Protestant" discussion of the operation of the sacrament; his participial wording leaves the link between baptism and confession undefined, allowing his readers to reach their own conclusions as

40. See J. E. Taylor, *John*, 34, 40-41, for similarities between John and Bannus and the suggestion that Bannus may have "known of John's example and copied him."

41. See below, p. 427, n. 29.

42. For instance, Josephus, *Ant.* 20.97 (Theudas), 169 (the Egyptian); *War* 6.285-86.

43. See below on vv. 14-15, where, however, the specific issue of Jesus' sinlessness is not raised.

to the appropriate sequence of repentance, confession, forgiveness, and baptism. He avoids Mark's statement that the baptism was "for the forgiveness of sins," perhaps because he wants to stress that such forgiveness is the prerogative of Jesus (9:6) and especially derives from the cross (26:28).

Ritual ablutions were familiar in Jewish religious and social life, as may be seen from the remains of *miqwā'ōt* (ritual immersion pools) found around the south side of the temple and in the vicinity of several early synagogue buildings.[44] But *baptisma* as a ritual term is a distinctively Christian word, which is used both of John's practice and of later Christian initiation to refer not to regular ablutions to remove ceremonial impurity but to a single act of symbolic cleansing marking the entry into a new relationship with God.[45] There is no certain evidence for such a practice in contemporary Jewish life. A parallel has been claimed in one text from Qumran, but it is not clear that a single initiatory act is there in view.[46] More promising is the practice of "proselyte baptism," the ritual cleansing of a Gentile at the point of commitment to a new life as a Jew, but scholars do not agree whether this practice can be attested as early as the time of John.[47] Whether or not the baptism of proselytes was yet a recognized practice, however, it seems most likely that John's distinctive rite carried some such symbolism. These were people who were "repenting" (renouncing their former way of life) and committing themselves to a new way of life as the purified people of God. In the language of some of John's prophetic predecessors, they were enrolling in a holy "remnant" over against the ungodly life of their contemporaries.[48] The motivation was perhaps similar to that which led Jerusalem Jews to go down

44. A whole tractate of the Mishnah, *Miqwa'ot,* is devoted to the subject. For a very extensive study of ablution rituals in OT Israel and in subsequent Judaism see R. L. Webb, *John,* 95-162.

45. Note that John's baptism was concerned with "sins"; its motivation was ethical rather than ceremonial. Ritual "impurity" was an impediment to involvement in worship but not a moral problem; it required no "confession" or "forgiveness," merely ceremonial cleansing.

46. 1QS 3:4 refers to "purification by cleansing waters," and 1QS 3:9 to "flesh cleansed by being sprinkled with cleansing waters" in connection with someone entering the "community of truth." J. E. Taylor, *John,* 76-81, argues that this washing was not truly initiatory "since it was not the decisive step towards inclusion in the community, but only something resulting from a practice of righteousness accounted acceptable by God."

47. It was already established at the time of the Mishnah (*m. Pesaḥ.* 8:8). The classical argument for first-century proselyte baptism was by H. H. Rowley in his *From Moses to Qumran,* 211-35; cf. J. Jeremias, *Baptism,* 24-29. R. L. Webb, *John,* 122-30, argues that its introduction was probably post-70, while J. E. Taylor, *John,* 64-69, regards its use in the early first century as possible though not proven.

48. For "remnant" theology as a key element not only in John's message but also in that of Jesus see B. F. Meyer, *JBL* 84 (1965) 123-30; R. E. Menninger, *Israel,* 135-51.

into the wilderness to join the breakaway Qumran community, but there is no sign that John expected his followers to cut themselves off from ordinary life as did the sectaries of Qumran. It seems rather that, at least after the initial "revival movement" by the Jordan, John's converts returned to their homes to live out their repentant and renewed life (see 9:14; 14:12; 21:32).

The crucial difference between John's practice and "proselyte baptism" is that John baptized *Jews*. There was, therefore, inherent in his baptism an implied critique of contemporary Jewish society as no longer truly constituting the holy people of God. This critique, which will become explicit in v. 9, thus prepares the way for Jesus' subsequent encounter with the Jerusalem authorities in chs. 21–23 in which he will make it clear that there is a shift in the center of gravity of the people of God and that the time has come for the unrepentant leaders of "this generation" to give way to "a nation which produces the fruit of the kingdom of God" (21:43).

The verb I have translated "were baptized" could in itself be read as in the middle voice ("baptized themselves"), but the following "by him" makes it clear that it is in fact a passive, and the same construction will occur in vv. 13-14. This marks a change from familiar Jewish rites of ablution, which were normally self-administered.[49] Just how John baptized people is not certain. The fact that he chose a permanent and deep river suggests that more than a token quantity of water was needed, and both the preposition "in" (the Jordan) and the basic meaning of the verb "baptize"[50] probably indicate immersion. In v. 16 Matthew will speak of Jesus "coming up out of the water." The traditional depiction in Christian art of John the Baptist pouring water over Jesus' head may therefore be based on later Christian practice.[51] But we need not assume that the actual method was always the same, nor that John's method was necessarily the same as that of later Christian practice, especially where the latter took place away from a major river such as the Jordan.

7   John was a popular figure, but also a controversial one, and Matthew now goes on to speak of the response of official Judaism. Matthew is the only NT writer to bracket the Pharisees and Sadducees together (except as op-

---

49. See R. L. Webb, *John*, 180-81.

50. BDAG translates βαπτίζω as "plunge, dip, wash" as well as "baptize"; they mention non-Christian usage outside a ritual context as "to put or go under water in a variety of senses." The symbolism of death, burial, and resurrection found in later Christian baptism (Rom 6:3-4) also suggests immersion. See further R. L. Webb, *John*, 179-80. J. E. Taylor, *John*, 49-58, also argues for immersion (probably self-immersion) and translates John's title as "John the Immerser."

51. L. Goppelt, *TDNT* 8:332, argues, however, for affusion as the normal method of baptism both by John and in early Christianity. See also H. Schürmann, *Lukasevangelium* 1, 156, 176 for archeological evidence for affusion rather than immersion as the early Christian mode of baptism.

posing parties in Acts 23:6-10), here and in 16:1-12, and it is often alleged that he must have been ignorant of the profound division between the two.[52] But when he mentions Sadducees on their own in 22:23, he seems well aware of their distinctive stance and of their difference from the Pharisees (22:34). As the two main ideological groups in the Sanhedrin, both the Sadducees (the "politically" dominant group from whom the priestly and temple hierarchy were drawn) and the Pharisees (a self-conscious "party" grouping committed to rigorous observance of the law) represented key elements in the Jerusalem establishment, and the mention of them together probably suggests a sort of "cross-party delegation" who had come out to examine this disturbing new religious phenomenon down by the Jordan. The description of them as "coming to his baptism" rather than "being baptized" like the crowds in v. 6 suggests such a surveillance role, and the reception they received from John (vv. 7-10) makes it unlikely that any of them actually were baptized.[53] See 21:25, 32 for the refusal of the Jerusalem leaders to accept John's message. It is significant that the same grouping of opponents will later confront Jesus (16:1-12), while the "chief priests and scribes" who will be his chief opponents in Jerusalem represent a similar "coalition" of distinct groups.

John's words sharply combine an ironical description of them as part of the repentant crowd[54] with a remarkably strong epithet, "brood of vipers" (used also by Jesus in 12:34; 23:33), which makes it clear that he did not regard them as really repentant.[55] The language of judgment (here literally "anger") now singles out the negative aspect of the coming of God's kingship, and will dominate the rest of John's public address. The sarcastic imagery of snakes wriggling away from an encroaching fire (cf. Acts 28:3; or perhaps, in the light of v. 10, we should picture them as escaping from those felling trees, as in Jer 46:22) makes up in vividness what it lacks in diplomacy.[56]

52. See my *Matthew: Evangelist*, 106-7, in response to J. P. Meier, *Law*, 18-19, who uses the author's supposed ignorance on this point as an argument for a Gentile redactor of the gospel. Cf. also G. N. Stanton, *Gospel*, 135-37.

53. But Carter, 96-97, goes too far in suggesting that they were there "to oppose John's baptism and persuade others not to be baptized." This depends on reading ἐπί as meaning "against," a possible meaning where the context requires it, but here John's ironical depiction of them as seeking to escape judgment is hard to square with their being openly hostile to his message.

54. Irony seems to me a better explanation of John's words than that of Davies and Allison, 1:304: "inconcinnity . . . the outcome of imperfect editing."

55. R. Mohrlang, *Matthew*, 54-55, is perhaps a little too generous in stating that "this is one of the very few pericopes in which the possibility of repentance at least remains open to [the Jewish leaders]."

56. Keener, 122-23, suggests an even more insulting implication in the phrase γεννήματα ἐχιδνῶν in that in antiquity vipers were often thought to kill their mothers, so that the phrase in effect means "mother killers."

8 While this and the following verses are still appropriate to the insincerity of the Pharisees and Sadducees, they also fill out John's message to the people in general. True repentance is not a matter of words and ritual, but of a real change of life. The imagery of bearing fruit[57] will also be deployed in Jesus' teaching (7:16-20; 12:33-37; 13:8, 22-23) until it reaches its climax in the condemnation of the Jerusalem leadership as the tenants who have failed to deliver the produce of God's vineyard (21:43), a situation which has been vividly illustrated by the destruction of the fruitless fig tree outside Jerusalem (21:18-19).[58] It is by what we do in response to God's demands rather than by what we hear or say that we will be judged (7:15-27; 21:28-32). Josephus (*Ant.* 18.117) agrees with this assessment of John's message: those who sought his baptism were to "practice virtue, behaving with justice toward one another and piety toward God" since only so would their baptism be acceptable to God.

9 Abraham was the "father" par excellence of the Israelite people; note the use of this title for him in, for instance, Luke 1:73; 16:24, 30; John 8:39; Acts 7:2; Jas 2:21. For "children of Abraham" cf. also Luke 13:16; Acts 13:26. The Jews easily took it for granted that, as Abraham's descendants, they belonged to the covenant people, the heirs to the promises of God,[59] but NT writers argue (a) that not all those descended from Abraham are his true "children" (John 8:39-44; Rom 9:6-8), and (b) that Gentiles who share Abraham's faith are no less his children than Jews (Rom 4:11-18; Gal 3:6-9, 14), a position already adumbrated in the title "father of many nations" (Gen 17:4-6) and given fuller and more recent expression in, for example, Sir 44:19-21. John's words here anticipate this later Christian argument. His insistence that *Jews* need to be baptized (see on v. 6) has already pointed toward (a), while his words here make the charge explicit; and in the concept of God's creating "children of Abraham" from stones Matthew may also have seen a pointer toward (b) the inclusion of non-Jews among the chosen people, a theme which Jesus will later spell out in 8:11-12 (again in relation to Abraham). The choice of "stones" to represent Abraham's true children is no doubt prompted by the obvious Hebrew or Aramaic pun (in Hebrew *bānîm* is "children," *ʾᵃbānîm* "stones," in Aramaic *bᵉnayyāʾ*, *ʾabnayyāʾ*; the same wordplay may underlie 21:42 following 21:37),[60] but also rather brutally wounds the pride of unre-

---

57. Cf. also v. 10; the singular in each case might suggest a total lifestyle rather than individual acts, but see below, p. 291, n. 23.

58. B. Charette, *Recompense,* 121-40, argues that the theme of "fruitlessness" is one of the most prominent elements in Matthew's emphasis on judgment. D. Instone-Brewer, *Traditions,* 1:123-27, contrasts Jesus' use of the imagery of fruit with that of the rabbis, for whom it symbolized a reward received for good deeds in this life.

59. Keener, 125-27, surveys the theme of "personal and ancestral merits in Jewish texts."

60. See, however, J. Jeremias, *TDNT* 4:268, 270-71, who finds the background to

pentant Jews — even stones have more chance of being God's true people than they have (cf. Luke 19:40 for a comparable use of stones to represent God's people). Those who remembered Isaiah's description of Abraham as "the rock from which you were hewn" (Isa 51:1-2) might reflect ruefully on the possibility of God's substituting different "stones."[61]

10 One strong image of judgment succeeds another. The urgency of John's "already" matches the claim that God's kingship has now arrived (see on v. 2). For the chopping down of a tree as a metaphor for God's judgment on pagan nations cf. Isa 10:33-34; Ezek 31; Dan 4:14; now Israel, too, faces such judgment. In 7:19 Jesus will take up the metaphor with specific reference to the failure to produce fruit (see on v. 8); cf. also the parable of Luke 13:6-9. Cutting at the root indicates a final removal of the tree rather than pruning. Burning the tree is a natural extension of the metaphor, but fire is also in itself a common OT metaphor for judgment (cf. 13:30, 40-42, 50; 18:8-9; 25:41), and will recur (without reference to a tree) in the next verse, as well as in the comparable agricultural imagery of v. 12. The basis of judgment is not failure to belong to the natural family of Abraham, but the lack of the "good fruit" which comes with true repentance.

11 This verse contains the only part of John's proclamation according to Matthew and Luke which Mark also records It consisted of two major themes: (a) the coming of a "stronger one" whom John is not worthy even to serve, and (b) the contrast between John's own water baptism and the "baptism in the Holy Spirit" which the stronger one will bestow. Both themes occur also in the Fourth Gospel (John 1:26-27, 30, 33). The Christian presentation of John, therefore, unlike that of Josephus, consistently locates his importance primarily in his role as preparing the way for the Messiah's more effective spiritual ministry.

While vv. 8-10 may be understood at least in part as continuing the address to the Pharisees and Sadducees, now John's address is specifically to those whom he is actually baptizing.

The phrase "the person who follows me" (literally, "comes behind me") is ambiguous. Most readers here take it to mean one who comes later in time, but this is not a normal sense of the Greek *opisō,* "behind," whereas "to come behind" occurs in 4:19; 10:38; 16:24 as a quasi-technical term for being a "disciple" of Jesus (cf. Luke 21:8; John 12:19). Was Jesus, then, first a "disciple" of John before he began his own ministry? The Fourth Gospel uses such language particularly prominently (John 1:15, 27, 30), and its depiction

---

the saying in Isa 51:1-2 and argues for *kêpā'* rather than *'abnayyā'* as the Aramaic underlying λίθος here.

61. On the "children of Abraham" theme see further B. Charette, *Recompense,* 67-69.

of Jesus as at first leading a baptizing movement similar to that of John (John 3:22-24; 4:1-2) supports that interpretation. But each of these uses of "behind me" in John 1 is closely linked with a statement of Jesus' superiority, so that the use of disciple language becomes ironical: Jesus is the disciple who becomes the master. Here in Matthew the theme is less emphasized, but the exchange between John and Jesus in vv. 14-15 perhaps suggests the same paradoxical notion of the follower who takes the lead.[62]

The paradox is underlined by the phrase "stronger than I" and by the imagery of the slave taking off the master's sandals. The use of "stronger" rather than a more neutral term for "superior" suggests that John is speaking not so much about status as about the greater efficacy of his follower's mission (cf. 12:29, where the "strong man" is the one who is in control until someone stronger is able to subdue him).[63] The following clause, however, does focus on status: to take off the master's sandals was a task too low even for the lowest disciple.[64] One who is not worthy even to perform this menial role is the lowest of the low.

The superiority of the "stronger one" is explained in terms of two baptisms (clearly marked as a contrast by a classical *men/de* construction): John's water baptism is a preliminary ritual "with a view to repentance," clearing the way for the real thing, the "stronger one's" baptism in the Holy Spirit and fire.[65] Water is an outward sign, but the work of the Holy Spirit will be inward. Since fire occurs in both v. 10 and v. 12 (and probably also by implication in v. 7 in the imagery of the snakes escaping the fire) as a metaphor for God's judgment, it should probably be taken in the same sense here. The coming of the Holy Spirit will burn away what is bad and so purify the repentant people of God.[66] For a similar metaphor in the OT see Isa 4:4; Zech 13:9; Mal 3:2-4.

62. See my article mentioned on p. 99, n. 13, p. 104, and the references there to others who have taken this as "disciple" language.

63. J. H. Neyrey, *Honor,* 41, interprets this term against the background of ancient concern with "military prowess" as the basis of honor.

64. Taking off the master's sandals was a slave's role, specifically excluded from the otherwise menial duties of a rabbi's disciple (*b. Ketub.* 96a). Another rabbinic source goes further in regarding the task as too low even for a Hebrew slave (*Mek.* Exod 21:2). In the second century, however, we read that Polycarp was not used to taking off his own shoes because his disciples were always so keen to do it for him (Eusebius, *Hist. eccl.* 4.15.30).

65. R. L. Webb, *John,* 272-75, argues convincingly for this combination of Holy Spirit and fire being the original version of John's message, despite Mark's omission of πυρί and against the suggestion of some that originally only fire was mentioned, the Holy Spirit being a Christianizing of John's message of judgment. Note the use of the imagery of fire in connection with the coming of the Spirit at Pentecost (Acts 2:3).

66. Albright and Mann, 26-27, argue on the basis of Qumran evidence that πνεύματι ἁγίῳ καὶ πυρί is a hendiadys, and translate "with the fire of the Holy Spirit"; the

"Baptize in the Holy Spirit" is a phrase used in the NT[67] almost exclusively in the context of this contrast between John's water baptism and the salvation Jesus brings (cf. Mark 1:8; Luke 3:16; John 1:33; Acts 1:5; 11:16). Only in 1 Cor 12:13 does similar language occur outside that specific context, and the different phrasing there, "in one Spirit baptized into one body," does not suggest that "baptism in the Spirit" would have been recognized in NT times as a designation of something other than initial Christian baptism.[68] Thus the contrast between water and the Holy Spirit here is not between two stages in Christian initiation, but between John's baptism and that of Jesus. Christian baptism did of course adopt John's use of the outward symbol of water, but the use of the outward sign in no way detracts from the true spiritual significance of baptism into the Christian community; it symbolizes (as for John it pointed forward to) that same pouring out of the Holy Spirit which is the essence of the Messiah's saving ministry.

The background to the idea of a messianic "baptizing in the Holy Spirit" is found in the OT prophets, who speak of an eschatological outpouring of the Spirit of God (Isa 32:15; 44:3; Ezek 36:26-27; 39:29; Joel 3:1-2 [EVV 2:28-29]) to describe a time of spiritual refreshment and renewal leading to a closer and more obedient relationship with God; for the same idea, including a pronounced judgmental tone, cf. 1QS 4:20-22. But whereas the prophets all speak of God himself as the one who pours out his Spirit, John here attributes that role to the "stronger one" who follows him. The "stronger one" might of course also be understood in itself as a title for God, and the

---

Greek wording, which combines the two nouns under the single preposition ἐν, suggests the same. The case is more fully argued by Davies and Allison, 1:317. Matthew's wording does not support the assumption of some commentators that the Holy Spirit and fire denote the contrasting fates of different groups of people ("Those producing good fruit will receive the gift of the Holy Spirit. Those producing bad fruit will suffer unending punishment"; Gundry, 49). B. Charette, *Recompense,* 122, n. 4, supports Gundry's view on the grounds that John is still addressing the Pharisees and Sadducees, but the "you" of this verse denotes those baptized by John, not the critical bystanders.

67. The expression is always with "baptize" as a verb, not, as modern usage might suggest, with the noun "baptism."

68. While βαπτίζω ἐν is a natural phrase to use in connection with water (see p. 109, n. 50, for the meaning of the verb), it is less easily understood of the Holy Spirit. The OT language about "pouring out" the Spirit shows that "liquid" metaphors could be used for the Spirit, and similar usage is found in 1QS 4:20-22. Elsewhere in the NT also the Spirit is spoken of in terms of water, whether poured out or drunk (John 7:37-39; Acts 2:33; 10:45; 1 Cor 12:13; Titus 3:5-6). But these metaphors are not the same as immersion (see on v. 6). In this context the phrase is used in order to express the antithesis with John's water baptism rather than because it is in itself a natural metaphor. It would therefore be inappropriate to use βαπτίζω ἐν as a basis for explaining the nature of the Christian experience of the Spirit.

next verse will go on to speak of divine judgment. We have already noted in v. 3 that John is described in language which in the OT speaks of the forerunner of *God's* eschatological coming. With the exception of the phrase "who follows me" with its implication of "discipleship," the whole of vv. 11-12 could be understood to speak of the coming of God himself in judgment as the sequel to John's ministry. The Christian reader knows, and vv. 13-17 will go on to relate, that it is in fact Jesus who "comes" as Messiah and who is to be understood as the "stronger one," but those who heard John's words might well have been surprised to see them fulfilled in a human figure. The christological implication is powerful: in some remarkable sense, when Jesus comes, God comes.[69]

12   After speaking of snakes escaping the fire (v. 7), the tree cut down and burned (v. 10), and "baptism in the Holy Spirit and fire" (v. 11), John now adds another metaphor for judgment (also involving fire), that of the threshing floor. The threshed grain is thrown up into the air with a winnowing fork so that the wind can blow away the chaff while the heavier grain falls back onto the threshing floor. Only when all the chaff has been separated from the grain is the latter collected (using the "winnowing shovel") and stored away for use, while the chaff is burned. The metaphor is a familiar one (Pss 1:4; 35:5; Isa 41:15-16, etc.; cf. the burned stubble in Mal 3:19 [EVV 4:1]) and needs no explanation. It will in part be picked up in Jesus' parable of the weeds in 13:30, 40-44. But two of the words used point beyond the pictorial scene to the reality it signifies. The verb I have translated "clear" is more literally "completely clean" or "purify"; in the agricultural imagery it perhaps indicates the threshing floor left bare when all the chaff has been separated off and the grain stored,[70] but metaphorically the verb points to the purpose of God's judgment, the complete removal of all evil leaving a purified people. With the mention of a fire "that cannot be put out" we have moved beyond the agricultural scene, where the fire must die when all the chaff has been burned, to take up an aspect of God's judgment which will be repeated in 18:8 and 25:41, 46, the "eternal fire/punishment" which awaits the wicked. We shall discuss the significance of this language in ch. 25, but we may note here that the term "unquenchable" does not in itself resolve the debate over whether the wicked are to be understood as eternally suffering or as annihilated, since an unquenchable fire may be the result of new fuel being

69. See p. 105, n. 34, for Öhler's argument that John also saw himself as God's forerunner.

70. A detailed discussion of the agricultural background to this saying by R. L. Webb, *John*, 295-98, suggests that it is this last stage of the process, rather than the prior act of winnowing itself, which is being described. An alternative view is that ἅλων, normally "threshing floor," is here used by metonymy for the grain on the threshing floor, which is "cleaned" by the removal of the chaff (so BDAG 49b).

constantly added. Such language derives from the vivid imagery of Isa 66:24 (cf. Isa 34:9-10), and also perhaps from the Jerusalem rubbish dumps in the Ge Hinnom (hence Gehenna), where fires burned continuously (see below on 5:22). A further term which will be echoed in Jesus' teaching is "gather," which will occur in the same agricultural sense in 6:26; 13:30, but in 24:31 will describe the gathering together of God's people by the angels.

The strong emphasis on judgment should not cause us to forget the positive aspect of John's message, that while the chaff will be burned up, there will also be "grain," a continuing purified "remnant" of the true people of God.[71] It is the drawing together of that true nucleus of Israel which is the ultimate aim of the ministry of John, as it will be of that of Jesus. The judgment is only a means to that end.

D. THE MESSIAH REVEALED AS THE SON OF GOD (3:13-17)

13 *Then Jesus arrived[1] from Galilee to join John at the Jordan in order to be baptized by him.* 14 *But John tried to put him off:[2] he said, "I am the one who needs to be baptized by you, and yet you are coming to me!"* 15 *Jesus replied, "Let it be so for now, for this is the right way for us to fulfill all that is required of us."[3] Then John allowed him to be baptized.[4]*

16 *As soon as Jesus had been baptized, he came up[5] out of the wa-*

71. See p. 108, n. 48, for the remnant theme in Matthew.

1. See p. 96, n. 1, above for the verb παραγίνομαι, used here for the last time by Matthew to introduce an important new character onto the scene. Whereas in v. 1 it indicated the "appearing" of a prophet with a new mission in an uninhabited place, by now that place has become more frequented, and Jesus "arrives" to join an existing movement.

2. The imperfect tense of διακωλύω indicates a protracted but unsuccessful attempt.

3. For the possible implications of this enigmatic reply see the comments below. The translation attempts to capture as idiomatically as possible the twin ideas of "fittingness" in πρέπον ἐστίν and of "meeting God's requirements" which is the primary sense of δικαιοσύνη in Matthew.

4. See B. M. Metzger, *Textual Commentary,* 10-11, for a textual tradition going back to the second century which adds here that "When Jesus was being baptized, a great light shone from the water so that all who were gathered there were afraid." This addition to the story, while clearly not original, testifies to a developing tendency to read Jesus' experience at his baptism as a spectacular public event rather than a private revelation to him alone as in Mark.

5. Matthew has εὐθύς, "immediately," qualifying ἀνέβη, "he came up"; it functions in the sentence not so much to indicate an unusually prompt emergence from the water as to alert the reader that something remarkable is about to happen. (Davies and

116

*ter, and suddenly⁶ heaven was opened,⁷ and he saw the Spirit of God
coming down like a dove and coming upon him.⁸ 17 And a voice was
heard from heaven, saying, "This is my beloved Son, with whom I am
delighted."⁹*

The first appearance of the adult Jesus in Matthew's story takes place in the
context of John's baptism, with Jesus as John's Galilean "follower" (see on
v. 11) who receives baptism along with the repentant Judean crowds. The
"debate" between John and Jesus in vv. 14-15 explores the paradox of this
situation in the light of the fact already spelled out in v. 11 that Jesus is in fact
John's superior and himself the dispenser of a far more significant "baptism."
Later Christians would raise the more specifically theological problem of
why a sinless Son of God should receive a baptism which focused on repentance and forgiveness; this problem is imaginatively tackled by the *Gospel
according to the Hebrews* as quoted by Jerome, *Pelag.* 3:2, where Jesus responds as follows to the suggestion that he should be baptized by John:
"What sin have I committed, that I should go and be baptized by him? Unless
perhaps the very thing I have just said is ignorance [and therefore sinful]."
But the specific issue of Jesus' sinlessness is not raised as such here in Mat-

---

Allison, 1:328, take the placing of εὐθύς as an error by Matthew in editing Mark, where it
apparently qualifies εἶδεν.) I judged that εὐθύς was better left untranslated where it occurs,
and instead have aimed to produce the same effect by using "As soon as" at the beginning
of the sentence and "suddenly" for ἰδού in the next clause.

6. As in 1:20; 2:13, 19 (see p. 46, n. 19), this is an attempt to capture the force of
ἰδού. Stylistic considerations have led me not to repeat "suddenly" in v. 17, where the construction is different in that ἰδού functions (vividly but not very literally; cf. Rev 1:12,
βλέπειν τὴν φωνήν) as the main verb of which the subject is φωνή, so that I have represented it there by a verb, "was heard."

7. Most later MSS and versions add "to him," which would imply a private vision
as in Mark 1:10, "he saw heaven torn apart," rather than an objective event as in Luke
3:21, "it happened that heaven was opened." The textual arguments are evenly balanced,
but in the comments below I will argue that Matthew leans toward the Lucan reading of
the event.

8. Manuscript and versional evidence is divided over whether the "and" should be
omitted. Most Greek MSS include it, and there is no evidence for the feminine form
ἐρχομένην, which would be required if the participle directly described the dove "settling"
on him. Since the neuter participle must have the Spirit as its subject on either reading, the
presence or absence of the καί is essentially a stylistic matter, and I have followed the majority of witnesses in preferring to retain it.

9. ἐν ᾧ εὐδόκησα, literally "in whom I found pleasure," an expression of warm approval and love. The aorist tense reflects the tense of the phrase in Isa 42:1 on which these
words are based (see comments below); it expresses a settled opinion rather than a temporary pleasure (*pace* Gundry, 53, who explains it as "referring to God's pleasure in the baptism of Jesus").

thew.[10] The issue is rather a matter of relative status and of the contrast between the two baptisms.[11]

Jesus' enigmatic reply in v. 15 indicates that he sees a God-given appropriateness in his receiving baptism from John, but he does not clearly explain why it should be so. Some suggestions will be discussed below. But for Matthew the importance of the event is not in the baptism itself, but in the revelation which follows it, which culminates in the declaration that Jesus is God's unique Son, a theological position which has been assumed in 2:15 but is now brought into the open.

How open it was in the narrative setting depends on whether the revelatory events of vv. 16-17 are understood as phenomena witnessed by John and other bystanders or as an experience of Jesus alone (and therefore given to the readers as a privileged insight not available to people at the time). The latter reading seems clear in Mark 1:10-11, where we are told only of what Jesus himself "saw" and of a voice which addressed him in the second person. Luke 3:21-22 apparently envisages a more public event, in that he describes the opening of heaven and the descent of the Spirit as what "happened," not just what Jesus saw, and describes the Spirit's descent as "*in bodily form* like a dove," though the voice from heaven again speaks to Jesus in the second person. John 1:32-34 tells us that John witnessed the descent of the Spirit. A further "objectifying" of the event is found in the early tradition of a light shining from the water to the dismay of the crowds (see p. 116, n. 4). Matthew's wording of the first part of the scene is closer to Mark's than to Luke's in that he speaks of the descent of the Spirit as what Jesus *saw* (and there is no mention of "bodily form"), but closer to Luke in that heaven "*was* opened," not just seen to be opened. More significantly, in v. 17 Matthew presents the voice from heaven as a third-person statement *about* Jesus, as in the parallel revelation to the disciples in 17:5.[12] As such it was apparently intended for others (including John) to hear (as the addition of "Listen to him" in 17:5 suggests), though Matthew lays no emphasis on John or anyone else other than Jesus himself being the audience. It seems then that Matthew (like Luke but by different means) has adapted the account to allow his readers to

10. Gundry, 51, imaginatively finds such an idea implied in v. 16: Jesus came up "immediately" from the water (see n. 5 above) because he did not "stay in the river to confess his sins. He had none." Subsequent interpreters have not been convinced.

11. For some expressions of post-NT Christian embarrassment over the fact of Jesus' baptism see J. E. Taylor, *John,* 262-63. The survey of the history of exegesis by Luz, 1:174-76, explores more widely "attempts out of embarrassment to set the text into a 'high' Christology of the church."

12. D sy[s c] and one OL MS have the second-person form as in Mark and Luke, but it is more likely that this is a case of Synoptic assimilation than that an original second-person text was conformed in the vast majority of early MSS and versions to 17:5.

see this as a public revelation of Jesus as the Son of God, while maintaining the focus essentially on the experience of Jesus himself.[13]

13   We noted above (on v. 3) that Matthew has given the impression that John's clientele came only from the south of Palestine and Perea, but that John 1:35-51 also speaks of Galileans among John's followers. For Jesus to make a journey of around seventy miles from Nazareth to the area of John's activity in a "foreign" territory would require significant motivation, and v. 15 suggests that Jesus was already aware of God's special purpose for him, for which his baptism by John was an appropriate prelude. The wording of this verse indicates a firm sense of purpose.

14-15   This exchange, recorded only by Matthew, reflects the consistent NT conviction that John's role was subordinate to that of Jesus, and therefore perhaps some apologetic embarrassment over the acknowledged fact that Jesus' public ministry derived from his initial enrollment as a "disciple" of John and a recipient of his baptism. No indication is given of how John recognized Jesus as the "stronger one" whose coming he had predicted in v. 11 (contrast John 1:30-34, where John's recognition of Jesus follows and results from the events at his baptism). His words perhaps imply, "I need your Spirit-and-fire baptism, not you my water baptism."

The substance of Jesus' reply is clear enough: John is to overcome his scruples and carry out the baptism requested. Whatever may be their ultimate relationship, this is the right course "for now," and Jesus will be, now as throughout the gospel, perfectly obedient to the will of God. But the explanation given does not spell out *why* this is "the right way for us to fulfill all that is required of us."[14] The usage of *dikaiosynē* (which I have translated "what is required") elsewhere in Matthew's gospel indicates a basic meaning of the conduct which God expects of his people.[15] This might be taken to mean only

13. J. D. G. Dunn, *Jesus,* 62-65, discusses the significance of the event of Jesus' baptism from the point of view of Jesus' own spiritual awareness, with the focus on the twin themes of "Spirit and sonship."

14. Davies and Allison, 1:325-27, set out seven different views of what these words might mean; see also ibid., 321-23, for eight suggestions as to why Jesus wished to be baptized by John.

15. The detailed discussion by B. Przybylski, *Righteousness,* has firmly established this meaning. Note especially his conclusion from a study (pp. 78-99) of the seven uses of δικαιοσύνη in Matthew: "Righteousness is seen as God's demand upon man. Righteousness refers to proper conduct before God" (99). Cf. D. Hill, *Greek Words,* 125-30, who concludes that here the term "bears its Septuagintal meaning of 'righteousness of life' through obedience which is in accordance with the divine will" (127). R. Mohrlang, *Matthew,* 113-14, argues that δικαιοσύνη in Matthew "embraces both being and doing," motivation as well as action, but agrees that it remains "a strictly ethical concept" in contrast to the Pauline soteriological use. See, however, D. A. Hagner, in M. J. Wilkins and T. Paige, *Worship, Theology and Ministry in the Early Church,* 101-20, for an attempt to

that John's baptism is a divinely instituted ordinance which therefore it is "right" for everyone to submit to. But the statement that it is "fitting *for us*" to fulfill this *dikaiosynē* indicates that Jesus is thinking of something specific to his own and John's role rather than of a general principle: God requires *him* to be baptized by John. The word "fulfill," normally used by Matthew in his quotation formula in connection with the completion of a scripturally authenticated pattern (see further on 5:17), also suggests that this baptism has a role in the carrying out of Jesus' specific mission.[16]

The most obvious way in which Jesus' baptism prepares for his mission is by indicating his solidarity with John's call to repentance in view of the arrival of God's kingship. By first identifying with John's proclamation Jesus lays the foundation for his own mission to take on where John has left off. Further, as Jesus is baptized along with others at the Jordan, he is identified with all those who by accepting John's baptism have declared their desire for a new beginning with God. He thus prepares for his own role in "bearing their weaknesses" (8:17) and eventually "giving his life as a ransom for many" (20:28) through shedding his blood for their forgiveness (26:28). If he is to be their representative, he must first be identified with them.[17]

This representative role is reminiscent of Isaiah's "servant of Yahweh" who is to suffer for the sins of the people, and an echo of the "servant" prophecy in Isa 53 may possibly be discerned in the use of the term *dikaiosynē* here.[18] Isa 53:11 speaks of the servant as "the righteous one" who

---

modify the growing consensus around Przybylski's view by emphasizing also the place of grace in Matthew's theology; here Hagner finds the primary reference of δικαιοσύνη to be to "God's saving will" (ibid., 115-17).

16. J. P. Meier, *Law,* 79-80, argues for taking πληρῶσαι πᾶσαν δικαιοσύνην "in a prophetic or *heilsgeschichtliche* sense." The same point is rightly argued by Hagner, 1:56, though it is a pity that he feels it necessary to do so by denying that δικαιοσύνη here means "moral goodness." It is surely "morally good" to do what God requires of one in a given situation. His objection that baptism as such "cannot be thought of as fulfilling *all* righteousness" misses the point of Jesus' saying in its dialogue context, which is not that "the act is positively described as the fulfilling of all righteousness" but rather that if we are to fulfill all that God requires, then even this (apparently inappropriate) act must also be included. To recognize the salvation-historical focus of this saying does not therefore demand that we exempt this use of δικαιοσύνη from the general Matthean sense established by Przybylski.

17. J. A. Gibbs, *CBQ* 64 (2002) 520-26, building on his argument that Jesus is addressed as "son" in v. 17 because he takes the place of God's "son" Israel, argues that the baptism presents "Israel standing with Israel." He discerns a development through the three passages which present Jesus as God's "son" Israel in 2:13-15 ("very much like Israel"), 3:13-17 ("distinguished from Israel"), and 4:1-11 ("sharply contrasted with Israel").

18. See my *Jesus and the OT,* 124-25. Carson, 107, objects that this suggestion "reads Paul's use of 'righteousness' back into Matthew," but the term is drawn from Isa-

"will make many righteous" by bearing their iniquities, and the repeated Hebrew term *yaṣdîq ṣaddîq* perhaps prompted Matthew's echoing *dikaiosynē*.[19] The verbal allusion is not certain, but the servant ideology forms an appropriate background to this saying of Jesus.

16 The significance of the baptism hinted at in vv. 14-15 is distinguished from the revelatory event which follows it, which takes place after Jesus has come out of the river. Three elements are combined in vv. 16b-17, the opening of heaven, the descent of the Spirit, and the divine proclamation. The opening of heaven is familiar elsewhere in the NT as an expression for a visionary experience (John 1:51; Acts 7:56; 10:11; Rev 4:1; 19:11). There is a significant OT parallel in Ezek 1:1 where Ezekiel, standing beside a river, also sees heaven opened and receives a theophanic vision and hears God's voice commissioning him for his prophetic role and giving him the Spirit (Ezek 2:2). Isa 63:19 (EVV 64:1) asks God to tear (LXX *anoigō*, as here) the heavens and come down to redeem his people. The opening of heaven is the prelude to the divine communication which follows and especially to the visible descent of the Spirit.

The descent of the Spirit of God recalls well-known messianic prophecies in Isaiah which say that God will place his Spirit upon his chosen servant (Isa 11:2; 42:1; 61:1).[20] This is not to say that Jesus has hitherto been without the Spirit, since Matthew has attributed his birth to the Spirit (1:18, 20). But now as the Spirit "comes upon him" Jesus is visibly equipped and commissioned to undertake his messianic mission.[21] The one who is to "baptize in the Holy Spirit" (v. 11) must first himself be endowed with the Spirit. If the coming of the Spirit is to be visible, however, some visual form is needed.

When the Spirit comes upon people in Acts, the evidence is in their subsequent behavior, speaking in tongues and preaching boldly (Acts 2:4; 4:31; 10:44-46; 19:6) rather than in any visible "descent," but in Acts 2:2-3 we read of both audible and visible phenomena, wind and fire. This is the only occasion when we hear of the Spirit appearing in visual form "like a dove."[22] In-

---

iah, not from Paul, and Carson himself goes on to agree that the saying does in fact refer to Jesus' fulfillment of the role of the Isaianic servant.

19. The same repetition occurs in the LXX, δικαιῶσαι δίκαιον, though the LXX syntax is different, with God as the subject of δικαιῶσαι and δίκαιον as its object.

20. Cf. the coming of the Spirit upon certain people in OT times to equip them for a special task: Judg 3:10; 6:34; 1 Sam 16:13, etc.

21. Note that in 1 Sam 16:13 and Isa 61:1 the coming of the Spirit is linked with anointing.

22. It is sometimes rightly argued (e.g., by L. E. Keck, *NTS* 17 [1970/1] 63-67) that ὡσεὶ περιστεράν may indicate not the visual *form* in which the Spirit was seen but rather the *manner* of the Spirit's descent. A "dove-like manner" is, however, not easy to define (Keck's suggestion that it refers to "the gentle flight of a dove" does not tally with

terpreters have scoured the OT and other literature (Jewish[23] and pagan) for references to doves which might explain the symbolism, but without finding any consensus (Davies and Allison, 1.331-34, list sixteen options). The most promising suggestion is perhaps that which draws on Noah's dove flying above the waters of chaos (Gen 8:8-12)[24] in combination with the metaphorical language of Gen 1:2 which speaks of the Spirit of God "hovering" or "brooding" *(merahepet)* over the face of the waters at creation; in the latter case no specific bird is mentioned, but the metaphor apparently depicts a birdlike motion (the only other use of the verb, in Deut 32:11, is of an eagle "hovering" over its chicks).[25] Such an allusion would suggest a "new creation" typology underlying the baptism narrative. But there is no reason to assume that the species of bird here is significant, any more than it was in the imagery of Gen 1:2; the dove is simply a familiar bird, whose swooping flight formed an appropriate way of visualizing the descent of the Spirit (and so has been given an honored place in Christian art ever since, especially in attempts to present the Trinity in a visual form).

17 The "voice from heaven"[26] in this verse, together with its repetition in 17:5, offers to Matthew's readers (and, to judge from the third-person form in which Matthew alone records it, also to the bystanders at the Jordan) the most unmediated access to God's own view of Jesus. Following Jesus' acceptance of John's baptism as the will of God for him, it declares both God's

---

the experience of those who have contended with the pigeons in Trafalgar Square; cf. J. E. Taylor, *John,* 274-75, for a similar experience), and in any case *some* visual form must have been required to make the descent of the invisible Spirit visible, so little is gained by this suggestion. Luke's σωματικῷ εἴδει indicates that he did not take the dove imagery purely adverbially.

23. Appeal is sometimes made to the rabbinic use of the dove as a symbol of Israel (*b. Ber.* 53b; *b. Šabb.* 49a; *Cant. Rab.* 1:15.2; 2:14.1; 4:1.2), but why should the Spirit resemble Israel? The use of this imagery in the OT (Hos 7:11) is not encouraging: Ephraim is a silly dove ready to be caught. The use of "my dove" for the bride in Song 2:14; 5:2; 6:9 also provides no obvious basis for reference to the Spirit.

24. The link between the flood and baptism in 1 Pet 3:20-21 might support such an association. Keener, 132-33, notes the typology of the new world after the Flood "as a prototype of the coming age."

25. The identification of the "hovering" Spirit as a dove is made by R. Ben Zoma in the late first century A.D. (*b. Ḥag.* 15a). Cf. *b. Ber.* 3a, a second-century reference to "a divine voice, cooing like a dove." *Tg. Cant.* 2:12 interprets the voice of the turtledove as "the voice of the Holy Spirit."

26. Sometimes described as a *bat qōl,* a rabbinic term for a supernatural communication. The *bat qōl* was in rabbinic thought only an echo of the voice of God, and many recent commentators therefore declare the concept inappropriate here, where there is no reason to believe that Matthew intends us to understand anything less than a direct declaration by God himself about his Son. See to the contrary, however, Keener, 133-34.

pleasure in that obedience and also, more fundamentally, his own unique relationship with God.

The words of the declaration are usually understood to be derived from one or more of Gen 22:2; Ps 2:7; and Isa 42:1.[27] Isa 42:1 introduces a new figure in the prophecy with the words "Here is my servant, whom I uphold, my chosen one, in whom my soul takes pleasure," and goes on to say that God has put his Spirit upon him, which links closely with what we have seen in v. 16. The wording of v. 17 does not echo the LXX version of Isa 42:1, but when Matthew later gives a full quotation of that passage (12:18), he will use a Greek version which is closer to this verse;[28] the final clause, "with whom I am delighted," closely reflects the Hebrew *rāṣtâ napšî* of Isa 42:1. But Isa 42:1 does not provide the key term "son."[29] This is usually explained as an echo of Ps 2:7 in which God addresses his anointed king, "You are my son; today I have begotten you," but while the second-person version in Mark and Luke readily suggests such an echo, in Matthew's version it is only the words "my son" which are in common.[30] In Gen 22:2, however, we have "your son, your only son, whom you love," and the LXX version uses *agapētos* for the "only" son, thus offering a suggestive source for the wording of most of the divine declaration here. A combined allusion to Isa 42:1 and Gen 22:2 might thus account quite adequately for the OT background to the wording in its Matthean form.

But these words of God are not presented as an OT quotation, and it is questionable how far we are justified in seeking specific textual sources for every word. The link with the descent of the Spirit certainly makes an echo of Isa 42:1 strongly plausible, so that Matthew's readers would learn to see Jesus in the role of the "servant of Yahweh" who would die for the sins of the people (see above on v. 15). Matthew will return to Isa 42:1-4 when he quotes it in full in 12:17-21 to show how Jesus puts into practice the non-

27. A further allusion to Exod 4:22-23 is suggested by P. G. Bretscher, *JBL* 87 (1968) 305-11. This would depend on Jesus' being seen as inheriting the status of Israel as God's "firstborn son." But the verbal links are not impressive.

28. It includes both ἀγαπητός, "beloved," and the same tense of the verb εὐδοκέω, "take pleasure in," neither of which is in LXX.

29. J. Jeremias, *Theology,* 53-55 (cf. *TDNT* 5:701-2), argued that this, too, derived from Isa 42:1, since παῖς can mean "child" as well as "servant." But "child" is not the same as "son," and παῖς is not normally used in that relational sense (except possibly in John 4:51). There is a comprehensive response to Jeremias by I. H. Marshall in *NTS* 15 (1968/9) 326-36.

30. J. A. Gibbs, *CBQ* 64 (2002) 511-20, disputes any echo of Ps 2:7 here, and derives the term "son" from the Matthean theme of Jesus as the fulfillment of God's "son" Israel, an allusion which he traces especially to Jer 31:20 (LXX 38:20, where Ephraim is described as υἱὸς ἀγαπητὸς . . . ἐμοί).

violent style of the servant's work. It is also possible, though less likely, that some readers who knew the Genesis story well might have noticed the echo of the phrase "beloved son, whom you love" and reflected that God was now going to give up his own son to death just as he had once asked Abraham to do.[31] But neither of those allusions is the main point of v. 17. God is not quoting the OT, nor setting a puzzle for scripturally erudite hearers to unravel. He is declaring in richly allusive words that this man who has just been baptized by John is his own Son in whom he delights. From this point on Matthew's readers have no excuse for failing to understand the significance of Jesus' ministry, however long it may take the actors in the story to reach the same christological conclusion (14:33; 16:16; 26:63-64). It will be this crucial revelation of who Jesus is which will immediately form the basis of the initial testing which Jesus is called to undergo in 4:1-11: *"If you are the Son of God . . ."* (4:3, 6). And there, as in the account of the baptism, Jesus' sonship will be revealed in his obedience to his Father's will.

E. THE TESTING OF THE SON OF GOD:
THE MESSIAH AS THE TRUE ISRAEL (4:1-11)

> 1 *Then Jesus was taken up*[1] *into the wilderness by the Spirit to be tested*[2] *by the devil.* 2 *He went without food for forty days and forty nights, and in the end he was famished.* 3 *Then the tempter approached him and said, "If you are the Son of God, give orders for these stones to become loaves of bread."* 4 *But Jesus replied, "It is written,*

31. Some interpreters take the possible echo of Gen 22:2 here as evidence that Matthew was relating Jesus' mission to the Jewish Aqedah doctrine, which saw the binding (*'ăqēdâ*) and submission of Isaac as the vicarious basis for Israel's redemption. See, e.g., the versions of Gen 22 in *Targum Pseudo-Jonathan* (see J. Bowker, *Targums,* 224ff.); Josephus, *Ant.* 1.232; Pseudo-Philo 18:5; 32:2-4. G. Vermes, *Scripture,* 193-227, argues that this theology was current in the first century A.D.; see, however, the cautionary comments of E. P. Sanders, *Paul,* 28-29, and the fuller discussion by P. R. Davies and B. D. Chilton, *CBQ* 40 (1978) 514-46. The Christianized *T. Levi* 18:6-7 apparently understands Jesus' baptism in the light of Gen 22, but without obvious Aqedah connotations.

1. ἀνάγω, to "lead up," is used only here by Matthew. The "up" element denotes the geographically higher level of the surrounding wilderness as compared with the riverbank which has been the setting of 3:1-17. Keener, 137, suggests that Matthew uses ἀνάγω to echo OT descriptions of God "leading" his people in the wilderness at the time of the Exodus.

2. See the comments below for the range of meaning of πειράζω and for the essential sense of testing which underlies this story. Note, however, that in v. 3 the participle ὁ πειράζων is used to describe the devil, and there the meaning "tempt" (with malicious intent) is clear.

'A person is not to³ live on bread alone,
    but on every word that comes from the mouth of God.' "

5 Then the devil transported⁴ him to the holy city and made him
stand on a high corner⁵ of the temple, 6 and said to him, "If you are
the Son of God, throw yourself down; for it is written that

'He will make his angels responsible for you,
    and they will lift you in their arms
    so that you never hit your foot against a stone.' "
7 Jesus replied, "It is also written,
    'You are not to put the Lord your God to the test.' "

8 Again the devil transported him to a very high mountain and
showed him all the kingdoms of the world in all their glory, 9 and said
to him, "I will give you all this, if you will bow down and worship me."⁶
10 Then Jesus said to him, "Away with you, Satan; for it is written,

'You are to worship the Lord your God;
    he is the only one you are to serve.' "

11 Then the devil left him alone, and angels came to him and took
care of⁷ him.

---

3. Here and in the other two quotations from Deuteronomy in vv. 7 and 10 the future tense reflects the Hebrew imperfect, which in each case functions as a quasi-
imperative.

4. Up to this point all the narrative verbs in this story have been aorist. From here
on the tenses are mixed, with παραλαμβάνει here and in v. 8 in the present tense, as are
δείκνυσιν (v. 8) and ἀφίησιν (v. 11), while the aorist continues in ἔστησεν (v. 5) and
προσῆλθον (v. 11). The verbs of speech are similarly mixed, with the present λέγει in vv. 6
and 10, but the aorist in ἔφη (v. 7) and εἶπεν (v. 9). The historic present perhaps adds a note
of immediacy to the narrative, but the inconsistent pattern of its use makes it inappropriate
to attempt to render it in translation.

5. πτερύγιον, a "small wing," is not known elsewhere as the designation of a particular part of the temple buildings. See the comments below for possible identifications.
It is clear from the context that it is a high point which commands a substantial drop to
ground level.

6. The same combination, πέσων προσκυνέω, was translated "prostrated themselves
and paid homage to him" in 2:11. The idea of homage to a superior recurs here, but the supernatural character of the one making the demand, and the contrasting demand to worship
God in v. 10, indicate that the more specifically religious terminology is in place here.

7. After the mixed aorist and present tenses of the rest of the narrative (see above,
n. 4) this imperfect tense conveys the sense of a settled continuing care in place of the
rapid succession of testing and response. The sense of practical, even domestic, service
which is often inherent in διακονέω is particularly appropriate in this context of Jesus' extreme hunger.

All three Synoptic writers record an experience of Jesus in the wilderness in confrontation with the devil immediately after his baptismal revelation and before his return to Galilee. But while Mark presents only a brief tableau of the opposing forces, Matthew and Luke record a three-point dialogue between the tempter and Jesus which explores more deeply the nature of the "testing" involved, the details of which, if they are not purely imaginary, can only have come from Jesus' own subsequent recalling of the event.

Matthew and Luke present the second and third elements in the dialogue in a different order. Reasons for preferring each order can be suggested. Luke's order brings the series to a climax with the devil's subtlest ploy in that he in his turn offers a scriptural text in support of his proposal. Luke's special interest in Jerusalem may also have led him to prefer concluding the story there. In Matthew's account, however, the more subtle suggestions of the first two proposals are succeeded by a blatant challenge to God's authority when the devil "drops his disguise" (Schweizer, 58) and the central issue is brought into the open. Matthew's account thus ends on a more decisive note, which he will exploit at the end of his gospel with an allusion to this third temptation in Jesus' eventual claim to an authority greater than anything the devil could offer (28:18). The escalation of the issues posed is appropriately symbolized by the geographical escalation from the wilderness to a high point in Jerusalem and then to a very high mountain. Matthew's inclusion of "Away with you, Satan" in Jesus' third reply suitably brings the confrontation to a close. The majority of recent interpreters think that Matthew's order, which also brings the two "Son of God" temptations together at the beginning, is more likely to be original.[8]

This incident is traditionally described as "the temptation of Jesus." But the English language cannot represent the ambivalence of the key Greek verb *peirazō* and its derivatives. Insofar as the devil is portrayed as trying to induce Jesus to act against the will of God, "tempt" is the right meaning, but the same verb frequently means to "test" with no pejorative connotation. Its other uses in Matthew are of human subjects who come to Jesus with hard questions hoping to trap him or expose him (16:1; 19:3; 22:18, 35); the meaning is in each case pejorative, but the questions involved are not "temptations" to do wrong, but dialogue challenges from Jesus' enemies. Here the introduction to the pericope indicates that while the "testing/tempting" is to be carried out by the devil, the whole experience takes place under the guidance of the Spirit and therefore according to the purpose of God. Underlying

8. The arguments are well set out by T. L. Donaldson, *Jesus,* 88-90, 97-98 (Donaldson himself argues tentatively for the originality of the Lucan order). A further argument in favor of Matthew's order may be derived from the suggestion that it corresponds to the order of the three elements of the *Šᵉmaʿ;* see n. 11 below.

it, as we shall see, is an OT passage which speaks of Israel's wilderness experiences similarly as a "test" (LXX *expeirazō*) designed by God "to find out what was in your heart, whether or not you would keep his commandments" (Deut 8:2; cf. 8:16). In the interpretation that follows I shall try to show that it is primarily concerned with this divine "testing" rather than the Satanic "tempting" which was its means. The title given by B. Gerhardsson to his illuminating monograph on this pericope, *The Testing of God's Son,* seems to me to sum up its thrust admirably.

The focus of the "testing" agenda is indicated by the clause which introduces the devil's first two suggestions, "If you are the Son of God." The link with 3:17 is obvious. The special relationship with God which has just been authoritatively declared at the Jordan is now under scrutiny. The following clauses do not cast doubt on this filial relationship, but explore its possible implications: what is the appropriate way for God's Son to behave in relation to his Father? In what ways might he exploit this relationship to his own advantage? The actions suggested are ones which might be expected to put that relationship under strain. The devil is trying to drive a wedge between the newly declared Son and his Father.

This understanding of the story leaves little room for the popular notion that what is under scrutiny here is the nature of Jesus' messianic agenda. The suggestion that turning stones into bread would be a way of attracting a following by the provision of cheap food, and that an uninjured leap from the temple roof would demonstrate the Messiah's supernatural credentials to a stunned crowd, does not match the way the story is told: the loaves are to satisfy Jesus' own hunger, and there is no indication of any spectators for the proposed leap from the temple (even if this is understood as an actual physical event; see on v. 5). The third temptation, too, appeals to Jesus' own ambition, and does not mention a messianic agenda.

It will be in his passion in Jerusalem (the "holy city," v. 5) that Jesus' loyalty to his role as Son of God will be supremely tested, and some features of Matthew's wording link these two episodes at the beginning and end of his story. The devil's temptation will be echoed by the crowd who call on Jesus to come down from the cross "if you are the Son of God" (27:40). In 26:53 Jesus will claim, but refuse to exercise, the right to call on legions of angels to deliver him (cf. 4:6). And the final dismissal, "Away with you, Satan," will be deployed again against Peter when he tries to dissuade Jesus, whom he has just recognized as the Son of God, from going to the cross (16:23).

The most significant key to the understanding of this story is to be found in Jesus' three scriptural quotations. All come from Deut 6–8, the part of Moses' address to the Israelites before their entry into Canaan in which he reminds them of their forty years of wilderness experiences. It has been a time of preparation and of proving the faithfulness of their God. He has deliberately put them through a time of privation as an educative process. They have been learning, or should have been learning, what it means to live in trusting obedience to God: "As a father disciplines his son, so the LORD your God disciplines you" (Deut 8:5; for Israel as God's son cf. Exod 4:22; Jer 31:9; Hos 11:1-4).[9] Among the lessons they should now have learned are not to depend on bread alone but rather on God's word (8:3), not to put God to the test (6:16), and to make God the exclusive object of their worship and obedience (6:13). Now another "Son of God" is in the wilderness, this time for forty days rather than forty years, as a preparation for entering into his divine calling. There in the wilderness he, too, faces those same tests, and he has learned the lessons which Israel had so imperfectly grasped. His Father is testing him in the school of privation, and his triumphant rebuttal of the devil's suggestions will ensure that the filial bond can survive in spite of the conflict that lies ahead. Israel's occupation of the promised land was at best a flawed fulfillment of the hopes with which they came to the Jordan, but this new "Son of God" will not fail and the new Exodus (to which we have seen a number of allusions in ch. 2) will succeed. "Where Israel of old stumbled and fell, Christ the new Israel stood firm."[10] It is probably also significant that the passage of Deuteronomy from which Jesus' responses are drawn begins with the Šᵉmaʿ, the text from Deut 6:4-5 recited daily in Jewish worship which requires Israel to "love the LORD your God with all your heart, and with all your soul, and with all your strength"; it is precisely that total commitment to God that this wilderness experience is designed to test.[11]

The story of the testing in the wilderness[12] is thus an elaborate typological presentation of Jesus as himself the true Israel, the "Son of God" through whom God's redemptive purpose for his people is now at last to reach its fulfillment.[13]

9. For the concept of God's "testing" of Israel as an essential part of the covenant relationship see B. Gerhardsson, *Testing,* 25-28.

10. M. D. Goulder, *Midrash,* 245.

11. The link between the temptation narrative and the Šᵉmaʿ is explored by B. Gerhardsson, *Testing,* 71-79, with the conclusion that the three temptations (in their Matthean order) represent the three elements of Deut 6:5, "heart," "soul," and "strength," as they are expounded in *m. Ber.* 9:5. The first and third (the suppression of the evil inclination and the use of "mammon") can be made to fit the equation quite well, but the second depends on the "soul" being understood in relation to martyrdom, and this is less easy to relate to the second temptation, which is precisely *not* about God calling Jesus to lose his life.

12. While the whole pericope is set in "the wilderness," Donaldson, *Jesus,* 95-97, rightly points out that the transportation of Jesus to the temple and the mountain creates in fact a series of three locations. Donaldson argues that each of these (wilderness, temple, mountain) "was a place where eschatological events were expected to occur"; they were thus "entirely appropriate settings for the testing of the Son and his vocation."

13. For this understanding of Matt 4:1-11 see my *Jesus and the OT,* 50-53, with

1   The fact that Jesus was taken into the wilderness by the Spirit suggests a deliberate "retreat" away from other people, but the specific area of "wilderness" is no more defined here than it was for John in 3:1. The verb "lead up" (see p. 124, n. 1) indicates that it was away from the Jordan, and the story assumes solitude and a lack of food resources, but the mention of a very high mountain in v. 8 cannot determine the overall location since both the mountain and Jerusalem are places to which Jesus needed to be "transported" (see on v. 5). See on 3:1 for the very positive connotations of "wilderness" in Jewish thought at the time; to be in the wilderness was to be prepared for a new beginning with God.

We should not therefore read the presence of the devil as something uniquely appropriate to this area, despite the later monastic tradition of going out into the desert to contend with demons. Indeed, to judge from 12:43-45, "waterless places" are the last place a demon wants to be. The devil is present not because this is his domain, but because he has a vital role in the testing which is God's purpose for this retreat. In this passage we meet the same character under three names, "the devil," "the tempter" (v. 3), and "Satan" (v. 10). In 12:24 he will appear as "Beelzebul, the ruler of the demons," and in 13:19 as "the evil one." The terms "the devil" and "Satan" (which originate respectively from Greek and Hebrew terms for an "accuser" or "opponent") are virtually interchangeable in the gospel tradition, as throughout the NT. The figure of Satan as an individual spiritual enemy of God and his people is found only rarely in the OT (1 Chr 21:1; Job 1–2; Zech 3:1-2), but by the first century had developed (under a variety of names: Belial, Beliar, Mastema, Azazel, but most commonly Satan) into a standard feature of Jewish belief which the Christian church fully shared. Running through Jewish references to the devil is a tension between his total hostility to God and his people and his operation apparently within and subject to the ultimate sovereignty of God, a tension which Matthew here reflects in that the devil's intention to "tempt" Jesus to do wrong is subsumed under God's good purpose to "test" his Son.

2   "Forty days" is used in the Bible as an idiomatic expression for a significant but limited period (e.g., Gen 7:4; Num 13:25; 1 Sam 17:16; Jonah 3:4; Acts 1:3), but Matthew speaks more specifically of "forty days and forty nights," and in view of his interest elsewhere in Moses and Elijah it is possible that he intends that phrase to recall more specifically either the period spent without food by Moses on Mount Sinai (Exod 24:18; 34:28; Deut 9:9,

---

references to several earlier accounts, notably B. Gerhardsson, *Testing,* who describes the pericope as "an example of an early Christian midrash" (p. 11) based primarily on Deut 6–8. Gerhardsson's study provides rich comparative material from the OT and later Judaism for the midrashic nature of this pericope.

etc.)[14] or by Elijah in the wilderness (1 Kgs 19:8); the latter would be a particularly suggestive allusion in that Elijah's hunger during that period was miraculously solved by food provided by an angel (cf. v. 11). But in view of the clear background to this story in the pentateuchal narratives of Israel's wilderness experience (see above) Jesus' "forty days and forty nights" more obviously serve as a reminder of Israel's "forty years" of privation and testing.[15] Matthew gives us no means of knowing whether Jesus' fast for this period was deliberately self-imposed or simply the result of lack of available food in the wilderness (where, however, both John the Baptist and Bannus seem to have found adequate resources; see on 3:4). Jesus' fasting is not presented as a model for his followers' practice; this is an experience unique to the Son of God at the outset of his mission.

3 Having described Jesus' situation in the wilderness, Matthew now introduces the other principal actor in this scene. The only other NT reference to the devil as "the tempter" is in 1 Thess 3:5; in both places it is not so much an independent title as a functional description of his role in the context. The proposal to turn stones into "loaves of bread"[16] is an appeal to the miraculous power assumed to be available to a "son of God."[17] It is not only beneath the dignity of such an exalted figure to suffer hunger, but also unnecessary since he has the means to create food. In this proposal we already hear an echo of Israel's wilderness experience of hunger, which was met by God's supply of manna (picked up from the ground, like stones, Exod 16:14-16); history shows that there is no need for God's son to be hungry in the wilderness.

4 Jesus' first reply consists solely of a quotation from LXX Deut 8:3[18] — no further argument is needed. As the first part of Deut 8:3 ex-

14. D. C. Allison, *Moses,* 165-69, argues for an intentional allusion to Moses here, though not all his points are equally persuasive. He acknowledges that the typology of Israel in the wilderness is primary but attributes this to the Q tradition, which Matthew has "overlaid . . . with specifically Mosaic motifs" (166).

15. B. Gerhardsson, *Testing,* 42-43, attempts to bolster this conclusion by observing that in Num 14:34 the forty years in the wilderness are linked to the forty days of the scouts' mission, and notes that in Ezek 4:6 we find again "the principle that days can correspond to years," but this is surely to treat the idiom too mechanically. In any case, it is unnecessary: given the shared context of wilderness and hunger, the numeral alone suffices to effect the echo.

16. The round, flat loaves commonly used in Palestine at that time were roughly sufficient for a single meal for one person.

17. Morris, 70, n. 1, comments: "Turning stones into bread is not a temptation to us; it is a temptation only to someone who knows he can do it."

18. R. H. Gundry, *Use,* 67 (following G. D. Kilpatrick), favors a Western reading omitting ἐκπορευομένῳ διὰ στόματος; such an abbreviation, if accepted, would represent merely a stylistic clarification of the Hebrew idiom, not a change of sense.

plains, Israel's hunger had been a part of the educative process designed by
God; it was only after they had experienced hunger that they were fed, in
God's good time, not at their own convenience. This was to teach them that
there are more important things in life (and especially in the life of God's
people) than material provision. The contrast between "bread" and "every
word that comes from the mouth of God"[19] is of course paradoxical: God's
word does not fill the stomach. But it is a question of priority (which Jesus
will express in another form in 6:24-33). Obedience to God's will takes priority over self-gratification, even over the apparently essential provision of
food.[20] God will provide the food when he is ready — as indeed he will in
this case (see v. 11). Jesus' use of this OT text shows that he understood his
experience of hunger as God's will for him at the time, and therefore not to
be evaded by a self-indulgent use of his undoubted power as the Son of
God. To do that would be to call in question God's priorities, and to set
himself at odds with his Father's plan. As God's Son, Jesus must trustingly
and obediently comply with his Father's purpose (as he has just done at the
Jordan, 3:15).

Neither in the devil's suggestion in v. 3 nor in Jesus' reply is there any
hint of the miraculous provision of bread for others, still less of impressing
the crowds with a display of power. In due course Jesus will indeed miraculously provide bread for hungry crowds (14:13-21; 15:32-39), but here there
is no crowd, just Jesus alone with the tempter and God. It is Jesus' filial trust
that is under examination, not his messianic agenda.

5   The devil's first proposal needed no special setting: there in the
wilderness Jesus was surrounded by stones. But the remaining two proposals require different settings, and in each case we are told that the devil
"transported"[21] Jesus to a new location. The fact that no actual mountain
could provide a view of "all the kingdoms of the world" at once suggests
that this transportation was not physical but visionary. There in the wilderness Jesus "found himself" first on top of the Jerusalem temple and then on

19. "Word" is an LXX explanatory addition: the Hebrew simply says "everything
that comes out of the mouth of the LORD." In the Deuteronomy context what came from
the mouth of God would be understood primarily as his law communicated to Moses; the
phrase does not in itself refer specifically to the written Bible, but in this pericope Jesus
does in fact three times use words from the Pentateuch (the written form in which those
utterances of God had been passed down) as his guide to living.

20. For a similar sentiment see Wis. 16:26: "that your sons, whom you love, Lord,
may learn that it is not the produce of the crops that nourishes people but it is your word
that preserves those who trust in you."

21. παραλαμβάνει, literally "takes along with him," the same verb used for Joseph
taking the child and his mother on their journeys in 2:13-14, 20-21 and for Jesus taking
chosen disciples to be with him on special occasions (17:1; 20:17; 26:37).

an impossibly high mountain with a view of the whole world. Cf. the visionary visit of Ezekiel to Jerusalem while he was in fact in Babylon (Ezek 8:1-3; 11:24).[22]

It is therefore not very important to decide just which part of the actual Herodian temple was meant by Matthew's term *pterygion,* "little wing," which I have translated "high corner" (see p. 125, n. 5).[23] Apart from the parallel in Luke (and subsequent Christian references to this passage) the word is not used elsewhere of a building feature, though there are rare uses of it in classical literature for a projecting piece of a coat of armor or of a rudder or other machinery. The context makes it clear only that it is a high part of the temple from which a fall might be expected to be fatal. This might either be a part of the sanctuary building itself (which was some fifty meters high) or perhaps of the temple's outer portico, which on the east overhung the deep Kidron valley.[24] For "the holy city" as a term for Jerusalem see 27:53; Isa 52:1; Dan 9:24; Rev 11:2; 21:2, etc.

6 The devil's proposal again draws on the assumed privileges of a "son of God." If Jesus can quote Scripture, so can the devil, and Jesus' own formula "It is written" is thus deployed against him. The passage quoted from Ps 91:11-12 (in the LXX version, abbreviated)[25] is addressed to all who

22. L. Schiavo, *JSNT* 25 (2002) 141-64, interprets the whole temptation story as an "ecstatic experience" such as is narrated in some apocalyptic sources; his reading is founded especially on the distinctively Lucan phrase "led *in* the Spirit" (Luke 4:1), whereas Matthew's "led up *by* the Spirit" less clearly suggests mystical experience.

23. Some MSS of the Theodotion translation of the obscure vision of the eschatological abomination in Dan 9:27 use πτερύγιον to represent the enigmatic *kānāp,* "wing," of the Hebrew, and M. D. Goulder, *Midrash,* 246, suggests that this passage contributed to Matthew's wording here. It is not clear, however, that *kānāp* in Dan 9:27 refers to a part of the temple (that interpretation being usually suggested under the influence of Matthew's use of πτερύγιον), so that this is to explain *obscurum per obscurius.*

24. Today's visitor to Jerusalem can gain a limited impression of this feature by looking down from the top of the Herodian masonry making up the southeast corner of the temple area. But in the first century this was only the base of a huge portico which, according to Josephus, *Ant.* 15.415, rose a further thirty meters above today's ground level. Josephus's description of the effect of looking down from the top of the portico well illustrates this passage: "The ravine itself was so deep that no one could bear to lean over and look down to the bottom from above; but above it stood also an immensely high portico, so that anyone who looked down from the top of its roof, with the two heights combined, would become dizzy as he looked into the depths, his eyesight being unable to reach the bottom of such an unfathomable drop" (*Ant.* 15.412).

25. The second line of v. 11, "to protect you in all your ways," is omitted, but this does not affect the sense. LXX's ἐπὶ χειρῶν represents the strongly anthropomorphic Hebrew dual *'al-kappayîm,* "on their [two] hands," but since χείρ is sometimes used for the arm rather than the hand, I have translated it by the more natural English idiom, "in their arms."

have chosen to "live in the shelter of the Most High;"[26] how much more can it be expected to apply to God's special Son? A similar assumption lies behind the later "temptation" to come down from the cross "if you are the Son of God" (27:40). The vivid imagery of the psalm envisages some of the hazards which may be expected to confront God's people, and promises God's protection for them, but it does not suggest that they should take the initiative in courting such dangers. The devil's suggestion, however, is to test the literal truth of God's promise of protection by deliberately creating a situation in which he will be obliged to act to save his Son's life. In this way "man may become lord of God, and compel him to act through the power of his faith" (Schweizer, 63). It would be "to act as if God is there to serve his Son, rather than the reverse" (Keener, 141).

7 Jesus quotes Scripture against Scripture (his "also," literally "again," indicates a countertext), not because he disputes the validity of God's promise in Ps 91:11-12 but because he rejects the devil's use of it to support his proposal of forcing God's hand. Jesus selects his second Deuteronomy text (6:16, using LXX, which straightforwardly translates the Hebrew) in order to draw out the implications of such an act. It would be an attempt to "put God to the test,"[27] and as such it would demonstrate a lack of filial trust and a doubting of his Father's competence or dependability. It would be like the attitude of the Israelites "at Massah," as Deut 6:16 goes on to specify, using a Hebrew wordplay which the Greek cannot capture.[28] The allusion is to Exod 17:1-7, where the Israelites' thirst in the wilderness drove them to demand a miraculous provision of water, provoking Moses to respond, "Why do you test the LORD?"; and Moses "called the place Massah and Meribah, because the Israelites quarreled and tested the LORD, saying, 'Is the LORD among us or not?'" That same cynical challenge would be implied if Jesus were to force God into a physical rescue which he ought to be able to trust in without testing it.

Again, as in vv. 3-4, it is Jesus' relationship with God which is under scrutiny, and there is no suggestion that anyone else would observe the proposed "leap of faith" to use it as a proof of Jesus' messianic credentials.[29] If,

26. B. Gerhardsson, *Testing,* 56-58, argues that this psalm is particularly appropriate in this context because it relates to the theme of special divine protection within the temple. He goes on (p. 59) to suggest less plausibly that πτερύγιον (see on v. 5) is used because several such texts speak of protection "under God's wings."

27. For the theme of "testing God" in the OT cf. B. Gerhardsson, *Testing,* 28-31.

28. "Massah" is from the same verbal root as "test"; LXX simply translates it as "the Test," not as a geographical name.

29. A later example of such an idea occurs in *Acts of Peter* 31–32 (late second century A.D.?), where Simon Magus flies over the temples and hills of Rome to the amazement of the crowd, but then as a result of Peter's prayer falls and breaks his leg!

as we have discussed at v. 5, the whole experience was in any case a vision rather than an actual event in Jerusalem, that suggestion becomes even more inappropriate.

8-9 The devil's third attempt involves another "transportation," this time to an unspecified mountain,[30] which could be in the wilderness area (though in that case a vision of "all the kingdoms of the world" would be a wild exaggeration), but need not be since Jerusalem, the location of the last visit, was not. The mountain need be no more literal, and the traditional identification of the "Mount of the Temptation" above Jericho has no historical basis. For mountains commanding a view of promised territory cf. Gen 13:14-17; Deut 34:1-4,[31] but now much more than Canaan is in view.[32] "All the kingdoms of the world" form a telling contrast with the single "kingdom of heaven" which Jesus will soon proclaim (v. 17). The mention of the "glory" of the kingdoms of the world[33] confirms that what the devil is offering is not just a sphere for service, but paramount status, as "king of kings."[34] Universal dominion over all peoples is a theme of some OT hopes for the people of God or their royal Messiah (Pss 2:8;[35] 72:8-11; Dan 7:13-14; Zech 9:10), but the proposed route to this goal by prostration before God's enemy

---

30. T. L. Donaldson, *Jesus,* has constructed a whole Matthean theology around six references to a "mountain" in this gospel (4:8; 5:1; 15:29; 17:1; 24:3; 28:16), which he takes to indicate a typology of Mount Zion. The only mountain specifically identified, however, is not Mount Zion but the Mount of Olives (24:3), while in three cases (as also in 14:23, which Donaldson does not include in his list) the phrase εἰς τὸ ὄρος is better translated "into the hills" than taken as referring to a specific mountain (see on 5:1-2). The two unidentified "high mountains," here and in 17:1, are in different senses places of vision, but in neither case does anything in the text indicate a Zion typology.

31. D. C. Allison, *Moses,* 169-72, finds in this motif a further proof of a Matthean Mosaic typology. See p. 130, n. 14, for his parallel argument with regard to v. 2. The arguments adduced in this case are if anything less convincing, and Allison does not address the improbability of a divine revelation in the OT being used as a model for a Satanic revelation in the NT.

32. Cf. *2 Bar.* 76:3 for a mountain from which Baruch could see "all countries of this earth."

33. According to B. Gerhardsson, *Testing,* 66, the "glory" of the kingdoms indicates that Satan is offering "the whole might and wealth of the earth, all that the rabbis called '*mamon.*'"

34. M. D. Goulder, *Midrash,* 246-47, draws attention to the prominence of "kingdoms" and "glory" in the stories of Dan 2–6, which focus on the resistance of God's faithful people to the worship demanded by pagan rulers.

35. T. L. Donaldson, *Jesus,* 94-95, following K. H. Rengstorf, notes that three features of Ps 2:6-8 find an echo here: the king set on God's "holy mountain," the declaration that the king is God's son, and the promise of a universal dominion. The link is, however, weakened by the fact that this is the one temptation in which the title "son of God" is *not* explicit.

strikes a new and obviously unacceptable note. The change of tone is signaled also by the omission this time of "If you are the Son of God," which would have been blatantly at odds with this proposal to abandon Jesus' allegiance to God. When eventually Jesus is able to claim on another mountain (but see n. 30) that "all authority has been given to me," it will be as a result not of kowtowing to Satan but of suffering in obedience to God's purpose, and then it will be all authority not only on earth but also in heaven, an authority which the devil was not able to offer (28:18).

There is not much subtlety in this temptation: it is a simple choice of allegiance. It is an offer of the right end by the wrong means — if indeed even the end is right when it is expressed in terms of paramount glory in contrast with the obedient and self-sacrificing role which Jesus will be called to fulfill as God's chosen servant. We shall meet a similar contrast in 20:20-28 between the human ambition of James and John and the paradoxical role of Jesus the servant who gives his life as a ransom for many.

Should the devil's offer be read as sheer bluff, or was he understood to have some real authority over "the kingdoms of the world"? Several times in the NT he will be described in such language as "the ruler of this world" (John 12:31; 14:30; 16:11; 2 Cor 4:4; Eph 6:11-12; 1 John 5:19; Rev 12:9-17); in 12:26 he has his own "kingship." As such he is understood to have real power in the present age,[36] though always under the perspective of the ultimate victory of God. And as such he can offer power and glory, but not ultimate fulfillment, still less an authority in accordance with the will of God.

10   There can only be one answer, and again it is drawn from Deuteronomy. The wording of the quotation from Deut 6:13 differs from the LXX in substituting "worship" for "fear" in the first line and in drawing out the point more clearly by the addition of "only" in the second; the first change makes the intention of the OT text clear in the light of the devil's demand for "worship," and the second brings into the quotation what immediately follows in Deut 6:14, the prohibition of following any other gods. But this time the quotation is not left to speak for itself, but is prefaced by a curt dismissal of the tempter, showing clearly who is in control. "Away with you" (*hypage*) is an imperative occurring many times in Matthew, usually in the quite positive sense of sending someone to undertake a task or sending them away with their request granted. In 20:14 it is a brusque dismissal, but here and in 16:23 it carries an even sharper tone with in each case the vocative "Satan" ("Enemy") added, here literally appropriate but in 16:23 as a re-

---

36. There is no obvious basis in the text for the more specific deduction that "Satan controls the Roman empire" and thus that Jesus' refusal "signals his resistance to . . . Rome" (Carter, 106-7), making this temptation a warning against emperor worship (ibid., 111).

markably wounding epithet for Peter (see on 16:23 for the similarity between Peter's comment and the third temptation). Jesus is not just terminating the interview: he is sending his adversary packing.

11 The devil has been defeated and leaves the field. Matthew does not say, as does Luke, that his withdrawal was temporary, but the narrative that follows will contain many further encounters with the demonic, even though not again in a narrative confrontation with the chief demon himself (see, however, 12:28-29 for the implication of Jesus' continuing struggle with the "strong man"). Meanwhile Jesus, though victorious, is weak and hungry, and angels provide him with the sustenance he refused in v. 4 to commandeer for himself; compare the experience of Elijah in the wilderness (1 Kgs 19:4-8), though in that case the food was provided at the beginning of the forty days, not at the end. The angels thus fulfill their protective role as it was promised in the devil's quotation from Ps 91:11. Jesus will later claim to have legions of angels at his call in case of need (26:53), though again he will decline to call on them. For the "caring" role of angels cf. Heb 1:14: they are "ministering spirits sent to care for (*diakonia,* the same term as here) those who are to inherit salvation," though it is unlikely that Hebrews was thinking there of the provision of literal food.[37]

II. GALILEE: THE MESSIAH REVEALED IN WORD AND DEED (4:12–16:20)

In 1:1–4:11 we have been introduced to Jesus of Nazareth, Israel's Messiah and the Son of God. A rich profusion of scriptural quotations and allusions has traced a variety of prophetic themes and typological connections which together point to the coming of Jesus as the time of fulfillment of God's age-old purpose for his people. Jesus himself has come on the scene in the context of the exciting revival movement of John the Baptist and has been marked out as the one who will carry John's work forward into the era of effective judgment and salvation which God has promised. A period of personal preparation in the wilderness has proved his fidelity as the Son of God. We are now ready for the messianic mission to be launched.

As in ch. 2, Matthew first explains from Scripture what is to be the geographical setting of the mission: in conformity with Isaiah's prophecy it must be in Galilee (4:12-16) — despite the standard view expressed by the

---

37. B. Gerhardsson, *Testing,* 69-70, is probably right to insist that διακονέω here has a wider connotation than merely the provision of food, but in the narrative context this is naturally taken to be its primary focus.

priests and scribes in 2:5-6 and endorsed by the Jewish opinion cited in John 7:41-42, 52. Galilee and surrounding areas accordingly are the setting for the presentation of the Messiah's mission, which will take up nearly half the gospel until it reaches its climax near Caesarea Philippi (probably the most northerly point of Jesus' recorded travels) in 16:13-20. From time to time Jesus will move outside Galilee proper (8:28-34; perhaps 14:13-21; 15:21-39; 16:13-20), but all the time he remains in the north. It will be only from 16:21 that he sets off for Judea, where the climactic scenes of the gospel will be set, until the final triumphant return to Galilee in 28:16-20. The narrative from 16:21 to 28:15 will be cast in the form of a single journey from north to south culminating in a single week in Jerusalem. In contrast, the Galilean section of the gospel has no clearly defined framework of time and movement (though in some sections a coherent itinerary can be discerned) but is rather an anthology of events and teaching designed to convey an overall impression of an undefined period of largely public activity in the north. In this section we are given a broad impression of Jesus' ministry in and around his home province; after 16:21 he will go south into Judean territory for the confrontation with the Jerusalem authorities which will bring his ministry to its paradoxical climax.

It is therefore within this northern section of the gospel that the majority of the words and deeds of Jesus recorded by Matthew, especially those which envisage a public setting, must find their place. Matthew has his own distinctive way of arranging this collection of disparate material. Three of his five discourse collections (see pp. 8-10) occur in this section (chs. 5–7, 10, 13). Between the first two of these is found an equally carefully constructed anthology of the authoritative deeds of Jesus (chs. 8–9; see the introduction to that section). There is thus a clear plan to the first part of the Galilean section of the gospel:

4:18-22	The call of the first disciples, to form the essential audience
5:1–7:29	Teaching on discipleship, revealing the Messiah's authority
8:1–9:34	Anthology of actions revealing the Messiah's authority
9:35–10:42	The Messiah's authority shared with his disciples.

Thereafter, while some deliberate patterns and development can be discerned (see my section headings for 11:2–16:20), there is less sign of an overarching design, and at times one feels that the material is there simply because Matthew had to find somewhere to put it within the northern period of public ministry.

This whole section of the gospel corresponds broadly to the first main section of Mark's account (Mark 1:14–8:30), though considerably expanded with non-Marcan material at several points. In Mark's Galilean section there is only one main block of teaching, the parable discourse of ch. 4, which falls roughly halfway through the section and thus provides an opportunity for reflection on the implications of Jesus' announcement of the kingdom of God and the responses which it has met. Matthew 13 is a considerable expansion from Mark 4, but serves a similar purpose following the varied responses to Jesus recorded in chs. 11–12. But by his careful construction of the opening part of the section (chs. 5–10) Matthew has considerably enhanced the impression of Jesus' authority, thus providing fuller food for thought when the parable discourse is reached. In order to achieve this effect Matthew has not only constructed a substantial discourse out of almost entirely non-Marcan material (chs. 5–7) but also extensively reordered the narrative pericopes which he has in common with Mark, with chs. 8–9 mainly made up of a careful interweaving of two Marcan sections, Mark 1:29–2:22 and 4:35–5:43.

A. THE LIGHT DAWNS IN GALILEE (4:12-17)

12 *When Jesus heard that John had been arrested,[1] he withdrew[2] to Galilee.* 13 *He left Nazareth, and went and settled in Capernaum, beside the lake[3] in the territory of Zebulun and Naphthali.* 14 *This was to fulfill what had been declared through Isaiah the prophet, who said,*

15 *"Land of Zebulun and land of Naphthali,*
the way of the sea,[4] beyond the Jordan,
Galilee of the nations:
16 *the people who sat in darkness have seen a great light,*

1. παραδίδωμι, "hand over," has no expressed subject or indication of what he was handed over to. 14:3-4 will explain, but for now the menacing verb (which will be used frequently of Jesus' own subsequent arrest and conviction) is sufficient to convey the sense of danger.

2. See p. 76, n. 2, on 2:14 ("escaped"; cf. 2:22, "got safely away") for Matthew's frequent use of ἀναχωρέω for getting out of a place of danger. Here Antipas's hostility to John suggests that it is wise for John's "successor" to move away to a less exposed area than that of John's movement beside the Jordan, and the mention that Jesus had "heard" about the arrest indicates that this news influenced his movement.

3. Literally, "sea"; see the comments on v. 13 below.

4. The Hebrew idiom probably meant "toward the sea," but Matthew uses the LXX literal translation, perhaps because it reminds him of the major road which ran through Capernaum (see comments).

and on those who sat in the land of the shadow of death[5]
light has risen."[6]

17 *From that time Jesus began to proclaim this message, "Repent,[7]*
for the kingdom of heaven has arrived."[8]

Matthew sets the geographical scene more carefully than Mark, both by noting Jesus' removal from Nazareth to Capernaum[9] and by giving it theological significance by means of another formula-quotation. The effect of his reference to Isa 9:1-2 is to designate Galilee as the place of light, as opposed to the darkness which we shall eventually find to be settled over Judea. The dawning light is heralded in Jesus' proclamation, and the succeeding section of the gospel set in and around Galilee will be essentially one of light and hope, as light shines on the people at large and they respond gladly to it, despite the hostility of some whose special interest keeps them from welcoming it. Galilee is the place where the mission will be enthusiastically launched and developed (and from which eventually, after the conflict and rejection in Judea, the mission will be relaunched to reach all nations, 28:16-20). Even as early as this there is a further hint (cf. 1:3-6; 2:1-12, and the Abrahamic theme of 1:1; 3:9) that Jesus' messianic mission extends beyond Israel alone, in Isaiah's loaded phrase "Galilee of the nations."

See on v. 17 for the view that a new section begins with that verse. As a transitional passage it relates both to what precedes, the dawning of the light in Galilee (4:13-16), and to what follows, the whole Galilean proclamation as set out in 4:18–16:20. There is an obvious new narrative beginning in v. 18, so one must either let v. 17 stand as a paragraph on its own or else rec-

---

5. The LXX phrase which Matthew reproduces is literally "the land and shadow of death"; it represents the Hebrew idiom 'ereṣ-ṣalmāwet, traditionally translated in English as "land of the shadow of death," though modern versions prefer "land of deep darkness" or "land as dark as death."

6. Matthew's Greek version adds a redundant αὐτοῖς, reflecting the Hebrew construction of the sentence, whereas LXX, which treats the whole verse as a second-person address to the people in darkness, here has ἐφ' ὑμᾶς.

7. μετανοεῖτε (and the following γάρ) is omitted by one OL MS and by the Old Syriac versions. It is in all our Greek MSS (though a few Greek fathers either omit it or indicate that it was absent in some MSS known to them), so that if it was a harmonistic addition based on 3:2 it was very early; most critics conclude that it was original. The omission is intriguing: was it an attempt to differentiate the positive message of Jesus from the negative preaching of the Baptist? In the parallel message of the disciples in 10:7 the call to repentance is also omitted.

8. For the sense of ἤγγικεν see p. 96, n. 3, and the comments on 3:2.

9. Mark simply mentions Galilee at this point and lets us infer as the story develops in the lakeshore area that Jesus has now settled in Capernaum.

ognize its link with the Galilean agenda of vv. 12-16 and its function as an overall summary by including it within the same introductory paragraph. In my view more is gained by the latter approach.

12 Again (cf. 3:1) Matthew gives no indication of the time which has elapsed between the events of 3:1–4:11 and Jesus' return to Galilee, nor is the arrest of John which triggers that return narrated at this point (see 14:3-4); neither the gospels nor Josephus tells us how long John's public activity was allowed to continue. That Jesus stayed in the south for some time is indicated by John 3:22; 4:1-3.

The continuity between John and Jesus is recognized by the link made here, and yet there is a clear sense of discontinuity, of a new and different ministry beginning in a new location. This "withdrawal" (see above, n. 2) was in part a matter of political wisdom: in view of John's conflict with Antipas (see on 3:1 for his probable location in Antipas's Perean territory) his "successor" could not expect to be safe in the same area, especially if, as Josephus tells us (*Ant.* 18.118), Antipas saw the baptizing movement as a potential source of sedition. Galilee was, of course, also under Antipas, but an itinerant preacher touring the Galilean villages was a less obvious target for political concern than John's centripetal campaign by the Jordan. News of John's fate will again cause Jesus to "withdraw" in 14:13.

13 Jesus' relocation (the combination of *kataleipō* and *katoikeō* indicates a decisive move away to a new home) took him from the rather remote hill village in which he had been brought up (see on 2:23 for Nazareth)[10] to a busy lakeside town set among other thriving villages which depended largely on the productive fishing industry of the Lake of Galilee. He thus gained a more public platform for his proclamation, as well as escaping the suspicion attaching to a local boy who becomes a celebrity (see on 13:54-58).[11] Matthew records only one return to Nazareth, whereas Capernaum and the neighboring lakeshore communities will be the setting for most of the Galilean ministry. It is sobering to note, however, that even Capernaum, favored with so much of Jesus' presence, will be denounced as unresponsive in 11:23-24.

Capernaum was an important settlement on the northwestern shore of

10. There is some variation in NT texts with regard to the form of the name. The form Ναζαρά, strongly attested here and in Luke 4:16, was apparently a recognized variant for Ναζαρέτ or Ναζαρέθ (see M. D. Goulder, *NovT* 45 [2003] 366-71). For similar variations in the transliteration of Semitic endings see BDF 39(2); cf. B. D. Chilton, *God in Strength,* 311-12.

11. G. D. Kilpatrick, *JSNT* 15 (1982) 3-8, argues from Mark that Jesus' going to live in Capernaum marked a decisive break not only with Nazareth but also with his own family, and finds confirmation of this view in Matthew, especially the present passage (ibid., 8-9).

the lake, and the presence there of a centurion (8:5) and a customs post (9:9) indicates that it was a local administrative center. The population in the first century was perhaps as high as ten thousand,[12] substantially bigger than Nazareth. While Capernaum had its resident Roman officials, it was a traditionally Jewish town, very different from the newly established Hellenistic city of Tiberias a little further down the western shore. While Luke and Josephus more correctly speak of the "Lake" of Galilee, Matthew, Mark, and John consistently refer to this inland freshwater lake as a "sea" (reflecting the OT name *yām-kinneret*, Num 34:11 etc.); in my translation (except in v. 15, see comments below) and in the commentary, however, I have thought it less misleading to modern readers to use "lake."

In the traditional tribal allocation after the conquest the tribes of Zebulun and Naphthali shared the area between the Lake of Galilee and the territory of Asher along the Mediterranean coast. The lakeshore area originally belonged to Naphthali, while Nazareth was in Zebulun, but tribal areas had little actual relevance by NT times. Matthew combines the two tribes in order to echo Isaiah's prophecy.

14-16 The central emphasis in this pericope again falls on the "fulfillment" of Scripture: Jesus' move to Capernaum is the cue for one of Matthew's longest formula-quotations. For the quotation formula see on 1:22, and for the attribution to a specific prophet see on 2:17. Matthew gives an abbreviated quotation of Isa 8:23–9:1 (EVV 9:1-2) in a form closer to the Hebrew than to the LXX, but not fully corresponding to the sense of either.[13] By leaving out all verbs from the first part of the quotation he has, like LXX, produced a string of geographical terms which give the setting but do not relate grammatically to the statement that follows; they serve to fill out the identity of the "people who sat in darkness." His abbreviation throws the focus on the geographical terms which are appropriate to Jesus' new home in

12. E. M. Meyers and J. F. Strange, *Archaeology,* 58, suggest twelve to fifteen thousand on the basis of the discernible area of building and the density of housing. Others offer considerably lower estimates, some as low as a thousand; see Keener, 145, n. 210.

13. G. M. Soares Prabhu, *Formula-Quotations,* 86-104, painstakingly examines the textual character of the quotation in relation to the Hebrew, LXX, and targum texts. He concludes that it is "an *ad hoc* christologically oriented translation, made directly from the original (proto-Masoretic) Hebrew, but influenced in its language by that of the LXX." R. Beaton, *Isaiah's Christ,* 110 (drawing on his textual analysis, ibid., 97-102), concludes that "Matthew's citation of 4.15-16 suits his context perhaps too well, suggesting editorial work on some level." M. J. J. Menken, *Matthew's Bible,* 15-33, prefers (in accordance with his overall thesis) to understand the deviations from our LXX text as due to Matthew's use of a (hypothetical) earlier revision of the LXX which aimed to assimilate the Greek more closely to the Hebrew.

Capernaum (note "way of the sea") rather than Nazareth. It also emphasizes the link between his Galilean location and the dawning of the light, which in the Isaiah context is the prelude to the great messianic prophecy of the child "born to us" who is called "wonderful counsellor, mighty God, everlasting father, prince of peace" — a prophecy which is remarkably never directly referred to in the NT.[14]

Isaiah's geographical terms raise interesting questions. While Matthew apparently understood "way of the sea" as referring to the Lake of Galilee (hence his description of Capernaum as, literally, "beside the sea"), it is more likely that Isaiah was referring to the major route from Damascus to the Mediterranean which ran along the northwest shore of the Lake of Galilee, past Capernaum; if that road was known in Isaiah's time as the "way of the sea" (the Romans later called it *Via Maris*), the "sea" was the Mediterranean. In Isaiah's text the three terms "way of the sea, beyond the Jordan, Galilee of the nations" stand in apposition to each other, but in contrast to "land of Zebulun and Naphthali"; Matthew's abbreviation has put all four terms in apposition. "Beyond the Jordan" depends, of course, from which side of the river one is speaking. From a normal Palestinian viewpoint it would mean the east side as it does in v. 25, whereas Matthew here clearly understands the text to refer to the west (the territory of Zebulun and Naphthali)[15] where Capernaum was located. Did he then understand Isaiah to be speaking not from his own Palestinian standpoint but from that of the Assyrian invader? A related problem arises at 19:1; see the comments there. On this basis it has been argued that Matthew's gospel originated in Trans-Jordan,[16] but that is a lot to load onto a phrase included in a quotation from Isaiah when Matthew himself uses it in a different sense in 4:25 (and probably in 19:1).

"Galilee of the nations" reflects the region's greater openness to surrounding Gentile populations, and perhaps especially Isaiah's Judean awareness of the deportation of Israelites from Galilee by the Assyrians both be-

---

14. W. Carter, *JBL* 119 (2000) 513-18, rightly draws attention to the whole context of Isa 7–9 for understanding Matthew's choice of this text, and notes that it is the second formal quotation from this section of Isaiah (cf. 1:23; see p. 57, n. 63). Here, as in 1:23, Carter finds a predominantly political, antiimperial motive in Matthew's choice.

15. The LXX, presumably aware of this problem, has inserted καί before πέραν τοῦ Ἰορδάνου, thus making it a separate district. Matthew is here apparently dependent on the Hebrew rather than on the LXX, and so does not have this convenient solution available.

16. H. D. Slingerland, *JSNT* 3 (1979) 18-28; so also P. Luomanen, *Entering,* 275-77. Slingerland acknowledges Matthew's more conventional use of πέραν τοῦ Ἰορδάνου as a "semitechnical" term for Perea in 4:25, but rather lightly dismisses this as "only indirectly relevant" (n. 22). See, in response to Slingerland, D. C. Sim, *Gospel,* 41-45.

fore (2 Kgs 15:29) and after the Assyrian conquest (2 Kgs 17:24-34), to be replaced by foreign populations. By NT times southern Jews were suspicious of Galilee's mixed population; indeed, by the Maccabean period the region had become so paganized that its remaining Jewish population was evacuated to Judea (1 Macc 5:14-23); the subsequent incorporation of Galilee into the Jewish Hasmonean kingdom resulted again in a substantial Jewish population, particularly in Lower Galilee, but the total population remained mixed and by the first century included the new Hellenistic cities of Sepphoris and Tiberias. By including "Galilee of the nations" in his quotation Matthew gives a further hint of the direction in which his story will develop until the mission which will be launched from Galilee in 28:16 is explicitly targeted at "all nations" (28:19), even though for the time being Jesus' ministry will be largely (but not entirely: 8:5-13, 28-34; 15:21-39) focused on the Jewish population of Galilee — a principle which will be explicitly stated in 10:5-6; 15:24, but breached in practice in the latter pericope.

The imagery of darkness and light is clear and conventional (cf. 6:23). It speaks in Isaiah of the transformation from hopelessness to hope, in the immediate context of the devastation caused by the Assyrian invasion.[17] Matthew (perhaps encouraged by the messianic prediction that follows in Isa 9:6-7) takes it in a more eschatological sense, and will immediately ground this new hope in the Messiah's preaching of the kingdom of heaven.[18] Matthew's aorist tenses (LXX has an imperative and a future) make it clear that for him the prophecy has now found its fulfillment in Jesus. It is possible that Matthew uses "rise" *(anatellō)* rather than simply "shine" (so Hebrew and LXX) to recall the "rising" *(anatolē)* of the star in 2:2, 9, especially if the latter carried an echo of Balaam's prophecy of the rising star (Num 24:17). But the imagery speaks for itself without that echo.

17 Hitherto Jesus has been a largely passive figure in Matthew's story. "From that time," however, the situation is changed, as Jesus takes the initiative. This simple broad summary of his public ministry in Galilee uses exactly the same words as the account of John in 3:2; see the comments there for the meaning of the terms. Since this verse is an abbreviated version of the fuller summary with which Mark introduces Jesus' Galilean ministry (Mark 1:14-15), whereas Mark has no comparable account of John's proclamation,

17. Where both Hebrew and LXX speak of the people "walking" in darkness, Matthew has brought forward the idea of "sitting" from the next clause. There is no appreciable difference between the two metaphors in context; "sitting" here implies "residing."

18. Consistently with his politicizing agenda, Carter, 115, asserts that Matthew "transfers the Isaiah text from one situation of imperial aggression to another." This can be maintained as Matthew's intention only if, with Carter, we take "the kingdom of heaven" as opposition to Roman rule, and "Galilee of the Gentiles" as meaning "Galilee under Gentile oppression" (see his discussion in *JBL* 119 [2000] 516-18).

it seems more likely that Matthew has taken the traditional account of Jesus' preaching and extended it back to John than that he began with John and then chose to introduce Jesus in the same terms. He will soon add a rich variety of additional themes to Jesus' message for which John had no equivalent, but it remains a remarkable testimony to Matthew's positive estimate of John that he is willing to allow him to share Jesus' core message verbatim.

In recent years there has been a good deal of support for the proposal of N. B. Stonehouse, developed by E. Krentz and adopted by J. D. Kingsbury,[19] that the opening five words of this verse, "From that time Jesus began," constitute an introductory formula to a new main section of the gospel; the repetition of the same "formula" in 16:21 then provides the marker for Kingsbury's third (and last) main section. There is no doubt that the two phrases do serve to introduce a fundamental change in the pattern of Jesus' activity at these two points, and their placing corresponds quite closely with what I have designated on grounds of content as the beginning and end of the longest main section of the work (see above, pp. 2-5). But a five-word phrase repeated once at a distance of twelve chapters is not an impressive basis for claiming a structurally significant "formula" indicating a deliberate three-part presentation of the story by Matthew. The five words are an effective transitional idiom, but they do not compare with Matthew's frequently repeated formulae of quotation (1:22 etc.) and of discourse ending (7:28 etc.) as markers of literary design.

B. THE FOUNDING OF THE MESSIANIC COMMUNITY (4:18-22)

18 *As Jesus was walking beside the Lake[1] of Galilee, he saw two brothers, Simon (also called Peter) and his brother Andrew, throwing their casting net into the lake; for they were fishermen.* 19 *He said to them, "Come and follow me,[2] and I will send you out to fish for people."[3]* 20 *Immediately they left their nets and followed him.* 21 *He went*

19. N. B. Stonehouse, *Witness,* 129-31; E. Krentz, *JBL* 83 (1964) 409-14; J. D. Kingsbury, *Matthew: Structure,* 1-37. See the discussion in my *Matthew: Evangelist,* 151-52. Kingsbury's student D. R. Bauer, *Structure,* has given fuller expression to the theory; see Bauer, 84-88, for the significance of 4:17a for this structural scheme.

1. Literally, "Sea"; see on v. 13 above.

2. Literally, "Come behind me." See on 3:11 for "to come behind" as "a quasi-technical term for being a 'disciple' of Jesus." The normal verb for "follow" is used in vv. 20 and 22 with no difference in sense.

3. This famous verse is one of the most difficult in the NT to translate satisfactorily in a way which reflects modern sensitivity to the "exclusive" effect of a generic mas-

on from there, and saw two other brothers, James son of Zebedee and his brother John, who were in the boat with their father Zebedee, preparing⁴ their nets. He called them, 22 and they too immediately left the boat and their father, and followed him.

Hitherto Jesus, while briefly involved with John and others by the Jordan, has been presented as operating alone. But it is significant that his first recorded action is to gather a group of followers who will commit themselves to a total change of lifestyle which involves them in joining Jesus as his essential support group for the whole period of his public ministry. From this point on we shall not read stories about Jesus alone, but stories about Jesus and his disciples. Wherever he goes, they will go; their presence with Jesus, even if not explicitly mentioned, is assumed. While the Twelve will not be formally listed until 10:1-4, the stories from here on will assume a wider group of disciples than just these first four. They will be the primary audience for his teaching (5:1-2) and witnesses of his works of power, but they are also called to be his active helpers in the task of "fishing for people," as we shall discover in ch. 10. The first time Jesus will be left alone after this point will be when eventually the disciples desert him in the garden of Gethsemane (26:56). Until then, Matthew's story is not only that of the Messiah, but also of the messianic community which is being formed around him. The placing of this incident right at the beginning makes it clear that that was Jesus' intention.

Within that close-knit group of disciples it will become clear that three of the four whose call is recorded first will form an "inner circle," chosen to be with Jesus in moments of special significance (17:1; 26:37), and mentioned by name from time to time whereas the rest of the Twelve receive little or no individual mention beyond the listing of their names in 10:2-4. The proximity here of the two pairs of brothers suggests (as Luke 5:7, 10 states explicitly) that the four were already colleagues in the fishing business. The association of the mother of James and John with the other women at the cross according to 27:56 (see comments there), as well as her intervention on

---

culine. Not only has the traditional masculine phrase "fishers of men" become firmly entrenched in Christian usage, but any nonmasculine rendering also loses the echo (in English, not in Greek) of the preceding clause, "for they were fishermen." Nevertheless, the attempt must be made if we are to avoid the sort of misunderstanding which reputedly caused *Fishing for Men* (a paperback on evangelism) to be listed among recent publications in the *Angling Times,* while a young woman of my acquaintance was disappointed to discover that the same paperback was not a guide to dating. Simply to add "and women" invites the response, "What about children?" I adopt the TNIV rendering as the least unsatisfactory.

4. καταρτίζω means to prepare the nets for use, both by cleaning and repair and by folding them ready for the next catch.

their behalf in 20:20, has led some to suppose that the family of Zebedee was in some way related to Jesus' own family,[5] so that this sudden summons may not have come quite so much out of the blue as it appears, but the inference of kinship is very uncertain, and Matthew does not indicate it. Rather, the suddenness with which Zebedee is left behind in the boat suggests an unpremeditated action. Matthew betrays no awareness of the previous meeting of some of this group with Jesus near the Jordan which is mentioned in John 1:35-42.

This call story portrays a sudden and complete change of lifestyle, involving "leaving" both work and family.[6] Details later in the story suggest a modification of this impression of total renunciation,[7] but in 19:27-29 we shall be reminded of the radical dissociation which their discipleship entailed. The repetition of similar language with regard both to the call of Matthew in 9:9 and to the abortive call to the rich man in 19:21-22 shows that Matthew's understanding of discipleship was ideally of "giving up everything" to follow Jesus. Cf. 8:19-22 for Jesus' uncompromising demands on would-be followers. While Matthew does not record the call of any others of the Twelve except Matthew, we are left to assume that all of them were similarly expected to give up everything to follow Jesus (as indeed Peter will assert in 19:27).

If the announcement of "God's kingship" in v. 17 might lead the reader to expect some dramatic development in world history, the character of these first recruits offers a different perspective: four local fishermen do not sound like a world-changing task force. The parable of the mustard seed (13:31-32) will spell out the paradoxical character and insignificant beginnings of the kingdom of God.

18 As Simon was one of the commonest names in first-century Palestine[8] (we shall meet four other Simons in 10:4; 13:55; 26:6; 27:32), the nickname by which Jesus later distinguished this Simon (10:2; 16:18) is used here to identify him (and especially to distinguish him from the other Simon among the Twelve, 10:4). Simon is a Semitic name, but Andrew is Greek; the family, though now settled in Capernaum (8:14), originated from Bethsaida according to John 1:44, and their names reflect the mixed culture of that Hel-

---

5. So most boldly J. A. T. Robinson, *Priority,* 119-22, suggesting that Jesus and the sons of Zebedee were first cousins.

6. Keener, 151-53, documents the extensive and economically significant fishing industry of the Lake of Galilee and the economic sacrifice which would be involved in leaving it. Successful fishermen, even if not high on the social scale, were far better off than the peasantry.

7. Note the use of Peter's house and concern for his mother-in-law (8:14), and the availability of a fishing boat for the group's travels around the lake (8:23; 9:1; 13:2; 14:13, 22; 15:39).

8. See p. 34, n. 27.

lenistic settlement just across the river from Jewish Capernaum. The "casting net"[9] could be thrown by a man wading from the shore or, more effectively, from a boat. Matthew mentions that the sons of Zebedee were in a boat, but no boat is mentioned in connection with Simon and Andrew, and the different term for the "nets" of the sons of Zebedee has been taken to suggest a different type of fishing. But *diktyon* in v. 21 is not a very specific term (unlike *sagēnē*, the large "drag net" of 13:47, which required one or more boats), and in any case the same term *diktya* is also used in v. 20 for the nets which Simon and Andrew leave. So to use this difference of terminology to propose a social stratification, with Simon and Andrew belonging to the poorer shore fishermen while the Zebedee family were more affluent and owned a boat,[10] goes well beyond any clear hint in Matthew's wording (and is of course incompatible with Luke 5:1-11).

19-20 Etiquette required a rabbi's disciple to walk literally "behind" his teacher.[11] But when Jesus calls Simon and Andrew to "come behind him," they will soon find that he is far from a conventional rabbi,[12] especially in that those who wished to follow a rabbi generally took the initiative themselves, rather than being summoned in this way. What Jesus issues here is not even an invitation, but rather a demand. Such a summons is more typical of a prophet than of a rabbi (cf. Elijah's call of Elisha, 1 Kgs 19:19-21, a passage which bears fruitful comparison with this incident). Moreover, the task to which he is calling them is described not primarily as one of learning from a teacher, but of active "fishing." The metaphor follows naturally from the description of their previous occupation, but leaves open the nature of the "catching": from what and into what are people to be "fished"? Jer 16:16 uses the same metaphor of "catching" sinful people for judgment[13] (cf. also Amos 4:2; Hab 1:14-17), and indeed from the fish's point of view that is a more natural sense: it is no blessing for a fish to be caught! But following Jesus' proclamation of repentance in view of the coming of God's kingship, it seems more appropriate in this context to take the "catching" in a positive sense, of recruiting new subjects to God's kingship (cf. the parallel metaphor of seeking out the "lost sheep of Israel," 10:6). When the metaphor of fishing is used again in 13:47-50, the same "catching" will lead for some to judgment and for others to salvation. It is a metaphor for the time of decision, and Simon and Andrew will have a role in bringing people to that decision (10:5-15; 28:19-20).[14]

---

9. ἀμφίβληστρον, that which is "cast around," a circular net with a weighted edge which is drawn together to enclose the fish.
10. So H. C. Waetjen, *Reordering,* 10 and 79.
11. M. Hengel, *Leader,* 52-53.
12. Ibid., 42-57.
13. For this allusion cf. M. Knowles, *Jeremiah,* 194-97.
14. The background and meaning of the metaphor are exhaustively discussed by

Matthew is less prolific than Mark in his use of "immediately"; its use here and in v. 22 emphasizes the extraordinary readiness of these working men to abandon all that was familiar and secure for the sake of a charismatic stranger. The unique authority inherent in Jesus' teaching and actions which will be emphasized repeatedly in chs. 5–9 is already displayed both in the radical boldness of his demand and in the instinctive and uncharacteristic response of four ordinary men.

21-22   The call of the second pair of brothers closely echoes that of the first, and there is no need for the specific task of "fishing for people" to be repeated. But the inclusion of the boat and the men's father makes the radical nature of their renunciation even more graphic. For the priority of discipleship even over family ties cf. 8:18-22; 10:21-22, 34-37; 12:46-50; the tension between such demands and the proper concern for parents which Jesus will defend in 15:3-6 underlines the radical urgency of his call.[15] Zebedee may be mentioned frequently in the gospels (whereas Simon and Andrew are never referred to jointly as the "sons of John," John 1:42) because he (and his wife, 20:20; 27:56) became a familiar figure in the first-century church, though since James and John frequently feature together (usually along with Simon but not Andrew), this may rather reflect the need for a convenient joint title to denote them.

C. AN OVERVIEW OF THE MESSIAH'S REVELATION IN GALILEE (4:23-25)

> 23 *And he began*[1] *traveling around throughout the whole of Galilee, teaching in their synagogues*[2] *and proclaiming the good news of the kingdom and healing all sorts of illnesses and disabilities*[3] *among the people.* 24 *Reports about him spread out into the whole of Syria, and people brought to him all who were suffering from all kinds of ill-*

W. H. Wuellner, *Meaning;* cf. more briefly M. Hengel, *Leader,* 76-78. C. W. F. Smith, *HTR* 52 (1959) 187-203, argues for the more negative sense here.

15. See S. C. Barton, *Discipleship,* 129-30 (and passim).

1. The imperfect tense of this introductory verb (all the remaining verbs in vv. 23-25 are aorist) indicates a broad setting for the itinerant ministry which is now beginning and which will be narrated throughout the following chapters until Jesus sets off for Jerusalem in 16:21. "He was traveling" would suitably describe this background activity, but in this context the inceptive sense of the imperfect is probably also present.

2. Or "assemblies"; see the comment and n. 6 below.

3. μαλακία, literally "weakness," a term used in the NT only by Matthew in these general summaries (cf. 9:35; 10:1); it may be intended to distinguish physical impairments from more specific diseases.

nesses and afflicted by pain, and[4] those possessed by demons, and those subject to fits,[5] and those who were paralyzed; and he healed them. 25 *And great crowds followed him, from Galilee and the Decapolis, from Jerusalem and Judea, and from across the Jordan.*

Now that Jesus' entourage has been established, Matthew expands on the brief introduction to the Galilean ministry which he has given in 4:17, and fills in both the nature of Jesus' peripatetic activity and the phenomenal response with which it was met, even beyond the bounds of Palestinian Judaism. This general account of Jesus' immense popularity and "success," which will be repeated in an abbreviated form in 9:35, provides the essential background to the chapters that follow. While Jesus will be most immediately associated with his close circle of disciples, we shall be reminded constantly of a wider "crowd" who surround him, eager to witness and benefit from his power as well as to hear his teaching. Verses 18-22 have introduced the inner circle; these verses now add the outer periphery. Both groups will be important as the setting for the teaching which will immediately follow (see comments on 5:1-2; 7:28-29). In view of the various sources of opposition to Jesus which we shall encounter in chs. 11–16 (even including the Galilean communities of Nazareth, 13:53-58, and of Chorazin, Bethsaida, and Capernaum, 11:20-24), it is important for Matthew's readers to keep in mind this overall impression of general enthusiasm for Jesus' Galilean ministry which he has provided at the outset.

23 While Matthew will record several specific locations in Galilee, and many further Galilean incidents without a defined place, "the whole of Galilee" should be understood as describing a widespread ministry rather than quite literally. For instance, we have no record of Jesus ever visiting the two Hellenistic cities of Sepphoris and Tiberias which both served as capitals for Antipas's Galilee. Jesus' visits seem to have been primarily to the more traditionally Jewish parts of the province. The mention of "synagogues" reinforces this focus; in first-century Galilee the term may denote village assemblies rather than buildings erected for worship as such,[6] but its usage focuses

---

4. The omission of this καί in a few important MSS is apparently a stylistic "improvement" designed to read the three following descriptions as in apposition to the preceding general categories, specifying three particular afflictions. Most interpreters retain the καί, which has the effect of distinguishing demon-possession from purely physical ailments, in accordance with general (though not universal) NT usage (see comments on this verse).

5. σεληνιαζόμενοι, literally "those affected by the moon." See the discussion at 17:15 on what sort of affliction Matthew might have intended this rare verb to indicate.

6. The general assumption that NT συναγωγή denotes a religious building is strongly disputed, e.g., by R. A. Horsley, *Galilee,* ch. 10; *Archeology,* ch. 6. Horsley ar-

on Jewish communities.[7] "The people" (*laos;* see p. 53, n. 47 and p. 70, n. 46) in Matthew also normally denotes especially the people of Israel. Jesus will himself describe his mission as "only to the lost sheep of the house of Israel" (15:24), and when he is recorded as being involved with Gentiles, the narrative makes clear that this is exceptional (8:5-13; 15:21-28).

The mention of "proclaiming the good news" alongside "teaching" in the synagogues is perhaps not simply repetition but rather distinguishes informal preaching to gathered crowds from the more formal opportunity to speak by invitation in a regular weekly assembly; the content is, however, unlikely to have differed significantly.[8] Teaching, proclamation, and healing (with exorcism, mentioned in the next verse) constitute the bulk of Jesus' recorded activity in Galilee, and will be comprehensively illustrated in the anthologies of teaching and healing in chs. 5–7 and 8–9 respectively. Similar terms will be used for the disciples' derivative ministry in 10:7-8, though it may be significant that whereas they, too, are to "proclaim," Matthew never uses the verb "teach" of the disciples until after Jesus (the "one teacher," 23:8, 10) is no longer present (28:20).

This is Matthew's first use of *euangelion,* "good news." Unlike Mark (and Luke, who prefers the verb *euangelizomai*), he uses the term only four times, here and in the parallel passage 9:35 to summarize Jesus' message, and in 24:14; 26:13 to denote the church's proclamation about Jesus after his death; Matthew apparently intends his readers to perceive a simple continuity between the message of Jesus and that of his followers. In three of

---

gues that archeological and literary evidence suggests that by the first century most Galilean villages would not yet have had a "synagogue" building in the later sense (though Capernaum did, according to Luke 7:5). Schürer, 2:439-47, gives a less radical view of the situation than Horsley, but also cautions against the assumption that a *building* was always involved. The study of the nature and origin of the Palestinian synagogue by L. I. Levine, *JBL* 115 (1996) 425-48, is more inclined to accept synagogue buildings in the first century. For a summary of evidence for "synagogues" (both the building and the assembly) in the first century see Keener, 156-57; J. A. Overman, *Gospel,* 56-62; H. C. Kee, *NTS* 41 (1995) 481-500 (the latter disputed by K. Atkinson, *NTS* 43 [1997] 491-502).

7. The wording does not require the conclusion commonly drawn that by referring to "their" synagogues Matthew, reflecting later church-synagogue hostility, is deliberately distancing himself from official Judaism. This implication may more easily be found in some of Matthew's later uses of this distinctive expression (9:35; 10:17; 12:9; 13:54), especially 10:17, but here the reference is to assemblies in which Jesus and his disciples were welcome, and the use of αὐτῶν here is a perfectly natural way to refer to the synagogues *of Galilee.* See further my *Matthew: Evangelist,* 107-8.

8. Luz, 1:206-8, discusses the relationship between "teaching" and "preaching" in Matthew, and concludes that they are not essentially different. His discussion focuses, however, on their content rather than on the context of delivery.

these four cases the word occurs in the apparently stereotyped phrase "the gospel of the kingdom." Matthew is the only one of the three Synoptic evangelists to abbreviate "the kingdom of God/heaven" (see on 3:2) to simply "the kingdom" in this way. Modern usage has unfortunately adopted this abbreviation to the extent that "the kingdom" *tout court* is now commonly used to summarize the Christian message (a usage supported in the NT only by Acts 20:25); the word "kingdom" is sometimes used these days even as an adjective (e.g., Keener, 155: "kingdom works")! The effect of this abbreviation is to reinforce the common misunderstanding, already fostered by the unfortunate English translation "kingdom" instead of, for example, "reign," that *basileia* means a "thing" called a "kingdom" rather than being a verbal noun to describe God ruling.[9] Matthew does not use the phrase in that absolute way. He omits "of heaven/God" six times, but only where *basileia* already depends on another noun: "the gospel of the *basileia*" (4:23; 9:35; 24:14), "the sons of the *basileia*" (8:12; 13:38), "the word of the *basileia*" (13:19), where the gospel context makes clear that it is *God's* rule that is in view; he never uses *hē basileia* alone in the manner of Acts 20:25 and modern usage.

The mention that Jesus healed (literally) "every disease and every weakness," following the mention of "the whole of Galilee," suggests that Matthew is generalizing rather than asserting that no single case of illness was left untreated; cf. v. 24, the bringing of "all" the afflicted, apparently from the whole Roman province of Syria. He is describing a phenomenally successful and popular program of healing, not counting cases.

24 The Roman imperial province of Syria included not only the Syria (Aram) of the OT but also Palestine (Syria Palestina); the Herodian rulers and the prefect of Judea, as well as the cities of the Decapolis, were subject to the overall authority of the legate of Syria. Matthew's "all Syria" here, while even less likely to be meant literally than "all Galilee" in v. 23, serves to indicate that Jesus' reputation spread far beyond the area of his actual travels. For his reputation outside Palestine cf. 15:21-22. For the list of complaints cf. pp. 148-49, nn. 3-5. The three terms which conclude the list will all be illustrated by specific cases in 8:28-34; 17:14-21; and 9:1-8 respectively. Exact medical diagnosis is not to be expected or attempted on the basis of such a general summary, but we should note that demon-possession, often regarded by modern interpreters as a prescientific explanation for what we would describe as physical or mental disorder, is in fact listed as a separate category. In using the verb "heal" to cover all the complaints listed, Matthew is not as careful as Mark in 1:32-34 (cf. 3:10-12) to differentiate possession, with "expulsion" as its cure, from physical illnesses which are "healed,"

---

9. See above, p. 102, especially n. 24; more fully my *Divine Government,* 11-14.

but in his other general summaries he maintains the distinction clearly (8:16; 10:1, 8); where he mentions physical symptoms in a case of demon-possession in 9:32-34, the language remains clearly that of exorcism, though in 12:22 a more abbreviated account speaks simply of "healing."[10] See on 17:14-20 for the suggestion that one case of demon-possession was linked with what we call epilepsy.

25 While Matthew specifies Galilee as the area of Jesus' own travels (v. 23), the wider currency of his reputation (v. 24) results in people coming to him from the whole of Palestine and the immediately surrounding area. Cf. the similar but more limited statement of the extent of John the Baptist's following in 3:5. Galilee and the Decapolis cover the northern area, on both sides of the Jordan valley, while the south is represented by Judea on the west bank of the Jordan and Perea on the east bank. Jerusalem is included because of its importance as the main center of population, though it does not extend the geographical area. The striking omission geographically is Samaria: while Luke and John describe Jesus' activities in Samaria and the response of Samaritans (Luke 9:51-56; 17:11-19; John 4:4-42), Matthew not only omits any such record but also specifically excludes Samaria from the area of the disciples' mission (10:5-6); even though Jesus himself will from time to time move outside Jewish circles, his openness appears not to extend to Samaritans in Matthew's understanding.

These large "crowds" are said to "follow" Jesus, the same term which in vv. 20 and 22 denoted the first disciples' total change of lifestyle and will in 8:19-22 similarly indicate a radical commitment to accompany Jesus. Yet as the narrative progresses, we shall find only a few who are Jesus' constant and committed companions, while a less easily defined "crowd" comes and goes. This wider group represents a pool of possible "full-time" recruits, but generally their "following" seems to be more sporadic and temporary, and when Jesus sets off for Jerusalem in 16:21 it is apparently only the Twelve (and the women mentioned in 27:55-56) who are prepared to leave Galilee to accompany him. The distinction between "disciples" and "crowd" will be clearly maintained in 5:1-2; 7:28-29, and so on. The verb "follow" alone is not therefore a sufficient indication of full-scale discipleship.[11] Mark 3:7-8 is perhaps more exact in describing this interprovincial crowd as simply "coming to" Jesus.

10. See the discussion of the distinction between healing and exorcism in the gospel accounts by G. Theissen, *Miracle-Stories,* 85-94; more fully, and with reference to ancient thought more generally, E. M. Yamauchi, in *GP* 6:89-183.

11. See my *Matthew: Evangelist,* 262-64 for the breadth of Matthew's use of ἀκολουθέω.

D. THE MESSIAH'S AUTHORITY REVEALED IN HIS TEACHING: *THE DISCOURSE ON DISCIPLESHIP* (5:1–7:29)

As I have already published an overview of some of the issues raised by this memorable discourse,[1] I trust that I may be allowed here to introduce it quite briefly.

The scene has been well set: Jesus the Messiah has begun to preach in Galilee, as Scripture foretold (4:12-17), and large crowds are being attracted to his teaching (4:23-25). Matthew therefore now presents a lengthy collection of that authoritative teaching. A parallel collection of his authoritative deeds will follow in chs. 8–9. But the teaching is addressed, initially at least, not to the crowds, but rather to the narrower circle of his committed disciples, to whom we have been introduced in 4:18-22, and who are now taken apart from the crowds to be instructed on what their new commitment involves. The focus of these chapters is not then the wider proclamation of the "good news of the kingdom" (4:23), but the instruction of those who have already responded to that proclamation and now need to learn what life in the "kingdom of heaven" is really about. The teaching will frequently describe them as a special group who stand over against, and indeed are persecuted by, people in general. They are those who have entered into a new relationship with "your Father in heaven," and who in consequence are called to a radically new lifestyle, in conscious distinction from the norms of the rest of society.[2] They are to be an alternative society, a "Christian counter-culture."[3]

It is because of this distinctive focus of chs. 5–7 that I have preferred to call this "The Discourse on Discipleship" rather than to use the familiar but non-descriptive title "Sermon on the Mount," a term which too often conveys to modern hearers the concept of a general code of ethics rather than the specific demands of the kingdom of heaven.[4] As has often been pointed out (and sometimes discovered in experience, notably by Tolstoy), the demands of this discourse do not easily translate into a practical, day-to-day morality;

---

1. *Matthew: Evangelist,* 160-65.

2. See J. A. Overman, *Gospel,* 94-101, for the function of chs. 5–7 in "ordering and directing the life of the Matthean community," which saw itself as distinct from the surrounding society.

3. This was the title of the exposition of Matt 5–7 by J. R. W. Stott, subsequently retitled less memorably as *The Message of the Sermon on the Mount.*

4. For the history of the interpretation of the Sermon on the Mount see W. S. Kissinger, *Sermon.* There is a brief survey in G. N. Stanton, *Gospel,* 289-95; rather more fully R. A. Guelich, *Sermon,* 14-22, and much more fully H. D. Betz, *Sermon,* 6-44. H. K. McArthur, *Understanding* 105-48, interestingly discusses alternative approaches to drawing ethical guidance from the Sermon; G. Strecker, *Sermon,* 15-23, does the same more briefly but with reference to more recent approaches.

see especially the comments below on 5:39-42. The standard set is nothing less than perfection, being like God (5:48). Jesus' typical use of extreme, black-and-white categories lays down a challenge which cannot simply be converted into a set of rules and regulations for life in the real world. The essence of life in the kingdom of heaven is in fact the antithesis of a legalistic code, as 5:20 will state and 5:21-48 will repeatedly illustrate. The discourse is indeed intended as a guide to life, but only for those who are committed to the kingdom of heaven, and even they will always find that its reach exceeds their grasp.[5]

In the Introduction (pp. 8-10) I have outlined the nature of Matthew's five major discourses, with their distinctive concluding formula, of which this is the longest.[6] While the Synoptic substructure on which each of the others is based is found in Mark, in this case there is very little material in common with Mark and the basic Synoptic parallel is Luke 6:20-49.[7] The two "sermons" share a great deal of common material (all but eight verses of Luke 6:20-49 are paralleled, though not always closely, in Matt 5-7) in roughly the same order (the only exceptions are the placing of Luke 6:27-28, 31), and each begins with beatitudes and ends with the parable of the two houses. The opening and closing pericopes are, however, instructive in that while the subject matter is similar, in each case the wording is conspicuously different, to such an extent that at least in the case of the Beatitudes it is easier to explain the Matthean and Lucan sets as deriving from two separate traditions (see comments on 5:3-10). So while some of the common material is verbally very similar, at other times Matthew's "parallel" material appears to derive from a separate tradition, and it is the overall structure of the "sermon" rather than its specific content that links Matthew with Luke.

Roughly 27 percent of Matthew's discourse is shared with Luke 6:20-

---

5. Keener, 161-62, aptly comments that while "modern interpreters must let Jesus' radical demands confront us with all the unnerving ferocity with which they would have struck their first hearers," the gospel as a whole is not one of rigorist rejection of those who fail to reach the ideal standard, but of forgiveness and of grace. He also points out, however, that that grace is "not the workless grace of much of Western Christendom"; rather, "the kingdom message transforms those who meekly embrace it, just as it crushes the arrogant, the religiously and socially satisfied."

6. To speak of the Sermon on the Mount as a discourse composed by Matthew conflicts with the argument of H. D. Betz, *Essays* (especially pp. 17-22, 90-93), that it came to Matthew ready-made as a Jewish-Christian epitome of Jesus' teaching compiled probably in the fifties of the first century. This view is presupposed rather than argued again in Betz's Hermeneia commentary on the Sermon (1995). For a careful and convincing rebuttal of this theory see G. N. Stanton, *Gospel*, 307-25. The similar way in which the five discourses are compiled (see pp. 9-10) seems to me a strong argument against Betz's proposal that this one did not derive from Matthew.

7. For a chart of the Synoptic parallels see my *Matthew: Evangelist,* 161.

49, a further 33 percent has parallels elsewhere in Luke, and 5 percent in Mark, while the remaining 35 percent has no parallel in either Mark or Luke. These data, together with the preceding observations, are consistent with, and indeed provide the clearest illustration of, Matthew's method in compiling his five major discourses. A traditional unit of Jesus' teaching is adapted and massively expanded by the inclusion of other traditional sayings on related themes, some of which Matthew shares with Luke, but many of which he has derived from sources otherwise unknown to us. This discourse is thus properly described as an anthology of the teaching of Jesus relating to discipleship, compiled by Matthew into his own distinctive structure (though using as a basis the sermon outline of Luke 6:20-49), but aiming to provide an overview of the authoritative teaching of the Messiah himself. We shall see in chs. 10, 13, 18, and 24–25 similar anthologies based on traditional units found also in Mark, each of which, like this one, will conclude with the formula "And it happened, when Jesus had finished these [words]. . . ."

The subject matter of chs. 5–6 covers four main themes:

5:3-16   The distinctiveness of disciples
5:17-48 Fulfilling the law
6:1-18   Piety, true and false
6:19-34 The priority of trust in God over material security.

In 7:1-12 the structure of the discourse is less clearly coherent, with a collection of sayings on a number of loosely related themes, though reaching in 7:12 a summary which brings to a head much of the content of the discourse so far. Then a series of four challenging contrasts (7:13-27) brings the whole to a rhetorically powerful conclusion.[8]

The concluding verses (7:28-29) not only reintroduce the crowd as a secondary audience but also sum up the overall impact which Matthew intends this discourse to produce, that of the unparalleled authority of the teacher. From time to time throughout the discourse Jesus has spoken in the

---

8. An interesting structural analysis of the Sermon by Luz, 1:211-13 (following J. Kürzinger and R. Riesner), proposes that it is "built symmetrically around a center, namely, the Lord's Prayer." It is, however, not clear in what way, e.g., 5:21-48 and 6:19–7:11 correspond to each other, except in the purely formal sense that each occupies "59 lines in Nestle." As with similarly concentric structures sometimes proposed for Matthew as a whole (see my *Matthew: Evangelist,* 146-49), it is remarkable that if this were intended by Matthew the alleged "architectonic symmetry" should have been noticed by so few of his readers. Luz's proposal is to be distinguished from earlier suggestions that the Lord's Prayer is in effect expounded clause by clause in the Sermon (so W. Grundmann, *Matthäus;* cf. Schweizer, 202-3; and in a different way G. Bornkamm, *NTS* 24 [1977/8] 419-32).

first person, indicating that he himself is to be the focus of the disciples' allegiance (5:11) and the one who determines their lifestyle (5:17-18, 20, and the "I say to you" formula of 5:22, 28, 32, 34, 39, 44; cf. 6:25, 29) and their destiny (7:21-23, 24, 26). Thus, far from being a philosophical discourse on ethics, this is a messianic manifesto, setting out the unique demands and revolutionary insights of one who claims an absolute authority over other people and whose word, like the word of God, will determine their destiny. No wonder the crowds were astonished, not only by the teaching but even more by the teacher.[9]

1. Teaching in the Hills (5:1-2)

> 1 Seeing the crowds, Jesus went up into the hills; and when he had sat down, his disciples came to him. 2 He opened his mouth and taught them as follows:

The introduction to this discourse has in one sense already begun in 4:23-25,[10] since the crowds, introduced in 4:25, are cited as the reason for Jesus' move up into the hills. But the audience of the discourse is specified not as the crowds but as "his disciples," a term used here for the first time in Matthew, but presumably intended in context to denote those who have been called to follow him in 4:18-22, together with others who share the same calling and commitment.[11] The crowds are thus deliberately distinguished from the audience of the discourse, even though in 7:28-29 we shall find that they have been listening to it, perhaps as an outer circle "eavesdropping" on what he has to say to his disciples. It is explicitly to the disciples ("them," v. 2) that the discourse is addressed. While the crowds are themselves often the object of Jesus' concern both as a teacher and a healer (9:36; 13:2; 15:30; 19:2), there are also times in Matthew when he deliberately moves away from the crowds in order to be with his disciples (8:18; 13:36; 14:22). Sometimes he "withdraws" (4:12; 12:15; 14:13; 15:21) in contexts of hostility or danger; but this is simply the search for a quieter environment for teaching.

I have translated *eis to oros* as "into the hills" because here and in

9. For the christological focus of Matt 5–7 cf. R. A. Guelich, *Sermon,* 27-29.

10. So T. L. Donaldson, *Jesus,* 105-6.

11. See further on 8:21 for the meaning of μαθητής in Matthew. J. A. Draper, *JSNT* 75 (1999) 28-32, 45-47, argues that because only four disciples have so far been introduced, and the Twelve will not be listed until 10:1-4, the Sermon is specifically directed to the four named disciples and serves to legitimate them over against other claimants to leadership. Other interpreters assume that when Matthew speaks of "his disciples" he expects his readers to take these four as representative of the wider circle of followers who will increasingly feature in the story.

14:23; 15:29 (and, I shall argue, also in 28:16) I take *to oros* to be a general term for the hill country to the west and north of the Lake of Galilee, where the hills rise steeply from the lake. So the phrase need not denote a specific mountain; contrast the specific mention of "a (very) high mountain" in 4:8; 17:1 and the named mountain of 24:3.[12] To that extent "Sermon on the Mount" is a misleading description, and no specific "mountain" can be safely identified as the site of this teaching. The setting of the sermon of Luke 6:20-49, apparently on a "level place" to which Jesus descends (Luke 6:17), supports a reference to a setting generally in the hill country rather than on a mountaintop. But despite this geographical sense of *eis to oros* Matthew may well have intended *to oros* also to suggest a typological parallel with Moses,[13] who went up on "the mountain" (Sinai) to receive and then deliver God's law.[14] For a New Moses typology already in the prologue to the gospel see above, pp. 63-64, 79, 81-83, 89. For the possibility of a similar typology underlying the "very high mountain" of 4:8 see the comments there and see also below on 17:1-8. We have also noticed other exodus motifs in 2:15 and 4:1-11. In the light of this repeated theme, Davies and Allison, 1:427, make the rather exaggerated comment that "Mt 1–5 in all its parts reflects a developed exodus typology . . . every major event in Mt 1–5 apparently has its counterpart in the events surrounding Israel's exodus from Egypt." If such a typology was in Matthew's mind here, however, he must have intended his readers to reflect not only on the similarity but also on the contrast between Moses, who spoke only the words he was given, and Jesus, who, in explicit contrast to what was said "to the people of old" (through Moses), simply declares, "I say to you" (5:21-22 etc.). Moses gave them the law; Jesus "fulfills" it (5:17).[15]

The portrayal of Jesus as seated with "disciples" gathered around him casts him in the role of a rabbinic teacher; sitting was the posture for authori-

12. For the meaning of εἰς τὸ ὄρος see my *Matthew: Evangelist,* 313, especially n. 82.

13. For a recent defense of this traditional typology see D. C. Allison, *Moses,* 172-80, rightly modifying the more sceptical verdict of his colleague W. D. Davies, who famously (*Setting,* 25-93) concluded that the New Moses typology was only a minor element in Matthew's portrayal of Jesus, even in the Sermon on the Mount; for Allison's direct response to Davies see *Moses,* 298-306. The alternative suggestion of T. L. Donaldson, *Jesus,* 116-18, that ὄρος here, together with five other pericopes where Matthew uses the word, represents a "Mount Zion" typology has not been widely accepted (see above, p. 134, n. 30).

14. The phrase ἀνέβη εἰς τὸ ὄρος occurs repeatedly in the LXX accounts of Moses at Sinai (Exod 19:3; 24:15, 18; 34:4; cf. 24:12, 13; 34:1, 2; Deut 9:9: 10:1, 3 for related verbal forms).

15. R. J. Banks, *Jesus,* 229-35, in order to maintain this superiority of Jesus to Moses the lawgiver and to deny that the Sermon on the Mount is merely a new law, unnecessarily feels obliged to deny a Moses typology altogether.

tative teaching (cf. 13:2; 24:3; 26:55), as also in the synagogue (23:2; Luke 4:20).[16] The verb *didaskō,* "teach," reinforces that impression, while "opened his mouth" is a familiar OT idiom to introduce a significant pronouncement (Job 3:1; 33:2; Ps 78:2; Dan 10:16; cf. Matt 13:35; Acts 8:35; 10:34). Matthew thus sets up the model of the authoritative teacher with which the discourse will also conclude (7:28-29).

2. The Good Life: the Paradoxical Values of the Kingdom of Heaven (5:3-10)

> 3 *"Happy*[1] *are those who are poor in spirit, for it is to them*[2] *that the kingdom of heaven belongs.*[3]
>
> 4 *Happy are those who mourn, for it is they who will be comforted.*[4]
>
> 5 *Happy are the meek, for it is they who will inherit the earth.*[5]

---

16. D. C. Allison, *Moses,* 175-79, traces a Jewish tradition that Moses *sat* on Mount Sinai, but such a tradition is hardly necessary to explain Matthew's reference to Jesus sitting *in order to teach.*

1. No English word fully captures the sense of μακάριος in this traditional form of "beatitude"; see the comments below. I have chosen "happy" for the translation, despite its inappropriately psychological connotations, as the least inadequate option in current English.

2. "For it is to them," "for it is they,"and the like are intended to capture the emphatic ὅτι αὐτῶν/αὐτοί which introduces the second half of each line, identifying the people described in the first half, and only them, as the ones to whom the promised benefit will come.

3. αὐτῶν ἐστιν ἡ βασιλεία τῶν οὐρανῶν could also be translated "it is of them that the kingdom of heaven consists"; i.e., they make up its membership. The effect would not be greatly different, but insofar as the latter rendering suggests a more "concrete" view of the βασιλεία τῶν οὐρανῶν as comprising a group of people, it is less consistent with Matthew's usage generally. God's kingship ("the kingdom of heaven") belongs to them, of course, not in the sense that they exercise royal authority, but that they benefit from it.

4. The order of vv. 4 and 5, the second and third beatitudes, is reversed in D and most Latin versions, and this order is reflected in many patristic citations. The reversal has the effect of sharply juxtaposing heaven (v. 3) and earth (v. 5), and may have been made for that reason. The close similarity in meaning between "poor" and "meek" would also suggest that they should stand together. But the much wider attestation of the less "obvious" order which places the mourners before the meek suggests that it is original, though several interpreters have favored the Western order (see G. R. Beasley-Murray, *Kingdom,* 158).

5. ἡ γῆ can mean either "the land" (usually understood as Israel) or "the earth" in the broader sense, and it is the context which must decide. Here, while in Ps 37:11 the meaning is probably "the land," it is likely that Matthew intended a less territorial sense, which is better represented by "the earth." See the comments below, especially p. 166, n. 25.

6 *Happy are those who are hungry and thirsty for righteousness,*
for it is they who will be satisfied.

7 *Happy are those who show mercy, for it is to them that mercy*
will be shown.

8 *Happy are the pure in heart, for it is they who will see God.*

9 *Happy are the peacemakers, for it is they who will be called*
God's children.

10 *Happy are those who are persecuted because of righteousness,*
for it is to them that the kingdom of heaven belongs.

The discourse begins with a manifesto on the values of the kingdom of heaven which is carefully constructed for easy memorization and maximum impact. The sharply paradoxical character of most of its recommendations reverses the conventional values of society[6] — it commends those whom the world in general would dismiss as losers and wimps; compare the presentation of disciples as "little ones" in 10:42; 18:6, 10, 14; 25:40 (cf. the "little children" of 11:25). The Beatitudes thus call on those who would be God's people to stand out as different from those around them, and promise them that those who do so will not ultimately be the losers. While the promises in vv. 4-9 do not specifically mention God as subject, the implication of the passive verbs is that it is *God* who will comfort, give the inheritance, satisfy, show mercy, and call them his children.

a. The "Beatitude" Form

Beatitudes (statements of the form "Happy is/are . . .") occur in both pagan and Judeo-Christian literature.[7] For some OT examples see Pss 1:1; 32:1-2; 40:4; 119:1-2; 128:1. In the NT compare Matt 11:6; 13:16; 16:17; 24:46, and many instances in Luke (1:45; 10:23; 11:27-28, etc.).[8] The Greek adjective *makarios* ("happy"; see below) has spawned the verb *makarizō*, "to call happy" (Luke 1:48; Jas 5:11; the verb occurs frequently in classical Greek),

---

6. This is demonstrated at length by J. H. Neyrey, *Honor,* 164-89. His basic thesis (concerning the whole Sermon on the Mount, but focused especially on 5:3-12) is set out on pp. 164-65: "Jesus changed the way the honor game was played and redefined the source of honor, namely, acknowledgement by God, not by neighbor." Neyrey's discussion draws out an important aspect of this pericope, but the fact that his thesis finds no place for one of the beatitudes ("Blessed are the pure in heart," v. 8) suggests that it may not go to the heart of the message of the passage as a whole.

7. A wide range are collected in Davies and Allison, 1:431-34.

8. The beatitude form is continued in the *Gospel of Thomas,* sayings 7, 18, 19, 49, 54, 58, 68-69, and 103, most of which have little in common with the canonical beatitudes, though sharing the form.

and the derivative noun *makarismos,* a "calling happy," a beatitude (Rom 4:6, 9). Such "macarisms" are normally single statements, and there is no close parallel to Matthew's carefully structured set of eight beatitudes. Sir 25:7-11, with its list of nine or ten types of people whom the sage "calls happy," resembles Matt 5:3-10 in range but not in regularity of form (Sirach uses the verb *makarizō* once and the adjective *makarios* only twice); in Sir 14:20-27 there is a similar description of a (single) person whom the sage designates *makarios* (using the adjective once only, to introduce the series of descriptive clauses).[9] But in comparison with Matt 5:3-10 the lists in Sirach are strikingly conventional: they lack both the paradoxes of the Matthean list and the regular inclusion of explicit reasons for the commendations in the "for it is they . . ." clauses (a feature which is lacking in most other biblical beatitudes apart from Luke 6:20-22).[10]

b. The Meaning of Makarios

"Macarisms" are essentially commendations, congratulations, statements to the effect that a person is in a good situation, sometimes even expressions of envy.[11] The Hebrew equivalent of *makarios* is *'ašrê* rather than the more

9. The fragmentary Qumran text 4Q525 begins with what appears to have been a set of beatitudes outlining the character of God's true people in a way similar to that in Ps 15. In the surviving text *'ašrê* (which corresponds to Greek μακάριος) introduces four short commendations (there may have been more originally), which are followed by a more discursive portrait of the "happy" person, but without continuing the use of *'ašrê*. E. Puech, *RB* 98 (1991) 80-106, discusses this text in relation to Sir 14:20-27 and Matt 5:3-10, and suggests that they reflect a recognized stylistic form; on this basis he suggests that the Qumran text originally had eight beatitudes, like Matthew.

10. There is a set of nine beatitudes which in some ways resembles those of Sirach in *2 En.* 42:6-14 (repeated with variations in 43:6-14). It, too, lacks the regularity in form of the Matthean beatitudes; its date is quite uncertain, but is likely to be well after the NT period.

11. A good secular example is the exquisite little poem attributed to Anacreon (sixth century B.C.) addressed to a cicada:

"We call you happy (μακαρίζομεν), cicada,
when up on the treetops
after you have drunk a little dew
you sing like a king.
Yours are all the things
you can see in the fields,
all that the woods produce.
You are honored by all people,
sweet prophet of summer.
The Muses love you,

theologically loaded *bārûk,* "blessed (by God)." The traditional English rendering "blessed" thus also has too theological a connotation in modern usage; the Greek term for "blessed (by God)" is *eulogētos,* not *makarios.* The sense of congratulation and commendation is perhaps better conveyed by "happy," but this term generally has too psychological a connotation: *makarios* does not state that a person *feels* happy ("Happy are those who mourn" is a particularly inappropriate translation if the word is understood in that way), but that they are in a "happy" situation, one which other people ought also to wish to share. "Fortunate" gets closer to the sense, but has inappropriate connotations of luck. "Congratulations to . . ." would convey much of the impact of a "macarism," but perhaps sounds too colloquial. The Australian idiom "Good on yer" is perhaps as close as any to the sense, but would not communicate in the rest of the English-speaking world! My favorite translation of *makarios* is the traditional Welsh rendering of the Beatitudes, *Gwyn eu byd,* literally "White is their world," an evocative idiom for those for whom everything is good. Beatitudes are descriptions, and commendations, of the good life.[12]

c. The Structure of Matthew's Beatitudes

These eight statements[13] are clearly designed as a coherent group. The epigrammatic form of the eight pronouncements,

> "Happy are those who . . . [a quality or activity in the present tense], for it is they who . . . [a future verb, except in vv. 3 and 10]"

is repeated each time with only very minor variation. The first and last of the group both have the same second clause, "for it is to them that the kingdom of heaven belongs," thus forming a framework which sets the tone for the promises which come between. The first four qualities all begin in Greek with *p,* which might be merely coincidental, but suggests to many a deliber-

---

and so does Apollo himself
who gave you your shrill song.
Age cannot wear you down,
you earthborn sage and musician.
Free from the suffering of flesh and blood,
you are almost like the gods."

12. J. H. Neyrey, *Honor,* 165-67, reading the text against the background of ancient values of honor and shame, argues for the sense "honorable," "esteemed."

13. What is sometimes referred to as the "ninth beatitude," vv. 11-12, is formally distinct: it is longer and more complex, and is cast in the second person — and its content merely expands on the eighth beatitude rather than introducing a ninth quality.

ate alliteration; in that case, however, it is perhaps surprising that no attempt was made by the Greek translator[14] to carry the alliterative pattern through the remaining four. The effect of this tightly controlled structure is to produce an easily memorable unit of teaching, a pocket guide to life in the kingdom of heaven.[15]

d. Matthew's Beatitudes Compared with Luke 6:20-26

While both discourses begin with beatitudes, the two sets are very different:

(i) Luke has four beatitudes against Matthew's eight, corresponding roughly to Matthew's first, fourth, second, and eighth (though the last is in fact much closer to Matt 5:11-12 than to Matt 5:10).
(ii) Luke has four balancing "woes," to which Matthew has no parallel.
(iii) Luke's are cast in the second person, "Happy are *you* . . . ," rather than the third; in this they correspond to Matt 5:11-12 rather than to 5:3-10, which use the more traditional third-person form.[16]
(iv) The "tone" is quite different. Whereas in Matthew the qualities commended are essentially spiritual and ethical, in Luke they are concerned with the situation in which disciples find themselves, particularly in contrast with the security and satisfaction which the rest of society seeks. There is nothing to suggest that "poor," "hungry," "weeping," and "hated" in Luke are to be understood as anything other than literal, and their counterparts in the woes ("rich," "well fed," "laughing," and respected) maintain the same emphasis. Even where the same words occur in the Matthean beatitudes, they are explicitly qualified in a "spiritualizing" direction: "poor *in spirit*," "hungry and thirsty *for righteousness*." Thus while the Matthean beatitudes commend in general terms the qualities which promote the good life of the kingdom of heaven, the Lucan beatitudes and woes speak di-

---

14. I am assuming that Jesus spoke in Aramaic and that the alliteration would not work in that language.

15. Some commentators point out a further structural feature in that if the Beatitudes are regarded as two groups of four (one alliterative, the other not), each group consists of exactly thirty-six words. This observation may help to illustrate the carefully balanced nature of the structure, but I find it difficult to imagine Matthew counting the words (and adding or deleting a word or two to achieve symmetry?). The proposed division into two groups of four is examined and approved by M. A. Powell, *CBQ* 58 (1996) 459-79.

16. The observation that it is only in the second half of the first three of Luke's beatitudes that the second person is explicit is hardly significant, since the second person in the "because" clause determines the person of the first clause; in any case, both the fourth beatitude and the first, second, and fourth woes are all explicitly second person throughout.

rectly to the disciples of their own material and social disadvantage as a result of their following Jesus.[17]

(v) The cumulative effect of these observations is to cast serious doubt on the common assumption that there was a single original set of beatitudes which either Matthew has "spiritualized" or Luke has "radicalized." Jesus may well have used the familiar beatitude form on various occasions in the course of his teaching and for various purposes — as indeed the substantial number of other beatitudes scattered singly through these two gospels indicates. Matthew, aware that the sermon outline which he is using as the basis for this discourse began with a set of beatitudes, may well have used for that purpose a different tradition from that used by Luke. That he was aware of the second-person form (and indeed of the specific content of one of Luke's beatitudes) is clear from his "appendix" in 5:11-12, but he has chosen not to reproduce the distinctively socioeconomic manifesto of the second-person Lucan beatitudes and woes.

e. The OT Background to Matthew's Beatitudes

Not only is the beatitude form familiar from the OT, especially the Psalms, but the content of these beatitudes also echoes familiar OT passages and themes. Isa 61:1-3 tells of good news to the poor (cf. v. 3 — and note that in Matthew "good news" has already been defined in terms of the "kingdom of heaven" in 4:23) and of comforting those who mourn (cf. v. 4).[18] Verse 5 reproduces the LXX wording of Ps 37:11. Verse 8 reflects the "pure in heart" who "seek the face of God" in Ps 24:3-6. More generally, the qualities commended echo closely the character of the *ʿanāwîm* or *ʿanîyîm,* the righteous "meek" or "poor" (the two terms are used interchangeably) who feature so largely in the Psalms and elsewhere as the true people of God whom he will ultimately vindicate against the "proud" and "wicked" who oppress them.[19] In other beatitudes, while there may not be such direct verbal echoes, the teaching reflects that of the OT, especially the Psalms: for those who hunger and thirst for righteousness cf. Ps 42:1-2; Isa 55:1-2; for the reciprocal prin-

17. The view that Matthew's beatitudes, like Luke's, express the literal deprivation of God's people (and particularly "the terrible consequences of Roman power") and its literal reversal, and are not to be "spiritualized," is most consistently expressed by Carter, 130-37; but see also the comments below on Hagner's translation of the first and third beatitudes. In the comments below I shall give reasons for doubting this approach.

18. For the possibility of much more extensive dependence on Isa 61 see Davies and Allison, 1:436-39.

19. R. E. Menninger, *Israel,* 148-51, finds in this OT motif an indication that Matthew regarded the disciples as the true "remnant" of Israel.

ciple of mercy to the merciful cf. Ps 18:25-26; for the peacemakers cf. Ps 34:14. However paradoxical these blessings may seem to those who view things from the world's point of view, the divine perspective of the kingdom of heaven has been well prepared for already in the psalmists' accounts of the qualities and experience of the true people of God. Note also the comparable descriptions of those who may approach God's holy hill in Pss 15 and 24:3-6.

f. The Eschatological Character of the Promises

A distinctive feature of these beatitudes (and of those of Luke 6:20-22) is that they not only list the qualities commended, but they also explain that commendation by a promise appropriate to each quality. The second half of each line is as important as, and indeed is the basis for, the first. All but the first and last are expressed as promises for the future, and the question is often raised whether that future is envisaged as fulfilled within the earthly sphere, or whether it looks to compensation beyond this life. The third beatitude, with its echo of Ps 37:11, raises the issue particularly acutely: "inherit the earth" (or perhaps "the land"; see below) sounds more concrete than a purely heavenly reward. So are these beatitudes speaking of benefits "now in this age" and not only "in the age to come"? That is the language Jesus uses in Mark 10:30, but we shall note that Matt 19:28-29 avoids such an explicit dichotomy, and is worded in such a way that it can be read as speaking only of heavenly reward. On the other hand, the present tense used in vv. 3b and 10b, "it is to them that the kingdom of heaven belongs," warns against a purely futuristic interpretation, and suggests that the simple dichotomy between "now" and "then" may miss the breadth of Matthew's conception of the blessings of the kingdom of heaven. The kingdom of heaven has already arrived (4:17, and see on 3:2), and so these are people who are already under God's beneficent rule. The advantages of being God's people can then be expected to accrue already in this life, even though the full consummation of their blessedness remains for the future. The tension between "now" and "not yet," so familiar from much of the rest of the NT, may appropriately be seen as running also through the promises of Matt 5:3-10.[20]

3 "Poor in spirit" recalls the *ʿănîyîm* or *ʿănāwîm,* the "poor/meek" of

20. One of the more imaginative suggestions of M. D. Goulder, *Midrash,* 252-68, is that the eight beatitudes of 5:3-10 are expounded in reverse order throughout 5:11–7:11. Several links between aspects of 5:3-10 and later parts of the discourse will be noted below, and the link between 5:11-16 and 5:10 is of course transparent, but some of Goulder's other links take considerable ingenuity, notably the proposal that the discussion of lust, divorce, and swearing (5:27-37) is an exposition of the beatitude on the pure in heart, or that the section on criticism (7:1-6) expounds the beatitude on mourners. As Goulder himself remarks on one of these proposed links, "Matthew is never obvious" (p. 259)!

the Psalms (see above, section 5), who, while they do experience material poverty, are also, and primarily, presented as God's faithful people, humbly dependent on his protection in the face of the oppression which they endure from the ungodly rich. For "poor in spirit" cf. also Isa 66:2, "the poor/humble (*'ānî*) and contrite in spirit, who trembles at my word." "Poor" continues to be used in this positive sense in later Jewish literature, particularly the *Psalms of Solomon* and the Qumran literature (where the phrase *'anîyî-rûaḥ*, "the poor in spirit," occurs in a similar sense, 1QM 14:7; cf. *rûaḥ 'anāwâ*, "a spirit of meekness," 1QS 4:3).[21] The bold NEB translation of this verse, "How blest are those who know their need of God," while it may have been too specific (and was abandoned by REB), well reflects this background of thought. "Poverty in spirit" is not speaking of weakness of character ("mean-spiritedness") but rather of a person's relationship with God. It is a positive spiritual orientation,[22] the converse of the arrogant self-confidence which not only rides roughshod over the interests of other people but more importantly causes a person to treat God as irrelevant. To say that it is to such people that the kingdom of heaven belongs means (not, of course, that they themselves hold royal authority but) that they are the ones who gladly accept God's rule and who therefore enjoy the benefits which come to his subjects. The second clause of v. 3, repeated in v. 10 (see above, section 3), thus establishes the general context for the more specific blessings promised in vv. 4-9. This is the "good news of the kingdom" (4:23) announced in 4:17, and poverty of spirit is the product of the repentance which was there declared to be the appropriate response to the coming of God's reign.

4 This verse illustrates the danger of treating the first half of a beatitude in isolation from the second half. To say simply that those who mourn are "happy" (see above, section 2) would clearly be nonsense. Their "happiness" consists in the fact that they will be comforted. The echo of Isa 61:2-3 (following the echo of Isa 61:1 in the "good news to the poor" in v. 3) indicates that the "mourning" envisaged is not primarily, as modern use of the verb might suggest, that of personal bereavement, but rather of those whose situation is wretched. Isa 61:2-3 goes on to contrast their "ashes" with "a garland" and "the oil of gladness," "the mantle of praise instead of a faint spirit."

---

21. D. Flusser, *IEJ* 10 (1960) 1-13, explores a number of other links between Matt 5:3-5 and passages in the Qumran literature. Note especially 1QH 18:14-15, where God's blessings are proclaimed to "the meek (*'anāwîm)*," "those of a "contrite spirit," and "those who mourn."

22. This element seems to be lost in Hagner's decision (87, 91) to translate οἱ πτωχοὶ τῷ πνεύματι simply as "the oppressed." His version rightly recognizes the OT background, but οἱ πτωχοί alone would have sufficed to convey this; the addition of τῷ πνεύματι changes the focus, though Hagner is perhaps right to object to calling this simply a "spiritualizing" of the Lucan beatitude.

Its message is of the restoration of oppressed Israel (cf. Luke 2:25, "the consolation of Israel"). For those who, as God's people, find their current situation intolerable and incomprehensible, there are better times ahead. When they will be is not stated (see above, section 6); experience indicates that while for some there will be a reversal of fortunes in this life, this is not always so. The statement in 9:15 that the wedding guests (the disciples) cannot mourn while the bridegroom (Jesus) is with them speaks of the specific contrast between the period of Jesus' earthly ministry and the time to follow, whereas this beatitude speaks of a general characteristic of God's people: there will be times of rejoicing, but their situation in the world is generally one of disadvantage and therefore of mourning.

5 "Meek," like "poor in spirit," speaks not only of those who are in fact disadvantaged and powerless, but also of those whose attitude is not arrogant and oppressive.[23] The term in itself may properly be understood of their relations with other people; they are those who do not throw their weight about. But "meek," as well as "poor," is used to translate *ʿanāwîm* in the Psalms, where the emphasis is more on their relationship with God. It is the *ʿanāwîm* who, according to Ps 37:11, will inherit the earth (or "land") when the "wicked" who have oppressed them have been cut off. They are further described in Ps 37:7-9 as "those who wait for the LORD" instead of fretting and scheming to right their own wrongs. In echoing this psalm so closely, Jesus clearly intended to promise a reversal of fortunes such as the psalm envisages, but whereas the "inheriting of the land" in the psalm seems to be understood in terms of earthly reversal,[24] the overall tone of these beatitudes does not encourage us to interpret his words here quite so literally (see above, p. 164). Cf. Isa 61:7, where the "poor" and "mourning" of 61:1-3 (see on vv. 3-4) are promised inheritance of the land; if the promises to them in the first two beatitudes apply to the kingdom of heaven, the same should presumably apply to their inheritance. There is a general tendency in the NT to treat OT promises about "the land" as finding fulfillment in nonterritorial ways,[25] and such an orientation seems required here

---

23. As in v. 3, Hagner disagrees, and has translated οἱ πραεῖς with "those who have been humbled"; they are "not persons who are submissive, mild and unassertive, but those who are humble in the sense of being oppressed." Again, the OT background is appropriately recognized, but Matthew's use of πραΰς also to describe the character of Jesus' ministry (11:29; 21:5, which apart from 1 Pet 3:4 are the only other uses of the adjective in the NT; in 1 Pet 3:4 the reference is clearly to behavior, not to status) suggests that he understood it as not only or even primarily a description of social status.

24. Ps 37:25-26 speaks of their blessed life on earth, and v. 29 of their "living in the land forever."

25. This is comprehensively demonstrated in W. D. Davies, *Gospel.* He summarizes on p. 336: "A growing recognition that the Christian faith is, in principle, cut loose

too.[26] The focus is on the principle of reversal of fortunes rather than on a specific "inheritance." For "meek" as a characteristic of Jesus himself see 11:29; 12:15-21; 21:5.[27]

6 *Dikaiosynē,* "righteousness," is the term used in LXX to translate Hebrew *ṣᵉdāqâ,* which is often better translated "deliverance" or "salvation," sometimes even "victory," referring to God's putting right what is wrong. On this basis many interpreters have suggested that *dikaiosynē* here represents not the behavior of the disciple but rather the action of God, understood either as his exercise of "justice" in the world, especially as his intervention on their behalf,[28] or as his saving gift of "justification" in the Pauline sense. NEB's translation, "those who hunger and thirst to see right prevail," represents the former option. But in Matthew's usage *dikaiosynē* is overwhelmingly concerned with right conduct, with living the way God requires (see on 3:15), and in 5:20 *dikaiosynē* will be used emphatically in this sense. 5:10 follows closely on this beatitude, and the "righteousness" which is there the cause of persecution can hardly be understood as divine action. It is thus better understood here not of those who wish to see God's will prevail in the world in general or on their own behalf in particular, but of those who are eager themselves to live as God requires,[29] those who can say, as Jesus himself is recorded as saying in John 4:34, "My food is to do the will of the one who

---

from the land, that the Gospel demanded a breaking out of its territorial chrysalis. . . . Christianity increasingly abandoned the geographical involvement of Judaism." Jesus' "concentration on a loving, universal community suggests that the land itself played a minor part in his mind" (354). With regard to Matt 5:5 Davies (362) suggests that "it is necessary to divorce Matt. 5:5 from its meaning in Ps. 37:11" so that "for Matthew 'inheriting the land' is synonymous with entering the Kingdom and that this Kingdom transcends all geographic dimensions and is spiritualized." B. Charette, *Recompense,* 85-88, seems to agree completely with Davies' interpretation, but then, following Brueggemann, adds a comment that "the image of land not simply be absorbed into that of kingdom"; his desire to retain in some sense "its original, historical referent" is not clearly explained. In his discussion of 5:12 (ibid., 88-91) Charette suggests that the land is again in view, but he is unable to find any earthly element to the "reward in heaven" in that saying.

26. Jesus' understanding of Ps 37:11 is thus in contrast to that of the writer of the Qumran commentary on Ps 37, who takes the parallel v. 22 as referring to "the congregation of the poor" who will "possess the high mountain of Israel and delight in his sanctuary" (4Q171 3:10-11); see D. Flusser, *IEJ* 10 (1960) 7-9.

27. D. C. Allison, *Moses,* 180-82, considers, but is ultimately unpersuaded by, the suggestion that this beatitude alludes to the "meek" Moses (Num 12:3) who nonetheless was denied his inheritance of the land.

28. See, e.g., J. P. Meier, *Law,* 77-78, for the proposal that in 5:6 and 6:33 δικαιοσύνη is used in a different sense from its ethical use in 5:10, 20: 6:1, and means God's justice exerted on behalf of his people. Similarly Gundry, 70.

29. So especially B. Przybylski, *Righteousness,* 96-98.

167

sent me." The metaphor of hunger and thirst here recalls 4:4, the idea of living not on physical food but on every word that comes from God. It is a matter of priorities. Such hunger and thirst will be fully satisfied: *chortazomai,* a graphic word used also for fattening animals, implies being well filled, as in 14:20, colloquially being "stuffed."[30]

7 For "mercy" as God's requirement cf. 9:13; 12:7; 23:23. The principle of reciprocity embodied here comes to fuller expression elsewhere in Matthew. In connection specifically with mercy and forgiveness see 6:14-15 and its "commentary" in 18:21-35. It is expressed more generally in the "measure for measure" epigram of 7:2, while 7:1-5 fills out the principle with regard to the specific issue of criticism. The golden rule of 7:12 establishes the same principle at the heart of Jesus' ethic. "Mercy" is closely linked with forgiveness, but is broader here than just the forgiveness of specific offenses: it is a generous attitude which is willing to see things from the other's point of view and is not quick to take offense or to gloat over others' shortcomings (the prime characteristic of love according to 1 Cor 13:4-7). Mercy sets aside society's assumption that it is honorable to demand revenge. The passive verb here (as in vv. 4b, 6b, and 9b) speaks primarily not of how other people will respond to the merciful person, but of how God will deal with those who live by his standards.

8 Again the OT passage which this beatitude echoes fills out its meaning. Those who are qualified to "ascend the hill of the LORD" and "stand in his holy place" are characterized by "clean hands and a pure heart," which is then defined in terms of truthfulness and of an active "seeking" for God (Ps 24:3-6). The meaning is thus not far from that of v. 6, with its emphasis on a longing to live the life God requires. In the context of first-century Judaism, with its strong emphasis on ritual "purity," the phrase "pure in heart" might also be understood to imply a contrast with the meticulous preservation of outward purity which will be condemned in 23:25-28 as having missed the point of godliness;[31] but no such connotation is likely in Ps. 24, on which this beatitude is based. The vision of God which is the goal of the pure in heart (Ps 24:6; cf. Pss 11:7; 17:15; 27:5; 42:2 for this aspiration), and which is here promised to them, is sometimes expressed in the OT in terms of an actual "seeing" (Exod 24:10; Isa 6:1), though these are clearly marked out as exceptional. More often the invisibility of God is stressed (Exod 33:18-23), and

30. H. D. Betz, *Sermon,* 132, understands the metaphor as pointing to "the eschatological banquet" which is to "occur after the faithful enter through the gate into heaven (7:13-14)." But we may question whether this eschatological hope exhausts the significance of the promise, or whether there may also be a degree of satisfaction even in this life.

31. Cf. also the debate on purity in 15:1-20, where it is the state of the heart (vv. 8, 18-19) which matters rather than ritual observance.

this is strongly reinforced in the NT (John 1:18; 1 Tim 1:17; 6:16). There may be visionary experiences in this world which include "seeing" God, as for John on Patmos, but "seeing God's face" is a privilege reserved for the new Jerusalem (Rev 22:4; cf. 1 Cor 13:12; 1 John 3:2). Meanwhile, it is the "angels" of God's people, not those people themselves, who see his face in heaven (18:10; see further discussion there). Here on earth the people of God may find strength "as if seeing him who is invisible" (Heb 11:27), but such "seeing" remains only a foretaste of the true vision of God in heaven.

9 It is a characteristic of God's true people to "seek peace and pursue it" (Ps 34:14). This beatitude goes beyond a merely peaceful disposition to an active attempt to "make" peace, perhaps by seeking reconciliation with one's own enemies, but also more generally by bringing together those who are estranged from one another. Such costly "peacemaking," which involves overcoming the natural desire for advantage and/or retribution, will be illustrated in the extraordinary demands of 5:39-42 which overturn the natural human principle of the *lex talionis.* (We will be reminded in 10:34, however, that not all conflict can or should be avoided; the issue there is not interpersonal relationships but faithfulness to God's cause in the face of opposition.) While the focus here is probably primarily on personal ethics, the principle of peacemaking has further implications. H. D. Betz (*Sermon,* 140) well comments that the discourse "recognizes war, persecution and injustice as part of the evil world. . . . Peacemaking is a means of involvement in the human predicament of warlike conditions" which "implies assuming responsibility against all the odds, risking peacemaking out of a situation of powerlessness, and demonstrating the conviction that in the end God's kingdom will prevail." Peacemakers "will be called God's children" (the passive probably implies that God himself will recognize them as his true children) on the basis that God's children reflect God's character (5:44-45), and God is the ultimate peacemaker. The Semitic idiom "sons of . . ."[32] often indicates those who share a certain character or status; for varied examples in Matthew see 8:12, "sons of the kingdom"; 9:15, "sons of the wedding hall"; 13:38, "sons of the evil one"; 23:31, "sons of those who killed the prophets." Here and in 5:45 "sons of God" similarly expresses the idea of sharing God's character, but a more relational sense is probably also implied since, while Matthew generally reserves "son of God" language for Jesus and does not elsewhere reflect the Pauline language of "becoming sons of God" as a term for salvation (e.g., Rom 8:14-17), he will frequently record Jesus as speaking to his disciples of "your Father in heaven" (5:16, 45, 48, etc.).

10 The pursuit of "righteousness" (v. 6) can arouse opposition from

---

32. The masculine is of course generic, hence my translation "children" to avoid a gender specificity which is inappropriate in modern usage.

those whose interests or self-respect may be threatened by it. Already in the commendation of the merciful and the peacemakers these beatitudes have marked out the true disciple not as a hermit engaged in the solitary pursuit of holiness but as one engaged in society, and such engagement has its cost. As the following verses will spell out more fully, to live as subjects of the kingdom of heaven is to be set over against the rest of society which does not share its values, and the result may be — indeed, the uncompromising wording of this beatitude suggests that it *will* be — persecution. Cf. 1 Pet 3:14, which echoes this beatitude, and for the likelihood of persecution for God's people cf. in this gospel 10:16-39; 22:6; 23:29-36; 24:9-13.[33] In vv. 11-12 the further element of an explicit allegiance to Jesus himself will be added to the cause of persecution, but already in the light of 3:15 and 5:6 "righteousness" sums up his distinctive mission and ethic.[34] For the persecution of those who "know righteousness" cf. Isa 51:7.

3. The Distinctiveness of the Disciples (5:11-16)

11 *"Happy are you when people insult you and persecute you and make all sorts of [false]¹ accusations against you because of me;* 12 *be glad and celebrate, because you have a great reward in heaven; remember, that was how they persecuted the prophets who came before you.*

13 *"You are the salt of the earth. If salt itself becomes tasteless,² what else is there to salt it with? It is no good for anything any more except to be thrown out and trampled under people's feet.*

14 *"You are the light of the world. A town built on top of a hill cannot be hidden.* 15 *Nor do people light a lamp only to put it under a bowl; they put it on a lampstand so that it gives light to everyone in*

---

33. The theme of the deliberate persecution of the "righteous poor man" by the ungodly is memorably expressed in Wis 2:10-20.

34. For the ethical sense of δικαιοσύνη here see B. Przybylski, *Righteousness,* 98.

1. The overwhelming majority of MSS include ψευδόμενοι, "lying," but its absence in D, several OL MSS, and the Sinaitic Syriac, as well as in a large number of early patristic citations, is striking. It is much easier to understand its insertion than its deliberate omission (since it is to be hoped that Christians would not be subject to *true* allegations of misconduct and certainly would have no cause to rejoice over them), and there is no obvious reason why it should have been lost accidentally. But such an "improving" insertion would have had to be made very early and very widely to be so well represented in the tradition. The reading must remain uncertain. See M. W. Holmes, *NTS* 32 (1986) 283-86, in support of the longer reading.

2. The context requires that μωραίνομαι (normally "to become foolish") here means to lose the distinctive character of salt, but neither Greek nor English can adequately represent the probable Aramaic pun involved (see comments).

the house. 16 *In the same way your light must shine in front of other people, so that they can see the good you do and give glory to your Father in heaven.*

I have pointed out above (p. 161, n. 13) that the so-called "ninth beatitude" (vv. 11-12) is in fact a repetition and expansion of v. 10, and stands from a literary point of view outside the tightly structured unit of eight beatitudes. It lacks the epigrammatic conciseness of vv. 3-10, nor does it repeat their regular formula "for it is they / to them. . . ." Moreover, its change to a second-person form links it directly with the verses that follow rather than with vv. 3-10. Like vv. 13-16, vv. 11-12 speak of the sharp contrast between the disciples (whose "good life" has been spelled out in the third person in vv. 3-10) and other people around them. I therefore think it more appropriate, despite the repetition of the opening *makarioi,* to treat the "ninth beatitude" not as a part of the Beatitudes as such but as the linking introduction to this following section which comments on the effect of living the good life on the rest of society.

At this point, then, the discourse turns from a general statement about the good life to a specific address to the disciples gathered around Jesus on the hillside. Because they have committed themselves to follow Jesus and so to adopt the new values of the kingdom of heaven, they are now going to stand out as different from other people. The address is in the second-person plural not only because more than one person is being addressed, but because it is the corporate impact of the disciple community, as an alternative society, which is here in view. The hilltop town of v. 14 is a symbol not of a conspicuous individual but of the collective impact of a whole community. Modern Western individualism is such that we easily think of the light of the world as a variety of little candles shining, "you in your small corner, and I in mine," but it is the collective light of a whole community which draws the attention of the watching world.[3]

The statement about persecution and the two (or three, if the town on the hill is seen as separate; see below) metaphors that follow embody two complementary features of the distinctiveness of the disciple community. On the one hand, they are different from those around them. Salt has its effect only because, and for as long as, it has a distinctive saltiness. Light is effec-

---

3. The intuitively corporate understanding of these verses which is natural to a non-Western culture is movingly expressed in the words of Marcelino, a Nicaraguan peasant, quoted by A. Kreider in *Third Way* 11/10 (October 1988) 14: "A lit-up city that's on top of a hill can be seen from far away, as we can see the lights of San Miguelito from very far away when we're rowing at night on the lake. A city is a great union of people, and as there are a lot of houses together we see a lot of light. And that's the way our community will be. It will be seen lighted from far away, if it is united by love. . . ."

tive because of its contrast with surrounding darkness. It is this visible distinctiveness which arouses the hostility of others and leads to the slander and persecution which the "ninth beatitude" celebrates. But, on the other hand, it is only those who are involved with other people who will be seen to be different and so attract persecution. Salt is of no use as long as it stays in the salt cellar. Light is of no use under a bowl. It is the town conspicuously sited on the hill which people notice. And the outcome of distinctive discipleship is intended to be that other people will notice and, though sometimes they may respond with cynicism and persecution, ultimately the light will have its effect and they will recognize and acknowledge the goodness of the God who is its source. Disciples, therefore, must be both distinctive and involved. Neither the indistinguishably assimilated nor the inaccessible hermit will fulfill the mandate of these challenging verses.

11 Verses 11-12 are closely parallel in sense and structure to the expansive fourth beatitude of Luke 6:22-23, though Matthew's wording is less graphic. Two of his verbs relate to verbal attack ("insult," "make [false] accusations"), though the outcome of the accusations might well be more than verbal. "Persecute" (the same verb as in v. 10) is broader, and would also cover physical or economic ill-treatment. A significant new note in comparison with v. 10 is that the cause of persecution is not simply "righteousness," the distinctive lifestyle of the disciples, but more specifically "because of me," a phrase which makes it clear that this discourse is not just a call to moral conduct but is grounded in the unique authority and radical demands of Jesus himself. The theme of this verse is expanded in 1 Pet 2:12; 3:13-17; 4:3-5, 13-16, where it is clear that first-century disciples in a non-Christian environment were subject to persecution not only because of their distinctive behavior but also more specifically "as a Christian," "sharing Christ's sufferings"; 1 Peter repeatedly emphasizes the possibility of being abused for good conduct.

12 The call to be glad about persecution (1 Pet 4:13 again picks up the thought; cf. also 1 Pet 1:6) sounds paradoxical, particularly in the exuberant terms Matthew uses. But as with the beatitude concerning those who mourn, the blessing is not in the suffering in itself but in its promised outcome. The beatitudes of vv. 3-10 have pronounced people happy "because" they are the ones to whom good things are promised, and here again there is a "because." The concept of a reward to compensate for the disadvantages of the disciples now becomes explicit. Unlike many modern Christians, Matthew is not coy about the "reward" that awaits those who are faithful to their calling.[4] He will use the word again in 5:46; 6:1, 2, 5, 16; 10:41, 42, and the concept of a heavenly recompense is built into several of his parables (nota-

---

4. See my *Matthew: Evangelist*, 268-70.

bly 20:1-15; 24:45-47; 25:20-23) as well as more broadly into the teaching of Jesus (6:4, 6, 18; 19:27-29; 25:34-40), though the parable of 20:1-15 will warn us against a crude "quid pro quo" concept of repayment which can be earned; God's "reward" is far more generous than that.[5] The source of the disciples' celebration is the recognition that the good which is promised to them far outweighs the bad that they may experience now. What form the "great reward"[6] will take is not spelled out here, beyond the fact that it is "in heaven," and that phrase is probably best understood not of a location so much as of a relationship with God (note Matthew's use of "kingdom of heaven" where others use "kingdom of God"). For the eschatological orientation of the Beatitudes, see above, introduction to 5:3-10, section 6.

The persecution of the prophets was an established feature of Jewish folk-memory, stated in general terms in 2 Chr 36:16 and Neh 9:26 and amply illustrated within the OT itself, notably in the case of Jeremiah (Jer 20:10; 26:10-19; 36–38, etc.) and his contemporaries (Jer 26:20-23; cf. 1 Kgs 18:4; 19:1-3; Amos 7:10-12). It was further developed in postbiblical traditions such as those alluded to in Heb 11:36-38.[7] Jesus will incorporate the theme in his parable of the vineyard (21:34-36; cf. 22:6) and develop it more fully in 23:29-36 (cf. also 13:57; 17:12). Those who have spoken out for God have always been liable to the violent reprisals of the ungodly. In the light of that heritage, to be persecuted for the sake of Jesus is a badge of honor. The phrase "the prophets who came before you" perhaps suggests that Jesus' disciples are now the prophetic voice on earth (cf. 10:41; 23:34).[8]

13   The call to accept persecution with joy is now followed in vv. 13-16 by a series of images which explain why it is important that disciples should both be different and be seen to be different. Sir 39:26 lists salt as one of the essentials for human life; cf. *Sop.* 15:8, "The world cannot endure without salt." Disciples are no less essential to the well-being of "the earth," which here refers to human life in general. For other metaphorical uses of

5. The same implication is found in the "hundredfold" of 19:29 and in the formula of 25:21, 23, "trustworthy over *a few* things; I will put you in charge of *many.*"

6. B. Charette, *Recompense,* 26-27, 90, sees the phrase as an allusion to LXX Gen 15:1, which he interprets as part of the Genesis theme of the promise of land to the patriarchs, and so as taking up the promise of "inheriting the land" in v. 5. The fact that this reward is explictly "in heaven" thus casts doubt on Charette's attempt to retain an earthly dimension to the promise in v. 5.

7. For some references in Jewish tradition and in the NT see Davies and Allison, 1:465.

8. The statement of W. D. Davies, *Setting,* 289-90, that here "the two groups emerge as Christians and Jews" reads too much into the text. The persecution of the prophets was a natural illustration for a Jewish teacher to take, but it does not in itself restrict the reference of vv. 11-12 to persecution of Christians *by Jews.*

salt in the NT cf. Mark 9:50; Col 4:6; in both cases it symbolizes a beneficial influence on human relationships, but the precise nature of the symbolism is not certain. The two most significant uses of salt in the ancient world
were for flavoring and for the preservation of food,[9] and either or both of
those uses would provide an appropriate sense here: the disciples are to provide flavor to the world they live in (perhaps with the thought of salt as wisdom, as in Col 4:6 and in some rabbinic sayings), and/or they are to help to
prevent its corruption. The two ideas are not incompatible; disciples are to
make the world a better place.[10] "The earth" (like "the world" in v. 14) thus
represents the sphere of their influence and is not itself part of the metaphor.[11] A further nuance may be found in the use of salt in the OT in relation
to the covenant; on this basis it has been suggested that there is a more specifically Israelite focus, in that "the disciples are seen as in prophetic succession, and thus like their OT counterparts as covenant witnesses and guarantors to their age."[12]

Unsalty salt is a contradiction in terms ("like water losing its wet-
ness"; Betz); if it is not salty, it is not salt. But salt as used in the ancient
world was seldom pure sodium chloride. The "salt" collected around the
Dead Sea[13] contained a mixture of other minerals,[14] and it is possible to

9. See N. Hillyer in *NIDNTT* 3:443-45 for the background. Davies and Allison,
1:472-73, list eleven possible uses or significances of salt.

10. Schweizer, 101, suggests a further nuance in that the pinch of salt is small and
insignificant but yet has great effect. The idea fits well with the poor and despised status
of the disciples as seen in the Beatitudes, but the wording here does not indicate it; the
metaphorical use of salt elsewhere focuses on its value and indispensability rather than on
its size.

11. It is sometimes suggested (e.g., Gundry, 75 and n. 56) that salt might be used
to improve the fertility of the soil, so that it is here part of the metaphor: "you are salt for
the soil." N. Hillyer, *NIDNTT* 3:444, refers to such a belief in Cato, Virgil, and Pliny, but
without giving references, and Luke 14:35 ("useful . . . for the soil") perhaps supports the
idea. M. D. Goulder, *Midrash,* 282, claims that "the use of salt in this way in Palestine is
unevidenced" but nevertheless states (again without references) that it represents "Greek
farming practice." According to E. P. Deatrick, *BA* 25 (1962) 44-45, "agricultural literature abounds in references to the use of salt as a fertilizer." When salt is applied to the
ground in the OT, however, it renders it barren rather than fertile (Deut 29:23; Judg 9:45;
Ps 107:34; Jer 17:6). The eleven possible uses or symbolic meanings of salt listed by
Davies and Allison do not include the idea of fertilization. Throwing this salt literally on
the earth in the second part of the verse symbolizes its failure, not its proper role.

12. W. J. Dumbrell, *NovT* 23 (1981) 11-13.

13. W. D. Davies, *Setting,* 250, exploits this location to suggest tentatively that in
choosing the metaphor of salt Jesus is deliberately contrasting his disciples with the Dead
Sea community of Qumran. The common use and importance of salt make any such specific connotation unlikely.

14. Luz, 1:250, n. 30, gives a chemical analysis of Dead Sea water.

imagine the true salt content being washed out, leaving a useless residue.[15] In any case, Jesus is not teaching chemistry, and the ludicrous imagery of trying to "salt" that which should itself be the source of saltiness is a powerful indictment of disciples who have lost their distinctiveness and so no longer have anything to contribute to society. The verb which I have translated "becomes tasteless" more literally means "becomes foolish." The apparently inappropriate verb points to the metaphorical role of the salt here, to symbolize the wholesome flavor of wisdom which disciples are to contribute. We use "taste" to speak of an aesthetic rather than an intellectual quality, but "tasteless" perhaps goes some way toward catching what may have been a more obvious double entendre in Hebrew and Aramaic, where the verb *tāpēl* can mean both to be tasteless and to be foolish.[16] The trampling of the tasteless "salt" does not have to imply that it then finds a useful role as surfacing for a path; it is simply thrown out into the street as refuse.[17]

14   We have already met the metaphor of light and darkness in the Isaiah quotation in 4:16, where the light symbolized the new hope which arose through Jesus' preaching of the coming of God's reign. Where there is light people can find their way and everything is clear; where there is darkness they stumble and are lost; the imagery is strongly developed especially in the Fourth Gospel, where it is Jesus himself who is "the light of the world" (John 8:12; cf. 1:4-5, 9). Here the light which Jesus brings is also provided by his disciples, who will soon be commissioned to share in his ministry of proclamation and deliverance. Cf. the mission of God's servant to be "a light to the nations" (Isa 42:6; 49:6). The world needs that light, and it is through the disciples that it must be made visible. The world (*kosmos;* not the "earth," *gē,* as in v. 13)[18] again refers to the world of people, as the application in v. 16 makes clear; cf. the call to Christians to shine in the *kosmos* (Phil 2:15).

15. See J. Jeremias, *Parables,* 168-69; E. P. Deatrick, *BA* 25 (1962) 41-44. Contrast Schweizer, 102, who declares such "explanations" to be as absurd as trying to explain how a camel can go through the eye of a needle. Of course it can't — that's the point! That seems to be the intention of the intriguing saying attributed to R. Joshua ben Hananiah (c. A.D. 90) in *b. Bek.* 8b comparing the resalting of unsalted salt to the afterbirth of a mule (something impossible). Was R. Joshua commenting directly on Jesus' saying?

16. *M. Soṭah* 9:15 lists as one of the preludes to the coming of the Messiah that "the wisdom of the scribes shall become insipid."

17. M. D. Goulder, *Midrash,* 255, takes the "garden path" as the cultural equivalent to our "garbage can."

18. The context does not suggest that either γῆ or κόσμος is intended to raise the issue of taking the gospel to Gentiles as well as to Jews, even though in Matthew's day both might have been used that way. Still less do the terms require the inference drawn by W. D. Davies, *Setting,* 249, that Matthew is here drawing a contrast "between Jesus' understanding of the mission of the New Israel and that of the Scribes and Pharisees of theirs."

The metaphor of light, and of the need for it to be where it can be seen, will be further developed in vv. 15-16, but first the apparently separate metaphor of the hilltop town[19] intrudes. It is in itself another effective metaphor for visibility,[20] but its presence in the middle of the sayings about light is surprising. See, however, the quotation from "Marcelino" on p. 171, n. 3 above: the combined impact of the many lights which make up a town at night illustrates more appropriately than the single lamp of v. 15 the corporate effect of the disciple community on the surrounding darkness.

15 A domestic lamp was a shallow bowl of oil with a wick. It would normally be stationary, placed on a fixed lampstand, rather than mobile like the "torches" of 25:1. The "bowl" is literally a grain measure holding about nine liters, probably made of earthenware or basketwork. While it may be true that a lamp placed under such a receptacle would soon go out for lack of oxygen,[21] the point seems to be rather the absurdity of hiding a lamp when its whole raison d'être is to be visible.[22] Similar sayings of Jesus are found in Mark 4:21 (par. Luke 8:16, and cf. *Gos. Thom.* 33) and Luke 11:33. In the former the lamp illustrates the revelation which comes through the preaching of the kingdom of God, while in the latter the saying is linked with Luke's parallel to Matt 6:22-23, which is concerned with inward "light." The metaphor thus suited a variety of applications, but here the context indicates that it is about the effect which the life of disciples must have on those around them. It thus takes for granted that the "job description" of a disciple is not fulfilled by private personal holiness, but includes the witness of public exposure.[23]

---

19. The contention of G. von Rad, *The Problem of the Hexateuch,* 232-42, adopted with enthusiasm by J. Jeremias, *Theology,* 106, 168-69, 230, 246 (cf. K. M. Campbell, *SJT* 31 [1978] 335-63; T. L. Donaldson, *Jesus* 116-18), that the reference is specifically to Zion, "the eschatological city of God," while it is based on a significant prophetic theme of the exaltation of Jerusalem, lacks any purchase in the text here, and would intrude quite inappropriately into the quite general tone of the illustrations in vv. 13-15. It is also rendered improbable by the lack of any definite article, as well as by the Galilean setting of the saying (*pace* H. D. Betz, *Sermon,* 161-62, who argues that the sermon originated from Jerusalem, even though it only once mentions the city, 5:35). πόλις does not demand a large settlement; it is used even for Nazareth (2:23)! Modern tourist guides point to the hilltop town of Sefat, clearly visible from the Lake of Galilee, but the proverbial saying requires no specific identification.

20. This simple metaphor is developed in a new direction by *Gos. Thom.* 32: "A city built on a high mountain and fortified cannot fall nor can it be hidden."

21. J. Jeremias, *Parables,* 120-21, sees this as the main point: "They do not light a lamp in order to put it out again immediately."

22. The use of empty jars as a temporary cover for torches (not lamps) by Gideon's men (Judg 7:16-20) is not comparable to the domestic scene envisaged here.

23. W. D. Davies, *Setting,* 250, suggests that Jesus is contrasting his disciples with the Qumran sect, who called themselves "the sons of light" but "hid their light under

16 The metaphor of v. 15 is now explained more prosaically, with the "light" shed by disciples interpreted as the good that they do. The phrase "good deeds" conveys the qualities set out in the Beatitudes, and especially the "righteousness" of life which is to be characteristic of disciples (cf. vv. 6, 10, 20); the phrase and the concept are echoed in 1 Pet 2:11-12. It is only as this distinctive lifestyle is visible to others that it can have its desired effect. But that effect is also now spelled out not as the improvement and enlightenment of society as such, but rather as the glorifying of God by those outside the disciple community. The subject of this discourse, and the aim of the discipleship which it promotes, is not so much the betterment of life on earth as the implementation of the reign of God. The goal of disciples' witness is not that others emulate their way of life, or applaud their probity, but that they recognize the source of their distinctive lifestyle in "your Father in heaven." This phrase, which is distinctive of Matthew's gospel and will be repeated throughout the discourse (5:45, 48; 6:1, 9, 14, 26, 32; 7:11; cf. "your Father" also in 6:4, 6, 8, 15, 18), reflects not a universal concept of the fatherhood of God toward all his human creatures but the distinctive relationship which exists between God and those who, through their response to Jesus' message, have become subjects of his kingdom. The metaphor of father, superimposed on that of king, imparts a new depth and richness to the concept of discipleship already set out in the beatitudes of 5:3-10.

There is a *prima facie* discrepancy between this verse and the principle of 6:1, amplified in 6:2-6, 16-18, that religious observance should not be undertaken "in front of other people so that they will notice you." But the discrepancy is only on the surface: the ostentatious performance of religious acts *in order to* win approbation is not at all the same thing as a life of conspicuous goodness lived in the public arena so that people cannot help being impressed. The effect (and the intention) of the former is a reputation for piety; the result of the latter is the glory of God. See further on 6:1.

4. Fulfilling the Law (5:17-48)

While we shall subdivide this section of the discourse for the purpose of commentary, it is important to recognize its coherence as a concentrated section of teaching on a single theme, the fulfillment of the law. It is the most extensive discussion of this issue anywhere in the gospel tradition, and raises important questions about Jesus' teaching on how his disciples are to do the

---

a bushel at Qumran and in enclosed communities." Even if Davies' suggestion that "salt" also alluded to the Dead Sea sect is doubted (see above, n. 63), this contrast would be a valid one, though it is questionable how far either Jesus' hearers or Matthew's readers would be familiar with the special ethos of the Qumran sect or with their terminology.

will of God. It raises acutely the issue of Jesus' messianic authority in relation to the existing authority of the Torah and of its authorized interpreters at
the time, and illustrates the tensions which were to lead to the ultimate decision of the Jewish leadership that Jesus was a dangerous influence who must
be eliminated. But its tone is not primarily polemical or negative. It sets out
by means of a series of graphic examples the sort of obedience to the will of
God to which the OT law could only begin to point the way. This radical approach to discipleship goes far beyond the best righteousness that the scribes
and Pharisees could envisage (5:20); its goal is nothing less than sharing the
perfection of God himself (5:48).

The apparently abrupt change of subject in v. 17 is to be understood in
the light of the concept of a new people of God which has emerged throughout the first part of the discourse. The question of the continuity of this people with the old Israel and its institutions will be a recurrent theme throughout the gospel, and the role of the OT law is a central aspect of that question.[1]
Here is a presentation of the law of the new covenant, as both in continuity
and in contrast with the OT law.[2]

These verses may be conveniently divided into three main sections:

5:17-20   Fulfilling the law: general principles
5:21-47   Fulfilling the law: six examples
5:48   Fulfilling the law: summary (to be reinforced later by a
          further summary of the law and the prophets in 7:12).

a. Fulfilling the Law: General Principles (5:17-20)

17 *"Do not suppose that I came to abolish the law or the prophets;
I did not come to abolish them but to fulfill them.* 18 *I tell you truly: until heaven and earth pass away, not one small letter or a single stroke
of the pen[3] will pass away from the law until everything has taken
place.* 19 *So anyone who sets aside one of these smallest command-*

1. P. Foster, *Community,* 161-64, notes the difficulty commentators have in finding a meaningful link between vv. 3-16 and vv. 17ff., and develops the suggestion of
Davies and Allison, 1:481, that these verses aim to answer the objection of other Jews that
this new messianic community was in effect rejecting the Torah; cf. also ibid., 182-83.

2. See the stimulating study by W. J. Dumbrell, *NovT* 23 (1981) 1-21.

3. Ἰῶτα represents *yôd,* the smallest letter of the Hebrew alphabet, written above
the line and sometimes little more than a dash; it was sometimes optional in spelling.
κεραία ("horn") perhaps denotes the small projection (like the crossing of our letter *t*)
which distinguishes some Hebrew letters from others of similar shape, but may refer to
some other small feature of writing; G. Schwarz, *ZNW* 66 (1975) 268-69, argues that it refers to the letter *waw,* which was similarly inconspicuous and sometimes optional.

In the light of the comment just made about the tension between vv. 19 and 20, there is a *prima facie* case to be made that Matthew is conscious of two opposite tendencies with which he is concerned, on the one hand a tendency to claim, in line with Paul's "freedom from the law" teaching, that the OT laws no longer matter and can be abandoned,[9] and on the other hand a tendency to emulate the scribes and the Pharisees in careful literal observance of the law as if nothing had changed with the coming of the Messiah. The former of these tendencies is confronted in vv. 17-19, the latter in v. 20 (illustrated by the examples which follow in vv. 21-47). It is likely that the material Matthew has brought together for this two-pronged attack is derived from teaching which Jesus gave on different occasions and in relation to different groups. What we must investigate is whether in bringing these contrasting strands of teaching together in this discourse he has produced an incompatible mixture, or whether there is a consistent principle with regard to Jesus and the law which underlies the correctives which he offers to the two opposite extremes. The key to this issue must be what is meant by Jesus "fulfilling" the law and the prophets.

17   For "the law and the prophets" (the "or" here results from the negative form of the sentence) as a way of referring to what we now call the OT see 7:12; 22:40; Acts 24:14; 28:23; Rom 3:21; the third element in the Hebrew scriptures, the "writings," does not need to be specifically included.[10] The repetition of the phrase in 7:12 marks the end of the central teaching of the discourse, though the teaching between 6:1 and 7:11 is not explicitly formulated in relation to the OT.

"Do not suppose . . ." might be no more than a teaching device to draw attention to Jesus' positive statement by first setting out its opposite (cf. 10:34), but it is not unlikely that there were in fact some who did suppose that Jesus was against the law and the prophets.[11] His disagreements with the scribes over the correct way to observe the law (notably with regard to the sabbath; see 12:1-14) would easily have given them the impression that he

9. G. Barth, *Tradition,* 159-64, summarizes his view that Matthew was confronted by the "antinomian" tendency of a group of Hellenistic libertines. J. Zumstein, *Condition,* 199-200, further defines the "heresy" Matthew confronted as a charismatic strand of Christianity which focused on the risen Lord even to the virtual exclusion of Jesus' own earthly teaching, while the OT law had no further interest for them. Most recent interpreters are more reluctant to trace such specific "opponents." W. D. Davies, *Setting,* 334-36, discusses and dismisses the view that these verses are "anti-Pauline."

10. Cf. Luke 24:27 with 24:44; for Jewish uses of "law and prophets" in this way cf. 2 Macc 15:9; 4 Macc 18:11, the latter of which introduces a list of scriptural themes including some from Daniel, Psalms, and Proverbs; see also the prologue to Sirach.

11. H. D. Betz, *Sermon,* 174-76, argues that what is being opposed is a "false saying of Jesus" which was actually in circulation when the sermon was composed.

sat light to the authority of the law itself; the same charge persisted with regard to his followers (Acts 6:11, 13-14; 21:28). By the time Matthew was writing, the "freedom from the law" message of some of Christianity's leading teachers would have strengthened this impression.[12] Jesus, it seemed, had set himself up against the written word of God. The issue is not simply an accusation of failing to keep the law in practice, but of aiming to "abolish" scriptural authority. The verb *katalyō* is used of dismantling and destroying a building or institution (24:2; 26:61; 27:40); with reference to an authoritative text it means to declare that it is no longer valid, to repeal or annul.[13] The issue is thus not Jesus' personal practice as such, but his attitude to the authority of the law and the prophets.

It is therefore improbable that when he contrasts "abolish" with "fulfill" he is speaking simply about obeying the requirements of the law and the prophets.[14] "Fulfill" (rather than "obey," "do," or "keep") would not be the natural way to say that, and such a sense would not answer the charge of aiming to "abolish." In Matthew's gospel the verb *plēroō,* "fulfill," plays a prominent role, most notably in its ten occurrences in the formula quotations (see on 1:22 and above, pp. 11-14) where it denotes the coming into being of that to which Scripture pointed forward (whether by direct prediction or understood typologically). The same sense appears in 26:54, 56, where Jesus' suffering is seen as "fulfilling the Scriptures," and in 13:14, where a compound form of the same verb *(anaplēroō)* again speaks of an OT prophecy coming true in contemporary experience. In 3:15 to "fulfill all righteousness" appears to denote the action which will bring about God's redemptive purpose through Jesus (see discussion there). Apart from a single non-metaphorical use (of "filling up" a net, 13:48), its only other use in Matthew is in 23:32 of the hostile actions of the scribes and Pharisees "filling up the measure" of their ancestors, where again the sense of reaching a destined conclusion seems to be dominant. In the light of Matthew's use of this verb elsewhere, and the evident importance it has for his understanding of the relation between the authoritative words of the OT and their contemporary outworking, the sense here is not likely to be concerned either with Jesus' actions in relation to the law or even his teaching about it, but rather the way in which he "fulfills" the pattern laid down in the law and the prophets. It is important to

12. For continuing Jewish attack on Christianity as a "lawless" movement in the early Christian centuries, and the relevance of Matt 5:17 to this apologetic debate, see G. N. Stanton, *Gospel,* 244-46 (= *NTS* 31 [1985] 383-84). Cf. Keener, 176-77, especially n. 46.

13. See P. Foster, *Community,* 184-85, for the meaning of the verb in this context.

14. The classic study by C. F. D. Moule, *NTS* 14 (1967/8) 293-320, remains of value in this discussion. On pp. 313-17 he argues that in Matt 5:17 πληροῦν "properly implies more than mere implementation or discharge."

note that this verse does not speak of Jesus "fulfilling the law," but rather of his "fulfilling the law and the prophets." His fulfilling of the prophets is amply illustrated in the formula-quotations: his life and ministry has brought that to which they pointed forward. Is it possible to understand his fulfilling of the law in the same light?

There is an intriguing little saying of Jesus recorded in 11:13 which throws light on this issue. In speaking of the pivotal role of John the Baptist as the point at which the time of fulfillment has dawned, Jesus is recorded as commenting that "All the prophets and the law prophesied until John." The law is thus linked with the prophets as looking forward to a time of fulfillment which has now arrived.[15] The Torah, then, is not God's last word to his people, but is in a sense provisional, looking forward to a time of fulfillment through the Messiah.[16]

In the light of that concept, and of the general sense of "fulfill" in Matthew, we might then paraphrase Jesus' words here as follows: "Far from wanting to set aside the law and the prophets, it is my role to bring into being that to which they have pointed forward, to carry them into a new era of fulfillment." On this understanding the authority of the law and the prophets is not abolished. They remain the authoritative word of God. But their role will no longer be the same, now that what they pointed forward to has come, and it will be for Jesus' followers to discern in the light of his teaching and practice what is now the right way to apply those texts in the new situation which his coming has created. From now on it will be the authoritative teaching of Jesus which must govern his disciples' understanding and practical application of the law. Verses 21-48 will go on to show how this interpretation can no longer be merely at the level of the literal observance of regulations, but must operate at the deeper and more challenging level of discerning the will of God which underlies the legal rulings of the Torah. If in the process it may appear that certain elements of the law are for all practical purposes "abolished," this will be attributable not to the loss of their status as the word of God but to their changed role in the era of fulfillment, in which it is Jesus, the fulfiller, rather than the law which pointed forward to him, who is the ultimate authority.

Such an understanding of "fulfilling the law" has gained a considerable degree of assent in recent decades,[17] over against the older view of a le-

---

15. J. P. Meier, *Law*, 73-81, concludes from a full study of the usage of πληρόω that "the Law in Mt must be interpreted in a prophetic light."

16. W. D. Davies, *Setting*, 183-90 (also 446-47), summarizing the results of a lengthy survey of rabbinic literature, finds significant evidence for a Jewish expectation that the messianic age would be marked by a new level of obedience to the law, and in some circles the belief that the Messiah would bring a new Torah to replace the old, though the evidence falls short of a general consensus.

17. See, e.g., R. J. Banks, *Jesus*, 203-35 (= *JBL* 93 [1974] 226-42); J. P. Meier,

gally conservative Matthew. It is this understanding of "fulfillment" which will underlie the following comments on vv. 18-19 and which will, I believe, be vindicated by the contrast which Jesus draws in v. 20 between the righteousness of the scribes and Pharisees and that of the kingdom of heaven and also by the illustrations which will follow in vv. 21-47.

Jesus will use the phrase "I came to . . ." to speak of the purpose of his ministry again in 9:13; 10:34-35; 20:28 (cf. 11:19). In the Fourth Gospel this sort of language represents Jesus as a preexistent figure who has "come into the world" (John 1:9; 9:39; 18:37) from heaven (John 3:13, 31), and it is tempting to find the same implication in Matthew. In a variety of ways Matthew implies or indeed openly states that Jesus is "God with us," but he does not elsewhere use language which specifically states his preexistence, and the fact that the same verb ("came") introduces the distinctive ministry of John the Baptist in 11:18 and 21:32 suggests caution in reading too much into it. It conveys a sense of mission rather than a metaphysical claim.[18]

18 In vv. 18 and 19 we have the strongest statement in Matthew of the undying significance of the law; the focus has narrowed down to the law alone, and the prophets will not be mentioned again in ch. 5.

This is the first occurrence in Matthew of the phrase *amēn legō hymin,* "I tell you truly," which will appear a further thirty times in this gospel, thirteen times in Mark, six in Luke, and (with the *amēn* doubled) twenty-five times in John. It is widely recognized as an authentic and distinctive feature of Jesus' teaching style,[19] with the *amēn* conveying the personal authority of the one who utters it. The Hebrew root *'mn* denotes faithfulness, reliability, certainty. In the OT and in later Jewish writings *'āmēn* is used responsively to affirm a solemn pronouncement just made by someone else or to conclude a doxology, and in Isa 65:16 God is called "God of *'āmēn*" (cf. the title "the Amen" in Rev 3:14). But Jesus' introductory use of *amēn* to confirm his own words is unique. The formula is used in the gospels to emphasize pronounce-

---

Law, 41-124 (and summary, pp. 160-61, showing how this exegesis also fits with the thrust of vv. 21-48); R. A. Guelich, *Sermon,* 134-74; D. J. Moo, *JSNT* 20 (1984) 3-49; R. T. France, *Matthew: Evangelist,* 191-97; Y.-E. Yang, *Jesus,* 106-20, 128-29, and the commentaries of Carson, Davies and Allison (on v. 17; they do not agree with the above on vv. 18 and 19), Blomberg, Hagner (with some variations), and Carter. Cf. also J. Jeremias, *Theology,* 82-85 (Jesus as "the concluding revelation").

18. W. Carter, *CBQ* 60 (1998) 44-62, discusses how this group of "I came" sayings fits into Matthew's purpose, and concludes that they serve to specify how Jesus is to fulfill the commission set out in 1:21-23, "to save from sins and to manifest God's presence."

19. J. Jeremias, *Prayers,* 108-15, remains the classic presentation of this view, which has been generally accepted despite the protests of V. Hasler, *Amen;* K. Berger, *Amen-Worte;* and *ZNW* 63 (1972) 45-75. See Jeremias's response in *ZNW* 64 (1972) 122-23.

ments which are meant to be noted, particularly those which the hearers may be expected to find surprising or uncomfortable.[20]

The pronouncement thus marked out is a striking and puzzling epigram. It is clearly a statement of the permanence of the law — notice that the "prophets" of v. 17 have now dropped out of the discussion: it will be the law which is the focus of the rest of ch. 5. The preservation of every least mark of the pen[21] is a vivid way of conveying that no part of it can be dispensed with. But the saying is complicated by two "until" clauses; it is not clear how these two clauses relate to one another, or whether they are making the same or different points. "Until heaven and earth pass away" is a conventional way (cf. our "until hell freezes") of saying for all practical purposes, "never" (cf. Jer 31:35-36; 33:20-21, 25-26; Job 14:12; also positively Ps 72:5, 7, 17), and the repetition of the verb "pass away" links the law closely with heaven and earth as being equally permanent; in 24:35 Jesus' own words are stated to be *more* permanent than heaven and earth.[22]

But if this saying is intended simply to assert the permanence of the law, why is a second "until" clause added? Some interpreters assert that the second "until" clause merely repeats the sense of the first and speaks of the (unimaginable) end of the world, but in that case why is the thought repeated before and after the main clause, and why is it expressed in terms of something "happening" *(ginomai)* when the point of the first clause was to propose something which *could not* happen (heaven and earth passing away)? "Everything happening"[23] is rather the language of eschatological fulfillment (as in the similar saying of 24:34), and if we were right to understand the "fulfilling" of the law and the prophets in terms of a future situation to which the law pointed forward, this clause could be saying that the smallest details of the law would be valid only until the time of fulfillment arrived.[24] This

20. J. A. Gibbs, *Jerusalem,* 107-8, outlines "six ways in which the amen-statements of Jesus may be said to function with respect to material that immediately precedes them."

21. See p. 178, n. 3. See J. P. Meier, *Law,* 50-52, for the terms used in the light of rabbinic discussion.

22. C. Fletcher-Louis (see p. 931, n. 120) argues, however, that "heaven and earth" is symbolic language for the temple, so that this verse requires the preservation of the law only until the temple is destroyed. He also goes on to argue that the same words might also be understood of Jesus' death and resurrection, and even of his life, ministry, and teaching, "as the embodiment of the new creation and the setting-up of the messianic Torah which His new community follows" (163).

23. See J. P. Meier, *Law,* 53-54, 61-64, for the sense of γίνομαι here.

24. It seems clear from Matthew's persistent "fulfillment" language that it is with the coming of Jesus that this fulfillment has arrived. It is probably unwise to be more specific, as, e.g., in the contention of W. D. Davies, *Origins,* 31-66, that ἕως ἂν πάντα γένηται refers specifically to the cross as the point of fulfillment.

would be a natural understanding of "not . . . until . . . ," which seems to suggest a temporary situation. There would then be an undeniable tension with the first "until" clause, since heaven and earth do not pass away when "everything has taken place." It would be necessary to take the first clause as a conventional statement of inviolability rather than a specific time-designation, with the second "until" clause providing the actual terminus envisaged.

But in the light of Jesus' claim not to be abolishing the law (v. 17) and of the insistence in v. 19 that even the least of the commandments remains important, v. 18 can hardly be stating that the "jots and tittles" have in fact been invalidated by the coming of fulfillment in Jesus, unless Matthew has done a remarkably poor job of editing these sayings. The jots and tittles are there to be fulfilled, not discarded, and that is what Jesus has come to do. They are not lost, but taken up into the eschatological events to which they pointed forward. The second "until," then, is not speaking of the time of their abandonment but of their intended goal. The double "until" is admittedly awkward, but we might paraphrase the whole saying as follows: "The law, down to its smallest details, is as permanent as heaven and earth, and will never lose its significance; on the contrary, all that it points forward to will in fact become a reality." Now that that reality has arrived in Jesus, the jots and tittles will be seen in a new light, but they still cannot be discarded.[25] It will be the function of vv. 21-47 to illustrate how they may function in this new situation in which they serve not as simple rules of conduct but as pointers to a "greater righteousness" which Jesus has brought into being and which supersedes the old type of lawkeeping.

19 The "So" which links this saying with the last rules out the convenient suggestion of some interpreters[26] that the "commandments" here

---

25. Keener, 178, attributes to J. P. Meier and to my 1985 commentary the view that "Jesus' death and resurrection is the 'goal of the world,' thus allowing the law to be set aside as fulfilled," and rightly complains that such a view "violates the whole thrust of the passage." Meier must speak for himself, but I neither stated nor implied that fulfillment involves "setting aside," which would indeed directly contradict v. 17. My comment was that "The law is unalterable, but that does not justify its application beyond the purpose for which it was intended." To speak of a change in application of the law is not to regard it as now discarded.

26. R. J. Banks, *Jesus,* 222-23, taking up a suggestion of G. D. Kilpatrick, *Origins,* 25-26; cf. S. Byrskog, *Jesus,* 291-94, 325; H. D. Betz, *Sermon,* 186-87; R. E. Menninger, *Israel,* 112-13. This proposal can be entertained only if v. 19 is interpreted as an isolated logion without reference to the context in which Matthew has placed it (unless, like Menninger, ibid., 108-11, one has taken v. 18 to imply that the law has "ceased to be in force" for Christians, thus creating a sharp tension with the denial of "abrogation" in v. 17). Even so, it has to contend with the fact that all other uses of ἐντολή in Matthew refer to OT commandments. The use of the verb ἐντέλλομαι for Jesus' teaching in 28:20 is a weak basis for proposing a different usage of the noun here; after the reference to the smallest points of the OT law in v. 18 it is surely impossible. The idea that there are "mi-

spoken of are those of Jesus, not those of the OT law. The context demands that "these smallest commandments" (cf. the rabbinic distinction between "light" and "heavy" commandments) are the same as the jot and tittle of v. 18: because they are as permanent as heaven and earth, no one has the right to set them aside. The verb is *lyō,* which I have translated more literally as "untie" in 16:19; 18:18;[27] it is the root of the verb *katalyō,* which was trans- lated "abolish" in v. 17. In John 10:35 Scripture cannot be invalidated (pas- sive of *lyō*). The issue is thus again not primarily obedience to the command- ments, but undermining their authority by teaching that they can now be ignored.[28] The translation "breaks" in NRSV and NIV (but not TNIV), or "disobeys" in GNB, thus misses the essential point, which is not so much about behavior as about teaching. Behavior is not excluded, of course, and the converse statement in the second half of the verse includes "doing" the commandments as well as teaching them, but it is teaching the value of the commandments which is the true converse of setting them aside.

But are the commandments to be "done" in the same way as before Jesus came? To insist on their value as pointers to Jesus does not in itself en- tail observing them literally as regulations. The use of the verb "do" in v. 19 is easily read as meaning that the rules of the OT law must still be followed as they were before Jesus came, and thus as reinforcing the "righteousness of the scribes and Pharisees" which the next verse will disparage. But if that is what Matthew intended these words to mean, he would here be contradicting the whole tenor of the NT by declaring that, for instance, the sacrificial and food laws of the OT are still binding on Jesus' disciples — and surely by the time Matthew wrote Christians were already broadly agreed that they were no longer required. In the light of the emphasis on fulfillment which has in- troduced this passage and which will be central to what follows we can only suppose therefore that he had in mind a different kind of "doing" from that of the scribes and Pharisees, a "doing" appropriate to the time of fulfillment.[29] That will mean in effect the keeping of the law as it is now interpreted by Je- sus himself,[30] and it will be the role of vv. 20-48 to explain what this means

---

nor" commandments among Jesus' teaching would also be unique (Betz can only explain it as ironical; ibid., 187-88), whereas rabbinic discussions of "heavy" and "light" com- mandments of the Torah are well known.

27. See the comments on 16:19 for the meaning of such language in relation to law and conduct.

28. Cf. *Did.* 11:2, where a visiting teacher is to be rejected if he presents a new teaching εἰς τὸ καταλῦσαι ("with a view to abolishing") the church's received teaching.

29. Y.-E. Yang, *Jesus,* 115-16, argues that αἱ ἐντολαὶ αὗται refers not to "the νόμος as it was" (which was the subject of vv. 17-18), but to "the νόμος as fulfilled," "the messianic νόμος."

30. Cf. P. Foster, *Community,* 197: "Such fulfillment was not equivalent to that

in practice. See further on 28:20, where it is the "commandments" of Jesus, not those of the OT, which are to be the basis of Christian discipleship.

Those who belittle the details of the OT law will be called the smallest in the kingdom of heaven. Unlike the scribes and Pharisees of v. 20, they are at least envisaged as being within the kingdom of heaven,[31] the new regime which Jesus has brought into being and whose values this discourse is setting out, but they are scarcely worthy of it. The graphic language derives from a play on words between the "smallest" commandments and the "smallest" reputation of the careless disciple. It is not helpful to press it into supporting a view of the kingdom of heaven as a social structure within which there are first- and second-class citizens, a view which Matthew seems at pains to discourage in 20:1-16 — cf. the idea that the greatest in the kingdom of heaven are the lowest (18:1-4; 20:25-27). The dynamic sense of the kingdom of heaven as God's rule (see on 3:2) suggests rather that to be called great or small in the kingdom of heaven means to be high or low in God's esteem, to be a more or less worthy representative of those who acknowledge him as king. Disciples should delight in and learn from every word that God has written (cf. 4:4) rather than picking and choosing between them.

20 Another "I tell you," though this time without the *amēn,* marks this out as a further significant pronouncement, and one which takes the discussion in a new direction.[32] Whereas vv. 18-19 have reinforced the value of every single aspect of the law, and have declared that a true disciple is one who honors it both in teaching and in practice, this saying sets out a radically new understanding of what it means to live under the rule of God.

We have met "scribes" in association with the chief priests as the recognized theological experts in 2:4, and "Pharisees" in association with Sadducees as members of a Jerusalem delegation in 3:7. This is the first time the two titles have occurred together, as they will most notably throughout ch. 23. The two groups together form the opposition to Jesus in 12:38; 15:1, but

---

expected by his opponents, it achieved observance of even the least of the commandments through following the new way of righteousness. In this sense Matthew's ploy is a rhetorical strategy. He agrees with the words of his opponents, but gives them a new meaning that allows him to claim both fulfillment of the law and a new way of fulfilling it."

31. J. P. Meier, *Law,* 92-95, convincingly argues this against the suggestion of G. Schrenk, *TDNT* 2:548 (cf. Schweizer, 105), that to be least in the kingdom of heaven means to be excluded from it.

32. N. J. McEleney, *CBQ* 41 (1979) 552-70, argues that 5:20 functions as a statement of general principle which will be applied in the second half of the discourse (6:1–7:12), parallel to 5:17-19 as a general principle applied in 5:21-48. This is a valuable observation, but is taken too far if it is implied that the principle set out in v. 20 is not relevant to what follows in the rest of ch. 5. The new approach to the law in these verses is as much part of the "greater righteousness" as are the ethical issues discussed in 6:1–7:12.

more often it will be Pharisees alone (or in conjunction with the Sadducees in 16:1-12) who fill this role, while scribes will eventually be noted as part of the Jerusalem coalition which plans and effects Jesus' death (16:21; 20:18; 21:15; 26:57; 27:41). While there is considerable scholarly debate over the precise meaning of the terms,[33] it is generally agreed that scribes were professional students and teachers of halakhah, the elucidation and practical application of law ("bureaucrats and experts on Jewish life," Saldarini), while "Pharisee" was the title of a reformist movement or school within Judaism to which individuals voluntarily adhered, and which was devoted to the meticulous practice of the law, with special emphasis on such matters as ritual purity, tithing, and sabbath observance. The two terms thus represent distinct categories, but in practice the aims and lifestyle of the two would coincide closely, with many professional scribes also being members of the Pharisaic movement.

The scribes and Pharisees would have approved of what Jesus has just said in vv. 18-19, except perhaps the note of eschatological fulfillment which underlies "until everything has taken place." For them every detail of the law was precious, and the aim of their rapidly developing legal traditions in addition to the OT law was not to supplant it as a rule of life but to guide God's people in observing its demands in more and more meticulous detail. 15:3-6 will show how in practice it could work the other way, and ch. 23 will spell out many ways in which their zeal for legal correctness could prove misguided, but in their own intention and, as far as we can tell, in the eyes of the people at large, they were staunch defenders and eager exponents of the role of the law as a practical guide to holy living, and people respected them for it.

To speak of a "righteousness which goes far beyond that of the scribes and Pharisees" might therefore seem to be an impossible, even ridiculous, ideal. As long as "righteousness"[34] is understood in terms of literal obedience to rules and regulations, it would be hard to find anyone who attempted it more rigorously and more consistently than the scribes and Pharisees. The paradox of Jesus' demand here makes sense only if their basic premise as to what "righteousness" consists of is put in question. Jesus is not talking about beating the scribes and Pharisees at their own game, but about a different level or concept of righteousness altogether. Ch. 23 will contain a series of illustrations of the inadequate principles of the scribes and Pharisees.

33. For a convenient overview see A. J. Saldarini, *ABD* 5:289-303 (Pharisees), 1012-16 (scribes). For a full account of scribes see D. E. Orton, *Scribe,* especially pp. 20-38 on the scribes in Matthew's gospel.
34. See above, p. 119, n. 15, for the sense of δικαιοσύνη in Matthew as the conduct required of God's people rather than the Pauline sense of a gift bestowed by God. B. Przybylski, whose argument we followed there, discusses 5:20 on pp. 80-87.

For all their scrupulous observance of OT (and other) regulations, the scribes and Pharisees are seen as still standing outside the kingdom of heaven. Within that new regime different standards apply. Those who are to belong to God's new realm must move beyond literal observance of rules, however good and scriptural, to a new consciousness of what it means to please God, one which penetrates beneath the surface level of rules to be obeyed to a more radical openness to knowing and doing the underlying will of "your Father in heaven." J. P. Meier describes Jesus' demand as "a radical interiorization, a total obedience to God, a complete self-giving to neighbor, that carries the ethical thrust of the Law to its God-willed conclusion, even when this means in some cases abrogating the letter of the Law."[35] Only those who thus "go far beyond the righteousness of the scribes and Pharisees" will be true subjects of God's kingdom. Those who can do no more than simply keep the rules, however conscientiously, haven't even started as far as the kingdom of heaven is concerned.[36]

Among the rich variety of language associated with the kingdom of heaven, the phrase "enter the kingdom of heaven," which occurs again in 7:21; 18:3; 19:23-24; 23:13 (cf. 21:31), is the most strongly spatial metaphor. The understanding of "kingdom" as a dynamic term for God's kingship (see on 3:2) requires that it be treated as what it is, a metaphor, rather than importing inappropriately concrete ideas of "place." To enter the kingdom of heaven does not mean to go to a place called heaven (though the eternal life of heaven will be its expected outcome; see on 18:8-9),[37] but to come under God's rule, to become one of those who recognize his kingship and live by its standards, to be God's true people.[38]

This lengthy attempt to unpack the significance of vv. 17-20 and to find a coherent ideology running through them may best be summed up in an expanded paraphrase:[39]

"Do not suppose that I came to undermine the authority of the OT scriptures, and in particular the law of Moses. I did not come to set them aside but to bring into reality that to which they pointed forward. I tell you truly:

---

35. J. P. Meier, *Law,* 110.

36. Carter, 143, colorfully refers to Matthew's "'bully' approach in using eschatological threats to procure compliance."

37. B. Charette, *Recompense,* 83-84 and passim, therefore includes this phrase (and "entering life," 18:8-9; 19:17) along with "inheritance" language as part of the theme of reward in Matthew.

38. The force of this metaphorical language is helpfully discussed by J. Marcus under the title "Entering the Kingly Power of God," *JBL* 107 (1988) 663-75.

39. For a similar but much more extended paraphrase see J. P. Meier, *Law,* 123-24.

the law, down to its smallest details, is as permanent as heaven and earth and will never lose its significance; on the contrary, all that it points forward to will in fact become a reality (and is now doing so in my ministry). So anyone who treats even the most insignificant of the commandments of the law as of no value and teaches other people to belittle them is an unworthy representative of the new regime, while anyone who takes them seriously in word and deed will be a true member of God's kingdom.

"But do not imagine that simply keeping all those rules will bring salvation. For I tell you truly: it is only those whose righteousness of life goes far beyond the old policy of literal rulekeeping which the scribes and Pharisees represent who will prove to be God's true people in this era of fulfillment."

The division of this paraphrase into two paragraphs indicates what I take to be a significant shift of emphasis, taking the battle onto a different front. While vv. 17-19 have confronted those who are tempted to set the law aside, v. 20 confronts those who are so preoccupied with its literal observance that they miss the whole point of the fulfillment to which it is pointing. It is this latter emphasis which will determine the direction of vv. 21-48.

b. Fulfilling the Law: Six Examples (5:21-47)

21 *"You have heard that it was said to people long ago, 'You shall not murder,' and that*[40] *anyone who committed murder should be liable to judgment.* 22 *But I tell you that everyone who is angry with their brother or sister*[41] *will be liable to judgment; whoever calls their brother or sister stupid*[42] *will be liable to trial;*[43] *and whoever calls them a fool will be liable to hellfire.*[44] 23 *So if you bring your offering*

40. The following words, while expressed in the same direct form as "You shall not murder," are in fact a paraphrase of the OT rule of capital punishment rather than a direct citation of a specific text.

41. See the comments on v. 22 below for this translation of ἀδελφός. The majority of MSS and versions add εἰκῇ, "without cause," but since this is so natural a softening of an impossibly hard saying it is generally regarded as a deliberate addition to the text, especially as it does not appear in the earliest Greek MSS (though its presence in almost all early versions and in many patristic citations shows that it was very early). D. A. Black, *NovT* 30 (1988) 1-8, argues for retaining εἰκῇ.

42. Literally, "calls them 'Ρακά"; see the comments below on the relatively inoffensive Aramaic epithet *rêqâ*, "empty[-headed]."

43. συνέδριον, "council," probably refers here not to the Great Sanhedrin of Jerusalem but to the appropriate local judicial court as in 10:17.

44. Literally, "the Gehenna of fire," a phrase which recurs in 18:9. See the comments below on the Jewish understanding of Gehenna.

to the altar, and there remember that your brother or sister has a complaint against you, 24 leave your offering there in front of the altar, and go first and make it up with your brother or sister, then come and make your offering. 25 Get on good terms with your opponent quickly, while the two of you are still on the way; otherwise your opponent will hand you over to the judge, and the judge to the officer, and you will be thrown into prison; 26 I tell you truly: you will not get out of there until you have repaid the last penny.[45]

27 *"You have heard that it was said, 'You shall not commit adultery.' 28 But I tell you that every man who looks at someone else's wife*[46] *and wants to have sex with her*[47] *has already committed adultery with her in his heart. 29 But if your right eye causes you to stumble, tear it out and throw it away: you are better off losing one part of your body than having your whole body thrown into hell. 30 And if your right hand causes you to stumble, cut it off and throw it away: you are better off losing one part of your body than having your whole body go to hell.*

31 *"It was said, 'Anyone who divorces his wife must give her a divorce certificate.' 32 But I tell you that everyone who divorces his wife for any reason except sexual unfaithfulness makes her the victim of adultery,*[48] *and anyone who marries a divorced woman himself*

---

45. κοδράντης represents Latin *quadrans,* a quarter of an *as;* there were sixty-four *quadrantes* to the Roman denarius (for which see on 20:2). Mark 12:42 tells us that the Jewish λεπτό" (the smallest coin in circulation, used in Luke 12:59 in the parallel to this passage) was half a *quadrans.*

46. Only the context can decide where γυνή has the more specific sense of "wife" rather than simply "woman"; here the specific mention of adultery indicates that the reference is to someone else's wife, and I have added "someone else's" to make this sense clear.

47. This phrase represents what I take to be the sense in this context of πρὸς τὸ ἐπιθυμῆσαι αὐτήν, "so as to want her," "covet her." The suggestion that the accusative αὐτήν should be understood as marking the subject rather than the object of the verb, producing the translation "so that she lusts" (so Carson, 151-52, following K. Haacker, *BZ* 21 [1977] 113-16), depends on the fact that ἐπιθυμέω normally takes a genitive of object; but there are numerous instances of its use with the accusative, particularly in the LXX, and the alternative translation has an oddly oblique effect which fits uncomfortably in this context (Davies and Allison, 1:523, consider it "just possible"; H. D. Betz, *Sermon,* 233-34, finds this view "not warranted by the text").

48. This is the natural meaning of the passive of μοιχεύω, which is generally used in both classical and biblical Greek as an active (or middle) verb with the woman as direct object (where the woman is the subject in Jer 3:9; Hos 4:13-14 the verb is active, not passive as here); note LXX Lev 20:10, where the man and the woman are described as ὁ μοιχεύων καὶ ἡ μοιχευομένη (the previous clauses having spoken of a man who μοιχεύσηται

commits adultery.[49] [50]

33 *"Again, you have heard that it was said to people long ago,
'You shall not swear falsely,'*[51] *and 'You shall fulfill*[52] *your oaths to the
Lord.'* 34 *But I tell you: do not swear at all, either by heaven (because
it is God's throne),* 35 *or by the earth (because it is the footstool for his
feet), or by*[53] *Jerusalem (because it is the city of the great king);* 36 *and
do not swear by your own head, because you cannot make a single
hair white or black.* 37 *Rather, let your words be simply 'Yes' and
'No';*[54] *anything more than that comes from evil.*[55]

38 *"You have heard that it was said, 'Eye for eye and tooth for
tooth.'* 39 *But I tell you: do not resist a bad person, but instead if anyone slaps you on the right cheek, turn the other cheek to them as well;*

___

someone else's wife, accusative case); the verb has just been used in that way in v. 28, with
the woman (αὐτήν) as direct object. The more traditional translation "causes her to become
an adulteress" (on the assumption that her assumed subsequent remarriage makes her party
to an adulterous act; so BDAG 657a) thus depends on an unnatural sense for the passive.
See the comments below.

49. The middle form μοιχᾶται (μοιχάω, unlike μοιχεύω in the previous note, is not
used in the active in biblical literature) may have here a reflexive sense, expressing the effect of the man's action on himself: while the effect of the divorcing husband's action is
expressed as it affects the woman, the one who marries a divorced woman also himself in-
curs the stigma of adultery.

50. Some MSS follow Luke 16:18 in using a participial construction instead of an
adverbial "if" clause, but the sense is not affected. The omission of the whole final clause
(from "and") in D and some Latin versions may be due to pastoral sensitivity or perhaps
more likely to a desire to simplify the pronouncement, but is very unlikely to represent the
original.

51. ἐπιορκέω can mean either to make a false statement on oath ("perjure yourself") or to break an oath by failing to do what you have sworn. The former is the more
common meaning, though the following clause might suggest that the latter is intended
here. Either sense is possible; see the comments below on the OT passages likely to underlie the use of the term.

52. Literally, "repay," the oath being taken as creating a "debt" which then must
be settled.

53. Literally, "toward" (εἰς rather than ἐν), possibly referring to orientation rather
than merely use of the name? Carson, 153-54, suggests that the term reflects a rabbinic
distinction between oaths "by Jerusalem" and "toward Jerusalem." *T. Ned* 1:3 lists "Jerusalem," "to Jerusalem," and "in Jerusalem" as equally binding formulae.

54. Literally, "Let your word be 'Yes, yes,' 'No, no.'" The doubling of ναί and οὐ
is probably best understood as a distributive idiom as in δύο δύο (Mark 6:7), "two at a
time"; so each utterance is to be "Yes" or "No" without addition.

55. Here, as in 6:13, the fact that the genitive form is the same in the masculine
and neuter allows either "evil" or "the Evil One" (the devil). See the comments below. In
13:38 a similar ambiguity is probably resolved by the explicit mention of the devil in the
following clause, but there is no such indication here.

40 *and if anyone wants to take you to court to get your shirt, let them have your coat as well;* 41 *and if anyone dragoons you as a porter for one mile,*[56] *go with them for two miles.* 42 *Give to someone who asks you, and don't turn a cold shoulder to someone who wants to borrow from you.*

43 *"You have heard that it was said, 'You shall love your neighbor and you shall hate your enemy.'* 44 *But I tell you: love your enemies and pray for those who persecute you,*[57] 45 *so that you may be true children of your Father who is in heaven; for he makes his sun rise on both the bad and good, and sends rain on both the just and unjust.* 46 *If you love those who love you, what reward will you get? Don't even tax collectors do as much?* 47 *And if you welcome only those of your own circle,*[58] *what is so special about that?*[59] *Don't even Gentiles*[60] *do as much?*

These six quite varied topics[61] illustrate the concept of a righteousness which goes beyond the legal correctness of the scribes and Pharisees (v. 20).[62] Each is presented in the form of a contrast (hence the frequent description of this section as "the antitheses")[63] between what "was said" and Jesus' own more

56. μίλιον represents the Roman *mille*, a thousand (paces), rather less than our mile.

57. This is the reading of the oldest Greek MSS and most of the earliest versions, but many MSS and versions either add further clauses ("bless those who curse you," "do good to those who hate you") or expand on the existing second clause ("those who abuse you and persecute you"). The additions reflect the fuller wording of Luke 6:27-28, and the considerable variety in the extent and order of the additional wording points to secondary accretions under Synoptic influence.

58. Literally, "your brothers," but the reference is probably intended to be wider than literal family relationships. The term functions similarly to "neighbor" in Lev 19:18.

59. Literally, "What extra (or what in excess) do you do?"

60. Many later MSS have "tax collectors" again instead of Gentiles, but the bracketing together of the two groups in 18:17 suggests that the earlier witnesses are right in preserving both here.

61. See, however, the discussion by J. H. Neyrey, *Honor*, 190-211, which attempts to explain the six topics as all aspects of "aggressive and conflictual relationships" set in the context of ordinary village life with its conventional values of honor and shame.

62. I discuss these pronouncements, as Matthew presents them, as the teaching of Jesus. They may also be studied from the point of view of the Christian community within which Matthew wrote, as a pointer to the nature and ideals of that community as a self-consciously distinct group over against "the synagogue group, which held a more traditional understanding of the interpretation of the Torah" (P. Foster, *Community*, 141). The results of Foster's study of 5:21-48 from that perspective (ibid., 94-139) are summed up in ibid., 140-43.

63. A term to be used with caution since it was apparently first applied to them by the Gnostic heretic Marcion, who saw them as marking Jesus' decisive break with the OT law (so H. D. Betz, *Sermon*, 200-201).

demanding ethic. So demanding are Jesus' alternative rulings that those who fully grasp his intention often declare them to be unworkable in the real world. Even allowing for the element of exaggeration, and a tendency to speak in black and white with no allowance for gray, which characterized much of Jesus' teaching, this section of the discourse poses formidable problems for those who wish to treat it as a straightforward code of conduct. It is only the most sanguine of disciples (or those with little self-awareness) who can comfortably attempt simply to put into practice this teaching, with its culmination in the requirement that our lives should be "perfect as your heavenly Father is perfect" (v. 48).

The formula with which Jesus' demand is made is unvarying: "But I tell you." The other side of the contrast varies from the full formula "You have heard that it was said to people long ago" (vv. 21, 33) to the more abbreviated forms "You have heard that it was said" (vv. 27, 38, 43) and even simply "It was said" (v. 31). But there is no discernible difference in intention: the full formula, once introduced in v. 21, does not need to be repeated in order to make the same point. Two aspects of the wording of this formula are important. First, "it was said" represents a relatively rare passive form of the verb *errethē,* which is used in the NT specifically for quotations of Scripture or divine pronouncements, the same form which I have translated "declared" in the quotation-formula of 1:22 and the like.[64] This is thus not a reference to human teaching but to divine declaration. Secondly, this declaration was made to[65] "people long ago" (literally, "the ancients"); the reference cannot then be to any contemporary or recent tradition. These features suggest strongly that in the first half of each contrast we should expect to find a quotation of the Mosaic law, as it would be heard read in the synagogues. And, in fact, in each case what is quoted is based on an identifiable passage or theme of the Pentateuch, though the form in which it is quoted is sometimes more paraphrase than exact citation, and in one case (v. 43) it incorporates a supplementary clause which the pentateuchal passage does not contain.[66]

Is Jesus here then setting his teaching in opposition to the divine law, in direct contradiction to his claim in v. 17? Quite apart from the improbability of Matthew allowing his compilation to produce such a direct contradiction, two other factors suggest a different view. One is the peculiar nature of the "quotations" of the law. While the first two are straightforward quotations

---

64. See above, p. 55, n. 54.

65. It is occasionally suggested that the dative τοῖς ἀρχαίοις might mean "*by* the ancients," but the Greek for this would be ὑπὸ τῶν ἀρχαίων (the NT provides only a single instance of an instrumental dative, Luke 23:15), and in any case the use of ἐρρέθη makes it clear that the speaker is God (or Scripture).

66. See further on the formula J. P. Meier, *Law,* 129-33.

of two of the ten commandments (in the first case supplemented by an additional pentateuchal principle), the third is significantly different from the text of Deut 24:1 and is angled in a different direction from the Deuteronomy text, the fourth merely summarizes pentateuchal guidelines on oaths and vows, the fifth quotes the text exactly but the discussion suggests that it was being quoted for a purpose other than that of the original in context, and the nonpentateuchal addition to the sixth places a negative "spin" on the commandment of Lev 19:18 which that passage in no way supports. The comments below will fill out each of these points, but the general impression they create is that Jesus is here presented as citing a series of "legal" principles based indeed on the pentateuchal laws but in several cases significantly developing and indeed distorting their intention. In other words, the dialogue partner is not the OT law as such but the OT law as currently (and sometimes misleadingly) understood and applied.

The second factor which suggests that this is not a simple contradiction of the OT law is the wording of the formula of quotation, "you have heard . . . ," "but I say. . . ." David Daube[67] has suggestively compared a rabbinic convention whereby what is "heard" is set over against what you must "say," where the contrast is between a literal but inadequate understanding of the OT text and a more enlightened, though possibly more creative, interpretation which is thus recommended as superior. What Jesus *says* ("But I tell you") is thus contrasted with what the disciples have hitherto *heard,* a superficial and potentially misleading reading of the OT texts as rules of conduct, whereas Jesus is now going to indicate the right (and deeper) interpretation and use of those same God-given texts.

The way in which Jesus' new reading of the OT laws differs from and goes beyond current understanding varies from one example to another.[68] In the first two examples (murder and adultery), while there is no suggestion that the literal ethical ruling is set aside, Jesus goes far beyond its outward observance (which can be observed and judged) to the thoughts and attitudes which underlie the action, whether they are carried into effect or not. In the

---

67. D. Daube, *Rabbinic Judaism,* 55-62. Cf. W. D. Davies, *Setting,* 101-2. See, however, for some cautionary comments, J. P. Meier, *Law,* 133-34, n. 21. The point is not that Matthew is deliberately citing a specific (and probably later) rabbinic formula, but that this is a natural connotation of the contrasting terms used. There is not, of course, any parallel in this rabbinic usage to Jesus' uniquely authoritative "*I* say to you" (see J. Jeremias, *Theology,* 251-53).

68. Contra the absolutism of R. E. Menninger, *Israel,* 118: "Either Jesus retains the Law or sets it aside, we cannot have both." Why not, if the principles involved in the different laws considered demand different treatment? Menninger, ibid., 116-18, argues that even in the first example, drawn from the Decalogue (and restated without modification by Jesus in 19:18), "Jesus' teaching replaces the Law" rather than merely "extending" it.

third and fourth examples (divorce and swearing) Jesus declares that the actions which the OT law presupposes and for which it provides regulation should never have occurred in the first place; where the law recognized and attempted to mitigate human failure to maintain the standard of life God requires (marital fidelity and truthfulness), Jesus goes to the root of the issue and challenges the initial actions themselves. In the fifth example (retributive punishment) an OT judicial ruling is stated to be inapplicable to personal ethics, to which it was presumably being applied by Jesus' contemporaries as a justification for retaliatory action; in its place Jesus declares a principle of nonresistance which leaves no room for the calculation of proportionate retribution. In the sixth example Jesus extends the principle of love far beyond the explicit purview of the OT law and in direct contradiction of what was presumably a contemporary "corollary" from the love of neighbors, the hatred of non-neighbors.

If there is a common pattern to these varied examples of "going beyond" both the OT law and the righteousness of the scribes and Pharisees, it might be characterized in a number of ways. (1) It promotes an "inward" concern with motive and attitude above the "outward" focus on the visible and quantifiable observance of regulations. (2) It goes behind specific rules to look for the more far-reaching principles which should govern the conduct of the people of God. (3) It is concerned not so much with the negative goal of the avoidance of specific sin but with the far more demanding positive goal of discovering and following what is really the will of God for his people. (4) It substitutes for what is in principle a 100 percent achievable righteousness (the avoidance of breaking a definable set of regulations) a totally open-ended ideal (being "perfect as your heavenly Father is perfect") which will always remain beyond the grasp of the most committed disciple. Such a radically searching reading of the will of God in the light of the OT law establishes a righteousness of the kingdom of heaven which is in a different league altogether from the righteousness of the scribes and the Pharisees — and of any other religious traditions which understand the will of God in terms of the punctilious observance of rules.[69]

What then happens to the jots and tittles of the OT law? They are taken

---

69. Contrast the view of B. Przybylski, *Righteousness,* 81-83, that "Matthew is applying the Rabbinic principle of making a fence around Torah in 5:21-48." This implies that Jesus' primary concern was that the laws themselves should not be infringed, whereas on the understanding here followed it was not the laws themselves which mattered to him so much as the true understanding of the will of God toward which they pointed. It is true, as Przybylski well demonstrates, that in each case Jesus' more radical teaching keeps the disciple away from the area where the law could be broken, but this is at the cost of rendering some of the laws themselves essentially irrelevant to the ethics of the kingdom of heaven.

197

up into a far more demanding "fulfillment" which leaves some of them on one side as having no role in the true life of the kingdom of heaven. This applies to the regulations for divorce, when divorce itself does not happen; the rules for oaths, when swearing is itself ruled out; the judicial limitation of retribution, when not only retaliation but even resistance is declared unworthy of the kingdom of heaven. Is this then, after all, to "abolish" them as v. 17 declared Jesus would not do? No, it is rather to bypass them, to leave them behind as no longer needed when the life of the kingdom of heaven is fully implemented.[70] In the real world it may be that there will still be divorce, untruthfulness, and judicial retribution, and for these purposes the regulations of the OT law may retain a practical role. But insofar as they are needed, that is a mark of the failure of the more radical ethic which Jesus here sets out. When people live according to the principles of the kingdom of heaven, those jots and tittles are no longer needed. They remain, no doubt, as part of the God-given revelation of the law which points forward to a better way, and in that sense they are not abolished. But the disciple should now have moved beyond them under the guidance of the Messiah in whom that fulfillment has come. His sovereign pronouncement, "I tell you," is not a contribution to exegetical debate, but stands alongside the law on which it is based as a definitive declaration of the divine purpose.[71] As such it provokes the question "Who is this?"[72] and Matthew's

70. R. J. Banks, *Jesus,* 203, makes this point with vigor: "It is a surpassing or transcending of the Law that is the keynote throughout. His teaching cannot be regarded merely in terms of the 'exposition' or 'completion' of the Law, its 'radicalisation' or 'sharpening,' or the 'abrogation' of some or all its commandments. He neither moves out from the Law in expounding his demands nor relates these, whether positively or negatively, back to it."

71. P. Foster, *Community,* 80-93, makes an interesting comparison between Matt 5:21-48 and the early Qumran document known as the "Halakhic Letter" (4QMMT = 4Q394-99), which sets out the community's understanding of various points of law over against what others ("they") teach and practice. He notes a marked difference in the tone of debate, the Qumran document being more conciliatory, that in Matthew more confrontational and dismissive of the opposing view. It should also be noted (more clearly than Foster does) that the degree of *literary* similarity is very limited. The Qumran document (insofar as it can be reconstructed from a collection of fragmentary texts) is not set out as a series of "antitheses," does not cite specific texts (whether scriptural or adapted), and has nothing comparable to the "I tell you" of Jesus. The predominant formula is "And concerning . . . we say/think . . . ," with the opposing view or practice left to be inferred. So the Qumran document reads more like a contribution to debate, whereas Matthew's Jesus lays down the law on the basis of a personal authority which is not claimed by anyone at Qumran.

72. S. Byrskog, *Teacher,* 294-96, argues that Jesus' authoritative use of ἐγώ in the antithetical formula alludes to "divine categories. It corresponds to a divine passive. It . . . shows that Jesus' teaching carries an importance to be compared with what God himself has said."

comment at 7:28-29 rightly characterizes the impact of the discourse as a whole as one of unparalleled messianic authority.[73]

(1) Murder (5:21-26)

Jesus' radical interpretation of the sixth commandment (and of the death penalty for murder which is its OT corollary) is stated in the three sharply paradoxical statements of v. 22. The remainder of this paragraph consists of what appear to have been two originally independent sayings (vv. 23-24 and 25-26; note the change to second-person singular) concerned with repairing broken relationships, which offer a positive counterpart to the negative verdicts of v. 22.

The principle of v. 22 is that the actual committing of murder is only the outward manifestation of an inward attitude which is itself culpable, whether or not it actually issues in the act of murder.[74] Angry thoughts and contemptuous words (which equally derive from "the heart," 12:34) deserve equal judgment; indeed, the "hellfire" with which the saying concludes goes far beyond the human death penalty which the OT law envisaged. Jesus in no way sets aside the simple correlation of the observable act of murder and its humanly imposed penalty — our modern questions concerning the appropriateness of capital punishment for murder are not raised — but adds a far-reaching new dimension by turning attention also to the motives and attitudes which underlie the act, and which are not susceptible to judicial process. No one can testify to the anger itself, only to its physical or verbal expression, and the everyday insults of "stupid" and "fool" do not provide the matter for court proceedings.[75] But, in the words of 1 Sam 16:7, "The LORD looks on the heart," and in his court its thoughts are no less culpable than the act itself. A similar view is attributed to R. Eliezer ben Hyrcanus (c. A.D. 100): "One who hates his neighbor is among those who shed blood" (*Der. Er. Rab.* 57b [11:13]). Cf. the tannaitic principle in *b. B. Meṣiʿa* 58b, "Anyone who publicly shames a neighbor is as though he shed blood," with the following comment of R. Hanina that such people will not escape from Gehenna. Cf. 1 John 3:15.[76]

---

73. See D. C. Allison, *Moses,* 182-90, for the theme in this passage of a new Moses setting out a "messianic Torah" for the new age.

74. For murder and other wrong actions originating in "the heart" cf. 15:18-19. The connection is spelled out by *Did.* 3:2: "Do not be angry, for anger leads to murder."

75. See, however, 1QS 6:25–7:9 for such proceedings within the tight-knit "monastic" community of Qumran.

76. The wording of this pericope may carry a deliberate echo of the story of Cain (alluded to also in Matt 18:22 and 23:35), who, because he was angry (Gen 4:5-6), murdered his brother (Gen 4:8), the problem having arisen from their respective offerings (Gen 4:3-5; cf. here v. 23); but, if so, the parallel is not exploited.

21 The direct quotation of one of the Ten Commandments leaves no doubt as to who were the "people long ago" to whom "it was said." Jesus is going to the heart of the Mosaic law itself. The LXX wording of Exod 20:13; Deut 5:17 correctly uses *phoneuō,* which, like the Hebrew *rāṣaḥ,* refers specifically to "murder," the intentional and unlawful taking of life, rather than a more general word for "kill."[77] The following clause does not cite a specific text but summarizes the OT prescription of the death penalty for murder, as expressed, for example, in Gen 9:6; Exod 21:12-14; Lev 24:17; Num 35:30-31. The use of "judgment" rather than a specific term for execution is perhaps intended to emphasize that the killing of a murderer was not to be through an unofficial blood-feud but through due process of law;[78] but the OT allows no doubt over what form that "judgment" must take.

22 The "brother or sister"[79] *(adelphos)* of vv. 22-24 is probably to be understood as a fellow disciple rather than a literal family member;[80] a similar concern with good relationships among fellow disciples will be the theme of the fourth discourse in ch. 18, where the term *adelphos* will recur in 18:15, 21, 35; cf. 12:46-50 for the concept of Jesus' "family" of disciples. It would, however, be pedantic to suggest that Jesus' ruling applies *only* to relations with fellow disciples and not to people in general; vv. 44-47 suggest otherwise.

It is possible to find an ascending scale of severity in the descriptions of the punishment in this verse, from an unspecified "judgment" to the more specific "trial"[81] and then to the final extreme of "hellfire." Certainly the

---

77. It is therefore inappropriate to cite this commandment, in its misleading KJV translation "Thou shalt not kill," as applying directly either to war or to capital punishment, the latter of which is in fact envisaged in the "judgment" specified in the next clause.

78. See Deut 17:8-13 for the process of "judgment" envisaged in cases of bloodshed.

79. Here and in all comparable cases I have followed the example of most recent translations in treating ἀδελφός as generic rather than as a gender-specific reference to a male sibling. In the absence of a suitably gender-inclusive English term ("sibling" is stilted and does not easily fit a metaphorical use) I have resorted to "brother or sister" to avoid misunderstanding. For the presence of women among the disciple group see 27:55.

80. This "community" use of ἀδελφός is more characteristic of Matthew than of the other gospels. See 5:23, 24, 47; 7:3, 4, 5; 12:49-50; 18:15, 21, 35; 23:8; 25:40; 28:10, most of which are peculiar to Matthew.

81. Both terms are appropriate to human judicial procedures, and the "judgment" in v. 21 referred to a humanly imposed penalty (J. Jeremias, *TDNT* 6:975, suggests that in each case the death penalty is implied). If they are taken in that sense, the shift to "hellfire" in the third clause is particularly remarkable, but since neither anger nor everyday abuse is a likely subject for human trial (though Gundry, 85 and n. 61, rightly points out that insulting speech was tried and punished at Qumran), it is possible that in fact God's

most striking and powerful image is kept to the last. But there is no such clear escalation in the offenses cited.[82] The first (anger) is in the mind and the second and third in speech, but the speech is cited not so much as a clearly actionable utterance but rather as an indication of attitude. The two words of abuse, "stupid"[83] and "fool"[84] (the latter used by Jesus himself in 23:17),[85] are not readily distinguishable in either meaning or severity; both are everyday utterances, significant enough in a society which took seriously public honor and disgrace, but not the sort of exceptional abuse which might conceivably form the basis of litigation. The deliberate paradox of Jesus' pronouncement is thus that ordinary insults may betray an attitude of contempt which God takes extremely seriously. The effect of the saying is therefore to be found not in a careful correlation between each offense individually and the respective punishment assigned to it, but in the cumulative rhetorical force of a series of everyday scenes and the remarkable range of expressions used for their results; the totally unexpected conclusion in "hellfire" comes as a shocking jolt to the complacency of the hearer, who might well have chuckled over the incongruous image of a person being tried for anger or for conventional insult, only to be pulled up short by the saying's conclusion.[86]

---

judgment is in view already in the first two clauses, as it certainly is in the third. In that case συνέδριον must be understood as a metaphor, using the human institution to stand for the more ultimate judgment of God.

82. M. D. Goulder, *Midrash*, 257-58, attempts to find a parallel escalation in both offenses and penalties, as follows: "Anger in the heart will be punished in the local court, rudeness at the central assize, insult at the bar of heaven." For a different attempt see Gundry, 84-85.

83. The Greek term ῥακά is not found elsewhere. The third-century-B.C. Zenon Papyrus, sometimes cited as a parallel (see E. C. Colwell, *JBL* 53 [1934] 351-54), uses ῥαχᾶς, not ῥακά, as an uncomplimentary epithet for a certain Antiochus. The spelling ῥαχά is found here in ℵ* D W, but not in other Greek MSS. ῥακά here is usually assumed to represent the Aramaic *rêqâ*, "empty," which occurs in rabbinic writings as a term of personal abuse and differs little from "fool." Basil describes it as "a vernacular word of mild abuse, used in the family circle"; see MM.

84. The fact that the Greek vocative μωρέ could also serve as a transliteration for the Hebrew *môreh*, a "rebel," has led some to suggest that this is Jesus' meaning here, but when the meaning of the Greek word is both obvious and appropriate, this seems an unnecessary subtlety.

85. R. Mohrlang, *Matthew*, 181, n. 45, rather casuistically explains the tension by the fact that 5:22 is about one's attitude to Christian "brothers," whereas in 23:17 Jesus is addressing "outsiders" (similarly Gundry, 463). But is this passage really laying down rules for addressing fellow disciples in contradistinction from others? How could that square with 5:43-47? Jesus' own use of the term simply serves to show what an everyday epithet it was.

86. An alternative reading of the text was suggested by McNeile, 62 (following B. W. Bacon) — though I have found no more recent commentary which notices it —

"Hell" *(geënna)* will be referred to again in 5:29-30; 10:28; 18:9; 23:15, 33 as the place of final destruction of the wicked; its use in this sense is well attested in Jewish apocalyptic literature. It is not the same as Hades, the place of the dead, which is not usually understood as a place of punishment or destruction but rather of shadowy existence. The name *geënna* derives from the Valley of Hinnom (Hebrew *gê hinnōm*) outside Jerusalem which had once been the site of human sacrifice by fire to Molech (2 Kgs 23:10; Jer 7:31). There is a later tradition that the city's rubbish was dumped and burned in this valley; if true,[87] this would provide a vivid image of "the eternal fire prepared for the devil and his angels" (25:41). See on 25:46 for the nature of the "eternal punishment" envisaged. To invoke this awesome concept in relation to the use of an everyday abusive epithet is the sort of paradoxical exaggeration by which Jesus' sayings often compel the reader's attention; contrast 1QS 6:25–7:9, where abusive language and attitudes are punished by a graded range of periods of exclusion from the assembly.

23-24 The change from second-person plural to second-person singular for vv. 23-26 (as also in vv. 29-30, 36, 39b-42) indicates that these are individualized illustrations of the general principle just enunciated. Verses 23-24 and 25-26 are in effect two little parables about reconciliation. The saying in vv. 23-24, while quite different in form, conveys a message similar to that of Mark 11:25, "When you stand praying, if you have anything against anyone, forgive it."[88] Cf. also the comment on the Lord's Prayer in 6:14-15. But

---

which takes v. 22a as Jesus' response to v. 21b, and v. 22c as his response to a further quotation of what "was said" in v. 22b, thus:

It was said, "Whoever murders will be liable to judgment";
But I say to you, "Whoever is angry with their brother or sister will be liable to judgment."
[It was said,] "Whoever calls their brother or sister stupid will be liable to trial";
[But I say to you,] "Whoever calls them a fool will be liable to hellfire."

This reading is most improbable for the following reasons. (i) Nothing in the text suggests that there is a second quotation. (ii) Verse 22b and v. 22c are introduced by the identical clause ὃς δ' ἂν εἴπῃ, which suggests parallel rather than contrasting clauses; there is no "but I tell you" in v. 22c. (iii) There is no discernible difference between the two types of abuse in v. 22b and v. 22c to provide a basis for Jesus' supposed contrasting of them. (iv) There is a lack of symmetry between the two supposed contrasts, in that the first sets "judgment" simply against "judgment," while the second moves from "trial" to "hellfire." (v) Such a double antithesis in a single paragraph and on the same subject would be out of keeping with the literary pattern of these six contrasts.

87. G. R. Beasley-Murray, *Kingdom,* 376-77, n. 92, casts doubt on it.
88. The difference between this verse and Mark 11:25 in the subject of "have against" implies that the worshipper here recognizes that the other is the offended party,

here the situation envisaged is not prayer in general but the more specific and relatively rare experience of making an offering in the temple. The only "altar" at which an offering could be made was that of the temple in Jerusalem.[89] This saying, presumably uttered in Galilee, thus envisages a worshipper who has traveled some eighty miles to Jerusalem with his "offering" (probably a sacrificial animal), who then leaves the animal in the temple while he makes a journey of a week or more to Galilee and back again in order to effect a reconciliation with his offended brother or sister before he dares to present his offering. The improbability of the scenario emphasizes Jesus' point, that the importance of right relationships demands decisive action.[90] This, then, is the positive counterpart to the anger and abuse condemned in v. 22. It puts in the form of a vivid practical example the principle which Paul lays down in Eph 4:26: "Do not let the sun go down on your anger."

25-26 This is another illustration of the importance of reconciliation, set in a different and more threatening scenario. In the preceding saying the disciple is seen as freely taking the initiative to effect a reconciliation. Here he is under duress. The "opponent" is apparently a legal plaintiff who has a case likely to lead to the disciple's conviction, probably for debt. A settlement out of court is a more prudent option, and the prospect of imprisonment until the debt has been cleared provides a compelling incentive. This little cameo is designed, like many parables, not to give practical advice for legal disputes (no indication is given as to what sort of settlement might be possible if the money is not available) but simply to reinforce an ethical message: do not allow bad relationships to remain unresolved. It is linked with vv. 21-22 by the theme of good relationships rather than bad, though the prudential focus of the parable-story sounds almost banal by comparison. But the inclusion of "I tell you truly" (see on 5:18) alerts us to a more ultimate purpose than merely avoiding imprisonment; like the other parable of debt and imprisonment (18:23-35), it is a pointer to the divine judgment on those whose earthly relationships do not conform to the values of the kingdom of

---

leaving the onus of reconciliation on himself or herself, whereas Mark 11:25 speaks of forgiving an offense against oneself.

89. Matthew's preservation of this saying indicates either that he wrote while the temple was still standing (see above, p. 19) or, if he wrote after A.D. 70, that he did not feel the need to contemporize the sayings he recorded so as to fit them into the world of his own day, when there was no altar at which an offering might be made. Cf. H. D. Betz, *Sermon,* 222-23, who, believing the sermon to have an origin independent of Matthew, finds here "important information about the Temple worship around 50 CE by Jerusalem Christians."

90. The same principle is applied to the Eucharist in *Did.* 14:2: "Let no one who has a quarrel with his fellow join you, until they have been reconciled, so that your sacrifice may not be defiled."

heaven. Luke similarly sets his parallel to this saying (Luke 12:58-59) in a context of eschatological readiness.[91]

(2) Adultery (5:27-30)

The basic treatment of the seventh commandment in vv. 27-28 is in principle the same as that of the sixth in vv. 21-22; the visible and punishable act forbidden by the commandment is only the outward expression of an inward desire which is, in this case, adultery "in the heart" — and presumably therefore liable to the same punishment, though in this case neither the OT quotation nor Jesus' interpretation refers explicitly to the punishment (which in the case of adultery was also death). Here, too, an originally independent saying of Jesus (again changing to the second-person singular) is added in vv. 29-30 to reinforce the seriousness of the warning. This additional saying will reappear in a fuller form in 18:8-9, where it is parallel to a rather longer version in Mark 9:43-48. In this additional saying the punishment of *geënna* is again explicit, as in 5:22.

27-28   The commandment is again quoted verbatim from LXX Exod 20:14; Deut 5:18. It is concerned specifically with a man who has sexual relations with another man's wife. The "woman" in Jesus' declaration is thus to be understood also as another man's wife (see p. 192, n. 46), and the looking "in order to desire her," specifically of wanting (and planning?) sexual relations (hence my translation "wants to have sex with her" above). The focus is thus not (as some tender adolescent consciences have read it) on sexual attraction as such, but on the desire for (and perhaps the planning of) an illicit sexual liaison (cf. Exod 20:17, "you shall not covet your neighbor's . . . wife," where LXX uses the same verb, *epithymeō*).[92] The famous sin of David (2 Sam 11:2-4), where such a desire led not only to adultery but also to murder, would naturally come to mind as a lurid scriptural example. The danger of looking lustfully at women is the subject of many Jewish sayings (e.g., Job 31:1, 9; Prov 6:25; Sir 9:5, 8; *T. Benj.* 8:2), and the idea that the desire is tantamount to the deed is hinted at in, for example, *T. Reu.* 5:6; *T. Iss.* 7:2 and explicit in the extracanonical tractate *Kallah* 7 ("whoever gazes intentionally at a woman is as though he had intercourse with her"); according to *b. Yoma* 29a it is even worse.[93]

---

91. See, however, G. B. Caird, *ExpT* 77 (1965/6) 36-39, for the suggestion that in its Lucan context, and probably in Jesus' original intention, it was a warning to Israel in the light of its current political crisis.

92. Keener, 187, comments: "Jesus reads the humanly unenforceable tenth commandment as if it matters as much as the other, more humanly enforceable commandments."

93. For other Jewish examples see H. D. Betz, *Sermon*, 234-35. Luz, 1:296-97, discusses the special relevance of this teaching in the light of Jesus' own relaxed attitude toward relations with women, in contrast with the defensive stance of most rabbis.

29-30 As in vv. 23-26, second-person singular illustrations reinforce the radical implications of Jesus' interpretation of the law, and as in v. 22 he exaggerates to make his point, this time by the use of a shocking but well-recognized metaphor[94] of self-mutilation.[95] In its Marcan context (Mark 9:43-48) and in its fuller Matthean use (18:8-9) this metaphor does not have a specific reference to sexual desire. It may be the need to fit it to this more specific purpose that has led Matthew this time to put the eye first (following the lustful "look" of v. 28), and to omit the foot as an offending member, since "the feet are not much used in adultery"![96] The other notable difference in this form of the saying is the specification of the *right* eye and the *right* hand. The latter strengthens the impact of the saying in that the right hand is assumed to be of greater value and usefulness, but the right eye is not obviously more important than the left.[97] We shall note a particular contextual reason for specifying the right cheek in v. 39, but here the right eye is probably singled out to provide a literary balance to the right hand. For poetical uses of parts of the body to represent sins see Job 31:1, 5, 7; Prov 6:16-19.

To "cause to stumble" *(skandalizō)* is a recurrent metaphor in Matthew; see 11:6; 13:21, 41, 53; 15:12; 16:23; 17:27; 18:6-7, 8-9; 24:10; 26:31-33. In some of these cases the passive denotes "being offended" by a person's behavior or teaching (11:6; 13:57; 15:12; 17:27), a relatively mild sense of the verb. But often it denotes something more catastrophic, a stumbling which deflects a person from the path of God's will and salvation (13:21; 18:6; 24:10; 26:31-33), and a "stumbling block" is a person or thing which gets in the way of God's saving purpose (13:41; 16:23; 18:7). In the case of the disciples' stumbling in Gethsemane (26:31-33) the effect was not terminal, but here and in 18:8-9 (and by implication in 13:21) the stumbling involves the final loss of salvation *(geënna);* cf. the drastic penalty appropriate to one who causes stumbling in 18:6-7. The term therefore goes beyond a

---

94. J. D. M. Derrett, *Audience,* 201-4, argues that these sayings are not metaphorical, and that Jesus was calling for literal self-mutilation. He is right to point out that literal punitive amputations did take place in the ancient world, even occasionally in Judaism (though the only such legal provision in the OT is the very unusual case of Deut 25:12), but this is not at all the same thing as self-mutilation (which is forbidden in Deut 14:1). Derrett regards Pesch's metaphorical interpretation here as "timid"; fortunately most other commentators are equally timid! Luz, 1:297, offers some sensible comment.

95. H. D. Betz, *Sermon,* 238-39, provides ample evidence that in both Hellenistic and rabbinic literature "exaggerated demands to cut off limbs from the body as a sign of seriousness about morality were commonplace."

96. M. D. Goulder, *Midrash,* 259.

97. See, however, 1 Sam 11:2 and the comment on it in Josephus, *Ant.* 6.69-70; also Zech 11:17.

mere pictorial image of physical mishap — which in any case would not follow easily from the action of the hand, though rather more appropriately from the eye. The theme is impediments to ultimate salvation, and the importance of eliminating them at all costs, a theme which could have many different applications to relationships, activities, mental attitudes, and the like, certainly not only to sexual temptation. It is probably not helpful to speculate whether the eye and the hand were chosen to represent specific sins or temptations. As "removable" parts of the body they serve to make the point that any loss, however painful, is preferable to the total lostness of *geënna*. The throwing of the "whole body" into hell belongs to the pictorial imagery as the alternative to physical amputation; it is not the basis for a doctrinal debate over either the nature of human existence after death or the physicality of hell. Nor should this passage be used to suggest that amputees will be raised in an imperfect body.

(3) Divorce (5:31-32)

This very brief statement on divorce poses a problem for the commentator, in that a fuller discussion of the issue, explaining Jesus' opposition to the principle of divorce, will occur later in 19:3-12, but since many of the same questions arise in both passages it seems better to deal with the issue more generally here, and to ask the reader of the commentary at 19:3-12 to refer back to this section.

The third example of Jesus' new interpretation of the law follows from the second in that it is also concerned with sexual ethics, and more specifically marriage, and in that it also speaks of "adultery," but in other ways it is very different. Not only are there no supporting sayings as in vv. 23-26 and 29-30, but the debate concerns not one of the Ten Commandments but a single piece of regulatory law which occurs in Deut 24:1-4. This, the only pentateuchal passage which directly speaks of divorce, served perforce as the basis for subsequent Jewish teaching on the subject, even though it was not concerned with the rightness or wrongness of divorce in itself, nor with permissible causes of divorce, but only with the aftermath of a divorce which is assumed to have taken place. The "quotation" which provides the first half of the contrast is not in fact a direct quotation of the Deuteronomy text but an inference from it, in that Deut 24:1 does not instruct the divorcing husband to provide a certificate, but rather states that *if* this has in fact occurred, certain consequences follow: the divorced wife, having married another man and been divorced also by him (or he has died), may not then be taken back by her first husband. This rather tortuous scenario assumes that both husbands in the case have the right to divorce the woman, but the basis of that right (and of the certificate which is the specific focus of Jesus' "quotation") is not spelled out either here or anywhere else in the OT. That assumption is taken by Jesus' questioners in 19:7 to mean that Moses "commanded" not only the certificate but also the divorce itself. On this basis subsequent Jewish teaching developed a detailed body of legal teaching on divorce; a whole tractate of the Mishnah, *Gittin,* is devoted to provisions for a valid divorce certificate. Divorce was, of course,[98] purely a male prerogative, which required no legal hearing, merely the husband's decision; Jewish law made no provision for a woman to initiate divorce (Josephus, *Ant.* 15.259).[99]

The main area of rabbinic dispute was not the legitimacy of divorce in itself, which everyone seems to have taken for granted,[100] but the permissible grounds of divorce, and here Deut 24:1-4 provided fruitful material for debate, since the first husband's decision is said to be based on his finding "something shameful"[101] in the woman, while the second husband is simply said to have "disliked" her (*śānā',* a quite general word for "hate"). On this basis rabbinic teaching, as set out in *m. Gi*ṭ. 9:10, ranged from the "hard-line" position of Shammai that only "unchastity" was a valid ground for divorce to the "liberal" position of Hillel which allowed a man to divorce his wife for such a trivial offense as spoiling a meal, or even (according to R. Akiba) simply because he had found someone he preferred (cf. the "hate" of Deut 24:3?).[102] In practice it seems clear that the Hillelite position pre-

98. Doubt has been cast on this hitherto universal assumption by the recent publication of what seems to be an official divorce certificate from the early second century issued by a woman to her husband; see D. Instone-Brewer, *Divorce,* 85-90.

99. This is, however, envisaged in Mark 10:12, perhaps on the basis of Roman law, where the woman did have this right, or perhaps reflecting the *de facto* assumption of the right by certain prominent Jewish women in defiance of the law: for Herodias see Mark 6:17-18; Josephus, *Ant.* 18.136; for Salome wife of Costobarus see Josephus, *Ant.* 15.259. For a useful survey of marriage and divorce in the ancient world see W. Carter, *Households,* 72-82.

100. Two Qumran texts (CD 4:21; 11Q19 [*Temple*] 57:17-19) have been taken to suggest that the community did not allow divorce, but neither certainly supports that view. CD 4:21 is followed by a reference to Deut 17:17 which suggests that the prohibition of "taking two wives in one's life" relates primarily to polygamy rather than to divorce and remarriage. 11Q19 57:17-19 may equally refer to polygamy rather than to divorce and remarriage; it should be balanced against 11Q19 54:4, which makes provision for the vow of a divorced woman. It is not clear whether the Qumran sectaries themselves married (see below, p. 722, n. 28).

101. *'erwat-dābār,* literally, "nakedness/shame of a thing," a phrase which allowed a wide variety of specific interpretation. In the original context the phrase cannot have meant simply adultery, since the penalty for that was death, not divorce. But by the time of Jesus, when the death penalty for adultery was apparently no longer applied, it was possible for the phrase to be interpreted in that sense. Jewish debate on the phrase is summarized by P. Foster, *Community,* 110-12.

102. To this standard division should be added the likelihood that both

vailed among most Jews, of whom Josephus's laconic comment is probably typical: "At this time I sent away my wife, being displeased with her behavior. . . . Then I took as wife a woman from Crete. . . ." (*Life* 426-27). In commenting on Moses' legislation in Deut 24:1-4 Josephus adds a significant aside: "The man who wishes to be divorced from his wife for whatever cause — and among people many such may arise — must certify in writing . . ." (*Ant.* 4.253). Cf. Sir 25:26: "If she does not accept your control, divorce her and send her away" (NEB; literally, "cut her off from your flesh").[103]

We shall return to this question in 19:3, where Jesus is asked specifically about the permissible grounds of divorce. Here, however, he raises the issue not to discuss the grounds (though his phrase "except for sexual unfaithfulness" inevitably raises that question for us) but in order to query the assumption that any divorce could be acceptable in the first place. He does not comment on the aftermath of divorce which was the focus of the pentateuchal text, but sweeps its trouble-shooting provisions aside with the assertion that the original divorce itself was not permissible. We shall note below the question whether the provisions of Deut 24:1-4 retain any practical relevance in an unideal world where divorce does in fact happen, but that discussion falls outside the scope of Jesus' teaching both here and in 19:3-12 where the issue is more fully addressed. His concern, which will be explicitly set out in 19:4-8, is with getting back to first principles, to God's original intention for marriage, not as in Deut 24:1-4 with regulating what follows after those principles have already been broken. His quarrel with current ethical teaching is that it is basing its standards on an assumption of failure (Moses' provision only for "your hardheartedness," 19:8) rather than on God's original purpose for marriage.

Jesus' teaching on divorce in Mark 10:2-12 and Luke 16:18 (cf. also 1 Cor 7:10-11) is clear-cut; divorce is simply forbidden. Matthew, both here and in 19:9, apparently blurs the stark opposition between Jesus' teaching and that of all Jewish tradition by inserting the clause *parektos logou porneias* (19:9, *mē epi porneia*), which appears to allow a single cause for divorce, *porneia,* which I have translated "sexual unfaithfulness."[104] The

---

Shammaites and Hillelites permitted, though not necessarily required, divorce in the case of continued infertility; see D. Instone-Brewer, *Divorce,* 91-93.

103. For rabbinic evidence on grounds for divorce see D. Instone-Brewer, *Divorce,* 91-114.

104. H. Baltensweiler, *TZ* 15 (1959) 340-56, followed by J. P. Meier, *Law,* 147-50, and several other Catholic commentators (and also in the translation of NJB, "except for the case of an illicit marriage"), suggests that πορνεία here refers to marriage within the prohibited degrees of Lev 18. So also B. Witherington, *NTS* 31 (1985) 571-76. But clear parallels to such a use of πορνεία are lacking (notably in LXX Lev 18). Its use in

noun more strictly refers to relations with a prostitute (traditionally, "fornication"), but its usage was wider, covering various kinds of sexual irregularity. Here as applied to a married woman it most likely applies either to adultery or to the discovery of premarital intercourse with someone other than the husband,[105] or more likely to either or both.[106] It is clearly used for adultery in Sir 23:23; Hermas *Mand.* 4.1.5 (cf. *T. Jos.* 3:8).[107] Since this was probably the primary[108] meaning of the "unchastity" which for Shammai also constituted the sole ground for divorce, Matthew's Jesus thus appears to hold a Shammaite position — though a particularly strict one, in that his term *porneia* is more clearly limited to actual sexual misconduct than the wider range of immodest acts which some Shammaites included in "unchastity."[109] The phrase *logos porneias* in the exceptive clause here is probably

---

1 Cor 5:1, sometimes to support this interpretation, relates if, as seems likely, the father was still alive, not to marriage but to an adulterous (even if also incestuous) relationship with his wife. The proposal to read πορνεία in this sense in Acts 15:29 is equally debatable; the broad range of usage of the noun makes it unlikely that it could have been expected to be understood in this technical sense when used without explanation. J. A. Fitzmyer, *Advance,* 79-111, argues for this sense on the basis of Qumran usage, but the evidence relates of course to the Hebrew *zᵉnût,* not to its Greek "equivalent" πορνεία. See further Keener, 467-69; S. C. Barton, *Discipleship,* 195-97.

105. As in 1:18-19, where divorce was assumed to be required. D. C. Allison, *JSNT* 49 (1993) 3-10, helpfully discusses the light which the Joseph story sheds on first-century Jewish attitudes and practice.

106. The case for this sense is well made by D. Janzen, *JSNT* 80 (2000) 66-80.

107. The use of πορνεία rather than μοιχεία (the normal term for adultery) may be due to the fact that it is the wife's action which is referred to, whereas adultery was thought of primarily as a male sin against another man (as in vv. 27-28); after all, μοιχεία is not used in LXX Deut 24:1 either. Davies and Allison, 1:531, appeal to J. B. Bauer's finding that "in biblical Greek the μοιχ- root tends to be used of men, the πορν- root of women."

108. See J. P. Meier, *Law,* 143-44 (and n. 44), for a wider range of acts of "impurity or immodesty" which the Shammaites sometimes held to constitute the *'erwat-dābār.* They include "going outside with hair unfastened, spinning cloth in the street with armpits uncovered, and bathing in the same place as men." It is thus misleading to state, as most commentators do, that the Shammaites allowed divorce *only* in the case of adultery.

109. See the previous note. It is sometimes objected that a restatement of the Shammaite position, even in this more rigorous form, would not represent a righteousness which goes far beyond that of the scribes and Pharisees, as this context requires. But it must be remembered that even the broader Shammaite position was in all probability itself an extreme minority view even in Jesus' day, and by the time Matthew wrote his gospel it was probably largely forgotten. Certainly a strict principle of no voluntary divorce and remarriage (while allowing that where a marriage has already been broken by adultery it cannot be allowed to continue) would stand out as radical in the light of the dominant rabbinic teaching.

intended to recall[110] the *'erwat-dābār* of Deut 24:1,[111] which was also the basis of the Shammaite position.[112]

If Mark and Luke preserve Jesus' actual teaching on divorce, Matthew's version, even if close to the "hard-line" Shammaite position, would seem to represent a substantial softening of the radicalism of Jesus' total prohibition of divorce. It is often assumed that this represents the beginning of a process of pragmatic adaptation by a church which found Jesus' absolute ethic unworkable in practice, an adaptation which in many modern Christian circles has resulted in something like a Hillelite liberalism. But it may be worth inquiring how far Matthew would in fact have understood himself to be differing from the total prohibition of divorce in Mark and Luke. The concept of man and wife as "one flesh" which will be the basis of Jesus' rejection of divorce in 19:4-9 stands in tension with the fact that an act of adultery sets up a "one-flesh" relationship with a different person.[113] In Jewish thought this second "one-flesh" union was understood to violate the original one so radically that the subsequent continuation of the original marriage was unthinkable; it was officially dissolved (*m. Yebam.* 2:8; cf. *Soṭah* 5:1; *Ketub.* 3:5).[114] In the OT the marriage was terminated by the death penalty

---

110. It is not a literal translation, as it reverses the order of the two terms (as did some rabbinic interpretation of the passage), but these words used in a context of divorce would naturally be heard as an echo of the terminology of Deut 24:1. J. P. Meier, *Law,* 143-44, regards the allusion as "not certain."

111. *Dābār* more often means "word" than "thing," and is regularly translated by λόγος, even though not here in LXX.

112. R. J. Banks, *Jesus,* 156-57 (following B. Vawter, *CBQ* 16 [1954] 163-65; though Vawter abandoned this position later in *CBQ* 39 [1977] 534-35), recognizing the allusion to Deut 24:1, suggests that "πορνεία had become, at least in Matthaean circles, a technical term for the Deuteronomic provision," and so takes the exceptive clause as relating not to the verb ἀπολύω but rather to the whole clause. The resultant translation reverses the normal understanding of the passage by allowing no exception: "Whoever dismisses his wife — the permission of Deut 24:1 notwithstanding — and marries another, commits adultery." This radical solution to the problem of discrepancy between Mark and Matthew depends on an unnatural reading of the term πορνεία and is even harder to square with the wording in 19:9 (μὴ ἐπὶ πορνείᾳ) than it is with the natural meaning of παρεκτός ("except for") here. Luz, 1:304, comments that such interpretations which attempt to avoid the exceptive sense "have today just about disappeared from the discussion, because the philological finding is unambiguous."

113. Paul draws this conclusion concerning intercourse with a prostitute (1 Cor 6:16).

114. The point is well spelled out by Luz, 1:306. For the rabbinic requirement (not merely permission) of divorce following adultery see M. Bockmuehl, *NTS* 35 (1989) 291-95, pointing out that the same principle is also implied at Qumran. D. Instone-Brewer, *Divorce,* 95-97, however, questions whether this was yet an absolute requirement in the early first century.

for adultery, but by Jesus' time the death penalty was not normally imposed; instead the marriage was legally dissolved. The termination of a marriage already destroyed by the act of adultery was thus not so much "divorce" (a man's voluntary repudiation of his wife) as the necessary recognition that the original marriage no longer existed, that a new "one-flesh" union was already a *fait accompli*. Joseph's dilemma in 1:18-19, for instance, was not over whether to repudiate Mary or not, but only over whether this duty should be carried out publicly or privately; until otherwise directed by the angel, it did not occur to him that the betrothal (and the marriage to which it must otherwise lead) could be regarded as still valid. Against such a background it can be argued that when in Mark and Luke Jesus forbids divorce *tout simple* this is understood to mean the voluntary breaking of a marriage which is hitherto intact, it being assumed that in the case of *porneia* by the wife the marriage was already destroyed and could not be allowed to continue. On that view, Matthew is merely making explicit what was assumed by Mark and Luke to be already obvious to their readers.

This interpretation perhaps gains support from the way the prohibition of divorce is here expressed, as the initiation of adultery. With regard to the woman, it makes her the victim of adultery,[115] either in that the husband's repudiation of a marriage which is intact is itself equated with an act of adultery (since adultery destroys a marriage), or in that when she subsequently remarries (as is provided for in the divorce certificate and is assumed as the sequel to her divorce) she will be placed by her husband's act in an adulterous relationship, since the original marriage remains valid in the sight of God. So both the divorced wife (the victim of the first husband's unjust act) and her subsequent husband are involved in an act of adultery — and thus in breaking the seventh commandment, which in its OT context carried the death penalty. Moreover, to terminate a marriage where adultery has not in fact occurred is to treat the repudiated wife as if she had herself committed adultery (after which annulment of the marriage would have been automatic); to thus brand her unjustly as an adulteress may also be part of what is meant by to "make her the victim of adultery." 19:9 will add that if the original husband remarries, he, too, is committing adultery.[116]

Modern discussions of divorce in the light of Jesus' teaching sometimes suggest that Jesus recognized the necessity of divorce after adultery,

115. See p. 192, n. 48; cf. the even more striking parallel in Mark 10:11, "commits adultery against her," a phrase which contrasts sharply with the accepted Jewish understanding of adultery as an offense against the husband, not the wife.

116. See D. Instone-Brewer, *Divorce,* 125-32, for the Jewish view that remarriage after an invalid divorce is adultery.

but forbade remarriage.[117] But such a view does not fit the Jewish context, where divorce consisted of the provision of a certificate which explicitly granted the right to remarry: the standard wording, according to *m. Giṭ.* 9:3, was, "You are free to marry any man." Without that permission it was not divorce. Divorce and the right to remarry are thus inseparable, and the Jewish world knew nothing of a legal separation which did not allow remarriage.[118] There is nothing in Jesus' words, here or in the Mark and Luke parallels, to suggest that he intended to initiate any such provision. His condemnation of remarriage as adultery is simply on the grounds that the divorce (unless for adultery) was not legitimate and so the original marriage remains valid in the sight of God.

What effect, then, does Jesus' new teaching have on the understanding of Deut 24:1-4? Ideally it makes it obsolete, if God's purpose for marriage is truly honored, since the prior divorce for which it legislates will not in fact occur in the ethics of the kingdom of heaven. In opposing current divorce legislation Jesus is rescuing Deut 24:1-4 from misuse for a purpose for which it was never intended. It was not meant to provide a positive basis for the ethics of God's people, but only a trouble-shooting provision in case things went wrong. In 19:4-5 he will ground his positive understanding of marriage on a different pentateuchal source, and if that prior principle is observed there will be no divorce and therefore no use for the remedial legislation of Deut 24:1-4.

But Matthew's version of the saying, by specifying the possibility of *porneia* and therefore of the ending of a marriage otherwise than by death, at least entertains the possibility of a world in which God's ideal is not always met. In such a world the very undeveloped damage-limitation provisions of Deut 24:1-4 may continue to have a place, and indeed it may be necessary, as the rabbis had already found, for such contingent legislation to develop over a much wider front. That is what has happened ever since, and still continues with our divorce laws today. Such laws have their place in a well-ordered society, but they cannot claim to have the direct sanction of Jesus, and can only claim to fall within the spirit of his teaching if it is their aim not to accept and accommodate human "hardness of heart" but rather to uphold the standard of

117. A clear statement of this position is by G. J. Wenham, *JSNT* 22 (1984) 95-107, with a follow-up in *JSNT* 28 (1986) 17-23 focusing more specifically on the grammar of Matt 19:9. Cf. more fully W. A. Heth and G. J. Wenham, *Jesus.* See in response the comments of Keener, 469, especially n. 29. Wenham's articles appear to suggest that Jesus described divorce except for πορνεία as in itself "adulterous" on the part of the husband; but it is not at all obvious how the term "adulterous" could be applied to the dissolution of a marriage if it does not result in subsequent sexual activity — who would be committing adultery with whom?

118. See D. Instone-Brewer, *Divorce,* 117-25.

unbroken, lifelong marriage which God designed and to oppose the human tendency to make it easier to "separate what God has joined together" (19:6).

(4) Swearing (5:33-37)

While the subject is completely different, the principle by which Jesus responds to "what was said" in this case is very similar to that of vv. 31-32. A law which aims to control human failure (in vv. 31-32 the destruction of marriage, here the unreliability of people's word, even under oath) is set aside in favor of a bold reassertion of the way God intended things to be, lifelong faithfulness in marriage and simple truthfulness in speech without the need for oaths to undergird it. In each case the laws quoted may still have a trouble-shooting function, but they are being misused if they are made the basis of ethical thinking. The kingdom of heaven operates on a more radical level of essential righteousness. In thus going back to first principles Jesus leaves the remedial legislation of the Torah on one side, not so much abrogated as declared unnecessary where the greater righteousness of the kingdom of heaven obtains.

Two different but related subjects are at issue here. *Oaths,*[119] invocations of God or of some sacred object to undergird a statement or promise, shade into *vows,* solemn promises to God of an action to be performed. The OT passages summed up in v. 33 apparently relate to both issues, though Jesus' response focuses on the use of oaths to support one's word rather than on vows (he will touch on the latter question in 15:3-6). His simple command not to use oaths at all (v. 34a) is illustrated by a number of possible oaths each of which is shown to be inappropriate (vv. 34b-36), and explained in the pronouncement of v. 37 that any elaboration of a simple affirmation or denial is "from evil." Since the OT law not only provided for but in some cases demanded such elaborating oaths (e.g., Num 5:19-22), there is a *prima facie* case to be made that Jesus is here opposing the intention of one aspect of the law. At least he is doing what he did in v. 32, declaring that these provisions should never have been needed if people practiced the uncomplicated truthfulness which is what God desires.[120]

---

119. See H. D. Betz, *Sermon,* 259-62, for a survey of the nature and significance of oaths in the ancient world.

120. This pericope has obvious similarities with the longer text of *2 En.* 49:1, where Enoch says that he is not using an oath since God does not use oaths, but goes on, "If there is no truth in human beings, then let them make an oath by means of the words 'Yes, Yes' or 'No, No.'" He then proceeds to "make an oath" using the words "Yes, Yes." This passage seems likely to reflect Christian influence, and may well be derived from Matt 5:33-37, but whereas "Yes, Yes" and "No, No" are for Jesus the alternative to oaths, in *2 Enoch* they seem to have been made themselves into pseudo-oaths to counter human

33   The repetition of the full "quotation" formula from v. 21, with the addition this time of "again," is often taken to indicate that Matthew understands the series of six contrasts as falling into two equal parts. From a literary point of view that may be so, but it is not easy to see any difference in principle between the first three and the last three,[121] and the close similarity in principle between the third and the fourth which we have just noted cautions us against reading too much into this "new beginning."

The words quoted are again not an exact citation; this time they represent the gist of a number of passages in the law and elsewhere in the OT which require oaths and/or vows to be taken seriously. "You shall not swear falsely"[122] probably represents the prohibition on false swearing in Lev 19:12 (cf. Lev 6:3-5; Ps 24:4), while the command to "repay" your oaths reflects a recurrent OT theme that vows must be carried out, exemplified in Num 30:2; Deut 23:21-23; Ps 50:14; Eccl 5:4.[123] Vows were undertaken voluntarily, but once undertaken they were binding. Since the first two contrasts have involved two of the Ten Commandments, it is possible that the prohibition of false swearing here is meant to echo either the ninth commandment concerning bearing false witness (though there is no verbal echo since Exod 20:16 does not mention an oath) or the third concerning misusing God's name, of which a false oath would be a specific instance (though again not specified in Exod 20:7).

34a   Jesus' prohibition of all swearing (its comprehensiveness is indicated by the emphatic *holōs,* "at all") will be explained in principle in v. 37. With regard to vows, which were voluntary, Jesus is not so much opposing OT legislation as telling his disciples not to take up an option which the law offered but did not require. His words recall the comment of Deut 23:22 that, while vows once undertaken must be fulfilled (vv. 21, 23), if you do not make a vow at all "there will be no sin in you." Oaths, too, could be voluntary (Lev 5:4; Num 30:3-15), and such oaths are found frequently throughout OT history, but

---

untruthfulness. Cf. *b. Šebu.* 36a for the idea that the repetition of "Yes" and "No" makes them into oaths (cf. *b. Meg.* 32a).

121. The suggestion of Davies and Allison, 1:504, that the first three examples are regarded as derived from Deuteronomy and the last three from Leviticus drastically oversimplifies the actual nature of the quotations, only two of which (vv. 31, 43) come from a single pentateuchal source.

122. See p. 193, n. 51, for the meaning of the verb, which occurs in the LXX only in apocryphal books.

123. These passages are all about vows, and LXX uses εὐχή in all of them rather than ὅρκος as in Jesus' "quotation," though in LXX Num 30:3 the two terms are used in parallel. The "quotation" thus appears to deal with the subject of vows but under the related term ὅρκος. For confusion of the two terms in popular Greek see W. D. Davies, *Setting,* 240.

there were also occasions when the law required an oath (Exod 22:11; Num 5:19-22; cf. the general expectation that oaths will be taken in Yahweh's name, without specific context, in Deut 6:13; 10:20), and these, too, are swept aside by Jesus' blanket prohibition if it is taken as a literal regulation.[124]

34b-36 The general principle that disciples should not take oaths is now illustrated by series of examples of specific oaths which are inappropriate. Cf. 23:16-22 for a similar discussion of oaths. Oaths normally invoked God as the guarantor of the person's word, and it was this which made it so serious a matter to break them: it was a misuse of God's name (Exod 20:7), a profanation (Lev 19:12). In response some Jews had already developed the habit, which underlies much of our "social swearing" today, of finding more innocuous substitutes for the actual name of God; here Jesus lists oaths by heaven, earth, Jerusalem, and one's own head, while in 23:16-22 he will add a further list (the temple, the gold of the temple, the altar, and the gift on the altar). Such casuistry, of which the Mishnah provides numerous examples,[125] receives very short shrift since heaven, earth, and Jerusalem are inseparably linked with God as his dwelling and possession; the point is made by allusions to Isa 66:1 ("Heaven is my throne and the earth is my footstool") and Ps 48:2 ("Mount Zion, the city of the great King"). The oath by one's head[126] might have been given parallel treatment, since the head, too, is God's creation, but the point is made more obliquely by pointing out that you have no power over your own head; the implication is that it is God, not you, who determines the color of your hair (some early patristic interpreters took this verse as a ruling against the use of hair dye!) since he is its creator and sustainer. All such surrogate oaths display not reverence but theological superficiality.

37 Jesus' prohibition of swearing is based on the assumption that God requires truthfulness. A simple Yes or No should be all that is needed.[127] As soon as it is necessary to bolster it with an oath in order to persuade others

---

124. P. Foster, *Community*, 115-22, argues that this "authoritative rejection of oaths by Jesus" should be seen as abrogating the law in this respect.

125. Notably in the tractates *Nedarim* and *Nazir* on vows and especially *Šebu'ot* on oaths. *M. Šebu.* 4:13 is a good example, including "by heaven and earth" as a less binding oath. For swearing by Jerusalem cf. *m. Ned.* 1:3, and for swearing by one's head *m. Sanh.* 3:2.

126. Note the reversion to the second-person singular for the illustrative example in v. 36, as in vv. 23-26, 29-30; the basic commands of vv. 34 and 37 remain in the plural.

127. See Jas 5:12 for a restatement of this principle. While Jas 5:12 reflects the *sense* of Jesus' words here, 2 Cor 1:17, with its doubled ναὶ ναί and οὒ οὔ, is closer to their *form*. It uses the phrases in a quite different sense, however, in that the utterance side by side of ναὶ ναί and οὒ οὔ represents the *unreliability* of someone who says sometimes one thing and sometimes another; in that case the repetition of the particle probably indicates emphasis intended to gain credence.

to believe what is said, the ideal of transparent truthfulness has been compromised.[128] The need for such an addition is "from evil";[129] it betrays our failure to live up to God's standard of truthfulness. The option of translating "from the Evil One" (see p. 193, n. 55) would not essentially change the sense: whether the moral failure is blamed on an abstract principle of "evil" or on the personal intervention of the devil (the "father of lies," John 8:44) does not affect its evil character. The context here gives us no obvious reason for preferring the personal to the abstract sense.

The majority of references to oaths in the OT, especially in the book of Deuteronomy, are to God's oath by which he has committed himself to bless his people under his covenant with their ancestors. Is God's oath then also "from evil"? In one sense it is, in that if people were prepared to trust God's simple word there would be no need for an oath. But insofar as God's oath is a powerful statement of his own dependability ("By myself I have sworn, says the Lord"), it differs from human oaths which attempt to enlist God in support of their less dependable words.

A more pertinent question for us is whether Jesus' words here are intended as a literal regulation for all human circumstances, including oaths of political allegiance or the oath required in many courts of law: should Christians refuse to take such oaths?[130] The issue is similar to that with regard to divorce: Jesus' absolute pronouncement sets out the true will of God, but in human life that will is not always followed, and there is still a place for legal oaths (as for divorce regulations) to cope with the actual untruthfulness of people, even sadly sometimes of disciples. They should not be needed, but in practice they serve a remedial purpose in a world where the ethics of the kingdom of heaven are not always followed. Refusal to take a required oath can in such circumstances convey quite the wrong impression. Jesus' illustrations of the "greater righteousness" are not to be treated as if they were a new

128. Jesus' teaching here bears a striking resemblance to Josephus's account of the Essenes: "Every declaration they make is stronger than an oath, and indeed they avoid swearing since they regard it as worse than perjury on the grounds that anyone who cannot be believed without an appeal to God is already condemned" (*War* 2.135). However, in *War* 2.139-42 Josephus goes on to describe the solemn oath which was *required* of a new adherent to the Essene sect; it seems, then, that the "avoidance" of oaths related to everyday affairs, not to the formal oath of commitment. This "oath of the covenant" is described also in CD 15:1-10; cf. 1QS 5:8. An oath is apparently also required in a judicial context in CD 9:11-12. For further details on oaths at Qumran see W. D. Davies, *Setting*, 242-44. For criticism of oaths in Hellenistic literature and Philo see Luz, 1:314.

129. Cf. Sir 23:11: "The one who swears many oaths is full of iniquity." Sir 23:9-11 is a strong invective against swearing as inevitably linked with sinfulness.

130. Luz, 1:318-22, gives a fascinating historical survey of Christian views on this issue.

set of literal regulations to replace those of the scribes and Pharisees. For Jesus' own response when "put on oath" by the high priest see below on 26:63-64, and for other NT oaths cf. 2 Cor 1:23; Gal 1:20; 1 Thess 5:27.[131]

(5) Retribution (5:38-42)

Here Jesus' teaching moves even further away from the spirit of the OT law quoted than in any of the previous examples. The law of Moses, like other ancient (and modern) law codes, regulated the extent of retributive punishment. The principle of retribution was accepted, but it must be proportionate to the offense: one eye in retribution for an eye destroyed, one tooth for a tooth (see comments below on how far this was understood and implemented literally). That seems to be the main thrust of the words quoted. They provide guidance in sentencing for those responsible for trying a case of physical assault.

In response Jesus does not comment on the appropriateness of such judicial rules. His concern is only with the inappropriateness of such a formula to personal ethics. Applied to that context it becomes a justification for "getting your own back," and thus ultimately for the relentless perpetuation of the traditional blood-feud with no hope of escaping the cycle of reciprocal violence — which is still sadly evident in many cultures, not least in the Middle East today. Jesus' position is shockingly radical: not only no retaliation, but even no resistance to one who is admittedly "bad." The series of four personal examples which make up vv. 39b-42, and which are partially paralleled in Luke 6:29-30,[132] illustrate the principle of not even standing up for one's own rights (three of the four examples involve legal principles), of not defending one's own honor,[133] of allowing others to take advantage. They portray an unselfish and uncalculating benevolence which thinks only of the other's needs or desires, not of protecting one's own resources or even one's honor. Those who have understood the true thrust of Jesus' teaching here have often declared it to be not only extreme and unwelcome, but also practically unworkable in the real world. You cannot live like this. It would be to encourage the unscrupulous and the feckless and so to undermine the proper ordering of society.

Here more than anywhere in this section we need to remind ourselves that Jesus' aim is not to establish a new and more demanding set of rules to

---

131. J. A. Brant, *JSNT* 63 (1996) 3-20, shows how in the three instances in Matthew where an oath is introduced into the narrative (14:7; 26:63, 72-74) it proves to be "infelicitous."

132. In the Lucan context these examples are linked with the theme of loving enemies which Matthew will take up in the next section.

133. This aspect of vv. 38-42 is brought out by J. H. Neyrey, *Honor,* 203-8.

supplant those of the scribes and Pharisees. It is to establish a "greater righteousness," a different understanding of how we should live as the people of God, an alternative set of values.[134] In place of the principle of retribution he sets nonresistance; in place of the defense of legal rights he sets uncalculating generosity; in place of concern for oneself he sets concern for the other. The disciple may be forced to conclude that in an imperfect human society Jesus' illustrations of these principles could not work as literal rules of conduct, that unlimited generosity to beggars would not only undermine the economic order but also in the end do no good to the beggars themselves. But instead of therefore dismissing Jesus' teaching as starry-eyed utopianism, a proper response to this challenging section is to ask in what practical ways Jesus' radical principles *can* be set to work in our very different world. Our answers will vary, but if they are true to Jesus' teaching they will represent an essentially non-self-centered approach to ethics which puts the interests of the other before personal rights or convenience. We should note also, however, that a willingness to forgo one's own rights and even to allow oneself to be insulted and imposed on is not incompatible with a firm stand for justice in principle and for the rights of others.

Does this teaching contradict or abrogate the law? Rather, insofar as "an eye for an eye" had come to be used to justify personal retaliation, it is simply declared to be irrelevant to personal ethics. The principle of proportionate retribution should not guide us in our relations with others. But then that was not its intention: it was a judicial guideline, not a license to get one's own back. In its place Jesus lays out an ethical approach which simply sets aside legal considerations and goes far beyond anything the law, as law, either did or could promote. The "fulfillment" of the law (v. 17) here consists in leaving it behind in favor of something of a different order altogether, the righteousness of the kingdom of heaven. But, as we have already noted in relation to divorce and to oaths, in the real world where people do oppress and take advantage of others, society will still have need for guidelines on how to deal judicially with such cases, and a standard of proportionate retribution (even if not in the physical terms of the OT rulings) may continue to serve as a useful guide for the judiciary.[135]

---

134. Luz, 1:326-29, discusses the function of vv. 39b-41 not as practical advice but as a passage in which "the contrast between kingdom of God and world breaks open."

135. J. Piper, *Love,* 89-91, helpfully discusses the links between the third, fourth, and fifth of Jesus' examples as all dealing with Mosaic regulations to govern "hardness of heart," which Jesus now sets aside on the basis of "a change of heart which makes superfluous the written law of Moses." On pp. 95-99 Piper goes on, however, to suggest that in the real world of human sinfulness the Mosaic regulations (and specifically the *lex talionis*) still have a valuable role, though recognizing that this is a question "which Jesus neither asked nor explicitly answered."

38 "Eye for eye, tooth for tooth" (quoted from the LXX) occurs three times in the Pentateuch: Exod 21:24; Lev 24:20; Deut 19:21, in each case as part of a longer list of equivalents (beginning with "life for life"), and in a context of formal trial. Such stipulations of proportionate retribution occur in other ancient law-codes, notably in the much earlier Babylonian code of Hammurabi where the same examples of eye and tooth are used (paragraphs 196-201). They may have been intended originally to limit the extravagant vengeance associated with an oriental blood-feud, but the OT texts do not express this intention; rather, in Deut 19:21 the list is preceded by "Show no pity," to ensure that judges did not mitigate the full penalty required. The pentateuchal rulings are clearly intended to be applied literally: "Anyone who maims another shall suffer the same injury in return . . . the injury inflicted is the injury to be suffered" (Lev 24:19-20). But by the time of Jesus appropriate financial compensation had generally taken the place of physical mutilation,[136] so that it is probably not physical brutality as such which Jesus is here opposing, but rather the essential principle of even legitimate retribution.

39 Jesus is often quoted as opposing retaliation,[137] a stance for which there are several parallels in the OT and other Jewish writings (see, e.g., Lev 19:18; Prov 20:22; 24:29; 25:21-22; Sir 28:1-7, and the principle of leaving vengeance to God, not exacting it oneself, Deut 32:35; Isa 50:6-9; 1QS 10:17-18) and among pagan philosophers. But Jesus' words go further than that: even resistance[138] is forbidden, and no distinction is made between

---

136. See Str-B 1:337-41; D. Daube, *Rabbinic Judaism,* 255-56, but cf. also the cautionary comments of J. P. Meier, *Law,* 158, n. 78, pointing out the evidence for some continuing physical application of the law (as Str-B also illustrates). Philo, *Spec. leg.* 3.181-204, continues to argue for literal, physical application. Josephus, *Ant.* 4.280, indicates that there was discretion as to whether financial damages were accepted (but Daube rules this out on the grounds that Josephus was out of touch with Jewish law and is drawing instead on Roman). Cf. *m. B. Qam.* 8:1.

137. H. D. Betz, *Sermon,* 280, insists that since "total nonresistance to evil constitutes an irrational and unjustifiable position incompatible with the rest of early Christian teaching," the phrase must be translated "Do not retaliate" (whatever the lexical meaning of ἀντιστῆναι!). He goes on (281-82) to cite critics, especially Jewish, of the idea of nonresistance, and then to argue passionately (282-85) that nonretaliation (not nonresistance) is the true way to establish justice. He also cites many examples of the commendation of nonretaliation from Greco-Roman ethicists (286-88). The effect is to align Jesus closely with the best of current pagan ethics ("reasonable and ethically justifiable") rather than to present him as distinctive within his own environment.

138. In view of the legal tone of the first two illustrations that follow, ἀνθίστημι probably here includes the sense of "to oppose in court" and thus to insist on one's legal rights, but the verb is in itself quite general, and not all the following illustrations concern legal situations. See R. J. Banks, *Jesus,* 196-98; J. P. Meier, *Law,* 157, n. 77. R. A. Guelich, *Sermon,* 219-20, argues for the legal sense as the only meaning here.

active and passive resistance, violent and nonviolent,[139] legal and illegal.[140] Nor is this because of any doubt over the injustice of the offense: the person who is not to be resisted is "bad." The term is the same as in v. 37, but here the context rules out the translation "the Evil One," that is, the devil (see p. 193, n. 55) since the following examples are of human opponents or exploiters. The same consideration weighs against the abstract translation "Do not resist evil," quite apart from the improbability of Jesus or Matthew ever countenancing such an amoral attitude. The startling teaching of this passage is that these are bad people, intent on getting the better of the disciple, but even their admitted badness does not justify the disciple in resisting them. The issue, then, is not whether one should stand up for good in principle (or as it affects other people), but whether one should stand up for oneself when under threat.

Four illustrations follow, all, as in vv. 23-26, 29-30, and 36 above, in the second-person singular, envisaging specific personal dilemmas which in different ways exemplify the principle of nonresistance. The first results from a slap on the right cheek. To slap another's cheek was a serious insult (2 Cor 11:20; cf. Lam 3:30) for which legal redress could be claimed (the code of Hammurabi deals with this too, in paragraphs 202-5, with penalties ranging from a small fine to the cutting off of an ear, depending on the social standing of the two parties involved), but to slap the *right* cheek required (if the assailant was right-handed) a slap with the back of the hand,[141] which was far more insulting and would entail double damages (*m. B. Qam.* 8:6). This is more a matter of honor than of physical injury,[142] and honor required appropriate recompense. Yet Jesus tells the disciple to forgo the financial benefit to which he is legally entitled, to accept the insult without responding,[143] and

139. Carter, 151, following W. Wink, *RevExp* 89 (1992) 197-214, boldly translates ἀντιστῆναι as *"violently* resist" and reads Jesus as positively commanding "active nonviolent resistance." The case may be argued exegetically, but lexical study of ἀνθίστημι does not support this as a *translation,* despite Wink's correct observation (199) that it is frequently used in military contexts. An interesting contrast to Wink's study is provided by S. D. Currie, *HTR* 57 (1964) 140-45, who argues that ἀνθίστημι should be translated "protest against" (i.e., *nonviolently* resist!) and takes it as a reference to legal action: "Don't file a complaint; don't make a court case of it; don't seek damages."

140. See Luz, 1:331-35, for the history of Christian interpretation and application of this principle, with special reference to pacifism.

141. Alternatively, it entails the use of the left hand, which was also regarded as particularly insulting (1 Esdr 4:30).

142. J. Jeremias, *Theology,* 239-40, suggests that the context envisaged is of Christian messengers being abused as heretics by non-Christian Jews; cf. the physical ill-treatment of Jesus as a blasphemer in 26:67.

143. John 18:22-23 records Jesus' own response when unjustly slapped: his situation would in any case not allow retaliation, but he points out the injustice. Paul's

even to offer the left cheek for a further, if less serious, insult. Such a response follows the model of God's servant, who "gave my back to those who struck me, and my cheeks to those who pulled out the beard [LXX has "to slapping"]; I did not hide my face from insult and spitting" (Isa 50:6).[144] In a culture which took honor and shame far more seriously than ours, this was a paradoxical and humiliating demand.[145]

40 The second illustration is even more clearly located in the law-court, with the opponent suing for possession of the disciple's "shirt."[146] To forfeit the shirt would be bad enough, but the disciple is to voluntarily give up his "coat" (the *himation,* the larger, heavier, and more valuable outer garment) as well. Whatever the legal rights with regard to the shirt (perhaps claimed as pledge for the payment of a debt), there could be no question of legally forfeiting the coat, since this was explicitly prohibited on humanitarian grounds in the OT law (Exod 22:25-27; Deut 24:12-13, showing that the *himation* could double as a sleeping blanket). What the opponent could not have dared to claim, the disciple is to offer freely, even at the cost of leaving himself with nothing to wear or to keep warm with. Cf. Paul's exhortation to be wronged and defrauded rather than to institute a lawsuit (1 Cor 6:7).

41 The third illustration takes up a specific grievance of subject people under the Roman occupation. "Dragoons you as a porter" is an attempt to capture the military force of *angareuō,* a rare term originally used for the stages ridden by officers in the Persian postal service, but in first-century Palestine referring especially to the Roman soldier's right to enlist a member of the subject population for forced labor, in this case presumably

---

more hotheaded response in a similar situation (Acts 23:2-5) does not quite match Jesus' injunction!

144. M. D. Goulder, *Midrash,* 293, points out many coincidences of vocabulary between the present pericope and LXX Isa 50:6-9, though the way the words are used does not support his view that Matthew has compiled the pericope as a midrash on Isa 50. Cf. also R. H. Gundry, *Use,* 72-73. D. C. Allison, *CBQ* 56 (1994) 703-5, finds in these verbal links evidence that Matthew intended his readers to think here of Isa 50:4-9, and thus also to reflect on how Jesus' experiences at his passion (26:67; 27:30) fulfilled his own injunctions.

145. Carter, 152, suggests rather that by this unexpected initiative the disciple refuses to be humiliated: "The chosen action refuses submission, asserts dignity and humanness, and challenges what is supposed to demean." Carter finds similar defiance, designed to shame the oppressor, rather than meek submission in the actions enjoined in vv. 40 and 41 as well. See to the contrary, however, J. H. Neyrey, *Honor,* 204-5, who insists rather that "Jesus requires his disciples to step apart completely from the honor game. . . . They are not in any way seeking to win, even by passive aggression."

146. The χιτών was the basic garment worn next to the skin, without which one would be naked apart from a loincloth.

as a porter[147] for his equipment; the only other NT use of the verb is for Simon of Cyrene forced to carry Jesus' cross (27:32). This oppressive practice was of course deeply resented by the people of occupied Palestine, but it was a Roman legal provision and they would have no choice about complying up to the limit required ("mile" was a Roman, not a Jewish measure). But Jesus calls on the disciple not only to accept the imposition but also to volunteer for a double stint.[148] To do this for anyone would be remarkable, but to do it for the enemy was unheard of. This cameo thus serves not only to illustrate Jesus' demand to renounce one's rights, but also prepares us for his equally revolutionary command to love one's enemies (v. 44), and suggests that Jesus advocated a response to the Roman occupation which not only full-blown Zealots but even the ordinarily patriotic populace would have found incomprehensible.

42 The fourth illustration is a more everyday situation, a request for money or goods, whether from a neighbor or a beggar — and Jesus' comprehensive wording does not allow us the luxury of distinguishing. Jesus' injunction reflects the remarkable generosity of the provisions in Deut 15:7-11 for helping a fellow Israelite in need, but is more open-ended (and even more obviously so in the parallel in Luke 6:30). Our natural resistance to such a request, especially from a stranger, is scarcely lessened when it is ostensibly for a loan rather than for an outright gift. This "beggar's charter" is the most obviously impractical of all these illustrations, just because it does not speak of an exceptional situation. Few are in so fortunate a position as to be able to obey it literally for more than a few days, and it is easy to marshal arguments to prove that it is in the long-term interest of no one, not even the beggar, for us to do so. The principle of discrimination set out in 7:6 seems to offer a welcome refuge. But none of these illustrations sets out a prudential maxim; all of them (like the Beatitudes) challenge us to unnatural behavior, and all must seem crazy to a secular world (and indeed have often been denounced as such). The point they are making is that in the kingdom of heaven self-interest does not rule, and even our legal rights and legitimate expectations may have to give way to the interests of others. It is for each disciple to work

147. E. A. Judge, in G. H. R. Horsley (ed.), *New Documents,* 1:36-45, prints and discusses a contemporary Roman edict setting out the acceptable limits of *angareia* by the army in Pisidia. Since the edict deals only with the requisitioning of donkeys, mules, and carts, not personal porters, Judge suggests that the reference here is also to the requisitioning of one's donkey. Josephus, *Ant.* 13.52, uses the term for the requisitioning of beasts of burden by the army. But the *angareia* in 27:32 was clearly personal.

148. Note the contrast with the superficially similar advice of the Stoic philosopher Epictetus, *Diss.* 4.1.79: "If there is an *angareia* and a soldier seizes your donkey, let it go. Do not resist or grumble, or you will be beaten — and lose your donkey just the same!"

out for themselves how this principle can most responsibly be applied to the issue of giving and lending in the different personal and social circumstances in which we find ourselves.

(6) Love (5:43-47)

Here there is no question of Jesus contradicting what "was said" in the Pentateuch; indeed, he might be thought rather to be defending it in that the words "quoted" include not only the OT command to love one's neighbor (Lev 19:18) but also an additional clause which is not part of that text and which Jesus goes on to repudiate. But while the additional words draw a corollary which the OT text does not state, they represent what would be naturally understood to be the counterpart to its intended application, whereas Jesus' contrasting statement goes far beyond the purview of Lev 19:18 and introduces a concept of undiscriminating love which cannot easily be derived from the Pentateuch at all. The key (as the lawyer of Luke 10:29 rightly perceived) lies in the meaning of "neighbor." For most contemporary interpreters the term was restrictive, leaving non-neighbors outside the command to love; hence the popular addition "and hate your enemy." The general use of "neighbor" in the OT suggests that Lev 19:18 has this restrictive sense, applying specifically to fellow members of the Israelite community. For Jesus, however, the love of neighbor was broadly inclusive, as is spelled out in vv. 44-47 and more graphically in Luke 10:30-37.

In these verses, which are paralleled but in different words and order in Luke 6:27-35,[149] the paradoxical values of the kingdom of heaven reach their climax in what is virtually an oxymoron, "Love your enemies"; an enemy is by definition not loved. Perhaps even more than turning the other cheek, this command has attracted the incredulity, and often the scorn, of many interpreters, as a utopian policy[150] which makes no sense in a world characterized by conflict and self-interest.[151] But it is at this point that Mat-

---

149. This passage includes Luke's parallel to the case studies which Matthew has already used in vv. 39-42 to illustrate nonresistance.

150. See Luz, 1:349-51, for discussion, with historical examples, of the charge that Jesus' ethic is here unnatural and impractical.

151. As with nonretaliation (see last section) there are examples, both Jewish and pagan, of an attitude of benevolence toward personal enemies or persecutors (see Davies and Allison, 1:551-52 and 553, for parallels to "pray for those who persecute you"), but Davies and Allison conclude that the simple, unqualified form of Jesus' exhortation represents something "fresh and unforgettable." J. Piper, *Love,* 19-49, surveys the attitude to enemies in both Hellenistic philosophy and Jewish sources, and fails to find a parallel to Jesus' open-ended demand. The texts cited exhibit "one or more of the following features: a command or permission to hate another person; a qualification of enemy love so that it is

thew's Jesus plays his strongest ethical card: to love those who do not love you is not offered as a piece of pragmatic wisdom, but as a reflection of the character of God himself (v. 45). This final example thus prepares the way for the breath-taking final summary in v. 48, where the "greater righteousness" of v. 20 is revealed in all its otherness. The purpose of the whole of the discourse so far has not been to provide a suitable ethic for getting along alright in the world but to challenge those who have accepted the demands of the kingdom of heaven to live up to their commitment by being different from other people. The rhetorical questions of vv. 46-47 therefore sum up the thrust of all these examples of the greater righteousness: it is to live on a level above that of ordinary decent people, to draw your standards of conduct not from what everyone else is doing, but from your heavenly Father. This teaching of Jesus on the love of enemies formed one of the most distinctive traits of the early Christian movement,[152] and has been widely influential ever since.

43 It may seem surprising that Lev 19:18, which is here quoted as the less-than-adequate first half of a contrast with Jesus' new teaching, will later appear with no hint of criticism as the OT text which Jesus uses for half of his eventual summary of the law in 22:37-40 and which he puts on a par with the Ten Commandments in 19:19.[153] But the addition of "and hate your enemy" shows that he is quoting it in its popularly understood form, which goes in quite the opposite direction to his own inclusive reading of "neighbor." "Neighbor" is a frequent OT term for a fellow member of the covenant community, and the associated terms in Lev 19:17-18 ("your kin," "one of your people") leave no doubt that that is its meaning there. The related question of the Israelite's attitude to non-Israelites is not raised there. But it is raised elsewhere, often in a form which suggests that the addition "and hate your enemy" was not so far wide of the mark. Some passages in the law did call for benevolent treatment of a personal enemy (Exod 23:4-5; cf. Prov 24:17; 25:21) as well as a welcoming attitude to

---

not always or in every case demanded; an ambiguous mixture of unrelated directions to love and hate; a ground and aim in 'loving' which is irreconcilable with the NT paraenesis" (ibid., 64). Cf. also M. Reiser, *NTS* 47 (2001) 411-27, who concludes that the ethical level of loving one's enemy "is reached only by Socrates, a few Roman Stoics, Lev. 19:18 and Jesus" (426).

152. J. Piper, *Love,* 100-133, traces the influence of Jesus' love commandment in the NT epistles. For the view in the early church that it was "*the* Christian distinction and innovation" see Luz, 1:340, and his treatment of the "history of influence," ibid., 347-48.

153. All other quotations of Lev 19:18 in the NT include the words "as yourself." Their omission here is probably because to include them would destroy the balancing structure of the double saying (though H. D. Betz, *Sermon,* 302-3, also suggests a theological reason for the omission).

well-disposed foreigners (Lev 19:34; Deut 10:19), but the attitude to the non-Israelite enemy is probably more typically expressed by the verdict on neighboring peoples in Deut 23:3-6, by the treatment of the indigenous peoples of Canaan prescribed in Deut 7:1-6; 20:16-18 and illustrated in the book of Joshua, and by the violent nationalistic invective of Ps 137:7-9 and the hatred of God's enemies in Ps 139:21-22. Such "hatred" would be felt by many to be a patriotic duty which appropriately complemented the communal loyalty expressed by Lev 19:18. We cannot now know whether the extended version of Lev 19:18 quoted by Jesus came from a recognizable source, but there is little doubt that many would have taken it as the natural sense. The nearest approximation to it in surviving literature is probably the Qumran rule "to love all the sons of light . . . and to hate all the sons of darkness,"[154] where of course the "sons of light" represents a far narrower group than the "neighbor" of Lev 19:18.[155] While it is true that in biblical language "hate" sometimes carries the connotation of "not love" or even "love less" as opposed to positive hatred (Gen 29:30-31; Matt 6:24; Luke 14:26; Rom 9:13), J. Jeremias is stretching this linguistic elastic to its limit when he translates here "You shall love your compatriot (but) you need not love your adversary."[156]

44 Jesus' radical new precept, "Love your enemies," does not specify whether he is talking about personal hostility or about political enemies — which at that time would mean primarily the Roman occupying forces. The following verses focus on the former ("those who persecute you"; "those who love you"; "your own circle"), but even to raise the question is probably to engage in the sort of casuistry Jesus' simple demand was intended to sweep aside. The change from the singular "enemy" of v. 43 to the plural here may be intended to underline its comprehensiveness: no class of enemy is excluded (cf. the very general "bad person" in v. 39). To "love" (*agapaō*) in the NT is not only a matter of emotion but also of an attitude which determines our behavior, acting for the good of the other (7:12 well sums up its implications), and is therefore appropriately expanded by the following clause, "pray for those who persecute you." The expectation of persecution for Jesus' followers is a recurrent theme in Matthew's gospel (5:10-12; 10:16-39; 13:21; 16:24-26; 23:34-36; 24:9-13). His demand here goes even beyond v. 39: not only are they not to retaliate, nor even to resist, but even positively to seek the good of their persecutors and to pray for

154. 1QS 1:9-10; cf. 1:3-4; 9:21-22; cf. Josephus, *War* 2.139, the Essene oath to "hate the unjust."
155. W. D. Davies, *Setting,* 245-49, 427, considers the possibility that vv. 43-48 may have had the attitudes of Qumran in mind.
156. J. Jeremias, *Theology,* 213-14, n. 3.

them. The example of Stephen (Acts 7:60) was followed by many of the early Christian martyrs.[157] Prayer is mentioned primarily as an expression of goodwill toward the persecutors, without specifying its content, but presumably it would at least include the request that they, like Saul of Tarsus, might see the light.[158]

A realistic assessment of what "loving enemies" might mean in practice must of course take account of the very robust way in which Jesus reacted to the opposition of the scribes and Pharisees in the diatribe of ch. 23. His concept of love is apparently not at the level of simply being nice to people and of allowing error to go unchallenged. Love is not incompatible with controversy and rebuke.

45 Love for enemies is a reflection of the character of God himself.[159] The thought is not that such behavior will by itself make the disciples into God's children,[160] since that status is already implied in the term "your Father who is in heaven" (see on 5:16). Rather, it will be the proper outworking of that relationship and demonstrate its legitimacy (as with the peacemakers in 5:9, a beatitude which is strongly reflected in this passage). Like father, like son (as v. 48 will further require). Both bad and good are part of God's creation, and his provision of natural resources[161] is not targeted toward his "favorites"[162] — a thought which should give pause to some con-

---

157. Jesus' prayer according to the majority text of Luke 23:34 would, if original, be the inspiration for Stephen's attitude, and illustrate Jesus' observance of his own precept. If it is not part of Luke's original text, it nonetheless testifies to the early influence of this principle.

158. J. Piper, *Love,* 143-44, argues this on the basis of the content of the Lord's Prayer, which he regards as "a proper source for Matthew's understanding of the sermon's many imperatives."

159. B. A. Reid, *CBQ* 66 (2004) 237-55, finds a tension between this passage and the endings of several Matthean parables which appear to depict God as inflicting cruel punishment on his opponents; she resolves the tension by noting that the parables are about eschatological judgment, and are not to be taken as a model for present ethical behavior.

160. As could be understood from J. Piper's insistence (*Love,* 76-80) that the love of enemies is presented as a *condition* for entering the kingdom of heaven. B. Charette, *Recompense,* 93, is more circumspect, but accepts the term "condition."

161. The impartiality of God's provision in nature does not, of course, indicate that he is indifferent to people's behavior, nor does it obviate the reality of divine judgment. In a passage interestingly "parallel" to this verse Josephus says that it is "madness to expect God to treat the just as he treats the unjust" (*War* 5.407), but he is speaking not of natural provision but of God's judgment in history, explaining that God does not destroy the Romans as he did the Assyrians in Isaiah's day because their imperial policy was "just" in a way the Assyrians' was not.

162. A suggested parallel from Seneca, *Ben.* 4.26.1, is in context not so positive

temporary patterns of prayer for God's discriminatory benevolence to his own people whether in matters of weather and natural resources or with regard to health, prosperity, and the like. The disciple's benevolence should be equally open and uncalculating.[163]

46-47   Two pairs of rhetorical questions underline the point: benevolence restricted only to members of one's own circle is no more than what the rest of the world expects and practices. "Love" and "welcome"[164] refer not only to feelings and words, but to an accepting attitude which determines the way we treat other people. For the use of "tax collectors" (see on 9:9) and "Gentiles" to characterize the world outside the disciple community cf. 18:17 and comments there (and cf. 6:7 for a similar use of "Gentile").[165] By using traditional Jewish terms for those whom they regarded as at the bottom of the moral scale Jesus underlines how basic a human instinct this is: everyone looks after their own. Underlying the form of these questions is the assumption first that the life of the disciple is meant to be different, special, extraordinary, and secondly that there is a reward for a life lived by this higher standard of love. The first of these assumptions has been amply displayed throughout this discourse, in the distinctive "good life" of the Beatitudes, the images of the salt of the earth and light of the world, the "greater righteousness" of v. 20, and the series of increasingly unconventional demands which have illustrated it. The second (rewards for discipleship) has also already come to the surface in 5:12 (see comments there), and will do so increasingly in the next chapter. The reward of the children of God is for those who live as the children of God.

---

as Jesus' illustration since Seneca is quoting someone whose position he goes on to criticize as simplistic: "If you are imitating the gods, confer benefits also on the ungrateful, for the sun rises even upon the wicked and the seas are open even to pirates." Schweizer, 133, reads Seneca's words as illustrating "the indifference of the gods toward men."

163. In the light of vv. 39-42 there is perhaps a grain of truth in Lord Bowen's satirical comment on this verse (which betrays a European rather than Middle Eastern attitude to rain!):

"The rain it raineth on the just
And also on the unjust fella —
But chiefly on the just, because
The unjust steals the just's umbrella."

164. Or "greet"; the same verb is used in 10:12; the traditional greeting "shalom," if taken seriously, was itself an expression of concern for the other's good.

165. The word used in 5:47; 6:7; 18:17 is not the normal τὰ ἔθνη (as in 6:32) but the adjectival οἱ ἐθνικοί, which more strongly emphasizes their belonging to a different category and thus reflects a traditional Jewish feeling about non-Jews.

c. Fulfilling the Law: Summary (5:48)

48 *"So you are to be perfect, as your heavenly Father is perfect.*

While this verse appropriately rounds off the final example in vv. 43-47, picking up from v. 45 the theme of the children's imitation of their heavenly Father (see on 5:16 for this Matthean phrase), its comprehensive phrasing also serves to sum up the nature of the whole new way of living which the six examples have together illustrated, and thus to put into a neat epigram the essential nature of the "greater righteousness" introduced in v. 20. This saying thus fulfills a more climactic function than the parallel in Luke 6:36, which has "merciful" instead of "perfect" and serves to underscore only Luke's parallel to Matthew's last two antitheses. The disciple's lifestyle is to be different from other people's in that it draws its inspiration not from the norms of society but from the character of God. Even the God-given law had been accommodated to a practical ethical code with which Jewish society had come to feel comfortable, but Jesus is demanding a different approach, not via laws read as simply rules of conduct but rather by looking behind those laws to the mind and character of God himself. Whereas any definable set of rules could, in principle, be fully kept, the demand of the kingdom of heaven has no such limit — or rather its limit is perfection, the perfection of God himself.[166]

The wording of this summary recalls the repeated formula of Leviticus, "You are to be[167] holy, for I, the LORD your God, am holy" (Lev 19:2; cf. 11:44, 45; 20:26). God's people were to reflect his character, and the same is now true for those who are subjects of the kingdom of heaven. The use of *teleios* (perfect)[168] instead of "holy" may derive from the requirement of total loyalty to God in Deut 18:13, where the Hebrew *tāmîm* (complete, unblemished, blameless, perfect) is rendered by *teleios* in LXX. It is a wider term than moral flawlessness, and is used for spiritual "maturity," for example, in 1 Cor 2:6; 14:20; Phil 3:15, and frequently in Hebrews.[169] Matthew will use

---

166. To recognize this dimension is to rule out of court the theoretical debate still sometimes heard as to whether it is possible for a disciple to reach "perfection" (understood as freedom from moral failure) in this life. However completely the rules may be kept, "perfection" (understood in relation to the nature of God) remains a goal, not an achievement.

167. The future tense echoes that in LXX Lev 19:2 etc.; here, as there, it is best understood in context in an imperative sense, though H. D. Betz, *Sermon,* 321, rightly points out that a prediction or promise of their ultimate perfection cannot be ruled out.

168. R. A. Guelich, *Sermon,* 177, 233-36, here renders τέλειος as "whole," which picks up a significant component in the meaning of τέλειος but reads oddly in context, not only in that "Be whole" is hardly a natural way to phrase an exhortation, but especially when God is referred to as "whole."

169. W. D. Davies, *Setting,* 209-15, notes the prominence of "perfection" lan-

teleios again in 19:21 to denote the higher level of commitment represented by the rich man's selling his possessions in contrast with his merely keeping the commandments (including again Lev 19:18).[170] It is thus a suitable term to sum up the "greater righteousness" of v. 20, a righteousness which is demanded not only from an upper echelon of spiritual elites but from all who belong to the kingdom of God. It is in the promotion of this standard of perfection, going far beyond the literal requirements of the OT law, that Jesus "fulfills" it.

5. Piety, True and False: Three Contrasts (6:1-18)

1 *"Be careful not to practice your righteousness in front of other people so that they will notice you. Otherwise you cannot expect[1] any reward from[2] your Father who is in heaven.*

2 *"So whenever you are giving alms, do not blow a trumpet in front of you as hypocrites do in the synagogues[3] and in the streets, so that they will be applauded by other people; I tell you truly, they have had all[4] their reward.* 3 *But as for you, when you give alms, your left hand must not know what your right hand is doing,* 4 *so that your almsgiving is in secret. Then your Father, who sees in secret, will repay you.[5]*

---

guage at Qumran, but also draws out significant differences between the kinds of perfection envisaged; at Qumran it denoted primarily complete fidelity in keeping the law. See further R. A. Guelich, *Sermon,* 234-35.

170. The link between 5:48 and 19:21 is helpfully explored by J. Piper, *Love,* 146-48.

1. Literally, "But if not indeed (γε), you do not have." In the light of the future tense of "repay" in vv. 4, 6, and18 it seems that the reward here, though expressed in the present tense, refers to what may or may not be expected as a result of present behavior. The particle γε, which occurs rarely in NT Greek (and mainly in this particular idiom εἰ δὲ μή γε), serves here to draw attention to the contrast; my translation by "you cannot expect" attempts to convey its force.

2. παρά with the dative properly means "with," "in the presence of," but it may also convey the sense of "in the judgment of." The sense of God as the one who determines the reward is clear in vv. 4, 6, and 18.

3. Or "assemblies," here and in v. 5; see above on 4:23 and n. 6 there.

4. ἀπέχω, rather than simply ἔχω as in v. 1, is often a technical commercial term for receiving payment in full: the transaction is concluded and there is nothing more to expect.

5. Many of the later MSS and versions add ἐν τῷ φανερῷ, "openly," here and at the end of vv. 6 and 18. The addition, which clearly appealed to a sense of "poetic justice," must have been made quite early, but it detracts from the teaching of the passage that God's rewards are not for public approbation. Cf. *Gos. Thom.* 6, where Jesus' answer to his disciples' question about how to fast, pray, and give alms concludes by saying that "there is nothing hidden which shall not be made manifest."

5 *"And whenever you[6] are praying, you are not to be like the hyp-ocrites: they love to pray standing in the synagogues and at the cor-ners of the streets[7] so that people will notice them; I tell you truly, they have had all their reward. 6 But as for you, when you pray go into your most private room, shut the door and pray to your Father who is in secret. Then your Father, who sees in secret, will repay you.*

7 *"When you[8] pray, do not babble on like the Gentiles, for they think that the more they speak the more likely they are to be heard. 8 So don't be like them, since your Father[9] knows what you need be-fore you ask him. 9 This, then, is how you should pray:*

'Our Father in heaven,
May your name be held in reverence;
10 *May your kingdom come;*
May your will be done,
        as in heaven so also[10] on the earth.
11 *Give us today the bread we need for the coming day.[11]*
12 *And forgive us our debts*
        as we, too, have forgiven[12] our debtors.

6. The "you" of vv. 5 and 16 is plural, unlike the singular of v. 2, but in each case the following verse reverts to the singular when prescribing the disciple's behavior. The difference may be that almsgiving is envisaged as an individual initiative, whereas the prayer and fasting are conceived as corporately prescribed, even though individual se-crecy is required for those taking part. (Several MSS and versions here have "Whenever you are praying, you are not" in the singular, but there is no parallel singular reading in v. 16, and the evidence is not strong enough to support this as the original reading; it ap-pears to be an assimilation to the singular of v. 2.)

7. The "streets" of v. 2 are ῥύμαι, narrow streets or alleys, while these are πλατεῖαι, wide streets more like public squares. But the difference is more likely a matter of stylistic variation than because narrow streets are somehow more appropriate to public almsgiving; it is not obvious why in a narrow street one "could not make a gift without it being noticed" (Morris, 137).

8. Verses 7-15, which interrupt the matching sequence of individual exhortations in vv. 1-4, 5-6, and 16-18, address the disciples entirely in the plural.

9. A few MSS have either "our Father" or "God your Father" or "your heavenly Father" (repeating the phrase already familiar from 5:48 which will come again in 6:14, 26, 32). The first is most unlikely in this second-person context (but might have been in-fluenced by the following verse); the other variants do not affect the sense.

10. For καί following ὡς and doing duty for οὕτως see BDF 453 (1).

11. See the comments below on the possible meanings of the rare adjective ἐπιούσιος.

12. The majority of witnesses have a present tense here (using either of the forms ἀφίομεν or ἀφίεμεν), but most commentators see this as a deliberate alteration of an origi-nal aorist, ἀφήκαμεν, which appears in B and ℵ and a few minuscules (though a corrector

13 *And do not bring us into testing,*[13]
but rescue us from the Evil One.'[14] [15]

14 *"For if you forgive other people their offenses, your heavenly Father will forgive you as well;* 15 *but if you do not forgive other people,*[16] *neither will your Father forgive your offenses.*

16 *"Whenever you are fasting, do not look miserable as the hypocrites do: they hide*[17] *their faces so that everyone can see they are fasting; I tell you truly, they have had all their reward.* 17 *But as for you,*

---

of ℵ has substituted ἀφίεμεν), partly by assimilation to Luke 11:4 (where almost all witnesses have the present tense) and partly to avoid the stringent requirement that the one praying must *first* have forgiven the sins of all others.

13. See above, pp. 126-27, on the range of meaning of πειρασμός, including both "testing" and "temptation"; here the proximity of a reference to "the Evil One" (see next note) might suggest that temptation is the primary factor, but in 4:1-11 the temptation by Satan also proved to be the means of God's testing of his Son. See the comments below on which sense is more likely to be in focus here.

14. See p. 193, n. 55, on the ambiguity of the genitive case τοῦ πονηροῦ. Here a personal reference is perhaps more likely in view of the preceding reference to πειρασμός, an experience which has already been associated with the devil in 4:1, 3. Cf. 13:19, 38 for Matthew's use of ὁ πονηρός for the devil in a similar context. The traditional rendering "Deliver us from evil" would come to the same thing, but with a less personal understanding of the conflict. H. D. Betz, *Sermon,* 412-13, argues for the neuter reading as more appropriate in this context.

15. The doxology, "For yours is the kingdom and the power and the glory forever. Amen," or variants of it occur in a wide variety of later MSS and versions, but seem to derive from a conventional liturgical ending (reflecting the doxological tradition witnessed in 1 Chr 29:11-13) which became customary as the prayer was used in the second-century church. The citation of the prayer without this conclusion in a wide range of early patristic sources confirms the evidence of its absence from the earlier MSS in Matthew (it has no support in Luke either). See further H. D. Betz, *Sermon,* 414-15. W. D. Davies, *Setting,* 451-452, argues that Jesus as a Jewish teacher is unlikely to have taught the prayer without some sort of doxology, though J. Jeremias, *Theology,* 202-3, thinks that it might originally have been left for those praying to conclude it in their own words, with a fixed doxology becoming established late in the first century.

16. Most MSS add "their offenses," but since several of the most important earlier witnesses do not repeat the phrase here, it is likely that it was a natural filling out of an originally more terse (and chiastic) form of expression.

17. ἀφανίζω is literally to "make invisible" (a play on words with their being "seen," φανῶσιν, to be fasting). The same word is used in vv. 19-20 for what moths and vermin do to treasure. It is not clear whether the term envisages those who were fasting literally veiling their faces (cf. the covering of the head as a sign of shame and dismay, Jer 14:3-4) or perhaps leaving them unwashed (as the contrast in v. 17 may suggest), smearing them with ashes, or even "pulling a face," to give the impression of holy misery. Schweizer's "go around with a hungry look" (139) owes more to context than to lexical meaning!

when you are fasting anoint your head and wash your face, 18 *so that other people cannot see that you are fasting, but only your Father, who is in secret.*[18] *Then your Father, who sees in secret, will repay you.*

The last main section of the discourse (5:20-48) has been devoted to setting out a "righteousness" greater than that of the scribes and Pharisees (5:20). The discourse now goes on to warn against a wrong kind of "righteousness" (6:1), which is undertaken not to conform to the will of God and to imitate his perfection, but to gain human approval. The people who practice this kind of righteousness are described as "hypocrites," a term which occurs frequently in Matthew for the official (or self-appointed) representatives of national religion, and more specifically, six times over in ch. 23, for the scribes and Pharisees. Some of the failings with which the scribes and Pharisees will be charged in ch. 23 focus on a similar concern for externals and lack of inward depth. The contrast with the righteousness of the scribes and Pharisees which underlay 5:20-48 is thus continued in this passage; the disciples are not to be like them. But the focus has moved from ethical distinctives to the practice of religion, the "righteousness" of 6:1 being not so much a moral orientation as a religious one, practical piety.

The basic framework of the passage is an introductory exhortation (v. 1) illustrated by three matching contrasts (vv. 2-4, 5-6, 16-18) setting out the wrong and the right way to undertake three prominent religious duties, almsgiving, prayer, and fasting. These three duties are recognized by most religious traditions;[19] together with the two more specifically Muslim requirements of recitation of the creed and the pilgrimage to Mecca, they constitute the Five Pillars of Islam. The wording of the three contrasts follows a standard pattern (don't be like the hypocrites who . . . but as for you [singular], when you . . .), with verbatim agreement in the concluding clauses ("I tell you truly, they have had all their reward" . . . "in secret. Then your Father, who sees in secret, will repay you"). The wrong way in each case is a matter of outward show, looking for human approval; the right way is that of secrecy, which only God can see. It is only the latter kind of "righteousness" that God, who is strikingly described as "being in secret," will reward, whereas the ostentatious piety of the hypocrites has received the only reward

---

18. This and the following clause do not use κρυπτός, "hidden," as in vv. 4 and 6, but the cognate adjective κρυφαῖος. There is no discernible difference in meaning.

19. In Tob 12:8 Raphael sets out the essential religious duties as "prayer with fasting and almsgiving and righteousness." His words go on to focus especially on almsgiving, which "rescues from death and itself purges away all sin." The three duties are often commended by the rabbis, though Keener, 207, is right to maintain that other such religious duties were also listed, so that this is not a fixed list but rather a series of selected examples of a wider principle.

it will get (and is looking for), the approval of other people. The nature of God's reward for secret piety is not stated, but since he is their Father "in heaven" (v. 1) we should probably think of the "reward in heaven" which was promised to the persecuted in 5:12 (see comments there on the theme of rewards in Matthew); cf. also the "treasure in heaven" of vv. 19-20 below.[20] For the superiority of "secret" religion cf. Paul's contrast between the person who is a Jew "in appearance" and the one who is "secretly" a Jew, "whose praise is not from other people but from God" (Rom 2:28-29).[21]

This carefully balanced tripartite unit of teaching is, however, interrupted in vv. 7-15 by an extended discussion of prayer, consisting of (a) a further wrong way / right way contrast (vv. 7-8), (b) the pattern prayer (vv. 9-13), and (c) a pastoral comment on one clause of the pattern prayer (vv. 14-15). Matthew has apparently decided that the subject of true prayer is too important to be passed over as briefly as almsgiving and fasting and so has inserted other sayings material on the subject, parts (b) and (c) of which have inexact parallels in different contexts in Luke 11:2-4 and Mark 11:25. The centrally important tradition of the Lord's Prayer thus finds its way into the center of the discourse (fifty-four verses before it, forty-eight after), though by means of what is in effect a literary digression!

a. The General Principle: Avoiding Ostentation in Religion (6:1)

This verse is expressed in the plural, as compared with the singular focus of the following examples (see p. 230, n. 6). It is thus a general exhortation, which introduces 6:2-18 in much the same way as 5:20 introduced 5:21-48, and in each case the key term is *dikaiosynē*, "righteousness."[22] Here it is concerned not with personal or social ethics but with matters of religious

---

20. See D. Instone-Brewer, *Traditions,* 1:123-27, for the contrast between Jesus' concept of reward and rabbinic notions of "fruit" as reward in this life, which he suggests Jesus is here deliberately criticizing.

21. *Gos. Thom.* 6 has the disciples asking Jesus about how they should fast, pray, and give alms. His response is that they should not speak a lie or do what they hate "because everything is manifest before heaven." But there is no explicit commendation of secrecy, and indeed the saying goes on to declare that "there is nothing hidden which shall not be made manfest."

22. Some MSS here read ἐλεημοσύνην, the term which will be used for "almsgiving" in v. 2, in place of δικαιοσύνην. While the evidence is not sufficient to overturn the majority reading, the alternative (which would have the effect of taking v. 1 as part of the opening illustration rather than as the introduction to vv. 2-6, 16-18 as a whole) testifies to the behavioral force of δικαιοσύνη in this context. Ṣ*edāqâ,* the OT equivalent to δικαιοσύνη, often carries the sense of righteous action, and especially "deliverance"; it is sometimes translated by ἐλεημοσύνη in the LXX. See B. Przybylski, *Righteousness,* 78, 99-101.

observance, but it remains something to be "done."[23] See on 3:15 for the essentially behavioral sense of *dikaiosynē* in Matthew, as opposed to Paul's more theological and soteriological use of the term. The three examples of almsgiving, prayer, and fasting are thus categorized as activities which God requires of his people. Jesus' quarrel is not with the doing of them[24] — indeed, he assumes that the disciple will do them — but with the manner and the motive. The manner to which he objects is "in front of other people," that is, publicly; the motive is "so that they will notice[25] you," that is, aiming for human approval. Cf. 23:5-7 for a similar criticism of the scribes and Pharisees, using the same verb *theaomai* in 23:5.

In 5:16 we were told that the result of the disciples' way of life should be that other people "can see the good you do and give glory to your Father in heaven." The secret "righteousness" of 6:1-6, 16-18 seems to negate that expectation. But there are two significant differences. First, 5:16 was talking about the whole character and lifestyle of disciples, while the subject here is specifically religious duties. The latter offer more fruitful ground for the development of a false piety leading to a reputation for otherworldly "holiness." It is easier to be a religious hypocrite than to gain by false pretenses a reputation for overall goodness. In a society which values piety, as did first-century Judaism, people are more easily conned by religious ostentation. Secondly, and more importantly, this passage is about a deliberate search for public recognition, whereas 5:16 summed up a searching character study of true disciples which focused on essential qualities; those who live like that will inevitably be "a town built on top of a hill which cannot be hidden," whether they like it or not. And whereas the outcome of religious ostentation is the desired "reward" of human applause,[26] the result of the shining light of the disciples' lifestyle is that people glorify God, not them.

23. "Practice" here translates ποιέω, the regular verb for "do." B. Przybylski, *Righteousness,* 88, defines it here as "the practical side of man's religion." The phrase ποιέω δικαιοσύνην is used to describe right conduct in 1 John 2:29; 3:7, 10; Rev 22:11.

24. Jesus' attitude as presented here is remarkably contradicted by *Gos. Thom.* 14 (unconnected with the logion quoted in n. 21 above): "If you fast, you will beget sin for yourselves; if you pray, you will be condemned; if you give alms, you will do evil to your spirits." The intention may have been, as in this passage, to warn against dangers inherent in the abuse of these acts, but the stark wording has the effect of forbidding the very practices of which Jesus is here guarding against abuse, and it is more likely that the *Thomas* text represents a reaction against "ritual."

25. The verb θεάομαι, as opposed to the more neutral "see" in 5:16, usually implies watching carefully, taking notice.

26. Or, to use the term preferred by anthropologists, "honor." See J. H. Neyrey, *Honor,* 212-22, for an interpretation of the whole passage 6:1-18 as a call to men to challenge the conventional honor code and to "vacate the playing field" by absenting themselves from the public arena where honor was sought and achieved and staying at home like women.

But there is a "reward" from your Father in heaven, not like the reward which the hypocrites have already received (vv. 2, 5, 16) but one which remains in the future, to judge from the future tense "will repay" in vv. 4, 6, and 18, which recalls the future tenses of the "because" clauses in the Beatitudes, 5:4-9 (see comments there on the tension between present and future fulfillment). This "reward in heaven" (5:12) is on a quite different level from the hypocrites' public approval and self-congratulation. It is perhaps most fittingly summed up in the formula of acceptance in 25:21, 23: "Enter into your master's joy." It is that reward which the disciples risk losing if they allow their allegiance to be diverted from their Father in heaven to their human contemporaries.

b. Secret Almsgiving (6:2-4)

The general principle expressed in the plural in v. 1 is now more specifically applied to the practice of the individual disciple (see p. 230, n. 6). Giving to the poor was an important part of Jewish social life,[27] one which Jesus has already endorsed in 5:42 and will require in 19:21, and one which is taken for granted in 25:35; 26:9. It was a religious duty enjoined on the people of God in such passages as Deut 15:7-11 and endorsed in, for example, Ps 112:9; Tob 1:3; 4:7-11; 12:8-10. Some specific means of relief for the poor are set out in Lev 19:9-10; Deut 14:28-29; 24:19-21; 26:12-13. By the first century there was a well-organized system of relief for the poor based in the synagogues,[28] providing something of what our modern state-sponsored welfare systems aim to offer. The funding of this system depended on contributions from members of the community, some of them laid down under the regulations for the "tithe for the poor,"[29] but also involving a great deal of private initiative,[30] which could reach such an extent that there were rabbinic regulations to prevent a man from impoverishing himself and his family by giving away more than 20 percent of his income.[31]

2 "Applauded" here translates the same verb *(doxazō)* which was used in 5:16 for people "giving glory" to God as a result of the disciples' good living; the repetition of the verb but now with the almsgiver, not God, as the object (God is also the object in Matthew's two other uses of the verb in

27. *M. 'Abot.* 1:2 quotes Simeon the Just (third century B.C.) as declaring that "By three things is the world sustained: by the law, by temple-service and by acts of generosity."

28. See Schürer, 2:437. See further W. D. Davies, *Setting,* 308, for the importance of almsgiving in the period after A.D. 70.

29. For this provision, based on Deut 14:28-29; 26:12, see Schürer, 2:264-65, n. 23; J. Jeremias, *Jerusalem,* 134-38.

30. See J. Jeremias, *Jerusalem,* 126-34, with many examples focused especially on Jerusalem.

31. M. Hengel, *Property,* 20-21.

9:8 and 15:31) speaks eloquently of the different perspectives in the two passages. There is no evidence for a literal blowing of trumpets[32] in connection
with almsgiving, and the phrase may be used purely metaphorically here,
though it would not be atypical of Jesus to conjure up the image of such a
crass piece of self-advertisement.[33] It is in any case likely that significant donations were publicly announced in the synagogues.[34] The impression of ostentation is increased by speaking of almsgiving not only in the synagogues,
where it was expected but would probably go into a distribution system
rather than straight to the beneficiaries, but also out in the streets, presumably
directly to beggars, who could be expected to respond enthusiastically. The
fact that the rabbis also warn against ostentation when giving alms (see Str-B
1:391-92; Davies and Allison, 1:579-80) indicates that it was a familar problem.[35]

   Hypokritēs (the word originally meant a theatrical "actor") is used by
Matthew not only here in vv. 2, 5, and 16 but also for a critic who does not
criticize himself (7:5) and as a general term for those subject to ultimate
judgment (24:51; in the LXX *hypokritēs* is used for the godless). Its main
use, however, is for those with whom Jesus will be engaged in controversy in
15:7; 22:18, and six times in ch. 23. In several of these uses it probably carries the sense of insincerity, of consciously acting a part, which is close to

---

32. In a Jewish context the term probably refers to the *šôfār,* or ram's horn, though
they also had metallic trumpets (Num 10:1-10). The *šôfār* was used not only in battle
(Judg 7:16-18; Job 39:25) but also on various ceremonial occasions, such as the proclamation of a new king (1 Kgs 1:34, 41), and at certain solemn religious ceremonies (Lev
23:24; 25:9; 2 Chr 15:14; Ps 81:3; Joel 2:15), including the daily temple sacrifice (Sir
50:16; *m. Tamid* 7:3). A use of trumpets to announce some special relief collection is possible, but not directly attested in our literature. In any case, Jesus seems to be speaking
here of a private initiative, not a public ceremony.

33. Cf. his even more grotesque image of straining out a gnat and swallowing a
camel (23:24). When there is so obvious a sense, it is unnecessary to suggest some sort of
pun or mistranslation based on the fact that the donation chests in the Jerusalem temple
(where it was possible to watch people giving money, Mark 12:41-44) were known as
"trumpets" because of their shape (so S. T. Lachs, *JQR* 69 [1978] 103-5), still less to conjecture that σαλπίζω here denotes the sound of the coins falling into these "trumpets" (so
N. J. McEleney, *ZNW* 76 [1985] 43-46). And, as Gundry, n. 71, points out, these "trumpets" were in the temple, not in the synagogues and streets. They were also in Jerusalem,
not in Galilee.

34. Cf. Sir 31:11, "the assembly will proclaim his acts of charity."

35. *M. Šeqal.* 5:6 describes two rooms in the temple where donations were made,
one of which was known (Harry Potter fans, please note) as the "Chamber of Secrets,"
where "worshipers used to put their gifts in secret and the poor of good family received
support from them in secret." The ideal of secrecy was thus well established, even though
not always observed in practice.

what "hypocrite" means today. But in general, notably in 7:5; 15:7; 23:15, 23, 25, the focus is not so much on a conscious attempt to deceive as on a false perspective or sense of values which prevents the "hypocrites" from seeing things as God sees them; they are not so much deceivers as disastrously self-deceived (like the enthusiastic but misguided followers of 7:21-23).[36] In this passage there is no necessary allegation of deceit as such — they presumably *did* give alms, pray, and fast; the problem was that they wanted everyone to know it. These religious show-offs are "actors" in that they aim to impress others, but at the same time their behavior demonstrates how far they are out of touch with God's understanding of "righteousness."

For "I tell you truly" see on 5:18. For "they have had all their reward" see p. 229, n. 4; the choice of the single word *apechō* contrives to convey both a sense of receipt in full (they have not been cheated) and the threat of nothing still to come. It thus underlines their sadly limited perspective: they cannot see, and have no aspirations, beyond the applause of their peers.

3 The change from the plural hypocrites to a singular disciple here and in vv. 6 and 17 underlines the fact that these religious duties are not undertaken corporately but are between the disciple and God. In the cases of prayer and fasting (which are introduced by a plural, "When you pray/fast") the individual disciple's action may be seen as falling within an agreed pattern of prayer or fasting undertaken by the community corporately, but how it is done is up to the individual, not for public awareness. In the case of alms-giving, even that degree of corporateness is apparently lacking (hence perhaps the singular introduction, "When you give alms"). It is entirely a matter of private decision. The lack of communication between left and right hands[37] is a delightfully grotesque but vivid way of describing absolute secrecy:[38] no one is to know about it. Compare 25:35-40, where the righteous are themselves unaware of the good they have done.

4 In the phrase "your Father" in Matthew the "your" is normally

---

36. *Pace* Gundry, the second edition of whose commentary contains an appendix (pp. 641-47) in which he takes issue with the argument of D. O. Via, *Self-Deception,* that "hypocrisy" in Matthew is self-deception. As so often in a polarized argument, the attempt on either side to find a single all-embracing use of the term fails to do justice to the range of Matthew's usage. While there is a clear sense of dishonesty and/or play-acting in several Matthean uses of the term, Gundry's term "audience-deception" is no more an adequate characterization of all of them than is Via's "self-deception." The full study of the term by D. E. Garland, *Intention,* 96-117, concludes for a more varied sense; see below, p. 869, n. 24.

37. The suggestion by Gundry, 102, that Jesus envisages giving with the right hand only rather than more visibly with two hands seems unnecessarily literal.

38. The image seems to be original with Jesus (see H. D. Betz, *Sermon,* 358-59). *Gos. Thom.* 62 takes it up to describe secret teaching, without reference to almsgiving.

plural; only here and in vv. 6 and 18 is it singular, because the scene has been set up in terms of the individual disciple's private relationship with God. That God "sees in secret" reflects the OT understanding that nothing is hidden from him, expressed so eloquently in Ps 139; cf. Deut 29:29; Ps 90:8; Eccl 12:14; Jer 23:24; Sir 17:15-20; 23:18-19. In the OT it is often a threatening rather than a comforting thought, but here it is good deeds, not bad, which are to be "repaid." The reference is apparently to the "reward" mentioned in v. 1 (and forfeited in v. 2) as well as earlier in 5:12, 46, which has been more fully outlined in the "because" clauses of the Beatitudes. The commercial term "repay" here and in vv. 6 and 18 may suggest a "quid pro quo" transaction which sits uncomfortably alongside a Pauline doctrine of salvation by grace and not by merit. It is, however, counterbalanced by the wider Matthean understanding of God's disproportionate rewards which comes to the surface in 19:29; 20:1-15; 25:21, 23 (see above on 5:12).[39]

c. Secret Prayer (6:5-6)

The second example of religious practice is prayer, which will be dealt with in vv. 5-6 in the same way as almsgiving and fasting in vv. 2-4 and 16-18, before the theme is taken further in the additional sayings of vv. 7-15. For the standard formulae repeated in each of the three illustrations see above on vv. 2-4. The hope that other people will witness the public prayers of the "hypocrites" probably indicates that prayers were said aloud, not just that they were visibly engaged in prayer. Just as even private reading in the ancient world was done out loud, so, too, people generally prayed audibly. Even the call to secret prayer in v. 6 does not necessarily mean silent prayer: the point of going into a secret place is so that no one else will be in a position to hear. If *synagōgē* here refers to the gathering for worship (see on 4:23), prayer would of course be expected there, but the privilege of leading it was not open to everyone. But the following mention of praying out in the streets perhaps supports a more secular sense of "assembly" here; wherever people are gathered as a potential audience, the "hypocrites" will make sure that their prayers are heard and seen. We should probably think of something more obtrusive than the silent prayer on a mat in the street or in a corner of a public room which is so familiar in Muslim countries today. Devout Jews prayed three times a day (Dan 6:10), not necessarily at fixed times (*m. Ber.* 1:1-2; 4:1),[40] though the ninth hour (3 p.m.) seems to have been normal (Acts 3:1;

39. See B. Charette, *Recompense*, 99-100, against the desire of some interpreters to play down the element of "reward."
40. Luz, 1:359, points out how this differs from Islam, where everyone is expected to pray at the same set time. Jews would therefore not normally need to stop to

10:30). Standing was the normal Jewish posture for prayer (cf. Mark 11:25; Luke 18:11, 13),[41] though sometimes people knelt (2 Chr 6:13; Dan 6:10; Luke 22:41) or even, in special circumstances, prostrated themselves (Num 16:22; Matt 26:39).

The "most private room" is probably an inner storeroom, which is likely to have been the only lockable room in an ordinary Palestinian house (the same term is used for a secret place in 24:26; Luke 12:3). Cf. 2 Kgs 4:33 for shutting the door before prayer, and Isa 26:20 for locking oneself in the storeroom (LXX uses the same word *tamieion*) for secrecy, though in the latter case the aim is not prayer but safety from God's judgment on other people. In such a secret place[42] the disciple encounters the God who "is in secret." This remarkable phrase[43] (not just who *sees* in secret, as in the following clause), used here and in v. 18, suggests not only that God is omnipresent, even in the secret place, but also that he is himself invisible, in stark contrast to his pretended worshippers, who are only too visible.

This passage is not intended to prohibit audible prayer in public as such. While Jesus is often portrayed as praying privately (Mark 1:35; 6:46, etc.), he also on occasion prayed aloud where others could hear (11:25; 14:19; 26:39, 42; Luke 11:1). The pattern prayer given in vv. 9-13 is worded in the plural, as a corporate rather than a private prayer, and gatherings for prayer together were a regular feature of the life of Jesus' disciples from the beginning. The issue here is not the prayer but the motive.

---

pray at street corners, and those who did so would be the more conspicuous. While *m. Berakot* gives directions for praying at places of work, on journeys, and the like, and about not interrupting prayer once begun, these do not amount, as Morris, 140, argues, to insisting on prayers at specific times, only within the prescribed periods of the day. J. Jeremias, *Theology,* 187, is therefore perhaps taking Jesus' vivid language (cf. the trumpet of v. 2) too literally and assuming too fixed a pattern of prayer when he suggests that they deliberately timed their movements to bring them to the most public places at the afternoon hour of prayer. See also D. Instone-Brewer, *Traditions,* 1:63-64.

41. Hagner, 1:141, therefore goes too far in translating ἑστῶτες by "positioning themselves conspicuously," even though of course the context indicates that intention.

42. The focus is of course on the secrecy rather than the specific location. Keener, 211, regards the mention of the storeroom as a "humorous hyperbole," pointing out that there is no record of Jesus praying in a storeroom! J. H. Neyrey, *Honor,* 220-21, argues that such a room would be extremely small, like our "broom closet."

43. The same phrase ἐν τῷ κρυπτῷ is used to describe the genuine Jew as opposed to the merely professed Jew in Rom 2:28-29. In such usage the phrase indicates not so much concealment as such but rather the genuineness of that which is inward and unseen as opposed to what is put on for others. God himself is the model of that essential genuineness which he requires in his people.

d. Further Teaching on Prayer (6:7-8)

The "digression" on prayer, which breaks into the tripartite unit of teaching on religious secrecy (see above, p. 233), begins with a similar contrast between the wrong and the right ways of praying, in which "the Gentiles" take the place of the "hypocrites" in v. 5.[44] The focus this time is not on prayer performed with a view to human approbation but on an attitude and practice in prayer which betrays a misunderstanding of how God expects to be approached by his people.

The term for "Gentiles" is the same as that used in 5:47 (on which see below on 18:17) to denote the world outside the disciple community. The emphasis here is not so much on their not being Jewish as on their being religious outsiders, people who do not understand what it means to know God as a heavenly Father.[45] So instead of trusting a Father to fulfill their needs, they think they must badger a reluctant Deity into taking notice of them (cf. the expressive modern term "God-botherer"). Their approach to prayer is characterized by two colorful terms, first "babbling,"[46] a noisy flow of sound without meaning, and *polylogia*, "much speaking," "many words." It is an approach to prayer which values quantity (and perhaps volume?) rather than quality. It is not necessarily purely mechanical, but rather obtrusive and unnecessary. It assumes that the purpose of prayer is first to demand God's attention and then to inform him of needs he may have overlooked. The terms used do not prohibit the use of liturgical forms as such (after all, a formulated prayer follows in vv. 9-13), nor do they denigrate persistence in prayer, as the unfortunate KJV rendering "vain repetitions" has often been taken to suggest.[47] The issue is not the

---

44. Two significant MSS (B sy^c) have "hypocrites" here too, perhaps mechanically reproducing the formula of the surrounding pericopes (vv. 2, 5, 16), but perhaps also in order to avoid offending non-Jewish readers.

45. Schweizer, 146, suggests that the reference is particularly to the long lists of divine names which characterize the magical papyri, "so that the correct name of God might not be omitted during the incantation." H. D. Betz, *Sermon*, 364-67, rightly points out that Greco-Roman philosophers also criticized unintelligible or thoughtless prayer, so that Jesus' broad characterization does not apply to all "Gentiles."

46. Greek βατταλογέω, which like the English word "babble" seems to be an onomatopoeic coinage. MM, 107, imaginatively link the D reading βλαττολογέω with "provincial English *blether*," while suggesting that βατταλογέω may relate to Βάτταλος, "gabbler" or "stammerer," a nickname of the orator Demosthenes, who stammered as a young man (Herodotus 4.154-45 tells of King Βάττος of Thera, whose name was traditionally explained as derived from his stammer; there is a verb βατταρίζω, "to stammer"). All such "derivations" are conjectural; the meaning of the word lies in its sound rather than in its etymology. The similarity to the Hebrew *bāṭal*, "to be idle, ineffective" (Aramaic *bāṭēl*), might have added an extra nuance for some readers.

47. Repetition is, however, frowned on in the interestingly parallel saying in Sir

method or the frequency of prayer (Jesus himself repeated his prayer in 26:44, apparently spent a whole night in prayer in 14:23-25, and taught his disciples to keep on praying in Luke 18:1), but the attitude of faith which underlies and inspires it.

The reason why "you" (plural, the disciple community united in prayer) are not to be like them lies in a theology which attributes to God both the benevolent concern of a Father and an omniscience which makes the prayer apparently unnecessary (cf. Isa 65:24: "Before they call, I will answer"). But if God does not need to be informed of our needs, why does he expect us to tell him about them? Christian spirituality has traditionally found the answer in a concept of prayer not as the communication of information, still less as a technique for getting things from God (the more words you put in the more results you get out), but as the expression of the relationship of trust which follows from knowing God as "Father." The pattern prayer which follows illustrates how such a relationship works.

e. The Pattern Prayer (6:9-13)

In contrast to the empty prayers of "hypocrites" (v. 5) and "Gentiles" (v. 7) we are offered a model of how to pray in the form of the Lord's Prayer, which Matthew presents in a form close to that which is most widely used today. The significantly shorter form in Luke 11:2-4 and the textual accretions following v. 13 here (see p. 231, n. 15) indicate a text which was in frequent use and thus subject to liturgical variation and expansion. *Did.* 8:2-3 gives evidence of this trend around the latter part of the first century: the full wording of the Lord's Prayer (in the expanded form familiar in modern use) is set out with the instruction "Pray thus three times a day," where "thus" is normally taken to envisage liturgical repetition of the words rather than simply praying in the spirit of the pattern prayer. Such set forms of liturgical prayer were already familiar from the synagogue liturgy.[48] The Lord's Prayer has been used liturgically, with local variation and in different translations, ever since.

It is sometimes suggested that the introductory formulae in Matthew

---

7:14: "Do not prattle among the assembled elders, and do not repeat a word in your prayer." For commendation of brevity in prayer cf. Eccl 5:2; *b. Ber.* 61a. The Lord's Prayer itself is remarkably brief in comparison with what we know of set prayers both within and outside Judaism.

48. *Did.* 8:2-3 aims to distinguish Christian prayer from that of "the hypocrites." Since in 8:1 Christian fasting is to be on Wednesday and Friday as distinct from that of "the hypocrites," who fast on Monday and Thursday, it seems likely that the *Didache*'s term "the hypocrites" denotes the practice of the synagogue or of a more specific Jewish group. In that case the Lord's Prayer may well be understood here as a deliberate alternative to the synagogue liturgy.

and Luke point to different conceptions of the nature of the prayer, Luke's "When you pray say" (in answer to the request "Teach us to pray") indicating a set form of words to be repeated, while Matthew's "This, then, is how you should pray" (following a comment on the right attitude in prayer) suggests a pattern for right praying rather than a liturgical formula.[49] But that is probably too artificial a distinction, and it is likely that when Jesus taught these words (in whichever form) he would have been content for them to be used either way. Christian tradition has always found them to be suitable either for simple repetition or as a template for more extended prayer or a basis for thinking (and teaching) about prayer and its priorities. The fact that the early church seems to have been content for the prayer to be preserved in different forms does, however, suggest that it was more concerned with the content of the prayer than with its exact form.

The question which form of the prayer is "the original" is of course unanswerable. On the one hand, the tendency for such a prayer to be expanded in use, as witnessed by the additions after v. 13, might suggest that the shorter Lucan form is the earlier. On the other hand, the Matthean wording has been judged to be closer to a likely Aramaic original.[50] In any case, the instinctive critical assumption that any piece of Jesus' teaching could have been given only on a single occasion, after which it became altered to different forms in transmission, is here more than usually suspect. If any aspect of Jesus' teaching is likely to have been repeated, perhaps with varying wording, on a number of occasions and perhaps to different audiences, it must surely be so central a unit as this pattern prayer. There is then no basis for judging one or the other version to be "more authentic"; each in its own way (and the differences are not at a fundamental level) may appropriately be taken as demonstrating Jesus' concept of true prayer.[51]

The pattern of the Matthean form is essentially as follows:

Opening address:

Our Father in heaven

49. This inference is, however, cast in doubt by the fact that Matthew's wording (οὕτως προσεύχεσθε ὑμεῖς) is very close to that of *Did.* 8:3 (οὕτω προσεύχεσθε), which, as mentioned above, is normally understood of liturgical repetition.

50. J. Jeremias, *Theology,* 195-96. See, however, the cautionary comments of H. D. Betz, *Sermon,* 374-75, who suggests that the prayer originated in Greek.

51. See, however, M. D. Goulder, *Midrash,* 296-301, for the radically simple solution that Jesus did not teach this prayer at all, but that Matthew composed it "from the traditions of the prayers of Jesus in Mark and the teaching on prayer by Jesus in Mark, amplified from the Exodus context of the sermon, and couched in Matthaean language," and that Luke simply abbreviated it.

Three clauses about God and his worship:

May your name be held in reverence;
May your kingdom come;
May your will be done,
    as in heaven so also on the earth.

Three petitions for our own needs:

Give us today the bread we need for tomorrow.
And forgive us our debts
    as we, too, have forgiven our debtors.
And do not bring us into testing,
    but rescue us from the Evil One.

This balancing structure in itself speaks strongly against the "Gentile" view of prayer condemned in vv. 7-8. The first half of the prayer is concerned with God's honor, kingdom, and purpose, and only after that do our own needs find a place. The first three clauses are cast in the form of wishes, using the third-person imperative form; they are in effect a doxology, an act of worship, associating the praying community with God's purpose in the world. The second-person imperatives of the following clauses are thus set within the overall priority of God's will rather than our desires.

Not all aspects of prayer are included in this pattern prayer. There is no explicit confession of sin, no direct thanksgiving for blessings already received, no intercession for the needs of the world or for those to whom disciples are sent (or for their persecutors, 5:44). All of these may be developed through meditation around the clauses of the prayer individually. But the fundamental starting point is worship and petition.

The first three clauses of the prayer are strongly reminiscent of the Aramaic Qaddish prayer or doxology which was already in regular synagogue use by the time of Jesus. J. Jeremias[52] translates the earliest accessible form of this prayer as follows:

Exalted and hallowed be his great name
    in the world which he created according to his will.
May he let his kingdom rule
    in your lifetime and in your days and in the lifetime of
    the whole house of Israel, speedily and soon.
Praised be his great name from eternity to eternity.
    And to this say: Amen.

---

52. J. Jeremias, *Theology,* 198-99.

The first part of Jesus' prayer may be regarded as a distillation into a more concise form of this familiar expression of eschatological hope, and as such would have caused no surprise to his disciples.[53] Where Jesus' prayer differs from the Qaddish is first in the second-person address to God as "Our Father in heaven" and secondly in the continuation of the prayer to include the community's petitions.[54]

In the light of the clear sense of eschatological expectation in the Qaddish, many interpreters have argued for a similar orientation not only in the opening clauses of the Lord's Prayer but in the prayer as a whole.[55] I shall comment on this contention with regard especially to vv. 11 and 13 below. But even if vv. 9b-10 are understood as focused on a coming time of crisis rather than on the working out of God's purpose in the present, it would not necessarily follow that the provision of daily needs, material and spiritual, would be inappropriate to such a prayer. In fact, as we shall see, even vv. 9b-10 deal with matters which should be the constant concern of disciples in the present as well as with a view to the future: they desire to see God's name reverenced, his rule established, and his will done in the world as it is. While the synagogue prayer was necessarily forward-looking, for Jesus and his disciples the kingdom of God has already been announced and is working its way into the world through Jesus' ministry. In the light of that perspective, every clause of this prayer has an immediate relevance to the present situation and concerns of those who are praying.

9 The connecting "then" indicates that the following words will express the trust in a heavenly Father which has been stated in vv. 7-8 to be the basis of true prayer. The instruction is addressed to the disciples corporately, and the whole prayer will be phrased in the plural. It is the prayer of a community rather than an individual act of devotion, even though its pattern would also appropriately guide the secret prayers in the storeroom (v. 6).

The simple "Father" with which Luke's version of the prayer begins

---

53. The thoroughly Jewish character of the Lord's Prayer as a whole is recognized and explored in an interesting collection of essays by Jewish and Christian scholars, J. J. Petuchowski and M. Brocke (eds.), *Lord's Prayer.*

54. In this last respect the Lord's Prayer finds closer parallels in some clauses of the much longer Tefillah (or "Eighteen Benedictions"), another Aramaic prayer of the synagogue in Jesus' time (though there is some uncertainty over the date at which it attained its preserved form), but because of the different scale of the Tefillah and the Lord's Prayer, the parallel is less striking overall than in the case of the Qaddish; see further Davies and Allison, 1:595-97. D. Instone-Brewer, *Traditions,* 1:54-59, notes, however, that shorter "abstracts" of the Tefillah were also in use, and suggests that the Lord's Prayer may be understood better in that light.

55. A good example is R. E. Brown, *NT Essays,* 217-53.

reflects the Aramaic vocative *'abbā'* which was Jesus' distinctive approach to God in prayer (in this gospel see 11:25, 26, and for the Aramaic term see Mark 14:36), which his disciples were subsequently privileged to share (Rom 8:15; Gal 4:6).[56] Matthew's addition of "our" makes the echo of the form *'abbā'* less obvious, but the implication of privileged access to God is equally clear.[57] For God as the heavenly Father of disciples see, within this discourse, 5:16, 45, 48; 6:1, 4, 6, 8, 14-15, 18, 26, 32; 7:11. The same language will recur more rarely in the rest of the gospel (10:20, 29; 13:43; 23:9), and instead from 7:21 onward Jesus will speak frequently of God as his own Father in a way which seems to exclude others from that special relationship (notably in 11:25-27; see comments there), and which correlates to the title "(my) Son" applied uniquely to Jesus from 2:15 and 3:17 on. When Jesus prays to God as "Father" (11:25, 26), it is sometimes explicitly to "*my* Father" (26:39, 42; Jesus speaks of God as "my Father" a further fourteen times in Matthew) and never in the form "our Father" which he here teaches his disciples to use. Here are the raw materials for a theological system which posits a unique filial relationship for Jesus and a derivative relationship for God's other "children" into which Jesus introduces them (cf. 11:27) but in which he does not share with them on the same level. While such a doctrine may be more fully developed from other parts of the NT, Matthew is content to allow it to emerge by implication from his usage. But it is primarily here, in the discourse on discipleship, that this privileged status of the disciples emerges, and in the family prayer which is at the heart of the discourse it is most appropriately expressed as their corporate address to God. In well over half the references to "your Father" in the discourse, "in heaven" or "heavenly" is added. It not only underlines the metaphorical nature of the concept but also prescribes the disciple's attitude to God: he is on the one hand all-powerful and therefore completely to be trusted but on the other hand to be approached with the reverence which the following clauses of the prayer will express.

The first three clauses of the Lord's Prayer are expressed as third-person imperatives, two of them passive. In a prayer such an imperative is in

---

56. J. Jeremias, *Prayers*, 54-62; idem, *Theology*, 61-68; J. D. G. Dunn, *Jesus*, 21-26. For the debate on Jeremias's claim that this was Jesus' distinctive usage see R. E. Brown, *Death*, 172-75; briefly my *Mark*, 584. Luz, 1:375-77, adds the important consideration that while Jesus' usage was distinctive in its familiarity of approach, it was not "un-Jewish," since the thought of God as Father is well attested in Judaism. Keener, 217, provides ample evidence that the idea of God (or the chief god, Zeus or Jupiter) as a father was also familiar in Greek and Roman religion.

57. For "our Father" as a description of God (not a vocative form of address) in the OT see Isa 63:16; 64:8; cf. Tob 13:4; "our Father in heaven" occurs in *m. Soṭah* 9:15; cf. *m. Yoma* 8:9 (again not as a vocative).

effect a plea for God's action to bring about the desired state of affairs, hence Hagner's paraphrastic version using second-person imperatives: "Set apart your holy name; Bring your eschatological kingdom; Cause your will to be fulfilled" (Hagner, 1:144). But perhaps something is lost when the third-person form is concealed, since the hallowing of God's name, the acceptance of his kingship, and the doing of his will involve human response (including that of the ones praying). To speak as Hagner does simply of "the divine passive" runs the danger of obscuring this human dimension, even though the point of including these wishes in a *prayer* is that it is by God's intervention that they are to be fulfilled.

God's "name" is a recurrent OT term for God himself as he is perceived and honored by people. It is frequently described as "holy" (Pss 30:4; 97:12; 103:1; 111:9, etc.) since holiness is a prime characteristic of God himself. The present clause is not then a request that it be made holy, as the traditional translation "hallowed" properly means — it is holy already. Rather, it is that people may recognize and acknowledge its holiness by giving God the reverence which is his due; cf. Isa 29:23, where to "keep God's name holy" is further explained by "stand in awe of the God of Israel." Compare the concern of the prophets that God's name should not be profaned as a result of his people's sinful behavior and its punishment (Ezek 20:8-9; 36:20-23; cf. Isa 48:11; 52:5-6). This clause, then, is not merely a petition that people in general may come to acknowledge God, but is itself an expression of that reverence which his holiness requires.

10 For God's "kingdom" see on 3:2. There and in 4:17 (and in other places throughout the gospel) the coming of God's reign is something already announced. Its actual presence is required by the wording of 12:28, though the sense of being caught unawares in that saying suggests that even when God's kingdom is present not everyone recognizes and acknowledges it. The parables of ch. 13 will repeat this point, notably those of the mustard seed and the yeast (13:31-33) where the hidden presence of God's kingdom is preparing for a future more public demonstration. It is probably in that sense that we are to understand this petition, perhaps the most clearly futuristic reference to God's kingdom in Matthew. The "already–not yet" tension which underlies the Synoptic uses of the term is vividly illustrated by the doxology later added to the end of this prayer, which requires the disciples who have just prayed that God's kingdom may come to declare immediately afterward that it is already a reality. As with the "making holy" of God's name, this petition is not so much asking that something may become true which is not true already (that God may become king) but rather that his actual kingship *de jure* may be fully implemented *de facto* as people submit to his sovereignty. In so doing the disciples echoed the prayers of many faithful Jewish people in the Qaddish (see above) and the hopes of those who, like Joseph of Arimathea, were "expecting the kingdom of God" (Mark 15:43).[58]

The third of these clauses builds on the second: the essence of the coming of God's kingship is that he is duly obeyed and his purpose fulfilled. The "already–not yet" tension is here more explicit, as the situations in heaven (where God's kingship has been eternally honored) and on earth (where it is yet to be fully acknowledged) are compared. The time must come when God's human creatures join his angelic forces in honoring and serving their king. "Doing the will of God" is for Matthew a potent summary of disciples' lives[59] (7:21; 12:50; and parabolically in 21:31), and even Jesus himself in prayer must submit his own will to that of his Father (26:42).

The final words, "as in heaven so also on earth," can be seen to apply to all three of the preceding clauses. In heaven (among the angels) God's name is already honored, his kingship acknowledged, and his will done, and the prayer is that this heavenly state of affairs may also be reflected on earth. In the Lucan form of the prayer the first two clauses occur without this rider, but when it is added as part of the third its relevance to the preceding two also becomes obvious.[60] To pray such a prayer is, of course, to be committed oneself to honor God's name, accept his kingship, and do his will.

11   The first of the petitions for the disciples' own needs concerns material provision (cf. Prov 30:8, "feed me with the bread I need").[61] In vv. 25-33 we will be told that part of what it means to recognize God as our heavenly Father is to be prepared to trust him for food and drink and clothing, and this petition expresses that trust in its simplest form. Even bread, the most basic of survival rations, comes by God's daily provision (cf. Ps 104:14-15, 27-28), and is thus a proper subject for prayer rather than to be taken for granted. If this is true even for bread, how much more for all our other physical needs.

The traditional term "daily" represents the Greek adjective *epiousios,* which occurs nowhere else in extant[62] Greek literature and whose etymol-

---

58. For a number of other Jewish texts which look for a future manifestation of God's kingdom see D. C. Allison, *End,* 103.

59. See B. Przybylski, *Righteousness,* 112-15, for the centrality of "doing the will of God" (as compared with δικαιοσύνη) in Matthew's presentation of the disciple life. Cf. also my *Matthew, Evangelist,* 265-68; D. J. Verseput, *Rejection,* 288-93.

60. So G. R. Beasley-Murray, *Kingdom,* 151-52.

61. See R. H. Gundry, *Use,* 74-75, for this echo, noting the Targum version, "bread of my requirement."

62. It was allegedly found in a papyrus fragment from an Egyptian account book which was published in the nineteenth century by A. H. Sayce but subsequently lost; it is said to have referred there to a daily "ration." But the accuracy of the original transcription has been questioned, and an article by M. Nijman and K. A. Worp in *NovT* 41 (1999) 231-

ogy and meaning have been variously explained. The ancient Syriac versions have either "continual" or "for our need"; earlier Latin versions have "daily," while Jerome's Vulgate coined *supersubstantialis,* which probably meant "supernatural." Among modern interpreters some derive it from *epi* and *ousia,* giving a meaning "needed for existence," some from *epi tēn ousan (hēmeran),* "for the present day," but most recent interpreters prefer to see it as an adjective formed from *hē epiousa (hēmera),* which occurs in Acts 7:26; 16:11; 20:15; 21:18 for "the following day" (in a sequence of events or traveling stages). In these uses *hē epiousa*[63] means the day after the one just described; in Acts 23:11 *hē epiousa nyx* means the ensuing night. The sense probably depends on the time of speaking: in the morning *hē epiousa* would mean the day then beginning (classical usage supports this sense), but later in the day it would mean "tomorrow." If *epiousios* derives its meaning from *hē epiousa,* "for the coming day" may well have a similar range of meaning.[64] The bread requested is therefore for the near future, which may be "today" or "tomorrow" depending on the time of utterance. This petition would remind a Jewish hearer of the provision of manna in the wilderness, enough for each day at a time, except for an extra supply when the following day was a sabbath (Exod 16:4-5).

To ask for such bread[65] "today" is to acknowledge our dependence on God for routine provision. In modern Western culture where the provision of food is usually planned and assured for a good time ahead, such immediate dependence seems remote from our experience. In many other parts of the world today, as in Jesus' world, it is not so; Carson, 171, rightly reminds us of "the precarious lifestyle of many first-century workers who were paid one day at a time and for whom a few days' illness could spell tragedy."[66] Similarly for Jesus and his disciples during their itinerant mission, the daily provision of material needs could not be taken for granted (see 8:20; 10:9-14, 40-42).[67]

---

34 claims to have rediscovered the original papyrus and that Sayce's transcription cannot be justified.

63. A participial form from ἔπειμι, "to come upon," "come after," which has come by the NT period to function virtually as a noun in its own right.

64. Jerome, *Comm. Matt.* 6:11, quotes an Aramaic version of the prayer from the *Gospel of the Hebrews* which uses *māḥār,* "tomorrow," to translate ἐπιούσιος. C. J. Hemer, *JSNT* 22 (1984) 81-94, usefully discusses and illustrates the wider usage of ἡ ἐπιοῦσα and provides solid support for the translation of ἐπιούσιος as "pertaining to the coming day."

65. The singular ἄρτος can mean a single loaf, the normal daily ration for one person (see 7:9), but since this is a corporate prayer it is better translated simply "bread" rather than trying to bring in the idea of a loaf *each* for all those praying.

66. E. M. Yamauchi, *WTJ* 28 (1966) 145-56, provides an interesting survey of ancient Near Eastern references to the importance of "daily bread."

67. D. Instone-Brewer, *Traditions,* 1:158-61, explains this petition in the light of

The instruction not to worry about material provision in vv. 25-33 (which seems equally remote from most modern Western experience) is dependent on all such needs having been trustfully committed to God as this prayer requires. Jesus himself had to depend on God for food rather than taking the matter into his own hands (4:3-4).

I have assumed hitherto that this petition is concerned with the literal provision of everyday material needs. Those who emphasize an eschatological dimension to the Lord's Prayer suggest rather that "bread for tomorrow" is a shorthand expression for eschatological provision, perhaps with special reference to the messianic banquet (see on 8:11; cf. Luke 14:15), or more specifically to the eschatological hope of a return of manna (*2 Bar.* 29:8; *Sib. Or.* 7:149; Rev 2:17). Some support this sense by deriving *epiousios* not from *hē epiousa (hēmera)* but directly from the verb *epienai,* so that it is the bread itself rather than the day which is "coming," "future."[68] Hagner, 1:144, expresses this view in his "interpretive paraphrase," "Give us today the eschatological bread that will be ours in the future." Whatever may be the case for the prayer as a whole, however, an eschatological sense does not suit the wording of this petition (Hagner's paraphrase has added a lot to the actual wording of the Greek!). "Bread" carries its literal meaning elsewhere in this gospel, even when the context indicates that the literal bread is being used to convey a symbolic message (15:26; 16:5-12; 26:26), and the everyday dimension implied by *epiousios* (if derived, as is more linguistically probable, from *hē epiousa)* seems to require that meaning unless anything in the context suggests a nonliteral sense. Further, the request for bread to be supplied "today" (and even more the Lucan version "every day") sits uncomfortably with an eschatological perspective.

12 The petition for forgiveness is the only clause of the prayer which is singled out for comment at the end (vv. 14-15). The point of that comment, as indeed of the balancing structure of the clause itself, is that forgiveness is a reciprocal principle,[69] a point which will be more fully underlined in the parable of 18:23-35. That parable, like the present petition, will be about debt, though the introductory question and answer in 18:21-22

---

the rabbinic "distinction between the itinerant poor (who were given enough for one day at a time) and the local poor (who were given enough for a week)"; Jesus and his disciples came into the former category.

68. This derivation of ἐπιούσιος faces the difficulty that, first, the verb ἐπιέναι is used in biblical Greek only in the participial form noted above to identify the "coming" day, night, or time, not as a verb in its own right, and secondly that the formation of an adjective ending in *-ousios* from such a verb (rather than from the participial form ἐπιοῦσα) would be unusual. On the philological question see further C. J. Hemer, *JSNT* 22 (1984) 82-84.

69. See R. Mohrlang, *Matthew,* 52-54, for "Matthew's concept of reciprocity."

makes it clear that debt is a metaphor for offenses which need to be forgiven. Here, too, any purely monetary understanding of debt is ruled out by the fact that it is debts *to God* for which forgiveness is asked.[70] The substitution in vv. 14-15 of "offenses"[71] (and cf. the "sins" of Luke 11:4a) gives a more prosaic but undoubtedly correct interpretation of the graphic metaphor of debt.[72] Matthew's version, unlike Luke's, by keeping the same metaphor in both halves of the clause ensures that a close parallel is maintained between God's forgiveness and ours. We should note that it is the debtors rather than the debts which we have forgiven; our concern, like God's, is to be with personal relationships.

The *hōs* ("as") which links the two halves of this clause leaves open the question whether the forgiveness of our fellow humans is to be understood strictly as a prior condition of our being forgiven.[73] The variation in the MSS as to the tense of the verb (see p. 230, n. 12) perhaps reflects uncertainty on this issue, the aorist tense properly indicating that our forgiveness of others is prior to God's requested forgiveness of us, while the present may be thought to allow a less precise relationship. But perhaps precision on this point is not necessary; the issue is whether the forgiveness sought from God is mirrored in the attitude of those pray.[74] In the parable of 18:23-35 God's forgiveness comes first, but it is withdrawn when the person forgiven fails to forgive another. There is then something inevitably reciprocal about forgiveness. To ask to be forgiven while oneself refusing to forgive is hypocritical.[75] Those who ask for forgiveness must be forgiving people, whether the offenses concerned

70. Further, as Keener, 223, points out, "most of Jesus' hearers would have been borrowers rather than lenders," and therefore the question of remitting the monetary debts of others would not arise.

71. The term παραπτώματα is used in Mark 11:25, with which vv. 14-15 are related, so that Matthew's choice of the term there may have been due to the Marcan tradition. But a deliberate "unpacking" of the debt metaphor may well be intended.

72. The metaphor is already supplied in the single Aramaic word *ḥôbāʾ*, which covers both "debt" and "sin." But Greek does not afford the same ambiguity, and Matthew's deployment of the two different Greek words in his version of the prayer and in the comment on it allows the παραπτώματα of vv. 14-15 to control our understanding of the metaphorical sense of ὀφειλήματα in v. 12.

73. Contrast the more specifically conditional language of Sir 28:2: "Forgive your neighbor's wrongdoing, *and then* your sins will be forgiven when you pray."

74. C. F. D. Moule, *Essays*, 278-86, helpfully distinguishes here between "deserts" and "capacity." It is not a matter of earning forgiveness, but of being capable of receiving it.

75. The point is eloquently developed in Sir 28:1-5; see especially vv. 3-4: "One person cherishes anger against another; and does he then seek healing from the Lord? He has no mercy on a person like himself; and can he then pray about [ask for forgiveness for] his own sins?"

are past or future. J. Jeremias[76] suggests that *aphēkamen,* "we have forgiven," represents an Aramaic perfect with performative force: "as *herewith* we forgive our debtors." It may be doubted whether the Greek aorist can naturally be taken in quite this sense, but Jeremias's rendering offers an appropriately challenging perspective on what this clause of the prayer should involve for those who pray it.

13   After a petition for the forgiveness of past sin comes one for protection from future sin. The final clause of the prayer is again in two parts, but this time the two lines are both petitions whose theme is closely related, so that the second may be understood as an expansion or elucidation of the first. If the translation of *tou ponērou* as "the Evil One" is correct (see p. 231, n. 14), the parallel between the two lines is clear, since we have seen *peirasmos* ("testing") as the role of the the devil already in 4:1-11 (where he is actually described as "the tempter," *ho peirazōn*). It is possible to see a progression between the two lines, the first being a request to be kept free from testing, the second for rescue if it does occur (a "worst-case scenario"). But that is perhaps to be too pedantic concerning the meaning of the phrases "not bring into" and "rescue from." Both are vivid ways of saying that the disciples are aware of the need for God's help and protection in the face of the devil's desire to lead astray.

The question is sometimes raised how the notion of God's "bringing us into *peirasmos*" is compatible with his absolute goodness,[77] but this involves two mistakes. First, a negative request does not necessarily imply that the positive is otherwise to be expected — a husband who says to his wife, "Don't ever leave me," is not necessarily assuming that she is likely to do so. Secondly, *peirasmos* is not in itself always to be understood as a bad thing: it was after all the Holy Spirit who took Jesus into the wilderness "to be tested" (4:1). When James says that God "does not tempt anyone" (Jas 1:13) he is presumably using *peirazō* in its more limited sense of "tempt to do wrong," but the idea of God "testing" his people is a biblical one (Gen 22:1; Deut 8:2, etc.).[78] If *peirazō* is here taken in that more positive sense, the point of the petition would be not that the testing is in itself bad, but that the disciples, aware of their weakness, would prefer not to have to face it.[79] As in 4:1-11, it

---

76. J. Jeremias, *Theology,* 201.

77. See H. D. Betz, *Sermon,* 406-11, for an account of some of the ways that have been found of tackling "the theodicy problem" as it arises in relation to this petition.

78. In view of this usage, it is unnecessarily subtle to find in this clause a petition that God will not lead his people into the situation where they will "test" him, as at Massah/Meribah (Exod 17:7; Ps 95:8-9; so Carter, 168, following C. B. Houk, *SJT* 46 [1963] 216-25).

79. The language is echoed in what was perhaps already a familiar Jewish prayer, subsequently preserved in *b. Ber.* 60b: "Bring me not into the power of sin, and not into

is possible to discern in the same circumstances both the devil's "tempting" and God's "testing" of his people.

Those who understand the petitions of this prayer as having a primarily eschatological focus tend to read this "testing" as referring to a specific event, the tribulation which was to introduce the end times.[80] But the lack of a definite article before *peirasmon* suggests that the focus is not so specific (nor is *peirasmos* a recognized term for this idea). Moreover, a community eagerly looking for the eschatological consummation could hardly pray to be spared this "time of trial," without which the final dénouement could not come. Their prayer would rather be to be preserved safe through it (the second line of v. 13 rather than the first). As in the prayer as a whole, while this petition might be made with an eschatological reference, its wording does not suggest that that is its main purpose. It relates rather to the testing experiences which are the normal lot of disciples who try to live according to the principles of the kingdom of God in a world which does not share those values. The sort of persecution envisaged in 5:11-12 comes to mind. In 26:41 Jesus will again exhort his disciples to pray for deliverance from *peirasmos,* with reference to their immediate danger rather than an eschatological threat.

f. Comment on the Lord's Prayer (6:14-15)

Here is one of the few echoes of Mark in this discourse; see Mark 11:25 for the same principle of reciprocal forgiveness in relation to prayer. This expansion of the principle underlying the petition of v. 12 reflects the typically Matthean concern, which will be developed especially in the discourse of 18:1-35 (and cf. 5:23-24), that the disciple community should function properly as a group whose values have been transformed by their acceptance of God's kingship in their life together. It puts into simple propositional form the message of the parable of the two debtors in 18:23-35. In 26:28 Jesus will place the forgiveness of sins at the heart of his mission. But if the disciple community which results from that mission is to be and to function as a community of the forgiven, its members cannot themselves begrudge forgiveness to others. In these verses the conditional element which was apparently implicit in v. 12 becomes quite explicit, and is emphasized by being stated both positively and negatively. Only the forgiving will be forgiven.

---

the power of guilt, and not into the power of temptation, and not into the power of anything shameful" (see J. Jeremias, *Theology,* 202).

80. Albright and Mann, 74, even render πειρασμός by "*the final* test" — hardly a straight *translation*!

The stark simplicity of this pronouncement raises uncomfortable questions. First, how does this conditional forgiveness relate to the gospel of free and unmerited grace which Paul proclaims? Does our act of forgiving earn our forgiveness from God? The same problem arises elsewhere in Matthew, notably in 25:31-46, where we shall have to consider how far the salvation of the "righteous" is dependent on their behavior toward other people in need. It is neatly encapsulated in the parable of 22:1-14, where apparently undeserving people ("both bad and good") are drafted into the wedding feast, and yet one of those is subsequently ejected for being improperly dressed. Salvation according to that parable may be undeserved and unexpected, but it is not without conditions. Like the debtor of 18:23-35, one of the recipients of grace turns out not to meet the expectations on which the continuation of that salvation depends. So also here, if the forgiveness of sins which is achieved through the saving death of Jesus (26:28) is not matched by an appropriately forgiving attitude on the disciple's part, it cannot be presumed upon. Such a theology of salvation fits Matthew's primarily ethical use of *dikaiosynē* ("righteousness") over against Paul's more "theoretical" use of the same term to denote a salvation ("justification") independent of "works." As with the traditional antinomy between Paul and James, there is not perhaps a simple contradiction, but there is certainly a clear difference of perspective on what the forgiveness of sins involves, though the parable of 20:1-15 will make it clear that Matthew has no room for a crudely mechanical view of salvation earned in proportion to human effort.

A second problem relates to the breadth of the forgiveness required. Its object is literally "people" without any further specification. So is there no limit to what and whom we must forgive? Should disciples forgive war criminals, serial murderers, and abusers of children? What does "forgive" mean in such circumstances? In 18:21-22 the issue is discussed specifically with reference to a brother who sins "against me," and in that case Jesus insists that there is no limit. The parable which follows in 18:23-35, by contrasting the unimaginable debt remitted by the king with the relatively paltry sum demanded by the debtor, indicates that no offense we may suffer can even get close to the weight of sin we have already been forgiven by God. Hard as it may be for human nature, there is to be no limit to disciples' willingness to forgive those who offend them. The phrase "against me" in that passage perhaps gives us a guide to the intention of this passage as well. While the reference to the offenses of "people" could hardly be more general, the clause of the prayer which these verses are explaining uses the metaphor of debt specifically of those who are indebted *to us* (v. 12). It is where there is personal offense that the concept of "forgiveness" properly applies. Those who commit evil by which we ourselves are not affected should be the object of our prayerful concern and (as far as possible) sympathetic understanding, but it is properly speaking not for us to "forgive" them: that is God's prerogative. The concern of these verses, as of 18:21-35, is with the disciples' response to those whose offense is against them. It is our own enemies whom we are to love (5:44).

g. Secret Fasting (6:16-18)

The pattern established in vv. 2-4 and 5-6 is now resumed with the third type of secret religious observance. For the standard formulae again see above on vv. 2-4. As with almsgiving and prayer, it is assumed that disciples will fast; the issue is not whether to do it but how. In a culture where few now give serious attention to fasting as a religious discipline (as opposed to token acts like giving up chocolates in Lent) this assumption causes surprise. In the NT as a whole there is little explicit instruction on fasting; it is simply mentioned occasionally (and never in the epistles) as something Christians sometimes did. Jesus himself fasted (involuntarily?) in the wilderness (4:2), but there is no other record of his doing so subsequently, and indeed it was the lack of fasting by him and his associates which was commented on in 9:14, though in his reply Jesus does envisage his disciples fasting at a future date (9:15).[81] In Acts we are told of prayer and fasting on two occasions as an accompaniment to important decisions (Acts 13:2-3; 14:23), but not of any regular pattern of fasting. When Paul speaks of "fasting" as part of his apostolic sufferings (2 Cor 6:5; 11:27), the reference is to involuntary shortage of food rather than to deliberate abstention. It is not until *Did.* 8:1 (late first century?) that we find instruction on regular fasting for Christians — twice a week, like the Pharisee in Luke 18:12. In view of the paucity of evidence, it is hard to decide whether the fasting Jesus here assumes is expected to be a regular practice (as in the *Didache*) or only on special occasions as in Acts. He simply comments on the familiar Jewish practice with the expectation that his disciples will continue it.

Fasting is often mentioned in the OT, usually together with prayer and/or penitence. Normally it is a response to a special situation, whether by an individual alone (2 Sam 12:16-23; 1 Kgs 21:27; Neh 1:4; Ps 35:13; Dan 9:3) or by the nation as a whole (Judg 20:26; 2 Chr 20:3; Ezra 8:21-23; Neh 9:1; Jonah 3:5-9). The only regular fast laid down in the Pentateuch is that

---

81. See below, p. 657, n. 8, for the mention of fasting in some texts of Matthew as a prerequisite for success in exorcism. While the reference is almost certainly not part of the authentic text of Matthew, a good case can be made for its authenticity in Mark 9:29, despite the tendency of modern editions to reject καὶ νηστείᾳ there (see my textual note in *Mark,* 361).

on the Day of Atonement (Lev 16:29-31; 23:27-32), but during the exile additional fast-days were established in memory of the destruction of Jerusalem (Zech 7:3-5; 8:19). But it is not until NT times that we find evidence of regular fasting by the Pharisees (9:14; twice a week according to Luke 18:12) and the disciples of John the Baptist (9:14). What had been a special provision for times of penitence or emergency had thus been turned into a matter of routine religious duty, despite the protest of Isa 58:3-7 against assuming that fasting had an automatic efficacy of its own. The asceticism of John the Baptist (and of the slightly later Bannus; see above on 3:1) displays the sort of approach to religion in which routine fasting might flourish, though it is interesting that the "monastic" community of Qumran does not seem to have had a regular regime of fasting. The implication of *Did.* 8:1 that (some) Jews observed Mondays and Thursdays as days for fasting is confirmed by *m. Ta'an.* 2:9. For the importance and prevalence of fasting in post-OT Jewish religion, and in outsiders' impression of Judaism, see J. Behm, *TDNT* 4:929-31.

The sort of fasting envisaged here is presumably that of choice rather than of routine, since there would be little point in putting on a show to impress people with one's fasting if it was already known and expected. In 9:14-17 we shall find the voluntary fasting of the Pharisees used as a stick with which to beat the Jesus movement, which is thus alleged not to take its religious obligations sufficiently seriously; the argument of course assumes that other people knew the Pharisees were fasting. Just how the "hypocrites" made their fasting visible (by making their faces "invisible"!) is not clear (see p. 231, n. 17), but there is a delicious irony in the play on words between *aphanizō* ("hide") and *phainomai* ("everyone can see"; cf. also v. 18). Their "miserable" look was felt by some, then as now, to be a suitable expression of religious devotion.[82] By contrast, the disciples' washing and anointing are part of the everyday bodily care which were sometimes forgone as part of the self-affliction involved in fasting (*m. Ta'an.* 1:6). Anointing, like the washing of the face, represents normal cosmetics[83] (Luke 7:46; cf. Ruth 3:3; 2 Sam 14:2; 2 Chr 28:15; Dan 10:3), not an artificial show of gaiety; everything is to be outwardly normal. Fasting, like almsgiving and prayer, is to be between the disciple and God. No one else should know. (Perhaps that is why we know so little of early Christian practice in this regard!)

---

82. H. D. Betz, *Sermon*, 420-21, traces this theme (and the use in this connection of σκυθρωπός, "sullen," "scowling") in ancient society.

83. See Keener, 227-28, for the prevalence of the cosmetic use of oil in the ancient Mediterranean world.

6. Treasure in Heaven (6:19-24)

19 *"Do not store up treasures for yourselves on earth, where moths and vermin[1] ruin[2] them, and where thieves break in[3] and steal them. 20 Rather, store up treasures for yourselves in heaven, where neither moths nor vermin can ruin them, and no thieves break in and steal them. 21 For where your[4] treasure is, there your heart will be too.*

22 *"The eye is the lamp of the body. So if your eye is sound,[5] your whole body will be illuminated; 23 but if your eye is bad, your whole body will be in the dark. So if the light which is in you is darkness, how great that darkness is!*

24 *"No one can be the slave[6] of two owners; either he will hate the one and love the other, or he will take the side of[7] one and have no regard for the other. You cannot be slaves of both God and wealth.*[8]

1. Βρῶσις means "eating" (as in Rom 14:17; 1 Cor 8:4; 2 Cor 9:10; Col 2:16) or sometimes "food" (John 4:32; 6:27, 55) or a "meal" (Heb 12:16). What sort of "eating" treasure is subject to depends on the nature of the treasure. The traditional rendering "rust," based on the Vulgate and on comparison with Jas 5:3, assumes that it is metal, but ἰός would be the normal term for rust (as in Jas 5:3), whereas βρῶσις would better suit an animal pest (it is used in LXX Mal 3:11 for a devouring locust), perhaps mice or rats nibbling at rich fabrics, or even woodworm destroying the treasure chests. Cf. *Gos. Thom.* 76, where moth and worm are linked in the parallel to this saying. It might also be taken as a term for the effect of the moths themselves, so that σὴς καὶ βρῶσις would be a hendiadys, "moth-eating," but this is less likely in view of the disjunction in the next verse, "*neither moths nor vermin.*"

2. For the meaning of ἀφανίζω see p. 231, n. 17. Here the treasure is "made invisible" by gradual deterioration and eventual destruction by vermin.

3. Literally, "dig through," a vivid description of the burglar's forced entry through a mud-brick wall as in Ezek 12:5, 7; Job 24:16 (cf. Matt 24:43; in Mark 2:4 a similar term is used for entry through the roof!). Josephus, *Ant.* 16.1, uses τοιχωρύχος, "wall digger," for a person who broke into a house. Hagner also notes the possibility of treasures being buried under a house floor.

4. The "you"s of v. 21 (and of vv. 22-23) are singular, unlike those of vv. 19-20 and v. 24. The plural reading in most later MSS is an obvious attempt at stylistic tidying.

5. It is impossible in English to find a single word which conveys the wordplay of the Greek; see the comments below. While the basic meaning of ἁπλοῦς is "single," as applied to an eye "single" would convey a quite inappropriate sense of being one-eyed. "Sound" attempts to do justice to the contrast with "bad" (unhealthy, ineffective), but the further nuances of generosity and, perhaps, single-mindedness must be left to the commentary.

6. The saying requires the full sense of δουλεύω as being owned by and therefore totally responsible to a single master. See the comments below.

7. ἀντέχω means to "hold fast to," "be devoted to" a person or truth. Here the context requires that it be understood of loyalty to one of two rivals.

8. Greek μαμωνᾶς is a transliteration of Aramaic *māmôn(ā'),* a neutral (non-

There is a clear continuity of thought between the idea of a secret, heavenly reward in vv. 1-6, 16-18 and the subject of treasure in heaven which opens this section of the discourse with its focus on the disciple's attitude to material security. The theme of a heavenly reward for those who are disadvantaged on earth also recalls 5:3-12.

Three separate sayings (on treasure, the eye, and slavery), which have parallels respectively in Luke 12:33-34; 11:34-35; 16:13, are here grouped together, probably on the basis that all contribute in different ways (vv. 22-23 rather obliquely, as we shall see) to an understanding of the disciple's attitude to material possessions, a theme which will then be taken up in the more unified section of teaching which forms the rest of ch. 6, and to which this short collection thus provides an introduction. The separate origin of the sayings in vv. 19-24 is indicated by the alternation between plural and singular second-person pronouns (see n. 4). The thought which connects them is of single-mindedness, which comes to the surface in the subtle wordplay on *haplous,* "single, sound," in v. 22. Disciples, as subjects of God's kingship, are totally committed to his service, and must allow no other concerns to distract them from this prior aim (see 6:33).

The relationship between discipleship and wealth or possessions is a recurrent theme in the gospels,[9] particularly in Luke, who has included three substantial sections of material (most of it found only in his gospel) on issues relating to affluence and the affluent (Luke 12:13-34; 14:1-33; 16:1-31). In Matthew, in addition to the present section of the discourse on discipleship (6:19-34), the issue will recur in 19:16-30, in a section shared with the other Synoptic evangelists, while other sayings will raise it more briefly (5:42; 6:2-4; 8:20; 10:8-11; 13:22; 26:6-11), and several parables and other teaching units can also be applied specifically to one's attitude to possessions (7:7-11; 13:44-46; 25:14-30, 31-46). Recurrent themes are the expectation that disciples will not be among the affluent, the priority of spiritual allegiance to material security, the assurance of God's care for his people's material needs, and the call for uncalculating generosity.

A cue for the inclusion of this topic at this point in the discourse may be found in the petition of v. 11, where "bread" may appropriately be taken to represent all the material needs which disciples are expected to commit to their heavenly Father. When that prayer has been sincerely prayed, the disciple is set free from material anxiety and can instead concentrate on the kingship and righteousness of God (6:33) which are the prayer's primary focus.

---

pejorative) term for "wealth" or "property"; in Luke 16:9, 11 it is the addition of τῆς ἀδικίας / ἄδικος which conveys the pejorative sense. See further comments below.

9. Note the monograph on the subject by T. E. Schmidt, *Hostility.* I have addressed it briefly in "God and Mammon," *EQ* 51 (1979) 3-21.

"Treasures on earth" and the demands of "mammon" are thus put into their proper place.

19-20 The instruction "Do not store up for yourselves" might better be rendered "Stop storing up for yourselves";[10] this is a call to reorientation away from one type of acquisition to another. In a culture where banking was embryonic and little used or trusted (see 25:25-27), "treasures" were normally kept in goods or hard currency in the home or in a supposedly safe place; see 13:52 for the former and 13:44; 25:25 for the latter. They were thus liable to physical deterioration (see p. 256, n. 1 for the nature of the damage)[11] or theft, and the insecurity of material goods is a recurrent theme of the wisdom writers (Prov 23:4-5; 27:24; Eccl 5:13-17; cf. Jer 17:11); for the role of the "moth" in this cf. Ps 39:11; Job 13:28.[12] Equally obviously, however carefully it may be preserved, material wealth is of no use beyond this life on earth (Pss 39:6; 49:16-19; Eccl 2:20-26; this is the point of the parable in Luke 12:16-21). In place of such dubious acquisitions, "treasures in heaven" are a much more desirable alternative; cf. Isa 33:1-6, where the stable "treasure" of the fear of the Lord is contrasted with the short-lived triumph of Zion's enemies. The nature of these heavenly treasures is not spelled out here, but later in the gospel we shall hear of "inheriting eternal life" as the compensation for loss of earthly advantages (19:27-29; cf. 16:25-26), of "entering the master's joy" (25:21, 23), and of "inheriting the kingdom prepared for you from the foundation of the world" (25:34), which is further identified as "eternal life" (25:46). "Heaven" can of course serve as a surrogate for the name of God (as in "the kingdom of heaven" and, e.g., in 21:25), so that "treasures in heaven" might be taken to mean "treasures with God" rather than as referring specifically to a future life, but here the direct contrast with "on earth" and the sense of provision for the future implied in "store up for yourselves" strongly suggest an otherworldly focus. Cf. the similar metaphor of 1 Tim 6:19.[13]

The verb "store up for yourselves" (literally, "make a treasure for

---

10. A present imperative in the negative often implies that the act prohibited is already occurring, as against an aorist subjunctive, used to prevent something contemplated but not yet actual.

11. An interesting parallel to this saying is found in Sir 29:10-11, where the sage points out how much better it is to use your wealth to benefit a brother or a friend (and thus to "deposit your treasure according to the commandments of the Most High"; see n. 14 below) than to leave it to rust away under a stone.

12. Most OT references to the destructive capacity of the σής are specifically of clothing, but BDAG 922a note that in Hermas, *Sim.* 8.1.6-7 etc. the σής destroys wood, so that there perhaps the reference is to woodworm.

13. Cf. *4 Ezra* 7:77, where the "treasure of works stored up with the Most High" is shown by the context to belong to life after death; similarly *2 Bar.* 14:12; 24:1.

yourselves") might suggest that these heavenly treasures are to be earned by the disciples' own efforts, and the frequent language of "reward" in this gospel easily conveys the same impression (see above on 5:12, and compare the "reward" language of 6:1-6, 16-18); in 19:21 it is by giving to the poor that "a treasure in heaven" is to be secured; in 19:29 eternal life is spoken of as compensation for earthly losses, and in 25:21, 23, 34, 46 the heavenly rewards are directly linked to the disciples' use of earthly opportunities.[14] But while the theme of reward is important in this gospel, we must remind ourselves again that in the parable which most directly addresses the issue (20:1-15) there is a deliberate discrepancy between the effort expended and the recompense received: God does not leave anyone unfairly treated, but his grace is not limited to human deserving. In a kingdom in which the first are last and the last first (19:30; 20:16) there is no room for computing one's "treasures in heaven" on the basis of earthly effort. Those treasures are "stored up" not by performing meritorious acts (and certainly not only by almsgiving) but by belonging to and living by the priorities of the kingdom of heaven.

The focus of this saying is on priorities: heaven rather than earth (for these two contrasting spheres cf. 6:10; 16:19; 18:18; 23:9). It is going beyond the intention of the saying to use it as a basis for ruling out all material possessions and all provisions for the (earthly) future on the part of disciples. For a positive valuation of material possessions if properly used see, for example, 1 Tim 4:3-5; 5:8; 6:18; the itinerant and dependent lifestyle of Jesus and his disciples depended on the support of those who had not divested themselves of all their possessions (Luke 8:3; 10:38-42; John 12:1-2, etc.).

21 The singular "you"s and singular "treasure" of this verse suggest a separate origin from vv. 19-20, but the content of the verse could hardly be more appropriate to round off their message: each disciple's priorities will be determined by his or her comparative valuation of earthly and heavenly benefits. The sequence might suggest that the orientation of the "heart" follows from the determination of where the treasure is to be, but that is to be pedantic; the valuing of the treasure both follows from and reveals the orientation

---

14. A similar principle appears in the OT wisdom writings, notably Prov 19:17: "Whoever is kind to the poor lends to the LORD, and will be repaid in full" — though Proverbs does not indicate that the repayment will be in heaven. Sir 29:9-13 describes alms-giving as "depositing a treasure (θησαυρόν) according to the commandments of the Most High," while in Sir 3:3-4 honoring one's parents is compared with "storing up treasure"; in neither case, however, is there any clear link with a heavenly rather than an earthly reward. The theme is more fully developed in Tob 4:5-11, where almsgiving is described as "storing up (θησαυρίζω) for yourself a good deposit against the day of need," which is then further specified as rescue from death and going into darkness; cf. Tob 12:8-10. See also *Ps. Sol.* 9:5.

of the heart. For the "heart" as a term for what is of central importance in a person, what constitutes their true character, cf. 5:8; 11:29, and especially 12:34; 15:18-19; 22:37. For the unhelpful effect of wealth on the "heart" cf. Deut 8:17; 17:17.

22-23 The singular address continues in this enigmatic saying, which has a parallel, differently developed, in Luke 11:34-36. The imagery of treasure gives way to that of light as another way of speaking of a healthy orientation in the disciple's life, but the metaphor of light is complicated by its linkage with the function of the eye as "the lamp of the body," and a further nuance is added by the adjectives which I have rendered "sound" and "bad," which allow a play on the usage of the Greek words to introduce the further theme of generosity and meanness. It is this last element in the saying which best explains its inclusion in this context dealing with the disciples' attitude to material possessions.

The use of light and darkness as imagery for spiritual health or failure is familiar from, for example, John 3:19-21; 8:12; 11:9-10; 12:35-36, and cf. "sons of light" in Luke 16:8. In Matthew the disciples have been described as themselves a light to others (5:14, 16), but this is the only place in this gospel where the metaphor is used in the "Johannine" sense.[15]

But while the imagery of light may be familiar and easily understood, that of the eye as "the lamp of the body" is not so obvious. In the OT and later Jewish writings we hear of the "light of the eyes" as a mark of happiness,[16] of eyes being enlightened or darkened as a mark of vigor or decline,[17] and of light shining from the eyes, which may then be compared with torches or lamps.[18] Ancient writings contain a variety of ideas about how the eye functions,[19] but modern commentators have not been able to agree on how the image works here in relation to the body. A common view that the eye is the "window" through which light enters the body suggests the surprising notion that light is needed inside the body.[20] Or the idea might be that our awareness

15. A partially parallel saying in *Gos. Thom.* 24 inclines rather toward the "light of the world" imagery: "There is light within a man of light, and he (or 'it') illumines the whole world; when he (or 'it') does not shine, there is (or 'he is') darkness." The relation between this saying and Matt 6:22-23 is explored by T. Zöckler, *JBL* 120 (2001) 487-99.

16. Prov 15:30; cf. the expression "the light of my eyes" for a favorite son (Tob 10:5; 11:14).

17. 1 Sam 14:27, 29; Ezra 9:8; Lam 5:17; Bar 1:12.

18. Dan 10:6; Rev 1:14; *1 En.* 106:2, 5; *2 En.* 1:5; *T. Job* 18:4; cf. the seven lamps which represent the seven eyes of the Lord in Zech 4:2, 10.

19. See H. D. Betz in E. Best and R. McL. Wilson (eds.), *Text and Interpretation,* 43-56; idem, *Sermon,* 442-49; D. C. Allison, *NTS* 33 (1987) 61-87. The material is summarized and discussed in Davies and Allison, 1:635-37.

20. Davies and Allison, ibid., 1:635-37, strongly reject this notion as a modern

of light around us comes through the eye,[21] but "lamp" is not the most obvious way to say that. The lamp metaphor more naturally suggests the function of the eye in providing the light which shows the body the way to go,[22] but the following adjectives appear to indicate that it is the body itself, not its surroundings, which is either "illuminated" or "in the dark" depending on how well the eye functions — cf. the final comment on "the light *which is in you*" being darkness. Perhaps we can be no more definite than to say that the imagery depends on light being necessary for the proper functioning of the body (person) and that this light is in some way dependent on the condition of the eye.[23]

To convey this sense we might expect an adjective meaning "healthy," but that is not in itself a normal meaning of *haplous,* "single," and the choice of this term suggests that something more is being said about what makes an eye "healthy." One obvious sense would be "single-minded," "undistracted,"[24] and this would fit admirably with the emphasis on spiritual priorities already expressed in vv. 19-21 and soon to be given memorable epigrammatic form in v. 24 as well as an extended exposition in vv. 25-33. But *ponēros,* "bad," is not a natural opposite to *haplous* in that sense. There is, however, another probable sense of *haplous* which does provide a natural opposite to *ponēros:* the meaning "generous" is suggested by the use of the derivative noun *haplotēs* for "generosity" in, for example, Rom 12:8; 2 Cor 8:2; 9:11, 13, and the adverb *haplōs* in Jas 1:5 for God's giving "generously" (cf. LXX 1 Chr 29:17; Prov 11:25). If generosity is to be understood as the outworking of the "sim-

---

anachronism. It is, however, the position reached by H. D. Betz, *Sermon,* 451, as a result of his survey of ancient theories of vision: "the body is understood as something like a vessel that is dark inside unless it is illuminated; the eyes serve as the instruments of such illumination."

21. Hagner, 1:155, assumes this sense in his paraphrase: "The eye enables a person to see light." In v. 23 his "translation" continues, "If therefore the very organ that should bring you light is the source of darkness in you."

22. D. C. Allison, *NTS* 33 (1987) 61-83, argues for this sense on the basis of Jewish as well as pagan ideas about the functioning of the eye. It is apparently supported by *Gos. Thom.* 24 (see n. 15 above).

23. "Just as the heart follows the treasure (v. 21) and service follows the choice of master (v. 24), so the body follows the eye" (T. E. Schmidt, *Hostility,* 126). Davies and Allison, 1:637-38 (and more fully Allison, *NTS* 33 [1987] 74-76), argue that these conditional sentences should be read (on the analogy of 12:28) as citing the brightness or "badness" of the eye as *evidence of,* rather than the cause of, the light or darkness within; their proposal depends on a greater confidence in identifying the nature of the imagery than most commentators feel able to claim. B. Charette, *Recompense,* 102-3, supports their interpretation, and appositely cites 5:16 as a parallel.

24. For ἁπλότης in this sense as a key moral term in Greek Jewish literature see T. Zöckler, *JBL* 120 (2001) 489-90.

plicity" or "openness" denoted by *haplous,* this would form a direct counterpart to the phrase *ophthalmos ponēros,* "bad eye,"[25] which is used for a jealous stinginess in 20:15. In view of the recognized meaning of the "bad eye" to denote selfish greed or meanness,[26] it seems likely that this saying is meant to indicate that one indication of a person's spiritual health is their generosity or lack of it in the use of their material possessions.[27]

So this rather obscure little saying seems to be using a wordplay[28] which the English translator cannot reproduce without extensive paraphrase in order to commend either single-mindedness (in pursuing the values of the kingdom of heaven) or generosity, or more likely both, as a key to the effective life of a disciple. The final comment then underlines how spiritually disoriented is a life which is not governed by those principles, but rather aims to amass and hold on to "treasure on earth."

24 The connection of this saying to vv. 22-23 is perhaps to be found in the idea of "single-mindedness" suggested by the adjective *haplous* in v. 22; v. 24 portrays the sort of "double-mindedness" which spells spiritual disaster. The traditional translation "No one can *serve* two masters" is patently untrue; we do it all the time, whether by combining part-time jobs or by "moonlighting." But a *slave* was not employed under contract, but was normally wholly owned by the person who had bought him or her (though see Acts 16:16 for the possibility of joint ownership). It is that total commitment which Jesus uses to illustrate the demands of God's kingship and to show the impossibility of combining those demands with the pursuit of "mammon."

Milton's use of "Mammon" as the name of a fallen angel[29] takes to the extreme this personification of wealth as a master making claims to rival those of God. But it is here merely a literary personification; there is no evidence that anyone in the ancient world thought of an actual being called "Mammon." Nor is the term in itself pejorative, as may be seen from the use

---

25. In many cultures an "evil eye" denotes a magical influence or curse, but a study of such usage by F. C. Fensham, *Neot* 1 (1967) 51-58, concludes that the phrase does not generally carry this sense in biblical literature. See J. H. Elliott, *BTB* 22 (1992) 52-65, for the primary sense of envy in ancient use of the phrase.

26. Cf. Mark 7:22, and for wider Greek usage LXX Deut 15:9; Sir 14:10; 31:13. In Prov 22:9 the Hebrew translated "generous" is literally "good-eyed," while in Prov 23:6 and 28:22 the stingy are the "bad-eyed."

27. For similar imagery cf. *T. Benj.* 4:2, where a good man does not have a "darkened eye" (σκοτεινὸς ὀφθαλμός) in that he shows mercy and does good even to his enemies.

28. "A cleverly constructed riddle which can be read on two different levels" (Davies and Allison, 1:639).

29. Milton, *Paradise Lost* 1.678ff.; a similar personification is found in Spenser (who describes the "Cave of Mammon," the god of wealth), and as early as Piers Plowman, but it has no foundation in ancient sources. It is an extrapolation from the "personified" use of the term here.

of *māmôn* in the targums of Deut 6:5 ("love the Lord your God with . . . all your *māmôn*")[30] and Prov 3:9 ("honor the LORD with your *māmôn*"); in Gen 34:23 it represents the Hebrew for "livestock," the principal "wealth" of the Shechemites. When wealth is referred to pejoratively, *māmôn* is commonly qualified by *dišᵉqar,* "of falsehood" (cf. "the mammon of unrighteousness," Luke 16:9, 11; *1 En.* 63:10), though sometimes the word alone is shown by the context to carry a pejorative connotation. The term is not used in OT Hebrew;[31] in the Hebrew of Qumran and of the Mishnah *māmôn* denotes money or property without any pejorative connotation;[32] in *m. Sanh.* 1:1 *dînê māmô-nôt* is a technical term for legal cases concerning property.

Jesus' warning here is thus not specifically against ill-gotten wealth but about possessions as such, which, however neutral their character, can become a focus of concern and greed which competes for the disciples' loyalty with God himself.[33] The principle of materialism is in inevitable conflict with the kingship of God.[34]

7. Trusting Your Heavenly Father (6:25-34)

25 *"I tell you, therefore, don't worry about your life, what you are to eat,[1] nor about your body, what you are to wear. Isn't life more im-*

---

30. So both Targum *Pseudo-Jonathan* and *Targum Neofiti* I.

31. In the Hebrew text of Sir 31:8, however, there is the interesting commendation of a *rich* man who does not pursue *māmôn;* here the word does seem to carry a negative connotation.

32. 1QS 6:2; CD 14:20; 1Q27 2:5; *m. 'Abot.* 2:12. Note, however, *m. Yad.* 4:3, where R. Eleazar accuses R. Tarfon of giving people *māmôn* but allowing their souls to die (see D. Instone-Brewer, *Traditions,* 1:162-66).

33. T. E. Schmidt, *Hostility,* 126-27, argues against those commentators who explain the "love" and "hate" of this saying "as comparative rather than absolute opposites, as in Gen 29.31-33; Deut 21.15" since in those contexts even the "less loved" wife is retained, but here only one master is possible. Compared with Matt 10:37, Luke 14:26 demonstrates that μισέω can be used in NT times in the sense of "love less than," but the antithetical form of this saying indicates a choice between two options rather than a comparative ranking.

34. A version of this saying appears in *Gos. Thom.* 47, as part of a series of statements of incompatibility (including sayings about new wine and patching a garment which resemble 9:16-17).

1. Most MSS add either "or drink" or "and drink." The addition is a natural expansion, especially in the light of v. 31, where drink is included, but both the balance of the saying (with only food mentioned in the following rhetorical question) and the parallel in Luke 12:22 suggest that the shorter reading, which has early versional as well as MSS attestation, is original. The variation between "or" and "and" in the MSS which give the longer reading also suggests that it is an expansion.

portant than food, and the body more important than clothing? 26 Take a good look at² the wild³ birds: they do not sow seed or harvest crops and store them in barns, and yet your heavenly Father feeds them. Aren't you more important than they? 27 Which of you by worrying can add a single cubit to your life span?⁴ 28 And why worry about clothes? Take a lesson from the wild flowers;⁵ see how they grow: they do not have to work or spin, 29 but I tell you that not even Solomon in all his splendor was clothed as magnificently as one of them. 30 If God gives such clothing to the wild plants that are here today and will be thrown into the oven tomorrow, will he not do much more for you, you faithless⁶ people? 31 So don't worry,⁷ 'What are we to eat?' or 'What are we to drink?' or 'What are we to wear?' 32 (all the things the Gentiles are searching for) since your heavenly Father knows you need all these things. 33 Rather, make it your priority to find God's⁸

2. This rendering reflects the stronger compound verb ἐμβλέπω which is used here, as καταμανθάνω is in v. 28, to indicate a searching look in order to learn, rather than just casually noticing something. John Stott, himself a noted bird watcher, paraphrases Jesus' command as "Watch birds" (*Message,* 164). Following Luther's comment that "he is making the birds our schoolmasters and teachers," Stott has subsequently coined (only half in jest) the term "orni-theology" for the science of drawing theological lessons from the observation of nature (*The Birds Our Teachers* [London: Candle, 1999]).

3. The Hebraic phrases "of the sky" here and "of the field" in vv. 28 and 30 serve not so much to specify location as to indicate the natural order rather than the results of human domestication or cultivation.

4. Ἡλικία can mean "height" (as in Luke 19:3) but normally means "age," and in this context the latter meaning is required; see the comments below.

5. The common flower-name κρίνον, traditionally translated "lily," was probably not used with the botanical precision that "lily" implies to us; see p. 269, n. 18. Cf. Matthew's general reference to "birds" in v. 26, rather than the more apparently specific κόρακας of Luke 12:24.

6. While ὀλιγόπιστος strictly means "having *little* faith" or trust, its use in Matthew does not focus on little faith as against none, but rather on those who do not have the faith which is needed to trust God in the situation concerned (see further on 17:20); the English term "faithless" best conveys its force in such contexts.

7. The participle λέγοντες serves here as an indication of direct speech or thought, spelling out the nature of the worry, and is better "translated" merely by quotation marks.

8. א and B omit τοῦ θεοῦ, and some scholars have taken this to represent the original text. Such an unqualified use of ἡ βασιλεία would, however, be unique in Matthew, who, unlike modern usage, does not speak of "the kingdom" except in the genitive as part of a compound phrase (see on 4:23). The presence of the unusual (for Matthew) τοῦ θεοῦ in the vast majority of witnesses is more likely to represent the original text, and the omission of τοῦ θεοῦ in א and B, like the substitution of the normal Matthean τῶν οὐρανῶν in a few late MSS, might reflect scribal sensitivity to this "non-Matthean" use. The omission of the phrase by א and B does not in any case affect the sense here, since the following

kingship and his righteousness; then all these other things will be
given you as well. 34 *So don't worry about tomorrow; tomorrow will*
worry about itself. Today's own troubles are enough for today.

This unit of teaching occurs (with the exception of v. 34) in a closely parallel
form (though not verbatim the same) in Luke 12:22-31, and its coherence of
subject matter and terminology suggests that the whole of vv. 25-33 belonged together in the tradition of Jesus' sayings, rather than being collected
together from individual sayings as we have seen in vv. 19-24. Verse 34,
which makes a rather different point from vv. 25-33, may well have been an
independent saying which Matthew added as a conclusion to this section of
the discourse on the basis of the shared exhortation "Don't worry."

The subject matter continues the theme of the disciples' attitude to
material needs and possessions, and the issue of priorities which underlies
vv. 19-24 is more fully articulated in v. 33. Verse 32, with its contrast between the anxious attitude of the Gentiles[9] and the disciples' dependence
on their heavenly Father's prior knowledge, closely echoes vv. 7-8. But
while the subject matter is familiar, the approach of this pericope is distinct
and memorable, with its direct application to the most basic human needs
and concerns, its insistent repetition of the term "worry" (six out of the
seven Matthean uses of the verb are here), and its striking lessons drawn
from God's more than adequate provision for his natural creation. The simple analogy with the birds and flowers is worth many paragraphs of reasoned argument ("stunningly naive but undeniable," Betz), and the assumption that God's people are more important to him than the rest of his
creation provides the disciple with an attractive basis for filial trust. For a
similar emphasis on trusting God for daily needs cf. Phil 4:6-7; Heb 13:5;
1 Pet 5:7.

The lessons are clear and simple, and many disciples have found them
of great help and comfort. But they also raise problems in the modern world
(and surely also in the world of Jesus' day) which the discourse does not address and which leave many readers feeling that idealism has here triumphed
over reality.[10] Does God really provide so bountifully for the birds, which die

αὐτοῦ would unambiguously refer back to ὁ πατὴρ ὑμῶν in v. 32 and could be read as governing both βασιλείαν and δικαιοσύνην; it may be that τοῦ θεοῦ was omitted because it was
therefore felt to be redundant.

9. See H. D. Betz, *Sermon,* 461-64, for an illuminating survey of the themes of
anxiety and of divine providence in Greco-Roman philosophy and literature.

10. W. D. Davies, *Setting,* 299-300, suggests that this pericope, and especially
v. 34, would have similarly struck the rabbis as irresponsible, "the enthusiasm of a Galilean movement over against the realism of the Jamnian." Davies and Allison, 1:658, coyly
describe this pericope as "not filled to overflowing with level-headed common sense"!

or are killed in huge numbers every year, often for lack of suitable food, and many of which face the probability of extinction in our shrinking world? Even more pertinently, how are we to maintain the relevance of this teaching to those large numbers of human beings, many of them devout disciples, who simply cannot obtain enough food and die through famine while the affluent part of the world lives in excess? It would be a grossly insensitive and blinkered expositor who would dare to suggest that it was simply because they did not trust God enough. This teaching seems to envisage the world as it should be rather than the world as it is, and while it is true that much of both human and animal suffering can be blamed on human selfishness and greed and our disastrous mismanagement of God's world, it is not easy to trace a human cause for every famine or disaster, ancient or modern.

Such philosophical and apologetic problems are simply not raised here. The focus is on the disciples' trust in a heavenly Father, whose concern and ability to meet their needs are taken for granted. We must look elsewhere for a more wide-ranging theodicy. In the specific situation of Jesus' first disciples the issue was one of direct existential importance: their itinerant and dependent lifestyle made the questions of daily provision constantly relevant, and worry about material needs a recurrent possibility. These were the people for whom the petition "Give us today the bread we need for the coming day" (v. 11) rang true each day, and it was the confident offering of that prayer to a "Father in heaven" that was their essential safeguard against worry.

Worry *(merimna)* is the antithesis of the practical trust in God which is the essential meaning of faith *(pistis)* in this gospel (8:10; 9:2, 22, 29; 15:28; 17:20; 21:21). Those who worry show their "lack of faith" (see on v. 30). Outside this passage Matthew contains only two other uses of *merimna(ō):* in 13:22 the thorns which choke the good seed represent "the worry of the world and the deceit of wealth" (a close parallel to the competing interests set out in this passage and already in vv. 19-21, 24), while in 10:19 disciples under pressure are again exhorted "not to worry," this time not over material provision but over how they should respond to hostile accusation. In that situation, as here with regard to material needs, "it will be given to you in that hour." The resultant impression of a carefree life of confident dependence on a caring and generous Father is an attractive one, but one which is less easy to relate to the lifestyle of a modern Western disciple with a nine-to-five job and a mortgage than it was to Jesus' itinerant companions in Galilee. The concern for tomorrow which v. 34 condemns is firmly built into our commercial and economic structures, and even within the NT we find harsh words for those who do not make appropriate provision (1 Tim 5:8). Of course sensible provision and "worry" are not the same thing, and perhaps we may responsibly claim that the focus of this passage is on faith and its opposite rather than on the specifics of economic planning. It is, after all, *worry* about tomorrow, not provision for tomorrow, which v. 34 condemns.[11] In normal circumstances our cushioned Western lifestyle leaves little scope for the sort of "worry" about basic provisions which this passage envisages. It is perhaps at times of economic catastrophe or of drastically changed personal circumstances that its message applies most directly, and that it becomes clear how far our essential priorities enable us to trust rather than to worry.

25 The "therefore"[12] suggests a connection with v. 24: those who accept the demand to be slaves of God rather than mammon might well wonder how their material needs are to be met if they have forgone the wealth that would provide for them. The parallel mention of *psychē* ("life," "soul")[13] and *sōma* ("body") may seem initially to suggest that here, unusually in the NT, a distinction is drawn between two "parts" of a human being, "soul" and "body." But the *psychē* and the *sōma* are mentioned here rather as the different aspects of our existence to which equally *material* worries might relate.[14] Food maintains the "life" (continued existence), and clothes protect the body. But neither food nor clothing is an end in itself; it is the "life" and "body" for which they provide which ultimately matter, and it is those that the following verses will show to be the object also of God's concern (as indeed they are the result of his creation). There is, however, a further nuance in the use of *pleion*, which I have translated "more important" but which literally means simply "more." Not only is the life more important than the food which sustains it, but it also *consists of* much "more." A life which is dominated by worry about food is missing out on that "more," which will be spelled out in v. 33 as the pursuit of God's kingship and righteousness. A life which does

11. This distinction would be undermined if the contention of J. Jeremias, *Parables,* 214-15, were to be accepted, that μεριμνάω denotes not just mental anxiety but the practical efforts which result from it. Jeremias offers no lexical support for this assertion, and it is not supported by wider usage of the word group. His argument from the context here and in the Luke parallel assumes that the birds and flowers are themselves to be taken as examples of how not to μεριμνᾶν, which begs the question; they are more naturally taken as illustrations of God's provision, which is the reason why mental anxiety is out of place. Of course it is true that efforts to make provision would be a normal result of anxiety, but it is not the function of μέριμνα(ω) to denote those efforts. See further T. E. Schmidt, *Hostility,* 128; Gundry, 116.

12. See D. E. Orton, *Scribe,* 141-42, on the rhetorical force of διὰ τοῦτο as more than a merely conventional conjunction in Matthew.

13. See on 10:39 and 16:25-26; also p. 399, n. 4.

14. The datives are best understood as "datives of advantage," indicating the thing worried about (so BDF 188[1]: "the person whose interest is affected"). μεριμνάω τῇ ψυχῇ does not here mean "worry *in* your soul," any more than μεριμνάω τῷ σώματι means "worry *in* your body."

not give priority to these higher concerns has fallen prey to materialism, as the third type of seed in the parable of the sower will illustrate (13:22). It is a life enslaved to mammon (v. 24).

26   The first of the concerns mentioned in v. 25 (food) is addressed by means of an illustration from nature; the second (clothing) will be similarly addressed in v. 28. For similar lessons from nature in the OT cf. Job 12:7-10; Prov 6:6-11; Jer 8:7. Solomon was famous for them (1 Kgs 4:32-33). For a close rabbinic parallel see *m. Qidd.* 4:14. For God's provision for his animal creation see, for example, Ps 104:10-15, 27-30. While it is true that God's creation provides the food which birds need, the statement that "your heavenly Father feeds them" should not be misunderstood. As Luther famously put it, God provides food for the birds, but he does not drop it into their beaks. More obviously than the flowers of v. 28, birds have to work for their food by searching and hunting, even if not in the human way of sowing, reaping, and storing.[15] This is not a charter for laziness, for birds or for humans. The argument is *a fortiori:* if God provides for the birds, how much more for you? The assumption that God's human creation is of more importance to him than the non-human (cf. 10:31; 12:12) echoes the pattern of the Genesis creation narrative, where human beings constitute the final and climactic act of creation and are given authority over the rest of the animal creation (Gen 1:26-28; cf. Adam's naming of the animals in Gen 2:19-20). While the idea of the "dominion" of humanity over the rest of creation has been seriously abused, especially in recent generations, the contention of some more extreme proponents of animal rights that humanity has no special place in God's order for his world finds little biblical support and is here clearly contradicted. It is interesting to observe that the same assumption with regard to the vegetable creation in v. 30, while equally taken for granted, is less explicitly stated than here.

27   The series of rhetorical questions continues with a different argument against worry — it does no good. Indeed, worry is more likely to shorten a person's life than to extend it, though that point is not made here as it is in Sir 20:21-24. The use of the spatial term "cubit" (a standard measure of length, rather less than half a meter), together with the fact that *hēlikia,* "life span," can also occasionally refer to physical height, has led some to imagine that Jesus is here speaking literally of physical growth, but quite apart from the fact that for the vast majority of people an extra half-meter of

---

15. These would normally be male occupations; in v. 28 the correspondingly female work of spinning will be contrasted with the growth of flowers; so especially J. H. Neyrey, *Honor,* 176-77. (The alternative view of some commentators, that in v. 28 the "toiling" represents male activity and the "spinning" female, shows a remarkable lack of sensitivity to gender issues and to the realities of life!)

height would be a major problem, not a benefit,[16] the surrounding context is concerned with survival, not with stature. The cubit is being used here to represent the extension of life beyond the allotted "span" — an equally physical measure of length which in English also serves to indicate length of time; cf. the similar idiom in Ps 39:5. Our life span, no less than our food and clothing, is a gift of God, and is outside human control. Worrying about it changes nothing.

28-30 The second illustration from nature[17] is even more far-reaching, in that not only are the wild flowers[18] more obviously passive than the birds, but what is drawn to our attention is not their mere survival but their magnificence, beyond the best that human art can achieve. Indeed, their survival is not at issue; they are here today and gone tomorrow. Yet God lavishes on them a craftsman's care which the most ostentatious monarch can only envy. For the proverbial magnificence of Solomon see 1 Kgs 10:1-25 (which will be referred to in 12:42).[19] The short duration of wild vegetation is equally proverbial (cf. Job 8:12; Ps 103:15-16; Isa 40:6-8). Once dead, the

---

16. This applies even more obviously to the parallel in Luke 12:25-26, where the adding of the cubit is described as the "smallest" matter. BDAG 812a comment that "a cubit of bodily stature is monstrously large"!

17. The expanded version of *Gos. Thom.* 36–37 found in P. Oxy. 655 (see Aland, *Synopsis* §67) has a parallel to this saying, but not to that on the birds; the question of food is mentioned, but the focus is on clothing. While much of the content is clearly related to this Matthew text, the wording of P. Oxy. 655 is independent, and the conclusion goes in a radically different direction (clothing is to be dispensed with!).

18. The argument does not depend on the exact species of flower intended, and ancient terms for flowers are not usually as specific as ours; it need only be one that is strikingly beautiful and abundant, and even today the wild flora of Galilee allow a wide choice of species which would fit that description. In addition to the traditional "lily" (which would itself cover more than one showy species) other favored suggestions have been various types of anemone, iris, crocus, or gladiolus. Anyone who has seen the spring flowers of Galilee will have no difficulty in grasping the point, whatever the species originally intended. D. Instone-Brewer, *Traditions,* 1:236-38, argues that the reference here is to the arum lily, whose roots were a major source of food for the poor; but the balance of the passage and the terms used indicate that while the birds represent food, the flowers represent clothing.

19. The suggestion of Carter, 178 (drawing on his article in *JSNT* 65 [1997] 3-25) that the reference to the glory as Solomon's rather than God's means that Solomon is here portrayed negatively as "the model distrustful and anxious person" depends on a modern assessment of Solomon's reign rather than on any indication in the wording here or in ancient Jewish attitudes to Solomon more generally. The negative elements in the OT portrayal of Solomon's reign which Carter highlights (ibid., 16-22) are not the whole story, and the story of the Queen of Sheba in 1 Kgs 10:1-13, which Jesus will take up in 12:42, contains no hint of criticism; in 12:42 Solomon is a positive rather than a negative model, surpassed only by the "greater one" who has now come.

wild plants provided a regular fuel for the *klibanos,* a domestic oven for cooking food. If God creates with such extravagant and loving care something which is destined so soon for such an ignoble end, his care for his "higher" creation (see on v. 26) may confidently be expected to be "much more." It would, of course, be pressing the rhetorical language too far to find in this saying a promise that all God's people may expect to be more magnificent than Solomon. The point is rather that such a God, author and sustainer of a lavishly beautiful universe, can be trusted to meet his disciples' essential needs. Those who cannot exert such practical trust in God's care and provision are *oligopistoi,* literally "of little faith," a term used especially in Matthew for those who are afraid instead of trusting God to provide for their survival or need (cf. 8:26; 14:31; 16:8). In 17:20 we shall see that *oligopistia* means having faith less than a mustard seed, in effect no faith at all. "Faith," in Matthew, means the confidence that God can and will act on his people's behalf; without that, however much a person may "believe" intellectually, they are for practical purposes "faithless."[20]

31-32   The "worry" which this passage forbids is here set in contrast with God's prior knowledge of his people's needs, since it is our awareness of that knowledge and our reliance on it that creates the faith which is the antithesis of worry. So, at least in theory, God's people are characterized by faith, and thus by a calm confidence in their heavenly Father, while the "Gentiles" are characterized by worry.[21] That is the reason for their constant babbling in prayer, badgering a reluctant deity to take notice of them (v. 7). For Matthew's use of "Gentiles"[22] for people outside the community of God's people see on 18:17. As in 6:8, it is of course his people's *needs,* not necessarily their wants, that are the object of God's fatherly concern and provision.

33   The language of priority which underlies vv. 19-21 and 24 is now again made explicit by the call to "make it your priority to find" (literally, "seek first")[23] God's kingship and righteousness. The verb "seek" *(zēteō)*

---

20. M. J. Wilkins, *Disciple,* 182, describes ὀλιγόπιστος as "a faith which has failed or is bankrupt."

21. There is an interesting Jewish parallel to the characterization of Gentiles in this passage in *Let. Aris.* 140–41, where "those who worship the true God" are distinguished from "those who are concerned with meat and drink and clothes, their whole attitude being concentrated on these concerns."

22. This is the normal noun, which means literally "the nations," rather than the less common adjective used in 5:47; 6:7; 18:17.

23. T. E. Schmidt, *Hostility,* 129-30, argues that πρῶτον, which occurs here in Matthew but not in Luke, denotes not so much priority (allowing a legitimate secondary concern for material things) as an exclusive concern; cf. Gundry, 118: "emphatic rather than permissive." As Schmidt himself points out, however, twenty-five out of twenty-six other Matthean uses of πρῶτον do indicate priority, and even the one other exception he claims

echoes the stronger compound verb *epizēteō,* which was used for the Gentiles' anxious quest for material provisions in the previous verse. Disciples, by contrast, have a different orientation, a higher purpose in life. We have already seen "righteousness" used several times for living in the way God requires (see p. 119, n. 15). In 5:10, 20 it represents the distinctive lifestyle of disciples. As such it is something which is "done" (3:15; 6:1), but also the object of eager desire comparable to hunger and thirst (5:6), and the language of this verse points the same way. The disciple's deepest wish and resolve must be to live in God's way.[24]

In that case the idea of "seeking God's kingship" is best understood as another way of saying the same thing, resolving to live under God's direction and control, just as in 5:10 it is those who stand out for their pursuit of "righteousness" to whom the "kingdom of heaven" belongs. God's kingship means God's people living under God's rule. This sense of "seeking the kingdom of God," rather than any idea of "trying to bring in God's kingdom" as an eschatological event, is indicated both by the present imperative of *zēteite,* "seek" (this is to be a constant preoccupation, not a specific aim for the future), and by the use of this verb, which in this context would not naturally mean "try to bring about," even if such a view of human effort were consonant with the NT concept of *God's* reign. One must pray for the coming of God's reign (6:10) because it is *God* who will bring it into being. Such prayer is, of course, part of the "seeking" here required.

This is one of only five places where Matthew uses "kingdom of God" rather than "kingdom of heaven." In each case it seems likely that he departs from his normal usage because the context requires a more "personal" reference to God himself rather than the more oblique language of his heavenly authority.[25] In v. 32 we have heard of God as a "heavenly Father" who is per-

---

(23:26) does not in fact exclude the other side of the equation. The "seeking" of good things from God in 7:7-11 (and indeed the prayer of 6:11) hardly allow an implied "do not seek" here. But the legitimacy of such secondary concerns is not here raised as such; it is confidence in God's provision which allows the undistracted pursuit of God's will.

24. B. Przybylski, *Righteousness,* 89-91, demonstrates how this sense fits into both Matthew's general use of δικαιοσύνη and the development of thought in this discourse. On the latter point note especially the links with 6:1 (where the wrong sort of δικαιοσύνη finds no reward from God, whereas here the pursuit of God's δικαιοσύνη results in the "reward" of "all these other things") and with 5:48 (in that to seek *"God's* righteousness" is not far different from aiming to "be perfect as your heavenly Father is perfect").

25. This seems to me a more probable explanation than that of P. Luomanen, *Entering,* 163-64 (following M. Pamment), that Matthew uses "kingdom of God" with regard to the present reality of God's reign, and "kingdom of heaven" for its future manifestation; the use of the two phrases in parallel in 19:23-24 is a major problem for that suggestion. The proposal of R. Foster, *NTS* 48 (2002) 494-95, that "kingdom of God" is used when Jesus is speaking to the Jewish leaders who do not share the relation to

sonally concerned for his people, and a reference to *"God's* kingship"[26] follows naturally from this. Nothing in the context requires any more subtle reason for the change of terminology.

"All these other things" refers to the material needs which are not to be the object of worry (v. 31). Following immediately after the priority given to "God's kingship and righteousness," the passive "will be given you" is most naturally understood as the Semitic "divine passive": the Father who knows your needs and whose way you seek to follow will himself supply those needs. Perhaps we should note, however, that it is *these* things (basic material needs) which are to be supplied, not "all things" as in one MS of Luke! The disciple is promised survival, not affluence; this is no *carte blanche.*

34 This additional saying[27] has the ring of popular proverbial wisdom.[28] The thrust of its first clause is fully consonant both with the summons not to worry about provisions in vv. 25-33 and with the preceding petition for "bread for the coming day" in 6:11; once you have asked God for tomorrow's needs there is no need to worry about them. But the following clauses speak not of God's fatherly concern but, in a quite pragmatic way, of the pointlessness of anticipating tomorrow's problems. Taken out of its current context, this could, then, be read as simply a piece of cynical advice to live only for the present — the attitude condemned by Paul in 1 Cor 15:32 (following Isa 22:13; cf. 56:12), and indeed also by Jesus in Luke 12:19-20. In speaking of "tomorrow worrying" and of "troubles" as the likely experience of each day v. 34 strikes a more pessimistic (or at least realistic) note than the preceding verses. By including it along with vv. 25-33 Matthew has perhaps deliberately put a sobering question mark against an unthinkingly euphoric attitude which vv. 25-33 might evoke in some hearers. God's care and provision are assured, but that does not mean that the disciple's life is to be one long picnic. Each day will still have its "troubles"; the preceding verses simply provide the assurance that by the grace of God they can be survived.

"heaven" which characterizes disciples (see above, p. 101, n. 21) works for its uses in 12:28; 21:31, 43, but not here and in 19:24.

26. See p. 264, n. 8, for the omission of τοῦ θεοῦ in some MSS. If it is omitted, the sense would need to be derived from the αὐτοῦ, which refers back to "your heavenly Father" (v. 32), so that the personal connotation would remain.

27. Cf. the independent logion in *Gos. Thom.* 36: "Do not be anxious from morning to evening and from evening to morning what you will put on yourselves."

28. H. D. Betz, *Sermon,* 484-85, refers to a wide range of examples, pagan and Jewish.

8. Criticism (7:1-6)

> 1 *"Do not judge, so that you may not be judged; 2 for you will be judged by the same standard by which you judge others, and the same measure which you measure out will be measured out to you. 3 Why do you[1] focus on the splinter which is in your brother's[2] eye, and fail to notice the plank[3] which is in your own eye? 4 How can you say to your brother, 'Let me get the splinter out of your eye,' when all the time you have a plank in your own eye? 5 You hypocrite, first get the plank out of your own eye, and then you will be able to see clearly to get the splinter out of your brother's eye.*
>
> 6 *"Don't give sacred things to dogs or throw down your pearls in front of pigs, or they may trample them under foot and turn round and savage you.*

After the extended section of the discourse which has dealt with the disciples' attitude to possessions, a number of shorter sections deal with apparently unrelated issues before a further summary verse (7:12) brings the main body of the discourse to a close. Verses 1-5 and 7-11 deal with the two separate subjects of criticism (as an aspect of relationships between disciples) and of the disciples' trust in God's generous provision. Each is a self-contained unit, and there is no obvious link between them; vv. 7-11 are linked rather with the preceding section on God's provision of his people's needs. Between these two short sections stands an enigmatic saying (v. 6) which does not closely relate to either of its neighboring pericopes,[4] but which I have linked with vv. 1-5 because it may be understood to provide a balance over against what could be seen as a too uncritical attitude to the failings of others in vv. 1-5. This difficult saying will be dealt with below.

Verses 1-5, by contrast, convey an obvious message. They address the very down-to-earth issue of unfairly[5] critical attitudes to others, which,

1. The "you"s of vv. 1-2 (and of v. 6) are plural; but in vv. 3-5 they are singular, as an individual situation is envisaged.

2. In 5:22-24, where ἀδελφός also refers generally to a fellow disciple, I translated it "brother or sister"; in the tête-a-tête scenario of this illustrative cameo that translation would fit awkwardly, but there is of course no suggestion that this instruction applies only to male disciples.

3. In this humorous scene from the carpenter's workshop, whereas the κάρφος, a tiny chip of wood or perhaps a speck of dust, in the eye describes a real-life possibility, the contrasting problem is deliberately grotesque: δοκός is a large piece of timber, normally fashioned for building, as in a roof beam.

4. See, however, nn. 12 and 13 below for some suggested exegetical links with vv. 1-5, and n. 15 for a suggested link with vv. 7-12.

5. Hagner actually inserts "unfairly" into his translation of κρίνω in v. 1.

combined with a naive lack of self-criticism, threaten to disrupt a close-knit community such as that of Jesus' first disciples. A simple negative instruction (v. 1) is supported by an explanatory comment (v. 2) and by a parable which uses broad humor to show up the ludicrous inappropriateness of such behavior (vv. 3-5). Underlying the whole pericope is a principle of reciprocity such as we have noted above in 6:14-15, which will be taken up again in the summary in v. 12. We must expect to be treated as we treat other people (cf. Sir 28:1-7 for an earlier statement of the same principle). Verses 1-2 do not specify who will do the judging of those who judge others; it would be possible to read this merely as a warning about the way society may be expected to react to those it perceives as hypocrites. But in the light of 6:14-15 we should probably read these as "divine passives" (cf. also 6:33); just as God will forgive only the forgiving, so he will judge his people as they judge others.

See, however, 18:15-17, and the comments there, for a proper desire to correct a "brother who sins." The balancing of such pastorally responsible criticism against the dangers set out in this pericope calls for a rare degree of self-awareness combined with unselfish concern for others.

1 The verb *krinō* is used for technical legal decisions, but also more generally for forming judgments and reaching conclusions about both things and people. The verb is not in itself necessarily negative, but the following illustration shows that here the emphasis is on criticism of other people's failings, and the warning "so that you may not be judged" makes it clear that this sort of "judging" is not something to be welcomed. For the warning that criticism can be turned back against the one who criticizes compare our proverb, "People who live in glass houses should not throw stones." It is this reciprocal principle which is the focus of the whole pericope, rather than a prohibition of any use of the critical faculty in itself. Verse 6, as we shall see, appears to call for a proper discrimination which must be based on some "judgment" as to who are and are not fit recipients for "sacred things" and "pearls"; cf. the call to judge people by their fruits in vv. 15-20, and the requirement to draw a fellow disciple's sin to their own and, if necessary, other people's attention in 18:15-17. But what is forbidden here is the sort of faultfinding mentality and speech which is likely to rebound against the one who exercises it (cf. Jas 2:13; 4:11-12; 5:9).[6]

6. While most modern commentators assume that the saying applies to personal relationships, this has not always been assumed. See Luz, 1:414-15, for a range of more radical interpretations which have included questioning the right of the state to operate secular courts. Luz himself favors an interpretation which is "not limited to the personal realm"; in the kingdom of God "there must in principle be an end to the judging of human beings by others" (Luz, 1:416). Carter, 181, goes for a much more limited application: what is forbidden is usurping God's role as the eschatological judge by "condemning

2 The reciprocal principle is stated both directly with regard to judgment and indirectly using the metaphor of measuring out commodities in the market.[7] In both cases you must expect the same standards of measurement to be applied to both parties (Rom 2:1 makes a closely similar point). The critic who is blind to his or her own failings is living in a make-believe world where one can exempt oneself from standards to which others are expected to conform. Society will not tolerate that, and still less can the disciple community afford to operate by such double standards; it is a recipe for the breakdown of relationships. Still more seriously, behind the passive verbs lies the judgment of God, who maintains impartial justice. "You will be judged" looks beyond social criticism to God's ultimate verdict.

The proverbial form of the "measure for measure" saying allows a number of different applications. In Mark 4:24 it encourages careful listening to Jesus' parables (what you put in is what you will get out), while in Luke 6:38, in a slightly different form, it apparently encourages financial generosity (God will give to you as you have given to others). Similar proverbs occur in Jewish literature to indicate the appropriateness of God's judgment, in which the punishment fits the crime (e.g., *m. Soṭah* 1:7; *b. Sanh.* 100a).[8] The point here is similar; cf. the parable of 18:23-35, where the final condemnation of the obdurate slave stems from the way he has treated his fellow slave.

3-5 The general instruction of vv. 1-2 is now supported by a parable in which we change to the second-person singular, as an individual disciple's action is portrayed. The robust imagery from the carpenter's workshop[9] makes two related points, the inappropriateness of drawing attention to another's failing when your own is much greater, and the impracticability and insincerity of an offer to help until your own greater problem has been dealt with. It is not wrong to notice or to try to help with another's failing (cf. 18:15-17), but the person who is unaware of their own greater failing is not in a position to do so. The scenario is deliberately ridiculous: like the equally impossible picture of a camel going through the eye of a needle (19:24; cf. also 23:24), its very incongruity commands the hearer's attention and highlights the untenable position of the insincere critic.

[others] to hell." The removal of the splinter in the parable which follows in vv. 3-5, however, portrays attempted correction, not final condemnation.

7. B. Couroyer, *RB* 77 (1970) 366-70, points out parallels in the language of commercial grain contracts.

8. For further Jewish parallels see B. D. Chilton, *Rabbi*, 123-25, and more fully H. P. Rüger, *ZNW* 60 (1969) 174-82.

9. The similar imagery of a speck and a plank in the eye found in *b. 'Arak.* 16b; *b. B. Bat.* 15b, attributed to R. Tarphon, c. A.D. 100, may reflect a knowledge of Jesus' saying; or both may be derived from a popular figure of speech. For other comparable sayings see J. D. M. Derrett, *NTS* 34 (1988) 271-72.

For the meaning of *hypokritēs* in Matthew see on 6:2; this is the only time Matthew uses it of a disciple rather than of those outside the group. While it is possible that the critic here is to be understood as aware of his own failings but concealing them, it is more likely that he is criticized for failing to apply the same standards to himself that he applies to others (like David in his response to Nathan's parable, 2 Sam 12:1-7), and thus being unaware of the inconsistency of his behavior; v. 3 speaks of "failing to notice" rather than of deliberate deception. It is other people, and especially God, who can see the "hypocrisy" of his self-righteousness for what it is.

The person being criticized is described as the critic's "brother." As in 5:22-24, the term is probably used here for a fellow disciple (and not necessarily a male one) rather than literally for a member of the same family, though it might be argued that the term belongs merely to the setting of the parable, with two siblings working together in the family workshop. Here is another example of Matthew's sustained concern for good relationships within the disciple community which we have already noted in 5:22-26 and which will come to the fore in ch. 18.

6 Whereas vv. 1-5 carried a clear and simple instruction for disciples, this apparently independent saying is couched only in metaphor, with no indication how it might be applied to real-life contexts. The imagery of sacred things given to dogs and precious pearls to pigs is clearly about mismatch, about the inappropriate use of what is special. But what are the holy things and pearls, and from whom are they to be withheld? A very early interpreter (*Did.* 9:5) applied this saying to the Christian Eucharist, which was to be available only to the baptized, but there is no indication in context of any such restricted relevance, and the eucharistic application would be anachronistic for a saying of Jesus to his disciples during his lifetime.[10] The choice of dogs and pigs, both regarded by the Jews as unclean animals,[11] provides a suitable contrast with "sacred things," but does not identify what sort of people they represent. In 15:26-27 "dogs" will be used to represent Gentiles, as opposed to the Jewish "children," and pigs were of course immediately recognizable as Gentile food, forbidden to Jews. Such a reference might suit the "anti-Gentile" element in the mission of Jesus and his disciples according to 10:5-6 and 15:24, but would conflict sharply with the much

10. H. D. Betz, *Sermon,* 494-96, rightly judges that the metaphors depend on a shared assumption of writer and readers which is no longer available to us, and finds that esoteric setting in the life of an early Jewish-Christian community rather than in the ministry of Jesus. He thus regards the eucharistic interpretation as possible, but also proposes that the reference may be to the content of the discourse as a whole, which is "insiders' literature, not to be divulged to uninitiated outsiders." He cites (ibid., 497-98) passages from the Pseudo-Clementine *Recognitions* which take the saying in this sense.

11. They are similarly linked as unclean in 2 Pet 2:22; cf. Isa 66:3.

more pervasive ideal of the inclusion of Gentiles among the people of God which will culminate in 28:19, and the conclusion of 15:21-28 is that the "dogs" will in fact receive their bread. A more likely setting for the saying is perhaps in the mixed character of the disciple community, in which weeds grow alongside the wheat (13:24-30, 36-43), bad and good together (22:10), and in which there are prophets and miracle workers whom Jesus does not recognize (7:21-23).

Perhaps we can be no more definite than to say that disciples are to be discriminating in sharing the "sacred things" of the gospel and the treasures of their Father in heaven, so as not to lay them open to abuse, but to avoid offering a more specific identification of who are to be regarded as unsuitable or incapable of receiving them (cf. Paul's insistence in 1 Cor 2:13-16 that only the "spiritual" can receive spiritual teaching). Compare the ostracism of the unrepentant disciple in 18:17. So understood, this saying serves to counterbalance the prohibition of one-sided criticism in vv. 1-5:[12] there may nonetheless be times and situations when a responsible assessment of the likely response requires the disciple's instinctive generosity to be limited, so that holy things are not brought into contempt. The disciples' response to those hostile to their mission (10:14) is a possible example (and cf. Paul's policy in Acts 13:46; 18:6; 19:9). It is a principle which can easily be abused through an inappropriate use of the labels "dog" and "pig," but we can all think of situations where it might apply, and where a totally "unjudging" attitude would be a recipe for disaster. Keener, 244, rightly points out that while one should not "prejudge who may receive one's message," neither should one try to "force it on those who show no inclination to accept it."[13]

The imagery is compressed. The "sacred things" to be kept from the dogs may well be consecrated food (which in the OT was to be eaten only by the priests and their families); Exod 22:31 directs that unclean food should be thrown to the dogs. The incongruity of pearls (cf. 13:45-46 for their high value) thrown to pigs reflects the "gold ring in a pig's snout" of Prov 11:22. The animals' reaction is perhaps to be read chiastically: the pigs trample the

---

12. T. J. Bennett, *WTJ* 49 (1987) 371-86, disagrees with this almost universal assumption, arguing that Jesus uses this proverbial language as a sarcastic way of reinforcing v. 1: if you make judgments about what is holy and who is worthy, you must expect them to rebound on yourself.

13. M. D. Goulder, *Midrash,* 265-66, however, mounts a spirited argument for a quite different interpretation which links v. 6 directly with vv. 1-5: "Don't expose what is precious, your brother's character, to the malice of the godless." He locates this saying in the tradition of Jewish invective against backbiting and slander and concludes modestly, "It is the chief glory of my interpretation to have made sense of [these words] in their context, I think alone of all proposals."

pearls and the dogs attack those who feed them,[14] though pigs are quite capable of a violent attack if provoked. The last clause indicates that the saying is aimed not only at keeping sacred and precious things safe from misuse, but also more prudentially at the disciples' own safety: those who fail to exercise a proper discrimination are liable to get hurt themselves.[15]

9. Expect Good Things from God (7:7-11)

> 7 *"Ask and it will be given to you; seek and you will find; knock and the door will be opened to you. 8 For everyone who asks receives, and everyone who seeks finds, and to everyone who knocks the door will be opened. 9 Who[1] is there among you who, if his son asks for a loaf of bread,[2] will give him a stone?[3] 10 Or if he asks for a fish, will he give him a snake? 11 So if you, bad as you are, know how to give good gifts to your children, how much more will your Father in heaven give good things to those who ask him?*

While these sayings do not link clearly with the sense of vv. 1-6, they pick up directly from the sense of 6:25-34, with the language about the Father in heaven who gives to his children (v. 11) echoing vv. 32-33 and thus returning us to one of the overriding themes of the whole discourse; the invitation to

---

14. Contrast *Gos. Thom.* 93, where the dogs are oddly envisaged as throwing the sacred things "on the dungheap" and no attack on the giver is mentioned; the reaction of the pigs is unfortunately missing from the text, but it is apparently also directed at the pearls rather than at the giver.

15. A quite different approach is adopted by G. H. Stassen, *JBL* 122 (2003) 289-95, who takes v. 6 as the first part of a "triad" consisting of vv. 6-12, focused on the theme of whom the disciple should rely on. The dogs and pigs represent Roman imperial power; rather than trusting the Romans, who will only destroy them, disciples should rely on the heavenly Father, who gives good things. This exegesis depends on the surprising interpretation of "holy things" as "prayer, trust and service to God" (293); nor does the inclusion of v. 12 in the "triad" ("as God gives good gifts . . . therefore you should give good gifts of love to others") produce a convincing coherence of theme.

1. Literally, "what ἄνθρωπος," where the use of ἄνθρωπος, "human being," points up the contrast with God, the heavenly Father, in v. 11. To express this nuance in English would require an unacceptably artificial sentence.

2. The singular ἄρτος, which can mean simply "bread," as in 4:4 (compare the plural ἄρτοι in 4:3), here requires the more specific sense of a single "loaf" (enough for one meal for one person) in contrast with a single stone.

3. The phrasing of the Greek question, using the μή question construction which requires the answer No, does not translate naturally into English: "What human being is there among you whom his son will ask for a loaf of bread, he will not give him a stone, will he?" Similarly in v. 10.

"seek" (vv. 7-8) echoes the call to "seek first" in 6:33.[4] It is also possible to suggest a less direct link with the following v. 12, which envisages disciples doing good to other people, but the family imagery of these verses is not repeated there, and a comparison with God's generosity can be found there only by inference. Verse 12 is about how we should relate to other people, vv. 7-11 about how we relate to God, with interhuman relations introduced here only as the foil for a "how much more" argument. I shall therefore deal with v. 12 as a separate unit of teaching summarizing the main body of the discourse.

The antidote to worry (vv. 25-34) is a robust confidence in God's willingness to give his people all that they need. In vv. 25-34 the focus was explicitly on need rather than desire, and here, too, the son's requests are for basic food, not for luxuries. It is therefore perhaps wise to read the unqualified offer of vv. 7-8 against that background: the "good things" which God will surely give do not necessarily include everything that his children might like to have. The *carte blanche* approach to petitionary prayer does not find support from the NT as a whole. It is God as the Father in heaven who knows what is "good" for his children, and as with a human parent his generosity may not always coincide with the child's wishes. But for all that necessary caution, there is an openness about vv. 7-8 which invites not merely a resigned acceptance of what the Father gives, but a willingness to explore the extent of his generosity, secure in the knowledge that only what is "good" will be given, so that mistakes in prayer through human short-sightedness will not rebound on those praying. There is, fortunately, nothing inevitable or mechanical about God's answers to his people's requests (cf. 6:7-8). Perhaps we should note, too, that even in this gospel there are in fact circumstances when the door will not be opened to someone who knocks (25:10-12; cf. 7:21-23), just as there are prayers which will not be answered (6:5, 7; and cf. Jesus' own "unsuccessful" request in Gethsemane, 26:39). The childlike confidence of vv. 7-8 is the prerogative only of disciples who, as vv. 9-11 illustrate, have a true relationship with their Father in heaven.[5]

4. Among many more or less desperate attempts to suggest a coherent sequence of thought through the latter part of the discourse, so that 7:7 is not an arbitrary change of subject, perhaps the most attractive is that of Davies and Allison, 1:625-27, which parallels 7:7-11 with 6:25-34 as two periods of encouragement and of respite from the "constant bombardment by uncompromising demands" in the rest of the discourse. See, however, G. H. Stassen, *JBL* 122 (2003) 267-308, for a proposed overall structure of the sermon which takes 7:6-12 as a coherent "triad" contrasting reliance on Roman power (v. 6; see p. 278, n. 15) with reliance on the Father in heaven (ibid., 289-95).

5. H. D. Betz, *Sermon,* 506-8, argues that the passage is not primarily concerned with trust in *God,* but with "a general approach to life, an approach based on the assumption that one can trust life as good." Such an interpretation can be sustained only by taking

7-8 This double saying (triple imperative followed by triple assurance in the indicative, the two neatly balanced to form a memorable saying) is not explicitly limited to any one aspect of prayer, such as the material needs which were the focus of 6:25-34. The imperatives are in the present tense, indicating a continued activity, and the "everyone" which introduces v. 8 increases the impression of generality. This is an invitation to prayer which matches the extraordinary openness of the promises in the Fourth Gospel (John 14:13-14; 15:7, 16; 16:23-24), as well as the confident expectation of 17:20; 18:19; 21:22 that prayers offered in faith, however improbable, will be answered. It is the context, and the general pattern of NT teaching on prayer, which suggests caution in applying it too indiscriminately (see introductory comments above) rather than any limitation in the wording of these verses themselves. It should, however, perhaps be noted also that the present imperatives imply something more than a passing, ill-considered request, though it is probably overtranslation to render v. 7, "Keep on asking . . . keep on seeking . . . keep on knocking. . . ." Cf. the qualification in Jer 29:13, that those who seek God will find him if they seek with all their heart. The three verbs function as synonyms, as do the three responses; there is thus no need to seek a specific point of reference for the "door" (which does not appear as such in the Greek anyway); the saying simply uses the "rule of three" as a memorable means of communication. The "divine passives" serve as in 6:33 to indicate the response of the God to whom prayer is offered.

A further nuance, not explicit in either Matthew or Luke, may be hinted at in the version of this saying in *Gos. Thom.* 92: "Seek and you will find. But those things about which you asked me during those days, I did not tell you on that day. Now I am willing to tell them, and you do not inquire about them." The notion of a previous period of concealment followed by open revelation does not well fit the Matthean context here, but that asking is a prerequisite to receiving may well be part of what this saying was originally intended to convey; it is not only a promise of response, but an encouragement to ask. As Jas 4:2 puts it, "You do not have because you do not ask."[6]

9-10 The frequent characterization of God as "your Father in

---

this passage out of its context, where the demonstration of God's fatherly care in 6:25-34 has set the agenda. Even this pericope taken on its own climaxes in the affirmation that good gifts come from "your Father in heaven" (v. 11).

6. There is no need, with J. Jeremias, *Parables,* 159-60, to take πᾶς ὁ αἰτῶν λαμβάνει as an observation about life in general, that persistent beggars are rewarded in the end (K. E. Bailey, *Poet,* 135, points out that the observation would apply not only to beggars but to "life in the East in general," with its emphasis on asking and giving). As such it would form an appropriate parable to encourage persistent prayer, but in its context following a call to pray (to God) it is surely better taken as a direct statement about the effectiveness of prayer.

heaven" prompts an analogy from human parenthood. While the "how much more" of v. 11 will emphasize the contrast between human and divine parenthood, such an analogy is justified by the regular biblical use of this metaphor to point to the nature of God's care for his people. God's care is of course far more than even the best human parent can give, but it is never less. The point is not that human parents are incapable of cruelty or neglect of their children, but that our inbuilt assumption of what parenting *ought* to be like is a valid pointer toward the greater parental concern of the heavenly Father. The rhetorical questions depict what should be an unthinkable response to a child's request, not merely the denial of the food they properly ask for (bread and fish, the Galilean staple diet as in 14:17; 15:34), but the cynical substitution of something which is superficially similar but is either useless (a stone; cf. 4:3 for the visual similarity to loaves of bread) or positively harmful (a snake, which might resemble an eel or the common catfish of the Lake of Galilee).[7]

11 Human parents, even at their best, are "bad" in comparison with the heavenly Father,[8] and the adjective forms an effective contrast with the "good" things which even they will give to their children; the gifts of the wholly good Father must therefore be even more truly "good." In Matthew's version the promise is broad and unspecific, whereas in the otherwise close parallel in Luke 11:13 the Father's gift is specified as "the Holy Spirit." The lack of any reference to the Spirit in the context suggests that it is more likely that Luke (whose special interest in the Holy Spirit is often noted) has given a more specific application to the originally more general promise which Matthew records; "good things" follows more naturally both from the "good gifts" of the first half of the verse and from the preceding teaching of 6:25-34, where "all these things" (6:33) relates to material rather than to spiritual endowment.[9] That does not mean that this saying relates *only* to material provision, even though the parables of vv. 9-10 are concerned with food; the wording is broad enough to cover anything "good" for disciples, but a spe-

---

7. In Luke 11:11-12 the bread/stone contrast is replaced by egg/scorpion, which more closely matches the harmful nature of the snake instead of a fish, but offers a less obvious possibility of visual confusion. Commentators vary in their explanations of how the saying came to exist in these two different forms, but it is probably simplest to assume that all three options were in the tradition of Jesus' teaching, and Matthew and Luke (or their sources) made different selections of what seemed to them the more effective pairing, Matthew's choice being governed by the common pairing of bread and fish, and perhaps also influenced by the stones/bread imagery of 4:3-4 and/or the mention of bread in the Lord's Prayer.

8. It would be going beyond the function of this comparison in context to use it as the basis for a theological argument for a Pauline doctrine of original sin.

9. For the contrary view that Matthew has adapted Luke's version see Gundry, 124-25.

cific focus on "giving the Holy Spirit" (an idea which has no close parallel in Matthew, though see 3:11) seems less appropriate to the context.[10]

10. Fulfilling the Law and the Prophets (7:12)

12 *"So whatever you would like other people to do for you, you, too, are to do for them; for this is the law and the prophets.*

This striking saying does not directly relate to vv. 7-11,[1] which were concerned with our relationship with God rather than with other people — though they included human parental care as an illustration for God's concern for his people. The second part of the saying rather echoes 5:17, which introduced a major section of the discourse dealing with the disciples' relationships with other people under the rubric of "fulfilling the law and the prophets." While most of the more recent part of the discourse has focused on the disciples' relationship with God (the whole of ch. 6 and 7:7-11), the way we treat other people has been an even more prominent theme of the discourse as a whole, not only in the discussion of fulfilling the law and the prophets in 5:17-48, but also in the beatitudes of 5:3-10, the metaphors of salt and light in 5:13-16, the requirement to forgive in 6:14-15, and the strictures on unfair criticism in 7:1-5. All this material is now incorporated in a far-reaching and memorable summary of the ethics of discipleship (the "greater righteousness" of 5:20), which thus serves to conclude the main body of the discourse: what follows in vv. 13-27 is a coda calling for decisive response rather than adding further instructions on the requirements of discipleship.

In 22:34-40 we shall find Jesus specifically challenged to provide a summary of the law by identifying its "great commandment," and we shall note then the popularity of such a quest among Jewish teachers. Jesus' response, then, will be to single out two OT texts to summarize the law,[2] but the summary he offers here is of the spirit rather than the actual words of the law. It is a principle so all-embracing that he can declare not so much that it is the greatest commandment but that it actually "is" the law and the prophets. It does not, of course, cover every aspect of OT law, such as the sacrificial ritu-

---

10. J. Jeremias, *Parables,* 145, argues here (as he often does elsewhere) for a specifically eschatological reference on the grounds that τὰ ἀγαθά "frequently designates the gifts of the Messianic Age"; but it also has many other possible meanings!

1. See, however, J. Piper, *Love,* 204, n. 80, who takes the οὖν which introduces 7:12 as grounding this verse's demand in the antecedent generosity of God: "We are called to fulfill the love command precisely *because* the Father is generous and will give us the necessary resources." Similarly Gundry, 123, 125.

2. Note the similarity of his formula there, "the whole law and the prophets hang on these two commandments," to the concluding clause of this verse.

als or indeed the love for God himself which is the first of Jesus' two commandments in 22:37-40; rather, it draws out the principle enshrined in Jesus' second commandment (cf. also 19:19), "You are to love your neighbor as yourself" (Lev 19:18), which underlies the ethical demands both of the law and of the prophets. Cf. Paul's teaching that love for the neighbor fulfills the law so that "Love is the fulfillment of the law" (Rom 13:8-10), and that "the whole law is fulfilled in this one saying, 'You are to love your neighbor as yourself'" (Gal 5:14); note also James's singling out of the love of neighbor as "the royal law" (Jas 2:8).

The famous summary of the law by R. Hillel (*b. Šabb.* 31a) provides an instructive parallel. Challenged by a Gentile to "teach me the whole Torah while I am standing on one leg" (a challenge curtly refused by Hillel's rival Shammai), Hillel reputedly replied: "Do not do to your neighbor what is hateful to you. This is the whole Torah; the rest is commentary." The setting is roughly contemporary with that of Jesus, and the question in effect the same as that put to Jesus in 22:36. Hillel, like Jesus (and unlike Shammai), accepts the possibility of putting the law in a nutshell, and his comment, "This is the whole Torah," is strikingly similar to Jesus' saying here. Moreover, his summary is on the same lines as Jesus' summary here (and indeed the call to "love your neighbor as yourself" in 22:39), but with the interesting difference that Hillel's formula is negative where Jesus' is positive. Other less exact parallels are found in both Jewish and pagan literature,[3] but again the focus is predominantly negative, the call to avoid hurting others rather than positively to aim to please them. Surprisingly, even the *Didache,* normally thought to be dependent on Matthew, also has only the negative form, "Whatever you would like not to be done to you, you also must not do to others" (*Did.* 1:2, following an abbreviation of Jesus' other summary in Matt 22:37, 39), while in *Gos. Thom.* 6 (= P. Oxy. 654) the simpler "Do not do what you hate" appears without specific emphasis as one member in a list of ethical maxims. Jesus' positive version of the formula, even if not unprecedented,[4] represents a more demanding

3. Tob 4:15; *T. Naph.* (Hebrew) 1:6; Isocrates, *Nic.* 49 (positive) and 61 (negative). Seneca, *Ep. mor.* 47.11, has the socially nuanced version, "Behave toward your inferior as you would like your superior to behave to you." Other parallels are collected in A. Dihle, *Die goldene Regel,* representing a variety of religious and philosophical traditions. For a wide-ranging survey of the use of the Golden Rule in both ancient and modern ethics, see H. D. Betz, *Sermon,* 509-16. Betz sees Jesus' use of the principle as "appropriated . . . from the tradition" (515).

4. There is a similar principle, though differently formulated, in Sir 31:15. *Let. Aris.* 207 begins with a negative formulation, but a more positive injunction follows: "In so far as you do not wish evils to come upon you, but to partake of every blessing, put this into practice with your subjects." The saying in Sextus, *Sent.* 89 (third century A.D.), "As you wish your neighbors to treat you, so treat them," probably reflects Christian influence.

interpretation[5] of love of one's neighbor than was normal among other teachers of the time.

The common description of this saying as the "Golden Rule" is traditionally traced to the Roman Emperor Alexander Severus (A.D. 222-35), who, though not a Christian, was reputedly so impressed by the comprehensiveness of this maxim of Jesus as a guide to good living that he had it inscribed in gold on the wall of his chamber. Its influence in Victorian Britain is illustrated by the name given by Charles Kingsley in *The Water Babies* to the good fairy "Mrs Do-as-you-would-be-done-by" (in contrast to Mrs Be-done-by-as-you-did). As a guide to how unselfish love should work itself out in our relations with other people, this simple principle would be hard to improve on.

11. Responding to Jesus' Words: Four Warnings (7:13-27)

13 *"Go in through the narrow gate, since the gate[1] is wide and the road spacious which leads[2] to destruction, and those who go in by it are many.* 14 *But how[3] narrow is the gate and how restricted[4] the road which leads to life, and those who find it are few.*

15 *"Be on your guard against false prophets, who come to you dressed up as sheep while inside they are savage wolves.* 16 *It is by*

---

5. Carson, 187, appositely comments: "The goats in 25:31-46 would be acquitted under the negative form of the rule, but not under the form attributed to Jesus."

1. There is good attestation (א*, some OL, and a good number of early citations) for a reading which omits ἡ πύλη here, and it would be easy to understand its addition in order to provide a balance with v. 14 (where the omission of ἡ πύλη is less well attested). The effect of that reading would be to attach both adjectives here to ἡ ὁδός, giving the meaning "The road is wide and spacious," and envisaging a gate only on the road to life, not on the wide road to destruction. See the comments below.

2. The verb here and in v. 14 is ἀπάγω, properly to "lead *away*," but to make that explicit would be overtranslation. Here the sense of "leading *away* to destruction" would sound appropriately threatening, but there is no such connotation in the same verb in v. 14. Rather, the two roads are envisaged as going away in different directions from the viewpoint of the observer.

3. The best-attested reading is the interrogative τί, which must here have an exclamatory rather than an interrogative sense (BDF 299[4]); the change to ὅτι in א*, B*, and other MSS would be a natural assimilation to the construction of the parallel clause in v. 13.

4. τεθλιμμένη probably refers to the lack of space on this road, hence the fewness of those who travel it. The verb is also used for suffering, and cognates of the two descriptions used here, θλῖψις καὶ στενοχωρία, are used together of suffering in Rom 2:9; 8:35; but "road of sorrows" (U. Luz, *Theology,* 58, following A. J. Mattill, *JBL* 98 [1979] 531-46, "way of tribulation"; see also Luz, 1:436-37) may read too much into the participle in this context. The parallel with εὐρύχωρος, "spacious," in v. 13 indicates that the primary reference here is to the width of the road rather than its character.

their fruits that you will recognize them. People don't pick grapes from thornbushes or figs from thistles, do they? 17 *In the same way every good tree produces good⁵ fruit, while a rotten tree produces bad fruit.* 18 *A good tree cannot produce bad fruit, or a rotten tree good fruit.* 19 *Every tree which does not produce good fruit is cut down and thrown into the fire.* 20 *Well then, it is by their fruits that you will recognize them.*

21 *"Not everyone who says to me, 'Lord! Lord!' will come into the kingdom of heaven, but only the person who does the will of my Father who is in heaven.* 22 *On that day many will say to me, 'Lord! Lord! wasn't it in your name that we prophesied, and in your name that we threw out demons, and in your name that we performed many miracles?'* 23 *Then I will declare to them, 'I never knew you; get away from me, you lawbreakers.'⁶*

24 *"So everyone who hears these words of mine and puts them into practice will be like a sensible man who built his house on the rock;* 25 *then the rain poured down, the rivers rose, and the the winds blew and attacked⁷ that house, but it did not collapse, since it had been founded on the rock.* 26 *But everyone who hears these words of mine and does not put them into practice will be like a foolish man who built his house on the sand;* 27 *then the rain poured down, the rivers rose, and the winds blew and hammered against⁸ that house, and it collapsed — and its collapse was dramatic."⁹*

The Golden Rule of 7:12 concludes the substantive content of the discourse on discipleship. What follows is a series of four short sketches which underline the importance of an existential response to what has been heard and warn of the consequences of failing to respond. There is no uniformity in their literary form (unlike, e.g., the six examples of the greater righteousness in 5:21-47 or the three examples of misdirected piety in 6:1-18), but each in a

---

5. While the adjective used for the tree is each time ἀγαθός, that for the fruit is equally consistently καλός. The two adjectives are often synonymous, but it may be that καλός is chosen here because of the "fine" or "noble" deeds which the good fruit represents. In English, however, to speak of "fine fruits" would be stilted.

6. Literally, "you workers of lawlessness." See the comments below.

7. προσπίπτω has a "human" sound. It probably represents here the effect not only of the wind but of all the elements, mounting a concerted assault on the house. It also provides a wordplay with οὐκ ἔπεσεν: they "fell upon it," but it did not "fall."

8. While the rest of the description of the storm is the same as in v. 25, the verb προσκόπτω, "to hit against," is even more violent and deliberate.

9. The emphatic position of μεγάλη, "great," as the final Greek word of the discourse perhaps justifies this overtranslation!

different way draws out the contrast between a right and a wrong response, between the true and the false, the saved and the lost. This is, then, a rhetorical conclusion to the discourse,[10] aiming to motivate the hearers to take appropriate action.[11] A key word which runs through the last three of the four sections is *poieō*, "to do," though English idiom does not allow the repetition of the same verb in translation: it is represented above by "produce" (fruit) in vv. 17, 18, and 19, by "do" (the will of God) in v. 21, by "perform" (miracles) in v. 22, and by "put into practice" (Jesus' teaching) in vv. 24 and 26. In each case except v. 22 it is those who "do" who are commended; in v. 22 the wrong sort of "doing" is contrasted with the right sort in v. 21. In vv. 24 and 26 both men are described as "hearing" Jesus' words, but only the first "does" them; the message is clear, that those who have now "heard" Jesus' teaching receive no benefit from it unless they also put it into practice.

Some interpreters treat the third scene, vv. 21-23, as a subsection of the second dealing with false prophecy. Apart from a single use of the verb "prophesy" as one of a series of charismatic activities claimed in v. 22, however, the two sections have little in common, and v. 20 with its repetition of v. 16a looks like the conclusion of a section, after which a new group is introduced in v. 21. As we shall note below, the nature of the deception in vv. 21-23 is quite different from that in v. 15. Whereas that was deliberate deception of disciples by those outside the group, the people of v. 22 are, at least in their own understanding, insiders; they are not so much deceivers as self-deceived. Their situation is closer to that of the non-practicing hearer of v. 26 than to that of the wolves dressed up as sheep.[12]

The resultant four sections therefore press increasingly closer to home: the first is a simple contrast between saved and lost, the second con-

---

10. I. H. Jones, *Parables,* 173-89, treats 7:24-27 as a "summary parable," one of four which have a concluding and summarizing role at the end of four of Matthew's five main discourses; see his discussion of the function of these four parables (ibid., 115-23).

11. D. C. Allison, *Moses,* 190-91, points out several thematic links between these verses and aspects of the book of Deuteronomy, and tentatively suggests that Matthew may have designed this final section of the discourse to correspond to the closing section of the Pentateuch. The links are all plausible (though few of them verbally close enough to have been noted by most commentators), but the vast majority of Deuteronomy which is not represented in the comparison suggests that Allison was wise to refrain from a more definite claim.

12. D. Hill, *Bib* 57 (1976) 327-48, argues convincingly that two separate groups (which he calls "false prophets" and "charismatics") are in view in v. 15 and in vv. 21-23. The statement of B. Charette, *Recompense,* 124, n. 3, that Hill's argument "has not met with wide acceptance" is not borne out by my survey of recent commentaries on Matthew, which shows a preponderance in favor of two separate groups, even if Hill's terms to characterize them are not always followed. The point is well demonstrated by H. D. Betz, *Sermon,* 539-41.

cerns outsiders who merely pretend to be insiders, the third looks at those who think they are insiders but are not, and the fourth draws a line even within the group of insiders (who hear Jesus' words) between those who respond and those who do not. In each of the four cases, the result of a failure to respond is catastrophic: "destruction" (v. 13), "cut down and burned" (v. 19), excluded from the kingdom of heaven (vv. 21, 23), and the total collapse of the house (v. 27).

a. Scene 1: The Broad and Narrow Roads (7:13-14)

The first contrast is stark and clear, between "destruction"[13] and "life." This is not a matter of more and less successful attempts to follow the lifestyle of the kingdom of heaven, but of being either in or out, saved or lost. The two routes lead in opposite directions, and their destinations are totally apart. Without using those words, this saying sets before us the radical alternative of heaven or hell.

The choice is set out in the imagery of two roads, contrasted in their character (broad and narrow), in their popularity (followed by many and few), and in their destination. Cf. "the way of life and the way of death" in Jer 21:8; cf. Ps 1:6; also Deut 11:26-29 etc. This traditional Jewish teaching on the two ways[14] is developed at length in *Did.* 1-6. The nature of the imagery depends on which textual reading is adopted in v. 13 (see p. 284, n. 1). On the majority reading, translated above, each road has a gate leading onto it,[15] appropriately wide and narrow respectively; on the alternative reading there is no gate on the

---

13. One of the more remarkable reinterpretations of gospel sayings proposed by J. D. M. Derrett (*JSNT* 15 [1982] 20-29) is to take ἀπωλεία here as meaning "(financial) loss," not eternal destruction, and to read a presumed original saying of Jesus underlying vv. 13-14 as advice to look for the secret postern gate rather than the main gate of the city where the toll collectors would be lying in wait and you would be fleeced! Derrett takes this to be a prudential maxim intended (like Luke's parable of the dishonest steward) to provide a tongue-in-cheek model for the spiritual priorities of disciples. Whatever the merits of this reading of a supposed original saying, it cannot help us with the actual text of Matthew with its two roads leading respectively to ἀπωλεία and ζωή, nor does it offer a sense which could fit into the context in which Matthew has set it.

14. Davies and Allison, 1:695-96, list a large number of Jewish examples both pre- and post-Christian, together with a few pagan parallels. H. D. Betz, *Sermon,* 521-22, finds the motif "traditional in all of the ancient world." See also Keener, 250.

15. The relationship between gate and road is not made clear: is the gate at the beginning or the end of the road? I have assumed the former on the basis of the order in which they are mentioned, but the sequence may not be important. In the "parallel" in Luke 13:24 there are no roads, and in the Jewish two-ways teaching no gates; each metaphor contributes to the total effect in Matthew's version, but the reader is left to puzzle out how the two are to be envisaged together.

wide road. The latter reading offers the appropriate sense of the majority route as a way of life which has no entrance requirement, onto which people find their way without effort or thought, simply drifting with the crowd; it is only those who make the effort to turn aside through the unattractively narrow gate who can find the alternative road which leads *away* (see p. 284, n. 2) from the crowd to real life. Such imagery lends itself to a preacher's elaboration in terms of the need to fight one's way through the thoughtless, contented crowd on the broad road in order to make a decisive break by going through the gate of commitment to discipleship and undertake the hard, uphill struggle of the road to heaven. But unfortunately most textual scholars opt for the majority reading; it may even be that the popularity of the shorter reading among some ancient interpreters may have more to do with its homiletical possibilities than with its textual authenticity.

Whichever way the imagery is read, the saying offers a stark choice between two totally opposed orientations and their respective outcomes, and takes for granted that those who find the way to life will be a minority.[16] In Luke 13:23-24 the imagery of the narrow door is a response to the question "Are those who are saved few?"; the answer is clearly meant to be Yes.[17] This is consistent with the repeated assumption in this discourse that disciples stand out from the majority of the society in which they live (5:3-10, 13-16) and as such are subject to persecution (5:11-12, 39-47); see p. 284, n. 4, for the possibility that the wording here also envisages persecution for those on the narrow way. To envisage the majority as on the broad road to destruction adds a sense of urgency to the call to "seek first God's kingship and righteousness" (6:33). A similar contrast between the saved and the lost underlies several of the parables in ch. 13, and again there the impression may be gained that those who are saved are a minority taken out from a generally corrupt society (13:19-23, 37-43, 49-50). Cf. the imagery of the disciples as sheep among wolves in 10:16. Matthew's Jesus does not seem to envisage the general conversion of society; those on the road to life are only those few who have "found" it.

16. A similar image in *4 Ezra* 7:6-9 speaks of the path to the (heavenly) city, running between the twin dangers of fire and water, being so narrow that only one person can go on it at a time. While the need for a choice is implied in Matthew's contrasting of the two ways, his concern is more with the total numbers than with any concept of individual responsibility.

17. Cf. 22:14: "Many are invited, but few are chosen," and the "many" who will be repudiated here in v. 22. "Many" and "few" are of course relative terms, depending on the context; by contrast, in 8:11 and 20:28 we hear of the salvation of "many" (cf. also the "plentiful harvest" of 9:37-38), though in the former case those "many" are contrasted with the "sons of the kingdom" who are excluded (in the terms of 22:14, "invited" but not "chosen").

b. Scene 2: False Prophets: Good and Bad Fruit (7:15-20)

The second contrast focuses on the danger posed by false prophets, who are, by implication, contrasted with true prophets who may be trusted. The term "prophet" locates these people within the disciple community, and the imagery of wolves dressed as sheep indicates that that community may contain impostors. The specific focus on prophecy is found only in v. 15, while the imagery of trees and fruit in vv. 16-20 could apply to any other people who purport to be godly. Indeed, the same imagery will be used in 12:33 with reference apparently to the current Jewish leadership; the parallel in Luke 6:43-45 lacks the reference to prophecy and follows immediately upon the saying about the splinter and the plank, indicating that it there concerns hypocrisy on the part of any disciple. So perhaps Matthew has brought together in vv. 15-20 two originally separate pieces of teaching. But in that case he clearly intends them to be taken together: in his construction the clear antecedent of "their" and "them" in v. 16 (and therefore also in v. 20) is the false prophets, to whom the common-sense test of genuineness "by their fruits" must therefore especially apply.

15   False prophets are a recurrent problem in the OT, and Matthew's term here, *pseudoprophētes,* occurs in LXX Zech 13:2 and often in Jeremiah, who found himself frequently pitted against the more popular prophets who proclaimed "Peace" when there was no peace (Jer 6:13-14; 28:1-17, etc.). Cf. the classic story of Micaiah ben Imlah and the four hundred court prophets in 1 Kgs 22:5-28. We shall hear more warnings against false prophets in 24:11, 24, and *Did.* 11:2–12:5 provides graphic evidence of the nuisance they soon became in the postapostolic church.[18] The false prophets of *Did.* 11–12 were apparently more mercenary than actively destructive,[19] but we find the metaphor of wolves used again for false teachers in the church as early as Acts 20:29, and the NT is full of warnings against the damage that false teaching could do to the life and health of Christian congregations. The added authority claim implied in what purported to be prophecy (and so received directly from God) made false *prophets* even more dangerous. There is of course no evidence that "prophecy" as such featured in the disciple group during Jesus' ministry, but it quickly became a prominent feature of early Christian congregational life, and almost as quickly became subject to abuse. The warnings of 24:11, 24 indicate that Jesus was aware of this future hazard, as indeed OT experience might lead one to expect. By the time Matthew wrote his gospel the issue had already taken on much more immediate relevance.

---

18. The warning to "beware of (προσέχετε ἀπό) such people" (*Did.* 12:5) echoes this verse.

19. But see also *Did.* 16:3, which echoes Matt 7:15, warning of the coming "in the last days" of "false prophets and destroyers," when "sheep will be turned into wolves and love into hate."

These false prophets are described as "coming to you," and so apparently as people from outside the disciple group who nonetheless wish to represent themselves as on the same side. The contrast between their appearance and what they are "inside" makes it clear that, unlike the self-deluded charismatics of vv. 22-23, they are consciously putting on an act. The imagery of wolves dressed as sheep[20] not only indicates that their destructive intentions are hidden behind a mild facade but also draws on the common OT metaphor of God's people as his flock (cf. 9:36; 10:6, 16; 15:24; 18:12-13; 25:32-33; 26:31): they want to be accepted as belonging to God's people. For wolves as a metaphor for those who abuse their position of leadership among God's people cf. Ezek 23:27-28; Zeph 3:3-4, in each case in association with false prophets. The instruction to "beware" of them implies the same need for discrimination on the part of God's people as we saw in v. 6. People cannot always be taken at their face value, and the more so when they claim to speak for God. The testing of purportedly divine communications is a prominent and necessary concern of the NT writers; cf. 1 Cor 14:29, 37-38; 2 Thess 2:1-3; 1 John 4:1-6.[21] Such wariness coexists in the NT, however, with a recognition of and welcome for prophecy as a genuine divine gift, and Matthew shares that recognition (10:41; 23:34); after all, the reason why false prophets can pass themselves off as "sheep" is presumably that genuine prophecy is a familiar and welcome phenomenon in the church.

16-20 The test of "fruits" is set out at some length, from a variety of aspects. (1) The basic principle is in vv. 17-18: trees produce only the kind of fruit which reflects their basic character, good or bad. (2) That general point is illustrated by the specific instance of thornbushes and thistles (v. 16b), which from the point of view of human usefulness are "bad"[22] and therefore cannot produce the useful ("good") fruits of grapes and figs. This illustration depends on the species of the plant rather than its condition as "good" or "rotten," but the principle is the same. (3) Verse 19 adds a note which is parenthetical to the issue of testing as such, the ultimate fate of the unfruitful tree, but in context this additional note fits into the general pattern of these four warnings (see introductory comments above) by indicating what is in store for the false prophets and for any who like them do not produce the

---

20. The famous fable of the wolf in sheep's clothing attributed to Aesop (sixth century B.C.) may have been familiar around the Mediterranean world by this time. In Thomas Bewick's edition of 1818 it carries the moral, "We ought not to judge of men by their looks, or their dress and appearances, but by the character of their lives and conversation, and by their works. . . ." For the appeal of the imagery cf. our Little Red Riding Hood.

21. For a survey of the evaluation of prophecy in early Christianity see D. E. Aune, *Prophecy,* 217-29.

22. The two occur together in this negative sense in Gen 3:18; Hos 10:8; Heb 6:8.

"fruits" they promise (cf. the destruction of the unfruitful fig tree in 21:18-20, and comments there on its symbolic intention). Verse 19 repeats word for word the warning by John the Baptist in 3:10 (see comments there). (4) Finally, the pericope is framed by the repeated practical guideline which the fruit metaphor was introduced to support, "It is by their fruits that you will recognize them" (vv. 16a, 20).

The OT suggests a variety of tests for prophets. In Deut 18:21-22 we find the test of subsequent events: if what they have predicted does not happen, they are false prophets. But in Deut 13:1-6 there is also a theological test: even if a prophet's words do come true, they are to be rejected if they call God's people to follow other gods. In Jer 23:9-15 and elsewhere there is the ethical test: their ungodly behavior gives them away. This last seems the closest to what is intended here. The "fruits"[23] are not specifically identified, but the metaphor recurs several times in Matthew. In 3:8 it represents behavior which demonstrates true repentance, in 12:33 probably the words by which a person's true allegiance is revealed, in 13:8, 23 a lifestyle which responds to the preaching of the word; in 21:19 fruitlessness illustrates the failure of the temple establishment, and in 21:33-43 the fruit of the vineyard represents the life and loyalty which God expects of his people. It is thus predominantly an ethical metaphor, based on the assumption that true loyalty to God will issue in appropriate behavior by his people. However plausible their words, it is by the life they live that you can recognize those who are not true prophets of God. Thus this pericope, like those that follow in vv. 21-23 and 24-27 (each of which also gives prominence to the verb *poieō;* see above), is concerned, as the discourse as a whole has been, with the way disciples live. The word "righteousness" does not occur in these concluding pericopes, but that is what they are about. Only those prophets whose lives reveal the righteousness of the kingdom of God are to be credited. The constant refrain of the NT is that bad teaching is reflected in bad living; it is by their fruits that you will recognize them. Carson, 191, adds the pertinent comment that while the test of fruit is reliable, it is "not necessarily easy or quick"; fruit may take some time to develop, and the pernicious results of false teaching may not be obvious at first.

---

23. Apart from v. 19 (which is an exact copy of 3:10), the plural is used throughout these verses, as it is in 21:34-43; it might be understood of their actual deeds rather than of a general character (as in the "fruit [singular] of the Spirit," Gal 5:22-23), but the contexts where the singular is used (3:8, 10; 7:19; 12:33; 13:8) do not indicate a clearly different sense.

c. Scene 3: Insiders and Outsiders: Things May Not Be as They Seem (7:21-23)

The third contrast[24] presses even closer to home. Whereas v. 15 warned the insiders against interlopers who would pretend to belong to the group, here there is apparently no pretense. We meet people who profess their allegiance to Jesus as "Lord,"[25] and who can back up that claim with impressive spiritual achievements ("fruits"?) all carried out explicitly "in his name." Unlike the consciously fraudulent prophets of v. 15, these people are apparently themselves more surprised than anyone when they find themselves rejected from the kingdom of heaven. They really thought they had made the grade; like the "goats" of 25:44 they are quite unaware of where they have failed. But the basis of their rejection is expressed not in terms of what they have done or not done, still less in terms of the allegiance they professed, but in the poignant words, the more desolating when addressed to professed disciples, "I never knew you."

This is the more surprising when v. 21 has contrasted merely professed adherents with those who *do* God's will. "Doing" and "being known" sound like quite different criteria. And it is on their "doing" that they base their claim in v. 22, listing a series of charismatic activities done in Jesus' name, surely in themselves all appropriate marks of those who belong to the kingdom of heaven, and indeed characteristics of Jesus' own ministry and that expected of his disciples (10:7-8); the repetition of the verb *poieō* in v. 22 echoing v. 21 seems to clinch the point. Yet when they are rejected in v. 23, it is not merely on the basis that they have not been known, but that what they have *done* is itself no more than "lawlessness."

It seems, then, that a new dimension is now added to the question of "fruits." Even good works by themselves are not enough. Prophecy, exorcism, and miracles can hardly be described as "bad fruit," but even these spiritual activities can apparently be carried out by those who still lack the relationship with Jesus which is the essential basis for belonging to the kingdom of heaven. There are good people who claim to follow Jesus as "Lord" and who do good works and think they are doing them in Jesus' name who are nonetheless on the broad road. "Doing the will of my Father in heaven" is not a merely ethical category; that will also includes to know and be known by Jesus the "Lord." A professed allegiance to Jesus falls short of that, and so even does the enthusiastic performance of charismatic activities "in his name."[26]

---

24. See above, p. 286, for the view that vv. 21-23 are a separate section rather than a continuation of vv. 15-20.

25. Elsewhere in the NT the acknowledgment of Jesus as "Lord" is recognized as the mark of a true disciple (Rom 10:9; 1 Cor 12:3). Matthew, like James (Jas 2:14-26), warns his readers that even that distinctive confession is not enough in itself.

26. It is quite possible that v. 21 and vv. 22-23 were originally separate sayings,

This is, then, a profoundly searching and disturbing pericope for all professing disciples. It raises sharply the issue of assurance of salvation, and taken alone it can be a cause of great distress to some more sensitive souls. But such questioning is not a new phenomenon. It was apparently in the light of just such painful spiritual self-examination that the pastoral treatise we know as 1 John was written, with its recognition of the need for reassurance when "our hearts condemn us" (1 John 3:19-22) and its painstaking examination of the grounds for assurance: "by this we know . . ." (1 John 2:3, 5; 3:16, 19, 24; 4:2, 6, 13; 5:2).

21 This is the first use in Matthew of "Lord," *kyrie,* as an address to Jesus. God has been referred to frequently, both in OT quotations and in Matthew's own editorial style, as *ho Kyrios,* the regular LXX translation of the divine name "Yahweh." Matthew, unlike Luke, does not use *ho Kyrios* to refer to Jesus in his narrative or as a title used by Jesus for himself (21:3 is not an exception; see notes there), but the vocative *kyrie* will be the most common form of address to Jesus in the narrative from here on, used both by disciples and by strangers seeking Jesus' help. The vocative in itself carries no necessary theological connotation, but simply recognizes a superior social status: *ho kyrios* in the parables often denotes an employer or slave owner, and we find the vocative so used in 13:27; 21:30 (to a father); 25:11, 20, 22, 24. Pilate is so addressed in 27:63. But in Matthew's narrative, addressed to Jesus as a Galilean villager of no social prominence, and frequently in the context of expecting miraculous help, *kyrie* clearly carries more weight, and the fact that Matthew uses it substantially more than the other Synoptic evangelists indicates that he was well aware of this more than purely social dimension. In the present context this dimension is very clear, where the use of *kyrie, kyrie* (the doubling of the address draws attention to it as important in its own right, not merely polite) for Jesus is linked with entry to the kingdom of heaven and with the working of miracles. Cf. 25:11, where this same double vocative similarly accompanies an appeal for entry to the eschatological wedding feast, and 25:37, 44, where Jesus as the eschatological judge is addressed as *kyrie.* While it would go beyond the philological evidence to claim *kyrie* as in itself an attribution of divinity, in these contexts it fits well with Jesus' presentation of himself as the ultimate judge.

It is not only the address *kyrie, kyrie,* however, which makes this pericope christologically remarkable. The Jesus who in 5:21-47 repeatedly

---

v. 21 setting doing God's will over against a mere profession of allegiance, and vv. 22-23 setting being known by Jesus over against charismatic activity in his name. If so, Matthew (or some earlier transmitter of Jesus' teaching) will have brought them together on the basis of the shared appeal "Lord! Lord!" and the shared theme of acceptance over against exclusion. But in that case Matthew clearly saw their themes as complementary rather than in conflict.

matched God's OT laws with his own "but I tell you" now presents himself as the one who decides who does and does not enter the kingdom of heaven, and even more remarkably the basis for that entry is people's relationship with *him,* whether or not *he* "knew them." Further, the essence of their rejection from the kingdom of heaven is that they must go away *from him.* This pericope therefore stands alongside 25:31-46 in making the most exalted claims for Jesus as the eschatological judge and the personal focus of salvation.

For the meaning of "enter the kingdom of heaven" see above on 5:20. For "doing the will of God" see on 6:10. In 12:50 the same phrase "do the will of my Father who is in heaven" is used to describe those who truly belong to the disciple group, and the use there of family imagery (Jesus' brother, sister, and mother) gives further depth to the requirement of v. 23 that those admitted to the kingdom of heaven are those whom Jesus "knows"; cf. also 21:28-31, where, as here, "doing the father's will" is contrasted with mere profession of obedience. Hitherto God has been spoken of frequently as "*your* Father in heaven," but from now on Jesus will several times refer to God as "*my* Father" (10:32-33; 12:50; 16:17; 18:10, 19, 35; 20:23; 25:34, 41; 26:29, 53), and the special relationship indicated by this phrase will be further explained in 11:25-27 and its depth explored in Jesus' experience in Gethsemane (26:39, 42). Here, as in 25:34, 41, it is appropriate as the basis for Jesus' role, acting as judge on his Father's authority.

22 "On that day," like the idea of exclusion from the kingdom of heaven, indicates that this scene is set at the final judgment (which will be more fully described in 25:31-46). For "that day" cf. 24:36; Luke 10:12; 17:31; in the OT it frequently denotes "the day of Yahweh" (e.g., Isa 10:20; Hos 2:21; Amos 9:11; and throughout Zech 12–14). The three activities claimed are all accepted parts of early Christian discipleship, all practiced by Jesus himself, and all mentioned with approval elsewhere in Matthew. That there should be false claimants to the gift of prophecy comes as no surprise after v. 15, but exorcisms and miracles are less easily counterfeited, and it is not indicated here that the claims were false. Matthew himself mentions apparently successful exorcists outside the disciple group (12:27), and in Mark 9:38-41 and Acts 19:13-16 we find that such exorcists used Jesus' name as a source of power; perhaps the same sort of scenario underlies this saying. Matthew omits mention of the non-disciple exorcist of Mark 9:38-41, perhaps because the generous inference there, that his use of Jesus' name guarantees his acceptability, would conflict with this saying. Matthew's nearest equivalent to Mark 9:40, "Whoever is not against us is on our side," has a very different tone: in 12:30 the scribal detractors of Jesus' own exorcisms are dismissed with the verdict "Whoever is not with me is against me." Matthew, it seems, is more cautious about fringe supporters, and is unable to accept charismatic activity, even charismatic activity "in the name of Jesus," as itself evidence of being on the right side. After all, there were other exorcists and miracle workers around. The striking threefold repetition of "in your name" is the more remarkable in that elsewhere what is done "in Jesus' name" is taken to be a mark of genuineness (10:22; 18:5, 20; 19:29; 24:9), but cf. 24:5 where again we find impostors coming "in my name." The use of Jesus' name, like the reiterated address *kyrie,* can be a merely outward profession which does not guarantee genuine discipleship. And even the successful performance of miracles can be traced to other causes (as indeed Jesus' enemies will allege with regard to his own exorcisms in 9:34; 12:24); see 24:24. There is no substitute for personal discipleship.

23   To "know" is commonly used in biblical literature for much more than acquaintance or recognition; it denotes a relationship (see further on 11:27). In 1:25 it was used following the Hebrew idiom for the sexual relationship, but here it reflects rather the OT idiom for God's special relationship with his people, as in Amos 3:2 (cf. 1 Sam 2:12; Jer 22:16; 24:7; 31:34 for God's people "knowing" him). "I never knew you" means in effect that he does not acknowledge them as part of his true family (to use the imagery of 12:50); for its use as a formula of repudiation cf. 25:12; 26:70, 72, 74. The resultant verdict, "Get away from me, you lawbreakers," echoes Ps 6:9a (EVV v. 8a), where the psalmist dismisses his opponents and turns to the Lord for support; Matthew reproduces the LXX phrase which translates "workers of evil" as "workers of lawlessness." To describe those who claim to have practiced prophecy, exorcism, and miracles as "lawbreakers" is extraordinary: if Matthew is not simply mechanically reproducing the LXX term, the implication is apparently that all this charismatic activity, like their profession "Lord! Lord!" was merely a veneer on a life fundamentally opposed to the will of God, rather like those whom Jeremiah famously accused of turning from fervent devotion to "the temple of the LORD" which was "called by my name" to a catalogue of ethical and religious offenses (Jer 7:4-11). The focus here is on such ethical failure rather than their attitude to the law as such; for Matthew's use of *anomia,* "lawlessness," as a fairly general term for behavior displeasing to God rather than with specific reference to the breaking of laws cf. 13:41; 23:28; 24:12.[27] That these professed disciples did not even realize their religious failure, and would no doubt have rejected the term "lawbreakers" with indignation, only makes the verdict the more poignant.

27. See W. D. Davies, *Setting,* 202-6. Davies is there arguing against the view that this language was specifically directed against Gnostics; his arguments apply equally to the well-known contention of G. Barth, *Tradition,* 73-75, to the effect that the target was specifically "antinomians," a view which depends on a too precise reading of ἀνομία. See further R. Mohrlang, *Matthew,* 16-17. Other attempts to define the composition of the group more specifically are equally debated, and equally unnecessary.

d. Scene 4: Two House Builders: Hearing and Doing (7:24-27)

The parallel sermon in Luke 6:20-49 ends with a version of this same parable, which is similar in content but almost as different in wording and in the way the story is constructed as it would be possible to be while relating the same teaching.[28] This powerful image was apparently reshaped, perhaps several times, but retained its function as the striking conclusion to a challenging discourse which has left Jesus' hearers with a simple but demanding choice: to hear and ignore, or to hear and put into practice.[29] It is a make-or-break choice with eternal consequences. And as we noted in v. 21, it is Jesus himself who is the key to this choice; it is *his* words (and not, as one might have expected, God's words) which must be done. Indeed, to do *Jesus'* words here seems to be the equivalent of "doing the will of my Father in heaven" in v. 21. To ignore his words, therefore, will result in total spiritual disaster.

Unlike the image of the two roads in vv. 13-14, this parable does not draw a line simply between outsiders and insiders. Both men represent people who have "heard" Jesus' teaching. In terms of the narrative setting we must remember the surrounding crowds of 5:1, whom we shall find in v. 28 to be there listening apparently on the fringe of the disciple group to whom the discourse is specifically addressed — though of course any of the inner circle of "real" disciples who fail to take up the challenge of this teaching must stand similarly at risk. In terms of Matthew's church we are no doubt to envisage a typically mixed gathering such as we shall find depicted in 13:24-30, in which not all who hear are equally ready to respond. But to be there in the audience is no more guarantee of salvation than to have called Jesus "Lord! Lord!" and performed miracles in his name. It all comes down to "doing" what Jesus has now set out before them. The alternative is, in the imagery of the parable, total collapse.

The parable itself is simple and self-explanatory in a country where heavy rain can send flash floods surging down the normally dry wadis with devastating effect. For the contrast between "sensible" and "foolish" cf. 25:1-12.[30] No particular building site or type of construction need be specified, though a mud-brick house such as was envisaged also in 6:19 would be particularly susceptible to the effects of flooding. The point is not, as in 1 Cor 3:10-15, the suitability of the building material, but the solidity of the foundation. Cf. Isaiah's image of the firm foundation stone which provides the

---

28. M. D. Goulder, *Midrash,* 88, calls Luke's a "prose version."

29. Compare those who appreciated Ezekiel's eloquence, yet "they hear what you say, but they will not do it" (Ezek 33:32).

30. Note that that parable also contains in vv. 11-12 a strong echo of 7:22-23 in the useless plea "Lord! Lord!" outside the closed door and in the response "I don't know you."

only security when the floods sweep through (Isa 28:15-19), the foundations washed away by a flood in Job 22:16, and the wall which collapses under the pressure of the elements in Ezek 13:10-16 (where the target of the imagery is the false prophets who proclaim peace when there is no peace). The importance of a solid rock foundation will be echoed in 16:18, where again the resultant building will remain secure against all threats. The total collapse of the house with a bad foundation probably suggests that, as in vv. 21-23, the final judgment is particularly in view, but that setting is not emphasized, and the imagery applies equally to the testing which discipleship will repeatedly encounter before the final consummation.[31]

12. The Authority of the Teacher Recognized (7:28-29)

> 28 And then,[1] when Jesus had come to the end of these sayings, the crowds were astonished at his teaching, 29 because he was teaching them as someone who had authority and not as their scribes taught.

This brief conclusion forms with 5:1-2 a framework around the discourse on discipleship. Again we see Jesus as the teacher, but this time it is not the disciples, the primary audience of the discourse, who are in focus, but the crowds, away from whom Jesus had deliberately taken his disciples in 5:1, but who are now found to have been a secondary audience in the background. They have heard enough of this teaching, even if it was not directed toward them, to be mightily impressed. This response to Jesus' teaching, added to the general enthusiasm for his healing ministry already outlined in 4:24-25, will form the essential background for the narrative which now takes over from the discourse and will be a continuing feature throughout the Galilean phase of Jesus' activity.

The transition from discourse to narrative is marked by the formula which will conclude each of the five main discourses (cf. 11:1; 13:53; 19:1; 26:1);[2] the first six Greek words are identical in each case, while the teaching which is the object of the verb "come to the end of" is expressed in slightly

---

31. To derive a purely eschatological reference from "will be like" in vv. 24 and 26 (so Schweizer, 190-91) loads too much onto the natural use of the future tense to describe the future response of someone currently hearing Jesus' words.

1. The Semitic idiom καὶ ἐγένετο, "and it happened," to introduce a new phase of the story is a distinctive feature of the stereotyped formula which concludes each of Matthew's main discourses (see comments below). There is no contemporary English idiom which quite corresponds to it, and modern translations tend to leave it unrepresented. "And then" is an attempt to convey something of its function rather than its lexical meaning.

2. See pp. 2-4 for the role of this formula in relation to the total structure of Matthew's gospel.

different phrases to correspond to the content of the discourse just concluded. The distinctiveness of this formula derives from its rather formal wording.[3] The opening *kai egeneto,* "and it happened," has an archaic ring (like the KJV phrase "and it came to pass"), representing the familiar OT Hebrew introductory phrase *wayyᵉhî;* it is not a natural Greek idiom and occurs elsewhere in Matthew only at 9:10.[4] Nor is the verb *teleō,* in the sense of "to complete, come to the end of," part of Matthew's normal vocabulary: it occurs outside this formula only in 10:23. The whole clause thus looks like a set formula[5] deliberately designed to mark the end of each main block of teaching and to lead back into narrative.[6] In three of its five occurrences it is immediately followed by a main clause describing Jesus' movement to another location; here that relocation (8:1) is separated from the formula only by the need to comment first on the crowd reaction.

The periphrastic tense "he was teaching them" (rather than "he had taught them") suggests that Matthew intends us to think of the crowd's astonishment as applying not only to this discourse but to Jesus' continuing teaching in Galilee. The astonishment of both the crowds and the disciples at Jesus, already implied in 4:24-25, will be frequently noted as the story progresses. Often it will be Jesus' miracles rather than his teaching which evoke it; the particular verb used here, *ekplēssomai,* is used especially of the effect of his teaching (cf. 13:54; 19:25; 22:33), but that teaching is linked with miracles in 13:54. In both the feature which will impress them is his *authority* (cf. 8:9; 9:6, 8; 21:23-27; 28:18). To set the authority of his teaching in contrast with that of the scribes[7] is a bold claim, since the scribes were the

---

3. For its essentially Semitic character see D. P. Senior, *Passion,* 10, n. 1.

4. Even 9:10 is not an exact syntactical parallel, since there the main verb following καὶ ἐγένετο is introduced by a second καί.

5. It echoes the wording of LXX Josh 4:11; 1 Sam 13:19, καὶ ἐγένετο ὡς συνετέλεσεν . . . . Even closer to Matthew's wording in Hebrew (not LXX) are Num 16:31; Jer 26:8, where the formula also marks a transition from speech (though not a long discourse as in Matthew) to narrative.

6. D. C. Allison, *Moses,* 192-94, also draws attention to a repeated formula in Deut 31–32 which, though lacking Matthew's καὶ ἐγένετο, is otherwise close to his transitional formula, as it speaks of Moses completing (συνετέλεσεν) the speaking or writing of his words just recorded (Deut 31:1, 24; 32:45). But what follows in each case in Deuteronomy is not a move to narrative but rather further words of Moses.

7. The phrase οἱ γραμματεῖς αὐτῶν (cf. αἱ συναγωγαὶ αὐτῶν, 4:23; 9:35, etc.; see p. 150, n. 7) is sometimes taken to indicate the distance between the Christian community and the rabbinic establishment at the time Matthew wrote, but in this context the pronoun naturally picks up on the crowd's familiarity with "their" scribes as compared with the surprise caused by this new teacher whom they did not yet know. It may also serve to protect the Christian scribes whom we shall meet in 13:52; 23:34 from this negative assessment. Cf. D. E. Orton, *Scribe,* 30-31.

authorized teachers of the law who in virtue of their training and office had a right to expect the people to accept their legal rulings. When Jesus comes to Jerusalem it will be with the scribes that he must debate, and against them that his tirade in ch. 23 will be delivered. It will be a contest of authority, that of the established guardians of legal tradition against that of the upstart Galilean preacher. But here already the people, perhaps remembering how in 5:20 Jesus has declared the "righteousness of the scribes and Pharisees" inadequate, sense a new dimension in Jesus' teaching. Whereas scribal rulings were based on the tradition of earlier interpreters of the law, Jesus has in 5:17-48 set himself up as an authority over against that interpretive tradition, on the basis not of formal training or authorization but of his own confident, "*I* tell you." It was that sort of inherent "authority" that the people missed in their scribes, even though their office commanded respect. When to that remarkable claim is added Jesus' assumption that he himself is the proper object of people's allegiance and the arbiter of their destiny (5:11-12; 7:21-23, 24, 26), the crowd's astonishment is hardly out of place. W. D. Davies' comment on the modern reader's response to the Sermon on the Mount must apply at least as strongly to those who first heard this teaching: "The Sermon on the Mount compels us, in the first place, to ask who he is who utters these words."[8]

E. THE MESSIAH'S AUTHORITY REVEALED IN HIS ACTION: AN ANTHOLOGY OF WORKS OF POWER (8:1–9:34)

Matthew's overview of the messianic work of Jesus in Galilee has begun in chs. 5–7 with a lengthy and impressive collection of his teaching on discipleship. The conclusion of that discourse has commented on the astonished but presumably approving reaction of the crowd, who recognize in Jesus "someone who had authority, not like their scribes." But Jesus did not come only to teach, and the introductory paragraph in 4:23-25 has focused even more strongly on his acts of power, primarily in healing and exorcism, as both one of the main components in his ministry and the basis of his widespread reputation in and around Galilee. Matthew therefore now goes on to present in chs. 8–9 a parallel collection, almost as long as the discourse just concluded, of stories of Jesus' miraculous activity in the area, before he introduces his second discourse collection in ch. 10. That second discourse will be introduced by an account of the mission of the disciples (10:1; cf. 10:7-8) which closely echoes central aspects of Jesus' ministry as set out in these chapters. This anthology also provides the narrative basis for Jesus' christological

8. W. D. Davies, *Setting*, 435.

299

claim based on his miraculous acts in 11:2-6. These two chapters have thus been designed to play a foundational role in the building up of Matthew's account of Jesus as the Messiah.

Chapters 8–9 thus present "a 'slice of life' view of Jesus' overall ministry."[1] They contain fully half of Jesus' miracles individually recorded in Matthew's gospel. The collection consists of nine separate miracle stories comprising ten individual miracles (since one of the stories, 9:18-26, contains two intertwined miracles of healing), which are arranged in three groups of three (8:1-17; 8:23–9:8; 9:18-34). Between these three groups are two narrative interludes (8:18-22; 9:9-17) each of which focuses on the call to discipleship and the response of a variety of individuals to that call. The discipleship theme of the discourse in chs. 5–7 is thus fleshed out in a number of case studies which enable readers to think more deeply about their own response to the challenge issued in 7:13-27, and to do so against the backdrop of a sequence of stories which increasingly underline the unique authority of the one who has issued that call.

Of the nine miracle stories which Matthew has collected here, six are paralleled in both Mark and Luke, one (8:5-13) in Luke but not in Mark, while the other two (9:27-31, 32-34) are similar to stories which Matthew himself tells elsewhere (12:22-24; 20:29-34) and which also have their Synoptic parallels at those points. The collection of miracles is thus different in composition from the discourse of chs. 5–7, which contained virtually no Marcan material, and more than one third of which had no parallel in Luke either. The process of compilation, however, appears again to be a deliberate "anthologizing" on the part of Matthew, in particular by weaving together material most of which occurs in two separate sequences in Mark and Luke.

The chart on page 301 shows how Matthew has interwoven this material together with some Q material and his own pair of "doublets." The parallels printed in **bold** comprise the first Marcan sequence (Mark 1:29–2:22; Luke 4:38–5:38), while those underlined comprise the second Marcan sequence (Mark 4:35–5:43; Luke 8:22-56); *italic* represents Q material.

We may note the following features of Matthew's compositional method:

1. The only element in this whole complex of material which is peculiar to Matthew is the formula-quotation which concludes the first set of stories (unless one counts the two "doublets" as peculiar to Matthew; but each has a Synoptic parallel in one of its occurrences). Formula-quotations are of course recognized as a distinctive feature of Matthew's style, providing an editorial comment on the narrative to which they are attached.

2. Matthew has brought together two narrative sequences which occur

1. D. J. Weaver, *Discourse*, 67.

Matthew	Mark	Luke
8:1-4	**1:40-45**	**5:12-16**
8:5-13		*7:1-10*
(8:11-12)		*(13:28-29)*
8:14-16	**1:29-34**	**4:38-41**
8:17 (formula-quotation)		
8:18-22		*9:57-60*
8:23-27	4:35-41	8:22-25
8:28-34	5:1-20	8:26-39
9:1-8	**2:1-12**	**5:17-26**
9:9-17	**2:14-22**	**5:27-38**
9:18-26	5:21-43	8:40-56
9:27-31 (cf. 20:29-34)	10:46-52	18:35-43
9:32-34 (cf. 12:22-24)	(3:22)	*11:14-15*

separately in Mark and Luke, and has not only interwoven them but also altered their sequence by moving the story of the leper (Mark 1:40-45) to the beginning of the first group.

3. While the second "interlude" (9:9-17) occupies the same place in Matthew's sequence as in the Synoptic parallels, following the story of the paralyzed man, the first (8:18-22) introduces Q material which in Luke is not connected with any of this collection of narratives.

4. This complex of miracles includes some of the most spectacular examples of Matthew's abbreviated narration of stories told at more luxuriant length by Mark: note especially the seven verses of 8:28-34 compared with the twenty verses of Mark 5:1-20, and the nine verses of 9:18-26 compared with Mark's twenty-three (5:21-43). Where Mark apparently enjoys telling these dramatic stories for their own sake, in Matthew they serve a more disciplined function within an overall framework setting out Jesus' acts of power, and are pared down to contain only what is required for that purpose.

All this suggests that these chapters contain a careful and original arrangement of traditional material by Matthew to serve his editorial purpose.[2]

2. D. C. Allison, *Moses,* 207-13, considers sympathetically the view of B. W. Bacon and others that the miracle-working power of Jesus in chs. 8–9 is deliberately paralleled with that of Moses in Exodus (just as his teaching in chs. 5–7 presents him as a new lawgiver like Moses), and also suggests that the arrangement into three groups of three matches that of the Mosaic plagues (if the tenth plague, which "has no natural grounding," is discounted); Allison had not yet noticed this last possibility in Davies and Allison, 2:1-2. In the end, however, he remains sceptical on both points; W. D. Davies, *Setting,* 86-92, is even more sceptical. For a survey of other suggested structural schemes in these chapters see Davies and Allison, 2:1-4.

The provision of interludes on discipleship in order to divide the nine stories into three groups of three is also closely parallel to the arrangement of the parables of ch. 13 into groups of three with intervening explanatory material, an arrangement which is equally peculiar to Matthew. As in ch. 13, it is easier to suggest a thematic coherence within the first group of three than it is subsequently, and it does not seem that this was a necessary part of Matthew's plan, though he welcomed such thematic coherence when it occurred — and in this case underlined it by supplying a concluding formula-quotation for the first group but not for the others. See further below on 8:1-17.

The impact of the Messiah's teaching has been expressed in terms of a unique *authority* (7:28-29), and the same may be said of this account of his deeds. The crowd express themselves again as amazed by Jesus' God-given "authority" in 9:8, and it is that same "authority" which has persuaded the centurion to expect healing from Jesus (8:9), an expectation which proves amply justified. While the actual term *exousia* does not occur elsewhere in this section, the theme is seen both in the expectation of miraculous deliverance on the part both of individuals and of crowds, even in the extreme case of a dying daughter, and in the reaction of disciples and onlookers to Jesus' miraculous response. Note especially 8:27: "What sort of person is this?" But it is not only in his acts that Jesus' authority is seen in these chapters. The two interludes present us with a man who issues sudden and all-embracing calls to discipleship and expects to have them instantly obeyed, and who regards his presence among his disciples as sufficient authority for them to be exempt from the pious duty of fasting. The cumulative effect of these various displays of God-given authority is no less powerful than that of the teaching in chs. 5–7. The two anthologies, though very differently constructed, form a matching pair, and together they leave no doubt that the story of Jesus in Galilee is, as the prologue to the gospel has told us to expect, that of the Messiah, the Son of God, breaking in upon the humdrum lives of his fellow countrymen and calling them to decision. As the crowds appropriately comment at the end of this anthology, Israel has never seen anything like this before (9:33).[3]

1. Three Miracles of Healing and Restoration (8:1-17)

1 *When Jesus had come down from the hills,*[4] *great crowds followed him.* 2 *And up came a leper,*[5] *who approached Jesus with a low*

---

3. For the theme of "authority" in Matthew's presentation of Jesus see J. H. Neyrey, *Honor,* 135-38.

4. See the comments on 5:1 for this translation of what is traditionally rendered "the mountain."

5. While the disease was probably not what is now technically called "leprosy"

bow[6] and said, "Lord,[7] if you are willing, you can make me clean."
3 Jesus stretched out his hand and touched him. "I am willing," he
said; "Be clean." And immediately the man's leprosy was made clean.
4 Jesus said to him, "See that you do not tell anyone, but off you go
and show yourself to the priest, and make the offering which Moses
laid down, as a witness to them."

5 When Jesus had returned to Capernaum, a centurion ap-
proached him with an urgent request:[8] 6 "Lord, my servant is lying[9] in
my house paralyzed and in terrible pain." 7 Jesus replied, "Am I to
come and heal him?"[10] 8 "No, Lord," replied the centurion, "I am not
fit to have you come under my roof. Just issue a command,[11] and my
servant will be cured. 9 For I, too, am a man under authority, and I
have soldiers under me. If I say to one, 'Go,' he goes, and to another,
'Come,' he comes; if I tell my slave, 'Do this,' he does it." 10 When Je-
sus heard this he was amazed, and he said to his followers, "I tell you

---

(see p. 305, n. 17), the words "leper" and "leprosy" appropriately convey the social stigma attached to it in an age when precise medical diagnosis was not to be expected.

6. I have translated προσκυνέω with "pay homage to" in 2:2, 8, 11 where it is the act of visiting dignitaries, and with "worship" in 4:9, 10 where it implies divine honors. Here, and generally in Matthew's narrative (9:18; 15:25; 18:26; 20:20), it represents the conventionally deferential posture of a suppliant to someone of recognized authority whose help is sought. It probably involved actual prostration on the ground in front of the potential benefactor; in a culture which is less physically demonstrative a "low bow" perhaps best conveys the social nuance. The word does not in itself imply the recognition of the one approached as divine, though sometimes the context may suggest that, as probably in 28:9, 17 and in the disciples' words in 14:33.

7. See on 7:21 for Matthew's use of the vocative κύριε. In view of the strong christological overtones Matthew finds in it as an address to Jesus, at least on some occasions, I have used the traditional rendering "Lord" in all such cases, but "Sir" or "Master" (in the case of slaves) when it is addressed to other people. The term does not in itself demand a recognition of Jesus as divine, any more than προσκυνέω does (see previous note), and in the narrative context the "leper" may have used it in a socially conventional way, but Matthew probably intends us to read more into it.

8. This rendering tries to convey the force of Matthew's sequence of verbs: προσῆλθεν αὐτῷ παρακαλῶν αὐτὸν καὶ λέγων, "came to him entreating him and saying."

9. The use of βάλλομαι, "to be thrown," here, in v. 14, and in 9:2 is an idiom for lying down in connection with illness or recovery (cf. Mark 7:30; Rev 2:22; similarly Luke 16:20). There is no necessary nuance of violence, but rather of the person's inability to get up.

10. For the interrogative reading of this reply and the emphatic ἐγώ, see the comments below.

11. The dative λόγῳ is more than simply an object of εἰπέ; it designates the unexpected means of the requested healing, by speech rather than by physical presence and action: "say it *by a word*." The usage will be echoed with regard to exorcism in v. 16.

truly, I have not found anyone in Israel with faith like this.[12] 11 *And I tell you that many will come from the east and west and join Abraham, Isaac, and Jacob at the feast*[13] *in the kingdom of heaven,* 12 *while those who belong to that kingdom will be thrown out into the darkness outside, where there will be weeping and gnashing of teeth."* 13 *Then Jesus said to the centurion, "Off you go; as you have believed, so let it be done for you." And his servant was cured at that moment.*[14]

14 *Then Jesus went to Peter's house, where he saw Peter's*[15] *mother-in-law in bed with a fever.* 15 *He took hold of her hand, and the fever left her, and she got up and waited on*[16] *him.*

16 *In the evening they brought to him many people who were possessed by demons; he threw out the spirits with a command, and healed all the people who were suffering.* 17 *This was to fulfill what had been declared through Isaiah the prophet, who said,*

"He himself took up our weaknesses and carried our illnesses."

The first group of three miracle stories seems to be treated as a connected whole in that here, in contrast to the following two groups, there is a concluding general summary of Jesus' work of healing (v. 16) which then prompts Matthew to add a formula-quotation (v. 17) encapsulating the motif of deliverance which underlies these healings. Matthew's rearrangement of the traditional order of the healings recorded in Mark 1:29-45, so that the story of the leper comes first, is perhaps also designed to highlight Jesus' work of deliverance by putting up front a more striking instance of Jesus' restoration of the distressed and excluded than the relatively mundane fever of Peter's mother-in-law.

12. The "milder" version of this comment in Luke 7:9, "Not even in Israel have I found faith like this," appears here in an impressive range of MSS and versions, but is rightly regarded as an assimilation to Luke, perhaps motivated by the harshness of Jesus' verdict on Israel in its Matthean form.

13. ἀνακλίνομαι, "recline," is the posture expected at a banquet; they are not just sitting with the patriarchs, but feasting with them. See the comments below.

14. Literally, "in that hour," but the Greek idiom does not suggest, as our word "hour" more naturally does, an extended period of sixty minutes within which the cure took place. The phrase (in the form "*from* that hour") is a standard Matthean idiom for an immediate cure (cf. 9:22; 15:28; 17:18).

15. It is theoretically possible, though idiomatically unlikely, that Matthew's αὐτοῦ refers to Jesus rather than Peter, but this would be a very precarious foundation on which to build a theory that Jesus was married! Mark and Luke are both clear that she was *Peter's* mother-in-law.

16. Among the range of possible meanings of διακονέω the basic domestic sense of providing food and/or drink best fits this context. To translate it "serve" here might suggest an inappropriately religious sense.

The three individual accounts are of the healing of people who for different reasons were from a Jewish point of view disadvantaged: the leper was by virtue of his illness an outcast from normal society, the centurion (and presumably also his servant) was a Gentile, and the third patient was a woman — though in this latter case the issue of social status is not explicitly raised. So the "weaknesses" (v. 17) which Jesus is here portrayed as responding to involve social as well as physical dimensions. The leper is restored to normal society, while the Gentile and the woman, even if their objective status cannot be changed, have found not only physical healing but also an acceptance with Israel's Messiah which they could not have taken for granted. The point is strongly emphasized in Matthew's telling of the story of the centurion, with its elevation of this Gentile's faith above any in Israel and its revolutionary vision of outsiders welcomed to take their place alongside the Jewish patriarchs at the messianic banquet.

a. The Leper (8:1-4)

The Greek *lepra* in biblical literature denotes a disfiguring skin condition[17] which was believed to be contagious and which, following the instructions of Lev 13–14 (extensively developed in Mishnah *Nega'im*), rendered the affected person ritually unclean and thus excluded them from normal life and worship. Other types of uncleanness, for example, through contact with unclean creatures, dead bodies, or bodily discharges, were temporary, and once the prescribed period was past and the appropriate offerings made the person concerned could re-enter normal life without stigma. With this condition it was different: as long as the condition persisted, the person had no place in society and had to contrive to exist away from other people's dwellings (Lev 13:45-46). No other disease carried this stigma,[18] hence the horror with which the "leper" was regarded.[19] If the condition was cured, a careful examination by the priest and an appropriate offering and cleansing ritual (de-

17. It is generally agreed that the "leprosy" described in the Bible covers a wide range of skin conditions which may have included what is technically known as leprosy today (Hansen's disease; the more specific Greek term ἐλεφαντίασις seems to have described symptoms like those of Hansen's disease) but also other less serious conditions. All were, however, treated under the same regulations in Lev 13–14, which were designed to distinguish malignant from nonmalignant conditions; only the malignant incurred long-term ritual uncleanness. For a useful, nontechnical summary of the medical evidence see S. G. Browne, *ExpT* 73 (1961/2) 243-45. Also J. Wilkinson, *SJT* 31 (1978) 153-66.

18. See, however, below on 9:20-22. In that case what should have been a temporary impurity was rendered permanent by her irregular medical condition.

19. Blomberg, 138, suggests a parallel with current attitudes to AIDS, a point worth pondering.

scribed in detail in Lev 14:1-32) were required before they could be pronounced clean and allowed back into society. The NT consistently describes
the cure of "lepers" as "making clean," whereas other diseases are "cured";
see especially 10:8; 11:5 where the two are carefully distinguished. The terminology suggests that the physical suffering was not regarded as the most
serious aspect of a "leper's" problem. OT accounts of "leprosy" indicate that
it was regarded as practically incurable by medical means (Exod 4:6-8; Num
12:9-15; 2 Kgs 5:1-27; 2 Chr 26:16-21; to cure it is on a par with raising the
dead, 2 Kgs 5:7); for lepers to be made clean is a mark of the Messiah's coming (11:5).

In comparison with Mark's remarkably strong language about Jesus'
emotional reaction to the "leper's" approach (including his unexplained anger), Matthew's telling of the story is restrained. He says nothing of Jesus'
emotions nor of the disobedience of the man to Jesus' demand for silence
(Mark 1:45). But even in this more concise version it is a striking account
when read against the cultural setting described above. The man's confident
approach[20] contrasts with the self-isolation prescribed in Lev 13:45-46. His
recognition of Jesus' unique status is reflected not only in his deferential approach (a "low bow," "Lord") but also in his assumption that Jesus "can"
make him clean. His uncertainty, derived no doubt from the general attitude
toward "lepers," is whether this remarkable healer will be *willing* to respond
to his request. Jesus' response is straightforward, "I am willing," but is reinforced when he breaks the biblical taboo by touching the unclean man. The
immediate disappearance of a long-standing and disfiguring condition is
clearly miraculous. And with that the story, as an account of physical healing, is complete. But Matthew was well aware that there was more to "leprosy" than that, and Jesus' instructions in v. 44 ensure that the man is not
merely cured but also restored to society through the proper procedure. By
recounting Jesus' response to the most feared and ostracized medical condition of his day, Matthew has thus laid an impressive foundation for this collection of stories which demonstrate both Jesus' unique healing power and
his willingness to challenge the taboos of society in the interests of human
compassion.

1 Jesus' physical relocation following his period of teaching in the
hills[21] corresponds to similar relocations at the end of each of the other dis-

20. Keener, 260, speaks of a "holy chutzpah."
21. There is not much in Matthew's text to encourage the view that he is alluding
to Moses' descent from Sinai. The most that can be said is that if Jesus' going up on the
"mountain" to teach (5:1) was intended to recall Moses on Sinai, the same may be presumed to be true of his descent. But Matthew's wording does not closely echo LXX Exod
19:14; 32:1, 15; 34:29, and the events of these chapters bear no relation to what happened
in those chapters of Exodus.

courses (though that in 26:6 is delayed by the need to set the scene for the passion narrative in 26:1-5); a new phase of the story is beginning. The specific location of this first narrative scene is not given; a "leper" would not be found in a town or village, and we are left to assume that it is somewhere in the countryside on the way back from the hills to Capernaum (v. 5). The approach of the "leper" must assume that Jesus is at this point away from the crowds, who would not have tolerated the presence of the unclean and supposedly contagious person, but Matthew does not feel the need to explain such details. As in 4:25, the "following" by the crowd carries no technical sense of discipleship as it will do in vv. 19-23;[22] they are there to listen and to watch, not yet to commit themselves to join the "disciples" of 5:1.

2 Several of those coming to Jesus for healing or other miraculous help are said to have "bowed low" (see p. 303, n. 6; cf. 9:18; 15:25) and addressed him as *kyrie* (see p. 303, n. 7; cf. 8:6, 25; 14:30; 15:22; 17:15; 20:30). Neither term in itself need involve more than a polite recognition of the superior status of the one addressed, but see on 7:21 above for the fuller sense clearly intended in at least some Matthean contexts.[23] The man's assumption that Jesus *can* cure his disease, reflecting Jesus' popular reputation as set out in 4:23-25, indicates that he is doing more than merely being polite. More unusual is the explicit raising of the question of Jesus' *will* to heal,[24] which perhaps reflects the general horror with which "leprosy" was regarded. A Jewish teacher with a proper concern to maintain ritual purity might be expected to refuse to have anything to do with him.

3 Physical touch is a frequent (but not essential, 8:5-13) element in accounts of Jesus' healings, but here it has an unusual significance and is emphasized by the double expression "stretched out his hand and touched him." Other people who were ill might naturally be touched, but to touch a "leper" was to contract defilement (Lev 5:3 etc.). If anyone else was near enough to see what happened, they would have been horrified. Cf. 9:20-22 and 9:25 for other instances where Jesus is in contact with the "unclean." The narrative does not explain whether Jesus simply ignored the ritual consequences of this defiant mark of acceptance (as the principle enunciated in 15:11 might suggest), or whether the instant healing of the disease through the touch made the issue irrelevant. For the instant, visible cure of "leprosy" as a miraculous act cf. Exod 4:6-8; 2 Kgs 5:14. The reader is left to ponder the

22. For Matthew's use of ἀκολουθέω see my *Matthew: Evangelist,* 262-63.

23. C. F. D. Moule, *Origin,* 175-76, usefully discusses the implications of προσκυνέω; cf. also ibid., 35-44, on the developing meaning of κύριος.

24. In my commentary on Mark (*Mark,* 117) I inclined to the view that ἐὰν θέλῃς here is simply a polite formula, "if you would be so kind," rather than expressing a real doubt. That Matthew has retained it in his slimmed-down version of the story suggests that for him at least it had a more substantial significance.

christological implications of Jesus' remarkable reply, "I am willing" (rather than "God is willing").

4 The demand that those healed should not talk about it is not so prominent a feature in Matthew as in Mark, but will recur in 9:30 and as a generalization in 12:16, where Matthew will explain it by a lengthy quotation from Isa 42:1-4 concerning the nondemonstrative nature of the Servant's acts of deliverance. There it appears to be a general policy of not encouraging popular enthusiasm for a wonder-worker, and Mark's additional comment here on what happened when the instruction was disregarded (Mark 1:45) points to the pragmatic value of such secrecy.[25] But Matthew gives no such explanation here, and the immediately following instruction to go and show the priest that he was cured would suggest that this is not so much a blanket prohibition as a matter of priorities: *first* show the priest, and so gain official sanction for reentering "clean" society; to tell others before the priest had been informed and had ratified the man's new status would have been pointless as well as contrary to established law. Once that was done, we may assume that others would be told, since a former "leper" could hardly be expected to reappear as a healthy member of society without people needing to know how it had happened. The visit to the priest and the sacrifices would take a long time: the ritual covers eight days (Lev 14:8-10) and the offerings would have to be made in the temple, necessitating a journey to Jerusalem and back before the man could rejoin his Galilean society.

The examination by the priest and the resultant cleansing ritual and offering (Lev 14:1-32) would be a "witness to them" (the people, to whom the man has been forbidden to go directly with the news) that the cure was complete and the ostracized person might safely be accepted back. That is probably all that the final phrase of the pericope implies. On two further occasions Matthew will speak of future events (the disciples' appearance before rulers and kings, 10:18, and the worldwide preaching of the gospel, 24:14) occurring "as a witness to [them and] the Gentiles," and it is therefore sometimes suggested that the "witness" here relates not only or mainly to the man's own reintegration into society, but to increasing public awareness of Jesus and his special role — in other words, witness to the gospel.[26] But that is a lot to build on just three occurrences of the phrase *eis martyrion*. While it is true that this and other healings did contribute substantially to the development of the gospel message of deliverance through Jesus, in this context and in direct connection with the visit to the priest (in Jerusalem, not in Galilee

---

25. Keener, 261-63, gives a valuable perspective of the issue, pointing out that the avoidance of overt claims to a messianic or prophetic status is well attested elsewhere in Jewish and pagan culture.

26. So R. J. Banks, *Jesus,* 103-4.

where for now the "witness" to the gospel is focused) the phrase is more naturally interpreted in the less theological sense outlined above. Still less is there any hint of the idea sometimes floated that the man's visit is seen as a witness *to the priest*[27] that Jesus is a genuine healer or that in sending the man to make his offering he is duly observing the laws of purity; the plural "to them" tells decisively against that interpretation, since only one priest is mentioned. It is of course true that here we see the Jesus who in 5:17 felt the need to defend himself against the charge of "abolishing the law" actively encouraging a man to follow the prescriptions of that law, but this was a formal necessity for the man's readmission to society, and should not be pressed as an indication of Jesus' principled observance of the purity laws. When the issue is raised directly in 15:1-20, we shall meet a much less conventional approach; and it will be an issue between Jesus and the scribes, not a confrontation with the priests.

b. The Centurion's Servant (8:5-13)

The next appeal for miraculous help comes from a Gentile, and Matthew tells the story in a way which emphasizes the significance of an approach to the Jewish Messiah from a non-Jew. The only other such appeal from a Gentile in Matthew is in 15:21-28, and there are important similarities between the two stories, both of which explore the paradox of a Gentile's expectation of help from a Jewish healer, and in both of which Jesus' initial reluctance to respond is overcome by the faith of the suppliant, which refuses to be put off and which in each case draws Jesus' admiring comment. Significantly, these are also the only two stories in Matthew involving a healing from a distance.

This is the only miracle story which Matthew shares with Luke (7:1-10) and not also with Mark.[28] The basic story line is the same, but Matthew typically omits material which he regards as unessential to the narrative, the

27. Or even "against the priest[s]." In Mark 6:11 εἰς μαρτύριον αὐτοῖς has this threatening sense, but only the context indicates that. Here and in Matthew's other two uses of the phrase (10:18; 24:14) a positive sense fits better.

28. There are also similarities to the story of the distant healing of the royal official's son in John 4:46-54, and it is commonly assumed that the two stories are variants of the same tradition, but the differences are considerable. The Johannine story does not involve the racial issue which is central to the two Synoptic distant-healing stories, since the βασιλικός there was presumably a Jewish official of Herod Antipas, not an officer of the Roman army. It involves a son, not a servant (see on v. 6), and there is little verbal similarity. John's story is located not in Capernaum but in Cana, though the official's son is in Capernaum. If the two are variant traditions deriving from a single incident, the Johannine version has diverged too far from the Synoptic to be of any exegetical help for Matthew. It is probably more likely that two separate incidents lie behind the traditions.

warm relations between the centurion and the local Jewish community, and his use of Jewish elders as intermediaries (Luke 7:3-5). We shall note below that Matthew may have omitted this element not only in order to abbreviate but also because the inclusion of the Jewish elders would distract attention from the direct confrontation between the Gentile officer and the Jewish healer which is important for Matthew's version of the story. The focus of that confrontation in Matthew, not in Luke, is a challenging and apparently discouraging question, "Am *I* to come and heal him?" which resembles Jesus' dismissive reply to the Gentile woman in 15:24. In the dialogue that follows there are two significant differences in Matthew's version. Whereas "Not even in Israel have I found such faith" (Luke 7:9) suggests that there may be great faith in Israel but that this man's is even greater, "I have not found anyone in Israel with faith like this" (Matt 8:10) is far less complimentary to Israel. And following that pronouncement Matthew introduces (vv. 11-12) a saying which occurs in a different context in Luke (13:28-29), which makes explicit the salvation-historical significance of this Gentile's faith in relation to the unbelief of the "sons of the kingdom." All this indicates that what for Luke was a story of a good and humble man whose extraordinary request was granted is in Matthew more a paradigm for the extension of the gospel of Israel's Messiah to include also those who had no natural claim on him.[29]

The introduced saying in vv. 11-12 is one of the clearest statements of Matthew's understanding of the relation between Israel and the new community which results from the ministry of Jesus, and it gains added emphasis by its inclusion in this context of the Gentile officer's faith, which no one in Israel could match. Its vision of "the kingdom of heaven" combines elements of continuity (in that the Hebrew patriarchs remain at the head of the table in the messianic banquet) and of discontinuity (in that new people come in from east and west, while "those who belong to the kingdom of heaven" find themselves outside, exiled to the place traditionally reserved for the Gentiles). Here is the basic outline of a theology of the people of God which will be worked out through the confrontation with the Jewish leadership in chs. 21–23, explained in symbolic language in the discourse concerning the end of the old order in chs. 24–25, and triumphantly summed up in the command to go and make disciples of all nations in 28:19. This initial confrontation with a man of faith who is not a Jew also prepares us for the narrative of Jesus' extension of his ministry to Gentiles in 15:21-39. We should not be surprised, in the light of the Gentiles who were among the first to welcome his coming (2:1-11).

29. I have argued at greater length for this interpretation of Matthew's version of the story over against Luke's in I. H. Marshall (ed.), *NT Interpretation*, 253-64.

For all its salvation-historical symbolism, however, this is also in it-self a memorable story of the authority of Jesus to heal. That authority is the explicit basis of the centurion's confidence (vv. 8-9). In this case it is accen-tuated by the need to effect the healing from a distance, simply "by a word." That is all the centurion dare ask, since he cannot expect the Jewish healer to enter his Gentile home, but it is a remarkable request, and Matthew ensures that we notice its literal fulfillment by pointing out that the healing took place "at that moment," with Jesus still at a distance.[30] The only other distant heal-ing in Matthew also involves a Gentile who comes to Jesus to beg for help for a person left at home; it seems that it was taken for granted that while Jesus could not be expected to go into a Gentile home, this was no barrier to his ability to heal.

5 We have been informed in 4:13 that Jesus has made his base in Capernaum, and he now returns home after his trip into the hills. Here he is easily found by a local army officer who has heard of his reputation as a healer (4:23-25). There was no Roman legion stationed in Palestine at this time, but Herod Antipas had a small force of auxiliary troops at his disposal.[31] We have no means of knowing how large a force may have been stationed in Caper-naum, but the centurion (commander of a unit of theoretically a hundred troops) may well have been the senior officer in the area; his prominence in the local community according to Luke 7:3-5 suggests this. The auxiliaries, unlike the legionaries, would not be Roman citizens but drawn from the non-Jewish population of surrounding areas such as Phoenicia and Syria. Both the centurion and his servant may therefore be assumed to be non-Jewish, as in-deed the following dialogue requires (and as Luke underlines by explaining how well he got on with the Jewish community, Luke 7:4-5). By omitting Luke's mention of the Jewish friends whom the centurion used as intermediar-ies, Matthew has ensured that the reader will not be distracted from the direct, face-to-face confrontation of the Gentile officer and the Jewish healer which is the essential basis for Matthew's version of the dialogue which follows.

6 The Greek term *pais* can mean "child" as well as "servant," and

---

30. This point is spelled out more prosaically in the "parallel" story of distant healing in John 4:51-53. The rabbinic story of the distant healing through prayer of Gamaliel's son by R. Hanina ben Dosa (*b. Ber.* 34b) testifies to the strong impression such a healing would make. The uncertainty over the date of Hanina (and over the date of Mat-thew's writing) casts some doubt on the suggestion of D. Instone-Brewer, *Traditions,* 1:71, that Matthew's account is intended to be compared with that story, inviting the reader to contrast the status of the patients, the Gentile servant with the son of a prominent Jewish rabbi.

31. For the military situation in Palestine see Schürer, 1:362-67. With specific ref-erence to this centurion see A. N. Sherwin-White, *Roman Society,* 124; A. H. Mead, *JSNT* 23 (1985) 69-72 (Mead takes him to be the same as the βασιλικός of John 4:46).

the fact that in the partially parallel story in John 4:46-54 the patient is the official's *son* has led many to suggest either that Matthew is using *pais* in that sense or that the ambiguity of the word has led to a story which originally concerned a son becoming in the course of transmission a story about a servant. The usage of *pais* in the NT does not encourage the former option. The only use in the sense of "son" is John 4:51 (where it is parallel to *huios,* "son," in vv. 46-47, 50, and 53 and to *paidion* in v. 49). In eight other cases it means "child," but without implying any relationship to the speaker or to any character in the narrative. In twelve cases it means "servant," including the parallel to this narrative in Luke 7:7 where it denotes the same person who is called a *doulos,* "slave," in v. 2. For Luke the patient was clearly not the centurion's son, and there is no reason to think that Matthew disagrees. Moreover, it is questionable whether the conditions of service in the Roman auxiliaries allowed a centurion to be accompanied by his family.[32] We may reasonably suppose that the *pais* was a soldier detailed to act as personal aide to the commanding officer, though the term could also cover a domestic slave. At any rate, we may be fairly sure that for Matthew *pais* here means "servant," not "son"; it is only the "parallel" with John 4:46-54 which might suggest otherwise, and we have seen (n. 28) reason to doubt whether that story can help us in understanding Matthew's account.

We can only guess the nature of the "paralysis." What we would call polio or a stroke might be possible causes;[33] in either case there would be no prospect of medical cure. In appealing to Jesus as *kyrie* (see on 7:21) here and in v. 8 the man makes clear that he is looking for something beyond normal help. Even if the term is simply conventional politeness, it would be remarkable as addressed by an officer of the occupying forces to a socially insignificant member of the subject race. But the assumption of Jesus' unique authority in the centurion's words in vv. 8-9 makes it clear that it is more than mere politeness.

7 The nature of Jesus' response to the centurion's approach depends on how this verse is translated. While commentators generally recognize that

32. The οἶκος of Cornelius (Acts 10:2) is not further specified and need not include family members, though he had συγγενεῖς within inviting distance (10:24). Caesarea is in any case likely to have been a more permanent posting than a small town like Capernaum. Keener, 266, is prepared to be more definite: "Roman soldiers were not permitted to have legal families." He cites a variety of evidence, which is, however, weakened by the fact that he curiously assumes that this centurion was a Roman legionary rather than an officer in the auxiliary forces, even though he accepts that there was no legion in Palestine at the time (n. 15).

33. The suggestion of Carter, 201, that it was the result of beating or torture, and so that "Jesus' healing counters the short-term damage inflicted by imperial power," is more imaginative than derived from anything in the narrative.

both the wording and the flow of the dialogue require that it be construed as a question,[34] English versions have been slow to catch up with this exegesis: among earlier versions I have found this translation only in E. V. Rieu and in the NEB margin; more recently see TNIV.[35] The traditional translation as a statement or promise, "I will come and heal him," takes no account of the pronoun *egō,* which is not only grammatically unnecessary and unusual when the subject is already expressed in the first-person verb, but is also given added emphasis by being placed first in the sentence. If this is a statement, the emphasis requires a translation such as JB's "I will come myself and cure him," but such emphasis sounds surprisingly pompous on the part of Jesus; there is no suggestion here or elsewhere that he might have sent someone else to do the healing for him! If, however, this is a question, the *egō* performs an obvious and important function: it draws out the surprising nature of the request apparently implied in the Gentile officer's appeal to a local Jewish healer, and the emphatic *"I"* draws attention to the highly irregular suggestion that he, a good Jew, should visit a Gentile house — "You want *me* to come and heal him?"

The flow of the dialogue confirms this interpretation. So far the centurion has made no request, but merely stated the situation. Jesus' question thus draws out the request which was implicit. But the emphasized *egō* ensures that the boldness of the implied request is not passed over. Matthew's narrative has not so far seen the adult Jesus in contact with Gentiles, and the only time in the whole gospel (or indeed in any of the gospels) when he will enter a Gentile building is when he has no choice in the governor's headquarters in Jerusalem at his trial. Acts 10–11 shows us the repugnance felt by even a relatively open-minded Jew to such "defilement" (cf. John 18:28); for a Jewish teacher in the public eye it would be an even more defiant breach of taboo than even Jesus' controversial mixing with "tax collectors and sinners" (9:10-11). Is that really what this army officer is expecting of him? The centurion's remarkable reply follows naturally from such a probing question: "Of course not; I couldn't expect you to come under my roof; all I am asking for is a word of healing, spoken here where you are."

Jesus' question thus places the racial issue firmly in the forefront of the reader's understanding of the story, and the implied reluctance (indeed, more than "implied," in that Jesus did not in fact *"come and heal him"*)[36] produces

34. I have argued the case more fully in I. H. Marshall (ed.), *NT Interpretation,* 256-57. See also H. J. Held, *Tradition,* 193-94: Held refers to "the astonished or indignant question of Jesus, whether he as a Jew would be expected to enter into a Gentile house."

35. The Nestle-Aland and UBS Greek texts both give the interrogative punctuation in the margin, the latter quoting the *Traduction Oecuménique de la Bible* (1988) as adopting it.

36. A further argument against the noninterrogative interpretation of v. 7 is that it has Matthew attributing to Jesus a promise which he does not in fact keep.

the same tension between Jesus' mission as Jewish Messiah and his concern for all peoples which will be even more starkly raised in his reply to the Canaanite woman: "I was sent only to the lost sheep of the house of Israel" (15:24). The two Gentile-stories follow the same line of development: request met by a racial rebuff, which in turn provokes a remarkable declaration of faith in the light of which Jesus' apparent reluctance is overcome and the Gentile is restored. It is not the least virtue of the exegesis that recognizes v. 7 as a question that it enables these two stories to be read so closely in parallel.

8 In what way did the centurion feel himself not "fit" to have Jesus in his house?[37] The issue cannot be his social status: he was socially the more highly placed of the two, and in his following comments he deals with Jesus as an equal at a "man-to-man" level. It is possible that he feels some sense of personal inadequacy at a moral or spiritual level, not because he was an especially bad man (Luke, who also reports this comment, has gone out of his way to emphasize the man's goodness and kindness, Luke 7:2-5) but because he recognizes "the majesty and authority of Jesus, which lift him above everything human, especially in the non-Jewish sphere."[38] But it is most likely in context, as we have noted on v. 7, that Jesus' question has made him acutely aware of the impropriety from a Jewish point of view of a religious teacher visiting his Gentile (and therefore "unclean"; see *m. 'Ohal.* 18:7) home. Like the Canaanite woman in 15:27, he is prepared to allow for Jewish religious sensibilities in this area, but he sees no reason why they should interfere with his request, which, it now transpires, was not dependent on a personal visit from Jesus. All he needs is a "word"; in v. 16 we shall find the same expression used for Jesus' normal method of exorcism as opposed to physical healing, by a simple command and without touching the person affected. The gospel accounts of physical healings, however, elsewhere depend on the presence of Jesus and frequently involve his touching the patient or their touching him. The healing requested here is therefore atypical, probably on account of the racial barrier involved, and is a more clearly miraculous method. The simple confidence that as a result of such a command "my servant will be cured" is explained in the centurion's following words.

9 A military man recognizes "authority" when he sees it. The centurion has both superiors and inferiors in the military hierarchy; he both receives and issues orders, and orders are expected to be obeyed. The orders

---

37. The unusual Greek word order (ἵνα μου ὑπὸ τὴν στέγην εἰσέλθῃς) probably emphasizes "my" (though for an opposite view see BDF 473[1]), perhaps in response to the ἐγώ of Jesus' question.

38. K. H. Rengstorf, *TDNT* 3:294, s.v. ἱκανός. Some such sense would correspond well to John the Baptist's use of οὐκ εἰμὶ ἱκανός in 3:11. For similar uses of ἱκανός see 1 Cor 15:9; 2 Cor 2:16.

which he issues at the human level are compared with those he expects Jesus to issue at the spiritual level, and he sees no reason why physical disability should resist Jesus' authority any more than his own subordinates resist his. His is the no-nonsense faith of a practical man.

It would be pedantic to use the clause "For I, too, am a man under authority" as the basis for a christological argument; the point of comparison is in the issuing of effective commands, not in the respective hierarchical status of Jesus and this (subordinate) officer. There is in any case no problem in the recognition of Jesus as a "man" (which he was!), and if the centurion was sufficiently well informed to understand that Jesus was operating under the authority of the God of Israel as he himself was operating under the authority of his military superiors, Matthew would have no problem with this. But this pericope is not about defining Jesus' christological status, but about the recognition of his unquestioned authority.

10   Jesus recognizes something unique in this man's grasp of the situation. This is the only time the verb *thaumazō*, "to be amazed," which typically describes people's reaction to Jesus (8:27; 9:33; 15:31; 21:20; 22:22; 27:14), is used by Matthew with Jesus himself as the subject. The man's simple statement of confidence in his supernatural authority has mightily impressed him, and draws out an appreciative comment to "his followers," probably not now the following crowd whom we met in v. 1, since Jesus has meanwhile arrived back in Capernaum, but his more regular entourage of disciples. The following words challenge them, and through them the readers of the gospel, to think radical thoughts about where true "faith" may be expected to be found. The formula "I tell you truly" (see on 5:18) marks this out as a pronouncement to be noted. The relatively few references to "faith" and "believing" in Matthew are mainly concerned with the practical faith which expects miracles from Jesus and in answer to prayer.[39] Matthew uses the verb predominantly either in this sense or more generally of "believing" a person or a report, though there are two cases of the idiom (more familiar from John or Paul) of "believing in" Jesus (18:6; 27:42); the noun *pistis,* apart from a single use in the sense of "faithfulness" (23:23), always denotes the practical faith which expects a miracle, and in several cases, as here in v. 13, such "faith" is explicitly cited as the reason for a miraculous healing (9:2, 22, 29; 15:28). The remarkable "faith" of this centurion, then, is to be understood not in the Pauline sense of a soteriological commitment, but as the practical conviction that Jesus has the authority to heal. It is in this sense that he surpasses everyone in Israel. Matthew has told us in 4:23-25 of widespread Jewish enthusiasm for Jesus as a healer, and the numbers brought to him for healing in

---

39. It is in this connection, too, that Matthew uses his special word ὀλιγόπιστος, "faithless"; see on 6:30.

v. 16 will confirm that reputation. But this soldier's instinctive recognition of authority and his bold request for healing at a distance have sounded a new note. He points the way forward toward a level of response to Jesus which no Jew has yet been able to match.

11-12 If the "faith" of v. 10 was of an essentially practical nature, it is now taken, in the saying which Matthew has added here (see introductory comments), as a symbol of something more "Pauline": the vivid imagery of this saying of Jesus conveys a message similar to Paul's explanation in Rom 4 of how all who believe, Gentile as well as Jew, are now children of Abraham. So here this believing Gentile represents the "many" who will now come within the sphere of salvation; his story provides a preview of the insight which was to come from the faith of another centurion in Acts 11:18: "Then to the Gentiles also God has granted repentance leading to life." This saying concerns who does, and who does not, ultimately belong to "the kingdom of heaven." The imagery of reclining at table with the Hebrew patriarchs would inevitably speak to Jewish readers of the messianic banquet which was a popular way of thinking of the ultimate blessedness of the true people of God. In popular Jewish thought it would be taken for granted that, while not every Jew might prove worthy of a place at the banquet, it would be a Jewish gathering, while non-Jews would find themselves outside in the darkness; to be the people of God meant, for all practical purposes, to be Jewish. Jesus' saying dramatically challenges this instinctive assumption, both by including "many" others from foreign parts ("east and west") on the guest list, and also daring to exclude those who were assumed to have a right to be there, the "sons of the kingdom." To add insult to injury, the fate of these "sons of the kingdom" is described in the terms traditionally used in Jewish descriptions of the fate of the ungodly (and therefore, predominantly, the Gentiles), "darkness outside," "weeping and gnashing of teeth." The reason they are rejected is not explicit within this saying, but in the context in which Matthew has placed it, it must be linked with the fact that Jesus has not found in Israel faith like that of the centurion. Thus belonging to the kingdom of heaven is found to depend not on ancestry but on faith.

Such, in brief, is the traditional understanding of this saying. It is, to my mind, one which fits well both with the narrative context into which Matthew has placed it, the "faith" of a Gentile which is greater than that of anyone in Israel, and with the wider theology of the reconstituted people of God which will develop throughout this gospel and which is one of its most distinctive motifs. But not all interpreters agree. Three issues need to be addressed: (a) Does the language justify a reference to the messianic banquet? (b) Are the "many from the east and west" really to be understood as Gentiles? (c) Who are the "sons of the kingdom"?

(a) The setting is explicitly "the kingdom of heaven," which we have

316

seen to be a term with a broad range of reference (see on 3:2). It is that situation where God is recognized as king, his will is done, and his purpose achieved. While the term in Matthew normally refers to the situation on earth where God's people live under his sovereignty, there is an important strand of usage in which "entering the kingdom of heaven" functions as a term for ultimate salvation (5:20; 7:21; 18:3; 19:23-24; 21:31), and in 13:41, 43 the kingdom of the Son of Man and of the Father denotes the state of final blessedness from which the wicked are excluded and in which the righteous shine. The closest parallel to this usage, however, is in 26:29, where Jesus envisages drinking new wine with his disciples "in the kingdom of my Father" after his death. There is no explicit mention of food and drink here, but "reclining" (anaklinomai) suggests a meal, probably a more formal or festive one.[40] The presence of Abraham, Isaac, and Jacob lifts this above any ordinary meal; Jewish tradition not surprisingly gave them a leading role at the messianic banquet (b. Pesaḥ. 119b; Exod. Rab. 25:8). The imagery of the messianic banquet derives from Isa 25:6 (cf. 65:13-14) and was elaborated in Jewish literature both in the apocalyptic and the rabbinic traditions, but whereas in Isaiah it was a feast "for all peoples," Jewish tradition soon made it a blessing specifically for Israel.[41]

(b) While most interpreters follow the line adopted here, that the "many from the east and west" are Gentiles, Davies and Allison, 2:27-28, argue that the reference is to "unprivileged Jews," just as in 21:31-32 it is *Jewish* tax collectors and prostitutes who will go into the kingdom of God in front of those of the religious establishment who have failed to respond to the call of John the Baptist and of Jesus. That would undoubtedly be a theme congenial to Matthew, but here the context is decisively against it: the faith commended in v. 10 is that of a Gentile in specific contrast to Israel.[42] The chief arguments offered for a Jewish reference here are that this saying draws on language which in the OT depicts the regathering of Israel after exile and that in the OT the messianic feast is associated with the return of diaspora Jews rather than with Gentiles. These points may be granted, but to establish what OT expressions referred to in their original context is not to determine

---

40. See J. Jeremias, *Words,* 48-49; R. T. France, *NIDNTT* 3:587-89; in relation to the messianic banquet BDAG 65 suggests for ἀνακλίνομαι the translation "*dine in style* (or some similar rendering, not simply 'eat')." C. L. Blomberg, *Holiness,* 95-96, argues, however, that this Greco-Roman style of eating had become so widely adopted in Jewish circles that one cannot be sure from the terms themselves what sort of meal is in view.

41. See Str-B 4/2:1154-56; J. Behm, *TDNT* 2:34-35.

42. The rather desperate suggestion of Davies and Allison that "in Israel" here is a purely geographical term (a usage for which it is hard to find any NT parallel) makes the phrase redundant, in that, as they themselves point out, that is the only area Jesus has yet operated in! In speaking of a Gentile's faith, the racial sense is surely undeniable.

the way Jesus or Matthew may have developed such language (see Gundry, n. 89). It is precisely the force of this saying that it takes familiar OT categories and deploys them in a new and shocking direction. The OT gathering of the people of God "from the east and west" (Ps 107:3; Isa 43:5-6; 49:12; cf. Deut 30:4) provides the model for the ingathering of a new people from all over the world (see further on 24:31), but that model is no longer restricted to ethnic Israel.[43] Such a reangling of OT motifs is entirely in accord with the consistent NT hermeneutic which understands the nationalistic and territorial promises of the OT in terms of a new supranational people of God, a theme which Davies has himself been in the forefront of expounding.[44] The inclusion of Gentiles in the (Jewish) messianic feast is part of the same theological reorientation. The argument of Davies and Allison that if the "sons of the kingdom" are Jews in contrast to Gentiles, the saying "consigns all of Israel to perdition" is remarkably literalistic: it is not said that *all* the "sons of the kingdom" are excluded, and the presence of the Hebrew patriarchs at the feast makes it clear that what is here set out is not a Gentile takeover to the total exclusion of Jews, but a messianic community in which ancestry has ceased to be the determining factor.[45]

(c) The paradoxical force of the saying depends on these "sons of the kingdom" being those whom everyone would expect to be included.[46] When the same term is used in 13:38, it denotes those who will be saved in distinction from the "sons of the evil one" who will be rooted out. Here, however, they are those who *should* have been saved but who are shockingly declared to be consigned to the place of the ungodly. Again we are in familiar Matthean territory, those who are in the position of privilege but who have failed to live up to their calling, and who will be symbolized by the disobedient son of 21:28-32, the defaulting tenants of 21:33-44, and those who despised their invitation to the feast in 22:1-10. All these will be Jewish groups, but the issue as to how far they represent the whole nation or only its discred-

43. I have explored this theme in the sayings of Jesus in my *Jesus and the OT,* 62-65, 95. The wording of this saying echoes these visions of *Jewish* regathering rather than those which envisage Gentiles either worshipping Yahweh where they are (Isa 45:6; 59:19; Mal 1:11) or coming to Jerusalem (Isa 2:2-3; 60:3-4). For criticism of J. Jeremias's well-known identification here of the OT theme of the eschatological pilgrimage of the Gentiles to Jerusalem (J. Jeremias, *Promise,* 55-63) see G. R. Beasley-Murray, *Kingdom,* 170-72.

44. W. D. Davies, *The Gospel and the Land.*

45. B. Charette, *Recompense,* 69-72, rightly insists that this saying includes Gentiles along with faithful Jews rather than excluding all Jews from the banquet.

46. For the familiar idiom "sons of . . ." in the sense of "belonging to . . .," "destined for . . .," cf. 9:15, "sons of the bridechamber"; 23:15, "son of gehenna"; and Luke 16:8 (cf. 20:34-35), "sons of this age; sons of light."

ited leadership will remain an important exegetical question when we come to those chapters. We shall note then the need for a new "nation" to take over the vineyard (21:43), and yet it is clear that Jesus and his disciples, whom we must assume to represent that new "nation," are themselves also Jewish. Here, as there, it is not a simple matter of "Jews out; Gentiles in." Rather, we are to think of a reconstitution of the true people of God which is no longer on the basis of racial ancestry, but, as symbolized by the Gentile centurion, on the basis of faith in Jesus. The words of John the Baptist on the uselessness of an appeal to Abrahamic ancestry (3:9) have prepared the way for this radical rethinking of what it means to be the people of God.[47]

The "many from the east and west" are pictured here not merely as sharing the residue of Israel's eschatological blessings (eating the crumbs that fall from the children's table, 15:27), but even as reclining at the same table as the Hebrew patriarchs who, we are to assume, do not fear ritual defilement by eating with those who do not share Israel's purity. It is not suggested apparently that they come in as proselytes, but that they are accepted simply as Gentiles, on equal terms with the patriarchs. But if that side of the paradox is shocking to a traditional Jewish theology, what follows is worse: the "sons of the kingdom" will find themselves in the place they had reserved for the ungodly. For "darkness outside" see, for example, *1 En.* 103:7; 108:14-15; *Pss. Sol.* 14:9; 15:10; *Exod. Rab.* 14:2 describes darkness as covering the wicked in Gehinnom. For "weeping and gnashing of teeth"[48] (a favorite Matthean phrase; cf. 13:42, 50; 22:13; 24:51; 25:30) see *1 En.* 108:3, 5; *2 En.* 40:12.[49] In *1 En.* 108 the punishment of the wicked is increased by their being able to see the bliss of the righteous, and the phrase "darkness outside" may be intended to picture the bright lights of the banquet visible to those who are excluded (cf. "you will see" in the parallel to this saying, Luke 13:28).

13 The narrative is resumed with a simple closure which brings together two key elements in the story, the "faith" of the centurion and the im-

---

47. The following summary by J. Jeremias, *Promise,* 48, underlines the shocking nature of such language: "According to the popular view in the time of Jesus, Israel's superiority over the Gentiles consisted in the fact that Israel, by virtue of its lineal descent from Abraham, enjoyed the benefits of the vicarious merits of the patriarchs, and the consequent assurance of final salvation. It was the current belief that no descendant of Abraham could be lost."

48. Gundry's suggestion (146; cf. *Use,* 77) of a specific allusion here to the wicked gnashing their teeth in Ps 112:10 is unnecessary. The phrase is conventional, and the contexts are not similar.

49. Many further Jewish texts about Gehenna are collected by Str-B 4/2:1029-1119. D. C. Sim, *Apocalyptic,* 140, however, finds few parallels in Jewish apocalyptic to this actual phrase, and concludes that "Matthew oversteps a boundary which few of his contemporaries had crossed."

mediate effect of Jesus' authoritative word, spoken from a distance. The third-person imperative, "so let it be done for you," indicates not merely a prediction but, like Jesus' other words of healing and exorcism, an effective pronouncement. It is what the philosophers call a "performative utterance," not stating that something will happen, still less merely wishing it, but making it happen. This is the cure "by a word" which the centurion had asked for (v. 8) and which Matthew will again emphasize as Jesus' method in exorcism in v. 16. The close similarity of this verse to 15:28 further underlines the links between these two accounts of Jesus' response to a Gentile request.

c. Peter's Mother-in-Law (8:14-15)

After the high drama of the meeting with the "leper" and the remarkable healing of the centurion's servant by a word of power, this is a simple little narrative. Whereas in those incidents we were alerted to their wider implications with regard to ritual uncleanness and racial segregation, the banal domesticity of this scene invites no such theological extrapolation. If Matthew had in mind that a woman was also an underprivileged or even in some senses "excluded" person (see introductory remarks on 8:1-17), he does not draw this out in his narrative. It is simply a story of Jesus meeting with illness and responding with effective healing power. Among the many miraculous healings noted in summaries such as v. 16 and 4:23-24; 14:34-36 the only distinctive feature which justifies this one being individually related is the family connection with the leader of the disciple group. That is no doubt why it was remembered and narrated in a church where Peter remained a dominant figure.

The setting is still Capernaum (v. 5), and in Mark's narrative this incident is part of a sequence set on a sabbath day in Capernaum. Matthew does not have the same narrative framework, but the mention of Peter's house (see 17:24-27) confirms the location.[50] This incident and that in 17:24-27 suggest that the house of Simon and Andrew (as Mark 1:29 designates it) may have served as Jesus' base in Capernaum, though the note that Jesus had "settled" there before his meeting with the fishermen (4:13) might more naturally mean that he had his own residence in the town. Matthew has told us in 4:18 of Simon's nickname, Peter, and uses that distinctive name rather than the

---

50. The first-century-B.C. building identified by the Franciscans as underlying the octagonal Byzantine church (the remains of which have been covered since 1990 by a vast "suspended" memorial church) near the synagogue in Capernaum may well be the house of Peter, subsequently developed in the later first century A.D. as a Christian place of meeting. The identification has gained an impressive range of support among archeologists. See, e.g., E. M. Meyers and J. F. Strange, *Archaeology*, 59-60, 114-16, 128-30; V. C. Corbo, *ABD* 1:867-68.

common Simon throughout his narrative (for a partial exception see 17:25) even though he will not recount Jesus' giving of that name until 16:16-18. The fact that Peter has a home and family in Capernaum places an important caveat against a too radical understanding of the renunciation involved in following Jesus: Simon and Andrew left their nets, but not their home and (extended) family. For Peter's wife cf. 1 Cor 9:5.

The "fever" is no more specific than the "paralysis" of v. 6; we have no means of knowing how seriously ill she was. This time Jesus is actually there in the house, and so this healing employs the more normal element of touch. The aorist tense of "left her" implies an immediate cure, and this is underlined by her getting up and resuming her household duties without any time for convalescence.

d. Conclusion of the First Group of Miracles (8:16-17)

This more general healing session "in the evening" follows immediately after the healing of Peter's mother-in-law also in Mark and Luke. The time of day is significant in Mark, since he has said that the exorcism in the synagogue and the healing in Peter's house took place on the sabbath, so that it was only after sunset that people could properly come for healing. But Matthew has not mentioned what day it was. His summary of Jesus' ministry of exorcism and healing (the two types of deliverance being as usual carefully distinguished in the terms used for both diagnosis and cure) is brief and lacking in detail. The one notable feature here is the mention that, in contrast with the elaborate incantations and techniques used by other exorcists at the time,[51] Jesus drove out demons[52] simply "with a command," the same wording which was used by the centurion in v. 8, thus again emphasizing Jesus' unquestionable authority. But in Matthew this brief traditional summary is also made to serve a special purpose as the introduction for a formula-quotation which draws out the significance of this aspect of Jesus' ministry, an editorial comment on the story so far.

As usual when the quotation is drawn from one of the major prophets, the formula includes the prophet's name. The passage from which it is drawn, the fourth "servant song" in Isa 52:13–53:12, is one which may well have been framed originally in reference to the suffering of the people of

---

51. See, e.g., Josephus, *Ant.* 8.46-48; *Pesiq. Rab Kah.* 40a-b; Philostratus, *Vit. Apoll.* 4.20; Lucian, *Philops.* 16.

52. The reference to the expelled demons simply as πνεύματα is unusual. Matthew elsewhere sometimes uses Mark's term πνεῦμα ἀκάθαρτον (10:1; 12:43-45) but usually refers to them as δαιμόνια. Here the meaning of the unqualified πνεύματα is determined by the immediately preceding δαιμονιζομένους.

God, or more probably of some group within them (since Israel corporately is often addressed or described in Isa 40–55 as God's "servant"), but which is expressed in terms of an individual "servant" whose suffering benefits the people as a whole. As a result some early Jewish interpretation took it as presenting a messianic figure, whose suffering was variously interpreted (or evaded — see the remarkable rewriting of the passage in *Targum Jonathan*). Early Christian interpreters were accustomed to find this prophecy fulfilled in Jesus, but the verse here singled out for quotation is not the normal focus of christological interest, and when it is alluded to elsewhere in the NT it is understood not, as here, in relation to Jesus' healing ministry, but of his dealing with his people's sin (1 Pet 2:24; cf. Rom 4:25). The parallelism in Isa 53 suggests that this metaphorical interpretation represents what the prophet's language about "weaknesses and illnesses" was intended to convey, but Matthew has also seen in the literal sense of the Hebrew terms used ("illnesses" and "pains") a pointer to Jesus the healer. The LXX correctly interpreted the terms in context, and so rendered the clause "He carries our sins and is distressed on our behalf" (similarly also the targum), but Matthew either knows a different Greek version[53] or has produced his own more literal rendering of the Hebrew.[54] It thus seems that for Matthew the figure of the Servant of Yahweh in Isaiah, which other early Christians looked to only for an explanation of Jesus' suffering and death, was a more holistic model for Jesus' ministry as a whole.[55] His only other formal quotation from the relevant Isaiah passages (12:17-21, quoting Isa 42:1-4) also relates to the style of Jesus' ministry, not to his passion. Not that Matthew is uninterested in the traditional use of the Servant figure in connection with Jesus' messianic mission and death; we have seen possible allusions in 3:15 and 3:17, and the Servant model will become central to Jesus' explanation of his death in 20:28; 26:28 as well as probably underlying the whole concept of messianic suffering which will be developed from 16:21 on. But here and in 12:17-21 we see evidence of a more wide-ranging meditation on that scriptural model than elsewhere in the NT.[56]

53. M. J. J. Menken, *Matthew's Bible,* 35-49, takes this option, as consonant with his thesis that Matthew generally used a "revised LXX" (which of course is not otherwise available to us). Here, as elsewhere, the matter seems to defy clear demonstration either way.

54. So R. Beaton, *Isaiah's Christ,* 111-14.

55. L. Novakovic, *Messiah,* 131-32, suggests that Matthew's understanding of the Servant's mission as including (messianic) healing was influenced by Ezek 34:23, which combines the themes of David, "servant," and shepherd (the shepherd being one who "cares for and cures his flock," 132).

56. The lengthy attempt by Carson, 205-7, to show that even in this text Matthew is thinking of Jesus' redemptive suffering (that "Jesus' healing miracles pointed beyond

In Isaiah the Servant's "lifting" of illnesses and "carrying" of pains speaks in context of his sharing those experiences himself and so removing them ("by his stripes we are healed"); on that basis one Jewish tradition took Isa 53:4 to mean that the Messiah was to be a leper.[57] But the Hebrew verbs used, and Matthew's Greek versions of them, need mean no more than that he took them away, and Matthew does not suggest that Jesus himself became ill in order to heal.

2. Following Jesus: Two Contrasting Case Studies (8:18-22)

18 *Seeing a crowd[1] around him, Jesus told his disciples to go away with him to the other side of the lake.[2] 19 A certain[3] scribe said to him, "Teacher, I will follow you wherever you may be going away to." 20 Jesus replied, "Foxes have dens and the birds of the sky have roosts,[4] but the Son of Man has no place where he can lay his head." 21 Then another of his[5] disciples said to him, "Lord, give me per-*

---

themselves to the cross") seems unnecessary. Matthew will explore that aspect of the Servant model elsewhere, but here his focus is on the healings in themselves. R. Beaton, *Isaiah's Christ*, 114-19, looks more cautiously for a dimension beyond physical healing, but finds it in "the character and demeanour of the healer, who as a servant compassionately identifies with a broken humanity and offers wholeness," rather than specifically in the cross.

57. J. Jeremias, *TDNT* 5:690, 697: this tradition goes back to Aquila's translation of Isa 53:4, according to Jerome.

1. Many MSS read the plural ὄχλους and most add "many," reflecting Matthew's standard phraseology. The simple, anarthrous ὄχλον of B best explains the variety of expanded readings, and its very unusualness in Matthew suggests that it may be the original.

2. Several words need to be suppied in translation to convey the force of Matthew's terse expression ἐκέλευσεν ἀπελθεῖν εἰς τὸ πέραν: the addressees (the disciples) and the destination (the eastern shore of the lake) need to be deduced from the context, as well as the fact that Jesus himself intends to go with the disciples.

3. The use of εἷς rather than τις to represent the indefinite article has one clear parallel in Matthew at 9:18. In 21:19 and 26:69 we shall see that the numeral μία adds a significant emphasis in context. Here and in 18:24 εἷς introduces the first of two parallel characters (here there are two potential followers, the second introduced as ἕτερος; in 18:24 it introduces the first of two debtor slaves). But the suggestion of D. E. Orton, *Scribe*, 36, that here it indicates that this *one* scribe is exceptional among scribes is probably reading too much into the idiom.

4. κατασκήνωσις means simply a "lodging," a place to sleep. The traditional translation "nests" would apply only during the relatively brief breeding season.

5. αὐτοῦ does not appear in several significant textual witnesses, including ℵ and B, but the omission is probably deliberate, caused by the fact that this "disciple" does not seem yet to be part of the Jesus circle, and also by the fact that after ἕτερος it appears to say that the scribe of v. 19 was also one of Jesus' disciples. See p. 328, n. 19.

mission first to go away and bury my father." 22 But Jesus replied, "Follow me, and leave the dead to bury their own dead."

There is a change of scene between 8:18 and 8:28, when Jesus disembarks on the other (east) side of the lake, and vv. 23-27 will portray Jesus and his disciples during the crossing by boat — the first of several such crossings (see 9:1; 14:13, 22-34; 15:39–16:5). Jesus' intention to leave his home territory for "foreign" parts is signaled in v. 18 (and note the repetition of the verb "go away" in vv. 19 and 21), and this inevitably requires a separation between the few who can go with Jesus in the boat and the crowd as a whole whom he will leave behind. In this situation two[6] potential followers declare their intention to go with him. But the interest of the story is not in these two men in themselves (we are told nothing about them, not even whether they in fact joined Jesus or not), but in Jesus' remarkable responses to them both, which raise an abrupt challenge to any easy understanding of discipleship.[7] They express both the uncompromising authority of the demand Jesus makes on his followers and the radical change of lifestyle which such following must involve. Verse 22 has been taken by M. Hengel as the paradigm for his portrayal of Jesus as the "charismatic leader" whose call to follow him expresses here by its "unique offensiveness" an authoritative demand which "sharply runs counter to law, piety and custom."[8]

This brief interlude in the series of miracle stories thus prepares the ground for the account of the storm on the lake (vv. 23-27), where, as we shall see, the basic miracle story is heavily overlaid with a symbolic depiction of the nature of discipleship. The language of discipleship runs prominently through these two brief cameos: "follow" (vv. 19, 22, then picked up in v. 23), "disciple" (v. 21, also picked up in v. 23), "teacher," and "lord." The two case studies are of men who wish to join Jesus when he separates himself from the "crowd." They are thus at least potentially "disciples" (see on v. 21), though nothing in context suggests that either of them belonged to the group who were later to be distinguished as the Twelve (10:1-4). We are not told that either of them did in fact follow Jesus after his sobering response to their initial enthusiasm. In these two tantalizing scenes, therefore, we are reminded of the grey area which existed between the uncommitted "crowd"

6. Luke's version of this pericope (Luke 9:57-62) has three potential disciples. If Matthew knew the pericope in this threefold form (rather than Luke having expanded a double scene), his omission of the third is probably a typical Matthean abbreviation, since he did not find any significantly different principle in the final exchange. *Gos. Thom.* 86 is even briefer, giving merely the saying of v. 20, with no narrative setting.

7. There is an interesting parallel in 2 Sam 15:19-22, where David tries (unsuccessfully) to dissuade a supporter from joining him in his refugee life.

8. M. Hengel, *Leader,* 14 and passim.

(cf. 5:1; 7:28-29) and the fully committed Twelve, an area which will be further delineated in the range of responses set out in the parable of the sower (13:3-8, 18-23).

18 Already before we are formally introduced to the Twelve as a coherent inner circle of Jesus' followers this verse assumes that the "disciples" to whom the discourse of chs. 5–7 was addressed are a group distinguished from the crowd, who are expected to be Jesus' traveling companions and to whom it is now natural for him to give instructions (note the authorittative verb *ekeleusen,* "gave orders").⁹ The decision to cross the lake appears to be related to the presence of the crowd, and we may reasonably assume that Jesus' intention is, as in 5:1 and later in 14:13, to get away from their pressure so as to be alone with his disciples. "The other side" of the lake from Capernaum suggests somewhere on the eastern shore, on the other side of the Jordan inflow, and their eventual arrival in the Gadarene area (see on v. 28) confirms this general area, even if the storm may have affected their actual landfall. This was the largely non-Jewish area known as Decapolis, a loose confederation of self-governing Hellenistic city-states outside the control of the Herodian rulers, to which Jesus will apparently return in 15:29-39. Its non-Jewish culture is indicated by the large herd of pigs being pastured in the area (v. 30). Jesus is thus at this point deliberately withdrawing from his Jewish environment. It is a "foreign" journey on which it could not be expected that his Jewish supporters outside the disciple group would wish or be able to "go away" with him.

19-20 It is thus remarkable that we hear of "a certain scribe" (see above, n. 3) wishing to follow him. Unlike most of the scribes we meet in this gospel, this one is at least for the moment in favor of Jesus;¹⁰ scribes who are also disciples are mentioned as well in 13:52; 23:34, but these are notable exceptions to the strongly negative tone of all Matthew's other references to scribes. But even this scribe, despite his expressed enthusiasm, does not speak as a true disciple. He addresses Jesus as "Teacher," a form of address which in Matthew (unlike Mark) is used only by people outside Jesus' group, never by the disciples (with the significant exception of Judas Iscariot, who twice uses the Hebrew equivalent, "Rabbi").¹¹ His scribal training leads him to take it for

---

9. *Pace* S. C. Barton, *Discipleship,* 142-44, who argues that it is the *crowd* that Jesus instructs (unsuccessfully) to cross the lake with him.

10. See D. E. Orton, *Scribe,* 36-37, for this positive connotation in the light of the parallel with 13:51-52.

11. For a comparison of the different uses of διδάσκαλε in the Synoptic Gospels see my *Matthew: Evangelist,* 257, and more fully *GP* 1:106-9. C. Deutsch, *Lady Wisdom,* 43-45, suggests on the basis of the terms "scribe" and "teacher" that Jesus is here associated with Wisdom, and so reads v. 20 as reflecting the theme of Wisdom's rejection and homelessness on earth.

granted that it is for him to choose to follow Jesus, as did the disciples of rabbis, rather than for Jesus to call him as he has done in 4:19, 22; cf. 9:9. Jesus' response assumes that the scribe has not yet thought out the commitment involved in discipleship, and probably suggests that he is unlikely to be willing to face it. The wording of the scribe's declaration (which I have translated literally above — he does not simply say "wherever you go") perhaps indicates that his interest is only in the proposed journey across the lake, whose destination he does not yet know, rather than in a long-term commitment.

Jesus' reply, however, focuses not on the immediate boat trip, but on the itinerant lifestyle to which his disciples were to be committed. As "the carpenter's son" in Nazareth (13:55) Jesus presumably had a reasonably secure place in society, but he had left that behind (4:13). Even in Capernaum it seems that Jesus did have "a place where he could lay his head" (whether his own house or that of Peter; see on vv. 14-15), and sometimes on his travels he seems to have been able to find hospitality (e.g., in Bethany, 21:16; 26:6), as indeed he expected his disciples to do (10:11). But the itinerant ministry (4:23) which now required their crossing the lake would allow no certainty of lodging, and many nights must have been spent in more exposed locations even than those of the foxes and the birds;[12] the coming night will find Jesus sleeping in a boat (v. 24). The first use of the phrase "the Son of Man" in Matthew thus gives unusual weight to the literal meaning of the Aramaic phrase, "a human being," by contrasting this human being's material insecurity poignantly with the relatively better provision available to the non-human creation.[13]

This is not the place for a full study of Matthew's use of the title "the Son of Man," still less for entering the continuing and complex debate as to the origin and significance of that term in the light of its wider context. I have sketched out my understanding of these matters elsewhere,[14] and here I offer only a brief, unadorned summary, well aware that virtually every clause of it is open to dispute. Matthew's use of the term is not markedly different from that in the other gospels. It is always used by Jesus himself, not by others

12. S. C. Barton, *Discipleship,* 147, n. 85, lists texts to illustrate that foxes and birds were despised in Jewish thought.

13. K. E. Bailey, *Peasant Eyes,* 24-25, following T. W. Manson, suggests a secondary political nuance, in that Jesus the true Israelite contrasts his situation with that of the Romans ("birds") and their puppets ("foxes") who have made themselves at home in Palestine. Such an undertone can seldom be proved or disproved, but it is doubtful whether the imagery (especially "birds" = Romans) would have been sufficiently self-evident for most people to grasp it without further indication in context.

14. *Matthew: Evangelist,* 288-92. Carson, 209-13, provides a useful brief survey of discussion of the issue up to about 1980; it is doubtful whether much of substance has been added since. Fuller and more recent is Davies and Allison, 2:43-52.

about him, and it functions as a self-reference — note, for instance, how in 16:13 it corresponds to "I" in Mark, while in 16:21 the process is reversed. It is the only title by which Jesus refers to himself when speaking with people outside the disciple group.[15] Its primary OT source is the vision of Dan 7:13-14, where the "one like a son of man" (who represents Israel) is a victorious figure enthroned by God in heaven to rule over all nations, and in several of its occurrences in the gospel the language and imagery of that passage are present. But it is clear that Jesus, having coined[16] his chosen title from this biblical source, then used it much more widely, with reference to aspects of his ministry far removed from his future heavenly glory. In Matthew, as in the other Synoptic Gospels, it is customary to speak of three main areas of reference for the title "the Son of Man": to his future heavenly glory, to the earthly suffering which must precede it, and, less frequently, to his current earthly status and authority. It seems that the reason why Jesus found this title convenient is that, having no ready-made titular connotations in current usage, it could be applied across the whole range of his uniquely paradoxical mission of humiliation and vindication, of death and glory, which could not be fitted into any preexisting model. Like his parables, the title "the Son of Man" came with an air of enigma,[17] challenging the hearer to think new thoughts rather than to slot Jesus into a ready-made pigeonhole.

Here in 8:20 the reference is to Jesus' current status, but whereas in 9:6 and 12:8 the title will denote a figure of unique authority, here it speaks paradoxically of a state of earthly deprivation which is sharply contrasted with the heavenly glory of Dan 7:13-14. As Matthew's gospel progresses, it will be the future, heavenly authority of the Son of Man which will be in-

---

15. The phrase "a son of man" was sometimes used in Aramaic as a (usually deprecating) self-reference, rather like our English "one," but Jesus' use of the phrase with the definite article is distinctive and justifies describing the phrase as, for him, a "title"; the point is well argued by C. F. D. Moule, *Origin,* 11-17. See further the next two notes.

16. There is no evidence that ὁ υἱὸς τοῦ ἀνθρώπου or its Hebrew or Aramaic equivalents was already in use as a recognized title. Its prominent use as such in the *Similitudes of Enoch* may represent an independent coinage on the basis of Dan 7:13-14, since the evidence currently available suggests that that part of *1 Enoch* was not earlier than the time of Jesus (see G. R. Beasley-Murray, *Kingdom,* 63-68), and the title does not occur in the earlier *Enoch* literature. Elsewhere in Jewish literature Dan 7:13-14 is used as a model for eschatological and sometimes specifically messianic visions, but the "one who came in the clouds" is not referred to by the title "the Son of Man" (see my *Jesus and the OT,* 169-71, 179-83, 185-88).

17. In Greek the phrase ὁ υἱὸς τοῦ ἀνθρώπου is as unnatural as "the Son of Man" in English: whatever may have been true of the Aramaic usage, the Greek phrase as we meet it in the gospels can have been intended to be taken only as a title, its very foreignness ensuring that it challenged the hearer to think out what Jesus meant and whom he was talking about.

creasingly in focus, but this first use of the title brings out the contrast between its literal meaning and its specifically Danielic connotations: the one who is to rule over all first shares with his disciples in all the insecurity of their human condition.[18]

21-22 A second potential recruit is met by an even more off-putting demand from Jesus. The phrase "another of his disciples" suggests that both the potential follower of these verses and the enthusiastic "scribe" of v. 19 are in some sense to be understood as "disciples";[19] this one even uses the more committed form of address, "Lord," rather than "Teacher." Yet neither is identified as one of the Twelve, and we should probably assume that neither in fact became one of Jesus' traveling companions. Whereas in Mark the term *mathētēs* is probably restricted to the Twelve,[20] Matthew, like Luke, also uses it sometimes more widely of anyone who is committed to following Jesus. Note, in addition to this passage, its use in 10:24-25, 42. In 5:1, while it denotes people who are separated from the crowd, there is no reason to restrict it to those who would later be identified as the Twelve; the discourse is addressed to anyone who has become part of the kingdom of heaven. Matthew's use of the verb *mathēteuō* (not used in the other gospels) confirms this broader usage, being applied to a "scribe who has become a disciple to the kingdom of heaven" (13:52), to Joseph of Arimathea (27:57), and to the people from all nations who will become followers of Jesus as a result of the

---

18. The suggestion that here the term is used *only* in its generic sense, and that Jesus is talking of the insecurity of all humanity, not only makes nonsense of the saying itself (human beings in general *do* have homes) but also makes it irrelevant to this context: it is precisely and only the material deprivation of Jesus and his disciples which makes this reply relevant to the scribe's offer. M. Casey, *JSNT* 23 (1985) 8-9, suggests that it *could* be read as a general truth in the sense that foxes and birds find their shelter ready-made in nature, while human beings have to build homes, but goes on to recognize (10-13) that in context the reference is specifically to Jesus' own (atypical) situation. Even so, Casey denies any titular sense to the phrase in Jesus' usage, whatever it must have meant to Matthew and his readers.

19. The REB rendering "another man, one of his disciples" avoids calling the scribe of v. 19 a disciple, but is hardly a natural reading of the phrase. Even more tendentious is Albright and Mann, 95, "Another, (not one) of the disciples," postulating without any evidence that δέ originally read οὐδέ. Nor can the implication that the scribe was a "disciple" be evaded by citing the popular "rule" that ἕτερος means one of another kind whereas ἄλλος means one of the same kind, since Matthean usage generally shows no such distinction. For the debate on which of the two inquirers is to be regarded "positively" and which "negatively," see S. C. Barton, *Discipleship,* 144-46, who supports Orton's view (against that of Kingsbury, adopted by Davies and Allison, 2:39) that both are introduced in positive terms. The pericope does not, however, tell us the *outcome* of either application.

20. See my *The Gospel of Mark,* 158.

mission of the "eleven disciples" (28:19).[21] It seems then that here (and by implication also in vv. 19-20) Matthew is using the term for a potential committed follower, a volunteer who is thinking of leaving the "crowd" in order to travel with Jesus. Jesus' response is then designed to draw out the radical implications of such a commitment.

The potential disciple's words are usually understood of the immediate and pressing responsibility of arranging the funeral for his father who had just died. Burial took place within twenty-four hours of the death, so he would not be asking for a long postponement, though subsequent ceremonies could last up to a week. The arrangements were the responsibility of the eldest son (Gen 50:5-7; Tob 4:3; 6:15; 14:11-12; Sir 38:16), and Jewish custom and piety demanded that they take priority over all other commitments, even the most essential prayers (Lev 21:1-3; *m. Ber.* 3:1). The request would thus be entirely reasonable, indeed essential. If his filial duties prevented him from joining the group in the boat just now, he could catch up with Jesus as soon as his responsibilities had been discharged; the word "first" implies that that was his intention. No Jew, especially one who took religious obligations seriously, could have expected him to do otherwise. Jesus' refusal to allow so essential a filial duty would then be profoundly shocking.

But K. E. Bailey,[22] drawing on the insight of Arabic commentators and on his own experience of cultures and idioms of the Middle East, insists that such a scenario results from a "western" reading of the text and is culturally impossible. If the father had just died, the son could hardly be out at the roadside with Jesus; his place was to be keeping vigil and preparing for the funeral. Rather, to "bury one's father" is standard idiom for fulfilling one's filial responsibilities for the remainder of the father's lifetime, with no prospect of his imminent death. This would then be a request for indefinite postponement of discipleship, likely to be for years rather than days. In that case Jesus' reply would be less immediately shocking — the man's proposed "discipleship" was apparently not very serious.[23]

But, even so, Jesus' demand would still cut across deep-rooted cultural expectations, and the reference to those who can be left to fulfill the filial re-

21. For Matthew's use of μαθητής / μαθητεύω see further B. Przybylski, *Righteousness,* 108-10; R. Mohrlang, *Matthew,* 74-78; M. J. Wilkins, *Disciple,* passim and especially 166-69 on Matthew's extension of the term beyond the Twelve.

22. K. E. Bailey, *Peasant Eyes,* 25-27, commenting on the Lucan parallel. Cf. Keener, 275-76.

23. Keener, 276, following B. R. McCane, *HTR* 83 (1990) 31-43, suggests that what was in view was not an indefinite postponement while the father remained alive, but the customary "second burial" a year after the original death and burial, when the bones were transferred to an ossuary. It is doubtful, however, whether "bury my father" would naturally be understood in this sense.

sponsibility as being themselves "the dead" is harsh.[24] Like v. 20, it is an epi-grammatic formulation designed to pull the man up short. The cultural "insen-sitivity" of Jesus' demand underlines the radical newness and overriding importance of the message of the kingdom of heaven; even the most basic of family ties must not be allowed to stand in its way (cf. 4:22; 10:37; 12:46-50; 19:29). Compared with those who have found true life in the kingdom of heaven, those who remain outside it are "the dead." This metaphorical use of *nekros* (literally, "a dead person," "corpse") for those without spiritual life does not occur elsewhere in the gospels,[25] but it is a metaphor readily understood in the light of sayings like 10:39; 16:25-26, and occurs elsewhere in the NT (Eph 2:1, 5; Col 2:13; Rev 3:1).[26] A disciple's business is with life, not with death.

Whether the metaphor is immediately grasped or not, Jesus' reply is a stark refusal to allow filial duty to take priority over discipleship. No rabbi would have been so cavalier, and normal Jewish piety would find such an at-titude incomprehensible,[27] a prima facie breach of the fifth commandment, even though Jesus himself elsewhere endorses it (15:3-6; 19:19).[28] If this is

24. Most commentators assume this metaphorical sense here. It would not be out of character for Jesus to suggest the ludicrous image of the literally dead burying one an-other as a vivid way of saying, "Leave such matters alone" (so, strongly, Luz, 2:19-20), but the imagery of spiritual life and death was probably familiar enough to make the meta-phorical sense more likely. C. H. T. Fletcher-Louis, *JSNT* 26 (2003) 48-52, rightly inter-prets it as a forceful way of "redefining God's family."

25. The nearest equivalent is the father's description of the prodigal son as "dead and alive again" (Luke 15:24, 32).

26. For Jewish parallels see M. Hengel, *Leader,* 8; Keener, 275; C. H. T. Fletcher-Louis, *JSNT* 26 (2003) 54-57.

27. C. H. T. Fletcher-Louis, *JSNT* 26 (2003) 57-66, provides evidence for the de-liberate refusal of burial even by pious Jews, but the instances he cites are of vengeance on enemies or as an ultimate expression of dissociation from someone regarded as outside the true people of God. The relevance of this material to the present text seems limited, since Jesus is talking not about enemies and outsiders but about the man's father, and says nothing about refusal of burial, only about who should do it. He does not command the dishonoring of the dead father, but asserts the priority of discipleship above the (proper and desirable) filial duty of burial.

28. M. Hengel, *Leader,* 8-15, explores at length the "break with law and custom" involved in Jesus' demand. See also A. E. Harvey, *Jesus,* 59-61, who interprets the inci-dent in the light of God's instructions to certain prophets not to observe normal conven-tions of mourning (Jer 16:5-7; Ezek 24:15-18) and takes it as indicating "an exceptional demand signalled by the arrival of a prophetic figure empowered to authorise even serious dispensations from the demands of law and custom." Harvey, following Hengel, also draws attention to the rather cryptic account of the call of Elisha in 1 Kgs 19:19-21; he thinks it likely that Elijah refused permission for Elisha to say good-bye to his parents be-fore following him (so also M. Hengel, *Leader,* 16-18), but if Elisha did first return home (as the passage most naturally reads, and as it was apparently understood in Jesus' time

what "authority not like their scribes" (7:29) involves, most people would not want to have anything to do with it. The kingdom of heaven apparently involves a degree of fanaticism which is willing to disrupt the normal rhythms of social life.[29] Jesus can hardly have been surprised that true discipleship remained a minority movement, and that popular enthusiasm for his teaching and healing generally stopped short of full discipleship. Many are invited, but few are chosen (20:16; 22:14; cf. 7:14).

3. Three Further Demonstrations of Authority (8:23–9:8)

23 *And when Jesus had gotten into the boat, his disciples followed him.* 24 *Suddenly[1] there was a great storm[2] on the lake, so that the boat was being swamped by the waves — but Jesus went on sleeping.* 25 *So they[3] came and woke him, saying, "Lord, save us;[4] we are sinking."* 26 *He said to them, "Why are you scared, you faithless[5] people?" Then he got up and rebuked the winds and the lake, and there was complete calm.* 27 *The men were amazed, and said, "What sort of[6] person is this? Even the winds and the lake obey him!"*

[Hengel, 16]), the parallel would be even more significant: Jesus does not allow his potential disciple even the basic "family leave" which Elisha could take for granted.

29. M. Bockmuehl, *JTS* 49 (1998) 553-81, disputes Hengel's view that Jesus is here flouting the law, and suggests rather that he is calling the inquirer to undertake something like a Nazirite vow (Nazirites were not allowed contact with a dead body, even of their immediate relatives, Num 6:6-8). While recognizing that Jesus himself was not a lifelong Nazirite like John the Baptist, Bockmuehl demonstrates the popularity of this or similar ascetic practices in the Jewish world, and proposes that Jesus' demand here might have been understood to carry "a broadly Nazirite symbolism." Even such asceticism, within the law, would of course still have been a radical challenge to normal social and family values. See, however, C. H. T. Fletcher-Louis, *JSNT* 26 (2003) 43-48, for a critique of Bockmuehl's proposal (and Bockmuehl's response, ibid., 241-42).

1. An attempt to convey the dramatic force of ἰδού; see p. 46, n. 19.

2. σεισμός, a "shaking," normally denotes an earthquake, but on the water it presumably denotes the effect of a violent wind. Hagner's rendering, "a great earthquake *under* the sea," is unnecessary and reads oddly with Jesus' rebuke of the *winds,* resulting in complete calm.

3. Many MSS identify "they" as the disciples, but after v. 23 the subject is not in doubt. We have no reason to think that there was anyone else in the boat.

4. There was probably no object in the original text; the addition of "us" is stylistic, a need felt also by many MSS and almost all versions, which add ἡμᾶς. The staccato original is dramatically effective but perhaps too stark in English.

5. See p. 264, n. 6, for the meaning of ὀλιγόπιστος.

6. While ποταπός is essentially a neutral interrogative, "what kind of?" in some contexts, it carries the implication "how wonderful!" (Mark 13:1; 1 John 3:1), and such a nuance is clearly appropriate here.

28 *When he had reached the other side, in the territory of the Gadarenes,*[7] *he was confronted by two demon-possessed men who came out from the tombs; they were really unmanageable, so that no one was able to travel that way.* 29 *They shouted out at him, "Leave us alone,*[8] *you Son of God. Have you come*[9] *here before the proper time to torment us?"* 30 *Now there was a herd of many pigs feeding some distance away.* 31 *The demons began to plead with Jesus, "If you are going to*[10] *throw us out, send us into the herd of pigs."* 32 *"Off you go,"* *he replied; and they came out and went off into the pigs, and suddenly the whole herd stampeded down over the cliff into the lake and were drowned.*[11] 33 *The swineherds ran away, and went off to the town, and told the whole story, including*[12] *what had happened to the possessed men.* 34 *There and then*[13] *the whole town came out to meet Jesus; and when they saw him, they urged him to go away from their area.*

9:1 *Jesus got into the boat, and crossed the lake, and came to his own town.* 2 *And some people arrived, bringing*[14] *to him a paralyzed man lying*[15] *on a bed. When Jesus saw their faith, he said to the paralyzed man, "Take heart, son; your sins are forgiven."* 3 *But there were some scribes there who muttered among*[16] *themselves, "This man is*

7. For this reading and the variants see the commentary below.

8. Literally, "What to us and to you?" a biblical formula of dissociation (2 Sam 16:10; 19:22; 2 Kgs 3:13; cf. A. H. Maynard, *NTS* 31 [1985] 582-86), which when addressed to a potential aggressor has the effect of "Go away and leave me alone" (Judg 11:12; 1 Kgs 17:18; cf. Matt 27:19; Mark 1:24, and in a different context John 2:4).

9. The sentence could also be read as an accusatory statement or complaint: "You have come here to torment us before the proper time."

10. The verb is in the present tense, but in English the "going to" idiom better expresses a course of action now decided on but not yet implemented.

11. Literally "died in the water," but no other cause of death is suggested. The subject is the pigs, not the demons; see the comments below.

12. The phrasing is unusual: ἀπήγγειλαν πάντα καὶ τὰ τῶν δαιμονιζομένων, literally "reported everything and the things about the possessed men." The point seems to be that they reported not only the fate of the pigs but also, and especially, what had caused it.

13. Another attempt to convey the dramatic force of ἰδού, as was "suddenly" in v. 32. ἰδού occurs three times in this paragraph to mark dramatic developments in the story, but I have left it untranslated at the beginning of v. 29.

14. Here and in v. 3 I have rephrased to get the force of ἰδού; here it is literally, "And look, they [unspecified] were bringing," and in v. 3, "And look, some of the scribes said among themselves."

15. As in 8:6 and 14, the passive of βάλλω is used for someone confined to bed by illness.

16. ἐν ἑαυτοῖς could mean either (silently) within themselves or (vocally) among themselves as a group. Jesus' "seeing their thoughts" could follow either, but perhaps

blaspheming." 4 *When Jesus saw*[17] *what they were thinking, he asked,
"Why do you harbor evil thoughts in your hearts?* 5 *For which is easier: to say, 'Your sins are forgiven,' or to say, 'Get up and walk'?* 6 *But
so that you may know that the Son of Man has authority on earth to forgive sins" (he said to the paralyzed man),*[18] *"Get up, pick up your bed,
and off you go to your house."* 7 *And the man got up and went away to
his house.* 8 *When the crowds saw this, they were afraid,*[19] *and they
gave glory to God, who had given such authority to human beings.*

The second group of miracles (see pp. 300-302 for the grouping of miracles
in these chapters) are linked both geographically and thematically. Geographically they are grouped around the crossing of the lake, which was signaled in v. 18. The first miracle takes place during the crossing, the second on
arrival on the other side, and the third on their return to Capernaum. The explicit mention of the boat in 8:23 and 9:1 reinforces this connection. The first
two miracles are similarly linked in Mark and Luke, but the third is added to
them by Matthew's combining of two Marcan miracle catenae (see pp. 300-
301); it occurs in Capernaum as in Mark, but whereas in Mark Jesus has just
returned from a preaching tour in Galilee, in Matthew he has been across the
lake.

The thematic connection between these three miracles is in the unparalleled authority displayed by Jesus, which is the explicit focus of the third
(9:6-8), but it is also expressed in the reaction of the disciples to the first
(8:27) and of the people of the Decapolis to the second (8:34). The miracles
in the first group were physical healings (though exorcisms were also included in the general summary in 8:16). In this group the third (9:1-8) is also

more naturally indicates that they were visibly sharing their disapproval but without stating it openly.

17. The reading εἰδώς, "knowing," instead of ἰδών, "seeing," which occurs in B, Θ
and a number of later witnesses and versions, probably represents a tendency to make Jesus' supernatural knowledge more explicit, and was perhaps designed to assimilate Matthew's text more closely to those of Mark and Luke, who both have ἐπιγνούς. See the
comments below on how he may have "seen" their thoughts.

18. This clause is usually set off by a dash as if the former sentence had been left
unfinished and a new development introduced. In fact Jesus' speech continues after the inserted clause, the instruction to the paralyzed man being itself the means by which they
will know about the Son of Man's authority. All that is signaled by the inserted clause is a
change of addressee, within the same sentence. Its function as a "stage direction" is best
represented by putting it in parentheses outside the quotation marks.

19. Many later MSS read ἐθαύμασαν, "they were amazed," which is more normal
Matthean language for a crowd reaction. Matthew does not elsewhere use φόβος and cognates in the sense of "awe," and his surprising choice of that term here should be represented in translation.

a physical healing, but that is not the main focus of the pericope which contains it. Rather, we now see Jesus' authority revealed in three new ways, different from one another but all equally astounding. He has authority to quell wind and water, to expel demonic spirits, and to forgive sins. The question "What sort of person is this?" (8:27) thus becomes ever more insistent.

We noted above (p. 301) Matthew's remarkably concise narration especially of the story of the Gadarene demoniac(s) — 135 words to Mark's 330. The luxuriant details of Mark's description of "Legion" (Matthew does not mention the name) in Mark 5:3-5 are summarized in the two almost banal words I have translated "really unmanageable," and Mark's account of the subsequent condition and response of the demoniac after the exorcism (5:15, 18-20) finds no place in Matthew's version. Similarly in the Capernaum story, what is for many the most memorable feature of Mark's account (the breaking open of the roof to let the bed down in front of Jesus) is not mentioned, and while the story of the storm is less drastically abbreviated, both the storm and its cessation are more economically told and we miss the account of Jesus sleeping "in the stern on the cushion." Matthew, as usual, is less concerned with providing an entertaining story, and includes only what will serve his purpose of underlining the unique authority of the one whom the demons instinctively recognize as the Son of God (8:29).

a. The Storm on the Lake (8:23-27)

In its setting in chs. 8–9 this is clearly first and foremost a miracle story, and a very striking one at that, involving for the first time Jesus' control over the natural world. Its theme and in some ways even its wording recall the recurrent OT theme of God's control over wind and waves (e.g., Job 38:8-11; Pss 65:5-8; 89:8-9), with a specially clear echo of the storm scene in Ps 107:23-30. Further "nature miracles" in 14:15-21, 23-33; 15:32-38; 21:18-22 will reinforce the message that Jesus is able to do what normal human beings cannot do, and while the christological implication is here drawn out only in a rhetorical question (v. 27), a similar miracle will evoke in 14:33 the disciples' first explicit recognition that Jesus is the Son of God. When to this is added Jesus' authenticated claim to a further divine prerogative, the forgiveness of sins (9:3-6), there is no doubt that Matthew intends his readers to perceive what only gradually became clear to the disciples, that there was a more literal dimension to the title "God with us" (1:23) than perhaps Isaiah himself had intended.[20]

---

20. This implication is well brought out by W. D. Davies, *Setting*, 88-90. Keener, 279-80, lists several Jewish and pagan accounts of similar nature miracles attributed to famous people, but points out that they were normally credited to people long ago, while similar contemporary events were "nearly always ascribed directly to the gods."

That might be thought to be more than enough theological freight for a short story of only seventy-three words to carry, but modern interpretation of Matthew, inspired by a famous redaction-critical study by G. Bornkamm, has generally agreed that Matthew has added another symbolic dimension to this story. The experience of the disciples in the boat is also "a kerygmatic paradigm of the danger and glory of discipleship."[21] The context, immediately following the two cameos of potential disciples who had proposed to share in this boat journey, suggests this symbolism, as does the way Matthew introduces the story, not only by the repetition of the words "follow" and "disciples" which have been the focus of the preceding verses, but also by including in this severely economical pericope an apparently quite unnecessary description of Jesus getting into the boat first and the disciples following him in; moreover, on this point Matthew differs sharply from Mark (4:36), where the disciples are already in the boat and take Jesus in with them. There is no explicit allegorizing of the boat or the storm,[22] but the "prayer" of the disciples, "Lord, save," followed by Jesus' rebuke for faithlessness (compare 6:30 for this term applied to disciples), fits well with such a reading. A significant contrast with Mark's telling of the story is the different order of events: in Mark the appeal is immediately followed by Jesus' remedial action, only after which does he comment on their fear and lack of faith, whereas in Matthew the comments immediately follow the appeal — Jesus deals with the disciples before he deals with the storm. This order is perhaps intended to underline Jesus' control of the situation (there is no need to panic), but also serves to highlight the significance of the disciples' failure in trust.

To recognize this "paradigmatic" function of the story is not, however, to devalue the sheer miraculousness of the event itself, which is the reason for Matthew's including the story at this point, nor the clear echoes which the pericope provides of OT accounts of the power of the Creator God. Matthew, as we have seen before especially in ch. 2, is quite capable of maintaining multiple levels of meaning at the same time, so as to provide symbolic bonus meanings for the attentive reader.

23 The embarkation announced in v. 18 now takes place. By separating Jesus' embarking first from the disciples' following him, Matthew em-

21. G. Bornkamm, *Wort und Dienst,* 49-54; English version in G. Bornkamm et al., *Tradition,* 52-57. Most recent commentators have accepted the main lines of Bornkamm's study, but M. D. Goulder, *Midrash,* 324, n. 34, regards it as "a piece of serious overinterpretation."

22. Bornkamm, *Tradition,* 56, suggests that Matthew's unusual use of σεισμός for a storm on the lake is intended to echo its use to describe "apocalyptic horrors," as in 24:7; 27:54; 28:2. In all these cases, however, the reference is to literal earthquakes; it is the context, not the word itself, which gives it an "apocalyptic" nuance.

phasizes the social priority: the disciples are literally "followers," and it is Jesus who is in charge in the boat, even though he is presumably not its owner. Matthew does not at this point define how large a group of "disciples" Jesus took with him, but he will later list the Twelve as Jesus' closest associates (10:1-4), and thereafter "the twelve disciples" will be mentioned as the group who travel with Jesus and share his experiences (11:1; 19:28; 20:17; 26:20). While there were no doubt more significant symbolic reasons for the choice of twelve (see on 10:1), one practical factor may have been the size of boat available for trips such as this. If the first-century-A.D. boat recovered from the mud of the northwest shore of the lake of Galilee in 1986 (now preserved in the Yigal Allon Center at Ginosar) is typical of the normal working boats of the period, its dimensions (8.20 meters long by 2.35 wide) would suggest that the boat might be overcrowded with more than thirteen people. There might have been practical problems if the two potential disciples of vv. 19-22 had in fact joined the group!

24-25 The Lake of Galilee, situated well below sea level in the steep-sided rift valley of the Jordan, is subject to sudden, violent squalls, and the resulting turbulence could be dangerous to a relatively broad and shallow boat such as the one found at Ginosar (its depth is only 1.25 meters). Jesus has taken the opportunity for a rest, since the boat is in the competent hands of the Galilean fishermen who are the only disciples so far identified (4:18-22); his continuing to sleep in such circumstances may be attributed to natural exhaustion as much as to supernatural confidence, but it provides the setting for a remarkable reversal of roles, in that the experienced fishermen appeal for help to a man who as far as we know had little experience of boats (Nazareth is up in the hills, a long day's walk from the lake). The reader might recall the story of Jonah, who also had to be awakened in a storm (described in Jonah 1:4 in words similar to v. 24 here) to pray for his God's help for the boat and its crew (Jonah 1:5-6); but unlike Jonah, Jesus will prove to be in charge of the situation, by his own authority rather than by praying for God's help. As we shall read in 12:41, "something greater than Jonah is here." The wording of the disciples' appeal has more the tone of a prayer than Mark's brusque "Teacher, don't you care that we are sinking?" — compare Jonah 1:14 (addressed to Jonah's God), "Please, Lord, do not let us perish."

26 Jesus is sufficiently in control of the situation to be able to deal with the disciples' fear before taking action on the storm. The previous use of *oligopistos,* "faithless," in 6:30 provides the background for Jesus' rebuke here: if disciples are not to be concerned about their survival in terms of food and clothing, surely they must expect their heavenly Father to protect them from danger as well. Cowardice in such a situation shows that they do not take God's fatherly care seriously, which is the essence of practical faith. It is not that the danger is not real (for surely experienced Galilean fishermen would know when they were in serious danger), but that God is not limited by the natural forces which he created. Jesus' confident "rebuke"[23] to the storm, expecting it to recognize his authority, and the immediate calm which resulted, show that he wields the Creator's power (for God's "rebuke" of the sea cf. Pss 18:15; 104:7; 106:9;[24] Isa 50:2; Nah 1:4).

27 Matthew's use of "the men" here instead of "the disciples" is unusual, and has sometimes been taken to suggest that there were other people in the boat,[25] perhaps a crew unconnected with Jesus and his group (like the crew of Jonah's boat, whose awed reaction is related at Jonah 1:16) who as outsiders recognize something unique about Jesus. But nothing in the story suggests that there was anyone else in the boat, and the comments above on the size of fishing boats suggest that this is unlikely; nor has Matthew mentioned the "other boats" of Mark 4:36. The awed reaction fits well with the disciples' earlier panic and Jesus' rebuke to them, and their designation as *anthrōpoi,* "human beings," underlines the contrast between them and Jesus, who is thus seen as more than human. It is precisely as "human beings" that they must recognize a unique and non-human authority. Their rhetorical question must be understood in the light of the OT passages cited above, which make the control of winds and water the special and sole prerogative of God himself. It is enough at this stage that the question be posed. In due course it will be answered by the disciples themselves (14:33; 16:16), but already in the next pericope the answer will be provided from a very different source (8:29).

23. There is little to commend the suggestion that ἐπιτιμάω, which also occurs in an exorcism account in 17:18 (and cf. Mark 1:25; 3:12), is used because the storm was regarded as a demonic force, personally rebuked by Jesus. Even in the Marcan parallel, where the verb φιμόω, "be muzzled," also occurs, it is a tenuous suggestion; see my *Mark,* 224. Nothing else in the narrative supports such a suggestion here, and the verb ἐπιτιμάω occurs frequently in Matthew with no demonic connotations. The choice of the verb here may be ascribed not only to dramatic anthropomorphism, but more significantly to the OT usage mentioned above.

24. This reference is specifically to the drying of the Red Sea at the Exodus, and on this basis D. C. Allison, *Moses,* 209, notes a possible "new Moses" typology in this story. But the expression is used more widely, and nothing else here suggests a specific allusion to Moses.

25. Luz, 2:21, suggests that these ἄνθρωποι are not in the story at all, but that here "the evangelist steps out of the story as it were and lets the people to whom his church proclaims the gospel speak as if they were reacting to Jesus' miracles." Not only would this be an unparalleled literary technique in this gospel, but when the disciples are the natural referent in the story, and the context suggests a good theological reason for characterizing them precisely as ἄνθρωποι, there seems no basis for so surprising a proposal.

b. The Gadarene Demoniacs (8:28-34)

Jesus' reputation as an exorcist has already been mentioned in 4:24; 8:16, but this is the first of five specific exorcisms narrated by Matthew (cf. 9:32-33; 12:22; 15:21-28; 17:14-20). Three of these are recorded more for the surrounding controversy or dialogue than for the details of the exorcism itself; only 17:14-20 compares with the present pericope as a narration of an exorcism as such.

Jesus will also expect his disciples to act as exorcists (10:1, 8; cf. 17:16, 19-20), and recognizes the reality of exorcism carried out by others outside his group (12:27); other exorcists outside the Jesus circle are referred to in Mark 9:38; Acts 19:12-16. Both the controversy surrounding Jesus' exorcisms (12:22-32) and his cautionary tale about demonic repossession (12:43-45) indicate that the reality of demon-possession and the need for it to be addressed by exorcism were taken for granted by both Jesus and his audience.[26] Accounts from both the Jewish and pagan worlds of the time show that exorcism was an accepted feature of the ministry of those who claimed to be men of God,[27] though there are relatively few narratives of specific exorcisms[28] in comparison with the prominence of this feature in the ministry of Jesus, who thus appears in Christian sources as the exorcist par excellence.[29] In his exorcisms, and especially in Matthew's abbreviated version of this one, there is a striking lack of the quasimagical formulae and techniques (including the control of the demon by discovering its name) which seem to have been characteristic of other exorcists. A simple command suffices; indeed, in Matthew's concise narration here even the command is not directly reported, but assumed in the demons' response in v. 31.

This story, though drastically abbreviated (see above), is one of powerful

26. It is also taken for granted in much of the world today, including by many in the supposedly "scientific" Western world, both inside and outside the Christian churches. There is thus no need for the apologetic stance adopted by some commentators who try to justify this widely recognized phenomenon in terms of modern psychology (e.g., Davies and Allison, 2:77-78, including the remarkable understatement that "Exorcism is even occasionally practised in contemporary Christian circles in North America and Europe").

27. For an excellent brief (but very well-documented) account of ancient views on demons and exorcism see Keener, 283-86. P. S. Alexander has collected much relevant material with regard to Jewish belief and practice in this area in Schürer, 3:342-79.

28. The best known are Josephus, *Ant.* 8.46-48; Philostratus, *Vit. Apoll.* 4.20; Lucian, *Philops.* 16.

29. This comparative absence of actual exorcism narratives outside the NT is pointed out by E. F. Kirschner, *Place,* 29. He notes that even the charismatic rabbi Hanina ben Dosa, who had a reputation for being able to deal with demons, is never recorded as actually performing an exorcism in extant rabbinic texts.

confrontation between a formidable array of demons[30] and the single individual who, as Son of God, has authority over them. It is a direct confrontation between two spiritual authorities. The two men who were involved as the "hosts" of the demons are little more than part of the scenery: Jesus' dialogue is with the demons, not with the men, and nothing is said of the fate of the men after the demons have been expelled. The fate of the pigs, however, which might seem to be the sort of picturesque detail Matthew would omit as part of his normal literary abbreviation of Marcan stories, is retained, both in order to illustrate dramatically the reality of the exorcism and the actual scale of the problem solved, and also to explain the awestruck but apparently hostile reaction of the locals.

The most striking peculiarity of Matthew's account is that what is in Mark and Luke a single individual (though possessed by multiple demons) has become in Matthew "two demon-possessed men." If this case stood alone, it might be possible to explain this duplication as a rather clumsy way to alleviate the idea of many demons in a single individual — though 12:45 shows that multiple possession was not an unfamiliar concept; cf. also Luke 8:2. But the same thing occurs in 20:30-34, where one blind man in the other gospels becomes two blind men in Matthew, and in that case the duplication is further compounded by Matthew's telling a similar story of two blind men in 9:27-31, so that Mark's single blind man has become four altogether! An arguably similar case is 12:22, where a deaf demoniac in Luke 11:14 is parallel to a *blind and* deaf demoniac in Matthew; in that case the person remains single, but the complaint is doubled. I do not know of any really satisfactory explanation of Matthew's tendency to see double[31] (Davies and Allison, 2:80, list nine, none of which satisfy them). Among the most popular are (1) that he thus seeks to magnify the scale of Jesus' healing and exorcistic ministry; (2) that he doubles up in order to compensate for other stories of exorcism and the healing of the blind which he has omitted from the tradition as we know it from Mark (Mark 1:21-28 and Mark 8:22-26 have no parallels in Matthew); (3) that he is influenced by the OT legal principle that "two or three witnesses" are needed for valid testimony (Num 35:30; Deut 17:6; 19:15), and since both incidents give rise to important testimony to Jesus as Son of God (8:29) and as Son of David (20:30, 31; cf. 9:27), this is his way of ensuring that that testimony is heeded.[32] Of these the first two seem extraordinarily mechanical, and the sec-

---

30. Their large number may be inferred from the "many" pigs affected: it is Mark, not Matthew, who has the demons claim explicitly to be "many" (Mark 5:9) and gives the actual number of pigs (Mark 5:13).

31. The presence of two donkeys in 21:1-7 as against one in each of the other gospels is not quite the same phenomenon, and is more easily explained on the basis of Matthew's use of the underlying Zechariah text; see the comments at that point.

32. See J. M. Gibbs, *NTS* 10 (1963/4) 456-57; W. R. G. Loader, *CBQ* 44 (1982) 580-85.

ond is also put in doubt by Matthew's addition of a further story of two blind men — far from merely compensating for the omission of the blind man of Bethsaida, he has finished up with four blind men (five if we include 12:22) to Mark's two! The third does at least provide a theologically credible motive, and may be further supported by Matthew's specification of *two* witnesses in 26:60, where Mark speaks of an unspecified number of *false* witnesses (see on 26:60). But it remains speculative, and it accounts only with difficulty for 8:29, where the "testimony" is that of the multiple demons rather than of the two men. No less speculative is the traditional harmonistic view that both here and in the Jericho story two men were involved, and that Mark and Luke have mentioned only one of them (the same has also been suggested of the two donkeys, in that case with better reason since presumably Jesus rode on only one of them); such harmonizations can seldom be proved impossible, but most interpreters prefer to look for a literary explanation of what seems to be a tendency of this one author. The reason for Matthew's "seeing double" remains a matter of speculation.

28 The location is somewhere on the eastern shore of the lake, most of which fell in the region of the Decapolis and had a largely non-Jewish population (hence the presence of pigs, which were unclean to Jews; Lev 11:7; *m. B. Qam.* 7:7). In all three Synoptic Gospels there is a variety of readings here, but most scholars agree that Mark and Luke originally read "Gerasenes," while Matthew had "Gadarenes."[33] Both Gerasa and Gadara were important and well-known cities of the Decapolis, but neither was itself by the lake, Gadara being some six miles southeast of the lake, and Gerasa some thirty miles further away. According to Josephus, *Life* 42,[34] however, Gadara controlled territory reaching to the shore. Many later MSS of all three gospels have the reading "Gergesenes," and this is reflected in several early patristic citations, following Origen, who argued for this reading on the grounds of geographical plausibility and of local tradition. There is no clear evidence of a town called Gergesa in the first century, but the modern village of El Koursi near the northern end of the eastern shore has been claimed to represent its site, and the presence there of a fine fifth-century church probably testifies that this was the Gergesa which Origen and Eusebius claimed to be the site of the miracle, an identification supported by the fact that this is the only part of the eastern shore where there is a steep bank running down into the lake. But El Koursi is well to the north of the area likely to have been controlled by Gadara (and separated from it by the territory of Hippos), so that if Matthew wrote "Gadarenes" he was speaking impressionistically

33. Most of the OL versions read "Gerasenes" in Matthew as well, but that is probably a mechanical harmonization.
34. Cf. Schürer, 2:136.

rather than with geographical precision, using a more familiar name in place of the little-known Gergesa.[35]

While Matthew has eliminated most of Mark's description of the demoniac(s), he retains a mention of the tombs which Mark says were their home, since it was appropriate that unclean spirits should live in an unclean place, just as they will later go into unclean animals (pigs).[36] If the possessed men had been forced out of normal society, tombs, perhaps using hillside caves, would provide the best alternative shelter. The village was some distance away (v. 33), and the two men maintained a reign of terror in this unwholesome area near the lake.

29 Since two men are involved, Matthew's plural verb most naturally refers to them rather than to the demons, who have not yet been explicitly mentioned. But the men's voices convey the demons' thoughts, since in v. 31 the dialogue will be continued explicitly by "the demons," and here, too, the wording better suits them: they express a supernatural recognition of Jesus as the Son of God, and are aware that he is likely to bring trouble for them. For Jewish belief that the demonic forces, currently confined but still active, would eventually be punished see, for example, *1 En.* 12–16; *Jub.* 5:6-10; 10:1-13. The intriguing phrase *pro kairou,* "before the proper time," implies a recognition by the demons that their time of opportunity to trouble human beings is limited, and that the arrival of Jesus signals the beginning of the end, which they had hoped would not come yet; for the final judgment of evil spirits as the role of the Messiah see *1 En.* 55:4; *T. Levi* 18:12. Jesus in his earthly ministry is already introducing the eschatological "cleanup" of the forces of evil. Mark has repeated references to demons knowing and declaring who Jesus is (Mark 1:24, 34; 3:11-12; 5:7), a theme which serves to offset the deliberately incognito style of Jesus' public appearance in Mark. But this is the only time Matthew records such a declaration, though he has of course already spoken of Satan's testing of Jesus' status as the Son of God in 4:1-11. The title will come as no surprise to Matthew's readers after 2:15 and 3:17, but we have no indication here of whether the disciples heard the declaration or what they made of it — it will not be until 14:33 that they reach the point of making the same assertion themselves.

30-32 According to 12:43-45 demons do not like to be homeless. The pigs provide a suitable alternative home for them if they are forced out

---

35. For full discussion of the reading and its likely location see T. Baarda in E. E. Ellis and M. Wilcox (eds.), *Neotestamentica et Semitica,* 181-97. R. H. Gundry, *Mark,* 255-56, defends the less popular reading "Gergesenes" in Mark.

36. Is there an echo of Isa 65:4, where sitting in tombs and eating pigs' flesh are mentioned together?

from their present hosts.[37] But even for this they apparently need (and receive) Jesus' permission; he is in total control of the situation. The drowning of the pigs, however, is not part of the deal, and probably not part of the demons' plan either, since it will leave them homeless again. Matthew does not say, and probably does not imply, that the demons were destroyed when the pigs were drowned — the subject of the plural verb "died" must be the same as that of the preceding verb "stampeded," even though the latter is singular referring to the "herd" collectively:[38] demons, as supernatural beings, could not be destroyed by drowning. The behavior of the pigs, caused by the entry of the demons,[39] is recorded as visible proof that the demons have in fact left the men; similar visible proofs of exorcism are mentioned by Josephus, *Ant.* 8.48 (a basin of water overturned) and by Philostratus, *Vit. Apoll.* 4.20 (a statue knocked over). The account is concise, with no concession to the fact that the steep bank of the lakeshore near El Koursi hardly amounts to a "cliff," nor to the fact that pigs can swim if necessary and so could have climbed back up out of the water. Matthew is not recording natural history. Nor is he concerned with ethical issues of the destruction of animal life or of the economic loss of the owners. To point out that it was the demons, rather than Jesus, that caused the stampede (and even they perhaps not intentionally; see above) may be true, but it is hardly relevant to Matthew's purpose in telling the story. Nor does it seem to have been the conclusion drawn by the locals, who were keen to get rid of Jesus as soon as possible.[40]

33-34 Whereas Mark gives a touching account of the rehabilitation of the former demoniac, of his wish to join Jesus' party, and of his commission in-

---

37. J. M. Hull, *Magic,* 38-41, provides fascinating details of Hellenistic beliefs about demons and their preferences. A Babylonian exorcistic incantation actually offers a pig as an alternative host for the expelled demon (R. C. Thompson, *The Devils and Evil Spirits of Babylonia* [London: Luzac, 1903/4], 2:10-15).

38. Carson, 219, explains the change to the plural verb on the basis that "it would be awkward to speak of a herd's dying." The same change from singular to plural occurs in Mark, where the verb πνίγομαι is even more clearly appropriate to pigs, not to demons. But see contra Gundry, n. 98.

39. J. D. M. Derrett, *JSNT* 3 (1979) 5-6, assures us, on the basis of consultation with experts in pig behavior, that pigs do not naturally act as a herd, still less stampede over a cliff. "If such a thing happened, any onlooker would say they were bewitched."

40. Beare, 219, comments: "For a Jewish story-teller, and a Jewish audience, the destruction of a herd of swine would be no calamity, but rather a cause for merriment. Not surprisingly, the reaction of the owners is not the same." Carter, 213, goes further and finds in the destruction of the pigs "a coded depiction of Rome's demise," so that "the story celebrates Jesus' liberating reign, which subverts claims made by religious and imperial powers and points to God's sovereignty over Rome." Matthew, on the other hand, betrays no hint either of nationalistic merriment or of political symbolism! For him the pigs are merely incidental to the demonstration of the unique authority of Jesus.

stead to tell his own people about Jesus, Matthew is concerned rather with the impression left on the local population by Jesus' awesome authority. This is not a story about mission but about power. But whereas among the Jews his miracle-working power has attracted people to follow Jesus, here in the Decapolis they want to get rid of him. For them he is not a messianic figure, but a wandering Jewish "holy man" whose activities have already caused a great deal of damage; he will be safer back among his own people. It is a strangely unflattering ending to the story, but it has reinforced Matthew's message that Jesus is not like other people. Before long we shall hear of similarly unflattering reactions to Jesus' exorcistic activities even among his own people: his power is not doubted, but its source is called into question (9:34; 12:24).

c. The Paralyzed Man (9:1-8)

We are now back in more familiar territory, with Jesus in Capernaum responding to a request to heal a physical complaint. But the story takes a surprising turn. The paralysis will indeed be cured and the man instantly restored to normal health, but the healing itself is only a subplot, as Jesus asserts and then demonstrates his authority to forgive sins in the face of the scribal assumption that to make such a claim is blasphemy. The healing itself is brought into the service of this overriding theme, as the visible proof of the invisible authority Jesus claims. The reaction of the spectators this time is not merely amazement but fear. Their comment is on Jesus' authority, but it is not made clear whether this is with reference primarily to the spectacular healing itself or to the spiritual authority which it has been used to demonstrate.

This is the first time in this gospel that we find Jesus in controversy with scribes and/or Pharisees, a theme which will be taken further in the immediately following pericopes (9:11-13, 14-17) and will become a central motif of Matthew's story. Jesus' own words in 5:20 and Matthew's editorial comment in 7:29 have already laid the foundation for this conflict of interests, which will develop in the Jerusalem phase of the story into a serious power struggle, as the "new wine" of Jesus' introduction of the kingdom of heaven comes into confrontation with the accepted authority structures of first-century Judaism, resulting in their mutual repudiation. For now that confrontation remains relatively undeveloped, but the scribal objection here serves to highlight the boldness and uniqueness of Jesus' claim concerning the spiritual authority of "the Son of Man."

The combination in one narrative of physical healing and the forgiveness of sins seems to some modern commentators unnatural, and it has often been suggested that an originally simple healing story has been overlaid with a secondary layer of controversy about the authority to forgive. Proof of this has been claimed in the awkward syntax of v. 6, where Jesus' statement to the

343

scribes about forgiveness is interrupted by a stage direction and a change of addressee after which we hear only of physical healing, not of forgiveness. I shall suggest below that the syntactical awkwardness is the result not of literary stitching but of the logic of the scene, where the command to the paralyzed man is in itself the proof of the authority to forgive sins. The connection would be more easily perceived in a culture which did not draw so sharp a distinction between spiritual and physical dysfunction as the Western world tends to do today, and which would not necessarily have perceived it as a *non sequitur* when Jesus responded to a request for healing with a declaration of forgiveness. Matthew's readers may well be reminded of the original declaration of Jesus' mission in 1:21: "he will save his people from their sins."

1   This verse both concludes the preceding pericope and introduces the next. It is interesting that the disciples, whose presence with Jesus in the boat was emphasized in 8:23 and who were themselves the recipients of Jesus' powerful protection in 8:24-27, have dropped out of sight once the crossing was completed: since 8:28 Jesus has been spoken of in the singular, and this will remain the case until the disciples come into the picture again in 9:10. Their presence is assumed, but they have nothing to contribute to the story; all the attention is on the personal authority of Jesus. "His own town" is of course Capernaum (4:13); he is returning to the scene of his former healing miracles (8:5-17), and the people are ready to take advantage of his presence again.

2   Matthew does not situate this incident, as do Mark and Luke, inside a house; the presence of the scribes (v. 3) and of "crowds" (v. 8), as well as presumably the disciples, is more easily envisaged out in the street than in the relatively small and private space of a Capernaum living room. In that setting there is no need for extreme measures on the part of the bearers to bring their patient to Jesus, and Matthew thus omits the graphic account of forced entry through the roof which is the most memorable (and most improbable!) part of the story as told by Mark and Luke. The bearers are indicated only by the verb "they brought" without an expressed subject, and play no further part in the story. Matthew does, however, retain the comment that Jesus "saw their faith" as the basis for his response of forgiveness and healing; perhaps the mere act of bringing the man to Jesus was enough to demonstrate their faith, but it is possible that Matthew thus signals his awareness of the story of their determined and unorthodox entry which he has decided not to relate as such. For faith as a significant component in healing stories cf. 8:10, 13; 9:22, 28-29; 15:28, and for the principle involved see 17:20; 21:21-22. In 8:10, 13 and 15:28 the faith rewarded is not that of the sufferers themselves, and here, too, it seems that the faith of those who brought the man to Jesus plays a significant part, though of course "their" faith may be understood as including the patient himself as well as his bearers.

As in 8:6 (see comments there), it is impossible to determine the medical cause of the "paralysis"; we can deduce from the story only that the man was incapable of walking, and that his immediate restoration to health and strength could only be interpreted as an act of supernatural authority. The term does not in itself explain Jesus' unexpected assurance of forgiveness — there is no such reference to sin in the only other gospel account of the healing of "paralysis" (8:5-13). While a close connection between sin and physical illness or disability would have been assumed by many people at the time (cf. 1 Cor 11:28-30), the connection is made in only one other gospel healing story, and there it is in order to *dismiss* the idea of sin as the cause of blindness (John 9:1-3).[41] Here the connection is left unexplained; it is not stated that the paralysis was caused by sin. Other gospel accounts of healing do not mention the forgiveness of sins as if this were a necessary means to physical restoration; faith rather than forgiveness is the normal requisite.[42] We can only speculate as to whether in this case Jesus was aware of what we would call a psychosomatic element in the man's condition, or whether we should understand Jesus as addressing a separate spiritual problem of which the man's friends may have been unaware. Sin and disability are linked in this story in that the curing of the latter will be taken as proof of authority to deal with the former, but this does not in itself require us to regard the paralysis as *caused by* the sin which Jesus forgives, even though many of those present would probably have so understood it.

"Take heart" is a formula of reassurance, where we might say "It's alright" (cf. 9:22; 14:27; Mark 10:49). It may suggest that the paralyzed man himself was less confident of Jesus' help than his friends. *Teknon*, "child," is not often found in the gospels as a form of address to someone other than one's own son or daughter (elsewhere only in Mark 10:24; Luke 16:25; in the latter case the Jewish rich man is, theoretically, the descendant of the speaker, Abraham); its informality strengthens the tone of reassurance: "It's alright, lad" (cf. "Take heart, daughter," also to a stranger, in v. 22). The present tense[43] of Jesus' assurance (literally, "Your sins are being forgiven") reads like a performative utterance (BDF 320): Jesus is not merely stating a fact, but is there and then forgiving the sins by his own authority, without any formal atonement having been made. That is what the scribes will object to.

---

41. In John 5:14, however, Jesus instructs a healed man not to sin any more so that nothing worse may happen to him, even though his previous condition has not been attributed to sin.

42. Cf. Jas 5:14-16, which envisages the possibility that someone who is ill may also need to have sins forgiven, without making this in itself the basis of the healing process.

43. Many later MSS have the perfect ἀφέωνται here and in v. 5, but this is probably an assimilation to Luke. In Mark the evidence for the perfect is stronger than in Matthew, but there, too, most editors agree that the present was original. The performative sense would be less pronounced, though still possible, with the perfect tense.

3 For "scribes" see on 5:20. Here we are dealing presumably not with the Jerusalem establishment[44] but with local Galilean legal teachers. Most of the opposition to Jesus in Galilee will come from Pharisees (whom Luke includes here too), and in 12:38 it will be scribes and Pharisees together who challenge Jesus' credentials. As we noted at 5:20, the two terms overlap, and there is no real difference between scribal and Pharisaic opposition in the Synoptic accounts.[45] The charge of blasphemy,[46] which will later become the justification for Jewish condemnation of Jesus (26:65-66), is explained in Mark and Luke by the statement that only God can forgive sins. Matthew assumes that his readers do not need that explanation. Jesus has taken upon himself, without explanation or apology, a divine prerogative.

4-5 Jesus "saw" rather than "knew" (see p. 333, n. 17) their thoughts presumably by observing the "body language" and whispering together of the disaffected group. Matthew would have no hesitation in ascribing supernatural knowledge to Jesus (cf. 12:25; 22:18), but here his wording does not require it. For "evil thoughts" originating in the heart cf. 12:34-35; 15:19. The rhetorical question of v. 5 implies that if the "harder" of the two options can be demonstrated, the "easier" may be assumed also to be possible.[47] It might be suggested that to forgive sins is the harder, since only God can do it, but Jesus' question is not about which is easier to *do*, but which is easier to *say*, and a *claim* to forgive sins is undoubtedly easier to make, since it cannot be falsified by external events, whereas a claim to make a paralyzed man walk will be immediately proved true or false by a success or failure which everyone can see. This will be the logic of what follows: Jesus' demonstrable authority to cure the disabled man is evidence that he also has authority to forgive sins.

6 The argument is spelled out by a broken sentence in which the

44. In 15:1 we shall meet in Galilee scribes who have come up from Jerusalem (cf. also Mark 3:22), but no such note is made here.

45. The suggestion of D. E. Orton, *Scribe,* 31, that τινες τῶν γραμματέων (a phrase Matthew shares with Mark) is intended to set this group apart as exceptional and so to exonerate the scribes as a whole depends on his view that it is only *Pharisaic* scribes, not scribes per se, that Matthew treats as opponents of Jesus. Nothing in this context suggests such a distinction.

46. Clearly Jesus has not committed blasphemy in the later (Mishnaic) technical sense of actually pronouncing the divine name (*m. Sanh.* 7:5), but it is clear that in the pre-Mishnaic period the term was used more broadly for words or actions deemed to infringe on the divine prerogative. See D. L. Bock, *Blasphemy,* 110-12, summarizing a detailed discussion on pp. 30-110. Cf. the "definition" of blasphemy in John 10:33, "that you, being a man, make yourself God."

47. This use of the comparative εὐκοπώτερον, "easier," to express an *a fortiori* argument seems to be a distinctive usage of Jesus; it occurs in Greek only in the sayings of Jesus (cf. 19:24 pars.; Luke 16:17). Cf., however, Sir 22:15 for a similar use of the positive form εὔκοπον.

first (subordinate) clause addressed to the scribes leads into a main clause which is in fact an imperative addressed to the paralyzed man. In the narrative setting this change of addressee would be made perfectly clear by the speaker's physical movement or gesture, and the logic of the two-part sentence would thus be obvious: what the man is being told to do is itself the proof of the claim Jesus has made. But it is not easy to represent such a movement within reported speech in written form, and all three Synoptic writers have resorted to a parenthetical "stage direction" (see p. 333, n. 18). It is a sensible, if not elegant, device.[48] Those editors and translators who insert a dash, implying that the sentence is left incomplete, in fact obscure the logic of Jesus' reply; the sentence is indeed completed, but its main clause, while still intended for the attention of the scribes, is an imperative necessarily directed toward the man who is to be healed. As the sequel will show, the imperative is no less a "performative" utterance than the indicative "Your sins are forgiven" in v. 2.

The use of "the Son of Man" here can again only refer to Jesus himself (see above on 8:20): it is *his* authority to forgive sins that is specifically in question. A generalized sense ("Human beings have authority on earth to forgive sins") would only compound the blasphemy, and would only be relevant in this context if it was open to anyone equally to cure a paralyzed man. Jesus is not arguing that it is not God's prerogative to forgive sins, but rather than he himself, uniquely, shares it. The Son of Man, who according to Dan 7:13-14 will be enthroned in heaven to share God's sovereignty over all peoples, is already during his earthly ministry (hence the addition of "on earth," in distinction from his future heavenly sovereignty) authorized to dispense God's forgiveness. The forgiveness of sins as such was not, of course, a part of Daniel's vision of the authority of the Son of Man. Jesus is not expounding Dan 7, but boldly extrapolating from that vision to make a claim for his present status, as he will do again in 12:8.

The "bed" was presumably a simple, light-weight structure, sufficiently rigid to allow it to be used as a stretcher, but able to be carried by one

---

48. Much more awkward is the suggestion, argued in relation to Mark 2:10 by C. P. Ceroke, *CBQ* 22 (1960) 369-90, and tentatively supported with reference to Matthew by Davies and Allison, 2:93-94, that the whole of the first part of v. 6 is an editorial aside addressed to the reader as "you." On this view two asides of different kinds would be clumsily placed side by side, interrupting the flow of Jesus' speech. But Matthew nowhere else addresses the reader as "you." Moreover, this reading would create an unparalleled editorial use of "the Son of Man," a term conspicuously confined to the words of Jesus throughout the gospels. And by transferring to the editor the one clause which states openly Jesus' claim to have authority to forgive sins, it leaves Jesus' own reported saying incoherent, and takes out of the narrative context the primary basis for the crowd's reaction in v. 8.

person. By carrying it to his own home the man will demonstrate his complete and immediate cure.

7-8　The cure is related with a minimum of detail. What matters is rather the response of the crowd. Fear (see p. 333, n. 19) is not the usual reaction to a healing miracle in this gospel, and since the explanation is in terms of "authority" we should probably understand their response as triggered not so much by the miracle itself as by the claim to have authority to forgive sins which the miracle has now demonstrated to be valid. Fear in 14:26-27; 17:6-7; 27:54; 28:4-5, 8 is a response to supernatural phenomena, and that sense would be appropriate here: Jesus has just demonstrated that he wields suprahuman authority. They rightly acknowledge God's hand in what they have seen, but the particular focus of their awe is the means by which he has done it, by "giving such authority to human beings." The plural is surprising, since it is only one human being to whom this particular authority has been given. The phrasing has been thought to pick up Jesus' use of "the Son of Man" in v. 6 and to reflect on the normal sense of the Aramaic term: it is to Jesus as a (the) "human being" that this authority has been delegated. But there is little to indicate that the original meaning of the phrase played any significant part in Matthew's usage generally. For him it has become a title with a specialized meaning of its own, so that he would not regard the plural "human beings" here as an echo of the phrase "the Son of Man."[49] It is more likely therefore that the unexpected *tois anthrōpois* here is a generalizing plural used idiomatically to express surprise that this special prerogative of God has been shared with *any* human being. The reference is still to Jesus alone, since a more general sense that God now allows any human being to forgive sins on his behalf would be a *non sequitur* after Jesus has just claimed and demonstrated a special personal authority (see on v. 6). It is true that in 16:19; 18:18 Jesus will share his special authority "on earth" with a few carefully selected human beings (the Twelve), but that is far from being a blanket authorization for "human beings" in general to dispense God's forgiveness. The view of several commentators that the plural is intended to indicate that the church shares in Jesus' authority to forgive introduces an element which is extraneous to this pericope and which would detract from its emphasis on Jesus' unique authority.[50]

49. It would be possible to argue that in the historical situation Jesus' words about "the Son of Man" were understood by some of the crowd as a general statement about humanity, but surely inconceivable that Matthew could have recorded such a misunderstanding without comment and as the climactic declaration of this demonstration of Jesus' special authority. Hagner, 1:234, suggests that this is Matthew's "deliberate attempt to show the failure of the crowd to understand the title and thus to indicate their inadequate understanding of Jesus despite the logic of the narrative." Perhaps, but that is a lot to expect the reader to infer without the assistance of any editorial hint in that direction.

50. E. Schweizer's comment, in G. N. Stanton (ed.), *Interpretation,* 152, that "it is

4. Following Jesus: Tax Collectors and Sinners (9:9-17)

9 *As Jesus went on from there, he saw a man called Matthew sitting at the customs booth,[1] and he said to him, "Follow me." Matthew got up and followed him.*

10 *Now[2] while he was at a meal in the house, along came[3] many tax collectors and sinners and joined Jesus and his disciples at the meal.* 11*The Pharisees saw this, and said to his disciples, "Why does your teacher eat with tax collectors and sinners?"* 12 *Jesus heard them, and said, "It is not those who are well who need a doctor, but those who are ill.* 13 *Go and learn what this means, 'I desire mercy and not sacrifice.' That is why[4] I came to call not the righteous but sinners."*

14 *Then the disciples of John came to him and said, "Why do we and the Pharisees fast a lot,[5] while your disciples do not fast?"* 15 *Jesus replied, "Surely the wedding guests[6] can't be sad as long as the bridegroom is with them, can they? But a time will come when the bridegroom has been taken away from them; then they will fast.*

certain that Matthew has the community in view, where forgiveness of sins is still practised," claims a "certainty" which needs to be demonstrated rather than asserted. A similarly misplaced certainty is found in Gundry's comment that "'the men'... can hardly be different from the disciples whom Matthew strikingly called 'the men'" in 8:27; the definite article is much more likely to be read here as generic than anaphoric as it is in 8:27, since there is no plural group of human beings mentioned in this pericope to whom such an anaphoric use might refer — the disciples have been strikingly absent from the narrative since 8:27.

1. See the comments below on the nature of Matthew's profession and where it would be exercised.

2. Here, for the only time outside the five transition formulae (see on 7:28), Matthew uses the Semitic καὶ ἐγένετο as a narrative introduction, but in this case, unlike in 7:28; 11:1; 13:53; 19:1; 26:1, it is followed by a καί to introduce the main clause. The clause sets the scene for an important new development.

3. An attempt to represent the force of καὶ ἰδού which, following the καὶ ἐγένετο at the beginning of the sentence, draws attention to a significant new development in the story.

4. The Greek γάρ, "for," here explains the Hosea quotation as providing the justification for Jesus' mission.

5. The inclusion of πυκνά (parallel to Luke 5:33) in ℵ[1] (supported by most Latin versions) and of πολλά in ℵ[2] and most other witnesses may well represent an original element in the text; the two adverbial adjectives would have the same meaning in context. The omission of any qualification in ℵ* and B may be explained either by the influence of the Mark parallel or by the feeling that it was redundant since the issue is not the frequency of fasting so much as whether to fast at all.

6. The υἱοὶ τοῦ νυμφῶνος, literally "sons of the wedding hall," may be either wedding guests in general or a special group of men attached to the bridegroom, as bridesmaids are today to the bride (like the "best man," but plural), for which there is no current English expression unless it be the stilted "groomsmen."

16 *"No one patches an old coat with a patch of unshrunk cloth: the patch would[7] tear away from the coat[8] and a worse tear would result. 17 Nor do they put new wine into old wineskins; otherwise[9] the wineskins would burst, and both the wine would be wasted and the wineskins ruined. No, they put new wine into new wineskins, and so both are preserved."*

The previous interlude in the sequence of miracle stories which make up chs. 8–9 illustrated the demanding nature of discipleship by two examples of volunteers who apparently failed to meet Jesus' high standards (8:18-22). This one also begins with a case study, but this time it is Jesus who takes the initiative by calling Matthew, the first and only such call story in this gospel after the initial calling of the four fishermen in 4:18-22. The authority of Jesus' call cannot be refused, and Matthew becomes one of Jesus' close companions who will become the Twelve (10:1-4). We are left to assume that the other seven, of whom we have no biographical details, had similar experiences.

But Matthew the tax collector represents a wider group of "undesirables" who are also interested in Jesus and his message and who join him and his disciples at a meal in Matthew's house. Their interest, and Jesus' acceptance of them, even to the extent of sharing table fellowship, give rise to some pungent comments of Jesus in response to Pharisaic criticism (vv. 11-13) which sharply characterize the sort of people Jesus is looking for as his followers. Discipleship is not for the comfortable and respectable, but for those whom conventional society would rather keep at arm's length. The Pharisees can see only their failures, but Jesus sees their need, and the fact that they acknowledge it themselves gives him the opportunity to fulfill his calling to "save his people from their sins" (1:21).

There is no explicit connection between the call of Matthew and the encounter with John's disciples in v. 14, but perhaps we are meant to understand that their question was provoked by seeing Jesus and his entourage feasting in Matthew's house. Jesus' extended response to it (vv. 14-17) then adds a further dimension to the portrait of discipleship which is gradually

7. The two verbs in this clause are simple indicatives, but English idiom requires a "would" for an unreal situation. Similarly in v. 17.

8. Literally, the clause probably means "its filling (not the same word as "patch" in the preceding clause, but πλήρωμα, that which fills it [the coat] up) will take [something] away from the coat." It is possible that the surprising use of πλήρωμα is intended to evoke thoughts of Jesus' "fulfillment" of what had gone before (3:15; 5:17, and the formula of 1:22 etc.), but it could equally be due to a desire to vary the wording.

9. The idiom εἰ δὲ μή γε, "but if indeed not," fits awkwardly after a negative statement; presumably the "not" envisages that the implied (negative) advice of the previous sentence is not followed, so that the effect in context is "but if they *do.*"

building up in preparation for ch. 10. Following Jesus is not like "discipleship" as it was experienced in other pious circles at the time. It is characterized, at least for the present, by joy rather than solemnity, by feasting rather than fasting, and the two graphic sayings of vv. 16-17 indicate a fundamental incompatibility between the dry formality of existing religious traditions and an exuberant vitality in the Jesus circle which cannot be confined within conventional forms. To follow Jesus is to find life on a new level.

Here then is a pair of episodes which are narrated not so much for the intrinsic significance of what happened (though the call of Matthew is an exemplary story in itself) as for the radical pronouncements by Jesus to which they give rise. Together they provide a startling perspective on the new values of the kingdom of heaven which will increasingly put Jesus and his movement on a collision course with traditional Jewish piety. The overt criticism of Jesus by the religious leaders which we first encountered in 9:3 is here developed and further explained. Matthew is preparing his readers for the parting of the ways which will reach a threatening climax as early as 12:14.

9 A "tax collector" *(telōnēs)* in Capernaum would be responsible for the collection of a variety of taxes levied by Herod Antipas,[10] prominent among which would be customs duties on goods carried through and traded in this border town: the separate tetrarchy of Herod Philip began on the other side of the Jordan, which reaches the lake two or three miles east of Capernaum, while further south across the lake from Capernaum was the non-Jewish community of the Decapolis. The presence of "many tax collectors" (v. 10) indicates that Matthew did not work alone, so that his abrupt departure would not leave the customs booth unguarded. Mark 2:13-14 indicates that it was by the lakeshore, where boats would land their cargoes.[11]

By working for an unpopular government sanctioned by Rome a *telōnēs* incurred the hatred and disdain of Jewish patriots, quite apart from any economic grievances resulting from their reputation for exacting more than was officially necessary. The conventional pairing "tax collectors and sinners" (v. 10; cf. 11:19; Luke 15:1; 18:9-14) shows how society regarded them; cf. also 5:46; 18:17; 21:31-32.[12] For Jesus to call such a man to follow him was a daring breach of etiquette, a calculated snub to conventional ideas of respectability, which ordinary people no less than Pharisees might be expected to balk at. Fishermen may not have been high in the social scale, but at

10. Galilee was not yet subject to direct Roman taxation as Judea was; see on 22:15-22.

11. For the taxation system in Galilee see H. Hoehner, *Herod,* 73-79, and more widely Schürer, 1:372-76. See also J. R. Donahue, *CBQ* 33 (1971) 39-61.

12. For Jewish evidence to this effect see J. Jeremias, *Jerusalem,* 310-12. See also Keener, 292-93.

least they were not automatically morally and religiously suspect; Matthew was. Almost as remarkable as Jesus' decision to call him is Matthew's confident response; he does not seem to have felt uncomfortable at being included in a preacher's entourage, though we are not told what the other disciples thought. Jesus was by now a well-known figure in Capernaum, so Matthew would need no lengthy explanation. The very concise account of his call and response echoes those of 4:19-20, 21-22, and the emphasis on the verb "follow" recalls 8:18-23.

In Mark and Luke the tax collector of Capernaum is called Levi, even though the name Matthew (and not Levi) appears in their lists of the Twelve (Mark 3:18; Luke 6:15; Acts 1:13). Inevitably the discrepancy has been linked with the fact that this is traditionally the Gospel of Matthew, in two incompatible ways: either the appearance of the name here has been traced to the actual author's deliberate self-identification, or the traditional attribution of the gospel has been explained from the fact that the name Matthew appears here (so Luz, 2:33). Neither is a necessary or indeed a likely explanation. Within Matthew the use of the name is consistent, including the identification of Matthew as a *telōnēs* in 10:3 (in the disciple lists of Mark and Luke the name Matthew appears without qualification). It is of course possible that Jesus called more than one *telōnēs,* but since the call narratives for Matthew and for Levi are clearly the same, the appearance of the two names Levi/Matthew in Mark and Luke is better explained as parallel to the cases of Simon/Cephas (Peter), Joseph/Barnabas (Acts 4:36), or Jesus/Barabbas (see on 27:16-17), each of whom, like Levi/Matthew, had two Semitic names,[13] not just a translation of a Semitic name into Greek as with Thomas/Didymus.[14]

10-11 While only Matthew has been called to be a disciple, we now find that he represents a much larger number of people who have been attracted to Jesus. The pronoun "he" could refer to either Jesus or Matthew,

---

13. One of the names might be either a given nickname like Cephas or a family name or "surname" like Barabbas. For other examples of a person having two Semitic names see W. L. Lane, *Mark,* 100, n. 29. Another example known from the NT is the high priest Caiaphas, whose personal name was Joseph (Josephus, *Ant.* 18.35; cf. also 20.196; in each case Josephus uses the term ἐπικαλούμενος, "surnamed"). The suggestion that Levi was a tribal rather than a personal name ("the Levite") is awkward since the name occurs in Mark and Luke only on its own, not as a qualification to the name Matthew. Levi was in any case one of the most common personal names in first-century Palestine (there are three or four people called Levi in Josephus's *Life;* only Simon and Jesus are more common), and the more common the personal name the more likely it is that a person would be identified by a second name.

14. Saul/Paul is different, since the latter is not a translation of the former; similarly, Jesus/Justus (Col 4:11). These men were diaspora Jews, and Saul a Roman citizen as well, so that a Roman name alongside a Jewish would be normal. In Acts 1:23 Joseph, a Palestinian, has both a Semitic "surname" (Barsabbas) and a Roman name (Justus).

and "the house" is not identified, so that it is possible to read Matthew's account (and Mark's) as describing Jesus inviting Matthew and his friends to a meal at his (Jesus') house. But Luke says that this is a celebratory meal provided by Levi at his own house (which is likely to have been larger and more affluent), and that is the more likely reading here too: for Jesus and his disciples to be guests in the house of such a man sharpens the Pharisees' objections. The offense is compounded by the presence of "many" such undesirable people. "Sinners" has been taken here to mean simply the 'am-hā 'āreṣ, the common people who did not observe the scribal rules of tithing and purity,[15] but the term usually carries a more clearly moral sense, as in Luke 7:36-50, and the recent focus on the forgiveness of sins in vv. 2-8 points that way.[16] Even worse is the fact that they are not merely meeting with Jesus and his disciples, but sharing a meal as well.[17] In the ancient world generally a shared meal was a clear sign of identification, and for a Jewish religious teacher to share a meal with such people was scandalous, let alone to do so in the "unclean" house of a tax collector.[18] The attentive reader of the gospel might recall the vision of the messianic banquet in 8:11-12: here, as there, the guest list is not at all what most Jews would have expected.[19]

For "Pharisees" see above on 3:7 and 5:20. This is the first of several times they will appear as the chief opponents of Jesus during his Galilean ministry.[20] The scribal objections in 9:3 were "among themselves"; this time

15. Albright and Mann, 105, translate ἁμαρτωλοί here as "non-observant Jews."

16. Keener, 294-96 ("Who were the 'sinners'?"), argues convincingly against the view that the term means simply members of the 'am-hā 'āreṣ. After all, Jesus and his disciples themselves apparently belonged to the 'am-hā 'āreṣ, yet they are expected to keep apart from ἁμαρτωλοί.

17. ἀνακείμενος, which I have translated "at a meal" in v. 10a, is literally "reclining," the normal posture for a more formal or special meal (see on 8:11); Luke's mention of a δοχὴ μεγάλη corresponds to this implication. In v. 10b the compound συνανάκειμαι, "co-recline," underlines the Pharisees' objection.

18. J. Jeremias, Theology, 110-11, argues that the house of a τελώνης was not technically "unclean," but see to the contrary R. P. Booth, Purity, 80-81, 110-11. See further J. R. Donahue, CBQ 33 (1971) 39-61. To be the guest of an 'am-hā 'āreṣ jeopardized a person's purity in the matter of tithes (m. Demai 2:2-3). For the uncleanness of tax collectors see also m. Ṭehar. 7:6.

19. Carter, 220, following K. Corley, suggests that the presence of women at the meal may have added to the offense. This cannot be proved, but it is likely and would be in keeping with Jesus' more accepting attitude toward women generally.

20. In 15:1 the Pharisees who confront Jesus in Galilee are specifically identified as having come from Jerusalem, which was certainly the focus of the Pharisaic movement. It is sometimes argued that there would have been no Pharisees based in Galilee at this period, but Josephus's accounts of first-century Palestine do not indicate such a restriction. See the cautious comments of M. Hengel, Leader, 45, 55 (and nn. 26 and 64).

the Pharisees speak openly, but to the disciples rather than to Jesus himself, so that in each case Jesus has to "see" (v. 3) or "hear" (v. 12) what was not addressed directly to him. In 12:1-2 and 15:1-2 the Pharisees will tackle Jesus directly, but with reference to his *disciples'* actions. This curious indirectness may be intended to indicate some hesitancy in tackling this formidable teacher, but in the present case it need only mean that, unwilling to enter the house themselves, they address the nearest members of the party. The phrase "your teacher" carries an implied sarcasm: what sort of "teacher" would behave like this?

12 Jesus' first response is in the form of a proverb which uses physical illness as a metaphor for spiritual need. Plutarch quotes a similar saying of the Spartan king Pausanias when he was criticized for neglecting his own people: "It is not the custom of doctors to spend time among people who are healthy, but where people are ill." The philosopher Diogenes is quoted as saying that as a doctor must go among the sick, so a wise man must mix with fools.[21] The point is obvious: any effective "healer" must expect to get his hands dirty.

13 Two further sayings underline the argument. The first is simply a quotation (using the rabbinic formula "Go and learn") from Hos 6:6 in a form close to that of the LXX. The text is not directly expounded, but the context makes clear what Jesus expects them to "learn" from it.[22] The same text will be cited in 12:7, in the next encounter of Jesus with Pharisees, though in that case the issue is their demand for the disciples to adopt their strict understanding of a particular law rather than the more basic character of Jesus' mission which is here in question. Hosea 6:6 is one of several prophetic sayings[23] which challenge people's instinctive reliance on correct ritual while ignoring the moral demands of their religion. The principle is applied here not to sacrifice as such (which Jesus does not rule out, 5:23-24) but to the Pharisees' preoccupation with ritual purity, which overrides concern for those in need; the specific application to a concern for those whom society despised is perhaps sharpened by the LXX version, which uses *eleos,* "mercy," for the more wide-ranging Hebrew term *hesed,* covenant love and faithfulness.[24]

---

21. Plutarch, *Apophth. Lac.* 230F; Dio Chrysostom, *Orat.* 8.5. Another proverb about doctors in Luke 4:23 has a more literal application.

22. D. Hill, *NTS* 24 (1977/8) 111, rightly argues that the formula "does not mean 'go and find out what you do not already know' but rather 'go and discern the *sense* of Scripture' or 'go and make a valid inference from the scriptural statement.'"

23. E.g., Isa 1:10-17; Jer 7:4-11; Amos 5:21-24; Mic 6:6-8; cf. 1 Sam 15:22; Pss 50:7-14; 51:15-17.

24. D. Hill, *NTS* 24 (1977/8) 116-17, comments that "ἔλεος denotes, in part, the content which Matthew desires to give to the 'better righteousness' which disciples must

For "I came to . . ." as a formula of mission see on 5:17. To "call" was the verb used for the recruitment of James and John in 4:21, and even though that verb was not used in v. 9 the reader would naturally think of Matthew as the prime example of Jesus "calling sinners." But the principle is not restricted to Jesus' closest companions, but also includes the "many" of v. 10, and many more who in due course would be drawn into the Jesus movement; cf. the "calling" of "both bad and good" into the kingdom of heaven in 22:9-10. Righteousness is not of course in itself a bad thing; indeed, properly understood it is the goal of discipleship (5:6, 10, 20; 6:33). But the sort of "righteousness" which puts sacrifice before mercy is not the righteousness of the kingdom of heaven (see on 5:20), and those who rely on such correctness of behavior[25] are not likely to find their way through the narrow gate. It is hard for the "righteous" in that sense to recognize their need for a Messiah whose role is to "save his people from their sins" (1:21). Cf. 8:11-12 for a similar reversal of Jewish expectations as to who is in and who is out. The point of "calling sinners," of course, is not that they should remain sinners[26] but that they may find true righteousness.

14 We are now introduced to a third group (scribes in v. 3; Pharisees in v. 11; now John's disciples) who express their disapproval of Jesus' practice. John had attracted crowds to the Jordan (3:5-6), but this is the first we hear of a continuing group of his disciples after his imprisonment (4:12).[27] They will appear again in 11:2; 14:12, and a "Baptist" movement which continued after John's death is indicated in John 4:1-2; Acts 18:25; 19:3.[28] Cf. 21:26, 32 for popular response to John's message in Judea. We know nothing specifically of John's teaching about fasting, but an ascetic regime would fit John's own lifestyle (3:4) and his dour popular image (11:18, with specific

---

possess if they are to see the Kingdom of God." He goes on to argue (p. 118) that ἔλεος for Matthew does not exclude the "Godward meaning" which is primary in the Hebrew *ḥesed,* a "love to God which manifests itself in the attitude of identification with those whom a legalistic religion debarred from their rights as children of Israel."

25. B. Przybylski, *Righteousness,* 102, takes δίκαιος here as primarily meaning "law-keeping," as in 1:19.

26. Luke (followed by many later MSS and versions of Matthew and Mark) adds εἰς μετάνοιαν, "to repentance." It seems likely that Matthew and Mark would also have taken it for granted that this was the purpose of calling sinners, since repentance was the stated aim of the ministry of both Jesus and John in 3:2; 4:17. E. P. Sanders has argued in *JSNT* 19 (1983) 5-36 (cf. *Jesus and Judaism,* 174-211) that the scandalous element in Jesus' mission was that he accepted sinners *without repentance* and, where necessary, restitution. Others have not been convinced. There is a difference between welcoming sinners as they are and allowing them to remain subsequently unchanged.

27. J. E. Taylor, *John,* 102-6, discusses the nature of this movement; cf. ibid., 28, 209 for their remaining in normal society rather than setting up a separate community.

28. See C. H. H. Scobie, *John,* 187-202, for the "Baptist sect."

mention of John's own fasting); cf. the ascetic lifestyle of Bannus and his disciples in the wilderness a few years later (Josephus, *Life* 11–12). They may well have adopted the Pharisaic pattern of fasting twice a week (Luke 18:12; *Did.* 8:1), which went far beyond anything the OT required.[29] See above on 6:16-18 for Jesus' attitude to fasting, and the likelihood that the fasting which he there assumes for his followers was of an occasional rather than a routine nature. It was also to be kept secret from other people (unlike that of the Pharisees). Certainly the impression gained by those outside his group was that they did not fast, and Jesus does nothing to remove that impression. For John's disciples that indicated a movement which did not take its religious commitment seriously, and the feasting in Matthew's house only deepened their suspicion. In their different ways the Pharisees, John's disciples, and the Jesus circle were all renewal movements within first-century Judaism, and this brief encounter serves to draw out their distinctive approaches and priorities.

15 The festivities in connection with a wedding, which usually went on for several days, are a symbol of joy and celebration, and provide a natural image for the new life of the kingdom of heaven (22:2-13; 25:1-12, where again the bridegroom represents Jesus himself; cf. also John 3:29). Here that joy is not just a future hope, but characterizes the whole of Jesus' earthly ministry. Cf. 11:18-19 for a similar contrast between John's asceticism and Jesus' reputation as a *bon viveur.* Fasting does not fit naturally into such a setting. But the focus of this festivity is Jesus himself, and when he, like John, is removed from the scene it will be time for a more sober discipline to be considered; as in 6:16-18, Jesus assumes that fasting will then have its proper place in the normal life of his followers.

This is the first hint that Jesus will be "taken away" (the verb suggests a violent and unwelcome removal, with a possible echo of Isa 53:8), a theme which will become dominant after 16:21. No details are yet given, but in a response to John's disciples it would naturally be taken as linking his fate with that of John, already imprisoned for his opposition to the authorities (4:12; 11:2) and soon to be unjustly executed (14:1-12); in 17:12-13 Jesus will explicitly say that he is to be executed "by them" as John has been. The agents and the circumstances will in fact be different, but the principle of official suppression is the same.

16-17 Two little parables pick up the theme of a new and joyful pattern of religion which is incompatible with the old traditions represented by the fasting regimes of the Pharisees and the followers of John.[30] The pointer

---

29. For the importance of fasting in Judaism after the OT period see J. Behm, *TDNT* 4:929-31.

30. The sayings do not specifically relate to fasting, and may have been preserved independently before becoming attached to this narrative context in the Synoptic tradi-

toward Jesus' death is not explicitly taken further, but the reader who knows what is to come might well reflect that this very incompatibility was to be at the heart of the eventual repudiation of Jesus by the religious establishment in Jerusalem — though it would be excessive allegorization to read the spilled wine as a symbol of the cross and the burst wineskins as pointers to the subsequent destruction of the temple.

The "unshrunk" cloth is literally "unfulled": the fuller cleaned and combed the cloth to remove natural oil and gum, and bleached it ready for use in making garments. Cloth not pre-shrunk in this way would shrink when washed, and so would have a disastrous effect if sewn onto an old, and there-fore already shrunk, coat.[31] Wineskins were made of leather, which was at first soft and pliable but became hard and brittle with age so that it was un-able to withstand the pressure of fermentation (the first stage of fermention of new wine was in a vat, but it was transferred to jars or skins to complete the process after the lees were strained out).

The parable of the wineskins explicitly sets out the answer to this in-compatibility of the new with the old: new wine must be put into new skins. The parables are not decoded for us, and we can only speculate about what sort of new religious structures Jesus, or Matthew, may have had in mind as the appropriate context for the new wine of the kingdom of heaven. But in the light of this saying, perhaps Matthew and his readers would not have been surprised when the early Christian movement, which at first continued to worship in the temple and synagogues, increasingly developed its own "church" structures, not only because of hostility from the rabbinic establish-ment but also because the two patterns proved to be ultimately incompatible. A modern reader might observe that the principle was not exhausted by that early parting of the ways, but that the history of the church ever since has been punctuated by the bursting of old wineskins and the need to find suit-able new containers for the new wine.[32]

---

tion. In *Gos. Thom.* 47 they occur in reverse order attached to other sayings about incom-patibility (an expanded version of Matt 6:24 and the "old wine" saying of Luke 5:39).

31. The version of this saying in *Gos. Thom.* 47 intriguingly reverses the adjectives: "no one sews an old patch on a new garment," a more improbable scenario which is presum-ably designed to warn against going back to old ways after a new religious experience.

32. There is a curious tendency among some commentators to read "and so both are preserved" as including the *old* wineskins, and so to suggest that Matthew is trying to find a continuing role for Jewish tradition alongside the new wine of the kingdom of heaven; so, e.g., J. P. Meier, *Law,* 163, linking this saying with 13:52; cf. Keener, 301. But that is not what the text naturally means: it is the *new* skins which are preserved along with the new wine which is put in them, whereas when old skins are used, both wine and skins are lost. The only way the old skins can survive is if they are *not* brought into contact with new wine!

5. Three Further Stories of Deliverance (9:18-34)

18 *As Jesus was saying this to them, up came a certain[1] official[2] who bowed low before him[3] and said, "My daughter has just died, but come and lay your hand on her, and she will live." 19 Jesus got up and followed him, and his disciples came too. 20 Just then[4] a woman who had had a hemorrhage for twelve years came up behind and touched the fringe of his cloak, 21 because she said to herself, "If I can only touch his cloak, I shall be saved."[5] 22 But Jesus turned around and looked at her, and said, "Take heart, daughter; your faith has saved you." And the woman was saved from that moment.[6] 23 When Jesus reached the official's house, he saw the pipers and the wailing crowd 24 and said, "Go away; the girl is not dead but asleep." And they laughed at him. 25 But when he had thrown out the crowd, he went in and took hold of her hand, and the girl was raised.[7] 26 Then the news of this spread around all that region.*

27 As Jesus went on from there, two blind men followed him, shouting, "Show mercy on us, Son of David." 28 When he had gone

---

1. See p. 323, n. 3, for Matthew's occasional use of εἷς rather than τις to introduce a new character into the story. Here there is no obvious reason why he should not have used τις.

2. "Ruler," the traditional rendering of ἄρχων, is a political term hardly appropriate for a man who, according to Mark and Luke, held a leading position in the local synagogue. Matthew does not mention the synagogue, but his use of the unqualified ἄρχων does not require us to think of a member of the Herodian political establishment. Luz, 2:40, n. 2, finds "official" too formal, and commends the French *"un notable."*

3. See p. 303, n. 6, for this translation of προσκυνέω.

4. Another attempt to represent the force of ἰδού (as is "up came" in v. 18 and "along came" in v. 32). Here it serves to introduce a new story within the one currently being narrated.

5. The verb here and twice in v. 22 is σῴζω, "save" (as in 1:21; 8:25, etc.). Mark and Luke more frequently use it of physical healing, but this is the only case where Matthew does so (though see διασῴζω in 14:36), and this unusual (for him) vocabulary choice should be recognized. See the comments below on why he may have used it here.

6. For the idiom see p. 304, n. 14.

7. ἐγείρομαι occurs very frequently simply in the sense of "get up" (from sitting or lying down), and is used in that sense in healing narratives where there is no question of raising from death (8:15; 9:5-7); it is also used of being roused from sleep (8:25; 25:7), which may be relevant here in the light of Jesus' comment in v. 24. But in this context we should probably also detect the more specialized NT sense of "be raised" from death, which will occur in 10:8; 11:5 with a probable reference back to this passage and is Matthew's regular term for Jesus' own resurrection (16:21; 17:9, 23; 20:19; 26:32; 27:63-64; 28:6-7). All three senses ("got up," "woke up," "was raised") are appropriate here, but English does not allow us to retain the wordplay.

into the house, the blind men came to him, and Jesus asked them, "Do you believe that I have the power to do this?" "Yes, Lord," they replied. 29 Then Jesus touched their eyes and said, "According to your faith, so let it be done for you." 30 And their eyes were opened. Jesus warned them fiercely, "Make sure no one knows about this." 31 But they went out and told people about him all over that region.

32 As the blind men went out, along came some people bringing to Jesus a man who was dumb[8] and demon-possessed. 33 When the demon had been thrown out, the dumb man spoke. The crowds were amazed and said, "Nothing like this has ever been seen in Israel." 34 But the Pharisees said, "It is by the ruler of the demons that he throws the demons out."[9]

A third group of miracles further extends the range of afflictions which must bow to the authority of Jesus. First and foremost is death itself, for despite Jesus' teasing words in v. 24 Matthew makes it clear from the beginning that the girl was already dead, not just *in extremis* as at the beginning of the story in Mark and Luke. But each of the other three miracles also introduces a new element. The woman with the hemorrhage represents not only a longstanding and therefore presumably incurable condition, but also one with social and religious implications through the Jewish purity laws; it is interesting that only in this case in Matthew is the terminology of "salvation" used in relation to physical healing (see n. 5). Blindness and dumbness add instances of severe disability cured, the former in terms of directly physical healing, the latter in association with exorcism. This section thus provides the factual basis for including the blind, the deaf/dumb,[10] and the dead among those Jesus claims to have delivered in 11:5; and since 11:5 is partly based on Isa 35:5-6, these pericopes serve to demonstrate the fulfillment in Jesus' ministry of that prophecy of eschatological deliverance for the blind, the deaf, and the dumb.

All these acts of deliverance are narrated without much detail. The

8. κωφός can mean "deaf" or "dumb" or both (the two conditions being often associated). It is the mention of "speaking" in v. 33 which prompts the rendering "dumb" here.

9. Verse 34 is omitted in a few Western witnesses, but this is probably due to a desire to avoid duplication of the offensive charge which will recur in 12:24. Without this verse the brief pericope 9:32-33 would have little to contribute to Matthew's anthology in chs. 8–9; it also provides a background (though without the name "Beelzebul") for 10:25, which would otherwise refer only to a still future accusation. G. N. Stanton, *Gospel*, 174-76, argues strongly for the originality of the verse here.

10. The same word, κωφός, is used in 9:32 and in 11:5, though the cure is expressed in terms of speaking in 9:32 and of hearing in 11:5.

double healing of 8:18-26 is a further spectacular example of Matthew's narrative abbreviation: Matthew needs a mere 48 words for the woman with the hemorrhage, compared to Mark's 154, and for the dead girl 90 as against Mark's 192. The story of the blind men contains more detail, but its resemblance in some ways to 20:29-34 means that it is usually dismissed (unfairly, as I hope to show) as a colorless doublet of that other, better-known story of the healing of the blind. The deaf man is dealt with so briefly that one has the impression that the story is told for the sake of the contrasting reactions in vv. 33 and 34 rather than for its own sake.

Two more general themes come to the surface in these last two pericopae. The story of the blind men is set inside the house (as is that of the dead girl) and leads to a more explicit comment on Jesus' desire for secrecy than we have seen hitherto (cf. 8:4). The account of the exorcism suggests a more public arena, and gives rise to the charge of Jesus' collusion with "the ruler of the demons" which will be further developed in 12:22-32. So while the primary focus may be on the deliverance of specific individuals, Matthew intends us to set these stories against the wider background of how people are responding to the authoritative deeds of the Messiah ("Son of David," v. 27), with a clear hint that the (unwanted?) publicity given to his acts of power will have a significant part to play in the eventual official rejection of his messianic identity.

With this final triad of miracle stories Matthew brings to a close his comprehensive collage of the authoritative activity of the Messiah in chs. 8–9, both in his unquestioned power over a wide variety of threatening forces, natural and supernatural, and in the uncompromising demand which he makes on those who are called to follow him. But the overriding note is not one of hard power but of deliverance and joy, as people are set free from danger, disease, demonic powers, and death, and called to share with Jesus in enjoying the new wine of the kingdom of heaven.

a. Two Women Restored (9:18-26)

These two incidents are combined in the same way in all three Synoptic accounts: the encounter with the woman with a hemorrhage provides a dramatic pause which keeps the reader in suspense as Jesus is on his way to a dead (or dying — Mark and Luke) girl. The interweaving of the two stories is usually attributed to Mark's penchant for "sandwiching" stories, but the other Synoptic writers do not reproduce several of Mark's other sandwich patterns, so that their agreement in this case might be explained by an interweaving already in the underlying tradition rather than as the adoption of a specifically Marcan intercalation. Whether or not the two incidents originally occurred together in this way, they are linked by more than dramatic considerations.

Each is concerned with a woman (though of very different ages), and each raises the issue of ritual purity, since both a woman with a discharge of blood and a dead body rendered unclean anyone who touched them. The issue of impurity is not directly raised in either narrative,[11] but a Jewish reader could hardly have been unaware of it, and Jesus' disregard of the taboo would be noticed. He is, as always, concerned with need rather than ritual ("mercy" rather than "sacrifice," v. 13). In a sense, each of these women is restored to life, the one literally, the other metaphorically in that she is freed from twelve years of social restriction,[12] and the use here of the language of "salvation" (see n. 5) perhaps draws attention to this aspect of her deliverance. See Luz, 2:42-43: "the saving is more than the healing." The association of the language of "salvation" with faith perhaps also allows Matthew's readers, if so inclined, to find in this story a parable of spiritual salvation.

Matthew says clearly that the girl was dead before her father approached Jesus, and the customary mourning rituals (v. 23) also indicate this. In Mark and Luke, where she "dies" while Jesus is on the way, it might be possible to argue that Jesus' words about sleep rather than death are simply the correction of a false diagnosis,[13] but Matthew will have none of that explanation, and the inclusion of the raising of the dead among the works of the Messiah in 11:5 confirms that that is what this story is about. Compared with the massive literary focus on the raising of Lazarus in John 11, this story (and Luke's account of the widow's son at Nain, Luke 7:11-17) seems to us surprisingly low-key, hardly differentiating the resuscitation of the (recently) dead from other kinds of physical healing. Even more surprising is the almost casual inclusion of "raise the dead" among the disciples' roles in 10:8. (Did it happen in Matthew's church? one wonders.) There are memorable OT precedents (1 Kgs 17:17-24; 2 Kgs 4:18-37; cf. 2 Kgs 13:21) where the rais-

---

11. A.-J. Levine, in D. R. Bauer and M. A. Powell (eds.), *Treasures,* 379-97, argues, against the consensus of most commentators, that purity is not at issue here at all. A mediating position is suggested by S. Haber, *JSNT* 26 (2003) 171-92: purity was an issue, but it is the woman's health which is the focus of the story. Haber rejects the view of some feminist critics that the story is intended as an attack on the concept of menstrual impurity as such.

12. A.-J. Levine, ibid., 386-92, mounts a strong challenge to the normal modern understanding of the social effects of menstrual impurity. She makes several important points, both with regard to the way such impurity was regarded (not as a fault or an illness, but as a ritual restriction primarily affecting temple worship) and with regard to the practical impact on social relations for a menstruating woman. But even if her historical reading is accepted, the situation of a woman with an abnormal and apparently continuing menstrual discharge would surely have been both difficult and embarrassing if the regulations of Lev 15:19-33 were in force. Levine questions whether they were, but offers no specific evidence to the contrary.

13. I have discussed, and disagreed with, this exegesis in my *Mark,* 234, 239.

ing of the dead authenticates true prophets, and here the incident adds a climactic note to the demonstration of Jesus' messianic authority. But even so, Matthew's understatement is remarkable.

18-19 Matthew continues to tie his collected pericopes into a continuous narrative by means of literary links, so that the scene remains in Capernaum, and we are to envisage the official approaching Jesus as he concludes his response to John's disciples, though it would probably be attributing too much to this formal link to suggest that Matthew intends us to see the new life given to the girl as an illustration of the new wine Jesus has just been speaking about. Matthew mentions neither the man's name nor his synagogue connection; he is simply a person of some consequence in the local community. Matthew's version of his request is on a different level from that of Mark and Luke, not a natural appeal for medical help to prevent a girl dying, but the assumption that even death itself is subject to Jesus' authority. We have been given no basis in the narrative so far for such an assumption; like the "faith" of the centurion in 8:8-10 it is entering uncharted waters. It is therefore surprising that whereas the faith of the woman is commended in v. 22 and that of the blind men in vv. 28-29, the word is not used of this man's even more remarkable ability to see beyond a natural impossibility. The facts are left to speak for themselves.

The specific request for Jesus to lay his hand on the girl shows a surprising disregard for the taboo on touching a dead body; is the man thinking of Jesus' touch as life-giving and therefore "canceling out" the impurity of death? Or has his grief simply not considered the problem? Nor do Jesus and his disciples show any hesitation in responding. Note the contrast with 8:5-9, where there was the issue whether Jesus should go to a Gentile house; here in this Jewish context there is no problem and so no need for a distant healing.

20-21 The urgent summons to the official's house is interrupted by an unexpected encounter en route. This woman's twelve-year hemorrhage is usually understood to have been a menstrual disorder,[14] and so to come under the purity regulations of Lev 15:19-33.[15] In addition to the physical discomfort and debility there was the relentless inconvenience of impurity, whereby anyone who touched not only the woman herself but also anything she sat or

14. J. D. M. Derrett, *Bib* 63 (1982) 476-79 points out, however, that the text does not say this, and that there are other forms of hemorrhage. Similarly, and with more passion, A.-J. Levine, in *Treasures* (n. 11), 381-86, accusing Christian interpreters of an obsession with Jewish purity laws which a Jewish reader does not feel. Levine is right about the silence of the text, but she does not offer an alternative understanding of the "hemorrhage" to set against the very wide consensus of other interpreters; her subsequent argument appears to accept the likelihood that it was menstrual.

15. See Keener, 302, n. 102. For the substantial body of rabbinic legislation with regard to menstrual impurity see the Mishnah tractate *Niddah*.

lay on became unclean. The result could only be a serious measure of social restriction.[16] For her to touch even Jesus' cloak[17] risked making him unclean; hence perhaps her surreptitious approach "behind." It is an interesting question, however, whether the same touch which healed, as she believed it would, would be held to convey the impurity of the unhealed condition. For what seems to us a rather magical belief that healing could be secured "automatically" by touching a garment without the healer's express intention cf. 14:36; Mark 3:10; Luke 6:19; Acts 5:15; 19:12. In 14:36 Matthew allows that concept to stand without comment; here, however, Jesus will not leave the matter at that level. Indeed, in Matthew's version, unlike Mark's, the healing is reported following Jesus' words in v. 22 rather than as a direct result of the touch. For the "fringe" (or tassel) see on 23:5; his objection there is to ostentation, not to the fringe itself, which was an OT requirement (Num 15:38-39; Deut 22:12) which Jesus observed (cf. 14:36).

22 The comment that Jesus "turned around and looked at her" (since she had come up behind him, v. 20) perhaps presupposes Mark's account of her attempt to avoid detection. But there is no challenge or rebuke in Matthew's account. Far from repudiating her "unclean" approach, Jesus encourages her with words which echo his reassurance to the paralyzed man in v. 2,[18] though the issue here is not sin but ritual impurity. The commendation of her faith (in the sense of recognizing Jesus' power to save; see on 8:10) follows appropriately on the confidence expressed in v. 21, but it is notable that this is the only occurrence in Matthew of the alliterative formula, *hē pistis sou sesōken se,* "Your faith has saved you," which appears in the other Synoptic gospels not only in the parallels to this passage but also in relation to Bartimaeus (Mark 10:52; Luke 18:42), the sinful woman (Luke 7:50), and the Samaritan leper (Luke 17:19). If this is not simply a by-product of Matthew's policy of narrative abbreviation, it may reflect his view that the restoration to normal life of this "unclean" woman was best reflected in the language of "salvation" (see introductory comments above). The immediacy of the healing is in this case particularly significant in view of the long period of previous suffering.

23 After the interruption Jesus now arrives at the official's house. But whereas in Mark and Luke his arrival there is overshadowed by the news that the girl has now been pronounced dead, in Matthew this has been known

16. *Pace* A.-J. Levine (see n. 12). The problems are well illustrated in Keener, 302-4 (with due acknowledgment to Levine's argument). See further M. J. Selvidge, *JBL* 103 (1984) 619-23, for the extent of Jesus' challenge here to accepted social convention based on ritual purity.

17. Cf. 1 Sam 15:27 for taking hold of the edge of a garment in supplication; see also Zech 8:23.

18. For a similarly encouraging use of "daughter" cf. Ruth 2:8; 3:10-11.

from the beginning, and the customary mourning rites are already well under way. For professional mourners see Jer 9:17-20; Amos 5:16. Even the poorest Jewish families were expected to hire "not less than two pipers and one wailing woman" (*m. Ketub.* 4:4). For the suitability of pipes for mourning cf. Jer 48:36; Josephus, *War* 3.437 (though they could also accompany festivities, 11:17; Rev 18:22). Burial took place within twenty-four hours of death, so there was not much time for ceremonial. But in this case it is unnecessary, and Jesus dismisses the mourners curtly.

24 His pronouncement is in tension with what both the girl's father and the (presumably experienced) mourners have observed. Moreover, if the purpose of this pericope is to show Jesus' power even over death, these words introduce an incongruous element. Is she dead or isn't she? Had they mistaken for death what was in fact only a coma? But then how was Jesus, who had not yet seen the girl, to know that? The mourners have no doubt, and they scornfully dismiss Jesus' words, understood literally. But if that was what he meant, and the girl really wasn't dead, why was this story singled out for preservation among many other healings of gravely ill people, and where is the basis for the pronouncement of 11:5 that "the dead are being raised"? And, in any case, Matthew has not allowed even a hint of doubt about the girl's death from v. 18 on. So it seems that he, unlike the mourners, understood Jesus' words in a nonliteral sense. Even so, the wording is obscure. The common use of "sleep" as a metaphor for death does not directly help us, since it would produce the nonsensical declaration "not dead but dead"; in any case, when sleep is used as a metaphor for death in the LXX and the NT, the verb used is *koimaomai*,[19] not, as here, *katheudō,* which usually denotes literal sleep (except in Dan 12:2 and possibly 1 Thess 5:10), but is sometimes used metaphorically for spiritual inertia. Rather than using a standard metaphor, Jesus is drawing a thought-provoking parallel between death and literal sleep: if death is "sleep," then it allows the possibility of waking up. Death is not the end, and in the case of this girl it will prove to be only a temporary experience. Her death is real, but it is not final. Of course what happens in this story is only the resuscitation of someone who will later die again, merely a postponement of death. But the Christian reader of Matthew will be aware that in a much deeper sense Jesus' resurrection has overcome the finality of death itself, and given a new force to the metaphor of "sleep" which can apply to all those who die, not just to the very few whom Jesus will resuscitate during his earthly ministry. With hindsight, then, these enigmatic words can be seen to teach a great truth which can hardly have been grasped by those present at the time.

25-26 The dismissal of the crowd may be explained as much by

---

19. See especially the use of this verb in John 11:11-14; it is the root of our word "cemetery."

their derisive laughter as by a desire for secrecy, but the latter element will be explicit in the next pericope (vv. 27-30) and may be intended here too. This is a private act of deliverance, not a public spectacle. Even the presence of the girl's parents and of three disciples (Mark 5:40) is not mentioned in Matthew's concise account, resulting in a closer parallel to the private miracles of Elijah and Elisha (1 Kgs 17:19-23; 2 Kgs 4:33). The miracle is simply narrated, with specific mention of the physical touch which the father had requested (v. 18). If anyone thought about the impurity contracted by touching a dead body, this is not mentioned, and in any case, as in vv. 20-22, the touch itself brought the life which canceled the impurity. See p. 358, n. 7, for the possible significance of "was raised" as a pointer forward to Jesus' own return from death, even though the verb need mean no more than "got up."

As in vv. 31 and 33, if Jesus wanted to keep the event secret, he failed — inevitably, when a girl previously known to be dead was back in normal circulation! "All that region," repeated in v. 31, probably denotes the northern shore of the lake and perhaps more widely the Jewish areas of Galilee, the area where Jesus' own continuing mission (v. 35; cf. 15:24) and that of his disciples (10:5-6) will be focused. It is a sobering reflection that it will be precisely the towns of that area which will soon be condemned for their failure to respond to the miracles Jesus has performed in them (11:20-24).

b. Two Blind Men Healed (9:27-31)

This episode has no parallel in the other Synoptic narratives, but it is usually explained as a doublet of the story of the blind man (Matthew: *two* blind men) healed at Jericho in 20:29-34. It has in common not only the healing of two blind men but also the appeal, "Show mercy on us, Son of David." Most of this pericope, however, is conspicuously *not* parallel to 20:29-34: the men following Jesus, the location inside the house, the question about faith and their response, the word of healing, Jesus' "fierce warning" (a remarkably strong word not found elsewhere in Matthew) to keep the healing secret, and the men's disobedience to it. With so much that is distinctive, it seems to me more likely that this is an independent tradition preserved only by Matthew (just as another healing of the blind is preserved only by Mark, Mark 8:22-26), and that the similarity in the men's initial address to Jesus results from the natural process of assimilation of miracle stories (especially since "Son of David" finds its way into another Matthean miracle story in 15:22), than that the one story was created out of the other.

Since the two blind men in 20:29-34 correspond to a single man in the same story in Mark and Luke, it may well be that this story also originally concerned one blind man, though of course there is no way of checking this. In that case the same considerations (and the same bafflement!)

apply here as with the doubling of the demoniacs in 8:28-34; see the comments on pp. 339-40.

27 Again Matthew links this story with the preceding narrative, so that we find Jesus on his way from the official's house, with two blind men following him along the street until they arrive at "the house" (v. 28), presumably this time Jesus' house in Capernaum (4:13). They then follow him into the house (perhaps at his invitation, responding to their noisy appeal in the street), so that the healing takes place in private, away from the crowd who have witnessed other miracles (8:16; 9:8, 26). This private setting will make it possible for Jesus to attempt to keep their healing a secret.

Like the blind men at Jericho (20:30-31), they appeal noisily and insistently for help, though in this case we do not hear of the crowd turning against them. "Show mercy on us" is an appropriate appeal to a powerful stranger, but perhaps Matthew also intends his readers to catch an echo of 9:13, where it is "mercy" that God requires: Jesus is about to practice what he has preached. This is the first occurrence of "Son of David" as a form of address to Jesus, though the theological foundations for it have been well laid in ch. 1, both in the Davidic focus of Jesus' genealogy and in his adoption by Joseph, "son of David" (1:20). The title will be used of Jesus six more times in this gospel, whereas in Mark and Luke it is used only in the story of Bartimaeus. The NT generally accepts and asserts Jesus' Davidic origin as a given (e.g., Acts 2:29-36; 13:22-23; Rom 1:3; 2 Tim 2:8), but the title "Son of David" seems to have a special resonance for Matthew.[20] It is used by others about Jesus, usually as here when approaching him to ask for help (cf. 15:22; 20:30, 31), but also in discussing (12:23) or proclaiming (21:9, 15) his messianic status.[21] The only

---

20. See my *Matthew: Evangelist,* 284-86. G. N. Stanton, *Gospel,* 180-85, points out that the title is usually linked in context with expressions of hostility to Jesus, and argues that its prominence in the gospel reflects the church's apologetic stance at the time Matthew was writing.

21. For a full study of "Son of David" as a messianic title see L. Novakovic, *Messiah.* Her study explores the relation between Messiahship and healing, recognizing that we have no firm evidence of a pre-Christian Jewish expectation of a *healing* Messiah (though see below, p. 424, n. 20). She examines and rejects (96-109) the theory that this could have arisen from the tradition of Solomon as an exorcist (see next note), and the much less favored suggestion that healing was associated with the expectation of a "prophet like Moses" in Deut 18:15, 18 (109-18), and argues (briefly on 118-22, and more fully in her fourth chapter, 124-84) that the connection is best traced to certain Isaianic passages which Matthew quotes or alludes to in connection with Jesus' healing ministry in 8:17; 11:2-6, and 12:15-21 (see further below on 11:2-6, especially nn. 18-20). Not that any one passage explicitly said that the Messiah would be a healer, but Matthew has provided a scriptural basis for this belief by "applying certain midrashic techniques to the selected texts from Isaiah that speak either about the servant of Yahweh or an anointed bearer of good tidings" (183).

time Jesus himself uses it is to raise a question over its christological adequacy (see on 22:41-45), yet it is apparently not in itself inappropriate, since Jesus is prepared to defend its use in 21:15-16. He is in fact the Messiah (which is what the title primarily means),[22] however much his messianic role may be misunderstood by those who cannot see him as anything *more* than just another David.[23]

28-29 Faith has been mentioned as a key factor in previous healings, but this is the first time (and the only time in Matthew; he does not have a parallel to Mark 9:23-24) when it is explicitly set before the suppliant as a condition of healing. The centurion voluntarily declared his faith in Jesus' authority to heal (8:8-10; so also the leper in 8:2, the official in 9:18, and, secretly, the woman in 9:21), but these men are *required* to do so. There is no obvious reason why this additional element should be present in this case, since it does not occur in the similar story of the healing of blind men in 20:29-34. But the faith, once declared, is made the basis of their healing, as Jesus uses another third-person imperative as a "performative utterance" (see on 8:13, and cf. 15:28). Physical touch is an element in many of the gospel healing narratives, but when Jesus touches the eyes of blind people (cf. 20:34; Mark 8:23, 25; John 9:6), they would find special significance in this physical contact with a healer they could not yet see.[24]

22. The fact that "Son of David" is used in Matthew predominantly in connection with healing, either requested or experienced, has led some to argue that there was a popular hope of a "son of David" whose role would be particularly to bring healing; so D. C. Duling, *HTR* 68 (1975) 235-52; B. D. Chilton, *JSNT* 14 (1982) 92-97; followed by Davies and Allison, 2:135-36. Their arguments (anticipated by L. R. Fisher, in F. T. Trotter [ed.], *Jesus and the Historian,* 82-97) depend on the later Jewish tradition that Solomon, David's son, had power over evil spirits, which is especially developed in the (second-century-A.D.?) *Testament of Solomon* (see also below, pp. 477-78, nn. 17-18); but there is no specific connection of either David or Solomon with physical healing (a survey of Solomon's areas of knowledge in Wis 7:17-22 includes "the varieties of plants and the virtue of roots," but with no emphasis on how he used them). Of course the messianic age would be a time of healing (Isa 35:5-6), but this hope is not linked with the name of David. For a more political messianic connotation for "son of David" cf. *Ps. Sol.* 17:21. See further my *Matthew: Evangelist,* 285; L. Novakovic, *Messiah,* 96-109.

23. A further aspect of Matthew's use of "Son of David" is noted by J. M. Gibbs, *NTS* 10 (1963/4) 463-64; J. D. Kingsbury, *JBL* 95 (1976) 598-601; W. R. G. Loader, *CBQ* 44 (1982) 570-85. Those who use the title are people of no social or theological importance, the blind, the lame, the dumb, a Canaanite woman, Galilean pilgrims, and children in the temple. It is these "no accounts" (Kingsbury's term), in their need, who best perceive the messianic significance of Jesus, rather than the theologians and dignitaries of Jerusalem. What is obvious to a blind beggar and a Canaanite woman remains hidden from Israel's leaders (cf. 11:25). Cf. U. Luz, *Theology,* 73: "The 'little people' in Israel recognize Jesus for what he is."

24. J. M. Hull, *Darkness,* 135-37, emphasizes the significance of touch for a blind

30-31 "Warned fiercely" represents a verb which occurs only here in Matthew. Elsewhere it denotes a strongly emotional reaction of indignation (Mark 1:43; 14:5) or grief (John 11:33, 38) which is hard to explain in this context, but its use also in Mark's account of Jesus' demand for the leper's silence (Mark 1:43-44) suggests that it may have had a traditional role in such stories. Does Matthew intend his readers to see in it an anticipation of the men's disobedience in v. 31? The demand for secrecy after healing occurs in Matthew in specific cases only here and in 8:4, and in a general summary in 12:16. Only here are we told that the command was not obeyed. In Matthew it seems more like an occasional relic of a prominent Marcan theme than an issue that was also important to Matthew himself; see the comments on 8:4. Here it is difficult to find a specific reason in the circumstances of the case why this healing rather than any other should be kept quiet. But these are the first people to have addressed Jesus as "Son of David" (i.e., Messiah), so the secrecy may have less to do with the healing itself than with their perception of Jesus' role (as with the "messianic secrecy" of 16:20, and cf. 17:9). In any case, the reappearance of formerly blind men in the community with their sight restored could hardly be kept quiet for long. Perhaps rather than looking for an ideological principle we should read this in Matthew's narrative context and think simply of Jesus needing a brief respite from popular pressure until he is able to leave Capernaum (which he will have done by v. 35). In the event, despite the men's address to Jesus as "Lord," they disobey his command: there is no secrecy and no respite. The repetition of "all that region" (cf. v. 26) underlines the point.

c. Conflicting Responses to an Exorcism (9:32-34)

The exorcism itself is quite perfunctorily told; more than half of this little pericope deals rather with the subsequent responses. Both responses pick up themes with which we are already familiar, the enthusiasm of the general populace (vv. 8, 26, 31) and the hostility of scribes and Pharisees (vv. 3, 11). Contrasting reactions to Jesus (and especially to his ministry of exorcism) will continue to be portrayed throughout chs. 11–12, providing the basis for the discourse in ch. 13, where the significance of the varied responses is analyzed. The accusation of v. 34 will be repeated in 12:24 (again by Pharisees and in contrast to popular acclaim, 12:23), leading into a fuller debate on the significance of Jesus' exorcisms. And the specific exorcism which sparks off that debate in 12:22 is as briefly narrated as this, and in similar terms. In this whole short pericope, then, more appropriately than in relation to the preced-

---

person; cf. ibid., 155-57 on "Jesus as a tactile person." For the personal response of a blind writer to the present pericope, see ibid., 34-39.

ing pericope, it is customary to speak of a Matthean doublet, though it is interesting that the demoniac in 12:22 is blind as well as dumb, and further new dimensions will there be added by the introduction of the title "Son of David" and the naming of Beelzebul. Here in 9:32-34, by contrast, there is little that is distinctive in relation to the later and more developed account.

32-33a This pericope, too, is linked to the one which precedes it, with the blind men going out of the house and succeeded by "people" (unspecified) who bring to Jesus (presumably now outside the house, since there are "crowds" including Pharisees present) a dumb[25] man whose problem is traced to demonic possession. For the distinction between physical disability and possession see on 4:24; here, in contrast to 8:28-34, demonic possession has resulted in physical disability, but Matthew still speaks of exorcism rather than of healing, and the Pharisees will go on to speak of the source of Jesus' success as an exorcist. The terminology used here is therefore consistent, as compared with 12:22 where in a similar situation Matthew uses the verb "heal." Cf. the case of the demoniac often described as "epileptic" in 17:14-19, where the description is clearly of an exorcism and yet the verb "heal" is twice used; in that case Mark includes dumbness among the demoniac's symptoms (Mark 9:17, 25). But dumbness was not necessarily explained as the result of demonic possession; see 15:30-31, where it is included among other physical complaints which are "healed" without a mention of demons (cf. also Mark 7:32-37).

33b-34 The crowd's comment on a routinely narrated exorcism seems excessive if, as we shall see in 12:27, exorcisms were in fact an accepted feature in Jewish life; and, indeed, Jesus himself is already known as an exorcist (4:24; 8:16, 28-34). But perhaps, as this is the final crowd reaction in this anthology of works of power, we should read it as an evaluation not merely of this one exorcism but of the whole range of Jesus' miracles which these two chapters have set out: others might perform the occasional exorcism, but this man's ministry of deliverance is on an altogether different scale. A similarly climactic effect, but in an ominously different direction, is achieved by the Pharisees' accusation. They do not deny Jesus' power, but question its source. Such a total and offensive repudiation of his authority brings the growing hostility to a new level, and suggests a breach which is now irreparable. Jesus' response to the same accusation in 12:25-32 will make this clear. See on 12:24 for the "ruler of the demons."

25. See p. 359, n. 8, for the meaning of κωφός; he may have been deaf as well as dumb (so Gundry, n. 107).

F. THE MESSIAH'S AUTHORITY SHARED WITH HIS
DISCIPLES: *THE DISCOURSE ON MISSION* (9:35–11:1)

The second discourse, like the first (chs. 5–7), is marked off by a narrative setting and a formal conclusion.[1] The setting is the sending out of the disciples, who were also the primary audience of the first discourse, on a mission to bring the message of Jesus to a wider area of Galilee. From being the recipients of his ministry they are to become its agents, sharing not only in the proclamation of the kingdom of heaven but also in the works of mercy and power which the preceding chapters have shown to characterize the authority of the Messiah himself. With the formal recognition of the Twelve as Jesus' immediate entourage, his renewal movement takes its first steps toward becoming a structured group within which the radical new values of the kingdom of heaven, set out in chs. 5–7, can begin to be lived out.

But while mission is the primary setting and subject of this discourse, a prominent subtext is the hostile response which that mission is to meet, so that this also becomes a discourse on persecution. The preceding chapters have given mounting evidence of hostility to Jesus himself (9:3, 11, 14, 34), and those who share his message and authority can expect no less. Some will welcome them (10:11-13, 40-42), but the dominant impression of this section of the gospel is of a minority movement facing a predominantly hostile society, and following chapters will increasingly underline this perspective.

This second discourse, like the first, appears to be the result of a complex process of compilation from among the teaching of Jesus available in the Synoptic tradition. Not much of this discourse, unlike the first, is peculiar to Matthew (only vv. 5-6, 8, 16b, 23, and 41), but the Synoptic parallels are widely scattered. The basis of the composition is the mission charge recorded in Mark 6:7-13 and in two forms in Luke 9:1-6 and 10:1-12 which between them account for most of the material up to 10:16, but the rest of the discourse finds its parallels in a section of the Marcan "apocalyptic discourse," Mark 13:9-13, and in a variety of unconnected passages in Luke.[2] Many of the parallels are far from exact, so that it is sometimes difficult to say whether the same tradition lies behind them or whether characteristic motifs of Jesus' teaching are independently represented. In all, we seem to have here a typically Matthean anthology of Jesus' teaching on the realities of being a disciple with a mission to an indifferent or hostile world. Much of the compilation relates appropriately to this initial mission of the disciples during Je-

---

1. For the coherence of 9:35–11:1 as a unit, and its "interruption" of the sequence from the "deeds" set out in 8:1–9:34 to the mention of the "deeds of the Messiah" in 11:2, see, e.g., S. C. Barton, *Discipleship,* 157-58.

2. For details of the parallels see my *Matthew: Evangelist,* 159.

sus' lifetime (though v. 18 envisages a wider sphere of mission than is set out in vv. 5-6 and 23), but its relevance to Christian disciples in subsequent generations would have been as obvious to Matthew's first readers as it presumably was to the author himself.[3]

1. The Context of Mission (9:35-38)

35 *And Jesus was traveling around all the towns and villages, teaching in their synagogues,[4] and proclaiming the good news of the kingdom, and healing all sorts of illnesses and disabilities.[5]* 36 *When he saw the crowds, his heart went out to them,[6] because they were harassed and dejected[7] like sheep that have no shepherd.* 37 *Then he said to his disciples, "The harvest is great, but the workers are few;* 38 *so ask the Lord of the harvest to send out workers into his harvest."*

This transitional paragraph serves both as a summary of the ministry in word and deed which has been depicted in chs. 5–9 and as an introduction to the theme of mission which follows. Its first verse closely echoes the language of 4:23 which introduced the Galilean ministry, thus forming a framework around the anthology of words and deeds which Matthew has put together. Its closing verses provide the basis for the sending out of the Twelve as "workers in the harvest." The paragraph as a whole could thus with equal appropriateness be bracketed either with what precedes it or with what follows, but I have chosen the latter because it provides the necessary justification for the

3. D. J. Weaver, *Discourse,* 17-24, surveys different "historical-critical approaches" to the coherence of the discourse in relation to its narrative setting, including that which finds its coherence not in its reported narrative setting but in the situation of Matthew's church for which it was designed. She concludes, however, that none of these approaches does justice to Matthew's intention. Her thesis therefore sets aside the question of historical context in favor of reading the text from a literary perspective within the context of Matthew's communicative enterprise.

4. Or "assemblies"; see the comments on 4:23 above.

5. μαλακία, literally "weakness"; see p. 148, n. 3.

6. For this rendering of σπλαγχνίζομαι, traditionally "had compassion on them," see the comments below.

7. The passive of ῥίπτω, "to throw (down)," is sometimes used of lying on the ground without any connotation of violence (the active of the same verb is used in 15:30 for "laying" people who were ill in front of Jesus), though in the LXX it is more commonly used of corpses thrown down on the ground. Here the metaphor perhaps suggests sheep lying listlessly around with no shepherd to get them moving. The traditional translation "helpless" is derived more from the context than from the verb itself. Hagner, 2:258, suggests a further nuance with "confused." Luz, 2:64, goes for the more violent sense, "beaten down," and Carter, 230, characteristically amplifies this sense: "oppressed, downtrodden, beat-up, and crushed" (by "Rome and the religious elite").

sending out of the Twelve, and thus together with that pericope (10:1-4) provides the setting and the audience for the discourse that follows, in much the same way that 4:23–5:2 introduces the first discourse. Note, too, the repetition in the following discourse of the imagery of sheep (9:36; 10:6, 16) and of workers (9:37-38; 10:10).

These verses, like the discourse that follows, look like a Matthean compilation of traditional themes which find their parallels in Mark 6:6, Mark 6:34 (sheep without a shepherd), and Luke 10:2 (the harvest and the workers). The result is a remarkable change of metaphor between vv. 36 and 37. Having used the sheep/shepherd imagery here, Matthew will not repeat it in the introduction to the feeding of the five thousand where it occurs in Mark.

35 The wording of v. 35, including the Matthean abbreviation "the gospel of the kingdom," closely matches that of 4:23; see the comments there. The further specification here of the "towns and villages" as the scene of Jesus' mission prepares for the disciples' itinerant mission around the "towns and villages" (v. 11) and the expectation that they will be working their way through "the towns of Israel" (v. 23). Such generalizing terms confirm that what we have read so far in chs. 5–9 represents only a selection from a much more wide-ranging mission to Galilee. The phrase "heal all sorts of illnesses and disabilities" will be repeated verbatim in 10:1, showing that the mission of the disciples is to be a continuation of that of Jesus.

36 The "crowds," who have so far been noted primarily as the astonished audience of Jesus' teaching (7:28-29) and the witnesses of his miracles (4:25; 9:8, 33), now become the object of his direct concern. But whereas previously we have read of his response to physical need and demonic oppression by healing and exorcism, the description here moves to what sounds like a deeper and more universal level. The two participles translated "harassed and dejected" may imply oppression or exhaustion or lack of direction, or probably all of these together, but it is the following metaphor which gives them focus. The sheep/shepherd image is frequent in the OT, primarily for the relationship between God and his people but also with regard to their need for human leadership under God; in this gospel the metaphor has already occurred in 2:6, and it will be picked up in the mission to "the lost sheep of the house of Israel" in 10:6; 15:24; cf. also the parable of the shepherd in 18:12-14. Such a description is reminiscent of Ezek 34:1-16, where the sheep are oppressed and scattered because of the failure of the "shepherds of Israel," so that it is necessary for God himself to seek out and rescue the lost sheep. The wording also echoes two other OT passages: in Num 27:17-18 Joshua is appointed as Moses' successor so that the people "may not be like sheep without a shepherd," and in 1 Kgs 22:17 Micaiah's vision of Israel "scattered on the mountains like sheep that have no shepherd" is a prediction of the death of their king Ahab. Zech 10:2-3 uses similar language of a lack of prophetic leadership, and in Zech 13:7 the loss of their messianic shepherd leads to the sheep being scattered. Jesus sees the ordinary people of Israel as similarly in need of direction and leadership. Chapter 23 will make explicit the criticism of their current leadership which this implies. Cf. the similar implication in Jesus' offer of relief to those who are "toiling and heavily loaded" in 11:28-30.

His response is described by the strongly emotional Greek verb *splanchnizomai,* which speaks of a warm, compassionate response to need. No single English term does justice to it: compassion, pity, sympathy, and fellow feeling all convey part of it, but "his heart went out" perhaps represents more fully the emotional force of the underlying metaphor of a "gut response." A further feature of this verb appears through a comparison with its other uses in Matthew (14:14; 15:32; 18:27; 20:34). In each case there is not only sympathy with a person's need, but also a practical response which meets that need; emotion results in caring and effective action, in this case the action of sending out his disciples among the people. It is a verb which describes the Jesus of the gospel stories in a nutshell.

37-38 A different metaphor takes that response further, using an image which also introduces the mission charge to the seventy in Luke 10:2. These distressed people constitute a "harvest" waiting to be reaped.[8] Where the OT speaks of "reaping" people, it is usually a metaphor for judgment (Isa 17:4-6; 24:12-13; Jer 51:33; Hos 6:11; Joel 3:13; cf. Rev 14:14-20), though in Jer 2:3 Israel is God's "harvest" in a positive sense. Here, following the reference to Jesus' "compassion," it can hardly refer to judgment. Rather, as with the fishing metaphor of 4:19,[9] the focus is now on bringing people in for their own good. The metaphor will be developed in 13:24-30, 36-43, where it will become clear that in the process of bringing in the good grain there will also be the need to separate out the weeds, so that the judgment aspect of the metaphor is there preserved. But here, as in John 4:35-38, that aspect is not in focus; the harvest is the bringing in of new recruits to the kingdom of God.

Hitherto the reaping of that harvest has been the responsibility of Jesus himself; "the workers are few" is in fact an understatement — there has been

---

8. Most interpreters assume that the harvest here, like the catch of fish in 4:19, consists of people who are themselves "reaped" for the kingdom of God. B. Charette, *JSNT* 38 (1990) 29-35, suggests that the imagery is rather of a harvest *for* the people, consisting of the good things of the kingdom of God which the workers are to gather for the benefit of the helpless sheep. He is right to note that the OT contains references to a harvest of blessing *for* God's people in the future (Joel 3:18; Amos 9:13-15, etc.), but Matthew's use of harvest imagery for the gathering *of* people in 13:37-43, as well as the preceding fishing metaphor, makes it less likely that he intended a different sense for the same imagery here.

9. See the comments there on the contrast between Jesus' fishing imagery and that of Jer 16:16.

only one (unless Jesus is thinking here also of John the Baptist, who also proclaimed the kingdom of heaven, 3:2). It was Jesus alone who set out to proclaim the coming of the kingdom of heaven in 4:17 and who has continued to proclaim it through the intervening chapters. But in 4:19 he had given warning to his first disciples that they, too, would share this role, and now is the time for them to take up their responsibility as fishers and harvesters of people for God's kingship. Yet the immediate and explicit appeal to them is not as yet to go out and reap, but to pray for reapers. The one will lead to the other, and those who pray (or at least some of them: "disciples" here may be wider than the Twelve who are yet to be singled out) will turn out in the next pericope to be the ones who go in answer to that prayer.[10] The eschatological reaping by angels (13:39, 41; cf. 24:31) must be preceded by the sending of human messengers. The term "Lord of the harvest" is in itself merely a part of the human imagery, the man in charge of the harvest operation, but in this context, and following a command to "ask," the reader is expected to recognize the *Kyrios* as God, whose harvest of people is ready for gathering.

2. The Mission of the Twelve (10:1-4)

1 *And he called his twelve disciples to him, and gave them authority over unclean spirits so that they could throw them out and heal all sorts of illnesses and disabilities.* 2 *These are the names of the twelve apostles: first Simon (also called Peter) and Andrew his brother, and James the son of Zebedee and John his brother,* 3 *Philip and Bartholomew, Thomas and Matthew the tax collector, James the son of Alpheus and Thaddeus,*[1] 4 *Simon the Zealot*[2] *and Judas Iscariot, who also betrayed*[3] *him.*

10. In Luke 10:2-3 the sequence is even more immediate: "ask the Lord of the harvest. . . . Go, I am sending you. . . ."

1. Most later MSS have Λεββαῖος either in place of Θαδδαῖος (so D and a few other Western witnesses, both here and in Mark 3:18) or as an alternative name for the same person, in which case it usually precedes Θαδδαῖος. The NT tells us nothing further about either name, and this obscure twelfth member of the group appears in both Luke's lists as Ἰούδας Ἰακώβου (cf. the "Judas, not Iscariot" of John 14:22). Since the name Θαδδαῖος seems secure in the textual tradition of Mark 3:18, it is probably the original reading here too (and is attested by the earliest MSS); Λεββαῖος may have originated in an attempt to find a place among the Twelve for the Levi whose call story in Mark and Luke corresponds to that of Matthew in Matthew.

2. Καναναῖος is probably best understood as a Greek formation from *qan'ān*, which is the Aramaic equivalent of ζηλωτής, the title Luke uses for this same man (Luke 6:15; Acts 1:13). "Canaanite" (KJV) would be Χαναναῖος (see 15:22), for which there is no MS support here. Another early reading, quite well supported, is Κανανίτης, "man of Cana."

3. παραδίδωμι means simply "to hand over," leaving the context to supply the na-

Whereas 9:37, like the rest of the story so far, referred simply to "his disciples," the time has come to be more specific. We have been told of how five of them were specifically called to follow Jesus (4:18-22; 9:9), and those five names will be included in the list which follows. But we have not been told how many others have been accompanying Jesus up to this point, nor how they were recruited. See the discussion at 8:21 of the meaning of "disciple" in Matthew; it seems to be wider than just the Twelve, but narrower than the sympathetic "crowd." The specification now of an inner circle of twelve men[4] from among these more committed followers will give a clearer shape to the nature of Jesus' entourage throughout the rest of the story, and it will be to them that the term "disciple" will be generally (though not exclusively) applied from now on. Sometimes the term "the Twelve (disciples)" will be used to make the reference clear. In v. 2 we also find, for the only time in Matthew, the term "apostle," which for Luke becomes a regular term for the Twelve as a group; Mark uses the term once[5] in 6:30 but with immediate reference to the function of the Twelve as "envoys" rather than as a term of office. It is surprising that Matthew does not use again what must have been, by the time he wrote his gospel, a familiar title for this inner group, but perhaps this indicates his awareness of a difference in function between the "apostles" as church leaders in his day and the role of the Twelve as companions of Jesus during his ministry.

This is not an account of the initial calling of disciples; that has al-

---

ture and motivation of the act; but its frequently negative connotation can be seen in its two occurrences so far in Matthew, at 4:12; 5:25. Despite attempts to rehabilitate Judas by emphasizing the use of this verb rather than the more specific term for "betray," προδίδωμι (see below on 26:14-16), it is most improbable that Matthew (and the other gospel writers) could have used it in a neutral sense in view of the role for which Judas was famous. παραδίδωμι will become a prominent term in the predictions and accounts of Jesus' arrest and execution, within which Judas's role in "handing him over" to the authorities will be a central element (26:15, 21, 23-25, 45-46, 48; 27:3-4) and one which may properly be described as "betrayal."

4. The all-male character of the group is inevitably noted in this age of sexual politics. In the culture of Jesus' day a close-knit traveling group which included women would probably have been socially inappropriate, but we shall discover in 27:55-56 that women, while not mentioned in the earlier narratives, have all the time been part of the Jesus movement (Luke does mention women followers earlier: Luke 8:2-3; 10:38-42). They are described there as having "followed him" during the Galilean period, the same term which we have seen to carry the connotation of discipleship in Matthew (see 4:20, 22; 8:19, 22, 23; 9:9). So the absence of women among the specific task force of the Twelve does not indicate that there were no women disciples. See also the comments below on 12:50.

5. It also appears in many MSS of Mark at 3:14, but there it echoes Luke's formulation and is suspect as a textual assimilation.

ready taken place in chs. 4 and 9. Nor are we told that he first selected the members of the inner circle at this point (Matthew has no parallel to Mark 3:13-15; Luke 6:13); they are summoned as an existing group, "his twelve disciples." The verb here is not "called" (as in the initial summons in 4:21) but "called to him" (proskalesamenos; cf. its use in 15:10, 32; 20:25). Here Matthew takes the opportunity of their mission charge to list the names of Jesus' already selected traveling companions, whom he now wants to send out as his representatives.

The listing of their names is clearly a matter of some importance since both Mark and Luke also do so in their gospels (Mark 3:16-18; Luke 6:14-16), and Luke again in Acts 1:13. With the exception of Thaddeus[6] (see n. 1) the names are the same in all these lists, though the order of the names and the descriptions of the individuals vary a little. Matthew's list has two distinctive features: it is arranged in pairs (perhaps reflecting the tradition that they were sent out in pairs, Mark 6:7; cf. Luke 10:1), the first two being pairs of brothers, the others apparently arbitrarily grouped for literary effect; and Simon (Peter), who comes first in all the lists and whose leading role among the Twelve is clear in all the gospels, is explicitly designated in Matthew as "first," even though no further numbering follows. This is consistent with Matthew's emphasis on the special importance of Peter (16:16-19).

Jesus' choice of twelve as the number of his inner circle has, and must surely have had at the time, obvious symbolic importance as the number of the sons of Jacob and thus of the tribes of Israel. People might have remembered Moses' choice of twelve tribal leaders in Num 1:1-16, and it is even possible that Matthew's phrase "These are the names of . . ." is a deliberate echo of Num 1:4, "These are the names of the men who shall assist you."[7] The symbolism will become explicit in 19:28, where these twelve disciples are given an eschatological role when, alongside the Son of Man seated on his own glorious throne, they, too, "will sit on twelve thrones judging the twelve tribes of Israel." There is no reason to believe that these twelve Galilean men were in fact drawn from all twelve traditional tribes; their significance was in their number, not in their ancestry. When one of the Twelve was lost (note the emphatic "the *eleven* disciples" in 28:16, after Judas's death), the number was sufficiently important for him to need to be replaced (Acts

---

6. There is possible support for the name of Thaddeus in the rabbinic list of *five* alleged disciples of Jesus preserved in *b. Sanh.* 43a: "Matthai, Neqai, Netzer, Buni, and Thodah," to which the only names in the NT lists which even remotely correspond are Μαθθαῖος and Θαδδαῖος. But the source of the rabbinic names is unknown, and their function in context is not to supply biographical information but as the basis for a polemical wordplay.

7. See D. C. Allison, *Moses,* 215-16, following W. Horbury, *NTS* 32 (1986) 503-27.

1:15-26), though even before that Paul continues to refer to them as "the Twelve" (1 Cor 15:5). So from an early point in his ministry Jesus was apparently thinking in terms of an alternative "Israel" with its own leadership based now not on tribal origin but on the Messiah's call.[8]

1 The commission of the Twelve is spelled out in strictly functional terms: Matthew does not mention the primary purpose of their original selection according to Mark 3:14, "to be with him," though his narrative will continue to make clear that this was in fact their essential role. But at the moment the focus is on the immediate mission on which they are about to be sent, which will be spelled out more fully in vv. 7-8. It is an extension of Jesus' own ministry as chs. 8–9 have described it, the last few words of this verse being an exact repetition from 4:23; 9:35. Here only their role in exorcism and healing is mentioned, the former unusually taking precedence, whereas in v. 8, as in Jesus' own ministry as Matthew portrays it, physical healing receives more attention. The present statement is compressed, and by itself would suggest that "authority over unclean spirits" was the basis of their ability to heal as well as to exorcise, but see above on 4:24 for Matthew's general pattern of drawing a distinction between exorcism and physical healing and using different terminology for the two. In v. 8 the inclusion of exorcism as the last of four acts of deliverance, the first three being purely physical, is more typical of Matthew's approach when he is not giving an abbreviated summary as here.

Both exorcism and healing are regarded as taking place by supernatural power, and so as requiring a gift of "authority" (rather than of medical training). That Jesus not only has such authority himself (7:29; 8:9; 9:6, 8) but is also able to give it to others implies a divine authority which is the more impressive for not being spelled out. Matthew's usual term for possessing spirits is *daimonia,* "demons" (so already in 7:22; 9:33-34), and this will be the term used in 10:8. His use here of the Marcan term "unclean spirits" (used elsewhere in Matthew only at 12:43) has no obvious special motivation; it is simply an acceptable synonym.

2-4 The use of the term "apostle" here (the only use in Matthew; see above) is appropriate to the setting, as the term means properly an envoy and these twelve men are about to be sent out (*apostellō,* v. 5, the verb from which "apostle" is derived) on a mission in which they will represent Jesus and his message.

The first four names in the list have been introduced to us in 4:18-22, where we have already been informed of Simon's nickname and of the name of the father of James and John. They are listed in the same order as in 4:18-

8. There was probably a similar symbolism behind the appointment of twelve men, together with three priests, to form the ruling council of the Qumran community (1QS 8:1).

22, as pairs of brothers (as in Luke 6:14), rather than grouping together the "inner circle" of Peter, James, and John (as in Mark 3:16-17; Acts 1:13). In specifying that Peter is "first" Matthew reflects not only that he was the first to be called, but also his prominence throughout the story as leader of the group, which will be strongly underlined in 16:17-19. By Matthew's time the first apostle was generally known as "Peter" rather than "Simon," and so Matthew uses "Peter" even before that name is formally given in the narrative sequence at 16:18; his narrative uses "Simon" (always in connection with "Peter") only when he is being introduced, here and in 4:18, and on the occasion of his renaming in 16:16-17. But on the two occasions when Jesus addresses him by name (16:17; 17:25) it is by his personal name "Simon," even though he has been described in the narrative as "Peter."[9] It seems, then, that the evangelists recognized a distinction between Jesus' historical usage and that of their own day.

Apart from Matthew (see 9:9) the list in vv. 3-4 consists of men who are not mentioned anywhere else in Matthew's gospel except for the last, Judas Iscariot. The corporate role of the Twelve was obviously more important and more remembered than the individual contribution of most of the members of the group. Only three names receive even the briefest expansion: Matthew's previous life as a tax collector reminds us of the story of his call; the father of the second James is mentioned in order to distinguish him from his better-known namesake; and the second Simon is also given with his nickname, "Zealot," in order to distinguish him from Simon Peter. "Zealot" did not become a technical term for members of the revolutionary party until the time of the Jewish War, so that Simon's nickname may derive more from his reputation for religious zeal (for "zealot" in this sense see Acts 21:20; 22:3; Gal 1:14; cf. Phil 3:6) than from involvement in an insurrectionary group,[10] though by the time Matthew wrote his gospel at least some of his readers would have been likely to take the term in the latter sense. The title raises the interesting question how a man so described would enjoy being part of the same group as a tax collector, his ideological opposite, but that can only be speculation. All the names except Andrew and Philip are Jewish in form, suggesting that Jesus' disciples were drawn mainly from the more conservatively Jewish part of the mixed population in Galilee (see also on the names of Jesus' brothers in 13:55 below). Andrew and Philip, like Simon Peter, were originally from Bethsaida (John 1:44), on the other side of the Jordan and so strictly outside Galilee in the territory of Herod Philip; their Greek names perhaps reflect the more Hellenistic milieu of that area.

---

9. Mark's only vocative address also uses "Simon" (Mark 14:37); cf. also Luke 22:31.

10. So, e.g., C. Mézange, *Bib* 81 (2000) 489-506.

Judas's betrayal of Jesus will be fully narrated later (26:14-16, 21-25, 47-50; 27:3-10); here it is mentioned only because it is the one thing about him every Christian would remember. He comes, appropriately, at the end of all the gospel lists (just as Peter comes first in all of them) — and is of course absent from the list in Acts 1:13. His second name, "Iscariot," is usually included, partly to distinguish him from the other Judas of John 14:22, but also because his notoriety made his full name familiar. Many derivations of "Iscariot" have been proposed,[11] including the suggestion that it is a corruption of *sicarios,* a member of the most notorious of the revolutionary groups (which would make for an interesting collocation with Simon the "zealot"), but perhaps more likely is the traditional notion that it derives from *îš-qerîyôt,* "man of Kerioth";[12] if so, this raises the interesting possibility that Judas was the one non-Galilean among the Twelve, since the only two towns called Kerioth that we know of are in Moab and in southern Judea. But that, too, is speculation, and since Hebrew *qiryâ* ("town") occurs in several other place names, it cannot be relied on.

3. Instructions for the Mission (10:5-15)

5 *These twelve Jesus sent out with the following instructions:*

"Do not go off to visit the Gentiles,[1] *and do not go into any town of the Samaritans;* 6 *rather, go to the lost sheep of the house of Israel.*

7 *"As you go, proclaim this message: 'The kingdom of heaven has arrived.'*[2] 8 *Heal those who are ill, raise the dead, make lepers clean, throw out demons. You have received without cost; give without cost.*

9 *"Do not get*[3] *any gold, silver, or copper to put in your money belts,* 10 *no pack for the journey, no spare clothes*[4] *or sandals or staff.*

---

11. Among the more interesting are "liar," "dyer," "carrier of the leather bag," and "redhead" (Judas has red hair in much traditional Christian art). For a full list and explanation of the suggestions see R. E. Brown, *Death,* 1410-16.

12. Luz, 2:67-68, prefers "man from Iscaria" on philological grounds, but he does not identify Iscaria.

1. Εἰς ὁδὸν ἐθνῶν, literally "into a way of Gentiles," which presumably means on a journey which will take them to where Gentiles live.

2. For the meaning of ἤγγικεν see p. 96, n. 3, and the comments on 3:2.

3. κτάομαι is properly to "obtain" rather than simply to "take," suggesting that the items listed in this verse (and the next?) are not ones ready to hand which are to be left behind, but rather ones which would need to be acquired especially for the journey.

4. Literally, "no two tunics" (χιτών, the basic inner garment), which is taken to mean no change of clothes (though it could also mean not taking a second garment for warmth; see Josephus, *Ant.* 17.136 for two χιτῶνες worn at the same time, and cf. Mark 14:63, where the high priest apparently was wearing more than one χιτών). δύο, "two," is not repeated with the following nouns (sandals and staff), but since it is not likely that Je-

> *For the worker is worthy of his keep.* 11 *Whichever town or village you*
> *come to, make inquiries as to who in it is worthy, and stay with them*
> *until you leave.* 12 *When you go into the house,*[5] *wish peace on it,*[6]
> 13 *and if that household is worthy of it, let your peace come upon it,*
> *but if it is not worthy, let your peace return to you.* 14 *And if anyone*
> *will not welcome you and listen to your message, as you go out of that*
> *house or town shake off the dust from your feet.* 15 *I tell you truly: on*
> *the day of judgment it will be more bearable for the land of Sodom*
> *and Gomorrah than for that town.*

This first part of the discourse,[7] in which Matthew develops the traditional
form of the mission charge found also in Mark 6:7-11; Luke 9:1-5; 10:1-12,
deals in the narrative context specifically with a given mission of the Twelve
in Galilee. From v. 16 on he will add more general principles concerning
Christian witness in a hostile world, and at least in v. 18 a wider range of mission will be envisaged than is set out here in vv. 5-6. But even in vv. 5-15,
while the situation is specific to the Twelve themselves, it is likely that Matthew regarded these instructions as applicable, *mutatis mutandis,* to later disciples as well. There are principles here as well as specific instructions; the
problem for the interpreter is to know which is which (e.g., are all Christians
exhorted to "raise the dead" or to travel with only the barest of equipment?),
and on this problem Matthew gives us no explicit help.

The pericope covers three aspects of their mission: to whom they are
to go (vv. 5-6); the nature of their mission in both word and deed (vv. 7-8);
and how they are to be fed and housed (vv. 9-15, developing the principle of
v. 8b, "Give without cost"). The last section, which raises the possibility of
rejection as well as a hospitable welcome, leads naturally into the consideration of hostility to Jesus' messengers which will follow in vv. 16-39.

They go as representatives of the Messiah. Verses 7-8 carefully repeat
both the message and the activity of Jesus as we have been told of them in

---

sus intended them to go barefoot (and v. 14 indicates that they had some footwear which
could collect dust), it is probably to be understood at least with "sandals." See the comments below on the staff.

5. οἰκία means both "house" (the building) and "household" (the people who live
in it), and both senses are deployed in these verses. On entering the "house" they greet the
"household," whose worthiness or lack of it will determine whether the greeting is effective.

6. Literally, "greet it," but the following verse makes it clear that the greeting
would be of the form "Peace be on this house" (*šālôm,* "peace," being the conventional
form of greeting, still regularly used in both Hebrew and Arabic). In Luke 10:5 this form
of greeting is spelled out.

7. On the structure of the discourse see below, p. 400, n. 10.

chs. 5–9; the disciples are to say and do what he has already said and done. At the end of the discourse (vv. 40-42) it will be made clear that how people respond to them also reveals their response to Jesus the Messiah. That is why the welcome or lack of it which they will encounter in the villages of Galilee is so strongly emphasized in vv. 11-15; the villagers will be welcoming or rejecting their Messiah. The "peace" which will rest on the "worthy" is not just a social formality, but a real mark of God's blessing or judgment. This is a moment of spiritual decision, however little some of the people of Galilee may yet recognize it as such.

Such a mission has an urgency all its own. While Matthew does not include Luke's prohibition even of conventional greetings on the road (Luke 10:4), the sense of a restless compulsion also underlies Matthew's restrictions on material provision. They are to travel light and to keep moving. There is the whole of Israel to be reached (v. 23).

5-6   Jesus is the Messiah of God's people Israel (2:6), coming in fulfillment of Israel's scriptures (as we have seen repeatedly in chs. 1–2 and since) to save "his people" from their sins (1:21). So it is at first sight not surprising that it is specifically to Israel that his disciples are also sent. That will be more than enough to keep them busy until "the Son of Man comes" (10:23). He will define his own area of mission in the same terms in 15:24, in specific contrast with a non-Jewish woman's plea for his help. But natural as such a restriction may seem, it strikes a surprising note[8] in the wider unfolding of Matthew's story, which has seen Jesus already welcomed by non-Israelite magi (2:1-12), located in fulfillment of scripture in "Galilee of the nations" (4:15), celebrated not only in Jewish areas but in "all Syria" and Decapolis (4:24-25), responding to the plea of a Roman soldier (8:5-13), and delivering a Gentile demoniac on the other (non-Jewish) side of the lake (8:28-34), while Jesus' own comments in response to the faith of the centurion (8:10-12) have pointed decisively away from any idea of an exclusively Jewish presence in the kingdom of heaven. This openness to non-Israelites will recur in many ways throughout the gospel until it reaches its culmination in 28:19: "Go and make disciples of all nations" (cf. 24:14; 26:13). So why are Gentiles and Samaritans excluded from the disciples' mission here?

The geographical terms used here ("*way* of the Gentiles," "*town* of the

---

8. M. D. Goulder, *Midrash*, 339, somewhat melodramatically refers to vv. 5-6 as "a famous conundrum, a citadel of contradiction." He discusses (339-42) four ways of accounting for the paradox, and concludes (342-44) that these verses reflect the known historical fact that the mission of the Twelve, as opposed to that of Paul, was specifically to Jewish Palestine, while the commission of 28:19 was given, Goulder argues, not to the "eleven" of 28:16 alone, but to a wider group whom he believes (questionably; see comments there) to have been present as well on the mountain and who represent the whole church.

Samaritans"; cf. "*towns* of Israel," v. 23) indicate a restriction on the area to be visited rather than a total ban on contact with Gentiles and Samaritans as such. Galilee was surrounded by Gentile territory on all sides except the south, which bordered Samaria; they are thus in practice restricted to Galilee. This limited scope of mission was to apply (though with some exceptions in Jesus' own practice) for the initial period of proclamation until the undeniably primary focus of Jesus' mission as Messiah of Israel had been established; only after that, and after Jesus' own ministry within Palestine has culminated in his death and resurrection, would it be appropriate to widen the scope deliberately to include Gentile and Samaritan areas,[9] even though in the mixed society of Galilee there would inevitably be some earlier contact with Gentiles. Progress toward a wider perspective was no doubt a gradual one, and in 15:21-28 we shall see Jesus himself, in non-Jewish territory, being obliged to broaden his own initially conservative reaction to a Gentile's need. But the geographical limitation remained essentially in force as long as Jesus himself was there as the focus of the mission. After his death and resurrection the worldwide mission predicted in 24:14 and 26:13 could be launched in the disciples' commission in 28:19-20.

This is the only mention of Samaria and Samaritans in Matthew's gospel. Its negative tone suggests a more conventionally Jewish perspective[10] than the openness to Samaritans in Luke (9:52-55; 10:30-37; 17:11-19) and John (4:4-42), though in all those passages the acceptability of Samaritans in the kingdom of God is noted as a matter of surprise. For Matthew they simply represent, together with the Gentiles, the wider world outside "the house of Israel" which for now remains outside the disciples' jurisdiction, but there is no reason to believe that Matthew would have had any difficulty in recognizing Samaritans as included in "all nations" who are ultimately to be summoned to discipleship. For "lost sheep" see the comments on 9:36 above; cf. Isa 53:6; Jer 50:6 for similar imagery. There, as here, it is used to describe the condition of Israel as a whole rather than a specific group within Israel.

7 The message to be proclaimed by the disciples is exactly the same as that of John the Baptist (3:2) and of Jesus himself (4:17), though the call to repentance which explicitly introduces those earlier summaries is here left unspoken. Mark 6:12 tells us that the disciples called for repentance; Matthew takes that for granted as the corollary of the coming of

9. Note, however, that this extension of the preaching of the gospel was still regarded as irregular by some members of the Jerusalem church in Acts 8:14-15 (Samaritans); 11:1-18, 22 (Gentiles).

10. Sir 50:25-26 lists two nations which the author loathes, together with "a third which is not a nation": the Edomites, the Philistines, and "the foolish people that lives at Shechem" (the Samaritans).

God's kingship.[11] See the comments on 3:2. The message is to be proclaimed "as they go"; as vv. 11-15 will make clear, this is to be an itinerant mission, not a settled ministry in one place.

8 The verbal message is to be complemented by actions which also correspond to Jesus' own miraculous activity: the four acts of deliverance specified are carefully worded to reflect the miracles in chs. 8–9 (cf. also the summary to come in 11:5). Their mission is an extension of his, and (with the exception of the calming of the storm, which was an occasional response to circumstances, not a regular response to human need) what he could do they are given the power to do too. Healing through divine power (even the curing of "leprosy," though this was at the extreme end of treatable conditions; see on 8:1-4) was widely regarded as an appropriate activity of holy men, and even exorcism was an accepted part of the Jewish scene (12:27, but see introductory comments on 8:28-34). Given Jesus' wide reputation already for such supernatural acts, people would have expected his representatives to do likewise (as indeed some of the disciples will find to their cost in 17:16). But within this list the unobtrusive inclusion of "raise the dead" is remarkable. Its very matter-of-fact tone raises the stakes significantly. Only two great men of the past were credited with such a feat (Elijah, 1 Kgs 17:17-24; Elisha, 2 Kgs 4:32-37; cf. 13:21), and Jesus' resuscitation of the official's daughter has introduced a new element into the demonstration of the Messiah's authority (see comments on 9:18-26, and cf. 11:5). We have no record that the disciples did in fact "raise the dead" during Jesus' lifetime, though subsequent miracles of Peter (Acts 9:36-42) and Paul (Acts 20:9-12) would no doubt be taken as fulfilling this charge. But if Matthew's church was used to seeing the dead raised, it has left remarkably little evidence of it, and one can only speculate as to whether Matthew or his readers might have expected a literal application of this clause. Its function here is perhaps more to tighten the link between the disciples' mission and what their Messiah has already been doing than to provide a blueprint for subsequent Christian practice.[12]

"Without cost" translates *dōrean,* "as a gift," an expression which sometimes means "for nothing" in the sense of "in vain" (Gal 2:21) or "without cause" (John 15:25), but usually connotes generosity (for God's generosity, see Rom 3:24; Rev 21:6; 22:17), in their case by not charging for their services. Paul makes a point of not having charged for his missionary labors (*dōrean,*

---

11. For this and other explanations of why repentance is not mentioned here see D. J. Weaver, *Discourse,* 193, n. 68.

12. νεκροὺς ἐγείρετε is missing in many later MSS and versions; while the omission could have been accidental, as one of a list of brief clauses with the same imperative ending, it is more likely that it reflects the embarrassment of later church circles which did not expect to see the dead raised.

2 Cor 11:7), in contrast with the common practice of itinerant philosophers and teachers who expected not just board and lodging but fees as well;[13] Paul himself refused even free board (*dōrean,* 2 Thess 3:8; cf. 1 Cor 9:3-18). So Jesus' disciples, having received the message of the kingdom of God "free of charge" through Jesus himself, are to offer their services in both teaching and healing without expecting any material reward. The following verses show, however, that unlike Paul they are to accept board and lodging, since they are to take no money with them to pay for it, and "the worker earns his keep." For the development of mercenary "prophets" and "apostles" not long after the NT period see *Did.* 11–12. For rabbinic comments on the same problem see *m. 'Abot* 1:3; *m. Bek.* 4:6; and cf. 2 Kgs 5:26 for a similar principle in the OT.

9-10   The essence of this instruction is to travel light by not making special provision for their material needs while on the mission;[14] here is an opportunity to exercise the practical trust in God's provision which they have been taught in 6:25-33. If the Son of Man has nowhere to lay his head (8:20), his representatives can expect no material security except in God. All the items listed are in Matthew objects of the verb "Do not get *(ktaomai),*" which does not naturally refer to what they are to carry[15] but rather to fund-raising and acquiring special equipment for the journey.[16] If they are not to go barefoot (see p. 379, n. 4), basic clothing and equipment are assumed; it is additional provision which is forbidden. Money[17] will not be needed, as they are to expect to receive appropriate hospitality en route. The "pack" *(pēra)* is a sort of traveling bag, probably simply for carrying their food for the journey, though the *pēra* was also associated with Cynic itinerant teachers who used it when begging for food;[18] the disciples will not need to carry, still less beg for,

---

13. For debates about fees charged by healers and teachers in the Greco-Roman and Jewish worlds see E. C. Park, *Mission,* 101-3.

14. Cf. Josephus's account of Essene travelers, *War* 2.125-26; see E. C. Park, *Mission,* 104.

15. That would be the more natural sense of αἴρω, "lift," "take," which both Mark and Luke use here.

16. Gundry, 186 (and n. 109), takes it as referring to "acquisition *from* the itinerant ministry," and thus sees these verses as an extension of the prohibition of charging in v. 8b (similarly D. J. Weaver, *Discourse,* 85), but this is to put Matthew unnecessarily at odds with Mark and Luke, who speak of "taking *for* the journey." Moreover, Gundry rightly goes on to understand the pack, clothes, sandals, and staff, which are governed by the same verb, as equipment *for* the journey.

17. Matthew specifies "gold, silver, and copper," where Mark has only "copper" and Luke ἀργύριον (probably in the general sense of "money" rather than specifically silver). M. D. Goulder, *Midrash,* 61-62, draws attention to Matthew's liking for large sums: "Matthew moves among the millionaires"! But Luz, 2:71, points out that this threefold designation of valuables echoes an OT formula (Exod 25:3).

18. E. C. Park, *Mission,* 106-13, quotes ancient accounts of itinerant Cynics and

food.[19] The prohibition of spare clothes and sandals[20] (see p. 379, n. 4) probably suggests a mission of limited duration, though no doubt these, too, could have been supplied by well-wishers en route if necessary.

The "staff" is sometimes raised as an issue in gospel harmonization,[21] since while Matthew and Luke forbid it, Mark 6:8 allows "only a staff," together with sandals (6:9). The difference in the verbs used by Matthew and Mark (see above) may seem to offer an attractive basis for harmonization (take the staff you have but don't acquire a second one), but unfortunately Luke uses the same verb as Mark. Moreover, while to carry spare clothes and sandals makes sense, it would hardly seem necessary to forbid anyone to carry *more than one* staff; so perhaps Matthew might have in mind acquiring a new one to take *instead of* the old? Most readers, however, do not find it easy to get excited about this "gospel discrepancy," especially since the three "parallel" passages are far from identical otherwise; whether the tradition actually forbade the disciples to carry a staff or not, the thrust of the passage is hardly affected. Overall Mark's wording seems the more likely, in that it would be taken for granted in that culture that most travelers would have a staff (cf. Exod 12:11); Essene travelers, who carried nothing else, had a weapon (unspecified, but presumably a staff) in case of brigands (Josephus, *War* 2.125), and even Cynics, known for their asceticism, carried a staff (Keener, 318); cf. *m. Ber.* 9:5 for "staff, sandals, and money belt" as the basic equipment of the traveler, to be left behind on entering the Temple Mount.

---

argues that this discourse deliberately differentiates the disciples from "the popular caricature of the Cynic philosophers" as mere beggars. C. Deutsch, *Lady Wisdom,* 115-16, argues that here "Matthew imposes upon his wandering preachers a lifestyle more radical even than that of the Cynics." But it is questionable how far Cynics, a Greek philosophical school, would have been a familiar sight in first-century Galilee; see R. F. Hock, *ABD* 1:1221-26; Keener, 317-18.

19. For the prevalence of "religious begging" in the Mediterranean world see Luz, 2:78, nn. 60-61.

20. Matthew and Luke use the term ὑποδήματα rather than Mark's σανδάλια. Luz, 2:77, suggests that what is here forbidden is "good shoes," "shoes with leather on top" *as opposed to* sandals. But this sense for ὑπόδημα, based on Pollux's *Onomasticon* which represents second-century usage in Greece, is improbable in first-century Palestine, where sandals are the only footwear known to have been commonly worn by men. BDAG define ὑπόδημα as "a leather sole that is fastened to the foot by means of straps, sandal," in other words, a synonym for σανδάλιον, for which they give the same definition. The etymology of the term suggests this meaning, and indeed Mark correctly uses the phrase ὑποδεδεμένους σανδάλια.

21. B. Ahern, *CBQ* 5 (1943) 332-37, lists some proposed harmonizations. The plural ῥάβδους which appears in some later MSS and versions of Matthew is probably an early and rather clumsy attempt to allow for Mark's *one* staff.

The specific application of these instructions to the mission of the Twelve in Galilee, rather than as rules for all subsequent Christian mission, is indicated by Luke 22:35-36, where they are rescinded for the new situation following Jesus' arrest.

"The worker is worthy of his keep" has a proverbial sound,[22] and in 1 Tim 5:18 the same statement (in the Lucan form with *misthos,* "wages," instead of *trophē,* "food")[23] is quoted as justification for the payment of church "elders." There it follows a quotation of what "Scripture says" in Deut 25:4, and it would be natural to read it as a further scriptural quotation; but it has no obvious OT source, and it is possible that by the time 1 Timothy was written the recorded sayings of Jesus were themselves being treated as in effect "scripture"; it is also possible, however, that Paul is citing it simply as a familiar proverb. But in 1 Cor 9:14 he is clearly aware of teaching to this effect by Jesus himself. This saying is cited in *Did.* 13:1-2. The distinction between "being worthy of one's keep" and "giving without cost" (v. 8) is presumably that between accepting needed hospitality and profiting from payment for services rendered, though the distinction may not always be easy to apply in practice.[24]

11   The disciples can travel light because they will be able to rely on hospitality from strangers (the need to "make inquiries" indicates that the potential hosts are not yet known to the disciples). This expectation belongs naturally in a Middle Eastern culture; see Gen 18:1-8 for the classic example (cf. Gen 19:1-8; Judg 19:15-21). The search for somebody "worthy" is further explained in vv. 13-14: there will be suitable and unsuitable hosts, depending on their openness to the disciples' message. The word "worthy" is a repeated motif of this section: the worker is "worthy" of his keep, and potential hosts are "worthy" or "unworthy." The discrimination required reminds us of Jesus' maxim in 7:6 about placing treasure only before those who are able to appreciate it. By this time there were no doubt people in most Galilean villages who had been among the crowds following Jesus, and such sympathizers would be likely to be willing hosts for his disciples.[25]

12-13   For the announcement of peace as an aspect of the coming of

---

22. E. C. Park, *Mission,* 116, notes parallel ideas in Plato and in a later rabbinic midrash.

23. D. J. Weaver, *Discourse,* 194, n. 77, argues that τροφή, "food," here stands (by synecdoche) for "all those things which are essential for daily living."

24. Luz, 2:80-81, gives an interesting (and rather cynical?) overview of the way this passage has (or more often has not) been applied to the issue of the payment of Christian ministers.

25. Josephus, *War* 2.124-27, describes the practice of hospitality among Essenes in very similar terms; it is, however, directed specifically to fellow Essenes, whereas the circle of Jesus' supporters was probably not by this stage so well defined and organized.

the kingdom of God see Isa 52:7. The greeting "Peace to this house" (Luke 10:5 spells out what Matthew's "greet" assumes) is thus no mere formality. It is envisaged as an effective blessing which goes out and takes effect provided that it is suitably received; if not, it will have no effect, but will "return" like an uncashed check. Cf. Isa 55:11 for God's word which goes out and will not "return empty" but will accomplish its task (cf. Isa 31:2; 45:23). For similarly vivid language about God's word as an "independent" agent sent out to do God's work see Pss 107:20; 147:15, 18; Isa 9:8; Jer 23:29. But even human words, uttered with intent and with God's sanction, can be effective and irrevocable; see Gen 27:33-38. Some of the more remarkable statements of human authority in the gospels depend on this concept of the effective word spoken with divine approval (Matt 16:19; 18:18; John 20:23). To be the willing hosts of such messengers is indeed a blessing, but to oppose them is to forfeit God's peace, because to receive them is to receive Jesus, and to receive Jesus is to receive God (v. 40).

14-15   The latter part of this discourse will recognize that not everyone will welcome Jesus' representatives, and some will actively oppose them. So they are now prepared for what they must do if hospitality is refused. Shaking off the dust from one's feet is an obvious symbol of dissociation;[26] they want nothing more to do with the place (Luke 10:11 spells it out more fully).[27] This dissociation may be from an individual household, but it is also possible that a whole town or village will turn against them, as Jesus will accuse Chorazin, Bethsaida, and even Capernaum of turning against him in 11:20-24. The prophets had customarily proclaimed God's judgment against whole communities, but the mention of Sodom reminds us of Abraham's question (Gen 18:22-32) whether the communal wickedness (or, in this case, rejection of God's messengers) was on the part of every individual or household in the community, or whether, as in Sodom, there might be a few who stood out against the common attitude. But even the presence of "righteous Lot" (2 Pet 2:6-8) in Sodom was not enough to save the city, and Jesus now takes that exemplary judgment on Sodom and Gomorrah (Gen 19:24-29) as a model for what awaits those who reject him and his messengers. Indeed, their fate will be worse because the fuller light of the dawning kingdom of God is now being rejected; to reject Jesus' messengers is thus to reject God and to incur his final judgment.[28]

---

26. Cf. Acts 13:51 and for a comparable gesture Acts 18:6; Neh 5:13.

27. Carrying the earth of Gentile territory conveyed uncleanness (*m. 'Ohal.* 2:3; *m. Ṭehar.* 4:5). No one may enter the Temple Mount with dust on their feet (*m. Ber.* 9:5), presumably because the sacred place must not be touched by uncleanness from outside.

28. See D. J. Weaver, *Discourse,* 88-89, and ibid., 196-97, n. 98, for the eschatological nature of the judgment.

4. The Expectation of Persecution (10:16-23)

16 *"Look, I am sending you out like sheep among wolves; so be as cunning[1] as snakes and as harmless as doves.* 17 *Be on your guard against people: they will hand you over for trial[2] and flog you in their assemblies,[3]* 18 *and you will even be brought before governors and kings because of me, as a witness to them and to the Gentiles.* 19 *But when they hand you over, don't worry about what to say or how to say it: what you are to say will be given to you at that time,* 20 *for it is not you who are speaking, but the Spirit of your Father speaking in you.* 21 *A brother will hand over his brother to be killed, and a father his child; children will rise against their parents and put them to death.* 22 *You will be hated by everybody because of my name; but it is the person who remains faithful[4] to the end who will be saved.* 23 *But when they persecute you in one town, flee to the next.[5] I tell you truly: you will not go through all[6] the towns of Israel before[7] the Son of Man comes.*

1. φρόνιμος in itself has the positive meaning of "prudent" or "sensible," but the metaphor of snakes suggests that the proverbial "craftiness" of the snake (Gen 3:1) is in mind as a deliberate contrast with the vulnerable "guilelessness" of doves.

2. Literally, "hand you over to councils." For συνέδριον with reference to a local court rather than to *the* Sanhedrin in Jerusalem see on 5:22. Here the use of the plural (as well as the Galilean setting) confirms that the reference must be to the former.

3. For the meaning of συναγωγή see on 4:23 and n. 6 there. Whereas previous uses of the term in Matthew (4:23; 6:2, 5; 9:35) have focused on assemblies for teaching and worship, the apparently judicial function of the assembly here justifies that translation rather than "synagogue." See the comments below.

4. Literally, "who endures," but in a context of persecution because of their loyalty and witness to Jesus the sense of maintaining that loyalty undeterred seems required.

5. Literally, "when they persecute you in this town, flee to the other one." Many MSS substitute ἄλλην for ἑτέραν (making no significant difference to the sense), and some add a further stage of persecution and flight from the second town to a third, probably a rather pedestrian attempt to fill out the sense of "completing the towns of Israel."

6. Literally, "you will not complete (τελέω) the towns of Israel." See the comments below.

7. J. A. Gibbs, *Jerusalem*, 71-72 (following C. H. Giblin), states that ἕως means "until" rather than "before," but his discussion strangely takes little account of the presence of ἄν, the effect of which is to make the temporal link indefinite. "You will not have completed the towns of Israel *until* the Son of Man comes" would imply that the process *will* be completed at that (definite) time, whereas the force of the saying is rather that the task will *not* have been completed by the (indefinite) time the Son of Man comes (as Gibbs himself recognizes; the coming "will effectively prevent the completion of the mission activity . . ."). That sense, in my idiom, is better conveyed by "before" than by "until." For a similar usage cf. p. 636, n. 5.

These verses[8] begin and end in the context of the mission of the Twelve as set out in vv. 5-15: see "I am sending you out" in v. 16 and the mission to the "towns of Israel" with its limited duration in v. 23. But much of what falls between these two verses has a wider perspective, involving a witness to "governors," "kings," and "Gentiles" in v. 18, and speaking of universal rejection and of family divisions which suggest a more developed form of the confrontation between the gospel and the unbelieving world, including the prospect of actual martyrdom, while v. 22b seems to introduce an unexpectedly eschatological note. Whether that eschatological perspective is maintained in the reference to the "coming of the Son of Man" will depend on how that phrase is understood here and elsewhere in Matthew; see the discussion below. Moreover, vv. 17-22 are closely parallel to Mark 13:9-13 (and less closely to Luke 21:12-19), a part of what is normally understood to be Mark's "apocalyptic" discourse,[9] which will find a further but much less close parallel within Matthew's version of the same "apocalyptic discourse" (24:9-14). When we come to ch. 24, I shall argue that the focus of that part of the discourse is much less "eschatological" than is often assumed, and is concerned with the experience of discipleship between the lifetime of Jesus and the destruction of the temple in A.D. 70, but even so it deals with a situation beyond that of the initial Galilean mission from which the present discourse has set out. It seems, then, that Matthew's discourse, having begun with the immediate mission of the Twelve in Galilee, is now expanded to consider more widely the implications of the Christian mission and to guide disciples in how to respond to the rejection and hostility which vv. 14-15 have led them to expect. The degree to which these verses will apply directly to the immediate mission of the Twelve is limited; Matthew has a wider and later audience in his sights.[10]

A persistent feature of these verses is the repeated assertion that persecution arises not out of sociological factors but "because of me." The disciples are sent *by Jesus* to face the wolves (v. 16); they will be hauled up before the authorities "because of me" (v. 18), and what they say in that context will take the form of "witness" (presumably to Jesus and his message); the hatred they experience will be specifically "because of my name" (v. 22). It is as representatives of the coming Son of Man (v. 23) that they will be delivering their message to the towns of Israel. The conclusion of Matthew's story al-

8. For vv. 16-23 as a distinct section of the discourse see below, p. 400, n. 10.

9. I have discussed the interpretation of Mark 13:5-37, and the inappropriateness of labeling the discourse as a whole as "apocalyptic," in my *Mark,* 497-505. Cf. ibid., 513-14, for comments on the perspective of Mark 13:9-13.

10. See above, p. 371, n. 3, for D. J. Weaver's survey of different approaches to the coherence of the discourse in relation to its historical setting(s).

ready casts its shadow over this phase of its development with the assumption that the name of Jesus will provoke opposition and a violent response from the world at large.[11] This less optimistic assumption contrasts markedly with the general enthusiasm for Jesus' Galilean mission which has been the dominant note of the story so far, and has been (in 9:35-38) the setting for the disciples' mission at this point in the story. At the same time, however, this repeated emphasis on the significance of Jesus himself and his "name" carries similar christological overtones to those we noticed in the discourse of chs. 5–7, underlining the personal authority of the Messiah.

16 This verse is a bridge between the more immediate focus on Jesus' sending out the Twelve in vv. 5-15 and the more general treatment of the persecution of disciples in the remainder of the discourse. Its immediate trigger is the expectation in vv. 14-15 that there will be some who reject the Twelve and their message, and some interpreters prefer to treat it as part of the same paragraph. But its application is apparently wider than that, as the rejection of the Twelve at this stage in Galilee is unlikely to have been sufficiently violent to justify the vivid simile of sheep among wolves. It acts rather as a pointer to the eventually more serious vulnerability of disciples confronting a hostile world. For sheep threatened by wolves see 7:15, but here there is no pretense: the threat is real and open. As in John 10:12; Acts 20:29, the sheep are helpless in the face of an attack by wolves.[12] It is an image of the Christian presence in the world which sits uncomfortably alongside much of the subsequent history of the church, as a power structure and itself often the agent of persecution.

Two further animal similes fill out the picture. The vulnerability of sheep is enhanced by their proverbial stupidity, but disciples are not to be like that. The snake's instinct for self-preservation (by getting out of the way when trouble threatens) is a more helpful model. As a result of the Eden story, the snake was proverbial for cunning,[13] and the term used here *(phronimos)* is the same as that used for the "craftiness" of the snake in LXX Gen 3:1. Disciples under threat are not to be helpless and gullible, but must maintain the initiative. Cf. the shrewd self-preservation of the steward in Luke 16:1-8, also described as *phronimos*. But in popular thought snakes are feared rather than admired (cf. 3:7; 7:10), and it is as a threat to God's people

11. D. J. Weaver, *Discourse*, 101-2, draws attention to the parallel between the situation of the disciples in these verses and the experience of Jesus himself. "If the disciples are sent out to minister as Jesus is ministering, they are also sent out to suffer as Jesus will suffer."

12. For Jewish use of the metaphor of sheep for the people of God, often with emphasis on their vulnerability to predators, see H. Preisker and S. Schulz, *TDNT* 6:690.

13. E. C. Park, *Mission*, 129-30, also cites a few non-Jewish examples of this view.

that they appear more often in biblical literature. So Jesus here offsets that more obvious connotation of snakes by a balancing animal image, the harmlessness of doves;[14] the disciples' cunning is to be directed not to harming their opponents, but to their own survival and the commendation of the gospel. They need the cunning of snakes without the venom. Cf. Paul's instructions not to repay evil with evil and to overcome evil with good (Rom 12:17-21; and cf. Rom 16:19 for a close parallel to this saying).

17 The potential enemies (the "wolves") are described broadly as "people" rather than a specified class or group; opposition may come from any quarter. Matthew will use the same term for the opposition in vv. 32-33. But it seems here to have at least a quasi-official status, since it results in judicial trial and authorized punishment in the public assembly;[15] for flogging in Jewish assemblies cf. 23:34; Acts 5:40; 22:19.[16] The local "councils" of up to twenty-three members[17] in Jewish towns had responsibility for the maintenance of public order, and one of their powers was the imposition of a judicial penalty of flogging such as Paul describes in 2 Cor 11:23 ("countless floggings"), 24 ("five times I received the thirty-nine lashes"). For the "thirty-nine lashes," the maximum flogging permitted under Jewish law, see Deut 25:1-3 and more specifically *m. Mak.* 3:10-11; this punishment was applied for a variety of moral and ritual offenses against the Mosaic law, including breaking the food laws (*m. Mak.* 3:1-9), and it is perhaps on this point that later Christians, such as Paul, fell foul of the authorities.[18] But at the time of the mission of the Twelve that particular issue had not arisen, and we have no evidence of such judicial proceedings against Jesus' disciples before his death. Jesus' words here are looking further into the future.

---

14. BDAG 806b explains the use of the dove as a symbol of virtue by an ancient belief that it has no bile. It is probably also due to the observation that doves, one of the commonest and most noticeable bird families in Palestine, are, as vegetarians, always prey rather than predator. Cf. Song 2:14; 5:2; 6:9 for "dove" as a term of endearment, and Ps 74:19 as a metaphor for the vulnerable people of God. Keener, 322, quotes ancient references to doves as "weak and timid," and the imagery of Ephraim as a "silly dove" running into trouble in Hos 7:11 shows why the cunning of snakes needs to be added to the harmlessness of doves!

15. This sense seems more probable in this context than "synagogue," more narrowly understood as a building for worship and instruction; see above on 4:23 and n. 6 there.

16. For flogging as an official punishment among both Jews and Romans see D. J. Weaver, *Discourse,* 199, nn. 115, 116.

17. For the rules c. A.D. 200 see *m. Sanh.* 1:1-6; fewer members of the council were needed for less serious cases, but twenty-three in potentially capital cases, and according to some authorities where a sentence of flogging was incurred (*m. Sanh.* 1:1-2).

18. For the practice and causes of Jewish corporal punishment see Keener, 322-23.

18 While v. 17 maintained the focus on the Jewish situation in Galilee, here we apparently move onto a wider stage. At the time of Jesus' ministry Galilee had neither "governor"[19] nor king: Herod Antipas, though he liked to be known as "king" as Matthew entitles him in 14:9, was officially only a tetrarch. Nor is there any evidence for disciples of Jesus attracting the hostile attention of the governing authorities at this period. The plural "governors and kings" seems therefore to require the wider canvass of the subsequent mission of the church as it spread outside Palestine and encountered official opposition at the highest levels; for appearances before "governors" cf. Acts 13:6-12; 18:12-17; 23:23–25:12, and for "kings" see Acts 12:1-4; 25:13–26:32 (in the latter case Paul appears before "governor" and "king" together); in many of these cases it was hostile Jews who brought the Christian missionaries before the Gentile authorities. The local opposition which the Twelve can expect in Galilee is thus a foreshadowing of the more serious and official hostility which Jesus' followers will meet in the wider world.

Such unsought and unwelcome encounters will, however, also contribute to the mission, as they will result in "witness." In 8:4 this term probably meant no more than the visible "proof" to the people that the leper was cured. But here and in 24:14, both of which mention the "Gentiles" as the recipients of the witness, it has a stronger sense. In 24:14 the "witness" is the result of the worldwide proclamation of the *euangelion,* and here too, as vv. 19-20 will explain, verbal proclamation is involved. It is "because of Jesus" that they have been brought before the authorities, and their verbal explanation of their mission in that context will inevitably take the form of a presentation of the claims of Jesus (who himself was also to stand trial before both the Jewish council and the Roman governor). The governors and kings will be the immediate audience of the disciples' "witness," but from this prominent platform it will find its way to the consciousness of the "Gentiles" at large. Persecution and official opposition will thus contribute to the spreading of the gospel rather than stifling it, as the book of Acts will amply illustrate.

19-20 The same verb ("don't worry") which governs the disciples' attitude to material provision and security in 6:25-34 is here applied to their situation on trial, and the same principle applies: don't worry, but leave it to God. The right words to speak in that situation are as much a necessity as food and clothing, and God can be trusted to deal with both because he is "your Father." As in 6:25-34, this assurance is not an excuse for failure to make responsible provision for foreseeable needs; to take this assurance as an excuse for lazy preachers, insisting that all Christian utterance must be spontaneous and unprepared, is to take it seriously out of context. But in the

---

19. ἡγεμών, the term normally used for Roman provincial governors such as the prefects of Judea; it is the title used for Pilate throughout chs. 27–28.

crisis situation which demands a verbal defense and proclamation in an intimidating setting (particularly given the low social status of most of Jesus' early followers), disciples have a resource beyond their own intellectual or rhetorical powers. That resource is "the Spirit of your Father speaking in you," but it is not necessary to press the expression "it is not you who are speaking" to the point of envisaging a sort of ecstatic utterance in which the disciple's own mind is not engaged. More relevant is the language of John 14:26; 15:26-27; 16:13-15 about the Spirit "teaching," "reminding," and "guiding" disciples, where again the context is of "witness" to Jesus.

Matthew's relatively few references to the Holy Spirit (in comparison with Luke and Acts) include references to the Spirit as active both in the ministry of Jesus (3:16; 4:1; 12:18, 28) and in various ways in the experience of God's people (empowering Mary's conception, 1:18, 20; inspiring David's words, 22:43), but this is the only passage which gives practical substance to the promise of 3:11 that Jesus would baptize his people with the Holy Spirit, in that only here is a particular gift or ability said to come to disciples through the Spirit "in you." Matthew's gospel contains much more about their relationship to God as "your Father in heaven," and even here the work of the Spirit in directing their speech is explicitly the means by which "your Father" operates in their lives. The result is one of those incidental hints in the NT of a trinitarian way of thinking such as will be spelled out more explicitly in the farewell discourses of John 13–16: the Father gives his Spirit to empower the disciples' witness to his Son. Of course there is no formal trinitarian theology at this point, but such apparently unplanned collocations are the stuff of which later trinitarian theology was made, so that when the apparently formal trinitarianism of 28:19 bursts on the scene the careful reader may not be as completely unprepared as is often assumed.

21   The penalty for loyalty to Jesus in v. 17 was restricted to flogging, but now actual martyrdom is in view — a further sign that the perspective of these verses extends beyond the Galilean mission of the Twelve. Jesus expected families to be divided on the basis of loyalty to him; see vv. 34-37, where the prediction is grounded in a quotation of Mic 7:6. Here the same text is perhaps more loosely in view, though the only verbal echo of the LXX is in the verb *epanistamai epi,* "rise against" (which is strangely not used in the more direct quotation in v. 35), and the relationships are differently expressed (Matthew's "children will rise against their parents" sums up two clauses in Mic 7:6 which specify son against father and daughter against mother). But in Mic 7:6 the focus is only on enmity and contempt within the family, as a symptom of the breakdown of social order, and there is no mention of family members bringing about each other's deaths. Jesus' words present a much more extreme and shocking scenario. Both the expression "hand over to be killed" and the verb *thanatoō,* "put to death," suggest an of-

393

ficial execution by the governing authorities; Christian discipleship has apparently become itself a capital offense, as it certainly was by the time of Pliny's correspondence with Trajan in the early second century (Pliny, *Ep.* 10.96-97), and for a time at least in Rome in the mid-sixties under Nero (Tacitus, *Ann.* 15.44). Both Pliny and Tacitus mention Christians convicted on the testimony of others, and the phrase "hand over to be killed" here suggests a similar use of informers. The nearest equivalent to such official persecution in Palestine that we know of in the NT period is the apparently short-lived persecution of the Christian leadership by Herod Agrippa I in the early forties, though the brief account in Acts 12:1-4 mentions only James as an actual martyr at that time.

22 The mutual hostility within the family is only part of a more general hostility to Jesus' disciples. Verse 22a will be repeated verbatim in 24:9, with the addition of "all the nations." The broad expression "hated by everybody" is reminiscent of the famously ambiguous statement of Tacitus (*Ann.* 15.44) attributing Nero's persecution of Christians to *odium humani generis* ("hatred of the human race") — either because they were alleged to hate all other human beings, or because the whole human race hated them.[20] Such hatred of disciples "because of my name" is explained by John as an extension of the world's hatred for Jesus himself (John 15:18-25; 1 John 3:13-14). It must be balanced against the positive response of other people to the disciple's "light" which was presented in 5:13-16, though there, too, persecution (vv. 11-12) coexists with admiration. Here we hear only one side of the love-hate relationship of the world to the gospel.

The world's response is put in perspective by a reference to salvation at the "end." Verse 22b will be repeated verbatim in 24:13, and in that context the "end" is related to the events predicted in 24:1-3, the destruction of the temple, the *parousia* of Jesus, and the "close of the age"; which of those events is referred to by the word "end" in 24:6 and 14, and whether "to the end" in 24:13 has the same "end" in view, will be discussed when we come to ch. 24. Here there is no such context to define it, and the phrase *eis telos,* "to the end," can hardly have such a specific reference, but simply means persevering for as long as may be necessary. The "end" is defined more by the future "salvation" which terminates the period of "remaining faithful" than by a specific historical or eschatological reference. The thought loosely echoes Dan 12:12-13, a beatitude on those who remain faithful and will receive their reward "at the end of the days." *Sōzō,* "save," is used by Matthew in a wide range of senses; often it refers to physical deliverance from death or disease (8:25; 9:21-22; 14:30; 24:22; 27:40, 42, 49), but it is also used of salvation

20. See E. C. Park, *Mission,* 136-38, for this and similar statements, more generally by Romans about the Jews.

from sins (1:21), and in 19:25 it stands in parallel with "entering the kingdom of God," while in 16:25 the disciple's "life" is paradoxically saved by losing it. These latter uses are the most probable pointers to the meaning here. Jesus is talking not about the preservation of physical life, but the ultimate well-being which is compatible with the loss of physical life. In the face of persecution and possible martyrdom disciples must remain true to their loyalty to Jesus; if they do so "to the end," they will be "saved," even though they may be executed. Cf. the wordplay in 27:42, where Jesus' failure to "save" himself (from physical death) is contrasted with his "saving" other people, a fact which the evangelist, unlike the mocking authorities, wishes to affirm.

23   The prospect of being driven from town to town by the hostility of the inhabitants takes us back to the scenario of the mission of the Twelve in Galilee as set out in vv. 11-15. When they find themselves unwelcome, they should not waste time throwing the pearls of their message of the kingdom of God before the unresponsive pigs and dogs of the towns which refuse them (7:6) — a principle which later was central to Paul's mission and contributed to the rapid spread of the gospel in the wider world (Acts 13:45-51; 14:5-7, 19-20; 17:5-10, 13-15, etc.).

Given that Galilean setting, it is natural to understand "go through all the towns of Israel" as the completion of the mission of the Twelve; it is hard to see what else the phrase "*complete* the towns of Israel" could mean in this context,[21] where the visiting of "towns" by the Twelve has been specifically mentioned in vv. 11, 14-15 and where their geographical limits have been set in terms of "towns" to be visited (vv. 5-6; see comments there).[22] Two aspects of the wording seem to conflict with this view, however. First, "Israel" may seem to suggest a wider area than simply Galilee, and there is no indication that Jesus intended his disciples at this stage to go down to Judea. Note, however, that the term used in Jesus' instructions in v. 6 is "the house of *Israel*"; the narrative setting shows that "Israel" here means in effect Galilee. Secondly, to speak of "the Son of Man coming" leads most Christian readers to assume an eschatological *"parousia"* setting which is far removed from a

---

21. The reference might be to their exhaustion of all possible places of refuge, rather than to having nowhere left in which to preach, but the difference in context is not great. See G. R. Beasley-Murray, *Kingdom,* 283-85.

22. See D. J. Weaver, *Discourse,* 100. The geographical connotation of "the towns of Israel" in this context makes unlikely either the view that Jesus' words include the subsequent mission to the diaspora or the contention of, e.g., J. M. McDermott, *BZ* 28 (1984) 230-40, that this verse is speaking of the mission to the Jewish *people* ("the entirety of the Jewish nation, not just Palestinian Jews"), which is to continue until the *parousia.* Both of these interpretations are attempts to accommodate the wording of the verse to the assumption that "the coming of the Son of Man" refers to the *parousia,* a view which I shall dispute in what follows.

mission of the Twelve in the early thirties A.D. As such language will recur several times in Matthew, and has an important bearing on exegesis, it is appropriate here, where it first appears, to consider its implications.[23]

It is widely agreed that the wording of these passages is based on Dan 7:13, "one like a son of man coming with the clouds of heaven." The vision of the "one like a son of man" in Dan 7:13-14 was probably the major source of Jesus' chosen self-designation, "the Son of Man," and the language of that vision recurs several times in the Synoptic tradition, but especially in seven passages in Matthew (10:23; 16:27-28; 19:28; 24:30; 25:31; 26:64; 28:18). Daniel's vision is of one who is brought before God's throne in heaven and there given an everlasting kingship over all peoples. It is thus a vision of granting the ultimate authority to the people of God, who are symbolized by the "human figure" in contrast to the beasts which represent the preceding empires (Dan 7:3-8, 17), and who are thus vindicated after their oppression by the last of those empires (Dan 7:19-22). In this individual representation of the corporate experience of the "holy people" Jesus found a foreshadowing of his own experience on behalf of his people. In Dan 7:13-14 this "son of man" *comes* before God to be enthroned as king. There is nothing in the imagery of Daniel to suggest a coming *to earth,* as Christian interpretation has traditionally found in these passages; he *comes* in the clouds of heaven *to God.* The verb used both in Daniel and in the NT allusions is the very ordinary verb "come," which is not related to the more technical NT term for Jesus' eschatological return, *parousia.* The term *parousia* in fact occurs only four times in the gospels, all in Matthew 24, where we shall see that that future *parousia* is carefully distinguished from the "coming in the clouds of heaven" described in Matt 24:30. This means that, despite centuries of later Christian interpretive tradition, when the gospels speak of "the Son of Man coming" the presumption must be that they are speaking not of an eschatological *parousia* but of a heavenly enthronement, the vindication and empowering of the Son of Man after his earthly rejection and suffering, when God will turn the tables on those who thought they had him in their power. This emphasis will emerge clearly in several of the passages listed above where the vision of Dan 7:13-14 has molded Matthew's language, perhaps most clearly in 26:64, where Jesus stands before his supposed judges and predicts that instead God will make him "from now on" the judge over them.

"The coming of the Son of Man" is thus not a description of a particular historical event but evocative language to depict his eventual vindication

---

23. I have discussed the three Marcan passages where such language is used at some length in my *Divine Government,* 64-84; the arguments presented there apply, *mutatis mutandis,* to the more extensive use of this imagery in Matthew. See also more briefly my *Matthew: Evangelist,* 290-22, 311, 314-16.

and sovereign authority. As such it can be applied to different stages in the outworking of Jesus' mission. In 28:18 the echo of Dan 7:14 indicates that already immediately after his resurrection the Son of Man has received his kingly authority. In several passages the fulfillment of Daniel's vision is linked to a specific time-frame within the living generation: "some standing here will not taste death before they see . . ." (16:28); "this generation will not pass until . . ." (24:34); "from now on you will see . . ." (26:64). The fulfillment is thus apparently linked with the vindication and enthronement of Jesus after his resurrection; it is, to use Lucan terminology, ascension language. In 24:30, however, even though the time scale is limited to the living generation (v. 34), the context links the coming of the Son of Man to the latter part of that period, when the temple will be destroyed. But, on the other hand, the same Danielic imagery is applied in 19:28 to what appears to be a more ultimate situation, "the regeneration," when the Twelve will join Jesus in exercising authority over Israel, while in 25:31 it introduces what is generally taken to be a vision of the final judgment. It seems, then, that the sovereign authority envisaged in Dan 7:13-14, first inaugurated when Jesus has risen from the dead, works itself out in successive phases throughout history until it finds its ultimate fulfillment in the last judgment.[24] Just how each of the seven Matthean allusions to Daniel's vision fits into this historical trajectory will be discussed at the appropriate points in the commentary.[25]

In the light of this wider usage of Daniel's language, at what point in the historical trajectory should we set the uniquely Matthean text 10:23? Is it speaking of a mission to Israel continuing throughout history until the final consummation, or of an earlier terminus within history such as the events of the Jewish War[26] (to which Daniel's language will be applied in 24:30), after which it will no longer be appropriate for Jesus' disciples to "go through the

24. See my *Jesus and the OT*, 139-48 for a general discussion of the Synoptic allusions to Dan 7:13-14 (all of which are represented in Matthew) and their significance in understanding Jesus' view of his own mission.

25. A. I. Wilson, *When*, 161-72, surveys "Matthew's 'Coming Son of Man' Sayings outside Chapters 21-25" (he deals with 24:30 and its surrounding context, ibid., 144-61). He concludes that none of them require a reference to the *parousia*, and takes them as supporting the perspective which he has also demonstrated in chs. 21-25, that "Jesus is bringing judgement on his contemporaries and their society."

26. Hagner, 1:279-80 (following Carson, 252-53), presents an attractive argument for this possibility, with special reference to the significance of the destruction of Jerusalem for "the shift of salvation-history from the Jews to the Gentiles," so that the mission to Israel no longer takes priority. I leaned toward this interpretation in my *Jesus and the OT*, 140, 142, 145, but now find the link with 28:18-19 more compelling in this context. J. A. Gibbs, *Jerusalem*, 65-75, argues for a reference to the destruction of Jerusalem on different grounds; his argument depends too heavily on the "implied reader" understanding this text in the light of what is still to come in later chapters.

towns of Israel," or of a nearer point in time which would be more immediately relevant to the mission of the Twelve? In view of the use of Daniel's imagery (though not the same part of his wording) in 28:18, could we also interpret this text as looking forward to the resurrection and ascension of Jesus? It is interesting that the claim of 28:18 is immediately followed by a charge to make disciples of "all nations," not only of Israel. Are we then to understand the "coming of the Son of Man" here as marking the end of a mission specifically to Israel, when the universal kingship of the Son of Man is established after his resurrection[27] and his church's mission is accordingly widened beyond the narrow bounds set in 10:5-6? Until then, they will have more than enough to keep them busy in preaching to "the towns of Israel."

Perhaps this is to press the evocative imagery of this verse too far, to seek for too specific a point of reference. But some such scenario makes better sense of the Danielic imagery in the context of its wider use in this gospel than to assume, as popular (and often scholarly) interpretation has too easily done, that this is *parousia* language, and therefore either that Jesus mistakenly expected an immediate *parousia*[28] or that his words here had no bearing on the situation of the Twelve sent out on a mission among the towns of Galilee around A.D. 30 and no meaning for the first-time reader of Matthew who at this stage in the gospel story has heard nothing about a *parousia* of Jesus.[29]

5. How to Respond to Persecution (10:24-33)

24 *"A disciple is not greater than[1] his teacher, nor a slave greater than his master. 25 It is enough for the disciple to become like his teacher, and the slave like his master. If they have called the master of the house Beelzebul, how much more will they do so to the members of his household?*

26 *"So don't be afraid of them. Nothing is covered that will not be revealed or hidden that will not be known. 27 What I tell you in the dark, you are to speak out in the light, and what is whispered in your ear,[2] you*

---

27. Albright and Mann, 125, take the reference to be to "the exaltation of the Messiah in passion-resurrection."

28. So, famously, Albert Schweitzer, *Quest,* 357-58.

29. G. R. Beasley-Murray, *Kingdom,* 283-91, provides a useful recent survey of interpretations which have assumed that the reference is to the *parousia.* Beasley-Murray himself takes the verse as a traditional saying of Jesus which "belongs to a later period of time," attached by Matthew to a discourse whose setting it does not fit.

1. ὑπέρ, "beyond," "more than," here and in the second clause of this verse, denotes the relative status or importance of the two social roles.

2. Literally, "what you hear into the ear."

are to proclaim on the rooftops. 28 *And do not be afraid of* [3] *those who kill the body but cannot kill the soul;* [4] *you should be afraid rather of the one who can destroy* [5] *both soul and body in hell.* 29 *Aren't two little birds* [6] *sold for a few pence?* [7] *Yet not one of them falls to the ground without your Father's knowledge.* [8] 30 *But even the hairs of your head are all numbered.* 31 *Don't be afraid; you are worth more than a lot of little birds!*

32 *"So everyone who acknowledges* [9] *me before people, I, too, will*

3. Here, unusually in the NT, φοβέομαι is followed by ἀπό; this construction, found in both classical and LXX Greek, probably has no real difference in meaning from φοβέομαι with a direct object (which is used in the balancing clause that follows). If there is a special nuance, it might be overtranslated by "shrink in fear from" (hence the lack of ἀπό in the second clause, since fear of God is not like that; LXX never uses φοβέομαι ἀπό when the object is God), but that is implicit anyway in the context.

4. ψυχή is normally more appropriately translated "life," but it often refers to *real* (spiritual) life as opposed to mere animal existence, and this will be the basis of a telling wordplay in the epigram of v. 39 (cf. 16:25-26). Here the saying requires a term which denotes the continuing life of the person after the life of the body has been terminated, and "soul," despite its Greek philosophical connotation of an entity separable from the body ("the ghost in the machine," as philosophers have parodied the idea), is probably the best English word to denote that continuing life. R. H. Gundry, *Sōma,* 87-160, argues that Jews, like Greeks, typically spoke of the soul as leaving the body at death. For a wealth of literary references to the same effect, Greek, Roman, and Jewish, see Keener, 326-27, n. 40. For a survey of Jewish usage in relation to Greek cf. A. Dihle and E. Lohse, *TDNT* 4:632-37.

5. While the noun ἀπῶλεια can mean "loss" or "ruin" rather than "destruction," the active verb ἀπόλλυμι (which can mean "lose" when it has a thing as its object, as in v. 42) can hardly be translated other than "destroy" here, where the object is a person and where it is parallel to "kill" in the first clause.

6. στρουθίον, a diminutive form of στρουθός, a general term for small birds. While scientific identification is not usually possible for such biological terms in biblical usage, the traditional "sparrow" may well be right as sparrows are common throughout the Near East and were among the small birds sold as food for the poor (and as pets for the rich; Catullus, *Carmina* 2, 3).

7. Literally, "for an *as,*" the *as* being four times the *quadrans,* which I translated "penny" in 5:26 (see p. 192, n. 45). An *as* was a sixteenth of a *denarius,* which could be a day's wage (see on 20:2).

8. Literally, "without your Father," but that phrase alone would not be idiomatic in English. What noun is added to it will depend more on theological than linguistic considerations; see the comments below.

9. The verb ὁμολογέω occurs frequently in the sense of "confess" in the context of religious affirmation, often with an emphasis on public declaration. The unusual construction here (in both clauses) with ἐν rather than a direct object is usually explained as an Aramaism (BDF 220[2]) but does not seem to convey any different meaning. In the first clause it could be paraphrased "confesses *their faith* in me," but that nuance would not fit the second clause.

acknowledge them before my Father who is in heaven; 33 *but whoever denies me before people, I, too, will deny them before my Father who is in heaven.*

Divisions within the second part of this discourse are to some extent arbitrary, imposed for the convenience of writing a commentary rather than clearly intended breaks in Matthew's composition.[10] After v. 23 the mission to the "towns of Israel" drops out of focus, and the theme of persecution and the response to it, which has already been sharply raised in vv. 17-23, is developed by means of a series of sayings which have parallels in a variety of places in Luke (there are few parallels to Mark in this discourse after v. 22) and so probably had a separate existence in the tradition before Matthew brought them together into this discourse. Verses 24-25, which have a partial parallel in Luke 6:40 (cf. also John 13:16; 15:20), are treated by many interpreters either as a small, self-contained unit or as an extension of vv. 16-23, spelling out the relationship which makes it appropriate for disciples to suffer "because of Jesus." Verses 26-33, on the other hand, contain a series of sayings about "whom to fear" which also occur together in a quite closely parallel form in Luke 12:2-9. Many of the sayings included in this section, and in the following sections, vv. 34-39 and 40-42, are strongly marked by a parallelistic style reminiscent of Hebrew wisdom literature or of proverbial aphorisms, and well suited to memorization and catechetical instruction. Brought together in this context, they balance warning and encouragement as an incentive to disciples under pressure to remain faithful to their Lord rather than succumbing to the human opposition which threatens to dominate their horizon so that they lose their grip on the eternal realities.

24-25   Neatly balanced parallel clauses spell out the relative status of disciple and teacher and of slave and master. The former relationship is not surprising in context: it is as "disciples" of Jesus the "teacher" that the Twelve have been sent out. But the latter is more unexpected.[11] It is true that Jesus has been frequently addressed in this gospel as *kyrie,* "Lord," a term

10. My divisions are based on perceived coherence of subject matter within each section. D. J. Weaver, *Discourse,* 74, finds a formal structural marker in the repetition of the formula "I tell you truly" which occurs in vv. 15, 23, and 42. The use of this common formula throughout the gospel leads me to doubt whether it was intended to be noted as a structural marker (rather than a way of emphasizing key pronouncements), but it is interesting that her resultant division of the discourse into vv. 5-15, 16-23, and 24-42 coincides with my thematic division up to this point, while my subdivision of her third section, vv. 24-42, is perhaps more a matter of taste.

11. The disciples of a prophet or rabbi were in effect his servants (K. H. Rengstorf, *TDNT* 4:428-29, 434-35), but δοῦλος, "slave," would be a surprisingly strong term for this conventional relationship (see on 3:11 and n. 64 there).

which in itself need carry no more than polite deference, but which for Matthew probably has stronger connotations, as Jesus' own comments on the title in 7:21 indicate (see comments there). But for Jesus during his ministry to speak of his own disciples as his *douloi,* "slaves," is an extension of the metaphor which is unique in this gospel, though the apostolic writers were of course happy to describe themselves as *douloi* of the risen Christ (Rom 1:1; Gal 1:10; Phil 1:1 etc.; Jas 1:1; 2 Pet 1:1; Jude 1:1). Jesus has previously used the language of slavery to describe discipleship in Matt 6:24, but there they are slaves of *God.* He will also speak of being slaves of one another in 20:27. Here the terms *doulos* and *kyrios* do not directly describe the relationship between Jesus and his disciples; it is rather a parabolic analogy to the teacher/ disciple relationship. But it is nonetheless a striking turn of phrase which speaks strongly of Matthew's sense of the unique authority of Jesus in relation to those who have been called to follow him.

The higher status of the teacher and the master needs no argument.[12] The implication in context is that disciples can expect no better treatment than their teacher and master, whose experience will be shown as the story progresses to include all the areas of rejection, suffering, and death which vv. 17-22 have predicted for the disciples;[13] cf. John 15:20 for a similar inference. Verse 25a develops the same idea. The phrase "become like" may mean no more than that they must be content to share their teacher's lot, and that is the most obvious sense in this context, but the words might also be interpreted more positively in subsequent Christian reading as containing a promise: while they can never aspire to be *above* their teacher, they may hope one day to "become like" him. The disciples of a Jewish rabbi would certainly hope eventually to become like their teacher, but Matthew's sense of the uniqueness of Jesus suggests caution in simply transferring this aspiration to his disciples. Other NT writers do indeed develop a bold theology of Christian sanctification as "being conformed to the image of Christ" (Rom 8:29), of eventually "being like him" (1 John 3:2) as a result of putting off the old nature and "putting on Christ" (Rom 13:14; cf. Eph 4:20-24; Col 3:1-11). It would be pressing the metaphorical language of this saying too far to find in it a full-blown doctrine of eventual conformity to Jesus, but perhaps it is per-

---

12. The surprising comment of Blomberg, 176, that "verses 24-25a are simply false if generalized and applied out of context" is apparently a reflection on the possible *subsequent* progress of the disciple. But these aphorisms relate to the relative status of the two while the disciple/teacher or slave/master relationship is in force, not to the inherent worth or potential of the individual.

13. Gundry, 195, sees a more specific focus in this context: "Matthew directs these statements against falsely professing Christians who exalt themselves above their persecuted Teacher and Lord by evading persecution through keeping quiet (cf. vv. 26-33)."

missible to discover here a tantalizing pointer toward the Pauline theology which may already have been familiar to Matthew and his readers.

The sobering message of v. 24, expect no better treatment than I have received, is reinforced with a more specific example in v. 25b. For Jesus associated with Beelzebul see on 9:34 (where the name is not used) and 12:24 (where it is). For the meaning of the name "Beelzebul" see on 12:24. Neither accusation directly calls Jesus himself "Beelzebul," but we are dealing here with crude invective, not with sophisticated theological reasoning. Cf. 16:23, where Jesus actually calls Peter "Satan"! The "members of the household" probably means not so much the owner's family as the wider group of household slaves and clients who came under his patronage and control; this saying therefore picks up the slave/master imagery of v. 24.[14] They can expect no more respectful treatment by a hostile world than their master has already experienced.[15]

26-27 "Don't be afraid" prepares for the sayings about whom the disciples *should* fear in vv. 28-31 (note the repetition of "don't be afraid" in vv. 28 and 31), and the remainder of vv. 26-27 may seem something of an intrusion within that sequence. But v. 27 is about the disciples' duty to proclaim their message openly, and that proclamation would be the first casualty of a fear inspired by their opponents. The disciples' duty is not merely the negative one of avoiding fear, but the positive one of bold proclamation in the face of opposition. The epigram of v. 26b is paralleled not only in Luke 12:2 but also, less literally, in Mark 4:22 (= Luke 8:17),[16] where it is part of Jesus' teaching on parables and balances the declaration that parables leave some people in the dark (Mark 4:11-12, 33-34). What may need to remain secret for a time must ultimately be revealed. Here there is not the same balancing function in context; the saying serves rather to lead into the exhortation in v. 27 not to hide their light (cf. 5:14-16), but to proclaim their message so that everyone can hear it. Good news is not meant to be kept under wraps, how-

14. It is frequently suggested that οἰκοδεσπότης is used here in a deliberate wordplay on one possible derivation of the name Beelzebul, "lord of the house." (See further D. J. Weaver, *Discourse,* 204, n. 157, who finds a further wordplay with the "house of Israel" in 10:6, of which Jesus is the true "master of the house.") Such wordplay is certainly possible, but it would be lost on readers who did not know Hebrew and/or did not recognize this suggested origin of the name Beelzebul (even if Matthew himself did; see on 12:24). It is in any case not needed to explain the image, which follows naturally from the master/slave language which precedes it.

15. G. N. Stanton, *Gospel,* 176-77, sets this saying in the context of a wide-ranging polemic against Jesus as "a magician and a deceiver" (ibid., 171-80) which was continuing to be deployed in Matthew's day against his followers.

16. There are also parallels in *Gos. Thom.* 5, where it accompanies a promise that disciples will be shown what they do not yet know, and in *Gos. Thom.* 6, where it is linked to a warning against lying and concealment (as it is in Luke 12:1-2). On the varied applications of this epigram see my *Mark,* 209, and further B. W. Henaut, *Tradition,* 279-82.

ever little some people may wish to hear it. Even though for the time being Jesus' teaching to his disciples has to be "in darkness," "into the ear" (see further 13:10-17 for this element of secrecy), in the coming time of witness before governors and kings (vv. 17-18) and of worldwide proclamation of the *euangelion* (24:14) it must no longer be hidden. The flat roof of a Palestinian house was a place of rest (24:17) and prayer (Acts 10:9), but also a very visible platform for proclamation to people in the street below.[17]

28 The possibility of martyrdom for the cause of Jesus, already raised in v. 21, is now squarely faced. The body/soul contrast (see p. 399, n. 4), when used in relation to execution, presupposes that there is a true life which goes beyond mere physical existence, so that the real "self" is untouched by the death of the body alone. And that is all that human opponents can touch, whereas both body and "soul" are subject to God's power, and therefore also to his judgment. Under that judgment it is not only the body but the true life of the person which is liable to destruction in hell. See on 5:22 for *geënna,* "hell," in Jewish thought. In this passage it is spoken of as a place of destruction, not of continuing punishment, a sense which fits the origin of the term in the rubbish dumps of the Hinnom valley, where Jerusalem's garbage was destroyed by incineration. On the basis of this text alone it would therefore be better to speak of true life (the "soul") not as eternal but as "potentially eternal," since it can be "destroyed" in hell;[18] further comment on the contentious issue of "conditional immortality" must be postponed until 25:46. The "one" who has the power to destroy in hell is of course God himself; there is no suggestion in biblical literature that the devil has the power of judgment, nor that God's people should fear him, nor is the devil referred to at all in this context. But a healthy "fear" of God is a recurrent feature of OT spirituality which the NT in no way mitigates.[19] The theme will be taken up again in vv. 32-33, where the fear of human opposition rather than of God renders the disciple liable to eventual repudiation before God.

29 Fear of God is balanced by trust in God as the disciple's heavenly Father; the God who can destroy in hell is also the God who cares for the smallest bird. Within his fatherly care, there is nothing to fear from human hostility. The point is made, as in 6:26, by another comment on God's care for his animal creation (the cheapness of the little birds being emphasized to prepare for the contrast in v. 31b), this time concerning not their daily provi-

---

17. For an example see Josephus, *War* 2.611, and for the visibility of the rooftop see also 2 Sam 16:22.

18. See p. 399, n. 5, for the meaning of the verb in this context.

19. Luz, 2:102, aptly comments: "Our text is especially ill-suited to contrast a Jewish God of fear and a Christian God of love."

sion but, as the context of potential martyrdom here requires, the time of their death. That, too, falls within the Creator's care; cf. Ps 104:29 for the same idea. The pregnant phrase "without your Father" (see p. 399, n. 8) has been variously translated as "without your Father's knowledge" or "consent" or "will" or "care," depending on the view of divine sovereignty and providence which the translator holds: does God simply know about the death of the birds (and therefore also of his people), or does he allow it, or does it happen because he has decided on it, or is the point that even in their death they are not outside his loving concern? The issue can hardly be determined by exegesis of this text, with its cryptic ending — the theology needs to be imported from elsewhere.[20] The implication is apparently that nothing happens to the children of a loving Father which falls outside his providential care; it neither takes him by surprise nor frustrates his purpose. This saying does not, of course, promise immunity from death or suffering for God's people, only the knowledge that it does not happen "without your Father."[21]

30 The comparison with birds will be taken up again in the next verse, but first there is a further vivid image to convey God's providential care. The impossibility of counting the hairs of the head is proverbial (Pss 40:12; 69:4), but even the impossible is not impossible to God who made them. The Creator's intimate knowledge of those he has made is expressed movingly in other imagery in Ps 139:1-18. Equally proverbial is the saying "not a hair of his head will fall the the ground" to express a person's total security (1 Sam 14:45; 2 Sam 14:11; 1 Kgs 1:52; cf. Dan 3:27), which appears also in Luke 21:18; Acts 27:34.[22] The Father who knows the number of each disciple's hairs will make sure that none of them are lost.

31 The third repetition of "Don't be afraid" follows from the theology of divine providence in vv. 29-30, and the point is underlined by a clause

20. J. G. Cook, *ZNW* 79 (1988) 138-44, sets out the exegetical options and their theological implications. He prefers the rendering "without your Father's will/help." In contrast, see D. J. Weaver, *Discourse,* 206-7, n. 180, who argues from "the force of the logic in 10.29-31" that the focus is not on the will of God but on "the presence of God, which supports and sustains the disciples throughout their sufferings."

21. Schweizer, 249, comments: "This section derives its force from the fact that it does not try to sketch an illusory picture of a kindly God. Sparrows fall to earth and disciples of Jesus are slain, and Jesus never says that it hardly matters. What these sayings assert is that God is indeed God, that he is above success and failure, help and isolation, weal and woe, holding them in hands that Jesus says are the hands of the Father."

22. D. C. Allison, *ExpT* 101 (1990) 334-36, argues that the wording does not suggest the idea of protection (the reference is not to *one* hair nor to falling to the ground) but warns against presuming to question God's will, since he knows what human beings cannot know. But the immediate sequence from v. 29 suggests that in context this is more than an intellectual issue ("intellectual consolation for the problem of evil," as Allison puts it).

which again echoes the "Don't worry" passage in 6:25-34: you are worth a lot more than birds.[23] The point is not that birds do not matter — v. 29 rules out that conclusion — but that every one of God's people is important to him, even more important than the birds he looks after so carefully.

32-33   The question of priorities — whom to fear — leads to a radical choice of loyalty between Jesus and "people" (assumed to be in opposition to him). This saying has its most immediate parallel in the same context in Luke 12:8-9,[24] but it has a further, less exact, parallel (using the language of shame rather than of acknowledgment) in Mark 8:38; Luke 9:26, where it is set in the context of the future vindication of the Son of Man ("coming in his Father's glory"), a scenario which Matthew has already invoked in this context at 10:23. Davies and Allison, 2:214-15, find the vision of Dan 7 determinative for this saying too; note the appearance "before" God.[25] The context of judgment before God gives added urgency to the choice which this saying demands, between the short-term advantage of preserving human approval and the humanly risky but ultimately sound course of maintaining a prior loyalty to Jesus in the face of human opposition. The use of the broad term "people" (see on v. 17) here has the effect of contrasting human with divine approval. The issue is not merely obedience to Jesus' teaching, but the explicit "acknowledgment" of him as Lord before a hostile world. The saying, which Matthew introduces with an inferential "So," thus appropriately follows not only from vv. 26-31 about fearing God rather than people, but also from vv. 17-22 about the need to maintain a faithful witness to Jesus even when it means suffering "because of me." It provides the ultimate basis for the disciple's willingness to proclaim Jesus from the rooftops (v. 27). What ultimately decides a person's destiny is what Jesus himself will have to say about them "before my Father who is in heaven." Cf. 7:21-23 for a similar statement of Jesus' personal role in final judgment; the christological implications are as startling

23. Cf. 6:26b and comments there on the relative "value" of God's human and animal creation; also 12:12.

24. In Luke 12:8, however, the subject of the second clause is not "I" but "the Son of Man" (in Luke 12:9 the second clause is cast in the passive, so that no subject is stated). The apparent contrast in Luke 12:8 between the "me" of the first clause and the "Son of Man" of the second has suggested to many that Jesus originally spoke of someone other than himself as the ultimate judge and that Matthew, by taking "the Son of Man" in its normal usage as a title of Jesus, has distorted the sense. But Synoptic variations between "I" and "the Son of Man" occur elsewhere (see on 16:13, 21), and the very obvious parallelism of Matthew's version of the saying does not sound like a secondary adaptation. See further G. R. Beasley-Murray, *Kingdom,* 224-29.

25. Cf. Dan 7:13, though Matthew's ἔμπροσθεν is not the same as Theodotion's ἐνώπιον.

here as there.[26] His verdict will be on a reciprocal basis,[27] with acknowledgment or denial depending on whether they have acknowledged or denied him.[28] The later experience of Peter (26:69-75) is an object lesson in denying Jesus under the pressure of public opinion, but Peter's subsequent rehabilitation adds a reassuring suggestion that the stark verdict of this saying may be understood to refer to a settled course of acknowledgment or denial rather than to every temporary lapse under pressure.

6. The Radical Effects of Jesus' Mission (10:34-39)

> 34 *"Do not suppose that I came to establish[1] peace on the earth; I did not come to establish peace but a sword. 35 Indeed, I came to divide 'a man against his father, and a daughter against her mother, and a daughter-in-law[2] against her mother-in-law; 36 and a person's[3] enemies will be the members of their own family.'[4] 37 Anyone who loves*

26. See J. Jeremias, *Theology*, 250-55, for "the emphatic ἐγώ" in Jesus' teaching, a claim to personal authority which Jeremias declares to be "without parallel in the world of Jesus" (254).

27. Cf. 1 Sam 2:30, "Those who honor me I will honor, and those who despise me will be despised."

28. See on 25:31-46 (a passage with equally strong christological implications concerning Jesus as the ultimate arbiter of human destiny) for an apparently different basis of judgment, irrespective of people's conscious acknowledgment of Jesus.

1. While βάλλω has a wide range of uses, and is not always as vivid as the traditional English version "throw" suggests, the Semitic idiom βάλλω ἐπί here (with βάλλω repeated in the second clause) probably has more of the sense of a forceful imposition than can be conveyed merely by "bring."

2. In Jewish Greek, echoing the usage of Hebrew *kallâ*, νύμφη, which originally meant only "bride" (still its normal sense in the NT), was also used to mean "daughter-in-law," and the context here suggests that meaning (J. Jeremias, *TDNT* 4:1099).

3. It is not easy to decide where a nonmasculine rendering ("a person," "anyone," "their" rather than "a man," "his") is appropriate in these verses. The ἄνθρωπος of v. 35 corresponds to a clearly male "son" in Mic 7:6 (both Hebrew and LXX), and the parallelism also suggests that meaning in Matthew; but in v. 36, where Matthew uses the same ἄνθρωπος in place of the normally male terms used in Mic 7:6 in both Hebrew and LXX (ʾîš and ἀνήρ), there is no such parallelism and the context suggests a more general reference which then continues through vv. 37-39.

4. οἰκιακός occurs in the NT only here and at v. 25 above. In that context the reference to the "master of the house" and the parallel language about slaves and their master indicated that the οἰκιακοί were the members of the wider "household," including the slaves. Here the specifically family relationships spelled out in the preceding lines of the Micah quotation suggest rather that the οἰκιακοί (corresponding to LXX οἱ ἐν τῷ οἴκῳ αὐτοῦ) are the family. Wider Greek usage supports both senses for derivatives of οἶκος and οἰκία.

their father or mother more than me is not worthy of me, and anyone who loves their son or daughter more than me is not worthy of me. 38 And anyone who does not take their cross and follow after me is not worthy of me. 39 Anyone who finds their life will lose it, and anyone who loses their life because of me will find it.

The prospect of persecution and death because of their loyalty to Jesus has left an uncomfortable impression on those who have heard his words about what it means to represent Jesus. Is this what their message of the arrival of God's kingship (v. 7) was supposed to be about? Is this to be the result of letting their light shine before the world (5:13-16)? But already in 5:11-12 Jesus has made it clear that the good life will indeed result in hostility and persecution, and now he is in no mood to compromise. These are not just some unfortunate side-effects of a basically acceptable mission. The very purpose of Jesus' coming is "not peace but a sword," because the message of God's kingship is one which always has and always will lead to violent response from those who are threatened by it (11:12). As 5:11-12 has already reminded them, this has been true in the experience of God's prophets even before Jesus came, and a sobering quotation from Mic 7:6 underlines the point. To represent Jesus is to accept their share in the way he is treated by a hostile world (vv. 24-25), and now the lethal nature of that opposition is made explicit by the first reference in this gospel to the "cross." And it comes on the scene, startlingly, not only as *his* eventual fate, but as *theirs*. To follow Jesus is to embrace martyrdom.

This radical passage (marked like the preceding and following sections by the structural balance and parallelism which suggest material designed to be memorized) foreshadows the warnings about discipleship which will follow Jesus' first explicit prediction of his own rejection and death (16:24-28), and vv. 38-39 will be substantially repeated there. But vv. 34-37 set that grim prospect in a wider context of universal hostility and social division on the basis of Jesus' mission, which picks up and reinforces the predictions of vv. 17-22. Even one's one family will not be a place of refuge. But the cause of this hostility is not the disciples' own failures or lack of diplomacy. Even with the cunning of snakes (v. 16) they will be unable to avoid it if they are faithful disciples, because its cause is Jesus himself. These verses continue even more emphatically the focus on Jesus' personal authority which we have already seen throughout this discourse. The "I came to" formula sets out these distressing results as the intended outcome of Jesus' own mission (vv. 34-35). He demands of his followers a loyalty which transcends even the closest of family ties (v. 37). He expects them to follow him even to death (v. 38), and to incur that death simply "because of me" (v. 39). But those who die for him can look beyond that death to a true life which cannot be found by evading the disgrace and suffering of the cross. The "authority not like their scribes" which was perceived in Jesus' first discourse (7:29) is even more openly claimed in this one. To agree to follow Jesus is to sign away all rights to a quiet life of self-determination.

34 "Do not suppose that I came to" echoes exactly 5:17, and cf. 9:13; 20:28 for similar statements of the purpose of Jesus' "coming"; note that the verb "I came" is repeated three times in vv. 34-35. See above, p. 184, for the significance of this phrase as a statement of mission, which in Matthew need not carry the claim to preexistence which it probably implies in John. The "mission statement" here is meant to shock.[5] Not only is peace a basic human aspiration, but it was understood to be the purpose of the Messiah's coming (e.g., Isa 9:6-7; Zech 9:10) and the defining characteristic of God's eschatological rule (e.g., Isa 11:6-9). Matthew will draw attention in 21:4-5 to how Jesus presented himself as the messianic king who brings peace, and his nonconfrontational style will be commented on in 12:15-21 and demonstrated in chs. 26–27 in the story of his quiet acceptance of unjust accusation and condemnation. His coming was proclaimed as the dawn of "peace on earth" (Luke 2:14), and it is "peace" which the disciples are being sent out to offer (v. 13). Peacemaking is an essential part of the good life (5:9). But the way to peace is not the way of avoidance of conflict, and Jesus will be continuously engaged in robust controversy especially in chs. 21–23, while his whole experience will be the opposite of a "peaceful" way of life. His followers can expect no less, and their mission to establish God's peaceful rule can be accomplished only by sharing his experience of conflict. The "sword" can hardly be understood literally,[6] as the literal use of the sword is explicitly forbidden in 26:51-52; it is a metaphor for conflict and suffering, as in Luke 2:35. Cf. the saying about Jesus coming to "throw fire on the earth" in Luke 12:49, which is followed by a parallel to the present saying in Luke 12:51 but with "division" in place of the metaphor of the "sword."

35-36 If Mic 7:6 was implicitly echoed in Jesus' prediction of family division in v. 21, here the allusion becomes explicit. Micah spoke of the threatening situation in his own day, but the passage was commonly under-

---

5. Albright and Mann, 129-31, try to evade the problem by supposing a misunderstanding of the original Aramaic, as a result of which they translate: "Do not think that I have come to impose peace on earth by force; I have come neither to impose peace, nor yet to make war." Whatever may be said for their conjectural Aramaic "original," this is not what Matthew's Greek says!

6. For a survey of and response to a number of theories that Jesus did intend the sword literally, from S. G. F. Brandon's *Jesus and the Zealots* to Otto Betz's proposal of a supernatural "holy war" ideology, see M. Black in E. Bammel and C. F. D. Moule (eds.), *Jesus,* 289-94. See also Luz, 2:109-10, on the history of interpretation of this saying.

stood in Jewish interpretation to refer to the woes of the messianic age.[7] This distressing vision, like the "sword" of v. 34, is also presented as Jesus' purpose in "coming." The listing of the feuding parties in v. 35 is quite closely based on the LXX wording, but instead of Micah's separate verbs for the actions of the son and the daughter ("dishonor" and "rise against") Matthew supplies a single initial verb, "to divide" (extending the image of the sword in v. 34), which governs each of the following broken relationships. In each case, in contrast to v. 21, it is the younger member who is "against" the older, but any suggestion of a one-sided hostility on the part of the younger generation[8] is ruled out not only by v. 21 but also by the broad summary in v. 36 (which echoes the sense rather than the words of the final clause in the Micah text; see p. 406, nn. 3-4). No one can trust any other member even of their closest family circle. Like many prophetic oracles, this saying is cast in an absolute form which needs to be set alongside other contrasting aspects of Jesus' teaching. Family enmity is not a virtue in itself, nor is it the universal experience of Jesus' disciples, but it is a matter of priorities. Loyalty to Jesus and his mission comes first, and the result of that may be that family ties are strained to breaking point. But there is a new family relationship for disciples of Jesus which more than compensates for what may be lost by loyalty to him (12:46-50; 19:27-29).[9]

37 The disciple's prior loyalty is now explicitly spelled out.[10] Matthew does not go as far as Luke, who uses the startling Semitic idiom (cf. Gen 29:30-33; Deut 21:15-17; Mal 1:2-3) of "hating" the members of one's own family in comparison with love for Jesus (Luke 14:26). To "love more" is a less easily misunderstood idiom to express the same demand for a prior loyalty, but its practical effects are no less rigorous. The (perhaps well-meant, but still essentially selfish) attempts of either parents or children to dissuade the disciple from "seeking first God's kingship" (6:33) must be resolutely resisted, just as in 12:46-50 Jesus will distance himself from his natural family who, according to the most probable understanding of Mark 3:21,

---

7. See Davies and Allison, 2:219-20; Mic 7:6 is quoted in *m. Soṭah* 9:15 in this sense, with the telling addition, "On whom can we rely? On our Father in heaven."

8. So Luz, 2:111: "The issue is the alienation of the younger generation from the older ones; presumably the believing sons and daughters struggled with their parents."

9. S. C. Barton, *Discipleship,* 168, notes the repetition of οἰκιακοί in vv. 25 and 38, denoting the two different "families" to which disciples belong: "Discipleship involves membership of the household of Jesus and is likely to bring division between the disciple and the members of his natural kinship-group household."

10. For the rabbinic principle that the teacher takes priority over the father see *m. B. Meṣiʿa* 2:11. In 4Q175:14-17, based on Deut 33:9, Levi is held up as an example of piety because he abandoned his father, mother, brothers, and sons for the sake of his priestly calling.

wanted to take control of him because they had concluded that he was out of his mind. The same Jesus will later criticize the Pharisees and scribes for evading the force of the commandment to honor one's parents (15:3-9), and will take it for granted that that commandment remains of fundamental importance (19:17-19), but that "honor" needs to be exercised under God, and where God calls in a direction the parents oppose, the true disciple will know whom to "love more." Compare Jesus' shocking demand in 8:21-22 that discipleship should take priority over family responsibilities. Here and in v. 38 we return to the language of "worthiness" which was prominent in vv. 11-13. The modern idiom of "having what it takes" perhaps captures the sense of being "worthy" to be Jesus' disciple.

38 Verses 21 and 28 have raised the prospect of martyrdom resulting from loyalty to Jesus, and that prospect is now given more concrete form in the image of carrying the cross after Jesus (cf. 16:24, where this is explicitly commanded). Christian readers have become so used to the cross as a word and a symbol (and indeed a cause for "boasting," Gal 6:14) that it is hard now to recapture the shudder that the word must have brought to a hearer in Galilee at the time. Crucifixion was a punishment favored by the Romans but regarded with horror by most Jews,[11] and was by now familiar in Roman Palestine as a form of execution for slaves and political rebels. It was thus not only the most cruel form of execution then in use,[12] but it also carried the stigma of social disgrace when applied to a free person. To have a member of the family crucified was the ultimate shame. Crucifixion was an inescapably public fate, and drew universal scorn and mockery, as we shall see in 27:27-44. And that public disgrace, as well as physical suffering, began not when the condemned man was fixed to the cross, but with the equally public procession through the streets in which the victim had to carry the heavy cross-piece of his own gibbet, among the jeers and insults of the crowd.[13]

11. There are historical instances of Jews adopting this Roman practice (see M. Hengel, *Crucifixion,* 84-85), though the extent of this as a form of execution is sometimes exaggerated by failing to distinguish it from the traditional Jewish practice of exposing an already executed body on a pole (Deut 21:22-23). In 11Q19 (the *Temple Scroll*) 64:7-12, however, it seems clear that even in that conservative Jewish community "hanging on the wood" is the cause of death, not its sequel. See also the wider study of crucifixion in the Jewish world by J. Zias and J. H. Charlesworth, in J. H. Charlesworth (ed.), *Jesus and the Dead Sea Scrolls,* 273-89 (directed particularly toward denying that the Teacher of Righteousness was crucified).

12. Crucifixion was "the most cruel and revolting punishment" (Cicero, *In Verrem* 5.64.165), "the most pitiable of deaths" (Josephus, *War* 7.203). For full details of the use and nature of crucifixion in the Roman world see M. Hengel, *Crucifixion;* more briefly J. Schneider, *TDNT* 7:572-74; R. E. Brown, *Death,* 945-47.

13. The shame involved in crucifixion is well brought out by J. H. Neyrey, *Honor,* 139-40.

That is the prospect Jesus holds out before any "worthy" disciple: a savage death and public disgrace. Jesus himself will literally go through that experience, and he offers his followers the prospect of the same. The language of discipleship ("follow," "behind me"; see on 3:11; 4:19-20) thus takes on here the macabre sense of following Jesus on the march to execution. But when the opportunity eventually comes for one of the disciples to follow Jesus carrying his cross for him, they will not be there to take it up, and a stranger will fill the unwelcome role (27:32).

Popular usage has sanitized the language of having "a cross to bear" so that its challenge has evaporated. It is not of course true that every loyal disciple will be a martyr, but all must recognize and accept the possibility of dying for Jesus, and many who have not faced literal execution have nonetheless known well the social stigma implied in carrying the cross behind Jesus.

39 After the mention of the cross in v. 38 and the prediction of execution in v. 21, it seems clear that the reference in this paradoxical epigram to "losing life" is to be taken literally in the first instance, though of course, as with taking up the cross, the principle can also be extended to suffering and deprivation through loyalty to Jesus. But a play on two senses of *psychē* (see p. 399, n. 4) broadens the scope of this saying by contrasting the mere earthly existence, which can be preserved by evading martyrdom but at the cost of the real (spiritual) self, with the true life which does not depend on physical survival, and which may need to be preserved precisely by a willingness to go through literal death for Jesus. The addition of "because of me" ensures that the promise of true life is attached not to dying as such, but to dying as a loyal disciple. The same wordplay will be developed in a different way, but to the same effect, in 16:25-26. At its heart is the issue of priorities, which has been raised in various ways throughout vv. 26-39: to give greater weight to the visible human opposition and its very real but limited threats (to kill the body but not the soul, v. 28) than to the ultimate but invisible reward of acceptance by your Father in heaven (vv. 32-33) is to forfeit true life and court ultimate destruction (v. 28). Discipleship (to borrow the famous dictum of Bill Shankly about football) is not a matter of life and death — it is much more serious than that.

7. Supporters (10:40-42)

40 *"Anyone who welcomes[1] you welcomes me, and anyone who welcomes me welcomes the one who sent me.* 41 *Anyone who welcomes*

---

1. δέχομαι means to "receive," but in this context, where it echoes the contrast in vv. 11-14 between welcome (δέχομαι, v. 14) and the refusal of hospitality, the more positive sense of "welcome" is required.

a prophet as[2] a prophet will receive a prophet's reward, and anyone who welcomes a righteous person as a righteous person will receive a righteous person's reward. 42 And if anyone gives just one cup of cold water to[3] one of these little ones as a disciple, I tell you truly, they will certainly not lose[4] their reward."

The discourse since v. 16 has focused on hostility, persecution, and martyrdom. But there were also those who were prepared to offer hospitality to the disciples (vv. 11-13), and in these concluding verses of the discourse we turn with relief to consider them. In this context the "welcome" refers practically to the willingness to offer support and shelter to those who represent Jesus, though underlying this response is their positive attitude to the disciples and what they stand for. Such supporters would have made up the "crowds" whom we have repeatedly seen to be receiving Jesus with enthusiasm even though they were not committed to the more rigorous demands of discipleship (4:25; 7:28; 8:1, etc.). Such fellow travelers are a significant feature of the whole Galilean phase of Jesus' ministry, and Jesus is happy to recognize this less committed level of following him as the real thing, which deserves and will receive its "reward."[5] It is important to note that while Matthew does not include Mark's story of the exorcist who was not a disciple, with Jesus' telling comment that "Whoever is not against us is for us" (Mark 9:38-41), he has no problem with recording Jesus' positive comments on these fellow travelers, and these verses breathe the spirit of Mark 9:40.

These verses, like the two preceding sections, are strongly marked by parallelism and structural balance, and repeated terms and motifs link the three sayings together as a coherent unit. Verse 41 is cast in a "proverbial" third-person form, which might on its own be taken to apply to a wide range of situations, but v. 40 speaks of "you" and v. 42 of "*these* little ones" who are disciples, and Matthew's grouping of these three sayings together, as the conclusion to a discourse on the disciples' mission, indicates that he saw

---

2. The idiom εἰς ὄνομα (προφήτου/δικαίου/μαθητοῦ), repeated three times in these verses, is hard to represent in idiomatic English. The idea is probably that they are welcomed not simply as persons but in the light of their perceived role as God's prophets (righteous persons; disciples), and that it is that status which has triggered the welcome. TNIV's "welcomes someone known to be a prophet" is a rather wordy way of making the point.

3. There is no idiomatic English equivalent to ποτίζω as a transitive verb followed by a double accusative, to "cause someone to drink" something.

4. See above, p. 399, n. 5.

5. U. Luz, *Theology,* 78-79, notes that Matthew's gospel envisages "two fundamentally different groups or classes . . . the itinerant and the sedentary," though it is to the former (the "itinerant radicals") that this discourse is primarily addressed.

them as all having the same reference. In that case the collection of descriptions used in these three verses adds up to a remarkably high estimate of the standing of Jesus' disciples and the importance of their mission, "little ones" as they are: they represent Jesus, and through him "the one who sent him"; they come in the character of prophets and righteous people as well as in that of disciples, and those who respond to them as such will receive an appropriate reward (from God, understood).

40   For Jesus welcomed in the person of his disciples cf. 18:20: when they are together, he is among them. The chain of authority God–Jesus–disciples occurs elsewhere both in the Synoptic tradition (Mark 9:37; Luke 9:48; 10:16) and in John 13:20. Cf. also John 5:23; 12:44-45 for response to Jesus as equivalent to response to God, and Matt 18:5; 25:40 for response to the "little ones" as equivalent to response to Jesus. Underlying such sayings, with their repeated reference to being "sent," is the principle later enshrined in the Jewish legal institution of the *šālîaḥ,* the "one sent," an ambassador or representative who was understood to have the full authority of the one who sent them.[6] It is those who recognize such authority in the disciples who will welcome them, just as it is those who recognize Jesus as God's representative who will welcome him. The unspoken corollary (but spelled out in Luke 10:16) is that those who reject the disciples on their mission are guilty of a far graver fault than merely lack of hospitality to a fellow human being; they are rejecting God.[7]

41   By the time Matthew wrote his gospel the Christian "prophet" was a familiar figure (see on 7:15 and cf. 7:22), but at the time of Jesus' ministry the term was probably not so freely used; when John the Baptist and Jesus were hailed as "prophets" (11:9; 14:5; 16:14; 21:11, 26, 46), this was a mark of their distinctive role, rather than assigning them to a familiar class. But Jesus has already linked the disciples' experience of persecution (all of them, not just a special "prophetic" group) with that of "the prophets who came before you" (5:11-12), and he will later speak of sending out his "prophets" among the Jews (23:34), and here that later usage is anticipated. After all, in the light of the principle of v. 40, if Jesus is a prophet, so also are those he sends. And so it is in that capacity, with all its connotations of speaking with a direct authority from God, that people are expected to re-

---

6. Cf. *m. Ber.* 5:5, "a man's agent is as himself." The classic presentation of this tradition as the background to the NT concept of apostleship (the ἀπόστολος also being the "one sent") is by K. H. Rengstorf, *TDNT* 1:414-20. W. D. Davies, *Setting,* 97-99, finds that concept in this passage, and suggests that this and related passages in Matthew are the equivalent of Paul's teaching on Christians as constituting the body of Christ and being "in Christ."

7. "God himself enters houses with Jesus' messengers. What a statement!" (J. Jeremias, *Theology,* 239)

ceive Jesus' messengers[8] — "in the name of" a prophet implies recognition of the category to which the person belongs (see n. 2 above). The "prophet's reward" probably means either the sort of reward a prophet can give (perhaps thinking of the blessings conferred on those who welcomed prophets in the OT: 1 Kgs 17:8-24; 2 Kgs 4:8-37) or a reward on a scale appropriate to those who welcome a prophet — there is in effect little difference. It is less likely in this context to mean the reward which a prophet receives, since it is not the prophet but the welcomer who is to receive it, though it may be possible to take it as indicating that "to receive such a servant is to put oneself in the position of receiving the same reward as the person received" (Hagner, 1:296). "Righteous person" is a less specific designation than "prophet,"[9] and may indicate here no more than that the disciples are recognized by their welcomers as good people rather than bad, but in the OT the term "righteous" is often used specifically for the people of God over against "the wicked" who oppose him. In 13:17; 23:29 "prophets" and "righteous people" will again be paired as a way of speaking of the godly, there with reference to the period before Jesus' coming.[10]

For the prominence of the theme of "reward" in Matthew see on 5:12. The term is no more specific here than there, but here the section on rewards follows the saying about finding true life (v. 39), so that it is natural to read the reward in that light. In 25:31-46 the reward for those who have helped Jesus' "little brothers" and so helped him (in ways reminiscent of the cup of water given here to the "little ones" in v. 42) is spelled out as "the kingdom prepared for you from the foundation of the world," and as "eternal life" in contrast with the "eternal fire" reserved for those who have turned the "little brothers" away. In the light of that parallel passage the stakes are very high in relation to how Jesus' representatives are received.

8. Albright and Mann, 133-34, argue that the reference is not to Jesus' disciples but to people's reception of Jesus himself as "*the* Prophet" and "*the* Righteous One" (cf. Acts 7:52). While this reading would relate to the second part of v. 40, it is unlikely here where the parallel language of v. 42 refers to the reception of disciples (as does v. 40a), and the lack of articles with προφήτου and δικαίου seems decisive against it.

9. D. Hill, *Greek Words,* 135-38, drawing on his article in *NTS* 11 (1964/5) 296-302, discusses the Matthean use of δίκαιος in relation to "prophet" and "martyr" here and in 13:17 and 23:29, and suggests that this reflects an early church usage of δίκαιος in the more specific sense of a recognized teacher, so that here it would refer to "those in the community who witness, instruct and teach." See contra Carson, 258-59.

10. See D. J. Weaver, *Discourse,* 120-21, for the view that the three titles used here (prophets, righteous, little ones) denote distinct groups among the disciples. Her attempt to delineate "the righteous" as a distinct group, however, is unconvincing, since she recognizes that the "righteousness" by which they are designated is "the essential mark of life within the Kingdom of heaven" (and so is, or should be, characteristic of all disciples, not of a special group).

42 This saying is cast in a different syntactical form, but it closely echoes the themes of welcoming and reward in v. 41, and the "in the name of" formula continues the motif of recognizing the capacity in which a person comes ("as a disciple" thus refers to the "little one," not the one who gives the drink). This time that capacity is simply that of "disciple" (of Jesus, understood);[11] the issue is that of v. 40, the recognition of Jesus in his representatives, a theme which will be more fully explored in 25:31-46. Here we are introduced to a distinctive theme in Matthew's gospel, that of the disciples as "little ones."[12] In 18:6-14 it will become clear that this term, though introduced in relation to an actual child in vv. 1-5, is being used as a metaphor for all members of the disciple community,[13] old as well as young, in their insignificance and vulnerability (see comments there). Similarly, in 25:40, 45 the "smallest" brothers of Jesus are not children, but the members of his community perceived in the role and status of "little ones." Compare also the designation of true disciples as "little children" in contrast with the "wise and intelligent" in 11:25. So here there is no indication of a reference to children as such (though the saying would of course be applicable to a child no less than to an adult) or to any special subgroup; all disciples are "little ones."[14] Those who go out to represent Jesus in a hostile society have no status, and may easily be pushed aside.[15] It is only when people recognize

11. M. D. Goulder, *Midrash,* 352, suggests that the designations of the disciples in vv. 40-42 are cast "in the form of an anticlimax: apostle, prophet, saint, lay Christian." Several commentators see a similar gradation, but it is to be noted that not only is the term "apostle" not used, but the verb ἀποστέλλω is not applied to the sending of the disciples even though it is to that of Jesus (contrast the "parallel" saying in John 13:20, where πέμπω occurs in both halves). Against the view that the three designations προφήτης, δίκαιος, and μαθητής in vv. 41-42 refer to different categories see below, n. 14.

12. See my *Matthew: Evangelist,* 264-65, and more fully E. Schweizer in G. N. Stanton (ed.), *Interpretation,* 158-60, read in the context of his whole article, "Matthew's Church," ibid., 149-77.

13. See the comments of U. Luz in G. N. Stanton (ed.), *Interpretation,* 118 and n. 21 (p. 139) in response to G. Strecker.

14. *Pace* D. J. Weaver, *Discourse,* 121. See above, n. 10; her attempt to delineate a distinct group here ("the opposite end of the spectrum from that of 'prophet'") is no more successful than in the case of "the righteous," and is in tension with the leveling effect of Matthew's use of the terminology of "little ones" especially in 18:1-14 and of the subsequent discussion of "greatness" in 20:25-28 . There are no "great ones" in the disciple community! Weaver goes on to argue that these sayings in fact aim to subvert the "order apparently based on the outward honor associated with the respective designations" by "placing the crucial weight on the saying on the 'little ones' at the bottom of the list," but if the three categories are recognized not as a "hierarchy" (her word) but as parallel designations of the disciple community as a whole there is no need for such subversion.

15. On Jesus' paradoxically positive use of μικρός in contrast with Hellenistic and rabbinic disparagement of the "little," see O. Michel, *TDNT* 4:650-56.

the special significance of these "little ones" through their relationship to Jesus and to "the one who sent him" that they are willing to take them seriously, and so to welcome them with acts of basic hospitality. The cup of cold water is an essential though inexpensive provision in a hot climate, an act of expected hospitality as well as of kindness. It is not much, but even that little ("just one," representing *monon,* "only," emphasizes how little it is), because of the attitude it represents, is enough to bring the reward.[16]

8. Jesus Resumes His Mission (11:1)

> 1 *And then,*[1] *when Jesus had come to the end of instructing his twelve disciples, he moved on from there in order to teach and preach*[2] *in their towns.*

The formula which concludes the five main discourses in Matthew is here rather differently employed, in that the verb *teleō,* "come to the end of," is followed not by a noun ("these words," etc.) but by a participle describing the nature of the sayings just recorded. The effect is the same, and here more clearly than in 7:28-29 the formula functions not only as a closure but also as a transition to the next phase of the narrative. Matthew uses geographical relocation ("moved on from there"; cf. the same phrase in 12:9; 15:29) to signal a new narrative context, even though the precise locations are not specified, merely the general scene of going around the towns and villages of Galilee.[3]

"Teaching and preaching" summarizes the general nature of Jesus' mission, which has been more fully described in 4:23; 9:35. The disciples' role in this mission, which has been so carefully spelled out in ch. 10, is surprisingly not now mentioned. We are not told anything about what happened during their mission (nor even explicitly that they went at all,[4] though 10:5

---

16. U. Luz, *Theology,* 56, draws attention to the fact that "those who remain at home, practising hospitality . . . quite surprisingly and unpredictably receive God's infinite reward." Cf. ibid., 60: "The reward for a single glass of cold water is — paradise."

1. On this rendering of the formulaic idiom καὶ ἐγένετο, "and it happened," see p. 297, n. 1.

2. Where it has an object, κηρύσσω is better translated "proclaim," but English idiom does not favor "proclaim" used intransitively.

3. Read within this context alone, αὐτῶν should refer to the disciples, but it has been used in 4:23; 9:35 to denote the (Galilean) area of Jesus' mission, and here picks up from the preceding narrative setting in 9:35.

4. S. C. Barton, *Discipleship,* 173-74, argues that it is appropriate to the narrative flow of the gospel that at this point "the disciples do not go out because they are not ready to go out." As long as Jesus remains present the mission will be his, not theirs.

says they were "sent"), nor when they returned from it, and Matthew does not even include their report back to Jesus (contrast Mark 6:30; Luke 9:10; 10:17). In 12:1 we shall find the disciples still accompanying Jesus in his traveling ministry, and there is nothing in ch. 11 to indicate that they were not with Jesus during the events there recorded. Clearly Matthew is more interested in the principles underlying the disciples' mission (and therefore that of his readers) than in any contribution it makes to his narrative of Jesus' Galilean period; the only time we shall hear of any of the disciples operating independently of Jesus is in 17:16, where it was not a success. The mission, which has been that of Jesus from the beginning, continues in the same vein despite its theoretical extension to the disciples in ch. 10. It will be only after Jesus' resurrection (28:19-20) that Matthew's narrative will envisage the disciples actually going out on their own.[5]

G. VARYING RESPONSES TO THE MESSIAH (11:2-30)

The tight organization which has characterized Matthew's story so far, notably in the two great collections of the words and deeds of the Messiah in chs. 5–7 and 8–9 respectively and in the equally carefully compiled anthology of sayings on mission and persecution in ch. 10, now becomes less easy to discern in terms of major sections. The next prominent collection is the third discourse in ch. 13. In the two chapters which lead up to that we find a variety of narrative and dialogue sections, not so clearly structured as a whole, but together serving to provide the background to the discussion in ch. 13 of what happens when the kingdom of God is proclaimed. The parables which make up that discourse will speak of divided responses to the word of God, and of the problems of discerning the reality of God's kingship in a world where it is not yet universally acknowledged. So in chs. 11–12 we shall be introduced to a variety of people who are responding in different ways to what they are seeing and hearing, different ways of reacting to the coming of the Messiah.[1] There are the wholly

---

5. Cf. D. J. Weaver, *Discourse,* 125-26, for the literary function of the discourse in the light of Matthew's failure to narrate any subsequent mission activity by the disciples. On pp. 127-28 she goes on to outline the way this issue is taken up in the rest of the gospel. It will be only in the commission given to the disciples in 28:18-20 that "the implied reader finally discovers the answers to his/her questions concerning the disciples" (ibid., 151).

1. The thesis of D. J. Verseput, entitled *The Rejection of the Humble, Messianic King,* claims to find in chs. 11–12 as a whole "a solid, thematic unity dealing with the tragic fact of Jesus' rejection by the covenant people, Israel" (p. 1). This is undoubtedly the most prominent aspect of this section of the narrative, but Verseput's broad characterization hardly does justice to the strongly *contrasting* attitudes to Jesus which in fact

positive portraits of the "children" who have been given the ability to discern the truth (11:25-27) and of Jesus' true family who do the will of God (12:46-50). There is the puzzled John the Baptist, wanting to believe but still unsure (11:2-6), and of whom Jesus speaks in warm and yet slightly guarded terms (11:7-19). But there are also the local towns which have rejected Jesus' appeal (11:20-24), and in ch. 12 we read a succession of stories which illustrate the growing opposition to Jesus from the religious authorities, including not only the cynical demand for an authenticating sign (12:38-42) and the very threatening accusation that Jesus is in league with the devil (12:22-32) but also the beginning of an explicit threat to Jesus' life (12:14). These confrontations give rise to some uncompromisingly polemical sayings from Jesus, so that by the end of ch. 12 we are well prepared to think about the varying fates which may befall the good seed, including its total eradication by the evil one (13:19). There is thus in these two chapters a clear narrative development toward what is to follow, even though they do not have the overall structural sophistication of chs. 5–10. In chs. 14–16 we shall be shown a variety of further responses to Jesus, until the climax of the Galilean ministry is reached in 16:16 when Peter at last utters the true estimate of Jesus toward which even his warmest supporters have hitherto been feeling their way.

1. John the Baptist (11:2-19)

2 *John heard in prison about the deeds of the Messiah. He sent a message by his disciples,[2] 3 saying to him, "Are you the one who is coming, or should we look forward to someone else?" 4 In reply Jesus said to them, "Go and tell John what you see and hear: 5 blind people see again and lame people walk, lepers are made clean and deaf people hear, and the dead are raised and the poor are told the good news. 6 And happy is the person who is not caused to stumble because of[3] me."*

---

emerge (and which of course his detailed exegesis will fully recognize; cf. also the summary of his thesis, ibid., 295-300). It is this variety of response which forms the basis for the parables of ch. 13, notably that of the sower.

2. Several of the early fathers support the reading found in many MSS and versions, δύο τῶν μαθητῶν instead of διὰ τῶν μαθητῶν; if this is not simply a mechanical error, it may be an attempt to provide a direct object for πέμπω instead of the rather more awkward usage πέμπω διά, to "send (a message) by," perhaps influenced also by the mention in Mark and Luke (not in Matthew) that Jesus sent out his disciples in twos.

3. It would have been simpler, and more idiomatic, to translate σκανδαλίζομαι ἐν by "be offended by" (for this use of ἐν see D. J. Verseput, *Rejection,* 74), but the σκάνδαλον wordgroup plays such a significant role in Matthew's vocabulary that it seems better here to translate the metaphor literally so as not to obscure the verbal connections with passages such as 5:29-30; 13:21; 15:12; 16:23; 17:27; 18:6-9; 24:10; 26:31-33.

7 *As they were leaving, Jesus began to talk to the crowds about John: "What did you go out into the wilderness to look at? A reed swaying in the wind?* 8 *But what did you go out to see? A man dressed in soft clothes? Look, those who wear soft clothes are in royal palaces.* 9 *But what did you go out to see? A prophet?*[4] *Yes, I tell you, and more than a prophet.* 10 *For this is the one about whom it is written,*

'Look, I am sending my messenger before your face,
who will prepare your way ahead of you.'

11 *"I tell you truly: among those born of women no one greater than John the Baptist has arisen; yet the one who is less important*[5] *in the kingdom of heaven is greater than John.* 12 *From the days of John the Baptist until now the kingdom of heaven is subjected to violence,*[6] *and violent people plunder*[7] *it.* 13 *For all the prophets and the law prophesied until John came.* 14 *And if you are willing to accept it, he is the Elijah who is destined*[8] *to come.* 15 *Whoever has ears,*[9] *let them hear.*

4. It was perhaps the unexpected one-word answer "A prophet" which led some early copyists to reverse the word order so as to read "But why did you go out to see a prophet?" a reading which can hardly be original when the following ναί requires a Yes/No question, not a "Why?" It would, however, suit the alternative reading of all three questions as "Why did you go out? To see a reed/man/prophet?" which is supported by *Gos. Thom.* 78 for the first two questions. But the stronger attestation for the above reading of the third question (which does not have a parallel in the *Gospel of Thomas* saying), including most of the early versions and citations, supports the traditional rendering in which "to look at / see" is incorporated in each question, not in the proposed answer. The overall thrust of the series of questions is in any case not affected.

5. The term here is not "the least" (ὁ ἐλάχιστος) as in 5:19, but the comparative ὁ μικρότερος, "the smaller one," which can be used in a superlative sense (cf. 13:32), but perhaps here suggests a concern rather with *relative* importance.

6. Under the influence of the "parallel" (but in fact very different) saying in Luke 16:16 it is sometimes suggested that βιάζομαι is here to be read as middle voice, with a meaning something like "progresses forcefully." But in Luke 16:16 the subject is not the kingdom of heaven, but "people" who "force their way into" it. Here, with the kingdom of heaven as the subject, and with the cognate βιασταί ("violent people") following together with the equally violent and pejorative verb ἁρπάζω, such a positive sense is hardly possible, and the passive rendering seems required by the parallel clause in which the kingdom of heaven is the *object* of βία.

7. The basic meaning of ἁρπάζω is to "steal" or "seize," with the object taken (rather than the premises robbed) expressed in the accusative. The rendering adopted here is an extension of that usage, for which there is some support in classical Greek. But the idea that the kingdom of heaven itself is seized by force cannot be ruled out. See the exegetical comments below.

8. For this translation of μέλλω see p. 663, n. 2.

9. The fuller form of this formula, "Whoever has ears *to hear,* let them hear," is

16 *"But to whom shall I compare this generation? They are like children sitting in the marketplaces and shouting out to other children,* 17 *'We piped for you, and you didn't dance; we sang a dirge*[10] *for you,*[11] *and you didn't mourn.'* 18 *For John came neither eating nor drinking, and they say, 'He is demon-possessed.'* 19 *The Son of Man came eating and drinking, and they say, 'Look, what a greedy fellow who likes his drink,*[12] *a friend of tax collectors and sinners.' And wisdom has been justified by her deeds."*[13]

The first example of the varying responses to Jesus is that of John the Baptist, who last featured in Matthew's narrative in ch. 3, but whose imprisonment has been mentioned in 4:12 (and will be further explained in 14:3-5), and whose disciples have also appeared as critics of Jesus' practice in 9:14. Matthew now presents a collection of material (most of which is found together also in Luke 7:18-35) in which John's own dilemma and Jesus' response to it are the subject of vv. 2-6, but a number of sayings of Jesus about John and his significance follow in vv. 7-15, giving an intriguing insight into the development of salvation history from the time of the prophets through to that of fulfillment in the Messiah, with John himself occupying the hinge position between the two eras of promise and fulfillment. He is thus the greatest of the prophets and yet stands apparently outside the kingdom of heaven (v. 11). A

---

not surprisingly found in the majority of MSS and versions, but the omission of ἀκούειν in a number of significant early MSS (B, D) and versions (OL d, k; syrˢ) here and (with slight variations in attestation) in 13:9, 43 may preserve an originally shorter form which was naturally expanded to the more familiar form in the course of transmission.

10. θρηνέω can be a general term for mourning, but the parallelism here requires a musical performance to match the "piping," and both θρῆνος and θρηνέω commonly refer to a vocal lament.

11. ὑμῖν does not appear in several of the earliest MSS and versions here and in Luke 7:32, and would be a natural expansion to enhance the parallelism with ηὐλήσαμεν ὑμῖν; but since the evidence for its inclusion is rather stronger in Matthew than in Luke, it is possible that its omission here was due to assimilation to Luke. It is in any case the rhetoric rather than the sense which is affected.

12. οἰνοπότης is here often rendered "drunkard," but drunkenness as such is not the basic meaning of the word. He is a wine drinker, a *bon viveur,* as opposed to the ascetic John, whose Nazirite vow forbade alcohol. The gospels give no evidence that Jesus ever was, or was accused of being, drunk.

13. Most MSS and versions here read τέκνων, "children," which is the reading of the parallel in Luke 7:35. That ἔργων, "deeds," is the original reading here is indicated not only by the likelihood of assimilation to Luke, with his appealing image of John and Jesus as the "children of wisdom" as against the difficult concept of "wisdom's deeds," but also by the echo of "the deeds of the Messiah" in v. 2. A few MSS also add πάντων here, a further assimilation to most MSS of Luke.

420

final little parable (vv. 16-19) both contrasts the differing styles of the ministry of John and Jesus and yet links them closely together as prophets misunderstood, in opposite ways, by "this generation." It is a matter of debate how far Jesus intends the "deeds of wisdom" (v. 19) to cover John's ministry as well as his own; see below.

In this passage, then, we see clearly both aspects of the ambivalent estimate of John the Baptist which runs through all the gospels, and through all Christian theology since. On the one hand the continuity between John and Jesus (which is particularly emphasized throughout Matthew's account; see above, p. 98) is reinforced by the positive account Jesus here gives of John (note especially the explicit identification of him as Elijah, the precursor of the eschatological fulfillment, in v. 14), and by the association of the two misunderstood prophets in the parable of vv. 16-19. But, on the other hand, a more negative estimate is indicated by John's own uncertainty about Jesus as the Messiah (vv. 2-3), by Jesus' implied rebuke of his "stumbling" (v. 6), and by the relegation of John below the "less important in the kingdom of heaven" (v. 11). Despite his essential role as the forerunner of salvation (vv. 10, 14) and his status as the greatest of the prophets (vv. 9, 11), he remains outside the messianic community as one of the many prophets and righteous people who looked forward eagerly to the time of salvation but were not themselves privileged to experience it in their lifetime (13:16-17).

The section falls into three parts which may best be commented on individually, even though we must not forget that Matthew has deliberately presented them together to provide a more rounded theological assessment of John.

a. John's Estimate of Jesus (11:2-6)

In commenting on 3:11 we noted that John's prediction of the "stronger one" who was to baptize with the Holy Spirit and fire could have been understood purely of the action of God himself rather than of a human agent,[14] but that his use of the phrase "the one who follows me" pointed toward a Messiah figure, even though this was not required by the OT images used in his own prediction and in the scriptural authentication of John given in 3:3. The subsequent events at the Jordan (3:16-17) have made it clear to the reader that it is in the human figure of Jesus that this "stronger one" is to be found, and John's own response to Jesus in 3:14-15 indicates that he, too, saw Jesus in this light, as the "one who comes behind me." That phrase is partially echoed here in v. 3, "the one who is coming," and the reader is expected to make the

---

14. We shall note the same implication in the further scriptural authentication for John given here in vv. 10 and 14.

connection. The identification of Jesus as the "stronger one" which John had made in ch. 3 is apparently now less clear to him. His question is not hostile so much as uncertain, looking for confirmation of his previous insight.

The question is provoked by the account John has received of "the deeds of the Messiah" (v. 2). We can only speculate as to what it was in this account which fell short of John's own expectations of his successor.[15] The question from John's disciples in 9:14 suggests that John, like the Pharisees, may have found it hard to accept the free attitude of Jesus to religious propriety, and the company he kept.[16] Probably, too, the reports he has heard do not yet suggest the fiery judgment which his "coming one" was to bring (3:11-12). It is possible, too, that John, like many other Jews, understood the role of the Messiah in a more politically nationalist light than Jesus was prepared to countenance and that like many of those who followed Jesus during his ministry he was disappointed at the low-key nature of Jesus' village ministry of healing and teaching. But Matthew's account of John has not supported such an interpretation. The baptism of Holy Spirit and fire which he was looking for seems to have been more linked with the calling of a forgiven and renewed remnant than with the political restoration of the nation. Nor is the political interpretation required to make sense of John's question. He has heard much in Jesus' favor, but he would have liked to hear more. Jesus' reply does not change the agenda, but offers further evidence along the same lines ("the deeds of the Messiah"), with the additional element of a clear echo of OT prophecies of eschatological salvation. He expects such evidence to convince John, and the "rebuke" of v. 6 does not require us to believe that John's expectation was on the wrong lines, but only that he was slow to read the evidence.

2-3 For John's imprisonment see further on 14:1-12, and for his disciples see on 9:14. In the light of Jesus' reputation as described in 4:23-25 (where Perea, the site of John's imprisonment, is specifically mentioned) and

15. G. R. Beasley-Murray, *Kingdom,* 81, offers a suggestive, if overexpansive, reconstruction: "What was Jesus doing? Puzzling things from John's viewpoint: preaching, healing and driving out demons. And what is his message of the kingdom? Beatitudes, parables of the gracious rule of God, prospects of feasting in the kingdom of God. Where was the thunder of judgment? Where was the rebuke of the wicked? Why this use of power over demons but not over evil men? Why did Jesus consort with them in their feasting? Why did he allow the prophet of God's righteous wrath against sin to rot in Herod's jail without a word of protest? Could this possibly be the Messiah?" Over against such speculation, it is salutary to note the view of D. J. Verseput, *Rejection,* 60-66, that the thinking behind John's question is a matter of indifference to Matthew, who uses it only as a cue: it is Jesus' answer that interests Matthew, not John's question.

16. According to 21:31-32, "tax collectors and prostitutes" were also prominent among those who responded to John's call to repentance, but that does not necessarily require that he mixed with them socially — indeed, his lifestyle remote from civilization presumably did not allow it.

of his activity outlined in chs. 8–9 it is not surprising that John's disciples should bring him news about what Jesus was doing. Matthew describes this news as "deeds of the Messiah,"[17] reflecting perhaps not only his own estimate of Jesus' significance but also that entertained at least provisionally by John and his disciples. The "deeds" should probably be taken to include the teaching of chs. 5–7 as well as the miracles of chs. 8–9, since in vv. 4-5 Jesus will refer to hearing as well as seeing, and will include proclaiming good news to the poor in the list of his messianic acts. As throughout this gospel, *Christos* carries its full titular weight, rather than serving, as sometimes in other NT books, as virtually a substitute name for Jesus. Since his heavy emphasis on it in the prologue (1:1, 16, 17, 18) Matthew has not used the title with direct reference to Jesus, and will not again until Peter's declaration in 16:16. That will be the first time the title will occur in direct speech within the narrative, but Matthew's whole story so far has been geared to displaying Jesus' messianic credentials and authority, so that its editorial use here, where the question of Jesus' christological identity is specifically raised, is entirely appropriate. It is implicit, though not explicit, in John's words "the one who is coming." This phrase makes good sense in the historical context as a reference back to John's own prediction in 3:11; there is no need to claim that *ho erchomenos* was in itself a recognized messianic title, as some have supposed.[18] The question is, "We hear what you are doing; should we interpret this as the ministry of the Messiah I predicted?" The suggestion that it might be necessary to look for another candidate suggests that John was hoping for something more explicitly "messianic" and probably more judgmental, but we are not told what that might be.

4-5 John's disciples have already reported to him what they have seen and heard, according to v. 2, but this further report which Jesus asks them to take includes not only perhaps some further examples of the sort of actions they had already reported, but more importantly a theological frame-

17. While there is evidence that some Jews expected a Messiah who would work miracles (see below, n. 20; also *2 Bar.* 73:1-2), this is not a prominent theme in Jewish messianism (see p. 367, nn. 22-23; Luz, 2:132, n. 20, is more dogmatic: "There are in Judaism no particular concepts of 'messianic deeds'"; ibid., p. 134, "There are no Jewish texts that say that the Messiah will heal"), and is not required here. The reference is to the reported works of Jesus, whom John and others were considering as possibly the Messiah, not necessarily to works generally expected of the Messiah as such. It is interesting that the passages in Isaiah most obviously alluded to in Jesus' list of miracles in v. 5 (Isa 35:5-6; cf. 26:19; 29:18) concern the eschatological blessings brought by God himself, and do not envisage a separate Messiah figure.

18. Cf. the proposal of L. Novakovic, *Messiah,* 153-59, that the term here reflects its use in LXX Hab 2:3, so that John's problem, like Habakkuk's, is concerned with the delay of the promised end time.

work within which they are to be understood. The words of v. 5 not only list many of the more striking aspects of what has been narrated in chs. 8–9, but do so using words which closely echo several prophecies of Isaiah, especially Isa 35:5-6 and 61:1 (cf. also 26:19; 29:18; 42:18), the former a description of the blessings which will accompany the coming of God himself to judge and save, and the latter setting out the manifesto of the one anointed by God to proclaim his salvation.[19] The details selected focus on future blessings rather than on the eschatological judgment which is also found in these Isaiah passages (and which might have conformed more closely to John's expectations). The visible activity of Jesus thus conforms to the scriptural blueprints for God's eschatological deliverance, whether in his own person or through an anointed Messiah; the answer to John's question is Yes.[20]

For the narrative basis for the six individual claims (which Matthew has arranged in pairs) see: blind cured, 9:27-31; lame walking, 9:2-8; lepers cleansed, 8:1-4; deaf hearing, 9:32-33;[21] dead raised, 9:18-26. For the good news to the poor see not only 4:17, 23 but also chs. 5–7 as a whole, and especially the Beatitudes, which begin with the promise of the kingdom of heaven to the "poor in spirit." Isa 35:5-6 provides the scriptural basis for the cure of the blind, deaf (and dumb), and lame; Isa 61:1 is about good news to the poor and oppressed, with no reference to physical healing in most translations of the Hebrew text, though the LXX version also includes "recovery of sight for the blind."[22] The healing of lepers and the raising of the dead do not occur in these eschatological prophecies (or in others, except for the "resurrection" promise of Isa 26:19), so that Jesus' ministry is seen to exceed its scriptural models by catering also to the reputedly incurable conditions of leprosy and death (see 2 Kgs 5:7, and introductory comments on 8:1-4). The whole theological argu-

19. L. Novakovic, *Messiah*, 181, asserts that whereas "before the publication of 4Q521 [see next note], one could have easily concluded that a messianic interpretation of Isa 61:1 was a uniquely Christian development," it is now clear that its messianic reference was already more widely recognized.

20. L. Novakovic, *Messiah*, 169-79, draws attention to the remarkable similarity between Jesus' response to John and the recently published (1992) "Messianic Apocalypse," 4Q521, where the expected works of "his Messiah" include "freeing prisoners, giving sight to the blind . . . he will heal the wounded and make the dead live, he will proclaim good news to the poor." Novakovic goes on (179), "The main difference between 4Q521 and Q is that the former expects these events to occur in the future, whereas the latter maintains that they are already taking place in the present."

21. Deafness and dumbness are associated and are described by the same term, κωφός.

22. Luke 4:18-19 uses this LXX version. In my *Jesus and the OT,* 252-53 I argue for the possibility that LXX represents a valid understanding of the Hebrew phrase *la'ăsûrîm pᵉqaḥ-qôaḥ* (normally translated "release to the prisoners"), since *pāqaḥ* is elsewhere used exclusively of the opening of eyes or ears, not of doors or windows.

ment is achieved not by direct quotation of the relevant Isaiah texts,[23] but by an evocative drawing together of motifs of eschatological blessing which anyone familiar with Isaiah's prophecies could hardly fail to recognize. In the compassionate ministry of Jesus God is visiting his people as he had promised.

6   This little beatitude,[24] rather like John 20:29, commends those who can accept the reality of God's working without demanding undue proof. But, unlike the beatitudes of 5:3-10 and John 20:29, it is expressed in the singular, and in this context it must have reference to John's question: the evidence should have been enough for him. There may, however, be a special focus on the last item in the list of "deeds of the Messiah," if John's doubts about Jesus may have been prompted by the questionable company into which Jesus' mission to bring good news to the poor had led him. John's implied "stumbling" (see on 5:29-30 for this prominent theme in Matthew) need not be taken in the catastrophic sense which this verb will have in 13:21; 18:6-9 (cf. 5:29-30); 24:10; it is also used in a less drastic way, for instance, in 13:57; 15:12; 17:27; 26:31-33. But in all these cases it represents a degree of unbelief, even if not terminal. The verb does not in itself justify the conclusion that John is outside the scope of salvation, but it suggests that the attitude which led to his question is not conducive to spiritual insight. When he is declared in v. 11 to be outside the kingdom of heaven, the primary reference is to his place in the scheme of salvation history, but it may be that we are also meant to reflect on the scepticism concerning Jesus as the Messiah which his question implied. In this he was perhaps a prototype of the many who would find it hard to accept Jesus' concept of Messiahship as it became more evident (not least Peter in his response to Jesus' revelation in 16:21-23).

b. Jesus' Estimate of John (11:7-15)

All these sayings relate to John, but, particularly after v. 11, they do not seem to fit together as a coherent whole, and they present more the appearance of an anthology brought together on the basis of the man they all refer to. But if their literary structure does not flow easily, they share a central concern and perspective, to define John's position as the last and greatest of the prophets, fulfilling the role of the eschatological forerunner foretold in Mal 3:1 and 4:5-6, and as such ushering in the time of salvation to which he himself nonetheless remains to some degree an outsider. It is a role of high honor, but it remains that of a herald.

23. Though "the poor are told the good news" translates a two-word Greek phrase which is closely similar to the first clause of the manifesto in Isa 61:1 LXX.
24. "Happy" represents μακάριος; see the introductory comments on 5:3-10 for the beatitude form.

Verses 7-9 present a series of three matching questions with suggested answers which clearly belong together and build up to the climactic declaration of John's prophetic status. Verse 10 undergirds that declaration with a scriptural text more closely defining John's role as the eschatological forerunner. Verse 11 then summarizes the paradox of John's salvation-historical position. So far Matthew runs in parallel with Luke 7:24-28, but for the remainder of the section Matthew goes his own way. With v. 12, a saying with a partial parallel in a quite different setting in Luke 16:16, the logical sequence becomes obscure, resulting in one of the most controversial sayings in the gospel, which, though it mentions John, does not focus on his personal role. Verse 13 (still partially echoing Luke 16:16) returns to John's position as the climax of prophecy; v. 14 takes up another aspect of the forerunner motif from Malachi; and v. 15 appropriately rounds the section off with a formula indicating that it requires careful understanding.

7 The narrative link indicates a change of focus. Hitherto we have thought of John's estimate of Jesus. Now that his disciples are leaving to report back, Jesus widens the discussion by drawing in the listening crowd and asking for their estimate of John; while 3:5 does not mention crowds from Galilee, it is not likely that Jesus (and some of his disciples, John 1:35-42) were the only Galileans who had been drawn to John's preaching by the Jordan. But the questions are rhetorical, and it is Jesus' estimate, not that of the crowd, that we are about to hear. John had been a sensation in Judea and the surrounding area, drawing large crowds to the inhospitable area around the Jordan where he was baptizing (3:5-6). What drew them to make this improbable journey into the wilderness? Did they go to admire the scenery (reed grass being a very common feature of the area around the Jordan)? That may be all this first question and answer intends, an ironical statement that this was more than tourism. But the reed shaken by the wind is a natural symbol (sometimes used by the rabbis) for the type of man (and of preacher) whose message is adapted to fit the prevailing mood. If so, they would be disappointed, because John was not that sort of man.[25] His message as we have heard it in 3:1-12 was uncompromising and potentially very unpopular, and it was his very stubbornness and lack of tact which had now landed him in Antipas's prison.[26]

8 The second suggestion is equally improbable; if they wanted so-

---

25. It is less likely that the shaken reed was a metaphor for John's hesitations as expressed in v. 3 (so Albright and Mann, 136).

26. Other less plausible suggestions for the "shaken reed" include that it represents Herod Antipas, who used a reed as his symbol on some coins (see G. Theissen, *Gospels*, 25-42), or that the words recall God parting the "Sea of Reeds" by a strong wind in Exod 14–15, thus speaking of a new Exodus (so Davies and Allison, 2:247).

phistication and refinement, they had gone to the wrong place and to the wrong man. John's rough asceticism was legendary (3:4), and it fitted his wilderness location. You don't go into the wilderness to see a "smoothie," but to a royal palace.[27] The irony is, of course, that as Jesus spoke these words John was indeed in Antipas's royal palace at Machaerus (Josephus, *Ant.* 18.119), but as an unwilling guest and in the dungeon. All this was no doubt obvious enough to the people who had followed John; it was his inflexible, craggy character that had excited their reforming enthusiasm. He was as far as possible from the yes-men and courtiers of Antipas's court.[28] So what was it about him that had fired their imagination?

9   The answer would come as no surprise to the crowd, because not only had John's Elijah image (see on 3:4) constituted an implicit claim to be a prophet, but Matthew will tell us that it was in fact as a prophet that people had honored him (14:5; 21:26). This was a remarkable accolade in an age when prophecy was not taken for granted.[29] In declaring John "more than a prophet" Jesus is therefore using superlative language. He was not just a herald of the coming salvation, but was himself its immediate precursor, as vv. 10, 13, and 14 will go on to explain. He was the pivotal figure in the coming of the age of salvation, the one whose coming the last prophetic oracles of the OT (Mal 3:1-4; 4:5-6) said would mark the eschatological consummation.

10   This OT reference (like that of 3:3) does not have the regular formula of Matthew's fulfillment-citations (see on 1:22), but its effect is similar. The contemporary phenomenon of John "is" what Mal 3:1 was talking about; what God had spoken through the prophet has now been fulfilled. The quotation is almost the same as that with which Mark begins his account of John in Mark 1:2, where it is combined with Isa 40:3, which Matthew also introduced at that point (3:3). Both passages speak of preparing the way for God's eschatological coming, as does the Elijah prophecy in Mal 4:5-6 which will

---

27. The assertion by Luz, 2:137, that "The wilderness is a place where in those days one could find people in splendid apparel in the royal winter palaces" misses the point. Such people were in *palaces,* which were indeed in the area near the Jordan, but the palaces were *not* "the wilderness"!

28. *Gos. Thom.* 78 (a version of vv. 7-8 without the climax in v. 9) develops this idea: "Your kings and your great ones are those who are dressed in soft clothes, and they will not be able to know the truth."

29. The frequently cited rabbinic notion that prophecy had ceased with Malachi represents only one strand of Jewish thought, and there is evidence that various Jewish groups continued to speak of prophets in reality as well as in expectation (see D. E. Aune, *Prophecy,* ch. 5, especially pp. 103-6; R. L. Webb, *John,* 307-48), but there was nothing in first-century Judaism to match the groups of professional prophets known from the OT period, or the widespread exercise of prophecy in the NT church (1 Cor 14; *Did.* 11–12, etc.; cf. in this gospel 7:15, 22; 10:41; 23:34).

be alluded to in v. 14. What is different in the Christian application of the passages to John (in all three Synoptic versions) is that the first person of Mal 3:1 ("prepare the way before *me*") has become a second person ("before *you*"), thus allowing the possibility of taking the forerunner as preceding someone other than God himself.[30] This adaptation has been achieved by assimilating the wording of Mal 3:1 to that of Exod 23:20, where Yahweh speaks of sending his angel (the same Hebrew and Greek word as Malachi's "messenger") ahead of Israel in the wilderness; the wording of the first part of the resultant quotation is in fact closer to that of LXX Exod 23:20 than to Mal 3:1, even though it is surely the latter which is the prophetic passage primarily in mind (since the Exodus passage can only with difficulty be applied to the John/Jesus connection). The second half of the quotation reflects the Hebrew text of Mal 3:1 rather than the LXX. There is evidence that the two passages had already been connected in Jewish interpretation, so that this conflated form of words had become the standard form in which Mal 3:1 would be remembered and quoted.[31] This quotation, together with the identification of John in v. 14 as the Elijah of Mal 4:5-6, thus confirms what was already clear in 3:3 and 3:11, that John's significance lies in his being the immediate precursor of God's eschatological coming, which the Christian reader has been taught (and helped by the adapted wording of Mal 3:1) to recognize in the coming of Jesus the Messiah.

11 The argument of vv. 7-10 is brought to a resounding conclusion with a solemn "Amen" saying: John is the greatest of all human beings so far. In this context the focus has been on his role as a prophet, but this saying surprisingly declares him not simply the greatest of prophets but the greatest of all people (even Abraham, Moses, David?), so important is his pivotal role in the eschatological drama. After such a declaration the second half of the verse is the more striking, as it contrasts those hitherto "born of women" and the members of the kingdom of heaven.[32] The contrast is between two eras, that of preparation, culminating in John, and that of fulfillment, the arrival of the kingdom of heaven which Jesus has now inaugurated. John had proclaimed it

---

30. See above on 3:3 for the lack of an intermediary, "messianic" figure in the OT forerunner texts. For this interpretation of Mal 3:1 as containing only two figures, the forerunner and God himself, see my *Jesus and the OT*, 91-92, n. 31; also *Matthew: Evangelist*, 310.

31. See my *Jesus and the OT*, 242-43.

32. It would be overexegesis to find in the contrast between being born of women and belonging to the kingdom of heaven a suggestion of the Pauline and Johannine doctrine of regeneration, whereby belonging to the kingdom of heaven depends on being "born again," not of women but of the Spirit. "Born of women" is a conventional expression (as in Job 14:1; 15:14; Sir 10:18; see J. E. Taylor, *John*, 302-3, n. 85, for further Jewish examples) for humanity taken as a whole.

(3:2), but he apparently remains outside while even the less important (cf. 5:19 for "least" and "great" in the kingdom of heaven)[33] of those whom Jesus has now welcomed into the kingdom of heaven enjoys a privilege beyond that even of John himself.[34] See the introductory comments above for what this may imply about John's own spiritual status. The issue here is not John's personal salvation, but his place in the scheme of salvation history. For all his crucial role as herald of the kingdom of heaven, John (together with all the prophets and godly people of the OT) belongs essentially to the old era, not the new. This does not mean, however, that he, any more than the godly people of the OT, is ultimately excluded from the messianic salvation.

12   The link between John and the kingdom of heaven in explaining the development of salvation history in v. 11 now leads to a further and presumably originally independent saying (cf. Luke 16:16) which again links the two, but in a different way. The "days of John the Baptist" are clearly located in the past, and have been succeeded by the kingdom of heaven, which already has a history between John's time and the present. At the time of Jesus' ministry that history is still very short; by the time Matthew is writing it has extended another generation or two. That history, short or long, is not one of unmixed triumph for God's purpose, but paradoxically has been marked throughout by "violence." John himself has already suffered the "violence" of imprisonment,[35] soon to be followed by execution. Jesus and his followers have already been received with a hostility which, if it has not yet resulted in physical violence, will soon do so both for Jesus himself (16:21 etc.) and for his disciples (10:17-23, 28, 34-39). Cf. 17:11-13 for the continuity between John and Jesus in the experience of violent opposition.

That is the probable meaning of Matthew's version of the saying, tak-

---

33. In the light of the usage at 5:19 there seems nothing to be said for the common patristic view that the "smaller (younger?) one in the kingdom of heaven" is Jesus, despite the advocacy of B. T. Viviano, *CBQ* 62 (2000) 41-54, who somewhat improbably derives the terminology from Dan 4:17 (Heb. 4:14), where God sets up "the lowliest of human beings" over the kingdom of mortals (not "of heaven"). Matthew (unlike Luke) has given no indication that Jesus is "younger" than John.

34. *Gos. Thom.* 46 expands this saying by reflecting Jesus' teaching on "little ones" in such passages as Matt 18:3-4: "From Adam to John the Baptist there is none born of women who is greater than John the Baptist. . . . But I have said that whoever among you will become a little one will know the kingdom and will be greater than John." J. E. Taylor, *John*, 303-4, develops this idea by suggesting that this saying in Matthew does not place John outside the kingdom of heaven, but that because of its paradoxical values (expressed by Matthew's repeated references to the μικροί) even the great John is less than the least of its other subjects; but neither the context nor the Synoptic wording here supports this reading.

35. "John as a βιαζόμενος is in the prison of the βιαστής" (G. Schrenk, *TDNT*, 1:612).

ing the repeated language of violence *(biazomai, biastēs)* and of plunder *(harpazō)* in their normal negative sense.[36] There is nothing in Matthew (as against Luke 16:16) to suggest any other meaning for these strongly pejorative terms (see p. 419, nn. 6-7), and the concentration of negative language demands such an interpretation.[37] Whatever the process of transmission and adaptation which led to two such different sayings as Matt 11:12 and Luke 16:16 while still using some of the same terms and ideas, Matthew's text cannot be interpreted in terms of Luke's, where the one potentially violent term *(biazetai)* does not have the kingdom of heaven as its subject but rather speaks of people's attitude to it. The middle (and in Luke's saying perhaps commendatory) sense of *biazomai* as "to make forceful progress" or the like,[38] has no basis in Matthew's formulation of the saying. This is, in Matthew, a declaration that the kingdom of heaven has been and remains subject to violent opposition.

It remains unclear, however, in what sense these violent people "plunder," "ravage,"[39] or "seize" the kingdom of heaven. The literal, material sense of "plunder" is not appropriate to the spiritual nature of the kingdom of heaven and the material insignificance of the Christian community as we know it in the NT period — in contrast with the later affluence of the church, which has often invited literal "plunder." Metaphorically it might refer to those who try to steal away the members of the disciple community or perhaps to exploit its good name for their own ends — cf. the "wolves dressed up as sheep" in 7:15, and Paul's comments on fierce wolves in the Ephesian church (Acts 20:28-30).[40] "Ravage," even if not so common a sense of the verb, would fit well with the infliction of violence in the first clause and with the noun *biastai* and would require no more specific identification of the nature of their violence. If, however, we translate *harpazō* in its more normal sense of "seize," it might refer to a takeover bid aimed at the Jesus movement by people with an agenda of violence (against Rome?) rather than of spiritual salvation.[41] The phrase remains

---

36. See the recent summary of scholarly opinion by B. A. Reid, *CBQ* 66 (2004) 239-40.

37. See the full discussion of the meaning of these terms by W. E. Moore, *NTS* 21 (1974/5) 519-43; cf. also G. Schrenk, *TDNT* 1:609-14. The attempt to find a different meaning for the verb by appealing to a supposed Aramaic original underlying the different wording of Matthew and Luke (see G. R. Beasley-Murray, *Kingdom,* 92-94) is speculative; exegesis, here as everywhere, must proceed from the Greek text as we have it.

38. This sense is argued, e.g., by D. J. Verseput, *Rejection,* 94-99.

39. For this rendering of ἁρπάζω see G. R. Beasley-Murray, *Kingdom,* 93-95.

40. B. E. Thiering, *NovT* 21 (1979) 293-97, suggests on the basis of Qumran usage that "violent people" may refer to false teachers in the community.

41. Cf. the attempt of the enthusiastic crowd to "seize (the same verb, ἁρπάζω) Jesus and make him king" in John 6:15.

obscure, and such interpretations do not yet fit easily into what we know of the time of Jesus' Galilean ministry, though by Matthew's time they would have been more clearly pertinent.[42]

13 Another short saying underlines John's pivotal place in the fulfillment of God's purpose. This verse is partially parallel to the first clause of Luke 16:16 (the second part of which we have considered as parallel to v. 12), but in Matthew it takes a more developed form. In Luke it is a verbless clause which simply locates John at the end of the period of "the law and the prophets," but Matthew's special interest is shown by the addition of the verb "prophesy," the mention of the prophets before the law (an inversion of the usual order which is so unusual as to compel attention), and the addition of "all." Here then is a statement of Matthew's overriding sense of the fulfillment of Scripture in the period of Jesus' ministry. Until the time of John the Hebrew scriptures (with the prophets unusually placed in the foreground) were pointing forward to a time of fulfillment ("prophesying"); after John that fulfillment has come. We noted in the comments on 5:17 how this little statement helps to explain the "fulfillment of the law" as it is expounded in 5:17-48. It was not only the prophets who pointed forward to what was to come; the law, too, had this function, preparing the way for a fuller revelation of the will of God which was to come in the time of fulfillment, and which Matthew now finds present in the ministry of Jesus. Thus not only the prophets but even the law itself "prophesied." With the coming of John, the last and greatest of the prophets, that forward-pointing role is complete.

14 The expectation of an eschatological return of Elijah, derived from Mal 4:5-6 (the concluding declaration of the prophetic canon), was widely cherished in first-century Judaism. It had been taken up by Sir 48:10, and is referred to repeatedly by the rabbis.[43] The disciples can take this expectation as a given element in scribal teaching by the time of Jesus (17:10), and in 27:47-49 we shall hear an echo of it in popular thinking.[44] The narra-

---

42. Seven different interpretations of the saying (out of many proposed) are usefully listed by Davies and Allison, 2:254-55. For a full survey of interpretations see P. S. Cameron, *Violence;* Cameron finds the saying's primary setting in the violence experienced by John the Baptist, so that Antipas is the chief βιαστής.

43. See J. Jeremias, *TDNT* 2:931-34, supplemented with some Qumran material by J. E. Taylor, *John,* 283-87. But note also the important corrective by M. M. Faierstein, *JBL* 100 (1981) 75-86, who points out that while Elijah is expected to come eschatologically, Jewish sources hardly ever link that coming with the *Messiah* as such; similarly, M. Öhler, *JBL* 118 (1999) 461-64. The response by D. C. Allison, *JBL* 103 (1984) 256-58, fails to produce any counterevidence other than the distinctively *Christian* development of the Elijah hope in relation to Jesus, which begs the question.

44. Cf. 16:14, where Jesus himself is popularly identified as Elijah, as is John in Mark 6:15.

tive description of John the Baptist in 3:4 has given a strong hint that he is to be understood in relation to Elijah, and the quotation of Isa 40:3 (Matt 3:3) and Mal 3:1 (Matt 11:10) with reference to John would naturally point to the related prophecy of Mal 4:5-6, where the eschatological forerunner is named as Elijah. In 17:10-13 the discussion of the Elijah prophecy leads to Jesus' statement that Elijah has already come and been ill treated, and we are told that the disciples understood this of John the Baptist. But here for the only time in the gospels we hear Jesus making the identification explicit.[45] To do so is to make the same claim as was implicit in the quotation of Mal 3:1 in v. 10: if the forerunner has already come and finished his work, presumably "the great and terrible day of the Lord" for which Elijah was to prepare the way is now here. Perhaps it is the startling christological implications of this claim which explain the uncharacteristically coy tone of the opening clause, "If you are willing to accept it." To accept that John is the returning Elijah is to embrace a whole package of eschatological fulfillment in Jesus for which clearly most of those who heard him were not yet ready — cf. the unresponsiveness of "this generation" which will be condemned in vv. 16-19.

15 This formula (which echoes Jer 5:21; Ezek 12:2) will recur in 13:9, 43, where it will conclude a parable and a parable explanation (cf. similar uses in Luke 14:35; Rev 2:7). In relation to parables it constitutes a challenge to discern the meaning of a cryptic utterance, and its wording echoes the theology of revelation which will be spelled out in 13:10-17: not everyone does have "ears to hear," and it is only to those who do and who exercise them that revelation will be successful. Here, while the preceding sayings are not strictly parabolic, they contain deep matters which challenge the spiritual insight of those who hear, and their openness to receive new and surprising truth.

c. The People's Estimate of Both John and Jesus (11:16-19)

Verses 2-6 have explored John's estimate of Jesus, and vv. 7-15 have set out Jesus' estimate of John. Now the close link between the two is underlined by comparing the way in which they have been perceived by their contemporaries. Here is the first of several references in Matthew to "this generation." The term will recur in 12:41, 42; 23:36, and with the addition of various uncomplimentary adjectives ("wicked," "perverse," "unbelieving," "adulterous") also in 12:39, 45; 16:4; 17:17.[46] These passages focus on the failure of

---

45. It is also made explicit by the angel in Luke 1:17. In the Fourth Gospel, by contrast, John himself is portrayed as rejecting the identification (John 1:21), but no indication is given of either Jesus' or the author's view on the subject.

46. The term is also used in a more neutral chronological sense in 24:34.

Jesus' contemporaries to respond to his message, and so the term carries a strong tone of disapproval and warning, culminating in the climactic judgment on "this generation" in 23:36. At this earlier stage in the narrative the condemnation is less strong, but already the complaint is that "this generation" have failed to respond and have misconstrued the nature of Jesus' ministry, as they had already done that of John.[47]

The charge is launched in the form of a little parable from village life; the children are probably[48] playing at weddings (at which men traditionally danced) and funerals (at which women were the professional mourners).[49] Several commentators, following J. Jeremias,[50] therefore suppose the two groups of children to be the boys and the girls criticizing each other.

The verb *homoioō*, "to compare" (cf. 7:24, 26; 13:24; 18:23; 22:2; 25:1), and the adjective *homoios*, "like" (cf. 13:31, 33, 44, 45, 47, 52; 20:1), are Matthew's standard vocabulary for introducing parables. The comparison is perhaps not exactly drawn, in that "this generation" is apparently likened to the complainants rather than to those about whose lack of response they complain, but it is the scene as a whole rather than the specific equivalence which conveys the message.[51] It would be possible to understand the complaining children as "this generation," who piped to John but he refused to dance and who sang a dirge to Jesus but he refused to mourn[52] — the question and answer in 9:14-15 perhaps gets close to the latter scenario. But the

47. See Davies and Allison, 2:260-61 (following E. Lövestam, in J. Lambrecht [ed.], *L'Apocalypse johannique,* 403-13), for a helpful discussion of the theme of "this generation" in relation to its background in the OT, and especially the two notoriously corrupt generations of the Flood and of the wilderness wanderings, the latter being the subject of Deut 32:5, which clearly influences Matthew's use of the term.

48. In what follows I present the generally accepted reading of the scene. See, however, an interesting study by W. J. Cotter, *NovT* 29 (1987) 289-304, who points out that playing children seldom sit still and do not naturally use the formal address suggested by the verb προσφωνέω; Cotter argues that ἀγοραί often denotes a legal setting, so that the children here are purporting to pass formal judgment on their peers. "The parable is designed to expose self-righteousness as so much sham. [This generation]'s very judgments betray the superficiality it labours to hide."

49. "Mourn" translates κόπτομαι, literally "beat [one's breast]"; the game requires a physical display of grief to match the equally physical dancing at the wedding.

50. J. Jeremias, *Parables,* 160-62. So Gundry, 212; Davies and Allison, 2:261. Curiously these commentators ascribe to the boys and girls the opposite roles to those supposed by Jeremias, working from the same sociological data!

51. In many parables, as here, the point of comparison is loosely stated (using ὅμοιος / ὁμοιόω) by naming the most prominent figure in the story; see 13:24, 45; 18:23; 20:1; 22:2; 25:1, in each of which the kingdom of heaven is represented by the general scene, not by the specific figure named.

52. So Davies and Allison, 2:261-62.

explanatory comments that follow the parable fit better with the traditional interpretation[53] that it is Jesus who pipes and John who sings the dirge, and rather than join in the festivity or the lamentation "this generation" dismisses the one for his excessive exuberance and the other for his unnatural asceticism.[54] See on 9:23 for a more specialized use of "pipers" in connection with mourning rather than festivity; outside that specific context pipes more naturally call to jollity.

John's trademark asceticism (3:4; cf. Luke 1:15 for his abstinence from alcohol) had clearly appealed to some of the people, but the "disciples of John" remained a minority known for their regime of fasting which most people did not wish to follow (9:14). Jesus, though in many ways John's successor, did not follow him in this, and indeed made a point of the inappropriateness of fasting for his disciples (9:15). In Matthew's narrative sequence that dispute follows from Jesus' presence at a celebration meal in Matthew's house (9:10-13; Luke 5:29 calls it a "great banquet"), an incident which certainly justified his being labeled a "friend of tax collectors and sinners," and one which also illustrates his willingness to enjoy good fare when it was available, even though his normal lifestyle seems in fact to have allowed little such luxury (8:20). References to feasting in Jesus' teaching do not suggest a doctrinaire opponent of good food and drink (8:11-12; 22:1-14; 25:1-12; 26:29), though the common translation "drunkard" here goes further than the Greek term warrants (see p. 420, n. 12).[55] In the Cana miracle (John 2:1-11) Jesus provided a large amount of good wine, but we are not told how much of it he drank!

The reference to "wisdom's deeds" (see p. 420, n. 13) is unexpected. Following the "deeds of the Messiah" in v. 2, the "deeds" here are naturally understood as those of Jesus, that is, his criticized lifestyle, but in the light of the equal treatment of John and Jesus in the explanation of the parable it may also be understood to apply equally to the very different "deeds" of John. Each is equally justified in the context of their different roles, each offering a different application of the divine wisdom. When "wisdom" is used as the subject of a verb with a personal sense (to be "justified"), we should probably

---

53. Argued, e.g., by D. J. Verseput, *Rejection,* 112-15.

54. The charge that John is "demon-possessed" (cf. the same charge against Jesus in Mark 3:22, 30; John 7:20; 8:48; 10:20) is probably to be taken as popular invective against someone who does not fit into conventional life, rather than in the more theologically weighted sense of the allegation in 9:34; 12:24 that Jesus is using demonic powers.

55. The words "a glutton and wine drinker" may deliberately echo the description of the rebellious son by his parents in Deut 21:20 (thus many commentators), possibly used against Jesus by his Pharisaic opponents (so G. R. Beasley-Murray, *Kingdom,* 235), though the wording does not resemble that of the LXX; Luz 2:149, n. 37, is sceptical of the allusion.

take it in the sense widely developed in the postbiblical Wisdom Literature on the basis of the personification of the divine wisdom in Proverbs (notably but not only in Prov 8:22-31). That wisdom is essentially practical, guiding her followers in living the good life and avoiding the traps laid by folly and wickedness. Both John and Jesus in their different ways have displayed that practical wisdom, which is thus "justified" over against the criticism of those who represent a more conventional lifestyle.[56]

It has been argued, however, that Matthew sees more in the term "wisdom" in this saying. If the "deeds of wisdom" may be read as an echo of "the deeds of the Messiah" in v. 2, it is suggested that this is tantamount to identifying Jesus as Wisdom incarnate.[57] It is true that at the end of this chapter Jesus will speak words which closely echo the account of personified Wisdom in Sir 51:23-27 (see on 11:28-30), and a few other possible allusions to the tradition of personified Wisdom have been traced with less plausibility in other parts of Matthew. But in the present context, where John's actions are as much in focus as those of Jesus, a christological identification of Jesus as Wisdom is perhaps too extravagant a conclusion to draw from a term which in the OT Wisdom tradition refers primarily to practical guidance for living the good life rather than to a metaphysical personification of a divine attribute. Not that Matthew would have found the identification of Jesus with Wisdom unacceptable: it is clear in other parts of the NT which explain the cosmic significance of Christ in terms of the creative role of Wisdom in Prov 8 and the derivative traditions, and it is probably implied, as we shall see, in Matt 11:28-30. But the present context does not require it and indeed, if the parallelism between John and Jesus be given due weight, even militates against it.

56. This conventional interpretation is challenged by S. Gathercole, *NTS* 49 (2003) 476-88, who translates the last clause, "And wisdom has been absolved of her actions." He explains this as "a complaint by Jesus that this generation has zealously put Wisdom in the clear by denying that she has any connection with the ministries of John and Jesus" (480). This proposal offers an attractive explanation for the unusual phrase δικαιόομαι ἀπό (conventionally translated "justified by," even though this is not a normal use of ἀπό), but it requires a difficult mental adjustment by the reader to recognize that Jesus is here expressing his critics' view rather than his own. Gathercole also has to deny any connection between the "deeds" of wisdom and the "deeds" of the Messiah in v. 2.

57. The argument is based especially on the difference between Luke and Matthew: Luke's phrase "Wisdom's children" puts John and Jesus on a par as emissaries of the divine Wisdom, but Matthew's wording, with its echo of "the deeds of the Messiah" in v. 2, invites us to see Jesus as himself Wisdom. See M. J. Suggs, *Wisdom*, esp. 55-58 (and cf. J. D. G. Dunn, *Christology*, 197-98). So also C. Deutsch, *NovT* 32 (1990) 33-36; *Lady Wisdom*, 49-54. For a general discussion of Suggs' attempt to find Wisdom christology in Matthew see my *Matthew: Evangelist*, 302-6; also R. Pregeant, in D. R. Bauer and M. A. Powell (eds.), *Treasures*, 197-232.

2. Unresponsive Towns in Galilee (11:20-24)

20 *Then he began to reproach the towns in which his many[1] miracles had taken place, because they had not repented:* 21 *"Woe to you, Chorazin; woe to you, Bethsaida. For if the miracles which have taken place in you had taken place in Tyre and Sidon, they would long ago have repented in sackcloth and ashes.* 22 *And indeed[2] I tell you: it will be more bearable on the day of judgment for Tyre and Sidon than for you.* 23 *And you, Capernaum, will you really[3] be 'exalted to heaven'?[4] No, rather, 'you will go down[5] to Hades.'[6] For if the miracles which have taken place in you had been performed[7] in Sodom, it would have survived until today.* 24 *And indeed I tell you[8] that it will be more bearable on the day of judgment for the land of Sodom than for you."*

The response of John the Baptist to Jesus (positive but equivocal) has led on to Jesus' comments about "this generation," which refused to respond to both

1. For the superlative ὁ πλεῖστος used in this sense of "very large" or "very many" cf. 21:8 (and cf. BDF 245[1]). The more literally superlative sense would also be possible here: "most of his miracles."

2. While πλήν normally means "except" or "however," here as in v. 24 Matthew (reflecting LXX usage; "a formula of solemn affirmation," Luz, 2:151, n. 1) uses it not to introduce a contrasting idea but to change the focus of a saying by introducing a striking new dimension without, however, changing the overall thrust; "and indeed" captures this usage in context.

3. The construction with μή indicates an ironical question expecting the answer No. The "No, rather" supplied with the response is intended to draw out this rhetorical device.

4. The reading in some MSS and versions, "You, Capernaum, who have been exalted to heaven, will go down . . . ," may have been an attempt to alleviate the unexpected rhetorical question. It might also represent an accidental misreading, as the letters involved would be very similar, and the μ of μή might have been confused with the final μ of Καφαρναούμ.

5. The readings καταβήσῃ, "go down," and καταβιβασθήσῃ, "be brought down," are both well supported, the former being the LXX wording in Isa 14:15. It is possible that an original καταβιβασθήσῃ was assimilated to the LXX wording (see my *Jesus and the OT,* 243), but the sense is not greatly different, and the allusion to Isa 14:15 would be perceptible on either reading.

6. The two clauses marked out by quotation marks echo the LXX of Isa 14:13, 15, the second clause exactly, the first less closely. See the comments below for the point of the allusion.

7. While the wording of this clause otherwise matches exactly that of v. 21b, the translation here reflects the passive form ἐγενήθησαν, which is used here rather than the middle ἐγένοντο.

8. This "you," unlike that at the end of the verse, is plural: Jesus is speaking not so much to Capernaum as to whoever hears his pronouncement about its fate.

John and Jesus (vv. 16-19). It is that unresponsiveness rather than John's uncertainty which provides the cue for this pair of balancing sayings addressed to three of the most prominent towns of the area on the north of the lake where Jesus' ministry has so far been focused. They pick up the theme of 10:11-15: the towns which may be expected to reject the disciples are already failing to respond to Jesus himself. In the light of earlier accounts of widespread enthusiasm for Jesus in the area (4:23-25; 7:28-29; 8:1; 9:35-36), and particularly in Capernaum (8:16, 18-22; 9:8, 10, 26, 31, 33), the stark accusation that the communities as a whole have failed to repent is surprising. Is this due to a distinction between (superficial) enthusiasm and (life-changing) repentance? Or should we read these as broad generalizations about the attitude of the townspeople (and perhaps especially their leaders; 9:3, 11, 34), to which the crowds who followed Jesus (and still more his disciples, who are also local men) are exceptions? The general expectation of opposition and persecution which we have met in ch. 10, and which is apparently to come from the local Jewish population, suggests the latter, in which case we should probably read Matthew's earlier positive summaries of the response to Jesus as representing less than the majority of ordinary Galileans. For a time Jesus may have been the talk of the town, but interest has quickly waned, and Jesus' frustration with "this generation" finds expression in language nearly as strong as he will use more specifically for the scribes and Pharisees in Jerusalem in ch. 23. Even in Galilee, including Jesus' "own" town of Capernaum, the honeymoon period is apparently over. And when those who have been privileged to witness Jesus' ministry in their own communities fail to respond, they must expect to face a more serious judgment than the notorious pagan cities which had no such special revelation.

20   As in 11:7, "Jesus began to" indicates a change of focus, as Jesus turns from commenting to the crowds about John to a rhetorical address to the Galilean communities where his own ministry has been focused. Matthew uses *polis,* "town," for anything from the insignificant village of Nazareth (2:23) to the capital city of Jerusalem (4:5; 21:10). Here it applies to something in between, three of the larger Jewish communities which, while not rivaling the magnificence of the Hellenistic cities of Sepphoris and Tiberias, were the centers of provincial life north of the lake. Most of the miracles so far related, where any specific location is stated, have been in or around Capernaum, but the more general summaries of 4:23-24 and 9:35 (cf. also 11:1) indicate that other towns would also have witnessed miracles of healing and exorcism.[9] The expected response of "repentance" is more reminiscent of the ministry of John (3:2, 8, 11) than what we have so far heard of

---

9. According to a medieval commentary on Luke, the lost *Gospel of the Hebrews* recorded fifty-three miracles in Chorazin and Bethsaida (Hennecke, 1:151)!

Jesus' emphasis (and the contrast has been vividly drawn in vv. 16-19), but in 4:17 the demand of Jesus, as of John (3:2), was to "repent" in view of the coming of God's kingship. He is looking for a change, a new beginning, but these towns seem content to continue as if nothing was different. They have not grasped what God's kingship means.

21-22 Neither Chorazin nor Bethsaida appears elsewhere in Matthew, but archeology has shown both to have been substantial communities comparable in size and importance to Capernaum. Chorazin, less than an hour's walk from Capernaum, would have been a natural extension of Jesus' activity. Bethsaida, on the other side of the Jordan and so strictly outside Galilee in the territory of Herod Philip, is mentioned a number of times in the accounts of Jesus' ministry (Mark 6:45; 8:22; Luke 9:10) and, according to John 1:44; 12:21, was the original home of Jesus' disciples Peter, Andrew, and Philip. The traditional prophetic formula "Woe to you" (found twenty-two times in Isaiah alone)[10] marks out those whose actions and attitudes have aligned them against God and his purposes (note Luke's striking use of it as a counterbalance to the beatitude formula, Luke 6:24-26); in ch. 23 Jesus will use it repeatedly against the religious leaders in Jerusalem, and cf. 18:7b; 26:24. It can also be used of the innocent victims of disaster (cf. 24:19 and probably 18:7a), but here the formula certainly conveys blame rather than sympathy.[11] The expectation that the visible "deeds of the Messiah" should convince John the Baptist (vv. 2-6) also applies to these towns. Tyre and Sidon, usually mentioned in the NT as a conventional pair, were the leading cities of Phoenicia, their territory bordering Galilee to the northwest (15:21). Both are the targets of prophetic denunciation in the OT, but particularly Tyre (especially in Isa 23:1-17; Ezek 26-28); they represent arrogant opposition to Yahweh and his people. Yet even these pagan peoples (like Nineveh, 12:41; for the sackcloth and ashes cf. Jonah 3:6-8) would have been more likely to repent in the face of such evidence than Chorazin and Bethsaida. There may also be an oblique reference to the miracle of Elijah which took place in Sidon (1 Kgs 17:8-24), which brought a local woman to recognize God's prophet and the truth of God's word (v. 24), though nothing is said there of the reaction of other Sidonians. The comparison of fates on the day of judgment is a repeated motif (cf. 10:15; 12:41-42) which is designed to emphasize the guilt of the Jews who failed to respond to Jesus rather than to pronounce on the destiny of the Gentile peoples as such (cf. 10:15, where the destruction of Sodom and Gomorrah is not put in doubt by the comparison).

10. See further below, pp. 867-68 and n. 19 there.
11. D. J. Verseput, *Rejection,* 121-24, argues that these woes express Jesus' harsh reproach and the expectation of judgment, rather than in themselves pronouncing judgment, since Jesus will continue to be active in these towns.

23-24 Capernaum has hitherto been a place of revelation and response (4:13-16; 8:5-17; 9:1-34), but woven into those accounts has been an undercurrent of opposition and rejection (8:10-12, with special reference to its Jewish inhabitants over against the Gentile centurion; 9:3, 11, 34) provoking Jesus' comment that the old wineskins cannot accommodate the new wine (9:16-17). Capernaum, as the base of Jesus' operations, has received more of the light (4:16) than the other towns, and so its unresponsiveness deserves a greater condemnation. The comparison with Sodom (cf. 10:15) is therefore even more wounding than that with Tyre and Sidon, since at least the Phoenician cities, though captured by Alexander the Great, were still standing, whereas Sodom was the classic example of total destruction, its remains now buried under the waters of the Dead Sea. Even worse is the unmistakable echo in v. 23 (see above, n. 6) of Isaiah's taunt (Isa 14:13-15) against the ambitions and downfall of the king of Babylon, the traditional enemy and destroyer of Judah. The comparison seems remote, both in that Capernaum was no imperial power and was strongly Jewish in its population and sympathies and in that we have no information to enable us to identify any such desire on its part to "be exalted to heaven." The example of the king of Babylon is apparently being used not because of any specific equivalence, but as a proverbial example of pride going before a fall, the pride in this case being Capernaum's failure to recognize any need to respond to Jesus' call to repentance. Hades[12] is the place of the dead rather than a place of punishment; here, as in 16:18, its only other use in Matthew, it symbolizes destruction.

3. Revelation to the Little Ones (11:25-30)

> 25 At that time Jesus declared,[1] "I praise you, Father, Lord of heaven and earth, because you have hidden these things from the wise and intelligent, and revealed them to little children. 26 Yes, Father, that was your good pleasure.[2] 27 Everything has been entrusted[3] to me by

---

12. "Hades" is the regular Greek term for the Hebrew *Šeʾôl*, and should not be confused with Gehenna (see on 5:22, 29-30; 10:28).

1. The Semitic formula "answered and said" (when there is no preceding speech to "answer") is used to mark a significant new pronouncement (cf. 15:15; 17:4). Hagner, 1:315-16, adds "responding to this unbelief" to his translation here, but that is to look for too precise a focus in this common idiom.

2. Literally, "because thus was goodwill (εὐδοκία) before you," a Semitic idiom for deliberate choice and purpose. Cf. the cognate εὐδοκέω in 3:17, where again there is an element of choice as well as pleasure. For "before" in the sense of the Semitic idiom "pleasing in the eyes of" cf. 18:14, and see BDF 214(6).

3. For the more frequent negative sense of παραδίδωμι (to "hand over" with a view to punishment) cf. 4:12 ("arrest"); 5:25; 10:4 ("betray"), 17, etc. The essential sense

my Father, and no one recognizes[4] the Son except the Father, nor does anyone recognize the Father except the Son and anyone to whom the Son is willing to reveal him.[5]

28 *"Come here to me, all you who are toiling and heavily loaded, and I will give you rest.* 29 *Take my yoke on your shoulders[6] and learn from me, because[7] I am meek and lowly in heart; so you will find rest for your souls.* 30 *For my yoke is kind[8] and my burden is light."*

In stark contrast to the towns which had refused to respond to Jesus (because they did not "recognize the Son," v. 27), we hear now of those to whom the truth about Jesus has been revealed and who are encouraged to enjoy the benefits of being his followers. In ch. 12 we shall return to Jesus' opponents and those who refuse to respond to his message, before again turning with relief to a portrait of those whose commitment to do the will of his Father makes them Jesus' true family (12:46-50). 11:25-30 and 12:46-50 thus constitute two high points within an otherwise unpromising survey of Galilean responses, two instances of successful sowing within the otherwise unresponsive soil (13:1-9).

Within what is presented as a single speech of Jesus there are apparently two independent sections, the first (vv. 25-27) shared with Luke 10:21-22, where it similarly follows closely on the woes against Chorazin, Beth-

---

is to put something into someone's control. Also relevant here may be the use of this verb to denote the process of "tradition" within rabbinic Judaism, whereby truth was "entrusted" by a teacher to his pupil for further transmission (cf. 1 Cor 15:3 etc.).

4. The compound verb ἐπιγινώσκω can be used synonymously with γινώσκω, "know," and is frequently so translated here. But in his otherwise exact parallel to this saying (10:22) Luke uses not the simple γινώσκω but γινώσκω τίς ἐστιν, which is well represented by Matthew's ἐπιγινώσκω in its more specific sense of "recognize."

5. Several early church writers testify to a version of this saying in which the positions of Father and Son in the verse were reversed, with the result that the last clause was about the Father revealing the Son to those he chose. It seems that this version appealed especially to Gnostics, but in the almost complete absence of MSS and versional evidence for such a reading it can hardly be original. (See C. Deutsch, *Hidden Wisdom*, 34-35.)

6. The Greek says simply "on you," but this is not natural English for a yoke. The yoke worn by either humans or animals (see comments below) is placed across the shoulders.

7. It is also possible to translate ὅτι here as "that"; in that case the meekness and lowliness of Jesus is the subject of the learning. So U. Luz, *Theology*, 95, following G. Strecker, *Weg*, 174. But most interpreters see this clause as parallel to the γάρ clause of v. 30. In any case, as Strecker comments, the overall sense is not greatly affected.

8. χρηστός can mean simply "good" (Luke 5:39; 1 Cor 15:33), but it usually carries the sense of "good to other people" and so "considerate," "kind" (Luke 6:35; Rom 2:4; Eph 4:32).

saida and Capernaum, the second (vv. 28-30) peculiar to Matthew.[9] They are not of the same type, vv. 25-27 being an address to God,[10] vv. 28-30 an invitation to potential followers. Their coherence is not in their literary form but in their underlying subject matter, as they express in different ways the paradoxical values of the kingdom of heaven and the privilege of those who through Jesus have become its subjects. As in the Sermon on the Mount, Jesus' true disciples (for that is surely the reference of the "little children" of 11:25 as it is explicitly of the "mother and brothers" of 12:49) represent an alternative community. They are "little ones" in comparison with those whom the world thinks important, but it is they alone who can know the truth about God and his Son; the same theme will be developed further in 13:10-17. Moreover, Jesus himself represents that same paradoxical value-scale: his character as "meek and lowly in heart" reflects the values of the beatitudes in 5:3-10, and his "yoke" (traditionally a symbol of oppressive power) is in fact "kind" and a source not of misery but of "rest" for those who submit to his benign control.

These verses also contain some of the most remarkable christological teaching of the gospel. The theme of privileged revelation and of the uniquely close relationship of Jesus to his Father in vv. 25-27 provides a suggestive context for Matthew's clearest allusion to the Jewish figure of Wisdom in vv. 28-30.[11] Jesus' prayer reminds us of the portrayal of Wisdom in the OT and later Jewish literature as God's firstborn and only associate in creation (Prov 8:22-31) and as the one who alone mediates God's truth and instruction for living (Prov 8:1-21, 32-36 and passim). The wording of vv. 25-27 does not directly echo familiar Wisdom passages, though conceptual parallels to v. 25 can be traced in the tradition of a "hidden wisdom,"[12] and to v. 27 in the idea that only God knows Wisdom (e.g., Job 28) and only Wisdom knows God and can reveal his truth (e.g., Wis 9:9-11).[13] But in vv. 28-30 the echo becomes un-

---

9. An abbreviated version of vv. 28-30 (independently of vv. 25-27) appears in *Gos. Thom.* 90.

10. Note, however, that vv. 25-26 are in the second person while v. 27 is a third-person comment. Many commentators therefore treat vv. 25-26 and v. 27 also as originally separate sayings. But they are also together in Luke, and their subject matter (the hiddenness of truth except for those to whom it is specially revealed) is so closely related that, whatever the process by which they came together, they are better treated as a single unit.

11. See on vv. 16-19 for a previous passage in which it is suggested, though with less agreement, that Matthew portrays Jesus as Wisdom.

12. C. Deutsch, *Hidden Wisdom,* ch. 3, explores at length the possible Jewish conceptual backgrounds to vv. 25-27; see especially pp. 107-11 for the theme of privileged access to truth.

13. See C. Deutsch, ibid., especially pp. 103-7. In her *Lady Wisdom,* 54-60, Deutsch summarizes the Wisdom themes running through 11:25-30 as a whole.

mistakable, as not only the imagery of the yoke but also many other aspects of the wording are reminiscent of Sir 51:23-27 (and less directly Sir 6:23-30, where the imagery of Wisdom's yoke is first deployed).[14] For details of the echoes see the comments below. Their significance lies not only in Jesus' issuing of the sage's invitation to "come to me" for relief, but more remarkably in that he offers not Wisdom's yoke, but his own, and is himself the giver of the "rest" which the sage could only claim to have found for himself as a result of taking on Wisdom's yoke. Jesus is not then, like the earlier Jesus ben Sirach, merely Wisdom's messenger — he adopts in his own person the role of the divine Wisdom which the sage had commended.[15]

That alone would be enough to mark this pericope as a christological high point in the gospel, but no less important is the Father/Son imagery of v. 27 (as well as Jesus' first direct address to God as "Father" in vv. 25-26). The unique status of Jesus as God's Son has been explicit in 2:15 and 3:17, has formed the basis for the testing in the wilderness in 4:1-11, and has been declared by supernatural beings in 8:29, but here it achieves a new prominence in the private prayer of Jesus himself, and is made the basis for a statement unique in this gospel about the exclusive mutual knowledge of Father and Son, a Synoptic saying which has understandably been declared more in keeping with the language of the Fourth Gospel than with the rest of Matthew or Luke.[16] This is

14. R. Pregeant, in D. R. Bauer and M. A. Powell (eds.), *Treasures,* 214-15, surprisingly makes no mention of the Sirach texts in his analysis of what information a reader might have been expected to bring to the text of Matthew. His overall "reader-response" argument is well taken, that we must not expect Matthew's readers to derive their understanding of his text from matters extraneous to it with which the reader would not be familiar (in particular from a comparison of Matthew's wording with that of Luke; see below on 23:34). But Sirach was a widely circulated text which would surely be familiar to many of Matthew's readers, so that echoes of and contrasts with that text might be expected to draw their attention.

15. A further dimension to the christology of this passage is suggested by D. C. Allison, *Moses,* 218-33 (cf. Davies and Allison, 2:283-86, 296-97), who finds in various of its ideas and phrases echoes of the role of Moses in both the OT and later Jewish writings. It is clear especially from Exod 33:11-23; Num 12:1-8; Deut 34:9-12 (the passages at the heart of Allison's argument) that Moses had an especially close relationship with God and was the means of communicating God's mind to other people, and the description of Moses as exceptionally "meek" in Num 12:3 provides a suggestive parallel to v. 29. But Allison's lengthy and sometimes tortuous discussion does not seem to me to establish any other clear allusion to those passages, and the exclusive mutual knowledge of Father and Son in v. 27 goes far beyond what was said of Moses. Nor does rabbinic teaching about the "yoke of Torah" justify the suggestion that when Jesus speaks of his yoke he is likening himself to *Moses.* There is no "yoke of Moses" in the Jewish tradition.

16. For a cautious discussion of the likely origin of this saying see J. D. G. Dunn, *Jesus,* 27-34.

not, of course, a public declaration but a prayer, and there will be few occasions when Jesus himself will even hint publicly at his status as Son of God until the climactic declaration of 26:63-64; in 21:37-39 the claim will be conveyed only in the imagery of a parable, and in 24:36 it occurs almost in passing and in the hearing only of his disciples. But the truth declared in 3:17 (and to be repeated in 17:5) remains the basis for the reader's understanding of Jesus, and here it finds its expression appropriately in Jesus' first recorded prayer to his Father. What is said here of the exclusive relationship between "the Father" and "the Son" begins to prepare the reader for the climax of the gospel where "the Son" will take his place alongside the Father and the Holy Spirit as the object of the disciples' allegiance (28:19). This is not yet a formulated doctrine of the Trinity, but it is a decisive step toward it.[17]

25 In Luke 10:21-22 this saying begins with "In that same hour," which links it with the return of the missionaries and their rejoicing that their names are written in heaven. Matthew does not make that connection, and so instead here "At that time" links the following declaration with the unresponsiveness of the people of Galilee, who exemplify the "wise and intelligent" from whom the truth is hidden. The very unspecific term "these things" must be understood in the context of the whole revelatory process of Jesus' ministry, both the truths he has taught and the truth about who he himself is. The division in response to Jesus' message is here unambiguously traced to the will of God himself (see also the following verse); it is a matter of revelation to some and not to others, as 13:11-17 will more fully spell out. The basis of this division is not an arbitrary selection, but the fundamental principle of divine revelation, that it comes to those who are open to it, but finds no response with those who think they know better; with the "wise and intelligent" it is wasted like seed sown beside the path (13:4, 19). To describe this effect as God's actively "hiding" the truth reflects the Jewish tendency to ignore intermediate causes and to attribute the end result directly to the divine purpose; we shall have more to say on this in relation to 13:11-17. If God is indeed "Lord of heaven and earth," a form of address unique in the NT (though cf. Acts 4:24; Rev 10:6; 14:7) but typical of Jewish prayer,[18] it is understood that what happens on earth, even in the minds of the human beings he has created, comes under his sovereign will.

The strongly Hebraic tone of the prayer is seen also in the word for

---

17. See Luz, 2:159-60, for patristic interpretation of this passage in a trinitarian sense, and pp. 160-61 for subsequent reaction against this understanding. On pp. 169-70 Luz adds his own interesting comments on the validity of reading the text in a trinitarian sense today.

18. It occurs in the opening address of the regular synagogue prayer, the T^{e}fillâ; cf. also Jdt 9:12; Tob 7:17; 1QapGen 22:16.

"praise," *exhomologeomai,* which occurs in only one other place in Matthew, where it means "confess" (3:6). Its use here reflects LXX usage, where the verb not only means "confess," "acknowledge," but also regularly translates the hiphil of the Hebrew *yāda‛,* meaning to "make known" or "declare" the works of God, and hence to "praise" him.[19] But while the tone of the prayer is thus familiarly Jewish, the address to God simply as "Father" breaks new ground. The imagery of God as Father of his people is not new, but while Jewish prayers might occasionally refer to God as "our Father," as Jesus taught his own disciples to do (6:9), for an individual to address God simply as "Father" (presumably in the Aramaic form *Abba,* Mark 14:36) is, as far as extant records go, unprecedented.[20] The familial tone of the simple "Father" in combination with the reverential "Lord of heaven and earth" provides a telling insight into the nature of prayer for Jesus.

"Wise" and "intelligent" are not in themselves pejorative terms. Indeed, Jesus will speak in 23:34 of sending "prophets, wise people, and scribes" as his messengers to an unresponsive Israel. But the wisdom which he has just celebrated in 11:19 and whose tones he will adopt in this pericope is not that of human cleverness but of divine revelation. Even the best of human insight which relies only on its own resources cannot penetrate the divine wisdom; it is "hidden" from it. By contrast, "little children," precisely because they do not rely on their own resources, are open to receive the revelation; cf. the OT theme of wisdom given to the "simple" (Pss 19:7; 119:130 [in both of which LXX uses *nēpios*]; Prov 1:4, etc.). *Nēpios,* an "infant," even a "babe in arms," is a familar NT image for the immature who remain dependent on others (Rom 2:20; 1 Cor 13:11; Eph 4:14); it is the opposite end of the human value-scale from the mature, self-confident adult. The unresponsive world may despise the humble disciple, but in the matter of divine wisdom as in so many aspects of the kingdom of heaven the first will be last and the last first; for a similar contrast, again using *nēpios,* see 21:15-16. We have already met in 10:42 the Matthean motif of Jesus' true disciples as the "little ones," and the theme will be resumed more forcefully in 18:6-14 as well as in the "least of these brothers of mine" in 25:40, 45.

26 The reversal of roles set out in v. 25 (the little children receive the truth while the wise and intelligent remain in the dark) is not an accidental exception to the normal order of things; it is God's "good pleasure." It represents the basic reversal of human values which constantly recurs as the val-

---

19. A parallel use of ἐξομολογέομαι in Sir 51:1 is of interest in the light of the echoes of the latter part of that chapter in vv. 28-30, though attempts to trace the influence of Sir 51 as a whole on the composition of vv. 25-30 are not convincing.

20. See the comments at 6:9 (especially p. 245, n. 56) for the debate concerning the uniqueness of this form of address in prayer.

ues of the kingdom of heaven are explained in this gospel, and Jesus, as the Son who alone fully understands his Father (v. 27), can declare that this is the way God intended it to be. This theme is already clear in the OT, where prophets and wisdom writers delight to put the pretensions of human wisdom in their place (Isa 29:13-16; Jer 8:8-9; 9:23-24; Prov 1:2-7, etc.); it will be memorably developed by Paul in 1 Cor 1:18–2:16.[21] What human wisdom, with its self-centered viewpoint, finds paradoxical and humiliating is quite simply God's good pleasure. This is the way he has ordered his world. It should be noted, of course, that to say this is not to say that he has pre-selected individuals to be placed in each category; vv. 20-24 have already made it clear that people have a responsibility and a choice as to whether or not they receive his revelation. It is also important to note that this declaration is followed by Jesus' open invitation to any who are in need (not only the "chosen") to "come to me" (v. 28).

27 The direct address to God in vv. 25-26 now gives way to a third-person pronouncement about Jesus' own position. It provides the justification for his confident declaration of God's purpose in the preceding verses, but also draws out the wider christological dimensions of what it means for Jesus to be God's "beloved Son, with whom I am delighted" (3:17). In relation to the issue of divine revelation in vv. 25-26 it in effect makes Jesus the indispensable intermediary between God and the "little children": it is only through him that they have received and can receive their special knowledge of God's truth. In this context "everything" probably refers particularly to the revelation of truth,[22] but the term is not in itself restricted to that, and the wording anticipates the postresurrection pronouncement of 28:18, that "All authority in heaven and earth has been given to me." Jesus, the Son, is the one and only plenipotentiary of the one true God, his Father. The focus is on his possession of this authority rather than on when and how it was given. While this statement would be consonant with a doctrine of Jesus' preexistence, it does not in itself require it, any more than does the parallel aorist passive verb in 28:18, which in context should probably be taken of the empowerment of the Son of Man through his death and resurrection rather than of his eternal status.

The familiarity of Jesus' boldly distinctive address to God as "Father" in vv. 25-26 is explained by the teaching of this saying that only the Father truly knows the Son and only the Son truly knows the Father. This exclusive mutual knowledge[23] of Father and Son has the effect of placing them in a cate-

21. Note especially the use of εὐδοκέω in 1 Cor 1:21 compared with εὐδοκία here; cf. p. 439, n. 2.

22. Note the frequent use of παραδίδωμι elsewhere in the NT for "tradition"; see p. 439, n. 3.

23. D. C. Allison, *JTS* 39 (1988) 478-83, suggests an OT background to this idea

gory apart from other sentient beings, much as in 24:36 "the Son" (the same abbreviated title as here) is placed in a category above and separate from the angels and everyone else — though in that case, as we shall see, even the Son is not privy to one particular aspect of the Father's knowledge. Matthew's use of *epiginōskō,* "recognize," here (see p. 440, n. 4) may seem surprising in that in 8:29 demons have recognized Jesus as the Son of God (and cf. 4:3, 6), but such formal identification falls far short of the Father's intimate knowledge of his Son. In biblical literature to "know" is more a matter of relationship than of intellectual attainment; it is personal rather than formal. When both OT and NT writers speak of people other than the Son as "knowing God" (Jer 9:24; 31:34; Hos 6:6; John 14:7; 17:3; Gal 4:9, etc.), this "knowledge" is understood not as information available to all (except in a very limited sense in Rom 1:21), but as a special gift of God, and in the NT is specifically associated with faith in Jesus. Jesus' saying here provides the basis for that extension: "anyone to whom the Son is willing to reveal him." Here then is a Synoptic equivalent to the Johannine declaration, "I am the way and the truth and the life; no one comes to the Father except through me" (John 14:6). And just as the revelation of truth has been attributed to the Father's "good pleasure" in vv. 25-26, so now the knowledge of the Father depends on the "will" of the Son. It is freely given, not achieved by human cleverness. In that revelatory process the Son's will stands on a par with the Father's.

J. Jeremias[24] has suggested that the use of capital letters for "Father" and "Son" in the second part of this verse is inappropriate, since Jesus is making a general statement about fathers and sons, not a specific statement about himself and God. It would be linguistically possible (though probably not very natural) to read "the father" and "the son" in that generic sense, but this would be a highly questionable generalization: there are many fathers and sons who can hardly be said to know one another as well as some other people (especially spouses) know them. Moreover, the extension of this knowledge to others through the son, but not through the father, is hard to explain if it is simply a statement about human relationships. But even if Jeremias were right with regard to v. 27b alone, it is hardly possible that either Matthew or his readers could have read the saying in this parabolic sense, immediately after Jesus' address to God as "Father" in vv. 25-26 and his reference to "my Father" in v. 27a, and yet failed to recognize the specific "father" and "son" to whom in context the parable must refer — and indeed Jeremias had no desire to dispute this application or the christology which

---

in Exod 33:12-13, where Yahweh speaks of knowing Moses by name (cf. Deut 34:10, "whom Yahweh knew face to face") and Moses asks that he may know Yahweh (and a promise of "rest" follows in v. 14).

24. J. Jeremias, *Theology,* 58-61.

derives from it. The unique position of Jesus as God's Son is thus clear in this saying, whether the point is made parabolically or more directly by the use of recognized titles.

28 Jesus has spoken to God about the revelation of truth in vv. 25-26, and in v. 27 he has spoken in general terms about how the Father can be known only through the Son. Now this special revelatory role of the Son is expressed in a direct invitation to find the solution to life's problems by coming to Jesus. The terms he uses reflect the Jewish understanding of the divine Wisdom as the intermediary between God and his people. I mentioned above (p. 441) that already in vv. 25-27 it is possible to trace conceptual links with aspects of the Jewish Wisdom tradition, and so to see Jesus as, in Matthew's view, himself taking the place of the personified divine Wisdom, hidden from human cleverness, but able to communicate to those who seek her the truth about God which she alone truly understands. As the focus moves in vv. 28-30 from knowing the truth to finding rest, the echoes of Wisdom literature become even clearer. The most obvious source[25] for Jesus' language here is Sir 51:23-27 (cf. Sir 6:23-30), in which the sage invites the unlearned to come near to him to find Wisdom, to put their necks under Wisdom's yoke so that their souls receive instruction, and informs them that in this way he himself, having toiled only a little, has found much rest. The echoes of the Greek text are clear: the words for "to me," "toil," "yoke," "find," "rest," and "soul" are all the same. But the way these themes are combined is significantly different. Whereas the sage is himself the recipient of Wisdom's blessings, and invites others to share what he has received from her, Jesus is no intermediary but issues "Wisdom's" invitation in his own person. Wisdom's yoke is now his yoke, and it is he who offers rest to those who toil.[26]

---

25. For a wide-ranging survey of Jewish background to these verses see C. Deutsch, *Hidden Wisdom,* 113-30. She concludes that while there are a number of suggestive parallels to the themes of invitation, the yoke, and the promise of rest, Sir 51:23-27 offers the clearest parallel to this pericope as a whole. B. Charette, *NTS* 38 (1992) 290-97, chides Deutsch for neglecting the canonical background and argues that there is sufficient OT background to Jesus' words to make the Sirach reference unnecessary. His article exposes a rich seam of OT imagery involving the concepts of "yoke" and "rest" in connection with God's covenant with his people (imagery on which presumably Sirach has drawn), but these admittedly important echoes need not be set in opposition to the Sirach text, where so many of the terms used in this passage occur together in the same context.

26. G. N. Stanton, *Gospel,* 368-71, disputes the link with Sir 51:23-27 (as do Gundry, 220; D. J. Verseput, *Rejection,* 145; Davies and Allison, 2:292-93). Stanton is of course right in saying that the Matthean emphasis is very different from that of Sirach, as noted above, in particular with the inclusion of the portrait of Jesus as meek and lowly, which has no parallel in the Sirach text, but that does not mean that the verbal echoes (which Stanton understates) are coincidental. Rather, this is a deliberate reangling of a familiar text to say something wholly new about *Jesus,* which is in continuity but also and

The invitation to "come here to me" is an important counterbalance to the statement in v. 27 that the knowledge of God is open only to those to whom the Son "is willing" to reveal him. That willingness is here shown to be not restrictive but open-ended, the invitation being issued to "all." The only requirement is that those who come to him must recognize their need for help and be willing to accept his yoke and learn from him. This is an invitation which the "wise and intelligent" may well choose to ignore, while the "little children" come willingly. The invitation is there for all, but (as in vv. 20-24) not all will respond to it; many are invited but few are chosen (see on 22:14).

The "toiling" and "loading" which form the background to this invitation[27] are not explained. They may be metaphors for the difficulties and pressures of life in general,[28] but in 23:4 "heavy, cumbersome burdens on people's shoulders" is a metaphor for the legal and ethical demands made by the scribes and Pharisees. The metaphor of a yoke, which in the OT commonly denoted social or political oppression (Gen 27:40; Exod 6:6-7; 1 Kgs 12:4-14; Isa 58:6, 9; Jer 28:2-14, etc.) and had a strongly pejorative sense, came to be used in later Jewish literature for the demands of the law upon people's obedience, usually understood in a positive sense, an obligation freely accepted by "putting on the yoke of the Torah."[29] It is possible, then, that here we should understand the heavy burdens in the light of 23:4 as the unreasonable demands of the scribes with their excessive concern to regulate people's behavior; cf. Acts 15:10, where the "yoke" is an unreasonable legal demand. But the wording in this passage does not make that application explicit, and a wider reference to life's difficulties cannot be ruled out.[30]

---

more importantly in contrast with what Sirach said about Wisdom. I do not find it as hard as Stanton does to suppose that Matthew was capable of combining, and expecting his readers to combine, the different portraits of Jesus as Wisdom, the Son, and the humble Servant, all into a single christological package.

27. Note the repetition of "loaded" / "burden" (from the same Greek root φορτ-) and the two references to a "yoke."

28. Or, as Carter, 259, typically argues, more specifically "life under Roman imperial control and its unjust political and socioeconomic structures." He accordingly goes on to interpret Jesus' yoke as "freedom from Rome's reign" (260).

29. C. Deutsch, *Hidden Wisdom,* 115-16, 126-28. The metaphor is well illustrated by *m. 'Abot* 3:5: "He who takes upon himself the yoke of the Torah, from him shall be taken away the yoke of the kingdom and the yoke of worldly care; he who throws off the yoke of the Torah, on him will be laid the yoke of the kingdom and the yoke of worldly care." Despite the overwhelmingly negative connotations of "yoke" in the OT, there is slight OT precedent for this later Jewish usage in Jer 2:20; 5:5; Lam 3:27.

30. G. N. Stanton, *Gospel,* 372-75, discusses whether the "toiling and heavily loaded" are the wider crowds (note "harassed and dejected" in 9:36) or more specifically the disciples, whose tribulations in mission have been set out in ch. 10, and concludes that

448

29 The animal yoke, which harnesses two animals together to pull a plow or cart, is to be distinguished from the human yoke, which is worn by a single person to distribute the weight of a load across the shoulders.[31] Each is an unwelcome restriction which is gladly thrown off when the work is done, but the purpose of the human yoke is to make it easier to carry or pull a load. If there is a burden to be borne, it is better with a yoke than without. The pejorative use of "yoke" imagery in the OT, if it refers to the human yoke (as it apparently does in Jer 27:2), therefore focuses not so much on the function of the yoke itself as on the unwanted imposition of the burden and the servitude it implies; the rabbinic use, on the other hand, focuses on the willing acceptance of an aid to carrying. The animal yoke is the basis of two NT metaphorical uses which focus on joining two people together (2 Cor 6:14; Phil 4:3),[32] but here, as in most Jewish usage, it is more likely the single human yoke which is in view. However appealing the idea of being "in double harness with Jesus" may be, that is not the point. He is offering those who are finding their loads too hard to carry a new yoke which, far from adding to their oppression, will ease the burden and, paradoxically, will bring not further toil but "rest."

Jesus' yoke, like that of the Torah (and of Wisdom in Sir 51:26), is one of "learning." Discipleship (from the same Greek root, "learn") is a lifelong process of learning how to live as God requires. But this learning, unlike that of the scribes (23:4), brings not weariness but "rest for your souls." "Souls" here translates the same term *psychē* which I have normally translated "life" (2:20; 6:25; 10:39; see further on 16:25-26), but in 10:28 "soul" (see p. 399, n. 4). "Rest for your lives" would be an awkward English idiom; *psychē* denotes as usual the true being of the person, so here the reference is to rest at the deepest level.[33] If there is a specific reference in this passage to the "burdens" of scribal demands (see above), we should remember that the "rest" Jesus offers is not a relaxation of the demands of righteousness (rather the opposite: see 5:20 and the following examples), but a new relationship with God which makes it possible to fulfill them. It is not the removal of any yoke but a new and "kind" yoke which makes the burdens "light."

A "yoke" implies obedience, indeed often slavery (Gal 5:1; 1 Tim

---

the latter is the primary reference. The apparently unrestricted appeal, "Come to me, all who . . . ," convinces most interpreters that the intended audience is wider. Indeed, as Gundry, n. 123, points out, those who follow Jesus, far from being in distress, have a "kind yoke" and a "light burden."

31. See J. Jeremias, *Parables,* 194.

32. Other NT references to a yoke, however, use the metaphor in its OT sense of oppression (Acts 15:10; Gal 5:1; 1 Tim 6:1).

33. This dimension is probably not brought out clearly enough by Hagner's otherwise valid translation "rest for yourselves" (Hagner, 1.322).

6:1); what makes the difference is what sort of master one is serving. So the beneficial effect of Jesus' yoke derives from the character of the one who offers it.[34] Human convention finds it hard to envisage as "meek and lowly" one who can claim that everything has been entrusted to him by God and who has just been declaring in forthright terms God's judgment on those who have rejected his message. But in the kingdom of heaven meekness is not incompatible with authority,[35] and in 12:15-21 we shall be reminded of the nonconfrontational style of God's appointed Messiah. With those who are unresponsive and hostile to his message Jesus can be fierce (see ch. 23 passim), but to the "little children" to whom God has revealed the truth he is gentle and considerate, "lowly" not in the sense of being unaware of his exalted status but of not using it to browbeat those under his authority. His disciples will be called to adopt the same approach in 20:25-28 (as indeed they have been already in 5:3-10).

"You will find rest for your souls" echoes the Hebrew text of Jer 6:16 (LXX has "purification" instead of "rest"), where it is the reward Yahweh offers to those who find and walk in the good way.[36] That Jesus now issues the same promise under his own authority says much for the christology underlying this extraordinary pericope. As in the beatitudes of 5:3-10, there is no doubt an eschatological dimension to the rest which Jesus offers,[37] but that does not mean that the offer has no relevance to the problems encountered by disciples in this life; it is for the present as well as for the future, just as the "sabbath rest which still remains for the people of God" in Heb 4:1-11 is nonetheless one which its readers are exhorted to enter "today."

30 A comfortably fitting yoke and a light burden is the ideal combination. *Chrēstos,* "kind,"[38] is of course a personal term not appropriate literally to a yoke; it is transferred to the metaphor from the person whose service the yoke symbolizes. Contrast the "heavy, cumbersome burdens" imposed by the scribes and Pharisees (23:4). The lightness of Jesus' yoke depends not only on his personal character as described in v. 29 but also on his new inter-

---

34. D. J. Verseput, *Rejection,* 149-51, helpfully discusses the nature of Jesus' "meekness" and its relevance to this context.

35. In both 5:5 and 21:5 meekness is deliberately set in paradoxical connection with ruling.

36. M. Knowles, *Jeremiah,* 214-17.

37. S. Bacchiocchi, *AUSS* 22 (1984) 296-301, argues that the "rest" alludes to the sabbath, viewed as a foretaste of the messianic age, so that this invitation builds on the messianic claims implied in vv. 25-27.

38. In 1 Pet 2:3, χρηστὸς ὁ Κύριος, Peter is probably already exploiting the similarity of sound between χρηστός and Χριστός which became an irresistible source of wordplay for the early Christian apologists. The word is not common in the NT, but it is unlikely that any such wordplay was in view here.

pretation of the Torah, which, in contrast with the scribal concern for detailed regulation, enables a person to see beyond the surface level of dos and don'ts to the true underlying purpose of God (see the discussion of 5:17-48 above). A striking example of this difference of approach to lawkeeping will follow immediately in 12:1-14, which will reveal two contrasting ways of understanding the "rest" which the sabbath was meant to provide.

H. JESUS' AUTHORITY IS CHALLENGED (12:1-45)

In 11:25-30 the narrative has reached a high point, not only in the remarkable christological revelations contained in Jesus' brief prayer, declaration, and invitation, but also in that we have been reminded that not everyone has shared in the unresponsiveness which Jesus has castigated in 11:16-24. There will be a similar "high point" in 12:46-50, before the third main discourse of the gospel analyzes by means of parables the reasons for the varied response encountered by Jesus and his message of the kingdom of heaven. But before we reach that point, Matthew continues to set out the narrative basis for that discourse by further exploring the way people in Galilee (and especially now the leaders of opinion) have reacted to Jesus' claims. In ch. 11 we heard about the failure of people in general to recognize and respond to Jesus as the Messiah; now the narrative plumbs lower depths, as we hear of those who are not merely indifferent to Jesus but actively opposed to him. Three areas of controversy stand out in this chapter: Jesus' attitude to the sabbath (vv. 1-14), his exorcisms (vv. 22-37), and the basis of his authority as it is challenged in the demand for an authenticating "sign" (vv. 38-45). At each point we meet people in positions of religious leadership who confront Jesus and challenge his authority to act as he has been doing, "the Pharisees" in vv. 2, 14, and 24 and "some of the scribes and Pharisees" in v. 38. For them Jesus is a law-breaker (vv. 1-14), an agent of Satan (vv. 24-32), and a self-appointed "teacher" with no proper authorization (vv. 38-42). As a result, already at this relatively early point in the story we hear of a formulated plan to eliminate Jesus (12:14), even though it will not in fact be in Galilee and under Pharisaic auspices that Jesus will eventually be executed, but under the priestly regime of Jerusalem. Matthew will have more to say of Galilean opposition to Jesus in 13:53–14:2; 15:1-20; 16:1-4, but already by the end of ch. 12 the main lines have been laid down.

But in this section of the gospel we hear not only of the opposition but also, and at greater length, of Jesus' response to it both in overt justification of his mission (vv. 3-8, 11-12, 25-29, 39-42) and in polemical comment on his opponents and their attitude (vv. 30-37, 43-45). In the course of this teaching we shall three times meet the claim, in relation to the recognized au-

451

thorities of OT Israel, "something greater/more is here" (vv. 6, 41, 42; cf. the same idea without the phrase in vv. 3-4; see comments below), a phrase which occurs only here in the gospel. This is a pointer to the issue of authority which underlies this whole section and which comes into the open in the demand for a sign in v. 38. Jesus sets his own status alongside that of the highest authority figures of the OT, David the king, the priests in the temple, Jonah the prophet, and Solomon the king and wise man, and (implicitly in the case of David but explicitly for the others) claims that "something greater" has now superseded those recognized authorities. Here is one of the most striking examples of the typological character of Matthew's presentation of Jesus: king, priest, temple, prophet, and wise man all provide models against which Jesus stands as "something greater."[1] It is the failure of Israel's current religious leadership to recognize this new and decisive phase in God's dealings with his people which makes them more culpable even than Israel's old pagan neighbors (vv. 41-42), and leaves them perilously close to that fundamental rebellion against God which cannot be forgiven (vv. 31-32).

Set within this story of confrontation is Matthew's longest formula-quotation (vv. 17-21), comprising the whole introductory paragraph in Isaiah's portrait of the Servant of Yahweh (Isa 42:1-4). In context it serves as a counterbalance to the harshly polemical tone of much of the chapter. Jesus, even though he must denounce unbelief when it confronts him, is characterized essentially rather by gentleness and patient trust in God. His non-confrontational style is illustrated by his withdrawal in the face of the Pharisaic threat (vv. 15-16). At the same time, however, Matthew here adds a further strand to his messianic presentation of Jesus. He has already noted Jesus' role as Yahweh's servant in 8:17, and already the voice from heaven at his baptism has suggestively echoed the opening line of this long quotation. Now Matthew spells it out, and by continuing the quotation into v. 4 he points forward to the future triumph of this gentle Messiah, despite the seriousness of the opposition which he now confronts.

I described 11:25-30 as a christological high point in the gospel, and so it is in its concentrated presentation of Jesus as the unique Son of God and the embodiment of divine Wisdom. But here in ch. 12, in the more diffuse form of the continuing Galilean narrative, further christological reflections come thick and fast for the reader who is prepared to look below the narrative surface and try to understand what is at stake in the debate on Jesus' authority as it unfolds in confrontation with the Pharisees.

---

1. See further my *Matthew: Evangelist*, 189-91.

1. Conflicts over Keeping the Sabbath (12:1-14)

1 *At that time Jesus went through the grainfields on the sabbath. His disciples were hungry, and began to pick ears of grain and eat them.* 2 *When the Pharisees saw this, they said to him, "Look, your disciples are doing something which ought not to be done on the sabbath."* 3 *But he replied, "Haven't you read what David did when he and his companions were hungry,* 4 *how he went into the house of God and ate[2] the ceremonial loaves,[3] which[4] it was not lawful for him or his companions to eat, but only the priests?* 5 *Or haven't you read in the law that on the sabbath the priests in the temple violate the sabbath without incurring guilt?* 6 *But I tell you that something greater than the temple is here.* 7 *If you had known what this means, 'I want mercy, not sacrifice,' you would not have passed judgment on the guiltless.* 8 *For the Son of Man is the Lord of the sabbath."*

9 *And he moved on from there and went into their synagogue.[5]* 10 *And there was there a man with a paralyzed[6] arm.[7] So they questioned him, "Is it permissible to heal on the sabbath?" (they were planning to bring a charge against him).[8]* 11 *He replied, "Which man*

2. The two early MSS ‭א‬ and B have this verb in the plural; all others agree with Mark and Luke in giving it in the singular. Since Matthew does not, like Mark and Luke, go on to mention that he "gave them to those who were with him," the plural might be his way of including the rest of the group in the action, and the majority reading would then represent a mechanical assimilation to Mark and Luke. But it is equally possible that copyists might for the same reason feel the need to include the companions in the verb, and the singular ἔφαγεν follows more naturally from the singular εἰσῆλθεν which occurs in all three gospels. Two Alexandrian MSS, however august, should probably not be allowed to outweigh the rest of the textual tradition.

3. οἱ ἄρτοι τῆς προθέσεως, literally "the loaves of the presentation," is the term used in LXX 1 Sam 21:7 for the twelve loaves of consecrated bread regularly placed in the tabernacle/temple, and known in the OT as the "bread of the presence" (which is variously rendered elsewhere in the LXX).

4. Matthew's syntax is slightly awkward here, literally, ". . . loaves, which (singular) it was not lawful for him to eat or his companions." The neuter singular ὃ οὐκ ἐξὸν ἦν denotes the action, not the loaves ("loaf" is masculine), but the following φαγεῖν presupposes a plural antecedent, οὕς.

5. Or "assembly"; see the comment on 4:23 and p. 149, n. 6.

6. Literally "dry," a term sometimes used for diseased parts of the body, usually to denote their nonfunctioning rather than a physical deformity. The cause may have been polio, or a stroke (cf. 1 Kgs 13:4).

7. χείρ is used both for the hand alone and for the arm, especially the forearm (including the hand). The action described in v. 13 may suggest that in this case it was not only the hand which was affected.

8. The Greek clause continues as part of the same sentence, literally "in order that

453

among you, if he has one[9] sheep which falls into a hole on the sab-
bath, will not get hold of it and pull it out? 12 So how much more is a
human being worth than a sheep? Well then,[10] it is permissible to do
good on the sabbath." 13 Then he said to the man, "Stretch out your
arm." And he stretched it out, and it was restored to health just like
the other.

   14 The Pharisees went out and consulted together against him
with a view to[11] getting rid of[12] him.

These two stories are both concerned with the keeping of the sabbath, a matter not only of legal debate but of national pride, the sabbath and circumcision being the most obvious distinguishing marks of the Jews as the people
of God.[13] This issue was remembered as a recurrent point of conflict between
Jesus and the scribes (Luke 13:10-17; 14:1-6; John 5:9-18; 7:19-24; 9:14-
16), though Matthew (like Mark) treats it only here. It is probably not accidental that it follows the offer of "rest" in 11:28-30, since "rest" was the de-

---

they might bring a charge against him," a subordinate clause dependent on the main verb
"questioned." But the intrusion of quotation marks in English makes it awkward to reproduce that syntax; a parenthetical comment achieves the same explanatory function.

   9. Most interpreters take "one" here as simply a Semitic way of expressing an indefinite article (cf. p. 323, n. 3). Some, however (e.g., Luz, 2:187-88), suggest that it is
emphatic, "a single sheep," and depicts a poor man who has only one sheep and so is anxious to rescue it. The wording does not require this, and when "one" sheep is singled out
in 18:12, it is in fact one out of a flock of a hundred, singled out because of its individual
danger, not because its owner has no other. The "one" here perhaps functions similarly, to
draw attention to the plight of the one rather than to suggest that he has no others.

   10. ὥστε, "with the result that," here functions as a logical inference from the
premises just stated.

   11. I take ὅπως here in its normal Matthean sense of "for the purpose of," though
its other sense of "how" might also be appropriate here, meaning that the consultation was
on the appropriate *means* of getting rid of Jesus, the end having already been agreed.

   12. While ἀπόλλυμι usually means "destroy," often as a virtual synonym for "kill"
(2:13; 8:25; 10:28; 22:7; 27:20), it can also mean to "lose" in a milder sense (10:6, 42;
15:24). This range of meaning provides the basis for a telling wordplay in 5:29-30; 10:39;
16:25. Here the desire of the Pharisees is certainly to be rid of Jesus, to get him out of the
way; the verb probably suggests, but does not necessarily demand, that they are already
thinking of having him killed.

   13. It was still remembered how the pious Jews who resisted Antiochus
Epiphanes had been prepared to die rather than violate the sabbath by fighting (1 Macc
2:29-39); subsequent reflection, however, had convinced them that the preservation of life
took priority over the sabbath (1 Macc 2:40-41). The book of *Jubilees,* from around the
same period, enthusiastically promotes the sabbath (which God and the angels observed
in heaven even before it was instituted on earth, *Jub.* 2:18, 30) and continues to insist on
the death penalty for those who break it (*Jub.* 50:8, 13).

clared aim of the sabbath law (Exod 23:12; Deut 5:14, etc.). Jesus' arguments attempt to restore the "rest" to what was in danger of becoming, under the weight of scribal elaborations of the law, more a burden than a blessing.[14]

The controversy centers not on whether the sabbath should be observed (there is no suggestion that Jesus questioned that) but on what that observance entailed in practical terms. A key term in this section is the impersonal verb *exestin*, "it is permissible, lawful," which occurs in vv. 2 ("ought"), 4 ("lawful"), and 10 and 12 ("permissible"). The OT commandment was clear, that no work was to be done. But what is "work"? OT case law and narrative precedent provided a few guidelines,[15] but it was a major concern of the scribes to work out more specific rules so that everyone could be sure what was and was not permissible. Two lengthy tractates of the Mishnah (*Šabbat* and *'Erubin*) are devoted to such rulings, often in meticulous detail, and while these did not reach their present form until the end of the second century, they are agreed to represent in principle the sort of discussions and rulings in which Pharisaic scribes were engaged in Jesus' day. Anyone who has not read through at least some of those two tractates will have little idea of the meticulous care, and sometimes ingenuity, which went into ensuring that every eventuality was covered and nothing was left to private judgment.

On the specific aspects of sabbath regulations raised in these two stories, see the comments below on vv. 1-2 (picking ears of grain) and v. 10 (healing). Fundamental to the rabbinic discussion was the agreed list (*m. Šabb.* 7:2)[16] of thirty-nine categories of activity which were to be classified as "work" for this purpose, some of which are very specific ("writing two letters, erasing in order to write two letters"), others so broad as to need considerable further specification ("building, pulling down"), while the last ("taking anything from one 'domain' [normally a private courtyard] to another") is so open-ended as to cover a vast range of daily activities. The thirty-nine categories of work do not explicitly include traveling, but this, too, was regarded as "work," a "sabbath day's journey" being limited to two thousand cubits, a little over half a mile. These two rules together made sabbath life potentially so inconvenient that the Pharisees developed an elabo-

14. D. J. Verseput, *Rejection*, treats 11:25–12:21 as a unified "segment" of the gospel, which he entitles "God's Mercy in Jesus" (p. 132), and regards 12:1-14 (to which he gives the heading "The Yoke of Mercy") as "expanding the same themes" as 11:25-30 (153).

15. Gathering manna (Exod 16:22-30) and firewood (Num 15:32-36); plowing and harvest (Exod 34:21); kindling a fire (Exod 35:3); trading (Neh 10:31; 13:15-22; Amos 8:5); carrying loads (Jer 17:19-27).

16. A few other "culpable" acts of a different nature are listed also in *m. Beṣah* 5:2. For earlier such lists from different Jewish circles see *Jub.* 50:6-13; CD 10:14–11:18.

rate system of "boundary extensions" (*'erubin*)[17] to allow more freedom of movement without violating the basic rules. The *'erub* system illustrates an essential element of all this scribal development of sabbath law: its aim was not simply to make life difficult (though it must often have seemed like that), but to work out a way in which people could cope with the practicalities of life within the limits of their very rigorous understanding of "work." The elaboration of details is intended to leave nothing to chance, so that no one can inadvertently come anywhere near violating the law itself. Some rabbis spoke about this as "putting up a fence around the law."

Jesus' disagreement with this Pharisaic approach centers on two considerations. The first (which is in view in vv. 3-6 and 8) is that of authority: who has the right to declare what is and is not forbidden on the sabbath? For the christological implications of Jesus' claim to such authority see the introductory comments on 12:1-45 above. The second (developed in vv. 11-12, and cf. v. 7) is the issue of priorities: as in 5:21-48, Jesus is concerned to get behind the regulations to the original spirit and intention of God's law. Jesus' key pronouncements on these two issues are v. 8, "The Son of Man is the Lord of the sabbath," and v. 12b, "It is permissible to do good on the sabbath." The effect of these two positive principles together is to call in question the whole scribal industry of sabbath regulation; no wonder they wanted to get rid of him.[18]

Jesus' critics are described as "Pharisees" in vv. 2 and 14, and the indefinite "they" of v. 10 must in context have the same reference. While Matthew has a clear tendency to single out Pharisees (often combined with scribes) as Jesus' principal opponents both in Galilee and in Judea,[19] on this particular issue the charge rings true.[20] The Mishnaic regulations to which I have referred are the product of the rabbis who represented the continuing Pharisaic leadership after the destruction of the temple. The Pharisaic party existed to promote and practice the most rigorous observance of the Torah, and the scribal elaborations of the law derived from the same ideological sta-

---

17. For a brief explanation see Schürer, 2:485.

18. A valuable article by D. M. Cohn-Sherbok in *JSNT* 2 (1979) 31-41 demonstrates that the arguments here attributed to Jesus are at several points not valid according to the accepted conventions of rabbinic interpretation of the Torah. He rightly concludes that, rather than trying to play the rabbis at their own game and getting it wrong, Jesus is setting his own rules of interpretation and teaching on his own authority, and that it was this challenge to the accepted norms, no less than the specific conclusions drawn, that alienated the Pharisees.

19. For Matthew's characterization of the Pharisees see my *Matthew: Evangelist,* 219-22.

20. See Keener, 351-53, on the historical probability of Jesus' confrontations, especially with the Pharisees.

ble (see comments on "scribes and Pharisees" in 5:20). Jesus' "free" attitude to sabbath observance was a direct challenge to the Pharisaic understanding of what it meant to do the will of God.[21]

1-2 "At that time" links these stories with 11:25-30, as the same phrase linked those verses with 11:16-24. Both the theme of "rest" (see above) and that of Jesus' "kind yoke" in contrast with the burdens of scribal demands (23:4) will be illustrated as Jesus' understanding of the sabbath is contrasted with that of the Pharisees — note especially the "mercy" of v. 7. The grainfields (probably of wheat or barley) must have been close to the town, since the disciples are not criticized for exceeding a sabbath day's journey, and the Pharisees themselves are depicted as present in the fields to confront them.[22] The disciples' hunger is mentioned to provide a basis for the link with the story of David in v. 3. It can hardly be taken as in itself a justification for overriding the sabbath law,[23] since casual pickings from a grainfield would not have contributed much toward alleviating real starvation;[24] Jesus will justify their action not on the basis of need (he does not, like Mark, mention "need" in v. 3) but of his own authority. The OT law allowed the poor to go into someone's field and pick grain by hand and eat it (Deut 23:25; cf. Lev 23:22),[25] but that is not the issue here; it is specifically that of sabbath law. Picking the grain could be understood as "reaping,"[26] and in order to eat it they would also have to rub the grain out of the husks (as Luke 6:1 specifically mentions), which could be understood as "threshing"; both of these activities occur in the list of thirty-nine forbidden acts (see above); even within the OT law itself "harvesting" on the sabbath is forbidden (Exod 34:21). The

---

21. On the whole issue of the attitude to the sabbath in Matthew, and on the present passage in particular, see the very careful study by Y.-E. Yang, *Jesus and the Sabbath in Matthew's Gospel,* to which several specific references will be made in what follows. Yang's work takes up and develops the general perspective, and in some cases the specific proposals, of R. J. Banks, *Jesus,* 113-31.

22. On the plausibility of the historical setting see Y.-E. Yang, *Jesus,* 168-69. See also Keener, 351, n. 43, for further information about sabbath restrictions.

23. Keener, 353, points out that the sabbath was a day of feasting, and that fasting on the sabbath was forbidden, and suggests that the alleviation of hunger was therefore a sabbath duty (similarly Luz, 2:180). But there is a difference between "being hungry" and formal fasting, and the text gives no hint of the latter.

24. See below on v. 10 for the danger of death as a reason for suspending sabbath regulations — but "hungry" does not mean "in danger of death from starvation"! Carter, 262-67, lays unusually heavy stress on the mention of hunger, and argues that the point at issue is primarily that of "access to food": "Jesus resists controls on the sabbath which harm the poor by limiting access to food resources." Other interpreters have not been able to find this socioeconomic issue emphasized in Matthew's narrative.

25. For the *Pe'ah* regulations see M. Casey, *NTS* 34 (1988) 1-4.

26. For varying rabbinic views on this see Y.-E. Yang, *Jesus,* 170, n. 133.

Pharisees address Jesus rather than his disciples because it is understood that a teacher is responsible for his disciples' behavior,[27] and his reply will accordingly focus on his own authority, not theirs.

3-4 Jesus' reply, presented as a single speech, consists of two related OT analogies (vv. 3-4, 5-6) together with a prophetic quotation which exposes the underlying issue (v. 7), followed by a pronouncement (v. 8) which summarizes the thrust of the earlier analogies.[28] Both analogies are introduced by "Haven't you read?" (vv. 3, 5), a formula which also occurs elsewhere to introduce a polemical or argumentative quotation from the OT (cf. 19:4; 21:16, 42; 22:31); it suggests that what Jesus is about to say should have been obvious to anyone familiar with the OT text, though in fact in all these cases there is a considerable element of creativity about the way Jesus applies the familiar text. The second analogy is drawn explicitly from "the law" (see below); the first takes up a historical narrative.[29]

The first analogy is with the story of David at Nob (the temporary sanctuary set up after the Philistines destroyed Shiloh), as related in 1 Sam 21:1-6. The OT narrative does not state that David himself "went into the house of God," but that Ahimelech the priest gave him the ceremonial bread which was kept inside the sanctuary where only the priests could go. The assumption would naturally be that Ahimelech brought it out for David (or perhaps more likely gave David the old loaves which had just been replaced), but Jesus' account, by having David himself enter the sanctuary, makes his action even bolder than the OT original. David's irregular demand is explained by the comment that he and his men[30] were hungry, as Jesus' disciples also are (v. 1). The OT story does not mention the sabbath, but it could be inferred (and was by some later Jewish interpreters) that it took place on the sabbath since that was the day when the "bread of the presence" was regularly replaced (Lev 24:8). But what David infringed was not the sabbath law

27. This theme is helpfully explored by D. Daube, *NTS* 19 (1972/3) 1-15.

28. On the use of the OT in this pericope as a whole see my *Matthew: Evangelist*, 169-71.

29. Keener, 357, oddly speaks of Jesus' scriptural arguments in vv. 3-8 as drawn from "the law, the prophets, and the writings"; they are in fact from the former prophets (vv. 3-4), the law (vv. 5-6), and the latter prophets (v. 7).

30. The double mention of David's companions in vv. 3 and 4 makes the analogy clearer, in that Jesus, like David, is acting on behalf of hungry followers (see p. 453, n. 2, on whether Matthew mentions that the companions also ate the loaves). In the OT narrative David appears alone, but uses his intended rendezvous with his "young men" to persuade the priest Ahimelech to provide food, which it is understood that the "young men" will share with him. Since David is in the process of escaping to Gath, where he appears to arrive alone, commentators generally regard the "young men," as well as David's "secret mission" from the king, as a convenient fiction, but the OT narrative does not make this clear.

as such but the regulation that only priests were to eat the ceremonial loaves (Lev 24:9). It is David's authority to override a legal prescription, not his attitude to the sabbath as such, which is at issue in Jesus' argument. There would be little force in an argument which simply asserted that if the law has been broken once it can be broken again. The point is *who* it was who was, exceptionally, allowed to break it. Ahimelech's willingness to bend the rules must be related to his assumption that David, as not only the king's emissary but also himself the anointed successor to Saul, and now engaged on a holy mission (1 Sam 21:4-5), stood in a category apart from other Israelites. It was David, *as David,* who was permitted to do what was not lawful; and now Jesus places his own authority alongside that of David. Matthew, as the evangelist who most often portrays Jesus as the "son of David," is the more likely to have appreciated the force of this christological argument.[31] Such a logic seems required here by the following analogy (v. 5), which also speaks of those whose special position allowed them to do what others might not do. The concluding declaration that "something greater is here" (v. 6) may then be seen as implied here too: something greater than David is here.[32] In 22:41-45 Jesus will argue that the Messiah is more than just a son of David, and that claim is applied in a veiled form to establish his special authority here.

5-6 The second analogy is not with a specific narrative but with a principle in the OT legal code (note "in the law," as opposed to the lesser authority of the book of Samuel); in rabbinic terms, we move now from haggadah to halakhah. It is not stated what specific "violation of the sabbath" is in view here, but the regular duties of the priests serving in the temple involved them in what for others would have been classed as "work,"[33] particularly in the offering of sacrifices, with all the preparation and butchery involved (Num 28:9-10), and in the changing of the ceremonial loaves (Lev 24:5-8).[34] Their

31. This point is made by Y.-E. Yang, *Jesus,* 176, as part of an argument for a Davidic typology as the basis for the allusion to 1 Sam 21:1-6 (ibid., 174-77) which repays careful study.

32. This point is argued as an example of christological typology in my *Jesus and the OT,* 46-47. Such an interpretation seems more appropriate to the flow of Jesus' argument in vv. 3-8 and to the Davidic emphasis of this gospel than the proposal of D. J. Verseput, *Rejection,* 161-62, that Jesus' argument appeals only to the mercy of God.

33. For some minor acts which may be carried out on the sabbath "in the temple but not in the provinces" cf. *m. 'Erub.* 10:11-15. For Passover duties which "override the sabbath" see *m. Pesah.* 6:1-2.

34. E. Levine, *NTS* 22 (1975/6) 481, suggests a closer analogy to the situation in the grainfields in that the Pharisees defended against Sadducean opposition their right to reap the sheaves for the offering of the firstfruits on the sabbath (*m. Menah.* 10:3, 9). The situation is indeed more analogous, but this practice was clearly not regarded as "written in the law," or the Pharisees would not have needed to mount a special argument for it; indeed, the relevant OT text (Lev 23:10-14) speaks explicitly of presenting the offering on

"guiltlessness" does not need to be argued in the law: the mere fact that the law requires these actions indicates that they are in accordance with God's will. The basis for this exception is in who they are (the priests, appointed for this divine service) and the institution which requires it (the temple, as the focal point of God's presence among his people). It is a matter of priorities, the authority of the office and the necessity of the service overriding the sabbath rules which for other people and other purposes remain inviolable.[35]

This time the logic is explicit: "something greater than the temple is here." It is hard to overestimate the shock value of this pronouncement. The tabernacle set up under God's directions in the wilderness, and the fixed temple which had succeeded it, were understood to be the focus of God's relation with his people. The temple was more than a place of worship. It was a symbol of nationhood (and the more so since political power had been assumed by Rome). Its priestly establishment was the nearest thing Israel still possessed to a government of its own. To threaten the temple, as Jeremiah had discovered long ago, was to commit unpardonable treason. As the story of Jesus unfolds, his negative attitude to the temple and its activities (21:12-16, 18-22; 23:38; 24:1-2) will become the central symbol of his challenge to the status quo (see 21:23-27) and the issue which above all will unite the people against him. At his trial it will play a central role (26:60-61), and on the cross it will still be thrown against him (27:40). But in the discourse of ch. 24 Jesus will explain how the coming destruction of the temple symbolizes the end of the old order, and in 27:51 the tearing of the temple curtain shows that that time has now come. This preliminary comment in 12:6 is a pointer to a recurrent and disturbing theme in Matthew's portrayal of what the coming of the kingship of God must mean for Israel and for the sacred institution which lies at its ideological heart.[36]

But if the analogies concern the actions of people (David and the priests), why does Jesus speak in the neuter of "some*thing* greater"?[37] Here in v. 6 this might be explained formally by the fact that the immediate point of comparison is an institution, the temple, not a person. But when a very

---

the day after the sabbath, without specifying when it was to be reaped. Nor did the reaping of the sheaves take place "in the temple." The point of Jesus' argument does not depend on a similarity in the action, but on the recognition within the OT law of the principle of authorized work on the sabbath.

35. *T. Šabb.* 15:16 quotes R. Akiba as directly comparing the rules for the temple service and for the sabbath and concluding that the former were the more binding. In *b. Šabb.* 132b there is an explicit ruling that "Temple service takes precedence over the sabbath."

36. On the temple in Matthew see further my *Matthew: Evangelist,* 214-16.

37. Keener, 356, suggests an apologetic motive: "Jesus' self-claim is veiled enough to prevent accusations of blasphemy . . . but obvious enough to enrage them."

similar formula is used again in vv. 41 and 42, the point of comparison will be individual people of the OT, Jonah and Solomon, yet the neuter is found there as well. Both here and there it is the authority of Jesus himself which is immediately at issue, but not so much Jesus in his own person as in his *role,* as now (in comparison with priest, prophet, and king in the OT) the true mediator between God and his people; such a role is some*thing* new. Here in v. 6, where the contrast is with the temple rather than with a person, the neuter is perhaps also intended to point beyond Jesus himself to the new principle of God's relationship with his people which will result from Jesus' ministry, a principle which will remain embodied in the community of his disciples even when Jesus himself is no longer present. This at least seems to have been the conclusion drawn by other NT writers, who can speak of the church corporately as now constituting God's true temple (1 Cor 3:16-17; 1 Pet 2:5).

7 A third OT argument offers not an analogy but a basic prophetic principle which justifies Jesus' less formal approach to sabbath observance.[38] Hos 6:6 has already been quoted against the Pharisees in 9:13 when they objected to Jesus' loose attitude to the purity laws as shown in his eating with sinners. Here the specific issue is different, but the principle is the same: in God's scale of priorities a positive concern for the good of others ("mercy")[39] takes precedence over formal compliance with ritual regulations. Jesus quotes from Hosea a maxim which matches in its radical open-endedness his own pronouncement in the following story (v. 12): "It is permissible to do good on the sabbath." For the text quoted, and for the underlying principle with its wide attestation in the prophets and psalms, see on 9:13.[40]

The brief maxim, "I want mercy, not sacrifice," is given here without an explicit quotation-formula, and presented simply as a well-known saying.

38. The suggestion of D. J. Verseput, *Rejection,* that the central issue in this whole pericope is "the mercy of God" (see above, p. 455, n. 14 and p. 459, n. 32), finds more obvious support in this verse (see ibid., 166-71) than in the surrounding arguments, which focus on the personal authority of Jesus.

39. D. Hill's study, *NTS* 24 (1977/8) 107-19, of the significance of Matthew's uses of Hos 6:6 concludes that ἔλεος here carries much of the force of the Hebrew *ḥesed* which it translates, and so signifies "that loyal love to God which manifests itself in acts of mercy and lovingkindness" (110); this, Hill argues, is the "better righteousness" required in 5:20.

40. Further nuances are suggested by Y.-E. Yang, *Jesus,* 185-87: (i) a christological note to complement vv. 3-4 and 5-6, in that Jesus is the merciful one who fulfills God's will revealed in Hos 6:6 and as the one greater than the temple declares the priority of mercy over temple sacrifice; (ii) a direct link with the sabbath issue in that in God's original intention the sabbath was a merciful institution, associated with the redemption from Egypt. Luz, 2:181-82, suggests that the "something greater" in v. 6 is in fact to be understood as the "mercy" of v. 7, which takes precedence over the (temple) sacrifices.

No doubt the Pharisees "knew" it, but they had not grasped its practical implications. If they had, Jesus argues, they would not have raised this petty objection against his disciples' behavior. By calling his disciples "guiltless" Jesus assumes what he has not in fact argued directly, that their action was in
fact "permissible." His explicit argument has so far been concerned with his
own authority to declare what may and may not be done, and v. 8 will also
conclude on that note. But to call the disciples "guiltless" also suggests that
the Pharisaic interpretation of the sabbath law was in itself wrong. They had
found guilt where God saw none. The direct echo of the same word in v. 5
(the priests who work on the sabbath are also "guiltless") implicitly claims
for Jesus' verdict the same divine sanction as the law had provided for the
priests.[41]

8 For "the Son of Man" see on 8:20, where I argued that here it denotes Jesus himself, in his earthly ministry, as "a figure of unique authority."
Dan 7:13-14, from which the title almost certainly derives, is a vision of universal authority over all peoples exercised by the "one like a son of man"
from his heavenly throne. Here, as in 9:6 (see comments there), that future
authority is anticipated; the Son of Man is already "Lord." As in 9:6, some
interpreters have argued that in these references to authority on earth the
phrase "son of man" originally carried[42] its generic sense rather than being a
title for Jesus alone, so that this saying would have meant in effect, "Human
beings are in control of the sabbath." This is sometimes justified by comparison with the saying which precedes it in Mark (but not in Matthew), "the sabbath was made for man, not man for the sabbath" (Mark 2:27). But that saying does not use the phrase "the son of man." Moreover, Matthew's omission
of that saying suggests that he did not regard it as the basis for his v. 8; indeed, it is more likely that he omitted it because it seemed to him to be potentially in conflict with the unique authority attributed to "the Son of Man." After vv. 3-6 it would be a strange *non sequitur* to claim a general human
freedom to dispense with sabbath law. The argument has been that Jesus, as
Jesus ("something greater"), alone has the authority to interpret that law for
his disciples, and it is in that sense that he, not they (or the Pharisees), is
"Lord of the sabbath."

In that case this concluding pronouncement[43] is christologically even

41. Y.-E. Yang, *Jesus,* 182-83, adds the consideration that if the guiltlessness of
the priests derived from their being "in the temple," that of the disciples derives from their
being with Jesus, the one who is "greater than the temple."

42. There is surely no doubt that Matthew and his readers would have understood
"the son of man" to refer to Jesus; the issue is only whether this agreed Christian usage
has distorted what was originally a nontitular use by Jesus himself.

43. It is sometimes seen as an editorial comment (presumably originally by Mark)
rather than the continuation of Jesus' speech, but there is no obvious reason for believing

more daring than what has preceded it in vv. 3-6. Not only is the Son of Man greater than David and the temple, but he is "Lord" of the institution which is traced in the OT to God's direct command (Gen 2:3), enshrined in the Decalogue which is the central codification of God's requirements for his people, and described by God as "*my* sabbath" (Exod 31:13; Lev 19:3, 30; Isa 56:4, etc.; cf. the recurrent phrase "a sabbath to/for Yahweh," Exod 16:23; 20:10; 35:2, etc.). Against that background to speak of humanity in general as "lord of the sabbath" would be unthinkable; to speak of an individual human being as such is to make the most extraordinary claim to an authority on a par with that of God himself.[44]

9   The second sabbath story is presented as a direct sequel to the first, occurring on the same day and involving presumably the same group of Pharisees, who are introduced in v. 10 simply as "they" but again identified as "the Pharisees" in v. 14. We have heard of Jesus' presence and teaching in "their synagogues" more generally (4:23; 9:35), but this is the first account of a specific synagogue visit, even though this was presumably Jesus' regular practice (so Luke 4:16). In this case "their synagogue" should probably be taken as that of Capernaum, Jesus' normal base in Galilee (4:13; 8:5; 9:1). The use of "their" here for a single synagogue is perhaps more significant than in places where the plural has a more clearly geographical connotation (see p. 150, n. 7). Geographically the synagogue at Capernaum was as much Jesus' local synagogue as it was "theirs," but Matthew's use of the possessive probably begins to hint at the growing rift between Jesus and the synagogue establishment, which vv. 1-8 have just illustrated. The Pharisaic group no doubt had a leading role in the local synagogue (23:2, 6-7 and cf. 6:2, 5), and may not have been reluctant to have it described as "theirs"!

10   In this case the Pharisees, instead of criticizing after the event, take the initiative in raising the issue of sabbath observance in the form of a test case. This aspect of Matthew's telling of the story stands out in contrast

---

that Matthew so intended it, especially as the earlier commment on the earthly authority of the Son of Man (9:6) is clearly presented as part of Jesus' words. It would be unique in the gospels as an editorial use of the title "the Son of Man."

44. Y.-E. Yang, *Jesus*, 193-95 (and see also his more general discussion in ibid., 224-29), develops from this conclusion a view of the sabbath as "fulfilled" (in the sense of 5:17) in the coming of Jesus and therefore as no longer obligatory for his disciples; he thus understands Matthew as "encouraging his community to give up sabbath observance and instead to focus on Jesus, who is the Lord of the sabbath" (ibid., 229). It is arguable that this pericope potentially lends itself to such an inference, but perhaps more questionable whether, either in the narrative context of Jesus' dispute with the Pharisees or in Matthew's own church context, such a far-reaching conclusion was yet in view. Matthew's Jesus nowhere directly calls in question the sabbath principle as such; the issue is always how it should be translated into practical guidance for living.

to that in Mark and Luke, both of whom refer only to the Pharisees' unspoken criticisms, which Jesus then brings into the open. Matthew does not say that the Pharisees had brought the man with the paralyzed arm to the synagogue specifically for this purpose, but their question, though phrased as a general inquiry, is clearly a challenge as to how Jesus will deal with this specific case — there were presumably other people in bad health in the synagogue, but only one is mentioned. Matthew's parenthetical comment, "they were planning to bring a charge against him," does not allow us to read this as a purely academic debate.

In all the gospel accounts of sabbath controversies except the grainfield incident the specific issue is healing (though in John 5:10 there is also the issue of the healed man carrying his sleeping mat). Healing was not in itself included among the thirty-nine forbidden acts, and was less easy to associate with one of them, especially as Jesus' method of healing usually involved little or no physical action, and in this case was simply a word of command. But Mishnaic discussions assume, as do the scribes and Pharisees in the gospel stories,[45] that healing is not allowed on the sabbath,[46] and simply discuss when an exception might be permitted. This was normally only where there was imminent danger of death (*m. Yoma* 8:6); assistance in childbirth was also permitted (*m. Šabb.* 18:3), presumably because it could not be postponed until the next day.[47] There is no such urgency in any of Jesus' sabbath healings, and that is particularly obvious in the test case here chosen: a paralyzed arm, though very inconvenient, is not a threat to life, and the healing can safely be left until tomorrow.

11-12 Jesus appeals not to a legal authority but to the common sense which normal people would follow — "Which man among you?" while it is formally addressed to the Pharisees, is surely intended to be heard and reflected on by everyone in the synagogue. It so happens that we have extant records relating to just this situation both in rabbinic discussion and in a ruling at Qumran.[48] The latter (CD 11:13-14)[49] is unequivocal: "No one may help an animal to give birth on the sabbath; and if it falls into a well or into a pit he may not lift it out on the sabbath." But the rabbinic discussion, which

45. Cf. also Mark 1:32, where the people wait to bring people for healing until after the sabbath is over.
46. For a few specific medical rulings see *m. Šabb.* 14:3; 22:6; *m. 'Ed.* 2:5. According to *t. Šabb.* 16:22, the Shammaites (unlike the Hillelites) even forbade praying for healing on the sabbath.
47. See further E. Lohse, *TDNT* 7:14-15.
48. See Y.-E. Yang, *Jesus,* 201-3, for details of the Qumran and rabbinic evidence.
49. See the discussion of this text in Y.-E. Yang, *Jesus,* 62-67, and ibid., 67-68 for a disputed reconstruction of 4Q251 which treats the same subject.

comes from a later period (*b. Šabb.* 128b), shows a different spirit: some said that articles might be thrown into the hole to allow the animal to climb out, others that it might be fed on the sabbath but lifted out the next day, but a concluding ruling is that the relief of animal suffering should be allowed to override the sabbath regulation. The instinct which led to this later ruling (together with the less altruistic desire to protect a valuable asset!) was evidently already prevalent in Jesus' time in common practice, so that Jesus could take it for granted and assume that the Pharisees would not object to it. The further assumption, which appears to need no argument, that a human being is more important than an animal (echoing a point already made; see comments at 6:26 and cf. 10:31) then establishes *a fortiori* the permissibility of measures for human welfare, and thus of healing, on the sabbath. While it might be argued that there is a more urgent need for the rescue of the animal than for the healing of the arm, we are not told that the point was contested.

The corollary that "it is permissible to do good on the sabbath" goes far beyond the specific issue under discussion. Its very lack of specificity is in striking contrast to the rabbinic desire to leave nothing to individual judgment. As a guide to sabbath observance it could result in widely divergent practice, and it lends itself to use as a convenient self-justification for any chosen course of action. What especially distinguishes it from the rabbinic rulings, and indeed from most of the OT laws themselves, is that it is positive rather than prohibitive. Like Jesus' version of the Golden Rule (7:12), it puts the onus on the individual to decide what is "good" and how it may or may not be squared with the equally "good" aim of the sabbath law, to provide a day of holiness and rest.

13 As in several other healing stories (8:5-13; 9:1-8; 15:21-28), the actual cure is related quite briefly; the focus of interest is on the dialogue which leads up to it rather than on the healing in itself — or, to use the terms of traditional form criticism, this is a pronouncement story rather than a miracle story. But the dialogue has set up a dramatic tension, and Jesus' decisive command resolves that tension in favor of "doing good" over against the Pharisaic rules. The healing, as usual with Jesus, is instantaneous. It is also purely verbal, so that no visible "work" is involved. It results from the man's obedience to Jesus' command. How far that obedience is a sign of faith depends on the nature and extent of the paralysis: if the whole arm was paralyzed, Jesus has told him to do something impossible in stretching it out, but if it was only the hand, the stretching out was not in itself remarkable. Matthew does not satisfy our curiosity on this point.

14 The healing, in front of the synagogue congregation, was very public (a point which Mark and Luke make explicit: "Get up and stand in the middle"), and the Pharisees' challenge has drawn extra attention to it. We might then have expected to find here, as with previous miracles, a comment

465

on the crowd's reaction of astonishment and/or recognition of Jesus' unique authority. That will indeed be noted in v. 15, but Matthew's immediate interest is elsewhere. Jesus has taken up the Pharisees' challenge and thrown it back at them. He has further underlined his radical disagreement with their approach to sabbath observance and thus disputed their authority to pronounce on the subject. This is enough to extinguish any lingering respect they may have had for Jesus, and to set them on a collision course. "Went out" may be no more than a narrative link, but perhaps Matthew intends us to understand that they have lost control of "their synagogue" (v. 9) "because of Jesus' overwhelming authority in the synagogue after the healing."[50] How far their consultation might have reached at this stage is hard to judge. A group of local Pharisees in Galilee is a very different constituency from the formal body of "chief priests and elders of the people" (21:23; 26:3; sometimes also with "scribes," 21:15; 26:57) who will confront him and eventually bring about his condemnation and execution in Jerusalem. Even though in theory the penalty for sabbath breaking was death (Exod 31:14-15; *m. Sanh.* 7:4), it was hardly realistic for these Pharisees to think of having Jesus officially executed in Galilee, and Matthew's verb "get rid of" (see p. 454, n. 12) need not carry that specific sense. They are determined to silence him, to put an end to his influence on the people, but how that might be achieved would probably not yet be clear, though the intention to "bring a charge against" Jesus (v. 10) indicates one possible way forward. When eventually Jesus is "gotten rid of" in ch. 27, it will not be by these particular enemies, though their reports to their colleagues in Jerusalem may have helped to start the process.

2. Jesus Withdraws from Confrontation (12:15-21)

15 When Jesus knew of this, he withdrew[1] from there. Many people[2] followed him, and he healed them all, 16 and he warned[3] them not to tell others about him. 17 This was to fulfill what had been declared through Isaiah the prophet, who said,

50. Y.-E. Yang, *Jesus,* 210.
1. See p. 76, n. 2, on 2:14 ("escaped"), p. 88, n. 2, on 2:22 ("got safely away"), and p. 138, n. 2, on 4:12 ("withdrew") for Matthew's repeated use of ἀναχωρέω for getting out of a place of danger.
2. Many MSS read ὄχλοι πολλοί (a common Matthean phrase in such contexts) rather than simply πολλοί here; the evidence is not decisive either way, but there is little difference in meaning.
3. In 8:26 I translated ἐπιτιμάω by the term "rebuke," which is its more normal sense in Matthew as in Greek generally. But here apparently no rebuke is involved, but rather a strong prohibition against revealing the recently discovered truth about Jesus; "warn" conveys this better.

18 *"Look, this is my servant whom I have chosen,*
my beloved with whom my soul is delighted.[4]
I will put my spirit upon him,
and he will be a messenger of justice[5] to the nations.[6]
19 *He will not quarrel or shout aloud;*
no one will hear his voice in the streets.
20 *He will not break a damaged reed,*
and he will not put out a smoking wick,
until he has brought justice right through[7] to victory;[8]
21   *and in his name the nations will place their hope."*

Immediately after the two sabbath stories Mark has a lengthy summary of Jesus' continuing ministry and the popular reaction to it (Mark 3:7-12). Matthew offers a very much abbreviated version (see comments below on vv. 15-16), which he uses as the cue for his longest formula-quotation, a slightly abbreviated rendering of Isa 42:1-4 in a version markedly different from that of

4. For this rendering of εὐδόκησεν see p. 117, n. 9, and the comments on 3:17.

5. κρίσις, here and in v. 20, may be translated either "judgment" (its most common sense in Matthew; see 5:21-22; 10:15; 11:22, 24; 12:36, 41-42; 23:33) or, in a positive sense, "justice," as in 23:23, where it is a virtue linked with mercy and faith. Here in Isa 42:1-4 (where the LXX also uses κρίσις) the positive sense best fits the context. See W. D. Davies, *Setting,* 133-35; R. Beaton, *Isaiah's Christ,* 143-45; contra Luz, 2:193-94. (D. C. Sim, *Gospel,* 221-22, argues for the sense of "judgment" here on the basis of usage elsewhere in Matthew and because it would suit his thesis of a negative view of Gentiles in this gospel, but he is clearly ill at ease with this passage, especially v. 21: "Matthew's intended meaning for this verse is no longer clear" . . . "a difficult section of the Gospel to understand, and no interpretation is free from difficulties"!)

6. Here and in v. 21 (as in 4:15) ἔθνη can be translated either "the nations" or more specifically "the Gentiles," but as the servant of whom Isaiah speaks is an Israelite (or indeed is "Israel," Isa 44:1-2; 49:3), the reference would be the same.

7. This is an unusual use of the very flexible verb ἐκβάλλω ("throw out"), most commonly used in Matthew for the expulsion of demons, but more positively applied to "sending out" workers to harvest (9:38) and to "producing" good things from the heart (12:35) or from the storehouse (13:52). Here the LXX uses ἐκφέρω, "bring out"; Matthew's choice of ἐκβάλλω conveys the same idea more vividly, and his equally non-LXX rendering εἰς νῖκος, "to victory," suggests the sense rendered above. (On Gundry's view [see p. 470, n. 16] ἐκβάλλω would have to correspond to Hebrew *śîm,* LXX τίθημι, "establish," which would be a much more remote sense for the verb.)

8. R. Kraft, *Septuagintal Lexicography,* 153-56, shows that in the LXX εἰς νῖκος can be an idiom for "successfully" or "permanently." But here, where the εἰς picks up from the ἐκ- of ἐκβάλλω, it is probable that the term νῖκος has its own weight as the triumphant end result of the servant's patient mission. If the phrase here meant "permanently," the sense would appear to be something like "until he expels justice permanently," which is hardly likely!

the LXX. This is the passage which introduces the intriguing and very important figure of "my [Yahweh's] servant" into the deliverance oracles of
Deutero-Isaiah, and provides a broad overview of the nature of that servant's
role in Yahweh's purpose of salvation. Matthew has already included a "servant" quotation from later in the Isaianic prophecies to illustrate his account
of Jesus' healing ministry (8:17), and further allusions to Isa 53 will be included in Jesus' explanation of his own role in 20:28; 26:28. He has also already included a prominent allusion to the present passage in his account of
Jesus' baptism (3:17; see also on 3:15 for a further possible allusion to Isa
53), and the same allusion will be repeated at 17:5. Most of these allusions
are to Isa 53, which highlights the vicarious suffering of the servant which is
the main focus of NT interest in this figure. In Isa 42 this motif has not yet
been introduced, but, as we noted at 8:17, Matthew's interest in Jesus as the
servant is not limited to his redemptive death but also embraces the general
character of his ministry.

In view of this persistent influence of the "servant" ideology of
Deutero-Isaiah,[9] Matthew might have introduced a quotation of Isa 42:1-4 at
almost any point in his account of Jesus' ministry. Much of what these verses
contain (the servant as God's chosen, his endowment with the spirit, his mission of justice, and the hope of the nations) echoes themes which apply
broadly throughout the gospel.[10] But this portrait also contains (in vv. 19-20)
a less triumphant note: a gentle, nonconfrontational attitude, an avoidance of
publicity, and a patient ministry of encouragement rather than denunciation.
It is this aspect of the quotation[11] for which Matthew has prepared in his brief
précis of Mark's summary: Jesus has withdrawn in the face of hostility and is
anxious to prevent people from forcing the issue of his Messiahship by inappropriate publicity. Controversies will continue in vv. 22-45, and the atmosphere will become even more highly charged, but by inserting this quotation

9. In response to the attempt of J. D. Kingsbury, *Matthew: Structure,* chs. 2 and 3,
to subordinate Matthew's servant christology to his emphasis on the title "Son of God,"
D. Hill, *JSNT* 6 (1980) 2-16, gives a robust defense of the importance of the servant theme
in Matthew's presentation of Jesus.

10. For a stimulating study of the theological themes raised in this quotation see
R. Beaton, *Isaiah's Christ,* 151-64. Beaton argues that this pericope fits appropriately in
the total presentation of Jesus as the ideal son of David which develops through chs. 11–
13.

11. M. J. J. Menken, *Matthew's Bible,* 51-65, argues, however, that the whole
quotation is relevant to the immediate context in which Matthew has set it because v. 14
has provided the first direct reference to Jesus' coming death. Jesus' withdrawal and command to silence relate to that theme in that it is only in his death and resurrection that the
true nature of his mission can be revealed. Those parts of the quotation which do not directly relate to the servant's avoidance of confrontation (vv. 18, 20c-21) bear on the mission to be accomplished and revealed in the death which v. 14 has foreshadowed.

here Matthew helps his readers to put the confrontation in context: it is not of the Messiah's choosing.[12]

15-16 These verses perform a function similar to that of the summary in 8:16, which introduces the other "servant" formula-quotation. From Mark's longer general account (Mark 3:7-12) Matthew retains just four motifs, greatly abbreviated: Jesus' withdrawal, a large crowd of people following him (in contrast with the Pharisees), general healing, and the demand for silence. But Jesus' "withdrawal" (see 466, n. 1), which in Mark is left unexplained, is here attributed, as in 4:12, to his awareness that he is under threat. In 14:13 and 15:21 a similar point will be made, and the repeated motif seems too obvious to ignore: Jesus is taking precautions to avoid premature confrontation. When the time comes for the showdown in Jerusalem he will not hold back, but for now he has a wider ministry to fulfill. If controversy is forced on him he will respond vigorously, but he takes care to avoid initiating it. Jesus' withdrawal reflects the instruction he has already given to his disciples to move on when they meet a hostile reception (10:14, 23).

The mention of crowds and healing has a formulaic feel.[13] As in 8:16 (compare Mark 1:34) Matthew's "all" in place of Mark's "many" gives a more broadbrush impression; Matthew prefers not to suggest that there were any who failed to find healing with Jesus.[14] Matthew's summary has omitted any specific mention of exorcism, which in Mark 3:11-12 is the context for Jesus' demand for silence: it was the expelled demons who recognized him as the Son of God and had to be silenced. In Matthew, therefore, the demand for secrecy lacks an explanation. In 16:20 and 17:9 Matthew will emphasize as strongly as Mark Jesus' demand for secrecy with regard to his Messiahship, but, as we have noted at 8:4 and 9:30, in relation to healings and exorcisms this motif is much less important to Matthew than to Mark. Its almost perfunctory appearance here, with no indication of just what it was about Jesus that was to be kept secret, suggests, as we noted at 9:30, that it is "more like an occasional relic of a prominent Marcan theme than an issue that was also important to Matthew himself." In this context, however, Matthew has retained it because it provides a link with the assertion of Isa 42:2 that the servant will not make a lot of noise, and "no one will hear his voice in the streets."

---

12. R. Beaton, *Isaiah's Christ,* 174-91, explores the apparent tension in Matthew's christology between the meek and humble Messiah and the "aggressive polemicist," a tension revealed especially by the juxtaposition of 12:17-21 and 12:22-45.

13. L. Novakovic, *Messiah,* 142-51, argues, however, that the mention of healing is in fact the key to the quotation: "The entire quotation has the purpose of showing that Jesus' healings belong to the domain of Jesus' messianic chores and as such fulfill the Scripture" (142).

14. Cf. 13:58, "not many miracles," compared with Mark 6:5, "no miracle" — except the healing of a few who were ill!

Withdrawal from conflict and a desire for secrecy therefore provide the cue for the long quotation that follows. But Isaiah's portrait of Yahweh's servant goes far beyond that one element, and the length of the quotation makes it clear that Matthew wants his readers to see it all, not just the secrecy element, as a blueprint for Jesus' ministry. Indeed, the following section, vv. 22-37, when the controversy is resumed, will take up Isaiah's language about the Spirit resting on the servant (v. 18) as the role of the Spirit in Jesus' ministry becomes the object of scrutiny.[15]

17-21 This long formula-quotation relates to the specific situation outlined in vv. 15-16, but it also provides a fuller overview of Jesus' ministry as a whole, as it conforms to Isaiah's vision of God's ideal servant. Apart from the omission of Isa 42:4a-b ("He will not grow faint or be discouraged until he has established justice on the earth"),[16] Matthew quotes the whole of Isa 42:1-4, but in a version which at most points is almost as different from the LXX as it is possible to be while translating the same Hebrew. In v. 1 he is closer to the Hebrew in that he leaves the servant unidentified, whereas the LXX adds the names "Jacob" and "Israel," but generally his version is the more free[17] — "I have chosen" for "I uphold" in the first line of v. 1; "beloved" for "chosen" in the next line; "be a messenger of" for "bring out" in the last line; "quarrel" for

15. So O. L. Cope, *Matthew,* 35-40. Cope also argues that the following pasage about Jesus as greater than Jonah develops the Isaiah theme of the Messiah bringing justice to the nations. For a fuller attempt to trace the relevance of the Isaiah quotation to many aspects of the surrounding narrative see J. H. Neyrey, *Bib* 63 (1982) 457-73.

16. R. H. Gundry, *Use,* 110, 114-15, argues that Matthew's ἕως ἂν ἐκβάλῃ εἰς νῖκος τὴν κρίσιν represents Isa 42:4b ("until he has established justice on the earth") rather than 42:3c ("truly/faithfully he will bring out justice"). Matthew's wording shows links with both lines and does not exactly correspond to either of them; it is a summary of their common theme. But see 467, n. 7 above for my reason for seeing 42:3c as the more likely source at least of the verb (cf. also J. Grindel, *CBQ* 29 [1967] 112-15). In his commentary (230) Gundry has modified his view: Matthew "conflates the two clauses." M. J. J. Menken, *Matthew's Bible,* 78-80, likewise argues that in v. 20c "two lines from Isaiah have been woven together."

17. *Pace* M. J. J. Menken, *Matthew's Bible,* 71-82, whose general thesis that Matthew used a "revised LXX" more closely assimilated to the Hebrew seems to me particularly hard to establish in this case. Menken attributes these "free" renderings to "textual change based on ancient exegesis" rather than to Matthew's own ingenuity; but they can hardly be described as moving the LXX in the direction of the Hebrew, as his thesis seems to require. More judicious is the conclusion which R. Beaton, *Isaiah's Christ,* 141, draws from his "brief analysis" (139) of the textual character of the quotation (ibid., 123-41), that "Matthew's unique text-form demonstrates his use of either the Hebrew, or more likely a Greek (or Aramaic) text conformed to the Hebrew, which he then altered in the light of his own concerns." L. Novakovic, *Messiah,* 136-42, argues that the unique text-form is entirely attributable to the evangelist himself, who has adapted it "to conform the scriptural text to the career of Jesus" (142).

"shout" in v. 2; "to victory" for "truly/faithfully"[18] in v. 3. In v. 4c, however, he agrees essentially with the LXX's "In his name the nations will place their hope" against the MT's "In his law the islands will place their hope." None of these variations involves major differences of meaning, and Matthew's version, whether his own creation or drawn from a Greek version now unknown to us, is a reasonable independent rendering of the general sense of the Hebrew.[19] We shall note below the points where his version seems to have particular relevance to the story of Jesus.[20]

18 It is interesting that despite the widespread interest of Matthew and the other NT writers in Jesus as the Isaianic servant, the actual title *pais,* "servant," is used for Jesus only here and in Acts 3:13, 26; 4:27, 30.[21] We have noted at 3:17 the echo of the opening words of Isa 42:1 in the heavenly voice at Jesus' baptism, where the term "beloved" *(agapētos)* reflects the non-LXX version Matthew here quotes.[22] By moving the idea of choice from the second line to the first (in place of God's "upholding") Matthew's version emphasizes the special appointment of God's chosen servant,[23] and the dou-

18. Or for "on the earth," if Gundry is right (see n. 16).

19. Various features of Matthew's version not surprisingly have parallels in other known versions (especially Theodotion and the Targum), but none of these corresponds to Matthew's version as a whole. For details see K. Stendahl, *School,* 107-15; R. H. Gundry, *Use,* 110-16. It is of course always possible that some of Matthew's independent renderings, and some of those where he coincides with other versions, may represent a different Hebrew text tradition from that preserved by the Masoretes (Gundry is especially open to this view), but in the absence of any other Hebrew text this can never be more than speculation.

20. Stendahl, in accordance with his general theory, attributes the distinctive Matthean version to the work of a "school" which Matthew represented. B. Lindars, *Apologetic,* 144-52, sees it as the end product of a long period of apologetic development in the church. D. Hill, *JSNT* 6 (1980) 9-12, following O. L. Cope, argues that we should credit it to the evangelist himself (so also Davies and Allison, 2:323-24).

21. It is sometimes suggested that παῖς (rather than δοῦλος, "slave") is used here to translate *'ebed* because its ambiguity ("servant" or "child") is more accommodating to the view that Jesus is God's son. But the other meaning of παῖς is "child," not "son" (see p. 123, n. 29; cf. also p. 312 above). παῖς is the standard Greek rendering here, as seen in both LXX and Theodotion, and so needs no special explanation. In this quotation it is Jesus' role as the servant that is in view, not the title "Son of God" (see 468, n. 9 above).

22. L. Novakovic, *Messiah,* 147, asserts that ἀγαπητός "cannot be explained on the basis of the textual history of Isa 42:1," and has been put here by Matthew specifically in order to echo the voice of 3:17 and thus to establish that Jesus the servant is also God's beloved son, confirmed as Messiah at his baptism.

23. Matthew uses a verb not used elsewhere in the NT (though sometimes in the LXX), αἱρετίζω, which means to select for oneself (and sometimes to "adopt" a child), and suggests the idea of an exclusive relationship; its cognate αἵρεσις is used for a "sect" or "party" (Acts 5:17; 15:5; 24:5, 14; 26:5; 28:22) and is the root of our word "heresy"!

ble expression of love/delight in the second line then reinforces the unique closeness of the relationship in a way which reminds us of 11:27. God's "pleasure" in his servant is in marked contrast to the attitude of the Pharisees in vv. 1-14. The endowment with God's spirit (the importance of which will become clear in vv. 28-32), already visually enacted at 3:16, is linked in Isa 61:1 with the idea of anointing, and Matthew's readers would have had no difficulty in identifying the mysterious "servant" of Isaiah with the promised anointed one, the Messiah of whose work of deliverance and proclamation we have been reminded in 11:5. There may well also be an echo of Isa 61:1-2 in Matthew's version of the last line of v. 1, which makes the servant a *messenger* of justice; so also the anointed one of Isa 61:1 *proclaims* good news to the poor (cf. 11:5), release to the captives, and the year of God's favor. "Justice" (see p. 467, n. 5) here conveys that wider sense of the working out of God's good purpose for his people rather than merely the legal sense of giving a right verdict. But the messenger of Isa 61 is sent to Zion, and the message there is of national restoration, whereas in Isa 42:1 it is *the nations* who will be the beneficiaries of the justice which the servant brings.[24] By following the LXX in finding "the nations" also explicitly in v. 4 Matthew ensures that his readers do not miss the theme of a gospel for the Gentiles which has been steadily developing throughout his gospel and will reach its climax in 28:19. This extension of God's purpose beyond Israel was not a new decision by God at the time of Jesus, but part of his long-declared purpose of salvation which Jesus, his "beloved," has now come to implement.

19   The Hebrew uses two verbs as virtual synonyms for "shout" (the second being "lift" with "his voice" in the following clause as the understood object). By using *erizō,* "quarrel" or "wrangle," for the first verb Matthew makes clear how this text applies to Jesus, who has just withdrawn to avoid a further "shouting match" with the Pharisees. In Jerusalem in chs. 21–23 Jesus will not be reluctant to provoke argument and opposition as he lays down his final challenge to the authorities there, but here in Galilee his style is different. This is a time for discretion and secrecy; when controversy comes in Galilee, it will not be Jesus who initiates it. When the confrontation reaches its climax in Jerusalem, we will again be reminded of Jesus' nonviolence and silence in the face of official hostility (26:52-56, 62-63; 27:12-14).

20-21   A reed was used for measuring and for support, so that once its straightness was lost by bending or cracking it was of no further use. A strip of linen cloth used as a lamp wick, if it smokes, is of no use for giving light and is simply a source of pollution; it is in danger of going out altogether. Common sense would demand that both be replaced, the reed being

---

24. Cf. Isa 49:6 for a more explicit announcement of this wider ministry of the servant as "a light for the nations . . . salvation to the ends of the earth."

snapped and discarded or burned and the wick extinguished. The imagery thus describes an extraordinary willingness to encourage damaged or vulnerable people, giving them a further opportunity to succeed which a results-oriented society would deny them. The servant will not be quick to condemn and to discard, but will persevere until God's purpose of "justice" has been achieved.[25] Here Matthew finds a further portrait of the meek and lowly Jesus who offers a kind yoke and a light burden, the giver of rest to the toiling and heavily loaded (11:28-30). His rewording of the last clause of Isa 42:3 (see nn. 7 and 16 above) emphasizes the patient perseverance which will eventually bring success ("victory"), and thus compensates for his abbreviation of the quotation by omitting Isa 42:4a-b, "He will not grow faint or be discouraged until he has established justice on the earth." This positive orientation, and the note of "hope" with which the quotation ends, provides a wholesome contrast to the critical opposition which Jesus has been facing and will shortly encounter even more forcefully.

3. The Accusation of Using Demonic Power (12:22-37)

> 22 Then a demon-possessed man was brought to him who was blind and dumb,[1] and he healed him, so that the dumb man could both speak and see. 23 All the crowds were astonished and asked, "Can this man really be the Son of David?"[2] 24 But the Pharisees heard this, and said, "This man could not throw out demons except by the power of[3] Beelzebul, the ruler of the demons." 25 Jesus knew[4] what they were thinking and said to them, "Every kingdom which is divided against itself is laid waste, and no town or household which is divided against

25. R. Beaton, *Isaiah's Christ,* 157-61, usefully examines the meaning of "justice" in this text in the light of its wider OT usage. For the place of "justice" in Jewish conceptions of the Messiah's role see also ibid., 161-64. Cf. more briefly Beaton's article in *JSNT* 75 (1999) 5-23.

1. κωφός can mean "dumb" (9:32) or "deaf" (11:5), and often covers both these (associated) conditions. Here the meaning "dumb" is indicated by the fact that the cure is expressed in terms of speaking, but the nature of the disability is not the main focus of interest.

2. A question introduced by μήτι formally expects the answer No (as in 7:16), but is also idiomatically used to put forward a tentative suggestion which may prove controversial or unwelcome (cf. 26:22, 25). For a close parallel cf. John 4:29 (cf. also John 7:26).

3. Literally, "in Beelzebul" (similarly in v. 27); for ἐν in the sense of "by the power of" cf. v. 28; John 3:21.

4. Some MSS have "saw," perhaps to reproduce the formula used in 9:4. The subject "Jesus" is left unexpressed in most of the older MSS, but later copyists found it helpful to add it.

itself can survive. 26 And if Satan throws out Satan, he is divided against himself; so then how could his kingdom survive? 27 And if it is by the power of Beelzebul that I throw out the demons, by whose power do your sons throw them out? Therefore it is they who will be your judges. 28 But if it is by the power of the Spirit of God that I throw out the demons, then the kingdom of God has caught up with⁵ you. 29 Or how can anyone get into the strong man's house to steal his possessions if he doesn't first tie the strong man up? Then he can plunder his house.

30 "Anyone who is not with me is against me, and anyone who does not gather with me scatters.

31 "Therefore I tell you, people may be forgiven every [other]⁶ sin and blasphemy, but blasphemy against⁷ the Spirit will not be forgiven. 32 And if anyone speaks a word against the Son of Man, they will be forgiven, but if anyone speaks against the Holy Spirit, they will not be forgiven, either in this age or in the age to come.

33 "Either make the tree good and its fruit [will be]⁸ good, or make the tree rotten and its fruit [will be] rotten; a tree is known by its fruit. 34 You brood of vipers, how can you say anything good when you yourselves are bad? For the mouth speaks what overflows from⁹ the heart. 35 A good person produces good things from their store of good,¹⁰ and a bad person produces bad things from their store of bad.

5. φθάνω, which essentially means "to be ahead of, to precede," can also mean "to overtake," and hence "to catch someone unawares." While in Hellenistic Greek the verb came to be used to mean simply "arrive," the combination here with ἐπί, "upon," focuses attention not so much on the arrival itself as on the effect on those who have unexpectedly encountered it; it implies an unwelcome surprise. Cf. the similar usage in 1 Thess 2:16.

6. The bald statement that "every sin and blasphemy will be forgiven" functions in the rhetoric of the saying not as a declaration in its own right but as a foil to the one blasphemy which will not be forgiven. The addition of "other" and the preceding "may" are intended to make that rhetoric clear, and to avoid the very misleading impression which a literal translation of the first clause on its own would give.

7. Literally, "blasphemy of the spirit." The following verse both specifies that the Holy Spirit is intended and defines how the blasphemy relates to the Spirit as "speaking against."

8. The concise proverbial form of this saying (see comments below) does not translate well into English; the added "will be" in both clauses draws out the logical connection which is the basis of the concluding clause of the verse.

9. περίσσευμα is more than simply "fullness"; it denotes excess, more than enough (cf. Mark 8:8, "leftovers"; 2 Cor 8:14, "excess," in contrast to ὑστέρημα, "shortage"). It is what the heart can no longer contain which finds expression in words.

10. Literally, "from the good treasure" (and in the next clause "from the bad treasure"); θησαυρός, which I have translated "treasure(s)" in 6:19-21 and "treasure chest" in

36 *But I tell you that for every empty*[11] *word that people utter they will give account on the day of judgment;* 37 *by your*[12] *words you will be acquitted,*[13] *and by your words you will be condemned."*

After the brief respite of Jesus' withdrawal, the confrontation with the Pharisees is resumed. The trigger in this case is not an act which can be criticized in itself, but the demonstration of Jesus' authority over demonic possession leads to polarized opinions, the crowd in general discussing whether Jesus is the Messiah, but the Pharisees, unable to deny his power, questioning its source. It is their outrageous allegation which provokes Jesus into a withering response, in part consisting of reasoned argument (vv. 25-29), but leading on to a quite melodramatic warning of the possible consequences of their entrenched refusal to recognize his divine authority for what it is.

The allegation that Jesus is drawing on demonic power has already been briefly noted in 9:34 (though without naming Beelzebul), and Jesus' comment in 10:25 on people calling the master of the house (himself) Beelzebul has kept the issue alive. Now it is confronted head-on. Some such charge remained for some centuries a staple element in rabbinic Jewish polemic against Jesus as a magician who by his black arts "led Israel astray."[14] It assumes the reality of a supernatural power, but questions its nature and origin. We have therefore moved beyond "academic" debate on the validity of Jesus' teaching and practice to the realm of personal abuse and character assassination. The accusation of complicity with the devil is not only extremely offensive, but is intended to destroy Jesus' credibility in the eyes of a God-fearing public. It is also potentially extremely serious, since sorcery was, according to the Mishnah, a capital

---

2:11, does not always imply exceptional wealth, but is used for an ordinary person's collection of belongings and/or the place where it is kept, as also in 13:52.

11. The traditional translation of ἀργός here by "idle" misses the point. In our idiom an "idle word" means a casual utterance, to which no importance is attached. But ἀργός means "idle" rather in the sense of doing no work, accomplishing nothing; the reference is probably to words which are not backed up by actions (as in 21:30) and so are "empty," hypocritical. Cf. Jas 2:20, where (in the most likely reading) faith unaccompanied by works is declared to be ἀργή.

12. "Your/you" in both clauses of this verse are singular (in vv. 34 and 36 "you" is plural).

13. δικαιόω, translated "justify" in 11:19, is here shown by the parallelism and by the explicit reference to "judgment" to have its basic judicial sense, to "declare to be right/innocent," rather than a more "Pauline" theological nuance.

14. G. N. Stanton, *Gospel*, 171-80 (and cf. ibid., 237-43), documents this polemical motif and discusses its relevance for understanding these passages in Matthew. The more obvious talmudic examples are in *b. Sanh.* 43a, 107b; *b. Šabb.* 104b (taking Ben Stada as a pseudonym for Jesus); for early Christian references to this polemic see Justin, *Dial.* 69; Origen, *Cels.* 1.6, 68, 71, etc.

offense.[15] But it is a step too far, as Jesus' reply will warn them. Not only is the accusation in itself patently ridiculous (vv. 25-29); it also indicates a fundamental choice to take sides against Jesus (v. 30) and, even more seriously, against the Spirit of God by whose authority he acts (vv. 31-32); by making this accusation they have revealed their true character, and will be judged for it (vv. 33-37). The Pharisees are playing with fire.

The complex of sayings which make up the first part of Jesus' response (vv. 25-32) is essentially paralleled in Mark 3:23-30, though Matthew's version includes some additional material in vv. 27-28 and 30. Those additional sayings also appear in the more concise parallel in Luke 11:17-23, but Luke's equivalent to the Marcan saying about the unforgivable sin occurs in a different context in 12:10. It seems, then, that a number of apologetic and polemical sayings were preserved which related to this theme, and each of the evangelists put them together in a different way. Within Matthew's version there is a clear coherence to vv. 25-29, which respond directly, though in a number of different ways, to the Beelzebul charge, while v. 30 (which has a sort of parallel in Mark 9:40) and the saying about the unforgivable sin in vv. 31-32 may have been originally independent. If so, Mark certainly understood the latter to relate specifically to the Beelzebul accusation (hence his editorial comment in 3:30), and Matthew, by retaining it in the same setting, supports this interpretation. As we shall see below, to recognize the specific setting of this troubling saying may be important for its proper understanding.

Matthew then continues Jesus' speech with a further complex of sayings (vv. 33-37) which recall the warning against false prophets in 7:16-20, but which also include some further material which Luke has included in his parallel to Matt 7:16-20 (Luke 6:43-45), and which then conclude with a saying about judgment not paralleled elsewhere (vv. 36-37). It seems, then, that Matthew has added to the Beelzebul controversy a further compilation[16] of polemical sayings of Jesus in order to underline the seriousness of the warning Jesus has uttered in vv. 31-32. The Pharisees cannot shrug off their scan-

---

15. *M. Sanh.* 7:4; cf. for Qumran CD 12:2-3. A broad (and for many readers surprising) impression of the prevalence of magical ideas and practices within Judaism may be gained from P. S. Alexander's study, "Incantations and Books of Magic," in Schürer, 3:342-79. Even if many of the texts cited are later than the NT period, it seems clear that at the time of Jesus there was already cause to be concerned.

16. The complex origin of this little section is indicated by the changing form of the sayings included. The proverbial language of v. 33 is followed by a direct second-person attack in v. 34, and then by a general statement in the third-person singular (v. 35); then comes a new introductory formula, "But I tell you," leading into a third-person plural statement (v. 36), which is then supplemented by a warning surprisingly cast in the second-person singular, even though the narrative context offers no single person as its target (v. 37).

dalous accusation in v. 24 as "mere words," because words, no less than deeds, reveal the true nature of the person who utters them. So the catastrophic judgment implicit in the saying of vv. 31-32 can properly be based even on "mere words." The "words" of v. 37 help to link this little paragraph to the preceding context by recalling the "word" spoken against the Holy Spirit in v. 32 (vv. 34 and 36 also focus on speech as the basis of judgment).

22 As in 12:9-14, the miracle itself is related extremely briefly. Its importance is rather in the confrontation which results from it. The story here is like that already narrated in 9:32-34, repeated in order to introduce Jesus' response to the Pharisees' accusation, but now with the added complication of blindness. It is clear that Jesus was known as an exorcist as well as a physical healer, and Matthew specifically mentions exorcisms in some of his summaries of the ministry of Jesus and his disciples (4:24; 8:16; 10:1, 8; but not in 9:35; 11:5; 12:15). Specific exorcism stories have been included in 8:28-34 and 9:32-34, and more will follow in 15:21-28 and 17:14-20. The present case is therefore representative of a recognized aspect of Jesus' ministry, and the minimal detail given underlines its representative character. See on 4:24 for the distinction between "healing" a physical complaint and "throwing out" a demon; here (as in 9:32 and 17:15) the demon-possession is manifested in physical complaints, but whereas in those stories the expulsion of the demon is specifically mentioned (9:33; 17:18), here Matthew's abbreviated narrative mentions only the "healing" which was the visible effect. It is clear, however, from the following accusation and debate that neither Jesus nor the onlookers had any doubt that this was a case of possession and exorcism, not a physical healing alone.

23 The crowd's astonishment is a standard motif (9:8, 26, 33), though this time a stronger verb is used. This time, too, the crowd reaction goes beyond the broader comment that "Nothing like this has ever been seen in Israel" (9:33) to a more specific speculation. Much has been said of Jesus' unique authority (7:29; 9:8), but this is the first time specifically messianic language has been used in a crowd scene (though the blind men's use of the title "Son of David" in 9:27 already indicates at least one strand of popular reaction to Jesus). They are beginning to draw the conclusion which Jesus had expected John the Baptist to draw from his miracles (11:2-6). The immediate juxtaposition of this acclamation with the Pharisees' accusation suggests that the latter have recognized the dangerous state of public response to Jesus, and decide to stamp on it before it is too late. For the messianic implications of the title "Son of David" see the comments on 9:27, and see nn. 21-22 there for its association with healing.[17] The uncertainty expressed by the

---

17. The tradition that Solomon had power over evil spirits would be more relevant here than in 9:27, where only physical healing is mentioned. L. R. Fisher, in F. T. Trotter

form of the question (see p. 473, n. 2 above) may be in part owing to the fact that Jesus, for all his unmistakable authority in healing and teaching, has shown no inclination to fulfill the more political aspect of popular Davidic expectation.

24 The positive reaction of the crowd is set in stark contrast to the determined opposition of the Pharisees; the same phenomena lead them to an opposite conclusion, because their minds are already made up. "When they heard this" confirms that the Pharisees are deliberately (and presumably publicly) countering the messianic interpretation which the crowd have tentatively put on Jesus' miraculous power. The accusation made in 9:34 is repeated but more vividly and offensively (see 10:25) in that this time the "ruler of the demons" is named.

"Beelzebul" seems to be an alternative popular name for Satan (the term Jesus uses in responding to the charge, v. 26). The name does not occur in earlier Jewish writings;[18] the commonest name for the chief demon is Satan, but we find also Belial, Beliar, Mastema, and Azazel. The form *Beelzeboul* (some MSS omit the first *l*) suggests an original link with the Canaanite god Baal, and a possible Hebrew derivation of the name would be *Ba'al-z^{e}bûl*, "Baal (lord) of the height" or "of the house,"[19] but how such a title came to be applied to Satan is a matter of speculation.[20] There is no clear link with the Philistine god *Ba'al-z^{e}bûb*, "Lord of the flies," in 2 Kgs 1:2-16, though this could have been a derogatory corruption of *Ba'al-z^{e}bûl*.[21]

Supernatural power demands a supernatural source, and if they are not prepared to admit that it is divine, there is only one alternative. There is clear evidence of popular belief that sorcerers operated through a "familiar spirit" (see n. 15 above), but to identify that spirit as no less than the chief demon himself was to raise the charge to an ominous level.

(ed.), *Jesus and the Historian,* 82-97, illustrates the significance of Solomon in Aramaic exorcistic magic texts, and suggests that "son of David" would have been understood especially in relation to Solomon the exorcist. But Matthew's use of "Son of David" as a whole does not focus primarily on exorcism.

18. In the *Testament of Solomon* Beelzebul occurs frequently as the name of the ruler of the demons, but this is generally agreed to be a Christian work of between the first and third centuries A.D., so that the name is derived from the NT.

19. See p. 402, n. 14, for the suggestion that this derivation lies behind the jibe against the "master of the house" in 10:25.

20. See further L. Gaston, *TZ* 18 (1962) 247-55. Gaston notes that in OT and later Hebrew *z^{e}bûl* is used both for heaven and for the temple, and suggests that Beelzebul is a Hebrew version of the Aramaic *B^e'el-š^{e}māyin,* a title for Zeus, the chief Greek god (and so from the Jewish point of view the chief demon). He dismisses the popular speculation that the title was meant as a derisive echo of the late Hebrew word *zebel* (compost heap).

21. The form "Beelzebub," which the KJV uses in the NT, has no support in the Greek manuscript tradition, but derives from the Latin and Syriac versions of the NT.

25-26   "Jesus knew what they were *thinking*" is surprising after what sounds like a public charge (to counter the crowd's unacceptable suggestion) in v. 24; contrast 9:4, where the charge was apparently as yet unspoken. Does Matthew want us to understand that the Pharisees were merely muttering in a corner, or does he mean that Jesus not only heard the accusation but also discerned the motivation which gave rise to it? Probably the latter, since Jesus' response in vv. 30-32 will go beyond the specific charge made and deal with the underlying mind-set of his opponents. "Jesus sees through his opponents" (Luz, 2:203).

Jesus' first counterargument is the commonsense point that it is absurd to imagine that the demon king would attack and defeat his own demonic forces. This would mean civil war in the demonic kingdom, and that can only be a recipe for disaster, as human experience of divided loyalties illustrates. Note that Satan (for the name see on 4:1) is assumed to have a "kingdom," which we will hear in v. 28 is under attack from the "kingdom of God." The term "kingdom" here carries its normal dynamic sense of "rule": Satan cannot for long remain king if his forces are divided. For Satan's claim to kingship in the world see on 4:8-9; cf. also Rev 2:13, where Satan has a "throne."

27   The second argument is *ad hominem*. Jesus takes it for granted that genuine exorcisms are taking place in Jewish circles unconnected with himself; "your sons" need not mean the actual sons of those to whom he is speaking, but "members of your community." For NT examples of such exorcists see Mark 9:38; Acts 19:13-14, and see the introductory comments on 8:28-34 for the acceptance and approval of exorcism in the Jewish and pagan worlds of the time. The uniqueness of Jesus' exorcistic ministry (9:33, and implied here in the suggestion that he may be "Son of David" in v. 23) consists in the nature and authority of his exorcisms, not in the lack of any other exorcists. Exorcism, as distinct from physical healing, presupposes a hostile supernatural force which can be countered only by a more powerful spiritual authority, and Jewish exorcists were understood to be acting by the power of God. The Pharisees can be assumed to be as much in favor of the practice as other Jews; why then should Jesus' exorcisms be any more sinister?

28   The spiritual nature of Jesus' exorcisms is now made more explicit: it is by the Spirit of God that they are performed. In v. 18 we have been reminded of endowment with God's Spirit as the basis of the servant's ministry, and in 3:16 the visible coming of the Spirit upon Jesus has launched him on it. While actual exorcism narratives do not elsewhere refer directly to the Spirit, preferring to focus simply on Jesus' own authoritative word of command, within the framework of Matthew's story the reader naturally understands that Jesus' special authority derives from his endowment with the Spirit. Luke here has the vivid image of "the finger of God," an echo of the source of Moses' miraculous power in Exod 8:19, but Matthew needs the more direct reference to the Spirit not only as a pickup from v. 18 but also particularly as the basis for the charge which Jesus will level against the Pharisees in vv. 31-32: they are deliberately denigrating the work not just of a human being, but of the Spirit of God.

This deployment of the Spirit's power is not merely a means of combating demonic possession, but also a sign of something more far-reaching, the establishment of God's kingship in place of that of Satan (v. 26). This is the second of five[22] occasions where Matthew speaks of "the kingdom of God" rather than his normal phrase "the kingdom of heaven" (cf. 19:24; 21:31, 43). I suggested at 6:33 that such departures from normal usage are "because the context requires a more 'personal' reference to God himself than the more oblique language of his heavenly authority." That reference is required here not only to balance "Spirit of God" in the first half of the saying but also because of the preceding reference to "Satan's kingdom" (v. 26); Jesus' saying thus vividly contrasts the personal kings of the two kingdoms. But the coming of God's kingship, which is a cause for joy to those who embrace it, is a threat to those who oppose his will; so it has "caught up with" the Pharisees, breaking uncomfortably into their cozily controlled world of tradition and turning everything upside down. It is not they but Jesus, as the Messiah in whose coming God's kingship is established, who now represents the true focus of divine authority on earth. Note how the aorist tense of *phthanō*, "has caught up with" (see p. 474, n. 5), carries the same implication as the perfect of *engizō* in 3:2; 4:17; 10:7 (see comments on 3:2): God's kingship is already a reality.[23]

This powerful challenge follows strangely after v. 27. If Jesus' exorcisms have this eschatological significance, why does the same not apply to the other Jewish exorcists who equally, it is presupposed, operate by the power of God's Spirit (and have been doing so, presumably, long before Jesus came to announce the arrival of God's kingship)? We noted above (p. 338) that while other exorcists were operating at the time, there is no record in extant literature of anyone else who carried out exorcisms on such a scale and with such decisive authority, as opposed to the often bizarre rituals to which other exorcists resorted. This special character of Jesus' exorcisms ("something completely new and qualitatively different," Luz, 2:124), combined with the overall tenor of his ministry and its note of unique authority,

22. Probably; the MSS are sometimes divided, as in 6:33; see p. 264, n. 8.

23. See G. R. Beasley-Murray, *Kingdom,* 75-80, for the remarkable attempts of some earlier interpreters, for ideological reasons, to deny this obvious implication. Beasley-Murray's own study of the text, and especially of the meaning of φθάνω, dismisses such views decisively.

perhaps accounts for the boldness of this claim.[24] The following saying underlines the point.

29 The robbing of the strong man recalls the imagery of Isa 49:24-25, where it symbolizes God's rescue of his people from their oppressors. This little parable is left uninterpreted, but the context in which it is set leaves little doubt of its meaning for Matthew.[25] Jesus' exorcisms, far from being in collusion with Satan, are a direct assault on his "possessions"; his "kingdom" is under attack. The "strength" of Satan, as the "god of this world" (2 Cor 4:4; cf. John 12:31; 14:30; 16:11), is acknowledged (cf. 4:8-9), but now at last he has met his match. Jesus has "tied him up" and so is now free to appropriate his possessions — or, in the imagery of Isa 49:24-25, to release his captives.[26] The tying up[27] represents not an exorcistic technique,[28] but the comprehensive superiority of Jesus' authority over that of Satan, and so the coming into force of the kingship of God.[29] It is that "tying up" that distinguishes Jesus' all-out assault on Satan's kingdom from the little local forays of other exorcists of the time.

30 This pithy saying clarifies the position into which the Pharisees have put themselves. It divides humanity simply into two groups; there is no middle ground. A superficially similar saying in Mark 9:40, "Whoever is not

24. Davies and Allison, 2:339, argue that the difference between Jesus' exorcisms and those of other Jews lies in "his very presence as the Christ. What matters is that *Jesus* cast out demons." Quite so, but this still does not explain *how* his exorcisms are different from theirs, especially from the point of view of a neutral observer.

25. By contrast, it occurs in *Gos. Thom.* 35 as an isolated logion with no clue to its interpretation.

26. The strong man's "house" may be intended as a play on the possible meaning of Beelzebul as "lord of the house" (see on v. 24).

27. A hope that Satan would eventually be "bound" in chains and imprisoned (perhaps based on Isa 24:21-22) is found in some Jewish apocalytic writings (e.g., *1 En.* 54:3-5; 69:28; *T. Levi* 18:12) and taken up in Rev 20:1-3. This hope is an eschatological extension of the belief that the fallen angels have already been "bound" in prison awaiting their final judgment (*1 En.* 10:4-5, 11-12; 21:1-6; *Jub.* 10:7-9). In *Jub.* 48:15-16 the demon prince Mastema is "bound" (apparently temporarily) to prevent his acting against Israel at the time of the Exodus, while in Tob 8:3 a demon is "bound hand and foot" after being expelled. For later use of such language, especially in magical formulae, see Keener, 365, n. 78.

28. *Pace* the popular use of language about the "binding of Satan" in some charismatic circles today.

29. See my *Mark,* 174, for the debate as to whether the binding of Satan should be understood to have been decisively accomplished in Jesus' confrontation with him in the wilderness (Mark 1:12-13) or as an ongoing process throughout Jesus' ministry. Similar considerations apply in Matthew. Matthew's account does not suggest that after 4:1-11 Satan is already effectively neutralized; rather, the exorcisms testify to a continuing conflict, in which, however, the superiority of Jesus is never in doubt.

against us is for us" (also set in a context of exorcism), equally excludes the middle ground, but has a more inclusive tone — compare the optimism of a glass "half full" as against the pessimism of "half empty." In Mark 9:40 the subject is an exorcist who honored Jesus by using his name, even though not a recognized disciple, but here it is his most bitter opponents, who have questioned his God-given authority. The two sayings are not incompatible (Luke includes both); it is their different contexts which demand the sharply different tone. The second line of the saying makes the same point in more graphic form, possibly using the imagery of harvest or of sheep-herding:[30] Jesus' opponents are spoilers, trashing what he and his disciples have carefully put together.

31-32 The saying about an "unforgivable sin" has often been inappropriately, and sometimes disastrously, applied to contexts which have little to do with its original setting. As it appears here in Matthew, it is specifically concerned with what the Pharisees have just said. In 9:3 the scribes had accused Jesus of blasphemy; now the charge is returned. For the meaning of "blasphemy" see on 9:3 (especially n. 46). The term could also be used in a less technical sense for "slander" of fellow human beings (27:39; Luke 23:39; Rom 3:8; etc.), and the use of "speak against" as a synonym for "blaspheme" in v. 32 reflects that usage, but here the reference to the Holy Spirit as the object of blasphemy requires the full religious sense of the term. The opening "therefore" indicates[31] that in this context blasphemy against the Holy Spirit (see p. 474, n. 7) is to be understood in terms of the Pharisees' charge in v. 24, attributing what is in fact the work of God's Spirit (v. 28) to his ultimate enemy, Satan. It is thus a complete perversion of spiritual values, revealing a decisive choice of the wrong side in the battle between good and evil, between God and Satan. It is this which has shown these Pharisees to be decisively "against" Jesus (v. 30). And it is this diametrical opposition to the good purpose of God which is ultimately unforgivable. The point needs to be emphasized, since the language of this saying has sometimes been incautiously applied to real or supposed offenses "against the Holy Spirit"[32] which have nothing to do with the blasphemy of these Pharisees, and serious pastoral damage has thus been caused.[33] This

---

30. But cf. Eccl 3:5 for another type of gathering/scattering. *Pace* Luz, 2:205-6, there is no need to overload this simple image by bringing in the more theological concepts either of God's "gathering" his "scattered" people (cf. 24:31) or of the prophesied "scattering" of the disciples (26:31).

31. Mark 3:30 has a different way of clarifying the link, by adding the editorial comment "because they were saying, 'He has an unclean spirit.'"

32. *Did.* 11:7 applies a version of this saying, taken out of its gospel context, to those who question the authority of a prophet speaking "in the Spirit."

33. Among many examples, see the graphic account by George Borrow in *Lavengro,* chs. LXXII-LXXVII, of a Welsh preacher he met on his travels who believed

saying is a wake-up call to the arrogant, not a bogey to frighten those of tender conscience.[34]

Matthew's version of this saying combines elements found in those of Mark and Luke. Verse 31 roughly parallels Mark 3:28-29, which speaks of all other (see p. 474, n. 6) sins and blasphemies being forgivable except that against the Holy Spirit, while v. 32, like Luke 12:10 (in a different context), makes the point more specifically by contrasting the forgivable blasphemy against the Son of Man[35] with the unforgivable blasphemy against the Spirit. Matthew's use of "speak against" rather than "blaspheme" in both clauses of v. 32 (Luke has "blaspheme" in the second clause) produces a tighter comparison, but the link with v. 31 ensures that, at least with reference to the Holy Spirit, it is understood of blasphemy. But see the comments below on the possibility of a less formal sense with regard to the Son of Man.

The balance of the clauses in v. 31 requires the first to be read as a foil to the second, not as a declaration in its own right.[36] It is beside the point to question whether any worse sin could be imagined; the point is that blasphemy against the Holy Spirit stands out from the run of "ordinary" sins as being uniquely serious. It is to declare oneself against God.[37] It is to "call evil good and good evil" (Isa 5:20).

---

that as a child he had committed *pechod Ysbryd Glân,* "the sin against the Holy Spirit," and was now irrevocably damned. See also John Bunyan's account of his wrestling with this issue in *Grace Abounding* §§147ff.

34. For the history of the interpretation of this text, especially in earlier Christianity, see Luz, 2:206-8. Note his plaintive question: "Can exegesis protect our saying from its own history of interpretation?"!

35. The suggestion that Matthew has here manufactured a "Son of Man" saying out of the plural τοῖς υἱοῖς τῶν ἀνθρώπων in Mark's version of the saying (Mark 3:28) has little to commend it. (a) Matthew renders the Marcan phrase correctly by τοῖς ἀνθρώποις in v. 31a, not by τοῦ υἱοῦ τοῦ ἀνθρώπου in v. 32a; (b) οἱ υἱοὶ τῶν ἀνθρώπων in Mark is the subject, not the object, of the blasphemy; (c) Matthew's v. 32 is a parallel not to Mark 3:29but to the Q saying found in Luke 12:10, which also uses the title ὁ υἱὸς τοῦ ἀνθρώπου, and seems quite independent of Mark. Against the related (and more common) view that an original Aramaic *bar-ʿenāšāʾ* was variously translated as "people" and as "the Son of Man," resulting in the different versions in Mark and Q, see Gundry, 238-39.

36. *Pace* Carter, 274, who says that it "affirms Jesus' salvific mission"; see p. 474, n. 6.

37. D. J. Verseput, *Rejection,* 236-38, argues that "all blasphemies" must include blasphemy against God himself, and so feels obliged to offer a rather forced explanation as to why blasphemy against the Holy Spirit may be understood to be worse than blasphemy against God. But surely this is to treat "all" too literally, and to disregard the balance of the two halves of the sentence, which is designed to focus on the *one* unforgivable sin rather than to catalogue all others. If βλασφημία is understood in the first half of the verse in its broader sense of "slander," there is no need to drive such a wedge between the "blasphemies" in the two halves of the verse: to blaspheme the Holy Spirit *is* to blaspheme God.

But if the Son of Man is Jesus, who is also the Son of God (and surely in Matthew's gospel both these points can be taken as read), why is it less serious to speak against him? Perhaps such a question ventures too far into later trinitarian orthodoxy and too far beyond the historical circumstances of Jesus' mission in Galilee.[38] The very mysteriousness of the title "the Son of Man" (see on 8:20) indicates an element of enigma, of the truth about Jesus being not yet openly revealed (see 11:25-27), and in that situation it would be possible to "speak against" him (see above for "blaspheme" in the sense of "slander") without being aware that one was opposing the saving purpose of God. Note the excuse of ignorance in Acts 3:17 (and cf. the distinction between unwitting and deliberate sin in Num 15:27-31). Even Peter, in the heat of the moment, would "speak against the Son of Man" (26:69-75) and still be forgiven. But the significance of Jesus' exorcisms was plain for all to see (v. 28); there could be no excuse for misinterpreting this work of the Holy Spirit and attributing it to Beelzebul.

"This age" and "the age to come" are Jewish terms[39] which apply primarily to the contrast between this life and the next rather than to successive phases of life on earth. "This age *(aiōn)*" (or in 13:22 simply "the *aiōn*") denotes much the same as the term *kosmos,* "the world," thought of as earthly reality apart from God. In Matthew the term is used especially in the phrase "the end (or fulfillment) of the *aiōn*" which we shall meet in 13:39, 40, 49; 24:3; 28:20. What follows from that "end of the *aiōn*" is the "*aiōn* to come," which lies on the other side of the judgment. Here, then, the consequences of the unforgivable sin apply not only to this life but also to the life to come, when judgment will finally have been given.

33 The Pharisees' malicious charge now provides the setting for some further reflections on the power and significance of words (vv. 33-37); this complex of sayings is clearly applicable to what the Pharisees have said, but it may also be more widely applied, and may originally have been preserved independently of this particular narrative setting.

The imagery of the tree and its fruit recalls 7:16-20 (using the same terms "good" and "rotten"), but this saying is much more concise, and is expressed as a second-person imperative ("*make* the tree good/rotten") which

---

38. The danger of reading this saying in terms of later trinitarianism is shown by the version of it in *Gos. Thom.* 44: "He who blasphemes against the Father will be forgiven, and he who blasphemes against the Son will be forgiven; but he who blasphemes against the Holy Spirit will not be forgiven, either on earth or in heaven." This remarkable statement not only drives a wedge into the heart of the Trinity (apparently giving the third person a higher status than the other two), but also, by discarding the title "the Son of Man," eliminates the reference to the *incognito* of Jesus during his earthly ministry and so removes any basis for the difference.

39. For the background see H. Sasse, *TDNT* 1:204-7.

probably reflects a popular proverbial style, as in our "Give him an inch and he'll take a mile" or "Give a dog a bad name." It can hardly be intended as an actual commmand in view of the second clause: are we exhorted to create a rotten tree? The point of the proverb is the same as in 7:16-20: a person's true nature is perceived by how they behave. The relevance of this piece of proverbial wisdom[40] in context will be drawn out in the following verses with special reference to words, whereas in 7:16-20 (see comments there) it was probably more concerned with actions.

34   The address, "brood of vipers," seems to be a fairly general term of abuse, applied to different groups also in 3:7 and 23:33, though it may be significant that in each case Pharisees are involved. In 3:7 it is taken up into the imagery of snakes escaping the fire, but here its literal meaning has no specific application. In 7:11 Jesus spoke of his hearers (disciples) as "bad" in relation to the goodness of God, but here, addressed to a more specific and clearly hostile group, "bad" is used in a more absolute sense; their "badness" (the adjective is a general term of disapproval) is revealed in the stand they have taken against God and his Messiah. *Ponēros,* "bad," is also used to describe Satan as "the evil one" (13:19, 39 and see above, p. 193, n. 55, and p. 231, n. 14), so that it is particularly telling in this context where it is they who have just accused Jesus of being on the side of Satan.[41] For words as the expression of what is in the heart see 15:18-19, the focus there also being on the expression of bad attitudes (and contrast the "clean heart" of 5:8).[42]

35   This saying is similar to the one in 13:52, which uses the same verb and noun for the scribe-disciple who "produces from his store" both new and old.[43] The thought is again of bringing to light what is in the secret place, so that a person's words or deeds reveal what is really important to them, and so their true character. Compare the use of "treasure" language (the same Greek noun) in 6:19-21 to express what is most important to a person, in that case in relation to heaven or earth.

36   The same "I tell you" formula as in v. 31 also marks out this saying as a warning to be taken seriously, and it, too, speaks of ultimate judgment (for "the day of judgment" cf. 10:15; 11:22, 24; 12:41, 42). The Phari-

---

40. Cf. Sir 27:6 (also with reference to words rather than deeds): "The fruit of a tree reveals its cultivation; in the same way a spoken thought [reveals the cultivation] of a person's heart."

41. "Because they themselves are inherently evil and in league with Satan, they are the appropriate leaders of 'this evil generation' (12:38-42; 16:4) and in no small way are responsible for it" (Sim, *Gospel,* 170).

42. R. Mohrlang, *Matthew,* 112, usefully surveys Matthew's ethical use of "heart."

43. D. E. Orton, *Scribe,* 152, 173, suggests that 13:52 derives from the same source as 12:35. For the idiom see below, p. 546, n. 11.

sees' offensive words in v. 24 reveal their true nature, and on this they will be judged. For judgment based on a word of abuse cf. 5:22. It is typical of Jesus' teaching style to shock by exaggeration (see, e.g., comments on 5:22), and "every idle word" sounds like an impossibly harsh basis for judgment; but see p. 475, n. 11, for the adjective traditionally translated "idle," which I have rendered rather by "empty." The point is not the casualness of the utterance, but its fallaciousness: "not . . . 'thoughtless' words, such as a carefree joke, but deedless ones, loafers which ought to be up and busy about what they say, the broken promise, the unpaid vow, words which said, 'I go, sir' and never went (Matt. 21:29)."[44] The Pharisees' charge against Jesus, which was far from "casual" or "thoughtless," is such an utterance, purporting to be a defense of God's truth but all the time working against his saving purpose. Reading this saying in its context therefore helps to avoid the excessive rigorism which a literal rendering of these words out of context can promote, and which can easily turn conscientious disciples into humorless pedants who are afraid to relax or to join in social banter.

37 The courtroom language of this saying fits the judgment theme of v. 36, and its specific focus on "words" sums up the message of the whole paragraph.[45] The unexpected change to the second-person singular, when Jesus is speaking to and about a group, the Pharisees, perhaps marks this out as a saying with a separate origin. But for general ethical teaching expressed as an address to the individual hearer (though set among second-person plural instructions) cf., e.g., 5:23-26, 29-30, 36, 39-42; 6:2-4, 6, 17-18, 21-23; it is a typical aspect of Jesus' teaching style as presented by Matthew, encouraging the reader to consider the personal application of the teaching.

4. The Demand for a Sign (12:38-45)

> **38** *Then some of the scribes and Pharisees responded to him, "Teacher, we want to see a sign from you."* **39** *But he replied to them, "It is a wicked and adulterous generation which demands a sign. No sign will be given to it except the sign of Jonah the prophet.* **40** *For just as 'Jonah was three days and three nights in the belly of the sea monster,' so the Son of Man will be three days and three nights in the heart of the earth.* **41** *The men of Nineveh will rise up at the judgment with this generation and will condemn it, because they repented in re-*

---

44. G. B. Caird, *Language,* 22. J. Jeremias, *Theology,* 220, suggests that "the underlying basis for the adjective ἀργός is an Aramaic bᵉṭīl . . . 'deceptive (not corresponding to the truth) words.'"

45. For Jewish parallels see *m. 'Abot* 1:17; 3:14, warning that to multiply words promotes sin, so that silence is wiser.

sponse to Jonah's proclamation, and I tell you that¹ something more than Jonah is here. 42 *The queen of the South will be raised² up at the judgment with this generation and will condemn it, because she came from the ends of the earth to hear the wisdom of Solomon, and I tell you that something more than Solomon is here.*

43 *"When the unclean spirit is expelled from³ a person, it wanders through arid places looking for somewhere to settle, and does not find it anywhere.* 44 *Then it says, 'I will return to my own home from which I have been expelled.' So it comes and finds it unoccupied, swept clean, and tidied up.* 45 *Then it goes and recruits seven other spirits worse than itself, and together they come in and live there. So the final state of that person is worse than at first. That is the way it will be with this wicked generation."*

A new challenge from the religious authorities (v. 38) introduces a further polemical response by Jesus. The issue is now overtly christological, as the demand for a "sign" is, like the later challenge in Jerusalem (21:23: "By what authority do you act like this, and who gave you this authority?"), in effect a questioning of Jesus' special authority. Jesus is putting himself forward as someone of unique status ("something greater than the temple," v. 6; "the Lord of the sabbath," v. 8), who acts by the power of God's Spirit, and in whose activity God's kingship is being established (v. 28). Such a bold claim needs to be verified: if God has sent him, surely God will be prepared to authenticate him. "We want to see a sign."

Jesus' response is not very accommodating. The only sign he offers is cryptic and, worse, is still set in the future so that it can be of no help to them now. The demand is met rather by repeated (and indeed escalated) assertions of Jesus' special status, in relation even to those who in the past have had a key role as mediators between God and his people, and by the warning that to fail to recognize where God is now at work is to risk ultimate condemnation. For so obvious an authority no sign is needed. It is not so much an answer as a counterchallenge. In the narrative context it clearly does not satisfy, as the

---

1. "I tell you that" is intended to convey the declarative force of ἰδού, "look!" both here and in v. 42; ἰδού functions in these formulae much the same as λέγω ὑμῖν ὅτι does in the similar formula of v. 6.

2. While ἀνίσταμαι (middle) in v. 41 and ἐγείρομαι (passive) here are in NT usage effectively synonyms for "rise up" with reference to future resurrection, the fact that different verbs are used in these two otherwise identically formulated verses perhaps deserves to be marked in translation, even though there is no discernible difference in the meaning in context.

3. Literally, "goes out from," but the context requires the sense of forcible expulsion through exorcism.

demand will be repeated in 16:1, and Jesus' repeated refusal of a sign then will mark the end of dialogue between him and the Galilean authorities.

Just as in the previous section a further paragraph of polemical comment was added to Jesus' response (vv. 33-37), so now again we find an added paragraph (vv. 43-45), still presented as part of Jesus' response, but which does not directly deal with the demand for a sign. It is a curious little "case history," told with the light touch of popular storytelling ("a somewhat puzzling ghost story," Luz, 2:213), concerning what may happen after an exorcism. It thus relates to the theme of vv. 22-29 (and indeed in Luke 11:24-26 it follows directly after that episode), but Matthew has placed it after the demand for a sign because for him it illustrates the spiritual danger facing "this generation," and by adding the final clause of v. 45 (not in the Luke parallel) he makes that connection explicit. The repeated reference to the "generation" in vv. 39, 41, 42, and 45 thus binds this section together and links it to the critical comments on "this generation" which we have read in 11:16-19, and which will reach their threatening climax in 23:36-39.

38 Hitherto in this chapter Jesus' opponents have been described simply as "Pharisees" (vv. 2, 14, 24; similarly in earlier controversies, 9:11, 34). The inclusion of "scribes" this time may reflect the more overtly theological character of the challenge, but the pairing is one which comes naturally to Matthew (5:20; 7:29; 15:1, and throughout ch. 23), as the interests of the two groups were closely related (see on 5:20). As, in their own view at least, guardians of true religion, they cannot allow Jesus' outrageous claims to go unchallenged. "Teacher" (an address used in Matthew by outsiders, not by disciples; see on 8:19) draws attention to his challenges to the teaching authority of the scribes, though it is not only his teaching which is now in question. The idea of an authenticating "sign" (cf. John 6:30) has good OT pedigree.[4] Moses, in the expectation that his God-given authority would be challenged, was given miracles to perform (Exod 4:1-9, 29-31; 7:8-22); Gideon requested and received a sign to confirm God's promise (Judg 6:36-40); Elijah called down fire from heaven (1 Kgs 18:36-39); Ahaz and Hezekiah were offered signs to authenticate Isaiah's prophecies (Isa 7:10-14; 38:7-8). All these signs took the form of miraculous or otherwise inexplicable events, and even though "sign" is not used in the Synoptics, as it is in John, as a word for "miracle," it would be natural to assume that that is what Jesus is now asked for (as it is apparently in 16:1, "a sign from heaven"),[5] though in view

---

4. For the concept in both the OT and later Judaism see O. Linton, *ST* 19 (1965) 112-29. The evidence is usefully summarized by J. Gibson, *JSNT* 38 (1990) 38-40.

5. J. Gibson, *JSNT* 38 (1990) 37-66, argues that in the Marcan parallel the request had a more specific focus: "the 'sign' is a phenomenon whose content is apocalyptic in tone, triumphalistic in character, and the embodiment of one of the 'mighty deeds of de-

of the steady succession of miracles already recorded it is not easy to surmise what more they wanted — unless this particular group had not been present at any of Jesus' miracles. But even in the OT miraculous signs were not in themselves a guarantee of a prophet's authenticity (Deut 13:1-3; cf. also Matt 24:24), and the Pharisees have found another explanation for Jesus' exorcisms (v. 24). Are they then looking for something more unambiguous (cf. the recognition in v. 27 that Jesus was not the only exorcist around)?

39   In view of the OT precedent the request for a sign is not in itself objectionable, and indeed Jesus has already drawn attention to the evidential value of his miracles in 9:6; 11:4-6, 21, 23. But Jesus dismisses the present request because of the attitude of those who have made it. "A wicked and adulterous generation" is perhaps an echo of Moses' description of rebellious Israel in Deut 32:5 (cf. Deut 1:35); see 17:17 for a more direct echo of the same passage. Israel's "adultery" in going after other gods is a frequent theme of the prophets. Here the leaders' challenge is taken to represent the sceptical attitude of the people in general. Their demand[6] for a sign after so much clear evidence (note especially v. 28) betrays their fundamental opposition to God's purpose as it is now focused in the ministry of Jesus. If they have not been convinced by what has already happened, what sort of sign can hope to persuade them? The refusal of a sign is absolute in Mark's parallel passage (8:11-12), but Matthew and Luke (11:29-30) both qualify it by an enigmatic reference to the "sign of Jonah," which they then develop differently, Matthew by an explicit typological parallel (v. 40), Luke by stating more cryptically simply that as Jonah was a sign to the people of Nineveh, so will the Son of Man be to this generation.

It is the view of some commentators that Jesus originally left the nature of the "sign of Jonah" open and that it is Matthew who has tied it down to a typological comparison of the sort that clearly appealed to him. Just *how* Jonah was a sign to the Ninevites in this supposed pre-Matthean form of the saying must be a matter of conjecture, but many suggest that it was in his preaching, a call to repentance which formed a model for that of Jesus (4:17). But Luke does not say that, any more than Matthew does. Luke's insertion of the saying about the Queen of Sheba between the "sign" saying and the Ninevites' repentance (whereas Matthew puts the Queen of Sheba after the

---

liverance' that God had worked on Israel's behalf in rescuing it from slavery" (53). That is a lot to read between the lines. R. H. Gundry, *Mark*, 402, is less definite: they are looking not for a miracle, but "a different kind of display, one that resists attribution to satanic power, magic or any other source besides God himself. . . . Exactly what kind they leave open." But, even though σημεῖον does not *mean* "miracle," OT precedent suggests that a miraculous occurrence would have been the natural sort of sign to look for.

6. ἐπιζητέω, which I have translated "demand" here, is a stronger compound of ζητέω, "seek"; see the comments on 6:33 above.

Ninevites) suggests that he did not intend his v. 30 to be interpreted directly by his v. 32; moreover, his future tense in v. 30 indicates that the sign is something still future rather than the present preaching activity of Jesus — which, in any case, hardly constitutes a "sign." References to the book of Jonah in extant Jewish literature show that it was not his preaching that was their main interest, but his experience in and deliverance from the sea monster, so that an unadorned reference to "the sign of Jonah" would be more likely to be understood in that light.[7] In that case the interpretation given in Matt 12:40 may not be so far wide of the mark. If v. 40 was part of the original tradition, it is strange that Luke omitted it, though it is possible that he was embarrassed by the apparent factual discrepancy between the "three days and three nights" of v. 40 and the "third day" of his own passion predictions (Luke 9:22 etc.). But even if v. 40 is Matthew's elucidation of an originally cryptic saying, it is not as obvious as some interpreters have suggested that he has missed the point of Jesus' reference to Jonah.[8]

If the "sign" is in fact to be accomplished, as v. 40 states, through Jesus' death and resurrection, it will of course be too late to convince his present hearers. From their point of view, therefore, the refusal of a sign remains for the time being absolute despite the tantalizing "except." It is Matthew's readers who, with hindsight, can see what the exception means. After the resurrection had occurred, it became the primary evidence in Christian preaching for Jesus' messianic credentials (Acts 2:22-36; 4:10-12; 13:29-39; 17:31, etc.).[9]

40 The carefully balanced wording of the two clauses (the first being a verbatim quotation of LXX Jonah 2:1 [EVV 1:17]) draws the typological parallel.[10] So far it is simply a matter of *comparable* experience — the further typological element of repetition *on a higher level* will be added in v. 41.[11] The explicit point of comparison is between Jonah's confinement in

7. P. Seidelin, *ST* 5 (1951) 119-31, demonstrates this at length. Note how popular awareness of the story of Jonah today is similarly almost entirely limited to the "whale" rather than to his role as a preacher.

8. I argue this understanding of the tradition in my *Jesus and the OT*, 43-45, supplemented by an excursus on the authenticity of v. 40 (ibid., 80-82). See also G. R. Beasley-Murray, *Kingdom*, 252-57.

9. In the light of v. 40 there is no reason to interpret this saying in relation to the obscure reference to a "sign" in 24:30, where the reference is to a still later period and "sign" is probably used in a different sense, with no reference to Jonah (see comments there).

10. The omission of v. 40 by Justin when quoting this passage in *Dial.* 107:1 has been held, e.g., by K. Stendahl, *School*, 132-33, to show that this verse was not part of Matthew's original text, even though there is no MS evidence for its omission. See, to the contrary, my *Jesus and the OT*, 81-82.

11. I have discussed these aspects of NT typology in my *Jesus and the OT*, ch. 3, esp. pp. 38-43. See also ibid., pp. 43-45, for the Jonah reference as "probably the most obvious example of typology attributed to Jesus."

the sea monster and Jesus' confinement in the earth, but the "three days and three nights" points to the divine intervention which brought each confinement to a spectacular end (Jonah 2:10, and Jesus' resurrection). The different phrasing of the three-day period compared with the "third day" of Matt 16:21; 17:23; 20:19; 27:64 and the "after three days" of Matt 27:63 is due to the LXX wording, but in Semitic inclusive time-reckoning these do not denote different periods as a pedantic Western reading would suggest.[12] The resurrection of Jesus will therefore demonstrate a correspondence between him and the prophet Jonah, each miraculously released from death; in Jonah's case it was a virtual death (cf. Jonah 2:2, 6, "the belly of Sheol," "the Pit"), but in Jesus' case it would be actual death (whether "the heart of the earth"[13] refers to Sheol, the place of the dead, or merely to the tomb).[14] This is the most explicit anticipation of Jesus' death in the gospel so far (cf. 9:15).

But was Jonah's deliverance from drowning "a sign to the Ninevites" (Luke 11:30)? In the OT narrative it occurs before his arrival in Nineveh, presumably somewhere on the Mediterranean shore, far from Nineveh, and there is nothing to suggest that the people of Nineveh knew about it. It was his prophetic message, not his marine experience, which led to their repentance. But Jewish exegesis was not necessarily so precise; the fact that the proclamation followed the deliverance in the text was enough to allow the two to be con-

12. The same phrase, "three days and three nights," occurs in 1 Sam 30:12 to denote a period which began (literally) "today three days," the day before yesterday (v. 13). Similarly in Esther a period described as "for three days, night and day" (4:16) is concluded "on the third day" (5:1). It is worth noting that the partially Pharisaic delegation which requests the guard at the tomb, and which may reasonably be assumed to be recalling this, the only public pronouncement by Jesus about his resurrection, nevertheless uses the terms μετὰ τρεῖς ἡμέρας and ἡ τρίτη ἡμέρα to specify the period Jesus had spoken of (27:63-64). Underlying this flexible usage is the Jewish tendency to speak of a period of twenty-four hours as a day and a night, so that Jesus' time in the tomb can be said to embrace (parts of) three "day-nights."

13. G. M. Landes, in C. L. Meyers and M. O'Connor (eds.), *The Word of the Lord*, 666-67, claims that the expression is found nowhere else in biblical or pre-Christian Jewish literature, and suggests that it was coined on the model of "the heart of the sea" in Jonah 2:3. Landes goes on to suggest (669-71) that the point of comparison is not Jesus' resurrection, but his supposed proclamation of God's deliverance to the dead before the resurrection (which Landes finds presupposed in the resurrection of the people of God in 27:52-53), in comparison with Jonah's praise of God's deliverance while still in the fish (Jonah 2:9).

14. However "the heart of the earth" is understood, nothing in this verse supports the view of some early interpreters that it relates to the postbiblical Christian doctrine of Jesus' freeing the dead from Hades (*pace* Landes; see the previous note). The idea is clearly present in *Odes Sol.* 42:11-20, probably from the second century, but attempts to discover it in the NT (e.g., 1 Pet 3:19; 4:6) have not been convincing.

nected, and few would have noticed the improbability of the Ninevites' knowing about the deliverance.[15] On such a reading it is possible to conclude, with J. Jeremias, that in both Luke and Matthew "both the old and the new sign of Jonah consist in the authorisation of the divine messenger by deliverance from death."[16] Matthew, unlike Luke, by speaking of the repentance of the Ninevites directly after his typological explanation of the "sign of Jonah," underlines this connection between resurrection and proclamation. But whereas Jonah's deliverance preceded his proclamation, Jesus' will follow it. For his hearers, therefore, unlike Jonah's, the sign can only convey retrospective authorization. For the time being, they have more than enough evidence without it.

41-42 Jesus has already compared his generation's unresponsiveness unfavorably with that of pagans of the past (10:15; 11:22, 24). Now the mention of Jonah leads to a similar comparison but on a different level: the earlier references were to the judgment on wicked Gentiles, but now we are introduced to Gentiles who turned to God, and who can therefore appear for the prosecution against "this generation" at the day of judgment.[17] Even the notoriously godless Ninevites were persuaded by Jonah's call to repentance, but "this generation" has not responded to the call to repent (4:17; cf. 11:20) by the second Jonah. And yet this second Jonah is not just a repetition of the first, because (and here we come to the other essential presupposition of Christian typology) "something more than Jonah is here." Commentators have not been able to agree on any significant reason for the substitution here and in v. 42 (as in Luke) of "more" for the "greater" of v. 6; it is simply a stylistic variation in the same formula between the Q version of the sayings and Matthew's own formulation in v. 6. Both versions use the neuter (see on v. 6).

A parallel contrast, and a parallel declaration of "something more," follows in v. 42. We have noted probable echoes of the story of the Queen of Sheba[18] (1 Kgs 10:1-13) in the coming of the magi to look for the new king

---

15. So P. Seidelin, *ST* 5 (1951) 121-22. J. Jeremias, *TDNT* 3:409, n. 26, quotes later Jewish references to Jonah which assume that Jonah's hearers knew of his deliverance. See also E. H. Merrill, *JETS* 23 (1980) 23-30.

16. J. Jeremias, *TDNT* 3:409.

17. See p. 487, n. 2, for the different verbs for "rise up" in vv. 41 and 42. ἀνίσταμαι need in itself mean no more than "stand up" (in court), but ἐγείρομαι would not naturally mean this, and both verbs are used frequently in the NT with regard to "resurrection" after death. Since the reference here is to "the judgment," that sense seems required here too. The focus of the two sayings is not primarily on the ultimate fate of the pagans but on the unfavorable comparison with Jesus' hearers, but in view of Matthew's interest in the salvation of non-Jews elsewhere in the gospel, it seems probable that he here envisages the future resurrection to life of the repentant Ninevites and of the Queen of Sheba.

18. "Queen of the South" reflects the probable location of the OT Sheba in southern Arabia.

of the Jews in Jerusalem (2:1-12). It is one of the classic OT stories of non-Israelite interest in Israel and its God, and so forms a natural parallel to Jonah's Ninevites, and the two cases are presented in a closely parallel formulation. But Matthew's interest is not only in the responsive pagans, but in the nature of the Israelite leaders to whom they responded. As Jonah represented the prophetic office, Solomon, the son of David, represents not only Israel's wisdom tradition (and it was "to hear his wisdom" that the Queen of Sheba came, 1 Kgs 10:1, 3, 4) but also its monarchy.[19]

In these two declarations Jesus, while not offering any specific sign, goes a long way toward giving his own answer to the question about authority which underlay the demand of v. 38. Jonah and Solomon, the prophet and the wise man (the latter also the king, son of David), represent two of the principal authorities by whom God's message was communicated to his people in the OT; the third major authority was the priests and the temple cult, which has been the subject of a similar formula in v. 6. If "something more/greater" than all these key authorities is now present, and if, moreover, all their functions have now been brought together into a single person,[20] Jesus' questioners have a thought-provoking basis on which to consider the question of his authority. Temple and priesthood, prophet, king, and wise man — something greater is now here.[21]

43-45 This cautionary tale does not relate directly to any of the exorcisms recorded in the gospels, but is a comment on a danger associated with exorcism in general.[22] A person liberated from demonic possession remains vulnerable to further possession if they remain "vacant." Something else, which is not specified, must take the place of the demonic occupation. We can only assume in the light of Jesus' teaching elsewhere that the void is to be filled by discipleship,[23] and more specifically by the Spirit of God, a link which is suggested in this context by the Spirit's role in exorcism in v. 28.[24]

The story is told with wry humor. Contrary to the traditions of St. Antony of Egypt (and the remarks of most commentators here), this demon is

19. C. Deutsch, *Lady Wisdom*, 60-63, argues for the influence of the Wisdom tradition on this whole pericope: "It is as Wisdom itself that Jesus surpasses Solomon's wisdom."

20. Hagner, 1.355, draws attention to Josephus's comment (*Ant.* 13.299) on the unique privilege of Hyrcanus, to be at once ruler of the people, high priest, and prophet.

21. I have discussed this typological focus more fully in my *Matthew, Evangelist*, 189-90.

22. For the recognized danger of "repossession" see Mark 9:25; Josephus, *Ant.* 8.47.

23. Cf. Mary of Magdala, who became a disciple after the expulsion of seven spirits (Luke 8:2).

24. For the Spirit of God in relation to disciples rather than specifically to Jesus see, in this gospel, 3:11; 10:20.

not comfortable out in the desert (see on 4:1), and is only truly at home with a human host. But a home which has been cleaned out is not fit for an unclean spirit, and so he recruits seven (the number of perfection) others worse than himself to help him render it unclean enough to be habitable again.

It is probably unwise to use this folksy parable as in its own right a guide to demonology, since its function here is to illustrate the danger facing "this generation." There is no indication in context that the whole "genera-tion" has been possessed; only a number of individuals have been delivered by exorcism. But their experience suggests a model for wider reflection. The rhetoric requires only that the situation of "this generation" is *like* that of the newly exorcised person, not that they have themselves been possessed. Their "liberation" has been rather through seeing and hearing in the ministry of Je-sus a new power and orientation (summarized in the slogan "the kingship of heaven") which has set them free to make a new beginning; but if they now fail to take the road of discipleship, they are in danger of relapsing into a con-dition worse than before. Half-hearted repentance without a new commit-ment will not last. The message reflects that of v. 30: if they are not positively "for" Jesus, they will turn out in the end to be "against" him.[25]

I. JESUS' TRUE FAMILY (12:46-50)

46 *He was still speaking to the crowds when his mother and broth-ers came and[1] stood outside, wanting to speak with him.* 47 *Someone told him, "Look, your mother and your brothers are standing outside, wanting to speak with you."*[2] 48 *But he replied to the person who told*

25. Gundry, 246-47, suggests a more specific application to "the generation of scribes and Pharisees," so that the empty house represents their "mere appearance of righ-teousness" and the return of the spirits the "outburst of multiplied evil on the part of the scribes and Pharisees" which will result in the death of Jesus and the persecution of his followers. The context allows this suggestion, since "this generation" is specifically linked with the demand of the scribes and Pharisees in vv. 38-39, but the wider use of "this generation" language in the gospel as a whole is against so narrow a reading. For other at-tempts to specify the supposed historical application of the parable see D. J. Verseput, *Re-jection*, 274-76.

1. Yet another attempt to find an idiomatic rendering for Matthew's narrative ἰδού, "behold." Literally the sentence begins, "While he was still speaking to the crowds, be-hold his mother and brothers stood outside. . . ." Two further uses of ἰδού in vv. 47 and 49 are rendered by "Look," since they occur in direct speech.

2. This verse is omitted by several early and important witnesses. Without it Je-sus' question in v. 48 lacks a report for him to respond to (and a "person who told him," v. 48), and the reader would simply have to assume that Jesus had been informed of his family's arrival. It is easy to imagine v. 47 (which is a fairly straightforward rendering of

494

him, "Who is my mother, and who are my brothers?" 49 Then he
stretched out his hand toward his disciples, and said, "Look, here are
my mother and my brothers. 50 Anyone who does the will of my Father
who is in heaven is my brother and sister and mother."

This little cameo, apparently set inside a house,[3] concludes the narrative section which has prepared the way for the discourse of ch. 13. Chapters 11–12 have revealed a wide variety of reactions to Jesus among his Galilean contemporaries, and the parables of ch. 13 will explain how such a divided response has come about. Most of the reactions noted, especially in ch. 12, have been hostile, but at the end of ch. 11 the mood was lightened by a brief glimpse of the "little ones" who have been able to perceive the truth (11:25-30), and now another ray of light concludes the section. In addition to the seeds which have failed or are failing, there is also seed growing in good ground.

The primary focus is therefore on the "true family" of Jesus' disciples (Matthew, unlike Mark, makes their identification explicit), to which his natural family provides merely a point of comparison. This paragraph, though it begins with Jesus' mother and brothers, is not really about them. After the account of Jesus' childhood in chs. 1–2 we have heard nothing more of his family. We do not even know whether his move down to Capernaum in 4:13 involved any of them, though 13:56 tells us that his sisters at least stayed in Nazareth. Nor will they be mentioned directly again, though some have supposed that the mysteriously named "Mary the mother of James and Joseph" at the cross (27:56) was in fact Jesus' mother (this will be judged unlikely; see comments there). Even Mark's brief notice of the attitude of (probably)[4] Jesus' family to his activity in Mark 3:21 finds no place in Matthew. Matthew's narrative as a whole thus reflects the message of this paragraph: Jesus' natural family is not the family that matters.

---

v. 46 into reported speech) being created to smooth over that obvious unevenness in the narrative. But, on the other hand, it is possible that v. 47 was omitted by mistake since it is so similar to v. 46, and the eye skipped from the end of one sentence to the next. The minor variations between them (an additional σου after μήτηρ and the placing of ἔξω before the verb) tell against a simple construction of v. 47 from v. 46. Since Matthew is here following Mark, whose version has a verbal report at this point (3:32), it is perhaps more likely that v. 47 is original in Matthew too.

3. Jesus "goes out of the house" in 13:1; but the presence of "crowds" here is surprising in that case.

4. See my *Mark*, 164-67, on the interpretation of the notoriously obscure Mark 3:21. Most versions and commentators identify οἱ παρ' αὐτοῦ as Jesus' family, on the assumption that this verse prepares the way for the arrival of the family "to take control of him" in 3:31. Matthew gives no such preparatory notice.

The "disciples" referred to in v. 49 are primarily the Twelve, who might be expected to be with Jesus, but Matthew's usage allows for a wider group (see on 8:21), and the inclusion of "sister" in v. 50 demands it. It is these disciples who constitute Jesus' true family. In the itinerant life in Galilee it is they, rather than the Nazareth family, who share his day-to-day life, but the thought here is at a less mundane level than that. Those who follow Jesus have committed themselves to "do the will of my Father who is in heaven," and so have entered into a new relationship with God as also their "heavenly Father" — the term which so prominently expressed the essence of discipleship in chs. 5–7. And those who are children of the same heavenly Father are thus members of the same family, and are to regard one another as brothers and sisters; for "brother" used of fellow disciples see 5:22-24; 7:3-5; 18:15, 21, 35; 23:8. In place of the earthly families some of them have had to leave, they are promised a hundred-fold more brothers, sisters, parents, and children (19:29). And this extended family under the one heavenly Father (23:8-9) includes Jesus himself, who acknowledges the same Father in heaven, so that he can refer to his disciples as "my brothers" (cf. 25:40; 28:10).[5]

This familial view of discipleship and of the nature of the new community being formed around Jesus is vividly expressed in this little paragraph by contrast with the mother and brothers from Nazareth who now apparently form no part of the Jesus circle. The result is that on the one occasion when Jesus' natural family appear in the narrative outside the infancy stories they are dismissed in what many have taken to be an unfeeling manner. The Jesus who in 15:4-6 upholds the OT command to honor one's father and mother here seems to treat his mother and brothers with scant respect. He is putting into practice what he taught his disciples in 10:37, that even the most important earthly ties cannot be allowed to stand in the way of loyalty to the kingship of God. It is a matter of priorities. But it is unfortunate that this prior allegiance to the work of God and the call of Jesus (cf. also the case study in 8:21-22) is not balanced elsewhere in Matthew by words or deeds of Jesus which demonstrate appropriate filial respect and love, such as we find in Luke 2:51; John 2:3-5; 19:25-27, or by any acknowledgment that loyalty to God and to family are not necessarily incompatible. An unsympathetic reader might well conclude from Matthew's account that Jesus' "honoring" of his family, and his instructions to his disciples on the matter, left something to be desired.[6]

5. Apart from John 20:17, these are the only places in the gospels where Jesus speaks of disciples as his "brothers," even though he often speaks of God either as his Father or as their Father (but never as "our Father," including himself with them; John 20:18 conspicuously avoids the phrase). The idea is taken up and developed in Rom 8:29; Heb 2:11-12.

6. See J. H. Neyrey, *Honor,* 53-55.

46-47 It is widely assumed that the mention of Jesus' "mother and brothers"[7] without a father is evidence that Joseph has died by this time; cf. also the naming of his mother and brothers in the Nazareth pericope (13:55), whereas Joseph appears only obliquely in that Jesus is described as "the carpenter's son." The tradition fits the evidence and may well be correct, though it cannot be proved. In Matthew the arrival of Jesus' mother and brothers is introduced without the preparation given by Mark 3:21 (see above), and we thus have no indication of what they wanted to talk to him about. In Mark it is possible to explain Jesus' dismissive response by the unwelcome nature of their mission, but Matthew provides no such justification. What he is rebuffing is apparently normal family contact; they are not even welcomed into the house after their journey. The double mention that they were "standing outside" (see p. 494, n. 2 for the authenticity of v. 47) gives visual expression to their exclusion from Jesus' immediate circle, though Matthew does not go as far as Mark in emphasizing this (cf. the "circle" sitting around Jesus in Mark 3:32, 34) and does not exploit the term "outside" as Mark 4:11 goes on to do. They are not as yet included in the number of the "disciples," however broadly defined; there is no hint of the prominent role to be taken later by both Mary and James in the developing Christian movement.[8]

48-50 The implied repudiation of Jesus' own family[9] is a matter of priority rather than an absolute dissociation; see the comments on 10:37. But the focus here is not on their rebuff but on the positive assertion that Jesus' disciples are his true family. Following Jesus has created a new and far-reaching bond between them and him. But it is a commitment which must go further than a mere profession of allegiance. "Does the will of my Father who is in heaven" exactly repeats the words used in 7:21 to describe true disciples over

---

7. That Jesus' "brothers" (and sisters, 13:56) were children of Joseph and Mary born subsequent to Jesus is the natural reading of 1:25 (see comments there). It is dogma, not exegesis, which suggests that they were either cousins or Joseph's children by a previous marriage.

8. D. Sim, *Gospel,* 191-92, argues to the contrary that Matthew's omissions from the Marcan accounts here and in 13:53-58 are designed to "rehabilitate" James and the other relatives of Jesus; for Matthew, unlike Mark, the natural family of Jesus is included in those who "do the will of my Father," so that the disciples are not so much contrasted with but rather included "within his natural family." The only argument offered in favor of this remarkable rereading of the text (other than noticing what Matthew does *not* say) is that "the mother of Jesus is presented favorably in the Matthean birth narratives." Even if this were so (and Matthew's remarkable lack of interest in Mary herself, as compared with Luke, renders it doubtful), it could hardly overturn the natural sense of this passage and the perspective of the gospel as a whole.

9. The *Gospel of the Ebionites* allegedly used this pericope to prove that Jesus was not truly human: Epiphanius, *Pan.* 30.14.5 (Hennecke, 1:158). For similar early deductions see Luz, 2:226 and n. 21.

against those who merely profess to follow Jesus. See the comments there, and note how the same language is used again to distinguish between true and false in the interpretation of the parable of the two sons (21:31). While presumably all religious people, including the Pharisees and Jesus' family, would aim to "do the will of God," the phrase as used by Jesus, with the more relational title "my Father who is in heaven," clearly has a more specific focus on the sort of discipleship which he has outlined in chs. 5–7 and which was summed up as a "greater righteousness" than that of the scribes and Pharisees (5:20).[10]

The inclusion of "and sister" in v. 50 is a rare case of gender-inclusive language in the gospel accounts of Jesus' sayings (cf. 19:29). Since only his brothers are mentioned as being present here (his sisters having remained in Nazareth, 13:56), the addition of "sister" in the concluding pronouncement is the more significant.[11] It shows that there were women among Jesus' disciples at this stage, even if not among the Twelve; they remain otherwise invisible in the narrative of Jesus' ministry, but will be mentioned retrospectively in 27:55 (see comments there); cf. also 20:20.

J. THE KINGDOM OF HEAVEN — PROCLAMATION AND RESPONSE: *THE PARABLE DISCOURSE* (13:1-53)

This third main discourse differs from the others (chs. 5–7, 10, 18, 24–25) in that, while the others are presented as unbroken monologues by Jesus (with the one exception of a question and answer at 18:21-22), this one is punctuated throughout by narrative introductions. Twice the disciples ask a question and Jesus responds (vv. 10-11, 36-37); once Jesus asks a question, they respond, and he comments (vv. 51-52); three times Jesus' continuing speech is punctuated by the editorial formula, "He put before them / told them another parable" (vv. 24, 31, 33); and in vv. 34-35 the sequence of parables is broken by an editorial explanation and a formula-quotation. There is even a change of audience at vv. 10-11, and a further change of audience accompanied by a change of location in vv. 36-37 — and since the new audience in v. 36 is the same as that in v. 10, a further unmarked change of audience must be assumed, presumably at v. 24. All this might suggest that this section of the gospel should not be classified with the other discourses, but the factors

10. See B. Przybylski, *Righteousness,* 112-15, for the centrality of "doing the will of God" (as compared with δικαιοσύνη) in Matthew's presentation of the disciple life. Cf. also my *Matthew: Evangelist,* 265-68; D. J. Verseput, *Rejection,* 288-93.

11. Note the contrast with *Gos. Thom.* 99, an abbreviated version of this pericope, which not only puts the brothers before the mother but also omits all mention of sisters. The *Gospel of Thomas* does not commend itself to female readers (especially *Gos. Thom.* 114)!

which link it with them are greater than the differences. It is concluded (13:53) by the same set formula; it serves to separate two substantial narrative sections; it has a clear coherence of theme (the kingdom of heaven), and in this case there is also a coherence of rhetorical form in that it consists entirely of parables together with comments on the meaning of parables.

The difference in form may be accounted for partly by the fact that in this case the Marcan "parallel" is much more extensive than for the other discourses, and Mark 4 displays a similar pattern of repeated introductory formulae, audience change, and editorial comment. Matt 13:1-53 looks like a considerably expanded but essentially parallel version of Mark 4:1-34, omitting one of Mark's story-parables (Mark 4:26-29) and a series of parabolic sayings (Mark 4:21-25), and adding further parables which go beyond the theme of growth which unites all the story-parables of Mark 4. But a further reason for the narrative interruptions in Matt 13 (as in Mark 4) is that they in fact enhance the message of the discourse as a whole, both in that they emphasize the parabolic nature of the material presented (vv. 10, 24, 31, 33, 34, 36) and that the changes of audience and location serve to "dramatize" the distinction between the disciples as privileged recipients of revelation and the crowds who receive "nothing without parables" (v. 34), which is one of the main messages the discourse itself is designed to convey.

Following from the portrayal in chs. 11–12 of the varied responses in Galilee to Jesus and his preaching of the kingdom of heaven, the parables of this discourse tackle the natural question why this should be so. If the message is good, and it is being presented by someone whom the reader has by now learned to recognize as God's Messiah, why is it not being welcomed and acted on by all those who hear? Surely the very phrase "the kingdom of heaven" predisposes the reader to expect a triumphant proclamation and response. How can God's kingship be resisted by his own people? The parables provide a variety of models for understanding this conundrum, by highlighting sometimes the varied nature of the hearers (vv. 3-9), sometimes the unexpected nature of the message (vv. 31-33, 44-45), and sometimes the division which is an empirical reality of human society in relation to God (vv. 24-30, 47-50). All this is designed to help the disciples (and through them, of course, Matthew's readers) to be less naive in their expectations, to strengthen them to continue as heralds of God's kingship even in the face of disappointment and opposition.

The theme, then, is "the kingdom of heaven." That phrase is linked explicitly to each of the parables (vv. 11, 24, 31, 33, 44, 45, 47, 52), even though they illustrate quite varied aspects of this multifaceted concept. They challenge the hearer to think through how God is working out his sovereign purpose in his world, as this is now being implemented through the ministry of Jesus in Galilee, and to recognize his sometimes surprising methods and motives in a way the Pharisees have so conspicuously failed to do (and even

499

John the Baptist has found difficult) in the previous two chapters. Only so will they be among the "little children" to whom the truth is revealed (11:25-27), the true family of Jesus who "do the will of my Father who is in heaven" (12:46-50). So the theme of division runs through these parables: unproductive and productive soil, good grain and weeds, good fish and bad. Those who find the treasure and the pearl stand out from other people in the extravagance of their response, and the householder of v. 52 is distinguished from others by his ability to produce the new as well as the old.

The suitability of parables as a method of teaching in this situation is explored especially in vv. 10-17, and we shall consider there the problems of a theory of parables which appears to drive outsiders further away rather than lead them into truth. Modern readers are so used to thinking of parables as helpful illustrative stories that they find it hard to grasp the message of this chapter that parables do not explain. To some they may convey enlightenment, but for others they may only deepen confusion. The difference lies in the hearer's ability to rise to the challenge. Far from giving explanations, parables themselves need to be explained, and three are given detailed explanations in this chapter (vv. 18-23, 37-43, 49-50). But that explanation is not given to everyone, but only to the disciples (vv. 10 and 36), and Matthew not only makes the point explicit in v. 34 (only parables for the crowds, not explanations), but also confirms it by a formula quotation in v. 35: parables are "hidden things." In this way the medium (parables) is itself integral to the message it conveys (the secrets of the kingdom of heaven).

The discourse shows again the careful attention to structure which we have noted especially in chs. 8–9, though interpreters differ in detail as to how they analyze the structure. I find it most satisfactory to see it as focused on two sets of three parables (vv. 24-33, 44-50) separated by a comment on parabolic teaching and a detailed parable explanation (vv. 34-43), which itself reflects the pattern of an earlier comment and explanation in vv. 13-23. Framing the whole are an opening parable which provides the essential foundation for all that follows (vv. 3-9), and a concluding parable which challenges the hearers to appropriate response (vv. 51-52).[1] A narrative introduction (vv. 1-3a) and conclusion (v. 53, using the regular concluding formula) integrate the discourse into the surrounding narrative. The resultant structure may be set out as follows:[2]

1. For the classification of 13:52 as a parable, giving a total of eight parables, not seven as is often assumed, and for the resultant balancing structure of the discourse, see D. Wenham, NTS 25 (1978/9) 516-23. Wenham also explores the possibility of more elaborate chiastic patterns than I am assuming here. His basic approach is accepted and developed by D. E. Orton, Scribe, ch. 6, especially 137-40.

2. Davies and Allison, 2:370-72, treat the very brief interpretation of the parable of the net (vv. 49-50) as on a par with the long interpretive paragraphs vv. 18-23 and 36-43,

1. Teaching by the Lake (13:1-3a)

1 *That same day Jesus went out of the house and sat by the lake.*
2 *Large crowds gathered around him, so that he got into a boat and sat there, while the whole crowd stood on the shore.* 3 *And he said many things to them in parables:*

By specifying the same day and mentioning the house (which Jesus is presumed to have been in for the scene in 12:46-50, leaving his family "outside"), Matthew creates a closer link with the preceding narrative than the other Synoptists. Jesus has just spoken of the special privilege of his disciples, to be regarded as his true family, and this discourse will underline that privilege. It is they, and not the crowds "outside," who have been given the ability to perceive the hidden truths of the kingdom of heaven (v. 11), and their privilege will be underlined in vv. 16-17. To them private explanations of the parables will be given, but not to the crowds, and the narrative shifts within this discourse will underline this distinction (vv. 10, 36). In this introductory scene-setting the boat already serves that purpose: Matthew does not mention here that the disciples were in the boat with Jesus, but their private approach to him in v. 10 indicates that they were — though the introduction of a "house" in v. 36 complicates the scenario and indicates the composite origin of the discourse. The boat forms a convenient pulpit in view of the pressing crowd, but it also serves symbolically to distance Jesus (and his disciples) from the crowd (who, like Jesus' family in 12:46, are "standing" separate from the disciple group), and thus to underline the editorial distinction between public and private teaching. As in 5:1-2 (see comments there) and

---

and regard vv. 51-52 not as an eighth parable but as a "discussion of parables" to parallel those in vv. 10-17 and 34-35 (but in this case following rather than preceding the parable explanation). The result is a no less carefully patterned structure, but in three sections.

24:3, Jesus the teacher adopts the traditional seated posture, while the audience stands. The setting is probably intended to be the shore at Capernaum, where Jesus' home now was.

That Jesus "said many things in parables" might remind the reader of Solomon, who was compared with Jesus as recently as 12:42, who spoke "three thousand proverbs (LXX *parabolai*)" (1 Kgs 4:32). We have already seen a number of parables in Jesus' teaching in Matthew (5:25-26; 9:12, 15-17; 11:16-19; 12:29, 43-45), but this is Matthew's first use of the term *parabolē,* whereas Mark also uses it earlier to describe the form of Jesus' response to the Beelzebul charge (Mark 3:23). It occurs throughout this chapter, where the reference is to story-parables of the type normally associated with the English word "parable," and this is the predominant use elsewhere in Matthew (21:33, 45; 22:1), though it is also used for a simple comparison (24:32) and for a striking aphorism which involves no comparative element (15:15). That last use indicates that for Matthew, as for Mark (cf. also Mark's inclusion of a series of aphorisms in his "parable" chapter, 4:21-25), *parabolē* is wider than the English "parable," and also includes cryptic sayings or epigrams, so that it is closer to the Hebrew *māšāl* (which it regularly translates in LXX), which covers proverbs (like those of Solomon), fables, prophetic utterances, and even riddles, as well as allegorical parables like those of Ezekiel. So understood, a *parabolē* is an utterance which does not carry its meaning on the surface, and which thus demands thought and perception if the hearer is to benefit from it. Learning from and responding to a *parabolē* is not a matter of simply reading off the meaning from the words, but of entering into an interactive process to which the hearer must contribute if true understanding is to result. That is why the same parable which enlightens one may puzzle or even repel another. A parable is not an easy option for understanding, but a challenge to which not everyone will be able to rise. Parables without interpretation, which is all that are offered to the crowds in this discourse, will thus result in a divided response, depending on what degree of understanding and of openness each hearer brings to them. See further on vv. 11-13 for this understanding of parable.

2. Introductory Parable: The Sower (13:3b-9)

3b *"Once[1] a sower went out to sow,* 4 *and as he sowed, some of the seed fell beside the path, and the birds came and ate it up.* 5 *Other*

---

1. Representing ἰδού, which here aims to capture the reader's attention for the story. The romantic speculation that Jesus was pointing to an actual sower at work on the hill by the lake, so that ἰδού really does mean "Look!" has no basis in the text, and the aorist tenses throughout the parable do not suggest something happening as Jesus spoke.

*seed fell on a rocky area where it did not have much soil, and it grew
up quickly because it did not have any depth of soil, 6 but when the sun
came up, it was scorched, and it shriveled up because it had no root.
7 Other seed fell on a thorny patch, and the thorns grew up and
choked it. 8 But other seed fell on good soil, and produced a crop, one[2]
yielding a hundred-fold, another sixty-fold, and another thirty-fold.
9 Whoever has ears,[3] let them hear."*

The title "the parable of the sower" is supplied by v. 18, but while it correctly
describes the narrative scene, it does not help in the interpretation of the parable, whose four-part structure focuses not on the sower or even on the seed
(which is assumed to be the same in each of the four scenes) but on the different types of soil into which it falls.[4] The traditional German title, *Gleichnis
vom viererlei Acker,* "Parable of the Four Types of Ground," better reflects
the focus of the parable. The specific delineation of the four areas, and their
equally specific individual interpretation in vv. 18-23, requires the reader to
compare and contrast them, and to ask what sort of people and situations
each of them represents. Modern interpretation of the parable has increasingly recognized this implication of the literary form of this particular parable, over against the dogmatic assertion of earlier NT scholarship, following
Adolf Jülicher, that a parable has only a single point and that all the rest is
mere narrative scenery, which must not be "allegorized" to determine what
each detail means. In this case the way the story is constructed demands that
the detail be noticed, and to interpret those details individually is not arbitrary "allegorization" but a responsible recognition of the way Jesus constructed the story. To argue, as has often been done, that the parable is all
about the assurance of an ultimate harvest despite disappointments is to do
scant justice to the careful way in which the three unproductive areas are

2. Mark has singular seeds until the last scene, where three successful seeds balance the three individual seeds which failed, but in Matthew's version the "seed" is in
each case expressed in the plural (ἃ μὲν . . . ἄλλα δὲ . . . ἄλλα δὲ . . . ἄλλα δέ) followed in
classical style by singular verbs, so that when the last batch of seed needs to be differentiated, this can be expressed by singular pronouns (ὃ μὲν . . . ὃ δὲ . . . ὃ δέ). In English idiom
this is best expressed by a collective singular "seed" with singular verbs, followed by "one
. . . another . . . another."

3. As in 11:15, most MSS here add the familiar "to hear." While the breakdown of
MSS and versions here is not quite the same, the same considerations apply; see the note
there.

4. *Gos. Thom.* 9 equally preserves the fourfold shape of the parable, even though
Thomas tends to give an abbreviated version of some other parables and sayings as compared with the Synoptics. The *Gospel of Thomas* does not include an explanation of the
parable.

sketched and to the differentiation in the yields achieved by different seeds in v. 8. There is in the end a good harvest, of course, but the parable also explains why it is not as large as it might have been, and challenges the reader to think about the obstacles to growth as much as about the happy ending.

An interpretation of the parable will follow in vv. 18-23, and I will postpone until then comment on what it all means. Even if, as many have argued, the interpretation differs from Jesus' original intention in telling this story (see on vv. 18-23), within the literary context of Matthew's gospel (as also of Mark and Luke) it provides the definitive account, so that the commentator on *Matthew* cannot discuss the story without its explanation. Indeed, it is tempting to avoid repetition by dealing with both passages together (as I did in my earlier commentary on Matthew), but Matthew has not placed them together, and the intervention of a substantial section of teaching about parables in vv. 11-17 is presupposed in the way the explanation is framed. So we shall deal with the two sections as they come in the text, but I shall try as far as possible to focus here on the story itself, leaving discussion of its implications until we have Matthew's own input on the subject.

3b-4   In a primarily agrarian society the choice of agricultural imagery for parables needs no special explanation;[5] three of the parables in this chapter are set on the farm (and cf. 20:1-16; 21:33-43). The sowing envisaged is most likely of wheat or barley, the two principal grain crops of Palestine at the time. The seed falling on the beaten earth beside the path, where it could not penetrate, may be the few grains which inevitably go beyond the intended range in broadcast sowing, though it is also possible that the technique envisaged is of sowing before plowing,[6] in which case the birds reached the seed before the path could be plowed up and the grain buried (a familar hazard?; see *Jub.* 11:11). This seed is totally wasted.

5-6   The second scenario would be familiar to those who farmed the rocky land of Galilee, where the bedrock is often close to the surface. It is not clear why seed sown on thin soil should grow initially any quicker than elsewhere, as the wording of v. 5 suggests, but the point of the scene is rather in

---

5. Such as a reference to God as a sower in Jer 31:27-28; Hos 2:23. More relevant may be Isa 55:10-11, which describes the effectiveness of God's word going out in terms of seed and fruitfulness (see C. A. Evans, *CBQ* 47 [1985] 464-68). A closer parallel is the use of seed imagery in *4 Ezra* 4:28-32; 8:6; 9:30-37, and especially 8:41, but since *4 Ezra* is normally dated about A.D. 100, this is not a source of Jesus' imagery, but rather testifies to the natural use of a familiar aspect of rural life.

6. So J. Jeremias, *Parables,* 11-12. The point has been much debated, and it is more likely that plowing generally preceded sowing (as it clearly does, e.g., in Isa 28:24-25), but that the seed might then be plowed in. So K. D. White, *JTS* 15 (1964) 303-5; reply by Jeremias, *NTS* 13 (1966/7) 48-53. See also J. Drury, *JTS* 24 (1973) 368-70; P. B. Payne, *NTS* 25 (1978/9) 123-29.

the contrast between this apparently promising initial growth and the inability of the growing plants to sustain themselves when the heat is on and the shallow soil is quickly parched. Here there is initial growth,[7] but it doesn't last.

7   This third scene is similar, but this time the danger comes not from the inadequate resources in the soil, but from competition. The luxuriant growth of the thorns shows that there is nothing wrong with the soil here; the problem is that it is already occupied and there is no room for a new type of vegetation (another recognized hazard; Jer 4:3). The plants do not necessarily die, but they cannot produce grain because of the competition for light and nourishment.[8] There has thus been a progression in the first three scenes: the first seed never started; the second started well but did not survive; the third may even have survived, but produced nothing. But none of them are of any use to the farmer.

8-9   In contrast with the three scenes of failure we now consider the seed which grows and is productive. There is no indication of what proportion of seed meets with the various fates mentioned, so that it is not legitimate to state, as some commentators do, that only one quarter of the seed was successful. Presumably, unless this is an extraordinarily incompetent farmer, the majority of the seed falls into good ground and produces a crop. But even here there is variation. It is not certain how the yield is being computed. If "thirty-fold" means thirty bushels harvested for every bushel sown, it would be a good but not unimaginable crop, but if, as is more likely,[9] it means that each germinating plant had thirty grains, it is probably on the low side of normal. In that case sixty-fold is an average crop, and a hundredfold very good but not miraculous.[10] The inclusion of the three levels of

---

7. *Gos. Thom.* 9, by contrast, allows no growth at all: "they did not send a root down into the earth and did not send an ear up to heaven."

8. *Gos. Thom.* 9 adds a further hazard in this third scene: they are eaten by a worm

9. See K. D. White, *JTS* 15 (1964) 301-3; cf. P. B. Payne, *GP* 1:181-86; Luz, 2:241-42.

10. Contra J. Jeremias, *Parables,* 150, who finds in it "the eschatological overflowing of the divine goodness, surpassing all human measure." White and Payne (see last note) are very critical of Jeremias's assumptions; but see contra R. McIver, *NTS* 40 (1994) 606-8, who argues that a four- or fivefold yield would be more normal in Roman Palestine. In Gen 26:12 a hundred-fold harvest is a mark of God's blessing, but it is not presented as outside human possibility. Pliny, *Hist. nat.* 18.21.95, also speaks of a hundredfold harvest as very good, whereas four-hundred-fold would quite extraordinary. For further references to yields in ancient literature (mainly based on the criterion of yield per quantity sown) see Keener, 377-78. Ancient writers who wished to speak of miraculous yields were much less restrained: *b. Ketub.* 111b–12a lists various amazing yields, including fifty thousand *kōr* from one *sᵉʾâh* (i.e., 1,500,000-fold); Papias (in Irenaeus, *Haer.* 5.33.3-4) speaks of a single grain of wheat producing ten thousand ears, and each ear ten thousand grains, and each grain five double pounds of flour!

yield[11] seems likely to be intended to be noticed;[12] see further on v. 23. For
the parable-formula of v. 9 see above on 11:15; its relevance in this context
will become clear in vv. 11-17 when the consequences of the way one
"hears" are spelled out.

3. About Teaching in Parables (13:10-17)

10 *His disciples came to him and asked him, "Why do you speak to
them in parables?"*

11 *He replied to them, "Because[1] to you it has been given to know
the secrets of the kingdom of heaven, but to them it has not been given.*
12 *For whoever has, more will be given to them, and they will have
more than enough; but whoever does not have, even what they have
will be taken away from them.* 13 *That is why I speak to them in parables, because when they see they do not see, and when they hear they
do not hear or understand.*[2] 14 *And for them is fulfilled Isaiah's prophecy which said,*

'*As you hear, you will hear but never understand,*
and as you see, you will see but never perceive.[3]
15 *For the heart of this people has become fat,*
and with their ears they have heard heavily,
and they have shut their eyes,
so that they will not perceive with their eyes

11. Luke has only the hundred-fold; the *Gospel of Thomas* has two, sixty-fold and
120-fold.

12. It is not clear why Matthew records the three levels of yield in reverse order
compared with Mark. Mark's order achieves a sense of climax as the hundred-fold is
reached so that all the attention is focused on the best result; was Matthew perhaps more
concerned that his readers should notice the variety as significant in itself?

1. Sometimes in the NT, especially in Mark, ὅτι is used as a connective to introduce direct speech (rather like our quotation marks; "merely equivalent to a colon,"
Schweizer, 298), but this usage is uncommon in Matthew (BDF 407[1]); since the vast
majority of direct speeches in Matthew are introduced without ὅτι, it is more natural to
read it here as "because" in response to the disciples' question "Why?"

2. Some significant witnesses here support a purposive construction using ἵνα (in
place of ὅτι, "because") with μή and subjunctive verbs, but this is most likely due to assimilation to the construction used by both Mark and Luke in their rather different summaries of Isa 6:9-10 (see comments below).

3. The LXX version here quoted by Matthew uses βλέπω and ὁράω for the two
types of perception, and English "look" and "see" might render those verbs better. But in
Matthew's summary in v. 13 βλέπω is used for both, and "see" is the English word which
best captures this ambiguity. In that case "see" must represent βλέπω here too, and so
something else is needed for ὁράω.

and hear with their ears
and understand in their heart, and turn around
so that I might[4] heal them.'

16 *But happy are your eyes, because they do see, and your ears,*
because they do hear. 17 *I tell you truly that many prophets and righteous people were eager to see what you see and did not see it, and to hear what you hear and did not hear it."*

The first of two lengthy private "asides" to the disciples within this discourse (cf. also vv. 36ff.) will focus on a detailed interpretation of the parable just given (vv. 18-23), but before that we have a more general account of how parables are intended to work. This paragraph is thus set between the parable of the sower and its explanation, and the three sections are closely interwoven. In answer to the disciples' question these verses explain why Jesus teaches in parables, but that explanation is itself based on the content of the parable: the failure of some of the soil to receive the seed is a comment on the human condition which Isaiah's prophecy sets out. The point will be developed in the interpretation of the parable in vv. 18-23. And the fact that the disciples, and they alone, receive an interpretation of the parable puts into practice the teaching about their privileged position which is at the heart of vv. 11-17.

These verses, too, are addressed only to the disciples, and indeed the content focuses on their special situation over against the larger crowd on the shore. Here (as in 11:25-27) we find people divided sharply into two groups, the enlightened disciples and the others who cannot grasp the truth however much they see and hear. The parable itself has given a more nuanced account, with its four (not two) different types of hearer, but here the first three groups are treated as one. Though their failure is traced to different causes, none of them find "understanding" (vv. 19, 23; see comments on v. 19), and all in the end fail to produce a crop. As an empirical observation (that people respond differently, and only some will reach "understanding") this would not be surprising, but the point of this paragraph is that this is not just a fact of life but the purpose of God. The truth about the kingdom of heaven is "secret," and is

---

4. This last verb of the sequence is a future indicative, in distinction from the aorist subjunctives ("perceive," "hear," "understand," "turn") which have followed the conjunction μήποτε, "so that not." The last clause of the quotation could thus be read as a promise, "and I *will* heal them," to counteract the dire state of the people, but the flow of the Hebrew sentence more naturally makes the healing a hypothetical result of the turning, which they are *not* going to do, and it is probable that the LXX indicative verb reproduced here by Matthew was intended to be taken that way. The compressed sense then is "[If they do repent], I will heal them [— but they won't]."

perceived only by those to whom "it is given," while the experience of the others has already been predicted in Isaiah's terrible prophecy about people who are unable to grasp the truth and to respond and find "healing." In the Hebrew version of Isa 6:10 the prophet is actually instructed to "*Make* the heart of this people fat" and so on, and while the LXX has dulled the shock of this rhetoric by turning the verbs into passives describing the people's own self-insulation against the truth, it is hard even in that version to avoid the conclusion that this is the way God has planned it. Isaiah 6:9-10 is clearly important to Matthew,[5] since he gives us not only an abbreviated summary of its message such as Luke also has (v. 13), but also a full quotation of the LXX text with its own introductory formula claiming that this prophecy has now found its fulfillment in those to whom Jesus has been sent (vv. 14-15).

Readers of these verses — and even more of the Marcan version, that parables are given "in order that" some people may not understand — find it hard to avoid the conclusion that God has chosen some people to be enlightened and has deliberately left others in the dark, and that parables are designed to reinforce this divinely appointed separation. After all, that seems to be what Isa 6:9-10 was saying (except that it focuses entirely on the unperceptive, and does not mention *any* who do receive the truth!), and Matthew is enthusiastically endorsing its viewpoint. But a few points may modify the harshness of this doctrine, even if they do not entirely neutralize it.

(1) Davies and Allison, 2:389-90, rightly point out that our tendency to focus on the problem of the unenlightened misses the point of these sayings, which is the positive blessing of God's gift of knowledge graciously made available in a world which as a whole is characterized by "ignorance of God's eschatological secrets" (as in 11:25 and 16:17). The glass is half full rather than half empty!

(2) The distinction between divine and human causation which we find so necessary seems to have been less clear to the biblical writers. Nothing that happens can happen without God, and the same effect may thus be attributed both to human (or demonic) will and to the divine purpose (see above on 4:1 and comments on v. 19 below). So the LXX version of Isa 6:10, which attributes the people's unreceptiveness to their own self-hardening, is not in direct contradiction to the Hebrew, which attributes it to the divinely intended effect of Isaiah's proclamation; they are two sides of the same coin.

(3) Few would doubt that as a matter of fact there is a difference in the way people respond to spiritual truth. Some absorb it with delight, while others shrug it off, or even campaign against it. As a depiction of reality these verses ring true. The problem comes when we look for the reasons for the difference.

5. As it was generally in the early church; see, in addition to the Synoptic parallels here, John 12:39-40; Acts 28:25-27.

Modern thought is likely to find the causes in psychology, environment, formative influences, and the like, but in the ancient world they were likely to be seen in more personal terms, so that a depiction of empirical fact easily shades into an attribution of design, whether human, demonic, or divine.[6]

(4) Whereas Isa 6:9-10 gives the impression of a total lack of response to the prophet's message (apart from the cryptic reference to a "holy seed" in 6:13), these verses are set within a parable (the sower) which does envisage a positive response on the part of some of those who hear, as do the following parables; note especially the eventually huge growth predicted for the mustard seed in v. 32 and the leaven in v. 33. The "pessimism" of the Isaiah prophecy is only a part of the truth about the coming of the kingdom of heaven.

(5) Where there are "insiders" and "outsiders," it is presumably always possible for an outsider to become an insider. The object of Jesus' proclamation of the kingdom of heaven was that people should repent, and so become subjects of God's kingship. The disciples themselves represent those who have responded to this proclamation and so have become insiders. So the two categories are not hard-and-fast; the boundary can be crossed. It is not the purpose of these verses to explain how that crossing takes place, but only to depict the situation as it is, with some inside and some outside. In that case it is not appropriate to look for answers to our questions about predestination in this paragraph. As the discourse develops, we shall find ample cause to believe that good soil can be found: the kingdom of heaven will grow like mustard seed and penetrate like leaven, and people will rejoice at discovering it as at finding a treasure or a pearl; "hidden things" are meant to be revealed (v. 35). This paragraph must not be taken out of that context. It tells us that there will always be some who do not respond, but it does not prescribe who they are to be.

(6) This paragraph is about why parables are an appropriate medium for the proclamation of the message. It is because people are so different, and react so differently. A parable is a story or epigram which does not carry its meaning on the surface (see above on v. 3a). It challenges the hearer to engage with it in an educational process which, if the hearer brings to it the right attitude and openness, will result in their perceiving and responding to the truth. But it can equally be resisted, and dismissed as a mere story. So parables, given without explanation, are open-ended.[7] In a situation where

---

6. Note the warning of C. F. D. Moule, in E. E. Ellis and M. Wilcox (eds.), *Neotestamentica et Semitica,* 99-100, against reading the rhetorical style of Isa 6:9-10 with a "pitiful literalism" which takes it as "an instruction to the prophet to make sure that his message was unintelligible."

7. F. Kermode, *Genesis,* 23, describes parables as "narratives that mean more and other than they seem to say, and mean different things to different people."

some are open to truth and some are not, parables, as imaginative challenge rather than simple proposition, are an appropriate way to communicate new ideas. For some they will break through the barriers to understanding, and to such people (like the disciples) the "secrets of the kingdom of heaven" will be "given." But other hearers will remain impenetrable, and the seed will be lost, scorched, or choked. Putting truth before such people only in the form of parables is a way of implementing the principle set out in 7:6.[8]

These considerations do not remove the robust stress on the divine purpose in these verses, but they may perhaps help in accommodating it within our overall understanding of the mystery of revelation and human response.[9]

10 The setting of the discourse in v. 2 described Jesus as speaking from a boat. Since no change of location has been mentioned, Matthew presumably intends us to assume that the disciples were in the boat with him (as they have been in 8:23–9:1 and will be again in 14:13-34), though nothing is made of the physical location, and Jesus will go into a house in v. 36. The boat, separating them from the crowd on the shore, would provide a suitable place for this private inquiry and explanation. If so, the size of the boat (see on 8:23) perhaps means that we should envisage only the Twelve as present (contrast Mark 4:10, "those around him with the Twelve"), though the open-ended definition of discipleship in 12:50 means that what is said about the privilege of disciples applies more widely than only to the Twelve.

Mark 4:13 implies and Luke 8:9 states that the question was more specifically about the parable just given, not just about parables in general, and Matthew implies as much by supplying an interpretation of the parable of the sower after this more general paragraph. But the parable of the sower itself, as a parable about varied hearing of the message, already raises the wider question of why Jesus uses a method which produces such variation in response, and that broader question is tackled first. "In parables" in this context probably means simply "using the medium of parable," but because *parabolē* includes the sense of "cryptic saying" (see on v. 3a) the question could also imply, "Why do you teach them so cryptically?" Why not spell things out for them?

11 In the narrative context the contrast between "you" and "them" refers in the first place to the disciples and the crowds on the shore respectively, but the principle is wider than that. There are (as we saw in 11:25-27)

---

8. Keener, 378-79, cites a wide range of examples from ancient literature of teaching deliberately designed to be understood only by chosen people, and of the practice of private explanation after a cryptic public statement.

9. There has been extensive scholarly discussion of these verses, focusing primarily on the briefer Marcan version (Mark 4:10-12). For a useful survey of that scholarship up to 1989 see M. A. Beavis, *Audience*, 69-86.

two classes of people, those to whom the secrets are revealed and those to whom they are not. The former class are disciples, in the broad sense set out in 12:50, those who appeared in the tableau at the end of ch. 12 as the insiders; others are "outside" (the term Mark actually uses here), not part of the new family to which one gains entry by belonging to Jesus. The life of discipleship has been described especially in chs. 5–7 as belonging to "the kingdom of heaven," and so that phrase now sums up the principle which separates the two groups.

It is a "secret" in the sense that it is accessible only to the insiders. That does not mean that it is to be jealously guarded from others; indeed, Mark adds in this context the saying "Nothing is hidden except in order to be revealed, or concealed except to become visible" (Mark 4:22).[10] It means rather that until those people become insiders they will not be able to grasp it. Only as disciples share "the message of the kingdom" (v. 19) and it is fruitfully received will the secret be communicated.

The Greek *mystērion,* which I have rendered by "secret," should probably be understood against the background of its use in Dan 2:18-19, 27-30, 47 (LXX and Thdt) to translate the Aramaic *rāz;*[11] there God gives Daniel privileged access to the divine "secret" which other wise men have failed to penetrate, so that he can then communicate it to the king. Paul uses *mystērion* frequently for that which comes by revelation, not by natural insight. Cf. the "mystery religions" of the ancient world, which were characterized by carefully guarded secrecy, their "mysteries" being revealed only to initiates. *Mystērion* is therefore not well represented by the English word "mystery," since in our idiom a "mystery" suggests something which is obscure or unfathomable in itself, whereas the divine message once revealed is not necessarily obscure or "mysterious." "Secret" better conveys this idea in English idiom. Matthew and Luke put the term in the plural (in Mark it is singular), perhaps to indicate that what is at stake here is not a single item, but the whole new world of realities which opens up once one enters the kingdom of heaven. The passives "has been given," "has not been given" should probably be taken as "divine passives"; the whole tenor of the passage, as of Dan 2, is to focus on God as the one who reveals. Only when he does so does the truth become available.

10. See above on 10:26 for Matthew's use of a similar saying, and cf. the uttering of "hidden things" in v. 35 below.

11. This term became important in the writings of the Qumran sect (notably in the Habakkuk commentary), where *rāz* is used to describe the uninterpreted biblical text, and *pešer* denotes the authorized interpretation given by the expositor. See D. E. Orton, *Scribe,* 145-51, for Matthew's portrayal of the "understanding" disciples in the light of the *maśkîlîm* ("the wise") of Dan 11 and 12 and of the development of this theme in relation to the "wise teacher" at Qumran.

12   This saying, which will recur in 25:29 to sum up the message of the parable of the talents, has a proverbial feel, and in Mark's parable collection it occurs not at this point but as the last of a series of epigrams which reflect on the parabolic teaching method (Mark 4:21-25; the other sayings in that Marcan complex have already occurred in Matthew's gospel). We have a similar saying: "Nothing succeeds like success." It is a maxim drawn from the world of trade, and sums up all too well the capitalist system of economics and its effects on the "have-not" part of our modern world. But here it is not used literally. In the matter of spiritual perception, too, both gain and loss are compounded; it is the disciples, to whom the secret has already been given, who are now in a position to benefit from further teaching. Once you have started on the road of spiritual enlightenment, the blessings multiply, but those who do not accept the "message of the kingdom" will lose everything (v. 19).[12] Luke, aware of the paradox of losing what you do not have, has rather pedantically explained it as losing what they "seem to" have (Luke 8:18),[13] but proverbs thrive on paradox.

13   The disciples' question is now given a direct answer by an appeal to OT precedent. Isaiah's mission in Isa 6:9-10 was to speak to the people with the clear expectation, indeed the intention as the Hebrew text phrases it, that they would take no notice of the message and so would fail to repent and find the healing God could give. The second half of this verse summarizes the text by focusing on the key paradoxical phrases about seeing and hearing in Isa 6:9 (taken in reverse order, but reflecting the order of the second part of the chiasm in v. 10), with the important addition of the verb "understand," which is repeated in both vv. 9 and 10 of the Isaiah text and will play a key role in the parable explanation in vv. 18-23. The summaries in Mark 4:12 and Luke 8:10 are similar, all reversing the order of the clauses in the same way, so that this is probably a traditional Christian summary of the passage, but the three Synoptists vary in the degree of conciseness in their versions.

Much is often made of the different conjunctions used by Matthew (*hoti,* "because")[14] and by Mark and Luke (*hina,* "in order that"). It is assumed that Matthew's version is a deliberate softening of the original saying, making

---

12. It is possible to discern an echo of this saying in 21:43, "the kingdom of God will be taken away from you and given . . . ," though the verbs (ἀρθήσεται, δοθήσεται) are not uncommon.

13. Cf. *Gos. Thom.* 41, which reads "from him will be taken even the little which he has."

14. It is sometimes suggested that this is the so-called ὅτι *recitativum,* which would here function as in 2:23 to introduce the content which the previous clause has promised (where we might simply use a colon). But since what is being spelled out is the content of "that is *why* I speak to them in parables," the effect would be little different from a simple "because."

the use of parables a response to the people's obtuseness rather than the intended cause of it, a means of enlightenment for the otherwise unreachable instead of a means of concealing truth from outsiders. There may be some truth in this suggestion, but it is not the panacea for the problems of this passage which it is sometimes supposed to be. Matthew, no less than Mark and Luke, has the secrets given to some and not to others in v. 11, and his v. 12 has compounded the inequality. Moreover, his full quotation of Isa 6:9-10 in vv. 14-15 makes explicit what is only implicit in the summary, that the people's failure to understand keeps them from repenting and so from being healed. Set in that context, Matthew's "because" does not seem so different from Mark's "in order that"; intentions and results are blended into a scenario which is not at all hopeful for the enlightenment of the outsiders. "Because" does not in itself make the parables a means of *curing* the people's blindness, but only a form of teaching *appropriate* to it.[15] It will still be only the disciples who have the blessing of understanding (vv. 16-17). People will respond to parables according to their capacity, some with perception and some with dullness, and this is the way God intends it to be. See, however, the introductory comments above for what these verses do *not* say: it is possible for outsiders to become insiders, and we may assume that parables have a role, though not a guaranteed success, in this process of bringing sight to the blind and hearing to the deaf.

14-15 The paradoxical passage from Isa 6, on which v. 13 has been based, is important enough to be cited in full. Unlike the Matthean formula-quotations, which are given as editorial comments, this lengthy OT quotation is presented as part of Jesus' speech. In other ways, too, it does not fit the pattern of Matthew's formula-quotations,[16] both in that the introductory formula is different[17] and in that it uses the LXX text without variation, whereas the

---

15. C. A. Evans, *To See,* 110, suggests the paraphrase, "I speak parables to them, instead of plain teaching, because they are obdurate," and goes on, "The parables do not promote obduracy, they only make it easier to remain obdurate, and so to 'lose what one already has.'"

16. So G. M. Soares Prabhu, *Formula-Quotations,* 31-35. It has therefore been argued, e.g., by K. Stendahl, *School,* 129-32, that vv. 14-15 are not an original part of the Matthean text, but there is no MSS or versional evidence for their omission. R. H. Gundry, *Use,* 116-18, refutes Stendahl's case, though Davies and Allison, 2:393-94, continue to regard it as "slightly more likely." But my reading of recent commentaries suggests that the statement of G. N. Stanton, *Gospel,* 349, that "it is taken by most exegetes to be a later interpolation" is something of an exaggeration. It is not obvious why Matthew should be imprisoned within his own supposed rules of composition: if he does not present this quotation in the same way as his formula-quotations, it is perhaps because he did not intend it to be read in the same way.

17. Hagner, 1:375, suggests that the difference in the formula may be due to Matthew's desire to avoid the purposive sense of ἵνα which he has already eliminated from his version of Mark 4:12 (see above on v. 13).

formula-quotations typically display a mixed and creative form of Greek text. Instead of the verb *plēroō,* "fulfill," which introduces the formula-quotations, we have here the compound verb *anaplēroō,* not found elsewhere in the gospels, which is probably best taken here as a stylistic variant without difference of meaning.[18] It is possible, however, that Matthew added the prefix *ana-* to mean "again,"[19] or "to the top" (i.e., completely)[20] so that the idea may be of a second fulfillment or the completion of a hitherto partial fulfillment: Isaiah's prophecy was fulfilled in his own day (it was after all an instruction concerning Isaiah's own mission to Judah), but now it is being "re-fulfilled" or brought to completion in[21] Jesus' contemporaries. The "they" to whom the prophecy is now applied are still those in vv. 11 and 13 to whom the secrets are not revealed.

The LXX version of Isa 6:9 translates woodenly the Hebrew emphatic idiom "hearing hear" and "seeing see," which might better be conveyed by "Keep on hearing," or "Hear as best you can," but by putting it in the future indicative makes it into a prediction rather than a command.[22] The rhetorical effect is, however, not very different. But in Isa 6:10 the LXX has made a more significant change, in that the command to the prophet to "*Make* this people's heart fat" and the like has become in the LXX simply a statement of fact, introduced by "for": this is the way the people already are, so your message is bound to leave them unenlightened. This not only blunts the sharp rhetorical effect of the Hebrew command, but also avoids the uncomfortable implication that it is the prophet's job to ensure that the people will not respond. Even in the LXX form the text is a devastating indictment of the people's condition, but at least it places the responsibility on them rather than on God and his prophet. Thus the robust Hebrew idiom, with its characteristic disregard of second causes, has been made more compatible with a Greek worldview.

Matthew uses the LXX form of the saying as the standard Greek form

---

18. See its use in Gal 6:2. In 1 Cor 16:17; Phil 2:30; 1 Thess 2:16 it means to "fill up" where something is lacking or incomplete.

19. Cf. the compounds ἀναβλέπω, "to see again"; ἀνακαινίζω/ἀνακαινόω, "to restore" ("make new again"); ἀνοικοδομέω, "to rebuild."

20. This is the sense of ἀναπληρόω in 1 Thess 2:16.

21. The simple αὐτοῖς, without a preposition, is probably to be taken as a "dative of disadvantage" (N. Turner, *Syntax,* 238) expressing those affected by the fulfillment. There is no grammatical basis for Gundry's rendering "by them," which he takes to emphasize "human responsibility."

22. *Targum Jonathan,* which *may* reflect conventional interpretation as early as the time of Jesus, turns v. 9 into a description of the antecedent state of the people rather than the result of Isaiah's preaching: "Go and speak to this people that hear indeed but do not understand, and who see indeed but do not know" (see B. D. Chilton, *Rabbi,* 91).

available to him, and not necessarily because it suits his purpose better than the Hebrew. But the LXX wording, "For the heart of this people . . . ," does in fact cohere well with Matthew's "because" in v. 13. Isaiah spoke as he did *because* the people were already unable to grasp his message, and Jesus likewise speaks in parables *because* of the crowd's incapacity to hear with understanding. As a result the "lest (in order that not)," which in Mark 4:12 complements the earlier "in order that" to express the *purpose* of Jesus' parabolic method, in Matthew expresses the inevitable *result* of the people's self-hardening; and their failure to repent and find healing follows from that self-hardening rather than from a divine refusal to allow them scope to return. So Matthew's full quotation of the LXX text has the same effect as his rewording of the summary in v. 13. But see the comments there on the question of whether the overall theology of revelation in vv. 11-17 is in the end any less stark than that in Mark and Luke. The basic theme of "to some and not to others" remains.

16-17   A further saying underlines the privilege of the disciples as Jesus has stated it in v. 11. A version of this saying also occurs in Luke 10:23-24, where it immediately follows Luke's equivalent to Matt 11:25-27, on the special insight granted to the "little ones," a passage with a message very similar to that of this paragraph. This beatitude (see introductory comments on 5:3-10 for the beatitude form, and for the translation "Happy are . . ."), like those of 5:3-10, differentiates those so congratulated from others who have not received the same privilege. The contrast is first with the crowds, whose condition has just been described in terms of Isa 6:9-10: the disciples have eyes which *really* see (as opposed to seeing without seeing) and ears which *really* hear (as opposed to hearing without understanding). But there is a further contrast in v. 17, with people in the past who were in no way hardened against the truth ("prophets" and "righteous people"[23] are by definition on the side of God and his truth rather than of human resistance to his word), but who lived too soon to see and hear what is now available to Jesus' disciples. The prophets looked forward to the day of eschatological restoration, to the coming of what Jesus now calls "the kingdom of heaven," but saw it only in prefiguration and promise, not in existential reality. For all their eagerness to see God's purpose fulfilled, they "could not without us be made complete" (Heb 11:40; cf. Heb 11:13). Like Abraham, who "rejoiced to see my day" (John 8:56), the prophets spoke of "the grace given to *you,*" aware that their service was not for their own benefit but for "yours," things which even angels are agog to get a glimpse of (1 Pet 1:10-12)! There is an incredulous wonder running through these NT reflections on the privilege of those who live at the time when God's saving purpose comes to fruition.

---

23. See B. Przybylski, *Righteousness,* 101-2, for Matthew's use of δίκαιοι for "those who were properly religious in the past," "the pious of the Old Testament."

Contrast the beatitudes in *Pss. Sol.* 17:44; 18:6, which are at first sight similar to the present text but which relate to those who will see an eschatological blessing still in the future. It is this eschatological secret that Jesus' disciples have now been let into, and so to them the parables of the kingdom of heaven convey not puzzlement but enlightenment. And to make sure that they do not miss it, Jesus will now go on to spell it all out for them.

4. Explanation of the Parable of the Sower (13:18-23)

18 *"So you must listen to [the meaning of]*[1] *the parable of the sower.* 19 *When anyone hears the message of the kingdom and does not understand it, the Evil One comes and snatches what was sown in their heart; this is the person*[2] *sown beside the path.* 20 *The person sown on the rocky area is the one who hears the message and quickly accepts it with enthusiasm,* 21 *but has no root in himself*[3] *but rather is short-lived and immediately stumbles when suffering or persecution arises on account of the message.* 22 *The person sown among thorns is the one who hears the message, but the worries*[4] *of this world*[5] *and the false lure*[6] *of wealth choke the message, and it cannot produce a crop.* 23 *The person sown in good soil is the one who hears the message and understands it; this one does indeed produce a crop, yielding in one case a hundred-fold, in another sixty-fold, and in another thirty-fold."*

We noted in the introductory comments on vv. 3-9 that earlier interpretation of this parable often tended to focus on the eventual harvest rather than on the details of the seed which failed. As long as it was assumed that this was Je-

---

1. The English "hear" or "listen to" does not in itself convey the sense of "really hear," i.e., grasp the meaning of, which is implicit in ἀκούω here (especially after the focus on true "hearing" in vv. 13-17). They have already "heard" the parable in vv. 3-9; what they must do now is understand it.

2. The masculine pronoun and participle require this rendering here and in vv. 20, 22, 23 even though the participle strictly refers to the seed, which would be neuter. See the comments below on Matthew's compressed way of moving from story to application.

3. This person is not of course specifically either masculine or feminine, but the individual nature of the description requires a singular pronoun here.

4. The singular μέριμνα (echoing the verb which was the basis of the exhortation not to "worry" in 6:25-34) is more naturally represented in English by the plural "worries."

5. See on 12:32 for the meaning of αἰών. There is no "this" in the oldest Greek texts here (though many MSS and versions add it), but English idiom requires it to distinguish this age from the age to come.

6. Literally, "the deceit," which in this context must convey both the desire for affluence and its false promise.

sus' intention in telling the story, the "allegorical" interpretation supplied in this paragraph was inevitably dismissed as an early *mis*interpretation — early enough to have found its way into all three Synoptic versions, while the supposedly original intention has left no trace. More recent interpreters have been less convinced of the dogma of the one-point parable, and have been more willing to take each parable on its own terms.[7] When the parable of the sower is approached in that way, an interpretation which takes up each of the four scenes in turn and explains how they relate to the realities of the proclamation of the kingdom of God appears much more plausible, not only as representing how the early church explained the parable, but also as reflecting the sort of application Jesus himself must have had in mind when he told it.[8]

Such a conclusion is the more compelling when vv. 18-23 are taken not as an isolated tract but as part of the development of the discourse as a whole. The fact that the explanation does not follow immediately after the telling of the parable alerts us to the significance of what has come between. The interpretive phrase "the message of the kingdom" (v. 19) takes up the theme of understanding the "secrets of the kingdom of heaven" in v. 11, and vv. 11-17 have explored the different ways in which that message has been received. So the explanation of the parable focuses on the theme of "hearing the message,"[9] and just as vv. 11-17 have given equal or even greater prominence to those who have failed to "hear" it properly, so also the explanation (like the parable itself) will deal at greater length with the seeds which failed. There is, then, a coherence about the whole section with which Matthew introduces the discourse, and the burden of proof must surely rest on those who continue to allege that he has himself failed to understand the parable. Increasingly in modern interpretation that position is being abandoned.[10]

7. The literature on parable interpretation is vast, and this is not the place to review it. For a recent nontechnical guide see R. N. Longenecker (ed.), *Challenge;* also C. L. Blomberg, *Interpreting.* A helpful brief survey in Davies and Allison, 2:378-82, concludes with a significant paragraph questioning the common assumption that parables are all of one kind, and require the same method of interpretation. One would think that this point was obvious enough to anyone who looks carefully at the NT parables, and even more in the light of the wide range of sayings described in the OT as *māšāl,* but the obvious sometimes needs to be stated.

8. B. Gerhardsson, *NTS* 14 (1967/8) 165-93, suggests that both parable and explanation were drawn up with the *Šᵉma'* in mind (the first three soils representing failure in "heart," "soul," and "strength" respectively), and on that basis argues that the Matthean parable fits the explanation "as hand fits glove."

9. Note how this phrase is repeated in each of the four scenes in vv. 19, 20, 22, 23.

10. For a detailed defense of the authenticity of the explanation of the parable of the sower (in its Marcan form) see P. B. Payne, *GP* 1:163-207. Davies and Allison, 2:397-99, judiciously summarize the debate. Cf. the wise comments of C. F. D. Moule in E. E. Ellis and M. Wilcox (eds.), *Neotestamentica et Semitica,* 106-13.

Another reason for claiming that this explanatory paragraph could not have come from Jesus himself is the common assertion that parables in the nature of the case need, and indeed allow, no explanation, and that Jesus always left them uninterpreted, leaving his hearers to work out for themselves what he was talking about. But the gospels do not support that assertion. Nor does the Jewish parable tradition, as exemplified in Nathan's famous, "You are the man" (2 Sam 12:7).[11] Even apart from the two lengthy explanations in this chapter (vv. 18-23, 37-43 and cf. the shorter explanation in vv. 49-50), parables in all strands of the Synoptic tradition often carry clear pointers to their application either in the wording of the parable itself,[12] or in the surrounding context,[13] or in accompanying editorial comments.[14] It is of course possible arbitrarily to declare all such hints unauthentic, but the device wears thin after a time. Clearly the gospel writers did not think that Jesus never gave any indication of what his parables were about. The point is not that they should not be explained, but that those explanations are not for everyone. That is precisely the point of this paragraph, directed as it is specifically to the disciples and not to the crowds.

In the narrative context the primary point of this paragraph is to explain the mixed response to the Galilean ministry of Jesus as chs. 11–12 have outlined it. The disciples were to take courage at that time from recognizing that there is fruitful as well as unfruitful seed, and that where the seed has not grown the fault lies in the soil rather than in the message itself. But the types of soil are described not in terms of any particular group or groups, whether during Jesus' ministry or subsequently, but in general categories which may be applicable in many different times and situations within Christian history. Even as "interpreted" the parable therefore remains open-ended in terms of its pastoral application. The careful spelling out of the successive agricultural hazards therefore probably justifies the use to which the parable has been most frequently put in subsequent Christian exposition, as a basis for those who hear it, even within the disciple community, to examine their own openness to God's message and the fruitfulness or otherwise of their response. The slogan "Whoever has ears, let them hear" (v. 9) invites such an application. Unreceptiveness, shallowness, and preoccupation with this age are

11. E. E. Lemcio, *JTS* 29 (1978) 323-38, demonstrates the currency in the OT of the sequence parable–question–explanation (e.g., Ezek 17:1-24; Zech 4:2-10, 11-14). See also D. Daube, *Rabbinic Judaism*, 141-50, for a similar pattern in rabbinic parables. For further ancient examples of the practice of explaining parables see Keener, 381-82.

12. E.g., in this chapter vv. 24, 31, 33, 44, 45, 47, 52 and elsewhere in Matthew 18:14, 35; 20:1, 16; 21:31-32, 43; 22:2, 14; 25:1, 13.

13. E.g., 24:45-51 and the parables which follow in ch. 25.

14. E.g., 21:45, and often in Luke (e.g., 18:1, 9; 19:11). For further references see P. B. Payne, *GP* 1:171-72.

problems not exclusively experienced by those outside the group, and even within the disciple community there are different levels of fruitfulness.

Each of the Synoptic writers seems to have found it difficult to express concisely how the scenes of the story relate to people who hear the message, and each has gone about the task slightly differently. The story is about the sowing of seed (the "message of the kingdom"), but its moral is found in the different fates which await that (same) seed in different types of soil. Matthew's way of expressing this is clear enough, but strictly inaccurate in that he speaks of each hearer as being the seed rather than the soil[15] but then speaks of how they "hear the message." In the first scene (v. 19) the identification of the person as seed comes at the end, but before that we hear of the seed sown *in the heart of* that person. In the rest of the scenes the identification comes first, followed by a description of the results of hearing, which is expressed sometimes in human terms ("enthusiasm," "suffering or persecution," "stumble," "the worries of this world and the false lure of wealth," "hears and understands") and sometimes in terms of the seed ("have no root," "choke," "produce a crop," "yielding a hundred-fold," etc.). The resultant blending of image and application might not satisfy a pedant, but it does communicate vividly.

18 The emphatic "You therefore" with which the explanation opens links it closely with vv. 11 and 16-17, where it is "you" (the disciples of v. 10) who have been given the privilege of knowing the secrets in explicit distinction from "them" (the crowds), and "you" who have the privilege of seeing and hearing what even God's special people in the past have not been able to perceive. By giving them the explanation which follows, Jesus will reinforce that privilege; the parable which others must work out as best they can is to be explicitly interpreted for them. And the parable itself is about their privileged position, since they, we may assume, are represented by the good soil in contrast to the rest of people who hear but do not understand. It is a parable about "understanding" (vv. 19, 23, taking up the key term introduced in vv. 13-15, for which see above). It is remarkable that, despite the title "parable of the sower," we are given no identification of the sower himself (probably in the first instance Jesus himself, as in v. 37, but in principle also applicable to any preacher of the gospel?); the focus falls entirely on the fate of the seed.

19 The key interpretive phrase is "the message of the kingdom" (repeated in the abbreviated form "the message" in vv. 20, 22, and 23), which is it-

15. The Jerusalem Bible attempted to solve the problem by translating ὁ σπαρείς as "the one who received the seed," but this approach was rightly abandoned in NJB. It is also argued by P. B. Payne, *GP* 1:172-77; even if he is right that this was the sense of an underlying Aramaic version, it is too unnatural Greek to be taken as the evangelists' intention.

self an abbreviation referring back to the full phrase "the kingdom of heaven" in v. 11.[16] It is this message which Jesus has been proclaiming since 4:17,[17] and which has been received in such a varied way in the narratives of chs. 11–12. This parable therefore aims to explain that varied response to Jesus' proclamation. In every case the message is "heard"; what matters is what happens next. The failure of the first seed to penetrate the earth symbolizes lack of "understanding," a term which has been prominent in the quotation of Isaiah's prophecy in the preceding verses (three times in vv. 13-15). It will occur several more times to denote that extra dimension which will take the disciples beyond merely hearing what Jesus says to grasping its true meaning (13:23, 51; 15:10; 16:12; 17:13).[18] The inability to get below the surface which Isaiah had prophesied is here attributed not, as it is apparently in Isaiah (and in Matthew's use of the Isaiah passage), to the purpose of God, but to the "Evil One."[19] See above, p. 193, n. 55, and p. 231, n. 14, for this title for Satan; its personal reference is clear here, where the nominative form is unambiguously masculine, and in vv. 38-39 it will be used in close parallel to "the devil." Mark here uses "Satan," and Luke "the devil." For the possibility in Jewish thought of the same effect being traced both to God and to Satan see on 4:1.

20-21 In the second scene the situation is initially hopeful. The "enthusiasm" of these hearers suggests the crowds who have followed Jesus so eagerly since 4:24-25, and who form the audience for the parables in this chapter, but who remain distinct from the disciples and do not share their "understanding." In Jesus' last days in Jerusalem nothing will be seen of these enthusiastic followers from the early days, while the disciples, even if they fail at the last moment, are at least still there with Jesus. Note that these people are said to "hear" and "receive" the message, but not to "understand." The problem is lack of roots "in themselves"; their enthusiasm is based on external stimulus, not on inner conviction, and so it will not last when the external is no longer there. The scorching sun represents the fact that following Jesus will not always be fun. It is no guarantee against "suffering" — the term often includes, but does not exclusively mean, trouble caused by other people. Indeed, it brings trouble of its own, since the same "message" which

16. See on 4:23 for Matthew's occasional abbreviation of "the kingdom of heaven" where it is a genitive depending on another noun; the most common such abbreviation, "the gospel of the kingdom," 4:23; 9:35; 24:14, is closely related to the present phrase.

17. While the sower is not explicitly identified, Gundry, 251, is probably right in seeing a deliberate echo of Jesus' "going out" (v. 1) in the sower's "going out" (v. 3).

18. For the significance of the theme of "understanding" in this chapter as a whole see D. E. Orton, *Scribe*, 137-53 (especially 143-45).

19. It is interesting that in *Jub.* 11:11 the eating of literal seed by birds is also attributed to the devil, Mastema.

brings enlightenment can also bring persecution from those who do not accept it (cf. 5:11; 10:16-33; 24:9-13). In such circumstances those without roots are liable to "stumble"; see on 5:29-30 for the range of meaning of this verb (here, expressed in the passive, they "are made to stumble"). Here, as opposed to 11:6, we should probably read the verb in its more drastic sense, which I described as "a stumbling which deflects a person from the path of God's will and salvation," since the imagery in the parable is of being completely shriveled up. These "rootless" people, for all their initial enthusiasm, are in the end no less neutralized than the "snatched" seed of v. 19 as far as the kingdom of heaven is concerned.

22 The hazard represented by the thorns is one which is a prominent feature of Jesus' teaching[20] and which will be exemplified in the story of the young man who turned back from following Jesus because he had "many possessions" (19:16-22); true disciples, by contrast, have "left everything" (19:27; cf. 4:20, 22; 9:9). The echo of 6:25-34 (cf. also Luke 21:34) in the word "worries" reminds us of the priorities set out in the discourse on discipleship. A concern with possessions betrays a focus on "this world" which is in tension with commitment to the kingdom of heaven; cf. 6:19-21, 24 on where the heart should be. That tension is symbolized in the "choking" of the grain; there is not room for both God and Mammon to take priority in a person's allegiance. The idea that wealth is "deceitful" is well established in Wisdom literature (e.g., Prov 11:28; 23:4-5); it promises a security which it cannot deliver. This grain too, while it may survive (though "choke" casts some doubt on that), will produce no crop for the kingdom of heaven.

23 Here is a direct antithesis to v. 19: the "understanding" which was explicitly absent there is now at last achieved. The bearing of a crop indicates that this "understanding" is not to be interpreted as a purely intellectual grasp of truth; it is rather the lifestyle commitment which the "message of the kingdom of heaven" demands and which has been thwarted by adverse circumstances and divided loyalties in the previous two scenes. But the fact that a singular person "sown in good soil" is then subdivided into three different levels of yield[21] suggests that we are intended to notice the variety of produc-

---

20. It has, e.g., been the subject of a monograph, T. E. Schmidt, *Hostility;* see pp. 105-7 on the present passage (in Mark). Cf. my article, "God and Mammon," *EQ* 51 (1979) 3-21.

21. See p. 503, n. 2, for the different way in which Mark tells the story, with three singular seeds in the first three scenes, and three successful seeds in the last (so six seeds in all), suggesting that we are meant to compare one group of three with the other, not simply to lump the successful group together. Mark's explanation, however, uses a plural description to identify the reference of each of the four scenes; Matthew's singular descriptions in the explanation thus have the effect of drawing attention in a different way to the unexpected plurality of the last scene.

tivity. Disciples are not all the same, and so equally genuine disciples may produce different levels of crop, depending on their different gifts and circumstances. A similar point will be made by the differing returns achieved by the two successful slaves in the parable of the talents (25:15-17), though in that case both returned a 100 percent increase; it was their initial endowment that differed. Cf. also the equal reward for unequal work in 20:1-15. Such parabolic motifs discourage an approach to discipleship which focuses on "keeping up with the Joneses"; the requirement is to produce the best crop each is capable of, and to recognize that not all will be the same. It should be noted that the variation here is in the disciples' "productivity," not in their heavenly reward — indeed, 20:1-15 does not allow us to extrapolate the imagery in that way.

In accordance with English idiom I have used the term "crop" in relation to grain (vv. 8, 22, 23), but the hearer of Matthew's gospel in Greek would not have failed to notice that the Greek term *karpos* is the same which has been translated "fruit" in 3:8, 10; 7:16-20; 12:33, and will be so translated again in 21:19, 34, 41, 43. It is an important Matthean image for the practical outworking of a commitment to God's service, and it is the mark of genuineness (see on 7:16-20). A fruitless hearer of the message (and the first three types of soil all proved fruitless in the end) is of no more use than a fruitless fig tree (21:19).

5. Three Further Parables of Growth (13:24-33)

24 *He put before them another parable: "The kingdom of heaven can be compared to*[1] *a man who sowed good seed in his field.* 25 *But while people were asleep, his enemy came and made a further sowing*[2] *of weeds among the wheat and went away.* 26 *When the plants*

1. All the rest of the parables which follow in this chapter are introduced by ὁμοία (ὅμοιος) ἐστίν, "is like" (vv. 31, 33, 44, 45, 47, 52). The aorist verb ὡμοιώθη (literally, "was made like") here and in 18:23; 22:2 (and cf. 25:1 in the future tense, as in 7:24, 26) is probably used because it introduces a more extended story with several characters, whereas the remaining parables are closer to a simple simile. That explanation does not, however, cover 20:1, where an equally extended story is introduced by ὁμοία ἐστίν. D. A. Carson, *NTS* 31 (1985) 277-82, argues for a distinction between the future and aorist uses of ὁμοιόω on the basis of whether the aspect of the kingdom of heaven being illustrated is in the future or in the present ("will be like" against "has become like"), but his categorization of the respective parables to fit this distinction is too rigid; few exegetes would be happy to eliminate any future reference from the parables of the weeds, the two debtors, or the wedding feast, all of which are parables of judgment.

2. The use of ἐπισπείρω here instead of σπείρω in v. 24 indicates a second sowing "on top of" the first.

sprouted and produced a crop, then the weeds became visible as well. 27 The slaves of the master of the house came to him and said, 'Master, didn't you sow good seed in your field? So where have the weeds come from?' 28 He replied, 'It is an enemy who has done this.' The slaves said to him, 'So do you want us to go and pull out the weeds?' 29 'No,' he said, 'in case while you are pulling up the weeds, you might uproot the wheat along with them. 30 Leave them both to grow together until harvest, and at harvest time I will tell the reapers, "First gather up the weeds and tie them in bundles to burn them up; but collect the wheat into my barn."'"

31 He put before them another parable: "The kingdom of heaven is like a mustard seed, which a man took and sowed in his field. 32 It is smaller than all other seeds, but when it grows, it is bigger than the vegetables and becomes a tree, so that the birds of the sky can come and roost[3] in its branches."

33 He told them another parable: "The kingdom of heaven is like leaven,[4] which a woman took and hid in three large measures[5] of flour until the dough had all risen."

The audience for vv. 10-23 was the disciples, in distinction from the crowds. No change of audience is indicated here,[6] but in v. 34 it will become clear

---

3. κατασκηνόω means simply to "settle" or "dwell" (see p. 323, n. 4); the reference is probably to finding shelter generally rather than to the more specific idea of building nests (for raising young) which some (myself included: *Mark*, 216, n. 33) have derived from the etymology of the verb (σκηνή, "tent"). In Dan 4:12 Thdt, which the verb echoes, κατασκηνόω is applied not to the birds but to the wild animals, which are hardly nesting, though in v. 21 it is used for the birds; both the underlying Aramaic words refer to dwelling or sheltering, not specifically nesting. *Gos. Thom.* 20 has σκέπη ("shelter") here. As Gundry, 267, rightly points out, nest-building would take place in early spring, too early for the annual mustard to have reached sufficient size.

4. The more normal term for the fermenting agent in bread is now "yeast," but the leaven used in biblical times was not quite the same as modern yeast; see the comments below.

5. According to Josephus, *Ant.* 9.85, the σάτον, here translated "large measure," was one and a half Italian *modii*, which would be rather less than half a bushel, i.e., about thirteen liters. (Ancient weights and measures were not uniform, however, and authorities vary in the equivalences given.) Three such measures of wheat flour would weigh about fifty-four pounds (hence the TNIV approximation "about sixty pounds," since most people now buy and use flour by weight, not by volume).

6. Unless we are meant to read "them" as picking up the "them" of vv. 3a, 10, 13, 14. But the same pronoun has been used for the disciples in v. 11, and it would normally take its antecedent from the more immediate context where the disciples have been the audience.

that these three parables, too, have been told to the crowds, and another change of audience will need to be stated in v. 36 for a return to private teaching for the disciples. We must therefore assume that at this point the public teaching which was broken off in v. 10 is resumed.

This group of parables[7] continues the theme of growth, two of them, like the parable of the sower, concerning seed, the third leaven which causes the growth of the dough. All are explicitly about "the kingdom of heaven," and describe different aspects of the new reality which has come into being through Jesus' ministry. All three include, though they do not necessarily focus on, the patience which is needed before God's purpose is fulfilled in all its glory. The parables of the mustard seed and the leaven form a natural pair which speak encouragingly of spectacular growth from insignificant beginnings, and they will be commented on together. But the parable of the weeds stands apart from them in that it, like the parable of the sower, draws attention to problems and division as well as to the ultimate harvest. It is also distinctive in that it, like that of the sower, will receive a detailed explanation in vv. 37-43, while the mustard seed and the leaven remain uninterpreted. I will therefore comment on this group of parables in two sections.

a. The Parable of the Weeds (13:24-30)

As with the parable of the sower, it will be appropriate to defer discussion of the meaning of the parable until we have Matthew's own input on the subject in vv. 37-43. At this point we will restrict comment to the story itself. This parable is recounted by Matthew alone.[8] It is a straightforward

---

7. All three parables appear, but not together, in the *Gospel of Thomas,* at 57, 20, and 96 respectively, in versions which are generally briefer than Matthew's but not significantly different. The *Thomas* version of the parable of the weeds has no explanation added, and its abbreviated form suggests a greater interest in the coexistence of good and bad until the harvest than in the imagery of the harvest itself, which is the focus of the explanation here in vv. 40-43.

8. Only a very restricted understanding of Matthew's access to source material could justify the view of some interpreters that this parable is Matthew's own adaptation of Mark's parable of the growing seed (Mark 4:26-29), even though in other cases where Matthew follows Mark in telling a parable his version is closely similar. The "nine reasons" amassed by M. D. Goulder, *Midrash,* 367-69, for derivation from Mark 4:26-29 depend on the assumption that Matthew is restricted to Mark for his subject matter (even though his discourse omits Mark 4:21-22, 24 as well as vv. 26-29, and contains five other parables not derived from Mark) and on the unsurprising recurrence of some common vocabulary in two parables each of which speaks of the growing and harvesting of wheat. The content and thrust of the two parables are quite different, leading Luz to suggest (2:254) that this parable was formulated as a deliberate *response* to Mark 4:26-29 in the light of experience which suggested that the latter gave too sanguine a picture.

and possibly familiar[9] account of agricultural sabotage: Roman law dealt specifically with the crime of sowing darnel in a wheatfield as an act of revenge.[10] The story is simply told at this point, with the wording little affected by the intended application;[11] even the tying up and burning of the darnel is a natural method of disposal, though it is certainly unusual for this to be done before the wheat has been safely stored. What is surprising is the extent of dialogue reported between the farmer and his slaves, suggesting an interest in the policy of "leaving them to grow together" which will not be taken up directly in the explanation in vv. 37-43, though it is implicit in the focus there on a drastic separation only in the final judgment (see comments on vv. 36-43).

24 The introductory formula is identical in vv. 24 and 31, while in v. 33 the verb is changed to "told." The verb here, *paratithēmi,* to "set before," while occasionally used in the LXX for presenting teaching or laws, is typically used in both LXX and NT for serving a meal (e.g., Mark 6:41; 8:6, 7; Luke 10:8; 11:6); might it be used here to suggest that parables are "set before" people for them to tackle as best they can in order to get the full nourishment, but that they are not spoon-fed? The opening sentence of the parable encounters the same sort of awkwardness which we saw in the explanation of the sower: the kingdom of heaven is not like the man himself, but like the situation which results from his action.[12] In the parable of the sower all the seed was good; it was the soil that was the problem. But in this story the problem arises not from the soil but from a second type of seed, so the first seed is declared to be "good."

25-30 The story itself needs little comment. This farmer, unlike the one in the parable of the sower, is a landowner with a workforce of slaves, so that when we are told that he sowed the seed we should probably understand that he had it sown by them. The weeds *(zizania)* are more specifically darnel *(Lolium temulentum),*[13] a weed related to rye grass which in the early stages of growth resembles wheat[14] though with narrower leaves, but which produces a

---

9. G. R. Beasley-Murray, *Kingdom,* 369, n. 66, collects references to similar incidents from a variety of cultures and periods. Luz, 2:255, is sceptical: "Who would keep darnel seeds at home?"

10. For the texts see A. J. Kerr, *JTS* 48 (1997) 108-9.

11. Luz, 2:255, disagrees. His argument that "several expressions easily lend themselves to metaphorical interpretation" is correct, but that interpretation is not developed at this point, and the "unusual kind of farming" which he finds in the story is surely related to the fact that the sort of sabotage depicted is itself unusual.

12. See above, p. 522, n. 1, for the way the wording may be designed to acknowledge this problem.

13. For the agricultural details see J. Jeremias, *Parables,* 224-25.

14. *M. Kil.* 1:1 lists wheat and darnel as the first of a set of pairs which are not

smaller ear. Its grains are poisonous, so that to have it mixed in with wheat renders the crop commercially useless as well as potentially harmful. Because of its similar growth the darnel infestation would not be readily apparent until the plants begin to form ears (hence the weeds "becoming visible" at the time when the wheat "produced a crop," v. 26), and by that time it is too late to eradicate the darnel without damaging the wheat with which its roots are intertwined. The only solution is to undertake the painstaking job of separating out the cut stalks. "Burn up" *(katakaiō)* is generally used of deliberate destruction, and so probably indicates incineration as rubbish, though dried vegetation might also be used for domestic fuel. For gathering wheat into the barn as a symbol for ultimate salvation cf. 3:12. In real life the slaves and the harvesters would no doubt have been the same people (though extra harvesters might be needed, 9:37-38), but separate terms are used in the story because, while the slaves are not identified in vv. 37-39, if they have a specific symbolic identity it is presumably as Jesus' disciples, whereas the reapers represent angels.

b. The Parables of the Mustard Seed and of the Leaven (13:31-33)

The first of these parables is shared with Mark and Luke, the second only with Luke (who also presents them as a pair, but not as part of this parable discourse). Mark's mustard-seed parable (Mark 4:30-32) is expressed as a simple simile, with no human agent, but Matthew (like Luke) introduces a "man" who sows the seed and a "woman" who bakes the bread, thus conforming them more closely to the narrative style of the preceding parables. Both speak of a small, barely perceptible beginning which results in a spectacular transformation (cf. our saying, "Great oaks from little acorns grow"). So also the kingdom of heaven, as presented in Jesus' ministry, may be unnoticed or disdained by most people for the time being, but the time will come when it will be impossible to ignore it. Despite the ambivalent and hostile reactions to Jesus and his message which we have seen in chs. 11–12, God's purpose will reach its triumphant fulfillment. Those who despised its small beginnings (cf. Zech 4:10) will have to eat their words. Meanwhile, those impatient to see the full outworking of God's kingship (such as John the Baptist, 11:3?) must be prepared to wait. The outcome may take time, but it is certain, for both the growth of the seed and the effect of the leaven are regular natural processes which, once begun, will surely bring about the desired result.

Along with this basic message the wording of these two parables suggests two further reflections. First, the account of the birds roosting in the branches of the tree recalls Nebuchadnezzar's vision in Dan 4:12, 21,[15]

---

counted as a mixture of "diverse kinds"; i.e., they are "similar enough to grow together" (so D. Instone-Brewer, *Traditions* 1:196-98).

which is interpreted in terms of Nebuchadnezzar's empire stretching "to the ends of the earth"; the birds are not directly identified in Dan 4, but it is likely that they would have been understood as the subject nations which had found shelter within the great empire of Babylon. If so, this parable invites a comparison between the great but short-lived earthly empire of Babylon and the far greater and more permanent kingdom of heaven. The inclusion of all nations in that kingdom might be a bonus point for the sharp-eyed reader who knew the Daniel text and understood the birds as symbolic of the nations, but it is not emphasized.

Secondly, the verb "hid" to describe the mixing of the leaven into the dough in v. 33 draws attention to, and invites reflection on, the hiddenness of the kingdom of heaven, hidden from the wise and intelligent (11:25), and given to the disciples only as a "secret" which is not available to others (13:11), the "hidden things" of v. 35; note also the hidden treasure of v. 44. The "messianic secret" which we shall encounter especially at 16:20 and 17:9 is thus woven into the wording of this parable.[16] The truth about the kingdom of heaven is not only inconspicuous; it is also deliberately kept hidden for the time being. But one day it will be plain for all to see. These two parables thus provide an important counterbalance to the "pessimism" of vv. 10-17 with regard to the revealing of the message outside the disciple group.

31-32 For mustard seed as proverbially tiny, the smallest of all seeds, cf. 17:20; *m. Ṭehar.* 8:8; *m. Nid.* 5:2.[17] Only a pedant would worry about whether there are in fact any smaller seeds or spores! The mustard plant hardly qualifies as a "tree," and the term may be a deliberate exaggeration designed to evoke the echo of Dan 4:12, 21 (see above), though some experts claim that the black mustard (*Brassica nigra,* grown in Palestine for oil and as a condiment), normally not more than two meters in height, could sometimes grow to as much as five meters (others limit it to three), which puts it well above most "vegetables." But the point of the parable does not depend on its botanical accuracy; parables often exaggerate for effect.[18]

---

15. The verb κατασκηνόω ("dwell" or "shelter") and the phrase ἐν τοῖς κλάδοις αὐτοῦ occur in Thdt in both verses (see p. 523, n. 3). Cf the similar tree imagery to describe an empire in Ezek 17:23; 31:3-9, both of which also mention the birds sheltering in the tree.

16. Note also that while vv. 31-32 do not draw attention to the seed *hidden* in the earth, the idea would also fit that imagery well.

17. According to C.-H. Hunzinger, *TDNT* 7:289, there are more than seven hundred seeds to a gram!

18. The proverbial smallness of the mustard seed is sufficient reason for this particular plant to be chosen to make the point about growth; there is therefore no need to follow M. Sabin, *JSNT* 45 (1992) 21, in regarding the choice of a garden vegetable rather than a noble tree as a deliberate "jolt, even a joke."

33 The normal method of bringing about fermentation in bread-making in the ancient world was to insert into the new dough a small amount of old, fermented dough reserved from the previous baking; it is this "leaven" (or sourdough) rather than "yeast" proper which the woman is here using.[19] The leaven is unlike the mustard seed in that it is not its own growth which is remarkable, but the expansion which it causes in the new dough. So the kingdom of heaven (and those who represent and proclaim it) has a dramatic effect on human society.[20] The wording of this parable is concise: we are not told how much leaven was used or what was the quantity of leavened bread which resulted, but the point is that a little leaven has a great effect.[21] The point is emphasized by the amount of flour used, an exaggeration comparable with calling the mustard plant a "tree": sixty pounds of flour (see p. 523, n. 5) would make enough bread to feed a small village![22] But the (presumably small)[23] amount of leaven is able to make it all expand into a huge quantity of bread.[24] The kingdom of heaven may be initially insignificant, but it is pervasive.

19. C. L. Mitton, *ExpT* 84 (1972/3) 339-43, usefully discusses the meaning and use of leaven, and its metaphorical significance in biblical literature.

20. Cf. the metaphors of salt and light for the influence of disciples on the world around them (5:13-16).

21. Cf. 1 Cor 5:6; Gal 5:9 for the same metaphorical point, there applied to the growth of evil. C. L. Mitton (see n. 19) argues that the symbolism of leaven is overwhelmingly negative. This parable therefore would be like that of the unjust steward, using a feature of something bad to illustrate something good: "the Kingdom of God shares with the power of evil one notable quality, the quality of infecting with its own nature whatever it has contact with" (342). While there would be nothing surprising in such a parabolic method, the fact that leaven was such a regular and neutral part of daily life surely means, however, that its negative symbolic connotations need not always be in mind. The point lies rather in its pervasive effect.

22. A typical estimate is that it would provide a meal for a hundred or 150 people. But the amount could be an echo of the "three measures (Hebrew *se'â,* the equivalent of the Greek σάτον used here) of fine flour" which Sarah prepared for the visitors in Gen 18:6 (itself a remarkable amount to feed a single household with three visitors) rather than chosen for its own sake.

23. Luz, 2:262, calculates that four pounds of leaven would be needed for forty liters of flour, and so argues that the point is not (as in the preceding parable) the smallness of the amount used but its pervasiveness. But again we need not assume that the parable envisages real-life dimensions. And even on Luz's calculation, it is a *comparatively* small amount.

24. *Gos. Thom.* 96 makes the point differently by saying that "large loaves" were made with a little leaven.

6. About Teaching in Parables (13:34-35)

34 *Jesus told all these things to the crowds in parables, and he did not tell them anything without a parable.* **35** *This was to fulfill what had been declared through the prophet,*[1] *who said,*

> *"I will open my mouth in parables;*
>   *I will utter*[2] *things hidden since the foundation of the world."*[3]

The second statement on teaching in parables is much shorter than vv. 10-17, and is presented entirely as an editorial comment, not as the words of Jesus. It is essentially a quotation formula preceded only by a brief descriptive sentence to justify it. Here, in contrast to 13:14 where Jesus was the speaker, the normal quotation formula returns, and we are invited to reflect on how Jesus' teaching method as it is set out in this chapter conforms to a pattern of revelation already established in Scripture. These two verses repeat some of the key themes of the chapter so far, that parables serve to reveal hidden truths, but that to the crowds (unlike the disciples) only the parables are given, not the explanations which enable those secrets to be grasped.

34 The principle of this verse will be confirmed in v. 36, when an explanation (i.e., teaching "without a parable") is again given to the disciples only when they are in the house away from the crowd (as it was, perhaps in the boat, in vv. 10-23). Matthew's statement can hardly be intended to apply to the whole teaching ministry of Jesus as recorded in this gospel, since

---

1. Some MSS identify "the prophet" as Isaiah, and some patristic writers testify to this reading. Since the quotation is not from Isaiah, it is possible that this was an original reading subsequently deleted as an error; but it is probably more likely a careless addition by scribes familiar with the occurrence of Isaiah's name in 3:3; 4:14; 8:17; 12:17; 13:14; 15:7 (by far the most common attribution in Matthew). According to Jerome some MSS had "Isaiah" while others substituted the "correct" name Asaph. See further R. H. Gundry, *Use,* 119, n. 2. But see M. J. J. Menken, *Matthew's Bible,* 89-104, for an argument in favor of the originality of the mention of Isaiah on the grounds that Matthew has introduced κεκρυμμένα in the second line from Isa 29:14, and so attributes the conflated quotation to Isaiah (cf. his attribution of the complex quotation of 27:9-10 to Jeremiah, even though the primary source was Zech 11:13).

2. An unusual and vivid word, originally meaning "to belch" or "to spew out," and used in the LXX especially of the roaring of a lion. It is not the LXX term here, but LXX uses it for the same Hebrew verb in Ps 19:2.

3. "Of the world" is missing in some significant MSS, but since "the foundation" alone would have been understood as the foundation of the world, the sense is not affected. It is probable that Matthew used the full phrase here, as he does in 25:34. See contra, however, Carson, 323-24, arguing that the shorter reading is closer to the less explicit wording of the psalm.

crowds have been part of the audience to a great deal of nonparabolic teaching in chs. 5–7 while 12:46 identifies the crowds as the audience for at least some of the preceding teaching. Nor does it seem likely that *all* the teaching which according to 22:33 impressed the crowds in Jerusalem took the form of parables. The diatribe of ch. 23 is addressed initially to the crowds as well as the disciples (23:1). What is observed here is not so much a watertight distinction of literary and rhetorical style, but rather that Jesus' public teaching, even when not cast in a form we would recognize as *parabolē*, remains elusive, challenging, and unsettling, leaving his audience in a dilemma as to what response they should make. And that is what parables do, when given without explanation.

35 We have already seen Jesus' teaching method explained by analogy with that of Isaiah in vv. 13-15; now another OT passage provides a precedent. The standard quotation formula is used even though in this case the OT passage quoted is not from a prophet but from Ps 78:2. The psalmist (traditionally Asaph) is understood as making a prophetic utterance; indeed, the words quoted are themselves a description of the prophet's role.[4] For the "prophetic" role of nonprophetic scriptures see 11:13 (cf. 5:17). But the relevance of the quotation for Matthew lies in the term *parabolē*, which occurs in the first line, quoted by Matthew in its LXX form (Matthew's second line is entirely independent of the LXX).[5] In Hebrew the first line uses *māšāl* (see on v. 3a above) and the second *ḥîdâ*, "riddle," "dark saying," a related idea. The psalmist claims to reveal things hitherto unknown; cf. the "secrets of the kingdom of heaven" (v. 11). In the psalm what is "revealed" is a theological account of the history of Israel, but Matthew is concerned not with the psalm as a whole[6] but with this introductory statement, focused in the term *parabolē*, about the utterance of God's hidden truth by one specially empowered to communicate it. So when Jesus taught in parables, that is what he was doing. He stands in the line of God's authorized spokesmen, and his chosen method of teaching has good OT pedigree. Note that "hidden things" are intended to be uttered (as in Mark 4:22); God's ultimate purpose is not that people be kept in the dark.

4. Asaph was regarded as a prophet, according to 1 Chr 25:2; 2 Chr 29:30.

5. See p. 529, n. 2. M. D. Goulder, *Midrash,* 371, sees here an example of "Matthew's acquaintance with the Hebrew, and his ability both to draw on the Hebrew and to write his own targum."

6. Carson, 321-23, mounts a spirited defense of the relevance of the whole psalm to Matthew's intention and to the overall perspective of ch. 13, based on the correct observation that Ps 78 is not just history but an interpretation of "the patterns of redemptive history." His point is well taken, but the nature of Matthew's quotation here, seen in the context of his formula-quotations as a whole, requires no more than a reflection on the meaning of the programmatic verse quoted.

7. Explanation of the Parable of the Weeds (13:36-43)

> 36 Then he left the crowds and went into the house, and his disciples came to him and said, "Explain to us the parable of the weeds in the field." 37 He replied, "The one who sows the good seed is the Son of Man; 38 the field is the world; the good seed is[1] the children of the kingdom; the weeds are the children of the Evil One;[2] 39 the enemy who sowed them is the devil; the harvest is the end of the age;[3] and the harvesters are the angels. 40 So just as the weeds are gathered and burned in the fire, so it will be at the end of the age: 41 the Son of Man will send out his angels, and they will gather out of his kingdom all the stumbling blocks and those who live lawlessly[4] 42 and will throw them into the burning furnace, where there will be weeping and gnashing of teeth. 43 Then the righteous will shine like the sun in their Father's kingdom. Whoever has ears,[5] let them hear."

This second detailed parable explanation takes a rather different form from the first. It divides into two parts, an item-by-item list of equivalences in vv. 37-39, followed in vv. 40-43 by a more discursive account of the meaning of the harvest which is the culmination of the parable. This second part of the explanation is similar to the briefer interpretation added to the parable of the net in vv. 49-50. But the detailed catalogue of equivalences in vv. 37-39 has no parallel in the Jesus tradition, and gives to this explanation a more "allegorical" feel than the explanation of the sower. It is not, however, a complete list: we are given no explanation of people's sleeping (v. 25), the slaves are not identified, nor are the fire and the barn — though the significance of

---

1. As in vv. 19-23, the expression of equivalence is slightly awkward. Matthew's wording is literally "The good seed [neuter singular] these [masculine] are the children of the kingdom."

2. Or "children of evil," since in the genitive masculine and neuter are indistinguishable, as in 5:37; 6:13; see the notes there. In this case the mention of the devil in the next verse indicates that the personal sense is more probable. For people described as children of the devil cf. John 8:44; Acts 13:10; 1 John 3:10.

3. The important phrase ἡ συντέλεια τοῦ αἰῶνος also occurs in vv. 40 and 49, and in 24:3, while in 28:20 it will be the concluding phrase of the gospel. συντέλεια indicates completion or fulfillment, and the αἰών is the present age as opposed to the age to come (see on 12:32); the two ages are separated by the judgment. Albright and Mann, 165, translate the phrase "the consummation of the natural order."

4. Literally, "those who do lawlessness," but ποιέω is also the term for "bearing (a crop)," so that in this harvest context it indicates the poisonous lifestyle of the "weeds."

5. As in 11:15 and 13:9, most MSS here add the familiar "to hear." Again the breakdown of MSS and versions is not quite the same, but the same considerations apply; see the note at 11:15.

these last two items will become clear in the description of the judgment in vv. 42-43. The function of this "glossary" is to provide the interpretive basis for the judgment scene that follows in vv. 40-43. Nor is it "allegorical" in the sense of making a surprising or arbitrary leap to a different area of discourse. Granted that the story of the weeds was told as a parable, and that the basic imagery of seed and harvest has already been established in vv. 3-23 as a model for the preaching of the "message of the kingdom" and its outcome, the specific identifications in vv. 37-39 occasion no surprise — indeed, they seem inevitable. The list is more a matter of pedantic explanation than of allegorical transference.

Once the equivalences have been established, the explanation in vv. 40-43 focuses only on the end of the story, the radical and public division of people into two categories, the lost and the saved, at the time of final judgment. While this is an important element in the parable's imagery, it does not place the emphasis on the aspect of the story which most modern readers instinctively focus on, the concept of a mixed community allowed to remain undifferentiated until the final separation. The dialogue between the landowner and his slaves within the parable draws attention to this initially surprising decision, and provides a justification for it in v. 29, but the explanation does not take up this issue and leaves the parable to speak for itself about the policy which refuses to impose a premature separation ("Leave them both to grow together until harvest"), and the patience which is required of disciples in the meantime.

Some interpreters, assuming (as many have done throughout the history of the church)[6] that the parable is aimed at problems within the church, find the absence of this theme from the explanation surprising in that the idea of the disciple community as a mixed body within which true and spurious disciples coexist is one that recurs several times in Matthew's gospel. See, for instance, the recruitment of "bad as well as good" guests to the wedding feast in 22:10, with the result that one of the new invitees had subsequently to be thrown out (22:11-13). The wicked will be picked out "from among the righteous" (13:49). There are false prophets who are wolves dressed up as sheep (7:15-20); there are those who call Jesus "Lord, Lord" with apparent sincerity, but who do not belong to him (7:21-23); there are foolish as well as wise bridesmaids, waiting and sleeping together until the bridegroom arrives (25:1-12); there is a son who sounds more loyal than his brother, but who ultimately fails to deliver (21:28-32). All these passages are peculiar to Matthew, and more could be added.[7] The parable of the weeds is often seen as

6. See Luz, 2:271-74.
7. See my *Matthew: Evangelist*, 275-78, though there I wrongly took the present passage to relate primarily to that pastoral issue within the disciple community.

Matthew's most graphic presentation of this theology of a "mixed church," and so it seems strange that he fails to draw it out explicitly in the recorded explanation.

But it is unlikely that the theme of a mixed *church,* however important to Matthew elsewhere,[8] was in fact the main point of this parable, at least as Matthew understood it.[9] The field is identified in v. 38 not as the church but as "the world," which suggests that the parable has a wider perspective than simply the professing disciple community.[10] Within "the world" believers and unbelievers continue to exist side by side even after the proclamation of the kingdom of heaven and Jesus' assault on the kingdom of Satan, and some disciples may have found this apparently unchanged situation perplexing. Where was the new world order they had been promised? What sort of "kingdom" was this that allowed opposition to continue unchecked? Why did God not straightaway destroy the "sons of darkness" and so make his world a place fit for the "sons of light" (to use the language of Qumran)?[11] The parable answers that question by a call to patience, directing attention away from the current situation to the coming judgment, when it will be made plain who are the true people of God and who are the "children of the Evil One." God is not in a hurry, and they must be prepared to wait for his time.

So the explanation given in these verses rightly focuses not on the present unsatisfactory situation but on the judgment of "the world" at the end of the age, when the wicked will be destroyed and the righteous will "shine" for all to see. Verses 37-43 (together with the parallel explanation in vv. 49-50) provide us with one of the most explicit accounts of final judgment and of the ultimate fates of the bad and the good which we find in the gospels.[12] In 25:31-46 it will be spelled out in more detail, with the attention focused there on the basis of judgment, but with the same essential division into

8. Note, however, that P. Luomanen, *JBL* 117 (1998) 469-80, disputes the widespread use of *"corpus mixtum"* to describe Matthew's Christian community.

9. See, however, R. McIver, *JBL* 114 (1995) 643-59, for an attempt to establish the "ecclesiastical" over against the "universalist" interpretation of the parable, though with the recognition that this is a minority view in more recent discussion. See contra P. Luomanen, *JBL* 117 (1998) 471-72.

10. D. C. Sim, *Apocalyptic,* 210-11, argues nonetheless that the reference must be to a mixed *church* since the term "his kingdom" in v. 41 "seems more appropriate to the church than to the whole world."

11. W. D. Davies, *Setting,* 230-33, explores the conceptual links between this parable explanation and some Qumran texts.

12. D. C. Sim, *Apocalyptic,* 78-79, rightly singles out vv. 36-43 as "the most precise statement" of Matthew's essentially dualistic outlook. His comments (ibid., 85-87) on the embarrassment which this causes for some modern interpreters (represented by F. W. Beare) are worth pondering.

"good and bad," with the former finding eternal life and the latter eternal punishment (again envisaged as "fire").

36 The crowds who have been the audience of the parables (but not the explanation) until v. 33 are now "left" as Jesus embarks on another private explanation. Some interpreters regard this "leaving" as final, so that the remaining parables recorded in this chapter are addressed to the disciples only. But we have already noted that Matthew failed to make explicit at v. 24 a change of audience which his account presupposes, so that other unmarked changes of audience are possible. The parable of v. 52 is apparently addressed only to the disciples, in response to their claim to have "understood" (v. 51), but no indication of audience is given in vv. 44, 45, and 47, and the parable of the net (vv. 47-48) is so similar in its message to that of the weeds that it is hard to see why the one should be addressed to the crowds and the other only to the disciples — even though in the case of the net the explanation is attached directly to the parable rather than recorded as a separate "aside" to the disciples. It seems more likely that Matthew intends his general rubric of v. 34 to cover what follows as well as what has preceded it: parables are for the crowd, explanations for the disciples. Once he has made that principle clear, he does not need to spell out the audience changes which it entails.

The "house" appears unexpectedly after the setting in a boat in v. 2 (see comments on vv. 1-3a). For Jesus to leave the crowd and return to the house which he left in v. 1 might be taken to suggest that the discourse is finished, but in fact it will continue until v. 53, where it will be concluded by the regular formula. If, as I have suggested above, the crowd remain the audience for the following parables, the mention of the house here simply indicates the composite origin of the discourse; it reflects the tradition of private teaching given in a "house" (Mark 7:17; 9:28, 33; 10:10). This time the disciples ask not for a general theory of parables (as in v. 10) but for a specific interpretation of a parable they have just heard.[13] Their verb, "explain" *(diasapheō)*, fits the account we have been given of parables: the story does not carry its meaning on the surface; it needs to be "made plain."

37-39 The explanation begins with a "glossary," identifying the symbolic significance of the various features of the story. Each identification is expressed by the simple verb "is/are," which in such a context denotes what a symbol "represents." The point is worth noting in the light of the wars and martyrdoms which resulted from the intense debates of the sixteenth century over the meaning of the verb in the phrase "This is my body."

The sower, who remained unidentified in the previous parable, is now declared to be the Son of Man, confirming that the primary theme of

---

13. As they do in relation to the parable of the sower in Luke 8:9 (cf. Mark 4:13).

these parables in their narrative context is people's response to Jesus' proclamation of the kingdom of heaven. "The Son of Man," besides being the regular term used by Jesus to describe himself (see on 8:20), is particularly appropriate because of the judgment theme which dominates this explanation. "The world" *(kosmos)* is a broad term both for the created universe (13:35; 24:21; 25:34) and for human society in general (see on 5:14); in this context it does not raise the issue of the geographical extent of the proclamation to include Gentiles as well as Jews,[14] but simply refers to "people." For "children of the kingdom" see on 8:12; here it is a less surprising and ironical phrase than there, and means simply those who belong to the kingdom of heaven. The contrast with "children of the Evil One" (see p. 531, n. 2) reinforces the impression gained especially from 8:11-12 that what separates the saved from the lost is a personal relationship, in the one case to Jesus, the proclaimer of the kingdom of heaven, and in the other case to his chief opponent, Satan, from whose grasp he comes to liberate them (see on 12:29). The direct mention of "the devil" underlines this personal confrontation; cf. v. 19 for the devil's direct intervention when God's seed is sown. To depict Satan as a spiteful enemy trying to spoil the good work of the landowner and ruin his harvest expresses graphically his status in biblical literature: he is a spoiler, not a constructive authority in his own right. The "end of the age" (see above, p. 531, n. 3) is a familiar Jewish expression for the crisis which was expected to bring the present world order to a close and to inaugurate the "age to come." It will be the term used by the disciples to express what they take to be the implications of Jesus' prediction of the destruction of the temple, the time when all that is familiar will be swept away. Here its specific concern is with the judgment which concludes the present age and determines people's status for the age to come. In that judgment "the angels" will have the role not of judges[15] but of agents who implement the divine judgment.

40-43   Now that the symbolism has been clarified, the significance of the parable can be drawn out in more general terms, with the emphasis on its final scene of judgment. The "one like a son of man" in Dan 7:13-14 was a figure of universal authority and sovereignty, and it is in accordance with that vision, and its context of judgment (Dan 7:10, 22), that the Son of Man is here presented (as he will also be in 19:28 and in 25:31-46) as executing the final judgment (sending out *his* angels) and thus standing in the place of the divine

---

14. A geographical nuance is more likely in 26:13, where the phrase ἐν ὅλῳ τῷ κόσμῳ corresponds to the more clearly geographical ἐν ὅλῃ τῇ οἰκουμένῃ in 24:14. Here, as in 5:14, that issue is not yet in focus.

15. Judgment is in Jewish understanding the prerogative of God alone — but see the following comments on vv. 40-43 for its extension to the Son of Man.

judge himself.[16] Similarly, in 24:31 the Son of Man will send out *his* angels to gather in not the wicked, as here, but his chosen people; we shall argue at that point, however, that the reference there is not so much to the final judgment as to the gathering in of the people of the Son of Man within history. Even more remarkably, the Son of Man is himself the king in *his* kingdom (v. 41). The "kingdom of the Son of Man" is a distinctively Matthean concept, which will recur in 16:28; 19:28; 25:31-34 (cf. 20:21). It is a natural corollary of the enthronement of the "one like a son of man" in Dan 7:13-14, but it is only Matthew who explicitly extends the "kingdom of God/heaven" proclaimed by the Son of Man to be also the kingdom of the Son of Man himself.[17]

The rather ponderous description of those removed from his kingdom as "all the stumbling blocks and those who live lawlessly"[18] is probably an echo of the judgment scene in Zeph 1:3 where "the stumbling blocks[19] with the wicked" are among the things which God is going to "sweep away" from the earth.[20] The Hebrew expression is surprising, and translators vary in their rendering (or emendation) of it, while the main MSS of the LXX omit the

16. For the theme of angels who "belong to Jesus the Son of Man" as a distinctively Matthean theme see D. C. Sim, *Apocalyptic,* 76.

17. Some interpreters propose that the kingdom of the Son of Man is not the same as the kingdom of heaven (or "of their Father," v. 43), and identify the former as more specifically the church. But Matthew does not use "kingdom" language of the church elsewhere, and to find that meaning here does violence to the parable, which purports (v. 24) to describe "the kingdom of heaven," and makes no distinction between the field which is the world and the kingdom of the Son of Man from which the weeds then have to be removed. The world is now under the dominion of the Son of Man, as Dan 7:13-14 predicted (and as Jesus will himself claim in 28:18). To distinguish the "kingdom of their Father" from the kingdom of the Son of Man on the grounds of 1 Cor 15:24-28 is theologically unexceptionable, but contextually hardly necessary here.

18. The choice of ἀνομία, "lawlessness," to represent this group leads D. Sim, *Apocalyptic,* 211-27; *Gospel,* 204-7, to suggest that the reference is specifically to "the law-free or Pauline wing" of the Christian community. Quite apart from the probability that Matthew does not see this parable as restricted to the Christian community (see above), that is a lot to derive from a common word for behavior displeasing to God, which in its other Matthean uses (7:23; 23:28 [applied to scribes and Pharisees!]; 24:12) hardly allows so specific a reference. Still less likely is the suggestion of S. G. F. Brandon that in the original parable the enemy who sowed the weeds represented Paul.

19. In Zeph 1:3 the term is probably applied to people rather than things (for a similarly personal use see 16:23), though it could also be a reference to idols. Carter, 294, includes in it "persecution and the tribulation or woes that precede the end," but this idea suits neither the Zephaniah context nor the identification of the weeds as "children of the Evil One"; it derives rather from the phrase "causes of sin," which some English versions use to translate σκάνδαλα here.

20. On the allusion and its textual background see my *Jesus and the OT,* 156-57 (and 245).

phrase altogether, but Matthew's wording reflects its likely literal sense. If so, he envisages Jesus as taking over the role of God the judge in the OT prophecy. The "furnace of fire" (literally), which will appear again in v. 50, is not used elsewhere in the NT as an image for hell,[21] but the familar use of fire imagery for hell (see on 5:22) makes it unsurprising; the "furnace" or "oven" derives from the imagery of the incineration of unwanted vegetation, just as the rubbish dumps of Jerusalem provided the background for Gehenna.[22] See on 25:46 for the question of the duration of punishment; the imagery of the incinerated weeds here supports the view that the wicked are destroyed rather than that they are endlessly tormented. For the conventional phrase "weeping and gnashing of teeth" see on 8:12.

The "righteous" include not only the disciples but all God's true people from the past (see v. 17 and cf. 8:11). Their ultimate state, described in the imagery of the parable as being gathered into the barn of the landowner, is spelled out in terms of glory; when Jesus appears in heavenly glory in 17:2, he will also be said to "shine like the sun." The language reflects Dan 12:3, where after the prediction that some will be raised to everlasting life we read, "those who are wise will shine like the brightness of the sky, and those who lead many to righteousness like the stars forever" — Matthew's verb "shine" is the same as that in Theodotion. In contrast with the present hiddenness of the kingdom of God and its adherents, one day they will shine in heavenly glory for all to see (cf. Wis 3:7; *1 En.* 39:7).[23] The "kingdom of the Son of Man" (v. 41) has now become the "kingdom of their Father"; cf. the frequent reference by Jesus in the Sermon on the Mount to God as the disciples' Father in heaven. This is the goal to which the hard road of discipleship must eventually lead.

For the concluding formula see on 11:15. Here it is applied not to the parable itself, as in v. 9, but to the truths which it symbolizes. These, too, need careful thought and assimilation.

21. See, however, Rev 9:2 for the smoke from the abyss "like the smoke from a great furnace."

22. Many commentators refer to the occurrence of the same phrase in Dan 3:6ff., but the context does not suggest such an allusion, and if it had been intended, it is likely that the full phrase τὴν κάμινον τοῦ πυρὸς τὴν καιομένην (LXX and Thdt) would have been used. The language, though vivid, needs no OT explanation.

23. D. C. Sim, *Apocalyptic,* 142-45, surprisingly concludes from this description that Matthew believes (indeed, "is adamant"!) that "in the new age the righteous will become angels," even though Matthew never says that. The nearest he gets to it is to say that the people of the resurrection are "*like* angels" (22:30; see comments there for the basis of comparison).

8. Three Further Short Parables (13:44-50)

44 *"The kingdom of heaven is like a treasure hidden in the field, which a man found and hid; then in his delight he goes and sells all he has and buys that field.*

45 *"Again, the kingdom of heaven is like a trader who was looking for fine pearls;* 46 *when he had found one immensely valuable pearl, he went off and sold[1] all he had and bought it.*

47 *"Again, the kingdom of heaven is like a net[2] which was thrown into the lake and collected fish[3] of every kind.* 48 *When it was full, the fishermen pulled it up onto the beach, sat down, and collected the good fish into containers, but threw out those that were worthless.[4]* 49 *That is how it will be at the end of the age: the angels will come[5] and separate the wicked from among the righteous,* 50 *and will throw them into the burning furnace, where there will be weeping and gnashing of teeth."*

These parables are found only in Matthew. All the preceding parables have been introduced by a narrative clause, but these follow immediately after the explanation of the weeds with no further indication of audience. This, and the fact that vv. 49-50 contain an explanation of the kind hitherto given only to disciples, leads many to assume that these parables, too, are addressed only to the disciples. But I have argued above (see on v. 36) that Matthew's audience-specifications are sufficiently imprecise to allow us to assume that these parables, too, come under the rubric of v. 34, that parables are for the crowds. The similarity of the parable of the net to that of the weeds strongly suggests

1. The verb here is not πωλέω, which is the more common verb for "sell" and was used in v. 44, but πιπράσκω, which is also found (in the passive) in 18:25 and 26:9. The two verbs are apparently used as synonyms in Acts 4:34, 37; 5:1, 4, and here, too, there is no discernible difference in meaning.

2. σαγήνη, used only here in the NT, denotes a large seine or drag net, which needed several people to operate it either between two boats or by ropes from the shore.

3. Surprisingly there is no word for "fish" or "fishermen" either here or in v. 48; the object is left to be assumed from the mention of the net.

4. σαπρός properly means "rotten," as for fruit in 7:17-18; 12:33. Within the story it presumably refers not to fish that had gone bad (they had only just been caught) but to those which were considered inedible (see comments below).

5. Literally, "come out"; the compound verb usually has a clear contextual force, going out of a building (or in the case of demons, out of a person) or leaving a specified location, but it can be used more generally for going out on a mission; the latter usage may account for its use here (as for the sower in v. 3), without our needing to inquire where they have come out *from*. Cf., however, Rev 14:15, 17, 18 for angels "coming out" from the heavenly temple to harvest. Cf. also "send out" in v. 41.

that the two are designed for the same audience. In that case the appending of the explanation in vv. 49-50 to a public parable without an expressed change of audience should be ascribed more to literary convenience than to a deliberate change of policy. The only parable in this chapter addressed specifically to the disciples would then be that of the householder in v. 52, and in that case, in contrast to vv. 44, 45, and 47, the audience will be clearly indicated.

As in vv. 24-33, this trio of parables divides into two sections, the treasure and the pearl forming a natural pair, with a similar form and message,[6] while the net is different not only in that it carries an explanation but also in its focus, so that it finds its natural twin in the parable of the weeds.[7] I shall again, therefore, discuss the group in two sections.

a. The Parables of the Treasure and of the Pearl (13:44-46)

These parables are similar in form and message, differing primarily in the narrative specifics appropriate to the two analogies chosen, though the vivid present tenses of v. 44 are not repeated in v. 46. They are about enthusiastic and wholehearted commitment to the kingdom of heaven, with the secondary theme of costly renunciation for the sake of the greater good. It is only those who make the kingdom of heaven their top priority who will enjoy its blessings. These parables also continue the theme of the "secrets of the kingdom of heaven" in that the treasure is "hidden" from others and the pearl has to be "found" (it is not thrown before pigs, 7:6!).

The relevance of these parables to the disciples is obvious, especially in view of their having "left" their previous lifestyle and its material possessions in the call stories of 4:20, 22 (and cf. 9:9), a theme which will be taken up again in 19:27-29, where it is provoked by the example of the rich man who was unwilling to sell his possessions in order to gain "treasure in heaven" (19:16-22). The same contrast between earthly and heavenly possessions and security has been explored in 6:19-34,[8] where it is specifically

---

6. In *Gos. Thom.* 109, 76 they appear separately, and in widely divergent forms. But this is as likely to be due to independent interpretations of the Matthean tradition as to an originally separate origin of these two parables before Matthew combined them.

7. W. G. Morrice, *ExpT* 95 (1984) 269-73, wonders whether the parable of the wise fisherman in *Gos. Thom.* 8 (see below, p. 542, n. 17), which is similar to the parables of the treasure and the pearl, represents the original from which the parable of the net in Matt 13:47-50 was developed, so that originally this set of three parables would all have had a similar form and message. Most scholars, however, do not regard the *Thomas* parable as connected with Matt 13:47-50 (other than by the common use of fishing terminology). Even if Morrice is right, the text of Matthew as we have it has not preserved such a set of three.

8. It is interesting that the parable of the pearl, left uninterpreted by Matthew, is in *Gos. Thom.* 76 expanded by an exhortation which is a version of Matt 6:20.

commitment to God's kingship (6:33) which must take priority over other concerns. In the treasure finder and the pearl dealer, then, we find the opposite attitude to the "worries of this world and the false lure of wealth" which stood in the way of true discipleship in v. 22. To find the kingdom of heaven is to find the one treasure which outweighs all other valuation. It is worth any cost to seize this unique and unrepeatable opportunity. Note that in both cases the treasure comes into the purchaser's possession immediately, so that it is unlikely that the blessings of the kingdom of heaven are envisaged as purely future and eschatological.

Is this, then, a message only for disciples? Surely insofar as the crowd is made up of people who are at least potentially disciples, it applies to them as well. It obliges them to think seriously about the single-minded commitment which discipleship must involve, as well as about the immense value of the offered kingdom of heaven. It is a message which, like the parables as a whole, is designed to divide those who hear. There will, one hopes, be some who like the men in the parables are sufficiently captivated by the treasure on offer to be ready for the sacrifice of everything else. But human nature being what it is, those who rise to the challenge are likely to be few (like those who find the narrow way in 7:13-14). So these parables, like the others, will bring enlightenment and joy to some, but leave others "hearing but not understanding."

44 Buried treasure is the stuff of popular stories[9] (a more colorful equivalent of winning the lottery today), but in the ancient world a more realistic possibility than it is today, even with the help of a metal detector. Before banking was generally established, to hide wealth in the form of coins, metals, or jewels in a jar or box in the ground was a recognized way of securing it, especially in times of crisis; the famous *Copper Scroll* from Qumran Cave 3 lists the locations of huge caches of precious metals and other buried treasure (perhaps hidden in anticipation of the Roman invasion, but perhaps fictitious?). For a more realistic example in this gospel see 25:25, where a talent of gold (equivalent to some twenty years of daily wages) would have been a "treasure" worth finding. Presumably in this story the current owner of the field, to whom the treasure would legally belong, was unaware of it; perhaps it had belonged to a previous owner, now dead.[10] The finder (presumably a

---

9. Luz, 2:276-77, gives several examples, Jewish and Roman, which are quite similar to this parable. Cf. also a fuller listing and analysis of parallels by J. D. Crossan, *SBLSP 1976*, 359-79.

10. So *Gos. Thom.* 109, with a rather complicated explanation: the original owner did not know the treasure was there; he left the field to his son, who sold it, still unaware of the treasure; the purchaser found the treasure while plowing. Note that in this version the finder is already the owner of the field; he has no need to sell anything to acquire it. There is thus no theme of contrasting values, or of renunciation. The thoroughly mercenary tone of the *Thomas* version is underlined by the final comment that the finder used

worker employed by the landowner) therefore hides the treasure again until he has legal ownership of the field, so that the treasure becomes his.[11] The man's action is dictated by pure self-interest, as is that of the person who opts for the kingdom of heaven. The "sacrifice" of all that is sold is no hardship; it is done out of "delight," not out of a sense of obligation. Once the kingdom of heaven is truly understood, nothing else can compare with it in value. Cf. the OT theme of wisdom as being like hidden treasure (Prov 2:4; Job 28; cf., with a rather different twist, Sir 20:30).[12]

45-46 Pearls were as highly valued in the ancient world[13] as they are today, and before convincing synthetic pearls were invented they formed a conspicuous way of displaying wealth (1 Tim 2:9; Rev 17:4; 18:12, 16). Huge pearls form the gates in the symbolic new Jerusalem (Rev 21:21). Unlike the man in the previous parable, who could presumably live off his treasure once he had secured it, this dealer, though initially a man of some substance, is apparently impoverishing himself to acquire something supremely beautiful and valuable which he could admire and display but could not live off unless he sold it again.[14] It would, however, be too literalistic to read this parable therefore as a commendation of unpractical fanaticism (like Jesus' commendation of the "waste" of valuable ointment in 26:6-13). Its point is the same as that of the treasure, an issue of priorities. The fact that what the dealer had to sell included presumably other, lesser, pearls might, however, have led the hearers to reflect on the value of the kingdom of heaven in relation to other competing ideologies; once you have it, you need no other.

---

the treasure to "lend money at interest to whomever he wished." See I. H. Jones, *Parables,* 348-50, for discussion of the *Gospel of Thomas* version in relation to Matthew.

11. In *m. B. Meṣiʿa* 2 there is a lengthy rabbinic discussion of what finds may be kept and what must be publicly announced in order to discover the owner. The latter category includes "money in a bag . . . heaps of coins, three coins one on top of another" (2:2), so that by that later standard this man's action was of questionable morality. See, however, J. D. M. Derrett, *Law,* 1-16, for an explanation and defense of his action according to both Roman and Jewish law. This is, in any case, a parable, not an ethical model, and the point of the parable does not lie in the legal or ethical correctness of the action.

12. A striking feature of this parable is the sequence of three historic presents, a relatively rare stylistic feature in Matthew except for verbs of speaking. S. M. B. Wilmshurst, *JSNT* 25 (2003) 281-85, argues that they not only make the story more vivid, but that they also draw attention to a key element in Matthew's presentation of the kingdom of heaven, the overwhelming joy of its discovery: "The tense switch has the same effect as a light switch!"

13. See J. Jeremias, *Parables,* 199, with details of the extraordinary prices they could command. Cf. also F. Hauck, *TDNT* 4:472-73.

14. *Gos. Thom.* 76 commends the merchant as "prudent," but says only that he sold "the merchandise," not everything that he had! I. H. Jones, *Parables,* 352-53, discusses the two versions.

Hence the emphasis on the fact that this is just *one* pearl, whose value eclipses all others put together.

b. The Parable of the Net and Its Explanation (13:47-50)

The explanation in vv. 49-50 is closely similar to the account of the judgment of the wicked in vv. 40-42; indeed, v. 49a repeats v. 40b, and v. 50 is an exact repeat of v. 42, even though the burning of unwanted fish seems less appropriate than the incineration of the darnel.[15] This parable then, like that of the weeds, is one of judgment.[16] It echoes not only the separation and destruction of the wicked but also the motif of a mixture of good and bad until the time of final separation. The type of net specified (see p. 538, n. 2) is inevitably indiscriminate in what it catches. As long as the fish remain in the lake, and indeed in the net, they remain undifferentiated. It is only when they come up for final scrutiny that some will be preserved and others destroyed.[17]

47-48 The comparison of the kingdom of heaven to a fishing scene reminds us of the calling of the disciples to "fish for people" in 4:19. We noted there that the focus seems to be on catching people for salvation rather than, as in Jer 16:16, for punishment; but insofar as the disciples' "fishing" ministry belongs to the establishment of God's kingship, this parable adds the thought that there is a negative as well as a positive aspect to it. Their net is cast over a wide cross-section of people, and while the message saves some, it will leave others unconvinced; those who have failed to respond to it are presumably among the "bad fish" of this parable. The fishermen of v. 48 are of course identified as the angels, not as the disciples, but it is the prior announcement of the kingdom of heaven (with which the disciples have been entrusted, 10:7) which forms the basis of the separation between good and bad.

At least twenty species of fish are found in the Lake of Galilee, most of which could be eaten, though some were more favored than others. The

---

15. The imagery is different from that of v. 48, where the unwanted fish are simply thrown away, presumably back into the lake. Luz, 2:281, n. 5, finds the latter image less appropriate to the parable's message: "The useless fish are thrown back into the lake! They remain alive while the 'good' fish end up in the frying pan!"

16. We might have expected "throw away" rather than "throw out" (literally, "throw outside") in context (outside what?), but the imagery is characteristic of Matthew's judgment scenes: cf. 5:13; 8:12; 22:13; 25:30; cf. 21:39.

17. A parable about a (single) wise fisherman in *Gos. Thom.* 8 has some language similar to that of this parable, but with a quite different application, related rather to the treasure and the pearl. It is about human choice, not divine judgment. The fisherman pulls up his net full of little fish with one "big, good" one; he throws away the little ones and keeps the big one. See above, p. 539, n. 7.

Levitical rule that only fish "with fins and scales" could be eaten (Lev 11:9-12) would have ruled out eels and possibly catfish (common in Galilee) because of their resemblance to snakes (cf. 7:10). And of course some fish caught would be too small or diseased for human consumption. Hence the need to sort out the catch once landed. For "of every kind" cf. the weeds growing in with the wheat (vv. 24-30), and the inclusion of "bad as well as good" in the wedding feast (22:10). That the net is not pulled out of the lake until it is full is perhaps intended to emphasize, as in the parable of the weeds, that there will be no premature separation; it will wait until everything is ready in God's good time.[18]

49-50   There is little here that differs from vv. 40-42 (see notes there), though this time there is no account of the destiny of the righteous as in v. 43: the focus is entirely on the judgment of the wicked. But one significant detail is that the wicked are picked out "from among" (literally, "out of the middle of") the righteous. The phrase draws attention to the theme which we also saw implicit in the parable of the weeds, though not specifically drawn out in its explanation, that until the final judgment there can be no separate existence for the true people of God: the wicked will be in the middle of them, like the wolves among the sheep in 7:15.

9. Concluding Parable: The Householder (13:51-52)

> 51 *"Have you understood all this?" "Yes," they replied.* 52 *Jesus said to them, "For this reason every scribe who has been made a disciple for the kingdom of heaven is like the master of a house, who produces from his storeroom[1] things new and old."*

For the classification of this saying as the eighth "parable" of the discourse see p. 500, n. 1.[2] It uses the same introductory phrase "is like," though the object of the comparison here is not simply "the kingdom of heaven" but the scribe who has become its disciple.

---

18. A number of coincidences of vocabulary (θάλασσα, συνάγω, αἰγιαλός, "sit") lead some commentators (especially Luz, 2:283) to see this parable as commenting on the narrative situation set up in vv. 1-2, Jesus and the disciples in the boat representing the good fish, and the crowd on the shore the bad fish. But given the setting by the lake and the choice of fishing imagery, the coincidences of vocabulary are hardly impressive (note the use of different verbs for sitting), and the net does not recall the boat of v. 2.

1. For this rendering of θησαυρός, which was rendered "treasure" in v. 44, see p. 474, n. 10.

2. It is rightly treated by I. H. Jones, *Parables,* 189-211, as one of the four "summary parables" which conclude four of Matthew's five main discourses (see ibid., 115-23, for the literary function of these summary parables).

Again there is no narrative clause to introduce Jesus' question, so that it is naturally taken as addressed to the same people who have been the audience in the previous section. But, as we noted in the introductory comments on vv. 44-50, while those three parables are, in my view, still addressed to the crowd, they conclude in vv. 49-50 (without explicit change of audience) with an explanation of the sort addressed only to the disciples. Jesus' question relates, initially at least, to that explanation, and so should be understood as addressed to the disciples. The use of the verb "understand," which has been a prominent description of the state of disciples as opposed to the crowds in vv. 13-15, 19, and 23, confirms this. Jesus is checking with his disciples whether the explanations he has offered have given them the special understanding which they were designed to convey. This parable, then, unlike all the others in this chapter, is addressed to the disciples, and speaks of their special situation — as indeed the verb "made a disciple" in v. 52 requires.[3]

51 The disciples' claim to have "understood" should cause no surprise after the declaration that they have been given knowledge of the secrets of the kingdom of heaven (v. 11). Matthew has a more sanguine view on the subject than Mark, who in 8:17-21 will have Jesus rebuke the disciples for not yet understanding and will even apply to them the language from Isa 6:9-10 which has been applied at this point to "those outside." Matthew's equivalent to that passage, 16:5-12, while still expressing Jesus' frustration at their lack of faith, will avoid the offensive language from Isa 6:9-10, and will end up with them again "understanding" in 16:12 (cf. also 17:13). Matthew's disciples are far from perfect, but they are now firmly on the road to understanding, and Jesus' response apparently accepts their claim without irony.

52 "For this reason" in Matthew generally "introduces a solemn and resounding logion" linked with and bringing to a climax what has gone before.[4] The "scribe" is unexpected. If this is, as the context seems to require, a comment on the situation of Jesus' own disciples, one might expect it simply to speak of "*anyone* who has been made a disciple for the kingdom of heaven," or even "*you* who have. . . ." All that we are told about the background from which the Twelve have come gives us no ground to believe that any of them was a "scribe" in the normal NT sense of a trained interpreter of the Mosaic law, nor has there been any hint that such scribes have been among the wider circle of "those who do the will of my Father in heaven" (12:50) who constitute the circle of disciples in the wider sense. Mark does indeed tell

---

3. See M. J. Wilkins, *Disciple,* 160-62, for Matthew's use of the verb μαθητεύω (only here and in 27:57; 28:19); Wilkins argues that it denotes the commitment of discipleship, not just the process of learning.
4. D. E. Orton, *Scribe,* 141-42. I. H. Jones, *Parables,* 193-95, argues that it refers "to the whole chapter and not only to the previous conversation."

us of an understanding scribe who was "not far from the kingdom of heaven" (Mark 12:28-34), but Matthew's parallel in 22:34-40 concerns not a scribe but probably a "lawyer" (see p. 841, n. 2) and contains no such commendation. We have met one scribe who was a potential but probably not actual disciple (8:19), but otherwise scribes (usually in association with others, especially Pharisees)[5] are normally portrayed in Matthew's gospel as the opposition. Two possible explanations are worth exploring. (i) Jesus uses the term to designate his chosen disciples as a new "alternative" scribal school, trained not in the rabbinic schools but by his own instruction to bring his new and radical understanding of the law to Israel.[6] The clearest hint of this is in 23:34, when in the course of his diatribe against the traditional scribes and Pharisees Jesus claims to be "sending scribes" to them, whom they will persecute and kill, just as in ch. 10 he has sent out his disciples with the expectation of meeting persecution and possibly death at the hands of the establishment. (ii) The term is being used here not in its specialized religious sense but in the secular sense of a "writer," someone sufficiently educated to undertake writing and reading commissions for others and to compile records — something like our "civil servant." Those who espouse this view point out that Matthew must have been such a "writer" in his customs office,[7] and some have suggested that this verse, which is found only in Matthew, is the author's own self-identification as the paradigm "discipled writer"[8] — just as some find Mark's self-portrait in the young man in the garden (Mark 14:51-52).[9]

---

5. D. E. Orton's thesis, *Scribe* passim, is that while the "scribes" referred to in Matthew as opponents of Jesus are the rabbinic, Pharisaic, scribes, Matthew does not reject the concept of "scribe" as such, and in particular that he also recognizes another type of scribe, the "apocalyptic scribe," known to us from the apocalyptic literature, Ben Sira and Qumran, which he approves and uses as a model for the ideal disciple of Jesus. See further below, n. 10.

6. See, e.g., R. Mohrlang, *Matthew,* 15-16, also supporting the view, associated especially with E. von Dobschütz, that Matthew was himself "a converted scribe."

7. C. F. D. Moule, *Essays,* 67-74, expresses this view attractively: "The writer of the Gospel was himself a well-educated, literate scribe in this sense. But so must also have been that tax-collector who was called by Jesus to be a disciple. Is it not conceivable that the Lord really did say to that tax-collector Matthew: You have been a 'writer' (as the Navy would put it); you have had plenty to do with the commercial side of just the topics alluded to in the parables — farmer's stock, fields, treasure-trove, fishing revenues; now that you have become a disciple, you can bring all this out again — but with a difference." Moule is not arguing for Matthew as the author of the final gospel, but as the compiler of much of the tradition which formed its basis.

8. M. D. Goulder, *Midrash,* 375, also considers that in this verse "Matthew appends his own signature," but not as the civil servant so much as the "parabolizing scribe" who has included in ch. 13 both old (Marcan) parables and new ones of his own.

9. The view that 13:52 is Matthew's self-description is not necessarily in conflict

Each of these suggestions has its problems, and neither seems to me to account entirely satisfactorily for the way this saying is worded. But insofar as this is apparently intended to be a saying about disciples in general, not about Matthew in particular (note "*every* scribe"), the first seems to make better sense of a puzzling expression. In that case the saying envisages disciples in their "scribal" function, that is, as authorized teachers for the kingdom of heaven, in contrast with the Pharisaic scribes who have failed to grasp its message.[10] As such, they are to be like the good householder who makes suitable and varied provision for his household.[11] The scribal language may suggest that the "things new and old" are a deliberate contrast with the official scribes of Israel, who can produce only what is old[12] because they have not discovered the new secrets of the kingdom of heaven. Yet those secrets themselves are not really "new"; they are "things hidden since the foundation of the world" (v. 35), and it is only their revelation which is new. If Jesus' disciples have indeed "understood" these old/new truths (v. 51), they are now in a position to offer more adequate provision for God's household, and this parable challenges them to "bring it out" for the benefit of others.

If something like that is the intention of this puzzling little epigram, the specific combination of "things new and old" may have a further nuance as a warning against neglecting the old in the excitement of having discovered the new — as indeed the imagery of the parables of the treasure and the pearl might suggest. The message of the kingdom of heaven does not wipe the slate clean, but rather brings fulfillment to what has gone before, as Jesus has been at pains to demonstrate in 5:17-48. The "old" is not to be "abolished" (5:17), but to be judiciously integrated into the new perspective of the

---

with the view that he uses "scribe" as a more general term for disciples. D. E. Orton, who strongly argues the latter view, nonetheless also finds a self-reference in 13:52, and discusses (*Scribe,* 165-74) "Matthew as a scribe" — one who himself puts into practice the principle of this verse by his own creative input to the tradition of Jesus' sayings.

10. D. E. Orton, *Scribe,* 142, drawing on his extended discussion of "the 'apocalyptic' scribe" (ibid., 65-120), asserts that against the background of that nonrabbinic usage the term "scribe" is particularly appropriate in this context because it was a special role of such scribes to understand and interpret dark sayings; parables were their stock-in-trade (see, e.g., Sir 39:1-3). It is because Jesus' disciples have understood the parables (v. 51) that they can be characterized as scribes. He goes on (145-51) to link this idea with the motif of the *maśkîlîm,* "the wise" in Dan 11 and 12.

11. For the rather surprising verb (literally, "throws out from his storeroom . . .") cf. 12:35, where the same phrase ἐκβάλλω ἐκ τοῦ θησαυροῦ is used, again with no sense of violence. It is apparently an idiom in which the verb has lost much of its original force.

12. Rabbinic scribes themselves drew a distinction between "old" and "new," as in *m. Yad.* 4:3 ("the work of the Prophets" is old, "the work of the elders" new); *b. 'Erub.* 21b (the old and new fruit of Song 7:13 represent the Torah and the words of the scribes); but from the perspective of the kingdom of God even their "new" is old!

kingdom of heaven. One can only speculate whether any particular radical tendency in Matthew's church (based on the treasure and the pearl?) led him to conclude the discourse with this corrective note.[13]

10. Moving On (13:53)

> And then,[1] when Jesus had come to the end of these parables, he moved on from there.

As in 7:28-29 and 11:1, the standard formula (for which see on 7:28) both closes the discourse and launches the next stage of the narrative. Matthew speaks of "parables" here instead of simply "sayings" or "instruction" not because there will be no more parables in his gospel[2] but because that form of teaching has characterized and indeed been the subject of this discourse in a way that is not true of the other discourses within which parables may be embedded. The verb "moved on" will be given more concrete content in v. 54, where we find Jesus for the first time since 4:13 leaving the lakeside area to return to his area of origin in the hill country.

K. FURTHER HOSTILE RESPONSES (13:54–14:12)

A more miscellaneous collection of incidents fills up the rest of Matthew's account of Jesus' Galilean ministry, which concludes at 16:20. Three significant complexes of traditions occur within this section, a sequence of miracles around the lake in 14:13-36, a debate about ritual purity in 15:1-20, and a series of incidents set outside Galilee proper in 15:21-39. The two pericopae which precede these complexes are grouped together here more for convenience than because of any natural affinity, but both in different ways develop further the theme of hostility to Jesus which has already been a significant factor in the narrative preceding the parable discourse. It may be significant that the first of these incidents includes the last mention of Jesus teaching in a synagogue; from this point on Jesus will be seen increasingly outside the structures of traditional Judaism.

---

13. I. H. Jones, *Parables,* 204-6, surveys ten different suggestions for the significance of "new and old" here; they are not all mutually exclusive, and none is clearly wrong. It is a matter of the interpreter's view of the Matthean church situation.

1. On this rendering of the formulaic idiom καὶ ἐγένετο, "and it happened," see p. 297, n. 1.

2. For parables set within the remaining discourses in this gospel, see 18:12-14, 23-35; 24:32-33, 45-51; and 25:1-12, 14-30, 32-33.

1. Nazareth (13:54-58)

> 54 *And Jesus came to his own home village[1] and was teaching the people in their synagogue, with the result that they were astonished and said, "Where do this man's wisdom and his miracles come from?* 55 *Isn't this the carpenter's son? Isn't his mother called Mary and his brothers James, Joseph,[2] Simon, and Judas?* 56 *And aren't all his sisters here with us? So where has this man gotten all this?"* 57 *They took offense[3] at him. So Jesus said to them, "A prophet is not without honor except in his own homeland and in his own household."* 58 *And he did not do many miracles there, because of their unbelief.*

After the long parable discourse, the narrative picks up where it left off, with an incident which again focuses on Jesus' family as in 12:46-50, just before the discourse began. There it was Jesus' actual family who were alienated from him; now a similar alienation is revealed more widely in his home village, of which that family are a significant part (and so are named in vv. 55-56).

This is Jesus' only recorded return to Nazareth after his public ministry began down by the lake. Luke 4:16-30 tells the story at length and in a more dramatic form, culminating in an attempt on Jesus' life; he has moved it out of its natural place in the narrative[4] in order to use it as a "frontispiece" for his account of the Galilean ministry. But in Matthew and Mark it fits more naturally, with reports already having reached Nazareth of the "wisdom and miracles" which Jesus has been displaying down in the lakeside area and beyond. He comes back to them now as the "local boy made good," and they react with the predictable scepticism of a small village community. Nazareth

---

1. πατρίς often refers to the wide area of one's "homeland," but in that sense Jesus' πατρίς would be Galilee, and he is already in Galilee. It must therefore here have the narrower sense of one's specific place of origin (as "their synagogue," singular, also confirms); but "home *town*" would be too grand a term for a place so small and insignificant as Nazareth. When πατρίς recurs in v. 57, the proverbial form of the saying allows the wider sense.

2. There is considerable uncertainty in the MSS of both Matthew and Mark over the name of this man and of his namesake (the same person?) in 27:56 (cf. Mark 6:3 and 15:40, 47). In both passages in Mark the more likely form of the name is Ἰωσῆς, in both passages in Matthew Ἰωσήφ. Both are forms of the OT name Joseph, Matthew apparently preferring the more obviously Hebrew form, which also reminds the reader of the (now dead?) head of the family who is not otherwise named.

3. I have hitherto translated σκανδαλίζω literally by some form of "stumble" (5:29-30; 11:6; 13:21), but in this context English idiom hardly allows that rendering. Literally, "they were caused to stumble in him."

4. Luke's account assumes that Jesus has already been performing miracles in Capernaum (4:23), even though the Capernaum period will come later in Luke's gospel.

apparently joins Chorazin, Bethsaida, and Capernaum (11:20-24) in the inglorious roll of communities which failed to repent despite the evidence of the miracles.

54 Matthew does not need to name Nazareth specifically since he has informed us of Jesus' home village in 2:23 and 4:13 (cf. also 21:11; 26:71). Bethlehem, the place where he was actually born (2:1), could not be intended here since the narrative is still clearly centered in Galilee, and his family, who lived in Nazareth, feature in it. "Their synagogue" need have no pejorative connotation (see p. 150, n. 7). It simply denotes the synagogue of the people whom he is teaching, which, unlike that in 12:9, was "theirs" and not his since his move away to Capernaum — though it was, of course, the synagogue in which he himself had worshiped as he grew up. But this synagogue visit does not evoke a welcoming response, and from this point on we shall hear no more of Jesus teaching in synagogues. The imperfect tense, "was teaching," may indicate an extended period of teaching, or it could suggest (as Luke's account does) that he began teaching but was interrupted by their negative response. The word for "astonished" is the same which recorded the reaction of the crowd to Jesus' teaching in 7:28 (cf. also 22:33); there it denoted approbation, but here it quickly gives way to scepticism. The "wisdom" they can hear for themselves; the "miracles" are a matter of report.

55-56 Whatever the theological truth about Jesus' birth (see 1:18-25), to the people of Nazareth he is simply Joseph's son, and that is what determines his place in village society. The "carpenter" was a significant member of the community. *Tektōn,* traditionally translated "carpenter," is a general term for a "constructor," and probably denotes general building work including masonry as well as woodwork; he was a skilled craftsman, probably also dealing with agricultural and other implements.[5] In Mark 6:3 Jesus is himself called "the carpenter," perhaps because Joseph had now died (see on 12:46-47) and Jesus, as the eldest son, had taken over the business until he moved away. It is consistent with this view that Joseph himself is not listed with the members of the family here.

The mention of the brothers'[6] names may simply be a way of making the story more concrete, but by the time Matthew wrote certainly James (who was leader of the Jerusalem church until his martyrdom in A.D. 62) and probably the other brothers (see Acts 1:14; 1 Cor 9:5) were well-known

---

5. The classical study of τέκτων is by C. C. McCown in S. J. Case (ed.), *Studies in Early Christianity,* 173-89. See also P. H. Furfey, *CBQ* 17 (1955) 204-15. Albright and Mann, 172-73, translate here "builder," and speculate at length on the extent of Joseph's (and Jesus') itinerant construction work around Galilee and beyond; similarly, more recently R. A. Batey, *NTS* 30 (1984) 249-58.

6. See p. 497, n. 7, for the nature of the relationship.

members of the Christian community. James and Judas are traditionally the authors of the two NT letters of those names. All four names are taken from the patriarchs of Genesis, indicating the conservatively Jewish background of Jesus' own family. The mention that the sisters are "with us" may be because, whereas Jesus' mother and brothers have recently been down in Capernaum (12:46-50), and may even have moved to live down there after Jesus went, the sisters, having presumably married local men, have never moved away. The implication of this list of family details is that a man whose local pedigree is so well known can hardly be thought of as something extraordinary (cf. John 6:42: "Isn't this Jesus the son of Joseph . . . ? So how can he say, 'I have come down from heaven'?"). Even though rabbis normally supported themselves by a trade, the village carpenter is hardly the person to pose as a distinguished teacher if he has not received any formal training — cf. John 7:15: "How does this man know his letters, when he has not been taught?"

57 "Stumbling" (see p. 548, n. 3) need not here have the drastic sense of spiritual disaster which we have seen in 5:29-30 and 13:21; it is perhaps closer to John the Baptist's "stumbling" over Jesus' surprising style of being Messiah (11:6). But it puts the people of Nazareth clearly in the camp of the sceptics rather than that of Jesus' followers; they at least do not merit the beatitude of 11:6. Jesus' wry comment has a proverbial sound (cf. our "Familiarity breeds contempt"). Several similar sayings occur in ancient literature, particularly with reference to Greek philosophers.[7] Apart from the Synoptic parallels see also John 4:44 and *Gos. Thom.* 31, the latter expanded by the hardly self-evident statement that no doctor cures those who know him.

58 Matthew diplomatically avoids saying, as does Mark, that Jesus *could not* do many miracles there, but the effect of the "unbelief" of the people of Nazareth is consonant with the repeated emphasis in this gospel on the importance of "faith" for healing or other miracles (8:10, 13, 26; 9:2, 22, 28-29; 14:31; 15:28; 17:20; 21:21-22). Here the problem is not so much doubt over Jesus' ability to carry out any specific healing as scepticism as to his whole image as a miracle-working "man of God." In this the people of Nazareth compare very unfavorably with the crowds from other parts of Galilee and beyond (4:24; 8:16; 14:35-36). "Unbelief" *(apistia)* is used only of these people who reject Jesus; when disciples are rebuked for lack of faith, we find the less absolute term *oligopistia* ("little faith"; see above on 6:30).

---

7. For a convenient collection see Davies and Allison, 2:459-60.

2. Herod Antipas (14:1-12)

> 1 *At that time Herod the tetrarch heard what people were saying about Jesus,* 2 *and he said to his servants, "This is John the Baptist: he has risen from the dead, and that is why these powers are at work in him."*
>
> 3 *For Herod had seized John and bound him and had put him away in prison on account of Herodias, the wife of his brother Philip,*[1] 4 *because John kept on telling him, "You have no right to have her [as your wife]."*[2] 5 *Herod wanted to kill him, but he was afraid of the crowd, because they regarded John as a prophet.* 6 *But when Herod's birthday celebrations came around,*[3] *Herodias's daughter danced among the guests and pleased Herod* 7 *so much that he declared on oath that he would give her whatever she asked.* 8 *Put up to it by her mother, she said, "Give me here on a dish the head of John the Baptist."* 9 *Reluctantly, because of*[4] *his oaths and in deference to*[5] *those who were feasting with him, the king gave orders for it to be given to her.* 10 *He sent and had John beheaded in the prison,* 11 *and John's head was brought on a dish and given to the girl, who took it to her*

1. The omission of the name "Philip" in some Western MSS and versions, perhaps under the influence of Luke 3:19, may reflect some uncertainty about the identity of the various members of the Herod family (see comments below), but the large majority of witnesses include the name here (as in Mark 6:17).

2. Matthew never actually states what he assumed his readers would already know, that Antipas had married Herodias after she left his brother, and that this was the basis of John's accusation. Matthew's abbreviated wording does not require, as Gundry, 286-87, supposes, that he understood that the marriage had not yet taken place; it is perhaps more likely that he avoids the term because for him it was not a valid marriage. See the comments below for the historical data.

3. The dative phrase γενεσίοις δὲ γενομένοις, where a genitive absolute would be expected (and is found in most later MSS), if it is original is perhaps to be explained as a rather clumsy blend of the temporal dative ("on the birthday") with the participial form of the genitive absolute; see BDF 200(3), attributing it to "copyists who were interpolating from Mark." N. Turner, *A Grammar of NT Greek,* vol. 3: *Syntax,* 243, is content to describe it as a "dative absolute," of which "there may be examples in Greek" (possibly under the influence of the Latin ablative absolute?).

4. An equally well-supported reading could be rendered, "The king was sorry, but because of. . . ." This reading makes the logic of the sentence rather clearer, but for that reason it is perhaps more likely to be a correction of an originally rather less lucid wording, as translated above.

5. Matthew joins the two reasons together with a simple "and" — "because of his oaths and of those who were feasting with him." The implied logic seems to be, however, that in order not to lose face with his guests he had to keep his oaths (which he now regretted).

mother. 12 *Then John's disciples came and took his body and buried it; and they came and told Jesus about it.*

Only vv. 1-2 speak of Antipas's reaction to Jesus, and so belong at this point in the narrative. Verses 3-12 are a "flashback," needed to explain Antipas's extraordinary idea that Jesus is the resurrected John. Mark tells the same story at much greater length simply as a digression from his narrative when he mentions Antipas's ideas about Jesus, but Matthew ties this chronologically unconnected incident into his narrative by having John's disciples report the event to Jesus (v. 12), whose next move is then explained as a reaction to hearing the news (v. 13).[6] This is probably more a literary device than a deliberate chronological link, since Antipas's interpretation of Jesus as the resurrected John must obviously have developed after the death of John. On the other hand, John's death cannot have been too long before, since he has been still alive in prison during Jesus' quite recent ministry (11:2-6). There is no independent information on the date of John's death, since Josephus, *Ant.* 18.116-19, though he links John's death with Aretas's invasion of Perea in A.D. 36, does not say that the one event followed closely on the other, merely that popular opinion attributed Antipas's troubles to his earlier execution of John.

Even in Matthew's much abbreviated version (136 words compared to Mark's 249),[7] vv. 3-12 stand out as the one substantial pericope in the gospel after Jesus' adult appearance on the scene in 3:13 which is not directly concerned with him and his disciples. Formally speaking, it is thus a digression from the ongoing narrative, but the prominence of John in the gospel as a whole ensures that it is not an irrelevant aside. We have heard of John's imprisonment in 4:12 and 11:2, and this pericope completes John's story. Moreover, it provides the necessary basis for the words of Jesus in 17:10-13 comparing his own imminent fate with that of John, to whom "they did whatever they pleased." Just as Jesus continues the mission and authority of John (3:11-12; 11:2-6, 9-19; 16:14; 21:24-27, and see above, p. 98), so he will share his fate of unjust execution. In that sense this pericope is not just a flashback but also a foreshadowing of what is to happen to the "second John."[8]

6. O. L. Cope, *CBQ* 38 (1976) 515-19, argues, however, that what Jesus "heard" in v. 13 was the news of Antipas's conjectures about his own ministry reported in vv. 1-2, the intervening story in vv. 3-12 being a parenthetical explanation introduced by γάρ and the resumption of the narrative being marked by the δέ which follows ἀκούσας in v. 13. On that reading there is no chronological discrepancy — but it is a very long parenthesis for the reader (or hearer) to negotiate!

7. Gundry, 286-87, shows how Matthew's version is not merely abbreviated, but also redesigned in order to shift the focus away from Antipas to John as "Jesus' prototype."

8. D. C. Allison, *Moses,* 138, sets out a number of verbal and conceptual links be-

The careful reader of Matthew might reflect on the contrast between this degenerate scene of Antipas's lavish feast with its sordid and tragic outcome and the wholesome simplicity of the "feast" which will follow in vv. 13-21.

1-2 The "Herod" of this story is Herod Antipas, tetrarch of Galilee and Perea from 4 B.C. to A.D. 39, and thus the ruler of Galilee during Jesus' adult life. Confusingly for modern readers whose knowledge of Palestinian politics is not as good as that of the original readers, the gospel writers refer to Antipas (who is mentioned only here in this gospel) simply by the family name "Herod," which Matthew has also used for his father in ch. 2. But Matthew correctly describes this "Herod" as "tetrarch" not as king, though in v. 9 he will use the title "king" which Antipas wanted and campaigned for (it had been his father's title), and which was popularly used to flatter him, but which Rome never officially approved for him.[9]

As governor of Jesus' home province Antipas could hardly avoid hearing about the popular movement focused around Jesus; he may well have been concerned about the possible implications of Jesus' announcement of the coming of a "kingdom of heaven." The reports reminded him of the earlier popular movement led by John on the border of his other territory Perea, but with the difference that Jesus was popularly known as a miracle-worker rather than just a preacher and baptizer. Antipas accounted for the difference by the superstitious idea that Jesus was John returned from the dead — miraculous powers were to be expected of such a supernatural figure. The idea of a ghostly or even physical return of someone who has had a special influence, especially if that influence has been prematurely cut off by violent death, is found in various cultures (think of Elijah, Nero, King Arthur, Elvis). This is popular superstition[10] rather than a worked-out theology of resurrection such as that of the Pharisees. Matthew does not say explicitly that Antipas felt personally threatened ("haunted") by the returning John, but that is probably implied, and Jesus' "withdrawal" in v. 13 suggests that he regarded Antipas as a potential threat to himself (cf. Luke 13:31).

3 The "flashback" begins with John still in prison (cf. 4:12; 11:2). Josephus (*Ant.* 18.119) locates John's imprisonment and execution in Antipas' palace at Machaerus, in Perea, which would be consistent with the implication of this story that the prison was close to where Antipas's birthday

---

tween this pericope and the story of Jesus to illustrate the "obvious and extended assimilation of Jesus and John the Baptist" in Matthew. See also Davies and Allison, 2:475-76.

9. For Matthew's ironical presentation of Antipas's pretensions in contrast with his real powerlessness see D. J. Weaver, in D. R. Bauer and M. A. Powell (eds.), *Treasures,* 187-91.

10. Cf. the report of the appearance in Herod's palace of the ghosts (δαίμονες) of his murdered sons Alexander and Aristobulus (Josephus, *War* 1.599).

celebrations took place. Antipas maintained palaces both in his new city of Tiberias in Galilee and at Machaerus (one of his father's former palaces), and presumably moved between the two in order to control the two geographically separated parts of his tetrarchy.[11] Josephus attributes the imprisonment and execution to fear of John's political influence, but the more specific issue which Matthew mentions would be consistent with this since Josephus also speaks of the political implications of Antipas's marriage to Herodias, and the divorce of his previous wife which cleared the way for it; it was a brazenly irregular action which subsequently provoked a ruinous war with his former father-in-law, the Nabatean king of Petra (*Ant.* 18.109-15).[12]

The identity of the various members of the complex Herod family, and the other historical problems surrounding this account, are patiently unraveled in an exhaustive study by H. W. Hoehner.[13] Josephus names the (half-)brother from whom Herodias was taken simply as "Herod," and elsewhere says that Herod Philip, tetrarch of the neighboring area of Trachonitis, was married to Herodias's daughter, Salome (*Ant.* 18.136-37). Since "Herod" seems to have been used both as the general family name and as a personal name for some members of the family, there was room for confusion; it is possible that the "Herod" who was Herodias's first husband also bore the name Philip.[14]

4 John's objection to the marriage of Antipas and Herodias would have had wide popular support at least among Antipas's more conservative Jewish subjects. Not only did the marriage infringe the Mosaic restrictions on the marriage of relatives (Lev 18:16; 20:21),[15] but it had also been achieved only by means of two divorces. Antipas's divorce of his first wife, the daughter of the king of Petra, however diplomatically disastrous (see above), would probably have been religiously acceptable to the less rigorous school of Hillel, but not to the stricter Shammaite party who approved of divorce only in the case of the wife's sexual infidelity (see above on 5:31-32). But Herodias had also herself repudiated her first husband (not been divorced by him), and that was forbidden under Jewish law; she had probably invoked Roman law, which did allow a wife to divorce her husband, but that would not have made it any more acceptable to Jewish opinion. The whole scenario would have underlined how thin was Antipas's supposed Jewishness (his fa-

---

11. See R. L. Webb, *John,* 374, n. 57.

12. For the political implications of John's stance in relation to the neighboring Nabatean kingdom see R. L. Webb, *John,* 368.

13. H. W. Hoehner, *Herod,* 110-71.

14. So Hoehner, ibid., 131-36.

15. Herodias was also the niece of Antipas, as indeed she was of her first husband, but such a marriage appears to have been accepted within mainstream Judaism; see Hoehner, ibid., 137-39, n. 4.

ther, Herod, was Idumean, not really Jewish, and his mother Samaritan), and made him increasingly vulnerable to orthodox Jewish criticism,[16] of which John was clearly an outspoken and persistent representative — note the imperfect tense, "kept on telling him." The "telling" was presumably by public denunciation since John would hardly have had direct access to Antipas before his arrest.

5   John's criticism of his marriage adds a further dimension to the political danger which, according to Josephus, Antipas saw in John, the popular preacher, and makes his determination to eliminate him the more understandable. But John had public support on his side, as Josephus also makes clear by his account of people's reaction after John's death. For the popular estimate of John as a prophet cf. 11:9; 21:26 (also 21:31-32), and for his wide popularity cf. 3:5-6. The same comment will be made about Jesus, that his popularity stood in the way of the authorities' desire to arrest and execute him (21:46; 26:3-5), and that popularity, too, is attributed to the view that Jesus was a prophet (16:14; 21:11, 46). In the case of Jesus the problem of public support will be overcome by strategy and the recruitment of Judas; in John's case it happens apparently almost by accident, though there may have been as much planning as opportunism in Herodias's demand.

6-11   The story is familiar, especially in Mark's more colorful version — and still more so in subsequent popular elaboration of the "dance of the seven veils," with the unnamed dancer of the gospel accounts identified as Salome. The telling in Matthew is comparatively restrained, leaving the reader to imagine the debauched atmosphere of an oriental princeling's party.[17] The account may simply reflect a popularly circulated report, but it is possible that it derives from people in the Herodian court who had links with the Jesus movement (see Luke 8:3; Acts 13:1).

After the statement in v. 5 that Antipas wanted to kill John, it is surprising to read in v. 9 of his "reluctance," which was overcome only by his determination not to lose face after his ill-advised public oath (see above, p. 551, n. 5). It may be possible to explain his reluctance as relating not so much to the death

16. There may be also the issue of Antipas's ritual status since Lev 20:21 describes marriage with a brother's wife as "impurity"; see R. L. Webb, *John,* 366-67.

17. Antipas had a reputation for giving extravagant parties: Josephus, *Ant* 18.102. See J. E. Taylor, *John,* 247, for "Antipas' reputation as 'the host with the most.'" Keener, 399-402, provides much interesting comparative historical detail on ancient birthday parties, and on the reputation of the Herodian family in particular. See also Carter, 303-4, on the morals of the Herodian family. The account may be intended to recall the party of Ahasuerus in Esth 1:5-12, at which the queen (unlike Herodias's daughter) refused to appear before the male guests; R. D. Aus, *Water,* 41-66, draws out numerous links between the Marcan version of this story and that of Ahasuerus's banquet, especially in later Jewish tradition.

itself as to the means, a summary execution without trial;[18] such an infringe-ment of Jewish law, publicly witnessed, was not the way Antipas had intended to get rid of John. But the comment may also be a relic of the explanation given in Mark, but omitted by Matthew, that it was Herodias rather than Antipas who wanted John dead, and that Antipas retained a secret admiration for John and "was glad to listen to him" (Mark 6:20). Herodias comes across as the domi-nant personality in the story,[19] and it may well be that her daughter's dance was designed from the beginning to undermine Antipas's defenses. The dancer is referred to as a "girl," *korasion,* the same diminutive which has been used for Jairus's daughter in 9:24-25; the term would be appropriate to a younger teen-ager, and what we know of the family history supports such an age.[20]

12 We have heard of John's "disciples" already in 9:14; 11:2. They have continued as a group after his imprisonment, and indeed there is evi-dence that such a group continued for a considerable time after John's death distinct from the disciples of Jesus; note the mention in Acts 18:25; 19:3 of "disciples" who "knew only the baptism of John." Their action in burying John's body after execution (presumably having obtained permission from Antipas's court to do so) is like that of Joseph of Arimathea later (27:57-60); in each case there was some risk in being associated with an executed leader, but that risk was overriden by the Jewish horror at leaving a body unburied. In view of the close relationship which Matthew has depicted between John and Jesus, it is not surprising that on John's death some of his followers should look to Jesus as the natural successor to their leader; hence Matthew's statement that they reported to Jesus (see above, p. 552).

L. MIRACLES AROUND THE LAKE (14:13-36)

A further collection of miracle stories, closely following the series recorded in Mark 6:30-56, now continues the narrative until it is interrupted by the debate

---

18. It is also debated whether beheading as such was permitted as a Jewish form of execution. It is certainly envisaged in the Mishnah (*m. Sanh.* 7:1, 3) but this may repre-sent an academic rather than an actual possibility, especially at this time when the Jewish authorities themselves (unlike Antipas) had no right to impose a death penalty. See Keener, 401, n. 14.

19. For Herodias's ruthless ambition and her ability to manipulate Antipas see the account in Josephus, *Ant.* 18.240-46, of her instigation of Antipas's disastrous bid for the royal title.

20. See H. W. Hoehner, *Herod,* 151-57, for her identity (Salome, daughter of Herodias by her first marriage) and age (12 to 14 years), and the cultural likelihood of a princess of that age dancing before men. Hoehner does not support the more lurid specu-lations as to the nature of the dance.

about purity which will follow in 15:1-20. These stories are linked not by their content (one involves the multiplication of food, one the ability to walk on water, and the rest, in summary form, physical healings) but by their geographical coherence as parts of the same continuing itinerary. We last heard of Jesus in Nazareth (13:53-58), but now he is apparently back in his more normal lakeside area. The uninhabited area to which he now withdraws (v. 13) is near the lake, reached and left by boat (vv. 13, 22); the next miracle takes place on the crossing from that place toward "the other side" (v. 22); and the following scene of many healings is again back on the northwestern lakeshore at Gennesaret. After the debate in 15:1-20 (which is not specifically located, but is presumably to be read as in the same lakeside area) Jesus will leave this familiar territory, and the only return to Galilee will be for a brief encounter with the Pharisees and Sadducees in 15:39–16:4, after which a further lake crossing will take Jesus and his disciples away to the northeast, from where they will set off for Jerusalem. Thus the "withdrawal" of v. 13 and the sequence of events which flow from it mark almost the end of Jesus' public activity in Galilee.

1. Feeding the Crowd (14:13-21)

13 When Jesus heard this, he withdrew from there by boat to an uninhabited area to be alone.[1] But when the crowds heard, they left their towns and followed him on foot. 14 So when he went out, he saw a great crowd, and his heart went out[2] to them, and he healed those among them who were ill. 15 As evening came on, his disciples came to him and said, "This place is uninhabited, and it's getting late.[3] Send the crowds away so that they can go into the villages and buy themselves something to eat." 16 But Jesus replied, "They don't need to go away; you give them something to eat." 17 They responded, "All we have here are five loaves and two fish." 18 He said, "Bring them here to me." 19 And when he had given orders for the crowds to sit on the grass, he took the five loaves and the two fish, looked up to heaven, said a blessing,[4] and broke them; then he gave the loaves to the disci-

---

1. κατ' ἰδίαν describes the place rather than the purpose of the visit, but since Matthew has already said that the place was uninhabited, this additional phrase seems to indicate Jesus' purpose (which is more fully spelled out by Mark 6:31). "Alone" is not, however, to be taken literally, as the disciples were with him (see on v. 13 below).

2. For this rendering of σπλαγχνίζομαι see on 9:36.

3. Literally, "the hour has already gone by." "The hour" may refer specifically to the normal time for the evening meal, but the translation given assumes a less precise idiomatic sense.

4. For the meaning of εὐλογέω (praising God or blessing the food?) see the comments below, and n. 18.

ples, and the disciples gave them to the crowds. 20 And they all ate and had as much as they wanted.⁵ The disciples⁶ collected twelve baskets full of the leftovers from the broken loaves. 21 Those who ate were something like five thousand men, apart from women and children.

We move from Antipas's lavish but degenerate feast to one with a simpler menu but a more wholesome atmosphere. This, the first of two related feeding miracles in Matthew (cf. 15:32-38), is recorded in all four gospels, with an impressive similarity in all the essentials, both in the numbers of people, loaves, fish, and baskets and in the sequence of verbs which describe Jesus' action.

The consistency in reporting the numbers reflects the way oral stories are passed on, with the key elements maintained even when the surrounding narrative is differently framed. In this case there is the further consideration of comparison with the second feeding miracle, where the numbers are different (and again Matthew and Mark agree on them). The point was clearly significant, as both sets of numbers are taken up in the discussion in the boat in 16:9-10 — and in Mark's fuller version the numbers are repeated in greater detail.

The significance of the verbs used becomes clear when the five Synoptic feeding narratives are compared with the three Synoptic accounts of Jesus' eucharistic action at the Last Supper. In all eight pericopae we find the same sequence: "took . . . blessed/gave thanks . . . broke . . . gave."⁷ The same sequence of verbs also occurs in Luke 24:30, where Jesus "presides" at the meal at Emmaus. This can hardly be accidental, and suggests that the evangelists framed their accounts of the feeding (and of the Emmaus story) to reflect the wording of the eucharistic formula with which they and their readers were by now familiar. The feeding of the crowd is therefore presented as a "foretaste" of the central act of worship of the emergent Christian community, even though the menu was not quite the same.⁸ And since the Last Sup-

---

5. χορτάζομαι means to have enough, and more than enough, to eat (cf. 5:6). It was used primarily of fattening cattle (cf. Luke 15:16). A less elegant version might be "were stuffed."

6. The subject of the verb is not explicit, and the most recent subject is the crowds, but 16:9 will make clear that the disciples did the collecting. The thought thus looks back over the preceding clause about the crowds to the end of v. 19, where the disciples were the servers.

7. The verb for blessing varies between εὐλογέω and εὐχαριστέω (see n. 18 below). In John's account of the feeding of the crowd we find "took . . . gave thanks . . . gave out" — the breaking is not explicit but is implied by the compound verb διαδίδωμι, and is presupposed in the mention of κλάσματα, "broken pieces," collected. In 1 Cor 11:23-25 we find "took . . . gave thanks . . . broke," but the "giving" is left unexpressed.

8. C. L. Blomberg, *Holiness,* 103-4, is unusual in disputing a eucharistic dimension to this story.

per was itself a foretaste of the messianic banquet (26:29), that dimension, too, can legitimately be discerned in this story.[9]

At the time, of course, this eucharistic nuance could not have been known. The disciples (and the crowd, if they were aware of how the food had been produced) would have been more likely to understand the event in terms of OT precedent. An obvious parallel would be with the miracle of Elisha, who fed a hundred people from twenty loaves, with some left over (2 Kgs 4:42-44); there are also verbal echoes of the Elisha story in this pericope, and the nature of Jesus' miracle is the same, though the scale is vastly higher. But another precedent which might have been felt to be even more significant in view of Matthew's emphasis on the place being (literally) "wilderness" (vv. 13, 15) is that of Moses, under whose leadership a far greater number of people were miraculously fed in the wilderness not just on one occasion but for an extended period (Exod 16); the manna was given to supply their need of "bread" (Exod 16:4, 8, 12). The parallel is made explicit in John 6:25-34. Moses, however, is unlike Jesus in that he is not himself presented as performing a miracle, but simply as a spokesman for God; he describes the manna as "the bread that the LORD has given you to eat" (Exod 16:15; cf. Ps 78:25; 105:40). There is evidence that some Jews expected a return of manna in the messianic age (2 Bar. 29:8; Eccl. Rab. 1:28; cf. Rev 2:17).[10]

A belief that the event reveals Jesus as a new Moses, leader of God's people in the wilderness, may be a factor in the "political" enthusiasm which John associates with this event (John 6:14-15). Matthew does not directly draw attention to that aspect of the incident, though it is possible to interpret the urgency in the verb "compelled" in v. 22 as indicating that the disciples were infected with the unhealthy popular enthusiasm so that Jesus wanted to get them away from the scene before he himself dealt with the crowd (see comments below on vv. 22-23). For another suggested indication of a political flavor to the incident see below on v. 21.

But whatever the OT or other nuances which might have been perceived either by the disciples or the crowd at the time or by Matthew and his readers in recalling the event, the incident stands out primarily as a spectacular miracle in its own right, yet another staggering display of Jesus' "author-

9. C. L. Blomberg, *Holiness,* 105-8, points out that so large an ad hoc gathering of the common people of Galilee would be bound to include many who were ritually impure, so that this, like the meal in Matthew's house, is another example of Jesus' symbolic table fellowship with "sinners."

10. For the "new Moses" theme here see D. C. Allison, *Moses,* 238-42; he is surprisingly hesitant in claiming this pericope as support for his thesis. See his p. 242 for the helpful observation that "In Matthew's Jewish-Christian world the exodus from Egypt, the last supper, and the messianic banquet were not three isolated events," but linked together in a single chain of typological recapitulation.

ity" over nature as well as over human conditions. The gospel writers give no encouragement to naturalistic attempts to "explain" it by Jesus' persuading those in the crowd who had brought food to share it. Whatever exactly the disciples are supposed to have learned from the two incidents (see on 16:9-10), it was not at the level of psychological manipulation! The further suggestion that only a token amount was actually received by each person is ruled out by Matthew's wording in v. 20. And by recording another such miracle shortly afterward, Matthew and Mark make it clear that this was no fluke.

The miraculous provision of bread here is in striking contrast with Jesus' refusal to do so in 4:3-4. But, as we noted, the temptation then was for the newly declared "son of God" to satisfy his own hunger by the self-centered use of miraculous power. Here that power is used for the benefit of others.[11] The contrast between the two situations confirms our understanding that the temptations in ch. 4 were not concerned with Jesus' messianic agenda, aiming for popular approval by miraculous means, but with his own relationship with his Father. Even here there is in any case no indication that the crowd were even aware of how the bread was provided, and no crowd reaction is mentioned; see on v. 20.

13 In 4:12 we were told that Jesus "withdrew" when he heard about John's imprisonment by Antipas. Now the report of John's death has the same effect (see above, p. 552, for the chronological issue raised). As in 12:15 and 15:21, the withdrawal takes him away from a place of danger or confrontation; see the comments on 12:15 for this significant Matthean motif. A direct confrontation with Antipas would not advance Jesus' mission and, in the light of what had happened to John, was a risk to be avoided, especially in view of Antipas's view of Jesus as a new John.

The last location mentioned was Nazareth in 13:54-58, but it seems that Jesus did not stay there long, and we should probably understand him as now being back in Capernaum. A "withdrawal" by boat from Capernaum would take him outside the territory of Antipas if it took him to the other side of the Jordan inflow (only a couple of miles to the east), into the tetrarchy of Philip. The northeast corner of the lake offered plenty of "uninhabited" areas provided he avoided Bethsaida. Matthew makes it clear that Jesus is seeking not just safety but also solitude for himself and his disciples. The disciples are not mentioned at this point, but their presence is always assumed when Matthew speaks of Jesus traveling (not least by boat, which needed a crew),[12]

---

11. It is not clear, however, from what aspect of the passage Carter, 305, derives his interpretation that "Jesus' act attacks the injustice of the sinful imperial system which ensures that the urban elite are well fed at the expense of the poor."

12. *Pace* Hagner, 2:417, who takes κατ᾽ ἰδίαν to mean that Jesus was literally

and they will be present in v. 15. Mark 6:30-31 describes this attempted retreat as primarily for the sake of the disciples, whose mission Mark has just
described, but the different sequence of Matthew's narrative makes such a focus inappropriate here.

Matthew gives no more specific indication of where the following
event took place, but since it concludes with the disciples being sent off by
boat to "the other side" (v. 22) and then arriving in Gennesaret on the western
shore (v. 34), he presumably understands it to be somewhere on the northeast
shore — as the "escape" from Antipas's Galilee also implies. This would
tally with Luke's placing of the incident in the region of Bethsaida, but raises
the question how the crowd could reach the place on foot, with the Jordan in
between. Mark's geographical indications are not easy to interpret, but *might*
be met by the traditional site at Tabgha, west of Capernaum.[13] There is no
simple solution, but within Matthew's narrative the Bethsaida area seems
slightly more probable, in which case we must assume that there was some
adequate means for the pedestrian crowd to cross the Jordan (boats for five
thousand people? or a ford?; we do not know of a bridge in the area at that
time). Matthew, however, does not notice the problem.

The gathering so quickly of so large a crowd from a number of towns
in the area suggests a very effective "bush telegraph," unless this was a pre-
planned movement (see on v. 21). Once mobilized, however, the crowd need
not take any longer to cover a few miles on foot than it took in the boat. The
result was complete disruption of the planned retreat.

14 It would be pedantic to press Matthew's "when he went out" to
the point of asking whether a house is envisaged (in this "uninhabited" area?)
or whether it means at the point of disembarkation from the boat, with the
crowd already waiting on the shore (as Mark suggests by saying the pedestrian crowd "got there ahead of them"). What matters is that Jesus immediately shelved his own plans in favor of the needs of the crowd. For "his heart
went out" see on 9:36. His response is described only as healing, not teaching, though it would not be wise to argue from silence at this point. But the
focus on healing suggests that the popular interest in Jesus remains, as it was
in 4:24-25 and will be again in 14:35-36, concentrated on the desire to benefit from his miraculous power.

15-18 It is not likely that so large a number of people would have
been able to buy enough food in any "villages" close to this "uninhabited
area," but in the event the question will not arise, and so Matthew does not
need to explore the point, any more than he feels it necessary to explain why

---

alone, so that the disciples must have come on foot with the crowd. He does not explain
how Jesus operated the boat on his own.

13. I have discussed the issue in my *Mark,* 264.

people had not thought to take provisions for this sudden journey into an inhospitable region. Given the numbers involved, Jesus' response, "You give them something to eat," must have seemed like a hollow joke; cf. Elisha's similar command to his servant in 2 Kgs 4:42-43. Even their own provisions of five loaves and two fish[14] are not enough for a group of thirteen.[15] So had they been expecting to find hospitality (as in 10:9-13) somewhere nearby, despite the loneliness of the area? If so, the arrival of the large crowd had upset their calculations. To surrender even this meager provision to Jesus was either an act of reckless obedience or evidence of a more confident faith in Jesus' problem-solving ability than we have seen the disciples displaying elsewhere. Keener, 404, helpfully points out how this miracle fits the OT pattern of God taking what his people already had and transforming or multiplying it.

19 Jesus is clearly in charge of the situation, and his authority is apparently accepted by the crowd. They are seated as if at an impromptu open-air banquet,[16] the verb for "sit" being one which is normally used for the practice of reclining on couches in a *triclinium* in the Greek and Roman world and which in the Jewish context can suggest a more formal or special meal.[17] So the term may depict this picnic, despite its everyday menu of bread and fish, as a festive banquet, perhaps even as a foretaste of the "messianic banquet," though the wilderness setting suggests caution in drawing this conclusion: in the absence of chairs they had little choice but to "recline" on the ground! Jesus takes on the role of the head of the family at a Jewish meal (as he will also do in Luke 24:30) when he takes the food and utters the formal blessing before it is shared. His looking up to heaven indicates that the "blessing" is an act of praise to God the provider (as was usual at Jewish meals) rather than a "consecration" of the food itself.[18] See the introductory

14. For bread and fish as the Galilean staple diet see 7:9-10.
15. A single "loaf," probably like our pita bread, normally provided a meal for one person.
16. Matthew does not repeat Mark's graphic description of their quasimilitary organization (Mark 6:39-40).
17. See on 8:11, where the same verb is used (especially p. 317, n. 40).
18. There is no stated object for the verb εὐλογέω, "bless," and the syntax does not make it clear whether we should understand the loaves and fish as the object or whether we should understand a blessing of God's name. In view of the traditional form of blessing used over both food and wine at Jewish meals, "Blessed are you, Lord our God, king of the universe . . ." (*m. Ber.* 6:1-3; 7:3, etc.), the latter seems the more likely sense here, and the preceding mention of "looking up to heaven" supports this. To understand such a blessing as directly "consecrating" the food itself is probably to import too much Christian eucharistic theology (cf. 1 Cor 10:16) into a pious Jewish convention (Luz, 2:314, declares roundly that "in a Jewish milieu God is praised, the food is not blessed"), though in Luke 9:16 and (probably) Mark 8:7 the loaves do become the direct object of the act of blessing. The same ambiguity as here occurs when εὐλογέω is used without expressed ob-

comments above for the significance of the sequence of verbs used in this verse in the light of developing Christian eucharistic language.

20 Matthew allows no doubt as to the scale of the miracle. "All" ate, and each had all they could eat (see p. 558, n. 5) — and even then far more was left over than had been available at the beginning. The idea that each received only a token piece of food (as in most modern communion services) is not only unrealistic[19] but is also expressly ruled out by Matthew's wording. The collecting of the leftovers is probably mentioned not so much as an example of avoiding untidiness or waste,[20] but to underline how much food has been provided — hence perhaps the focus on this aspect of the two feeding miracles in 16:9-10. The Jewish setting of the incident (as opposed to the later feeding of the four thousand; see comments on 15:37) is indicated by the word used for "baskets," which is of a type of basket especially associated with Jewish use;[21] it is described by BDAG 563 as "prob. a large, heavy basket, probably of var. sizes, for carrying things."[22] Twelve such baskets would hold a lot more than five loaves and two fish. How they came by twelve such baskets out in the countryside is another of those little mysteries which Matthew does not choose to explain — or does he mean one basket filled twelve times?

Surprisingly, there is no mention of the crowd's reaction to the miracle here or in 15:38 after the second such feeding (contrast John 6:14). Are we to suppose that the crowd were unaware of where the food had come from, and simply accepted it without question? It is the disciples, not the crowd, who will be expected to have noted the miracle in 16:9-10.

21 All six gospel accounts of feeding miracles draw attention to the numbers involved. In this incident the four evangelists agree not only on the number five thousand but also on describing these five thousand as "men," using *andres,* which normally applies to adult males rather than to people in general (though the distinction is not hard-and-fast). Matthew, however, underlines the masculinity of the number estimated by adding "apart from

---

ject at 26:26; Mark 6:41; 14:22; Luke 24:30. In the other feeding narratives and eucharistic accounts the verb used is εὐχαριστέω, which cannot have the bread as its object.

19. However small the pieces, to get five thousand out of five small loaves and two fish would surely be in itself a miracle.

20. So Keener, 405, arguing from the tendency of pagan and Jewish moralists to condemn wasteful extravagance. D. Instone-Brewer, *Traditions,* 1:182, suggests, however, that these were the pieces broken off by the individual eaters as an elevation offering before eating the rest of the bread; such portions were not to be eaten but must be given to a priest or destroyed.

21. The Roman poet Juvenal (*Sat.* 3.14; 6.542) speaks mockingly of the κόφινος as the typical equipment of the poor Jew.

22. What else do you do with baskets?

women and children."[23] This would normally be understood to mean that women and children were also present, and that the number fed was thus considerably higher than five thousand. But the Greek phrase ("*without* women and children") could also be taken to mean "and there were no women and children," thus indicating an exclusively masculine gathering, as the use of *andres* in all the other gospels might also imply. This surprising suggestion could be written off as merely the result of the imprecise use of language, but it has also been argued that the evangelists may mean exactly what they say. The "political" reaction of the crowd according to John 6:14-15 (see introductory comments above) suggests to some interpreters that this was no chance collection of people, but a deliberate gathering of *men* who were determined to force Jesus, in view of his recognized power and charisma, into the role of a nationalist leader; their rapid and determined chase after Jesus into the "wilderness" (the traditional place of national uprisings) was a potentially military movement, in which women and children would therefore have no place. The "military" style of the organization of the crowd according to Mark 6:39-40 has also been taken to support this view. On this understanding the feeding in the wilderness was the turning point in Jesus' Galilean ministry, when he decisively rejected a popular demand that he assume a role of political leadership.[24]

There are enough hints in the different ways in which the four evangelists tell the story to enable a modern reader to reconstruct the event behind the gospel accounts in that way. But even if in the historical context at least some of the participants had such aims, it does not look as if that is the way the evangelists intended it to be understood. With the possible exception of John 6:14-15 (and even that can be read as a spontaneous reaction to the miracle rather than as indicating a political motivation for the gathering in the first place), none of the gospel accounts requires a political interpretation, nor does it appear to be a conscious determinant in the way they tell the story. What then of Matthew's "without women and children"? A simpler explanation is that he is merely following OT convention: in Exod 12:37 the tally of the people who left Egypt is given as "six hundred thousand men, besides children,"[25] where the term for "men" is firmly masculine (literally, "feet of males"), not inclusive. Such numberings in the OT are generally of the men

23. In 15:38 Matthew, and only Matthew, will use the same terms for the numbering of the four thousand, where Mark does not call them specifically ἄνδρες.

24. See, e.g., E. Bammel, in E. Bammel and C. F. D. Moule (eds.), *Jesus,* 211-40.

25. The Hebrew *taph,* usually translated "little children," is perhaps used for the whole dependent part of the community as opposed to the adult males, thus including women where they are not mentioned separately (cf. Gen 43:8). LXX renders it here by ἀποσκευή, normally "baggage" but defined here by J. Lust et al., *Lexicon of the LXX,* 55, as "all persons apart from the full-grown men or apart from the men fit for military service."

rather than of the whole population, even where no such explicit rider is added. If that is the pattern Matthew is following,[26] and if we have no other reason to assume that it was an exclusively male gathering, the number actually fed must be seen as well over five thousand (unless only the men received the food, which is hardly likely!). When such large numbers are involved, however, it is pedantic to attempt to calculate them; the traditional term "feeding of the five thousand" serves well enough.

2. Walking on the Water (14:22-33)

> 22 *Immediately Jesus made his disciples get into the boat and go ahead of him to the other side, while he himself sent the crowds away.* 23 *Then, when he had sent the crowds away, he went up into the hills by himself to pray. Well into the night[1] he remained there alone.* 24 *Meanwhile, the boat was now miles[2] out from the land, being buffeted by the waves since the wind was against them.* 25 *But in the fourth watch of the night Jesus came to them, walking on the lake.* 26 *When the disciples saw him walking on the lake,[3] they were terrified and said, "It's a ghost"; they cried out in fear.* 27 *Jesus spoke to them straightaway: "Don't worry," he said; "it is me. Don't be afraid."*

26. Note, however, a further suggestion by D. Instone-Brewer, *Traditions*, 1:79-81, that the male count is related to the rabbinic provision of different forms of "grace" to be said, depending on the number of eaters present (*m. Ber.* 7:3): only the men would be eligible to be counted for this purpose.

1. In v. 15 I translated the same phrase ὀψίας γενομένης (literally, "as it had become late") by "As evening came on." There is considerable flexibility in the time of evening or night to which this common phrase is applied. Here it must be several hours after the ὀψίας γενομένης of v. 15, since the feeding of five thousand people, the collection of the leftovers, the sending off of the disciples, the dismissal of the crowd, and Jesus' walk up into the hills have all taken place in the meantime. Moreover, the immediate sequel is placed in "the fourth watch of the night," the three hours preceding dawn. It seems, then, that by ὀψίας γενομένης here Matthew intends to indicate a time long after dark. See on 26:20 below for an incident where the flexibility of the phrase may be exegetically important.

2. Literally, "many stadia," a στάδιον being about one eighth of a mile (the Lake of Galilee is thirteen miles long by eight wide). Cf. John 6:19, "twenty-five or thirty stadia." The boat's location is expressed in various ways in the MSS and versions of Matthew, with the majority following Mark in saying "in the middle of the lake"; but all the variant wordings agree on their being far from land.

3. Curiously, Matthew (probably; the MSS vary) uses different cases after ἐπί in vv. 25 (accusative) and 26 (genitive). Given the range of usage of ἐπί with the three different cases, it would be unwise to postulate any difference in sense. The narrative leaves no doubt that Jesus is walking *on* the water, not just "by" it.

565

28 Peter replied, "Lord, if it's you, give me the order to come to you on the water." 29 "Come on, then," said Jesus. And Peter got out of the boat and walked on the water and came[4] toward Jesus. 30 But when he saw the strong wind,[5] he panicked, and, beginning to sink, he cried out, "Lord, save me!" 31 Immediately Jesus stretched out his hand and took hold of Peter, saying, "You faithless man,[6] why did you doubt?" 32 When they had climbed into the boat, the wind died away. 33 Then those who were in the boat bowed down before him[7] and said, "Truly you are the Son of God."

This incident is also recorded by John immediately after the feeding miracle, though Luke omits it. The apparently hurried aftermath of the feeding results in the disciples being out on the lake without Jesus in the boat (contrast 8:23-27), and it is this temporary separation which provides the setting for Jesus' coming independently across the lake. His walking on the water is thus presented, like the other nature miracles, as a practical response to a difficult situation rather than as a wonder performed for its own sake. Nor is there such clear indication here as there was in the case of the stilling of the storm and of the feeding of the five thousand that Matthew intends his readers to read the incident as a whole symbolically as an object lesson in faithful discipleship, though this element will become more evident in the added account of Peter's experience in vv. 28-32. Jesus' walking on water is recorded rather as a spectacular instance of his supernatural power, which evokes a suitably awed and theologically loaded response from the disciples (v. 33). Behind their reaction lies the OT imagery of God walking on or through the sea (Job 9:8; Ps 77:19; Isa 43:16), a potent symbol of the Creator's control over the unruly forces of his world.[8] It thus fol-

4. Alternative readings, both well supported, have καὶ ἦλθεν, "and came," or ἐλθεῖν, "to come"; the latter predominates in the later MSS and may be a correction to indicate that the walk was not the complete success which "and came" suggests. See the comments below on how these readings might affect our understanding of the incident.

5. Or "that the wind was strong." ἰσχυρόν, "strong," does not occur in ℵ and the first hand of B as well as in the Coptic versions. Its presence or absence makes little difference to the narrative, since the strength of the wind has already been indicated in v. 24.

6. See p. 264, n. 6, for the meaning of ὀλιγόπιστος.

7. See p. 303, n. 6, for the translation of προσκυνέω. Here the following words suggest that "worship," in the sense of recognizing a divine being, is implied, but the physical action of bowing down is perhaps the immediate focus in the narrative context.

8. J. P. Heil, *Jesus,* 37-56, surveys these and other OT and Jewish instances of "the sea-walking motif." The OT does not, however, supply any idea of human beings walking on water (rather, they pass *through* it: Exod 14:21-22; Josh 3:14-17; 2 Kgs 2:8, 14). Luz, 2:319-20, lists a number of pagan references which indicate that in antiquity, while the idea of walking on water was fascinating, it remained only a dream; only divine

lows naturally that when Jesus, like God, walks on the water, the storm yields to his authority.[9]

As with the feeding of the five thousand, all three evangelists go out of their way to eliminate the sort of rationalistic explanation which some modern scholars have proposed, such as that Jesus was walking on a hidden reef or sandbar.[10] Not only is this hardly likely to have impressed fishermen who knew the lake well, but all the evangelists emphasize that the boat was a long way from the shore. The Lake of Galilee is deep, and there are no such shallows away from the shores. Matthew's version throws further doubt on any such naturalistic explanation, in that he portrays Peter as sinking where Jesus was walking.

Peter's ill-fated attempt to emulate Jesus occurs only in Matthew. It is here, rather than in the account of Jesus' own miracle, that an element of symbolism seems to be indicated, especially as Peter is specifically chided for his lack of faith, a common Matthean complaint about disciples (6:30; 8:26; 16:8; 17:20). The faith which can move mountains (17:20) would have kept Peter safe, if he had not allowed his obedience to Jesus' call to be over-whelmed by his very natural perception of the danger to which he had rashly exposed himself. It is thus an illustration of the vulnerability of the disciple who allows doubt, the natural human perspective, to displace the faith which relies on the supernatural power of God.

It is not so clear, however, whether Matthew intends us to see Peter in this incident as an example of valid faith which went wrong, or as from the beginning taking a foolhardy risk either to impress the others or simply in a childish search for exhilaration. Peter's motivation for wishing to do as Jesus is doing is not explained. On the one hand, Jesus appears to endorse Peter's request (v. 29) and to imply that had he had sufficient faith it would have suc-ceeded (v. 31), but on the other, the eventual failure of the experiment per-

---

beings could walk on water, though this might be extended to heroes who were regarded as "divine men" or sons of gods. There is, however, a later Buddhist text which speaks of a man who started walking across a river while his mind was set on the Buddha, but who, like Peter, began to sink when he noticed the waves; unlike Peter, however, he set his mind again on the Buddha, and so continued the walk (see Luz, 2:321-22, for details).

9. It is possible to discern several echoes of OT language about God in what is said about Jesus in this pericope as a whole. Carter, 312, speaks of five "Godlike acts" here attributed to Jesus: "walking on water, talking as God, extending his hand, saving from water, calming the storm," for all of which he provides OT parallels. The second de-pends on interpreting ἐγώ εἰμι in v. 27 as the pronouncing of the divine name, on which see n. 14 below.

10. E.g., J. D. M. Derrett, *NovT* 23 (1981) 330-48. Derrett's argument is based on features of the delta area where the Jordan flows into the lake, and so has to discount the insistence of all three evangelists that the boat was not near the shore.

haps suggests that Matthew does not intend it to be taken as a model for others to follow, but rather as a cautionary tale. Peter's proposal might be regarded as coming rather too close to the "testing" of God which is forbidden in 4:5-7. Peter's leading role among the Twelve is particularly emphasized in Matthew, especially in this central part of his narrative (cf. 15:15; 16:17-19; 17:24-27; 18:21, all peculiar to Matthew), but he does not always appear as a model of true discipleship or an example to be followed (16:22-23; 26:33-35, 69-75).

22 The decision to get the disciples away from the scene even before Jesus dismisses the crowd, and the unusually forceful verb ("made," with the sense of force or compulsion, not just instruction) may be pointers toward the more "political" dimension of the event in the wilderness which is otherwise not brought out as clearly in Matthew as it is in John 6:14-15. See the introductory comments on 14:13-21 and also on the surprisingly male focus of v. 21. If there was a popular attempt, whether spontaneous or planned, to pressurize Jesus into adopting a more openly messianic role (as "king," John 6:15), we may suppose that the disciples would not have been slow to share the enthusiasm, and that Jesus found it necessary to isolate them as quickly as possible from this seductive movement which ran counter to his own messianic agenda as he will set it out in 16:21-28. But all that is reading between the lines on the basis of John's account. Matthew does not draw attention to any political nuance in the situation, and gives no reason why Jesus should wish to get rid of the disciples so quickly. Unlike John, who suggests that Jesus had to escape to the hills because the situation was out of control, Matthew portrays Jesus as firmly in command: when he sends the crowd away, they go.

The identification of "the other side" depends on where the feeding miracle took place (see on 14:13-21), but the fact that after the (extended) crossing they will arrive at Gennesaret, on the northwest shore (v. 34), supports a location for the feeding to the east of Capernaum.

23 For "into the hills" see on 5:1-2.[11] No specific location need be sought; this is, like 14:13, an attempt to get away from the crowd, whom he has left by the lake to make their way home. And this time his retreat is successful since he has specifically sent away both the crowds and, unusually, even the disciples. This is indeed the only place after the initial period in the wilderness (4:1-11) where Matthew specifically mentions that Jesus chose to

11. Davies and Allison, 2:502, find here, as in 5:1-2, a Mosaic typology. While this is possible, the situation is not like 5:1-2, where Jesus went up into the hills to teach a "new law." Here his purpose is to be alone to pray, and while of course Moses did speak to God on Mount Sinai, he did not primarily go up to pray. The context here lends less weight to the typological suggestion, based only on the phrase "went up into the hills."

be truly alone.[12] Even in Gethsemane he will keep three of the disciples with him (26:37). Matthew does not elsewhere mention Jesus' habit of praying alone, as in Mark 1:35; Luke 5:16; 6:12; 9:18, though he has of course recorded his instruction to his disciples to pray in this way (6:5-6). It would be possible therefore to read this unusual note as indicating a particular crisis at this point in Jesus' ministry. But that would be an argument from silence, and Matthew gives us no indication of the subject of Jesus' prayer. In the narrative context the solitary prayer in the hills serves rather to explain how Jesus comes to be so far away from his disciples on this occasion when they find themselves in difficulties.

24 From Jesus praying alone in the hills the spotlight shifts to the disciples in trouble (again) on the lake — and this time without Jesus in the boat to rescue them. If the disciples are rowing from somewhere in the region of Bethsaida (see on 14:13-21) to Gennesaret (v. 34), it is surprising to find them so far from the shore, but presumably they have been driven off course by the contrary wind. The situation seems to be similar to the storm in 8:24, though the focus in this narrative is on the wind (vv. 24, 30, 32) rather than the waves. The disciples' predicament this time is the inability to make headway rather than an imminent danger of sinking.

25-27 The fourth watch of the night[13] indicates that Jesus has spent most of the night in prayer, and the disciples in rowing (see p. 565, n. 1 for the time scale). He now "came to them" presumably to bring them help in their difficulty, as well as to join them before they got back to the western shore. But the means of his "coming" caused panic rather than help. That he walked on the water is a given element in the Jesus tradition, and Matthew sees no need either to explain or to comment on so remarkable a feat. Nor does he explain how they saw his approach in the dark, though the mention of the fourth watch might indicate that there was already a hint of pre-dawn light. In such circumstances the superstitious reaction of the disciples is hardly surprising. A disembodied spirit could appear where a physical body would sink. The term used here and in the Marcan parallel for a ghost or "apparition" does not occur elsewhere in the NT. It represents instinctive superstition rather than a theologically formulated belief, and may reflect the popular belief that evil spirits lived in the sea or that those who had drowned haunted the water. The disciples' irrational fear is met by the familiar voice of Jesus; considering the startling manner of his appearance, his words sound almost banal, but their very ordinariness contributes to the reassurance.[14] The

12. See on v. 13 for the inclusion of the disciples in the previous attempt to get away.

13. A Roman term covering the period 3 A.M. to 6 A.M.

14. In my earlier commentary I favored the suggestion that ἐγώ εἰμι, "It is me" is

inclusion of Peter's hasty response leaves Matthew no room at this point for comment on the reaction of the rest of the disciples; that must wait until v. 33, by which time the contrast with Peter's failure has added further depth to their initial amazement.

28-32 See the introductory comments above on why Matthew may have added this rider to the story as told by the other evangelists. That Jesus has authority to share with someone else his miraculous ability to walk on the water adds a further dimension to the supernatural power he has already displayed. But the focus of this story is on Peter, who displays a characteristic mixture of attitudes: he will not attempt the walk without Jesus' direct instruction, but given that instruction he is unable to carry it through because he lacks the necessary faith. Desire to emulate Jesus' miracle conflicts with the experienced fisherman's realistic assessment of the risk ("when he saw the strong wind").

The text as printed above suggests that at first Peter was successful in walking on the water and had already reached Jesus when he ran into trouble. But the alternative reading ("to come" instead of "and came"; see p. 566, n. 4) would express intention rather than actual achievement. In that case it has been suggested that the preceding aorist verb "walked" might be taken not so much as a simple statement of fact as an "inceptive aorist," so that the whole clause would mean "stepped onto the water intending to come to Jesus." On such a reading the attempt was a failure from the start, and Jesus had to rescue Peter as soon as he was in the water.[15] But the "inceptive aorist" normally denotes the beginning of a continuing state rather than a failed attempt;[16] the desired sense would have been better expressed by an imperfect, which often means "tried to." Most interpreters, whichever reading they adopt in v. 29b, agree that we are intended to see Peter's attempt as initially successful, until doubt overcame him.

The verb for "doubt" will recur in 28:17, its only other use in the NT. We shall note there that it denotes not so much a theological uncertainty or

---

"an echo of the divine name in Exodus 3:14, here connecting the one who has power over the sea with the God who made it." I now find that idea less plausible, despite the clearly "numinous" setting. ἐγώ εἰμι is the most natural form of self-identification, which is what the context here calls for; to trace the divine name in every NT use of this common phrase would produce absurd results. Cf. my *Mark,* 273, n. 71; 610, n. 34. The "divine name" interpretation is, however, regarded as "probable" here by Davies and Allison, 2:506, and assumed by many commentators; Carson, 344, draws a distinction between what the disciples would have understood at the time and what "any Christian after the Resurrection and Ascension" would detect in the phrase.

15. So Tasker, 145-46.

16. Standard examples of the "inceptive aorist" are ἐβασίλευσεν, "became king," and ἐσίγησεν, "fell silent." See BDF 318(1), 331.

unbelief as a practical hesitation, wavering, being in two minds. Peter's problem was not so much lack of intellectual conviction as the conflict between the evidence of his senses and the invitation of Jesus. To be "faithless" is (as in 6:30; 8:26) to lack the practical confidence in God and/or Jesus which is required in those who seek his supernatural provision. But here, as in 8:26 (note the same urgent appeal, "Lord, save!"), Jesus overrides that lack of faith, and saves Peter[17] as he had saved the "faithless" disciples in the previous storm.[18] The sudden dropping of the wind echoes the conclusion of that story as well.

33 The disciples' reaction is not in itself surprising, but the way they express it draws attention. In comparison with their comments in Mark and Luke, this declaration that Jesus is the Son of God seems premature, and seems to steal the thunder of Peter's declaration at 16:16 and its confirmation by the voice from heaven in 17:5. Why did that declaration evoke Jesus' fulsome comment and personal commendation of Peter in 16:17-19 if the disciples as a group[19] had already reached and expressed the same conclusion two chapters earlier? Perhaps the difference is between the instinctive recognition of Jesus' more-than-human nature here in the context of an overwhelming miracle (cf. the use of the same phrase by an impressed Gentile, prefixed again by "Truly," in 27:54)[20] and the deliberate formulation at Caesarea Philippi of a christological confession which balances the supernatural ("Son of God") element of this exclamation with a functional identification of Jesus' role as Messiah. It remains remarkable, however, that "Son of God" language, which has hitherto been largely confined to declarations by God (3:17) and demons (4:3, 6; 8:29) and editorial explanation (2:15), should now be used by the disciples without prompting. But if the disciples had heard and remembered Jesus' words about his special relationship with his Father in 11:25-27, that memory (together with Jesus' other references

17. As an experienced fisherman, presumably Peter could swim (cf John 21:7), so that all he was threatened by was a wetting (apart from "loss of face"). But perhaps we are intended to envisage the storm conditions as too severe even for swimming?

18. It is possible that Jesus' "stretching out his hand" to save Peter from the water is a deliberate echo of God's action as described in Pss 18:16; 144:7, thus adding to the impression that in walking on the water Jesus is acting as God acts in the OT (see introductory comments above). So Gundry, 300.

19. The phrase "those who were in the boat" might be taken as excluding Peter, who at this stage has just climbed back into it (so Gundry, 300-301; Davies and Allison, 2:510), in which case this "confession" would be by the other eleven, leaving Peter to make his own (fuller) statement at Caesarea Philippi. But Peter is now in the boat with the others, and the phrase does not seem designed to exclude him.

20. At 27:54 we shall note the possibility that θεοῦ υἱός is meant to echo the official title of the Roman emperor, but such an allusion is extremely unlikely in the mouths of Galilean fishermen.

to "my Father," as in 7:21; 10:32-33; 12:50) might well trigger such a response to the numinous character of this scene, especially as it followed so closely on the equally striking miracle of the loaves and fish. Note the contrast between this positive statement and the question "What sort of person is this?" which concluded the previous lake story (8:27). As Davies and Allison comment, "The disciples are beginning to catch up with the readers of the gospel"!

3. Many Healings (14:34-36)

> 34 *They completed the crossing and came to land at Gennesaret.* 35 *The men of that place recognized him, and sent into all the surrounding region, and brought to him all who were ill.* 36 *They begged him that they might merely touch the fringe of his cloak; and all who touched it were restored to health.*[1]

Gennesaret is probably the modern Ginosar, on the northwest shore of the lake only three miles southwest of Capernaum, so that it is not surprising that Jesus and his disciples were recognized and his reputation as a healer already firmly established. As in v. 14, only healing is mentioned, not teaching; this was apparently what people in general were looking for. For similar summaries of large numbers of healings, indeed of the healing of "all" who came to him, cf. 4:23-24; 8:16; 9:35; 12:15; 15:30-31. For the expectation of healing by the impersonal means of touching Jesus' cloak, see on 9:20-21. What was there presented as an exceptional expedient has now become an accepted method (cf. also Mark 3:10; Luke 6:19), and no indication is given that Jesus was reluctant to allow this apparently "mechanical" means of benefiting from his healing power. Surprisingly, the specific mention of "faith" which followed in 9:22 has no counterpart here. Indeed, the statement that "all who touched" found healing seems to encourage such a practice, and Acts 5:15; 19:12 testify to the continued expectation of such "automatic" healing through the apostles. But perhaps it is unwise to read too much into so brief a summary; where Jesus' healings are reported individually, his personal compassion and the recipients' faith are emphasized rather than any guaranteed "technique."

---

1. See p. 358, n. 5, for Matthew's use of σῴζω, "save," for physical healing. Here he uses the compound διασῴζω, which in other NT contexts indicates being brought safely through danger (Acts 23:24; 27:43-44; 28:1, 4).

M. A FURTHER CHALLENGE:
THE QUESTION OF PURITY (15:1-20)

1 *Then Jesus was approached by Pharisees and scribes from Jeru-salem, who asked,* 2 *"Why do your disciples go against the tradition of the elders? They don't wash their hands when they eat bread."*

3 *He replied to them, "Why do you for your part[1] go against God's commandment on the basis of your own tradition?* 4 *For God said,[2] 'Honor your father and mother,' and 'Anyone who speaks evil of their father or mother is to be put to death.'* 5 *But you say that if any-one says to their father or mother, 'Any help you might have expected from me has been set apart [for God],'[3]* 6 *they are not to honor their parent.[4] So you have made the word[5] of God void on the basis of your own tradition.* 7 *You hypocrites, Isaiah made an excellent prophecy about you when he said,*

8 *'This people honors me with their lips,*
   but their heart is far away from me;
9 *It is in vain that they worship me,*
   teaching people to obey merely human rules.'"[6]

10 *Then Jesus called the crowd to him and said to them, "Listen and understand this:* 11 *It is not what comes into the mouth that makes*

---

1. The καί before ὑμεῖς sets up a parallel between the disciples and the questioners in that both are said to "go against" a supposedly divine requirement, but at the very different levels of "the tradition of the elders" and "God's commandment." To translate it simply with "also" would miss this contrast.

2. Many MSS read "God commanded, saying," a natural attempt to strengthen the rather colorless "said," drawing on the term "commandment" just used in v. 3 (cf. also n. 5 below). Davies and Allison, 2:522, accept the longer reading.

3. Matthew's compressed sentence reads literally "Gift whatever from me you might be helped"; see the comments below for the meaning spelled out in my free translation.

4. The reading τὸν πατέρα without explicit mention of the mother is found here in several of the earliest witnesses. The addition of the mother (in varying wordings) in the majority of MSS and versions is a very natural correction since the sense seems to require both parents to be mentioned again. If the shorter reading is original, the mention of the father must be understood to imply the mother as well, so that πατήρ is here used without emphasis on the gender (cf. its use in the plural for "father and mother" in Heb 11:23).

5. Many MSS read "commandment" (reflecting v. 3) and some read "law"; both seem natural attempts to "beef up" a less specific term (cf. also n. 2 above).

6. The compressed wording of this last line (following but not exactly reproducing the LXX) might literally be rendered, "Teaching as teachings the commandments of human beings."

a person unclean, but what goes out of the mouth — that is what makes a person unclean."

12 Then his disciples came and said to him, "Do you realize that the Pharisees were scandalized by what you said?"⁷ 13 Jesus replied, "Every plant which my heavenly Father has not planted will be rooted out. 14 Leave them alone; they are blind guides,⁸ and if one blind person leads another, the two of them will fall into the ditch."

15 Peter spoke up⁹ and asked, "Explain this¹⁰ parable to us." 16 Jesus replied, "Even now¹¹ are you,¹² too, still not able to understand? 17 Don't you realize that everything that goes into the mouth makes its way into the belly and then is passed out into the toilet? 18 But what goes out of the mouth comes from the heart, and these are the things that make a person unclean. 19 Out of the heart come bad thoughts, murders, adulteries, sexual offenses, thefts, false testimonies, and slanders.¹³ 20 It is these things that make a person unclean; but to eat without washing one's hands does not make a person unclean."

This is the last substantial episode of Jesus' public ministry in Galilee, to be followed, after an extended journey outside Galilee (15:21-39), only by a further brief account (cf. 12:38-42) of the demand for and refusal of a sign (16:1-4) before Jesus sets off across the lake and northward to Caesarea

7. Literally, "hearing the word were caused to stumble." As in 13:57, the stumbling metaphor, which I have translated literally where possible, does not work well here in English. In this context the English derivative from the Greek word σκανδαλίζω conveys the sense well: Jesus has just made an outrageously unorthodox pronouncement.

8. Most witnesses add "of the blind," but it is more likely that this was added to reflect the thought of the following clause than that it was deliberately omitted in the early tradition represented by B D ℵ* and the Coptic versions. The omission might have been accidental, with four uses of τυφλός in seven words, but a pedantic scribal filling out of the sense seems more likely. The recurrence of the phrase ὁδηγοὶ τυφλοί (without addition) in 23:16, 24 suggests that this is Matthew's natural idiom.

9. For the idiom ἀποκριθεὶς εἶπεν to mark a new contribution rather than a "reply" to what has just been said cf. 11:25 and see above, p. 439, n. 1. Peter's request is a response to Jesus' pronouncement in v. 11 rather than to his comments on the Pharisees.

10. Some early witnesses read simply "the parable," perhaps because the "parable" in question is in v. 11, not in the immediately preceding words of Jesus. On either reading the reference is plain from the explanation that follows.

11. The unusual idiom ἀκμήν (meaning "up to this point," "right up to now"), and its emphatic position at the beginning of the sentence, expresses Jesus' frustration.

12. The "you" is plural, here and in v. 17.

13. For the range of meaning of βλασφημία see on 12:31. Here, where all the other offenses listed are against other people, the sense "slander" seems more appropriate than blasphemy (against God); see the comments below.

Philippi, from where the journey to Jerusalem will begin. Its climactic significance is marked first of all by the fact that the confrontation is not now with local Galilean scribes but with a delegation "from Jerusalem" (v. 1), thus providing a foretaste of the confrontation to come; and secondly by Jesus' most radical pronouncement on a matter of scribal concern (v. 11) which in effect undermines a significant principle of the Mosaic law itself. After this dialogue the breach between Jesus and the scribal establishment is irreparable.

The question of ritual purity has arisen in various ways already, notably in the miracle stories of chs. 8 and 9 where Jesus has touched a leper, been in contact with an "unclean" Gentile, visited Gentile territory with its herd of pigs and its "unclean" demons, been touched by a woman with a menstrual disorder and touched a dead body, and where more generally his social involvement with "tax collectors and sinners" has provoked Pharisaic indignation. The issue would have been constantly present for one known as a healer, and it is likely that among the large numbers healed at Gennesaret in 14:34-36 there would have been some who were ritually unclean because of their illness. The present discussion, therefore, though introduced by what seems to us a relatively trivial objection, went to the heart of Jesus' ministry, and the following pericopae will illustrate more fully Jesus' willingness to transcend the barriers of Jewish "purity" as he travels in non-Jewish territory, meets with a Canaanite woman and expels her daughter's "unclean" spirit, and goes on to share Israel's bread with the Gentile "dogs." His radical rewriting of the concept of purity here in v. 11 thus fits into a developing motif of his ministry.

It is commonly suggested that in two ways Matthew has drawn back from the full implications of Jesus' pronouncement on what it is that defiles, as compared with the Marcan account: (a) he does not include Mark's bold editorial comment that thus Jesus "made all foods clean" (Mark 7:19);[14] and (b) his concluding summary in v. 20 takes us back to the specific issue of handwashing which, however important to the Pharisees, was not a matter specifically regulated by the OT law as the matter of clean and unclean food was. It may be true that Matthew has been more cautious, and has restricted himself to Jesus' remembered words without also echoing Mark's comment on them, but he still records Jesus' key pronouncement (v. 11) and the following commentary on it (vv. 18-19) no less explicitly than Mark,[15] and in the light of the controversy over Christian observance of the food laws which had so occupied the church in the decades after Jesus' death Matthew can hardly have been unaware of the radical significance of the principle that de-

---

14. See, however, p. 583, n. 34, for Gundry's suggestion that Matthew has "advanced" this element of Mark's account by specifically mentioning the mouth in v. 11.

15. See below on v. 11, especially p. 583, n. 37.

filement comes from inside, not from outside. The powerful polemic against scribal tradition in vv. 3-9 surely also confirms that Matthew, no less than Mark, is aware that relations between Jesus and the scribes have reached the breaking point.

It is hard to exaggerate the significance of ritual purity for the Pharisaic ideology, which the majority of scribes supported, and which became the basis of later rabbinic orthodoxy. A large proportion of the halakhic traditions which later came to be codified in the Mishnah focus on this issue in one way or another (particularly in the last of the six main divisions of the Mishnah, entitled *Teharot*, "Cleannesses"). The principle, set out at length in the OT law, is that in order to participate in the life and worship of God's holy people a person must avoid "defilement" which might arise through eating or drinking unclean food, through unclean bodily conditions, especially those involving fluid discharges, or through contact with unclean things or people. Any such defilement must be purified by prescribed rituals and by the passage of stipulated periods of time before a person could be readmitted to the community and its worship. The purity of God's people separated them from all others, and the food laws thus became a barrier to social intercourse between Jew and Gentile. It was this that caused the long and painful dispute within the early church when Gentiles began to come in on equal terms with Jews; Peter's experience at Joppa and in the house of Cornelius (Acts 10:9-48) vividly illustrates the extent of the mental revolution required for a Jew to come to terms with the equal inclusion of "unclean" Gentiles. Even if it took some time for its full implications to be grasped, Jesus' pronouncement in v. 11 provided the theoretical basis for the major change of perspective which would soon be required of all Jewish Christians.[16] That the issue took so long to be resolved is to be attributed more to natural religious conservatism than to any lack of clarity in Jesus' pronouncement on the subject.

It is ironical that this radical declaration which undermines the food regulations of the Mosaic law (especially Lev 11; also Lev 17:10-16) should be contained in a pericope in which Jesus has just accused his opponents of undermining that same law by their own traditions (vv. 3, 6). It might be argued that the example by which he illustrates his charge relates to a fundamental ethical principle of the law, enshrined in the Decalogue, while the food laws which his pronouncement invalidates are of more peripheral significance. But that is to import a more recent categorization of the law into "central" and "peripheral" or into moral and ceremonial of which there is lit-

---

16. J. D. G. Dunn, *Jesus, Paul and the Law,* 37-60, shows how significant this pronouncement of Jesus was for the discussion which led to Christian abandonment of the Jewish dietary laws. For the direct influence of this saying on Paul's discussion of dietary disputes in Rom 14 (and possibly elsewhere in Paul) see D. Wenham, *Paul,* 92-97.

tle trace in first-century thinking. Jesus' pronouncement may perhaps be seen as the first pointer toward a new, Christian, reevaluation of the OT laws which will find fuller expression in the argument of the Letter to the Hebrews that the whole sacrificial system is now obsolete in the light of Christ's one, perfect sacrifice. But he gives his scribal opponents and his disciples no such basis on which to evaluate his rejection of the principle of externally contracted impurity, and it is not easy to see either in Jesus' own time or in that of the gospel's first readers how this might have been squared with his assurance that he had not come to abolish the law (5:17).[17] We see here the tension which runs through so much of NT Christianity (and which we have seen illustrated to a significant degree in Matt 5:17-48) between faithfulness to the scriptural tradition and acceptance of a radically new perspective on the service of God which cannot leave legal observance unaffected.

All of that relates to v. 11 and its exposition in vv. 17-19, with its unavoidable implications for the OT laws of purity. But handwashing[18] itself, the issue which has given rise to the debate, was not a legal requirement, at least for ordinary Jews. Whatever may have been the commonsense demands of hygiene (particularly when food was taken from a common dish), the only regular ritual handwashing required in the OT law is that of the priests before undertaking their cultic duties (Exod 30:18-21; 40:30-32) or eating the sacrificial food (Lev 22:4-7).[19] It was subsequent scribal rulings that attempted to extend this principle to the eating of ordinary food, and to people other than priests (on the principle that Israel as a whole was a "priestly nation"), and it is uncertain how far this process had advanced by the time of Jesus.[20] It is likely that ordinary

17. Y.-E. Yang, *Jesus,* 130, in responding to this point, follows R. J. Banks, *Jesus,* 141, in arguing that Jesus neither attacks nor affirms the food laws as such, but "expresses an entirely new understanding of what does and does not constitute defilement." Yang connects this with the type of fulfilment of the law illustrated in 5:21-48 and categorizes it as "fulfilment in terms of internalization." Cf. Gundry, 306: "The cleansing of all foods does not countermand the law, but intensifies it by transmuting the dietary taboos into prohibitions against evil speech, just as the so-called antitheses in the Sermon on the Mount did not destroy the law, but fulfilled it." While this is true as far as it goes, it is hard to see how such a "fulfillment" can leave the law still standing as a literal requirement.

18. The hands were a potential source of ritual impurity since they were "ever busy" and so likely to be in contact with unclean things (*m. Tehar.* 7:8). The principle is discussed in detail in the Mishnah tractate *Yadayim,* "Hands."

19. Handwashing was also prescribed after specific causes of defilement in Lev 15:11; Deut 21:6.

20. See the very full discussion by R. P. Booth, *Purity,* 117-87 (with a summary of conclusions, pp. 186-87). Davies and Allison, 2:521-22, think that ritual handwashing may have been more prevalent than Booth allows; cf. also D. Instone-Brewer, *Traditions,* 1:85-86. See also A. J. Saldarini, *Community,* 135-36, for continuing debate on the issue in rabbinic circles.

people would have found no problem with the practice of Jesus' disciples, and that this group of Jerusalem teachers are expecting of them a more rigorous standard than was yet recognized in Galilee. As a religious teacher, they perhaps imply, surely Jesus could not afford to allow his disciples more laxity than the Pharisees expected of their followers.[21] In roundly asserting that true purity does not depend on ritual handwashing (v. 20), Jesus would thus not only be himself in no tension with the OT law on this point, but would also challenge the right of the scribes to impose nonbiblical rules on others. All this falls within the scope of legitimate scribal debate; it is when Jesus goes on to question the very nature of purity in itself that he, not his Pharisaic opponents, opens up the issue of the continuing validity of the OT law.

The whole pericope is paralleled (in a rather more expansive form) in Mark 7:1-23. Apart from Matthew's less sharp focus on Jesus' radicalism (see above), there is an interesting difference in their structuring of the opening dialogue. In Mark Jesus responds to the scribal challenge by immediately calling them "hypocrites" and launching into the polemical quotation from Isa 29:13; the explanation for his onslaught then follows as he accuses them of allowing their tradition to override the Mosaic law. But in Matthew that charge is first set out, with the quotation following as a comment on it. Mark's version is more arresting, but leaves the reader unsure what is the basis of Jesus' charge of hypocrisy until after the quotation has been read; Matthew's is typically a less dramatic but more logical order.

1 This is the first time in Matthew that Jesus has been confronted by opponents from Jerusalem (contrast Mark 3:22, where the Beelzebul charge is also made by "scribes who had come down from Jerusalem"). While we are not told why they have come north, the nature of their accusation suggests that they are here to investigate the orthodoxy of this popular northern "rabbi" ("possibly a formal or semiformal delegation," Hagner, 2:430). We have seen the combination "scribes and Pharisees" already in 12:38; see the comments there. Here, as usual in Matthew, the emphasis falls especially on the Pharisees, who are therefore mentioned first (cf. v. 12, where the scribes are not mentioned at all); the issue raised is, as we have just noted, one which particularly suits the Pharisaic agenda.

2 As in 12:2, the behavior of the disciples is taken as an index to Jesus' own teaching and expectations, since it is assumed that they will behave as their teacher has instructed them.[22] See the introductory comments for the issue of handwashing in first-century Jewish discussion. If it was, for people other than priests, a relatively recent requirement, and one not universally

---

21. Cf. 9:14; 12:2 for the use of the disciples' behavior as a stick with which to beat their teacher.

22. See D. Daube, *NTS* 19 (1972/3) 1-15.

recognized, there is some irony in its description as "the tradition of the elders,"[23] and that irony is underlined when Jesus in response speaks rather of
"your own tradition" (vv. 3, 6). But the phrase (a technical term for Pharisaic
oral tradition, in contrast to the written Mosaic law) fits the rabbinic approach which focused on providing a respectable pedigree for any ruling
through quoting earlier rabbis in its favor, and no doubt within the Pharisaic
movement there was already a sufficient tradition in favor of this particular
provision, even if its origin was relatively recent. Such tradition would at this
stage be oral; its written codification into the Mishnah came at the end of the
second century.

3   Jesus' reply does not deal directly with the issue of handwashing
at all; it will not be mentioned again until his concluding comment in v. 20,
and that will be addressed not to the Pharisees but to the disciples, as the culmination of a much more wide-ranging statement about the purity principle.
In response to the Pharisees he takes up instead their term "tradition of the elders" and puts in question the whole concept of religious authority which it
embodies. The implication, unexpressed, is that if such a questionable "tradition" is the basis of their charge, it has no validity, and so there is no case to
answer. His counterquestion carefully echoes the terms of their original question, but in place of the tradition which is being flouted, he places God's
commandment (in this case the fifth commandment of the Decalogue), and
the tradition becomes instead the basis of the flouting. By describing the
(scriptural) commandment as "God's" and the tradition as "your own," he
makes clear where the ultimate authority must lie.

4   The contrast is made even clearer by what follows: what "God
said" is set over against what "you say" (v. 5), thus categorizing scribal tradition as a matter of "merely human rules" (v. 9) over against the divine revelation in the law. Mark at this point has "Moses said," but Matthew's version
makes explicit the assumption which every Jew would have shared, that the
laws come from God rather than simply from Moses. The two laws quoted
from Exod 20:12 (cf. Deut 5:16) and Exod 21:17 (cf. Lev 20:9) are in fact
presented within the pentateuchal framework as the very words of God uttered to Moses on Sinai, so that Matthew's formula is true to their original
narrative setting, but any part of the Mosaic law would equally have been
taken as "the commandment of God." The first law quoted is from the
Decalogue, and so would have been agreed to be of central importance for Israel's life as the people of God,[24] while the second, a more specific applica-

---

23. See J. A. Overman, *Gospel,* 62-68, for the claims to traditional authority made
in the first century by the "formative Judaism" which was represented especially by Pharisees, and the challenges to those claims by other Jewish groups.

24. It will again be included in Jesus' summary of God's requirements in 19:18-19.

tion of the same principle, underlines its importance by making it a capital offense to dishonor parents. The following argument assumes that the "honor" which is commanded is more than verbal, and includes making appropriate provision for one's parents in old age.[25]

5-6a Jesus now accuses his opponents of undermining this basic principle of OT law by a formal legal device of their own invention. The scribal practice with regard to "Qorban" is described so briefly as to be quite cryptic to those not familiar with it, but Matthew's readers were presumably well aware of this convenient manipulation of the rules for dedication of property. These rules are the subject of extensive rabbinic discussion, collected in the Mishnah tractate *Nedarim,* "Vows," where the term *qorbān*[26] and its equivalent *qōnām* occur frequently in formulae for dedicating food, money or property to God, which in practice meant to the temple treasury.[27] Anything so dedicated was thus placed out of reach of other people who might otherwise have a claim on it, and the formula seems to have been deliberately used for this purpose.[28] What is not so clear is how such a dedication could be made without the donor also losing the right to his own property (was it a pledge to be honored only at the donor's death?), but the rabbinic discussion makes it clear that in some way this could be achieved. A *qorbān* vow was regarded as binding unless specifically "released" by a rabbi, and in *m. Ned.* 9:1 there is discussion of whether the fifth commandment was a sufficient basis for such a release, with the balance of opinion tilting in favor of release; apparently Jesus was aware of a more rigorous ruling. The strong wording of v. 6a ("they *are not to,*" not just "they need not") perhaps reflects a case such as is recorded in *m. Ned.* 5:6 where a man who had excluded his father by means of a *qorbān* vow had to resort to giving his courtyard away to a friend so that his father

25. Cf. 1 Tim 5:3-8 for this aspect of the "honor" due to widows and the assumption that this is the primary responsibility of their own children. The obligation to care for parents, especially in old age, was strongly emphasized in both Jewish and pagan society (see Keener, 411, nn. 39-42). Note especially Sir 3:12-16, which follows a discussion of the application of the fifth commandment (3:1-11).

26. Matthew's term δῶρον, "gift" (see p. 573, n. 3), is the regular LXX equivalent for *qorbān* when it occurs in Leviticus and Numbers to denote a sacrificial "offering"; Mark gives both the Hebrew and Greek terms.

27. Matthew will use the term κορβανᾶς for the temple treasury in 27:6. For a useful overview of the rabbinic data on *qorbān* see K. H. Rengstorf, *TDNT* 3:861-66.

28. In *m. Ned.* 8:7 the formula "*Qōnām* be any benefit you would have from me," or "*Qōnām!* if she has any benefit from me" is a vow which is in effect an emphatic way of saying, "You (she) shall never have. . . ." A similar intention appears in the warning inscription on an early first-century ossuary from near Jerusalem: "All that a man may find to his profit in this ossuary is *qorbān* to God from him who is within it" (J. A. Fitzmyer, *JBL* 78 [1959] 60-65).

could be allowed to attend his grandson's wedding.[29] This shows both that the vow was regarded as irrevocable even when the son himself wished to withdraw it, and also that under the vow the son still retained the use of the property himself.

6b All this might have been justified under the OT principle that a vow once made must be kept (Num 30:2; Deut 23:21-23), though Jesus has already stated in 5:33-37 that it is better not to make such vows at all. The problem with the scribal approach was that it did not inquire whether the vow was appropriate in the first place (and made no provision for a subsequent change of heart on the part of the donor), and obstinately insisted on the validity of the vow regardless of the consequences. Such an approach lent itself to cynical manipulation by an undutiful son, and the result was that the clear principle of the Decalogue was overriden. This was to "make the word of God void," a technical term for legal invalidation (cf. Gal 3:17) which graphically expresses the perverse effect of their failure to put first things first: they have actually dared to rule the "word of God" to be unlawful! The explicit contrasting of "your own tradition" with "the word of God" suggests a robust view of the authority of Scripture[30] in relation to all human teaching, however venerable and however piously motivated.

7 The specific example of the Qorban regulations illustrated a more general failure in the scribal approach to lawkeeping, which Jesus now goes on to denounce by means of a telling quotation from Isaiah. For "hypocrite" see on 6:2. The accusation is not so much of conscious deception as of a fatally distorted sense of priorities in the service of God. They have put the cart before the horse, and so have missed God's way. The result is an empty profession of piety, and it is this that the words from Isaiah will express. Isaiah's prophecy was "about you" not in the sense that the prophet was consciously depicting a future situation — Isa 29:13 is directly aimed at Isaiah's own contemporaries — but that the description fits these Jerusalem scribes as well as it did the superficially pious people of eighth-century Jerusalem. As in 13:14-15, where Isaiah's description of his own contemporaries is seen as "fulfilled" in Jesus' audience, there is a typological correspondence between

---

29. The courtyard now technically belonged to the friend, who could thus allow the father to attend. But the story gets even more bizarre: the friend then made a similar *qorbān* vow in his own right so that the original owner's plan was frustrated!

30. "The word of God" was probably not yet, as it soon became in Christian usage, in itself a synonym for Scripture. The term is used only here in Matthew, and when it occurs elsewhere in the NT, especially in Luke-Acts, it normally refers to the Christian message. But a few uses referring to divine utterances in the past (and found in the OT), such as John 10:35; Rom 9:6; Heb 4:12; 2 Pet 3:5, provide a pointer to the later usage. The "word" referred to here is the divine commandments recorded in Scripture which are quoted in v. 4.

these two significant phases in the response of God's people to his word through his prophet.[31]

8-9 The text is a slight adaptation of the LXX of Isa 29:13; the last line (see p. 573, n. 6 for a literal rendering) tidies up the rather clumsy LXX wording "teaching commandments of human beings and teachings." The contrast between "lips" and "heart" prepares us for the emphasis of vv. 11-20 on the importance of the internal rather than the external; the significance of the "heart" will be prominent in those verses. The LXX differs from the Hebrew of Isa 29:13 by restructuring the last two lines: the concise Hebrew lines may be literally rendered "and their worship of me is a commandment of human beings, taught." The sense of a mechanical repetition of human formulae is the same, but the LXX also includes the statement that such worship is "in vain." This may be the result of a variant text, with *w^{e}tōhû,* "and in vain," in place of the similar-looking *wat^{e}hî,* "and it is." It makes explicit what our received Hebrew text clearly implies.[32] The whole quotation, in either its Hebrew or Greek form, speaks of worship which is superficial, empty, meaningless, because it derives from human invention rather than from God's instruction. God has been effectively excluded from his own worship — and that is also the effect of the displacement of the commandment of God by scribal tradition.[33]

10 The crowd, as elsewhere in Matthew, are present as a background audience to the dialogue, to whom Jesus now addresses himself rather than continuing in direct dialogue with the Pharisees. The latter, however, are still able to hear (v. 12; see comments there on what it was that scandalized the Pharisees), and indeed are intended to hear, since in v. 11 Jesus takes up the issue of purity which they had first raised and which Jesus has not hitherto tackled directly. Compare 23:1-12, where Jesus turns from dialogue with the Pharisees (22:34-46) to talk to the crowd *about* the scribes and Pharisees, before returning to address them directly in the denunciation of 23:13-39. The key pronouncement of v. 11 is thus presented as a deliberately public declaration, not simply part of a private debate. Jesus wants everyone to "understand," a verb which was prominent in ch. 13 to describe what people in general (as opposed to disciples) could not achieve (13:13-15, 19) but which is the distinctive response of true disciples (13:23, 51). It is such "un-

31. See my *Jesus and the OT,* 68-69, and for the typological principle that underlies this "contemporizing" use of Scripture, ibid., 38-43, 75-80.

32. See my *Jesus and the OT,* 248-50, for the textual data; I argue there that the relevance of the quotation in this NT context is not dependent on the LXX text form, even though this undoubtedly makes the polemical point more sharply.

33. The same Isaiah passage, apparently in almost the same Greek version, appears in Egerton Papyrus 2 as part of Jesus' response to the question about paying taxes to the state. It functions there as a comment on their insincere address to him as "teacher."

derstanding" that Jesus' parabolic teaching was designed to evoke, and he is now about to utter a further "parable" (as it will be described in v. 15). If people are to benefit from it, they must "listen and understand," so that they penetrate its true meaning and become true disciples.

11   This key saying, though described as a "parable" in v. 15, is not particularly cryptic. It is more in the nature of a proverb or epigram (which also fall within the range of meanings of Greek *parabolē*), a pithy statement of a general truth which then needs to be applied more prosaically to specific cases. Matthew's version is slightly more pithy than that of Mark, which specifies that the things coming in are things "outside the person," while those coming out are "out of the person"; Matthew, on the other hand, makes it clear that both the coming in and the going out are via the mouth[34] — food and words respectively (cf. 12:33-37 for the importance of the latter). Not all ritual defilement in the OT was by means of food, of course; one could also be defiled by disease (especially skin disease), by one's own bodily secretions[35] or by touching something or someone unclean. But the principle of externally contracted defilement is well illustrated by the Levitical food laws (Lev 11; cf. also 17:10-16), and it is this principle which Jesus is here setting aside,[36] no less explicitly in Matthew's rather smoother version than in Mark's.[37] True de-

---

34. Similarly, *Gos. Thom.* 14. Gundry, 305-6, suggests that Matthew's specific mention of the mouth here is his "way of advancing for emphasis Mark's editorial comment that Jesus was 'cleansing all food.'"

35. The specific mention of the mouth in Matthew's version may be intended to avoid the possible misunderstanding that Jesus is denying defilement by means of food but still affirming the OT idea (Lev 15) of defilement by means of bodily secretions through other orifices.

36. See, however, Davies and Allison, 2:528-31, for an argument to the effect that Jesus' original pronouncement, even in its Marcan form, was intended, and understood, in terms of "the Semitic idiom of relative negation," where the emphasis falls on the positive side of the contrast, not necessarily to the exclusion of the other (as in Hos 6:6, "mercy, not sacrifice," understood to mean that mercy takes *priority* over sacrifice, not that sacrifice is abolished). When, however, such a *relative* weighing of the "external" and the "internal" is presented in 23:23 (cf. 23:25-26), the stark "not . . . but . . ." contrast of this saying is not used, and indeed the continued validity of the tithing rules is made explicit. Luz, 2:332-33, while wishing to argue that Matthew took Jesus' saying as speaking of "the *priority* of the love commandment over the purity regulations," admits that the wording "can hardly be interpreted linguistically as a so-called dialectic negation ('Not so much what goes into a person as . . .')."

37. Some commentators suggest that Matthew's version is less radical and far-reaching than Mark's since he does not have Mark's οὐδὲν . . . δύναται . . . ("nothing . . . can . . .") and specifies only the mouth as the point of entry. But the difference is rhetorical rather than substantial. For the essential equivalence of the two versions see R. J. Banks, *Jesus,* 139-40; Banks regards the Matthean version as probably the "most genuine form." Hagner, 2:429, does not explain his surprising statement that Matthew's version would be

filement is not external and ritual, but internal and moral, as vv. 17-19 will explain further.[38] The statement is simple and clear; it is its practical implications for those brought up on the OT and rabbinic ideology of ritual purity which are far-reaching and which were bound to lead to controversy and division in a church which derived its heritage from Judaism.

12-14　The public pronouncement was very brief. Now, following the pattern established in ch. 13, there will be private explanation to the disciples of the public "parable." Neither the crowd nor the Pharisees and scribes are present for the remainder of the pericope, the latter group being referred to only in the third person in vv. 12-14. It would be possible to understand the "word" which scandalized the Pharisees as Jesus' direct attack on them (especially as "hypocrites") in vv. 3-9, after which they left in anger and so were not there to hear what Jesus went on to say to the crowd. But the flow of the narrative makes it more likely that we are to understand it as the pronouncement of v. 11, which is the only direct response Jesus makes to their original charge; the continuity between v. 11 and the request for its explanation in v. 15 makes it unlikely that the intervening verses hark back to the earlier polemic. The Pharisees' adverse reaction to Jesus' words (see p. 574, n. 7) neither surprises nor dismays him; so direct a challenge to an essential principle of rabbinic thought could hardly expect any other reaction. But they are irrelevant, plants not planted by God and blind guides. We shall hear much more of Pharisees and scribes before the gospel is over, and Jesus will be engaged in hot debate with them again in Jerusalem (22:15–23:39). But already from the new perspective of the kingdom of heaven they are sidelined: "Leave them alone."

The metaphor of God's "planting" perhaps echoes Isa 61:3, where the redeemed people of God in Zion are "oaks of righteousness, the planting of the LORD, to display his glory"; cf. the same metaphor in Isa 5:7; 60:21, and in many OT passages where the planting of vines, trees, and the like stands

---

"more acceptable to Jewish Christians who no doubt continued to observe the dietary laws." A similar position is advocated by A. J. Saldarini, *Community,* 134-41. D. Sim, *Gospel,* 135, even argues that in v. 11 Matthew still has in mind only the issue of handwashing, and that "the evangelist would doubtless agree with the leaders of formative Judaism that defilement can occur by eating unclean foods (and in other ways)." When the word "doubtless" is used to support an argument that the evangelist believed the opposite of what he wrote, we are perhaps entitled to smell a rat!

38. A similar principle is developed in an apparently independent but incomplete tradition preserved in P. Oxy. 840, where Jesus contrasts the purity claimed by "a certain Pharisee, a chief priest called Levi," on the basis of his correct ablutions in the Pool of David with his internal condition "full of scorpions and all wickedness," whereas Jesus and his disciples, whom Levi has accused of failing to carry out their ablutions before coming into the temple, have been "immersed in living water which comes down from above."

for God's establishment of and care for his people.[39] For the uprooting of false plants cf. God's destruction of his own vineyard when it failed to produce fruit in Isa 5:1-7;[40] a similar message is conveyed by different imagery in the fate of the tenants (rather than the vines themselves) in the parable of the vineyard (21:33-44); readers might also recall the fate of the weeds planted by an enemy in the field of God's kingdom (13:24-30). The OT imagery of God's "planting" is not a metaphor specifically for Israel's leadership, but for the people as a whole.[41] These leaders of Israel thus apparently represent the wider failure of the people to live up to its special status.

But a second metaphor focuses more directly on their role of leadership: they are blind guides, a charge which will be repeated in 23:16, 24.[42] The same metaphor is used in Luke's sermon on the level place, Luke 6:39 (one of the few parts of that sermon which has no parallel in Matthew's Sermon on the Mount), but there it has no specific application to Jewish leaders but rather relates to failures in discipleship. Its bearing here is obvious: if these leaders of Israel have themselves missed the way in their understanding of what it means to be the people of God (as vv. 7-9 have powerfully alleged), their influence on other Jews can only lead them into the same "ditch" of distorted religious values. It is to draw people away from that damaging influence that Jesus has launched his appeal over their heads to the crowd (v. 10), as he will do again in 23:1-12.

15-16 For the request to have a parable explained cf. 13:36, and for the description of Jesus' pronouncement as a "parable" see on v. 11 and more generally p. 502 above. Peter, who was described as "first" in the list of disciples in 10:2, acts as spokesman for the group here as he will in 16:16, 22; 17:4, 24-25; 18:21; 19:27. Jesus' reply in the plural recognizes that he speaks as representative of them all, and so all together are rebuked for their lack of that "understanding" which he had called the crowd to display in v. 10; see the comments there on the importance for Matthew of the theme of "understanding" in relation to discipleship. Jesus' exasperated question (see p. 574, n. 11) reflects his expectation that at least the disciples ("you *too*"), as those to whom "it has been given to know the secrets

---

39. The same image is taken up in several later Jewish works, e.g., at Qumran (CD 1:7; 1QS 8:5; 11:8) and in *Ps. Sol.* 14:3-4; *Jub.* 1:16; 7:34.

40. *Gos. Thom.* 40 explains that a vine planted "apart from the Father" will not flourish, and so will be uprooted. M. Knowles, *Jeremiah*, 190-92, suggests an allusion here also to Jeremiah's mission of uprooting and planting (Jer 1:10).

41. B. Charette, *Recompense*, 44-48, surveys the theme of "the planting and uprooting of Israel" in the OT.

42. Cf. Rom 2:19 for Paul's attribution to his Jewish reader of the claim to be a "guide for the blind," a role which Paul is at pains to show they are not in a position to fulfill.

of the kingdom of heaven" (13:11), should by now have been ahead of the crowd in grasping spiritual truth. Cf. 16:8-11 for a similar expression of frustration.

17 This earthy description of the alimentary system (a tighter version of Mark's rather sprawling formulation, Mark 7:18-19) makes the point that physical food, while it goes into and through the body, is merely an aspect of animal existence and does not affect the heart, understood here as generally in biblical literature as the seat of thought and will (rather than of emotion, as in our idiom today). And since Jesus is going on to locate true purity and impurity in the heart and its products, the nature and origin of that food cannot therefore affect the matter. It is not a matter of what you eat but who you are; for the same principle cf. Rom 14:14, 17; 1 Cor 8:8; Heb 9:10. The principle can clearly be extended beyond food as such to include any aspect of "external" circumstances or contacts (including the other sources of ritual uncleanness as specified in the OT), but Jesus' saying focuses specifically on food, which was to become such a contentious issue in the church's early years as it struggled to understand how the people of God could extend outside the observant Jewish community. Its relevance to the different concerns of the church today, which often judges a person by conventional standards of background or behavior, must be a matter of sensitive reapplication of the principle involved.

18-19 The moral nature of true "uncleanness" is now made plain. The "unclean" things which come from the heart are not only *words* (as "out of the mouth" in v. 11 might suggest) but more broadly matters of behavior. They are introduced, however, by the general category of "bad thoughts," since it is the thoughts entertained by the heart that give rise to the actions and words — as Jesus has explained already in 5:21-28; cf. 12:34-35. Four of the six items which follow are taken directly from the Decalogue[43] and occur here in the traditional order: murder, adultery, theft, and false testimony. They are all expressed in the plural, even though some of the nouns are more naturally used as abstract singulars, presumably to indicate that it is not abstract categories that are in view but specific acts. The remaining two items (sexual offenses, slanders) are extensions of the immediately preceding sins (adultery, false testimony), thus warning the reader against sheltering behind a too limited definition of "adultery" and "false testimony," in much the same way that 5:21-28 took us behind the specific acts of murder and adultery to a wider area of culpability. "Sexual offenses" translates *porneiai*, which at root applies specifically to fornication (sexual intercourse with a prostitute) but

---

43. This focus becomes more clearly visible in Matthew's much reduced list as compared with Mark 7:21-22, which has thirteen items ranging much more widely and not so clearly reflecting the order of the Decalogue.

was used more widely for unacceptable sexual liaisons (see pp. 208-9 above). It would be possible to translate *blasphēmiai* here as "blasphemies," as in 9:3; 12:31, thus adding to the list an offense against God drawn from the "first table" of the Decalogue (Exod 20:7), but the secular sense of the term, "slander," better fits the overall character of the list and the position immediately following "false testimonies." In view of this extension of two of the commandments by additional terms, it would also be possible to read "bad thoughts" as an extension of the following item, "murders," which would echo well Jesus' comments on murderous thoughts in 5:21-22; but that seems unlikely in view of its position *preceding* "murders." Its character as the only purely mental item in the list suggests rather that it serves to introduce all the items that follow, explaining how they originate in the heart.[44]

The fact that all the items listed as coming from the heart are bad does not mean that human beings are capable only of evil. The context is a discussion of what produces "uncleanness," and so inevitably only the bad are mentioned here. The heart can also produce good; see 12:34-35, and cf. 5:8; 22:37.

20   Jesus' pronouncement in v. 11 and its exposition in vv. 17-19 have moved the discussion of purity far beyond the specific issue raised by the objectors in v. 2. Matthew (unlike Mark) rounds off the pericope by returning to that issue and indicating how the intervening discussion bears on the Pharisees' question. See the introductory comments above on the frequent suggestion that he does so in order to soften the impact of Jesus' radical teaching by anchoring it in the relatively "safe" area of handwashing where the OT law itself was not in question. I think it more likely that his conclusion is governed by literary considerations, to provide an *inclusio* for the pericope as a whole.

N. THE MESSIAH'S MISSION EXTENDED BEYOND ISRAEL (15:21-39)

In Matthew's account of the Galilean mission so far, Jesus has met with and commented on the faith of a Gentile army officer within Galilee (8:5-13), and has deliberately made one trip across the lake into the Gentile area of Decapolis, where he has delivered two demon-possessed men (8:28-34). Otherwise he has been depicted as meeting only with Jewish people within Galilee, though there has been a passing mention of crowds from Decapolis coming to him there (4:25). His "escape" from Galilee after hearing of the hostility

---

44. Such lists of virtues and/or vices occur frequently in both Jewish and pagan literature as well as elsewhere in the NT; see, e.g., R. P. Martin, *NIDNTT* 3:928-29.

of Antipas (14:13), while it took him (probably) outside Galilee proper, did not take him away from the Galilean Jewish crowd, who followed and caught up with him; nor did it involve any contact with the local people. But now there is a marked change of focus. Jesus "withdraws" not merely outside Galilee but outside Jewish territory altogether. The first person he meets is pointedly described as a "Canaanite" who belongs to the Phoenician area into which he has now traveled (v. 22), and while his itinerary from there is not clear, the local crowd will respond to his miraculous power by praising "the God of Israel" (v. 31), an unusual phrase which suggests that Matthew is speaking of Gentiles. We shall note reasons for believing, too, that the following feeding miracle (vv. 32-38) is not just a repetiition of what Jesus had previously done for a Jewish crowd, but is a deliberate extension of their privilege to the Gentiles also. This little section is held together by the theme of "bread," metaphorically denied and then granted to the Canaanite woman (vv. 26-28), and then, in fulfillment of the agreement she has extracted, also made available literally to the Gentile "dogs." (The theme of bread will be further developed in 16:6-12, but there without explicit reference to the racial issue.) This section at the close of the Galilean phase of Matthew's story thus marks a decisive break from the previous pattern of Jesus' ministry, a deliberate extension of the mission of the Messiah of Israel to the surrounding non-Jewish peoples.[1] The whole new approach is a practical enactment of Jesus' radical attitude toward Jewish purity laws which has just been declared in vv. 11-20; he and his good news will recognize no such restriction of the grace of God.

1. The Faith of a Canaanite Woman (15:21-28)

21 *Jesus went away from there and withdrew into the region of Tyre and Sidon.* 22 *And out came[2] a Canaanite woman from that area[3]*

---

1. This narrative pattern is essentially shared with Mark. See E. K. Wefald, *JSNT* 60 (1995) 3-26, for Mark's presentation of a "separate Gentile mission." See p. 597, n. 7, for my response to the view that Matt 15:29-39 is not intended to speak of ministry to Gentiles.

2. Another attempt to represent the dramatic force of Matthew's ἰδού, which draws attention to a remarkable new development; literally, "And behold . . . came out."

3. It would be possible to construe Matthew's Greek as "a Canaanite woman came out from that region," thus suggesting that Jesus never in fact entered the Gentile area but rather went "toward" it and met the woman before he arrived there. This is not only far less natural Greek (especially the rather desperate suggestion that εἰς means "toward" rather than "into"), but also goes against the overall focus of the section 15:21-38 on Jesus' ministry *among* Gentiles (see introductory comments above). "Came out" is more naturally understood of her leaving her house or village when she hears that Jesus is in the neighborhood. See further Luz, 2:338-39.

who kept shouting,[4] *"Show mercy on me, Lord, Son of David. My daughter is severely tormented by a demon."*[5] 23 *But Jesus replied to her not a word, and his disciples came and begged him, "Send her away: she's coming after us shouting."* 24 *Jesus replied, "I was not sent to anyone except the lost sheep of the house of Israel."* 25 *But the woman came, and bowed down before him, and said, "Lord, help me."* 26 *Jesus replied, "It is not right to take the children's bread and throw it to the dogs."* 27 *"Yes it is,*[6] *Lord," she replied, "for even the dogs eat the crumbs that fall from their masters' table."* 28 *Then Jesus replied to her, "My dear woman,*[7] *you have great faith; your wish is granted."*[8] *And her daughter was cured from that moment.*[9]

This incident has much in common with the encounter with the centurion at Capernaum in 8:5-13.[10] In both the request for help comes not from the "patient" but from a concerned superior officer/parent; both suppliants are Gentiles; in each case there is an initial show of reluctance by Jesus as a Jew appealed to by a Gentile (see comments on 8:7); in each case the "faith" of the suppliant is more highly commended than that of any Jew; and in each

4. This iterative sense of the imperfect tense seems justified by the following context.

5. Literally, "is badly demon-possessed." This is the only NT example of an adverb qualifying δαιμονίζομαι, an idiom which does not work well in English. The verb denotes simply the condition of being possessed; elsewhere degrees of severity are expressed by speaking of multiple demons (12:45; Mark 5:9; Luke 8:2).

6. Ναί, "Yes," is not common in direct speech, and when it occurs normally conveys a positive answer to a preceding question. Its use here following a negative statement is striking and emphatic, and indicates disagreement with the negative statement Jesus has just made. (Davies and Allison, 2:555, declare that "The word is not intended to contradict Jesus' οὐκ," but give no reason for this surprising pronouncement.) The following γάρ then gives the reason for disagreeing rather than, as most versions take it, meekly accepting his negative verdict and pleading for an exception. Surely that would need a following "but" or "yet," not a "for" (as indeed many versions insert with no warrant in the Greek — so, e.g., GNB, NRSV, REB, NJB, NIV [but not TNIV]). See further comments below on the flow of the dialogue.

7. Literally, "O woman." The addition of ὦ before a vocative is unusual and emphatic (the only other occurrence in Matthew is 17:17; see p. 656, n. 4, there); here it probably expresses Jesus' surprised admiration (BDF 146 interpret it as showing "stronger emotion"). With or without ὦ, the Greek γύναι, used as a form of address, does not carry a pejorative or rude tone as "Woman" might in English (cf. Luke 13:12; John 2:4; 4:21; 19:26; 20:13, 15).

8. Literally, "Let it be done for you as you wish." For the "performative" force of the third-person imperative in such an utterance, see the comments on 8:13.

9. For the idiom see p. 304, n. 14.

10. Davies and Allison, 2:558-59, usefully draw out and discuss the parallel.

case (and only in these two cases in Matthew) the cure takes place by a word from a distance. But whereas in 8:5-13 the initial reluctance was quickly succeeded by admiration for the officer's faith, here the dialogue is more labored and painful from the woman's point of view, as Jesus apparently "plays hard to get." As a result, her eventual triumph is the more emphatic.

The narrative (especially in its Matthean form, where Jesus' negative attitude is more emphatic and harsher than in Mark) causes understandable concern to many readers,[11] as Jesus appears insensitive and downright rude not only in his refusal to act but also in speaking of Gentiles as "dogs" and implying that they can expect no consideration from him as the Jewish Messiah. If the pericope ended at v. 26, that impression would be unrelieved. But the story must be read as a whole: in the end Jesus does exactly what the woman has asked and commends her faith in stronger terms than he uses for anyone else except the centurion. It is the woman's bold reply in v. 27 which has turned the tide, and which is the basis for Jesus' commendation. In refusing to accept the traditional Jewish exclusion of Gentiles from the grace of God, she has shown a truly prophetic grasp of the new perspective of the kingdom of heaven, which is now to be open to "people from east and west" (8:11-12) on the basis of their faith rather than of their racial identity. It is that perception which has won the argument.

So is it true to say that her argument has changed Jesus' mind? Yes, in that the policy which he has declared in vv. 24 and 26 is then abandoned. So is this a substantive U-turn by Jesus, resulting in a new and hitherto unforeseen redirection of his ministry? If this pericope stood alone, that might well be a valid conclusion. But the reader who has remembered the encounter with the centurion, and especially the prophetic words of 8:11-12, knows that Jesus has already envisaged a multiracial people of God. The exorcism in Decapolis (8:28-34) has also provided a precedent for the present case by showing Jesus as not reluctant to deal with demon-possession in a Gentile context. And Matthew's reader can hardly be unaware by now of the persistent hints that God's ultimate purpose for Israel's Messiah is not restricted to Israel (1:3-6;[12] 2:1-12; 4:15, 24-25), even though a temporary restriction has been stated in 10:5-6 as it is here in v. 24 (see comments on 10:5-6). We can only speculate on why Jesus felt it appropriate in this case to raise the stakes so high in reminding the woman of the primarily Israelite focus of the Messiah's mission before even-

11. The comments on this passage in F. W. Beare's commentary (342-43) include the following characterizations of the attitude here attributed to Jesus: "brutal," "offensive," "the worst kind of chauvinism," "incredible insolence," "atrocious."

12. Keener, 415, points out that two of the women mentioned in the genealogy, Tamar and Rahab, were actually Canaanites, so that a careful reader might find a special resonance in this woman's being described as "Canaanite."

tually acceding to her feisty response. Cold print does not allow us to detect a quizzical eyebrow or a tongue in the cheek, and it may be that Jesus' demeanor already hinted that his discouraging reply was not to be his last word on the subject. Need we assume that when eventually the woman won the argument Jesus was either dismayed or displeased? May this not rather have been the outcome he intended from the start? A good teacher may sometimes aim to draw out a pupil's best insight by a deliberate challenge which does not necessarily represent the teacher's own view[13] — even if the phrase "devil's advocate" may not be quite appropriate to this context!

This is inevitably speculation. What is certain, however, is that the pericope does not end where it begins, in a racial standoff between the Jewish teacher and the Canaanite woman, and when eventually her appeal is granted, there is no sign of reluctance on Jesus' part, but rather an exceptionally warm commendation of her "faith." It is only when the pericope is read as a whole that it is properly understood, and the harsh racial language of the earlier part of the exchange is put in its true context, not as independent propositions but as thrusts in a verbal fencing match.

Nor was this ministry to a Gentile merely an exceptional concession by Jesus, for the following pericopes (vv. 29-38) will go on to depict the Messiah of Israel at work among non-Jewish people, including the literal sharing of "the children's bread" with the "dogs" (vv. 32-38). The whole of the second half of ch. 15 thus puts into practice the message of its first half, the relaxation of the Jewish "purity" culture which had hitherto kept Jew and Gentile apart. In that process, so essential to the eventual internationalization of the Christian movement, the cheeky persistence of the Canaanite woman plays a defining role.[14]

21   See on 12:15 and 14:13 for the significance of Jesus' "withdrawals" in Matthew's narrative. The confrontation in 15:1-20 has been with Pharisees and scribes "from Jerusalem." From 16:21 onward Jesus will deliberately move toward Jerusalem in full awareness that there he will meet with hostility, rejection, and death, but it seems that it is not yet time to initiate that confrontation, and again he "withdraws," this time outside Jewish territory altogether. Galilee was bordered on the northwest by the Phoenician ter-

---

13. Cf. my comment in *Mark*, 296: Jesus here "appears like the wise teacher who allows, and indeed incites, his pupil to mount a victorious argument against the foil of his own reluctance."

14. J. M. C. Scott, *JSNT* 63 (1996) 21-44, commends a "narrative reading" of the pericope which reaches essentially the same conclusion concerning its place in the overall development of Matthew's story. He comments that "even Jesus on occasion had to be 'converted,' to change his attitudes; to recognize that his boundaries were set too narrow" (43). Scott is, however, more ready than most commentators to recognize, and not to excuse, Jesus' "bad manners"!

ritory of which Tyre and Sidon[15] were the principal cities, both (but especially Tyre) frequently condemned by the OT prophets as inveterate enemies of Israel (see on 11:21-22).[16] Matthew is careful to say that Jesus entered only the "region," not the cities themselves — cf. 16:13, where the same term is used in relation to the pagan city of Caesarea Philippi. This was not a mission to the pagan cities (like Jonah's to Nineveh), but a retreat to a place where Jesus and his disciples could be away from Jewish opposition and Jewish crowds. There is no indication that he sought contact with the local people; it is the woman in v. 22 and the crowd in v. 30 who initiate the contact, and Jesus here shows no enthusiasm for the encounter.[17]

22 The woman's "coming out" (from her village, to waylay Jesus in the open country? see p. 588, n. 3 above) is mentioned so that the reader can understand that her daughter is not with her, but has been left at home (as Mark 7:30 makes explicit). There is thus again no question of Jesus entering a Gentile house (see on 8:7-8). But Matthew makes the racial context of the encounter explicit not only by describing the woman as "from that area," but especially by the term "Canaanite," which by this time was probably not a current ethnic term (like Mark's "Syrophoenician")[18] but a part of traditional biblical vocabulary for the most persistent and insidious of Israel's enemies in the OT period, those whom God had driven out before his people Israel, and whose idolatrous religion was a constant threat to the religious purity of the people of Yahweh. That a "Canaanite," of all people, should receive the compassionate ministry of Israel's Messiah would be a potent symbol to Jewish readers of the universality of the gospel (cf. p. 590, n. 12 above).

The woman's appeal, so insistently repeated as to annoy the disciples (v. 23), is addressed to Jesus as "Son of David." The same appeal has been

15. Some similarities can be traced between the present pericope and Elijah's visit to Zarephath, a village in the territory of Sidon, in 1 Kgs 17:8-24, which also results in the healing of the child of a Gentile woman (and includes some mention of bread). But the links are tenuous, and there is no sign of deliberate verbal allusion beyond the name Sidon itself.

16. Josephus, *C. Ap.* 1.70, describes the people of Tyre as "notoriously our bitterest enemies."

17. G. Theissen, *Gospels,* 65-80, gives a detailed account of the relations between Jews and their neighbors in the border area between Tyre and Galilee.

18. G. D. Kilpatrick, *Origins,* 132, cites a few references to suggest that "Canaan was still current as the Semitic equivalent of Phoenicia not so long before Matthew was written," but the case is hardly compelling. Luz's note (2:338, n. 27), simply asserting that "'Phoenician' is the Greek translation of 'Canaanite,'" hardly advances the case. See, however, G. Schwarz, *NTS* 30 (1984) 626-28, for the suggestion that both terms derive from an original Aramaic *kᵉnaᶜᵃnîtā'* which could be translated either "Canaanite" or "Phoenician," while the Συρο- prefix derives from a misreading of an original χήρα, "widow," which appears in the Old Syriac texts.

used by the blind men in 9:27 (see comments there), who are also depicted as repeatedly asking for "mercy." But here there are two further elements. The first is the addition of the title "Lord" alongside "Son of David"; the second is the fact that the speaker is a Gentile. "Lord," *kyrie,* might be taken as simply a polite address acknowledging Jesus' social superiority (see on 7:21), but it seems probable that Matthew intended his readers to find a greater depth in it. And even in the narrative context its combination with "Son of David" suggests that the woman is doing more than being polite. She clearly has some knowledge of Judaism, and in using a Jewish messianic title she is hoping to attract the interest of a Jewish teacher who would not have expected such a title in this foreign context. Presumably she had heard some account of his popular reputation within Israel. But by using this flattering title she, perhaps unwittingly, draws attention to the "irregularity" of a Gentile appeal for the help of the Jewish Messiah.[19]

23 Given the attitude of other Jews to "Canaanites," she could hardly be surprised to be met by silence — if not actual verbal abuse. So far, Jesus is acting the part of a traditional Jewish teacher. That she nonetheless persists in her appeal already indicates a remarkable willingness to challenge social convention (as well as a mother's desperation). The disciples, however, are not silent. They are not, as in 19:13, simply concerned to protect Jesus, but display a more self-centered annoyance ("coming after *us*"). Twelve strong men could presumably have driven the woman away themselves, so the fact that instead they ask Jesus to take action may suggest that by "Send her away" they meant "Do what she wants, so that she will go away"; Jesus' reply in v. 24 suggests that sense.[20] If so, they show unquestioning confidence in Jesus' exorcistic power, but no awareness of the racial issue which Jesus will raise in vv. 24 and 26.

24 Jesus' words are a reply to the disciples (the woman's "coming" to him in v. 25 will indicate a change of dialogue partner), though probably spoken so that the woman also could hear them. This is a negative response to the implied request of v. 23: the woman's plea falls outside the properly Jewish sphere of operation of Israel's Messiah. Jesus now applies to himself the same restriction which he imposed on his disciples in 10:5-6, using the same metaphor of the lost sheep. But that restriction was essentially geographical, whereas in the present context Jesus has already moved outside the geograph-

19. For "Son of David" in Matthew see further my *Matthew: Evangelist,* 284-86.
20. For a similar positive connotation in "send away" cf. 18:27; Luke 2:29 (also Matt 14:22-23; 15:39; Luke 14:4). This reading of the disciples' request is not suggested to exonerate the disciples from the charge of insensitivity, turning them instead into "prototypes for the intercession of the saints" (Luz, 2:339), but simply because it makes better sense of the flow of the dialogue.

ical area of Galilee. It might therefore be suggested that this declaration focuses on the purpose of this journey as a retreat, not as an extension of his mission: he has not come to this Gentile area to make contact with the people here. But the sequel in v. 26 makes it clear that it is ministry to Gentiles as such, rather than just the interruption of a retreat, which is the issue. Jesus is thus putting into words what was implied by his silence in v. 23: Gentiles have no right to the ministry of the Jewish Messiah. In the wider context of the gospel such a restriction can only be seen as temporary (see on 10:5-6), and in the light of 8:5-13 and 8:28-34 it can not be taken to be a rule without exceptions. In the context of this pericope as a whole, moreover, it can hardly be seen as intended to be Jesus' last word on the subject (see introductory comments). But, like his discouraging silence in v. 23, this conventional Jewish rebuff serves to test the woman's grasp of what her appeal involves. In vv. 27-28 she will rise to the challenge, and the Messiah's mission will be gladly extended.[21]

For Jesus' being "sent" (by his Father) see on 10:40. The phrase underlines the sense of a unique personal mission which is also expressed in 5:17; 9:13; 10:34-35 by the phrase "I came to. . . ."

25 The woman, who has hitherto been shouting from a distance, now comes up to Jesus with a personal approach. As yet there is no argument, simply an emotional appeal. It is backed by a deferential posture. For the combination of *proskyneō,* "bow down," and the address *kyrie,* "Lord," see on 8:2 and p. 303, nn. 6, 7. The terms do not in themselves imply divinity, though Matthew might well expect his readers to hear more in them than the woman necessarily intended.

26 After the negative tone of Jesus' silence in v. 23 and his statement in v. 24, this little parable, his first direct address to the woman, seems to add insult to injury. Not only does Jesus repeat and make more explicit the restriction stated in v. 24, but he does so now by another metaphor which in any culture would be demeaning to those depicted as dogs over against children, but which in that context also carried the force of Jewish invective which could use "dog" (an unclean animal; cf. 7:6) as a deliberately offensive term for Gentiles. It is true that the Greek term is a diminutive, but only a pet-loving Western culture would suggest that this reduces the offense;[22] a

---

21. Cf. my own earlier comments on this verse in *Matthew: Evangelist,* 234: "It is remarkable how often this verse is quoted out of context as a proof-text for the 'parochialism' of Matthew, but it is nothing of the sort. While it is indicative in form, it functions in the dialogue more as a question, a test of faith, a statement of position which invites (and receives) a counter-proposal. . . . The narrative itself negates the apparent absoluteness of 15:24. Jesus *is* sent to lost sheep outside the house of Israel; there is plenty of bread for the dogs as well!"

22. So particularly Gundry, 314-15. Cf. Luz, 2:340, n. 53: "'Little dog' . . . especially in a modern, animal-friendly society, sounds cute."

"little dog" is no less unclean than a big one! The woman's reply takes these to be house dogs[23] rather than street dogs, but that does little to alleviate the problem.[24] The children are in a position of right and privilege, which the dogs cannot hope to share; what is holy is not to be given to dogs (7:6). In Mark's version there is at least a hint of change to come, "Let the children *first* have all they want," implying that the dogs' turn may follow. But Matthew does not offer even that crumb of comfort.

27 The "debate" reaches its climax in an unexpectedly feisty response from this Gentile woman: see p. 589, n. 6, for the translation of her reply. Far from being the meek acquiescence which most versions imply, it is a robust refusal to accept the apparent implication of Jesus' words. She turns Jesus' own parable against him. If Gentiles are to be "dogs," then at least let the dogs have their due. The dogs *do* have a right to be fed, even if all they get is the leftovers. Jesus, as the Messiah of Israel ("Son of David," v. 22), must indeed first go to his own people, but that does not mean that his mission must stop there. Her reply, whether she knows it or not, thus encapsulates the important biblical theology of the election of Israel not for their own benefit alone but to be a means of blessing to all nations, a light to the Gentiles (Gen 12:3; Isa 49:6). "Yes, it *is* right, Lord!"

28 Jesus' reply appears to be a complete reversal of his stance so far in the dialogue.[25] He recognizes the justice of her case, and applauds the boldness of her refusal to accept defeat. She has won the argument, and her request is granted forthwith. See the introductory comments on how far this need mean that Jesus has actually changed his mind and embraced a new theology of salvation, or whether his earlier Jewish reluctance may be seen rather as a debating ploy to draw out the "great faith" which he now welcomes and rewards. This is the only time in Matthew when faith is qualified

---

23. Luz, 2:340, speaks of the feeding of house dogs with table scraps as "a regular topos in ancient literature"; see his n. 59 for references (mainly Greco-Roman).

24. References to dogs in biblical literature are overwhelmingly negative, and when the term is used metaphorically for human beings it is abusive and derogatory (e.g., 1 Sam 17:43; 2 Sam 16:9; Ps 22:16, 20; Prov 26:11; Phil 3:2); one specific usage is to describe male prostitutes (Deut 23:18). The dog which accompanied Tobias on his journey (Tob 6:1; 11:4) is the one indication of a dog as anything like a pet. See further O. Michel, *TDNT* 3:1101-4; the evidence he cites for dogs as pets within Judaism belongs only to the rabbinic period. It is true that Greeks sometimes had pet dogs (Keener, 416), but Jesus is speaking as a Jew. Keener's survey of attitudes to dogs in Greco-Roman culture (416-17) confirms the negative implications of the term in those cultures too (though his reference to the Jewish view of dogs as "troublesome *rodents*" [my italics] is puzzling!).

25. Davies and Allison, 2:541, rightly point out the significance of the change in terminology. Jesus' three previous negative responses (vv. 23, 24, 26) have been introduced by ὁ δέ, "But he replied." In v. 28, however, we have a climactic τότε, "Then [at last] he replied," this time positively.

as "great" (though the centurion's faith is favorably compared with any in Israel, 8:10); contrast Peter (14:31) and the other disciples (8:26; cf. 16:8), who have shown "little faith."

The conclusion of this story is closely similar to that of the parallel story in 8:5-13, though the commendation of the centurion's faith took place earlier in that story (8:10). This woman's insight, no less than the centurion's, foreshadows the time when the people of God will include Gentiles equally with Jews on the basis of their faith. The rather perfunctory account of the healing even uses the same verb as in 8:13, "cure," even though the previous story was of a physical healing, this one of an exorcism (see on 4:24); the nature of the problem has been only a minor interest in this pericope, where all the emphasis has fallen on the issue of Jew and Gentile. These two healings of Gentiles are the only ones performed by Jesus at a distance in the Synoptic Gospels; cf. John 4:46-54, where it is possible, but not so certain, that the patient is also a Gentile.

2. Many Healings (15:29-31)

29 *Jesus moved on from there and went along by[1] the Lake of Galilee; then he went up into the hills and sat there.* 30 *Great crowds came to him, bringing with them people who were lame, blind, crippled,[2] dumb,[3] and many others; they put[4] them down at Jesus' feet, and he healed them,* 31 *so that the crowd were amazed when they saw the dumb speaking, the crippled made healthy,[5] the lame walking, and the blind seeing. And they gave glory to the God of Israel.*

1. παρά with the accusative has a range of meanings including "along," "by," "to the edge of," "near"; the context normally determines which is more appropriate, but here, in view of the unclarity of Jesus' itinerary (see below), we cannot be sure. Carson's insistence, following C. F. D. Moule, that it must mean "to the shore of" is probably too precise for first-century Koine.

2. There is an overlap in meaning between χωλός, "lame," and κυλλός, which I have translated "crippled." But the words describing the healing of the two conditions in v. 31 suggest that κυλλός is being used in a broader sense than simply of a walking disability. The two terms are used together again in 18:8, where the parallelism requires that κυλλός refers to the loss of a hand or arm, not to a disabled leg.

3. κωφός is used of the deaf as well as the dumb, as in 11:5 (see also p. 359, n. 8, and p. 473, n. 1). Here the description of the cure in v. 31 requires that the primary reference is to speech rather than hearing (but see also n. 5).

4. Literally, "threw," but it is doubtful whether the verb need carry a stronger sense than simply "place" (cf. its use in LXX Gen 21:15).

5. There is considerable confusion in the MSS and versions on the precise wording and order of the phrases describing the effects of Jesus' healings (as also in the order of the four conditions listed in v. 30); some of the variations are caused by the desire to

At this point Mark mentions a single healing, but Matthew gives a second general summary of healings which recalls that given quite recently in 14:34-36. This repetition is the more striking when it is also observed that this summary is immediately followed by a second feeding miracle closely similar to that which preceded the previous one. A clue to Matthew's purpose in thus apparently repeating himself is perhaps found in the unusual comment in v. 31 that the crowds "gave glory to the God of Israel." This is never said about the Galilean crowds, and the terminology suggests that the crowd are Gentiles, recognizing the special power of the Jewish Messiah.[6] We shall note in the next pericope the likelihood that the second feeding miracle is to be interpreted as a Gentile counterpart to the Jewish feeding in 14:13-21. And the immediately preceding pericope has been explicitly concerned not only with Jesus' ministry in a Gentile context but also more specifically with the issue of the role of the Jewish Messiah with regard to the non-Jewish world. It seems therefore that the whole of 15:21-38 is presented as Jesus' ministry outside Israel, with the many healings and the feeding miracle deliberately balancing those already granted to the Jewish crowds, a point which is reinforced when it is noted that the healings listed in v. 31 parallel those performed in a Jewish context according to 11:5 (see below).[7]

---

mention hearing rather than (or as well as) speech by the κωφοί (see n. 3). A few MSS omit "the crippled made healthy," perhaps because the distinction between χωλός and κυλλός (see n. 2) was not felt to be clear enough. The variations make little difference to the effect Matthew intends.

6. The term occurs several times in the OT as an expression used by Israelites, but generally in the fuller and more naturally Israelite phrase "Yahweh the God of Israel." In Exod 5:1, where the phrase occurs (as here) without "Yahweh," it is used specifically to identify Israel's God to a non-Israelite audience. There is no other use of it by Jews in the NT, except for Luke 1:68, which echoes the full OT phrase "Yahweh the God of Israel." In Acts 13:17 the fuller phrase "the God of this people Israel" is used, rather as in Exod 5:1, to emphasize his distinctiveness over against their Egyptian oppressors. J. R. C. Cousland, *NovT* 41 (1999) 14-23, argues that Gentiles would have been more likely to speak of the "God of the Jews." But this is Matthew's summary of their reaction, not necessarily their chosen vocabulary. For *Matthew* to use the unusual phrase "the God of Israel" rather than just saying that the crowds praised "God" suggests that something special was involved here.

7. The reader familiar with recent commentaries will see that I am unmoved by the current fashion (well exemplified by J. R. C. Cousland, *NovT* 41 [1999] 1-23) to deny any Gentile element in vv. 29-38, especially when it is presented as by Luz, 2:344, with a simple statement that it is "impossible" on the grounds that these healings do not differ significantly from Jesus' previous healings of Jews. Precisely! It is the extension of Jesus' ministry to the Gentiles in such a way as to parallel closely what he has previously done among Jews that justifies the otherwise puzzling "redundancy" of this section. Hagner, 2:450-52, apparently feels obliged to bow to the current consensus, but then curiously strives to draw out Gentile symbolism from the feeding of a second *Jewish* crowd; his in-

If that is Matthew's intention, his description of Jesus' itinerary in v. 29, while not as explicit as one might wish, is consistent with such a non-Jewish location. When Jesus has been near the Lake of Galilee in earlier chapters, he has normally been in Jewish territory. But there was also the largely Gentile area of Decapolis on the east side of the lake, which Jesus has already visited in 8:28-34, and the fact that he needed a boat to return from the scene of the second feeding to the Jewish area of Magadan (see on v. 39) suggests that it is in the hills on the east side of the lake that vv. 29-38 have been set; Mark's parallel specifically mentions Decapolis (Mark 7:31). To reach Decapolis from "the region of Tyre and Sidon" would involve a journey around the north side of the lake, which would naturally bring Jesus back to its shore as v. 29 indicates, though presumably not in the area around Capernaum where he was well known. The "hills" into which he climbed (v. 29) would then be on the Golan (eastern) side of the lake rather than in the more familiar Galilean area. But Matthew's geographical indications are not very specific, and the Gentile setting of these verses is indicated as much by the content of the narrative as by what Mattthew says about their location. The statement that he "went up into the hills and sat there" may be intended to recall Jesus' previous involvement with a Jewish crowd in the hills (5:1), though this time we are not told that he did so in order to teach.[8]

The summary of Jesus' healings in this Gentile area is as comprehensive as among the Jews in 14:34-36, but this time it is expressed in terms of specific complaints rather than in purely general terms, though with a generalizing "many others" at the end of the list. The complaints mentioned recall Isa 35:5-6, the blessings promised as part of God's redemption of his people, a passage which was also echoed in Jesus' depiction of the "deeds of the Messiah" in 11:5; but now those messianic blessings are also being experienced outside the covenant people. The surprisingly vivid verb "threw them

---

stinct seems to me better informed than his exegesis! An exegesis which explains (without resorting to such subtlety) the otherwise pointless repetition of healing and feeding miracles recorded as recently as the previous chapter seems to me preferable, especially when it so naturally follows from and reinforces the conclusion of the previous pericope concerning the sharing of the children's bread.

8. D. C. Allison, *Moses,* 241-42, draws out several verbal echoes between 4:24–5:1 and 15:29-32; cf. also T. L. Donaldson, *Jesus,* 119-21. Davies and Allison, 2:566-67, follow Donaldson, ibid., 129-31, in interpreting the "mountain" as an allusion to the OT motif of Mount Zion. This view, together with much of Donaldson's thesis, depends on reading τὸ ὄρος as referring to a specific "mountain," which can then be compared with specific mountains in the biblical tradition, rather than as a general designation for the hill country. That is a lot to build on a relatively colorless geographical designation. See the comments on 5:1-2. A Zion-typology is, of course, incompatible with the view that the crowds here were Gentile, not Jewish (see previous note).

down"⁹ does not seem to connote either violence or impatience, but perhaps conveys something of the pressure Jesus was put under by this expectant Gentile crowd, who clearly had heard (like those from Decapolis in 4:25 and like the woman of 15:22) about the Jewish Messiah's healing powers, and expected him to treat them in the same way. We hear nothing now of reluctance on Jesus' part: the principle accepted in 15:27-28 does not need to be argued again. That they "gave glory" not to Jesus himself but to "the God of Israel" shows a good understanding of the source from which Israel's Messiah must draw his authority.

3. Feeding the Crowd (15:32-39)

32 *Jesus called his disciples to him and said, "My heart goes out¹ to the crowd, because they have already stayed here with me for three days² and have nothing to eat. I don't want to send them away hungry, or they may collapse on the way." 33 His disciples replied, "Where are we going to find in this uninhabited area so many loaves of bread that we can give such a large crowd all they want to eat?" 34 Jesus said to them, "How many loaves do you have?" "Seven," they replied, "and a few little fish." 35 Jesus told the crowd to sit on the ground; 36 then he took the seven loaves and the fish, gave thanks and broke them, and gave them to the disciples, and the disciples gave them to the crowds. 37 And they all ate and had as much as they wanted. The disciples collected seven baskets full of the leftovers from the broken loaves. 38 Those who ate were something like four thousand men, apart from women and children.³*

39 *When Jesus had sent the crowds away, he got into the boat and came to the area of Magadan.⁴*

---

9. See p. 596, n. 4 above.

1. For this rendering of σπλαγχνίζομαι see on 9:36.

2. Matthew's Greek here is very odd (and so is corrected by ℵ, Θ and other MSS) in that he appears to use a nominative case to express duration of time; BDF 144 suggest that he has conflated two constructions, the more normal accusative ἡμέρας τρεῖς and a clause ἡμέραι τρεῖς (εἰσιν καὶ) προσμένουσιν. See further Davies and Allison, 2:570, n. 34.

3. Most of vv. 35-38 is identical with 14:19-21, apart from the different numbers involved and some minor variations in wording and word order. See the notes to the translation there (except that the verb here in v. 36 is εὐχαριστέω, "give thanks," rather than εὐλογέω, "say a blessing," as in 14:19).

4. The otherwise unknown name Magadan was corrected by scribes to the more familiar name Magdala (so the majority of later MSS). That Μαγαδάν nevertheless survived in the early MSS ℵ B D and in a wide variety of ancient versions testifies to its firm place in the tradition.

The second feeding miracle closely echoes the first, the wording of the account of the miracle itself (vv. 35-38) being almost identical with that of 14:19-21 apart from the different numbers involved. The buildup to the miracle is differently framed, but includes the same key elements of Jesus' "heart going out" to a large, hungry crowd, an uninhabited area, the disciples' incredulity at the idea of finding enough food, and the detailing of the small amount of food that the disciples have available. But within this overall similarity there are important differences.

(1) The context this time suggests a Gentile instead of a Jewish crowd (see introductory comments on 15:21-39, and also comments above on 15:29-31, especially p. 597, n. 7). A difference in the wording of v. 37 reinforces that reading (see below).

(2) The numbers involved are different: fewer people (four thousand against five thousand), more loaves (seven against five), fewer leftovers (seven baskets against twelve). The scale of the miracle, though still far beyond natural possibility, is thus reduced. Is this an indication of the priority of the Jewish mission over that to the Gentiles?[5]

(3) The disciples, who in 14:15-17 merely stated the problem of the inadequate resources available, here make a more emphatic protest (v. 33) about the impossibility of the idea of feeding such a large crowd. This is the more remarkable because the narrative sequence of the gospel suggests that whereas in 14:13-21 they were taken by surprise, in the light of that experience they ought by now to be ready for such a miracle again. See further below on v. 33.

Why then has Matthew (like Mark) devoted a significant space in his gospel to a second closely similar miracle but with significant differences? And is it not surprising for the narrative sequence to move from the more impressive miracle to the less, rather than building up to a climax? It seems to me that two factors are required to account for the presence of this pericope. First, the belief of both Mark and Matthew that as a matter of fact two such miracles did take place; and, secondly, a deliberate intention to draw a parallel between Jesus' Jewish ministry and his ministry to Gentiles, such as we have already noted in the summary of healings in 15:29-31 to parallel that in 14:34-36. The latter point is given added force by the observation that between the two feeding miracles, both in Mark and in Matthew, we find the

---

5. Many interpreters have tried to find more specific symbolism in the numbers, such as that twelve (tribes) and five (books of the law) are Jewish numbers, and four (corners of the earth) and seven (completeness) represent the worldwide mission, including the Gentiles. For these and other even more imaginative suggestions of numerical symbolism see my *Mark*, 306, n. 1. Such suggestions are as hard to refute as they are to prove, but I see little in the way Matthew tells the story to encourage such speculation.

debate about purity, with its radical implications for Jew-Gentile relationships, and the encounter with the Gentile woman which focuses on the right of the Gentiles to "the children's bread." The literal provision of bread to a Gentile crowd, as previously to a Jewish crowd, vividly illustrates that principle and the extension of Jesus' messianic ministry which it entails. But the numbers are scaled down; the children's bread remains the prior commitment. Without this element of comparison and contrast between the Jewish and Gentile feeding miracles it is not easy to explain what seems otherwise to be a needless (and strangely less impressive) repetition of the previous story.

In theory this point could have been made by constructing a second, fictional, miracle on the model of the first, and the close similarity in both motifs and wording has been taken by many commentators to suggest that. But if form criticism has taught us anything, it is that similarity in the formulation of a miracle story does not in itself indicate that one story has been created out of the other, but rather that similar stories are naturally told in similar ways. If the purpose of the second story is to invite comparison with the first, it is only to be expected that it should be told in a way that recalls the first except at the points where a difference is meant to be noted; and that is just what we find in this pericope. But to create a second miracle out of whole cloth would seem an odd way to try to establish the point that Jesus did actually extend his miraculous ministry to Gentiles, and the way the two miracles are mentioned side by side in 16:9-10 shows that the author believed that two such miracles had occurred.[6]

For the significance of the feeding, and its various symbolic nuances with regard especially to Israel's experience in the wilderness[7] and to the future liturgical meal of the Lord's Supper, see on 14:13-21. The "eucharistic" wording of the miracle in v. 36 is as clear and detailed here as in 14:19, thus reinforcing the message of 8:11-12 that Gentiles are to share with Jews in the messianic banquet (cf. also again the festive "reclining" in v. 35); and the Lord's Supper which anticipates that banquet is thus for people of all races and backgrounds who share the woman's faith that there is also bread for the dogs.

The following comments will focus on points of difference from the earlier feeding narrative, rather than repeating what has already been said on 14:13-21 where the two run parallel.

32 The narrative sequence indicates that the "crowd" who will now be fed are the same who have come to Jesus in the hills to the east of the lake

---

6. J. Knackstedt, *NTS* 10 (1963/4) 309-35, argues in detail for two actual miracles as the basis of the tradition.

7. D. C. Allison, *Moses,* 240-41, suggests a further OT flavoring in this miracle by means of an echo of Ps 107:4-9.

bringing patients for healing and who have just expressed their praise to "the God of Israel." That they have "stayed with me" and that Jesus can apparently "send them away" at will indicates a remarkable degree of personal attachment to Jesus and recognition of his authority on the part of a non-Jewish crowd. Three days, even if understood inclusively to cover the period since the day before yesterday, is a long time to stay out in an uninhabited area (thus testifying further to the attraction Jesus exercised), and accounts for their hunger: presumably any food they may have brought is now exhausted. As in 14:14-16, Jesus assumes responsibility for their welfare, even though they have come of their own accord.

33 An expression of natural human helplessness in the face of inadequate resources serves as a foil for the miracle Jesus is about to perform; even the disciples' ironical comment about the possibility of giving so many people "all they want" to eat will be echoed in v. 37 by the same vivid verb for "stuffing."[8] But the protest reads strangely here, when the same disciples have so recently witnessed a similarly miraculous act, and when the number involved is this time rather smaller than on the previous occasion. In 16:7-10 Jesus will comment on the disciples' inability to learn the significance of both feeding miracles, as they again worry about not having enough food, and this second expression of incredulity suitably prepares the way for that rebuke. But the reader is left wondering how the disciples could have been so slow to learn.[9] Is this simply a literary motif required by the story which Matthew has included without thinking about the way it reflects on the disciples? Or is it possible that they take it for granted that while Jesus might use his messianic power to feed a *Jewish* crowd, it is outside his domain to do the same for Gentiles? If so, they have not yet grasped the significance of vv. 27-28 but have remained stuck at v. 24.

34 In 14:17 the disciples took the initiative in offering their few loaves and fish. This time they do not volunteer even the small amount they have, and Jesus has to ask them directly. The amount is only marginally larger, and the diminutive noun used for the fish emphasizes its inadequacy. Since fish carried for eating on a journey would normally be dried, the unusual phrase may mean "a few scraps of [dried] fish" rather than a few small [whole] fish.

35-38 Here the narrative closely echoes 14:19-21. The word for "sitting" is different, but its usage has the same connotation of reclining for a festive or grand occasion (see on 14:19). Jesus' looking up to heaven (14:19) before saying the blessing is not mentioned this time (this phrase not being

8. See p. 558, n. 5.
9. Unless we are to emphasize the "we" as their way of acknowledging their own impotence and turning the problem back to Jesus, who alone can solve it; so Gundry, 320.

part of standard eucharistic language). Instead of "said a blessing" in 14:19 we have here "gave thanks" (to God for the food, as was the custom in Jewish meals); see on 14:19 (especially 562, n. 18) for the interchangeability of the terms, especially in Christian eucharistic language. Otherwise, apart from the different numbers,[10] the story continues in the same words, with one intriguing exception: for the "baskets" in which the scraps were collected we find here not the more specifically Jewish word for baskets used in 14:20, but a more general term, another minor pointer to a different cultural setting for the two incidents. The difference between the baskets at the two feedings is maintained when the two miracles are recalled in 16:9-10, suggesting that it was more than a merely stylistic variation. These baskets may be larger than those of 14:20, since the same term is used for the basket in which Paul was lowered over the wall at Damascus (Acts 9:25).

Matthew's inclusion again here of the phrase "apart from women and children" casts further doubt on the proposal that this phrase in 14:21 indicated a military-style all-male gathering of Jewish patriots; the present context gives no scope for such an interpretation, and yet the same formula is used. It is thus much more likely that Matthew is simply using a conventional method of reckoning numbers, as in Exod 12:37 (see on 14:21).

39   This time there is no need to send the disciples away first, and after the crowds have been dismissed Jesus crosses the lake by boat,[11] presumably with the disciples as on other boat trips (see on 14:13). Their destination, Magadan, is not otherwise known; the parallel in Mark 8:10 has the equally unknown Dalmanutha. Both names have understandably been altered in the manuscript tradition, the favored alternative reading being Magdala, known in the NT as the home of Mary, a town on the west side of the lake north of Tiberias, not far from Gennesaret (see on 14:34). Even if the reading Magdala is secondary, Magadan must be supposed to be somewhere in the same area, since it is across the lake from the Gentile site of the preceding incident, and the meeting with "Pharisees and Sadducees" which follows in 16:1 requires a Jewish location.

O. THE END OF THE GALILEAN MISSION (16:1-12)

A brief return to the Jewish area of Galilee will be immediately followed by yet another crossing of the lake "to the other side" (v. 5), to a point from which Jesus will set off with his disciples for Caesarea Philippi (v. 13), far to

10. See above, p. 600, n. 5.
11. "The boat" appears unexpectedly after a long overland journey and on the "foreign" shore. Matthew does not explain.

the north and further away from Jewish territory than they have yet been. From there he will deliberately set off with them for Jerusalem (v. 21), where the remainder of the story will be set, after a lengthy account of the journey southward. On the way they will necessarily go back through Galilee (17:22, 24; 19:1), but this will be a stage on the journey, and Jesus' teaching given at that point will be directed specifically to the disciples. So there will be no more preaching and healing among Galilean crowds, and the confrontation with "Pharisees and Sadducees" in vv. 1-4 is Jesus' last meeting with Galilean opponents. It is not a happy encounter; the sceptical demand for yet another "sign" contrasts significantly with the enthusiastic response of the Gentile crowd to the "signs" in 15:29-31. As a result Jesus both denounces and abandons that "wicked and adulterous generation" (v. 4) and warns his disciples strongly against their ideology (vv. 6, 11-12). This is thus the end of the mission to Galilee, until it will be relaunched dramatically in the Galilean hills by the risen Jesus after his confrontation with the Jerusalem establishment has run its course (28:16-20).

1. Jesus Dismisses His Critics (16:1-4)

1 *The Pharisees and Sadducees came to test Jesus by asking him to show them a sign from heaven.* 2 *But he replied to them, "[In the evening you say, 'The sky is red: it will be fine weather,'* 3 *and in the morning, 'The sky is red and angry: there will be a storm today.' So you know how to interpret the appearance of the sky, but you can't interpret the signs of the times.]*[1] 4 *It is a wicked and adulterous genera-*

1. The whole section from "In the evening" to "signs of the times" is missing from a few MSS and versions (Jerome also mentions its absence from most MSS known to him). Since these include the earliest uncials ℵ and B, both surviving early Syriac versions, and the earlier Coptic versions, textual critics take the omission very seriously, even though the text as translated above is firmly established in the OL versions and in most Greek MSS after ℵ and B. Verse 4 is a direct answer to the request of v. 1, and since the same answer follows without interruption from the similar request of 12:38, it is perhaps more likely that Matthew followed the same pattern here. The change from second to third person between vv. 3 and 4 also makes vv. 2b-3 seem out of place. In that case this would be an early insertion, perhaps prompted by the extreme brevity of the exchange if it consisted originally only of vv. 1 and 4. There is a "parallel" to vv. 2b-3 in Luke 12:54-56 so that the addition of these verses in Matthew can be attributed to the influence of Luke, but the parallel is not close in detail, the weather signs quoted being quite different. An even looser "parallel" in *Gos. Thom.* 91 ("You test the face of heaven and earth, and you have not known what is before you, nor do you know how to test this time") reflects the influence of the Lucan passage rather than of these verses. The originality of the passage can, however, be argued on the basis that scribes might omit the weather signs in an area (such as Egypt) where they did not suit the different climate. Gundry, 323-24, argues for the

tion which demands a sign. No sign will be given to it except the sign of Jonah." Then he left them and went away.

1-2a, 4   If we ignore the textually disputed sayings in vv. 2b-3, this pericope is a close parallel to 12:38-39, with the following differences: (1) the questioners are now "the Pharisees and Sadducees" instead of "some of the scribes and Pharisees"; (2) their hostile aim of "testing" Jesus is this time made explicit; (3) the sign they demand is explicitly "from heaven"; (4) the "sign of Jonah" is left unexplained (compare 12:40-41); (5) the closing account of Jesus' going away is added. See the comments on 12:38-39, therefore, for the exchange as a whole, and for the nature and importance of the "sign"; the fuller phrase, "a sign from heaven," appropriately draws out the nuances we discussed there.[2] But the first and last of the differences listed deserve further comment here.

Whereas "scribes and Pharisees" made a natural pairing in 12:38, "Pharisees and Sadducees" is more surprising. Matthew is the only gospel to use this combination, here and in 3:7. The comments made there apply equally here, where we should probably understand some sort of "cross-party delegation" sent to investigate Jesus' claims and actions.[3] The fact that the power base of the Sadducees was in Jerusalem suggests that this group, like those we have recently met in 15:1, represent not local opposition to Jesus but the interest of the Jerusalem establishment in this northern teacher and miracle worker, just as they had previously investigated his predecessor in the Jordan valley. Jesus will go on in vv. 6, 11-12 to warn his disciples against the "teaching of the Pharisees and Sadducees." In view of the sharp ideological differences between the two groups, the most likely matter on which their "teaching" might have been at one would be in their common rejection of Jesus and what they understood him to stand for — just as in Jeru-

---

originality of the passage; Davies and Allison, 2:580-81, n. 12, do so much more hesitantly. The matter does not allow a confident decision, but the textual status of vv. 2b-3 must remain suspect; see T. Hirunuma, in E. J. Epp and G. D. Fee (eds.), *NT Textual Criticism,* 35-45, for a thorough discussion, concluding that the passage is probably an early gloss.

2. Keener, 421, argues that it means a (meteorological) sign "in the heavens," which would of course give added point to Jesus' following comments (if the longer text is read) about how their expertise in reading "the appearance of the sky" has not led them to discern the things that really matter. But in that case the use of "from" is odd, and in view of the common use of "heaven" to refer to God (which Keener amply illustrates), it is more likely that it here means "a sign from God."

3. On Matthew's combination of Pharisees and Sadducees, sometimes taken as evidence that the author was a Gentile, unaware of Jewish ideological disputes, see above on 3:7 and my *Matthew: Evangelist,* 106-7.

salem the opposition to Jesus will consist primarily of "chief priests and scribes," a similarly ill-matched pair in terms of their own party interests. That false "teaching" is clearly revealed in their sceptical demand for yet another "sign," when they have already been given so many.

The final sentence of v. 4 might be read simply as an editorial transitional formula, but since this is in fact the end of Jesus' ministry in Galilee and of his contact with Jewish leaders in the north, it probably carries more weight. Following the blunt refusal of their request and his denunciation of them as representing a "wicked and adulterous generation," his abandoning them and going away marks a decisive break (following the principle of 7:6 and of 10:14-15) and prepares the reader for a new phase in the story. Cf. the equally decisive departure in 24:1 from the temple and the public confrontation which had taken place there.

2b-3 For the textual uncertainty of this first part of Jesus' response, see p. 604, n. 1. If it is a genuine part of Matthew's text, its function is to explain the distorted perspective of "this generation" which Jesus will denounce in v. 4. Their weather lore[4] is perceptive, but when it comes to more important matters they do not show the same ability to read the signs. "The signs of the times" has become a proverbial phrase, often used with reference to eschatological expectation, but it occurs only here in the NT, where the reference is not to future events but to what is already there for all to see. "Times" translates *kairoi,* a term which often denotes specific or decisive times or events rather than simply the passage of time. They ought to be able to see that important things are taking place, that this is a time of decision, but they are oblivious to what is taking place through the ministry of Jesus the Messiah. They have all the signs they need, but instead of taking note of them, they are stubbornly demanding a further "sign."

2. The Disciples Begin to Understand (16:5-12)

> 5 When his disciples reached the other side, they had forgotten to bring any bread. 6 But Jesus said to them, "Look out; beware of the leaven[1] of the Pharisees and Sadducees." 7 But they were discussing among themselves, saying, "[He said that] because we didn't bring any bread."[2] 8 Jesus knew what they were saying, and said, "You

4. Cf. the traditional saying, "Red sky at night, shepherd's delight; red sky in the morning, shepherd's warning." Luz, 2:347, refers to this weather rule as one of "the most widespread and obvious ones of antiquity," and quotes Latin and Greek authors (as well as a comparable saying from "north of the Alps").

1. For the meaning of "leaven" in the biblical world see above on 13:33.

2. The ὅτι which introduces this statement could be taken either as above, as a causal connective contained within their statement, which then requires the addition of

faithless[3] men, why are you discussing among yourselves the fact that you have no bread? 9 Don't you yet realize? Don't you remember the five loaves for the five thousand men, and how many baskets you collected? 10 Or the seven loaves for the four thousand men, and how many baskets you collected? 11 How can you not realize that I was not talking to you about loaves of bread? But you must beware of the leaven of the Pharisees and Sadducees." 12 Then they understood that he had not been telling them to beware of leaven,[4] but of the teaching of the Pharisees and Sadducees.

Mark's parallel to this pericope (Mark 8:14-21) refers to "the leaven of the Pharisees and the leaven of Herod." Matthew does not mention Herod (Antipas, whose appearance here in Mark is surprising), and instead speaks of "the leaven of the Pharisees and Sadducees," thus linking this warning closely with the two groups whose demand for a sign Jesus has just repudiated (vv. 1-4). Matthew's version of the whole pericope is also simpler than the very obscure dialogue in Mark 8:14-21, and he has attempted to clarify the flow of thought, but it remains a puzzling little passage. Two topics are woven together, the disciples' concern about lack of a literal supply of food and Jesus' metaphorical use of "leaven" as a symbol for false teaching. The resultant misunderstanding is exploited to reveal the disciples as not yet on Jesus' wavelength, but by the end of the pericope understanding has dawned.[5] "Bread," which has been an important theme running through 14:13-21; 15:21-28, and 15:32-38, again holds this dialogue together, and the opportunity is taken to draw out the lessons of the two bread miracles of 14:13-21 and 15:32-38. Thus, although Jesus' metaphorical use of "leaven" makes no direct connection with the feeding miracles, the disciples' misunderstanding prompts him to use them as object lessons in true understanding, as opposed to the misleading "teaching" of the Pharisees and Sadducees. But the readers are left, like the disciples, to puzzle out for

---

"He said that" as the assumed main clause supporting the "because," or as the mark of direct speech, equivalent to our quotation marks, so that the clause would read simply "saying, 'We didn't bring any bread,'" See the comments below.

3. See p. 246, n. 6, for this translation of ὀλιγόπιστος, literally "of little faith."

4. This is the reading of a significant range of MSS and versions; others (the majority) add either τῶν ἄρτων or the singular τοῦ ἄρτου. A few add instead "of the Pharisees and Sadducees." The variation in the added phrases suggests that the added words represent pedantic attempts to clarify Matthew's terse comment by explaining that "leaven" here means *literal* leaven, as opposed to its metaphorical use in v. 6. Cf. Luz, 2:349, n. 1.

5. Contrast Mark 7:21, where the pericope ends with a frustrated question, "Don't you yet understand?" together with Mark 6:52, which specifically mentions the disciples' failure to understand "about the loaves."

themselves just what lesson the two feeding miracles are meant to have conveyed, and just what is the nature of the dangerous "teaching" of Jesus' opponents. The whole pericope remains at the level of a parable without an explanation!

Mark presents this dialogue as taking place in the boat on the way toward Bethsaida, the point from which they will set off on foot for Caesarea Philippi. Matthew omits the Bethsaida incident, and the only indication of another boat trip is the phrase "reached the other side" in v. 5. The dialogue appears to take place after the crossing rather than on the voyage as in Mark, but the location remains unidentified.

The theme of the disciples' "understanding" was introduced in 13:11-17, where their privileged access to the "secrets of the kingdom of heaven" was contrasted with the inability of others to understand. In 13:23 understanding is the mark of true disciples, while in 13:19 the lack of it marks those who are lost, and in 13:51-52 Jesus accepts and builds on their assurance that they have understood the parables. But in 15:16 they show themselves still without understanding, and that is also the basis of this dialogue. Eventually, however, understanding dawns (v. 12), and the ground is thus prepared for the climactic question and answer at Caesarea Philippi which will immediately follow. There at last their developing understanding will find full expression through Peter's declaration, though in what follows it will be revealed again and again how partial that understanding still remains, right up to the time in Gethsemane when they will all abandon Jesus and run away. Perception and dullness will continue to jostle in Matthew's portrayal of the disciples as they wrestle with the demanding new values of the kingdom of heaven, and the present pericope gives full expression to that paradox.

5 We have noted at 14:13 and 15:39 that even where Matthew speaks only of Jesus himself crossing the lake, it is to be understood that the disciples were with him (see on 14:13). Here it is the other way around: only the disciples are mentioned, but we should assume that Jesus was with them.[6] Jesus is there with them immediately in v. 6, without any indication that they have just met up. Unless we are told specifically to the contrary (as in 14:22), it is always assumed that Jesus and his disciples are traveling together. The reason why the disciples rather than Jesus are the subject of the verb here[7] is that at this point it is their forgetfulness and their material worries that give rise to the dialogue.

The lack of available food has been a recurrent theme (14:17; 15:34), the amounts mentioned before the two feeding miracles being not even

---

6. *Pace* several commentators, especially Gundry, 324-25, who also apparently supposes that Jesus operated the boat on his own in 15:39.

7. Syntactically the main verb is "had forgotten," not "reached."

enough for twelve disciples and Jesus, let alone for the crowds. That they should yet again have failed to take supplies with them on a journey[8] strikes the reader as remarkably negligent, unless they are still following Jesus' instructions for their missionary journey in 10:9-11 and depending on finding hospitality as they go. Matthew does not explain the situation, but it provides the context for the following dialogue.

6   Jesus' warning is presumably to be understood as a follow-up to the encounter with the Pharisees and Sadducees in vv. 1-4. Leaven here, in contrast to 13:33, is clearly a symbol for the pervasiveness of something bad, as it is also in 1 Cor 5:6-8 (cf. Gal 5:9), where the imagery derives from the removal of leaven from the house to prepare for the Passover season.[9] The metaphor will be explained in v. 12 as referring to "teaching":[10] the ideological opposition of the Pharisees and Sadducees to Jesus and his message (their "toxic cynicism," Keener, 422) must be resisted if it is not to influence others.[11] See further above on vv. 1-2a, 4; the sceptical demand for a "sign" exemplifies the closed mind of these opponents of Jesus.

In this brief account of the dialogue Jesus thus seems to introduce a topic quite unconnected with the disciples' predicament. There is no indication that their problem has yet even been brought to his attention, though it is possible that he has chosen this metaphor because he is aware of their concern. It is the coincidence of the themes of leaven and of bread that will spark the dialogue which follows, with Jesus and the disciples initially at cross-purposes.

7-8   The disciples completely miss Jesus' point. The ambiguity of Matthew's construction in v. 7b (see above, p. 606, n. 2) allows us to read

8. Mark says that they had just a single loaf with them in the boat. Matthew omits this detail as an unnecessary complication of the story.

9. Exod 12:15, 19; cf. also Lev 2:11, where leaven is not allowed in sacrificial offerings. For the metaphorical use of leaven in a negative sense, especially in Philo and in rabbinic usage, see H. Windisch, *TDNT* 2:903-6; D. Instone-Brewer, *Traditions,* 1:383-85. Also C. L. Mitton, *ExpT* 84 (1972/3) 339-43.

10. A. Negoita and C. Daniel, *NovT* 9 (1967) 306-14, suggest that this is a play on the Aramaic words *ḥᵃmîrā'* ("yeast") and *'ᵃmîrâ* ("teaching"); they suggest that Jesus used the latter word, but the disciples thought he used the former. But such mishearing is hardly necessary to understanding the pericope, since Matthew makes the symbolism explicit. Matthew may have enjoyed the Aramaic assonance, but he could hardly expect his Greek readers to be aware of it.

11. Jesus apparently recognizes the validity of the teaching of "scribes and Pharisees" in 23:3a; but that statement functions in context as a foil for the negative comment on their practice which follows in v. 3b rather than as a commendation in its own right (see comments there). But the issue here is not the general scribal teaching, but the specific reaction to Jesus which has united Pharisees and Sadducees (who are not in view in 23:3) against him.

their words either as simply a verbalization of the concern expressed in v. 5 or (as translated above) as a direct comment on what Jesus has just said. But in either case the sequence of the dialogue, as well as Jesus' conclusion that they had wrongly thought that his comment about leaven related to real bread (v. 11), requires us to conclude that it was his use of the metaphor of leaven which provoked this response. We might then expect him to go straight on to correct their misunderstanding, as he will do in vv. 11-12. But instead he takes up their (misplaced) concern about lack of food, and takes them to task on that issue, before going on to clarify his original warning. Their concern about food reveals their lack of faith, and vv. 9-10 will show how recent events should have made it impossible for them to worry on that score. The charge of lack of faith recalls especially 6:30, where the same epithet is used for those who worry about the provision of food and clothing instead of trusting their heavenly Father. Their knowledge of God's fatherly care should alone have been enough to allay their concern; but in fact they have recently been given more tangible proof, twice over, that God (through Jesus) can provide food when it is needed.

9-10   Not only have they failed to "remember" the two feeding miracles, but they have not yet "realized" what those miracles revealed about Jesus. At the lowest level they showed that he could miraculously supply food, so that the disciples had no need to worry. But they also added to the growing evidence for who Jesus was, for the source of his authority and the nature of his mission, and their understanding of that more fundamental issue will be probed in the next episode. We hear again here Jesus' frustration at their slowness in understanding, as it was expressed in 15:16-17. It is time for them to put two and two together.

The miracles are recalled more briefly than in Mark 8:19-20, but the key numbers emphasize clearly the "impossibility" of what they have witnessed. The focus falls on the disciples' own experience as the collectors of the scraps at the end (with the two different types of basket mentioned in 14:20 and 15:37 duly recalled). Surely they should have remembered and learned from that.

11-12   After an apparent digression on the meaning of the feeding miracles in vv. 8-10 Jesus now returns to the disciples' misunderstanding in v. 7, and clarifies what he had been talking about in v. 6. Matthew's own editorial comment in v. 12 then more pedantically unpacks the meaning of the leaven metaphor. But the repetition of the verb *noeō*, "realize," in vv. 9 amd 11 links the two bread-related themes together, and seems to imply that if the disciples had understood the message of the feeding miracles they would also not have misunderstood his warning in v. 6. Perhaps the suggestion is that, like the crowds in John 6:26-27, the disciples' understanding of the miracles has remained at the level of the satisfaction of material need; they are so preoccupied with literal bread that their minds are not open to the more important spiritual truths which Jesus' metaphor is meant to convey. At any rate, Matthew's conclusion indicates that Jesus' reminder of the deeper meaning of the miracles has had the desired effect, and now at last they understand what Jesus was talking about. And so now they are ready for the more searching test of their spiritual understanding which will follow in vv. 13-16.

P. THE MESSIAH RECOGNIZED BY HIS DISCIPLES (16:13-20)

13 *When Jesus had come to the region of Caesarea Philippi, he was asking his disciples, "Who are people saying that the Son of Man is?"*[1] 14 *They replied, "Some say John the Baptist, others Elijah, and others Jeremiah or one of the prophets."*

15 *He asked them, "But what about you?*[2] *Who do you say that I am?"* 16 *Simon Peter replied, "You are the Messiah, the Son of the living God."*

17 *Jesus replied to him, "Happy are you,*[3] *Simon bar-Jona, because flesh and blood did not reveal this to you, but my Father who is in heaven.* 18 *And I tell you that you are Peter, and on this rock*[4] *I will build my church, and the gates of Hades will not overpower it.* 19 *I will give you the keys of the kingdom of heaven, and whatever you tie up on earth will have been tied up in heaven, and whatever you untie on earth will have been untied in heaven."*

20 *Then he impressed on*[5] *the disciples that they should not tell anyone that he was the Messiah.*[6]

1. A large number of MSS and versions add με, giving the rendering "that I the Son of Man am." This clarification seems to have been prompted by the use of με (without the title "the Son of Man") in Mark 8:27 and Luke 9:18, as well as here in the corresponding question in v. 15. The fact that the third-person title was preserved here (except in D) alongside the με, and that the position of με varies where it is included, indicates that the third-person form was the original. Luz, 2:354, however, regards the longer text as original.

2. An attempt to render the effect of the upfront position of ὑμεῖς in contrast to οἱ ἄνθρωποι.

3. For this rendering of the traditional "beatitude" form see above, p. 158, n. 1, and pp. 160-61. A less literal rendering might be "I congratulate you" (or "Good on yer"!).

4. See the comments below for the wordplay on Πέτρος, "Peter," and πέτρα, "rock."

5. This is Matthew's only use of διαστέλλομαι, a strong term for giving orders: "to express in no uncertain terms what one must do" (BDAG 236b). Mark uses it five times for Jesus' injunctions to silence.

6. Several MSS and versions rather oddly add the name "Jesus" here. It is not his

Matthew has made no secret of his own view that in Jesus the purposes of God declared in the OT have now come to their fulfillment. This has been demonstrated throughout the opening four chapters of the gospel. Matthew has used the actual term "Messiah" sparingly (but decisively in 1:1, 16-18), but the idea underlying it has been richly elaborated. But Jesus has not used that title, leaving both the crowds and the disciples to draw their own conclusions from the unique "authority" which has so often evoked their "amazement" (4:24-25; 7:28-29; 9:8, 26, 31, 33; 13:54; 15:31). These have included the tentative identification of Jesus as "the son of David" in 12:23, and such popular speculation may well underlie the authorities' demand for a sign in 12:38; 16:1. The disciples have gone even further on the basis of their special experiences of Jesus' power, resulting on one occasion in the spontaneous use of the phrase "the Son of God" (8:29; 14:33). We have also heard the outlandish speculation of Antipas (14:1-2) and the more perceptive but still tentative assessment by John the Baptist (11:2-6). So now it is time for this central issue of the Galilean story to be clarified: who is Jesus?

This pericope, together with its unexpected sequel in vv. 21-23, thus forms the central turning point in Matthew's narrative, as it is in Mark's. Its geographical location marks the most northerly point in Jesus' travels during his ministry,[7] from which the southward journey announced in v. 21 will take him into the hitherto foreign territory of Judea. Peter's declaration in v. 16 marks the climax of the gradual recognition of the Messiah by his disciples during the Galilean period. And the new note of suffering, death, and resurrection as the messianic mission which is first sounded in 16:21 will set the tone for the rest of the narrative. Galilee with its enthusiastic crowds has been left behind, and Jerusalem with its hostile religious authorities lies ahead.

The two pericopes, vv. 13-20 and 21-23, are thus closely related, the latter following from and explaining the former (especially the unexpected note of secrecy in v. 20). It is nonetheless appropriate to place a major division between vv. 20 and 21 to indicate the climactic nature of vv. 13-20 and the programmatic change indicated in v. 21, with its formulaic new beginning, "From that time Jesus began . . . ," balancing the use of the same phrase to introduce the public ministry in Galilee in 4:17 (see comments there). The sharp change of tone is exemplified especially in the experience of Peter, first praised for his perceptive messianic declaration in vv. 17-19, and then re-

---

personal name which is the object of secrecy but his role as Messiah. The addition seems to be an unthinking and mechanical "filling out" of the phrase ὁ Χριστός, read not as a title but as a name.

7. Had Jesus gone to the cities of Tyre and, particularly, Sidon, that would have been further north, but the "region of Tyre and Sidon" in 15:21 denotes the general Phoenician region, which extended well to the south of those cities themselves.

buked in the strongest terms for his lack of sympathy with the divine agenda in v. 23.

Peter is the focal figure in vv. 13-20.[8] The question is addressed to all the disciples, as is the injunction to secrecy in v. 20, but the messianic declaration is spoken by Peter alone, and the following commendation is addressed to him in the second-person singular. It is likely that historically Peter was here acting as spokesman for the whole group (who have already corporately expressed their conviction that Jesus is the Son of God, 14:33), but by adding vv. 17-19 Matthew has made it clear that he regards Peter as more than simply a corporate spokesman; it is his personal role in the foundation of the emergent "church" which is highlighted, even though the formula of v. 19 will be repeated in the plural with regard to the whole disciple group in 18:18. Matthew thus takes this opportunity to underline the historical role of Peter as we know it from the book of Acts and from subsequent Christian tradition, as the leading figure in the postresurrection church and the initiator of the new direction which made the community of Jesus' followers distinct from its Jewish heritage (Acts 10–11) — *"my ekklēsia."* It is this foundational role which is highlighted by the famous play on the name "Peter" in v. 18, on which see below.

The addition of vv. 17-19 changes dramatically the impact of the whole pericope. In Mark and Luke Jesus' only response to Peter's declaration is to forbid the disciples to speak about the matter, so that the reader unaware of the wider christology of the authors might suppose that Peter had made a mistake — and the more so when in the immediately following verses in Mark he is rebuked for his misunderstanding. In Matthew, however, there is an immediate glad acceptance of what Peter has said, so that the reader is obliged to think out the paradox of why a correct and warmly welcomed declaration is yet not to be made the subject of public announcement. The way is thus prepared for understanding Peter's gaffe in vv. 21-23 as exemplifying the natural misunderstanding of what the title "Messiah" implies, which was only to be expected if the title were to be unguardedly proclaimed to the general public. It was not that his declaration was wrong, but that he and his fellow disciples had not yet attained a sufficiently unconventional grasp of the nature of Jesus' messianic mission to allow the term to be bandied about. If Peter could get it so badly wrong, how much more the wider public.

This does not necessarily mean that Matthew simply composed vv. 17-19 as a counterbalance to the negative impression of the title "Messiah" which might have been derived from the tradition as we find it in Mark. It would be typical of his method to insert a piece of traditional material within

8. For the importance of Peter in Matthew as a whole see my *Matthew: Evangelist,* 244-46.

an existing pericope in order to draw out a particular angle; see, for instance, the inclusion of 8:11-12 within 8:5-13, the expansion of the section on prayer in 6:5-6 by the addition of 6:7-8, 9-13, and 14-15, and more generally the anthological composition of the discourses. Thus it might be suggested that vv. 18 and 19 were originally a freestanding tradition of Jesus' special commission to Peter together with the explanation of the name Jesus gave him. But v. 17 is more closely tied to this context since it requires a prior declaration of an important truth by Peter, and it is v. 17 which explicitly counterbalances the negative impression in Mark. And we shall see below that v. 18 also reads most naturally as a deliberate echo of the form of Peter's declaration in v. 16. So it seems more likely that Matthew had a tradition (or memory?) that Jesus did first welcome Peter's statement and comment on his special role, even though he then went on to warn them against broadcasting the title Peter had just declared.[9]

The interplay of titles in these verses is instructive. "The Son of Man" appears, as customarily in the gospels, as a self-reference by Jesus. Its lack of ready-made conceptual meaning (see on 8:20) is indicated by its function here as the basis for an inquiry about people's views on Jesus' identity: clearly the title in itself leaves the question unanswered. The various suggested identifications in v. 14 all cluster around the idea of "prophet," the category popularly used to explain John the Baptist (11:9; 14:5) and thus naturally transferred to his perceived successor, Jesus; cf. Jesus' claim to the same term in 13:57. As far as it goes, it is not incorrect, but it is clearly not adequate since Jesus goes on to ask for a more informed opinion. It comes in the title "Messiah," hitherto in this gospel used only editorially (1:1, 16, 17, 18; 2:4; 11:2) to express the true assessment of Jesus' role, to which the readers are therefore privy but which has not yet been directly mooted by the actors within the story — though John the Baptist has raised it implicitly in 11:3, and the tentative "Son of David" in 12:23 carries the same force. Its

---

9. For a careful defense of vv. 17-19 as an integral part of the original tradition, against the then (1979) trend of NT scholarship, see B. F. Meyer, *Aims,* 185-97. More recently Davies and Allison, 2:602-15, have discussed the matter in detail, with reference to all major views, and conclude that the whole section vv. 13-20 is probably to be regarded as the result of Matthew's conflation of a shorter (Marcan) and a longer account of the same incident, both derived from tradition. They regard the redactional composition of vv. 17-19 as "the least probable" explanation of their origin (605). In a characteristically cautious final verdict on the historical issue they are prepared to say that "Mt 16:17-19 *may* preserve the original conclusion to the incident at Caesarea Philippi, and the text *may* give us an important glimpse into the life of Jesus" (615, their italics). See also Hagner, 2:465-66, for a slightly less cautious summary. Keener, who thinks that Matthew gives the original tradition which Mark (followed by Luke) has abbreviated, judges (425, n. 74) that in recent years "the debate has somewhat receded."

ringing declaration here by Peter sets the tone for the second half of the gospel, in which the paradoxical nature of that Messiahship will be explored and enacted. But added to that functional title is the more far-reaching "Son of (the living) God," with which the reader is familiar not only from its programmatic declaration by God himself in 3:17 and the exploration of its significance in 4:1-11 (and cf. its editorial use in 2:15), but also from the disciples' own (perhaps not fully thought out) exclamation in 14:33. Underlying it is Jesus' repeated reference to God as his own Father. See the comments below on how far "Son of God" is to be understood here as a theological statement in its own right, and how far it may have been a natural extension of the idea of "Messiah."

13 The rather unclear geography of 15:39 and 16:5 has probably left Jesus and his disciples somewhere on the northeast side of the lake; Mark's intervening incident at Bethsaida (Mark 8:22-26), unmentioned by Matthew, would fit such a location. From there to Caesarea Philippi would be some twenty-five miles on foot, though, as with Tyre and Sidon in 15:21, we are not told that Jesus went to the city itself, but only to its "region" (Mark has its "villages"). Philip's Caesarea,[10] though close to the site of the earlier Hebrew settlement of Dan, was in the first century an essentially pagan, Hellenistic city, even though under a Herodian ruler. There is no indication that Jesus and his disciples made any contact with the people of the area, and we are not told the purpose of their going so far north. The focus of the account is entirely on the interaction between Jesus and his disciples, unless we are to suppose that the episode of 17:14-21 is still set in the same area (see on 17:1 for the site of the Transfiguration), and even that encounter was not sought by Jesus.

The disciples, as they have mingled with the crowd, have been in a better position than Jesus himself to tune in to what people are saying about him; what sort of pigeonhole have they put him in?

On the use of "the Son of Man" as a self-reference by Jesus see the introductory comments. The interchangeability of "I" and "the Son of Man" in the gospel tradition is indicated by the fact that in this verse Matthew has the latter (see p. 611, n. 1 above) and Mark the former, but in v. 21 the situation is reversed. Matthew's decision to use "the Son of Man" here perhaps reflects his awareness of the open-ended and puzzling nature of this designation as used by Jesus during his ministry; as a title it invites the question "Who?" The title alone does not provide the answer.

14 We have already met the identification of Jesus as (the resurrected) John the Baptist in 14:2. Jesus, because of the nature of his preaching

---

10. So called to distinguish it from Caesarea Maritima on the Mediterranean coast, and because Herod Philip had been responsible for its recent enlargement.

and his popular influence, would naturally be regarded as a second John, even by those who had no knowledge of the previous connection between the two; cf. the association of the two men's ministries in 11:16-19, and see below on 21:23-27. For the place of (the returning) Elijah in popular expectation see above on 11:14 (also on 17:3 below). In view of Jesus' identification of John as Elijah (11:14, and further below in 17:10-13), the appearance of his name here alongside that of John causes no surprise. Both John and Elijah are prophetic figures, and the generalizing "one of the prophets" draws out this basic element in the popular reaction to Jesus; cf. his own linking of his mission with that of the prophet Jonah, with the comment that "something greater than Jonah is here" (12:40-41). All the prophetic figures mentioned belong to the past, and it might be argued that to identify Jesus with any of them must involve a belief in their resurrection or reincarnation, as it certainly did in the case of Antipas (14:2). But that is probably to be too pedantic: the use of these key figures as models to identify the nature of Jesus' ministry need not necessarily imply their personal return.

One surprising element, which is peculiar to Matthew, is the singling out of Jeremiah as a model for understanding Jesus.[11] Jeremiah was, of course, a prominent OT prophet, but why choose him rather than, say, Isaiah, with whom Jesus has himself implicitly compared his own ministry in the quotation in 13:13-15? The answer may be found in the peculiar nature of Jeremiah's message, which has made his name proverbial as a prophet of doom, and in the sustained opposition he encountered among his own people. In particular, Jeremiah incurred fierce hostility by predicting the downfall of Judah and the destruction of the temple, and a similar message will become an increasing feature of Jesus' ministry as Matthew relates it. The three parables directed against the current Jewish leadership in 21:28–22:14 will be followed by the denunciation of the scribes and Pharisees in ch. 23 with its warning of a climactic judgment to come, and the explicit prediction of the total destruction of the temple (23:34–24:2; note the echo of Jer 22:5 in 23:38). It will be as a threat to the temple that Jesus will be tried (26:61) and derided on the cross (27:40). While this remains in the future as far as the narrative sequence is concerned, we have already heard Jesus' cryptic comment that "something greater than the temple is here" (12:6), and his threat of judgment on Galilean towns in 11:20-24. It is not very surprising that some people, whether in admiration or in disparagement, might have seen him al-

11. There is no evidence of an expectation (as for Elijah) that Jeremiah would return, though in 2 Macc 15:12-16 Jeremiah appears *in a vision* to encourage Judas Maccabeus. A promise of the future sending of Isaiah and Jeremiah in *5 Ezra* 2:18 is later and probably dependent on Matthew (see G. N. Stanton, *Gospel,* 269-70). See further M. Knowles, *Jeremiah,* 85-90.

ready as a second Jeremiah; as the story continues, the identification will become even more apt.[12]

The quoted popular views all categorize Jesus as a prophet; cf. also the later acclamation by the Galilean crowd as Jesus comes to Jerusalem in 21:11. We noted at 11:9, where Jesus makes the same claim for John, that prophecy was not a common category in first-century Judaism.[13] If people saw Jesus as a prophet, they believed him to be a figure of great significance, and someone with a divine commission. The identification with the returning Elijah also adds a more explicitly eschatological dimension, and while there is no direct allusion here to the expectation of an eschatological prophet like Moses (Deut 18:15-19), the prophetic category would natural lend itself to such hopes. All this is highly honorific, but Jesus' subsequent question reveals that it still falls short of the true estimate of his mission. It leaves him only on a level with John.

15 Jesus' second question expects that the disciples themselves will have a more adequate view of his mission than the popular estimate they have quoted. Matthew's comment on their eventual "understanding" in v. 12 perhaps also alerts the reader to expect something better. After all, these are the people to whom "the secrets of the kingdom of heaven" have been revealed (13:11, 16-17).

16 The question was addressed to the disciples as a group, but the reply comes from their leading member. This is the only time Matthew gives "Simon Peter" his full title. When he was first introduced and when he was listed as the first of the Twelve (4:18; 10:2), he was identified as "Simon (also called Peter)," and when he is addressed in the vocative Jesus will call him "Simon" (16:17; 17:25), but elsewhere Matthew always refers to him simply as "Peter." The fuller name here thus has a more formal sound, as befits the man about to make a momentous declaration. It also prepares us for v. 18, where "Peter" will be explained as a significant nickname given to Simon by Jesus. Here, as already in 15:15 and later in 16:22; 17:4, 24-25; 18:21; 19:27, Peter probably acts as spokesman for the whole disciple group, and indeed the second part of his declaration simply repeats what the disciples as a group have already concluded in 14:33. But the personal commendation which follows perhaps indicates that Peter has been ahead of the rest not only in speaking but also in formulating their growing recognition of Jesus' unique status and mission (see introductory comments).

---

12. For a survey of explanations offered for the inclusion of Jeremiah here see M. Knowles, *Jeremiah,* 82-95. The view of Jesus as a "second Jeremiah" is strongly undergirded by Knowles' extended demonstration (ibid., 96-161) that Matthew presents Jesus in the light of a widespread Jewish "Deuteronomistic rejected-prophet motif." Cf. also his brief summary of "typological correspondences between Jeremiah and Jesus" in Matthew (ibid., 245-46).

13. See p. 427, n. 29.

While the title "Messiah" (see on 1:1) as such is not used in the OT in this sense, it is clear that by the first century it was current as a title of hope, to denote the human deliverer whom God was expected to send to his people.[14] This hope took various forms in the OT, and it seems likely that the term "Messiah" might in principle be applied to any of these, but there is little doubt that among most Jews in first-century Palestine its primary connotation would be of a "son of David" who would restore the nation to the glory and independence it had known under the first David. It was thus a nationalistic term, and one which was hard to separate from the political aspirations of a subject people.[15] We shall see in vv. 22-23 that Peter himself will find it impossible to associate Messiahship with Jesus' proclaimed mission of suffering and death (which takes up one relatively limited strand of OT expectation); for him apparently the title conveys glory and success, not defeat and execution. So we must not read into Peter's declaration here all that later Christian theology has found in the term "Messiah." His understanding of Jesus' way of "saving his people from their sins" (1:21) still has a long way to go. But, however limited his grasp of Jesus' actual mission, he has gone beyond the popular acclamation of Jesus as a prophet to the point of recognizing him as not just one among many, not even, like John the Baptist, the greatest of the prophets (11:11), but as the one climactic figure in whom God's purpose is finally being accomplished. In that he has made the crucial breakthrough.

The title "Son of God" in itself plays a central role in Matthew's presentation of Jesus (see introductory comments). It is a matter of debate whether it appears here as a distinct and additional part of Peter's declaration about the identity of Jesus, or whether the two titles "Messiah" and "Son of God" belong together as two ways of expressing the same messianic status; they are similarly combined by the high priest in 26:63. An important OT prophecy says of David's future son: "I will be a father to him, and he will be a son to me" (2 Sam 7:14), and according to what was probably the current interpretation of Ps 2 the Messiah is there addressed by God in the words "You are my son; today I have begotten you" (Ps 2:7). It is on this basis that the Messiah could be thought of at Qumran as God's son,[16] and while evidence for such language among other Jews of the period is lacking, it seems likely that the two well-known OT passages would have made it acceptable.

14. On messianic terminology in later Judaism see M. de Jonge and A. S. van der Woude, *TDNT* 9:509-27. Also, more briefly, N. T. Wright, *Victory,* 481-86.

15. G. Vermes, *Jesus,* 129-56, gives a useful overview of what the title might have conveyed within first-century Judaism.

16. 4Q174 *(Florilegium);* 4Q246 *(Aramaic Apocalypse)* 2:1; perhaps 1QSa(28a) 2:11-12. See, e.g., M. Hengel, *Son of God,* 43-45; D. Juel, *Messiah,* 108-14.

It is therefore possible that both Peter here and the high priest in 26:63 are using the two titles as virtual synonyms. But in view of Matthew's emphasis on the title "Son of God" elsewhere, and especially its emphatic reaffirmation which will follow shortly after this incident (17:5), it is more likely that he expected his readers to hear it as adding a further dimension to Peter's declaration, by supplementing the "functional" title Messiah with one which speaks more directly of who Jesus really *is*. If Peter may be assumed to have heard Jesus' exultant prayer at 11:25-27, he would have good grounds for adding this theologically loaded phrase.

The powerful OT phrase "the living God" appears in Matthew here and in 26:63 (though not there as part of the title "Son of God"), and in a dozen other places in the NT. In one sense the participle adds nothing, since if God is not living he is not God. But it is a powerful reminder that the God with whom Jesus is here being connected is not a philosophical abstraction but the dynamic God of Israel's faith and history. The supernatural dynamic of Jesus' miracles derives from a God who is himself alive and active in his world. It is the church of the living God which will be declared in v. 18 to be immune to the powers of death. In the region of Caesarea Philippi, a center for the worship of Pan (as it had been previously of the Canaanite Baal), the title would have a special resonance as marking out the true God from all other gods.

17 Jesus' initial response to what Peter has said is entirely positive, in striking contrast to what will follow in vv. 20-23. For the meaning and function of a "beatitude" see above on 5:3-10, where the Beatitudes, like this one, are explained by a "because" clause; Jesus congratulates Peter on his exceptional insight, not in the sense that Peter has himself puzzled out the truth but that, like all knowledge about God and his Son (11:27), it has been revealed to him by God himself (cf. 11:25). We should remember, however, that a similar beatitude has already been addressed to the disciples corporately in 13:16-17, where they have all been declared to be the recipients of special revelation. The description of God as "my Father who is in heaven" follows aptly from the declaration that Jesus is God's Son. For "flesh and blood" as a graphic way of describing humanity in contrast with God or other spiritual beings cf. 1 Cor 15:50; Eph 6:12; Heb 2:14. A particularly relevant parallel is Gal 1:16, where Paul insists that his gospel came to him by divine revelation rather than through consultation with "flesh and blood."[17]

---

17. D. C. Sim, *Gospel,* 200-203, argues that this coincidence of language, together with the idea of Peter as the foundation rock in v. 18, is evidence of a deliberately anti-Pauline polemic in this Matthean composition, so that "the material in Matt. 16:17-19 should be regarded as an early response to the claims of Paul by the followers of Peter." But it is salutary to observe that others (e.g., B. P. Robinson, *JSNT* 21 [1984] 89) are equally

Matthew transliterates the Aramaic *bar-Iônâ,* "son of Jonah." Simon's father's name is mentioned here and in John 1:42, the two places where we hear of Simon being given the nickname Peter; the use of Simon's full title gives added solemnity to the occasion. But in John 1:42 the father's name is probably *Iōannēs,* John (the majority of MSS there also read *Iōna,* but this was probably by assimilation to the Matthew text).[18] There is no obvious reason why Matthew should have changed the name in order to associate Peter or his father with the biblical Jonah;[19] it is Jesus, not Peter, who is the "greater than Jonah" (12:40-41), and the "sign of Jonah" (12:39; 16:4) does not relate to Peter. It is more likely that *Iōna* and *Iōannēs* are variant Greek forms of the same Semitic name; *Iōannēs* (representing the Hebrew Johanan) was in common use in NT times, but the Hebrew name Jonah ("dove")[20] is found only for the OT prophet, right through to the third century A.D.[21]

18 The Greek phrasing of this declaration, when compared with that of v. 16, conveys a reciprocity which can be rendered in English only by heavy overtranslation. Simon has declared, "You are the Messiah," to which Jesus now responds, "And I in my turn have a declaration for you: You are Peter." Each "naming" also goes on to mention the father ("Son of the living God"; "son of Jonah"). "Messiah" was a title which implied a functional role (though that has not yet been spelled out); now Jesus gives to Simon a "title," a nickname, which (like the famous renamings in the OT: Abram/Abraham, Sarai/Sarah, Jacob/Israel) also speaks of his future role, and that role is spelled out in vv. 18-19. While Matthew has used the now familiar name "Peter" to designate Simon throughout his narrative (see on v. 16), he has made it clear that Peter was a second, given name (4:18; 10:2), and now is the time to explain it. This new name, *Petros,* representing the Aramaic *Kēphâ,* "stone" or "rock,"[22]

---

sure that Paul in Galatians is already aware of the tradition we know from Matt 16:17, and is "consciously staking out for himself a claim comparable with that made for Peter." The same point is argued more fully by D. Wenham, *GP* 5:24-28; cf. idem, *Paul,* 200-203. The argument is apparently reversible, depending on the date assigned to the tradition.

18. Almost the same textual phenomena also appear at John 21:15-17, where Simon is again identified by his father's name.

19. For valiant (though very different) attempts to suggest suitable common themes see M. D. Goulder, *Midrash,* 387-88; Gundry, 332. R. W. Wall, *JSNT* 29 (1987) 79-90, suggests that Luke saw Peter as a second Jonah in his mission to Cornelius in Acts 10, but does not relate this idea to Matt 16:17 beyond saying that the name given here "might have suggested" the connection to Luke.

20. M. Rastoin, *Bib* 83 (2002) 549-55, suggests that it is this meaning that Matthew has in mind in including the name: Peter, whose insight comes not from flesh and blood, is in this respect the son of the Holy Spirit (who has been seen as a dove in 3:16).

21. See J. Jeremias, *TDNT* 3:406-7.

22. The Aramaic name is transliterated in John 1:42, and Paul gives Peter's name in the form Κηφᾶς in 1 Cor 1:12; Gal 2:9-14, etc.

is otherwise virtually unknown as a personal name in the ancient world,[23] which makes it the more probable that Jesus chose it for Simon with a view to its literal meaning. He is to be a "Rock."[24] And one important function of a rock, as 7:24-27 has reminded us, is to provide a firm foundation for a building. So on this rock Jesus will build his church, and it will be forever secure.

This is such a bold image that attempts have been made to evade its obvious force. One has been to point out that the feminine noun *petra*, "rock," differs from the masculine name *Petros*. This is obviously true, but of questionable relevance. The masculine noun *petros* occurs infrequently in classical poetic Greek to mean a stone (i.e., a broken piece of rock), though the distinction from *petra* is not consistently observed.[25] But *petros* as a common noun is unlikely to have been familiar to Matthew's readers, as it is not found in the LXX (except twice in 2 Maccabees) or in the NT and related literature. In these writings the term for a stone is *lithos*. The Greek reader would therefore see here a difference in form but not in meaning, since *petros* was not now (if it ever had been) the term for a "stone." If Jesus was speaking in Aramaic, there would be no difference at all, with *kēphâ* occurring in both places. The reason for the different Greek form is simply that Peter, as a man, needs a masculine name, and so the form *Petros* has been coined. But the flow of the sentence makes it clear that the wordplay is intended to identify Peter as the rock.[26]

23. The only known pre-Christian use is in Aramaic in the fifth century B.C.; see J. A. Fitzmyer, in E. Best and R. McL. Wilson (eds.), *Text and Interpretation,* 127-30. No pre-Christian use of Greek Πέτρος as a personal name is known (ibid., 131-32). C. C. Caragounis, *Peter,* 17-25, lists various names related to πέτρα, but has found no example of Πέτρος as a name. For the idea, but not a name as such, cf. Isa 51:1-2, Abraham the "rock," though the metaphor is not there used in relation to building; Davies and Allison, 2:623-24, suggest a deliberate allusion here to that text, making Peter a second Abraham.

24. That the image is used with reference to Peter himself is confirmed by the startling recasting of the same image to describe Peter as a "stumbling block" only a few verses later (v. 23). The same "rock" which was meant to be a foundation can also be a rock to trip over (cf. the combination of the same ideas in 1 Pet 2:6-8, where, however, the rock is Christ).

25. For a full study of usage see C. C. Caragounis, *Peter,* 9-16. He concludes, "not only in classical but also in biblical Greek no clear-cut distinction can be made between πέτρα and πέτρος."

26. Gundry, 334, basing his argument on the assumption that the saying was composed in Greek and has no Aramaic substratum, and supposing (questionably, as I have argued) that πέτρος would have been familiar as a common noun so that the name would have been heard as a *contrast* with πέτρα, identifies "this πέτρα" not with Peter but with the πέτρα of 7:24-25, so that the foundation here spoken of is Jesus' words. Despite Gundry's protestation (n. 137), that is a remote allusion to expect the reader/hearer to detect, just as it has eluded most commentators; in this context "this" could not naturally be

A second escape route, beloved especially by those who wish to refute the claims of the Roman Catholic Church based on the primacy of Peter as the first pope, is to assert that the foundation rock is not Peter himself, but the faith in Jesus as Messiah which he has just declared.[27] If that was what Jesus intended, he has chosen his words badly, as the wordplay points decisively toward Peter, to whom personally he has just given the name, as the rock, and there is nothing in his statement to suggest otherwise. Even more bizarre is the supposition that Jesus, having declared Simon to be *Petros,* then pointed instead to himself when he said the words "this rock." This would be consonant with subsequent NT language about Jesus as the foundation stone (see below), but in regard to this passage it is the exegesis of desperation; if such an abrupt change of subject were intended, it would surely require a "but" rather than an "and," and could hardly be picked up by the reader without some "stage direction" (as in 9:6) to indicate the new reference.

All such apologetic rewritings of the passage are in any case beside the point, since there is nothing in this passage about any successors to Peter. It is Simon Peter himself, in his historical role, who is the foundation rock. Any link between the personal role of Peter and the subsequent papacy is a matter of later ecclesiology, not of exegesis of this passage.

When the image of a foundation stone is used in relation to the Christian church elsewhere in the NT, that stone is Jesus himself, not Peter, as in 1 Cor 3:10-11 (where Christ is the foundation, and Paul's apostolic work merely the superstructure) and 1 Pet 2:4-8 (which, if written by Peter himself, is particularly telling!). But Eph 2:20 expands the metaphor to a corporate foundation of "the apostles and prophets," with Christ as the cornerstone, and in Rev 21:14 the names of the twelve apostles are inscribed on the twelve foundations of the heavenly city. We shall see in 18:18 how the declaration of Peter's special authority here in v. 19 will be repeated in the plural with reference to the disciples as a whole. And here, as we have noted, Peter is acting as spokesman for the whole group. Yet it is Peter, not the Twelve, who is declared to be the foundation rock. So how does this corporate apostolic foundation relate to a specific foundational role for Peter alone? Matthew has made it clear in 10:2 that Peter comes "first" among the Twelve. Throughout the gospel he is mentioned far more often than any other disciple, and he regularly takes the lead. In the early chapters of Acts it is Peter who leads the disciple group in Jerusalem, and it is he who takes the initiative in the key developments which will constitute the church as a new, international body of the people of God through faith in Jesus: note especially his

---

heard as referring to something mentioned nine chapters earlier, when there is an obvious Πέτρος here for it to refer to.

27. A detailed argument for this interpretation is offered by C. C. Caragounis, *Peter.*

role in the bringing in of Samaritans (Acts 8:14-25) and Gentiles (Acts 10:1–11:18; 15:7-11). By the time James takes over as president of the Jerusalem church, the foundation has been laid. In principle all the apostles constituted the foundation, with Jesus as the cornerstone, but as a matter of historical fact it was on Peter's leadership that the earliest phase of the church's development would depend, and that personal role, fulfilling his name "Rock," is appropriately celebrated by Jesus' words here.

The metaphors of (foundation) rock and of building go together, and the latter will be used frequently in the NT for the development of the church, often linked with the idea of a new temple to replace the old one in Jerusalem (e.g., Mark 14:58; 1 Cor 3:9-17; Eph 2:19-22; 1 Pet 2:5); the metaphor of a new temple has already been introduced by Matthew in the reference to "something greater than the temple" in 12:6, and will underlie much of the language about the destruction of the temple in ch. 24 and the charge that Jesus planned to destroy and rebuild the temple in 26:61; 27:40. But modern English usage, in which "church" often denotes a physical structure, is liable to obscure the way this metaphor works here. When Jesus speaks of "building his church," the foundation rock and the verb "build" are the solid images on which the metaphor relies, but the word "church" does not contribute to the physical imagery. The Greek term *ekklēsia* never denotes a physical structure in the NT, but always a community of people. The new temple is not a building of literal stones, but consists of "living stones" (1 Pet 2:5).[28]

Ekklēsia was a common Greek term for an "assembly" of people (political and social as well as religious), but in a Jewish context it would be particularly heard as echoing its frequent LXX use for the "assembly" of the people of God, which thus denotes the national community of Israel. But now Jesus speaks with extraordinary boldness of *"my ekklēsia"* — the unusual Greek word order draws particular attention to the "my." The phrase encapsulates that paradoxical combination of continuity and discontinuity which runs through the NT's understanding of Jesus and his church in relation to Israel. The word is an OT word, one proudly owned by the people of Israel as defining their identity as God's people. But the coming of Israel's Messiah will cause that "assembly" to be reconstituted, and the focus of its identity will not be the nation of Israel but the Messiah himself: it is *his* assembly. How much of this theology of fulfillment the disciples could have

28. There is an interesting parallel in 1QS 8:4-8, where the council of the community (consisting of twelve members and three priests) is spoken of as "a holy house for Israel, a foundation of the holy of holies . . . the tested rampart, the precious cornerstone . . . the most holy dwelling . . . a house of perfection and truth." The building metaphors are strong, but the reference is, as here, to a community of people rather than a literal new temple.

been expected to grasp there at Caesarea Philippi is debatable, but for Matthew and his readers, as members of the Messiah's *ekklēsia,* the phrase would aptly sum up their corporate identity as the new, international people of God.

Much is sometimes made of the fact that Matthew, here and in 18:17, is the only NT gospel writer to use the term *ekklēsia;* his is therefore often dubbed "the ecclesiastical gospel."[29] There may be grounds for such a designation on the basis of the gospel's contents and tone, but not in these two uses of *ekklēsia.* In using this familiar LXX term to describe the community which will derive from Jesus' ministry, Matthew is developing an important typological theme of the continuity of the people of God in Old and New Testaments,[30] but it conveys nothing of the formal, hierarchical structures which our word "ecclesiastical" now suggests. Indeed, as E. Schweizer has memorably shown, Matthew is remarkably free of evidence of any such formal structure in the Christian community of his time.[31]

"The gates of Hades" is a metaphor for death, which here contrasts strikingly with the phrase "the living God" in v. 16. In the OT the "gates of death" describes the place to which dead people go (Job 38:17; Pss 9:13; 107:18), and in Isa 38:10 the phrase "the gates of Sheol" is used in the same way (cf. also Job 17:16, "the bars of Sheol").[32] "Hades" is the NT equivalent of Sheol (see on 11:23), and the same Greek phrase as here is used in this sense in LXX Isa 38:10 as well as in Wis 16:13; 3 Macc 5:51; *Ps. Sol.* 16:2. The "gates" thus represent the imprisoning power of death: death will not be able to imprison and hold the church of the living God. The metaphor, when seen against its OT background, does not therefore encourage the suggestion of some interpreters that "Hades" represents not death but the demonic powers of the underworld, which are then pictured as making an eschatological assault on the church.[33] Still less does it support the romantic imagery, sometimes derived from the traditional but incorrect translation "gates of *hell,*" of

29. I discuss this view in *Matthew: Evangelist,* ch. 7 (pp. 242-79).

30. The term ἐκκλησία was of course already familiar to Matthew and his readers as a description of the *Christian* community, both in its local (as in Matt 18:17) and universal (as here) forms, as is evident from the letters of Paul. But there is no need to see this more specifically Christian usage as the source of the term here; it is one which (whether in Greek or Aramaic) Jesus could expect his disciples to understand on the basis of its OT background.

31. "Matthew's Church" (1974); ET in G. N. Stanton (ed.), *Interpretation,* 149-77.

32. The Hebrew term in Job 17:16 is obscure ("chambers" or "gates" have been suggested in addition to the traditional rendering "bars"); others amend the wording to eliminate the metaphor (so LXX). For pagan Greek parallels to "the gates of Hades" see Keener, 428-29.

33. So Davies and Allison, 2:632-34, following J. Jeremias, *TDNT* 6:924-28; also D. C. Sim, *Apocalyptic,* 100-101. Cf. Carter, 335: "The gates of Hades open to let the attacking demons out." Similarly, J. Marcus, *CBQ* 50 (1988) 443-55. See contra Luz, 2:363-64.

the church as a victorious army storming the citadel of the devil. The imagery is rather of death being unable to swallow up the new community which Jesus is building.[34] It will never be destroyed.[35]

19 A change of metaphor now highlights the responsible role Peter will play in the development of this new *ekklēsia*. Taking up the imagery of Isa 22:20-22, Jesus declares Peter to be the steward (the chief administrative officer) in the kingdom of heaven,[36] who will hold the keys, so that, like Eliakim, the new steward (cf. Isa 22:15) in the kingdom of David, "he will open, and no one shall shut; he will shut, and no one shall open." The steward is not the owner. He has both authority (over the rest of the household) and responsibility (to his master to administer the affairs of the house properly). The keys[37] are those of the storehouses, to enable him to make appropriate provision for the household,[38] not those of the outer gate, to control admission.[39] The traditional portrayal of Peter as porter at the pearly gates depends on misunderstanding "the kingdom of heaven" here as a designation of the afterlife rather than denoting God's rule among his people on earth.[40]

---

34. Formally speaking, the syntax allows "it" to be understood of the rock rather than the ἐκκλησία, and on this basis it has occasionally been proposed that this is a promise of immortality to Peter himself; so B. P. Robinson, *JSNT* 21 (1984) 90, who sees the promise fulfilled not in Peter himself but in his papal successors. This is an unnatural reading in that it rejects the immediate antecedent in favor of a more remote one, and few readers have even noticed the theoretical possibility. Even in the light of the wordplay it would be odd for Peter to be referred to by a third-person feminine pronoun rather than as "you."

35. C. Brown, in J. E. Bradley and R. A. Muller (eds.), *Church, Word, and Spirit* 15-43, surveys at length the proposed readings of "the gates of Hades" and the exegetical issues involved, and then adds his own suggestion that the "death" in view is especially Jesus' own death, so that "the hostile, persecuting powers that put Jesus to death will not prevail against the messianic community."

36. I.e., under God's sovereign authority, which is what "the kingdom of heaven" means.

37. Luz, 2:364, points out that the plural "keys" is more suited to the steward than to the porter controlling a single entrance.

38. Cf. the role of the steward in 24:45; also Luke 16:1-8.

39. J. Marcus, *CBQ* 50 (1988) 443-55, proposes a novel view that the idea is not of admission but of releasing the powers of heaven to come to earth to combat the demonic powers, which he understands (see n. 33) to be denoted by "the gates of Hades."

40. In 23:13 Jesus declares that the scribes and Pharisees are shutting people out of the kingdom of heaven; there the sense of inclusion and exclusion is prominent, but the means by which it is being done is by their teaching, which is what the metaphor of "tying" and "untying" here conveys (see next paragraph). It is perhaps pressing the similarity of metaphors too far to discover a deliberate link: "the keys of the kingdom [are] taken from the scribes and the Pharisees and given to Peter" (Davies and Allison,

The metaphor of "tying up" and "untying" also speaks of administrative authority. The terms are used in rabbinic literature for declaring what is and is not permitted.[41] When the same commission is given to the whole disciple group in 18:18, it will be specifically in the context of dealing with sin within their community (see comments there). Such authority to declare what is and is not permissible will of course have personal consequences for the person judged to have sinned, but it is the prior judgment in principle which is the focus of the "tying" metaphor, and there, as here, the objects of both verbs will be expressed in the neuter, not the masculine; it is things, issues, which are being tied or untied, not people as such.[42] The historical role of Peter in Acts well illustrates the metaphor, as it was to him that the responsibility fell of declaring that Gentiles might be accepted as members of the new *ekklēsia* (10:1–11:18), though of course the exercise of his disciplinary authority could also have dire personal consequences for those who stepped over the mark (Acts 5:1-11; cf. 8:20-24). Peter's personal authority remained, however, that of the first among equals, and the extension of this commission to the rest of the disciples in 18:18 will ensure that he is kept in his place (cf. comments on the corporate extension of the foundation metaphor in v. 18).[43]

The heavenly "endorsement" of Peter's decisions is expressed (both here and in 18:18, twice in each verse) in the unusual syntax of future perfect passive verbs, "will have been tied up," "will have been untied." The construction is sufficiently unusual and indeed awkward in Greek to draw atten-

---

2:639). "Keys" as such are not mentioned in 23:13 (κλείω can mean "shut" without necessarily including the idea of locking), though a similar passage in Luke 11:52 speaks of the "key of knowledge."

41. Cf. the use of the same metaphor of "untying" in 5:19 for "setting aside" commandments. The rabbinic idiom occurs particularly in connection with oaths, which are and which are not "binding"; see Z. W. Falk, *JJS* 25 (1974) 92-100. For wider background to the usage see J. D. M. Derrett, *JBL* 102 (1983) 112-17. See also the similar language from *Tg. Ps.-J.* on Num 30, cited by W. G. Thompson, *Advice,* 192-93. This well-known usage makes it unnecessary to follow R. H. Hiers, *JBL* 104 (1985) 233-50, in tracing the origin of the terms to usage in connection with exorcism (as in 12:29), subsequently expanded to the "authority to deal with whatever problems might arise in the continuing years of the church."

42. The common tendency to read this saying in terms of the personal forgiveness (or otherwise) of sinners derives from associating it with John 20:23, even though the wording of the latter is quite different and its setting is after the resurrection. Whatever the intention of that saying, it is not legitimate to use it to control the meaning of this quite independent saying in a different gospel. I have discussed the matter more fully in my *Matthew: Evangelist,* 247-49.

43. On the limitations of the authority thus committed to Peter and to the other disciples in 18:18 see my *Matthew: Evangelist,* 249-51.

tion. If Matthew had wished to say "will be tied up," "will be untied" (as many translations have it), he could have used the much more natural syntax of a simple future passive to say it.[44] It seems likely, therefore, that these repeated future perfects are there for a reason. They change the sequence of actions. With simple futures, Peter would take the initiative and heaven would follow. But with future perfects the impression is that when Peter makes his decision it will be found to have been *already* made in heaven, making him not the initiator of new directions for the church, but the faithful steward of God's prior decisions. In this syntactical form the saying becomes a promise not of divine *endorsement,* but of divine *guidance* to enable Peter to decide in accordance with God's already determined purpose.[45]

20   See the introductory comments on how this unexpected verse (unexpected, that is, in Matthew, where, in contrast to Mark and Luke, it follows a warm endorsement of Peter's messianic declaration) fits into the sequence of the passage as a whole. We have noted that in 8:4; 9:30; and 12:16 Matthew has preserved a few instances of Mark's more frequent and more systematic account of Jesus' demand for secrecy after healing, but that in his presentation this is no longer a prominent feature of Jesus' ministry. But this is different. The secrecy after healings might be ascribed to a prudential concern to avoid excessive popular attention, but here there is no healing and no crowd. And the subject is not Jesus' miracles, but his identity as Messiah. Here and in 17:9, the two such demands where there is a more specifically christological focus, Matthew is no less emphatic than Mark on the need for secrecy. The phrasing indicates (and v. 17 has clearly affirmed) that the problem lies not in the accuracy of Peter's assessment — Jesus *is* the Messiah — but in the danger of using such language in public. We have noted the potential misunderstandings of the term "Messiah" in the comments on v. 16 above. Right up to 26:63-64, when the question is finally put and answered directly (though still, in Matthew, with a degree of reservation), Jesus never publicly claims in so many words to be the Messiah;[46] the only time he uses

---

44. It is true that in Koine Greek future perfects were sometimes used with a simple future sense, but the examples listed by Davies and Allison, 2:638, contain only one from the NT, and that is a quotation from the LXX (Heb 2:13, where the perfect is active, not passive as here). Luke 12:52 would have been a better choice: it is the only other future perfect passive in the NT, compared with no fewer than four in the two verses here under consideration. J. Marcus, *CBQ* 50 (1988) 448-449, argues for the full future perfect meaning, though the exegetical implications he draws from it are different.

45. See further my *Matthew: Evangelist,* 247, n. 11, and the detailed discussion of both the grammatical and exegetical issues in Carson, 370-74. Davies and Allison, 2:638-39, briefly give some reasons against this view.

46. 23:10, though formally addressed to "the crowds and his disciples," is for the disciples' benefit.

the term publicly will be in 22:42, where the challenge is couched as an academic argument which strikingly avoids identifying the Messiah with Jesus himself. The sequel in vv. 21-28 will make it clear how little Jesus' understanding of his own mission has in common with the conventional connotations of the word "Messiah."

III. FROM GALILEE TO JERUSALEM: THE MESSIAH AND HIS FOLLOWERS PREPARE FOR THE CONFRONTATION (16:21–20:34)

The Galilean period of Jesus' ministry has reached its climax at the most northerly point of his travels. This substantial central section of the narrative, which essentially parallels that in Mark 8:31–10:52, now bridges the gap between north and south, bringing Jesus and his disciples out of their home territory in the north and, for the first time in the Synoptic plan, into Judea in the south, where they are in "foreign" territory (see pp. 5-7) and where they will confront the hostile power of the religious authorities of Israel.

This geographical transition coincides with a significant change in the pattern of Jesus' activity and teaching, signaled by the formula "From that time Jesus began . . ." (16:21; see on 4:17). The declaration that he is the Messiah (16:16) leads him immediately to clarify what his messianic mission must involve, and the plain declaration in 16:21 that he must suffer, die, and be raised again will be repeated in 17:22-23 and with added emphasis in 20:18-19. The shadow of the cross thus falls across this whole southward journey, as Jesus tries to get his disciples to understand the paradoxical and unwelcome nature of his mission. We hear little now of crowds or of public teaching, even when the southward route necessarily leads through Galilee (17:22, 24; 19:1), and only two miracles are recorded in this section, the exorcism in 17:14-20 and the healing of the blind men in 20:29-34.[1] Instead Jesus' attention is focused on teaching his disciples, trying to instill into them the new and radically different values of the kingdom of heaven, and to prepare them for what lies ahead in Jerusalem. They prove to be slow learners, their "human thoughts" (16:23) being constantly shown up by their reactions to what Jesus says and does.

In most of this Matthew runs quite closely parallel with Mark, with little more respect shown to the disciples and their ineptitude, and with the

---

1. See the comments below on 17:24-27 as to whether a miracle is presupposed in that incident; it is certainly not the focus of the pericope and is not narrated as having actually happened.

same emphatic reiteration of Jesus' mission of rejection and death. The most substantial Matthean addition is a lengthy discourse in ch. 18 which, like those in chs. 5–7, 10, and 13, "takes off from" a brief Synoptic base (in this case Mark 9:33-37, 42-47) and considerably expands it with Matthew's own tradition of Jesus' teaching on the mutual concern and behavior of disciples. The distinctive theme of this, the fourth of Matthew's five major discourses, thus fits appropriately into the new focus of Jesus' teaching within this section as a whole. It is for the internal consumption of the disciple group rather than for wider public airing. Matthew also includes in 20:1-16 a parable, found only in his gospel and addressed apparently to the disciples, which further underlines the paradoxical nature of the values of the kingdom of heaven.

All this prepares the reader for the climax, when Jesus will arrive with his disciples outside the walls of Jerusalem in 21:1-9, and the subsequent confrontation with the unwelcoming city (21:10-11) and its sceptical establishment will test the disciples' allegiance to their Messiah as his predictions of rejection and death come to their fulfillment.

A. A GLIMPSE INTO THE FUTURE:
MESSIANIC SUFFERING AND GLORY (16:21–17:13)

The primary emphasis of this first part of the journey narrative is on the declaration that the Messiah must meet with rejection, suffering, and death, and that those who follow him must expect to share his fate. But set within this depressing message is a persistent reminder that that is not the end of the story. The prediction of 16:21 also includes resurrection on the third day (cf. also 17:9); those who lose their lives do so in order to gain them (16:25-26); the same Son of Man who is to be killed will "come in his Father's glory" as judge (16:27), and be seen to be king (16:28); and this paradoxical reversal is underlined by a unique "vision" (17:9) in which the rejected Messiah is seen in heavenly glory (17:1-8). A brief explanation to the puzzled disciples (17:9-13) links eschatological fulfillment with human rejection and death by comparing the fate of the returning Elijah (John the Baptist) with that of the Son of Man. There is thus running through these few pericopes a deliberate paradox of death and life (vividly brought out in the wordplay of vv. 25-26), of messianic suffering and glory. It is the same Son of Man who is both to die and to reign, and the glorious heavenly being on the mountain is the same Jesus who is going to Jerusalem to die. And if that is true for the Messiah, it can be true also for his followers if they stand firm in their allegiance to him. They will not escape suffering and death, but they are being prepared to look beyond it.

There is thus a thematic coherence to this whole sequence of sayings and incidents which justifies grouping its individual pericopes into a single section. How close that connection is depends on the interpretation of 16:28, and whether the "six days" of 17:1 are to be taken as inviting the reader to find in the vision on the mountain at least a partial fulfillment of Jesus' prediction. This in turn depends on how we interpret gospel language about "the coming of the Son of Man" (see above on 10:23 as well as comments below). But even if the link between 16:27-28 and the event of the Transfiguration is less specific, the latter provides (for the readers as well as for the three disciples involved) a vital counterbalance to the gloomy prospect of rejection and death which otherwise dominates this section.

1. Messianic Suffering Asserted and Challenged (16:21-23)

21 *From that time Jesus² began to show his disciples that it was necessary for him to go away³ to Jerusalem, and suffer many things from the elders and chief priests and scribes, and to be killed, and on the third day to be raised. 22 And Peter took him aside and began to rebuke him, saying, "God forbid,⁴ Lord. This shall never happen to you." 23 But Jesus turned and said to Peter, "Away with you; get behind me,⁵ Satan. You are a stumbling block to me, because your thoughts are not those of God but human thoughts."*

2. The first reading of both ℵ and B, supported by some Coptic versions, adds Χριστός, though it was removed by subsequent correctors in both MSS. While the title would pick up well from the declaration in v. 16 (though less easily from the suppression of the title in v. 20), and might suit Jesus' declaration now of his paradoxical "messianic" mission, it may have been added by later scribes for that reason. The expression Ἰησοῦς Χριστός, with Χριστός as a sort of "surname," is more typical of later Christian usage than of Matthew. It would also blur the similarity of this (formulaic?) introduction to 4:17, where the simple ὁ Ἰησοῦς is not disputed. The simple ὁ Ἰησοῦς is Matthew's normal style, and is far better supported here.

3. The compound verb ἀπέρχομαι indicates a radical departure to a new and more threatening environment (cf. 16:4). It does not of course suggest, as the English translation might, that he would go without the disciples.

4. The idiom ἵλεώς σοι, literally "Gracious to you," is normally, and probably rightly, taken as an abbreviation meaning "May God be gracious to you," and hence in this context "God forbid," though some grammarians prefer to see it as a (surely rather clumsy) attempt in Greek to reproduce the sound of the Hebrew *ḥālîlâ*, "far be it from (me etc.)" (so BDF 128[5]); the resultant sense is in any case the same. For this idiomatic use of ἵλεως to express strong repudiation of a suggestion see LXX 1 Kgdms 14:45; 2 Kgdms 20:20; 23:17; Isa 54:10; all but the last correspond to *ḥālîlâ* in the Hebrew.

5. The phrase "Away with you" (see on 4:10) is needed to pick up the echo of the dismissal of Satan after the third temptation, but the additional phrase here "behind me" does not follow naturally from it in English, hence the added imperative "get."

For the continuity between 16:13-20 and this following section, despite the obvious new beginning in a literary sense, see the introductory comments on those verses.[6] It is here that we begin to see why the declaration of Jesus as Messiah which has been so warmly welcomed in v. 17 is nonetheless not to be broadcast; if even Peter, who has just been commended for his christological insight, can get it so badly wrong, what sort of "human thoughts" might have been provoked by a public airing of the claim that Jesus was the Messiah?

The brief exchange in vv. 21-23 thus sets the tone for this new section of the narrative, both in that Jesus' paradoxical view of his messianic mission is firmly asserted and in that Peter's response represents the inability of the disciples to grasp it. The resultant contrast between "God's thoughts" and "human thoughts" neatly summarizes the nature of the problem. The way the disciples react to the idea of messianic suffering and "defeat" (here as elsewhere the element of resurrection on the third day is apparently so overshadowed by the suffering and death which precedes it that it seems to pass unnoticed) is symptomatic of the natural Jewish response. This is a concept of Messiahship which is going to be very hard to get across.

21   For the formula "From that time Jesus began to . . ." see on 4:17. The use of *deiknymi* ("show") for verbal communication is unusual, but perhaps emphasizes that this is an important new revelation (as in Acts 10:28; 1 Cor 12:31; Rev 1:1), making plain what has hitherto only been hinted at in 9:15 and 12:40.[7] The rejection and death of the Messiah are presented as "necessary." The basis of that necessity will begin to emerge in 20:28, where it is grounded in an obvious allusion to the prophetic model of God's servant who suffers for the sins of the people (cf. also 26:28), and will be made more explicit in 26:24 ("as it is written of him"), 31 ("it is written"), 54 ("how then would the scriptures be fulfilled, which say it must happen in this way?"), and 56 ("that the scriptures of the prophets may be fulfilled").[8] The OT basis for Jesus' belief that he must suffer and die is most probably to be found in the theme of the suffering and death of God's faithful servant which is found in Pss 22 and 69 (both to be picked up by allusion in the narrative of the passion), in the paradoxical inclusion of the themes of rejection and death in the cumulative portrait of the Messiah's mission in Zech 9–14 (to be taken up in the formula-quotations of 21:4-5 and 27:9-10 as well as in Jesus' words in 26:31), and above all in the suffering of the servant of Yahweh in Isa 52:13–

---

6. Cf. the comment of Luz, 2:379: "The transition to the new main section takes place not with a caesura but with a connecting bridge."

7. Cf. Mark's comment that Jesus now spoke "openly" (Mark 8:32).

8. Davies and Allison, 2:656, comment that δεῖ "in Matthew is the functional equivalent of γέγραπται."

53:12, to which we shall note allusions especially in 20:28 and 26:28, but which underlies much of the NT's exposition of the purpose of Jesus' death.[9]

The specific mention of Jerusalem as the destined place of rejection and death picks up the mention of Jerusalem as sharing Herod's "alarm" in 2:3 and as the origin of the scribal opposition in 15:1. In 20:17-18 the same point will be emphasized, so that by the time the narrative reaches the capital city in ch. 21 the reader is well prepared for the confrontation which follows. The source of the opposition which Jesus will meet in Jerusalem is more specifically spelled out by the mention of the three main groups who made up the Sanhedrin: the chief priests, the elders,[10] and the scribes. Hereafter Matthew (unlike Mark) will usually mention only the chief priests and the elders (though in 26:57 he speaks of the scribes and the elders), but here the opposing coalition is first introduced by the full listing. The only other time all three groups will be mentioned together is in their triumph over Jesus on the cross in 27:41.

The nature of the Messiah's "suffering" is as yet undefined; 20:18-19 will spell it out more fully. The fact that it comes from those who made up the Sanhedrin indicates the official and judicial rejection of Jesus by those who had formal responsibility for the life of Israel as the people of God, and so presents us with the paradox of the rejection of Israel's Messiah by the official leadership of Israel. And the outcome is not left in doubt: he will be killed. We have had a cryptic hint of this outcome in 9:15 and 12:40, and we have heard of the plans of the Galilean Pharisees (a different group from those listed here) to do away with him in 12:14. But now the impending death of the Messiah, which will be the focus of so much of the latter part of the book, comes unmistakably before us not just as a possible outcome of official hostility, but as a divine "necessity."[11] It is this unthinkable prospect which triggers Peter's instinctive response in v. 22.

Each of the three predictions of Jesus' death here and in 17:22-23 and 20:18-19 concludes with the contrasting prediction that he will be raised on the third day. Matthew regularly uses the passive verb "be raised" *(egeiro-*

9. I have explored these themes in my *Jesus and the OT.* See especially pp. 103-10 and 205-10 for Zech 9–14 and pp. 110-32 for Isa 53. On the latter see more fully my article in *TynBul* 19 (1968) 26-52.

10. Members of influential lay families, generally allied with the priests.

11. R. E. Brown, *Death,* 1468-91, discusses the whole range of Jesus' predictions of his own passion (both Synoptic and Johannine) in the light of the dogmatic exclusion of such "superordinary" prediction by the so-called "Jesus Seminar." Brown's cautious discussion provides a more historically responsible basis for assessing the predictions in the light of the religious and political realities of the day. He has no hesitation in speaking of Jesus' "foresight" in the light not only of his "reading the signs of the times" but also of his own conviction of the nature of his mission.

mai) to refer to Jesus' resurrection, rather than the more active *anistēmi* ("rise").[12] He uses the same term also for the raising of the dead other than Jesus (9:25; 10:8; 11:5; 14:2; 27:52). The two verbs seem to be used interchangeably for Jesus' resurrection in the NT generally, so that any attempt to draw a theological distinction between them is implausible (see p. 487, n. 2): that Jesus "was raised" by the power of God is not to be set over against his "rising" victorious. But the passive formulation perhaps encourages us to see in this event God's vindication of his faithful Messiah. Jesus' resurrection is predicted not only in the three passion predictions but also in 17:9; 26:32, in both of which it is not so much announced as taken for granted. His expectation of personal resurrection is not explicitly derived from the OT, but may have owed something to the influence of passages like Isa 52:13-15; 53:10-12; Pss 16:10-11; 118:17-18, 22, which link rejection, suffering, and death with subsequent vindication. But despite these predictions the disciples still seem to have been unprepared for the event, perhaps because the idea of the personal return to life of the Messiah (or indeed of any other person except by temporary resuscitation as in 9:25; 10:8; 11:5) was so foreign to their worldview that they instinctively heard the words as a metaphor for future vindication rather than as a literal prediction. It was the suffering and death that stayed in their minds rather than the resurrection.

Such a nonliteral hearing might also be supported by the phrase "the third day," if the disciples understood it against the background of Hos 6:2, where Israel corporately expresses its hope that "on the third day God will raise us up that we may live before him." There it is a metaphor for national restoration (compare the famous "resurrection" metaphor of Ezek 37:1-14). It may, however, be misleading to focus on "the third day" when seeking the OT background for Jesus' expectation of resurrection, since the focus in NT references to "the third day" is not on an OT text but on the fact recorded in the gospels of Jesus' actual time of lying in the tomb. Moreover, if an OT background is to be sought, a much more obvious one is ready to hand in this gospel in the allusion to Jonah in 12:40, where Jonah's "three days and three nights" (see p. 491, n. 12) are explicitly offered as a typological basis for interpreting Jesus' "three days and three nights" in the tomb. But the fact that in all three passion predictions Matthew uses "the third day"[13] rather than echoing the phraseology of LXX Jonah 2:1 (or Mark's phrase "after three days,"

---

12. There are, however, significant textual variants supporting ἀνίστημι in 17:9, 23; 20:19, which indicates the interchangeability of the two terms in Christian language about Jesus' resurrection (see further *NIDNTT* 3:276). ἀνίστημι is used in both its active and middle forms, without any discernible difference in the active meaning "rise."

13. Note also the similar phrases διὰ τριῶν ἡμερῶν and ἐν τρισὶν ἡμέραις when Jesus' resurrection prediction is alluded to in 26:61 and 27:40.

which Matthew uses only in 27:63) suggests that the third-day motif is more a reflection of the actual event than a deduction from scripture.

22 Peter's typically forthright and immediate response is unlikely to have expressed his feeling alone. Just as he spoke for the other disciples in declaring Jesus to be the Messiah, so now he expresses the horror they all shared at Jesus' perverted idea of the Messiah's mission. But as the one who has just uttered the honorific pronouncement of v. 16, he feels particularly let down and indeed shamed by the idea that his Messiah should prove to be anything less than a public success. The strong verb "rebuke" (used elsewhere for Jesus' stern commands to the wind and waves, 8:26, and to a demon, 17:18) not only conveys the intensity of Peter's shock and his boldness in expressing it, but also prepares us for the even more severe language with which Jesus will respond in v. 23. Peter's words indicate that he regards the prospect Jesus has outlined not as a goal to be fulfilled but as a disaster to be averted; other people might suffer at the hands of the authorities, but certainly not the Messiah. The strong negative (translated above by "never")[14] conveys that it is not just undesirable but unthinkable.

23 Jesus' counterrebuke of Peter is remarkably severe. Even the body language adds to the effect: whereas Peter had confidentially "taken Jesus aside," Jesus now "turns on him" to issue a public reprimand. The opening words directly recall the dismissal of Satan in 4:10, here strengthened by the addition of the words "behind me," to emphasize Jesus' dissociation of himself from Peter's ideology.[15] But whereas in 4:10 the "Enemy" (which is what "Satan" means) was the chief demon himself, here it is Jesus' loyal follower. For Peter to be addressed by this obnoxious name must have been deeply wounding, especially after the accolade in vv. 17-19. There is no parallel to such an address to a human being. But this is not merely extravagant abuse; the choice of this epithet suggests rather that behind the "human

---

14. BDF 365 characterize οὐ μή with the future indicative as "the most definite form of negation regarding the future."

15. It is tempting to recall the use of ὀπίσω μου, "behind me," in 4:19 and 10:38 (cf. also 3:11, where see comments), especially in view of the repetition of the phrase in that sense here in the very next verse, and so to suggest that in some way Jesus' words relate to Peter's status as disciple. But whereas to be "behind Jesus" in discipleship is an honorable status, the context here hardly allows that option, *pace* Gundry, *Mark,* 433, who suggests that "Jesus tells Peter to go back to his position among the disciples, where he belongs, following after Jesus, not taking him aside by walking ahead of him or at least beside him" (several other commentators favor this nuance). With ὕπαγε rather than δεῦτε it is hard to take ὀπίσω μου as expressing anything but repudiation, and the semitechnical use of the phrase in v. 24 and elsewhere should not be imposed on this very different context. But F. Belo, *Materialist,* 158, goes too far the other way when he takes Jesus' words to mean "Stop being my disciple"; despite Belo's claim, it is hard to see how the Greek could mean that (cf. Keener, 433, n. 99).

thoughts" of Peter Jesus discerns an attempt to divert him from his chosen course similar to that which Satan himself had made in 4:1-11. The same Peter who had just spoken what God had revealed to him (v. 17) is now speaking for Satan. Just as the third temptation in 4:8-9 had been to achieve worldly power by accommodating himself to Satan rather than attacking him, so now Peter's vision of Messiahship represents the easier way to power and authority, the gains without the pains. As long as he holds such a view, the "rock" on which the church is to be built proves instead to be a stumbling block.[16] The image goes neatly with the demand "get behind me": as long as Peter stands in front of Jesus, he is in his way, stopping him from getting on with his mission. He gets in the way of God's purpose for Jesus by his unthinking acceptance of "human thoughts." Peter has expressed only what comes naturally to the human mind when presented with the idea of power and authority which the title "Messiah" suggests. But human thoughts are not God's thoughts (Isa 55:8-9), and if they are not questioned they can stand in the way of God's purpose and derail it. In much of the rest of this section of the gospel Jesus will be seen persistently trying to undermine the "human thoughts" of the disciples so as to get them to see things from the perspective of the kingdom of heaven (note especially 19:23-30; 20:20-28).

2. The Disciples' Loyalty and Its Consequences (16:24-28)

24 *Then Jesus said to his disciples, "If anyone wants to be my disciple,[1] they must deny themselves and take up their cross and follow me. 25 For anyone who wants to save their own life will lose it, while anyone who loses their life because of me will find it. 26 For what good will it be for a person to gain the whole world but forfeit their own life? Or what can a person give in exchange for their life?[2] 27 For the Son of Man is destined[3] to come in his Father's glory with his[4] angels,*

16. Cf. 1 Pet 2:6-8 for a creative drawing out of these two opposite functions of a "stone."

1. Literally, "come behind me." As in 4:19, ὀπίσω μου, "behind me," is used as a term for discipleship; cf. 10:38, where the phrase is combined with the verb ἀκολουθέω, "follow," "be a disciple of," which also picks up the sense in 4:20. See the comments on 3:11 for this quasitechnical sense. Here the more specific translation is more appropriate than simply "follow" since ἀκολουθέω will occur in a separate clause at the end of the sentence.

2. See the comments below on the wordplay throughout vv. 25-26 on ψυχή, often translated in English as "soul," but used here both for "life" in the sense of physical life as opposed to being dead and for the "real life" or "self" which transcends death.

3. For this translation of μέλλω see p. 663, n. 2.

4. The Greek sentence structure makes it more probable that the antecedent of this "his" is the same as that of the preceding "his," namely, the Son of Man; the alternative

and then he will repay every person according to what they have done. 28 I tell you truly that there are some of those standing here who will certainly not taste death before[5] they see the Son of Man coming in his kingship."

The explicit concern of vv. 21-23 was with Jesus' own future suffering and death, but now these verses draw out what is also likely to have been a significant factor in Peter's dismay at Jesus' prediction: the death of the Messiah is likely to have serious implications for those who are identified as his followers. So a new stage direction ("Then Jesus said to his disciples") broadens the scene from the personal debate with Peter to a general pronouncement about discipleship, the first part of it echoing what Jesus has already said to his disciples in 10:38-39.[6] Subsequent Christian use of the language of "self-denial" (and even of "cross bearing") has blunted the force of Jesus' words.[7] They are about literal death, following the condemned man on his way to execution. Discipleship is a life of at least potential martyrdom. It may be legitimate to extrapolate from this principle to a more general demand for disciples to put loyalty to Jesus before their own interests and comfort, but that can be only a secondary application of the passage. Jesus' words are not to be taken as merely metaphorical. The "cross" and "losing life" which he speaks of are literal, and it seems clear from v. 28 that he did expect at least some of his disciples to be killed because of their loyalty to his cause (as indeed they were). Such a demand makes sense only in the context of a firm expectation of life beyond death, and the teasing wordplay of vv. 25-26 explores the contrast between that true and lasting "life" and the temporary "life" which is lost in martyrdom.

---

reading, taking "his Father" as the antecedent of this "his," is less natural in the Greek than the English might suggest.

5. In this context "until" (the more normal translation of ἕως ἄν followed by a subjunctive verb; see p. 882, n. 3) would imply that they will die at the time when they see, but that is not the point of the saying, which lies in their seeing the Son of Man coming in his kingship while they are still alive rather than in predicting the time of their death. "Before" better conveys this sense in English. Cf. p. 388, n. 7, for a similar issue in 10:23.

6. Mark at this point (8:34) rather confusingly introduces a "crowd" as the audience alongside the disciples, thus making these words a warning to potential as well as actual disciples. Matthew, perhaps aware that such a "crowd" is unlikely in his narrative setting in the district of Caesarea Philippi where Jesus has gone for a "retreat" with his disciples, has kept it simple by focusing only on the actual disciples, even though no doubt he expected his readers also to identify with them and take the warning as applicable also to themselves.

7. Hagner's translation, "they must practice self-denial," unfortunately fosters this weakened sense. Luz, 2:384-85, traces the development of the Christian ideal of "self-denial" in this broader sense.

The reason why it is better to die for Jesus is then explained in vv. 27-28. The note of judgment hinted at in v. 26 ("forfeit") now becomes explicit, and the judge is the Son of Man himself, that same Jesus for whom they have been called to give up their lives. It is a judgment which takes place in a heavenly scene, where the same Son of Man who is to die in Jerusalem will now be vindicated and enthroned in glory. The earthly threat of suffering and death is thus put into perspective: Jesus himself will rise above it, and his disciple, too, must expect to be judged (and where appropriate rewarded) in a more solemn and ultimate court than any earthly tribunal. It is in that context rather than in earthly self-preservation that true life is to be found.

Jesus' words following Peter's declaration at Caesarea Philippi thus close on a very different note from where they began. The prediction of his coming rejection and death still stands, but over against and beyond it his disciples are to set the vision of his ultimate vindication and glory, as judge and king in the presence of his Father and the angels. To speak of "the Son of Man coming" echoes the language of Dan 7:13-14 (as it did in 10:23), and here the added themes of glory, angels, judgment, and seeing confirm that the words are to be interpreted in terms of Daniel's vision. This is, then, a prediction of the vindication and enthronement of the Son of Man after his suffering and death, and that prediction is here given an even more explicit and emphatic time-limitation: it will be while some of those present are still alive. This time-limit is a remarkably persistent element in the allusions to Dan 7:13-14 in this gospel: in 10:23 this "coming" will be before the disciples have gone through all the towns of Israel; here it will be before some of them die; in 24:30, 34 it will be before the present generation is over; in 26:64 it will be seen by those who are Jesus' judges; and in 28:18 it is, after the resurrection, already a *fait accompli.* All this weighs heavily against the traditional Christian view that such language is meant to refer to the *parousia.* Indeed, we shall see in ch. 24 that when the *parousia* is explicitly spoken of, it will be in clear distinction from the events described as the "coming of the Son of Man." The "coming" is, as in Dan 7, a coming to God to receive power and glory, not a coming to earth. See further on 10:23. We shall consider below on v. 28 at what point before their death "some of those standing here" may be understood to have seen the coming of the Son of Man as king.

Mark at this point speaks both of the Son of Man coming in his Father's glory with the angels (Mark 8:38) and immediately afterward of some of those present seeing that "the kingdom of God has come with power" before they die (Mark 9:1). Luke less specifically speaks merely of their "seeing the kingdom of God" (Luke 9:27). In Matthew the link with Dan 7:13-14 is more consistently maintained in that the subject of the "coming" is in both cases the Son of Man. As a result the *basileia* is ascribed not to God but directly to the Son of Man himself, enthroned and given universal sovereignty as Dan 7:14 predicts. For Matthew, it seems, the "kingship of God/heaven" *is* the kingship of the Son of Man (see further on 13:41, and cf. 19:28; 25:31-34).

24 Following his declaration of what it will mean to fulfill the role of Messiah, Jesus now spells out the consequences for those who aspire to follow him. The first two imperatives in this verse are aorist, and the last present, so that it may be inferred that "denying oneself" and "taking up the cross" are single, initiatory acts, to be followed by a continuing life of "following," though this may be to press the usage of tenses too far. To "deny" means to dissociate oneself from a statement or a person, as in 10:33, and most famously of Peter in 26:34-35, 70-75. This is the only time in the gospels when the verb is used reflexively; in the rest of the NT it occurs reflexively only in 2 Tim 2:13, where for God to "deny himself" apparently means to prove untrue to his nature. In the light of what follows it must mean here to dissociate oneself from one's own interests, which in this case means the willingness to risk one's own life. It means putting loyalty to Jesus before self-preservation. The demand to "take up one's cross and follow" has already been made in 10:38; see the comments there for the image this would convey in first-century Palestine. It is interesting that the specific term "cross" is thus twice used of the disciples' fate (following Jesus) before it is made explicit in this gospel that that is the way Jesus himself is to die; this will first be predicted in 20:19 and repeated in 26:2. The crucifixion of some of Jesus' followers is also predicted in 23:34. Crucifixion is thus not associated exclusively with Jesus; its widespread use by the Romans also makes it a realistic prospect for those who will come to the attention of the hostile authorities as his followers. The NT does not record the crucifixion of any of Jesus' disciples, but Christian tradition has filled the gap with reference at least to Peter, Andrew, and Philip.

25 The idea of "taking up the cross" is now more explicitly spelled out. The play on the range of meanings of *psychē* ("life," "soul") is similar to that in 10:39, but will be further developed in v. 26. See the comments on 10:39, and also p. 399, n. 4, for the meaning and translation of the word. 10:39 was a simple contrast between "finding" and "losing" the *psychē,* expressed reciprocally. Here the first clause speaks not of "finding" life but "wanting to save it," thus underlining the volitional aspect already expressed in v. 24, "If anyone *wants.* . . ." A clear choice is thus offered between self-preservation at all costs and the risky business of following Jesus. But the self that is preserved by such a "safe" option is not worth preserving since the *true* self is lost. By contrast, the loss of *psychē* (in the sense of physical life) is the way to find *psychē* (in the contrasting sense of the true life which transcends death). As in 10:39, the key to this conundrum is the phrase "because of me." Loss of life as such is no gain; it is life lost out of loyalty to Jesus which ensures that *true* life is gained.

26 The wordplay continues. The prospect of "gaining the whole world" relates closely to the third temptation in 4:8-10, and the means there proposed, the worship of Satan, would indeed result in the loss of the *psychē*. So here is someone who has succeeded not only in remaining alive but also in attaining everything this world has to offer (the word translated "gain" is normally associated with economic acquisition; cf. 25:16-17, 20, 22), and who yet is ultimately the loser. The loss of that person's true *psychē* is described as a "forfeit," a term which often implies a judicial punishment or fine; the term is perhaps intended to make the reader think of the judgment of God which determines the person's ultimate destiny.

In the second rhetorical question the metaphor of "exchange" perhaps continues that of "forfeit": once the *psychē* has been forfeited nothing can buy it back or persuade the judge to rescind the penalty. But that is probably to look for too much precision in proverbial language. The saying (perhaps modeled on Ps 49:7-9) simply underlines the supreme importance of the *psychē;* nothing else compares with its value.[8]

27 The "for" which introduces this saying links this judgment scene with the disciples' loyalty and martyrdom: it is worth remaining faithful even to the loss of earthly life *because* there is an ultimate judgment to come, and on the outcome of that judgment the enjoyment of *true* life will depend. In Dan 7:9-10 the judgment takes place at the throne of the Ancient of Days, surrounded by ten thousand times ten thousand angelic attendants; when the Son of Man "comes" to that courtroom scene, it is as the one in whose favor judgment is given. But the result of that judgment is that he in his turn receives "dominion, glory, and kingship" over all nations forever (Dan 7:14), and so Jesus' saying here merges the two roles, and he comes not to be judged but to judge. He thus shares "his Father's glory," and the angels who surround the throne of God become "his angels" (see p. 635, n. 4). There may also be an echo here of Zech 14:5, the vision of the eschatological "coming" of God "and all the holy ones with him." Thus here, as in 25:31-34, Jesus speaks of his future glory as the Son of Man in terms which merge his role and dignity with that of God himself. It then follows naturally that in v. 28 the "kingship" is ascribed not to God but to the Son of Man.

As judge, he will "repay every person according to what they have done." The whole clause closely echoes Ps 62:12 (cf. Prov 24:12), which speaks of God's universal judgment; again language appropriate to God himself is transferred to the glorified Son of Man. "Repay" is used for divine re-

---

8. Compare Sir 26:14: "There is no exchange [ἀντάλλαγμα, as here] for a well-disciplined ψυχή" — though in that context the reference seems to be specifically to a wife's character!

wards in 6:4, 6, and 18, and here, too, the primary emphasis in context is probably on the reward for loyalty even to the point of martyrdom, the reward which results in "finding one's *psychē*." But the term is no less applicable to punishment for disloyalty, and a judgment of every person "according to what they have done" must be expected to envisage either reward or punishment, as will be spelled out more fully in 25:31-46. This saying is thus not only an encouragement to the faithful, but also a warning to those whose loyalty may be wavering. "What they have done" is a broad term, but in the present context the focus is not on lifestyle in general,[9] but on whether or not they have maintained their commitment to Jesus in the face of hostility. A more focused perspective on the basis of final judgment will be provided in 25:31-46, and we shall consider at that point how this prospect of judgment on the basis of "what they have done" relates to the Pauline doctrine of justification by grace through faith.

28 This future authority of the Son of Man is now given a time scale. Some of those standing there as Jesus speaks[10] will still be alive to see it. The solemn introductory formula "I tell you truly" (see on 5:18) and the emphatic wording "will by no means taste death" mark this out as a pronouncement to be noted. The wording seems unnecessarily heavy: "there are some of those standing here who will" seems a long-winded way of saying "some of you will," and "will by no means taste death before they see" seems a complicated way of saying "will live to see," or "will see before you die." But it is the preceding words which have produced this solemn wording. Jesus has spoken in vv. 24-26 of martyrdom as a realistic prospect for those who follow him, but not all of them will "taste" that death[11] before his kingship is revealed to them. Some of them may be martyred before that, but not all.

So how and when might *some* of them expect to see "the Son of Man coming in his kingship"? Perhaps the simplest answer is to link these words with the further allusion to Dan 7:14 in 28:18, where after the resurrection eleven of them ("some," not all, following the death of Judas) will encounter

---

9. B. Charette, *Recompense,* 108, suggests that the singular τὴν πρᾶξιν αὐτοῦ is used to indicate that a person's life "is seen as a unity, not divisible into so many individual deeds," but goes on to propose that in context the reference is specifically to self-denial, which "epitomizes the life of discipleship."

10. *Pace* B. D. Chilton, *God in Strength,* 267-74, who suggests that "those standing here" are Moses and Elijah, "the deathless ones" who will appear at the Transfiguration. Chilton's view depends on a debatable reconstruction of the "original" text in its Marcan form which eliminates "some of" and "here." Carson, 380-82, discusses Chilton's proposal.

11. A Semitic idiom for experiencing death; cf. John 8:52; Heb 2:9; *4 Ezra* 6:26. *The Gospel of Thomas* contains repeated promises that the enlightened disciple "will not taste death" (sayings 1, 18, 19).

Jesus now endowed with "all authority in heaven and on earth." But that will be only the beginning of an extended period during which the newly established sovereignty of the Son of Man will be increasingly visible. The imminent "seeing" of v. 28 need not then be thought to exhaust the range of application of the fulfillment of Daniel's vision. Verse 28 speaks of a more specific focus for the more general and timeless authority expressed in v. 27.[12] See above on 10:23 for this range of application of the Daniel vision, and below on 26:64 on when Jesus' judges in the Sanhedrin might be expected to "see" him as king and judge. So it is probably inappropriate to this saying to posit a specific time and place. The point is that while some of them are still alive it will have become clear to those with the eyes to see it that Jesus the Son of Man is enthroned as king.

But the immediate context here suggests another possibility which perhaps better suits the surprising phrase "*some* of those standing here." Six days later (an unusually precise time-connection in Matthew, which suggests a deliberate linking of the two pericopae 16:24-28 and 17:1-8) just three ("some") of those who heard Jesus' words in 16:28 were to witness a "vision" (17:9) of Jesus in heavenly glory.[13] This was a unique experience granted to those three alone; the rest of the Twelve would not see anything like that before they died. It may be questioned whether the vision on the mountain fully matches the promise of "seeing the Son of Man coming in his kingship," as that kingship was yet to be established after his death and resurrection — hence, no doubt, Jesus' instruction in 17:9 to keep the vision secret until after the resurrection. But it is likely that Matthew (and Mark and Luke, who use the same awkward phrase about "some of those standing here" and equally closely link that saying with the following account of the Transfiguration) saw in this vision at least a proleptic fulfillment of Jesus' solemn words in v. 28, even though the truth of Jesus' kingship was to be more concretely embodied in later events following his resurrection.

3. Glory Revealed on the Mountain (17:1-8)

> 1 *And after six days Jesus took with him Peter and James and his brother John, and led them up onto a high mountain by themselves.* 2 *And he was transformed before them: his face shone like the sun,*

12. See J. A. Gibbs, *Jerusalem,* 107-8.
13. The mention of the Transfiguration in 2 Pet 1:16-18 perhaps supports this interpretation, since the apostles are there described as having been "eyewitnesses of his majesty" and of his "honor and glory," and are thus in a position to testify to his "power and *parousia.*" Keener goes unusually far in supporting this interpretation in that (as in the traditional chapter division in Mark) he separates v. 28 from the preceding paragraph and links it with the Transfiguration story.

and his clothes became as white as light.[1] *3 And suddenly*[2] *they had a vision of*[3] *Moses and Elijah talking with Jesus. 4 Then Peter spoke up*[4] *and said to Jesus, "Lord, it is good that we are here. If you wish, I will make*[5] *three shelters here, one for you, one for Moses, and one for Elijah." 5 Suddenly, while he was still speaking, a radiant cloud overshadowed them, and they heard*[6] *a voice speaking from the cloud: "This is my beloved Son, with whom I am delighted;*[7] *listen to him." 6 When the disciples heard the voice, they fell on their faces and were terrified. 7 But Jesus came to them and touched them, saying, "Get up; don't be afraid." 8 When they looked up, they could not see anyone except Jesus himself alone.*

This is a unique incident within Jesus' ministry. The only comparable moment of supernatural revelation in the gospel is before that ministry begins, at the baptism of Jesus, when the opening of heaven, the visible descent of the Spirit, and the voice from heaven (speaking the same words as here) create a similarly numinous atmosphere and offer readers a glimpse behind the earthly scene. Jesus' identity as the Son of God, first declared in 3:17, is now reiterated with the same heavenly authority just at the time when his declaration about his coming suffering and death might have led readers to question it. Three aspects of the incident contribute to its christological force: (1) the

---

1. D and many of the versions substitute the more prosaic "white as snow," which will also appear in 28:3. Both the wide attestation of "light" and the more unexpected nature of the simile support "light" as the original reading.

2. Here and in v. 5 "suddenly" attempts to convey the dramatic effect of ἰδού, "behold."

3. Literally, "was (sing.) seen to them." The singular verb perhaps focuses on Moses, to whom Elijah is then added, but the following participle "talking" is plural, and in fact it is Elijah rather than Moses whose presence will be commented on in vv. 10-13; it is perhaps better therefore to take the singular verb as introducing the vision as a whole rather than Moses specifically.

4. As in 15:15, this translation attempts to draw out the force of ἀποκριθείς where it denotes a new initiative rather than a "reply" to a preceding speech; cf. also 11:25 for a similarly introductory use of ἀποκρίνομαι.

5. The majority of MSS have "let us make" (and a few "we will make"), but this is not only an obvious "improvement" following "it is good that *we* are here" (three builders for three shelters) but is also naturally explained by assimilation to the better-supported reading in Mark and Luke. It would have been surprising for Peter's suggestion of a solo building enterprise to be introduced if the plural reading was already established.

6. Yet another ἰδού (cf. "suddenly" in vv. 3, 5a). Here the effect of (literally) "behold, a voice speaking" is to focus on the experience of the startled disciples, hence "they heard."

7. See p. 117, n. 9, for this translation of the identical phrase.

visible alteration of Jesus demonstrates that he is more than a merely human teacher; (2) his association with Moses and Elijah demonstrates his messianic role; (3) the voice from heaven declares his identity as the Son of God.

At 3:17 it was not clear who else might have heard the heavenly declaration; readers of the gospel are the most obvious beneficiaries of the revelation. But this time it is not only readers who gain a privileged insight into the identity and mission of Jesus, but also a chosen group of disciples, and the whole episode is narrated from their point of view: Jesus "took *them* with him" and "led *them* up" (rather than he went and they followed); he was changed "before *them*"; Moses and Elijah "appeared to *them*"; we hear of Peter's rash words rather than of the experience of Jesus himself; the cloud "overshadowed *them*,"[8] and the voice which came from it addressed *them* directly, speaking of Jesus in the third person and calling on them to listen to him; we hear of *their* reaction, of Jesus' reassurance to *them,* and of what *they* could see when they opened their eyes. It is clear that Jesus took them up the mountain in order for them to have this experience, which he intends them to remember for future reference (v. 9). If what happened there provided Jesus himself with reassurance for his coming mission, we are told nothing of this; it is the disciples' christological understanding which is being enhanced, and the discussion as they return down the mountain (vv. 10-13) similarly focuses entirely on their grasp of the eschatological timetable. This is, then, an experience of the disciples rather than (as in 3:16-17) an experience of Jesus. The reflection on it in 2 Pet 1:16-18 will stress the privilege (and therefore the reliability) of the disciples as "eyewitnesses of his majesty" who also heard for themselves the voice from heaven.

The experience is described in v. 9 as a "vision,"[9] and is narrated in vivid terms of the disciples' visual and auditory sensations. The location on a high mountain away from other people adds to a sense of otherness and marks this incident as of a different character from the dealings with ordinary people and situations which make up the rest of the Galilean and journey narratives. The otherworldly atmosphere is further enhanced by the visible presence of Moses and Elijah, men long since removed from the earthly scene, and by the supernatural aura of brightness in the appearance of Jesus and of

---

8. "Them" could be taken to refer to the three disciples, or to Jesus, Moses, and Elijah, or to all six. But the fact that this clause follows Peter's speech and is followed by the disciples' reaction of fear probably encourages us to take it that the disciples (at least) were covered by the cloud.

9. While ὅραμα can in itself refer to anything "seen," it normally denotes something extraordinary; most of its other NT uses (all in Acts) denote private, internal revelations from God to an individual (several of them being when the person was asleep). The only one which is comparable to this "external" vision is Moses' ὅραμα of the burning bush (Acts 7:31), though even there no other human witness was present.

the cloud. We cannot, and need not, know what a cinecamera on the mountain would have recorded;[10] in the experience of the disciples heaven has invaded earth and the superhuman glory of the Messiah has been revealed. They, unlike their nine colleagues ("*some* of those standing here"), have been privileged to "see the Son of Man coming in his kingship" (16:28), even while he has still to complete the earthly mission of suffering and death through which that kingship is yet to be established.[11] The discussion on the way down the mountain will underline that paradox.[12]

Several features of this pericope recall Moses' ascent of Mount Sinai[13] in Exod 24:9-18: a selected group of companions,[14] an overshadowing cloud, and the appearance of God's glory on the mountain; *possibly* also the "six days"; see below. And the reappearance of Moses in this scene further links the two mountain experiences, while the echo of Deut 18:15-19 in v. 5 identifies Jesus as the coming "prophet like Moses." All this suggests that the figure of Jesus as a new Moses is a factor in Matthew's account, though it is important to note that whereas at Sinai Moses was the recipient of revelation, here Jesus is its subject, and it is the disciples rather than Jesus

10. Davies and Allison, 2:689-93, survey a wide range of "explanations" of the origin of the story, ranging from the historicist to the frankly antisupernaturalist, and including many attempts to derive it from literary influences; their own conclusion is cautiously in favor of a real incident involving unnatural radiance such as has been recorded of saints and mystics.

11. In view of the otherwise unexplained reference to Jesus' coming resurrection in v. 9, we should note the contention of M. E. Thrall, *NTS* 16 (1969/70) 310-12, that the vision on the mountain is also to be understood as a "prefiguration of the Resurrection." She supports this suggestion by tracing verbal and conceptual links between the Marcan form of this pericope and Mark's account of the empty tomb. The presence of Moses and Elijah, the deathless ones (see below on v. 3), thus enhances the glory of the Son of God whose heavenly glory, unlike theirs, will be achieved through conquest of death (ibid., 314-15).

12. Davies and Allison, 2:706-7, offer a suggestive comparison between this pericope and the account of Jesus' crucifixion in 27:32-54, noting several literary links which contrast and yet connect the glory here and the humilation there, both of them culminating in a declaration that Jesus is the Son of God.

13. The clear and sustained allusion to the Sinai stories which we shall note below makes it very unlikely that Matthew intended the mountain to be seen in terms of Mount Zion, as the thesis of T. L. Donaldson, *Jesus,* requires. His discussion (ibid., 149-56) therefore focuses on seeing the Transfiguration "in the context of the whole gospel" rather than on features of the narrative itself, though he attempts (ibid., 146-48) to support the Zion identification by means of Ps 2:6, the verse prior to the one allegedly echoed in the declaration "This is my Son" (but see on 3:17 for the tenuous nature of this allusion given the third-person form of the declaration).

14. Three are singled out for mention in Exod 24:1, 9, though the group was in fact much larger, with seventy-three going up the mountain, while only Joshua went on with Moses to meet with God (vv. 9, 13-14).

who are in the position of Moses, seeing the heavenly glory and hearing the voice of God. Nor is Jesus on this "high mountain" presented as the law-giver, as he was in the scene in the hills in 5:1ff. The link is thus more one of motif and atmosphere than of direct typological correspondence. But this pericope reinforces the perception of the careful reader of ch. 2 that Jesus comes, as Moses did long ago, to fulfill God's purpose of deliverance for his people. At the same time, he is also clearly marked out as a greater than Moses, both by the heavenly voice which speaks of him alone in terms never used of Moses, and by the fact that Moses and Elijah soon disappear, leaving Jesus alone to carry out the final act of deliverance.[15]

1 Whereas the rest of this pericope is narrated in the aorist, here we have two historic presents, perhaps intended (like the threefold use of *idou,* "look," in vv. 3 and 5; see p. 642, nn. 2 and 6) to get the reader imaginatively involved in a dramatic new development. "After six days" stands out as a more precise temporal connection than Matthew provides elsewhere. In view of the themes of mountain, glory, and cloud which will follow, it is possible that it is intended to reflect the "six days" during which the cloud of God's glory covered Mount Sinai in Exod 24:16, but the parallel is far from close: here the six days are merely the interval before the next story begins.[16] It is more likely that this period of roughly a week (Luke says "about eight days") is mentioned to show that the experience on the mountain followed closely after Jesus' prediction about seeing the Son of Man coming in his kingship, so as to invite the reader to link the two together (see on 16:28 and introductory comments above). The specific time mentioned is as likely to be derived from memory/tradition as from an OT allusion.

The special place of Peter, James, and John as an "inner circle" within the Twelve will also appear in Gethsemane (26:37); see also the comments on 20:21. Mark has made more of this small group of Jesus' closest companions (cf. Mark 5:37 and, with Andrew, 13:3), but in Matthew, too, they with

15. The Moses typology is explored by D. C. Allison, *Moses,* 243-48 (cf. also the earlier treatment by W. D. Davies, *Setting,* 50-56). Allison takes the shining of Jesus' face (compared with Moses in Exod 34:29-35) as an essential element in that typology, and so has to recognize (and respond to) the objection that radiance is also attributed to other figures in Jewish (and indeed Christian and pagan) legend. It should be noted, however, that my presentation of the case for a Moses typology above does not even mention the change in Jesus' apppearance (see on vv. 2 and 6-8 below for some cautions against basing too much on the link with Exod 34:29-35), but depends on other features of the narrative. The primary OT background to this incident is found in Exod 24 rather than Exod 34.

16. A closer parallel may be suggested by pointing out that according to Exod 24:18 Moses "went up" on the mountain *after* the six days (so Gundry, 342), but unfortunately the same verb has already been used in vv. 9, 13, and 15, *before* the cloud's six-day presence has been noted. Matthew's six days have nothing to do with the duration of the cloud.

Andrew are the first four disciples called (4:18-22), and they appear first in the list at 10:2-4. This present expedition and the prayer in Gethsemane[17] are perhaps particularly intimate moments, at which the full group of the Twelve would have been too many. At any rate, the restriction to only three here is by Jesus' deliberate choice.[18] Only "*some* of those standing here" (16:28) are to have the vision.

The scene is "a high mountain by themselves"; Jesus is taking them as far as possible from other people and from everyday life. Contrast the occasions when Jesus has gone "into the hills" and there has been surrounded by crowds (5:1; 15:29).[19] Here (as in 4:8) we are to think of a specific "high mountain"[20] where they could be alone, but which actual mountain it was cannot and need not be determined. The last recorded location was "the region of Caesarea Philippi" (16:13), and Mount Hermon, which rises to the northeast of Caesarea Philippi, is by far the highest mountain in or near Palestine (2826 meters). But the fact that they will come down from the mountain to meet an apparently Jewish crowd aware of the healing reputation of Jesus and his group suggests a location further south, and the traditional site at Mount Tabor in southern Galilee would be easily reached in six days from Caesarea Philippi. Tabor is not nearly so high at 588 meters, but to one who has climbed up it from the plain below it certainly seems like "a high mountain."[21] But there are other heights, such as Mount Meron[22] (1208 meters), the highest

---

17. Luz, 2:399, characterizes these two episodes as the "high point" and the "low point" of the story of Jesus.

18. It is not likely to be a purely literary motif inspired by Moses' taking Aaron, Nadab, and Abihu with him up the mountain in Exod 24:1, 9; those three were only part of a total entourage of seventy-three, and none of them went the whole way with Moses, but only Joshua (vv. 13-14).

19. There is thus a fundamental difference between this episode, the only time when Jesus takes his disciples up a "high mountain" away from other people, and the other episodes in the gospel using the term ὄρος in a less specific sense with which Donaldson's thesis (see p. 644, n. 13) links it.

20. It is possible that Matthew intends us to remember the "very high mountain," also apart from other people, where Jesus refused Satan's offer of earthly kingship (4:8-10) — an episode just recalled also in 16:23. If so, this mountain reveals by contrast the true basis of Jesus' kingship as the Son in whom God delights.

21. It is often objected that there was a military fort on the top of Mount Tabor at the time, so that it was not a place to be "by themselves." There were military installations there at least from the time of Antiochus III and of Alexander Janneus, but it is unlikely that they occupied more than a small part of the extensive summit area. It was not until the outbreak of the Jewish War that Josephus built a defensive wall around the whole summit (Josephus, *War* 2.573; 4.54-56).

22. This location is attractively argued by W. L. Liefeld in R. N. Longenecker and M. C. Tenney (eds.), *New Dimensions,* 167, n. 27.

mountain in Galilee, which is more nearly en route for Capernaum (v. 24), and so might better fit Matthew's few geographical indications.

2 The description of Jesus' changed appearance recalls other biblical descriptions of heavenly beings who appear among humans. In this gospel note the appearance "like lightning" and the white clothes of the angel in 28:3, and cf. Mark 16:5; Luke 24:4 (clothes like lightning); John 20:12; Acts 1:10 (white clothes). For a fuller account of such an angelophany see Dan 10:5-6, and cf. the description of the risen Christ in Rev 1:13-16. God himself is "wrapped in light as with a garment" (Ps 104:2). Note also the ultimate glory of the righteous in heaven "shining like the sun" in 13:43 (cf. Dan 12:3).[23] The visual "transformation"[24] is not so much a physical alteration as an added dimension of glory; it is the same Jesus, but now with an awesome brightness "like the sun" and "like light." Or, one might better say, with the dullness of earthly conditions temporarily stripped away, so that the true nature of God's "beloved Son" (v. 5) can for once be seen.[25] Cf. the reflection on this incident in 2 Pet 1:16-18, which focuses on the disciples' perception of Jesus' "majesty," "honor," and "glory." Here on the mountain we have at least a foretaste of the coming of the Son of Man "in his Father's glory with his angels" (16:27), though the heavenly beings who accompany him here are not angels but glorified humans.

All this indicates that what the disciples saw on the mountain is on a different level from the shining of Moses' face when he came down from the mountain in Exod 34:29-35.[26] Moses shone for a time with a reflection of the divine glory he had seen; Jesus shone with his own heavenly glory. Moses' radiance was derivative, Jesus' essential. The voice in v. 5 will make a clear

---

23. Cf. Paul's expectation of a glorious transformation after death (1 Cor 15:51-53; Phil 3:21).

24. The verb μεταμορφόομαι does not in itself determine the nature of the "change" (nor does the traditional English rendering "transfiguration," derived from the Vulgate). Its derivation suggests a difference in "form," but it is used less literally in Rom 12:2. The "transformation" in 2 Cor 3:18, where it is a matter of enhanced "glory" rather than physical alteration, provides a probable analogy to the present use of the verb (possibly even "a deliberate allusion to the transfiguration story"; so Hagner, 2:492).

25. Is this what John 1:14 refers to: "We saw his glory, glory as of the Father's only Son"?

26. In view of the emphasis placed on this aspect of the story by Allison (see p. 645, n. 15) as a basis for discerning a Mosaic typology, it is interesting that there is no clear verbal allusion here (other than the word "face") to the shining of Moses' face on Sinai in Exod 34:29 in either Hebrew or LXX (*pace* R. H. Gundry, *Use,* 82-83). Davies and Allison, 2:685-86, are clearly uncomfortable with the lack of a "direct verbal allusion." It should also be noted that the account of Moses' face shining relates to his coming down from the mountain, whereas Jesus shone *on* the mountain but is not said to be visibly different when coming down from it.

separation between Moses and Elijah, the servants of God and witnesses to his glory, and Jesus, whom God uniquely designates as his Son.

3 Jesus' otherworldly appearance is underlined by the presence with him of two well-known inhabitants of heaven. Several levels of significance or symbolism may be suggested for the appearance of Moses and Elijah[27] here. Both are men of God whose earthly life ended in a supernatural way: Elijah was taken up to heaven without going through death (2 Kgs 2:11), and mystery surrounds the end of Moses on Mount Nebo.[28] So these two men, along with Enoch (Gen 5:24), became known as the deathless ones. This was no doubt a major factor in the belief that Elijah would come back in the last days (Mal 4:5, and see on vv. 10-11 and above on 11:14), and while there is less evidence of a clear expectation of a return of Moses himself,[29] the promise of a "prophet like Moses" in Deut 18:15-19 played a significant role in Jewish (and still more Samaritan) eschatological hope.[30] In John 1:21 Elijah and "the prophet [like Moses]" are suggested together as categories (alternative to "Messiah") to explain the role of John the Baptist as an eschatological figure.[31] These two men therefore also symbolize the coming of the messianic age, and their conversation with Jesus marks him out the more clearly as the Messiah who comes as the climax to their eschatological role. There are also further connections in that both Moses and Elijah went up on Mount Sinai (Horeb) to meet with God and see his glory (Exod 24:15-18; 33:18-23; 1 Kgs 19:8-13). Both men also suffered rejection and hostility from the people to whom they were sent, and so prefigured the experience of Jesus the Messiah. Some or all of the above may have come to the minds of the three disciples on the mountain, and to those of Matthew

---

27. Mark mentions Elijah before Moses, probably because it is Elijah, not Moses, who will be the subject of the following dialogue and whose eschatological return was most commonly expected. Matthew, perhaps influenced by the various Mosaic motifs in the story, puts the names in the more normal historical order.

28. Deut 34:5-6 records that he died alone with God on the mountain and that he had no known grave. Patristic writers speak of a book called *The Assumption of Moses* (perhaps the latter part, or a revised edition, of the extant *Testament of Moses,* which breaks off before Moses' death) which apparently spoke of his removal to heaven (cf. Jude 9). Josephus, *Ant.* 4.323-26, says that Moses "disappeared" in a cloud, but that he wrote about his own death so that people would not "presume to say that he had returned to the Divine because of his exceptional virtue." For Jewish belief that Moses did not die see J. Jeremias, *TDNT* 2:939, n. 92.

29. See J. Jeremias, *TDNT* 4:856-57; more commonly Moses is seen as a typological model for the coming Messiah (ibid., 857-64).

30. For traces of this expectation in the NT see John 1:21; 6:14; 7:40; Acts 3:22-23; 7:37.

31. Cf. also the "two witnesses" of Rev 11:3-13, who are generally, in the light of their powers described in v. 6, taken to be modeled on Moses and Elijah.

and his readers as they reflected on the meaning of the appearance of these heavenly visitors with Jesus and on what this implied for the nature of Jesus' messianic mission. It is less likely that they would have thought, as popular interpretation commonly suggests, of Moses and Elijah as representing the law and the prophets (Elijah, after all, was not one of the writing prophets of the OT); they are there rather in their personal and symbolic capacities as figures in Jewish eschatological expectation and as prefiguring aspects of the Messiah's role. It is in that light that the disciples will question Jesus about Elijah in v. 10.

4 Peter again takes the initiative, speaking on behalf of the other two disciples, though his actual proposal is (probably, see p. 642, n. 5) to build three shelters himself. "It is good that we are here" in context means not so much "we are glad/privileged to be here" but rather "it is a good thing that we are here because we are available to do what needs to be done." Peter intends to be not just a spectator but a useful contributor to the event. A bare mountaintop is no place to entertain such august visitors: Peter, as a practical man, will provide them with accommodation befitting their dignity, using the best materials the mountaintop affords. The "shelters" (from the heat of the sun) would presumably have been made with branches and leaves, like those regularly made for the festival of Tabernacles.[32] Peter's proposal indicates a surprisingly "concrete" interpretation of the vision, though Mark and Luke ("not knowing what he was saying") discourage us from regarding it as a thought-out response. If Peter was inappropriately placing Jesus merely on a level with Moses and Elijah, that mistake is to be quickly corrected by what follows. Matthew, unlike Mark and Luke, does not comment on the appropriateness of Peter's words, but simply allows them to be superseded by events and forgotten.

5 In the OT the presence of God in the wilderness (Exod 13:21-22) and in the sanctuary (Exod 33:9-10; 40:34-38; 1 Kgs 8:10-11) is symbolized by a cloud, not just any cloud but one associated with fire and glory. Matthew's description of the cloud here as "radiant" (*phōteinos,* "full of light") recalls that motif; cf. also the "cloud with brightness around it and fire flashing from it" which introduces the vision of God in Ezek 1:4. Later Jewish tradition developed this motif into the concept of the Shekinah, the visible glory of God.[33] On this high mountain the radiant cloud especially recalls the cloud

---

32. The Greek word used here is the same as LXX uses for those "tabernacles." Nothing in the context suggests, however, that this narrative is set at the festival of Tabernacles (as was argued by H. Riesenfeld, *Jésus transfiguré;* see contra T. L. Donaldson, *Jesus,* 144-46). To build a shelter against the sun was a normal action of those who found themselves in an exposed position (cf. Jonah 4:5-8).

33. For the rabbinic concept of the *šᵉkînâ* see, e.g., W. Van Gemeren, *ISBE* 4:466-468. In 2 Macc 2:8 we find the belief that "the glory of the Lord and the cloud" would

which overshadowed Mount Sinai when Moses went up to meet God (Exod 19:16; 24:15-18); not only did the cloud visually proclaim God's presence, but his voice was heard speaking from it (Exod 19:9; 24:16; 34:5). And as in Exod 19:9 God spoke from the cloud so that the people might recognize Moses' special relationship with God and thus trust him, so now the voice of God addresses not Jesus but the disciples, calling on them to "listen to him." When God spoke the same words at Jesus' baptism (3:17), Matthew's third-person form (in contrast with Mark's and Luke's accounts) seems to assume that people other than Jesus heard the words (see comments there); here there is a ready-made audience, and all three Synoptists agree on a third-person statement, followed this time by a direct, second-person command to the disciples, "listen to him."

For the divine declaration see on 3:17, where the words are identical. Its purpose at this point is to confirm the disciples in their newly discovered christological understanding (which has been severely tested by Jesus' declaration of the nature of his messianic mission in 16:21), underlining especially the truth that this Messiah is, in Peter's words, "the Son of the living God" (16:16). It also marks Jesus out as in a different category from even the greatest of God's OT servants, Moses and Elijah. At the same time, the echo of Isa 42:1 (see on 3:17) recalls again the figure of the suffering and dying servant of God and so reinforces Jesus' declaration that he must suffer and be killed.

The added command to listen to him (which in this context probably relates particularly to the unwelcome announcement he has made in 16:21-28) is probably to be understood as an echo of Deut 18:15, 19, the promise of a future prophet like Moses to whom the people are to listen. The presence of Moses on the mountain underlines this echo. The purpose of the sending of that prophet was so that the people would not need to undergo again the frightening experience of listening directly to the voice of God himself (Deut 18:16-18); so also God's people of the new age are to hear the voice of God through the words of Jesus. Here on the mountain, and only here, does God speak to them (or rather their three representatives) directly, and they, like their OT counterparts, find the experience terrifying.

6-8 The disciples' fear on hearing God speak recalls that of the Israelites at Sinai: Exod 20:18-21; Deut 4:33; Heb 12:18-21. For falling on one's face as a mark of awe or entreaty cf. 26:39; Luke 5:12; 17:16; 1 Cor 14:25; Rev 1:17; 7:11; 11:16; in the OT it is the human response to a meeting with God or with a heavenly being (Ezek 1:28; Dan 8:17; 10:9, 15). Matthew frequently speaks of people, including the disciples, "coming to" Jesus to ask

---

again appear in the eschatological age when the hidden tabernacle and ark would be finally revealed.

for his help or to raise an issue with him; but he uses the common verb *proserchomai* with Jesus as the subject only here and in 28:18, in each case when the disciples are overwhelmed by a supernatural event. Together with his touch, it conveys a reassuring sense of normality restored; the dazzling figure of v. 2 has become again the familiar Jesus, no longer conversing with numinous figures from the past, but back with his disciples in the present. His straightforward words of reassurance reinforce the point. The frightening vision is over.

The final three words of the pericope, *auton Iēsoun monon,* "Jesus himself alone," confirm the return to normality: Jesus is himself again, and the heavenly visitors are nowhere to be seen. Their presence was only temporary, and now the true Messiah, to whose coming they pointed forward, remains in possession of the stage. But his mission will be accomplished not in heavenly glory but in the normal conditions of earthly life; it is interesting that whereas Moses' face was shining when he came down from the mountain (Exod 34:29-35), the following context does not suggest that Jesus was in any way different in appearance after his temporary transformation.[34]

4. Glory and Suffering: Elijah, John, and Jesus (17:9-13)

> 9 *As they were coming down from the mountain, Jesus gave them this instruction: "Do not tell anyone about the vision[1] until the Son of Man has been raised from the dead."* 10 *The disciples asked him, "So why do the scribes say that Elijah must come first?"* 11 *He replied, "It is true that[2] Elijah is coming and will set everything to rights;[3]* 12 *but I tell you that Elijah has already come, and they did not recognize him but did to him whatever they wanted. In the same way the Son of Man*

34. Mark 9:15 says that when Jesus came down from the mountain the crowd ἐξεθαμβήθησαν, an unusually strong word for astonishment, which *might* be taken to suggest that they could still see a visual difference in him, as the people did with Moses (Exod 34:30-35), though in my *Mark,* 363-64, I question this inference. Matthew, however, omits any such comment.

1. See p. 649, n. 9, for the meaning of the word.

2. This phrase conveys the force of the particle μέν, which accepts the truth of the scribal teaching but only to set over against it (δέ) an outcome which the scribes had not envisaged. Hagner, 2:496, here adds "As the scriptures say," but this is surely inappropriate since the question has been about what the *scribes* teach, not about its scriptural authority.

3. The verb is ἀποκαθίστημι, usually translated "restore," whose essential force is conveyed in BDAG 111b by the paraphrases "to change to an earlier good state or condition"; "to return someone to a former place or relationship." It is the verb used in 12:13 for the "restoration" of a paralyzed arm.

is destined⁴ to suffer at their hands." 13 Then the disciples understood that he had spoken to them about John the Baptist.

This brief dialogue unpacks something of the meaning of the vision on the mountain. It concerns two subjects, the place of Elijah in the process of messianic fulfillment (vv. 10-12a, 13) and the fate of Jesus himself (vv. 9 and 12b). An apparently "academic" question from the disciples about the eschatological role of Elijah is turned by Jesus into a basis for understanding his coming suffering and death, once it is accepted that Elijah is not just a figure in a vision on the mountain but has also already taken his place as an actor in the eschatological drama. The return to the theme of persecution and suffering, both that of John the Baptist and that of the Son of Man, brings us back to the subject which had occupied the disciples before their experience on the mountain, and forces them to integrate this unwelcome concept somehow with the glory they have just witnessed. The resplendent Son of God of the mountain is the same as the suffering Son of Man. The death and resurrection which he has so recently predicted remains his paradoxical destiny.

Matthew's account makes the connection of the two subjects a little easier than Mark's unexplained alternation between Elijah and the Son of Man (Mark 9:11-13), his connecting particle (see on v. 10) attempts to ease the sequence of thought, and his explicit identification of John the Baptist as the returning Elijah (as in 11:14) helps the reader to follow the train of thought. But the whole paragraph remains a rather cryptic exchange.

9 Jesus had deliberately taken only three of his disciples up the mountain to experience this vision, and now he reinforces that selective intention by telling them not to divulge what they have seen, even to their fellow disciples. Their natural tendency to talk (and boast?) about their experience must be curbed. But here, in contrast to when he commanded them to be silent about his Messiahship, there is a time limit. After his death (which is presupposed) and resurrection they may talk about it. This suggests, as we have also seen with regard to 16:20, that the reason for the injunction is primarily to avoid popular misunderstanding, or indeed in this case also misunderstanding by the remaining disciples. As long as his mission of suffering, death, and resurrection remains to be accomplished, he does not want people distracted by an account of his heavenly glory which, even if it did not in itself encourage nationalistic hopes of a political Messiah, would be likely to turn their thoughts away from the cross to the glory. After the event, no such distraction would be possible, and Jesus would no longer be there to be a potential political leader. In the light of

---

4. For this translation of μέλλω see p. 663, n. 2.

their Easter experience, and only then, the disciples may be expected to have a clear enough grasp of what it all means to be able to talk responsibly about what they have just seen.

Jesus' confident expectation that he will be raised from death, repeated so soon after the prediction of 16:21, maintains the ultimate perspective of his vindication and kingship (as in 16:27-28), but it will be his suffering that, even after the glory on the mountain, forms the more immediate focus in v. 12b. So the paradox continues.

10 The disciples' question changes the subject. Rather than ask about the experience as a whole, they raise a question which has been brought to their minds by seeing Elijah on the mountain. In Mark the change of subject is abrupt, but Matthew's connective particle *oun,* "so," suggests some connection with what Jesus has just said. The link is not close, however: the "so" probably connects their question loosely to the experience itself rather than marking a specific inference from Jesus' instruction to keep quiet about it or from his mention of his resurrection.[5] Elijah was, in popular expectation as well as in scribal teaching,[6] expected to be a player in the eschatological drama (see on 11:14); that is why he, rather than Moses, is the subject of the disciples' interest. He "must" come first because this had been prophesied in Scripture (Mal 4:5-6); cf. the comments on the "necessity" of Jesus' predicted destiny in 16:21. So was Elijah's appearance on the mountain the fulfillment of that expectation? If he was to come "first" (Mal 4:5 says it will be "before the great and terrible day of the LORD comes"), what does his appearance at this point indicate about the coming of that great day, and how does it relate to the coming of the Messiah (who is not mentioned in Malachi's prophecy),[7] especially in the light of what Jesus has so recently said about his future destiny? Or have the scribes simply gotten it wrong? The disciples are understandably confused.

11 Jesus first endorses the scribal teaching. They are right in what

---

5. For some attempts to suggest a more specific connection underlying the οὖν here see Carson, 388-89. His preferred option, that the disciples find the idea of Jesus' death (presupposed when he speaks of being raised from the dead) inconsistent with Elijah's role of "restoring all things," suffers from the difficulty that that role is not mentioned until v. 11; the disciples' question is about Elijah's coming, not his mission.

6. For the source of this scribal teaching about the return of Elijah see D. E. Orton, *Scribe,* 32-33, who argues that the reference is not so much to scribes contemporary with Jesus as to "the authoritative Soferim of an earlier generation."

7. See above on 3:3 and on 11:10, 14 for the lack of a third (messianic) figure in the forerunner prophecies of Isa 40:3; Mal 3:1-4; 4:5-6, which envisage a voice / a messenger / Elijah as the direct precursor of *God's* eschatological coming. M. M. Faierstein, *JBL* 100 (1981) 75-86, demonstrates that there is little relevant evidence for belief that Elijah was to be the precursor *of the Messiah* as such (see p. 431, n. 43).

they predict, even though they have failed to recognize when that prediction has been fulfilled. The tenses ("is coming" . . . "will set") are those of the scribal perspective, still looking for the coming of Elijah and for his future work of reconciliation; it is Jesus' past tenses in v. 12a which will subvert that future expectation by stating what has actually happened already. The scribal teaching is closely based on Mal 4:5-6, which says that when God sends the prophet Elijah before the day of the Lord, his role will be to "turn the hearts of parents to their children, and the hearts of children to their parents." This work of family reconciliation is broadened in Sir 48:10 by the added clause "to restore the tribes of Jacob," and on this basis the scribal teaching includes a wider "setting to rights"[8] of *everything*[9] so that God's people are able to face the judgment of that day.[10]

12-13 As repeatedly in ch. 5, Jesus now sets over against the accepted scribal teaching what "*I* say to you." Where Jesus differs from the scribes is not in their reading of the scriptural promise, but in their failure to recognize when it has been fulfilled. After the strong hint of 3:4 and the explicit statement of 11:14 the reader cannot be surprised to know that Elijah has already come in the person of John the Baptist, as Matthew spells out again in v. 13 to ensure that no one misses the point.[11] The account of John's ministry in ch. 3 supplies clear links with the prophecy of Mal 4:5-6 and its extension in Sir 48:10: John preached the coming of judgment and warned people to repent so that they would escape its terror, and his requirement of baptism as a mark of that repentance and new beginning was a potent symbol of the "restoration" of those of the tribes of Israel who were willing to respond. So "Elijah has already come." But while some of the people had recognized the validity of John's message, most of those in positions of religious leadership in Jerusalem had not (see 21:25, 32), and "they" had gotten rid of him. The "they" is not specified. John's ultimate fate was not at the hands of those same religious authorities (14:3-12), but it is unlikely to have

---

8. See p. 651, n. 3, for the meaning of the verb, which is also used of Elijah's "turning" the hearts in LXX Mal 3:23 (= EVV 4:6).

9. Cf. the cognate phrase "the restoration of all things" in Acts 3:21 to express the Messiah's ultimate role.

10. The returning Elijah's role of "restoration" is further extended in the Mishnah to include adjudication of legal disputes: *m. 'Ed.* 8:7; *m. B. Meṣi'a* 3:4-5; the stereotyped phrase "remain until Elijah comes" in the latter passage shows how firmly his return had established itself in Jewish expectation. Keener, 439-40 n. 122, collects a wide range of rabbinic references to the returning Elijah and his role.

11. Another reference to the disciples as "understanding" reminds us of an important Matthean theme; see above on 13:13-15, 18, 23, 51; 15:10, and especially the introductory comments to 16:5-12. Cf. D. E. Orton, *Scribe,* 143-44, for the place of this reference within the unfolding theme.

displeased them as it disposed of a troublesome and too popular challenge to their authority — note how in 3:7 it is the "Pharisees and Sadducees" who are the immediate target of John's invective. Antipas's personal and political motives coincided at this point with the interests of the religious authorities, and so "they" did to him whatever they wanted.[12] The imprisonment and death of John were not part of the expectation for the returning Elijah, though the confrontation of the historical Elijah with Ahab and Jezebel and his narrow escape from death at their hands (1 Kgs 19:1-3, 10) might have suggested it; Matthew, however, omits Mark's statement that John's death was "written of him" (Mark 9:13).

Jesus posits a direct link between John's death and his own. The "necessity" for his own death (see on 16:21) will later be attributed to a scriptural pattern to be fulfilled, but it also arises from historical analogy. Just as Jesus' mission is closely linked with that of John (see above, p. 98, and cf. 11:16-19; 21:23-27, 28-32), so also are their deaths. If Jesus is carrying on where John left off, he cannot expect to meet with any better treatment at the hands of those who are threatened by their reforming zeal (though in Jesus' case they will in fact be different hands; the vague "at *their* hands" leaves the reader with a sense of generalized opposition). So the appearance of Elijah on the mountain, while it has testified to the heavenly glory and authority of the Messiah, is also (through the experience of John, the second Elijah) a pointer to the earthly fate of the Messiah which he has so graphically predicted in 16:21.

B. BACK TO THE PRESENT: FRUSTRATION AND ACCOMMODATION (17:14-27)

Ever since Peter's declaration that Jesus is the Messiah, the story has focused not on the present situation of Jesus and the disciples but on what is to come, as Jesus has talked about what awaits him in Jerusalem (and about what it will mean for those who choose to follow him there) and about his vindication and glory which is to follow, while the vision on the mountain has also lifted the disciples out of the present situation and shown them a foretaste of that future glory. Now as they come back down from the mountain, they are brought rudely back to the present as they find their fellow disciples in severe difficulties with an attempted exorcism which has gone wrong.

The three short pericopes which fill the remaining space before the

---

12. Gundry, 348, points out a number of places where this expression "indicates tyranny" (Eccl 8:3; Dan 8:4; 11:16, 36; Sir 8:15; 2 Macc 7:16).

beginning of the next major discourse in ch. 18 do not form a clearly coherent whole. The first speaks of the failure of the nine disciples, with some resultant reflections on the power of faith; the second conveys Jesus' second formal prediction of his coming passion; and the third narrates a brief exchange concerning the payment of the temple tax which does not seem at first sight to contribute a great deal to the developing portrayal of the nature of Jesus' ministry. Attempts to trace thematic connections between these three pericopes are not very convincing,[1] and it may be that they are brought together here on no higher structural principle than that Matthew wanted to include them somewhere in this phase of his narrative and so has fitted them together where he could within this first part of the journey to Jerusalem. In this he follows the same order as Mark and Luke with respect to the first two pericopes, but the third is in Matthew alone (though Mark has at the same point a different dialogue also set in Capernaum, Mark 9:33-37). The first episode must occur here because its narrative setting depends on the absence of Jesus and the three disciples up the mountain; the second passion prediction needs to be included at some point suitably distanced from the first in 16:21 and the third in 20:17-19; and the temple tax episode is set in Capernaum (and requires a lakeside setting, v. 27), and so must be included before Jesus and the disciples move further south (19:1).[2]

1. The Disciples' Failure in Exorcism (17:14-20[21])

14 *When they had come to the crowd, a man approached Jesus and knelt before him,* 15 *saying, "Lord, show mercy on my son: he is subject to fits[3] and suffers terribly, because he often falls into the fire and often into the water.* 16 *I brought him to your disciples, but they were not able to cure him."* 17 *Jesus replied, "You[4] faithless and perverted genera-*

1. See the comments of W. Horbury in E. Bammel and C. F. D. Moule (eds.), *Jesus*, 268-69, on reasons for placing the temple tax pericope where it is.

2. Matthew may also have decided that, since the collection of the temple tax away from Jerusalem took place in the month before Passover, the pericope fits well at this point in the narrative, before the beginning of the final journey to Jerusalem for the Passover festival.

3. See the comments below for the meaning of this rare word, used also in 4:24.

4. Representing the vocative "O," which is no longer current English. In Greek the use of ὦ in an address (rather than a simple vocative) can indicate an emotional tone (see p. 589, n. 7, the only other vocative ὦ in Matthew). Here it may also be suggested that it functions as an exclamation rather than a vocative ("What a faithless . . . !"), though the following second-person address renders this translation more awkward. Cf. BDF 146(2), suggesting reading this verse "against the background of Semitic exclamatory interjections, which introduce forceful or impassioned statements, often in the form of questions."

tion, how long am I to be with you? How long must I put up with you?[5]
Bring him here to me." 18 And Jesus rebuked him, and the demon came
out of him, and the boy was cured from that moment.[6] *19 Then the disci-*
ples came to Jesus privately and asked, "Why were we not able to
throw it out?" 20 He replied, "Because of your lack of faith.[7] *For I tell*
you truly, if you have faith as much as a mustard seed, you will say to
this mountain, 'Move from here to there,' and it will move; nothing will
be impossible for you."[8]

From the mountain of revelation Jesus and the three disciples come down to a
scene of demonic oppression and human weakness which evokes a remarkably strong emotional response from Jesus (v. 17). The parallel with Moses'
experience at Sinai is suggestive: he came down from the mountain with the
tablets of God's revelation and was faced by a scene of religious apostasy
which caused him to break the tablets in his anger (Exod 32:15-20).

The disciples' failure, which is the main focus of the pericope, reads
oddly after Jesus has explicitly authorized them to exorcise demons in 10:1,
8, though Matthew, unlike Mark 6:13; Luke 10:17, has not recorded that they
have actually done so. It would be possible, therefore, in Matthew's account,
to read this as their first attempt to put that authorization into practice, but it
is more likely that Matthew intends us to assume what Mark and Luke explicitly state, that the disciples have done as Jesus instructed them in 10:7-8,
and that their failure in this case was atypical; hence his exasperated response
in v. 17, and their embarrassed and puzzled question in v. 19. See below on
v. 20 for the question of what special circumstances in this case may have led
to their failure. The effect of the pericope is to issue a salutary warning to
them, and through them to all who seek to draw on the miraculous power of
Jesus, that there is nothing automatic about such power, and it may not be
taken for granted. The key, as has been stated so often in previous accounts of

5. The "you" in both questions is plural; this is not an address specifically to the
man making the request. The following imperative, "bring," is also plural.

6. For the idiom see p. 304, n. 14.

7. See on 6:30 (and p. 264, n. 6) for the meaning of ὀλιγόπιστος (-ία) in Matthew.
The literal meaning "little faith" is most clearly inappropriate here, since Jesus goes on to
charge them with having not even the smallest grain of faith. It is no doubt for this reason
(and possibly also under the influence of ἄπιστος in v. 17) that most of the later MSS and
versions here read ἀπιστίαν, "lack of faith," rather pedantically spelling out what the general
usage in Matthew shows to be the idiomatic meaning of ὀλιγοπιστία in this gospel.

8. Most later MSS and versions add here Mark 9:29, "But this kind will not come
out except through prayer and fasting" (the last two words are absent from some early
MSS of Mark but present in all those that add the clause here in Matthew), but the evidence seems clear that Matthew did not originally include this clause.

miracles, lies in faith (8:10, 13, 26; 9:2, 22, 28-29; 14:31; 15:28), but in this case the faith that is missing is not that of the one seeking help but that of the would-be miracle workers themselves. The sovereign authority of Jesus the Messiah in healing and exorcism is unique; his disciples can draw on it only by faith, and that is what they have failed to do in this case.

This is the only healing/exorcism story after the end of the Galilean ministry, except for the healing of the blind men of Jericho (20:29-34), which could not be recorded elsewhere because of its geographical setting.[9] Its appropriateness at this point in the narrative derives from its focus on the faith and failure of the disciples, so that it is told not primarily as an example of Jesus' miraculous power, but as a lesson in discipleship. As such it fits well into the dominant focus of the journey narrative. So now we hear nothing of the reaction of the crowd; it is the disciples who are meant to learn from this experience.

Here is another striking example of Matthew's drastic abbreviation of a traditional miracle story, which results in the miracle itself taking second place to the lesson about faith. Matthew's account, even after the addition of a saying about faith and prayer (see below), is less than half the length of Mark's, and while it is similar in length to Luke's, this is partly accounted for by the fact that Luke has omitted the whole of the private dialogue with the disciples which takes up more than a third of Matthew's pericope. The abbreviation has been achieved by cutting out almost all the vivid description of the boy's condition which makes this pericope in Mark such a graphic tale. Matthew also, like Luke, omits any mention of the father's struggle of faith (Mark 9:23-24). As a result, after the brief description of the boy's fits in v. 15, Jesus' successful exorcism is narrated with minimal detail in a single verse (v. 18), and all the emphasis falls on the disciples' previous failure, and on what this reveals about their lack of faith. Matthew then adds Jesus' pronouncement on the power of faith which neither Mark nor Luke includes at this point, and which will recur in an expanded form after the cursing of the fig tree in 21:21-22 (where there is also a parallel saying in Mark), while Luke has a similar saying in 17:6 without any narrative miracle to support it. This procedure of drastically abbreviating the narrative detail but expanding the didactic material is typical of Matthew's method; cf. the addition of 8:11-12 to the traditional story of the centurion's servant.

14 The presence of a crowd, and of a man aware of the healing power of Jesus and his companions, is surprising because the last location we have been given is the largely non-Jewish region of Caesarea Philippi

9. Since this story depends on the other disciples having been left alone while Jesus and the three have been up on the mountain, it, too, could not easily have been placed at any other point in the narrative.

(16:13), where it seems that Jesus went alone with his disciples. But see above on v. 1 for the possibility that the Transfiguration took place somewhere further south, in Galilee, an area more likely to produce such a crowd; the next pericope assumes that they have now returned to Galilee (v. 22), and the next specific location will be in Capernaum (v. 24). We should therefore probably assume that the "man" here is Jewish, since there is no qualifying adjective as there was in 15:22. The only other specific mention of kneeling *(gonypeteō)* in Matthew is of the mock homage of the Roman soldiers to the Jewish "king" in 27:29, but the term probably does not significantly differ in connotation from the "low bow" *(proskyneō)* which is Matthew's usual term for the posture of a suppliant (see p. 303, n. 6).

15 Both "Lord" and "show mercy" are recurrent features in this gospel in appeals for Jesus' help and healing. But here, as in 15:22, the appeal is not on behalf of the speaker himself/herself, but for his son/her daughter. It is significant that in both cases the problem is one of demon-possession. There is no instance in the gospels of a possessed person appealing for Jesus' help for themselves, presumably because it is the demon who speaks through the possessed person, and the demon does not want Jesus to take any action; normally the approach is rather one of defiance or of dissociation. When Jesus acts against a demon, it is either on his own initiative in response to that defiance or in response, as here, to a parent's appeal.

But in Matthew's abbreviated account (contrast Mark 9:17-18) it is not until v. 18 that it becomes clear that the problem here is demon-possession. The affliction is rather described by the rare verb *selēniazomai* (which by derivation should mean to be affected by the moon, hence KJV's "lunatick" here) and by a description of fits which sound like what we would call epilepsy (the fuller description in Mark and Luke makes the similarity more impressive). Commentators therefore regularly refer to this episode as "The Epileptic Boy," but we should note that in the ancient world, which was well acquainted with epilepsy, *selēniazomai* was not used at this time to mean epilepsy as such.[10] Among pagans epilepsy was known as "the sacred disease," which

---

10. The normal term was ἐπίληψις or ἐπιληψία; see P. G. Bolt, *Defeat,* 66, n. 82. Bolt mentions a single use of σεληνιάζομαι for epilepsy in the second century A.D. Galen 9.903 links epilepsy with the moon, but uses the term ἐπίληπτος to denote those suffering from it. Lucian, *Tox.* 24; *Philops.* 16, twice refers to people who "fall down" (καταπίπτω) in moonlight, but without using a term for epilepsy as such. The symptoms described in this passage are the only basis for supposing that σεληνιάζομαι could *mean* "to have epilepsy" in Matthew's time. The confident assertion of Davies and Allison, 2:722, that Matthew "has correctly diagnosed the boy as having epilepsy (σεληνιάζεται)" is based on their discussion at 4:24, where they claim only that σεληνιάζομαι *"seems* to refer to epilepsy" (my italics), supporting the claim only from its use here in 17:15! Hagner, 2:502, even refers to σεληνιάζεται as "the technical term 'be epileptic.'" J. M. Ross, *BT* 29 (1978) 126-

suggests a divine rather than a demonic cause. It is of course possible that first-century Jews, unaware of the electrical disturbance of the brain to which we now attribute the disease, might have attributed the frightening manifestations of epilepsy to demonic action, but we have no evidence for that other than assumptions based on this pericope, where in any case epilepsy as such is not mentioned.[11] It seems truer to the text to describe this as a case of demon-possession (which is how all three Synoptic evangelists describe it and its cure) which resulted in fits similar to those we know as epileptic.[12]

16 No doubt the man came looking for Jesus himself, knowing him to be a successful exorcist, but in his absence he hoped that his closest associates would share his skill. The disciples apparently assumed as much too (presumably on the basis of Jesus' authorization in 10:1, 8), since they have tried to effect an exorcism. The fact that their failure was immediately obvious underlines the "objective" nature of the cure expected; it was impossible to bluff their way out with an assurance that the boy would now be alright. Cf. 9:5-8, where a real cure is "harder" than a mere statement of forgiveness.

17 Jesus' surprising outburst is addressed not to the man (see p. 657, n. 5) but to the whole "generation." For similar characterizations of "this generation" as unbelieving and unresponsive cf. 11:16; 12:39, 41-42, 45; 16:4; it is a Matthean theme which will reach its culmination in the charge in 23:34-36 that "this generation" has reached the point of no return in its rejection of God's messengers. Previous criticisms have described this generation as "wicked" and "adulterous" (taking up the OT imagery of Israel as God's unfaithful wife). Here "faithless" prepares us for the attribution of the disciples' failure to their lack of faith in v. 20, while "perverted" introduces a direct

---

27, is more cautious, since "if we translate it as 'epileptic' we are probably narrowing down the meaning of the original and failing to make the classification clear," though his offered alternative, "moonstruck," is even more open to misunderstanding. My translation "subject to fits" attempts to avoid inappropriate medical precision.

11. H. C. Kee, *Medicine,* 48-50, gives an interesting account of the treatment of epilepsy by Rufus of Ephesus in the second century A.D., which indicates a purely physical understanding of both cause and treatment.

12. P. J. Achtemeier, *CBQ* 37 (1975) 481, n. 35, gives reasons for not identifying this as a case of epilepsy. J. Wilkinson, *ExpT* 79 (1967/8) 39-42, concludes that the symptoms are those of "the major form of epilepsy," but argues that such symptoms might have been caused by demon-possession. I should declare a personal interest in careful definition at this point, in that I have witnessed the deep pastoral damage caused to a couple whose son died in an epileptic seizure by those who thoughtlessly assumed, on the basis of this gospel narrative, that he must have been demon-possessed. It was important for them to know that, however similar the symptoms may have been in this case, a simplistic equation of epilepsy with demon-possession is as invalid as is the equally simplistic assumption of many commentators that this was merely a case of epilepsy, the demonic dimension in the story being attributed to primitive superstition.

echo of the LXX of Deut 32:5, 20, where Moses speaks of the Israelites of his day as the degenerate children of their just and faithful God, a "crooked and perverted generation," "in whom there is no faith." Moses is speaking of the people as a whole, and Jesus' complaint sounds similarly general. But it has been provoked by the failure of his own disciples, who in their lack of faith represent the failing of the people as a whole; if even they, from their position of special privilege (13:11-17), do not have the faith to draw on God's saving power, what hope is there for the whole generation?

The frustration Jesus expresses here stands out as unusual in this gospel just as does his exultation in God's revelation in 11:25-26; the two outbursts express the opposite poles of his paradoxical mission. It has added force at this point in the narrative just as Jesus and the three other disciples are returning from their "mountaintop experience," and it is possible that the echo of Moses' complaint reflects the recent meeting with Moses and Elijah, each of whom equally found the people of their day extremely trying (see, e.g., Exod 17:4; 1 Kgs 19:10). Jesus has accepted that he will be rejected by the official leadership of Israel (16:21), but to find himself let down even by his own disciples evokes a rare moment of human emotion on the part of the Son of God.[13] Cf. the "How long?" laments of the psalms (Pss 4:2; 13:1-2, etc.) and prophets (Jer 4:14, 21; 12:4, etc.).

The imperative "Bring him here to me" is plural, perhaps because the boy's condition requires more than just his father to look after him, but perhaps it is addressed rather to the disciples, who are now to bring to Jesus the patient they themselves have failed to help.

18 Matthew's very concise account of the actual exorcism surprisingly says that the person "rebuked" is the afflicted boy himself,[14] but it is presumably understood that Jesus is addressing the demon within the boy, which "comes out" in response to the rebuke. For the same verb "rebuke" used of Jesus' direct address to a possessing demon see Mark 1:25; 9:25; Luke 4:41. The cure (graphically described in Mark 9:26-27) is as immediately visible as was the disciples' failure.

---

13. It is also possible in the light of later Christian orthodoxy to detect behind the cry "How long am I to be with you?" the situation of the eternal Son of God temporally present on earth through the incarnation (Gundry, 350-51, further suggests that "with you" is meant to recall "God with us" in 1:23; similarly Luz, 2:408, following H. Frankemölle), but it is unlikely that Matthew's readers would have detected that nuance without further prompting, which Matthew's brief record does not offer.

14. Hagner, 2:504, suggests that αὐτῷ refers to the demon, but since no demon has yet been mentioned, this is improbable; when there is an obvious antecedent to the pronoun, it would be perverse to expect the reader, without any prompt, to wait for an antecedent yet to be announced, especially when a second αὐτός, clearly referring to the boy, will occur before the demon is mentioned.

19-20   For the disciples' request for explanation after a striking saying or incident cf. 13:10; 15:15; 19:10; 24:3. In this case they need help not
only with understanding but also with their own bruised self-esteem after
their public humiliation. It seems that the authority to throw out demons
(10:8) is not enough on its own; faith is also necessary.[15] Their lack of faith
(see above, p. 657, n. 7) is not explained. Perhaps they had become over-
confident in the authority Jesus had given them, so that they assumed they
could carry out an exorcism as a matter of course; the added comment in
Mark 9:29 (and in later MSS of Matthew; see p. 657, n. 8) that "this kind will
not come out except through prayer [and fasting]" implies that they had not
prayed for God's power over the demon. Or perhaps the problem was the opposite, that in the absence of Jesus and the leading disciples up the mountain
the remaining disciples did not have the faith to draw on God's power for
themselves, despite Jesus' authorization, and so their attempt had lacked conviction. At any rate, the "little faith" with which Jesus has several times
charged his disciples (6:30; 8:26; 14:31; 16:8) has now proved to have serious consequences. For another failed attempt at exorcism see Acts 19:13-17.

The added saying on the power of faith is meant to be remembered
(see on 5:18 for "I tell you truly"), and its vivid imagery of mountain moving
(cf. 21:21) ensures that it will be.[16] The same figure of speech is used by Paul
in 1 Cor 13:2,[17] and while there is no known contemporary parallel, it appears in later rabbinic writings as a term for "feats of an exceptional, extraordinary, or impossible nature."[18] Cf. Isa 54:10 for a similar usage.[19] The following assurance that "nothing will be impossible for you" underlines the
force of the imagery. But such results are not promised only to those who
have great faith, but even to those with the smallest amount of faith. See on
13:31-32 for the proverbial smallness of mustard seed; faith compared to
anything less than a mustard seed would be no faith at all. Faith is not a mea-
surable commodity but a relationship, and what achieves results through

15. On the faith expected of disciples in Matthew and his use of ὀλιγόπιστος(-ία)
see further my *Matthew: Evangelist*, 273-75.

16. Davies and Allison, 2:728, interestingly comment on the connection with
mustard seed: "The insurmountable is accomplished by the infinitesimal."

17. Did Paul know of Jesus' saying? D. Wenham, *Paul*, 81-83, argues that he did.
In *Gos. Thom.* 48 and 106 there is a similar reminiscence of this saying of Jesus. The
(probably) early Christian *T. Sol.* 23:1 interestingly has a demon claiming to be able to
move mountains.

18. W. R. Telford, *Temple*, 115; he sets out and discusses the relevant texts on
110-17. The reference is in several cases to the extraordinary exploits of rabbis in halakhic
debate!

19. See also p. 795, n. 17, for the possible influence of the "mountain" of difficulty in Zech 4:7 on the parallel saying in 21:21.

prayer is not a superior "quantity" of faith but the unlimited power of God on which faith, any faith, can draw. The disciples, Jesus implies, had failed to bring any faith at all to bear on this situation.[20] For the pastoral problems raised by such an apparently unlimited promise (and by the series of similarly open-ended statements about prayer in John 14–16) see above on 7:7-8 and the introductory comments on 7:7-11.

2. Second Prediction of the Passion (17:22-23)

22 *As they were gathering[1] in Galilee, Jesus said to them, "The Son of Man is destined[2] to be betrayed[3] into the hands of people* 23 *who will kill him, and on the third day he will be raised." And they were utterly dismayed.*

The journey to Jerusalem is punctuated with three formal announcements of what is to happen to Jesus when they reach the city (16:21; 17:22-23; 20:17-19). This second[4] announcement, set while they are still in Galilee and so not far into the journey, largely repeats in an abbreviated form what the first has said, but adds the important new element of betrayal.

22 If it is not just a rather eccentric use of the verb, "gathering" may be intended to remind us that after the splitting of the party in 17:1-20 Jesus and the Twelve are now again back in Galilee as a single united group, committed to the journey southward. The next scene will find them temporarily settled in a "house" in Capernaum, so that we may be intended to envisage them back at their home base making final preparations for the journey which was first announced while they were away in the far north.

This is the first hint of Jesus' betrayal by Judas (apart from the editorial comment in 10:4), though as yet no indication is given to the disciples of who

---

20. Note that a parallel saying in Luke 17:6 (though with a mulberry tree taking the place of the mountain; see on 21:21-22) is given as Jesus' response to the disciples' request, "Give us more faith." Their "quantitative" idea of faith is thus firmly set aside.

1. The verb (συστρέφομαι) is unexpected in this context, where Jesus and his disciples are already traveling together. Many MSS have understandably substituted a different compound of the same verb, ἀναστρεφόμαι, "spend time" or "move around."

2. While μέλλω need mean no more than that something will happen in the (near) future, in this gospel it often carries a stronger sense of what *must* happen, what is intended or destined (see, e.g., 2:13; 3:7; 11:14; 16:27; 17:12). In this context of a formal prediction of Jesus' passion that sense seems required.

3. παραδίδωμι in itself means simply "hand over"; see p. 343, n. 3 and the comments below for the justification for translating it here more specifically as "betray."

4. Jesus has also spoken about his coming passion in 17:12, but not in a formal announcement as here, and not to the whole disciple group.

will do it. *Paradidōmi* does not in itself mean "betray"; sometimes it has a to-tally positive sense (as in "entrust," 11:27; 25:14, 20, 22), and where it is re-lated to imprisonment and death it can be used without any sense of betrayal (4:12; 5:25; 10:17, 19; 18:34; 27:2, 26). But often the hostile motivation of the agent is understood (10:21; 24:9, 10; 27:18), and *paradidōmi* (rather than the more specific term *prodidōmi*) quickly became the standard term for Judas's "betrayal" (see p. 374, n. 3).[5] In view of that general usage it seems likely that the "handing over" predicted here is not simply Jesus' arrest and the process of his trials and condemnation to death,[6] but more specifically the role of Ju-das. It is also possible to find here an echo of the OT phrase "give into the hands of" denoting God's determining the result of human conflict (Exod 23:31; Num 21:2, 34, etc.), and such a divine passive would suit the NT insis-tence that what was done to Jesus was done by the will of God;[7] but the promi-nent use of *paradidōmi* in the gospels in relation to Judas's treachery suggests that that is the more immediate focus here. The "people" to whom Jesus will be handed over are not specified here,[8] though the reader who knows the story will have no difficulty in identifying them. But the description of them as *anthrōpoi,* "human beings," not only produces an effective wordplay (the Son of *anthrōpos* in the hands of *anthrōpoi*) but also draws a telling and paradoxi-cal contrast between the Son of Man (the figure of future glory and authority, 16:27-28) and those to whose will he is to be subjected.

23 The final two elements in the prediction are the same as in 16:21, but the statement of the disciples' emotional reaction is new. In 16:22-28 we could infer it from Peter's immediate response and from the warnings Jesus went on to utter, but now Matthew makes it explicit, using a strong expres-sion which he will use of the disciples again in 26:22. The fact that their dis-may follows immediately upon the prediction of Jesus' *resurrection* under-lines the point we noted above (especially on 16:21), that the repeated inclusion of the resurrection as the conclusion of Jesus' destiny in Jerusalem seems to have gone completely over the disciples' heads; the prediction of his

5. The prevalence of this usage is shown by the remarkable fact that προδίδωμι is never used in the NT in the sense of "betray," and the cognate noun προδότης is applied to Judas only once (Luke 6:16).

6. As in 10:17-22, where I have translated παραδίδωμι by "hand over" where its object is the disciples.

7. παραδίδωμι is so used, e.g., in Rom 4:25; 8:32. This usage may be influenced by the use of παραδίδωμι for the fate of God's servant in LXX Isa 53:6, 12, "the Lord has *handed him over* for our sins"; "his life was *handed over* to death" (where the relevant He-brew verbs might more normally be translated "sins *laid on* him" and "he *poured out* his life"; on the latter see my *Jesus and the OT,* 244).

8. Contrast the careful listing of the constituent groups of the Sanhedrin in 16:21 (and cf. 20:18).

rejection, suffering, and death so dominated their thinking that they could not see beyond the death to the vindication and glory.

3. Paying the Temple Tax (17:24-27)

> 24 *When they had come to Capernaum, Peter was approached by the collectors of the temple tax,[1] who asked him, "Doesn't your[2] teacher pay the temple tax?" 25 "Yes," he replied. When he came into the house, Jesus spoke to him first: "What do you think, Simon?" he asked. "The kings of the earth — from whom do they levy duties and tax,[3] from their own sons or from strangers?"[4] 26 When Peter replied, "From strangers," Jesus said to him, "Well, then, the sons are free. 27 But so that we don't cause them to stumble, go down to the lake and cast your fishhook; take the first fish that comes up, and when you open its mouth, you will find a silver coin[5] there; take it and give it to them for[6] me and yourself."*

This apparently rather trivial exchange in fact has significant implications for the reader's understanding of the status and mission of Jesus. The half-shekel temple tax was an annual levy on adult Jewish males, and one which, unlike Roman taxes (see on 22:15-22), might be expected to be paid as a patriotic duty, but the Sadducees disapproved of it as a relatively recent Pharisaic institution,[7] and the members of the Qumran community on principle

---

1. The term used twice in this verse is τὰ δίδραχμα, "the two drachmas," the Greek monetary equivalent to the half-shekel tax for the upkeep of the sanctuary. The Greek term was presumably a recognized idiom, which needs to be spelled out for English readers. For the suggestion that the "two drachmas" refer not to the temple tax but to a civil tax (a view widely held in patristic and later interpretation [Luz, 2:419], but now rejected by almost all scholars; see, however, R. J. Cassidy, *CBQ* 41 [1979] 571-80), and for arguments against it, see Davies and Allison, 2:738-41; D. E. Garland in D. R. Bauer and M. A. Powell (eds.), *Treasures,* 85-87.

2. The Greek is plural. Peter is being approached as the representative of a recognized group.

3. The Latin loanword κῆνσος is singular, and refers specifically to the Roman poll tax which will be the subject of debate in 22:15-22; see the comments there for its nature.

4. ἀλλότριος can mean a "foreigner," but more generally it refers to any person or thing which is not one's own. See the comments below for the likely reference here.

5. See the comments below for the specific coin and its value.

6. Literally, "instead of," perhaps reflecting the origin of the tax in a "ransom" payment (Exod 30:12, 15, 16).

7. There was, however, a similar annual tax of a third of a shekel in the time of Nehemiah (Neh 10:32-33).

paid it only once in a lifetime.[8] This approach from the tax collectors suggests a suspicion that Jesus also might not accept this as an obligation.[9] Their question[10] is of the form that expects the answer Yes, and Peter takes that answer for granted, but the fact that they had to ask it at all is surely significant. We have already seen a hint of Jesus' radical attitude to the temple in 12:6, and as the confrontation develops in Jerusalem, this will become increasingly clear, both in his demonstration in the temple courtyard in 21:12-17 (which will include an attack on those who changed money for the payment of this tax) and in the developing critique which culminates in his prediction that the temple will be destroyed (23:38; 24:2). So it may well be that he was already gaining a reputation as one who sat light to the authority of the temple and its functionaries, a reputation which would contribute significantly to his eventual trial and execution (26:61; 27:40). This approach from the collectors was therefore more than just an administrative question. And Jesus' response to Peter in the house confirms that he did not regard himself as standing in the same relation to the temple as other Jewish men; he, unlike them, is a member of the "family," and the word "sons" invites us to reflect on Jesus' special relationship with the God whose temple the tax was meant to service.

The implication of the dialogue with Peter seems to be then that since Jesus has the status of a "son" in relation to God, he is "free" and so should be exempt from paying the tax (though the last step of the argument is left unstated). If he nonetheless does pay it, therefore, it is as a matter of accommodation, to avoid giving offense (which is what the verb "cause to stumble" probably means in this context), rather than of obligation. We are not told that he did in fact pay it, but the instructions given to Peter in v. 27 allow us to

8. R. J. Banks, *Jesus,* 92-93. For detailed study of the origin of, and objections to, the tax see W. Horbury in E. Bammel and C. F. D. Moule (eds.), *Jesus,* 277-82. He concludes that "there were many who, for whatever reason, in practice did not pay." So also S. Mandell, *HTR* 77 (1984) 223-32, who argues that both the pre-70 temple tax and the post-70 *fiscus judaicus* were paid only by observant Palestinian Jews (who after A.D. 70 were regarded by the Romans as responsible for the revolt).

9. According to *m. Šeqal.* 1:3-4 priests claimed exemption, though the rabbis disputed the claim. For groups who did not pay the tax see also D. E. Garland, in D. R. Bauer and M. A. Powell (eds.), *Treasures,* 70-72; Garland's article conveniently collects a great deal of information and discussion relating to the pericope as a whole.

10. It would be possible to read it as an accusatory statement, "Your teacher does not pay the temple tax," to which Peter then replies with an emphatic rebuttal, "Yes, he does" (see p. 589, n. 6, for such a use of Ναί following a negative statement). But we have no reason to believe that Jesus had in fact failed to pay it, and all commentators and versions seem to assume that this is a question. J. B. Phillips, however, surprisingly takes it as a question expecting the answer "No": "'Your master doesn't pay Temple-tax, we presume?' 'Oh, yes, he does!' replied Peter."

assume that he did. If so, this is an interesting contrast to other matters of controversy on which Jesus was only too willing to stand up against practices and assumptions which he saw as wrong in principle, and so to incur the hostility of those of a more conventional outlook, as we shall see when he comes to Jerusalem. But where it is his own personal privilege that is at stake, he has no problem with accommodating himself to what is expected of him, and in this way identifying himself with the traditions of his people. Is there a parallel here with his baptism, which, according to 3:14-15, was undertaken not because he personally required it, but to identify with repentant Israel and so to "fulfill all that is required of us"? The Jesus of Matthew's gospel is not one to stand on his personal dignity, nor to dig his heels in on matters of secondary importance. His followers have not always been so perceptive in differentiating between matters of principle and *adiaphora*.[11]

The instruction to Peter in v. 27 is a puzzle. The pericope as a whole is not a miracle story but a debate, with the miraculous solution of v. 27 unexpectedly tacked on at the end. And while Jesus' words about the fish and the coin read like a matter-of-fact instruction which Peter is expected to carry out to the letter, there is no account of the proposed miracle actually taking place. In view of similar popular stories about treasure found in fish (see below) some interpreters read v. 27 as a legendary addition to an otherwise mundane discussion of economic policy, but in that case it is strange that the catch is not actually narrated. At the other extreme it may be read as a playful comment by Jesus, never intended to be taken literally, on how Peter might raise the necessary sum; it would thus be an ironic reflection of the lack of ready money in the disciple group. There seems no way to decide the matter definitively, but it would be as unwise to include this purely verbal instruction, with no statement that what was proposed actually happened, in a list of Jesus' miracles[12] as it would be to assume on the basis of v. 20 that the disciples did actually move mountains.

24 For the presence of Jesus and his disciples back in Capernaum before undertaking the journey to the south see on v. 22. If, as tradition holds (see on 8:14-15), it was in Peter's house that they lived while in Capernaum, the tax collectors naturally approach Peter as the householder and therefore as responsible for those living with him. Jesus, though not the householder, is recognized as "your teacher," the leader of the disciple group, and it is his attitude to the tax which is in question. It might be assumed that whatever line he himself took on the issue his disciples would also follow, but that is not

11. For a thoughtful survey of the theological messages conveyed by this pericope see D. E. Garland, in D. R. Bauer and M. A. Powell (eds.), *Treasures*, 89-98.

12. B. Gerhardsson, *Mighty Acts,* 59, is prepared to include it in his catalogue of Jesus' miracles only as "a doubtful borderline case."

made explicit (though in v. 27 Peter himself is included with Jesus in the proposed payment).

The temple tax, though probably quite a recent innovation as an annual levy, found its basis in Exod 30:11-16, a one-time payment of half a shekel by every adult male when a census was taken as "a ransom for their lives" to be used "for the service of the tent of meeting."[13] It was paid annually into the temple treasury using the special Tyrian currency (hence the need for money changers in 21:12). Those going to Jerusalem for the Passover paid it in person, but it was collected locally in the month before Passover from the rest of the Jewish population both in Palestine and in the diaspora (Josephus, *Ant.* 18.312-13).[14] A Jewish shekel was reckoned the equivalent of four Greek drachmas (which were equivalent to Roman denarii), hence the term "the two drachmas" used for the half-shekel tax (see 665, n. 1). This was roughly the equivalent of two days' wages (see 20:1-15 for the value of a denarius).[15]

25-26 We do not know whether Peter's confident "Yes" sprang from knowledge of Jesus' views on the issue or simply from his assumption that Jesus would do as other patriotic Jews did. If he intended to raise the issue with Jesus, he was forestalled by Jesus (through supernatural knowledge, or through having heard the exchange outside?) raising it first with him.[16] Jesus' argument is by analogy with the taxation policy of the "kings

---

13. For details about the temple tax see Schürer, 2:270-72, and the first part of the Mishnaic tractate *Šeqalim.*

14. It is perhaps a mark of the artificiality of the Synoptic outline of Jesus' itinerary that this issue is raised at a time when Jesus and his disciples are about to set off for the Passover festival in Jerusalem, where they might therefore have been expected to make their payments in person rather than to do so via the local collectors in Galilee.

15. After the destruction of the temple in A.D. 70 Vespasian replaced the temple tax with an equivalent levy on all Jews in the empire as a war indemnity (the *fiscus judaicus*) to be paid to Rome for the treasury of the temple of Jupiter (Josephus, *War* 7.218; see further E. M. Smallwood, *The Jews,* 371-76; D. E. Garland, in D. R. Bauer and M. A. Powell (eds.), *Treasures,* 78-85). It is one of the incidental indications that Matthew's gospel was written before A.D. 70 that he can record with approval Jesus' acceptance of the temple tax, which after A.D. 70 would have had a quite different connotation of the support of pagan worship. W. Carter, *JSNT* 76 (1999) 3-31 (summarized in his commentary), is unusual in trying to turn the allegedly post-70 date of the gospel to positive account by suggesting that Matthew is indeed encouraging his readers to pay the tax to Rome as (paradoxically) "a defiant testimony to God's sovereignty," since the money, being miraculously provided, costs them nothing. Is he then telling his readers to expect similar miracles to pay all their taxes?!

16. While Matthew regularly refers editorially to the first disciple as Peter (as in v. 24) here and in 16:17, the only two occasions where Jesus addresses him by name, we find his given name, "Simon."

of the earth," a phrase unique in this gospel, and probably intended to contrast human rulers with God as the Lord of the temple;[17] it prepares the way suggestively for the question about precedence in "the kingdom of heaven" in 18:1 (see comments there). "Duties" (*telē*, plural) is a general term for (normally) indirect taxation through customs duties and the like, while the "tax" (*kēnsos*, singular) would refer in Palestine specifically to the Roman poll tax levied on the subjects of an area under direct Roman rule (see on 22:15-22). All rulers, it is taken for granted, need to raise revenue; the question is from whom do they raise it. The specific referent of "sons" and "strangers" will depend on which governing authority is in view: for the Roman poll tax the crucial division was between Romans and subject foreigners (a possible meaning of *allotrios*, "stranger"), but not all rulers rule over foreigners, and where they are taxing their own people, the "sons" who are exempt are more likely to be their own family members as opposed to the wider populace.[18] But whatever the exact reference, the principle assumed by Jesus' question and Peter's response is that rulers exempt those closest to them from taxation. Whatever our modern democratic ideals may suggest, that seems a valid observation of the natural human tendency as it would have been experienced in the first century.

The analogy assumes that the temple tax (a uniform tax on all Jewish adult males, irrespective of their wealth) is similarly levied by a ruler from his subjects. But who is the ruler of the temple? No human could claim that title; the reference must be to God,[19] and the Jewish people are his subjects. Who then are the "sons" who are exempt? The obvious reference in context is to Jesus himself,[20] whose payment of the tax was the subject of the question, and who has recently again been declared "Son of God" on the mountain (17:5); the plural might then be explained as derived from the analogy rather than determining its application. But the plural raises the possibility that here, as in 12:1-8, his disciples are also understood to share in his privilege as (in that case) "Lord of the sabbath." The next verse will go on to include Peter's own payment of the tax along with that of Jesus, as if the two are on the same footing of accommodation rather than obligation. Just as Jesus had spoken of "some*thing* greater than the

17. "The kings of the earth" is used in the OT to contrast human kings with the true heavenly king; see Pss 2:2; 76:12; 89:27; 102:15; 138:4.

18. J. D. M. Derrett, *Law*, 253-55, points out the danger of restricting the reference to Roman practice rather than to "the normal situation in Near Eastern kingdoms."

19. Josephus, *Ant.* 18.312, says that this tax was paid "to God."

20. See, however, W. Horbury, in E. Bammel and C. F. D. Moule (eds.), *Jesus*, 282-85 (followed by Davies and Allison, 2:745), for the view that "sons" refers to Israel as a whole, so that Jesus' reply is in effect declaring the tax on Jews to be invalid altogether. Similarly Luz, 2.417-18.

temple," not just "someone" (12:6), so here, too, we perhaps glimpse the concept of a messianic community which in some sense shares the Messiah's special relationship with God.

27 The word for "cause to stumble" here is the same as for "scandalize" in 15:12. On that occasion Jesus seems to have had no qualms about "scandalizing" the Pharisees by his free attitude, so why is it different here? Probably simply because the saying which caused the "scandal" in 15:11 was a matter of fundamental principle for Jesus, and one which exposed the deep divide between his attitude to the law and that of the Pharisees, whereas here it is simply a matter of custom, where compliance, even if not necessary, will do no harm, and to flout it would serve no useful purpose. But R. J. Banks also notes the difference in the attitude of the people involved: here, in contrast with the settled hostility of the Pharisees in ch. 15, we have simply people "seeking genuine information concerning his attitude to their customary practice."[21] Whatever the reason, the principle at stake is one which can and should be more widely applied: while there are times when a disciple must make an unpopular stand and so alienate others, many of the issues and practices on which we might legitimately differ from conventional assumptions are not worth fighting over. Cf. above on 7:6, where the issue of discrimination is discussed. A Christian community which sets up "stumbling blocks" only when it is really necessary is likely to be more effective in mission. In 18:6-9 we will be warned about the danger of stumbling blocks in a pastoral context.[22]

Jesus' instruction to Peter presupposes that though they were willing to pay, they did not have the necessary money available[23] — the half shekel for Jesus alone was not a negligible sum (see above); if the tax was to be paid for all the disciples, a substantial amount would be needed. So Peter is to go out and get it by a miraculous catch. The "silver coin" is a *statēr*,[24] a Greek

21. R. J. Banks, *Jesus,* 143; cf. the fuller discussion in ibid., 92-94.

22. The above comments assume that the "they" who are not to be scandalized are the tax collectors. E. J. Carter, *JSNT* 25 (2003) 423-27, argues that the phrase should be translated "and so that we might not lead them astray," the "them" being Jesus' followers (even though they have not been mentioned in the context). This suggestion depends on Carter's proposal (which he links with Luther's "two kingdoms" doctrine) that the whole pericope is about political responsibility, and conveys a message similar to that of 22:15-22, which both maintains a distance from the political authority and accepts its right to levy taxes.

23. Others suggest that it is a matter of principle: Jesus is willing to pay to avoid misunderstanding, but since he is "free" he should not be expected to use his own money; God will therefore provide the money miraculously, and so both parties are satisfied. See, e.g., R. J. Bauckham, *GP* 6:224, 233. This assumes, of course, that Matthew intends us to understand that the miracle actually occurred (see below).

24. B. H. Streeter, *Four Gospels,* 504, argued that the use of this term indicates

coin normally equivalent to four drachmas, and so sufficient to pay the two-drachma tax for two people. See the introductory comments above for the surprising fact that Matthew does not tell us that the proposed miracle actually took place. A number of ancient stories tell of finding something valuable in a fish that has been caught; the most famous is the recovery of Polycrates' ring (Herodotus 3.41-42), but there are similar Jewish stories in *b. Šabb.* 119a; *Gen. Rab.* 11:4, and other cultures provide numerous examples.[25] Such a background in popular folklore makes it questionable whether Jesus would have issued such instructions in all seriousness, and Matthew's failure to mention that Peter did as he was told leaves the pericope hanging in the air if it was meant to be an actual miracle story.[26] Nor would a single *statēr* have gone far toward the total tax bill for thirteen men. It seems to me more likely that Jesus' words should not be taken at their literal face-value but read in the context of popular belief as an ironical comment on their lack of resources.[27] Whether Jesus and the Twelve did in fact pay the tax, and, if so, how the money was raised, are questions which Matthew tantalizingly leaves open.

---

that the gospel was written in Antioch, since only there and in Damascus was a Greek στατήρ exactly equivalent to two δίδραχμα. See my *Matthew: Evangelist,* 92-93, for the implausibility of this argument ("one of the tenaciously held apocrypha of NT scholarship," Luz, 2:415, n. 22), which also sits rather uncomfortably alongside the fact that it was the Tyrian coinage, not the Antiochian, which was required for the temple treasury.

25. Davies and Allison, 2:742, n. 18, mention a number of similar legends relating to medieval Christian saints. C. H. Dodd, *Historical Tradition,* 225, n. 7, adds an example from a newspaper story from Cyprus in 1961 and compares the Hans Andersen story of the Little Tin Soldier. See also *The Arabian Nights,* tale of the 499th night. For other examples see R. Eisler, *Orpheus — the Fisher* (London, 1921), 100-105; R. J. Bauckham, *GP* 6:237-44. Such stories normally refer to the recovery of something previously lost, and the find is usually inside the fish rather than in its mouth (so Horbury, in E. Bammel and C. F. D. Moule [eds.], *Jesus,* 274), but these are hardly material differences.

26. J. D. M. Derrett's imaginative explanation (*Law,* 258-60) as to *how* it might have happened (and what type of fish was involved) does not indicate whether it did — and, if so, why Matthew doesn't say so.

27. This seems to me more probable than the suggestion that Jesus meant that Peter should sell his catch and pay the tax with the proceeds (J. Jeremias, *NT Theology,* 87) or even that he, as a "fisher of men," should go out and make a rich convert! For a similar approach see M. D. Goulder, *Midrash,* 397: "The good Lord will provide: go and try with your rod, and the first fish you catch will have enough for two of us in its mouth! The suggestion is not meant to be taken literally." Goulder, however, attributes the saying to Matthew rather than to Jesus. Albright and Mann, 213, suggest that the saying may be "the remnant of a parable."

C. LIVING TOGETHER AS DISCIPLES:
THE DISCOURSE ON RELATIONSHIPS (18:1–19:2)

Following the same pattern as with 7:28-29; 11:1; 13:35, I have included the concluding formula and transitional notice which ends this fourth main discourse within the section it concludes rather than as the opening of a new section, though of course these transitional notices look both backward and forward.

This discourse falls into two main sections, each prompted by a question from the disciples (vv. 1 and 21).[1] Apart from the insertion of the second question, however, ch. 18 runs as a continuous discourse, like those of chs. 5–7, 10, and 24–25, rather than being punctuated by repeated narrative introductions as in ch. 13. While it is convenient to divide the text into sections for the purpose of commentary, apart from the second question which divides the discourse at v. 21 all other such breaks are relatively arbitrary (see especially comment on v. 6) and should not be allowed to obscure the connected flow of the discourse as a whole.[2]

The second section consists almost entirely of a single parable, which undergirds the pronouncement of v. 22 in answer to Peter's question. The whole of this second part of the discourse is peculiar to Matthew, apart from a rather remote parallel to vv. 21-22 in Luke 17:4. The first part, on the other hand, is as usual based on a briefer Synoptic parallel which occurs at the same point in the structure of Mark's narrative (Mark 9:33-37, 42-47), together with some material loosely paralleled in Luke 17:1-3, and the parable of the lost sheep, which shares the same motif, but not the same application, with Luke 15:4-7. All this material Matthew has, as in the previous discourses, molded and expanded with other material, notably the section on dealing with sin and on the authority of the disciple community in vv. 15-20, to produce a coherent collection of Jesus' teaching within a particular subject area.

The theme of this discourse is not so much individual discipleship (though several of the examples and instructions are expressed in the singular) as the corporate life of those who are joined by their common commitment as disciples, with special attention being given to the strains and tensions to which such a life is exposed through self-concern and lack of care for fellow disciples, through bad examples and errant behavior, and through an unwillingness to forgive as we have been forgiven. These are dangers which concern every dis-

---

1. The last discourse in chs. 24–25 will also be structured as the answer to a double question from the disciples, though in that case both questions are asked together at the beginning (24:3).

2. W. G. Thompson, *Advice,* 245-51, attempts to trace the "flow of thought" and to demonstrate the coherence of the whole section 17:22–18:35.

ciple, and there is no indication that this discourse is intended, as has often been assumed, specifically for the guidance of church leaders. It has been referred to as a sort of "Manual of Discipline" or "Community Rule," on the analogy of the Qumran document variously so titled. But the emphasis in the first part is on *self*-discipline, and when the subject turns to the issue of dealing with the sins of others, the instructions are expressed in the second-person singular in vv. 15-17; it is about what the individual disciple should do. That pastoral concern does indeed, if necessary, lead to the involvement of other disciples, and in extreme cases of the whole group (the *ekklēsia,* v. 17), but it should not come to that. So when the disciplinary authority of the whole body is discussed in vv. 18-20, it is in the context of backing up the individual disciple's attempts to help a fellow disciple who has gone astray. And even here, as in the discourse as a whole, no church leaders or officers are mentioned. To take this corporate focus of vv. 17-20 as the leitmotif of the whole discourse, thus constituting it a manual for church leaders, is to get it out of proportion.[3] The "community" aspect of the discourse consists not primarily in that it prescribes corporate action, but that it guides the individual disciple on how to live in relation to other members of the community to which he or she is assumed to belong.

Is this discourse then anachronistic when set during Jesus' ministry, in that it presupposes an organized "church"? We have noted above on 16:18 that the familiar LXX term *ekklēsia* used here in v. 17 does not in itself demand such a setting. Even during Jesus' itinerant ministry the Twelve (with possibly a wider group of supporters) formed a close-knit community through their common commitment to Jesus and in their traveling and living at close quarters with him and with each other. Such a common life inevitably creates tensions, and the two questions which prompt this discourse in vv. 1 and 21 express the sort of rivalry and self-concern which would occur naturally in any such group (and which will be graphically illustrated in 20:20-28). But one saying within the discourse does look beyond that temporary situation to a period when Jesus is present with them no longer physically but spiritually (v. 20). It would, however, be unrealistic to suppose that Jesus never looked beyond the period of his earthly presence, that he envisaged the alternative lifestyle set out in chs. 5–7 as applicable only to the period of his earthly ministry, that he had expected his disciples to disband once he was gone, and that the disciple-making community which he launches in 28:18-20 was purely an afterthought. In 9:15 he clearly envisaged his disciples continuing to live as a recognizable group after his death, and the whole of the fi-

---

3. The valuable study of this chapter by W. G. Thompson, *Advice,* questions an understanding of ch. 18 as specifically relating to the role of official leaders in the church. He concludes that its contents "are better classified as wisdom sayings or advice rather than as regulations or prescriptions for a 'community-order'" (p. 266).

nal discourse in chs. 24–25 presupposes that there will be a distinctive group of those who belong to the kingdom of God both before and after the destruction of the temple, and indeed until the *parousia*. To speak of this continuing Jesus movement as "the church" perhaps raises unnecessary connotations at this point, and (despite v. 17) such language is not needed to make sense of this discourse. It is about disciples getting on together, and that is an issue which was equally relevant both before and after Jesus' death and resurrection. It is of course to be expected that Matthew has designed this anthology of Jesus' teaching with a view to some of the pastoral issues of his own Christian community,[4] which may be particularly in his mind in using the word *ekklēsia* in v. 17, but that is not to say that the issues, and the way they are addressed, could have no place in the teaching of the earthly Jesus.

A prominent feature of this chapter is the theme of the "little ones,"[5] introduced via the example of an actual child in vv. 2-5, but developed in vv. 6, 10, and 14 in a way which clearly goes beyond literal children to include fellow members of the disciple community[6] in their insignificance and vulnerability.[7] The theme has already been announced in 10:42, where "one of these little ones" is offered help "as a disciple," and will be further developed in the "smallest" brothers of Jesus in 25:40, 45. Jesus' true followers are "little children" who have received God's revelation, which is hidden from the "wise and intelligent" (11:25). So here the relationship between such disciples must be one of mutual consideration and pastoral care such as "little ones" need. By becoming "like children" (v. 3) and accepting the lowest place (20:26-27), all true disciples become, and must be treated as, "little ones." There are no "great ones" in the kingdom of heaven.

"The portrait of the church which thus emerges is an attractive one. Status-consciousness and formally constituted authority have no place. The focus is on the relationship and mutual responsibility of all members of the community, each of whom matters, and yet all of whom must regard themselves only as 'little ones.' The resultant pastoral concern and action is not the preserve of a select few, but is the responsibility of each individual disciple, and, where necessary, of the whole group together. The structure is infor-

---

4. Luz, 2:479-83, has some thought-provoking comments on the relevance of this discourse to the situation of the Protestant churches of northern Europe today, in "the approaching post-Constantinian era," as they move away from being state churches to becoming again minority "sects" as Matthew's community was.

5. See my *Matthew: Evangelist,* 264-65.

6. Note that the change of vocabulary from παιδίον, "child," to μικρός, "little one," in v. 6 coincides with the designation of those referred to as "those who believe in me." On the transition from "child" to "little one" see Davies and Allison, 2:753-54.

7. For the concept, but not the specific terminology of "little ones," cf. the beatitudes in 5:3-10, especially those on the poor in spirit, the meek, and the persecuted.

mal, but the sense of community is intense. And overarching it all is the consciousness of the presence of Jesus and of the forgiveness and pastoral concern of 'your Father in heaven.'"[8]

1. The Disciples' Question about Status (18:1)

1 At that time the disciples came to Jesus and asked, "So[9] who is the greatest[10] in the kingdom of heaven?"

The question of comparative status within the disciple group is a recurrent one; cf. 20:26-28; 23:11-12, and, in addition to Marcan and Lucan parallels to these passages, Luke 22:24-27 (even at the Last Supper!). For the concept of comparative status in the kingdom of heaven cf. 5:19; 11:11. Usage so far in this gospel indicates that "the kingdom of heaven" here refers to the new values which Jesus is inculcating, and the communal life of those who embrace them, so that in effect the question means "Who is the top disciple?" The question has become more urgent as Jesus has made it clearer that he is to die; in that case, who is to take the lead when he is gone?[11]

But the opening "at that time" and still more the connective "So" (see n. 9) indicate a more specific link with the preceding pericope. How then has the issue of the temple tax provoked this question? Jesus' argument was one of comparative status, that of the "sons" in relation to "strangers," and the privileges that go with it. Moreover, this argument has been based on the accepted practice of the "kings of the earth": so does the kingdom of heaven operate along similar lines? If so, who are the privileged "sons"? We have noted in 17:24-27 the possibility that Jesus includes the disciples with himself in that special status, but they want the issue clarified.

8. R. T. France, *Matthew: Evangelist,* 252. Cf. E. Schweizer, in G. N. Stanton (ed.), *Interpretation,* 161, who sees in ch. 18 "a community which seems to know neither elders nor bishops nor deacons," in which "everyone is involved on a par with everyone else."

9. The particle ἄρα normally indicates some inference from a previous statement (as in 17:26, "Well then"; cf. 7:20; 12:28; 19:25, 27). See the comments below on the connection intended here.

10. The Greek comparative often does duty for the superlative (BDF 60, 244), and in the case of μέγας the "true" superlative μέγιστος appears in the NT only at 2 Pet 1:4 (where the sense is in fact elative rather than genuinely superlative). There is of course a comparative element here, in that the issue is that of relative status, but the superlative is the natural way to express the question in English. The comparative μείζων is used similarly in 23:11 and in the Synoptic parallels Mark 9:34; Luke 9:46; 22:24, 26; in some of these the comparative sense would be quite inappropriate.

11. Cf. *Gos. Thom.* 12: "The disciples said to Jesus, 'We know that you will go away from us; who is it that will then be great over us?'"

And there is a further factor which has sharpened the question: in the previous pericope, as in several other situations already in the gospel, Peter has been in the limelight, living up to Matthew's singling him out as "first" (10:2). His declaration at 16:16 has evoked Jesus' warm commendation of his insight (16:17) and a consequent statement about his special role and authority in the founding of Jesus' *ekklēsia* (16:18-19), and Peter with his two closest colleagues has been singled out for a special journey with Jesus up the mountain (17:1), leaving the rest of the disciples behind to face a difficult situation. In 17:24-27 it has been assumed that Peter speaks for Jesus, and Jesus' "solution" to the tax problem has included Peter along with himself, to the apparent exclusion of the rest of the Twelve. "*So* who is the greatest in the kingdom of heaven?"

2. The Example of the Child (18:2-5)

> 2 *Jesus called a child to him, and placed the child*[1] *in the middle of them* 3 *and said, "I tell you truly: if you don't turn around and become like children, you will never get into the kingdom of heaven.* 4 *And so it is anyone who will take the lowly position of*[2] *this child who is the greatest in the kingdom of heaven.* 5 *And anyone who welcomes*[3] *one such child in my name welcomes me."*

The example of the child will lead into a more general discussion about "little ones" in the following discourse, but in these opening verses the teaching will be focused on this one child, used as a model for true discipleship in vv. 3-4 and as a model for how one should treat other disciples in v. 5. The disciples' question sets the agenda for these verses: they are about status, as the repeated use of "little ones" in the following verses will underline. The instruction to "become like children" is thus not about adopting some supposed ethical characteristic of children in general (innocence, humility, receptiveness, trustfulness, or the like)[4] but about accepting for oneself a position in

---

1. Greek has the neuter pronoun αὐτό, taking up the grammatical gender of παιδίον, "child," so that it is not indicated whether the child was male or female; since "it" is not appropriate for a human subject in English, I have repeated "the child."

2. See the comments below for the meaning of the ταπεινός word-group. The traditional translation would be "humbles himself like this child," but the word "humble" in English too easily conveys the idea of a mental attitude, whereas what is at issue here is comparative status within the group.

3. See the comments on 10:40-41.

4. One wonders whether some commentators who speak of children as "unselfconscious," "unconcerned about status," and the like have ever been parents! Luz, 2:427, lists some quite remarkable examples from the (presumably unmarried) Church Fathers,

the social scale which is like that of children, that is, as the lowest in the hierarchy of authority and decision making, those subject to and dependent on adults.[5] The phrase "take the lowly position" in v. 4 (see n. 2) confirms this understanding of what the context already demands. Children are socially as well as physically "little ones" (v. 6). If the disciples' question about being "great" was prompted by a desire to exercise authority over others, they have started at the wrong end. Their "grown-up" sense of social position puts them out of sympathy with God's value-scale.

The Synoptic parallels to this pericope are complicated by the fact that both Mark and Luke have a separate saying, set in the context of the blessing of the children (Mark 10:15; Luke 18:17), which combines elements of vv. 3 ("I tell you truly," "will never get into the kingdom of heaven") and 5 ("welcome," "child") but relates not to welcoming a child but to welcoming the kingdom of God "as a child."[6] Matthew does not include that verse in his account of the blessing of the children (19:13-15), but here has a statement about becoming like a child (v. 3) to which Mark and Luke have no parallel. Matthew thus achieves a more coherent sequence of thought (both here and in 19:13-15) which also then leads naturally into the Matthean language about the "little ones" which follows in vv. 6-14 (see comments below on v. 6 for the continuity of the thought).

2 Jesus' love of parables and vivid illustrations here reaches perhaps its most striking expression in the use of a child as a "visual aid." In the Fourth Gospel a similar lesson about status is equally graphically illustrated by Jesus' own action of washing his disciples' feet (John 13:2-15). He is calling for so radical an inversion of their natural assumptions about leadership and importance that shock tactics are needed. We are given no indication of the identity of the child, and that is as it should be: the child's very anonymity helps to make the point.

3 This solemn warning[7] uses the same language about "getting into the kingdom of heaven" as we have seen in 5:20[8] and 7:21; it will recur in

---

such as the pronouncement of Euthymius Zigabenus that children "are not inquisitive . . . are free of malice and rivalry . . . and stubborn passion"!

5. W. Carter, *Households,* 95-113, provides a detailed survey of the status of and attitudes to children in the ancient world, noting a "dominant pattern of subordination, marginality and general impatience with children," which was by the first century, however, beginning to be offset by a more positive attitude in the Greco-Roman world.

6. The phrase is ambiguous, but in context I think it more likely that it means "as a child welcomes it" than "as one welcomes a child." In that case the sense would be similar to that of Matt 18:3.

7. For "I tell you truly" see on 5:18.

8. See the comments there; the saying is constructed similarly to the present verse.

19:23-24; 23:13 (cf. "entering into life" in 18:8-9 and 19:17). Its use here is surprising, since we have been led to assume throughout the gospel that the disciples are already within God's kingship, as opposed to those depicted in 5:20 and 7:21 who are in danger of never being true people of God; is Jesus here then suggesting that their position as disciples remains under threat? That is probably to import too rigid a typology of "saved" and "lost" into the phrase, but it strongly warns them that the concern for status which they have just displayed is not compatible with God's scale of values, and that true discipleship must involve the eradication of this natural human tendency. There is no room for complacency even for those who have become God's subjects, as the imagery of 22:11-14 will sharply remind us later.

The KJV rendering "except ye be converted" suggests, at least in our modern usage, too technical a sense for the quite ordinary verb "turn," but while the verb in itself is not technical,[9] to speak of conversion suitably draws out the radical nature of the change Jesus is calling for. To abandon human thoughts of personal status and to accept or even seek a place at the bottom of the pecking order implies as radical a change of orientation as our term "conversion" involves.[10] To turn around and become like a child is in effect to start again on a new footing; cf. the language of rebirth in John 3:3, 5.[11] To belong to the kingdom of heaven requires no less.[12]

4 The way has now been prepared for a direct answer to the disciples' question. The *tapeinos* word-group is traditionally translated by "hum-

9. It is the compound verb ἐπιστρέφω (rather than the simple στρέφω, as here) that is used to denote the turning to God which is the beginning of Christian commitment in Acts 3:19; 9:35; 11:21, etc., and cf. the noun ἐπιστροφή in this technical sense of "conversion" in Acts 15:3. But this usage, belonging to the period of apostolic preaching after Easter, does not belong here.

10. This sense of radical change is weakened by the suggestion of J. Jeremias, *Theology*, 155, that στρέφω here represents an Aramaic verb which does not function as a verb in its own right but as an auxiliary with the sense of "again." He therefore translates, "Unless you become like children again." But the Greek verb does not naturally function in that way. Its OT background in the verb *šûb* conveys rather the sense of repentance, of a reorientation of life. See further against Jeremias's proposal J. W. Pryor, *JSNT* 41 (1991) 82-84.

11. J. W. Pryor, *JSNT* 41 (1991) 71-95, discusses at length the possible relationship between these Johannine sayings and the Synoptic tradition. He concludes that they are particularly closely related to Matt 18:3, but is not convinced of a direct literary dependence.

12. A knowledge of this saying is reflected in *Gos. Thom.* 22, where Jesus compares young children to "those who enter the kingdom," and the disciples ask, "If we are children, shall we enter the kingdom?" (to which unfortunately Jesus gives a complicated Gnostic answer which effectively changes the subject), and in *Gos. Thom.* 46, "Whoever among you will become a little one will know the kingdom and will be greater than John."

ble," which in English normally has a strongly ethical implication denoting a mental attitude. The Greek adjective *tapeinos* can carry the same connotation (as in 11:29),[13] but the verb *tapeinoō* which is used here regularly denotes status, often in direct opposition to *hypsoō*, "to lift up" (as in 23:12); its meaning is thus closer to "humiliate," so that to "make oneself *tapeinos*[14] like this child" (the literal translation of the expression here) does not mean to attempt to gain the mental virtue of humility[15] which is supposed (by whom? — not by most parents or teachers!) to be characteristic of children, but rather to accept the low social status which is symbolized by the child, who in an adult world has no self-determination and must submit to the will of adults who "know best." The paradox expressed in this verse is therefore stark: the least are the greatest, as in 19:30, "the first last and the last first."

5 Jesus' second comment about the child he has set up as an example looks not now at the child's own position but at how other people regard the child. It thus moves us forward into the main area of concern in this discourse, how disciples should treat one another. The child is to be welcomed "in Jesus' name," just as in 10:40-42 we heard of welcoming a prophet, a righteous person, or a "little one" literally "in the name of a prophet/righteous person/disciple." We noted there (p. 412, n. 2) that the "in the name of" formula indicates that "they are welcomed not simply as persons but in the light of their perceived role as God's prophets (righteous persons; disciples), and that it is that status which has triggered the welcome." But here the child is to be welcomed not simply as a child, but "in Jesus' name," which implies that the child represents Jesus (just as in 25:40, 45 Jesus' smallest brothers represent him), so that to welcome them is to welcome Jesus himself. In this way Jesus gives to the least important person a significance out of all proportion to their human standing. The last is indeed first.

The welcome is to be given to "one such child." The word "such" suggests that already we are moving beyond the specific child introduced in v. 2 to a wider category of people whom that child represents. That category will no doubt include those who are literally children, but the wider reference of "little ones" in the next part of the discourse points us beyond children as such to all who, as instructed in vv. 3-4, have adopted the childlike position. Jas 2:1-4 dramatically calls for such a welcome to be given to the humanly unimportant.

13. This sense of personal attitude is often conveyed in the NT by ταπεινόφρων / ταπεινοφροσύνη rather than the simple ταπεινός.

14. Note the use of the same phrase in Phil 2:8, the most radical example of voluntary loss of status (there is no suggestion that Jesus achieved a previously absent quality of humility!).

15. I am reminded of an applicant who in response to the application form question "What are your greatest strengths?" replied, "My greatest strength is humility." (Yes, really!)

3. Care for the Little Ones: The Danger of Stumbling Blocks (18:6-9)

6 *"But if anyone causes one of these little ones who believe in me to stumble, it would be good for them to have a heavy millstone*[1] *hung around their neck and to be drowned in the deepest sea.*[2] 7 *Woe to the world because of stumbling blocks; for stumbling blocks are bound to occur, but woe to the person through whom the stumbling block occurs.*

8 *"But if your hand or your foot causes you to stumble, cut it off and throw it away: you are better off entering into life crippled*[3] *or lame than keeping both hands or both feet and being thrown into the eternal fire.* 9 *And if your eye causes you to stumble, tear it out and throw it away: you are better off entering into life with one eye than keeping both eyes and being thrown into hellfire.*[4]

These sayings, the second of which (vv. 8-9) is roughly parallel to 5:29-30, are held together by the repeated mention of stumbling, *skandalizō/skandalon* (see above on 5:29-30). In order to maintain this connection I have again translated the metaphor literally (as in 17:27, though the type of "scandal" involved there was different from this context of pastoral care within the disciple community). Here, as in 5:29-30 and 13:21, the "stumbling" envisaged is much more drastic than simply "being offended" or even "scandalized." It appears to envisage fatal damage to the disciple's relationship with God. They are caused to "trip" so as to be in danger of falling out of the race altogether. So serious a danger demands extremely serious measures, whether in the punishment of the person responsible (vv. 6-7) or in the elimination of the source of the problem when it is within oneself (vv. 8-9). The result is that these verses contain some of the most severe teaching on spiritual punishment in the gospels. They take hell very seriously.

Apart from the common theme of "stumbling" the two sayings have a different focus. The first is about causing trouble for other disciples, which fits well into the general theme of the discourse; the second seems less appropriate in this context, being about dangers in one's own life. But the two may of course be connected, as it is likely that the sort of ungodly behavior sym-

---

1. Literally, "a donkey millstone," the upper grinding stone of a mill worked by donkey power being much heavier than that of a handmill.
2. The Greek τὸ πέλαγος τῆς θαλάσσης is literally something like "the ocean of the sea"; πέλαγος denotes the deep, open sea as opposed to the shallow part near the shore. It is a place where there is no hope of rescue from drowning (even without a donkey millstone around your neck!).
3. See above, p. 596, n. 2, for the translation of κυλλός.
4. Literally, "the hell of fire," as in 5:22.

bolized by the offending hand, foot, or eye will have its effect not only on the person responsible but also on others within a close-knit disciple community, within which "no man is an island," and so may cause them, as well as oneself, to stumble. This community is, as vv. 10-14 will go on to spell out more fully, made up of "little ones," and that term implies not only their mutual pecking order but also their vulnerability, like that of the child presented in vv. 2-5. In such a community mutual pastoral concern, such as will be illustrated by the parable of the sheep in vv. 12-14, is a high priority, and it is this pastoral concern which makes the danger of "stumbling blocks" so acute.

6 I have made a break between vv. 5 and 6 in order to draw attention to the new vocabulary now introduced ("cause to stumble," "one of these little ones"), which will dominate the following section. There is no break in the sense, however: the present verse follows closely from v. 5, with the opening clauses of the two verses using the same Greek construction to contrast the two attitudes of "welcoming" one such child and causing one of these little ones to stumble.[5]

To "believe in me *(eis eme)*" is a very common Johannine phrase, and language about "believing in" Jesus recurs throughout the rest of the NT, but this is the only time the phrase occurs in the Synoptic Gospels,[6] the nearest parallel being in 27:42, the ironical proposal of becoming Jesus' disciples by those who had condemned him to death, where the preposition is (probably — there are textual variants) *epi* rather than *eis*. The phrase serves to define who are meant by the "little ones" here and in vv. 10 and 14, so that to "believe in Jesus" describes those who are disciples.[7] But the phrase is not necessarily used here in its later sense to mean simply, as we would say, "being a Christian"; it may carry more of the connotation of "trust" which *pisteuō* generally carries in Matthew — "believing in Jesus" would be a good description of the attitude of the centurion in 8:5-13. The seriousness of the charge lies in that these "little ones" have put their trust in Jesus but someone else (a fellow disciple?) has damaged that trust.

RSV and NIV translated *skandalizō* here (and elsewhere) by "cause to sin," but that is too specific (and has been rightly changed to "cause to stumble" in NRSV, TNIV); GNB probably gets closer to the sense with "cause to lose their faith," but other versions tend to prefer to keep the metaphor unspecified (e.g., "cause the downfall of," REB, NJB). To lead a person into sin

---

5. W. G. Thompson, *Advice,* 106-7, accordingly opts to connect v. 5 with vv. 6-9 rather than with vv. 1-4.

6. In the parallel in Mark 9:42 the phrase εἰς ἐμέ occurs in many MSS, but is probably an assimilation to the text of Matthew (and to later Christian usage).

7. W. G. Thompson, *Advice,* 119, sums up from his preceding discussion the reasons for understanding the "little ones" in this broad sense rather than as denoting a subgroup among disciples.

is one means of causing them to "stumble," but their life and development as disciples may equally be damaged by discouragement or unfair criticism,[8] by a lack of pastoral care, or by the failure to forgive which will be highlighted in vv. 21-35. The "despising" of the little ones in v. 10 is the attitude which promotes such damaging behavior toward them.

The punishment for so doing is not spelled out. If a quick drowning[9] is preferable,[10] the alternative must be terrible, and the "woe" which follows in v. 7 underlines its seriousness. The result of being caused to stumble by one's own fault is spelled out in vv. 8-9 in terms of eternal fire and hell, and it is unlikely that the penalty for bringing about another's downfall would be any less. The "little ones" are so important to Jesus that to cause spiritual damage to even one of them is a more than capital offense.

7 This double "woe"[11] underlines two aspects of the problem. One is the terrible fate of the offender, as we have noted above. But the other is broader: "the world" itself suffers from such behavior. "The world" *(kosmos)* here refers especially to the world of people rather than the physical creation as a whole; for this sense of *kosmos* cf. 4:8; 5:14; 13:38; 26:13.[12] People in general are bound to be confronted by stumbling blocks; the world is a dangerous place. The "necessity" of such problems *(anankē* speaks of inevitability) springs not from a specific divine purpose but from the nature of things in a fallen world; cf. 13:37-43 for this acceptance that evil (including "stumbling blocks," 13:41) will remain in the world until the final consummation. Discipleship was never going to be an easy proposition, but that is no reason for anyone to make it harder by irresponsible behavior toward fellow disciples. The idea that people are responsible for their actions even though these are "necessary" is one which runs through both OT and NT (most notably in the story of Judas Iscariot; note a similar "woe" specifically directed at him

8. Cf. 5:21-22 for the severe penalty merited by an apparently mild term of abuse.

9. The millstone ensures that there is no chance of survival. Cf. Rev 18:21, where a heavy millstone thrown into the sea symbolizes the total destruction of Babylon.

10. συμφέρει αὐτῷ, "it is to his advantage," is used without any comparative term here, but the same expression in 5:29-30 is followed by a "rather than" clause, and the same implication seems clear here, even though the alternative is not spelled out. Cf. also the sayings of vv. 8-9, which similarly set out alternatives, using the different but equivalent formula καλόν σοί ἐστιν . . . ἤ, "it is good for you . . . rather than."

11. For the "woe" formula see above on 11:21 and below, pp. 867-68. The second of these woes is of the more common denunciatory type, but the first, like 24:19, expresses sympathy rather than blame.

12. Hagner, 2:522, takes it pejoratively, and translates "Woe to the world for the stumbling blocks *it brings*" (ibid., 519), but this Johannine sense of κόσμος would be unique in Matthew. The more natural sense here is that the κόσμος suffers from, rather than is the source of, the σκάνδαλα. In the second half of the saying the source of the stumbling block is a specific person, not "the world" in general.

in 26:24). The fact that a person is operating within a determined structure does not excuse them for their personal choices and decisions.

8-9 This double saying is differently phrased and constructed from that of 5:29-30, but its thrust is the same. This is a rather fuller version, and corresponds more closely to the parallel in Mark 9:43-47, so that 5:29-30 is probably best seen as a slightly abridged and rearranged version of this saying. For the startling imagery of amputation as a preferable alternative to damnation see the comments on that earlier saying.[13] There the specific context was a warning against adultery (mental as well as literal), but here the scope is not limited, and the principles which applied there to the avoidance of dangerous behavior and attitudes can as well be applied to other areas of human sinfulness. The whole warning is expressed in the second-person singular:[14] it is for individual disciples to work out for themselves where their particular danger of "stumbling" lies and to take appropriate action.

The only significant difference from 5:29-30 in the wording of the conditional clauses and the imperatives is the inclusion this time of the foot along with the hand (following but abbreviating Mark 9:43, 45), which expands but does not alter the imagery. In the explanatory clauses there is more variation in wording, but not in content. The place of punishment now is not simply "hell" but "the eternal fire" and "hellfire." "Eternal" *(aiōnios)* will be used in 25:41, 46 for the ultimate fate both of the saved ("eternal life"; cf. also 19:16, 29) and the lost ("eternal fire," "eternal punishment"), and we shall discuss its implications more fully there. The adjective derives from the noun *aiōn,* which we have seen used in 12:32 to distinguish between the two "ages" of this present life and life after death; cf. also the description of this world as "this *aiōn*" in 13:22, and the frequent use of "the end of the *aiōn*" to denote the end of the present world order (13:39, 40, 49; 24:3; 28:20). The fire here therefore belongs to the "age to come"; the reference is to ultimate punishment, as the parallel use of "hell" in 5:29-30 would suggest. For fire as an image for the ultimate judgment see 3:10-12; 7:19; 13:40, 42, 50, and for the more specific expression "hellfire" see on 5:22 (cf. also destruction in hell, 10:28).

In 5:29-30 the alternative to hell was stated simply as the loss of one part of the body, but here it is more positively described as "entering into

13. Luz, 2:436 (and 1:297, n. 50), quotes a few instances of similar imagery used by pagan writers.

14. This fact stands against the interpretation, suggested by the corporate concern of the discourse as a whole, that these two verses are speaking metaphorically of the need for the community to cut out from its membership those individuals who are causes of stumbling to others. Such a reading (which goes back to Origen) would follow well from vv. 6-7, but could hardly have been expressed in the singular, and would be quite inappropriate to the parallel saying in 5:29-30.

life" without the affected part. While this life is not specifically said to be "eternal," analogy with the fire would suggest this, and the same phrase in 19:17 stands alongside the specific mention of "eternal life" in 19:16, 29 (cf. also 25:46). Coming so soon after the statement about "entering the kingdom of heaven" in v. 3, this phrase may reasonably be assumed to have a related meaning, eternal life being the prerogative of those who belong to God's kingship. "To enter the kingdom of heaven" does not *mean* "to go to heaven" (see on 5:20), but that is the ultimate destiny of those who are God's true subjects, and the phrase "enter into life" here appropriately spells out that heavenly destiny. As in 5:29-30, it is appropriate to warn against a too literal application of the imagery of this saying to suggest that amputees will find themselves disadvantaged in heaven.

4. Care for the Little Ones: The Parable of the Sheep (18:10-14)

10 *"See to it that you do not despise one of these little ones; for I tell you that their angels in heaven are always looking at the face of my Father who is in heaven.*[1]

12 *"What do you think? If someone has a hundred sheep, and one of them wanders away, won't he leave the ninety-nine on the hills and go and look for the one that is wandering?* 13 *And if he manages to find*[2] *it, I tell you truly that he rejoices over it more than over the ninety-nine that never wandered away.* 14 *In the same way it is not the will of*[3] *your*[4] *Father in heaven that one*[5] *of these little ones should be lost.*

1. Many MSS and versions include here "For the Son of Man came to [seek and] save the lost." The saying is well established at Luke 19:10, but it is hard to see why several of the most important witnesses should omit it here if it was originally present. It looks more like a well-intentioned addition reflecting on the message of the parable of the sheep, but rather awkwardly inserted before rather than after it.

2. The use of γένηται εὑρεῖν rather than simply εὑρῃ places emphasis on the successful outcome of the search; colloquially we might say "he gets to find it."

3. Literally, "there is not will before (ἔμπροσθεν, in front of) your Father." Cf. 11:26, "thus was good will before (ἔμπροσθεν) you," an awkward bit of Greek probably reflecting the Semitic idiom "pleasing in the eyes of" (see BDF 214[6]).

4. MSS and versions are divided between ὑμῶν, "your," and μου, "my" (with a few also opting improbably for ἡμῶν, "our," which would be a unique usage in Matthew except when Jesus is telling his disciples what *they* should say, 6:9). Both "my Father in heaven" and "your Father in heaven" are familiar expressions in Matthew. Here it is more likely that some scribes changed "your" to "my" under the influence of the latter expression in v. 10. The second-person expression is especially appropriate here where Jesus is calling on the disciples to learn from the example of "your Father."

5. In v. 6 "one" was masculine and in v. 10 the genitive could be either masculine or neuter, but here the generally accepted reading is the neuter ἕν. This is surprising, since

684

The thought of disciples (not restricted to children, though of course including them) as "little ones" (v. 6) continues. Verses 6-7 contemplated the possibility of a "little one" being caused to stumble and so lost from the life of discipleship. These verses underline how serious such a situation would be. The point is made explicitly in vv. 10 and 14 by emphasizing how much every single "little one" matters to God, and therefore should matter also to fellow disciples. In between these verses a short parable reinforces the message that the one matters just as much as the many, and by likening the "little one" to a wandering sheep reminds the disciples again of how vulnerable they all are. But it also reassures them that they have a "Father in heaven" who cares for each one, and whose pastoral concern is meant to be shared by all his people.

Whereas vv. 8-9 were expressed in the singular, the appeal here is to the disciples corporately; the disciple community should not merely be made up of caring individuals, but should be a caring body, with a corporate pastoral concern for the problems faced by each individual.

The "framing" verses 10 and 14 are peculiar to Matthew, but the parable looks like a reduced version of that in Luke 15:4-7.[6] Both have the theme of the effort made to recover a lost sheep and the joy of the shepherd when he finds it, and both contrast the one with the ninety-nine. But among the various differences in wording one may be significant: in Luke the sheep is already "lost," whereas here it is "wandering away" (the word is repeated three times). This may be no more than an idiomatic variation, but the contexts in which the two parables are set, and the audiences to which they are addressed, suggest that it may indicate a different focus. In Luke the parable is addressed to Pharisaic critics and justifies Jesus' outreach to the "lost" tax collectors and sinners who are outside the disciple group, whereas here Jesus is speaking to his own disciples and the emphasis is on disciples caring for one another so that none who are already "inside" will wander away. To oversimplify the difference, Luke's parable is evangelistic, and Matthew's pastoral. This may be to press a slight difference in wording too far, especially as in both parables the sheep is a former member of the flock. But in view of the section which follows here in vv. 15-17 about what to do if "your brother sins," it may be that Matthew's

---

it is clearly a *person* who is being talked about, and many MSS have replaced it with the more expected εἷς. The neuter presumably derives from the neuter noun παιδίον, "child" (see p. 567, n. 1), from which the whole discussion of "little ones" has developed (or, less probably, from the "one" [ἕν] sheep which in v. 12 symbolizes the "little one"). There is nothing to suggest a different reference within the three uses of "*one* of these little ones" in vv. 6, 10, and 14.

6. While the basic story line is the same, the wording is surprisingly different; on this basis Carson, 400, argues that the two parables are not the result of variation in the tradition but of Jesus using the same story on different occasions and for different purposes. Similarly but more cautiously I. H. Marshall, *Luke,* 600.

"wandering" sheep is meant to depict a situation where things have not gone quite as far as in Luke's version, where it is already "lost."[7]

10 To "despise" is the opposite of the "welcome" in v. 5. It is the natural way of the world to "despise little ones," in the sense of not taking them seriously or giving their interests priority. Here, as so often, Jesus attacks the values of the rat race. It is not just "little ones" as a class who must be respected and welcomed, but, as in vv. 6 and 14, every single "one" of them individually.

The thrust of the second half of the verse is apparently to state, as in v. 14, that every "little one" matters to God. Those who might easily be despised on earth are represented in heaven by angels who are important enough to have privileged access to God. To "look at the face of God" reflects courtly language for personal access to the king (cf. 2 Sam 14:24, 32; Esth 1:14); for the ultimate privilege of seeing the face of God see Rev 22:4, and see further the discussion of "seeing God" at 5:8 above.[8]

"Their angels in heaven" is an expression unique in biblical literature. Perhaps the nearest parallel to the idea of an angel linked with an individual human being is in Acts 12:15, where the presence at the door of Peter, who is assumed to be in prison or dead, is taken to be "his angel" (where we might have spoken of "his ghost"). There are hints of the idea of an individual guardian angel in Gen 48:16 (where the "angel" seems in the parallelism to be the same as God) and in the story of Tobias (Tob 5:4ff.), where the archangel Raphael acts as companion and guardian to Tobias during his journey, though there is no suggestion that he is permanently linked with Tobias as "his" angel. Dan 3:28; 6:22 speak of an angel sent for a specific act of deliverance (cf. Pss 34:7; 91:11-12; *1 En.* 100:5). There are also angelic representatives of nations (with Michael as Israel's representative) in Dan 10:13, 20; 12:1; and Rev 1:20 will speak of angels representing churches. But none of this gives a clear basis for the conception of angels in heaven representing individual people on earth.[9] Heb 1:14 talks of angels "serving" God's people, but without specify-

---

7. So, e.g., W. G. Thompson, *Advice*, 164, 168-74.

8. In commenting on 5:8 we have noted the psalmists' aspiration of seeing the face of God. But there is a contrasting strand in OT and later Jewish spirituality which says that no human being may see God's face (e.g., Gen 32:30; Exod 33:18-23; cf. John 1:18; 1 Tim 1:17; 6:16), and even that some angels may not look directly at God (Isa 6:2; *1 En.* 14:21), so that those angels who are permitted to do so are distinguished as (literally) the "angels of the face" (*Jub.* 2:2, 18; 1QH 6:13; 1QSb 4:26; and cf. the description of the four archangels in *1 En.* 40 and of Raphael in Tob 12:15 and Gabriel in Luke 1:19). If (and it is a big "if"; see Davies and Allison, 2:771) this is the background to the present saying, it would add even further to the prestige of the "little ones": their angels are superior to ordinary angels (cf. O. Michel, *TDNT* 4:651, n. 15).

9. For an alternative interpretation, which takes the "angels" to be the spirits of

---

ing any individual connection. Subsequent Christian devotion has developed the idea of a personal "guardian angel,"[10] probably influenced by this passage, and there are parallels in later Jewish writings (Str-B 1:781-83), but there is little evidence that the idea was already popularly accepted among Jews at the time of Jesus.[11] Hagner, 2:527, argues that the idea of an individual guardian angel (which most commentators assume) is not spelled out here as such; he finds here rather "a more general idea . . . that angels represent the 'little ones' before the throne of God" — thinking apparently of angelic representatives of the class of "little ones" rather than of each individual.

12-13   Care for the "little ones" is illustrated by a simple parable. Following the principle established in 13:10-17, 34, this parable, spoken to the disciples rather than to the crowd, comes with a clear explanation of its intended application in vv. 10 and 14. The straying sheep represents one of God's "little ones." The shepherd in the story is apparently the owner of the flock, not a hired helper[12] — John 10:11-15 draws out the importance of the distinction. So each sheep is important to him, not as a matter of sentimentality but as a financial asset, and to lose one would be serious. One that has wandered off becomes an easy prey to wolves or thieves, and so he takes action to recover it before it is too late.[13] We are not told how he secures the rest of the flock "on the hills" while he goes off: perhaps by leaving them with a colleague[14] or by enclosing them in a sheepfold?[15] The greater joy over the

---

the little ones after death, see Carson, 401. Evidence for such a use of "angel" is hard to find (though it would be a possible way of taking Acts 12:15); in 22:30 those who are resurrected are said to be "like" angels, not to be angels (see p. 537, n. 23). And the present tense, "are always looking at," fits very uncomfortably with this interpretation.

10. See Davies and Allison, 2:772.

11. Perhaps the earliest Jewish hint of individual guardian angels is in *Jub.* 35:17, which speaks of separate "protectors" for Jacob and for Esau. The idea is, however, apparently well established in such post-Christian writings as *3 Bar.* 12–13; *T. Adam* 4:1; *T. Jac.* 2:5. Davies and Allison, 2:770, n. 82, also list a number of Hellenistic examples of the idea of a δαίμων accompanying an individual, and Luz, 2:441, gives references for the comparable ideas of the *fravashi* (Persian) and the *genius* (Roman).

12. K. E. Bailey, *Poet*, 148, argues, however, that anyone wealthy enough to own a hundred sheep would not do his own shepherding, so that "has" must mean "has in his charge" rather than "owns." But Bailey concludes that the shepherd in such a case would be a member of the extended family rather than a hired stranger, so that the point that the sheep matter to the shepherd remains.

13. The "if" of v. 13a presupposes that not every straying sheep will be found, but it is not appropriate to the nature of a parable to press this detail of the story line into service for a discussion of the eternal security of God's people.

14. So K. E. Bailey, *Poet*, 149-50, pointing out that a hundred sheep would require more than one shepherd.

15. The mention of the number "ninety-nine" and the fact that he knows one is

one recovered sheep than over the ninety-nine "good" sheep emphasizes God's pastoral care: it is caused by the recovery, rather than by any inherent superiority in the sheep itself.[16] The natural tendency to regard such discriminatory joy as unfair is firmly repudiated in the figure of the elder brother in Luke 15:25-32.

The practical implications of the story will become clear from the verses that follow: if one member of the disciple community is in spiritual danger, action must be taken to "win" them back (v. 15). To do so is to share the pastoral care of God, the true shepherd of his people. The imagery is thus of an insider who has to be kept from straying outside the fold rather than (as seems to be the primary intention of Luke 15:4-7 in context) of an outsider to be brought in.

The Fourth Gospel develops the idea of Jesus as the good shepherd, and there are hints of this in the Synoptic tradition as well (2:6; 26:31, and see on 9:36), but the imagery here derives from the OT, where God the shepherd is a frequent theme (Pss 23; 95:7; Jer 23:1-4; Ezek 34:11-16, etc.),[17] and the wording of this parable reflects this OT shepherd language, particularly that of Ezek 34:11-16. The explanation of the parable in v. 14 will focus on God rather than Jesus as the one who owns and cares for the sheep. But there is of course no incompatibility between this OT-based concept of God as shepherd and the Johannine imagery of Jesus as the good shepherd — indeed, the two are explicitly brought together in John 10:27-30.[18]

14 For similar "explanations" of parables cf. not only the detailed interpretations in 13:18-23, 36-43, 49-50 but also 11:18-19; 21:31-32, 43; 24:33, 44, and the parable application which concludes this discourse in v. 35. Matthew (and Jesus?) seems to have been innocent of the modern scholarly dogma that a parable should not be explained or applied but left to speak for itself! The explanation given here focuses only on the direct application of the imagery of the parable to God as the shepherd, but the introduction in v. 10 made it clear that the disciples are expected to reflect the pastoral mind of

---

missing have been taken to indicate that the shepherd has just counted the rest of his sheep into the fold for the night.

16. *Gos. Thom.* 107 misses, and indeed reverses, the point of the parable: in its version the sheep which has gone astray is not a little one but "the biggest," and when the shepherd has recovered it he says, "I love you more than the ninety-nine"! For Gnostic interpretations of this parable, which may cast some light on the *Gospel of Thomas* version, see Luz, 2:444. W. L. Petersen, *NovT* 23 (1981) 128-47, argues, however, that the sheep in the *Thomas* version represents Israel.

17. For the tendency of God's sheep to "stray" cf. Ps 119:176; Isa 53:6.

18. K. E. Bailey, *Poet,* 147, discusses the interesting question of how this very positive use of shepherd imagery relates to the low social standing (even "uncleanness") of actual shepherds in the ancient Near East.

God, and it will be the individual disciple who is expected to take the necessary remedial action in vv. 15-17 to ensure that God's pastoral concern is implemented among his people. To be "lost" (the verb can also mean "destroy") is the potential end result of the sheep's "wandering away"; the term has been used of ultimate spiritual disaster in 7:13; 10:28, 39; 16:25. Its use following the parable of the sheep reminds us of the "lost sheep of the house of Israel" whom Jesus and his disciples are sent to bring back to God (10:6; 15:24).

5. Dealing with a Brother's Sin (18:15-17)

15 *"But if your[1] brother or sister[2] sins,[3] go and confront[4] them, just between the two of you. If they listen to you, you have won your brother or sister. 16 But if they do not listen, take with you one or two others as well, so that 'every charge[5] may be sustained on the evidence of two or three witnesses.' 17 If they refuse to listen to them, speak to the church; and if they refuse to listen even to the church, let them be to you like a Gentile and a tax collector.*

1. "You(r)" throughout vv. 15-17 is singular.

2. As in 5:22-24, where the reference is clearly to any fellow disciple, not specifically to a male one, it is appropriate in modern English to spell out "brother or sister" for Greek ἀδελφός; for women among the disciple group at this stage see 27:55. The "singular they's" that follow are needed to maintain the non-gender-specific reference in English, but the focus remains on one individual dealing with another.

3. The addition of εἰς σέ, "against you," at this point in the majority of MSS and versions changes an altruistic concern about a brother's spiritual danger into a personal grievance. That personal concern will be appropriate, and is made explicit, in Peter's question in v. 21 (εἰς ἐμέ), which leads into the discussion of forgiveness for personal wrongs, but to introduce it here, where it is the brother's welfare, not "your" interest, which is in focus, is premature; it is probably due to a mechanical reading back of the phrase from v. 21. The shorter reading of א and B (in agreement with the parallel in Luke 17:3, where there is less support for an added εἰς σέ) is thus to be preferred (so also W. G. Thompson, *Advice,* 176-77). The matter is complicated by the possibility of a mishearing, since the additional εἰς σέ would probably sound very much like the final two syllables of ἁμαρτήσῃ, "sins"; this could work both ways, either (as many commentators believe) causing the omission of an original εἰς σέ because it sounded like a repetition of -ησῃ or (as I think more likely) causing the insertion of the extra words because someone thought they heard εἰς σέ. The reading ἁμάρτῃ εἰς σέ in W and other MSS and quotations probably derives from this mishearing.

4. It is not easy to capture the force of ἐλέγχω here in a single English word. It includes the related ideas of reprimand, of bringing the wrong to light, of trying to bring the person to recognize that they are in the wrong, and of correcting them; see the comments below.

5. Literally, "every word (ῥῆμα)," but the context in Deut 19:15 is the establishment of a verbal charge in court.

689

The thought flows on naturally from vv. 10-14:[6] this is how a disciple is to act when he or she is aware that a fellow disciple is in spiritual danger, through sin. This is, then, a description of the practical outworking of the pastoral concern for the "little ones" which vv. 11-14 demand. It is addressed entirely to the individual disciple; even the "you" of v. 17 is still singular, so that that verse prescribes not communal ostracism but the attitude of the individual disciple who first noticed the problem. The disciple is envisaged as acting within the context of the whole community, but the focus is on the individual's attitude and action. In vv. 18-20, on the other hand, the "you" will be plural, and the focus will be on the authority of the whole disciple community and the nature of its spiritual fellowship. This change from singular to plural is sufficiently remarkable to justify treating vv. 18-20 as a separate section, even though here, as throughout the first part of this discourse, there is an important thematic link between the paragraphs.[7]

There is a remote "parallel" to v. 15 in Luke 17:3 in the instruction to "rebuke" a brother who sins, but that saying lacks the specific instructions given here and speaks simply of forgiving him if he repents, thus linking the theme of these verses with that of vv. 21-22 (which is, however, differently developed in Luke 17:4). Otherwise, this whole section is peculiar to Matthew, and reveals the practical pastoral concern which characterizes his presentation of Jesus' teaching (especially but not only in this discourse) and is likely to reflect something of the circumstances of the Christian community within which he wrote.[8]

The singular pronouns of this paragraph make it very unlikely, however, that these verses should be understood as guidance specifically for church leaders. The subject is dealing with sin within the disciple community, but, remarkably, it is the concerned individual, not an appointed leader or group, who is expected to act in the first instance; the wider community is involved only when that individual initiative proves inadequate, and then only to back up the individual's concern. It may be likely that the gathered community, whose warning has been ignored, will wish to share in the attitude described in v. 17b so that it becomes a community response to unrepented sin in its midst, but that can only be a matter of reading be-

6. W. G. Thompson, *Advice,* 187-88, effectively draws out the continuity of thought.

7. W. G. Thompson, *Advice,* 201-2, traces the continuity of thought through vv. 15-20.

8. A partially parallel piece of community regulation in 1QS 5:25–6:1 (cf. CD 9:2-4) envisages one member of the community bringing a charge against another before the assembly only after he has confronted him before witnesses, but the Qumran text has a more judicial sound than these verses in Matthew. It has no parallel to v. 17b, the outcome of the case not being described.

tween the lines; all that v. 17b actually says is that the person who initiated the pastoral action is then to adopt this attitude for themselves. Commentators who use the formal language of ecclesiastical discipline or even "excommunication" in connection with v. 17 seem regularly to fail to notice the singular "you."[9]

The person at risk is described as "your brother or sister" (*adelphos*; see 689, n. 2). This family language imports a note of personal care rather than objective censure. It has been used already in the gospel to refer to a fellow disciple; see 5:22-24, 47; 7:3-5, and especially Jesus' designation of those who follow him as "my brothers" in 12:49-50 (cf. also 25:40; 28:10), who are therefore also brothers to each other. The same usage will recur within this discourse at vv. 21 and 35 and later at 23:8. In view of such language we should be cautious about speaking in this context of "discipline," if that term is understood to connote one person exercising authority over another. The two brothers/sisters stand on an equal footing, and the motive for the approach is personal concern, a concern which the offending brother or sister is apparently at liberty to ignore or to reject. A biblical basis for such an initiative may be found in Lev 19:17, where the individual Israelite is instructed to "rebuke [LXX uses the same verb as v. 15 here] your neighbor, so that you will not share in their guilt."[10]

For the "church," which, if necessary, can be appealed to as a last resort, see on 16:18. Here the reference is clearly more local, so that the *ekklēsia* is the gathering of the brothers and sisters who are accustomed to meet in that place. No mention is made of any officers or leadership within the group; the added force of this third level of appeal derives from the greater number of people who agree in disapproving of the offender's action, not from any defined "disciplinary" structure. The group share corporately in the pastoral concern which motivated the individual disciple to raise the issue, and in the event of a rebuff we may reasonably suppose that they would share that individual's attitude of disapproval and even ostracism (see above), but to speak of anything so formal as "excommunication" is to import an anachronistically developed concept of ecclesiastical jurisdiction.[11]

In a formally constituted church with an appointed leadership it is easy for the "ordinary" disciple to hide behind that authority structure and to

9. Luz, 2:452, n. 36, rather lamely explains the inconvenient singular as "already given in the history of the tradition. Σοι simply functions to establish this consistent address rhetorically in v. 17 as well."

10. Davies and Allison, 2:786, usefully survey the development of this principle of reproof in Judaism.

11. W. G. Thompson, *Advice,* 176-88, argues strongly for a pastoral rather than disciplinary focus in these verses. "The regulations stress the threefold attempt at reconciliation rather than a juridical process of excommunication" (ibid., 186).

leave it all to the official leaders, appealing to Cain's question "Am I my brother's keeper?" with the comfortable assumption that the answer must be No. But this passage asserts that the answer is Yes. In a community of "little ones," each must be concerned about and take responsibility for the spiritual welfare of the other. Matthew's "church" is not a formal one. Of course such individual pastoral initiative, especially where the initiator has not been personally affected by the sin, is open to the response, "What right have you . . . ?" and the warning in 7:1-5 against finding fault with others while not noticing one's own failings is an important caveat to set alongside this passage. But with the sensitivity which properly marks the approach of one "little one" to another, the pastoral model set out here surely has a lot to teach the modern church in which attention to another's spiritual and ethical problems is too easily dismissed as "bad form" or meddling.

15 The scenario begins with one disciple aware that another disciple has sinned. The nature of the "sin" is not specified. See above, p. 689, n. 3, for the omission of "against you," a decision which significantly affects one's understanding of the whole passage. I understand this verse (unlike vv. 21ff.) to refer to sin in general, not injury specifically to the person concerned, so that to speak of "grievance" or of "conflict resolution" here is inappropriate. The concern may be with the spiritual welfare of the offender themselves or with the effect of their behavior on the rest of the group or on its reputation; the two are not mutually exclusive, but see below for the probable focus here on the danger to the individual. Sin, of whatever form, is not to be tolerated within the disciple community, but is to be dealt with when it is noticed. But this is to be done with sensitivity and with a minimum of publicity. The principle set out in these verses is of minimum exposure,[12] other people being brought in only when the more private approach has failed. The ideal solution is "just between the two of you." But it is to be explicit and robust: *elenchō* (see p. 689, n. 4) is not a gentle verb (see its uses in Luke 3:19; John 3:20; 16:8; Eph 5:11). It assumes, as this whole passage does, that the person raising the issue is in the right and that the behavior being criticized is self-evidently wrong (the verb "sin" assumes that). In practice matters are not always so straightforward, and it behooves the person taking the initiative to make sure that the "sin" is not simply a matter of personal preference; the eventual involvement of the "one or two" and then of the church should minimize that danger.

The pastoral purpose of the approach is underlined by the verb "win," which shows that the concern is not mainly with the safety and/or reputation of the whole community but with the spiritual welfare of the individual.

---

12. Keener, 453, usefully illustrates the same principle in a range of Jewish and other sources.

"Win"[13] suggests that the person was in danger of being lost, and has now been regained; it reflects the preceding image of the shepherd's delight in getting his sheep back. For the same verb used of the conversion of outsiders cf. 1 Cor 9:19-22; 1 Pet 3:1.

16 The initial one-to-one approach has not been successful, so more drastic action is needed. Again there is no suggestion that the "one or two others" hold any position of leadership, and no indication of how they should be selected. Their role is to back up the concern of the initiator and to endorse their assessment that the matter raised is really "sin." While the perception or the motives of an individual may be questioned, there is more authority in the united testimony of two or three. Deut 19:15 laid down the principle that multiple testimony is necessary for the judicial conviction of a person for "any crime or wrongdoing"; it is applied more specifically to capital punishment in Num 35:30; Deut 17:6. Verse 16b quotes directly (though more concisely) the LXX of Deut 19:15, with the necessary change of verb form to fit it into Matthew's sentence. This principle of multiple testimony was widely recognized (see on 26:59-60a) and is appealed to several times in the NT (John 8:17; 2 Cor 13:1; 1 Tim 5:19; Heb 10:28) in a variety of settings which make it clear that it was understood to apply more widely than in a strictly judicial setting. Here, too, the reference is not judicial: there is no court, nor is it suggested that the one or two others were present at the offense and so could testify as "witnesses" in the legal sense.

17 We now come to the last resort, which the earlier approaches have been designed to avoid. To "speak to the church" must presumably require a public statement when the community is gathered (rather than a whispering campaign). Such publicity must be avoided where possible, but it may prove to be inevitable if the problem is to be solved. The object of the gathering is not to pronounce judgment but to strengthen the pastoral appeal, in the hope that the offender may yet "listen." The offender, faced by the disapproval of the whole local disciple community, ought surely to recognize that this was not just a personal grievance on the part of the initiator. Anyone who is not willing to accept such united testimony may then properly be regarded as no longer a fit member of the community. "You" (singular, referring to the individual who raised the issue, not, at least explicitly, to the community as a whole) should then treat them as "a Gentile and a tax collector."

The terms "Gentile"[14] and "tax collector" were used together in 5:46-

---

13. κερδαίνω is often used of financial gain; cf. 25:16-22 and see on 16:26.

14. Here, where an individual is in view, the adjective ἐθνικός is used rather than the normal description of the Gentiles as a class by the noun τὰ ἔθνη. But in 5:47 and 6:7 Matthew has the plural οἱ ἐθνικοί where the term is used, as here, pejoratively, so that there may be a more pejorative connotation attaching to the adjective than to the noun.

47 to represent those of whom a high standard is not to be expected (those who were regarded as "at the bottom of the moral scale," as we noted there), and "Gentiles" functions similarly in 6:7. This usage represents the traditional Jewish assumption of superiority as the people of God, and the sense that the tax collectors, even if they were Jewish, were little better than Gentiles (see on 9:9). The terms thus seem to stand for a person who has no place among the holy people of God, and who is to be shunned, in particular by refusing table fellowship.[15] That would be the natural meaning if spoken by most Jews, but could Jesus (or Matthew) have used the terms in this way, since this gospel has emphasized and will continue to emphasize Jesus' sympathy for outsiders and his willingness to break conventional taboos in order to reach them?[16] After the welcome given to the Gentile's faith in 8:10-13 (greater than any in Israel) and to Matthew and other tax collectors in 9:9-13, would it not be more natural to take "treat as a Gentile or a tax collector" as an invitation to extend friendship and understanding to the offender? But that would make nonsense of the sequence of these verses, where every effort has been made to restore fellowship with the offender up to this point, but now their final repudiation of the consensus of the community has made any further accommodation impossible. We must assume therefore that here the terms are being used in their conventional Jewish sense,[17] and that the disciple is being instructed to suspend normal fellowship with the offender. See the introductory comments above on how far this may be supposed to extend to the attitude of the community as a whole, and on the lack of any formal "excommunication" language.

6. The Authority of the Disciple Community (18:18-20)

18 *"I tell you truly: whatever you tie up on earth will have been tied up in heaven, and whatever you untie on earth will have been untied in heaven.*

15. For table fellowship with Gentiles see on 8:7, and with tax collectors on 9:10-11.

16. D. C. Sim, *Gospel,* 226-31 (and in *JSNT* 57 [1995] 19-48, especially 25-30), argues, however, that the four "anti-Gentile statements in Matthew" (5:46-47; 6:7-8, 31-32; 18:17) are evidence for the real position of Matthew's community, who "viewed the Gentile world as a foreign place with foreign practices, and . . . had minimal contact with the local Gentile society." He goes on to speak of "this distinctive policy of the Matthean community to avoid or shun its Gentile neighbours." Few have been so willing to assert that, among the disparate strands which make up the Gospel of Matthew, the conventional language of these four sayings should be given such priority. For a brief response to Sim's article see D. Senior, *CBQ* 61 (1999) 8-11.

17. Much as in Britain we speak conventionally of "sending someone to Coventry" (UK idiom for ostracizing someone) even if we have no personal aversion to the actual city of Coventry.

19 *"Moreover[1] I tell you[2] that if two of you on earth agree about anything that they should ask for, it will be given to them by[3] my Father who is in heaven. 20 For where two or three have come together in my name, I am there among them."*

In these verses, as in vv. 15-17 (except for a rather remote "parallel" to v. 15 in Luke 17:3), Matthew's material has no parallel in the other gospels, though of course v. 18 is closely paralleled within this gospel by the commission to Peter in 16:19. While vv. 15-17 formed a single sequence, these verses have more the appearance of independent sayings (note the repeated introductory formulae in vv. 18 and 19) brought together by Matthew around the theme of the community's authority and the links between "earth" and "heaven" which undergird it.

The change from the second-person singular address of vv. 15-17 to the second-person plural in vv. 18 and 19 marks a broadening of the subject. The specific case dealt with in vv. 15-17 is left behind, and we are told now about the authority with which the disciple community as a whole has been entrusted. So here we find the theoretical background which justifies the practical appeal to the *ekklēsia* in v. 17. The corporate wisdom of the community as to what is and is not permitted ("tying" and "untying"; see on 16:19) represents not only their human judgment but the will of God in heaven; what they corporately declare to be "sin" God also disallows.

Verses 19 and 20, which are bound together by the "two of you" / "two or three" motif, do not directly link up with the discussion of dealing with sin in the community,[4] and may well have originally circulated sepa-

---

1. The normal English translation of πάλιν as "again" would be misleading here since it would suggest that what is about to be said is a repetition of something Jesus has already said; πάλιν functions here rather to add a further significant saying to the one just given (cf. similar uses of πάλιν to introduce an additional and comparable statement or event whose content is nonetheless new in 4:7, 8; 5:33; 13:45, 47, etc.).

2. MSS vary considerably in this opening clause, in particular as to whether ἀμήν, "truly," is repeated here. It is perhaps more likely that it was inserted under the influence of the preceding verse. Cf. 19:24 for a comparable sequence, where πάλιν λέγω ὑμῖν follows a statement introduced by ἀμὴν λέγω ὑμῖν, but without repetition of the ἀμήν.

3. Literally, "it will happen for them from."

4. J. D. M. Derrett, *ExpT* 91 (1979/80) 83-86, challenges the well-nigh universal assumption that vv. 19-20 are about prayer, and finds in them a continuation of the theme of discipline and disputes. He translates, "If two of you arrive at an accord on earth concerning any claim that they may be pursuing, it shall be allowed, ratified on the part of my heavenly Father. For where there are two or three convened in my name, there I am amongst them." The subject, he argues, is an agreement to compromise over conflicting legal claims, and the "two or three" are "unofficial dispute-settlers, peacemakers [who] perform a divine function" (cf. the delegation of divine authority to the assembled com-

rately from the context in which we now find them, but the "moreover" by which they are introduced indicates that Matthew intends us to see a connection, and the twin motifs of "on earth" and "in heaven" more explicitly link vv. 18 and 19 together. The authority exercised in dealing with the offending brother or sister is grounded in the privileged access of the agreeing community to God in prayer. No specific request to God has been mentioned, but we may perhaps envisage the community (or two or more of its members) praying either for the person whose sin has been brought to light or for guidance in their corporate decision as to how it should be dealt with.

At the risk of becoming repetitious, it is appropriate to point out again that no specific officers or leaders in the church are mentioned in these verses. The "tying" and "untying" of v. 18 are spoken of as the responsibility of the group as a whole — even though it has previously been attributed specifically to Peter as the foundation "rock." The access to God in prayer in v. 19 is promised to any two members of the community. And the "two or three" who experience the presence of Jesus are unidentified. What gives them their special privilege is not any appointment to office but the name of Jesus in which they meet. The authority and the answers to prayer come from "heaven," not via the channel of a formal church establishment but wherever some of God's people are together on earth.

18 The commission given to Peter in 16:19 is repeated almost verbatim except that the verbs are now plural, addressed to the disciples as a group, and the introductory "I tell you truly" (see on 5:18) gives it added weight.[5] See above on 16:19 for the meaning of "tying" and "untying," where I argued that they do not refer to condemning or forgiving a person but to making decisions about what is right and wrong. In this context, where the "sin" of a member of the community has been under consideration, the rabbinic use of these terms for "declaring what is or is not permitted" seems particularly relevant. Here, as in 16:19, the object of the "tying" is expressed in the neuter,[6] not the masculine: it is things, issues or actions that are tied or untied, not people — though of course, as v. 17b has made clear, the decision made in principle will have practical implications for the person involved. The individual who was at first

---

munity in v. 18). The chief drawback of this bold reinterpretation is that it hardly does justice to the language of asking and receiving from God.

5. This opening clause, with its plural pronoun, also suitably introduces a new section of teaching which is addressed to the disciples corporately rather than to the individual as in vv. 15-17.

6. It is also plural this time (ὅσα as opposed to ὅ); this may be no more than a stylistic variation, perhaps affected by the plural verbs for "tying" and "untying," but it makes it even more improbable that those verbs could be understood here as meaning to "condemn" or "forgive" the singular person whose sin has been under consideration in vv. 15-17.

concerned over the offender's action has, in v. 17, found it necessary to appeal to the gathered community, and the community has endorsed that individual's assessment that this was "sin." In so doing they have exercised the same authority to declare God's will which was given to Peter in 16:19, and that authority is now spelled out in exactly the same way as in that earlier saying; Peter's "power of the keys" is thus seen to be not an exclusive authority given to him alone, but one shared by the whole disciple group. See on 16:19 for the significance of the way this authority is expressed through the use of future perfect passives, and the effect this has on the apparently "carte blanche" endorsement of fallible human decisions. The fact that God has given his people the role of declaring his will on earth does not mean that he is bound to add his divine sanction to anything they may think up.[7]

19 Contemporary Judaism regarded ten males as the minimum number for corporate worship to be valid. Jesus' principle is much less restrictive: two in agreement are enough. The prayer envisaged in context is likely to be for the restoration of the sinner (see introductory comments), but this saying is not framed in such a way as to restrict it to only one kind of prayer, and, as we have noted above, it may not originally have been linked to this context. We have already heard sweeping promises of answers to prayer in 7:7-8 and 17:20; see the comments on those verses (and in the introduction to 7:7-11) for the limitations which the broader biblical context may be understood to impose on such apparently open-ended offers. Here a further limitation is explicit: the promise is made with respect not to the whims of the individual but to the agreed request of "two of you."[8] There is safety in numbers; cf. the principle of requiring the testimony of two or three witnesses in v. 16. Of course two people may also be mistaken or motivated by selfish concerns, and the experience of "unanswered prayer" is by no means limited to the prayers of individuals. But when two agree, and when Jesus himself is present in that agreement (v. 20), the risk is significantly reduced.

20 In v. 19 prayer was expressed as a direct transaction between the two on earth and God in heaven. But now a third party is introduced into the scene. The wording makes sense only as a forward look[9] to the presence of the

7. On this tension between divine authority and human fallibility see my *Matthew: Evangelist,* 250-51.

8. *Gos. Thom.* 48 interestingly links this saying with the earlier saying about prayer in 17:20: "If two make peace with each other in the same house, they will say to the mountain, 'Be moved,' and it will be moved."

9. That it is a "forward look" by Jesus rather than a saying coined by the post-Easter community is allowed as possible by Davies and Allison, 2:790, who point out that if Paul could also speak of his being spiritually present in Corinth when absent in body (1 Cor 5:3-4), it cannot simply be assumed that such a saying could not have come from Jesus himself. Similarly, B. Englezakis, *NTS* 25 (1978/9) 263-64. Keener, 456, n. 31, in-

risen Christ among his earthly followers.[10] Its thrust is thus similar to that of 28:20, but whereas there the presence of Jesus "with you" is expressed in relation to the new post-Easter situation, here it is, remarkably, already in the present. The perspective is thus that of Matthew's church rather than of the disciple group during Jesus' ministry. The saying is linked to v. 19 with a "for," which indicates that this is the basis for expecting united prayer to be answered: it is not just the prayer of the two who agree, but also that of Jesus who is "among them" because they have come together "in his name,"[11] that is, as his disciples representing him (cf. on v. 5, and cf. 10:40-42). While Jesus is on earth his disciples are his brothers and sisters (12:49-50), but even when he is no longer on earth he remains spiritually present as the focus of their unity.

This verse and 28:20 give fuller expression to the idea which we have seen to be probably implicit in Matthew's adoption (and translation) of the title Immanuel, "God with us," in 1:23. See above, p. 49, for this theme of being "with you" as a significant element in Matthew's christology and ecclesiology. It echoes the OT theme of God dwelling among his people (cf. Ezek 43:7; Joel 2:27; Zech 2:10-11). When Jesus is the subject, it depends on the expectation, already firmly set before us in 16:21; 17:9, 23, that his mission will not end with his earthly death but will be continued through his resurrection. The disciple community will continue even after that to be not merely the followers but also the companions of Jesus. His spiritual presence among them is the source of their authority to declare the will of God and to expect God to hear their prayers. And that presence is promised not to a formally convened ecclesiastical council, but to any two or three[12] of his people who meet as his disciples.[13]

---

terprets the saying as expressing the "wisdom Christology" which he claims to have originated with Jesus himself.

10. "The fact that the gathering is 'in my name,' and that it is specifically 'on earth' as opposed to 'in heaven,' suggests that he is speaking of a situation beyond that of his physical presence during the ministry — to comment on his being literally 'among them' in that context would be banal, and in any case could hardly be true of *every* gathering of two or three!" (R. T. France, *Matthew: Evangelist,* 312).

11. For the implications of such language in Matthew see D. D. Kupp, *Emmanuel,* 189-92. He concludes that here it represents "the allegiance, or identity marker, of this particular group." For the link between the idea of "receiving Jesus" (v. 5) and of his presence among his disciples here see also ibid., 196-98.

12. The phrase recalls the agreed witnesses of v. 16. It was a problem to some early Christian solitaries that the saying mentions "two or three" but not "one." See B. Englezakis, *NTS* 25 (1978/9) 262-72, for the possibility that this concern lies already behind the mysterious *Gos. Thom.* 30, which is normally read as "Where there are three gods, they are gods; where there are two or one, I am with him," but where a fragmentary Greek version suggests a different reading of the opening clause.

13. See D. D. Kupp, *Emmanuel,* 86-87, 185-88, for the theme of "coming to-

This saying is regularly compared to a rabbinic motif found especially in a saying from the early second century A.D. in *m. 'Abot* 3:2 (cf. 3:6): "If two sit together and words of the Law are between them, the Shekinah rests between them" (i.e., God is present with them). W. D. Davies, *Setting,* 225, therefore calls Matt 18:20 "a Christified bit of rabbinism."[14] The idea of spiritual presence is similar, and may represent a tradition of thought already present at the time of Jesus, but what makes the present saying remarkable by comparison is that the one present is not the more abstract concepts of the law or the Shekinah, but the human figure of Jesus.[15]

7. Peter's Question about Forgiveness (18:21)

21 *Then Peter came to Jesus and asked him, "Lord, how many times shall my brother or sister sin against me and I still forgive them? As many as seven times?"*

The question in v. 1 which gave rise to the first part of the discourse was about comparative status and so was appropriately asked by the disciples corporately. Now the focus is on an individual's response to personal injury, and so one disciple asks the question which leads into the section of the discourse which speaks of individual forgiveness. As usual, that individual is Peter, but the question he asks applies equally to any disciple. Here, in contrast to vv. 15-17, the issue is of personal grievance and personal forgiveness; one of the chief causes of disharmony within a group of disciples is the actions or attitudes of one individual which another member of the group perceives to be "against me." So personal forgiveness is the key to good relationships.

Some commentators notice a tension between vv. 21-22 with their demand for unlimited forgiveness and vv. 15-17 where the end result may be a

---

gether," συνάγομαι, in Matthew and its implications for the relations between the ἐκκλησία and the συναγωγή. Kupp understands the term to be used of the Jewish leaders "to draw uncompromising battle lines" (186), but in a more positive sense when referring to disciples. He resists any attempt to define the nature of the gathering here more specifically (as liturgical, judicial, or for prayer). See, however, W. G. Thompson, *Advice,* 197-98, for the view that the combination of συνάγομαι with εἰς τὸν ἐμὸν ὄνομα denotes the reason for the gathering, which he describes as "to invoke the name of Jesus."

14. Cf. Davies and Allison, 2:790: "a Christian reformulation of a rabbinic sentiment."

15. Carter, 369, rightly points out that the rabbinic sayings related to the issue of "where and how God's forgiving presence and will were encountered now that the temple was destroyed. Matthew's answer is Jesus." See D. D. Kupp, *Emmanuel,* 192-96, for the discussion of how this saying relates to *m. 'Abot* 3:2 and of the respective ideologies which underlie them.

breaking off of relationships. But that tension is caused by including the phrase "against you" in v. 15 (see p. 689, n. 3) and so failing to see that the subject has now changed. There is no incompatibility between a robust pastoral concern over another disciple's sin and willingness to forgive offenses against oneself. Verses 15-17 are about how to prevent the loss of a member of the disciple community; vv. 21-22 are about the danger of allowing personal animosity to poison that community. In vv. 15-17 the concern is with the spiritual well-being of the offending member; in vv. 21-22 it is with the willingness of the individual not to insist on his or her own right to redress. In each case the "sin" is assumed to be real and culpable, but in the first case what is considered is the effect on the sinner, in the second case the response of the one sinned against.

Jesus has given a high profile to the issue of personal forgiveness in the one rider added to the Lord's Prayer in 6:14-15. The principle is clear, but its practical outworking still needs to be clarified, since its open-ended demand may easily be exploited by a manipulative fellow disciple; surely there must be a limit? Peter's proposal of up to seven times is probably intended to express the outer limits of generosity. If a debate recorded in *b. Yoma* 86b–87a may be taken to represent earlier rabbinic teaching, a limit of three times was regarded as sufficient. To suggest as many as seven (the number of perfection?) would probably have been regarded as "over the top," and Peter is putting up an extreme proposal (possibly in deliberate contrast to Cain's sevenfold vengeance, Gen 4:13) for the sake of argument. In that case, Jesus' reply in v. 22 will be the more startling.

We noted that a partial parallel to v. 15 in Luke 17:3 combined elements of Matthew's v. 15 and the subject of personal forgiveness. Luke 17:4 continues with a saying about forgiving seven times, but in Luke there is no question-and-answer format, so that it is Jesus, not Peter, who speaks of forgiving seven times, and there is no contrasting seventy-seven as here in v. 22. In Luke the offender has apologized, which is not stated in Matthew. Luke has no parallel to the parable which follows. The whole effect is therefore quite different, even though the demand for generosity in personal forgiveness is similar. It is possible that Matt 18:15-17, 21-22 is a creative expansion of an originally simple saying about forgiveness represented in Luke 17:3-4 (just as vv. 1-9 have adapted the tradition found in Mark 9:33-37, 42-47, some of which also underlies Luke 17:1-2),[1] but the wording and structure of the two passages are so different that it may be as plausible to speak of separate traditions, each in its own way developing the theme set out in Matt 6:14-15.[2]

1. So W. G. Thompson, *Advice,* 227-37.
2. The number "seven" in both sayings would then derive not from direct dependence of one saying on the other but from independently citing it as either the number of perfection or an allusion to the sevenfold vengeance of Cain.

8. Unlimited Forgiveness: The Parable of the Debtors (18:22-35)

22 *Jesus replied, "I tell you, not just seven times, but as many as seventy-seven times.*[1]

23 *"Therefore the kingdom of heaven can be compared to*[2] *a human king*[3] *who wanted to settle accounts with his slaves.* 24 *When he had begun to settle up, one slave was brought to him who owed him ten thousand talents.* 25 *The man did not have the money to pay him, so his master ordered that he should be sold, together with his wife and children and all that he had, so that payment could be made.* 26 *So the slave fell down at his feet*[4] *and said,*[5] *'Be patient with me, and I will repay you everything.'* 27 *But the heart of that slave's master went out to him,*[6] *and he set him free and forgave him the loan.* 28 *But when that*

---

1. The KJV rendering "seventy times seven" (i.e., 490 times), still represented in some English versions, is a literal reproduction of the idiom ἑβδομηκοντάκις ἑπτά, which is better understood as an idiomatic way of expressing the adverbial form of the compound number "seventy-seven" in Greek (N. Turner, *A Grammar of NT Greek,* vol. 3: *Syntax,* 187-88; R. H. Gundry, *Use,* 140; Luz, 2:465, n. 1, regards the phrase as "not completely correct" for seventy-seven times, and as "even less correct" for 490 times). Its meaning here is determined by the clear allusion to Gen 4:24, where the same phrase ἑβδομηκοντάκις ἑπτά in the LXX translates the Hebrew *šib'îm wᵉšib'â,* "seventy-seven."

2. For this formula cf. 13:24; 22:2, and see p. 522, n. 1.

3. This may be overtranslation, but whereas the ἄνθρωπος, which I have generally left untranslated in the introduction to other parables (literally, "a man sowing," 13:24; "a man, a trader," 13:45; "a man, a householder," 13:52; 20:1; 21:33), seems a more natural way to introduce a less prominent character whose function is then defined, the use of "a man, a king" here and in 22:2 (instead of simply "a king") seems less natural, and the immediate juxtaposition of the matching words βασιλεία and βασιλεύς qualified by the contrasting terms οὐρανοί and ἄνθρωπος has the effect of contrasting "the kingdom of heaven" which is being illustrated with the human kingship which the story portrays.

4. The same combination of πίπτω with προσκυνέω was translated in 2:11 "prostrated themselves and paid homage" (where the object was the infant Jesus) and in 4:9 "bow down and worship" (where the object was Satan). Here the object is a human king, so that "worship" is not appropriate, and the slave is not a vassal paying homage but a terrified man acknowledging his master's absolute authority. The repetition of πίπτω (but not of προσκυνέω) in v. 29 draws attention to the similarity of the appeal, even though in the second case there is not the same social difference.

5. Most MSS and versions add the address "Lord" at the beginning of the slave's appeal. The vocative fits both the narrative context (slave to royal master) and the parable's implicit application (a sinner's appeal to God for mercy), but because it fits so well it is hard to see why it should have been omitted in a significant range of early witnesses if it was original. To include it would reduce the verbal similarity between the two slaves' appeals in vv. 26 and 29 (in the latter of which it would not be appropriate), but deliberate omission for that reason seems unlikely.

6. For this translation of σπλαγχνίζομαι see on 9:36.

slave had gone out, he found one of his fellow slaves who owed him a hundred denarii,[7] and grabbed him by the throat[8] saying, 'Pay me back what you owe me.' 29 So his fellow slave fell down[9] and begged him, 'Be patient with me, and I will repay you.' 30 But he refused and went off and threw him into prison until he should pay the debt. 31 His fellow slaves saw what had happened and were horrified,[10] and they went and reported to their master all that had happened. 32 Then his master summoned him and said to him, 'You wicked slave, I forgave you all that debt, since you begged me. 33 Wasn't it your duty to show mercy on your fellow slave, just as I for my part showed mercy on you?' 34 And his master was furious and handed him over to be tortured until he should pay all that he owed.

35 "And my heavenly Father will treat you in the same way, unless every one of you forgives your brother or sister from your heart."

The second part of Jesus' discourse, in response to Peter's question, consists of a striking epigram, supported by a long parable and enforced with a brief explanatory comment in v. 35. All of this is peculiar to Matthew (see on v. 21 for the relationship of vv. 21-22 with Luke 17:3-4).[11] The opening exhortation to forgive without limit (see comments below) is undergirded by a parable which compares God's forgiveness and ours; it is because there is no limit to God's generosity[12] to his undeserving people that they in their turn cannot claim the right to withhold forgiveness from their fellow disciples. A community of the forgiven must be a forgiving community.

7. In 20:1-15 a denarius is understood to be a normal day's wage for a laborer. See the comments below.

8. Literally, "grabbed him and was strangling / tried / began to strangle him" (imperfect tense).

9. See n. 4.

10. ἐλυπήθησαν σφόδρα, the same phrase which I translated "were utterly dismayed" in 17:23.

11. A short parable about two debtors in Luke 7:41-43 has almost nothing in common with this one in either construction or purpose except for the shared motif of the cancellation of debt and the vocabulary which necessarily goes with that (*pace* Gundry, 371, who regards the Lucan parable as the source of this one; I. H. Jones, *Parables,* 218, speaks only of "related traditions").

12. Some commentators find a problem in that whereas vv. 21-22 speak of repeated forgiveness, the parable speaks of only one remission of debt, and so speaks of God's forgiveness as unlimited in quantity rather than in frequency. This is surely to look for too pedantic a match between pronouncement and parable; both speak of uncalculating, unmerited forgiveness. No one who has understood the point about "all that debt" (v. 32) can then suggest that God's mercy should be imitated only once (or only seven times)!

The story is about a king and his slaves in order to explain how the kingship of God operates (v. 23). God has full sovereignty over those who as members of the disciple community belong to his kingship (note the repetition four times of the term "fellow slave"), but he chooses not to enforce his authority harshly but rather with unimaginable generosity because his "heart goes out" to them. Compared to the immeasurable extent of the divine grace which they have experienced (see comments below on the monetary sums around which the story revolves), any generosity his people may be called upon to exercise in forgiving their fellow disciples is insignificant. The parable is in the educational tradition of Nathan's parable of the ewe lamb (2 Sam 12:1-7); the hearer reacts (along with the fellow slaves in the story) with fury to the insensitivity and arrogance of the slave who could not see the inconsistency of his own behavior, and thoroughly approves of the gruesome punishment he receives in v. 34, but then the punch line in v. 35 turns the story back on the hearer: "You are the man!" The application, in keeping with the tenor of Peter's question, is to the individual disciple ("every one of you"); none are exempt from the demand to reflect the divine mercy.

This story about monetary debt picks up the language of 6:12, which uses "debt" for the sin which needs to be forgiven. This parable thus spells out what Jesus has stated in stark propositional form in his comment on 6:12 in 6:14-15, that forgiveness must be reciprocal, so that God cannot be expected to forgive the unforgiving. See the comments on 6:14-15 for some of the issues this raises for Christian soteriology. The parable assumes that disciples are, by definition, forgiven people. It makes unmistakably clear that the initiative is with God: it is because he has first forgiven[13] that we can be expected, and indeed enabled, to forgive. But the forgiveness we have already received may be forfeited by our failure to forgive in our turn. It was freely given, but it must not be presumed on. There is thus in this parable "a fascinating blend of the motive of fear of punishment (vv. 34-35) with the more fundamental motive of gratitude and imitation of the grace of God."[14]

The concept of the disciple as one who has been forgiven an incalculable debt fits well with the wider NT understanding that "Christ died for our sins, the righteous for the unrighteous, that he might bring us to God" (1 Pet 3:18), that "in him we have redemption, the forgiveness of sins" (Col 1:14), and so on. This parable does not explain, however, the role of Jesus himself in achieving that forgiveness. It is presented rather as the result of God's

---

13. Gundry, 371, rightly points out that the imagery of the settling of accounts is not therefore meant to represent the last judgment but "forgiveness that has already taken place."

14. R. T. France, *Matthew: Evangelist,* 270. For the Jewish doctrine of God's "two measures" of mercy and judgment see J. Jeremias, *Parables,* 213-14.

heart going out to the sinner and of his unmerited generosity.[15] The parable speaks not of the soteriological basis of forgiveness but rather of its after-effects. But while the issue is not raised here, we have already been told in 1:21 that Jesus' mission is "to save his people from their sins," and at the climactic moment of the Last Supper in 26:28 it will be explained how that mission is to be achieved. The careful reader may therefore be expected to read more into the presupposition of our forgivenness than the imagery of the parable in itself demands.

While a hundred denarii is a plausible amount for one man to owe another, ten thousand talents (see below for its value) is far beyond what any individual, still less a slave, might owe even to a king. The suggestion[16] that the first debtor is in fact a highly placed official responsible for handling the tax revenues of a large province may perhaps bring the sum closer to the bounds of possibility, but the way the rest of the story is told hardly encourages that supposition; note that the debt is described in v. 27 as a "loan," and that the debtor is a "slave" (see below, n. 21). But, in any case, there is no need to make the sum more possible. A parable is not necessarily a reflection of real life (see, e.g., comments on 7:3-5). It is an imaginary story designed to make a point in a striking way, and the more improbable the sums involved, the greater the audience's gasps of astonishment and the greater their amazement both at the unheard-of generosity of the master and at the obtuseness of the slave. Larger-than-life imagery makes for compelling listening and is not well served by pedantic explanation.[17]

22 If Peter's question reflected some conventional understanding of the reasonable limits of forgiveness (three times?, seven times? — see above on v. 21), the formula "I tell you" functions here as in 5:21ff., to set Jesus'

---

15. In this it is similar to the Lucan parable of the lost son (Luke 15:11-32), where the absence of the cross has often been remarked on. It is of course inappropriate to expect a single parable to contain the whole of Christian soteriology. That is not what either of these parables is about.

16. J. D. M. Derrett, *Law,* 32-47. Several commentators are attracted to Derrett's essential proposal, even if not to all the details of his argument.

17. "It is the nearest thing to a tale from the Arabian Nights in the teaching of Jesus. . . . Surely those exegetes who want to cut down the figures (e.g., from ten thousand talents to ten) have locked their imaginations in their filing cabinets" (G. R. Beasley-Murray, *Kingdom,* 115). Davies and Allison, 2:795-96, following M. C. de Boer, *CBQ* 50 (1988) 214-32, are willing to risk the charge of lack of imagination, and argue that the original story had a debt of only ten thousand denarii, which Matthew has arbitrarily turned into talents (displaying the same inflationary tendency which has made the minas of Luke 19:13 into talents, 25:15). They claim that this solves many problems, but the "problems" they cite arise only from trying to make the story realistic, which surely loses much of its point. Nor does their "solution" make any difference to the fantastic nature of the sum in the text of Matthew as it stands.

radical new standard over against the prudential conclusions of conventional wisdom.[18] Here, as there, the "righteousness of the scribes and Pharisees" is left behind altogether. The escalation from seven to seventy-seven reflects the boast of Lamech in Gen 4:24: "If Cain is avenged sevenfold [see Gen 4:13], surely Lamech is avenged seventy-sevenfold." (The reminiscence of Cain gives added point to the concept of forgiving a "brother.") The disciple must be as extravagant in forgiving as Lamech was in taking vengeance.

This is the language of hyperbole, not of calculation. Those who are concerned as to whether the figure should be seventy-seven or 490 (see p. 701, n. 1) have missed the point. The benchmark is provided by the unimaginable scale of God's forgiveness of his people illustrated in the huge debt of vv. 24-27. In other words, there is no limit, and no place for keeping a tally of forgivenesses already used up. Peter's question was misconceived; if one is still counting, however "generously," one is not forgiving.

23-24   The parable which makes up most of the rest of the discourse underlines the principle of unrestricted forgiveness which Jesus has just enunciated. Most of Matthew's parables are introduced as illustrations of "the kingdom of heaven" (13:11, 24, 31, 33, 44, 45, 47, 52; 20:1; 22:2; 25:1). Here that formula is especially appropriate since the parable concerns a king and his subjects:[19] this, then, is how God rules. That application of the story will be made explicit in v. 35: the king's action represents how "my heavenly Father" will deal with you. The king's dealings in this story are more specifically with his "slaves." In the ancient world slaves, while not free to determine their own lives or to offer their service to anyone but their owner, could become highly responsible and trusted members of the household;[20] a king's slaves might hold positions of authority which today might be taken by civil servants.[21] The concept of a king's slave owing a large sum of money to his

18. Luz, 2:466, interestingly documents the practical problems which subsequent Christian interpretation has found with the open-ended idealism of Jesus' pronouncement.

19. The "king" is referred to as such only in v. 23; thereafter he is simply the "master" in relation to the "slaves." This fact casts doubt on reconstructions of the story which depend on understanding the "slaves" as governors of provinces (see introductory comments); after v. 23 the story is not told in the terms of high politics; it is simply that the size of the debt does not belong to ordinary life, but on this see n. 17. Hagner, 2:534-35, is influenced by v. 23 to translate κύριος throughout as "sovereign" (and δοῦλος as "servant"), but that is not the most natural rendering of the terms (see n. 21).

20. See the discussion of "managerial slaves" by J. A. Glancy, *JBL* 119 (2000) 71-75.

21. It is sometimes suggested that the term δοῦλος here denotes not slaves as such but the "ministers" of an oriental king who were not in fact *owned* by him; so BDAG 260 (§2ba); J. Jeremias, *Parables,* 210, 212. But while the term is found in that sense, it may be doubted whether this usage would have been familiar to Palestinian Jews, for whom

master is therefore not implausible, even though the actual sum owed in the story belongs to the realm of fantasy.

A talent was originally a weight (probably about thirty kilograms) of metal; when used as a monetary term without specifying the metal involved, it would probably have been understood to be of silver. While the exact amount varied, a talent of silver was conventionally reckoned at six thousand denarii. If one denarius was an acceptable day's wage for a laborer (see 20:1-15), a single talent would then represent what a laborer might hope to earn in half a lifetime. It was, at all events, a very large sum of money. Ten thousand talents (sixty million denarii; or some three hundred tons of silver!) is therefore a sum far outside any individual's grasp.[22] Ten thousand (*myria,* hence our "myriad") is the largest numeral for which a Greek term exists, and the talent is the largest known amount of money. When the two are combined, the effect is like our "zillions." What God has forgiven his people is beyond human calculation.

25-27   As a slave, the debtor, together with his family and his belongings, belonged to his master, and so could be sold, though the total raised would not go far toward such an astronomical debt.[23] The slave's suggestion that, given time, he might be able to pay it off is equally unrealistic. But the ludicrous nature of the proposal only serves to underline the generosity of the master, who, far more than simply giving him time, freely writes off the whole debt. His decision derives not from calculation but from his "heart going out" (traditionally "compassion"), that quality which we have seen to be characteristic of Jesus himself when confronted with the need of those who cannot help themselves (9:36; 14:14; 15:32; 20:34). The parable thus speaks of the totally unmerited grace of God which forgives his people more than they could ever imagine because they are unable to help themselves.

28-30   The second scene of the parable moves us out from the king's

---

δοῦλος had a clear meaning as "slave," especially when linked with κύριος, "master" or "owner," as it is throughout this story after v. 23. To claim that the large sum involved entails that "δοῦλος *must* mean not 'slave' but . . . 'minister' or 'official'" (Davies and Allison, 2:797, my italics) is to fall again into the trap of trying to turn an extravagant story into a realistic scenario; the imagination remains locked in the filing cabinet (see n. 17). See further J. A. Glancy, *JBL* 119 (2000) 85-86.

22. By way of comparison, the total annual tax income from the whole of Galilee and Perea in 4 B.C. was only two hundred talents (Josephus, *Ant.* 17.318). The enormous sums contributed to the decoration of Solomon's temple according to 1 Chr 29:4-7 together add up to eight thousand talents of gold, seventeen thousand of silver, and eighteen thousand of bronze (and commentators suspect that the Chronicler's figures are exaggerated: they represent around 240, 510, and 540 tons respectively!).

23. J. Jeremias, *Parables,* 211, gives five hundred to two thousand denarii as the price of a slave.

audience chamber to the servants' hall, and the sums involved are accordingly more modest. The second slave's debt is not in itself insignificant (some three or four months' wages),[24] but it represents only one six-hundred-thousandth of the debt the first slave has just been forgiven. The second slave's groveling appeal to his creditor is described in almost the same words as that of the first slave to the king (see p. 701, n. 4), so that the hearer of the story does not miss the parallel. Does the similarity of wording suggest that the second slave is aware of what has just happened, and so has some confidence that he will be met with no less generosity than the other? Those who are listening carefully to the story may note, however, that whereas the first slave ludicrously offered to repay *everything,* the second slave is less specific but more realistic in his promise, even though his debt is more nearly within reach. But the first slave is not only violent[25] but implacable. He cannot sell his debtor, who belongs to the king, but he can have him committed to a debtor's prison (his ability to do so underlines the position of authority which the first slave held). He will have his rights.[26]

31-33   We are not told what motivated the other slaves to take up the case. Imprisonment for debt was not in itself illegitimate (cf. 5:25-26); the first slave was acting within his rights. What shocked them was his failure to exercise toward his fellow slave even a little of the generosity with which he himself had been treated (cf. 7:12). And that is the charge the king now puts into words. The phrase "all that debt" puts it all in perspective (note the repetition of "all" in relation to the first servant's debt in vv. 26, 32, and 34), and prompts the hearers to reflect on the extent of their own indebtedness to the grace of God. If the master had insisted on his rights, there would have been no mercy; he expects the same of his slave. The introduction in v. 33 of the term "mercy" adds a more theological nuance to the story. Remember 5:7, "Happy are those who show mercy, for it is to them that mercy will be shown." If mercy is the characteristic of God, it should also be the characteristic of his people (cf. Luke 6:36). Conversely, where God's people do not show mercy, they cannot expect to receive it (Jas 2:13).

---

24. The danger of offering a modern monetary equivalent is illustrated by the fact that here Gundry, 374, says a hundred denarii is "about $20," while S. C. Keesmaat, in R. N. Longenecker (ed.), *Challenge,* 269, reckons what she oddly describes as "a few hundred" denarii as "approximately ten thousand dollars in today's terms." Inflation must have been considerable in the eighteen years between the publication of these two estimates!

25. For an interesting parallel see *m. B. Bat.* 10:8, which envisages a creditor taking a debtor by the throat in the street; in that case the result is that a third party offers to pay the debt.

26. D. Instone-Brewer, *Traditions,* 1:251, suggests that the urgency of his demand may be due to the nearness of a Sabbath Year, when the debt would be cancelled.

34 The master was willing to forgive a debt the slave could never have paid, but will not forgive his refusal of an act of generosity which was within his power. If he is determined to insist on his just deserts, he shall have them. The forgiveness which was freely granted is now withdrawn, not because the slave is any more likely to be able to pay the debt, but because he has proved himself unworthy of his master's mercy. And this time it is worse: in place of being sold, he is to be tortured.[27] The squeamishness of the RSV, which turned the "torturers" (KJV "tormentors") into "jailers" (and so made his punishment no worse than what he had inflicted on his fellow slave), was misplaced; his destiny is not detention but painful punishment.[28]

35 For explanatory comments on parables in Matthew see above on v. 14. This one forms with vv. 21-22 a framework around the parable, with the repetition of the same keywords "forgive" and "brother (or sister)." As 6:15 has already made clear, God, whose generosity is beyond measure, will nonetheless not forgive the unforgiving. They must expect the punishment which their unforgiven sin deserves. And the forgiving-ness which he expects of his people is not a reluctant or merely verbal concession which leaves the underlying problem unresolved, but a genuine, warm forgiveness "from the heart" so that the broken relationship is fully restored.[29]

The statement is absolute and unqualified, as the story line of the parable has suggested. Is refusal to forgive therefore an unforgivable sin? In 12:31-32 we have been told that there is only one unforgivable sin, and that is not simply a refusal to forgive, so that to set the present passage against the wider spread of Jesus' teaching may suggest some qualification of its absolute language; even the unforgiving may not be beyond redemption. But such considerations, appropriate as they may be to the compilation of a systematic theology, must not be allowed to weaken the impact of this sobering parable and of the solemn words in 6:14-15 which it illustrates. Those who will not forgive must not expect to be forgiven; the measure they give will be the measure they get back (7:1-2).

27. On the non-Jewish practice of torture to extort payment see J. Jeremias, *Parables,* 212-13. J. A. Glancy, *JBL* 119 (2000) 67, provides evidence for the existence of professional "torturers" to whom slaves would be committed by their owners for punishment (and cf. ibid., 79-84, on the physical punishment of slaves more generally).

28. Cf. the "eternal punishment" of 25:46, also inflicted on those who have failed to show compassion on their neighbors. For torture language (using the same βασαν-word-group as here) in relation to the fate of the wicked after death see Luke 16:23, 28; Rev 14:10-11; 20:10.

29. For the "heart" as expressing a person's true inward nature cf. 5:8, 28; 6:21; 12:34; 15:8, 18-19.

9. Moving On toward Jerusalem (19:1-2)

> 1 And then,[1] when Jesus had come to the end of these sayings, he moved away from Galilee and came into the area of Judea across the Jordan. 2 And great crowds followed him, and he healed them there.

This is now the fourth use of the concluding formula which marks each of the five main discourses. See on 7:28 for its wording. The formula serves again both to conclude the discourse and to move the narrative on into its next phase. Within the narrative structure of this part of the gospel the next phase must be the approach to Jerusalem, which was announced as the ultimate goal of their journey in 16:21 and toward which they have been traveling since leaving the area of Caesarea Philippi. They have passed through Galilee again on their way southward (17:22, 24), but now the group finally leave their home province[2] and head for the unfamiliar territory of Judea and its threatening capital Jerusalem. They will not return to Galilee until 28:16, after all Jesus' predictions have been fulfilled.

Matthew does not make the route clear, but since the next specific location he mentions will be Jericho, we may reasonably assume that Jesus, like other Galilean Jews, took the route down the east side of the Jordan to avoid going through Samaria, finally crossing back at Jericho for the climb up to the capital. That route would fit the statement here that he went into the area "beyond the Jordan," but Matthew's wording is confusing[3] in that at this time[4] Judea proper (governed by a Roman prefect) ended at the Jordan, the east bank being the separate province of Perea (sometimes described as "beyond the Jordan," as in 4:25), part of the tetrarchy of Herod Antipas. It seems that Matthew is using "Judea" loosely to mean the southern part of Palestine as opposed to Galilee, so that "the area of Judea across the Jordan" would mean that part of Perea which one must pass through to reach Jerusalem

---

1. For this rendering of the Semitic idiom καὶ ἐγένετο, "and it happened," see p. 297, n. 1.

2. Cf. the previous departures from Galilee to go north in 15:21 and in 16:4.

3. In the parallel in Mark 10:1 there is textual uncertainty as to whether there was originally a καί between Ἰουδαίας and πέραν τοῦ Ἰορδάνου, which would have the effect of making them two separate regions (see my *Mark*, 386 and 389), but there is no such textual uncertainty here (so that D. C. Sim, *Gospel*, 44, can suggest only that it was Matthew, not a copyist, who "made a mistake . . . by accidentally omitting the καί").

4. It might be suggested that Matthew is using the terminology of his own day, when the whole of the former kingdom of Herod the Great (including Perea) had been reintegrated under Herod Agrippa I (A.D. 41-44), and in A.D. 44 became the single Roman province of "Judea." But Luz, 2:488, rightly points out that this is unlikely since that later expanded "Judea" also included Galilee, which hardly fits Matthew's language of *leaving* Galilee to go to "Judea."

without going through Samaria; perhaps its largely Jewish population helps him to include it in "Judea."[5]

The large crowds and the healing have a formulaic sound and do not contribute substantially to the narrative until the final approach to Jerusalem when the "large crowd" which accompanies Jesus and his disciples out of Jericho (20:29, 31) and witnesses the one specific healing still to be recorded (20:29-34) will become the supporters who hail the king outside the walls (21:8-9) and introduce "their" prophet to the sceptical city (21:11). We shall note then that they are likely to have consisted largely of other Galileans also following the pilgrim route to Jerusalem for the Passover.

D. THE REVOLUTIONARY VALUES OF THE KINGDOM OF HEAVEN: RE-EDUCATION FOR THE DISCIPLES (19:3–20:28)

The remainder of the journey narrative before the arrival in Jericho and the eventual climb up to Jerusalem consists of a series of episodes and sections of teaching some of which are provoked by people outside the disciple group, but the main focus of which is on the experience of the disciples as they are confronted by increasingly unsettling challenges to their conventional attitudes and values, especially as these relate to family and social life.[1] The sequence will be concluded with the last and most detailed prediction of Jesus' coming rejection, death, and resurrection, followed by the extraordinary request of the mother of James and John which reveals that the disciples' grasp of the values of the kingdom of heaven remains at best embryonic. Jesus' response to their continuing quest for positions of importance hinges on the key demand, "It shall not be so among you" (20:26); things do not work the same way in the kingdom of heaven as they do in the kingdoms of the world. 19:30 sums up the revolutionary values of the kingdom of heaven, "Many who are first will be last, and the last first," and the same slogan will be repeated in 20:16; it is this lesson which, in a variety of ways, the disciples must learn while Jesus is still with them. It will not be a comfortable experience, as one situation or pronouncement after another reveals how far they

5. There is a related problem in 4:15; see the comments there for the argument of H. D. Slingerland that Matthew wrote in Trans-Jordan, so that for him Judea was indeed "across the Jordan." In 4:15 Matthew took the phrase from Isaiah, but here no quotation is involved.

1. Davies and Allison, 3:1-2, interestingly compare the subject matter of the whole section 19:1–20:28 with a Pauline *Haustafel* such as Col 3:18–4:1, which they entitle "Instructions for the Christian Household." It is "a long *Haustafel* consisting of sayings of Jesus, a *Haustafel* in which traditional values are turned upside down. . . ." Similarly, and more fully, Carter, 376-77, drawing on his *Households and Discipleship*.

have still to go before they can see things as he sees them. Their "human thoughts" must be set aside in favor of "the thoughts of God" (16:23). It may be deliberately symbolic of the disciples' experience that the last event which occurs before they reach Jerusalem, after this period of re-education, is a miracle of the cure of blindness, which results in those who have been cured "following" Jesus (20:34).

This whole section follows the same outline as Mark 10, the only substantial addition being the parable in 20:1-16. Throughout this lengthy series of pericopes we are told little about the stages of the journey which is presupposed between 19:1 (leaving Galilee) and 20:29 (leaving Jericho for Jerusalem). Occasional pointers keep the journey motif alive ("he went on from there," 19:15; "on the way up to Jerusalem," 20:17), and a number of people outside the disciple group are encountered (19:3, 13, 16), but even in these encounters the emphasis continues to fall on the reactions and reorientation of the disciples, and from 19:23 on, the dramatis personae are only Jesus and his disciples (and the mother of two of them; see on 20:20). Specific locations are not important for this intensive interaction of teacher and learners. What matters is that they are on their way to Jerusalem, where the paradoxical values of the kingdom of heaven will be fully revealed and the disciples' grasp of them will be painfully put to the test.

1. Marriage, Divorce, and Celibacy (19:3-12)

> 3 *And Pharisees came to him with a test question: "Is it lawful for a man to divorce his wife for every[2] cause?"* 4 *He replied, "Haven't you read that the Creator[3] at the beginning 'made them male and female,'* 5 *and said,[4] 'For this reason a man will leave his father and*

2. This is a literal if not very idiomatic translation. See the comments below on the force of the question. It is not whether divorce is permissible *at all*, which is what would be implied by translating here "for *any* cause," but rather what is the extent of the permissible grounds; some versions have therefore used a phrase like "for any cause he pleases/whatever" (so GNB, NJB, REB) or expanded it to "any and every reason" (NIV).

3. The majority of MSS have ὁ ποιήσας ("he who made [them]") here instead of ὁ κτίσας ("he who created"), but this is probably an assimilation to the verb in the following quotation. ὁ κτίσας corresponds to the language of Mark 10:6, but is not a mechanical assimilation to that text since the construction there is different, ἀπὸ δὲ ἀρχῆς κτίσεως without explicit identification of the subject of ἐποίησεν.

4. Instead of reading καὶ εἶπεν as within Jesus' reported speech (as translated above) some have suggested that it might be a new speech opening, "And he [Jesus] said" (so REB, "And he added"; cf. Gundry, 378), in which case the question mark would come not at the end of v. 5 but at the end of v. 4. This would be an uncharacteristic idiom for Matthew — I can find no other case where he uses a simple καὶ εἶπεν without expressed subject to introduce a second speech from the same speaker. The immediate antecedent to

mother and be attached[5] to his wife, and the two will become one flesh'? 6 This means that they are no longer two, but one flesh. So what God has joined together, a man must not separate." 7 They said to him, "So why did Moses give the commandment to 'give her a divorce certificate and so divorce her'?"[6] 8 He replied, "It was in response to your disobedience[7] that Moses gave you permission to divorce your wives; but that's not how it has been from the beginning. 9 Rather, I tell you that anyone who divorces his wife except for sexual unfaithfulness and marries another woman commits adultery."[8]

10 The disciples said to him, "If that's the way it is[9] for a man with his wife, it's better not to marry." 11 He replied, "Not everyone can accept[10] this saying,[11] but only those who have been given [the abil-

---

εἶπεν is ὁ κτίσας, not ὁ δὲ ἀποκριθείς. Moreover, the words immediately following are a quotation from Genesis which on the REB reading lacks an introduction by Jesus. Nor would the quotation in v. 4, taken on its own, constitute an answer to the question of the Pharisees; it is the combined quotation of Gen 1:27 and 2:24, as a single speech by Jesus, which together provides the basis for the answer which follows in v. 6. See further comments below.

5. This translation attempts to capture the vividly physical metaphor of being "glued" or "cemented" together.

6. MSS vary as to whether "her" is explicit or left to be understood as in Mark 10:4 (or, in some Latin and Syriac versions, spelled out as "the woman"). The sense is not affected.

7. Literally, "hardness of heart." See the comments below on the reasons for this translation.

8. See p. 193, n. 49, for this translation. There is considerable textual variation here, largely as a result of attempts to harmonize the various Synoptic divorce logia, though pastoral concerns in the early church may also have been influential. The reading given above is that of ℵ and of the majority of later MSS, which, being the most distinctive over against 5:32, is likely to be original. B and some versions assimilate the text entirely to 5:32, while other MSS use other forms of words to bring in here the double formulation of that verse. But several (mainly Western) MSS assimilate only by reproducing the clause παρεκτὸς λόγου πορνείας from 5:32 instead of μὴ ἐπὶ πορνείᾳ. See further Luz, 2:486, n. 3.

9. The Greek idiom uses the same noun αἰτία which was translated "cause" in v. 3, so that a literal rendering would be "If thus is the cause of a man with his wife." English idiom does not allow the verbal echo to be reproduced easily.

10. The metaphor implied by the verb χωρέω is to "contain" or "have room for" something; this sense of the verb seems more probable here than its common use for to "go," "run," which prompts Goulder's tongue-in-cheek rendering (*Midrash,* 404), "He who can go it, let him go it." Here it might best be translated "cope with," but the double repetition of the same verb at the end of v. 12 cannot easily be rendered with that phrase, so that "accept" in both places best reproduces the verbal link.

11. λόγος does not always mean a verbal utterance, but may denote a "matter, concern." B and some versions omit "this," so that the text would read "the word" or even

ity].[12] *12 For there are eunuchs who were born that way from their mother's womb; and there are eunuchs who have been made eunuchs by others; and there are eunuchs who have made themselves eunuchs because of the kingdom of heaven. Whoever is able to accept this, let them accept it."*

While the main part of this pericope is a controversial dialogue with Pharisees similar to those which have been a feature of the Galilean ministry, its setting here within the journey narrative is perhaps explained by the following exchange with the disciples in vv. 10-12. The ethical stance which Jesus sets out in vv. 6 and 9 is in essence the same as what he has already taught in 5:32, but there it was subsumed within a wider discussion of discipleship in relation to the demands of the law, whereas here it stands alone and is more fully developed. This enables the disciples to express here their reaction to what they regard as an impossibly idealistic ethic. The contrast between their conventional ethical realism and the disturbingly new and demanding teaching of Jesus thus sets the tone for the process of re-education in the revolutionary values of the kingdom of heaven which runs throughout this part of Matthew's narrative (see introductory comments above). The specific mention of the "kingdom of heaven" as the motivation for the unconventional ethic advocated by Jesus in v. 12 draws out the contrast between human thoughts and God's thoughts (16:23), and the repetition of the same phrase in 19:14, 23, 24; 20:1 (together with the contrast with the rulers of the nations in 20:25) will maintain that focus throughout the remainder of the journey.

The commentary above on 5:31-32 has dealt extensively with the setting in Jewish attitudes to divorce and remarriage both in the OT and at the time of Jesus, with the nature of Jesus' distinctive teaching in this regard, and with its implications for pastoral ethics today. The meaning and implications of the clause "except for sexual unfaithfulness" (v. 9) were also discussed at that point. The reader is urged to consult that earlier discussion for the general issues raised in the present passage; it will not be repeated here except insofar as the specific details of this fuller pericope require it.

What is distinctive about this passage is that rather than simply mak-

---

"the matter." If the reference is to Jesus' earlier teaching, "this" would probably point to Jesus' pronouncements in vv. 6 and 9; without "this" the reference might be more generally to the teaching about marriage and divorce which he has been putting forward. On the interpretation adopted below, however, "this" seems necessary to refer back to the immediately preceding words of the disciples.

12. Literally, "to whom it has been given." The same phrase is used for the giving or withholding of revelation in 13:11. See the comments below on vv. 11-12 for the nature of the divine "gift" implied here.

ing a pronouncement over against currently accepted teaching, Jesus here grounds it in a hermeneutical argument set out in the form of a dialogue with the Pharisees, who represent current Jewish understanding of the matter. By setting Deut 24:1-4, the scriptural basis of all current Jewish teaching on divorce, over against the account in Gen 1–2 of God's original intention for marriage, Jesus raises a fundamentally important hermeneutical issue. He finds within the Pentateuch two different levels of ethical instruction, in Deut 24:1-4 a pragmatic provision for dealing with a problem that has arisen, but in Gen 1–2 a positive statement of first principles which, if observed, would have rendered the trouble-shooting legislation of Deut 24:1-4 unnecessary. His argument is that the original principle must take precedence over the later concession to human weakness,[13] and thus that current Jewish teaching which took Deut 24:1-4 as the basis for its teaching on divorce was starting in the wrong place.

This is a principle which applies much more widely than only to the specific issue of divorce: ethical norms should be sought not in legal texts which deal with the situation where things have already gone wrong, but in the most fundamental statements available of the positive will of God for human behavior. There is a saying, "Hard cases make bad law," and it may be suggested that they make even worse ethics. The ethics of the kingdom of heaven, as we have seen them illustrated in 5:21-48, seek not primarily how evil may be contained and alleviated, but how the best may be discerned and followed. It would make a huge and beneficial difference to modern debates on divorce if this priority were observed, so that the focus fell not on what grounds for divorce may be permitted (as in the Pharisees' question), but on how marriage may best live up to the Creator's purpose for it. There will, no doubt, always be a need for trouble-shooting legislation and pastoral help when things have gone wrong, but if that is where our ethical discussion *begins,* the battle is lost before it is joined. Those who start from Deut 24:1-4 will have as their basic presupposition that divorce is to be expected, the question being only how it is to be regulated. Those who start from Gen 1–2 will see any separation of what God has joined together as always an evil; circumstances may prove it to be the lesser evil, but that can never make it less than an infringement of the primary purpose of God for marriage.

Up to v. 9 Matthew's account runs parallel with Mark 10:2-12 (though with some significant differences, which will be noted below). But only Matthew gives us the disciples' response (v. 10) and the enigmatic pronouncement of Jesus which it evokes in vv. 11-12. Here the focus has

---

13. Note that whereas the Pharisees take the Deuteronomy text as a "commandment," Jesus will give it only the status of "permission."

shifted. The general subject is still marriage, but the issue of divorce gives way to that of celibacy,[14] unexpectedly introduced through the disciples' incredulous reaction that if marriage is as binding as Jesus says it would be better not to marry at all. Whether their comment was meant seriously or not, Jesus takes it so. It should not be taken for granted that everyone should marry; there is an alternative, even if it is not for everyone. The whole pericope therefore constitutes a double challenge to conventional attitudes to marriage: on the one hand God intends marriage to remain unbroken, and the current acceptance of divorce is a surrender to human failure; on the other hand, for some people obedience to God's will may properly mean that they do not marry at all.

3   The presence of Pharisees is not surprising as the group gets nearer to Jerusalem, which was the main power base of the movement. Matthew's lack of geographical precision does not allow us to know whether he sees this group as fellow travelers en route from Galilee to Jerusalem for the Passover or as based at some point on the journey. Jesus' most recent comments on Pharisees (15:12-14; 16:1-4, 6, 11-12) predispose the reader to expect an argument. This controversy comes out of the blue rather than arising from a recorded incident or teaching, but since it is presented as a "test" question (cf. 16:1; 22:15, 18, also involving Pharisees), we should probably understand the Pharisees to be deliberately broaching a controversial issue on which Jesus might be expected (especially if they were aware of his teaching already recorded at 5:31-32) to have radical views which could easily be represented as a contradiction of the Mosaic law of Deut 24:1-4. It is explicitly a "halakhic" question, about what is lawful, this being the primary concern of the Pharisees as well as the professional domain of the scribes. It is typical of Jesus that, as in 5:21-48, he will use current discussion about law as a springboard from which to launch a more fundamentally ethical pronouncement.

See above on 5:31-32 for Jewish assumptions and debates about divorce at the time. The question is not whether divorce was *ever* permissible (see p. 711, n. 2 above); that was accepted by all on the basis of Deut 24:1-4. It concerns the permitted grounds for divorce,[15] an issue which among Pharisees at that time would have been focused on the debate between the schools of Shammai and Hillel.[16] "To divorce his wife for every cause" might serve

14. For an alternative view that vv. 11-12 are concerned with remarriage after divorce, not with celibacy, see the comments below, especially p. 725, n. 38.

15. D. Janzen, *JSNT* 80 (2000) 72-79, illustrates from both Jewish and other Near Eastern law why the issue was important: only if "just cause" for divorce could be shown was a man not liable to return the dowry!

16. R. J. Banks, *Jesus,* 146-47, argues that this would not be a "test" question, since it would restrict the issue within the accepted area of rabbinic disagreement. He sug-

as a sweeping summary of the Hillelite view[17] (see above, pp. 207-8), which was probably the more influential among ordinary people. Would Jesus then support a more restrictive "Shammaite" approach,[18] which would not be popular among most Jewish men, who, it may be assumed, valued their "freedom" in this matter (and whose attitude is represented by the disciples' response in v. 10)? Moreover, the recent execution of John for questioning Antipas's divorce (14:3-12) made it a politically sensitive issue, particularly as Jesus was probably now in Perea, the area of John's ministry and of his death at Machaerus: was this "second John" going to maintain his predecessor's hard line?

4-5 In Mark 10 Jesus' answer begins with the discussion about Deut 24:1-4 (which here will come in vv. 7-8) and goes on to the more fundamental texts from Genesis. In Matthew the order is reversed (cf. a similar transposition in 15:3-9), so that Jesus starts by laying down the positive principle of unbroken marriage, and only in the light of that turns to Deut 24:1-4 as a permitted departure from that principle. Mark's order, which moves from the basis of current discussion to Jesus' new contribution to the debate, allows a neater transition between the statement that Deut 24:1-4 does not represent what was the case "from the beginning of creation" and the texts which support that statement. Matthew places the texts in perhaps a more logical order, which progresses from the higher principle to the lower level of accommodation, and which allows the key texts to be quoted before the inference is drawn from them. The resultant argument develops as follows: statement of basic scriptural principle (vv. 4-6); counterscripture (v. 7); resolution of how scripture B relates to scripture A (v. 8); resultant pronouncement (v. 9).

For the formula, "Haven't you read?" which occurs also in 12:3, 5; 21:16, 42; 22:31, see on 12:3. The texts are very familiar, but the inference which Jesus will draw from them is not one with which his Pharisaic hearers would have been comfortable. The two texts are both drawn from the account of the original creation, and so represent the situation of created humanity before the Fall. The first text, from Gen 1:27 (conforming to the LXX; the clause is also repeated in Gen 5:2), establishes the complementarity of male and female within God's created order, but does not in itself directly address

---

gests that the intention is, as in Mark, to ask whether Jesus approves of divorce *at all,* but that Matthew has worded the question in the terms of current debate. See, however, the commentary on 5:31-32 (especially p. 209, nn. 108, 109) for how Jesus' position even in its Matthean form differs from that of the Shammaites.

17. It may even reflect the standard formula used to characterize the Hillelite view; see D. Instone-Brewer, *Divorce,* 110-15.

18. The school of Shammai permitted divorce only in the case of "unchastity" (see above, pp. 207-10).

the issue of divorce or indeed marriage as such.[19] Jesus' argument depends on the combination of this text with Gen 2:24 (here quoted in a slightly adapted version of the LXX), still set within the story of creation — first-century readers would not have been aware of the modern critical division of Gen 1–2 between two sources! This combination results in a compelling sequence of thought: the God who first designed humanity in two sexes also laid it down (see next paragraph) that those two sexes should come together in an indissoluble union of "one flesh," a union which takes precedence over even the close relationship of a man with his parents. The union is depicted in the vivid metaphor of Genesis as one of "glueing" or "welding"[20] — it would be hard to imagine a more powerful metaphor of permanent attachment. In the Genesis context the "one flesh" image derives from the creation of the woman out of the man's side to be "bone of my bones and flesh of my flesh" (Gen 2:21-23); in marriage that original unity is restored.

This argument is the more compelling if, as I have argued (see p. 711, n. 4), the first clause of v. 5 is taken not as Matthew's editorial introduction of a further comment by Jesus, but as part of Jesus' own argument, attributing the saying of Gen 2:24 directly to the Creator himself. In Genesis it appears as an editorial comment, following on from words of Adam, so that it cannot be read as God's statement in that narrative context. But if the translation given above is correct, Jesus attributes this comment by the author of Genesis to God himself. Such an attribution would have caused no surprise in first-century Judaism, for which Scripture as a whole was the word of God, so that its contents, even if narratively spoken by someone else, are God's statements.[21] If the alternative translation of, for example, REB is followed, the argument would be less tight, but for Jesus himself to quote the text of Gen 2:24 as a supplement to his statement about God's creation of the two sexes would make sense only if he presupposed, as surely his hearers would have done, that these words of the author of Genesis truly convey the mind of God on the nature of marriage.

---

19. It is, however, used in CD 4:21 as a probable argument against polygamy (see p. 207, n. 100), and in *m. Yebam.* 6:6 as a proof-text for the duty of marriage and procreation.

20. This is the primary sense of Matthew's Greek κολλάω followed by dative (and of the LXX προσκολλάω πρός). The Hebrew *dābaq* is widely used metaphorically for "clinging to" as in the present passage, but its primary sense is of something "stuck" to another thing (bone to skin, or the joining together of Leviathan's scales, which "clasp each other and cannot be separated," Job 19:20; 41:17) and the cognate noun is used of "soldering" (Isa 41:7).

21. A clear example of this assumption is Heb 1, which presents words of Moses (v. 6) and of the psalmists (vv. 7, 8-9, 10-12) as what God says; in v. 6 the speaker is unambiguously identified as the one who "brings the firstborn into the world." Cf. Matthew's own attribution of prophetic sayings to God in 1:22; 2:15.

6 Jesus now draws out the ethical implications of the Genesis texts he has cited. The "one flesh" metaphor, if it is taken seriously, makes marriage indissoluble. To break it is like tearing apart a single body. Moreover, this union is not a matter of human decision or social convention. If it is *God* who has done the "cementing," it is not for a human being to try to undo it. Indeed, it might be argued that it is impossible, that there is something ontological about the "one flesh" union which no human decision can destroy: the man and the woman are no longer two independent beings who may choose to go their own way, but a single indivisible unit. We have noted in relation to 5:31-32 that the Matthean exceptive clauses probably derive from the view that when a new sexual union has been formed the previous marriage has been automatically destroyed; this position seems to presuppose an "ontological" view of the "one flesh" union.[22] But even if that is so, the argument here is expressed not in terms of what cannot happen, but of what *must* not happen: the verb is an imperative, "*let* not man separate." To break up a marriage is to usurp the function of the God by whose creative order it was set up, and who has decreed that it shall be a permanent "one flesh" union.

It may be objected that this is to press a metaphor too far, that husband and wife in fact remain two individuals and so can be separated. And in fact divorces and remarriages (and, indeed, polygamy) do happen; it is not in the strict sense *impossible*. But the point of the metaphor is that it *should* not happen, that God has created a union which is designed to be permanent, and that human action which purports to dissolve it is not legitimate. Thus Jesus' argument up to this point is one of total rejection of divorce: it is a violation of what God has created. The dispute between Shammai and Hillel over the grounds of divorce has been firmly set aside: there simply is no basis for divorce. It is this absolute statement of principle which provokes the understandable objection of the Pharisees in v. 7.

7 There is an obvious *prima facie* discrepancy between what Jesus has deduced from the texts in Genesis and the fact that Deut 24:1-4 (the only OT legal text on the subject) legislated for what may follow from a divorce. The Pharisees accordingly seize on that discrepancy. The "quotation" here is a summary (rather fuller than that in 5:32) of part of the preamble to the Deuteronomy ruling, phrased as if it were an imperative in its own right, and using the more technical term for "divorce" rather than the LXX's "send away." See above, pp. 206-7, for what Deut 24:1-4 does in fact say and how

---

22. See pp. 210-11. The view that one cannot be "one flesh" with two people at the same time assumes that sexual intercourse in itself sets up a permanent union, rather than being simply a passing relationship. Paul's argument in 1 Cor 6:16, again based on Gen 2:24, assumes that it is the act of sexual intercourse, rather than a private or public ceremony, which constitutes the "one flesh" union.

it was currently interpreted. The Pharisees read into it a "commandment" which is not in fact there: the giving of a divorce certificate[23] and the resultant divorce are not "commanded" but presupposed as having already taken place, while the actual legislation concerns a later stage in a particular divorce and remarriage scenario. But their assumption that this presupposition implies the acceptance of the original divorce is a reasonable one with which all current Jewish interpretation would have agreed; if it is not strictly a "commandment," it surely at least implies permission. Matthew's wording of this exchange carefully observes this distinction, with Jesus using the verb "permit" in response to their verb "command." In Mark the verbs are reversed in that Jesus asks what "command" Moses gave and the Pharisees reply only that he "permitted" divorce, while Jesus goes on to speak of the Deuteronomy text as a "commandment." Matthew's version puts the Pharisees more clearly in the wrong, and allows Jesus to withhold from the Deuteronomy text the status of "commandment" which would more nearly put it on a par with the Genesis principle. As merely a "permission," it can more appropriately be set aside.

8 Jesus accepts that Deut 24:1-4 does in effect *permit* divorce, even though it does not actually say so in so many words. How then is this permission to be squared with his absolute statement that divorce should not take place? The naming of "Moses" as the one who gave permission might suggest that a contrast is being drawn with the original principle of unbroken marriage which was explicitly attributed to the Creator himself in vv. 4-5; on that understanding what *Moses* permitted is downgraded to a merely human deviation from the divine purpose. But that would be a very modern inference. In first-century Judaism the laws given by Moses were understood to be the laws of God; "Moses" means the Pentateuch, the God-given body of law which is Israel's highest authority. The name "Moses" is used in v. 8 not to contrast Moses with God, but because Jesus is responding to the question of v. 7 in which Moses has already been named as the source of the Deuteronomic provision.

The contrast Jesus draws is not with regard to the authorship or authority of the two Pentateuchal texts, or even simply to the order in which they were given,[24] but with regard to their purpose. The Deuteronomic legislation is a response to human failure, an attempt to bring order to an already unideal situation caused by human "hardness of heart." This familiar biblical term refers not so much to people's attitude to one another (cruelty, neglect, or the like) as to their attitude to God, whose purpose and instructions they

---

23. See above, p. 212, for the wording of the certificate.
24. Cf. Paul's argument in Gal 3:17 that the promise takes precedence over the law, which came later.

have set aside. Its classical use is with regard to Pharaoh, whose "heart was hardened" to refuse God's call for the liberation of Israel (Exod 7:13 and a further dozen times in the Exodus narrative); it is a term for rebellion against the God to whom obedience is due. It was the fact that divorce was taking place in defiance of God's stated intention for marriage that made it necessary for Moses to make appropriate provision. But it should never have been so. The existence of divorce legislation is a pointer not to divine approval of divorce but to human sinfulness.

Was the provision of Deut 24:1-4 then a mistake? That does not follow from Jesus' argument. It was rather a mark of divine condescension. Even after his people had rejected his design for marriage, God gave them laws to enable them to make the best of a bad job. But the Mosaic "permission" was not a statement of the way God intended things to be. For that one needs to look in Genesis at the way God had set up his pattern for human sexuality "from the beginning," before the Fall. So the mistake in relation to Deut 24:1-4 is not that of Moses in making legislative provision for the problems which arise in a fallen world after divorce has taken place, but that of his interpreters who have taken this regrettable but necessary provision as the starting point for their ethical discussion in preference to the original purpose of God as expressed in Genesis. But if the latter is allowed its proper status, Jesus' pronouncement of v. 6 still stands: what God has united must not be divided.

9 The resultant pronouncement about divorce and remarriage is introduced not by a further reference to scripture but by the same formula, "*I tell you*," which introduced Jesus' authoritative restatements of the will of God in 5:21-47, and in particular his parallel ruling on divorce and remarriage in 5:32.[25] The commentary there should be consulted, in particular with regard to the assumption that remarriage follows divorce and the significance of the clause "except for sexual unfaithfulness." This is a shorter version, with a single main clause in place of the double statement of the effect of divorce and remarriage in 5:32. The results of divorce and remarriage are set out differently here, in that there is no statement of the effect on the divorced wife, and the man whose adultery is condemned is the divorcing husband

---

25. There are parallel sayings in Matt 5:32; 19:9; Mark 10:11-12; Luke 16:18. Quite apart from textual variations within each of these sayings (of which there are many), the normally accepted texts of the four passages, while all stating that divorce and remarriage constitute adultery, present a wide variety of structure and of forms of wording, probably reflecting some of the complexities of applying this radical teaching to pastoral issues within first-century churches. The most striking distinctives are Mark's presupposition that a wife might divorce her husband (a possibility under Roman but not under Jewish law) and the inclusion in both Matthean texts of the clause "except for sexual unfaithfulness."

who remarries rather than another man who marries the divorced wife; it is not stated that his second wife is herself divorced, which places the charge of adultery squarely on the man who has divorced his wife and married another. But these are different permutations on the same theme, that marriage should not be terminated except for sexual unfaithfulness, and that if it is, the subsequent marriage of either party will be adulterous.

See on 5:31-32 for the question whether the clause "except for sexual unfaithfulness" here has the effect of lining Jesus up with the Shammaite school, who allowed divorce only in cases of "unchastity." In that case it would seem that Jesus is here after all giving an answer to the question about the grounds for divorce in v. 3. In practice the two positions may indeed result in similar (though not identical, see p. 209, nn. 108, 109) policy, but if my comments there are valid, the way they are arrived at is quite different. The Shammaite position was based on Deut 24:1-4, and especially the interpretation of the phrase "something shameful," which some Shammaites took in a broader sense than Jesus' term "sexual unfaithfulness." Jesus' teaching starts rather from the "one flesh" of Gen 2:24, so that it is only because "sexual unfaithfulness" has already violated the unity of the one flesh that the marriage must be regarded as no longer intact. Shammai was concerned with a man's right to initiate divorce, Jesus with the formal recognition that the marriage has already been broken by the wife's action.

If all this seems very remote from our own society with its soaring divorce rate, divorce by mutual consent, and the widespread assumption that marriages cannot be expected to last for life, it is! But it was no less radical in the Jewish world of Jesus' day, where divorce was if anything easier in practice than it is for us now, except that it was in theory the prerogative of men only. Jesus is laying down a challenge to accepted norms, and demanding a complete rethinking of marriage, on the basis not of human convenience but of the purpose of God for his creation. See pp. 212-13 for how this divine standard may be maintained while still allowing for the fact of human sinfulness and failure. Our society cannot avoid the sad realities which resulted in the concessive legislation of Deut 24:1-4, and will always have to make its own provisions for failure, but if it is to be true to Jesus' understanding of God's purpose for marriage, it must not allow the failure to become the norm. Divorce and remarriage must be legislated for, but can have no higher ethical status than as the lesser evil.

10   Mark records that after the discussion with the Pharisees the disciples asked Jesus about his teaching about inseparability, but does not give their words; their question is simply the cue for Jesus' pronouncement on divorce and remarriage as adultery. In Matthew that pronouncement has already been made, and the disciples' response is now in reaction to the whole of his teaching about marriage and divorce. It serves to introduce a new theme to which Mark has no parallel. They comment rather humorously that in the light of Jesus' radical challenge to conventional thinking about marriage it would be better not to marry at all than to be saddled with a marriage from which you cannot escape.²⁶ This sounds like an instinctive reaction rather than a thought-out response, since in Jewish society at that time the possibility of remaining celibate was not a recognized option. With the one remarkable exception of Jesus himself,²⁷ there is little evidence that mainstream Judaism²⁸ contemplated the possibility of a man remaining unmarried;²⁹ marriage and the fathering of children were regarded as religious duties.³⁰ But, ironical as the disciples' words may have been intended to be, Jesus takes them as the basis for a serious response.

11 The interpretation of Jesus' response depends on how "this saying" (or "the word/matter"; see p. 712, n. 11) is understood. If, as some commentators believe,³¹ Jesus is referring back³² to his own radical teaching

26. See Keener, 471, for the prevalence of "escape clauses" in marriage contracts in the ancient world.

27. Even his unmarried state is an argument from silence, though it is a very loud silence. The nature of the evidence and the debate around it are well summed up by F. J. Moloney, *JSNT* 2 (1979) 42, 54-55. See more fully J. P. Meier, *Marginal Jew,* 1:332-45. It is often assumed that John the Baptist was also unmarried, but for this, too, there is no specific evidence.

28. Josephus states that Essenes did not marry but instead adopted other people's children (*War* 2.120-21; *Ant.* 18.21), but he mentions another group of Essenes who disagreed (*War* 2.160-61). The practice at Qumran remains a matter of debate in the absence of specific rules about marriage or celibacy in 1QS, though other Qumran documents seem to assume families within the community.

29. This is not the place to debate the marital status of Paul. When writing 1 Cor 7 he was apparently not in a marriage relationship, but it may be debated whether he may at that stage have been a widower, or even whether his comments in 1 Cor 7:12-16 reflect the experience of a man who had been deserted by a wife who did not share his Christian faith. And what about the "believing wife" who does not accompany him on his travels according to 1 Cor 9:5: is she hypothetical?

30. See *m. Yebam.* 6:6 for the rabbinic view.

31. I took this position myself in my 1985 commentary on Matthew (282-83). I then argued that to take "this saying" as the disciples' comment involved "setting vv. 10-12 against vv. 3-9" (by offering celibacy as an alternative to the "highly prized" God-given institution of marriage), whereas I now find a greater inconsistency in the implication (if "this saying" refers to Jesus' own teaching) that not everyone is able (or even required) to comply with his insistence that marriage is intended to be for life.

32. οὗτος normally refers to something already present or mentioned, usually in the immediately preceding context. Sometimes the context requires that it refers forward, and so it might be suggested that it refers here to the eunuch saying of v. 12, but such forward reference is usually marked by a following resumptive relative or participle, and here there is no such resumption; v. 12 is separated from τὸν λόγον τοῦτον by the final

which has provoked the disciples' wry comment, the "saying" referred to may be either of the key pronouncements in vv. 6 (prohibiting divorce) and 9 (declaring that divorce followed by remarriage constitutes adultery); or he may be speaking more generally of the "matter" or "principle" which has been the subject of his whole response to the Pharisees and which underlies those pronouncements, the indissoluble nature of the "one flesh" union which was God's intention for marriage. In the end any of these options comes to much the same result, that Jesus will here be conceding that not everyone is able to maintain God's high standard for the permanence of marriage — in other words, that divorce (other than as a result of *porneia*) may in some cases be permissible after all.

But it is more likely that "this saying" refers not to Jesus' own teaching but to the more immediate antecedent, the comment which the disciples have just made.[33] In that case Jesus is here taking quite seriously what was probably intended by them as an ironical comment: celibacy *is* a real option, but it is not for everyone. I prefer this interpretation for two reasons. First, for Jesus now to concede that the teaching he has given in vv. 4-9 is unworkable for some people would be a surprising climbdown from the absolute standard which he has so far insisted on maintaining against all current practice; to accept that for some the expectation of lifelong marriage is "not given" would undermine what he has just been arguing.[34] Secondly, the equally cryptic verse which follows, and which is linked to v. 11 by an explanatory "for," talks not about divorce but apparently about celibacy. In that case the discussion of divorce has ended, and the disciples' interjection has changed the agenda by raising (even if in their view facetiously) the option of voluntary celibacy.

For the concept of a divine "gift" given to some but not others cf. 13:11 concerning the gift of knowledge of the secrets of the kingdom of heaven. Paul uses similar language with regard to marriage or celibacy in 1 Cor 7:7. To speak of a "gift" of celibacy is to assume that marriage is the norm, but that God has given to some people the ability, perhaps even the inclination, to stand apart from that norm. Jesus himself, if indeed he was not married (see above), would be the prime example of this gift.

12 The opening "for" ensures that this extraordinary saying is understood as explaining how the divine gift of celibacy referred to in v. 11 is

---

clause of v. 11, and it is introduced by γάρ, which indicates that it is an explanatory addition rather than itself the content of the preceding τὸν λόγον τοῦτον. Luz, 2:500, n. 114, argues that "in the almost formulaic connection with λόγος in Matthew οὗτος *always* refers to what has preceded."

33. So, e.g., W. D. Davies, *Setting,* 393-95; Keener, 470.

34. Cf. Carson, 419: "After a strong prohibition, it is highly unlikely that Jesus' moral teaching dwindles into a pathetic 'But of course, not everyone can accept this.'"

conveyed. It uses the model of the eunuch to describe those who do not marry and have children. In the case of the literal eunuch this is a matter of necessity, but most subsequent interpretation has understood the "making oneself a eunuch" here not as a literal prescription[35] but as a metaphor for making the choice to remain unmarried (see comments on the nonliteral interpretation of the even more graphic mutilation texts in 5:29-30; 18:8-9 above).

To us the use of "eunuch" language seems unhelpfully extreme when talking about those who could marry but choose not to do so, and the fivefold repetition of the word (the noun "eunuch" three times and the verb "to make a eunuch" twice) within this one verse makes it the more uncomfortable. But the word would have been no less offensive in first-century Jewish culture, in which eunuchs were the object of pity if not of horror (see below). The choice of this striking metaphor perhaps reflects a culture where marriage and the procreation of children were so much taken for granted as the norm that strong language is needed to question that assumption. The "abnormality" in that culture of a man's not being married meant that there was little room in popular thinking for a middle way between marriage and being a eunuch. Jesus' saying is framed against that black-and-white background.[36]

The saying is framed (as was the disciples' comment) in terms of the man's situation; its application to celibate women must be a matter of inference. Three reasons are suggested why a man may not conform to the norm of marriage and fatherhood. He may be a "eunuch" by birth, by human interference, or by choice. Of these the second is the most easily understood. The deliberate castration of men, particularly in order to provide "safe" attendants of a married woman or custodians of a harem, was widely practiced throughout the ancient world. The practice is known, but not approved, in the OT (Isa 56:3-5; cf. Deut 23:1); specific instances are invariably associated with a pagan court (2 Kgs 9:32; 20:18; Esther passim; Acts 8:27).[37]

To be "born a eunuch" appears to refer to those who are physiologically incapable of procreation; cf. the standard rabbinic distinction between a "man-made eunuch" and a "eunuch by nature" (*m. Yebam.* 8:4; *m. Zabim* 2:1). In the context of modern discussions about homosexual orientation it

---

35. Eusebius, *Hist. eccl.* 6.8.1-3, says that Origen took it literally and castrated himself. Pagan religion provides examples of self-castration, especially where priesthood in some cults was reserved for eunuchs, and there have been other examples in a Christian context; for details see Davies and Allison, 3:23, n. 112.

36. F. J. Moloney, *JSNT* 2 (1979) 50-52, following J. Blinzler, *ZNW* 48 (1957) 254-70, suggests that the term may derive from Jesus' own experience of being abused as a "eunuch" because of his unmarried state.

37. For a postbiblical Jewish description of castration as a barbarous foreign practice see Josephus, *C. Ap.* 2.270-71; *Ant.* 4.290-91 (the latter also includes a condemnation of self-castration); cf. *T. Jud.* 23:4. See further J. Schneider, *TDNT* 2:765-68.

might be suggested that it also includes those who are psychologically disinclined to heterosexual intercourse and thus debarred from fatherhood, but evidence for such an understanding of homosexuality in the ancient world is hard to find. Most references to homosexual behavior in the ancient world are to what we now call bisexuality, the choice of some who are capable of heterosexual intercourse to find sexual fulfillment also (or instead) with members of their own sex. Such a choice could hardly be described as being "born a eunuch," and the idea of an innate and irreversible homosexual orientation belongs to modern Western psychology rather than to the world in which Jesus lived.

If to "make oneself a eunuch" is not to be understood literally (see above), it should probably be understood along the lines of some modern versions, "to renounce marriage" (NIV, REB), "do not marry" (GNB). The first two categories were incapable of marriage; this third group represents those who have voluntarily chosen celibacy.[38] Their choice is ascribed not to disinclination but to their perception of God's will for them: the "kingship of heaven" means God's sovereign authority, and it is in obedience to that authority that they have been prepared to stand apart from the normal expectation of marriage and fatherhood. The phrase does not in itself indicate what is the specific purpose for which God may have called and enabled such people to be celibate.[39] It does not denote specifically, for example, either an overriding imperative of evangelism or the call to a contemplative life.[40] These and other reasons[41] may explain God's call in certain cases, but Jesus' state-

---

38. Some commentators argue that the divorce context remains in view here, and that "making oneself a eunuch" refers to disciples who, having divorced their wives for πορνεία in accordance with v. 9, choose not to remarry (so Gundry, 377, 382-83 and n. 154; S. C. Barton, *Discipleship,* 194-99). This seems an improbably restricted interpretation of the metaphor, and one which follows with difficulty after the interruption of the disciples' comment in v. 10. It is, in any case, out of place if, as argued above (pp. 211-12), Jesus did not forbid remarriage after divorce for πορνεία.

39. Here most commentators miss the point by assuming (on the basis of the English term "kingdom" rather than the Greek βασιλεία) that the "kingdom of heaven" is a "thing" (a particular situation, state, or activity) for the sake of which, or in order to enter which, one may choose to remain unmarried. The phrase serves here, as elsewhere, not to denote something called "the kingdom" but to point to the fact that God is king and is recognized and obeyed as such. On this problem in the use of "kingdom" language see my *Divine Government,* 11-14.

40. In 10:34-37 Jesus spoke of loyalty to him taking precedence over family ties, but it should be noted that the husband/wife relationship is not mentioned there (as it is in Luke 14:26). In Matthew Jesus does not suggest that marriage as such is a distraction from loyalty to him. See, however, p. 740, n. 4, for the inclusion of this idea in much later Christian teaching.

41. Such as Paul's argument from the "impending crisis" in 1 Cor 7:25-35.

ment here is much more general: some are celibate because they believe this to be God's will for them.[42]

The final clause of this saying (taken together with v. 11) underlines that this is a matter of individual gift; it is not for everyone. There have been times within Christian history when it has been assumed that the monastic ideal is the *best* way of life, and that those who marry and have children are on a lower level of spiritual achievement, but Jesus' words give no sanction to that view. The ideal of marriage set out in vv. 4-9 remains God's standard for his people, but it is not, as many in Jesus' day would have assumed, the *only* way of faithfulness to the Creator's purpose. God's people are not all the same, and are not all called to the same path of obedience. As Paul wrote in connection with another matter of lifestyle on which believers had come to different conclusions, "Everyone should be fully convinced in their own mind" (Rom 14:5).

2. Children (19:13-15)

> 13 *Then children were brought to him so that he might lay his hands on them and pray; but the disciples rebuked them.* 14 *But Jesus said, "Leave the children alone, and don't stop them from coming to me; for the kingdom of heaven belongs to*[1] *such people."*[2] 15 *And when he had laid his hands on them, he went on from there.*

In the sequence of pericopae dealing with family and social values (see introductory comments on 19:3–20:28), after matters related to marriage we come to children. Here, too, the disciples have much to learn about the paradoxical values of the kingdom of heaven; the recurrence of that phrase here in v. 14 so soon after its use in v. 12 and preceding its use again in vv. 23 and 24 and in 20:1 keeps the primary focus of these chapters to the fore. The subject of the importance of children is not new, having been raised as recently as 18:1-5 (see comments there), but now it is sharpened by an actual encounter which

---

42. F. J. Moloney, *JSNT* 2 (1979) 47-49, argues that the reference is specifically to Gentile converts whose former marriages are no longer acceptable or viable, and who are therefore called to live as "eunuchs" because of their Christian conversion. His position depends on taking vv. 10-12 as still dealing with the divorce issue rather than introducing celibacy as a subject in its own right.

1. See p. 158, n. 3, for this usage, which here, as there, could also be translated "consists of."

2. No noun follows "such" in the Greek, but English idiom requires one. "Such children" would tend to restrict the reference only to children, while "such people" reflects the move in 18:2-6 (where again "such" is used) from the literal child to disciples whom that child represents.

again catches the disciples on the wrong foot and depicts them as out of sympathy with Jesus' value-scale.

13   While *paidion* is diminutive in form, in Matthew it is the normal word for children in general, without reference necessarily to the very young (cf. its use in 11:16; 14:21; 15:38). One may perhaps guess the age of these children from the fact that they are "brought," but Matthew does not speak (as does Mark 10:16) of Jesus taking them in his arms. Those who brought them are not identified, but we may reasonably assume that it was their parents. There is nothing unusual about the desire to have children blessed by a "holy man." The request here may be compared with the practice of bringing children to the elders for "blessing, strengthening, and prayer" in the evening following the Day of Atonement (*Sop.* 18:5), or the blessing of the child Jesus in the temple by Simeon according to Luke 2:28 (cf. Gen 48:14-20). Because the parents are not mentioned, Matthew's text reads as if the disciples' rebuke is addressed directly to the children, and that is quite possible if the children were old enough to be independently mobile; Jesus' response suggests that it was the children themselves that the disciples tried to turn away. But we might also think of the parents who had initiated the approach and who are implied by the passive "were brought." The disciples' motive is not explained, but Jesus' response in v. 14 suggests that they are wrongly assuming that children have no claim on their master's attention. Their memories are short: their attitude could hardly be more opposite to "welcoming a child in the name of Jesus" (18:5).

14-15   Children matter in the kingdom of heaven, which can be entered only by those who are like children and where those of the lowest status are the great ones (18:3-4). Here, as in 18:2, it is literal children who focus the issue, but here too, as in 18:5, the use of "such" rather than "these" indicates that the thought is broader than the literal children who are present in the narrative setting. Those who are to be welcomed and encouraged in Jesus' name also include those who are spiritually in the position of children, the unimportant, the dependent, the vulnerable; the statement that the kingdom of heaven belongs to such people reminds us of 5:3, 10, where the same statement is made about the "poor in spirit" and the persecuted. To keep such people away from Jesus is to run a risk worse than being drowned with a millstone (18:6).

The laying on of hands as a mark of blessing appears in a variety of biblical contexts. In this gospel we have met it in relation to healing (9:18, and cf. "touch" in 8:3, 15; 9:29), and in 17:7 Jesus' touch brought reassurance in panic. Laying on of hands for healing is also mentioned in Mark 6:5; 7:32; 8:23, 25; Luke 4:40; 13:13; Acts 9:12, 17; 28:8. But the gesture is also appropriate for commissioning someone for a special responsibility (Acts 6:6; 13:3; 1 Tim 4:14; 5:22; 2 Tim 1:6) and for conveying the gift of the Spirit

(Acts 8:17-19; 19:6), and it apparently held an unspecified place in the regular ministry of at least one branch of early Christianity (Heb 6:2). In view of this wide usage it is not appropriate to look for any more specific significance here than as a mark of blessing to accompany prayer. This pericope thus has no direct bearing on the issue of whether young children should be baptized, though those who debate that issue need to be sure that their conclusions and their practice enshrine an appropriate welcome to children to whom "the kingdom of heaven belongs," and do not turn them away.

3. Wealth (19:16-26)

16 *Now along came[1] a man who approached him with the question, "Teacher,[2] what good thing shall I do in order to have eternal life?" 17 Jesus replied, "Why do you ask me about what is good? There is one person who is good.[3] But if you want to enter into life, keep the commandments." 18 "Which?" he asked. Jesus replied, "These:[4] 'You shall not murder; you shall not commit adultery; you shall not steal; you shall not bear false witness; 19 honor your father and your mother,' and 'You shall love your neighbor as yourself.'" 20 The young man said to him, "I have kept all these.[5] Where do I still fall short?"[6] 21 Jesus said to him, "If you want to be perfect, off you go and sell all you have and give [the proceeds] to the poor, and you will have treasure in heaven; then come and follow me." 22 But when the young man heard this, he went away in distress, for he had a lot of property.*

23 *Then Jesus said to his disciples, "I tell you truly that it is hard*

1. Another attempt to convey something of the rhetorical function of καὶ ἰδού to draw attention to a dramatic new development.

2. Most later MSS have Διδάσκαλε ἀγαθέ, "Good teacher," assimilating to Mark and Luke. But Matthew's transfer of ἀγαθόν from the address to the content of the question and consequent rewording of Jesus' reply make it clear that he is deliberately avoiding the address to Jesus as himself "good" (see below).

3. Here, too, most later MSS assimilate to Mark and Luke, but there is also some confusion even among those which remain distinct. The most significant variation is in the addition of "God" after "who is good" in a number of Latin, Syriac, and Coptic MSS; this, too, may be an attempt to assimilate to Mark and Luke, but it could also result from a natural desire to clarify the oblique statement in the text as printed.

4. The list of commandments is introduced by the definite article Τό, which has the effect of marking out what follows as a quotation ("a kind of catechism," Gundry, 386); cf. the similar usage in Rom 13:9.

5. Again, most later MSS assimilate to the parallels by adding "from my youth."

6. Since ὑστερέω is constructed with its "object" in the genitive, the accusative Τί here must be an accusative of reference, "With regard to what am I deficient?"

for a rich person to enter the kingdom of heaven. 24 *Or to put it an-other way,[7] it is easier for a camel[8] to get through the eye of a needle than for a rich person to get into the kingdom of God." 25 When the disciples heard this, they were flabbergasted,[9] and exclaimed, "So who can be saved?" 26 Jesus looked at them intently[10] and said, "In human terms it is impossible; but for God everything is possible."*

Here is another approach from someone outside the disciple group, but this man's social standing[11] is in marked contrast to the social insignificance of the children. As a result, the same disciples who in 19:13 proved so unwelcoming to those who came to "bother" Jesus now appear to be so favorably impressed by this potential new recruit that they can hardly believe their ears when they hear Jesus send him away with his tail between his legs. Jesus, who has just confounded them by welcoming the "little ones," here makes matters worse by turning away a "great one." If ever there was a promising candidate for the kingdom of heaven, surely this was he: young (vv. 20, 22; only Matthew includes this description), moral (v. 20), spiritually in earnest (vv. 17, 20), and wealthy (v. 22). If such a man cannot be saved, who can?

The disciples' astonishment arises from the common Jewish assumption (reflecting an important strand in the OT, especially in the Wisdom tradition but also in the seminal passage Deut 28:1-14) that wealth is a sign of God's blessing and his reward for faithful service,[12] so that when Jesus instead declares it to be an impediment to salvation he is undermining a fundamental part of their religious worldview. It is true that the OT prophets and psalmists had spoken against the oppressive rich and championed the pious

---

7. Literally, "Again I tell you," a formula which here, in contrast to 18:19 (where I translated πάλιν as "moreover"; see p. 695, n. 1), introduces a restatement of almost the same point.

8. The famous conjecture (see comments below) that Jesus spoke not of a camel (κάμηλον) but of a rope (κάμιλον) has found its way into the text of a few later minuscule MSS and into the Armenian version (and the Georgian version of Mark).

9. Literally, "very much astonished"; the addition of σφόδρα to the verb ἐκπλήσσομαι, which in itself means "to be astonished," indicates the need for a stronger English expression.

10. In 6:26, the only other use by Matthew of the compound ἐμβλέπω, I translated it "take a good look." See p. 264, n. 2. The verb usually denotes looking carefully or searchingly.

11. For the link between affluence and social standing in relation to this pericope see J. H. Neyrey, *Honor,* 61-62.

12. For some examples of the rabbinic attitude to wealth see M. Hengel, *Property,* 19-22. For a fuller survey of the postbiblical Jewish material, which illustrates a wide variety of attitudes to wealth, see T. E. Schmidt, *Hostility,* 61-100. W. Carter, *Households,* 127-43, surveys attitudes to wealth more widely in the ancient world.

poor (see above, p. 163), and such hostility to the wealthy continues to be expressed especially within the apocalyptic tradition.[13] It seems unlikely, however, that in popular thought material possessions *as such* were distrusted. This pericope does not say, however, that this young man was guilty of oppression of the poor,[14] and Jesus' demand on him, while it includes giving to the poor, is expressed in terms of his own "perfection," "treasure in heaven" and discipleship. It is his actual wealth, and his attitude toward it, that is in focus rather than his social behavior; his affluence is a danger to the owner himself rather than a threat to others.

Matthew has already included in 6:19-24 a powerful section of teaching on the incompatibility of earthly and heavenly treasure, with the concluding maxim that "you cannot be slaves of both God and wealth." See above, p. 257, on the prominence of this theme in the Synoptic tradition as a whole. The pericope which follows it in 6:25-34 has also placed concern about material security in contrast with trust in a heavenly Father, and has defined discipleship in terms of a prior commitment to the kingship of God which overrides material concerns. Now a specific practical example focuses that more generalized teaching in the case of one rich man whom Jesus calls to choose between God and Mammon. There is no blurring of the clear either/or of 6:24: discipleship and the pursuit of wealth are fundamentally incompatible.

It is not only Jesus' original disciples who find his demand uncomfortably extreme. The history of the interpretation of this passage[15] is divided between the unconventional minority who take v. 21 as a literal prescription which applies to every disciple and so rules out the acquisition or retention of private property, and the "bourgeois" majority who look for exegetically responsible ways to avoid a literal application of v. 21 to disciples in general. Three features of the text have provided ammunition for the latter approach. (a) The word "perfect" in v. 21 has been taken to suggest a two-tier model of discipleship, with the "perfect" renouncing their possessions while "ordinary disciples" are allowed to aspire to a less ascetic standard. (b) The specific attention drawn to the man's extensive property in v. 22 has been taken to indicate that v. 21 is Jesus' prescription only for this individual who had a particular "wealth problem." (c) It is noted with relief that the impossibility of the wealthy being saved is modified by v. 26: God is not bound by this human impossibility.[16] Each of these points will be discussed below. Their cumula-

---

13. Notably in the repeated denunciation of oppressive sinners in the final section of *1 Enoch;* see especially 94:6-11; 97:8-10.

14. *Pace* Carter, 388, whose ideology takes it for granted that to be wealthy at all is in itself to be guilty of "greed, violence and oppression."

15. For which see Luz, 2:518-23.

16. A further and exegetically more questionable ploy has been the attempt, in de-

tive effect has been to allow most readers to conclude that v. 21 does not literally apply to them, and it has been noted in addition that the gospels themselves provide evidence of disciples who retained some of their possessions (house, boat, fishing tackle) and of other supporters who were, and remained, wealthy enough to provide for the needs of the itinerant group of Jesus and the Twelve.[17] There is, however, an undeniable element of self-justification in such exegesis of this passage by the wealthy (a category which in comparative terms includes almost all Western readers of the gospel), and we do well to note the waspish comment of Gundry, 388, "That Jesus did not command all his followers to sell all their possessions gives comfort only to the kind of people to whom he *would* issue that command." However differently the material detachment which Jesus requires (both here and in 6:19-34) may work out in different times and circumstances, the church will be parting company from Jesus' teaching at a fundamental level if it loses sight of the principle that affluence is in essential opposition to the kingdom of heaven.

The above comments apply broadly to all three Synoptic versions of this pericope. Matthew's version of the opening part of the dialogue raises a different and apparently unrelated issue. In Mark and Luke the man addresses Jesus as "Good teacher," and Jesus immediately repudiates the title on the grounds that only God is good — allowing the inference that Jesus himself is not good and therefore is not God. But in Matthew the adjective "good" has been transferred out of the vocative address[18] to become part of the question ("what *good* thing . . ."), with the result that Jesus' response concerns only the phrasing of the question ("about what is good") so that his own goodness and relation to God do not arise. It is of course very unlikely that either Mark or Luke *intended* to suggest that Jesus was not divine or even that it occurred to them that their wording could be so interpreted (the issue simply doesn't arise in that narrative context), but Matthew has apparently spotted a possible embarrassment in the traditional wording of the dialogue when seen in the light of subsequent Christian dogmatic development,[19] and his revised version looks like a deliberate apologetic device.[20]

---

fiance of the flow of the dialogue, to contrive to get a camel through the eye of a needle after all; see below on v. 24 for such conjectures.

17. I have summarized this evidence in *EQ* 51 (1979) 13-14.

18. See p. 728, n. 2.

19. Luz, 2:511, n. 20, is unusual in doubting this dogmatic motive for Matthew's distinctive version. See also P. Luomanen, *Entering,* 144-45, who sees the change as designed to discredit the young man by allowing him to use only an "outsider's" address, "Teacher."

20. For a spirited attempt to avoid this generally agreed conclusion see Carson, 421-23, based on his fuller harmonizing study in D. A. Carson and J. D. Woodbridge (eds.), *Scripture and Truth,* 131-37.

The verbal differences are the minimum required to achieve this shift of emphasis, which suggests that the difference derives from Matthew's editorial work rather than from an independent tradition.

16 Luke says that this man was a "ruler" (perhaps a deduction from his wealth?), but it will be his wealth rather than his specific social or political status that is at issue. The address to Jesus as "Teacher" is respectful but uncommitted; Matthew, unlike Mark, never has this term used of Jesus by his disciples, only by those outside the group — and in its Hebrew form "Rabbi" by Judas Iscariot after he has abandoned his allegiance as a disciple (26:25, 49). Jesus' advice is being sought as a recognized religious authority, but without the commitment to following it which would be expected of a disciple. The man's question, however, is not a matter of academic theology, but concerns his personal salvation. "Life" has been used for the desired ultimate end as opposed to destruction in 7:14 and as opposed to the "eternal fire" of hell in 18:8-9, and the phrase "eternal life" will recur in the same sense in 19:29; 25:46. For "eternal" see on 18:8-9, and below on 25:41, 46.

The questioner assumes that his ultimate salvation can be ensured by doing some "good thing." The Christian reader, alert to the danger of seeking salvation by works, is likely to find in the form of the question a clue to the man's spiritual problem: he is expressing the "Pelagian" view of salvation which comes naturally to those who have not had the benefit of a Pauline education. But that is not the agenda of Matthew's gospel, and it is striking that Jesus' response, both in his more predictable initial prescription in vv. 17-18 and apparently even in his more radical demand which follows in v. 21, remains within the thought world of the questioner by listing things to "do." We have seen, however, in 5:20 and in its exposition in 5:21-48 that simply to fulfill the requirements of the law as the scribes and Pharisees understood them is not yet to have met the demands of the kingdom of heaven, and in the light of that teaching we are probably justified in seeing "follow me" (v. 21) not simply as another thing to "do," but as the inauguration of a new and life-changing relationship with Jesus. To follow Jesus will lead the inquirer along the path of discipleship which entails the "greater righteousness" that God requires and which is the way to "eternal life."

17 The first part of Jesus' reply, as edited by Matthew (see introductory comments above), is unexpected. It is possible to read it with the emphasis on "me" in contrast with the "one person" who is good (and therefore, unlike Jesus, is qualified to answer such a question), but as Matthew's rewording seems to be designed to avoid such a comparison, that seems unlikely. The emphasis of the Greek sentence falls rather on the adjective "good," twice repeated; the man has asked what "good" thing he should do, and Jesus reminds him first that the term "good" as applied to human activity is relative and can be applied in its absolute sense only to God; see p. 728,

n. 3, for versions which have spelled out what is surely implied by Jesus' reference (possibly echoing the *Š^ema'*, Deut 6:4) to the one (unique) good person. This is a rebuke of theologically careless language and a pointed reminder that even the best of human efforts at "doing good" are inadequate,[21] but it does not directly contribute to the answer to his question.[22] That comes in the second half of the verse, where Jesus identifies where the good conduct required by the one good God may be found.

For the phrase "enter into life" cf. 18:8-9 and the comments on "enter the kingdom of heaven" in 5:20. To keep God's commandments is a necessary condition for salvation: Jesus has not come to abolish the law, and what God has declared still stands (see on 5:17-19). But Jesus does not say that it is also a *sufficient* condition, that if you keep the commandments *you will* enter into life, and the man's reply in v. 20 will rightly look for something more, which Jesus is happy to add in v. 21. It is perhaps significant that Matthew does not include here the words which Luke records in a similar exchange about the way to eternal life in Luke 10:28: "Do this, and you will live" (cf. Lev 18:5, "Whoever does them will live by them"). The keeping of the commandments is here only a first element in the search for salvation.

18-19 In response to Jesus' reference to "the commandments," the question "Which?" is not necessarily a purely rhetorical device. There are, after all, according to rabbinic calculation, 613 commandments in the Pentateuch, and while the Decalogue of Exod 20:2-17 and Deut 5:6-21 held a prominent place in Jewish spirituality, it was not the exclusive place which popular use of the term "commandments" has given to that particular code in some modern Christian usage. So this was a reasonable and appropriate question: to which of the many commandments of the law did this particular teacher give priority? But Jesus does in fact take the Decalogue as the basis of the first part of his reply. Already in this gospel he has affirmed the importance of three of its commandments (5:21, 27; 15:4), quoting respectively the sixth, seventh, and fifth. Now he repeats those three together with the eighth and ninth. The sixth to the ninth commandments (all negative) are given in the traditional Hebrew (not LXX) order, followed by the fifth, with its positive formulation. So far it is a reply which would have caused no surprise to any rabbinic teacher. The selection of these five from among the ten is probably because they all concern observable behavior toward other people rather

---

21. This sense of the surpassing goodness of God comes out below in 20:15, where the unexpected generosity of God is described as his "goodness" over against human standards of fairness.

22. O. L. Cope, *Matthew*, 111-15, suggests a more directly relevant sense by proposing to understand the "one" that is good as the Torah, but the masculine gender makes such a nonpersonal reference very unlikely.

than the more "inward" focus of the first four commandments about our attitude to God and of the prohibition of coveting. These five commandments (if not subjected to the radicalizing treatment which Jesus has given to two of them in 5:21-22, 27-28) can thus be used as an "objective" checklist for one's own behavior, as indeed the young man will use them in v. 20. Nor would the addition of "You shall love your neighbor as yourself" from Lev 19:18 (which only Matthew adds here) cause much surprise. It, too, has already been quoted by Jesus in 5:43, and he will use it again in 22:39[23] as a clear summary of the essential requirement of the law with regard to one's treatment of other people.[24] Taken at face value (rather than in the more nuanced way in which Jesus interprets the Decalogue commands in 5:21-30 and the neighbor-command in Luke 10:29-37), these OT precepts aptly sum up a conventional Jewish view of what it means to do good.

20 That is just how the young man takes them, and so he has no difficulty in claiming, probably in all sincerity (like Paul in Phil 3:6), that he has kept them; he has led a good life. Is that all there is to it? He deserves credit for the perception that there is more to serving God, and therefore to finding eternal life, than merely conventional morality, even when it is directly based on the requirements of the OT law. His initial question was looking for something more searching, and he is not prepared to be fobbed off with such an elementary ethic. He is more spiritually adventurous than that.

21 Jesus recognizes and responds to his spiritual ambition. He wants nothing less than the best in his service of God, and merely keeping commandments has not brought him to that point. He wants to be "perfect" *(teleios)*, a word that denotes not so much moral flawlessness as completeness, full maturity.[25] And that is what Jesus wants for him too, as he does for all his disciples according to 5:48. See the comments there on the meaning of the word, which there sums up the theme of a righteousness greater than that of the scribes and Pharisees (5:20). But perfection is, according to that same verse, the characteristic of God, who has just been declared in v. 17 to be the only one who is truly "good." The young man's request for some "good thing" to do has brought him face to face with goodness at a level which will prove too high for him. The "goodness" of keeping commandments is, as

23. See the comments on 22:39 on the use of Lev 19:18b as a summary in Jewish and Christian teaching.

24. Cf. the similar summary of the demands of the law in 7:12, which, while it does not cite Lev 19:18b, is close to its spirit.

25. Some commentators find a deliberate contrast between the man's status as a "young man" and the "maturity" Jesus calls him to. It is true that both terms occur only in Matthew's version of this episode, but no such contrast is found in Matthew's other use of τέλειος in 5:48; the "greater righteousness" which the term implies both there and here does not depend on a person's age. If any wordplay was intended, it is only at a superficial level.

v. 17 has reminded us, always relative; Jesus now replaces it with a demand which is absolute, the demand of the kingdom of heaven.

The practical outworking of the man's search for perfection thus takes an unexpected direction. Rather than some spiritual exercise or mystical pilgrimage, Jesus first prescribes a very practical action. But this is no token gesture, but the total disinvestment and irrevocable disposal of everything that has provided the basis for his "good" life so far. He has no doubt, like all pious Jews, made regular and generous contributions to the relief of the poor and disadvantaged within his community[26] (that is at least part of what he would understand by "loving your neighbor as yourself"),[27] but Jewish charity operated within prudential limits,[28] whereas Jesus puts no limit to his demand. To follow it will place this self-sufficient young man in the same position as the birds and the flowers in 6:25-32, depending directly on the provision of a heavenly Father for the essentials of life.

But even this radical action of dispossession is not simply another "good thing" to do; it is the prelude to something even more far-reaching. The imperatives "sell" and "give" are followed by "come" and "follow"; the essence of Jesus' demand is not disinvestment but discipleship. So the giving up of possessions is not presented as a sacrifice[29] desirable for its own sake, but rather as the means to something far better — treasure in heaven. See on 6:19-21 for this theme. We noted there that while the theme of reward is important in this gospel (and will come to the fore again in vv. 27-29), it is too simplistic to speak in terms of a transaction whereby the loss of earthly possessions "earns" treasure in heaven. The parable which follows in 20:1-16 rules out any crude idea of *quid pro quo* in this connection. It would be more appropriate to speak, in the language of 6:24, of a release from slavery to Mammon in order to be free to enjoy the treasure of slavery to God. The release from material preoccupation is not in itself the secret of eternal life; it is the introduction to a new way of life as a disciple of Jesus: "follow me." It is in this, rather than in the act of renunciation and generosity alone, that the eternal life which the man is looking for will be found. This is the treasure in heaven.

26. For the nature and importance of poor relief within Jewish society at that time see J. Jeremias, *Jerusalem,* 126-34.

27. The *Gospel according to the Hebrews,* as quoted by Origen, *Comm. in Matt.* 15.14, rather unfairly assumes that he had not done even this: Jesus asks him how he can claim to have kept "the law and the prophets" when the law includes "You shall love your neighbor as yourself," and yet his house is full of good things, none of which have been sent out to "your many brothers, sons of Abraham, [who] are covered in filth and dying of hunger."

28. See A. E. Harvey, *Commands,* 119-21, for Jewish almsgiving and its limitations.

29. Cf. the comments on 13:44-46 on the inappropriateness of the idea of "sacrifice" in this connection.

We noted above the suggestion that the command to sell everything and give applies only to a special elite among disciples who aspire to be "perfect," leaving the rest of us to continue to enjoy our material security with a good conscience. The monastic ideal has often fostered such a division among disciples, with the holy poverty of the "religious" supported by the worldly goods of rank-and-file believers. But such a reading is hard to square with 5:48, where Jesus has declared that "perfection" is the proper goal of *all* disciples.[30] Here, as there, the term is used to contrast true discipleship with the inadequate spirituality of this man's merely law-based ethic (v. 20), the "righteousness of the scribes and Pharisees"; and in 5:20 those who follow the latter are not "ordinary believers" but fail to get into the kingdom of heaven at all. In practical terms, some of those who followed Jesus were called to dependent itinerancy while other disciples supplied their needs (Luke 8:1-3 etc.), but this is a functional rather than a spiritual distinction, and neither here nor elsewhere in the gospel is it suggested that the former are "perfect" and the latter second rate. "Perfection" is the goal for all disciples.[31]

22 Jesus' demand in v. 21 indicates that he has selected this young man, if he is willing to become a disciple, to be one of the itinerant group who have also "left everything" to travel with Jesus (4:20, 22; 9:9), as they will remind him in v. 27. But his "great possessions" mean that the change of lifestyle will be more drastic for him[32] than it probably was for Peter, Andrew, James, John, and Matthew. Jesus' challenge thus sets the claims of God and Mammon in a direct opposition which proves too sharp for him. Why then has Jesus chosen to confront this man with a demand which he has not made on many of his other followers, such as the hospitable family of Mary, Martha, and Lazarus (Luke 10:38-42; John 12:1-3), the wealthy wife of Chuza (Luke 8:3), the "rich disciple" Joseph of Arimathea (27:57), or even Zaccheus, who gave away only half his wealth plus restitutions (Luke 19:8)?

---

30. This point is argued particularly by G. Barth, *Tradition,* 95-99, and by W. D. Davies, *Setting,* 210-15; almost all recent commentators accept that a "two-tier" understanding of discipleship is alien to Matthew. Davies draws an interesting parallel with the ideal of "perfection" at Qumran, but points out that there is no parallel at Qumran to the centrality of *following Jesus* as the essence of "perfection."

31. U. Luz, *Theology,* 111-12, struggles with the question whether all should therefore renounce their possessions, and concludes that "an itinerant existence and the renunciation of possessions are lofty goals. Not that Matthew asks all his readers to attain this goal. His point is, however, that one must take steps in that direction, and the steps should be as large as possible." "Steps in that direction" and "as large as possible" are comfortingly relative terms!

32. A. E. Harvey, *Commands,* 36, adds the suggestion that in twice describing this man as "young" Matthew allows his readers to deduce that he probably still has responsibilities for the support of his parents.

Was it because he saw in this man's spiritual earnestness the potential for a leading role in the disciple group (perhaps implied by Mark's comment that Jesus "loved him," Mark 10:21)? Or had he, as much interpretation has gratefully supposed, diagnosed this man as having a specific spiritual problem through an unhealthy attachment to his wealth, so that he would not have made the same demand on the rest of us? Possibly, but the text does not say so. The young men will serve in vv. 23-26 as an object lesson for the spiritual problems of the affluent, but it can only be a matter of conjecture whether he fills this role because his materialism was exceptional or simply as a typical representative of his class.

23   The story of one man's spiritual failure becomes the model for a general and emphatic pronouncement by Jesus (see on 5:18 for "I tell you truly"), which picks up and takes further the warning in the interpretation of the parable of the sower that "the worries of this world and the false lure of wealth [can] choke the message [so that] it cannot produce a crop" (13:22). Whatever the specific pressures faced by the young man, his experience is now universalized as the danger which faces "the rich" in general. To "enter the kingdom of heaven" has occurred several times as a term for salvation, understood both in the context of present discipleship and of eternal life (5:20; 7:21; 18:3; cf. 18:8-9). Here its essential meaning, becoming a subject of God the king, is especially appropriate, since what makes the salvation of the rich difficult is the power struggle between the rival "kings" God and Mammon which allows no divided allegiance (6:24). For the shock value of such a pronouncement in the context of Jewish attitudes to material possessions see the introductory comments above.

24   The pronouncement is repeated, this time in a more graphic, proverbial form. But two differences from v. 23 should be noted. First, this is one of the few places where Matthew uses "kingdom of God" instead of "kingdom of heaven" (see on 6:33). The parallelism of the two verses makes it clear that the reference is the same, and it may be that the change from "heaven" to "God" is merely for literary variation, but this consideration has not stopped Matthew from repeating "kingdom of heaven" three times in 5:19-20 (cf. 18:3-4), and it may be that here the more personal expression "kingdom of God" is chosen to emphasize the opposition between the two "kings," God and Mammon (see on last verse); cf. the similar effect in 12:28, where the opposition to the kingdom of Satan was in view. Secondly, whereas in v. 23 the salvation of the rich was merely "hard," now it is declared impossible. This is the clear sense of the grotesque imagery of the camel (the largest animal in Palestine)[33] going through the eye of a needle, as

33. Cf. the similarly proverbial use of the gnat and the camel (the smallest and the largest) in 23:24.

it is of a parallel rabbinic saying which speaks of an elephant (the largest animal known in Mesopotamia, where this rabbinic material originated) going through the eye of a needle.[34] Moreover, the disciples' response in v. 25 assumes that Jesus has ruled out the salvation of the rich altogether, and Jesus' reply in v. 26 confirms that that was his meaning: it is humanly "impossible."

This clear intention of the proverb in context has not prevented some interpreters from trying to make the impossible possible. See p. 729, n. 8, for the later substitution of *kamilon,* "rope" or "cable," for *kamēlon,* "camel." The word is not attested in Greek before this time, and LSJ suggest that it may have been coined in an attempt to evade the sense of this text. But if so, it was not a very clever attempt, since it is hardly less ludicrous to attempt to put a cable through the eye of a needle than it is a camel. More widely adopted has been a suggestion popularized in the nineteenth century that "the eye of the needle" was the name for a small gate within the large double gate of a city wall through which pedestrians could enter without the need for the large gates to be opened as they would be for a camel train. It is suggested that a camel might be forced through such a gate with great difficulty, and further spiritual lessons have then been extracted from the observation that in order to do so it would have to bend its knees and be stripped of its load. This romantic speculation has been repeated so often that it is sometimes treated as established exegesis. Unfortunately, while this suggestion was not new in the nineteenth century,[35] there is in fact no evidence at all for such usage of "the eye of the needle" either in nonbiblical sources or in ancient commentaries on the gospels.[36] Even if there were, such a scenario would be quite out of keeping with what the context requires: v. 23 spoke of difficulty, but v. 24 goes further and speaks of impossibility, as vv. 25-26 will confirm.

25-26 Jesus' radical statement has challenged one of the basic cultural assumptions that the disciples have hitherto taken for granted: can he really mean what he has just said? While "save" in Matthew normally refers to physical healing or rescue, see on 10:22 for its wider range of meanings. Here its meaning is defined by the context in which it stands parallel to "enter the kingdom of heaven/God" in vv. 23-24, which in turn picks up from the young man's question about gaining "eternal life." The form of the question

34. *B. Ber.* 55b; cf. *b. B. Meṣiʿa* 38b; *b. ʿErub.* 53a; a date palm made of gold is linked with it as another image of the impossible. LSJ (s.v. κάμιλος) mention a similar Arabic proverb using an elephant.

35. Lagrange attributes it to Poloner (fifteenth century), Gundry to Theophylact, Davies and Allison to Anselm (both eleventh), and Schweizer to an unnamed commentator in the ninth. Shakespeare was apparently aware of this proposal: "It is as hard to come as for a camel to thread the postern of a needle's eye" (*Richard II,* Act V, scene 5).

36. See K. E. Bailey, *Peasant Eyes,* 166, following G. N. Scherer.

suggests that in the disciples' view the rich are more, not less, likely to be candidates for salvation since their wealth is a sign of God's blessing on them; if they are excluded, what hope is there for anyone else? This reaction depends on seeing salvation in terms of human worthiness, and on that basis Jesus agrees with their interpretation of what he has said: if it depends on human qualification, salvation is beyond the grasp of any. But Jesus' good news is of the kingdom of *God,* and under his gracious sovereignty the situation is very different. Just as understanding the truth about the kingdom of heaven depends on revelation being "given" (13:11), so the salvation which depends on that understanding is possible with God. The specific subject is salvation, but the maxim of v. 26 (which echoes the spirit though not the words[37] of Gen 18:14; cf. also Zech 8:6) of course has much broader application: where humanity is helpless, God can.

This very terse epigram is thus compatible with a Pauline doctrine of salvation by grace, not by works, but in this Matthean context its theological basis remains undeveloped. The point is simply that salvation is ultimately a matter for God. This may seem something of a *non sequitur* after the young man has asked about gaining eternal life by doing something good and Jesus has replied in the same vein; vv. 18-21 seem to suggest that it *is* humanly possible to find eternal life by what one does. But what must be done was there understood in terms of submitting to God's sovereignty and following Jesus in a life of discipleship. It is people who do that who are in a position to experience the divine "possibility" which is here expressed (and which will be illustrated in 26:57 by Matthew's pointed description of Joseph of Arimathea as both "rich" and a "disciple"). The young man exercised his freedom to decline God's invitation, and it seems that the God for whom everything is possible is not prepared to override that decision. The pericope taken as a whole thus offers a salutary warning: anyone *can* be saved by God's grace, but this does not remove human responsibility. The possible becomes actual only when Jesus' call to "follow me" is freely obeyed.

4. Rewards (19:27-30)

27 *Then Peter spoke up,*[1] *"Look, we have left everything and followed you; so what will we get out of it?"*[2] 28 *Jesus replied, "I tell you*

---

37. Gundry, *Use,* 38-39, points out, however, that the unusual use in all three Synoptics of παρά with the dative in the phrase I have translated *"for God"* corresponds to the usage in LXX Gen 18:14; Gundry concludes that this is a mark of "slavish dependence on the LXX."

1. See the notes on the translation of 11:25; 15:15; 17:4.
2. Literally, "What then will be for us?"

truly that in the new age,[3] when the Son of Man takes his seat on his glorious throne, you who have followed me will also be seated on twelve thrones, judging the twelve tribes of Israel. 29 And everyone who has left houses or brothers or sisters or father or mother[4] or children or land because of my name will receive a hundred-fold[5] and will inherit eternal life. 30 But many who are first will be last, and the last first."

To divide this part of the narrative into sections is again rather arbitrary, as these verses have clear links both with what precedes and with what follows. Many commentators therefore keep vv. 27-30 in the same section as the preceding discussion of wealth, in view of the clear contrast between the rich man's failure to "leave everything" and the disciples' willingness to do so. But Peter's intervention has also changed the focus, and these verses cover the issue of reward more widely than simply in relation to material wealth; the change seems to me sufficient to justify a section break.[6] In 20:1

3. For the possible implications of the Greek term ἡ παλιγγενεσία, "the rebirth," see the comments below. The only other use of the term in the NT is for the "regeneration" of believers in Tit 3:5. The syntax here would allow "in the new age" to be taken with "you who have followed me" rather than with "when the Son of Man takes his seat . . . ," but its clearly eschatological sense (see comments below) surely rules this out. Hagner, 2:565, is unusual in even noticing this possible reading, which he translates "those who follow me in personal regeneration."

4. At this point in both Matthew and Mark many MSS and versions add "or wife." In Mark the evidence of the earlier witnesses makes it clear that this was a later insertion, but in Matthew it is much more widely attested, including ℵ W Θ f¹³ and the majority of Latin, Syriac, and Coptic MSS. It is hard to decide whether this wide attestation represents an original element in the text, which was omitted by B and a few other witnesses perhaps under the influence of the Marcan version (though assimilation of Matthew to Mark would be unusual), or an early insertion (from Luke 18:29?) resulting from the widespread movement toward celibacy in early Christianity. The list was subject to alteration, as is seen by the absence of "father" in D and the early Syriac versions and some early Latin (all of which except syrᶜ also omit "wife"). Most recent commentators follow the Nestle-Aland and UBS texts in omitting ἢ γυναῖκα, but Davies and Allison, 3:59, surprisingly include it without argument, following Huck-Greeven.

5. As in the case of "or wife" (see previous note), some MSS (notably B) here follow Luke 18:30, "many-fold," rather than Mark 10:29, "a hundred-fold," but this time the evidence for the latter is much stronger; the sense is not significantly affected.

6. Some of those who attach these verses to what precedes also separate vv. 16-22 from vv. 23-26, which seems to me a much less helpful division since the point of introducing the story of the rich man in this section of the narrative seems to be to draw attention to the disciples' problem in grasping the new values of the kingdom of heaven in relation to wealth; the discussion with the disciples in vv. 23-26 is therefore integrally bound up with the story of the rich man.

the introduction of a long parable marks what is formally a new section and one which, unlike the whole of ch. 19, is not paralleled in Mark 10; but the parable relates to the question of rewards which has been the subject of vv. 27-29 and may be seen as illustrating the principle set out in v. 30, which is then repeated in 20:16 so as to form a framework around the parable. Some therefore understandably do not have a section break after v. 30: Keener treats 19:30–20:16 as a single unit, Gundry 19:27–20:16, and Blomberg 19:16–20:16.[7]

In contrast to the man who has refused the way of discipleship because of the renunciation it entailed, the Twelve have left behind (though not apparently sold; see below) their possessions and their familiar surroundings in order to accompany Jesus on his mission. If the rich man was promised "treasure in heaven" as a recompense for his renunciation, Peter assumes that they, too, will not be the losers, and Jesus affirms that this is so. In Matthew's version the nature of the hundred-fold recompense is not spelled out as it is in Mark (houses, family, and land, though combined with persecution), and in particular he does not have Mark's contrast between these good things "in the present time" and eternal life "in the age to come," so that it is possible for the reader of Matthew to see the recompense as belonging entirely to the future life; indeed, after the promise of "treasure in heaven" this seems the more likely reading. This eschatological focus is strongly reinforced by the additional saying about sitting on thrones in the "new age" (roughly paralleled in Luke 22:30) which Matthew has included in this pericope.

See above on 5:12 for the importance of the theme of rewards in Matthew. The rewards promised to the faithful in the beatitudes of 5:3-10 probably have both a present and a future aspect (see above, p. 164). In other passages such as the section on religious observance in 6:1-6, 16-18 and on the reward for welcoming God's messengers in 10:41-42 the nature of the reward is less clearly indicated, though in both passages we have seen reason to think that it is to be found primarily beyond this life. In 5:11-12 and in 6:19-21, with the phrases "reward in heaven" and "treasure in heaven," that emphasis is stronger, and it is that heavenly dimension which is now most clearly in view in Matthew's version of this pericope.

27 Peter speaks as usual on behalf of the Twelve, and Jesus' answer will be directed to them in the plural. The grammatically unnecessary subject "we" adds emphasis to the contrast with the rich man. Peter's words sound both smug (*we,* unlike that young man, have done what you asked) and mercenary (God owes us). The reader is being prepared for v. 30 (and the parable that follows), where Peter's simplistic calculation will be challenged. But he

---

7. B. Charette, *Recompense,* 109-10, also argues for the unity of 19:16–20:16.

is at least partly right, as vv. 28-29 will accept. Those who put God's call first (as 6:19-34 has demanded) will not be the losers in the end. We should note, however, that Peter's claim does not quite match the demand made on the young man in v. 21. They have *left* everything to follow Jesus, but we have heard nothing of selling and giving. Peter apparently retained his house and family in Capernaum (see on 8:14-15), and the ready availability of a boat for the various lake crossings in Matthew's narrative suggests that at least one of the fisherman-disciples kept his boat.[8] For the period during which they shared Jesus' itinerant ministry they have left home, family,[9] and possessions behind, and the little we know of the subsequent history of the Twelve from Acts suggests that they would in fact have little opportunity to return to them, but it seems that they had not gotten rid of them. 1 Cor 9:5 suggests that in their subsequent lives they were able to rejoin their wives, if not return to their homes. What Peter here expresses is not an ideal of monastic poverty as much as pragmatically sitting light to possessions and family for the sake of the work Jesus has called them to.

28 Yes, says Jesus, there *is* a "reward" for leaving everything to follow him. It takes two forms: in v. 28 a position of unique authority (this is only in Matthew at this point) and in v. 29 (shared with Mark and Luke) a manifold recompense and eternal life.

The emphatic thrones saying (see on 5:18 for "I tell you truly") is a more elaborate version of the promise Jesus makes at the Last Supper in Luke 22:30, which itself picks up an earlier promise to the "little flock" that he will give them the kingship (Luke 12:32). Each of these Lucan sayings in its context similarly contrasts their present experience of sharing Jesus' renunciation and suffering with the royal authority they are also to share.[10] In Matthew's version that theme is further developed by a clear allusion to the language of Dan 7, the vision of the enthronement of the Son of Man.[11] In 25:31-34 that imagery will be even more fully deployed to describe the Son of Man as "king" on his glorious throne of judgment.[12] In 25:31-46 the scene is apparently of the final judgment, and that eschatological perspective seems required here, too, by the term *hē palingenesia*, "the rebirth" (translated

8. Cf. John 21:3, where boat and tackle are ready for use when the disciples get back to Galilee after the resurrection.
9. Note, however, the unexpected appearance of the mother of James and John apparently as part of the traveling group in 20:20, and again in 27:56.
10. Note the term βασιλεία, "kingship," in both passages, as well as the "thrones."
11. See above on 10:23 for the range and significance of such Danielic language in Matthew. For the "throne of glory" (literally) of the Son of Man cf. *1 En.* 62:3, 5; 69:29, where the imagery is likewise drawn from Dan 7.
12. For the christological implications of such passages, which put the Son of Man in the place of God as judge and king, see my *Matthew: Evangelist,* 308-11.

"new age" above),[13] a term which is more typical of Stoic philosophy than of Jewish writers,[14] but which aptly sums up the OT eschatological hope of "new heavens and a new earth" (Isa 65:17; 66:22, etc.).[15]

In that new age the Son of Man will be openly enthroned as king, but the remarkable new dimension in this saying is that Jesus' kingship will be shared.[16] The theme of believers sharing in Christ's kingly power is developed elsewhere in the NT in 1 Cor 4:8; 6:2; Eph 2:6; Rev 1:6; 3:21; 20:4-6. In the vision of Dan 7 the individual figure of the "son of man" represents the corporate "people of the holy ones of the Most High" (i.e., Israel as the people of God), to whom[17] in Dan 7:22 "judgment was given, and they possessed the kingdom." While Jesus generally used the figure of the son of man as a model for his personal destiny, as he does here in speaking of the Son of Man on his glorious throne, in this saying the original corporate dimension of that figure also comes

13. Cf. the "time of the restoration of everything" in Acts 3:21. J. D. M. Derrett, *JSNT* 20 (1984) 51-58, suggests that the phrase here means "at the Resurrection," but the fact that Matthew twice uses a different expression to convey that sense (22:28, 30) makes this less likely. F. W. Burnett, *JSNT* 17 (1983) 60-72, opts for a broader eschatological sense which might encompass both "new world" and "resurrection."

14. There is, however, a similar (Hebrew) expression in 1QS 4:25. which speaks of "the appointed end and the new creation ($^{a}s\hat{o}t\ h^{a}d\bar{a}\check{s}\hat{a}$)." The Greek παλιγγενεσία occurs in Philo, *Moses* 2.65, with reference to the renewal of life after the Flood, and in Josephus, *Ant.* 11.66, with reference to the "rebirth" of Israel after the exile; both these references illustrate the sense of a radical new beginning, but they are to past rather than eschatological events. In Stoic thought παλιγγενεσία was the term for the cyclical rebirth of the world as it rose from the ashes of its periodic conflagration. See further F. Büchsel, *TDNT* 1:686-89.

15. For wider Jewish evidence for such an expectation see D. C. Sim, *JSNT* 50 (1993) 5-7. He rightly asserts that such language denotes an end to the present cosmos and its replacement, but I am less convinced by his argument from 5:18 and 24:35 that this cosmic recreation was a significant part of Matthew's own eschatological belief (ibid., 7-12; cf. his *Apocalyptic*, 111-14); both texts use conventional OT language for permanence (see on 5:18), and in each the focus is not on the "passing away" of heaven and earth but on the permanence of (respectively) the law and Jesus' words. The point of the cosmic language is that such dissolution is unthinkable rather than that it is to be expected.

16. Does this new element explain the unexpected request which will soon be made by the mother of the sons of Zebedee in 20:21?

17. The wording of Dan 7:22 is ambiguous. If judgment is given "to" the people of God (the more natural meaning of the Aramaic *l^{e}* and the Greek dative following the verb "give"), this would imply that they receive the right to judge (an idea which also surfaces in 1 Cor 6:2). Most modern versions and commentators, however, regard it as more appropriate to the context to render it "for," meaning that judgment was pronounced in their favor. But the more natural reading "to" fits better with their also receiving the kingship: they become judges and kings. That reading of Dan 7:22 provides a more adequate basis for this saying of Jesus, though on either reading they "possess the kingship."

into view in the twelve[18] thrones of the disciples (cf. the plural "thrones" which were set up in Dan 7:9). Consistently with the imagery of Dan 7 the function of the enthroned disciples is to judge, but whereas in Dan 7 the son-of-man figure represented Israel itself exercising judgment over other nations, now it is Israel that is being judged. The significance of this shift of imagery depends on what sort of "judging" is intended. If the term carries the sense of an appointed ruler, as in the OT "judges" who led Israel before the time of Samuel, the disciples may be understood as the leading representatives of the community to which they themselves belong. But if it carries its more normal sense of judicial decision, the disciples (though themselves Jewish) are set over against Israel, with authority to pronounce judgment on it. In NT Greek there is no other example of the verb[19] "judge" being used in the sense of "rule,"[20] so that the normal sense of the verb should probably be understood here.[21] In that case, this saying reflects the distinctively Matthean ideology in which Jesus' disciples under the leadership of the Son of Man constitute a "new Israel" over against the old, failed regime, a theology which will reach its clearest expression in the parables of 21:28–22:14 and in the discourse of ch. 24. The choice of the Twelve as his task force was already a pointer in that direction, and now the significance of the number[22] as representing the tribes of Israel is made explicit[23] — cf. the linking of the twelve tribes with the twelve apostles in Rev 21:12, 14.

18. Some commentators are troubled by the mention of twelve thrones at a time when one of the Twelve was Judas Iscariot. But after their initial listing in 10:2-4 the Twelve appear throughout more as a "college" than as twelve specific individuals. The replacement of Judas by Matthias in Acts 1:15-26 shows that it was the (symbolic) number that mattered rather than the identity of the individuals who made up the group.

19. The noun "judge" is used with historical reference to the leaders before Samuel in Acts 13:20.

20. Luz, 2:517, vigorously dismisses this proposed meaning of the verb as "a philological fiction that is clearly false" despite its wide appeal to commentators on this passage!

21. See Davies and Allison, 3:55-56, for arguments against this conclusion. Their contextual arguments in favor of the sense of ruling in general are uncontroversial since this idea is, in any case, present in the mention of "thrones." But their arguments to exclude the sense of judgment (in sharp contrast to Luz's philological comment; see last note) depend on the assumption that this saying should fit into standard Jewish expectation and do not take account of the distinctively Matthean theology of the disciples of Jesus as taking the place of the national community as the people of God. The thrust of this saying is deliberately in contrast to the standard Jewish interpretation of Dan 7.

22. The Qumran community also had a leading council of twelve members (plus three priests), presumably for the same ideological reason (1QS 8:1-4). See W. D. Davies, *Setting,* 228-30, for comparisons and contrasts, notably that the Qumran council had a present governing role, whereas Jesus speaks here only of a future role as judges.

23. This point is valid without supposing a specific connection with Moses' choice of twelve tribal leaders in Num 1:1-16, as D. C. Allison, *Moses,* 215-16, suggests.

29 The first promise in v. 28 was specifically addressed to "you (Twelve)," but now the scope is broadened to include in the second promise *everyone* who has given up security for the kingdom of heaven. The list of things left behind includes both property (houses and land)[24] and family (the three generations of parents, siblings, and children). It is significant that (as in 10:34-37) it does not include wives (probably: see p. 740, n. 4, for the textual evidence), whereas Luke does envisage leaving one's wife in both Luke 14:26 and 18:29. Such separation, except for a temporary period, would hardly be compatible with the high view of marriage expressed in vv. 3-9 (and see p. 725, n. 40); Matthew may also have been influenced by the fact that the Twelve were later known to have taken their wives with them in their itinerant ministry (1 Cor 9:5). The phrase "because of my name" rather than simply "because of me" as in 5:11; 10:18, 39; 16:25 is probably not significantly different; cf. "in my (your) name" in 7:22; 18:5, 20, and "because of my name" (using a different preposition) in 10:22. The name variously represents identity, representation, and loyalty; here the latter is the main point. These things were abandoned in order to respond to Jesus' call.

As in 13:8, 23, "a hundred-fold" points to a disproportionately large "recompense," and the following parable will underline that God is more generous to those who serve him than human society might expect. But whereas Mark has spelled out the nature of the recompense by listing again the houses, family, and land and locating them specifically in "the present time," Matthew and Luke leave its nature unstated (perhaps because a hundred earthly houses, fathers, mothers, and children might appear a mixed blessing!). See the introductory comments above on the likelihood that the reward is envisaged as being heavenly rather than earthly, like the treasure promised to the rich man if he abandoned his possessions. In that case the hundred-fold receipt and the inheriting of eternal life (the very goal which the rich man had sought but failed to find, v. 16) are effectively synonyms. The life of heaven is far more than enough to compensate for any earthly loss.

30 This concluding slogan, which will be repeated in 20:16, recurs in different contexts in Luke 13:30 and (in a less developed form) in Mark

---

Jesus' words refer to the Twelve corporately, and do not necessarily suggest that each of them is assigned a specific tribe to judge.

24. The placing of land (literally, "fields") at the end rather than with "houses" at the beginning may be explained by the fact that while almost everyone will have a house and family to leave, only the more affluent will own land. This seems more likely than the suggestion of T. E. Schmidt, *Hostility*, 115 (more fully *NTS* 38 [1992] 617-20), that ἀγρούς derives from Aramaic ʾarᵉʿāʾ referring to the country (or countryside) as a whole, and so here indicates that the disciples have left not just their homes but "the very region."

9:35; a similar aphorism will be found in 23:12. It is possible to interpret it here as an entirely positive comment on the disciples' situation. By making themselves "last" through giving up their homes and families they have become "first," whereas the rich man, whom society would have classed as "first," turns out to be "last." Those who have faced persecution from Israel (10:16-23 etc.) will be judges over Israel. In the kingdom of heaven the tables are turned.

But, while the conjunction *de* is not strongly marked, it usually indicates some degree of contrast rather than a restatement of the same point, and in the light of the following parable which is framed by this saying, it is possible to detect a different nuance: it is a retort to the smugness of Peter's assumption that they at least have it right. Those whose renunciation has put them at the forefront of the Jesus movement might naturally expect to be the greatest in the kingdom of heaven, as their question at 18:1 has shown, but there is no such guarantee. Those who have borne the greatest weight of loyal service for the kingdom of heaven cannot assume that their reward will be greater than that of others (20:1-15). In the kingdom of heaven nobody earns their status, even by spectacular renunciation. They may rightly expect a reward, but not necessarily the reward of preeminence. The kingdom of heaven, which operates by divine grace rather than by human achievement, is a great leveler.

5. The Parable of Equal Wages for Unequal Work (20:1-16)

1 *"For the kingdom of heaven is like a landowner[1] who went out early in the morning to hire workers for his vineyard. 2 He agreed with the workers on one denarius for the day, and sent them off into his vineyard. 3 About mid-morning[2] he went out and saw others standing in the marketplace with no work to do, 4 and he told them, 'Off you go into the vineyard as well, and I will pay you whatever is fair.' 5 And off they went.[3] He went out again about mid-day and mid-afternoon, and*

1. Here and in 21:33 the term οἰκοδεσπότης, which I have translated more literally "master of the house" in 10:25; 13:27, 52, clearly designates someone who owns and farms his own land.

2. This phrase and "mid-day," "mid-afternoon," and "late in the afternoon" in the following verses represent the third, sixth, ninth, and eleventh hours in the Greek, which reflect a working day from dawn to sunset divided into twelve hours.

3. The clause οἱ δ᾽ ἀπῆλθον might more naturally be translated "But they went away" (so B. Charette, *Recompense*, 115, n. 2). This would not affect the ultimate outcome of the parable since only the first and last workers are involved, but it would be a strange and unexplained element in the story when all the other groups have accepted the offer of work.

did the same. 6 *Late in the afternoon he went out and found others standing there, and he said to them, 'Why are you standing here all day and not working?'* 7 *'Because no one has hired us,' they replied. He said, 'Off you go, too, into the vineyard.'* 8 *In the evening the owner of the vineyard said to his foreman, 'Call the workers and pay them their wages, beginning with the last and so on to the first.'* 9 *When those hired late in the afternoon came, they were given a denarius each;* 10 *so when the first came, they assumed they would get more, but they, too, were given a denarius each.* 11 *When they had received it, they began to grumble against the landowner:* 12 *'These who came last have worked only one hour, and you have made them equal with us who have put up with a whole day's work in the heat of the sun.'*[4] 13 *'My friend,'*[5] *he replied to one of them, 'I am not cheating you; didn't you agree with me on one denarius?* 14 *Take what you have earned and be off with you. It is my wish to give to this last person the same as to you;* 15 *or*[6] *don't I have the right to do what I choose with what belongs to me? Or are you jealous*[7] *because I am generous?'*[8] 16 *"So the last will be first, and the first last."*[9]

This parable, recorded only by Matthew, interrupts the Marcan sequence which Matthew has been following since the beginning of ch. 19 and which will continue after the parable until the end of ch. 20. It thus stands as a comment on the discussion of rewards for discipleship in 19:27-29 and on the saying about the last and the first which concluded that discussion and which is repeated after the parable in v. 16. It is therefore about the reversal of hu-

---

4. In the LXX καύσων sometimes means specifically the hot east wind (Job 27:21; Jer 18:17; Jonah 4:8, etc.), and that sense would also be appropriate here.

5. For the idiom see p. 1009, n. 4.

6. The "or" is missing from several early MSS, but it was probably omitted because it was felt to be unnecessary to the sense and awkward with a further "or" following in the next sentence (especially since the ἤ . . . ἤ . . . construction could be read as "either . . . or . . .").

7. Literally, "Is your eye bad?" See the comments below and more fully on 6:22-23.

8. Literally, "good," but the context suggests the more specific meaning.

9. Verse 16 could be read as still part of the landowner's speech, but the change to a general statement instead of a second-person address suggests that this is a comment on the parable, and the fact that it repeats the idea of 19:30 marks it out as part of an editorial framework. A further slogan-type comment, "For many are called, but few are chosen," is added in most later MSS and versions; this comes from 22:14, where it better fits the preceding parable; here it would be out of place since there is no suggestion of anyone being "not chosen" (see J. Jeremias, *Parables*, 34, for some suggestions as to how this addition came to be made).

man expectations in the kingdom of heaven — which, in various ways, has been the dominating theme of the whole of ch. 19.[10]

The story is as clear as it is unexpected. Whereas we take it for granted that harder work deserves a greater payment, this employer operates on a less conventional basis. The reader instinctively sympathizes with the aggrieved workers in vv. 11-12: it *doesn't* seem fair. The retort of the landowner is of course technically correct: no one has been cheated; the agreement has been scrupulously observed. Why then do we still feel that there is something wrong? Because we cannot detach ourselves from the ruling convention that rewards should be commensurate to the services rendered. When one man is "rewarded" far in excess of what has been earned while another receives only the bare sum agreed, we detect unfair discrimination. Any union leader worth their salt would protest at such employment practices. Anyone who took this parable as a practical basis for employment would soon be out of business.[11]

But the kingdom of heaven does not operate on the basis of commercial convention. God rules by grace, not by desert.[12] The "rewards" which this gospel has so persistently spoken of (see on 5:3-10, 11-12; 6:1-6, 16-18, 19-21; 10:41-42; 19:27-29) are not earned, nor are they proportionate to human effort. The God who lavishly clothes the flowers and feeds the birds (6:26-29) delights to give his servants far more than they could ever deserve from him. It is that principle, rather than the disappointment of the whole-day laborers, which is the main focus of the parable, but their very natural disappointment and sense of unfairness helps readers to reexamine how far their reactions are still governed by human ideals of deserving rather than by the uncalculating generosity of the kingdom of heaven. In the kingdom in which the first are last and the last first there is no room for envious comparisons.

The theme of divine generosity is enhanced by an awareness of the

10. For some other proposed meanings for the parable, either in Jesus' original intention or in Matthew's placing of the parable at this point, see below on vv. 8-12.

11. For the socioeconomic background to the story see especially J. D. M. Derrett, *JJS* 25 (1974) 64-91.

12. For an interesting contrast see a similar (but later) rabbinic parable in *Sifra* Lev 26:9, where God will give Israel a large reward for their long work for him, but the Gentiles who have only worked a little will receive a small reward. An early fourth-century rabbinic parable (*y. Ber.* 2:8 = *Eccl. Rab.* 5.11:5; *Cant. Rab.* 6.2:6) at first sight seems closer to that of Jesus, in that one man who worked only two hours is given the same pay as those who worked all day, but this is justified by the judgment that he had accomplished more in two hours than they had in a whole day! On the latter parallel see J. Jeremias, *Parables*, 138-39. For these and similar parables see also M. D. Goulder, *Midrash*, 407-8. I. H. Jones, *Parables*, 421-22, appropriately contrasts the more conventional concept of divine rewards in *m. 'Abot.* 2:16 with the Christian focus on "the generosity of God."

employment situation for day laborers ("involuntary marginals," Carter) in first-century Palestine. The day laborer did not have even the minimal security which the slave had in belonging to one master. There was no social welfare program on which an unemployed man could fall back, and no trade unions to protect a worker's rights. An employer could literally "do what he chose with what belonged to him" (v. 15). In such a setting no work meant no food for the family. The extraordinary behavior of this landowner in adding extra workers after he has already recruited all he needs in the early morning therefore probably indicates not that he could not calculate his labor needs in advance[13] but that he was acting compassionately[14] to alleviate the hardship of the unemployed.[15] It is unlikely that he *needed* the extra workers, and his excessive payment of them speaks for itself. Commercially, the man is a fool. And God is as uncalculating as that.

1   The opening "for" confirms that this parable refers to the issue of rewards and of first and last which has taken up vv. 27-30. The formula "the kingdom of heaven is like . . ." (cf. 13:31, 33, 44, 45, 47) here functions less obliquely than it did in ch. 13, in that the stated point of comparison here is not just a situation but a person,[16] the landowner, who himself represents God; this is how God rules. The setting of the story in a vineyard (which will recur in two further parables in 21:28-32 and 21:33-41) reflects not only one of the most common agricultural settings in Palestine, but also the familiar OT imagery of Israel as "God's vineyard" (Isa 5:1-7; cf Isa 3:14; 27:2-6; Jer 12:10); God's kingship over Israel continues in his kingship over the disciples of Jesus.

2-7   This parable incidentally provides evidence for the effective monetary value of the Roman denarius in first-century Palestine; the story depends on the audience agreeing that one denarius (equivalent to a quarter of a Jewish shekel) is a fair wage for one day's work by a laborer.[17] A Jewish

---

13. Nor, *pace* J. Jeremias, *Parables,* 136, "that the work was unusually urgent." What had changed since early morning?

14. J. Jeremias, *Parables,* 37: "the behaviour of a large-hearted man who is compassionate and full of sympathy for the poor."

15. There is an interesting parallel in Josephus, *Ant.* 20.219-20, where the people, aware that completion of work on the temple left the workers without work and so without pay, appealed to Herod Agrippa II to provide further work by raising the height of a portico, but Agrippa refused on the grounds of the cost.

16. As in 13:24; 18:23; 22:2, where the similar formula uses the verb "compare" rather than the preposition "like" which is used here.

17. Cf. the sum of two denarii paid to the innkeeper for an indefinite stay in Luke 10:35; also Tob 5:15, where the drachma is the Greek equivalent of the denarius. In Tacitus, *Ann.* 1.17, we hear of mutinying Roman soldiers early in the first century demanding a denarius a day as fair pay.

employer would be likely to pay in Jewish rather than Roman coins (see on 22:15-22), but the NT writers regularly use Greek and Roman rather than Jewish terms for money.

The sequence of groups of extra workers hired throughout the day enhances the story line by emphasizing the diversity of the different workers' experience (and perhaps the active generosity of the employer; see above), but only the first and the last groups will be noted in the second part of the story, in accordance with the framing formula of 19:30 and 20:16. The open-ended phrase "whatever is fair" poses a question for the reader which will be unexpectedly answered in the sequel.[18] The adjective *argos* in vv. 3 and 6 is translated literally above by "with no work to do" and "not working" rather than by the traditional "idle," since the latter often has a pejorative note (implying "lazy"), whereas these men could not be blamed for having been offered no work, though they had perhaps come into the marketplace too late for the early morning hiring.[19] They are victims rather than culprits. Hagner, 2:571, suggests, however, that in the case of the final group the statement that "no one has hired us" is included to indicate that these were the least desirable workers, passed over by other employers; they are thus the "last" in more than a purely temporal sense, which makes it the more surprising when they are eventually rewarded as well as any.

8-12 The unusual employment practices of the landowner have prepared us for an interesting conclusion to the story when the day's work is over. Day laborers were paid each evening after work (Lev 19:13; Deut 24:14-15). The unexpected order of payment, "beginning with the last and so on to the first" (echoing 19:30 and 20:16), already indicates that things are not going to happen along conventional lines. If hiring extra workers whom he did not really need was an act of generosity, the landowner's payment to them all of a full day's wage (we are left to assume that it was he who had instructed the foreman on how much each should receive) goes even further. The principle appears to be of payment according to need rather than desert. The complaint of the whole-day workers expresses a more conventional understanding of "reward."[20] The comparison between their whole day of hard, hot work and the short stint of the others in the cool of the evening proves tempting to interpreters who are looking for a specific group to whom to ap-

18. See the interpretation of the parable by W. Carter, *Households,* 152-57, as centered on the redefinition of "what is right": it sets aside "the hierarchical, patriarchal structure" in favor of "an egalitarian way of life in which human beings have an equal value" (ibid., 158).

19. Keener, 482, suggests that they had spent the morning on their own harvests, and were now looking for extra work.

20. Luz, 2:532, n. 72, comments: "That the first workers in the name of justice protest against 'equality' may be intentional irony."

ply the parable.[21] Is Jesus contrasting the Twelve, called at the beginning of Jesus' ministry, with more recent adherents such as the rich man of 19:16-22 would have been?[22] Or is Matthew contrasting the original Jewish disciples with more recent Gentile converts?[23] Or is the parable about deathbed conversions? None of these are clear in the way the story is told, and we do better to focus on the equality of the reward. The blessing of eternal life is the same for all.[24] Some are not more saved than others.[25]

13-15 The first part of the landowner's explanation reinforces the message of 19:29 that no one loses out by becoming a disciple; God is no one's debtor. The God who is generous far beyond what could be expected is also never less than just.[26] But to think in terms of contractual obligations is to miss the point of the kingdom of heaven. God's "goodness" (cf. 19:17) is far more generous than that. By contrast, the calculating comparison of rewards is a mark of the "bad eye" which is a biblical image for stinginess and jealousy (see above on 6:22-23).[27] This idiom results in a simple opposition of the two adjectives "bad" and "good" (which cannot be directly reproduced in English; see p. 747, nn. 7, 8), and so effectively sets human standards of "fairness" in

21. I. H. Jones, *Parables,* 418-20, suggests five possible interpretations which "shift to and fro across the page as the reader gives attention to it."

22. In the context in which the parable is set in Matthew, this seems more probable than the view of G. R. Beasley-Murray, *Kingdom,* 118 (following E. Fuchs), and of some commentators, that this parable, like 21:28-32, is contrasting the respectable Jewish leadership with the underclass who welcomed Jesus' ministry. This parable, unlike that of 21:28-32, does not depict people outside the kingdom of heaven, those for whom there is no reward at all. It is about equality among disciples rather than about insiders and outsiders. The suggestion of B. Charette, *Recompense,* 115, that it is about "why some in Israel inherit eternal life while others do not" is hard to square with the fact that *every* worker received a denarius.

23. So Gundry, 399. He labels the whole section 19:27–20:16 "Accepting Gentiles in the church."

24. Carter, 395, claims that 5:19 undercuts this theme of equality of reward, but this is to confuse "the kingdom of heaven" (God's rule) with heaven (= eternal life). 5:19 does not speak of rewards but of quality of discipleship; the "smallest" and the "greatest" in 5:19 may be appropriately compared with the "last" and the "first" here, all of whom receive the same reward.

25. Cf *4 Ezra* 5:41-42, where the problem is raised whether those alive at the end will have an advantage over those who lived earlier, and the response is given that judgment is like a circle: "those who are last will not be behind, and those who are first will not be in front."

26. Cf. the rabbinic concept of God's "two measures," justice and mercy, which are not in conflict. See Luz, 2:535.

27. See J. H. Elliott, *BTB* 22 (1992) 52-65, for a survey of "evil eye" language in the ancient world, and its relevance to this parable, which he concludes is essentially about envy.

contrast with God's uncalculating love. The theme is like that of the Prodigal Son (Luke 15:11-32), where the worthy elder brother who has been treated fairly resents the father's generosity to the one who deserves nothing. In that case the explicit application (Luke 15:1-3) was to Jewish religious leaders who objected to Jesus' openness to the undeserving; now the same principle is being applied to those within the kingdom of heaven who do not share God's generosity toward those who have not earned his favor.

16 For this slogan see above on 19:30. The reversed order of the clauses here (to fit the sequence in the story, vv. 8-10) makes no difference to the sense. If in 19:30 this epigram was directed partly against an assumption of superiority on the part of the original Twelve, the same note fits well with the parable in between. No one has a right to preeminence or to a higher reward in the kingdom of heaven. In the gloriously subversive words of the Dodo in *Alice in Wonderland,* "Everybody has won, and all must have prizes."[28] It is all by grace.

6. Third Prediction of the Passion (20:17-19)

> 17 *And as Jesus was going up to Jerusalem, he took the twelve disciples[1] aside privately, and on the way he said to them,* 18 *"Look, we are going up to Jerusalem, and the Son of Man will be betrayed[2] to the chief priests and scribes, and they will condemn him to death* 19 *and hand him over to the Gentiles to be mocked and flogged and crucified, and on the third day he will be raised."*

With this short pericope[3] we return to the Marcan sequence which Matthew has followed since 19:1 and which has been interrupted by the parable in

---

28. The suggestion of some commentators (e.g., D. Via, *Parables,* 153-54) that ὕπαγε, "be off with you," in v. 14 represents the dismissal of those who, because of their legalistic response, have forfeited the kingdom of heaven, reads far too much into a common verb (which also occurs in vv. 4 and 7) which comes naturally in the setting of the story for workers going home at the end of the day. All have been paid and all, presumably, go home.

1. Mark and Luke here have simply "the Twelve," and several important MSS of Matthew agree, but many MSS and versions add "disciples" (and a few also add "his"). Matthew does not generally use "the Twelve" alone as a title for the group as Mark and Luke more commonly do, so the shorter reading here is likely to be a later assimilation to the title familiar from the other gospels.

2. This is the same verb παραδίδωμι which I have translated "hand over" in the next verse. For the justification for translating it "betray" in this case see on 17:22, and also the comments on the meaning of the verb in p. 374, n. 3.

3. Carter, 399, rightly points out the continuity between these verses and the following pericope, especially in the focus on Jesus' impending death and on what it there-

20:1-16. The first prediction of the passion took place in the far north before the journey to Jerusalem began (16:21), the second after they had set off but while they were still in Galilee (17:22-23), but now they are "on the way," and Jerusalem (twice named explicitly in these verses) is closer and more threatening. This is, then, appropriately the most detailed of the three predictions, and the reader who is familiar with how the story is to unfold will recognize its accuracy point by point. The specific mention this time of the involvement of Gentiles adds a new note of rejection and of humiliation, with the Jewish Messiah subjected to the shame of Gentile mockery.

17   Three phrases set the scene for this important further forewarning. They are "going up[4] to Jerusalem," they are "on the way," and the revelation is made to the disciples, who have been taken aside "privately."[5] The rather awkward way in which these phrases are all fitted into a short introductory sentence suggests Matthew's concern that his readers should picture the scene, though he does not match the powerful cameo painted in Mark 10:32. The narrative focus is on the small group of Jesus and the Twelve, but Matthew has already hinted (19:2) that they were making their journey to the Passover festival in the company of a larger number of pilgrims, and in v. 29 we shall find that it is among a "large crowd" that Jesus will eventually set off up the road from Jericho to Jerusalem. Within that crowd of (presumably) fellow Galilean pilgrims, however, Jesus manages to find privacy for the special preparation of his closest disciples.

18-19   The previous passion predictions have spoken only of Jesus' own fate; now the verb "*we* are going up" adds what 10:38 and 16:24 have already indicated, that the disciples, too, are implicated in what is to happen to Jesus. The first passion prediction in 16:21 has mentioned the role of the Jerusalem religious authorities leading to Jesus' death and resurrection, and in 17:22-23 the theme of betrayal has been added. All those themes are now repeated, but with more precision. We are now told first that his death will result from a judicial decision by the Jewish authorities, but also secondly that in order for that decision to be carried out "the Gentiles" (the Roman occupying power) must also be involved. Verse 19

---

fore means to follow him to Jerusalem. But vv. 17-19 also stand apart as one of the sequence of passion predictions (16:21; 17:22-23; 20:17-19), and the "Then" which opens v. 20 marks a new beginning.

4. The use of ἀναβαίνω in vv. 17 and 18 is of course literally appropriate to the long climb up to Jerusalem from the Jordan valley, but it also carries a more ideological connotation of pilgrimage: "thither the tribes go up" (Ps 122:4; cf. Ps 24:3, Isa 2:2-3, etc.).

5. The same phrase is used for Jesus' deliberate withdrawals with a few disciples in 14:13; 17:1 and for their private questioning of him in 17:19; 24:3; in 14:23 it denotes Jesus absolutely alone.

therefore summarizes the story as we shall read it in ch. 27, when Jesus is "handed over" by the Sanhedrin to the judgment of Pontius Pilate and the mockery, flogging, and crucifixion which follow will all be carried out (though not in quite the same order) by the Roman soldiers under Pilate's directive. There is, however, no suggestion that it is really all the fault of the Romans, since Jesus is to be handed over by the Jewish authorities to the Romans *in order to* be mocked, flogged, and crucified, in pursuance of the verdict that the Jewish leaders have already reached. This corresponds to the historical reality (expressed in John 18:31) of the limited judicial competence of the Sanhedrin under Roman occupation (see below, pp. 1018-19). Previous predictions have spoken in more general terms of Jesus' "being killed," but now that the Romans have been explicitly brought into the scene the means of execution can be specified as crucifixion (for which see on 10:38). The careful reader will not be surprised, since Jesus has already called his disciples to "carry their cross" after him in 10:38; 16:24. After this comprehensive portrayal of rejection (both by his own people and by their imperial rulers) and of brutal suffering and humiliating death, the almost matter-of-fact concluding statement (already familiar from 16:21 and 17:23) that he will be raised on the third day reads even more incongruously.

7. Status in the Kingdom of Heaven: James and John (20:20-28)

20 *Then the mother of the sons of Zebedee came to Jesus with her sons, bowing before him and asking a favor.* 21 *"What is it you want?" he asked, and she replied, "Give me your word[1] that these two sons of mine may sit one on your right and one on your left in your kingdom."* 22 *Jesus replied, "You[2] don't know what you are asking. Are you able to drink the cup that I am soon to drink?"[3] "Yes, we are," they replied.* 23 *Jesus said to them, "You will indeed drink my cup, but to sit at my right and left is not for me to grant; rather, it is for those for whom those places have been prepared by my Father."*

24 *When the ten heard this, they became angry with the two brothers.* 25 *But Jesus called them to him and said, "You know that those who rule over the nations lord it over them, and their great men im-*

1. The Greek is simply εἰπέ, "say," but the request is surely for more than a simple statement; she is looking for a decisive declaration, a firm guarantee.
2. The "you's" in vv. 22-23 are plural, addressed to James and John, and it is they rather than their mother who will reply.
3. Many later MSS have added the further clause from Mark 10:38, "or (and) to be baptized with the baptism that I am baptized with," but the support for the shorter text among earlier MSS and versions is decisive.

pose their authority on them. 26 It is not to be[4] *like that among you; but whoever among you wants to become great is to be*[5] *your servant, 27 and whoever among you wants to be the first is to be your slave, 28 just as the Son of Man came not to be served but to serve, and to give his life as a ransom in place of many."*

The question "Who is the greatest in the kingdom of heaven?" was raised and answered in 18:1-4 and in the portrayal of the "little ones" which followed in ch. 18; it was more obliquely addressed in the passages about the blessing of the children (19:13-15) and the rich man (19:16-26), and has come to the fore again in the discussion of rewards in 19:27-29, especially in the repeated slogan "The first will be last, and the last first" in 19:30 and 20:16 together with the illustrative parable which comes between them. Now the same question arises in its most memorable form in the request of the sons of Zebedee and is dealt with definitively by Jesus in vv. 25-28; it will be broached again in 23:8-12. The natural human concern with status and importance is clearly one of the most fundamental instincts which must be unlearned by those who belong to God's kingdom. Verses 25-26 set out a sharp antithesis with the way earthly kingdoms and authority structures operate, and the contrast is clearly focused in the words "It is not to be like that among you." That clause could have been written over most of the preceding pericopes in which the disciples' "human thoughts" have been painfully contrasted with the values of the kingdom of heaven; it sums up in a slogan-like form the character of Jesus' disciples as an alternative society which was first set out in the discourse of chs. 5–7.

But to this exhortation is now added in v. 28 the explicit example of the Son of Man himself, whose messianic dignity is expressed not in being served but in serving, not in receiving but in giving, and whose messianic destiny is to be fulfilled in the ultimate paradox of his death for the salvation of others. We have known of the *necessity* of Jesus' death since 16:21, but here for the first time, almost in passing, is an epigrammatic explanation of its *purpose,* which will remain alone as an isolated outcrop of the theology underlying the passion predictions until it is taken up and given definitive expression in Jesus' words and actions at the Last Supper (26:26-28). Atonement theology does not take up a lot of space in the Gospel of Matthew, but these two brief pronouncements open a suggestive window onto how Mat-

---

4. Some significant MSS read ἐστίν, "it is not," rather than ἔσται, "it is not to be," but this is probably due to assimilation to Mark 10:43 (though the same variation is found also there, with stronger support for the present tense). The repetition of ἔσται in both the following clauses supports the same tense here.

5. Here and in v. 27 the simple future ἔσται is used, but the context suggests an imperative force, echoing the similar OT legal use of the future indicative ("You shall [not]"). A number of MSS have made this explicit by reading the imperative ἔστω.

thew and his church understood Jesus' mission to "save his people from their sins" (1:21).

20 In Mark the request is made directly by James and John themselves, and even in Matthew's account their mother disappears from the dialogue after her initial request: in vv. 22-23 Jesus speaks to "them" in the plural, and "they" reply similarly. It makes little difference whether their mother is to be understood as included in the plural "you" of v. 22a, "You don't know what you are asking." From there on the address is clearly to the two disciples, and it is they rather than their mother who are understood to be ready to drink the cup. Why then does Matthew include their mother in his account, and was it he who introduced her into the story, or did Mark omit her as an unnecessary complication? Such omission of detail is much more typical of Matthew than of Mark,[6] so that it seems likely that he included the mother here for a reason, but we can only guess what it was. It is often suggested that this was an attempt to protect the reputation of James and John: the request came not from their personal ambition but from a mother's misguided pride in her sons. But Matthew does not elsewhere seem to be averse to depicting even the chief of the apostles in an unfavorable light: no excuses will be made for Peter's far worse lapse in 26:69-75. In any case, it remains clear that the request is made with the brothers' full consent, and Matthew does nothing to modify the anger of the other disciples against them (not their mother). It is a more economical explanation to see the inclusion of the mother not as an ideological device but as a reminiscence that this was in fact how the request was presented.[7] If so, we can only speculate as to whether she herself took the initiative or whether the brothers, aware that their request was likely to be resented or misunderstood, had put her up to it.[8]

If, then, there may be a historical tradition behind the mother's involvement, her presence with the disciple group at this stage in the narrative deserves comment. In contrast with 19:29, here was one mother who had not been left behind! Matthew's focus has been on Jesus and the Twelve, but here is an indication that others were traveling with them. This will be confirmed near the end of the gospel where "the mother of the sons of Zebedee" will be

6. Cf. especially Matthew's omission of the centurion's Jewish friends as his spokesmen in 8:5-13.

7. Matthew might then have included this otherwise trivial detail because it reminded him of Bathsheba's request for the throne for her son Solomon (1 Kgs 1:15-21). Keener, 485, gives other references, both Jewish and pagan, for the ability of women to "get away with asking requests men dare not ask." K. E. Bailey, *Peasant Eyes,* 134-35, provides more recent cultural evidence for the same point.

8. A further nuance would be added if we accept the contention of some (see pp. 145-46) that James and John were Jesus' first cousins. In that case Jesus' aunt would be using her family influence to further their "careers."

named among the women at the cross (27:56), and she is presented there as one of "many women who had followed Jesus from Galilee and looked after him" (27:55). Those women will form part of the "large crowd" on the way to Jerusalem whom we shall meet in v. 29 (see above on v. 17).

Ironically, in view of the ideology of status and authority which is to be presented in vv. 25-28, Zebedee's wife approaches Jesus as a suppliant might approach an oriental monarch, and his "kingship" will be the basis of her request. The specific petition remains unstated while she attempts first to gain his favorable attention.

21 The request, once elicited, seems to ignore what Jesus has just said about his own destiny in vv. 18-19. Are we to assume that the mother, unlike her sons, had not been present when Jesus made this pronouncement to the Twelve "privately"? But if James and John themselves were behind her approach, that explanation does not work. More likely we are to discern here another, even more outrageous example of the ability of the Twelve to miss Jesus' point, and to filter out from his words what they want to hear. They now know that Jesus is the Messiah (16:16-17), and his use of the title "the Son of Man" also conjures up an image of victory and sovereignty (Dan 7:13-14). Now the approach to the royal city of Jerusalem brings the prospect of kingly authority closer. Indeed, Jesus has already spoken of his own future kingship (13:41; 16:27-28), and more specifically they have just heard his promise that the Twelve will sit on thrones along with him (19:28). How all that regal language relates to what Jesus has said of suffering and death they cannot as yet grasp, though it is even possible that the talk of "being raised on the third day" has encouraged them to see beyond the impending defeat. At any rate, they have reason to believe that somehow, some time, Jesus will be king and his disciples will reign with him. When that happens, they want to be sure that they will have the places of greatest honor. The request is incredibly badly timed after vv. 18-19, but it is based on clear elements in Jesus' teaching, however selectively grasped. The place on the king's right is traditionally that of highest honor and authority, but where two people are concerned that on the left is necessarily also included without any sense of inferiority (cf. 2 Kgs 22:19; Neh 8:4).[9] The well-informed reader of the gospel will notice the same phrase "one on the right and one on the left" to describe those crucified with Jesus in 27:38, and may reflect that the true nature of Jesus' kingship is such that to be on his right and left is not at all what the brothers envisaged.

James and John, the sons of Zebedee, have featured alongside Peter as,

9. In biblical literature there is some evidence of the traditionally pejorative connotation of the left side (Eccl 10:2), and this will be reflected in the imagery of the sheep and goats in 25:33, 41; but no such discrimination can be intended here since there is no debate as to which brother is on which side.

with Andrew, the first disciples called (4:18-22) and as the core group whom Jesus singled out to accompany him up the mountain in 17:1, as he will again in Gethsemane (26:37); Mark adds two further such occasions (Mark 5:37; 13:3). In 10:2 their names follow Peter (the "first") and Andrew at the head of the list of the Twelve. But only one of that leading group, Peter, has featured prominently in the story so far, and has been given a special accolade in 16:17-19, while James and John have not received any individual attention. Their open bid for leadership now is therefore a direct challenge to Peter's leading position: if James and John are at Jesus' right and left, where will Peter be? It may be that the brothers have detected in 19:30 a rebuke of Peter's assumption of a leading role in the kingdom of heaven (see comments above), and regard this as a good opportunity to press their counterclaim. Peter's gaffe in 16:22 and Jesus' sharp rebuke of him in 16:23 may also have raised their hopes of supplanting him.[10] At any rate, the egalitarian picture of the "twelve thrones" in 19:28 is now challenged by the brothers' concern for personal status.

22-23 For Jesus, kingship is intimately tied up with suffering; it is through the cross that the throne will be achieved. The "cup" is sometimes used in the OT as a metaphor of blessing (Pss 16:5; 23:5; 116:13), but more often for judgment (Ps 75:8; Jer 25:15-29; Ezek 23:31-34, etc.). In the latter sense it usually denotes the punishment of the wicked, but in Isa 51:17-23; Lam 4:21 it is used of the suffering of God's people. Here the context demands that it be understood of suffering rather than of punishment. It is reading too much into it to find in this context the theme of vicarious punishment, since there could be no question of that for James and John; but when the same metaphor is taken up again in 26:27-28, 39, that aspect will be added, and many of Matthew's readers, aware of that later imagery, might have found it reflected here in relation to Jesus' death even if not that of James and John.[11]

If James and John really understood the imagery of the cup, their prompt response sounds thoughtless. But there is no reason to believe that it is insincere: they have not been deterred by Jesus' challenge to carry the cross behind him (10:38; 16:24), and their loyalty has not yet been tested. In the event (26:56), they will prove less ready to "drink the cup" than they have glibly assumed at this stage.[12] But Jesus takes their response at face value, and his prediction that they will in fact "drink the cup" will eventually be ful-

---

10. Cf. the rivalry between Peter and the beloved disciple in John 21:20-23.

11. Matthew's omission of the parallel imagery of baptism which occurs in Mark 10:38-39 (see p. 754, n. 3) may be due to a concern not to dilute the specific symbolism of baptism by using it metaphorically without direct reference to the actual water rite. Matthew also has no parallel to the similar metaphorical use in Luke 12:50.

12. Cf. Peter's equally unrealistic but apparently sincere protestations in 26:33, 35; in the latter case James and John are included in the "all" who echoed Peter's self-confidence.

filled in James's martyrdom (Acts 12:2); what happened to John is less clear, but tradition has it that in his old age he was a prisoner on Patmos "because of the word of God and the testimony of Jesus" (Rev 1:9).[13]

To share Jesus' suffering is not, however, the criterion for the allocation of thrones in the kingdom of heaven. For the idea that these places have already been "prepared" by God cf. 25:34, 41 (and see comments on 25:34 for the "deterministic" language). That being so, they are not in Jesus' gift. The effect of this statement is to rule the brothers' request out of order, and perhaps that is all it is intended to convey. To the natural question who then will be given those places no answer is offered, but the slogan of 19:30; 20:16 warns us that the choice is unlikely to conform to any human expectations. The repetition of the phrase "at my right and left" again points the informed reader to the "honor" of being beside Jesus on the cross (27:38) rather than on a throne.

24 The anger of the remaining disciples is not to be attributed to a high-minded rejection of the brothers' worldly ambition. The fact that Jesus' next words will be addressed to them all, not just to James and John, suggests that all of them still suffer (as they did in 18:1) from the same concern for status. The anger of the other ten (and perhaps particularly of Peter?) is provoked rather by the fact that James and John have tried to steal a march on them. All of them would like to look forward to the most honorable places, and they resent being elbowed out of the way by this ambitious pair.

25 In response to the disciples' concern for status, Jesus sets out the radically different value-scale of the kingdom of heaven. First, the way of the world is illustrated from the example of those at the top of the social scale, the "great ones" — contrast the "little ones" of the kingdom of heaven (10:42; 18:6, 10, 14). As in 5:47; 6:7, 32, "the Gentiles" are taken to represent the natural human order as opposed to the people of God (see further on 18:17); if you wanted to see absolute power in operation in the world of Jesus' day, it was among the Gentiles rather than in subject Israel that it would be found. Human society needs properly structured authority, of course, but Jesus' emphasis here is on the way that authority is exercised.[14] The two

---

13. There are variant traditions about John. The Patmos tradition depends on the dubious identification of the author of Revelation with the son of Zebedee. John is not generally credited with a martyr's death, but one tradition, probably based on this passage, has him executed along with James; this account is first found in Philip of Side (fifth century), who claims to have it from Papias (see L. Morris, *Studies,* 280-83; and more fully J. II. Bernard, *John,* 1:xxxvii xlv). On the traditions about John more generally see Davies and Allison, 3:90-92.

14. D. Seeley, *NovT* 35 (1993) 234-45, provides evidence of a widespread philosophical ideal that rulers should be servants, but Jesus' reference is to the actual reality rather than to philosophical theory.

Greek verbs which I have translated "lord it over" and "impose their author-ity on" are both compounds beginning with *kata-,* "down":[15] they use their position at the top to "bear down on" those below them in the social scale.[16] This natural human pecking order is found, of course, not only among "the great," but at all levels in society, on the school playground, at the workplace, and even within the family.

26-27 In contrast with the world's social conventions Jesus lays down an alternative agenda. For the imperatival future tenses see p. 755, nn. 4, 5. The "you" who must operate by a different standard are initially, of course, the Twelve, but the principle applies to all who belong to the king-dom of heaven. The demand that such people should "become like children" and accept the lowest position in order to be great (18:3-4) is now rephrased in terms which more directly echo the social realities of the day, "servant" and "slave." The former term, *diakonos,* occurs here for the first time in Mat-thew, but its verb, *diakoneō,* has appeared in 4:11 and 8:15 for the practical "taking care" which focuses on household duties, especially the provision of food; it is about doing things for other people rather than for oneself. *Doulos,* "slave," has been more prominent, denoting someone who is not free to do what they wish, but is bound to obey a master (8:9; 10:24); note especially the verb *douleuō* in 6:24 for a person's being under the control of either God or wealth. The *doulos,* even more than the *diakonos,* is at the bottom of the pecking order;[17] they are the last, who under God's rule are the first. If there is to be ambition in the service of God (note the repeated "whoever *wants*"), it must be the ambition to serve others (cf. Paul's similar challenge in a dif-ferent context, 1 Cor 14:12).

28 The function of this much-discussed pronouncement[18] in context is to illustrate the attitude demanded in vv. 26-27: the Son of Man is the su-preme example of putting oneself at the disposal of others. By this stage in the

---

15. κατεξουσιάζω is a coinage "scarcely to be found in other Greek" (BDAG 531a); the only other NT uses of κατακυριεύω (Acts 19:16; 1 Pet 5:3) clearly indicate a pejorative sense.

16. This inference from the κατα- compounds is denied with regard to κατακυριεύω by K. W. Clark, in J. K. Elliott (ed.), *Studies,* 100-105, but the effect of the two compounds together supports it, especially in this context where the typical "Gentile" use of power is being criticized. See also Carter, 402-3, against Clark (whom Carter had previously supported, *Households,* 170).

17. W. Carter, *Households,* 172-89, provides a broad survey of the status of slaves in the ancient world.

18. For a survey of the issues discussed in relatively recent scholarship see Davies and Allison, 3:95-100; they include a careful response to the argument of S. K. Williams, *Jesus' Death as Saving Event,* that the idea of an expiating human death is alien to Jewish thought and must derive from Greek sources.

gospel no reader can be in doubt that "the Son of Man" is Jesus, but the title still carries the aura of the supreme authority granted to the "one like a son of man" in Dan 7:13-14. That authority is expressed in terms of the "service"[19] which all peoples, nations, and languages will offer him, yet he whose destiny it is to be served will be found in fact to take the place of a servant. Compare Phil 2:6-8 for the same paradoxical role, which there as here culminates in the death of the servant; there, too, the function in context is to provide a model for Christian living. The death of the Son of Man is therefore portrayed here as the supreme example of unselfish service; he will give himself for others. His specific role as a "ransom in place of many" is of course unique; what is to be imitated is the spirit of self-giving which inspires it.[20]

The nature of the benefit others will derive from Jesus' death is spelled out as a "ransom in place of," *lytron anti. Lytron* occurs nowhere else in the NT except in the parallel in Mark 10:45. It is, however, a cognate of *apolytrōsis,* "redemption," which plays a significant part in Paul's theology of salvation through the forgiveness of sins as a result of the death of Christ (Rom 3:24; Eph 1:7; Col 1:14, etc.). The same word-group occurs in a more literal sense in the LXX to denote the "redemption" by a monetary payment of things or persons dedicated to God (see especially Lev 27), but is more frequently used metaphorically to translate the recurrent OT idea of God's deliverance of his people from evil and oppression.[21] In this latter biblical usage the emphasis falls not so much on the "ransom" idea as such (a price paid to secure release, normally of a captive or a slave) as on the freedom which results from it.[22] So the primary sense here is that Jesus' death will bring deliverance to many, and the reader is likely to remember the earlier explanation of the name Jesus as the one who "will save his people from their sins" (1:21).

How far the terminology gives any indication of the *means* by which

---

19. The verbs are not the same. The Aramaic verb normally denotes religious service, even worship, and the LXX version picks up that sense with λατρεύω, but Thdt uses δουλεύω, which more closely approximates the sense of διακονέω, the verb used here in Matthew.

20. The authenticity of v. 28 as a saying of Jesus has been questioned partly on the basis that the introduction of atonement theology in the second half of the verse is an inappropriate change of subject, and partly because the "ransom" language is not otherwise found in Jesus' teaching. The comments above suggest that neither argument is persuasive. See further S. H. T. Page, *GP* 1:137-61. See also n. 18 above.

21. For a full survey of the uses of this word-group see C. Brown, *NIDNTT* 3:189-200.

22. There is therefore no place here for the questions, sometimes raised on the basis of the literal sense of "ransom," concerning how the equivalent sum is calculated or to whom the payment is made.

that deliverance is effected depends on whether a more specific OT allusion is recognized. Many commentators find in v. 28 a deliberate echo of the language of the portrait of the servant of Yahweh in Isa 53.[23] The verb "serve" in itself does not require this, as the LXX of Isa 53 uses *pais* for "servant" and *diakonos* (a very rare word in the LXX) does not occur in this chapter. But the *idea* of service is of course present in the portrait of the *pais*. More directly relevant are the three phrases, "give his life," "ransom in place of," and "many." "Many" is prominent in Isa 53:11-12 to designate the beneficiaries of the servant's work (*polloi* occurs three times in the LXX of those verses), and the phrase "for many" to explain the purpose of Jesus' death in 26:28 is again widely recognized as an echo of Isa 53.[24] "Give his life" sums up the theme of vicarious death which runs through Isa 53 and climaxes in "he poured out his life to death" in v. 12.[25] *Lytron* does not occur in the LXX of Isa 53, but the idea of "ransom in place of" appropriately represents the theme of vicarious punishment leading to deliverance: "he was wounded for our transgressions . . . upon him was the punishment that made us whole . . . the LORD has laid on him the iniquity of us all" (Isa 53:5-6). Even though *lytron* never translates *'āšām,* "sin offering," in the LXX, "a ransom in place of" describes well the nature of the *'āšām* (for which see Lev 5:17-19) which the servant became (Isa 53:10). The influence of Isa 53 is thus seen as much at the level of ideas as of specific verbal echoes in Greek, but this has been enough to convince most interpreters that Jesus here deliberately places himself in the role of the Isaianic servant, and thus explains his death in terms of that model of vicarious suffering. We noted at 16:21 that Jesus' belief that he "must" suffer and die may be attributed most plausibly to that OT background, and here the language brings us significantly closer to Isa 53. It would be hard to compose a better brief summary of the central thrust of Isa 53 than "to give his life as a ransom in place of many."[26]

23. For the extensive debate on this question see W. J. Moulder, *NTS* 24 (1977) 120-27; D. J. Moo, *The OT,* 122-27; G. R. Beasley-Murray, *Kingdom,* 278-83; R. E. Watts, *Exodus,* 258-87.

24. "The many" was also a term used at Qumran (e.g., throughout 1QS 6-7) to designate the community (reflecting perhaps the usage of Dan 12:2-3, 10 as well as Isa 53?); Albright and Mann, taking this to be the main background to the wording here, translate "as a ransom for the community," but is unlikely that Matthew's readers could have been expected to take it in that more technical sense.

25. In v. 10 the words seem at first sight even closer in that the LXX has δίδωμι and ψυχή, "give" and "life," together, but the verb is in the second person, and the LXX, unlike the Hebrew, does not have ψυχή as its object.

26. The echo of Isa 53 in this saying was the subject of considerable dispute at the time when I wrote my *Jesus and the OT,* and a substantial section of that book is devoted to demonstrating the influence of Isa 53 on Jesus (pp. 110-32; see also rather more fully my article in *TynBul* 19 [1968] 26-52). The argument there on this saying (pp. 116-21) is

This vicarious servant role is stated to be the *purpose* of Jesus' coming. Several such "I came to" sayings have already appeared in this gospel (see 5:17; 9:13; 10:34-35), and they are also found in the other gospels, notably in John (9:39; 10:10; 12:46-47, etc.). The vicarious death of Jesus is thus firmly placed before us not as a historical accident but as his deliberate goal. The one whose mission it was to "save his people from their sins" (1:21) and to "call sinners" (9:13) must tread the path of the servant whose suffering and death were to be for the sins of his people (Isa 53:5, 6, 8, 10-12).

That Jesus' death is "in place of *many*" should not be taken as a deliberate contrast to "a ransom for *all*" in 1 Tim 2:6 (cf., e.g., 2 Cor 5:14-15). The use of "many" derives from the Isa 53 background, and sets up a contrast between the one who dies and the many who benefit.[27] A theology of "limited atonement" is far from the intention of the passage and would be anachronistic in this context.

E. SIGHT RESTORED (20:29-34)

> 29 *And as they were going out from Jericho, a large crowd followed him.* 30 *There[1] by the roadside sat two blind men; when they heard that Jesus was going by, they shouted out, "Show mercy on us, Lord,[2] Son of David."* 31 *The crowd rebuked them and told them to be quiet, but they shouted out even more, "Show mercy on us, Lord, Son of David."* 32 *Jesus stopped and called them. "What do you want me to do for you?" he asked.* 33 *"Lord," they replied, "we want our eyes to be opened."* 34 *Jesus' heart went out to them,[3] and he touched their eyes;[4] and immediately they could see again, and they followed him.*

---

focused on Mark 10:45, but Mark's wording is identical with Matt 20:28. Nowadays there seems less need to argue in such detail for a conclusion which is now widely agreed.

27. Cf. Rom 5:12-19, where the beneficiaries of Christ's death are spoken of as "all" in vv. 12 and 18 but as "many" in vv. 15 and 19.

1. Another attempt to convey the rhetorical force of ἰδού.

2. Here and in v. 31 there is considerable variation in the MSS as to what form of address, if any, was used in addition to "Son of David." Some have "Jesus," a few "Lord Jesus," most "Lord," while some have simply "Show mercy on us, Son of David," as in 9:27. Several, especially in v. 31, have "Lord" before "show mercy," but this is probably the result of familiarity with the liturgical prayer κύριε, ἐλέησον (but Davies and Allison, 3:107, n. 23, disagree). Since Ἰησοῦ appears in the parallels in Mark and Luke, that reading here may be due to assimilation, and Matthew's more frequent use of κύριε, especially on the part of those appealing for healing, suggests that it may be the original reading here.

3. For this translation of σπλαγχνίζομαι see on 9:36.

4. This is a different Greek word for "eyes" from that in v. 33. ὄμμα is a rarer,

This healing outside Jericho[5] comes at the end of all three Synoptic accounts of the journey to Jerusalem. Its geographical location at the last stopping place before Jerusalem fixes its position in the narrative (though Luke also has a further incident set in Jericho and a lengthy parable before they reach Jerusalem). In Mark its position here is widely regarded also as symbolic, balancing the other (and less immediately successful) cure of a blind man which immediately preceded the journey section of Mark's narrative (Mark 8:22-26), the two framing incidents together inviting the reader to reflect on the gradual enlightenment of the disciples through Jesus' teaching.[6] Matthew's omission of the healing at Bethsaida makes any such symbolism less obvious in his account, though the concluding statement that the healed men "followed him" (v. 34) *may* perhaps invite the reader to see them as in some sense model disciples.[7] Nor does the use of "Son of David" draw attention in the same way here in Matthew as it does in Mark and Luke, for both of whom this is the only occasion when Jesus was so addressed; in Matthew others have already used the title in 9:27; 12:23; 15:22, so that it does not come to the reader as a new level of christological awareness, even though it provides here, as in Mark and Luke, an appropriate lead in to the messianic acclamation outside the city walls in 21:9.

Matthew typically tells the story more briefly than Mark, with less attention to the person(s) healed: Matthew does not tell us his name (Bartimaeus) or that he was a beggar, does not mention the crowd's reassurance or the man's throwing off his cloak and jumping up, and does not include the probably symbolic comment that he followed Jesus "in the way." The focus in Matthew thus falls on the act of healing. But Matthew does retain the subplot of the crowd's initially hostile reaction to the blind men's appeal, which serves to throw the attention and compassion of Jesus into sharper relief. Here it is the wider crowd rather than the disciples (as in 19:13-15) who act as a foil to the welcoming attitude of Jesus toward the "little ones." The story thus appropriately rounds off the journey section of Matthew's narrative by providing a practical example of the reversal of val-

---

more poetic term, which occurs only here in Matthew; in the NT elsewhere it appears only at Mark 8:23, also with reference to touching the eyes in healing. It seems to be used only to vary the terminology without any discernible difference in connotation, since in the parallel clause in 9:29 the more normal ὀφθαλμός is used.

5. Luke has the incident on the approach to Jericho, Matthew and Mark on the way out. The discrepancy is hardly of sufficient importance to justify the conjecture that "Jericho" at this time could be used both for the site of the OT city and for the new Herodian city about a mile away in the Wadi Qelt (*ABD* 3:737), and that this incident took place between the two (so P. Ketter, *Bib* 15 [1934] 411-18).

6. See, e.g., my *Mark,* 321-23.

7. W. Carter, *Households,* 198-203, expounds the pericope along those lines.

ues in the kingdom of heaven which has been the dominant theme of the last three chapters.

But Matthew's version is not just an abbreviated version of Mark's. It is distinctive in two puzzling ways, first in that Mark's single blind man has become two blind men, and secondly in that the whole episode (with its doubled beneficiary) has a parallel earlier in the gospel (9:27-31). Matthew thus has a total of four blind men to Mark's one (though no parallel to the other blind man of Mark 8:22-26). On the doubling of the beneficiary see the comments above at 8:28-34 (pp. 339-40), where the same surprising change has been made. The suggestion that the doubling is intended here to provide "two or three witnesses" to Jesus' status as "Son of David" is rather weakened by the fact that the title is not new here in Matthew; but I have no better explanation to offer.[8] On the parallel in 9:27-31 see the comments there, where I have pointed out that the differences between the two stories are sufficient to cast doubt on the assumption that the one story is simply a "doublet" of the other. That story is set in Galilee, this outside Jericho. The specific parallels are restricted to two blind men, "Show mercy on us, Son of David," and the touching of their eyes to restore sight; in all other ways the stories are different.

29   Jericho was the last settlement the Galilean pilgrim to Jerusalem would go through after crossing the Jordan from Perea (see on 19:1-2 for the likely route) and before setting off up the long climb to the capital, more than three thousand feet above. Anyone going to Jerusalem from the east would go through Jericho, and so now the small group of Jesus and his followers is part of a much larger crowd on their way up for the Passover. This "large crowd" will have an important role to play in 21:8-11, when they will bring Jesus up to the city walls with messianic acclamations. Their proud identification of him as "the prophet from Galilee" (21:11) indicates that the majority of this crowd, like Jesus and his immediate followers, are Galileans making the regular festival pilgrimage to Jerusalem. Matthew has regularly spoken of crowds "following" Jesus (4:23; 8:1; 12:15; 14:13; 19:2), so that it would be wrong to claim that his use of the term here implies that he sees the whole crowd as "disciples,"[9] but it will become clear in 21:8-9 that the crowd as a whole is strongly supportive of Jesus, like the enthusiastic crowds of the earlier Galilean period. After a time of deliberate seclusion with his closest disciples, Jesus is now again the leader of a substantial popular movement among his own Galilean people, even though they are now in the foreign territory of Judea.

8. M. D. Goulder, *Midrash,* 411, suggests that the two blind men represent James and John, the "two blind apostles" of vv. 20-23.
9. For Matthew's use of the verb ἀκολουθέω see my *Matthew: Evangelist,* 262-63.

30-31 Blind men sitting by the roadside were probably begging, as Mark indeed says explicitly; the traditional generosity of Passover season made this a good time for begging. That these southerners knew who Jesus was, expected him to be able to heal them, and felt it appropriate to address him as "Son of David" (Messiah)[10] suggests a greater knowledge of recent events in Galilee than we shall find among the Jerusalem crowd (21:10), but Matthew does not explain the source of their knowledge. No explanation is given for the crowd's attempt to silence them, and perhaps none is needed: crowds can be like that! But the result is that the reader is shown the men's persistence and is given a second chance to hear the title "Son of David," and perhaps to reflect on the ability of these Judean beggars to discern who Jesus is when the religious leaders in Jerusalem will so signally fail to do so.[11]

32-34 The rest of the story is told quite straightforwardly. That Jesus stopped among such a large, moving crowd to respond to the request of two insignificant individuals illustrates again the unconventional values of the kingdom of heaven, in which the good of a "little one" takes precedence, and in which compassion triumphs over the expectations of the many. At a time when his mind might be expected to be on his imminent arrival in Jerusalem and the fate which awaited him there, Jesus still has time to notice and respond to the need of a beggar. His power to heal is by now taken for granted, and requires no extra comment, even though this is the only individual healing miracle (17:14-18 was an exorcism rather than a healing) which Matthew has recorded since the end of the Galilean ministry. At this stage, with Galilee left behind and with Jesus about to approach Jerusalem in an openly "messianic" manner, there is no call for secrecy, as there was in the case of the other two blind men in 9:30.

The one extra note that is added is the statement that the healed men "followed" Jesus. Given the use of the same verb for the large crowd in v. 29, it does not necessarily carry the full weight of discipleship as the more circumstantial account in Mark 10:46-52 seems more likely to intend. It may be due simply to the itinerant atmosphere of the whole setting; they joined the cavalcade around Jesus. But it is an unusual ending to a healing story in Matthew, and it is possible that he intends us to see, both in their restored sight and in their immediate following, a model for discipleship.

10. The probable additional use of κύριε, "Lord" (see p. 763, n. 2), need not be so christologically significant at the narrative level, though for Matthew and his readers it would be more suggestive; see above on 7:21.

11. See p. 367, n. 23, for the significance of those who call Jesus "Son of David" in Matthew.

IV. JERUSALEM: THE MESSIAH IN CONFRONTATION WITH THE RELIGIOUS AUTHORITIES (21:1–25:46)

Here, for the first time in the Synoptic accounts[1] (except for a childhood visit in Luke 2:41-52), Jesus and his disciples come to the Jewish capital, the site of the temple which was the earthly focus of the religion of Israel. The visit will be brief. All the narrative of 21:1 to 28:15 appears to cover a period of only about one week, focused on the Passover festival which takes place as its climax and in the context of which Jesus will be executed. During this week the events which Jesus has so starkly predicted in 16:21; 17:22-23; and 20:17-19 will at last take place, and the fulfillment of those predictions will be carefully documented in these chapters. The shadow of those events has fallen across the whole of the journey narrative in chs. 16–20, and now with the arrival of Jesus and his Galilean followers outside the city walls we see the beginning of the decisive confrontation with the Judean authorities for which we have been well prepared.

I have divided this climactic part of Matthew's narrative into two major sections (21:1–25:46 and 26:1–28:15), even though in my commentary on Mark I treated the whole Jerusalem narrative together as a single final "act" of a deliberately three-act drama. Two distinctive features of Matthew's story have persuaded me to divide this section despite the fact that it contains no change in geographical location. First is the fact that a three-act structure is in any case ruled out by Matthew's inclusion of a further "act" in the contrasting location of Galilee as the conclusion to his story in 28:16-20; for him Jerusalem is not the end. Even if Mark originally planned (or indeed wrote) such a final Galilean scene,[2] it is not part of his gospel as we know it, and this difference in Matthew's narrative scheme must be honored. But secondly, and more significantly, Matthew's account of the period in Jerusalem before the last supper is considerably longer than the equivalent section in Mark 11:1–13:37. In his account of Jesus' confrontation with the authorities in the temple Matthew has included two additional parables and the whole of ch. 23 with its diatribe against the scribes and Pharisees, while the discourse of Mark 13 has increased in Matthew to more than twice its Marcan length by the addition of a substantial section of parables and other teaching about the messianic future. The result is that chs. 21–25 provide a much more extended

---

1. In contrast with the Gospel of John, which records frequent visits of Jesus to Jerusalem before the final week, normally at festival times. The artificiality of the Synoptic single-visit scheme (see pp. 3-4) becomes clear when Jesus speaks of a more extensive ministry in Jerusalem than they have reported (23:37) and when we note that some people in the area are already his supporters (see on 21:2-3, 17; 26:6, 18; 27:57).

2. I have argued this in my *Mark*, 670-74.

and theologically weighted account of the confrontation which precedes the passion narrative proper, in which Matthew has filled out his distinctive theology of the royal authority of the Son of Man in contrast to the failure of the existing regime and the temple on which its authority is centered. These five chapters are much more than simply an introduction to the passion narrative; they challenge the reader to think through, before the final dénouement of the story, who is now the true Israel.[3]

This whole section divides naturally into two parts: in chs. 21–23 Jesus confronts and debates with the Jerusalem authorities, while in chs. 24–25 he talks privately to his disciples about what is to come and what it all means in relation to the fulfillment of the OT vision of the kingdom of the Son of Man. The transition between these two parts is clearly marked by Jesus' leaving the temple (24:1). The repudiation of the misguided religion of the scribes and Pharisees leads up to a climax in 23:29-39 with the pronouncement that judgment is now to fall on "this generation" and in particular that "your house" is to be abandoned. The more explicit prediction to the disciples that the temple will be totally destroyed (24:2) then provokes a bewildered question as to how this prediction fits in with "your *parousia* and the close of the age," and it is this question which Jesus will deal with in the last great discourse of the gospel, which deals first with the coming destruction of the temple and secondly with the subsequent *parousia* and final judgment by the Son of Man.

But while in chs. 24–25 the audience has changed, the essential thrust of the narrative has not. Ever since Jesus has ridden up to the city as the "Son of David," the focus has fallen on the question of his authority. His openly messianic gestures have led inevitably to a confrontation between the self-proclaimed Galilean "king" and the Jerusalem authorities whose position he threatens. In the debates and polemic which follow, the reader is faced with a fundamental choice between the old, discredited leadership and the Son of Man who has come to fulfill his messianic mission. The three polemical parables of 21:28–22:14 all focus on the contrast between the true and the false, those who fulfill their responsibilities and those who do not; in all of them there is a surprise in store for those who were confident of their own position of privilege, a reversal of fortunes by which the first become last. After this the prediction of the destruction of the temple and the discourse which explains it do not change the subject. This temple is the visible symbol of the old regime; its fall is not just the loss of a building but the end of an era. The kingdom of the Son of Man will be established in its place,

---

3. A. I. Wilson, *When,* 67-71, argues for the coherence of chs. 21–25 as a distinct unit within the gospel. His thesis focuses on the theme of judgment, and of Jesus as the judge, which he regards as central to this section as a whole.

and the great discourse will reach its superb climax in the vision of the Son of Man ultimately enthroned in power and pronouncing judgment over all the nations.

It is against that perspective that Matthew's reader is then able to read the story of Jesus' rejection, condemnation, and death, and to perceive that the "defeat" of Jesus by his enemies is in fact the paradoxical way to the establishment of his kingship. Even on the cross he is king, and when death is itself defeated in the resurrection the reader will be able to recognize in Israel's rejected Messiah the one to whom "all authority in heaven and on earth has been given" (28:18).

I have spoken above generally of "the Judean authorities" or "the Jerusalem leadership." Matthew in fact uses a variety of more specific titles for the people with whom Jesus is in confrontation in chs. 21–23. We meet "the chief priests and the scribes" (21:15), "the chief priests and the elders of the people" (21:23), "the chief priests and the Pharisees" (21:45), "the Pharisees . . . with the Herodians" (22:15-16), "Sadducees" (22:23), and "the Pharisees" (22:34, 41), until in ch. 23 the focus finally narrows down specifically to "the scribes and Pharisees" who are the repeated target of Jesus' polemic in that chapter. It seems that Matthew wants us to recognize a wide "coalition" of different groups, who on other matters would not see eye to eye, coming together to oppose this northern preacher who in different ways threatened each of their positions of power and influence. When the actual process of the arrest and trial of Jesus begins in ch. 26, it will be predominantly the chief priests and elders who are mentioned as Jesus' opponents (see below on v. 23), but for now the base of opposition is much more widely drawn.[4]

The account of the public confrontation in chs. 21-23 follows a natural progression from the initial provocative arrival and gestures of Jesus to the authorities' challenge to his authority and on through a sequence of public encounters and challenges as Jesus teaches in the temple courtyard to the point where in ch. 23 dialogue becomes monologue and Jesus denounces the scribes and Pharisees without response. Within this overall development Matthew's distinctive style may be discerned in the way many of the episodes fall into groups of three: three symbolic actions (21:1-22), three polemical parables (21:28–22:14), and three hostile questions and responses (22:15-40).

---

4. For an overview of the extensive academic discussion of Matthew's terminology for the Jewish leaders see my *Matthew: Evangelist,* 219-23.

A. THE CONFRONTATION BEGINS:
THREE SYMBOLIC ACTIONS (21:1-27)

Jesus' arrival in Jerusalem is deliberately dramatic. It begins with two actions designed to draw attention and to provoke people to think about Jesus' messianic claim (the royal procession to the city walls and the attack on the traders in the temple courtyard), together with a further symbolic action (the miraculous destruction of the fruitless fig tree) which, though witnessed only by Jesus' immediate entourage, seems to be closely connected with his prophetic action in the temple.[5] In the first of these actions Jesus is supported and acclaimed by the pilgrim crowd who accompany him to Jerusalem, but in the second he apparently acts alone. In both cases, however, Matthew tells us of the hostile reaction of Jerusalem, in the first case in the response of "the whole city" (v. 10) and in the second as focused on the leading group of "chief priests and scribes" (v. 15). Jesus has publicly thrown down the gauntlet, and so this section concludes with the response of the "chief priests and elders of the people," representing the Sanhedrin, who publicly question Jesus' right to act in this high-handed way. That this challenge takes place in the temple courtyard where Jesus' most provocative action has been staged sets the scene for the continuing confrontation which will all be set in the same temple area until Jesus finally and decisively leaves the temple in 24:1.

Three aspects of the historical situation are important for understanding the significance of these and the following incidents in Jerusalem.

(1) The "temple." I have spoken of "the temple courtyard" (where Matthew speaks simply of "the temple") to make it clear that the location for these scenes is not the temple building itself, the place of sacrifice (into which only priests were allowed to go), but the much more extensive area surrounding the temple building, which we refer to as the Court of the Gentiles. The majority of the huge temple complex (about 13.5 hectares, thirty-three acres, roughly six times the size of Trafalgar Square) consisted of this open space, nearly a mile in circumference, surrounding the temple building and its inner courtyards and itself surrounded by porticoes, into which anyone could go so long as they did not pass the barriers which restricted the central area to Jews. It formed the natural meeting place for visitors and locals alike, especially at festival seasons, and the porticoes provided shaded areas for groups to gather and for teachers to collect a crowd, and in the days before the Passover also for the flourishing market in sacrificial animals and sacred money (see below). When Jesus "taught in the tem-

---

5. A. I. Wilson, *When,* 85-99, discusses these three incidents as "prophetic acts" comparable to those of the OT prophets Hosea, Jeremiah, and Ezekiel.

ple," he may well have been one of several such teachers, but he was in the place where people in general could best be reached.

(2) Passover. Of the three pilgrimage festivals when all adult male Jews were in theory expected to visit the temple in Jerusalem (Passover,[6] Weeks [Pentecost], and Tabernacles; Deut 16:16) Passover seems to have been the most enthusiastically observed. Passover pilgrims came not only from Galilee and other Palestinian provinces, but from all over the Mediterranean world where Jews were settled. The nearest modern equivalent is perhaps the Hajj to Mecca. Ancient and modern estimates of the numbers involved vary wildly, but the calculation of J. Jeremias[7] perhaps offers a reasonable approximation: he estimates the normal population of Jerusalem at the time as about thirty thousand, but the number present at Passover as something like 180,000. There were therefore many times more people than the city could properly accommodate, and Passover groups camped all around the city (see on 21:17). The official city limits were extended at Passover time to include the surrounding hillsides, Bethphage (v. 1) being the outer limit according to the Talmud. The temple courtyard would be the natural gathering ground for this huge throng of people during the festival.

(3) Galileans. See pp. 5-7 for the differences between Galilee and Judea and their importance for Matthew. A Galilean was essentially a foreigner in Jerusalem, and Jesus' entourage, being made up of Galileans, would normally stand out as distinctive among the Jerusalem crowd. At Passover time the cosmopolitan crowd would make this less obvious, and of course many other Galileans would be present. We have already noted (see on 20:29) that the "large crowd" which accompanied Jesus to the city were probably mainly Galileans, and no doubt others were already there or arrived during the week. We shall note below in vv. 10-11 the impact of this Galilean influx on the city. But Jesus' recorded dealings are not with the larger Passover crowd but with the Jerusalem authorities, and to them the challenge of the prophet from Nazareth and his Galilean movement (v. 11) represented an unwelcome threat. The comment on Peter's Galilean accent in 26:73 reveals something of the cultural background to this confrontation.

1. The King Comes to Jerusalem (21:1-11)

1 *And as they approached Jerusalem and reached Bethphage and the Mount of Olives, at that point Jesus sent off two disciples* 2 *with the instructions, "Go into that village over there,*[8] *and straightaway you*

6. With the associated festival of unleavened bread; see on 26:17.
7. J. Jeremias, *Jerusalem*, 77-84.
8. Literally, "into the village which is opposite to you."

will find a female donkey tied up, and her foal with her. Untie them, and bring them to me. 3 And if anyone says anything to you, you are to say, 'The Lord needs them.' Then he will let them go[9] immediately."

4 This happened to fulfill what had been declared through the prophet, who said,

5   *"Say to my daughter Zion,[10]*
'Look, your king is coming to you,
      meek and mounted on a donkey,
      and on a foal, the colt of an ass.'"[11]

6 The disciples went and did as Jesus had instructed them. 7 They brought the donkey and the foal, and put cloths[12] on them for Jesus to sit on.[13]

8 The huge crowd spread their own cloaks on the road, while others were cutting down branches from the trees and spreading them on the road. 9 And the crowds, both those who were going ahead of him and those who were following him, were shouting out:

"Hosanna to the Son of David!
Blessed is he who comes in the Lord's name!
Hosanna in the highest!"

9. Literally, "send them away," but in context this must mean "allow you to take them away." Cf. Luke 4:18 for a similar use of ἀποστέλλω.

10. The traditional translation "the daughter of Zion" is possible, since Σιών is indeclinable and so could be read as genitive. But this common OT idiom is now generally agreed to speak not of someone associated with the city but of the city itself addressed as a "daughter" (cf. "Virgin Israel" in Amos 5:2 etc.). Since the literal "Daughter Zion" is not a natural English idiom (*pace* TNIV), and since God is the speaker, "my daughter Zion" best conveys the idiom.

11. Greek, like English, is not so well supplied with terms for donkeys as Hebrew. Matthew's version, even though not following the LXX (which oddly does not use the standard Greek term ὄνος at all in this verse), uses its word ὑποζύγιον, a more general term for a beast of burden, to represent the second of two Hebrew terms for donkey in this verse (in this case more specifically a female donkey), which in the poetic parallelism function as synonyms.

12. Literally, "the cloaks/clothes"; the definite article probably indicates "the (expected) riding cloths," but the use of ἱμάτιον may indicate that the disciples' own cloaks were used for the purpose (they are unlikely to have been carrying saddle cloths!).

13. Literally, "and he sat on top of them." Common sense rather than Greek syntax requires that the "them" must refer to the cloths (the most recent antecedent) rather than the two animals. My free translation attempts to avoid the unhelpful impression of a circus act. See, however, Hagner, 2:595, for a rather labored explanation of how "them" could refer to the two animals without Jesus being required to ride both. G. M. Soares Prabhu, *Formula-Quotations,* 151-54, considers and dismisses the suggestion of resolving the problem by adopting the D reading ἐπ᾽ αὐτόν (i.e., the πῶλος) instead of ἐπ᾽ αὐτῶν.

10 And when he had come into Jerusalem, the whole city was in an uproar, asking, "Who is this man?" 11 And the crowds replied, "This is the prophet Jesus, who comes from Nazareth in Galilee."

In 20:29 we have seen that Jesus and his disciples are not traveling alone to Jerusalem. By now the "large crowd" of 20:29 has become a "huge crowd" (v. 8), and in vv. 1-9 we read of the approach of this pilgrim crowd toward the city from the Mount of Olives, which overlooks it on the east. Note that Jesus does not enter Jerusalem until v. 10. The traditional title for this pericope, "the triumphal entry," is thus misleading: the entry *follows* the royal acclamation, in which the people of Jerusalem are not yet involved. What happens in vv. 8-9 is outside the city walls, and the people who hail Jesus as the Son of David are specifically described as Jesus' traveling companions, "the crowds, both those who were going ahead of him and those who were following him" (v. 9). It is only in v. 10 that we are introduced to the people of the city, and their reaction is specifically contrasted in vv. 10-11 with that of the enthusiastic, mainly Galilean (see on 20:29) crowd. All this can be discerned by the careful reader of Mark 11:1-11, but Matthew, by his addition of vv. 10-11, has more clearly drawn the reader's attention to the opposing views of the Galilean pilgrims and of the people of Jerusalem. It is surprising how many readers, unaware of the "tribal" distinction between Galilee and Judea, have failed to notice this element of the story, and so continue to talk and preach about the fickleness of a crowd which could shout "Hosanna" one day and "Crucify him" a few days later. That is an unfortunate misreading both of the texts and of the historical situation: the Jerusalem crowd of 27:15-25 were not the same people as the pilgrims who had escorted Jesus into the city.

The acclamation of Jesus as "Son of David" is clearly messianic, and so royal. Mark, Luke, and John make this even more explicit by including "king" and "kingship" in the words of the crowd, but Matthew does not need to do so since the same theme has already been drawn out explicitly in his quotation of Zech 9:9, "your king is coming to you." In the view of the crowd Jesus comes as the messianic king. But was this how Jesus himself intended to be perceived? In 16:20 Jesus, while not denying his messianic role, has forbidden his disciples to talk about it, and he has spoken about himself consistently under the enigmatic title "the Son of Man" rather than as the Messiah. So has the crowd here jumped to a premature conclusion? Is their messianic fervor an embarrassment to Jesus? The story suggests otherwise.

Matthew (like John) explains Jesus' ride on the donkey as the fulfillment of Zech 9:9. Even without an explicit quotation of that prophecy in the text, any Jewish reader of the story could hardly fail to be reminded of it and of the royal ideology which underlies it. Zechariah's prophecy of a humble

and peaceful king coming to Jerusalem "vindicated and saved"[14] is based on
the story of David's return to the city after the defeat of Absalom's rebellion,
when he came in triumph as king, and yet humbly and in peace (2 Sam 19–
20). When the Son of David chose to ride down to the city from the Mount of
Olives on a donkey,[15] the acted allusion was unmistakable. A further messianic nuance is added by the "foal" and "donkey's colt" which feature in the
royal oracle of Gen 49:10-11,[16] and observers might also have remembered
how Solomon, the son of David, rode on a mule to his enthronement in 1 Kgs
1:38-40.[17] We shall note below (see on vv. 2-3) that Jesus' donkey ride was a
matter of deliberate choice, and indeed probably of careful planning, rather
than a matter of necessity. Among a crowd of pilgrims on foot the rider on
the donkey intended to be noticed and expected his supporters to draw the appropriate conclusion. He can not have been surprised or displeased when
they did. Such a deliberately provocative approach to the city is also consistent with the equally public and provocative action which Jesus was to take
on his arrival in the temple area (vv. 12-13). Among the Passover crowds
coming into the city it would have been possible for Jesus and his disciples to
arrive without drawing attention to themselves, but Jesus has not come to slip
quietly into Jerusalem.

So what has happened to the "messianic secret"? Jesus has been publicly hailed as "Son of David" in 20:30-31 and, in contrast with the similar
story in 9:27-31, has not asked the men to be quiet. It seems that the time for

14. This is the probable meaning of the Hebrew phrase ṣaddîq wᵉnôšāʿ, usually
translated rather misleadingly as "triumphant and victorious" or the like.

15. Zechariah's prophecy pictures David retracing his outward route over the
Mount of Olives (2 Sam 15:30) and riding on the donkey which has been provided for him
in 2 Sam 16:1-2. A donkey is a suitable mount for a king, but only for a king in time of
peace.

16. It is possible that the fact that the donkey was "tied up" (v. 2) is meant to
echo the "tying" of the donkey in Gen 49:11 (so Davies and Allison, 3:116), but the word
used is not the same as that of LXX, and so obvious a narrative feature hardly needs to be
explained.

17. D. R. Catchpole in E. Bammel and C. F. D. Moule (eds.), *Jesus,* 319-21, provides fuller background to this tradition of triumphal and royal processions in the ancient
world. Similarly Carter, 599, n. 5, following B. Kinman, *Jesus' Entry to Jerusalem*
(Leiden: Brill, 1995), 25-65. Note, however, the comment of Davies and Allison, 3:113;
recognizing this cultural background, they nonetheless point out how Jesus' approach to
Jerusalem breaks the pattern at several points: "Our story is as much an anti-*parousia* as a
parousia." Carter, 414-15, develops the same point at some length, adopting the title of
W. Tatum, *Forum* 1 (1998) 129-43, "On Making an Ass of the Romans." Cf. also P. B.
Duff, *JBL* 111 (1992) 55-71. In *NTS* 40 (1994) 442-48 (further developed in his *Jesus' Entry,* 159-72) Kinman imaginatively contrasts Jesus' coming to Jerusalem with that of Pilate a few days earlier for the festival.

concealment is over. Jesus is well aware that the decisive confrontation is about to take place in Jerusalem, and here, in the capital city, is where his messianic claim must be presented. It is still not done in his own words, and in 22:41-45 his teasingly oblique question and implied answer concerning the nature of Messiahship will still refrain from explicitly claiming that title for himself. But his actions here and in the temple speak as loudly as words, and the words of the crowd in v. 9, which Jesus appears not to have discouraged but rather deliberately provoked, are enough to throw down the challenge. His parable in 21:33-43 will not be explicitly applied, but its claim for his role in bringing God's last word to his people (and, in the imagery of the parable, as God's son) can hardly be mistaken. When eventually at his trial he is asked whether he claims to be Messiah and Son of God (26:63), this is not a shot in the dark but a reasonable inference from the way Jesus has been publicly presenting himself in Jerusalem in all but explicit words, and the element of verbal evasion in his reply in 26:64 in no way obscures the claim he is there at last openly making. The "messianic secret," it seems clear, was a temporary expedient, and now its time is over.

But in deliberately presenting himself before Jerusalem as its messianic king, Jesus has chosen an OT model which subverts any popular militaristic idea of kingship. The meek, peaceful donkey-rider of Zech 9:9 is not a potential leader of an anti-Roman insurrection. In 20:25-28 Jesus has spoken of a type of leadership which is completely opposed to the world's notions of kingship and authority, and now he models it in the "meekness" of his royal procession to the city.

1 The road into Jerusalem from the east came over the shoulder of the Mount of Olives, the hill which overlooks the city across the Kidron valley. Matthew's mention of the Mount of Olives in addition to the specific location of Bethphage may be intended not only for geographical clarity but because the area had its own messianic connotations (Zech 14:4; cf. Ezek 11:23 with 43:1-5), because it recalls David's exile and return (see above), and because it will soon be the site of Jesus' last great discourse (24:3). Bethphage, the outer limit of the "greater Jerusalem" designated for Passover (see above, p. 77), was on the slopes of the Mount of Olives, probably still a mile or two from the city walls, though its exact location is uncertain.

2-3 We never hear of Jesus riding an animal elsewhere in the gospels; he and his disciples seem to have walked everywhere, as most people except the wealthy did in first-century Palestine. His decision to ride a donkey[18] for the last mile or two into the city, when he has walked more

---

18. Donkeys were the most common animals for both transport and farm work. They were not only the transport of the poor, as some have alleged; indeed, Keener, 490, n. 91, points out that a donkey would cost from two months' to two years' wages; donkeys

than a hundred miles from Caesarea Philippi, can hardly have been a matter of physical necessity; his disciples apparently had no such need. It is the more remarkable in view of the probable implication of *m. Ḥag.* 1:1 that those arriving for Passover were expected to do so on foot.[19] In that case, to ride the last mile to the city among a wholly pedestrian crowd could only be a deliberate gesture, designed to present his claim as the messianic king (see above).

The move is presented as planned rather than spontaneous. The instructions to the disciples are precise and informed, suggesting that this loan of a donkey had been prearranged with a local supporter of Jesus;[20] cf. the similarly prearranged loan of the room in 26:18. The brief formula "The Lord needs them" would serve well as an agreed password, but would not persuade any but a very gullible villager to part with his animals to two strangers if he had not been forewarned. Matthean usage requires that the "Lord"[21] referred to must be God rather than Jesus: "the Lord" as a title in this gospel elsewhere always refers to Yahweh, never to Jesus.[22] The vocative *kyrie,* as we have noted at 7:21, does not carry a necessary titular force, and Matthew[23] does not use *ho Kyrios* as a title for Jesus even editorially. The password means simply "God needs them."

If the "Lord" here is God, that rules out the syntactically possible reading "The Lord needs them, and he [the Lord, i.e., Jesus] will send them straight back," which is sometimes proposed here on the basis of the Marcan

are found as mounts for members of the royal household and court (2 Sam 16:2; 17:23; 19:26; cf. Davies and Allison, 3:116-17 and n. 36).

19. This point is interestingly developed by A. E. Harvey, *Jesus,* 121.

20. Verse 17 and 26:6-7 suggest that Jesus already had contacts in nearby Bethany, and this is confirmed by John 11:1-53; 12:1-11 (the same family is mentioned in Luke 10:38-42, but their location there is merely "a certain village").

21. It is often suggested that κύριος here has its more basic sense of "owner" (of the donkeys), and therefore refers either to their actual owner (who is assumed to have joined Jesus' entourage) or to Jesus who is claiming the royal right to requisition transport (so J. D. M. Derrett, *NovT* 13 [1971] 241-58) and thus depicts himself as "*their* owner." It has even been suggested that Jesus was in fact the owner (R. G. Bratcher, *ExpT* 64 [1952/3] 93). But αὐτῶν is required to complete the sense of χρείαν ἔχει ("has need *of them*"); otherwise it would read strangely, "their owner is in need") and so cannot also serve to qualify κύριος; this leaves ὁ κύριος standing unqualified as the subject of the sentence, and as such it is most naturally read in its normal titular sense.

22. ὁ κύριος ὑμῶν in 24:42 is not an exception; the phrase derives from the parabolic imagery developed in 24:45-51 rather than standing as a title in its own right, and the possessive distinguishes it from a titular use of ὁ κύριος alone such as is suggested here. See also p. 1096, n. 7.

23. In contrast with Luke, who, however, also never uses it in reported speech except once after the resurrection (Luke 24:34).

parallel.[24] The use of *apostellō* to mean "send *back*" would in any case be very awkward.

4-5 This quotation of Zech 9:9 conforms to the pattern of the other formula-quotations (see pp. 11-14) in its set formula and in its character as an editorial comment inserted into the narrative. The formula leaves the prophet unidentified, as is always the case when it is not one of the major prophets, Isaiah or Jeremiah. As in most of the other formula-quotations, the text presented does not conform to either the LXX or the Hebrew text as we know it. The opening clause, "Say to my daughter Zion," uses the same idiomatic title for the city as the opening of the Zechariah oracle, but is shorter and less colorful; the words in fact correspond to LXX Isa 62:11, where this clause introduces a similar prophecy of the coming of salvation. Such conflation of related oracles occurs naturally among those familiar with the Scriptures, and is also found in other formula-quotations (see on 2:6; 27:9-10).[25] Thereafter Matthew's wording is based on that of the LXX but departs from it by (1) omitting the clause "vindicated and saved" (LXX's "righteous and saving") and (2) providing a more literal translation of the Hebrew description of the animal(s), where LXX has "on a beast of burden and a new foal" (see p. 722, n. 11). See below on vv. 6-7 for how Matthew's two animals relate to the meaning of the OT text.

Even if the reader did not notice the echoes of the story of David noted above, Zech 9:9-10 would be readily recognized as a messianic oracle, with a king coming to Jerusalem and establishing universal peace and worldwide dominion.[26] There is a subtle tension within Zechariah's description of this messianic king: he is victorious and yet meek, and his triumph is received rather than won ("vindicated and saved"). He rides a donkey rather than a warhorse, and his kingdom will be one of peace rather than of coercion. When Jesus chose this oracle to enact as he approached the city, he was

---

24. Even in the Marcan version that reading is doubtful; it depends on the textually doubtful addition of πάλιν; see my *Mark,* 432, and for the textual issue ibid., 428.

25. M. J. J. Menken, *Matthew's Bible,* 108-9, explains the use of Isa 62:11 on the grounds that in v. 11 Matthew will portray Jerusalem as hostile rather than welcoming, so that a command to announce the arrival to Jerusalem fits the situation better than a call to Jerusalem to "rejoice."

26. For rabbinic messianic interpretation of Zech 9:9 see my *Jesus and the OT,* 188-89 (and for possible Qumran interpretation ibid., 175-76). This is the first of several references to Zech 9–14 in connection with Jesus' mission within the Jerusalem phase of the narrative; cf. 26:31 (Zech 13:7) and 27:9-10 (Zech 11:12-13) as well as echoes in the expulsion of the traders (Zech 14:21), the mourning of the tribes in 24:30 (Zech 12:10), the thirty silver coins (Zech 11:12-13), and possible allusions in 25:31 and 26:28 (see comments ad loc.). See my *Jesus and the OT,* 103-10, and literature cited there; also below, p. 998, n. 8.

thus claiming to be the Messiah, but not the sort of Messiah much popular patriotism might have hoped for. Zechariah's vision prepares the reader well for a kingship which will be established without violence and indeed through submitting to the will of his enemies, so that his ultimate triumph will come only when he is "vindicated and saved" from death by the power of God. For "meekness" as a characteristic of Jesus' mission cf. 11:29, and the portrait of the servant in 12:18-21. Both Matthew and John probably omit "vindicated and saved" from the quotation in order to focus attention most clearly on the adjective "meek."

6-7   In the other three gospels only one animal is mentioned, a "foal" in Mark and Luke[27] and a "small donkey" in John — and John's version of the Zechariah quotation is abbreviated to mention only one animal. Matthew has explicitly mentioned two in both the instructions to the disciples (v. 2) and the Zechariah quotation (v. 5), and now two animals are brought to Jesus and prepared for riding, probably by the disciples' using their own cloaks as saddle cloths. Assuming that he rode on only one animal (and Matthew does not tell us whether it was the mother or the foal), the presence of the other is probably best explained at the narrative level by the comment of Mark and Luke that the "foal" had not been ridden before, so that its mother's presence would help it to cope with the new experience (and the frightening noise of the crowd); the festive occasion required that the mother, even though not ridden, should also be given a saddle cloth. But it is not typical of Matthew to add circumstantial detail to his narrative without a purpose, and it seems likely that, aware that two animals had been present,[28] he enjoyed the fact that the wording of Zechariah's oracle can be read as including both mother and foal, and so mentioned them both. That is not to say, as some have suggested, that Matthew simply invented a second animal because his wooden reading of the Hebrew parallelism told him that it was needed. The author of this gospel was not ignorant of OT idiom, and would surely have recognized parallelism when he saw it. His mention of the second donkey is due rather to a typically Jewish interest in the *form* of the text, so that even though he knew it referred to only one animal, its wording nonetheless lent itself to the men-

---

27. Neither Mark nor Luke mentions a donkey as such, and πῶλος can refer to the young of any member of the horse family. But assuming that Mark and Luke recognized the acted allusion to Zech 9:9, they must surely have intended their πῶλος to be understood as a young donkey, as it is explicitly in the Hebrew (though not the LXX) of Zech 9:9. For discussion of the meaning of πῶλος see further my *Mark*, 431.

28. That the second animal comes from Matthew's tradition rather than from his imagination is argued, e.g., by K. Stendahl, *School*, 200. B. Lindars, *Apologetic*, 114, attributes it to Matthew's assumption that of course a hitherto unridden foal would not yet have been parted from its mother, rather than to his arbitrarily creating it from the text. Cf. *m. B. Bat.* 5:3 for the assumption that a foal went with its mother.

tion of the other.[29] This is not, therefore, another example of Matthew's "doubling" of characters in the stories (as in 8:28-34 and 20:29-34); if the suggestion that those doublings were connected with the need for "two or three witnesses" has any merit, it could not apply here: the donkeys are not witnesses to anything. In those cases there was no OT text underlying the story, but here there is, and its expansive poetic wording has given Matthew scope for adding a further creative twist to his concept of "fulfillment."[30]

8 The crowd's response to Jesus' regal gesture is described in exuberant terms. The crowd itself is now "huge,"[31] and its acts of homage are extravagant, as the mention of "their own" cloaks emphasizes. For the use of cloaks as an improvised red carpet for a newly proclaimed king cf. 2 Kgs 9:13; the greenery (it is only John who specifies palm branches) presumably has the same intention of making this a special, royal progress.[32]

9 The shouting crowd is specifically identified as Jesus' traveling companions; so also Mark, while Luke says specifically that they were "disciples." Contrast John 12:13, who has people coming out (presumably from the city) to meet Jesus, and so misses the contrast between the enthusiastic crowds and the unwelcoming city which Matthew will develop in vv. 10-11. The four gospels give different versions of what the crowd shouted, but all focus on the formula "Blessed is he who comes in the Lord's name!" and all

29. D. C. Allison, *Moses,* 251-52, suggests that Matthew was also influenced by the LXX of Exod 4:20, which has the plural ὑποζύγια for the single donkey of the Hebrew; his suggestion draws on the late rabbinic association of the donkey of Zech 9:9 with that of Exod 4:20 (ibid., 249-50). This explanation is adopted in Davies and Allison, 3:121. Perhaps a little more probable is the proposal of M. J. J. Menken, *Matthew's Bible,* 110-11, that Matthew has been influenced by the "two donkeys" that were brought for David's "household" to ride on his return to the city in 2 Sam 16:1.

30. See further my *Matthew: Evangelist,* 105-6, in response to J. P. Meier, *Law,* 16-18. M. D. Goulder, *Midrash,* 22-23, explains how Matthew's procedure derives from "the midrashic mind . . . Nothing more Jewish could be asked." Hagner, 2:594: "This is precisely the detailed kind of agreement which would delight the rabbinical taste and inclinations of both Matthew and his readers." R. H. Gundry, *Use,* 197-99, provides further illuminating discussion.

31. An unusual use of the superlative πλεῖστος, "the most," to mean "very large." Cf. the possibly similar use in 11:20; see p. 436, n. 1.

32. In specifying that the branches were thrown on the road rather than carried and waved Matthew indicates that these were not the *lûlab,* a wand of palm, myrtle, and willow traditionally carried by the crowd at the festival of Tabernacles (not, as far as we know, at Passover) according to *m. Sukkah* 3–4 (cf. 2 Macc 10:6-7; also 1 Macc 13:51, but without specific mention of Tabernacles). This is an improvised celebration, perhaps inspired by the "branches" of Ps 118:27, not a set ritual. T. W. Manson's proposal that this incident took place at Tabernacles rather than at Passover (*BJRL* 33 [1950/1] 271-82) depends partly on the assumption, which as we have seen Matthew does not encourage, that the branches were *lûlabîm.*

except Luke record the cry "Hosanna!" which in Matthew as in Mark forms a framework around the central acclamation. All except Matthew also include "king" or "kingdom" (which Matthew has already included in the Zechariah quotation), and Mark and Matthew also include the name of David. There is nothing secretive about the crowd's messianic fervor. In Matthew's version they pick up and repeat the title "Son of David" already used by the blind men at Jericho, and here, as there, this messianic acclamation meets with no rebuke from Jesus.

"Hosanna!" and "Blessed is he who comes in the Lord's name!" both derive from Ps 118 (vv. 25 and 26 respectively), which was the last and longest of the Hallel psalms (113–118) traditionally chanted at the major festivals in Jerusalem. The latter part of Ps 118 apparently describes a joyful pilgrimage (with green branches, v. 27) into the temple, led by the king (the "one who comes in the Lord's name"), and it is from those verses that the crowd's shouts are drawn. "Hosanna" is a Greek representation of the Hebrew *hôšî'â-nā'*, "Save us now,"[33] which opens the plea for God's blessing in v. 25; the phrase seems to have passed into more general use as a shout of praise, like Hallelujah, and that is how it is used here, where the following dative "to the Son of David"[34] makes it clear that it is an ascription of praise rather than a prayer.[35] The same sense is required in the second Hosanna clause by the addition of "in the highest," a reverent way of speaking of God in heaven (cf. Luke 2:14).[36]

---

33. J. A. Fitzmyer, in G. F. Hawthorne and O. Betz (eds.), *Tradition*, 110-18, has given reasons to believe that the Greek transliteration may come more directly from an Aramaic form *hôša' nā'*.

34. Albright and Mann translate, "Hosanna! O Son of David!" and explain this by a vocative use of Hebrew *le-;* but since the crowds were probably shouting in Aramaic rather than in Hebrew and in any case Matthew records their words in Greek, this can hardly be what he intended by a Greek dative.

35. It appears as a set form of praise in *Did.* 10:6, "Hosanna to the God of David!" (perhaps based on this passage). "Hosanna" (as a prayer for rain) became a prominent feature of the liturgy of the festival of Tabernacles, its sevenfold repetition on the last day of the festival leading to this ceremony being called "the Great Hosanna." See E. Lohse, *TDNT* 9:682; Lohse supposes, though without clear evidence, that "Hosanna" had become "an expression of praise," "a shout of jubilation," already in pre-Christian Judaism; so also R. H. Gundry, *Use*, 42-43. M. H. Pope, *ABD* 3:290-91, is sceptical of this claim, but his arguments are well answered by Davies and Allison, 3:124-25. For the evolution from prayer to shout of jubilation Gundry, 411, compares "God save the king" (presumably in British usage!). J. A. Fitzmyer, in G. Hawthorne and O. Betz (eds.), *Tradition* (118), identifies the developed use of "Hosanna" as more specifically "a cry that Jerusalemites used to greet pilgrims coming to Jerusalem for feasts like that of Tabernacles and perhaps even Passover," from which "the original sense of the term . . . was in the course of time lost."

36. The idiom may derive from Ps 148:1, where LXX has the identical phrase ἐν τοῖς ὑψίστοις for the praise of God.

The fact that the same praise formula is applied to the Son of David and to God is interesting in the light of later christological developments, but that is probably to read too much into the instinctive exuberance of this pilgrim crowd. In the psalm "the one who comes in the Lord's name" was probably the king, leading the festival procession, and as such the acclamation fits well with Jesus' regal approach to the city. But in the light of the title "Son of David" it seems clear that for the crowd Jesus was not just any king, but the expected Messiah whose "coming" the prophets had foretold.

10-11   As a result of the exuberant behavior of the pilgrim crowd outside the walls, Jesus' arrival in the city causes a commotion. In 2:3 we read that "all Jerusalem" was alarmed along with Herod at the news of the birth of a new "king of the Jews"; now that king is presenting himself to the city, and again "the whole city" is disturbed (literally, "shaken"; cf. 28:4 for a similar figurative use of the verb). The demonstration outside the city walls has made it clear that this man is claiming some sort of royal authority, but he is a stranger unknown to the people of Judea. At this time Judea was no longer under a Herodian king but ruled directly by Rome through a prefect. Any suggestion of a Jewish "king" could only mean trouble with the Roman government, and the more so if that king were a Galilean (from the province which was still under Herodian rule) attempting to impose his authority on the southern province. The title "king of the Jews" will be used against Jesus at his trial (27:11, 29:37), and this incident has given strong grounds for attributing this ambition to him. Jerusalem is understandably worried.

The Galilean crowd, however, are not in a conciliatory mood. True, they do not use the word "king," but rather the less immediately political term "prophet." But "the prophet," as a title,[37] would be likely to be understood as a reference to the coming "prophet like Moses" (Deut 18:15-19) who played a significant role in the messianic expectation of many Jews (cf. John 1:21; 6:14; in the latter case the acclamation of Jesus as "the prophet" led to the attempt to "make him king").[38] And they are at pains to point out that this prophet is not a Judean:[39] he is known as Jesus "of Nazareth," and Nazareth is in Galilee; and it is in Galilee that he has until now been gathering his following. So Judea is under threat from the northern province. Moreover, as a "prophet" he claims, or the crowd claims for him, divine authority, so that his coming is a threat not only to the Roman political power but also

---

37. The word order suggests this, with ὁ προφήτης preceding the personal identification. One might paraphrase "This is The Prophet; he is Jesus, who comes. . . ."

38. Starting from this point, D. C. Allison, *Moses,* 248-53, rather imaginatively explores other possible Mosaic connections in this incident, especially the donkey.

39. While Matthew's readers know of Jesus' birth in Bethlehem, there is no reason why this should have been known to his Galilean supporters.

to the religious authority vested in the temple priesthood and the Sanhedrin. The people of the city have every reason to see trouble ahead as the unruly Galilean crowd bring "their" prophet into Jerusalem in a royal procession.

2. The Messiah Asserts His Authority in the Temple Court (21:12-17)

12 *And Jesus went into the temple[1] and threw out all who were selling and buying in the temple, and overturned the money changers' tables and the seats of those who were selling doves. 13 And he said to them, "It is written, 'My house shall be called a house of prayer'; but you are turning it into a bandits' cave."*

14 *And blind and lame people came to him in the temple, and he healed them. 15 But when the chief priests and the scribes saw the wonderful things he did and [heard] the children shouting out in the temple, "Hosanna to the Son of David!" they were angry 16 and said to him, "Do you hear what they are saying?" But Jesus replied, "Yes; haven't you ever read, 'You have caused your praise to come[2] out of the mouth of little children and infants'?"[3]*

17 *Then he left them and went out of the city as far as Bethany, and camped there.*

On arriving in Jerusalem from the east the first area reached was the temple precinct. The importance of this sacred area for Jewish ideology can hardly be exaggerated. It was not only the focus of the nation's religious life, but also a symbol of national identity and pride, particularly since the Maccabean revolt of the second century B.C. had succeeded in reclaiming it from the deliberate paganization attempted by Antiochus Epiphanes. The purification and rededication of the temple in 164 B.C. were commemorated annually

---

1. There is significant MSS and versional support for adding "of God," and the longer reading can be defended on the grounds that the omission of the phrase would bring Matthew into line with Mark and Luke here. But elsewhere Matthew does not so qualify τὸ ἱερόν (though cf. τὸν ναὸν τοῦ θεοῦ in 26:61), and it is possible that the phrase was added by scribes shocked at the profanation of the divine sanctuary which is described. The textual variant makes little difference to the sense, since the quotation of Isa 56:7 in v. 13 in any case identifies the temple as God's house.

2. Literally, "you have prepared for yourself praise." The same verb is used in 4:21 for fishermen "preparing" their nets. Here the reflexive sense of the middle voice ("for yourself") implies that the praise is not only received but also inspired by the one addressed. The Greek verb derives from the LXX, where it translates a Hebrew term for "establish," so that a causative element is prominent.

3. Literally, "those who suck (the breast)," but the focus is on the young age rather than the breast-feeding.

thereafter in the Festival of Dedication. The rebuilding and enlargement of the temple by Herod the Great had been on a scale to match its patriotic significance; as a later rabbi remembered, "It used to be said: He who has not seen the temple of Herod has never seen a beautiful building" (b. B. Bat. 4a).

Matthew's account reads as if Jesus went straight into the temple area and took action immediately, whereas Mark 11:11-15 inserts a day's delay. In Matthew's account Jesus' second dramatic gesture thus follows directly and appropriately from the first, and the effect is no less startling and provocative.[4] The day's delay mentioned by Mark suggests, however, that it was less a spontaneous outburst of anger than a planned act of defiance and public demonstration of the Messiah's authority.

The setting is the Court of the Gentiles (see above, pp. 770-71), where stalls were set up under the porticoes by those who sold animals for temple sacrifices and those who changed pilgrims' money into the special Tyrian coinage which was required for temple offerings, especially for the annual temple tax which was paid just before Passover (m. Šeqal. 1:1, 3; see on 17:24). Both services were in principle helpful, indeed necessary, for pilgrims, who could hardly be expected to bring their sacrificial animals all the way from Galilee or further afield; though no doubt the traders also made a healthy profit on their activities. But the location of the stalls actually within the temple precinct was more controversial, and it seems likely that they had only recently been given permission by the priests to move in there.[5] There may well, therefore, have been some popular support for Jesus' protest insofar as it related to the location of the stalls.

Jesus' explicit protest is against the misuse of God's house for trade instead of prayer.[6] The phrase "bandits' cave," traditionally translated "den of thieves," has sometimes been taken to mean that he was attacking unfair trade practices which exploited the poor pilgrims,[7] but that is not the most likely

4. In recent years there has been an extraordinarily large body of discussion of the historicity and significance of this incident, both from the point of view of its background in second-temple Judaism and as to what it indicates of Jesus' purpose. The studies referred to in the following notes are only a very small percentage of those published.

5. So V. Eppstein, ZNW 55 (1964) 42-58, who attributes the move (the stalls were previously on the Mount of Olives) to Caiaphas, c. A.D. 30, against the wishes of the Sanhedrin; see also C. A. Evans, CBQ 51 (1989) 265-67. B. D. Chilton, ABD 1:805b-6a, develops this insight into a personal confrontation between Jesus and Caiaphas, which was thus a major factor in Jesus' eventual execution, when "the collision of the two was finally adjudicated by Pilate, Caiaphas' protector."

6. This fact casts doubt on the contention of P. Richardson, SBLSP 1992, 507-23, that Jesus attacked the money changers because he objected to the use of Tyrian coinage for God's temple (it is acceptable for the emperor, but not for God; see 22:15-22).

7. C. A. Evans, Jesus, 319-44, collects ample evidence that there was in fact con-

reason for this allusion to Jer 7:11 (see below). Nor would it explain his expulsion of the buyers along with the sellers.[8] It is *where* the trade is being carried out rather than *how* that is the focus of his displeasure. And that means that the protest is directed not so much against the traders themselves but against the priestly establishment who had allowed them to operate within the sacred area. Commercial activity, however justified in itself, should not be carried out where people came to pray, and a temple regime which encouraged this had failed in its responsibility. This was, therefore, apparently a demonstration against the Sadducean establishment.

But Jesus was not leading a popular protest movement: the gospel accounts suggest that he acted alone (see below on v. 12). The significance of the action therefore focused on the credentials of Jesus himself: who was this Galilean visitor who dared to challenge the system?[9]

Those who had witnessed his overtly messianic arrival could hardly fail to read this action in the same light, as an assertion of messianic authority. They may have shared the hope of the Pharisaic writer of *Ps. Sol.* 17:30-32 that the Messiah would purify Jerusalem and make it holy again; it had been desecrated by pagan invaders (Antiochus Epiphanes, 167 B.C.; Pompey, 63 B.C.), but also by the impure worship of God's own people.[10] The vision of a new and purified temple in Ezek 40–48 played an important role in such hopes. The same book of Zechariah on which Jesus' donkey ride had been based also spoke of the messianic "Branch" who would build the temple of the Lord (Zech 6:12-13, perhaps reflecting the earlier prophecy about David's son in 2 Sam 7:12-14), and we shall see this hope echoed in the popular understanding of Jesus' claims in 26:61; 27:40.[11] At this stage there is no suggestion of *rebuilding* the temple, of course, but rather of its purification, but that, too, had been promised by OT prophets as part of the eschatological hope. The same book of Zechariah looks forward to the day when "there will no longer

---

cern about corrupt practices in the temple at this time; the question, however, is not whether such practices existed but whether that was the focus of Jesus' concern.

8. The argument of R. J. Bauckham, in B. Lindars (ed.), *Law and Religion,* 78, that the buyers must be temple staff and merchants, not ordinary worshipers "whom Jesus would not have driven out," rather begs the question; who is to judge what Jesus "would have" done?

9. There are suggestive similarities with the prophetic protest (apparently also single-handed) against the temple a generation later by Jesus ben Hananiah, whom Josephus disparagingly describes as an uneducated countryman up for the festival of Tabernacles (Josephus, *War* 6.300-305).

10. C. A. Evans, *CBQ* 51 (1989) 250-56, surveys scriptural and later Jewish expectations of temple cleansing.

11. For the new temple in messianic hope cf. Tob 14:5; *Jub.* 1:27-29; for further data see E. P. Sanders, *Jesus,* 77-90.

be traders in the house of the LORD of hosts" (Zech 14:21),[12] a vision which Jesus now enacts as literally as he had that of the king riding on the donkey.[13] And an onlooker would probably also recall Malachi's vision of "the LORD" coming suddenly to his temple to purify its worship and offerings, so that no one can stand before his anger (Mal 3:1-4). "The LORD" in that passage is God himself, but this would not be the only time when Jesus' coming is seen as fulfilling the OT hopes of an eschatological coming of God; see above on 3:3 and on 11:10 (where the same text from Malachi is quoted). Jesus' action thus points beyond the present priestly regime to the purified temple of the messianic era, and implicitly claims that he himself is the one whom God has promised to bring in that new age. Matthew's readers might remember Jesus' assertion in 12:6 that "Something greater than the temple is here."[14]

In vv. 10-11 Matthew has added to the messianic demonstration a short piece to highlight the reaction of the city. Now in vv. 14-16 he again adds a scene not found in the other gospels which tells us of the reaction of the temple authorities. The healings which give rise to the exchange are not narrated in detail, but the nature of the patients, together with the renewed acclamation of Jesus as "Son of David," allows the well-instructed reader to draw a suggestive parallel with the first David (see below on v. 14). But it is the acclamation itself, with its echo of the crowds' messianic enthusiasm in v. 9, which provokes the outrage of the priests and scribes. Jesus' response, however, is no more conciliatory than that of the crowd in v. 11. The self-effacing servant of 12:15-21 now has no qualms about allowing messianic enthusiasm to be expressed, and by his choice of text implies a further and even bolder claim. There is no "messianic secret" now.[15]

12. N. Q. Hamilton, *JBL* 83 (1964) 365-72, links this prophecy with the function of the temple as a bank, and so understands Jesus to be opposing "this ancient and accepted economic function of the temple."

13. For the significance of Zech 9–14 in Matthew's presentation of Jesus as the eschatological prophet see A. I. Wilson, *When,* 96-97, and see above, p. 776, n. 26, and below on 24:30; 26:31; 27:9-10.

14. J. Neusner, *NTS* 35 (1989) 287-90, argues that since the money changers were necessary for payment of the temple tax, and the tax was the essential basis for the regular daily sacrifices in the temple, Jesus was in effect repudiating "the most important rite of the Israelite cult" in favor of a new means of atonement. R. J. Bauckham, in B. Lindars (ed.), *Law and Religion* (78), links this action with Jesus' argument against the temple tax in 17:25-26.

15. The openly messianic, and so climactic, nature of this gesture throws light on the question whether it could have taken place at the beginning of Jesus' ministry, as John 2:13-22 appears to suggest (if John's arrangement is meant to be chronological — a big "if"!), or even, as some harmonizers have suggested, on both occasions. The latter suggestion can work only if the event is scaled down to a relatively innocuous protest rather than a messianic manifesto. If I may quote my own comment, *Mark,* 438, n. 34: "The sugges-

The disciples are not mentioned in vv. 12-17, so that Jesus' action stands out as his personal challenge to the authorities. The incautious reader might even assume from v. 17 that Jesus camped alone at Bethany, though the narrative will soon make it clear that the disciples who accompanied him to the city are also staying with him there (v. 20).

12 Scholars debate the scale of Jesus' protest. It was significant enough to provoke the chief priests and elders (a quasiformal Sanhedrin delegation? see on v. 23) to demand his authority for acting in this way. But, on the other hand, it is narrated in all the gospels as a one-man demonstration rather than a crowd event, and the lack of immediate practical response from either the temple police or the Roman authorities suggests something relatively small-scale. Within the large and crowded Court of the Gentiles it is possible that many would have been unaware of such a disturbance in one corner. Contrast Acts 21:27-35, where the Roman garrison, on the lookout for disturbance during a festival period (in that case Pentecost), took immediate action to stamp out a riot which was beginning in the temple courtyard.[16] Most recent interpreters therefore prefer to speak of a symbolic gesture[17] — an enactment of Zech 14:21, just as he had first enacted Zech 9:9? — rather than a serious attempt to reform the use of the temple courtyard for the future. It is quite possible that the traders were back in their places the next day. It is only John who mentions sheep and cattle as well as doves (the sacrificial offerings of the poor: Lev 5:7; 12:8) and who depicts Jesus wielding a whip; in the Synoptic account it is easier to envisage a relatively small-scale demonstration. But "threw out[18] all who were selling and buying" clearly depicts more than a token act.

13 Jesus justifies his protest by quoting from Isa 56:7. The quotation follows the LXX, but by abbreviating the quotation so as to omit the phrase "for all the nations," which Mark includes, Matthew makes it clear that he understands Jesus' act to be concerned with the proper use of the temple as such rather than with the fact that it takes place specifically in the Court of the

---

tion . . . that it happened twice is about as probable as that the Normandy landings took place both at the beginning and the end of the Second World War."

16. D. R. Catchpole, in E. Bammel and C. F. D. Moule (eds.), *Jesus,* 332-33, provides further evidence of the Roman tendency to crack down quickly on any potential disturbance.

17. A. E. Harvey, *Jesus,* 129-31, suggestively compares it with the acted prophecies of OT prophets.

18. Is the verb intended to recall Hos 9:15, where LXX also uses ἐκβάλλω: "I will throw them out of my house"? The fact that the same context includes the image of Israel as a fig tree (v. 10) and speaks of withered roots (v. 16) strengthens the connection in view of what is to follow in the next pericope. This is more likely than the suggestion of Carter, 418-19, that, because one of many uses of this verb is to describe exorcisms, Matthew presents Jesus' action in the temple as exorcistic (ibid., 418-19).

Gentiles,[19] even though the passage in Isa 56 is in fact concerned with the welcome to be given to foreigners when God's salvation comes. But within that passage the role of the temple as a holy place of prayer and sacrifice is emphasized, and that holiness is, Jesus complains, being destroyed by this commercial (and presumably noisy) activity.[20] Even so, selling doves and changing money are not in themselves "banditry."[21] But the phrase "a bandits' cave" is also an OT allusion, from v. 11 of the famous temple sermon in Jer 7.[22] God, through the prophet, contrasts the people's pious words of trust in the temple with their actual behavior, and accuses them thus of turning his house into a bandits' cave, a hideout for criminals. The commercial activity in the Court of the Gentiles does not match closely the crimes listed in Jer 7:6, 9, but the principle that pious words demand proper respect for God's house applies, and Jesus, who has already been compared with Jeremiah (see on 16:14) and who will soon, like Jeremiah, predict the destruction of the temple, joins the prophet in delivering his own brief "temple sermon."[23]

19. What we call the "Court of the Gentiles" (it did not have that name in antiquity) was not, of course, *only* for Gentiles; it was simply the only part of the temple complex open to Gentiles (see Josephus, *War* 6.124-26; *Ant.* 15.417 for the barrier preventing them from going further into the temple). But the majority of people in it, especially in the festival period, would be Jews.

20. Cf. *m. Ber.* 9:5 for rabbinic insistence on respectful behavior on the temple mount, which includes not bringing onto it staff, sandals, wallet, or dust on the feet.

21. The words chosen do not support the popular view that Jesus was protesting against unfair profiteering (such as is attested later in *m. Ker.* 1:7, and no doubt had always taken place). See Keener, 496-97. λῃστής means a violent robber or bandit rather than a swindler or extortioner, and its usage in Matthew (cf. 26:55; 27:38, 44), as by first-century Jews generally, usually has a more political angle, "insurrectionist." But the term here comes from the LXX, so that it is misleading to suggest that Jesus chose it with this later usage specifically in view in order to accuse them of making the temple into a "nationalist stronghold" (cf. C. K. Barrett, in E. E. Ellis and E. Grässer [eds.], *Jesus und Paulus,* 13-20). Still less must we conclude that they were actually using "violence in extorting money" (Carter, 420).

22. See M. Knowles, *Jeremiah,* 173-76, for a brief overview of discussion of this allusion.

23. R. E. Winkle, *AUSS* 24 (1986) 155-72, draws out the significance of this link in relation to Matthew's portrayal of Jesus as a new Jeremiah. N. T. Wright, *Victory,* 413-28, argues that not only the Jeremiah allusion but the whole of Jesus' action in the temple constituted "a dramatic symbol of its imminent destruction" (p. 424). C. A. Evans, *CBQ* 51 (1989) 237-70, on the other hand, represents many when he argues (against E. P. Sanders) that Jesus' action is better understood as a purification of the temple than a portent of its destruction. Davies and Allison, 3:135-37, provide a characteristically careful analysis of the opposing arguments for the act as a symbol of destruction or as an attempt to reform practice, and reach an equally characteristic and sensible conclusion that the two interpretations need not be opposed to each other.

14 This is remarkable as the only Synoptic reference to Jesus healing in Jerusalem, where he will be presented otherwise as a teacher and controversialist, not as a miracle worker — the emergency action of Luke 22:51 is hardly an exception. The notice lacks any specific narrative, and serves in context to provide the basis for the "wonderful things" witnessed by the priests and scribes and celebrated by the children in v. 15. Its brevity recalls the summaries of healing activity in Galilee and around (4:23-24; 8:16; 9:35; 12:15; 14:14; 15:30-31; 19:2), but whereas such summaries have typically been in quite general terms ("all who were ill," "the sick," etc.), the specific identification of the patients here as only the blind and the lame draws attention. In the light of the setting in the temple, the reader who has a good knowledge of the OT text is likely to recall that at David's first capture of Jerusalem he was taunted with the cry "Even the blind and the lame will keep you out," and in response declared his hatred for "the blind and the lame," resulting in the saying "The blind and the lame shall not come into the house" (2 Sam 5:6-8).[24] Yet here, in "the house," Jesus the Son of David is approached by the blind and the lame, and, far from dismissing them, he heals them. That Matthew expects his readers to make the comparison is indicated by the cry of the children in v. 15, "Hosanna to the Son of David!" He is the Son of David indeed, but at this point the connection with David is one of contrast rather than of similarity; cf. 22:41-45 when again the adequacy of the title "Son of David" will be put in question.

15 We were warned in 16:21 of the hostility of "the elders and chief priests and scribes" in Jerusalem, and here for the first time since 2:4 we meet the last two of those groups. In v. 23 it will be the chief priests and the elders who challenge Jesus, and it will be those two groups who predominate in Matthew's descriptions of the opposing authorities in chs. 26–27, but the variation in Matthew's abbreviations of the full list of the three groups which made up the Sanhedrin is probably not significant; it is the same body of opposition which is in view. What provokes their anger is not so much the healings as such but rather the messianic conclusions which the children are drawing, and in the repetition of the dangerously political language of the Galilean crowd outside the city they sense trouble in store. The "children," a natural part of any eastern crowd, will be described in Jesus' quotation in the next verse as "little children

---

24. This is not presented as a saying of David himself, but a subsequent deduction; the "house" is not identified. There is no OT evidence for such a rule being enforced (Lev 21:17-18 applies only to priests), but at Qumran the blind and the lame were among those who were excluded from the assembly because of the presence of holy angels (1QSa 2:3-9; CD 15:15-17; cf. 1QM 7:4-6 for the same rule for the army, and for the same reason). In *m. Ḥag.* 1:1 the blind and the lame are among those excused from the obligation to go to the temple for the festivals. But in none of these passages are the blind and the lame singled out as they are in 2 Sam 5:8.

and infants" (the first term echoing 11:25), but that is the language of the psalm, and they are clearly here at least old enough to give uninhibited expression to their enthusiasm for Jesus, even if the words they choose owe more to what they have heard adults saying than to their own theological deductions.

16 The question of the priests and scribes is presumably (following the statement that they were angry) to be taken as a call for action, like that of the Pharisees who according to Luke 19:39 called on Jesus to silence the messianic acclamations of his disciples. But far from apologizing for the children's misguided zeal, Jesus answers the question with a simple "Yes" and defiantly offers a scriptural justification for it. It comes from LXX Ps 8:3 (EVV 8:2). The psalm speaks of how God the creator silences his enemies by means of "strength" (so the Hebrew) which comes from the mouths of children. "Strength" is often ascribed to God in a formula of praise (e.g., Pss 29:1; 59:16-17; 68:34-35), and when that "strength" issues from mouths it is not hard to see why LXX translated it as "praise."[25] The LXX version makes the relevance of the text to Jesus' situation in the temple more explicit, but the underlying sense of the Hebrew also is of vindication by what children say, and it is that sense on which Jesus' quotation here depends.[26] The most striking feature of this quotation, however, is the bold assumption by Jesus that what the psalm says about the praise of *God* (in distinction from mere human beings, Ps 8:4) is applicable to the children's praise of *him.* I included this quotation in a study of places where Jesus' use of OT passages shows that he "was not averse to taking upon himself what in the OT was said of Yahweh," and commented that in this case "unless he is here setting himself in the place of Yahweh, the argument is a *non sequitur.*"[27] It may be objected that all his argument really requires is the recognition that sometimes children can perceive spiritual truths to which adults are closed, as 11:25 has already declared. But the fact that the children in the psalm vindicated *God*

---

25. See further my *Jesus and the OT,* 251-52, for other passages where the meaning of *'ōz* is close to "praise" (especially 2 Chr 30:21, where "instruments of *'ōz*" are used to accompany the praise of God), and for the connotation of praise frequently attached to the word in context. LXX translates it not only by αἶνος here but also elsewhere by δόξα and τιμή. The Syriac here has "glory." Cf. R. H. Gundry, *Use,* 121: "The divine attribute praised becomes so identified with the act of praise that it comes to mean the praise itself." K. Stendahl, *School,* 134, regards LXX αἶνον as "a peculiar, though possible, translation of the M.T."

26. D. C. Allison, *Moses,* 250-51, observes a later rabbinic use of Ps 8:3 to comment on the song of praise by Moses and the Israelites in Exod 15:1 (prompted by the use of *'ōz* in Exod 15:2?), and imaginatively finds here "yet one more attempt to conform Jesus to Moses" on Matthew's part. The same rabbinic use is noted by R. H. Gundry, *Use,* 121-22 (following Str-B), but without drawing Allison's conclusion.

27. *Jesus and the OT,* 151-52.

against his enemies remains strongly suggestive, particularly when this quotation follows an action of Jesus which could be seen as "the LORD" coming to his temple (Mal 3:1; see introductory comments above).[28]

17 See above, p. 771, for the situation at Passover, when because of the huge pilgrim influx most visitors needed to camp out, as Jesus and his disciples have probably needed to do already for most of the journey to Jerusalem. Bethany was outside even the extended limits of Jerusalem recognized by later rabbis, but their strict rules may not yet have been in force at this time,[29] and if Jesus already had contacts in the area (see p. 776, n. 20) it would be a natural place to stay, less than an hour's walk outside the city. It appears from 26:6 that the group remained based in Bethany during the week; that may also be what Luke 21:37 means in speaking of their staying each night "on the Mount of Olives," on whose further slope Bethany was located. The phrase "he left them" is the same as in 16:4 (see comments there), and perhaps already points to a growing hostility which will reach its climax in 24:1. As soon as he is back in the city, the confrontation will be resumed (v. 23), but Bethany will offer some respite each evening.

3. A Fruitless Tree Destroyed (21:18-22)

> 18 *In the morning, on his way back up to the city, Jesus felt hungry.*[1] 19 *Seeing a single*[2] *fig tree by the road he went up to it and found nothing on it except leaves. So he said to the tree, "May you never bear fruit again for ever!" Immediately the fig tree withered.*[3] 20 *When the disciples saw this, they were amazed and said, "How did the fig*

---

28. A similar implication may be found in Matthew's use of τὰ θαυμάσια, "the wonderful things," to describe Jesus' miracles in v. 15: the term occurs nowhere else in the NT but is familiar from the LXX (especially of the Psalms), where it denotes the wonderful works *of God.*

29. The requirement to spend the night within "Jerusalem" in any case applied only to Passover night itself (J. Jeremias, *Jerusalem,* 60-62), hence perhaps the later move to Gethsemane, closer to the city walls (but see on 26:17; this may not yet have been the official Passover night).

1. The use of the aorist rather than the imperfect tense suggests a specific sensation of hunger rather than a general state of being hungry.

2. Matthew occasionally uses εἷς simply where we would use an indefinite article, without emphasis on the number. For a clear example see 9:18. But see p. 323, n. 3, for other alleged examples of that usage where in fact there is a contextual reason for the use of εἷς. See the comments below for such a contextual reason in this case, where Matthew's addition of the term, which is not in Mark, may be assumed to have a purpose.

3. Literally, "was made dry," the same term which is used for the plants which die for lack of moisture in 13:6 and for the "paralyzed" arm in 12:10. It denotes the death of the tree rather than a temporary loss of leaves.

tree wither so quickly?"[4] 21 *Jesus replied to them, "I tell you truly: if you have faith and do not doubt, you will not only do what has been done to the fig tree, but even if you say to this mountain, 'Up with you*[5] *and be thrown into the sea,' it will happen. 22 And whatever you ask in prayer, if you believe, you will receive it all."*

Matthew tells this story more simply than Mark. In Mark it is split into two scenes which are inserted between Jesus' actions in the temple, so that the reader is invited to compare the fate of the fruitless tree with the denunciation of the failed temple. Matthew, however, leaves his readers to make this connection simply by noting the juxtaposition of this story with that of Jesus' temple demonstration the previous day and his return to the temple immediately after the fig-tree episode. It is probable, from the way the story is told (see below), that Matthew also intended such a symbolic interpretation, but the explicit lessons drawn from the incident are in Matthew, as in Mark, not symbolic but parenetic, taking the withering of the tree as an example of powerful prayer.[6] The compression of the story into a single incident allows Matthew to place greater stress on the immediacy and completeness of the effect of Jesus' words; note the repeated use of *parachrēma* (translated "immediately" and "so quickly" above) only in Matthew's version.

Two factors, however, suggest that this explicitly drawn moral, and the demonstration of Jesus' miraculous power which it presupposes, does not exhaust the significance of the event. One is the instinctive reaction of most Christian readers that such a raw display of power for a purely destructive purpose (and, it would appear, in a spirit of spiteful "revenge" on an inanimate object which could hardly be blamed for having no fruit out of season) is quite out of keeping with the character and behavior of the Jesus of the gospels,[7] whose power is deployed to heal and save, not to

---

4. This could also be read as an exclamation, "How suddenly the fig tree has withered!"

5. Literally, "be lifted up"; αἴρω can mean simply "remove" without the sense of lifting, but with reference to a mountain the latter sense seems more appropriate and graphic. What is envisaged is more than a landslide!

6. Mark also takes the opportunity of this, his only substantial account of Jesus' teaching on prayer, to add further sayings on the subject, but Matthew has already provided such teaching in the Sermon on the Mount.

7. The fate of the pigs in 8:28-32 is not really comparable, as it is a by-product of an act of human deliverance. Punitive miracles are a marked feature of some parts of the OT, beginning with the plagues of Egypt and the destruction of the Egyptian army and with a notable concentration in the stories of Elijah and Elisha (2 Kgs 1:9-12; 2:23-24; 5:25-27; 6:18); in the NT cf. Acts 5:1-11; 9:1-9; 13:6-12. But the destruction of an inanimate object can hardly be described as punitive.

destroy[8] or for personal gratification.[9] Such atypical behavior is strongly reminiscent of the bizarre acts of some of the OT prophets (e.g., Isa 20; Jer 27–28; Ezek 3:1-3; 4; 24:15-24; Hos 1:2-3), which were deliberately "out of character" in order to draw attention to their symbolic message.[10] The other factor is the setting of the story in the buildup to the confrontation with the authorities in Jerusalem, immediately following on two dramatic "acted parables" declaring Jesus' authority over the city and the temple. Apart from the almost formulaic reference to healing in v. 14, this is the only miracle of Jesus which Matthew records as taking place in or near Jerusalem; does its location (as well as the juxtaposition of this pericope to vv. 12-17) then provide the key to its significance as an acted symbol of judgment to come on Jerusalem?

Three aspects of the wording of vv. 18-19 support this interpretation:

(1) The phrase "nothing except leaves" stands out as a surprisingly emphatic way of saying "no fruit." At Passover time in Jerusalem (March-April) fig trees are beginning to come into leaf, but there is not yet a full covering of leaves. Once the leaves are fully developed, it is time to look for the early fruit (cf. 24:32; the topic there is also the fate of the temple), which can be picked from about the middle of May.[11] This "single fig tree" (see on v. 19) apparently stood out as having an unusually full coverage of leaves for Passover season, which encouraged the hope of early fruit even though, as Mark conscientiously reminds us, "It was not the season for figs" (Mark 11:13). It offered promise without fulfillment.

(2) "Fruit" has been, and will continue to be in this gospel, a prominent metaphor for the sort of behavior God requires of his people. See 3:8, 10; 7:16-20; 12:33; 13:8, and especially the parable of the vineyard which will follow in vv. 33-43 and which will emphasize that the failure of the Jerusalem establishment to produce the "fruit" due to the landowner will lead to

8. It would be more characteristic of the Jesus of the second-century *Infancy Gospel of Thomas;* see, e.g., *Inf. Gos. Thom.,* chs. 3, 4, 5, 8, 14; the story in ch. 3 clearly echoes this story of the withering of the tree but with reference to a person.

9. Hagner, 2:605, appropriately contrasts 4:2-4, the only other place where Matthew mentions Jesus' hunger, where he refused to use his miraculous power for his own convenience.

10. For this incident as a "prophetic act" see A. I. Wilson, *When,* 97-99.

11. Experts provide a variety of (not always compatible!) insights into the normal behavior of fig trees in Palestine. Some speak of the small green figs (*paggîm;* modern Arabic *taqsh*) which are already forming in early spring and which can at a pinch be eaten, though they are not very pleasant (as I can testify, having tried them at Passover time); perhaps that was what Jesus hoped to find at this premature season, but even that failed. But the focus on leaves suggests that this tree promised something more nourishing. See W. R. Telford, *Temple,* 2-4, for some of the suggestions based on fig cultivation; more briefly my *Mark,* 439-40.

their expulsion and the substitution of "another nation" which *will* come up with "the fruits of the kingdom of God."

(3) That the specific tree concerned is a fig tree would evoke symbolic associations in readers familiar with the OT, where the fruit of the fig tree is a prophetic symbol for the good life God expects from his people; for examples see Jer 8:13; 24:1-10; Hos 9:10, 16-17.[12] The passage most likely to come to mind from this story is Mic 7:1-6,[13] where the prophet's dismay over the corruption of Judah is described as his failure to find "the first-ripe fig for which I hunger." Following the explicit statement that Jesus was hungry in v. 18, his inability to find early figs to eat speaks powerfully of how the prophetic vision is fulfilled in the failure of contemporary Jerusalem and its temple. For the withering of fig trees as a symbol of God's judgment see Isa 34:4; Jer 8:13; Hos 2:12; Joel 1:7. For a similar symbolic use of the fig tree in one of Jesus' own parables cf. Luke 13:6-9; the present pericope, it may be suggested, provides an acted parable on the same theme.

These features suggest, then, that Matthew would be content for this story to be bracketed with those of the donkey ride and the temple demonstration as "three symbolic actions" which assert Jesus' authority over the city and temple and its coming judgment.[14] This action is witnessed only by the disciples, and its symbolism is not made explicit, but for the instructed reader it further develops the themes of the other two public acts and prepares us for the mutual repudiation of Jesus and the Jerusalem authorities which will follow and the explicit prediction of the destruction of the "fruitless" temple to which that confrontation inevitably leads. But exegesis of Matthew's text must recognize that all that symbolism remains unexpressed, while Jesus' uncharacteristic destruction of the tree is presented explicitly as a model of the power of prayer when uttered in faith, a power which is further illustrated hypothetically (echoing 17:20) by the equally destructive and ap-

12. See W. R. Telford, *Temple*, 132-63, for a full study of this symbolic use of the fig tree in the OT, which goes much further than just the few verses noted above. Telford also goes on (ibid., 179-96) to show how the same imagery continued in postbiblical Judaism. For Jesus' cursing of the fig tree as a "narrated prophecy" based on Hos 9:10-17 see D. Krause in C. A. Evans and W. R. Stegner (eds.), *Gospels*, 235-48.

13. M. Knowles, *Jeremiah*, 176-80, argues, however, for Jer 8:13 as the primary (though not the only) OT background. B. Charette, *Recompense*, 134-35, places the emphasis equally on Jer 8:13 and Hos 9:10.

14. *Pace* W. R. Telford, *Temple*, 69-94, who argues that Matthew's redaction of the story is designed to eliminate the Marcan symbolism and to make it a purely exemplary story about the power of faith. It is interesting to note that the same data lead Gundry, 415-16, to conclude that Matthew's adaptations "make the incident serve more dramatically its purpose of symbolizing God's rejection of the Jewish leaders in Jerusalem, whom the fig tree represents in Matthew."

parently useless feat of throwing a mountain into the sea. Matthew does not show any sign of the embarrassment with which many of his modern readers react to this incident.

18 Matthew presupposes the pattern of daily visits to the temple and nightly returns to Bethany which is more explicit in Mark 11:11-12, 19-20 and Luke 21:37. That Jesus was hungry is no surprise given the hand-to-mouth lifestyle of the disciple group and the lack of proper accommodation implied by the verb "camped" in v. 17, but his hunger is also mentioned in order to supply the background to his search for fruit and perhaps especially to underline the echo of Mic 7:1 (see above).

19 By speaking of "a single fig tree" rather than just "a fig tree" (see p. 790, n. 2), Matthew probably intends to alert the reader that this tree, perhaps standing on its own, was unlike others which at that season would not have fully developed leaves. Its precocious show of foliage promised, but did not provide, the fruit which normally came with the leaves (see above). Unlike the landowner in Jesus' own parable in Luke 13:6-9, Jesus does not give the tree a further chance; its failure is terminal. His words, though their effect is aptly described by Peter as a "curse" in Mark 11:21, are in form rather a negative wish. This is a performative utterance which, like his words of healing or exorcism in, for example, 8:13, 32; 9:6, 22, 29; 15:28, takes immediate and visible effect. The reader who recognizes the symbolism outlined above may reflect that the failure of God's people has reached a point of no return; as 23:29-36 will spell out, the culmination of centuries of rebellion is to come upon "this generation."

20 We have seen the disciples previously commenting on a saying or event with a view to eliciting some explanation from Jesus (see 15:15; 17:19; 19:10, 25). Here their response, whether framed as a question or an exclamation (see p. 791, n. 4), expresses their amazement, a reaction more typical in Matthew of the crowds but paralleled in the disciples' response to Jesus' calming of the storm in 8:27. Their words here, as in 8:27, imply that Jesus' power is unique, which will make it all the more remarkable when he goes on to suggest that they, too, can do what he has done.

21-22 This general statement about effective prayer is very similar in content to 17:20, though the wording is different. Both sayings are marked as important by the formula "I tell you truly" (see on 5:18). Both sayings raise the problem that not all requests made in prayer are in fact successful; on this issue see the comments on 7:7-11.[15] The key here again is "faith" (cf. the "faith as much as a mustard seed" in 17:20), and the insertion of "if you

---

15. In her discussion of the parallel sayings in Mark 11:22-25, S. E. Dowd, *Prayer,* 133-62, gives a helpful discussion of theodicy in relation to unanswered prayer, drawing attention especially to Jesus' own "unanswered prayer" in Gethsemane.

believe" into the otherwise unqualified promise of v. 22 underlines the point. Faith is further defined here by its negative counterpart, "and do not doubt." This is not the same word for doubt as Matthew uses in 14:31 and 28:17, but the sense is probably much the same (note that in 14:31 "doubt" is identified as lack of faith); see the comments at 14:31 on the sense of hesitation, being in two minds, a lack of practical trust in God, which also suits the NT use of *diakrinomai* for "doubt" in a practical rather than intellectual sense.[16] The "faith" which receives answers to prayer is characterized by practical confidence in God's power and willingness to respond. In view of what has been said in 18:19-20, it should also be noted that the verbs in these verses are all plural; the promise of effective prayer is made to the united praying community rather than to the private interest of the individual.

For the use of "moving mountains" to denote the impossible see on 17:20.[17] It is a proverbial image[18] like that of the camel going through the eye of a needle (also to denote the impossible; see on 19:24). That is probably all that Jesus intended by his reference to "this mountain"; note that the same phrase is used in 17:20, which is in a different geographical setting. In this context the phrase would most naturally be understood of the Mount of Olives, on the slopes of which this incident is set, and it is sometimes suggested that Jesus had in mind the eschatological vision of Zech 14:4 that when God's feet stand on the Mount of Olives it will be split in two to make a valley by which his people will escape from Jerusalem. But Zech 14:4 does not envisage the mountain being removed and thrown into the sea,[19] and the proverbial imagery is all that is needed to make his point without specific reference to that prophecy.[20]

---

16. Outside the NT the range of the meaning of the verb covers "distinguish," "divide," "dispute." Its use for "doubt" or "hesitate" is distinctive of the NT; BDAG 231b paraphrase as "to be uncertain, be at odds with oneself." See further F. Büchsel, *TDNT* 3:946-49; B. Gärtner, *NIDNTT* 1:503-5.

17. The temple context here suggests to Keener, 505-6, that Jesus has in mind especially another OT "mountain" saying, Zech 4:6-9, where the mountain represents the "impossible" obstacles facing Zerubbabel's building of the temple.

18. A. I. Wilson, *When,* 204, delightfully speaks of "a matter-of-fact comment on mountain removal"! The point is precisely that there is nothing "matter-of-fact" about it. Wilson tentatively prefers Telford's proposal (see below, n. 20) to so "matter-of-fact" a usage.

19. This inference might, however, be drawn from the confused geography of the LXX version, which has the mountain being split into four halves (!), one of which moves πρὸς θάλασσαν, whereas the Hebrew speaks of the mountain being divided toward north and south, leaving a valley running from east to west (Hebrew *wāyāmâ,* "to the sea"); hence the LXX version).

20. The alternative proposal that he meant the temple mount, which would be seen across the Kidron valley from the Mount of Olives (so W. R. Telford, *Temple,* 56-59,

There is possibly a loose echo of this story in Luke 17:6, where a parallel saying about effective prayer speaks of removing not a mountain but a "mulberry tree" into the sea (and the Greek for "mulberry" is *sykaminos,* which is easily linked with *sykos,* "fig").

4. Jesus' Authority Is Challenged (21:23-27)

> 23 *And when Jesus had come into the temple, the chief priests and the elders of the people came up to him as he was teaching and asked, "By what authority are you doing these things? Who gave you this authority?" 24 Jesus replied, "I will ask you just one question in return; if you can answer me, then I, too, will tell you by what authority I am doing these things: 25 Was the origin of John's baptism heavenly or human?"[1] They discussed it among themselves: "If we say 'heavenly,' he will reply, 'Then why didn't you believe him?'; 26 but if we say 'human,' we are afraid of the crowd, because they all regard John as a prophet." 27 So they replied to Jesus, "We don't know." Jesus said to them in return,[2] "And I will not tell you by what authority I do these things."*

These verses record the response to the provocative actions with which Jesus has arrived in Jerusalem, just as 21:45-46 will record the reaction to his equally provocative teaching which follows. "These things" which the authorities object to are the openly messianic manner of his arrival and the high-handed way in which he has interfered with the business of the temple, compounded by his refusal to silence his young supporters.[3] This northern

---

95-127), has the obvious attraction that it would link in with the theme of the destruction of the temple, but ὄρος is not used elsewhere in the gospels to refer to the temple (though it might have been inferred from Isa 2:2-3), and "*this* mountain" spoken en route from Bethany more naturally refers to the Mount of Olives. A reference to the temple is impossible when the same phrase, "this mountain," is used in a parallel passage (17:20) set far away from Jerusalem. The destruction predicted for the temple in 24:2 does not envisage the whole hill being thrown into the sea, nor that the disciples will be the agents! S. E. Dowd, *Prayer,* 72-75, criticizes Telford's proposal.

1. Literally, "The baptism of John, where was it from? From heaven or from human beings?"

2. "In return" represents καὶ αὐτός, "he too": Jesus is responding to their refusal to answer by his own counterrefusal.

3. Gundry, 419, suggests, on the basis that Matthew has introduced a reference to Jesus' teaching, that "these things" refers specifically to his teaching. No doubt this was equally a concern, but the focus of the narrative so far has been on his actions rather than his teaching, and the way the participle διδάσκοντι is introduced is not sufficiently marked to carry such weight, nor is "to do these things" a natural way to refer to teaching.

villager, proclaimed by his followers as a prophet (v. 11), is assuming an authority which challenges the duly constituted leadership of the official guardians of the temple and of the religious life of Jerusalem. They could hardly ignore such a challenge. His behavior is not only highly irregular; it is a threat to their position. Just who does he think he is?

Jesus' reply sounds evasive, and he does in fact refuse to give an explicit answer to their question. But the form of his response implies clearly what his answer would be. He links his authority to that of John, and we have been left in no doubt in this gospel that John was a true prophet, who like the OT prophets spoke with the authority of God (see on 3:1-4; 11:7-19). The link between Jesus and John has been established through John's prediction of the "stronger one" to come (3:11-12; cf. v. 14), through Jesus' own acceptance of John's baptism (3:13-16), through the summary of their respective proclamation in the same words (3:2; 4:17), through Jesus' response to John's question (11:2-6), and through his comments on their parallel ministries in 11:16-19. It has been confirmed by the perception of outsiders in 14:1-2; 16:13-14 that Jesus is another John; and Jesus has closely linked their roles and their prophetic fate in 17:11-13. The parable which follows in vv. 28-32 will be explained on the assumption that John was the authentic messenger of the kingdom of God.[4] If then John was a true prophet sent by God, and Jesus is his successor, the implied answer to the question about his authority is quite unmistakable. But it has been cunningly presented in such a way that it cannot be used against him as an explicit claim to divine authority. That claim will not be made openly until the climactic confrontation in 26:63-64, and then it will lead directly to his condemnation as a blasphemer and his execution as a political danger. For the moment it remains prudently unstated, but neither the priests and elders nor the listening crowd can have been in any doubt about the claim which was implied.

23 "The temple" (i.e., the Court of the Gentiles; see pp. 770-71) is the scene for all the remaining teaching and action until 24:1. The colonnades around the great courtyard offered ample shaded space for people to gather around a preacher. "As he was teaching" indicates that this was Jesus' normal practice during these days before the festival, even though Matthew's record of specific teaching will not begin until v. 28. We are therefore to assume a substantial crowd around Jesus when this official approach is made, so that the following dialogue takes place in public (as v. 26, "we are afraid of the crowd," confirms).

We have heard of the "chief priests and elders" (together with the

---

4. For Matthew's special emphasis on the continuity between John and Jesus see the introductory comments on 3:1-12 above.

scribes) in 16:21 as the body who will bring about Jesus' death. At this point Mark and Luke again give the full list of the component groups of the Sanhedrin, but Matthew abbreviates by mentioning only the two groups who were to take the "political" lead in responding to the threat Jesus posed to their official status as guardians of the temple and of the community affairs of Jerusalem. In chs. 26 and 27 he will regularly (except for 26:57) single out these two groups as the opponents of Jesus, though in 27:41 all three groups will again be mentioned as mocking him on the cross. Matthew, unlike the other evangelists, often gives the full title "elders of the people" (cf. 26:3, 47; 27:1), perhaps in order to emphasize their role in representing the whole people of God, just as it is only Matthew who in 27:25 will attribute the demand for Jesus' death to "all the people," using as here the term *laos,* which spoke especially of the communal privilege of the chosen people.

The challenge as to Jesus' "authority" is a more explicit expression of the suspicion which led the leaders in Galilee to ask for a "sign" (12:38; 16:1; see comments on 12:38). Jesus' actions imply a personal authority greater than that of a mere village preacher from Galilee. In particular, his action in the temple implies a claim to authority greater than that of the priests who were responsible for its affairs. *They* had given him no such authority, so who had?

24-25a In response to their double question ("what authority, and who gave it?") Jesus poses "just one"[5] question, which is in effect the same question but focused now not on himself but on John the Baptist: where did *his* authority come from? See the introductory comments above for the logic of Jesus' response. "Heaven" functions here as a reverent periphrasis for the name of God, as in 3:17; 16:1, 19; 18:18. The simple alternative between divine and human authorization will apply equally to Jesus, and the implied claim is that he, like John, comes with God-given authority, not by his own human initiative. John's ministry was recent enough and had been influential enough (see 3:5, and cf. Josephus, *Ant.* 18.118) to give a sharp point to the question, both for the officials and for the listening crowd. The focus specifically on John's baptism, rather than his call to repentance, picks out the element in his ministry which was likely to have been found most offensive by the Jewish establishment (see on 3:6), with its radical implications for the membership of the true Israel, a theme which will be explored further in Jesus' parables which follow in 21:28–22:14.

A counterquestion in place of a direct answer was an accepted pattern in rabbinic debate, where the second question further opens up the subject

---

5. For Matthew's use of εἷς where we might use an indefinite article see p. 323, n. 3, and p. 790, n. 2. Here, as in most other such uses in Matthew, there is contextual reason to suggest that the choice of εἷς is deliberate. Cf. Gundry, 419.

raised by the first.[6] We have seen an example already in 15:3, and another will follow in 22:20; cf. also Mark 10:3.[7] In none of these cases does Jesus' counterquestion change the subject, but it substitutes dialogue for simple assertion and so answers the question more obliquely where a direct pronouncement might have been used against him.

25b-26 The dilemma[8] of the questioners is not an intellectual one — their view of John seems to have been clear enough — but tactical, involving the danger of "loss of face." To voice their true view of John would have exposed them to popular anger, but to give an insincere answer would expose them to ridicule, since their rejection of John's message was well known, as Jesus will confirm in v. 32.[9] While there is some ambivalence about the popular response to John as Jesus describes it in 11:16-19, the presupposition is that they went out to him as a prophet (11:9), even if his style of prophetic ministry proved not to be to their taste. John's prophetic image is confirmed in 16:14, and his popular appeal, already mentioned in 14:5, is presupposed in v. 32.

27 Their decision that silence is the more prudent course allows Jesus to adopt the same approach without loss of face. But it is not true that "the whole dialogue has to do with nothing deeper than saving and losing face."[10] No one who heard Jesus' response could fail to understand the implied claim to continuity between his ministry and that of John, and therefore to a divine authority for it. The popular opinion that Jesus, too, was a prophet (v. 46) was a natural deduction from this exchange.

B. THREE POLEMICAL PARABLES (21:28-22:14)

See above, p. 769, for the groups of three around which the confrontation in chs. 21-22 is constructed. The other groups are shared with Mark, but at this point Matthew has taken the single parable which occurs at this point in Mark and Luke and expanded it by the addition of two others whose themes are closely related so that the three together form an impressive and startling

---

6. See D. Daube, *Rabbinic Judaism,* 151-55. Examples are set out in R. Bultmann, *History,* 42-45, though in some of them the response is interrogative in form rather than in substance.

7. Matt 19:3-6 is differently constructed, but the style of argument is similar.

8. Davies and Allison, 3:161, unnecessarily assume that their deliberation is silent. Their concerted response in v. 27 surely implies that they have discussed it together first.

9. Cf. John's harsh words about the "Pharisees and Sadducees" in 3:7-10. Luke 7:29-30 explicitly claims that "the Pharisees and lawyers" refused John's baptism.

10. R. H. Gundry, *Mark,* 667. But see J. H. Hellerman, *JETS* 43 (2000) 213-28, who argues that in that society "there *was* nothing deeper — nothing more important — than saving and losing face in public contests over honor."

body of teaching. All three parables focus on the failure of the current Jerusalem leadership to respond to God's call, and go on to explore the consequences of their failure for the future of the people of God. While the explicit target of the polemic remains the group of leaders who have just challenged Jesus' authority (further specified in 21:45 as "the chief priests and the Pharisees"), there are broad hints within these parables that the effect of their failure extends beyond their own role of leadership: 21:31 speaks of who is to "go into the kingdom of God"; 21:43 speaks of a "nation" which will take over from the evicted tenants; and 22:7 includes "their city" along with the reluctant guests as the object of the king's reprisals. In all three parables two groups of people are contrasted, those who assume that they have a right to their privileged position and those who instead find themselves unexpectedly promoted (and who, in 21:31, are the people most despised by those presently in power).

All three parables thus speak of a radical and unexpected reversal of roles, and so raise far-reaching and troubling reflections about how the Israel of Jesus' day relates to the people of God in the future. They clearly indicate that the current leadership is to be replaced, but hints of a wider effect on the city and the nation will continue to surface in the following chapters, especially in the lament over Jerusalem (23:37) and the prediction of the destruction of the temple (23:38; 24:2), which is then further developed in the discourse of ch. 24 to envisage the sufferings of "Judea" (24:16) in which everyone, not just the leaders, will be involved (24:15-22). While the attitude of the Jerusalem crowd will remain at least ambivalent during chs. 21–23 (see on 21:46), by the time of Jesus' Roman trial they will have turned decisively against him, and in 27:24-25 the chilling words accepting responsibility for his death will be attributed to "all the people."

Seen in the light of Matthew's distinctive development of this theme, the statement (in Matthew only) that the kingdom of God will be taken away from "you" and given to "a nation" that will yield its fruits (21:43) might be read as a manifesto for the total rejection of Israel and its replacement by Gentiles (see comments on 21:43). But that is a good deal too simple. The vineyard, after all, represents Israel, and it remains to produce its fruit after its original tenants are evicted. The tax collectors and prostitutes who will go first into the kingdom of God (21:31) are presumably as Jewish as the establishment they replace. What is envisaged seems to be more than merely a "regime change," but less than a total repudiation of Israel as the people of God. What appears to be in view is rather a reconstitution of Israel, such as we saw outlined in 8:11-12, with new and unexpected members drawn in to replace those rejected by their lack of faith, but with a recognizable continuity with the OT people of God. The balance is well expressed in some words of C. H. Dodd in relation to the NT theme of the new temple:

The manifest disintegration of the existing system is to be preliminary to the appearance of a new way of religion and a new community to embody it. And yet, it is the *same* temple, first destroyed, that is to be rebuilt. The new community is still Israel; there is continuity through the discontinuity. It is not a matter of replacement but of resurrection.[1]

Of the three parables here brought together, one (21:28-32) is found only in Matthew, one is shared with Mark and Luke but is given a distinctively Matthean application in 21:43, while the third, that of the wedding feast, shares a basic motif with the parable of the great dinner in Luke 14:16-24, but is so differently related as to be in effect a separate parable; its final scene in 22:11-13 has no parallel in Luke. The whole complex, therefore, bears the clear mark of Matthew's editorial work, and reflects his distinctive theology of Israel.[2]

1. The Two Sons (21:28-32)

28 *"What do you think? A man had two sons, and he went to the first and said, 'Off you go, my lad, and work in the vineyard today.'* 29 *'No, I won't,' he replied; but later he changed his mind and went.* 30 *He went to the other and said the same thing. 'Yes, sir,' he replied; but he didn't go.* 31 *Which of the two did his father's will?" "The first," they replied.[3] Jesus said to them, "I tell you truly that the tax collectors and the prostitutes will go into the kingdom of God before you.* 32 *For John came to you as a preacher of[4] righteousness, and you didn't believe him; but the tax collectors and the prostitutes did believe him. And even when you saw this, you did not change your minds later and believe him."*

I have placed a structural division after 21:27 in order to highlight the sequence of three parables, but formally speaking there is no break, as Jesus' address to the chief priests and elders continues uninterrupted into v. 28. There is also an important continuity in the thought, since the issue of the authority of John the Baptist which dominated vv. 23-27 will be the basis of the condemnation of the Jewish leaders which follows this parable in v. 32. The

1. C. H. Dodd, *Founder,* 90.
2. For Matthew's theology of the people of God see further my *Matthew: Evangelist,* ch. 6, especially pp. 223-38.
3. For the confusion in the textual tradition as to which son the leaders approved, see the comments below. The reading given here represents the majority tradition as against a Western tradition which has the leaders approve the son who promised but failed.
4. Literally, "In the way of righteousness"; see the comments below.

central importance of John's ministry is again underlined, even to the extent of declaring that people's response to John determines their entry to the kingdom of God — which was, after all, the burden of John's preaching according to 3:2. And since "entering the kingdom of heaven/God" is already familiar to us as an idiom for ultimate salvation (cf. 5:20; 7:21-23; 8:11-12; 18:3; 19:23-24), John's significance could hardly be more strongly endorsed.

The parable proper takes up only vv. 28b-30. It is framed by the two parts of Jesus' question, "What do you think? . . . Which of the two did his father's will?" and the Jewish leaders' answer, after which Jesus delivers a blunt verdict on their conduct and its consequences. The reversal of roles which we have seen to be a characteristic of this group of parables comes to expression in these final comments, which expound the contrast between the attitudes and actions of the two sons. See the comments below on v. 31 for the question how far Jesus' words may be read as *excluding,* rather than simply demoting, the Jewish leaders.

There is considerable confusion in the MSS and versional evidence for the form of the parable and the subsequent answer to Jesus' question.[5] There are three main options: (a [as translated above]) The first son refuses and then goes; the second promises and then fails; and the leaders approve the first. (b) The first promises and then fails; the second refuses and then goes; and the leaders approve the second.[6] (c) The first refuses and then goes; the second promises and then fails; and the leaders approve the second.[7] The first two of these versions clearly come to the same conclusion, and simply reverse the order of the two scenes. The third, however, is strikingly different

5. The issue is helpfully discussed by B. M. Metzger, *Textual Commentary,* 55-56, and more technically by K. and B. Aland, *Text,* 307-11; I. H. Jones, *Parables,* 393-96 (Jones argues for a pre-Matthean form of the parable, commending immediate obedience rather than a later change of mind, which differs from all preserved texts).

6. This option (adopted by NEB and REB) is found, with several variations in wording, in B, Θ, f¹³, and a number of versional MSS. It may have originated from scribes who knew the tradition taking the third option and in order to restore the "right" conclusion changed the sequence of the two sons rather than the leaders' answer. It might also have been motivated by interpreting the son who promises but does not perform as the Jews, and the one who initially refuses but then repents as the Gentiles, and then attempting to restore the "historical" order, Jews before Gentiles. J. D. M. Derrett, *ST* 25 (1971) 109-13, supports it on the cultural ground that these are the elder and younger sons, in that order, and that the younger is more likely to be the rebel (as in Luke 15:11-32). P. Foster, *NTS* 47 (2001) 26-37, also supports it as more likely Matthew's preferred version, with the second party in the story being approved rather than the first, as in the other two connected parables 21:33-44 and 22:1-14, but suggests that version (a) may represent a pre-Matthean form of the parable.

7. This option is represented by D, many OL MSS, and Sinaitic Syriac; it is known by Hilary and Jerome, and even appears in one version of the Vulgate.

in that it has the Jewish leaders approving words rather than deeds. This puts them in a bad light[8] even before Jesus comments on their behavior, and it may have been for that reason that some scribes and translators preferred this reading which makes the Jewish leaders speak as Jesus will charge them with having acted.[9] But this can hardly have been the original intention of the story since Jesus' response does not challenge their answer, but rather charges them with not having lived up to it. Their reading of the story, he implies, is right, but their correct thinking is belied by their actual behavior. The reading as translated above is agreed by most commentators to represent the original form of the story and response.

28-30 For "What do you think?" as the lead-in to a question with searching implications cf. 17:25; 18:12; 22:42; here the question will be completed in v. 31a. The little story on which it is based assumes a small family farm. Such farms often grew grapes, though the specific crop is not emphasized in this parable. But this is already the second vineyard parable (cf. 20:1-16), and another will immediately follow. There it will become clear that the vineyard is a symbol of Israel, based on Isaiah's famous analogy (see on v. 33), so that it would not be difficult for Matthew's readers to transfer the same symbolism to this story and so to apply it to God's plans for the care of his people. The implied fault of the chief priests and elders, then, is not simply the inconsistency of their behavior but their failure to fulfill their God-given role as leaders of Israel.

The wording of the story carries few surprises. Even the potentially theological term *metamelomai* has a quite normal secular sense of "change one's mind" or "regret" (cf. 2 Cor 7:8; see below on 27:3); to "repent" in a more theological sense is normally in the NT expressed rather by *metanoeō*, though in v. 32 *metamelomai* will be used in a sense closer to "repent" in order to echo the word used in the parable. Similarly, *kyrie* in v. 30 is a normal respectful address by a son to his father, "Sir," even though the father in the parable represents God, the *Kyrios*.

31 The question which Jesus posed in v. 28a is now filled out: the chief priests and elders are required to adjudicate between the two brothers. For "doing the will of" God cf. the comments on 7:21 and 12:50; it is in this

---

8. This almost universal Western assumption that deeds matter more than words is robustly challenged by W. E. Langley, *CBQ* 58 (1996) 228-43, who points out that in Palestinian culture the lack of respect shown by the son who says "No" to his father's face is arguably as bad as the other son's failure to obey after giving the "right" answer. Langley argues, therefore, that it does not much matter for Jesus' purposes which answer is given. Each son is partly obedient and partly disobedient!

9. Jerome discusses this reading and rather improbably suggests that the Jewish leaders deliberately gave a "wrong" reply in order to divert the obvious point of the parable (see Metzger, *Textual Commentary*, 55-56).

gospel an expression which distinguishes mere profession from active compliance,[10] and so here it suitably distinguishes between the attitudes of the two sons. Jesus' question thus allows only one reasonable answer,[11] which the Jewish leaders duly provide (see introductory comments above on the textual question), but, like David in his response to Nathan's parable (2 Sam 12:5-7), in so doing they provide Jesus with the ammunition he needs to mount an attack in v. 32 on their own inconsistency. First, however, he spells out its consequences.

The Jewish leaders (like the second son) claimed to be living in obedience to God's law, and kept themselves strictly apart from those who (like the first son) made no such claim. It was Jesus' interest in such "tax collectors and sinners" (Luke 15:1-2) which gave rise to another parable about two sons (Luke 15:11-32). In this gospel the "underclass" of Jewish society have also been described as "tax collectors and sinners" (9:10, 11; 11:19), and on two occasions the Jewish tax collectors have been even more dismissively linked with Gentiles (5:46-47; 18:17). The substitution of "prostitutes"[12] here for either "sinners" or "Gentiles" gives an even more offensive comparison,[13] especially in so male-dominated a society as first-century Palestine.[14] These are the people whom the "chief priests and elders of the people" would most despise and most heartily thank God that they were not like (cf. Luke 18:11). They had no place in respectable, religious Jewish society[15] — how much less in the kingdom of God.[16] So when Jesus speaks not only of their entering

10. See my *Matthew: Evangelist,* 265-68.

11. B. M. Metzger, *Textual Commentary,* 55, says of the D reading which approves the other son, "it is not only difficult, it is nonsensical — the son who said 'Yes' but did nothing obeys his father's will!" But this does not seem to have prevented some scribes from attributing such an objectionable answer to those whom they took to be the "villains" in the story!

12. Note that in Luke 7:36-50 Jesus accepts such a woman in the same way that he accepts tax collectors and sinners. There is, however, no biblical support for the later tradition that Mary Magdalene was a reformed prostitute.

13. For the sense of disgust conveyed by the term cf. the image of "the great prostitute" in Rev 17 and the early apocryphal gospel story P. Oxy. 840, where Jesus speaks of "prostitutes and flute girls" who adorn themselves outwardly "while inwardly they are filled with scorpions and all unrighteousness." Keener, 508-9, gives a useful survey of prostitution and the attitude to prostitutes at the time.

14. M. D. Goulder, *Midrash,* 414, attributes the "prostitutes" here to Matthew's tendency to complement a male term with a female (see ibid., 98, for other examples).

15. J. Gibson, *JTS* 32 (1981) 429-33, suggests that the surprising combination of these two disparate groups derives from the fact that both were regarded as collaborators with the Roman occupying forces.

16. Of Matthew's (probably) five uses of "the kingdom of God" rather than "the kingdom of heaven" (see on 12:28), this is the one least easily explained as contextually

God's kingdom but also going in there *first,* he is making a no less radical pronouncement than when he spoke of Gentiles coming into the kingdom of heaven to sit with Abraham, Isaac, and Jacob while the "sons of the kingdom" found themselves outside (8:11-12).

Comparison with that earlier saying also raises the question of how much is implied here by *proagō,* "go before." At least it means a reversal of priorities, with the chief priests and elders admitted but only after the riffraff have been welcomed in. In that case they must endure the humiliation of being led, "shown the way" (a possible sense of *proagō;* cf. 2:9) by those they have regarded as beyond the pale. But in 8:11-12 the fate of the "sons of the kingdom" was not merely demotion but exclusion, and while *proagō* normally implies that the other person will follow (cf. 14:22; 26:32; 28:7), in the wider context of Matthean statements about the future for Israel's leaders many interpreters conclude that it implies here "get there first" and so "take the place of."[17] In the parable of 25:1-12 those who go in first enjoy the feast, but the door is shut before the others get there. And in 7:21-23 the fate of those who do not "do the will of my Father" is to be excluded from the kingdom of heaven. Exclusion is not explicit here, but it would be hazardous to argue from the choice of the verb *proagō* that here there is, unusually, hope for the ultimate salvation of those who have rejected God's call — unless, of course, like the good son, they subsequently change their minds and respond to the preaching of righteousness as the tax collectors and prostitutes have done.

32 It is a remarkable testimony to the high view of John the Baptist in this gospel that whereas previously Jesus has condemned those who refused to believe and respond to his own message (11:20-24; 12:41-42), he now places rejection of John's ministry on the same level. Those previous denunciations were of unbelief in Galilee, where Jesus had himself been active; now he is in Judea, where according to this gospel's story line he has not hitherto been heard, and so he speaks now of John as his southern predecessor and "colleague," to whose call Jerusalem had responded before he himself took up the mission in the north (3:5). The "way of righteousness" (see p. 801, n. 4) which he has himself preached in Galilee was represented in Judea by John. For the meaning of "righteousness" as the

---

requiring a personal reference to God, but it is possible that it has been influenced by the personal father/son imagery of the preceding parable: the father's vineyard = God's kingdom (so, e.g., M. D. Goulder, *Midrash,* 414; cf. ibid., 332, n. 64).

17. J. Jeremias, *Parables,* 125, n. 48 (followed by BDF 245a[3]), argues from an alleged Aramaic original of προάγω that its meaning is "not temporal but exclusive." In the absence of clear evidence for such a sense of the *Greek* verb, this seems a tendentious argument, but it is surprising how many recent commentators accept it without further evidence. The argument from the wider Matthean context seems to me more substantial.

way of life according to the will of God see p. 119, n. 15, and the uses of the term in 5:6, 10, 20; 6:33.[18] The phrase "the way of righteousness" (a Semitic expression for "the right way"; cf. Prov 8:20 etc.)[19] occurs only here in the NT, but it well suits the behavioral sense of the term which we have seen to be dominant in Matthew. That John "came in the way of righteousness" no doubt implies that he lived a godly life, but that in itself gives no message to which to respond by "believing" him, and so the phrase here probably refers mainly to his message; hence my translation above, "as a preacher of righteousness."[20]

The repentance and its appropriate "fruit" which John demanded according to 3:7-10 match closely the Matthean sense of "righteousness." John came to show people how to live according to God's will, and those who "believed" him repented and were baptized. They included especially the less respectable members of Jewish society, for whom repentance was an obvious need, and perhaps for that reason his message was resisted by those who already considered themselves "righteous" (cf. Jesus' own mission according to 9:12-13). The obvious and enthusiastic response of the common people should have caused them to "change their mind later."[21] And if they refused John's call, it is clear that they will also refuse that of Jesus who comes with the same heavenly authority (vv. 23-27), as Jesus has already predicted (17:12-13). The kingdom of God is not for them. Cf. 11:18 for another statement of John's mission and the people's negative response, using the same phrase "John came . . ."; there, too, the missions of John and of Jesus are placed in parallel.

A comparable, but not closely parallel, saying in Luke 7:29-30 contrasts the positive response of "all the people and the tax collectors" to John with the refusal of "the Pharisees and lawyers" to accept his baptism, thus rejecting "God's purpose for them." That saying, with its focus on John's baptism rather than his message, is integrated into Luke's parallel to Matt 11:7-

18. Hagner, 2:614, links the phrase here more closely with the special use of δικαιοσύνη in 3:15, and concludes that it refers to "the process of the accomplishment of salvation in history." See p. 119, n. 15, for Hagner's special study of δικαιοσύνη; he deals with 21:32 (ibid., 117-18).

19. See Davies and Allison, 3:170, n. 43. See, however, B. Przybylski, *Righteousness,* 94-95, for some cautionary comments on the value of positing a direct link with the usage of Proverbs.

20. B. Przybylski, *Righteousness,* 95-96, discusses whether the reference is to John's behavior or to his message, and concludes that while the latter is more relevant in context, the two cannot be separated. "John practised what he preached."

21. This phrase, using the verb μεταμέλομαι, is picked up from the parable in v. 29, but it reminds the reader of the "repentance," μετανοέω, that John demanded and they refused.

19, Jesus' verdict on John, and lacks the link with the parable which this saying expounds.

2. The Vineyard (21:33-44)

33 *"Listen to another parable. There was a landowner[1] who planted a vineyard. He put a fence around it, dug a winepress in it, and built a watchtower. Then he let it out to tenant farmers and traveled away. 34 When the time came for the vintage, he sent his slaves to the tenant farmers to collect his fruit. 35 The tenants took his slaves and beat one up, killed another, and stoned another. 36 Again he sent a new lot of slaves, more than the first, and they treated them the same way. 37 In the end he sent his son to them, saying, 'They will respect my son.' 38 But when the tenants saw the son, they said, 'This is the heir. Come on, let's kill him and get hold of his inheritance.' 39 And they took him and threw him out of the vineyard and killed him.[2] 40 So when the owner of the vineyard comes, what will he do to those tenants?"*

41 *"He will bring those bad men to a bad end," they replied, "and let the vineyard out to other tenants, who will return the fruit to him when it is due."*

42 *Jesus said to them, "Haven't you ever read in the Scriptures:*

'The stone which the builders rejected
is the one that has become the head of the corner.
This is what the Lord has done,
and it is amazing to our eyes'?

43 *Therefore I tell you that the kingdom of God will be taken away from you and will be given to a nation which produces its fruit.* 44[3] *And*

1. See p. 746, n. 1, for this rendering; the phrase is the same.
2. Most MSS agree with Luke in having the throwing out before the killing, but D, Θ, and several OL MSS follow the Marcan order, where the killing precedes the throwing out. Since the latter is the more natural order, the D reading probably represents a deliberate correction.
3. Verse 44, which is almost the same as Luke 20:18, is omitted by D, 33, several OL MSS, and the Sinaitic Syriac (much the same Western grouping whose alternative readings we have seen reason to doubt in vv. 28-30 and 39). Here many scholars accept the Western omission as original, and regard the longer majority text as an assimilation to Luke. But the wording is not quite the same, and one would expect an insertion into Matthew to be made after v. 42 (which would correspond to its position in Luke) rather than after v. 43 where it is separated from the stone quotation to which it relates. (See, however, p. 818, n. 42, where a link between v. 43 and the Dan 2 allusion in v. 44 is suggested.) The

whoever falls on this stone will be smashed, but if it falls on anyone, it will scatter him like chaff."[4]

The second parable, together with the explanatory quotation from Ps 118:22 at the end, is shared with Mark and Luke.[5] The story itself is told in much the same way by the three evangelists,[6] though a few distinctive Matthean features will be noted below, but it is at the end that his version becomes most distinctive. He agrees with Mark against Luke in quoting v. 23 of the psalm as well as v. 22; he agrees with Luke against Mark in adding further OT allusions to a stone in v. 44; and between the psalm quotation and the other stone allusions he inserts in v. 43 an explanatory comment on the significance of the parable. This last is the most significant of his adaptations: the mention of another "nation" to replace "you" in the tenancy of the vineyard takes us to the heart of the issue of the true Israel which underlies this whole section of the gospel, and in conjunction with the other two parables in the group it enables the reader to reach a more far-reaching understanding of what the vineyard parable implies than is possible from Mark and Luke when they record it alone.

The story of an absentee landowner reflects a familiar economic situation at the time;[7] some of the chief priests and elders to whom Jesus is speak-

---

very awkwardness of its placing within the Matthean text, which would explain its omission, inclines me to accept v. 44 as original. See also I. H. Jones, *Parables,* 387-88; B. Charette, *Recompense,* 138-39.

4. This rendering reflects the derivation of λικμάω (which occurs in the NT only here and in the Luke parallel) from λικμός, a "winnowing fan." The verb is used literally for the winnowing process in classical and LXX Greek, but in the LXX it is also used metaphorically for scattering people; here it reflects Thdt Dan 2:44, where the effect of the stone is both to smash and to scatter the opposing kingdoms; in Dan 2:35 the imagery of scattered chaff is explicit, though different Greek words are used.

5. For a full study of issues in the interpretation of this parable in the light of scholarship up to about 1980 see K. R. Snodgrass, *The Parable of the Wicked Tenants.* For a rather earlier survey see M. Hubaut, *La parabole des vignerons homicides.*

6. There is a simpler version in *Gos. Thom.* 65, which stops with the killing of the son before any reprisals are taken, though it is followed by the stone-quotation from Ps 118:22 (see p. 814, n. 31). Several commentators have speculated whether the *Thomas* version, which has several independent features, represents an earlier form of the parable than any of the Synoptic versions. I have commented on that view in my *Mark,* 456-57. Now that it is no longer assumed that "allegorical" elements in Jesus' parables are a necessary sign of secondary development, the proposal has less support. See further K. R. Snodgrass, *NTS* 21 (1974/5) 142-44.

7. See J. D. M. Derrett, *Law,* 286-312, for helpful information on the social and economic background, though his ingenious attempts to explain every detail of the story as matching the real-life situation are hardly necessary in what is an imaginative story rather than a transcription of actual conditions. J. D. Hester, *JSNT* 45 (1992) 34-36, notes the de-

ing would probably have owned land away from Jerusalem. The landowner must be a wealthy man in that a newly planted vineyard could not be expected to produce fruit for at least four years, during which he would have no return on his capital outlay. Once the vines began to produce fruit, there would be an agreed proportion of the crop due to the owner, leaving the tenants to derive their living from the rest. The fault of the tenants in withholding the due produce (and in the violence perpetrated on the slaves) is massively compounded by their decision to murder the owner's son and so to attempt to take over the property. At this point the story has moved away from everyday reality,[8] and, as often happens in parables (notably in 22:7), the intended symbolism has apparently invaded the story line: the murder of the son represents the forthcoming execution of Jesus.

That last comment assumes the traditional interpretation that the story is a symbolic account of the history of Israel, whose leadership has rejected God's earlier prophetic messengers (cf. Jer 7:25-27) and is now on the point of rejecting and killing Jesus, his Son, an interpretation which is strengthened by the curious order of the clauses in v. 39 (see p. 807, n. 2) which reflects Jesus being taken outside the city to be executed. The continuity between the earlier leaders of Israel who killed the prophets and those who will now kill Jesus will be explicitly asserted in 23:29-36. Various alternative suggestions have been made for the original intention of the parable, for example, as a defense of Jesus' offer of the gospel to the poor,[9] an attack on the strong-arm tactics of the Zealots,[10] a commendation of resolute opportunism similar to that of Luke's unjust steward,[11] or an assertion of Palestinian land-rights against aristocratic expropriation.[12] Such proposals depend on reconstructing a supposed "original" form prior to what we actually find in the

velopment of popular unrest during the Herodian period owing to the growth of wealthy estates and the consequent expropriation of the peasantry, and goes on to suggest that the parable may originally have presented the tenants as popular heroes who stood up against the plutocratic landowner; only subsequent allegorization has turned them into villains.

8. Attempts to preserve verisimilitude in the story include the speculation of J. Jeremias, *Parables,* 75-76, that the tenants believed that the owner was dead (he is very much alive in vv. 40-41!), and the assertion of J. D. M. Derrett, *Law,* 300-306, that if the owner failed to collect rent for four years he forfeited his title to the property. The story says nothing about any other years.

9. J. Jeremias, *Parables,* 70-77.

10. J. E. and R. R. Newell, *NovT* 14 (1972) 226-37.

11. J. D. Crossan, *JBL* 90 (1971) 451-65.

12. J. D. Hester, *JSNT* 45 (1992) 27-57. E. H. Horne, *JSNT* 71 (1998) 111-16, accepts Hester's basic approach, but argues that the parable more directly addresses the Jewish leaders who as property owners would have taken action against rebellious tenants; so "Why, faced with your failure to produce the justice and mercy which God wills, and your subsequent murderous rebellion, will not God crush you?" (113-14).

text; as such they may be of historical interest but do not provide an exegesis of the gospel text as we have it.

The traditional interpretation is grounded in the fact that the parable's opening clearly echoes the vineyard allegory[13] in Isa 5:1-7 (see below on v. 33), in which the vineyard is explicitly identified as "the house of Israel" and "the people of Judah." Now that the old dogma that parables cannot be allegories has been abandoned, there is no problem in recognizing in the successive phases of and characters in the story a history of God's dealings with Israel,[14] even though there is no need to find allegorical equivalents for every circumstantial detail such as the fence, winepress, and tower.[15] This interpretation is strengthened by noting the insistent repetition of the word "fruit" (vv. 34 [bis], 41, 43) to describe what the owner requires of his tenants. This term has recurred throughout the gospel to describe the life which God requires of his people (3:8, 10; 7:16-20; 12:33; 13:8, 23, 26), and the lack of fruit has most recently in 21:18-20 symbolized the current failure of the temple regime.

The identification of the tenants as the current Jerusalem leadership is demanded both by the context in which this parable is set (as still part of Jesus' response to the chief priests and elders, which began in v. 27) and by the explicit comment in v. 45.[16] The whole parable might then be interpreted as a prediction of imminent regime change in Jerusalem, if it were not for the unexpected term *ethnos,* "nation," in v. 43. See above, pp. 800-801, for the question of how far-reaching a change these three parables represent. When a "nation" replaces the chief priests and elders, something more radical is implied, just as the withering of the fig tree symbolized the destruction of the temple, not merely its reorganization, and that same destruction ("deserted," 23:38; "not one stone on another," 24:2) is the conclusion to which the present confrontation is heading.

A further clue to what sort of new regime may be expected is provided

---

13. W. J. C. Weren, *Bib* 79 (1998) 2-6, describes it as a "juridical parable."

14. J. D. M. Derrett, *JTS* 25 (1974) 426-32, draws attention to a rabbinic parable in *Sifre Deut.* 312 (text in Davies and Allison, 3:176, n. 14) involving a king leasing a field to two successive groups of tenants whose dishonesty led to their being ejected in favor of his (newly born) son; it is explicitly interpreted in terms of the patriarchal history, with Jacob/Israel as the son.

15. The tower in Isa 5:2 was interpreted in the targum tradition as the temple, and it has been suggested that Jesus includes it in his parable in order to link it with his recent action in the temple; so C. A. Evans, *BZ* 28 (1984) 82-86; cf. J. Marcus, *Way,* 120.

16. C. A. Evans, *Ancient Texts,* 333, also suggests that the targum rendering (see last note) indicates that in the time of Jesus "Isaiah's Song of the Vineyard had come to be understood as directed against the temple establishment"; hence their recognition that Jesus' parable was directed against them.

by the quotation from Ps 118:22 which is an integral part of this parable as we find it in the Synoptic tradition.[17] After the tenants' rejection of the son in the parable the builders' rejection of the stone is not hard to interpret.[18] In that case the psalm quotation adds an element which is missing from the story: if the same stone which is rejected will become the cornerstone, then the son who is rejected may also be expected to be vindicated and to replace the present leadership. The addition of this quotation thus points us beyond the death of Jesus to his resurrection, which is the amazing thing which the Lord will do. In that case the new "nation" of v. 43 may be understood as the people who follow the risen Jesus, just as the "something greater than the temple" in 12:6 appears to point beyond Jesus himself to a whole new regime focused in him.

There is thus inherent in this parable with its appended psalm quotation a bold christology of rejection and vindication, of death and resurrection, and it is focused in the parable character of the owner's son. This is not yet an explicit public claim by Jesus to be the Son of God, but those who grasped the intention of the parable could hardly fail to notice this implication, and this parable is surely part of the high priest's source material when he charges Jesus with having claimed to be the Son of God (26:63).

33 Whereas Mark and Luke introduce this parable with an editorial link, in Matthew it is integrated into Jesus' extended reply to his questioners, and so he introduces it as "another parable," the second of a group of three. It is the third vineyard parable in Matthew, and its opening words recall 20:1, using the same phrase for "landowner." Thereafter this verse agrees with Mark 12:1 (against Luke) in echoing some of the agricultural details of LXX Isa 5:2.[19] While the agricultural procedures are commonplace, the wording is clearly allusive, and predisposes the reader to a story in which the disappointing vineyard represents God's frustration over his people's failure.[20] The alle-

---

17. The psalm quotation is more fully integrated with the parable by Matthew's insertion of his explanatory comment in v. 43 after the stone-quotation rather than following the leaders' response in v. 41, as one might have expected.

18. Mark and Luke make the connection more obvious by using ἀποδοκιμάζω, the LXX term for "reject" in Ps 118:22, in Jesus' first passion prediction (Mark 8:31; Luke 9:22); Matthew's abbreviation at that point has lost a suggestive echo.

19. The allusion is selective, and the wording not identical, but all three clauses are directly based on clauses in the LXX description. The LXX "fence" represents an OT *hapax legomenon* which is usually translated "hoe" or "dig around," but which in later Hebrew means "enclose"; see my *Jesus and the OT*, 247. I. H. Jones, *Parables*, 373-75, argues against M. Hubaut that the details are intended to recall the Isaiah passage, not to have individual allegorical symbolism.

20. The picture of Israel as God's vine is also familiar from other OT passages (Ps 80:8-16; Isa 27:2-6; Jer 2:21; 12:10; Ezek 15:2-6; 19:1-14), so that even the versions of

gories are not the same in that in Isaiah it is the fruit itself that fails, while here it is the tenants; in Isaiah the vineyard is itself destroyed, but here it is given to new tenants, so that in this parable there remains hope for the future, whereas in Isaiah all is disaster. But the echo remains unmistakable. Israel's failure to produce the fruit God required in Isaiah's day is now being repeated, but on a more disastrous level, as the parable will go on to explain.[21]

It is not important to the story how far away the owner's new home was (the verb suggests relocation, not just a temporary journey, and the long period of absence confirms this), but the apparently rapid succession of messengers suggests that he was not very far away.

34-36 In first-century society slaves were not necessarily of low social importance. Trusted slaves held important responsibilities in wealthy households (see on 18:23). The word for "fruit" twice in this verse and also in vv. 41 and 43 is plural, as it is in 7:16, 17, 18, 20, whereas it is singular in 3:8, 10; 7:19; 12:33; 13:8, 26; 21:19. Comparison of both wording and context in these passages does not indicate a clear idiomatic difference, especially in the light of the alternation between plural and singular in 7:16-20 (see p. 291, n. 23). For the metaphorical sense of "fruit" in this gospel see the introductory comments above.

The three Synoptic versions differ considerably in how the fate of the slaves is expressed.[22] Luke has three slaves sent individually, all of whom are ill treated but none killed. Mark also has three individuals, the third of whom is killed, after which the owner sends "many others," some of whom are beaten and some killed. Matthew's version typically abbreviates Mark's, with the result that we hear of two groups of slaves, the second larger than the first, with the same mixture of treatment (including stoning and death) given to each group. There is no obvious division of the OT prophets into two periods with the second group more numerous,[23] so Matthew's two groups of

---

this parable in Luke and in *Gos. Thom.* 65 which lack the direct echo of Isa 5:2 would naturally be understood as carrying the same symbolism (*pace* J. Jeremias, *Parables,* 70-71, who supposes an original nonallegorical parable).

21. C. A. Evans, *BZ* 28 (1984) 82-86, draws out the close links between this parable and Isa 5:1-7, especially as interpreted in later Jewish exegesis. Cf. also W. J. C. Weren, *Bib* 79 (1998) 6-26, who demonstrates the influence of the Isaiah text on Mark's version of the parable, and argues that Matthew has not only taken over that version but has also both modified it in the light of the LXX text and introduced further verbal echoes of Isaiah's parable.

22. The version in *Gos. Thom.* 65 is different again, with only two slaves sent, the first of whom is "nearly killed," prompting the owner to wonder whether he failed to recognize them *(sic)*.

23. Some commentators surprisingly refer to the "former" and "latter" prophets, but in normal Jewish usage these terms refer not to two phases of prophecy but to two types

slaves do not seem to be allegorically motivated. They are more simply explained as a tidy reorganization of Mark's version by combining the first three into a group, followed by "many others." The persecution and in extreme cases murder[24] of true prophets is a theme Matthew has already mentioned in 5:11-12 and will develop more fully in 23:29-36. Matthew's specific mention of stoning (cf. 23:37, explicitly with reference to prophets) may be a reflection of 2 Chr 24:21; Jeremiah was also stoned, according to *Liv. Pro.* 2:1.

37-39 The climax of the story comes with the unexpected involvement of the landowner's son. Cf. Heb 1:1-2 for "a son" as God's last word, following the prophets. Within the framework of the story the sending of the son is clearly a last resort, short of the owner returning himself (as he will eventually do in v. 40). When the son goes as his father's messenger, he goes with all his father's authority, and so deserves "respect" and obedience. To reject the son's demand is therefore the climax of rebellion. But to kill him is to add injury to insult. As a bid for independence[25] and an attempt to gain possession for themselves it was hardly likely to succeed in a society under the rule of law, and it reads more like a spontaneous and ill-conceived impulse than like a calculated policy.[26] But a parable does not have to fit into real life, and the points at which it becomes improbable are usually meant to draw attention. The Christian reader cannot fail to see here the status of Jesus as the Son of God,[27] the heir of the vineyard of Israel, and his death[28] as Is-

---

of "prophetic" book, the "former prophets" being the histories from Joshua to Kings. And the distinction between preexilic and postexilic prophets is one more familiar to modern scholarship than to Jewish usage, nor were the postexilic prophets more numerous.

24. The only OT prophets explicitly said to have been killed by their own people are Uriah (Jer 26:20-23) and Zechariah son of Jehoiada (2 Chr 24:20-22); the massacre in 1 Kgs 18:4 was by the foreign queen Jezebel. Jeremiah came close to being killed (Jer 26:10-19, 24; 38:4-13), and later legend attributed martyrdom to Isaiah, Jeremiah, Ezekiel, Amos, and Micah *(Lives of the Prophets);* cf. Neh 9:26. A more recent example would be John the Baptist.

25. Cf. a similarly over-the-top element in a different parable in Luke 19:14, "We do not want this man as our king."

26. See, however, p. 809, n. 8 above for attempts to make it more realistically plausible.

27. Mark and Luke refer here to the owner's "beloved" son, and thus introduce an unmistakable echo of the christological formula of 3:17; 17:5. Matthew's surprising omission of this blatant hint is perhaps due to his usual conciseness, mentioning only what the narrative requires, which is the status of the son rather than his father's love for him. Or does it mean that Matthew preserves an earlier version of the parable (so K. R. Snodgrass, *Parable,* 59)?

28. See p. 807, n. 2, and p. 809 above for the echo of the passion story in Matthew's order of clauses in v. 39 as compared with Mark.

rael's culminating act of rebellion, and may well reflect on how futile it was to try to escape from under God's rule. To kill the son is an act of defiance to the father, and he cannot be expected to let them get away with it.

40-41   The "coming" of the owner needs no allegorical interpretation (e.g., the destruction of Jerusalem); it is simply part of the story. It can hardly refer to Jesus' own *parousia* (so Gundry, 428): Jesus is the son, not the owner. As in the previous parable, Jesus asks for his hearers' verdict,[29] and here, as there, only one answer can be given, even though, again, it will be turned against them. The fate of the tenants is to be not merely eviction but "destruction," presumably referring to capital punishment for the murder they have committed. Matthew's vivid double addition of "bad" ("bring to a bad end" is literally "destroy badly") emphasizes that the punishment fits the crime. The replacement tenants are not at this point identified; all that matters is that they will "return"[30] what is due to the owner.

42   Since the fate of the tenants has been expressed in Matthew's version not by Jesus himself but in the reply of the chief priests and elders, Jesus' own comment on it is still awaited. It will come in v. 43, but that logical sequence is interrupted by what at first sight appears to be a change of subject. The quotation of Ps 118:22-23 is the concluding element of this parable tradition as represented by Mark and Luke,[31] but why could Matthew not delay it until after Jesus' direct comment on the fate of the tenants in v. 43? This would also have allowed the further stone allusions of v. 44 to follow directly from the original stone quotation in v. 42.[32] Matthew does not generally seem averse to reordering sayings material to give a more coherent sequence of thought, so that the bumpy sequence of vv. 41-44 stands out as atypical. This suggests that Matthew goes straight on to the psalm quotation

---

29. Matthew's version differs here from Mark's and Luke's, where Jesus answers his own question. Matthew thus avoids the problem which J. S. Kloppenborg, *NTS* 50 (2004) 495-518, notes in Mark 12:9, that Jesus is depicted as advocating "lethal self-help" rather than the recourse to the courts which would have been normal in contemporary society; it is not Jesus but his opponents who prescribe this high-handed action. It may be questioned, however, how far the hearers of this parable would have been concerned about legal propriety; this is a symbolic story (and at several points one which transcends the bounds of normal socioeconomic reality) rather than a reflection on correct practice.

30. The appropriate term for paying what is owed; cf. the same verb in 5:26, 33; 18:25-34; and see below on 22:21.

31. In the *Gospel of Thomas* the parable is followed by a saying of Jesus paraphrasing the same psalm quotation, though a concluding "He who has ears, let him hear" at the end of the parable and an introductory "Jesus said" before the psalm quotation have resulted in their being numbered in modern editions as two separate sayings, 65 and 66.

32. This point would of course not apply if v. 44 were not an original part of Matthew's text; see p. 807, n. 3.

here not simply mechanically because it follows in the tradition, but because he needs it at this point. See the introductory comments above on how the quotation fills out the message of the parable by providing the element of vindication which the story itself lacks. Without that element readers will find it difficult to understand who the "nation" of v. 43 can be. They are the people of the vindicated and resurrected Son of God who has become the cornerstone.[33]

For "Have you never read?" cf. 12:3, 5; 19:4; 21:16; 22:31, and see on 12:3. In each case the text quoted is well known, but Jesus is using it in a way his hearers would not have thought of. Psalm 118:22-23, here quoted exactly according to the LXX version, is part of the climax to the Hallel psalm which has already featured in Jesus' royal ride to the city (v. 9, alluding to vv. 25 and 26). The speaker is probably the king, speaking on behalf of the nation, and the vindication of the rejected stone represents Israel's triumph over the enemies who despised her. Thus the text does not in itself require a messianic application,[34] but we have seen in 2:15 and 4:1-11 how naturally it comes to Matthew (and presumably to the wider Christian tradition within which this parable was handed on) to present Jesus as the personal embodiment of Israel, the "son of God." If it was Jesus himself who linked this quotation with his vineyard story, that would go a long way toward accounting for the rapid development of such "new Israel" typology among his followers. The link would more naturally have been made by Jesus' speaking in Aramaic because of the well-known assonance of "son" and "stone" (see on 3:9);[35] in Greek there is no such echo.

The "head of the corner" is probably to be understood as the highest stone in a corner of the wall, which holds the two sides of the building together. It is thus both conspicuous and structurally indispensable. This imagery lies behind the description of Jesus as the *akrogōniaios*, "top cornerstone,"

---

33. G. N. Stanton, *Gospel,* 151-52, goes further and argues that in Matthew's understanding (as opposed to Mark's) the "stone" of Ps 118:22 is not Jesus himself but the new ἔθνος of v. 43, i.e., Matthew's own Christian community. I am not sure that Matthew would have wished to make such a clear distinction between the two, since it is the role of the Christian community to continue what Jesus has begun. Cf. J. Marcus, *Way,* 119-28, who argues that even in Mark, while Jesus is the stone, that stone is the cornerstone of the new temple which is the Christian community collectively. Similarly B. Charette, *Recompense,* 138: "This building . . . is essentially a metaphor for the new nation."

34. For eschatological interpretation of Ps 118 in Judaism, however, see J. Marcus, *Way,* 114-15. See further J. D. M. Derrett, *SE* 4 (1968) 180-86. See also the targum (next note).

35. The same assonance lies behind the targum version: "The *boy* whom the builders abandoned was among the sons of Jesse, and he is worthy to be appointed king and ruler." See C. A. Evans, *Ancient Texts,* 333-34.

of God's building, the church, in Eph 2:20; cf. 1 Pet 2:6, where the same term occurs in the LXX quotation from Isa 28:16, also applied to Jesus.[36]

43 As a result of Matthew's unexpected structuring of these final verses (see on v. 42), the "therefore" here does double duty. In the first place this verse is the sequel to v. 41 and applies to the chief priests and elders the verdict they have just pronounced on the defaulting tenants: in view of what you have concluded, you yourselves are to be dispossessed. But, in the second place, the "therefore" also takes up the theme of the psalm quotation: just as the builders rejected the stone only to find that their judgment was overturned and the stone given the place of highest importance, so you will see that the son you have rejected and killed is the one God has chosen to take your place. But instead of a single new tenant, or even a new ruling group to replace the current Jewish leadership, Jesus speaks of a "nation." See the introductory comments above on how this unexpected substitution may be related to the theme of a new people of God arising out of Jesus' ministry and characterized by faith in him, such as has been outlined in 8:11-12 and in the rabble of tax collectors and prostitutes who "go ahead of" the chief priests and elders into the kingdom of God (vv. 31-32). The term *ethnos,* "nation," demands some such understanding,[37] and takes us beyond a change of leadership to a reconstitution of the people of God whom the current leaders have represented. But, on the other hand, the singular *ethnos* does not carry the specific connotations of its articular plural, *ta ethnē,* "the Gentiles." We may rightly conclude from 8:11-12 that this new "nation" will *contain* many Gentiles,[38] but we saw also at that point that this is not to the exclusion of

36. In both 1 Pet 2:6-8 and here in v. 44 (cf. Luke 20:18) the same stone is one that can be stumbled over, which leads many commentators to understand it as a foundation stone at ground level. But "head" does not suggest that; nor does the sense of *height* in ἀκρογωνιαῖος. And in Eph 2:20 the foundation is the apostles and prophets, not Christ. The stumbling derives from a different OT stone metaphor in Isa 8:14 (see on v. 44), and must not be allowed to control the sense of Ps 118:22. See further J. Jeremias, *TDNT* 1:791-93; 4:274-75; also M. Barth, *Ephesians 1–3,* 317-19; J. D. M. Derrett, *SE* 4 (1968) 181.

37. *Pace* A. J. Saldarini, *Community,* 59-61, who attempts to show from a variety of sources that ἔθνος can mean "a voluntary organization or small social group," so that here it denotes "a new group of leaders, with their devoted followers, that can lead Israel well." Saldarini's discussion does not distinguish sufficiently clearly between the singular ἔθνος and the plural τὰ ἔθνη, and does not explain why Matthew should have chosen so apparently inappropriate a term if he simply meant a new group of leaders.

38. D. C. Sim, *Gospel,* 148-49, asserts that Matthew uses ἔθνος here to represent only "either the Matthean community alone or Christian Judaism in general," to the exclusion of Gentile Christians. This not only conflicts with Matthew's wider context, but also, even given Sim's translation of ἔθνος as "people," does not explain how the term "people" can designate such a group when set in contrast with the chief priests and elders, who were hardly in themselves "a people."

Jews as such but only of those whose lack of faith has debarred them from the kingdom of heaven. The vineyard, which is Israel, is not itself destroyed, but rather given a new lease of life, embodied now in a new "nation." This "nation" is neither Israel nor the Gentiles, but a new entity, drawn from both, which is characterized not by ethnic origin but by faith in Jesus. If there is a deliberate echo of Dan 7:27, "the kingdom . . . will be given to the people of the saints of the Most High," there is a poignant force in the transfer of this image to a different "people" which is not now simply Israel as Daniel had known it but which fulfills the role of the vineyard which is Israel.[39]

What is lost by the current leadership and gained by the new "nation" is "the kingdom of God." Here this more personal phrase, rather than "the kingdom of heaven," is more easily explained than in v. 31 (see p. 804, n. 16), since this verse is the direct application of a parable in which God's kingship has been represented by the personal authority of the landowner, and the quotation in v. 42 has spoken directly of what "the Lord" has done in vindicating his Son. Israel, they have assumed, is where God rules, but they have rejected his will and so will find themselves outside his domain, while he will rule over a reconstituted "Israel" which acknowledges his sovereignty.[40]

The old tenants lost their place because they failed to produce the required fruit, and it is the distinguishing mark of the new "nation" that it will produce it. The point is not developed here, but this qualification potentially carries a warning to the new "nation" as well. If it in turn fails to produce the fruit, it can not presume on its privileged position. The next parable will contain a sobering final scene to just that effect (22:11-13).

44 See p. 807, n. 3, for the textual uncertainty of this verse. If, as I think more likely, it is original here (as it certainly is in Luke 20:18), it takes further the OT imagery of a messianic "stone" which has just been discovered in Ps 118:22. The same passage will be taken up again in Acts 4:11, and two passages in the epistles (Rom 9:32-33; 1 Pet 2:4-8) testify to early Chris-

---

39. G. N. Stanton, *JTS* 28 (1977) 67-83, further developed in his *Gospel,* 256-77, has drawn attention to the influence of this Matthean text on the second-century Jewish-Christian work *5 Ezra* (which appears as chs. 1–2 of the apocryphal book 2 Esdras). This second-century Jewish-Christian work emphasizes strongly both the final rejection of Israel (with emphasis especially on Israel's rejection of the prophets) and the continuity between Israel and the "coming people," who are the Christian church; both communities have the same "mother," Jerusalem, but the church is *gens altera,* "another people" (Stanton, *Gospel,* 264-65, defends this reading of *5 Ezra* 1:24 against the plural of some MSS).

40. G. W. H. Lampe, in E. Bammel and C. F. D. Moule (eds.), *Jesus,* 164, defines "the kingdom of God" here as "God's special relationship to Israel, with its promises, blessings and obligations."

tian interest in developing this theme by searching for other references to stones in the OT which could be christologically applied;[41] it is likely that it was Jesus' use of Ps 118:22 which started the search. This saying contributes two further such allusions, one of which (Isa 8:14) will be used again in combination with Ps 118:22 in 1 Pet 2:8. In the absence of quotation marks it is impossible to be sure whether Matthew intends this verse to be read as the continuation of Jesus' speech or as his own editorial comment, but in the translation above I have opted for the former both because v. 45 appears to be a comment on a speech just concluded and because Matthew's editorial quotations are normally marked by an introductory formula.

The first clause reflects the imagery of Isa 8:14-15, where it is God himself who is described as a rock or stone which both provides sanctuary for those who trust him and forms a stumbling block for the unfaithful; those who stumble will fall and "be smashed." This last verb is not the same as LXX Isa 8:15, but it vividly conveys the sense of being broken to pieces which is in both Hebrew and LXX. The identification of this stone with that of Ps 118, and therefore with the Messiah rather than with God, is typical of the bold use of OT imagery which we have seen, for example, in 3:3 and 11:10, where the forerunner of God becomes the forerunner of Jesus (cf. the use of Ps 8:2 in 21:16).

The second clause introduces an OT stone which neither Paul nor Peter brought into their collections, but which is of obvious messianic significance. Daniel 2 describes the vision of a statue, representing a succession of pagan empires, smashed by a stone which represents a new kingdom[42] set up by the God of heaven which will replace all previous regimes and will last forever. When the stone hits the statue, the statue is "broken in pieces and becomes like the chaff of the threshing floor which the wind carries away" (Dan 2:35; cf. vv. 44-45), while the stone itself becomes a mountain and fills the whole earth.

These two stone passages together add a new dimension to Ps 118:22. The sense of ultimate vindication and triumph is echoed in the Daniel allusion, but this verse adds the destructive effect of the stone on all who do not value it. It thus ends Jesus' parable and interpretive comments with a severe warning of the consequences of rejecting the stone God has chosen, that is, rejecting and killing the son.

41. See B. Lindars, *Apologetic,* 169-86. More briefly but with strong arguments for the originality of this motif with Jesus himself, see N. T. Wright, *Victory,* 497-501.

42. Gundry, 430, points out that the new kingdom in Dan 2:44 "will not be left to another people" (LXX ἔθνος; Thdt λαός), and suggests that this text is already in mind in Matthew's v. 43, so that there is a deliberate contrast between the untransferability of the kingdom in Daniel and the threat of the kingdom of God being taken from you and given to another ἔθνος. Cf. P. Luomanen, *Entering,* 165-66.

3. Reactions to Jesus' Parables (21:45-46)

45 *And when the chief priests and the Pharisees heard his para-*
bles, they recognized that he was speaking about them; 46 *and they*
wanted to arrest him, but they were afraid of the crowds since they re-
garded him as a prophet.

The leaders' perception of the thrust of Jesus' parables is hardly surprising in
view of the obvious OT-derived symbolism of the vineyard, and their determination to put an end to such seditious teaching is the more understandable
if v. 44 with its threat of destruction is also part of his comments. The audience is apparently still the "chief priests and elders of the people" (v. 23);
Matthew's use of "Pharisees" rather than "elders" here brings in the group
who will feature prominently in the following controversies (22:15, 34, 41,
and throughout ch. 23). Pharisees also formed a substantial element in the
Sanhedrin (cf. Acts 23:6-10), though it is likely that they were represented
mainly among the scribes (the group whom Matthew has omitted in v. 23;
contrast Mark 11:27) rather than among the elders.

It is possible that the "crowds" here should be understood as largely
made up of Jesus' Galilean supporters who had accompanied him into the
city (see on vv. 1-11) and who then presented him as their "prophet" (v. 11).
But Galileans would be a minority in the Court of the Gentiles, and we
should probably think rather of the wider Jerusalem crowd, whose estimate
of John as a prophet (v. 26) is now also applied to Jesus. In chs. 21–23 the
"crowd" remain in the background as a wider audience for the controversy
between Jesus and the leaders, and their attitude appears to be generally re-
ceptive to Jesus. Their "amazement" at Jesus' teaching (22:33) is probably to
be taken in a favorable sense, and in 23:1-12 Jesus is able to appeal to the
crowds over the heads of the scribes and Pharisees, and to assume that the
crowd will support him rather than them. In 26:3-5 we find the leaders still
afraid of a crowd reaction in favor of Jesus. But we shall meet a very different "crowd" in Gethsemane (26:55); and in 27:15-25, and especially in
27:24-25, the attitude of the "crowd" will be one of total rejection. Historically speaking, of course, these various "crowds" would probably have
consisted of different people, but Matthew's repeated use of the term is probably intended to allow us to trace a movement in the response of the people
of Jerusalem, from an initial openness and indeed support for Jesus as a
prophet to their eventual acceptance of their leaders' view that he was a false
prophet.[1]

---

1. See my *Matthew: Evangelist,* 219, 225-27, for an analysis of Matthew's presentation of the "crowds" during this Jerusalem period.

4. The Wedding Feast (22:1-14)

1 *And Jesus went on to speak to them*[1] *again in parables:* 2 *"The kingdom of heaven can be compared to*[2] *a human king*[3] *who made a wedding feast*[4] *for his son.* 3 *He sent his slaves to summon those who had been invited to the wedding, but they were not willing to come.* 4 *So again he sent other slaves with the instructions, 'Say to those who have been invited, "Look, I have the meal ready; my bulls and fattened cattle have been slaughtered, and everything is ready. Come to the wedding feast."'* 5 *But they took no notice and went off, one to his own farm, and another to his business,* 6 *while the rest of them grabbed the king's slaves and abused and killed them.* 7 *But the king was furious, and sent out his troops, and destroyed those murderers, and set fire to their city.* 8 *Then he said to his slaves, 'The wedding feast is ready, but those who were invited didn't deserve it.* 9 *So go out to the street corners*[5] *and invite to the wedding whomever you can find.'* 10 *Those slaves went out into the streets and collected all the people they could find, bad as well as good; and the wedding hall*[6] *was filled with guests.* 11 *But when the king went in to inspect*[7] *the guests, he saw there a man who was not wearing wedding clothes,* 12 *and he said to him, 'My friend,*[8] *how did you get in here without wedding clothes?' The man was speechless.* 13 *Then the king said to his attendants, 'Tie him hand and foot, and throw him out into*

1. Literally, "And Jesus answered and said to them." See p. 439, n. 1, for the use of this expression to introduce a new contribution rather than a reply as such. Here, however, there is perhaps an element of "reply" to the unspoken hostility of the Jewish leaders in vv. 45-46.

2. For this formula cf. 13:24; 18:23, and see p. 522, n. 1.

3. See p. 701, n. 3, for this translation.

4. The plural γάμοι used in vv. 2, 3, 4, 9 and in 25:10 properly refers to the whole complex of wedding celebrations, but it is the meal that is the focus of the story, as it would have been of the celebrations. The use of the singular in v. 8 does not seem to have any different meaning.

5. The phrase αἱ διέξοδοι τῶν ὁδῶν, "the ways-out-through of the streets," perhaps refers to the places "where a main street cuts (through) the city boundary and goes (out) into the open country" (so BDAG 244a), but in context it refers to anywhere where ordinary people may be found.

6. The MSS tradition varies between ὁ γάμος, literally simply "the wedding," and the more specific term ὁ νυμφών, "the wedding hall" (as in 9:15; see p. 349, n. 6), but the meaning is not affected.

7. θεάομαι means more than just "see" or even "look at"; it implies a careful or searching look, "the implication being that he went in to 'look them over'" (BDAG 445b). Cf. its uses in 6:1; 23:5 (trying to attract attention); 11:7 (sightseeing).

8. For the idiom see p. 1009, n. 4.

the darkness outside.' There there will be weeping and gnashing of teeth.

14 *"For many are invited, but few are chosen."*

The third parable is still spoken to the same audience of chief priests and elders/Pharisees (21:23, 45). There is a partial parallel to this parable in Luke 14:16-24, but the audience there is more general (fellow guests at a dinner). There is the same essential story line of a lavish feast to which those previously invited refuse to come when summoned, to be replaced by a motley collection of people from the streets, and the conclusion in Luke 14:24 similarly focuses on the exclusion of those previously invited. But the story is very differently told: Luke has no king or wedding, focuses at some length on the reasons for nonattendance to which Matthew alludes only briefly in v. 5, and has two waves of replacement guests brought in (perhaps to represent Jews and Gentiles). He has nothing about the ill-treatment of the (single) messenger, and his host takes no punitive action other than excluding the original invitees from the feast. And Luke's parable stops short when the hall is full; there is no second scene with the expulsion of one of the new invitees. Luke's story is thus essentially simpler than Matthew's, but stylistically more expansive.[9] The situation is similar to what we will find with the parable of the talents in 25:14-30: a basically similar story line but in a different setting in Luke, and so differently constructed that it seems more economical to assume that Jesus told two related but separate parables on different occasions than to explain the one as an extraordinarily radical and complicated editorial revision of the other. From the point of view of an exegetical commentary it is more responsible to read Matthew's story on its own terms, and in its own literary context, than to look for its meaning primarily in terms of how it differs from Luke's.[10]

This parable, like the two which precede it, speaks of people who do not live up to expectation and so lose their place of privilege, to be replaced by a more surprising group; the first are last and the last first. There are obvious parallels between this story and that of the vineyard (two groups of slaves sent out, and the ill-treatment and murder of the slaves by those to whom they are sent), but many interpreters believe that there is also a historical pro-

9. That is even more true of *Gos. Thom.* 64, which covers much the same ground as Luke's version, without the Matthean distinctives noted above, but substantially expands the series of excuses beyond those in Luke. The search for replacement guests is, by contrast, quite perfunctorily mentioned at the end, and a concluding comment betrays the different focus of the story: "The buyers and merchants shall not come into my Father's place."

10. See R. J. Bauckham, *JBL* 115 (1996) 482-88, on the importance of respecting the "narrative integrity" of the parable in its Matthean version.

gression between them in that the slaves' mission in the vineyard parable ended with the killing of the son, whereas here the setting is the son's wedding, which most interpreters take to be a symbol of the Christian era. In that case the double invitation in vv. 3-4 may symbolize first the OT prophets preparing Israel for the coming of the Messiah, and then Christian preachers summoning the prepared people to enter the kingdom of heaven. Then, when Israel has refused the invitation and has accordingly been punished in the destruction of Jerusalem (v. 7), a new set of messengers are sent out to summon the Gentiles to take their place (vv. 8-10). That is an interpretation which would probably have come easily to Matthew's Christian readers, and it is possible that that is how he intended the parable to be read, but it would be much less obvious to the Jewish leaders to whom the parable is actually addressed. And certain features of the story may suggest caution in accepting this wholesale allegorical reading. The king's son, whose wedding is mentioned in v. 2 as the setting for the story, plays no further part in it; the double invitation of vv. 3-4 fits the cultural pattern of the time (see below) and requires no allegorical explanation; the replacement guests of vv. 8-10 are apparently recruited from the king's own city, and are not described as foreigners. It may therefore be more prudent to read this parable more generally as a warning, as in the preceding two parables, that those who refuse God's call face ultimate exclusion and replacement, and to leave the specific application to the setting within which the story is read. Its message to the original hearers is not necessarily the same as that discerned by a later Christian reader.

In this parable the symbolism invades the telling of the story even more blatantly than in the last, notably in vv. 6-7 in the gratuitous violence of the invited guests against the king's errand bearers and even more in the scale of the king's retribution — a military expedition launched while the meal gets cold, and the burning of their *city*, rather than simply their personal punishment — after which the festivities are resumed with new guests. There is also the improbability that all those originally invited live in the same city, which is apparently not that of the king himself. As usual, the more improbable the details of the story, the more likely they are to indicate the intended application. So just as the failure of the current leadership is going to open the way not just for new leaders but for a new "nation" (21:43), so now their refusal of God's call will lead to the destruction of Jerusalem itself.

This parable further clarifies not only the failure of the leaders and its consequence, but also the nature of the new "nation." They are symbolized now by an indiscriminate collection of people from the streets, people of no special standing, just as in 21:31 it is the lowest social groups who will get into the kingdom of God first. This feature of the story speaks of the universal proclamation of the good news of the kingdom of heaven. But this time

822

there is a new and jarring note from the point of view of the Christian reader. These new invitees contain "bad as well as good" (v. 10; cf. "of every kind" in a similar context in 13:47), and the second part of the parable focuses on one of those who turns out to be "bad"; when he is consigned to the "darkness outside" and the "weeping and gnashing of teeth" (cf. 8:12; 25:30), the symbolism again invades the story, as the punishment far exceeds the scale of the man's offense. So to be a member of the new "nation" is no more a guarantee of salvation than to be born into the old Israel; it still depends on producing the "fruit," here symbolized by the wedding clothes. The final epigram about the difference between being invited and being chosen applies to the church as well as to Israel.

The concept of a mixed community, within which not all will make it through to ultimate salvation, has been a recurrent feature of this gospel. See above on 7:13-27, especially the "impostors" of 7:21-23 who apparently thought they were all right, and below on 25:1-13, where both wise and foolish bridesmaids are invited but only the wise get into the feast. See also the introductory comments on 13:36-43, where the weeds and the wheat are allowed to grow together and are separated only at the final judgment (cf. also 13:47-50, good and worthless fish in the same net), though I there question the common assumption that that parable is primarily concerned with discipline within the professing church community. But the principle that bad and good are mixed together, and that it is dangerous to judge by appearances or to presume on privilege so far enjoyed, seems basic to Matthew's presentation of the gospel, and here that principle is applied to the new "nation" itself as well as to those whose place it takes.

1-2   This new parable is introduced by one of the standard parable formulae concerning the kingdom of heaven (cf. 13:24; 18:23, and see p. 522, n. 1). As in 18:23 (and as in many rabbinic parables), the chief character is a human king whose exercise of his kingship is a pointer to how God rules. The scale of the story (in comparison with Luke 14:16-24 and *Gos. Thom.* 64) is correspondingly grand, with many slaves and attendants deployed (as against a single slave in Luke and in the *Gospel of Thomas*) and with the king able to launch a military campaign to destroy another city. Another marriage feast parable in 25:1-13 will also symbolize the state of salvation, from which some will be excluded (cf. the imagery of 8:11-12, though there the messianic banquet is not specifically a marriage). Jesus has earlier used the same imagery for his relationship with his disciples in 9:15. The marriage celebrations would normally last for several days, but the focus here is on the initial meal.

3-4   For the social standing of slaves see on 18:23 (and cf. 21:34); a king's slaves are certainly not people to be despised. Their role is not to issue an initial invitation, but to inform those who have already been invited and have accepted that it is time to come.[11] They are sent, therefore, only to the "invited," a privileged group who symbolize the chief priests and elders/ Pharisees who, like the "sons of the kingdom" in 8:12, are expected to share in the feast. When they ignore this second invitation, having already accepted the first, they are going back on their word, like the second son in 21:30 and like the tenant farmers whose acceptance of their tenancy carried with it the obligation to pay the rent. For the social significance both of the invitation and of a refusal to honor it see Keener, 519-20: they are "insulting the dignity of the king." Their refusal, and the king's second appeal, remind the reader of the repeated approaches of the OT prophets to a recalcitrant Israel (and there- fore of the imagery of the preceding parable in 21:34-36). The fact that the second appeal is more fully recorded, and spells out how much the king (God) has already done for his guests (the elite of Israel), heightens the drama and increases the sense of betrayal.

5-6   The response of the first group is the same as that in Luke's par- able (Luke 14:18-20): they have better things to do. Matthew only briefly hints at their prior concerns, mentioning only two commercial interests as against Luke's three examples, but his wording "*his own* farm," "*his* busi- ness" emphasizes that they put their selfish concerns before their responsibil- ity to the king (God). They just don't care (the essential meaning of *ameleō*, translated "took no notice" above) about the will of God. But in v. 6 the stakes are raised: in another clear echo of the preceding parable, some of the messengers are subjected to violence and death.[12] See on 21:34-36 for the fate of the OT prophets, and of John the Baptist, the latest messenger sent to summon God's people. This parable has no separate "son" figure,[13] so that Jesus himself may also be understood to be among the martyred messengers.

7   The treatment of the slaves in v. 6 was already disproportionate to the story situation; now the account of the king's response to this act of defiance seems to take us right outside the wedding context, both in the sud- den transition to a military campaign and in the phrase "their city" — for it is surely likely that a king would have invited his own subjects to the wed-

---

11. The cultural background to this "double invitation" system is well explained by K. E. Bailey, *Peasant Eyes,* 94-95. Bailey points out that the decision on which animals should be butchered is based on the initial acceptances; this gives force to the king's com- plaint in v. 4. See also Keener, 519.

12. There is an interesting parallel in Josephus, *Ant.* 9.265, where Hezekiah in- vites the northern Israelites to come to Jerusalem to celebrate the Passover, and they mock and spit on the messengers and finally kill them. While this parable does not have the overtly political dimension of Josephus's story, it is clear that to refuse a king's invitation was more than just a social gaffe.

13. The "son" mentioned in v. 2 plays no part in the story, but simply provides the setting for the feast.

ding, and that if any of the guests were from elsewhere they would not all have lived in a single city which was not part of his kingdom. Most interpreters agree[14] that this is a specific allusion to the destruction of Jerusalem in A.D. 70, when large parts of the city were burned by the conquering Romans (Josephus, *War* 6.353-55, 363-64, 406-8). It is usually assumed that this must be a reflection by Matthew writing after the event.[15] But it would not have been difficult for a politically astute observer in the sixties to see what was likely to happen, so that this is not necessarily an argument for a post-70 date for the gospel (see above, pp. 18-19).[16] Whether Jesus himself is to be credited with the prophetic insight to know what would happen a generation later is a question which will concern us when we consider his predictions of the destruction of the temple in 23:38 and 24:2; this specific reference is of a piece with that tradition.[17] It is interesting to note that to speak of the burning of the city rather than the temple corresponds to Josephus's account of what the Roman army did in A.D. 70, whereas the burning of the temple is attributed to the Jewish defenders (*War* 6.165-68, 346). To attribute the Roman devastation to the troops of the king (God) echoes the robust theology of the OT prophets who hailed pagan conquerors as God's instruments (Isa 10:5-11; 44:28–45:7; Jer 25:9, etc.). The phrase "their city" thus depicts the devastating result of the failure of Jerusalem's current leadership; Jerusalem is now no longer God's city but "theirs," and the community as a whole is implicated in their rebellion and its punishment, as had so often happened in the past when Israel's sins had led to the city's destruction by invading armies.

8-10   After the murder of the earlier slaves (v. 6), a new group are now sent (hence perhaps the phrase "*those* slaves" in v. 10). The former invitees have proved not to be "worthy"[18] by their refusal to put into practice their professed acceptance of his invitation. They are replaced by others still from the king's own city, and so probably intended to represent the ordinary

14. Gundry, 436-37, is an exception. He argues that the wording is derived from Isa 5:24-25, and so needs no historical basis. There is little in the wording of Isa 5:24-25 to support this theory.

15. For a careful statement of this argument see D. C. Sim, *Gospel*, 33-40.

16. K. H. Rengstorf in W. Eltester (ed.), *Judentum*, 106-29, demonstrates that the terms used here are not uniquely appropriate to A.D. 70 but are typical of standard descriptions of punitive expeditions in a wide range of literature from ancient Assyria to the rabbis, and concludes that this passage cannot be used to date the gospel after A.D. 70. Cf. B. Reicke in D. E. Aune (ed.), *Studies*, 121-34.

17. Keener, 518-19, lists a number of considerations supporting the possibility "that Jesus spoke of the city being burned."

18. ἄξιος, the same term which has been used for those who receive Jesus' messengers in 10:11-13, and for disciples who risk their lives for him in 10:37-38.

people and the despised within Israel[19] (cf. 9:11-13), whereas Luke's two phases of invitation probably symbolize first Jews, then Gentiles; the Gentile mission is not drawn out in Matthew's parable,[20] though the reader might infer this from the wider context. These replacement guests are less apparently worthy, but, for all their lack of natural advantages, they are at least willing to come when they are invited and need no second invitation. The deliberately indiscriminate nature of this second wave of invitations reflects the open offer of the good news through the ministry of Jesus, and the fact that "bad as well as good" respond to it depicts the messy reality of church life (see introductory comments above). This is an uncomfortable parable for advocates of a "pure church" ecclesiology.

11-13   This final scene, with no counterpart in the Lucan version, is nonetheless expressed as a direct continuation of the story, not as a separate parable. The "coming in" of the king, like the "coming" of the owner in 21:40, does not require an allegorical significance, but the clear element of judgment in what follows at least allows the interpretation of his "inspection" of the guests as the final judgment; the description of the fate of the ejected guest supports the same reference.

When the guests have just been brought in from the street, it seems surprising that one of them can be faulted for not being properly dressed, but again we must remember that a parable is not obliged to reflect real life. However, the issue has troubled some readers, and is normally addressed by the traditional speculation (deriving from Augustine) that the host was himself responsible for providing a wedding robe, so that this man's fault was in his refusal to accept what was freely offered. That is good Augustinian theology, but it lacks any convincing evidence in terms of contemporary wedding customs.[21] The clothing expected at a wedding was not a special garment (like our "morning dress") but decent, clean white clothes such as anyone should have had available.[22] In that case the man's fault is that, even though invited to a royal wedding, he had not gone home to change into his best; to

---

19. Cf. Carter, 436: "When the elite do not come, they are replaced by those of the lower social orders, not of a different ethnicity."

20. D. C. Sim, *Gospel,* 239-40, argues that it is not envisaged at all.

21. M. D. Goulder, *Midrash,* 416, mentions Judg 14:12-13 and 2 Kgs 10:22, but the former refers to wedding *gifts* and the latter to vestments for worship. Gundry, 439, offers other equally irrelevant references, only one of which, Rev 19:8, refers to a wedding, but speaks of the clothing of the bride, not of the guests.

22. So J. D. M. Derrett, *Law,* 142. J. Jeremias, *Parables,* 187-88, quotes a parable of Johanan Ben Zakkai from *b. Šabb.* 153a where the wearing of dirty working clothes excludes the unprepared guests. A later version of the story identifies the clean clothes of the accepted guests as "fulfilment of the commandments, good works, and the study of the Torah" (ibid., n. 71)

turn up in ordinary, dirty clothes was an insult to the host.[23] The symbolism is of someone who presumes on the free offer of salvation by assuming that therefore there are no obligations attached, someone whose life belies their profession: faith without works. Entry to the kingdom of heaven may be free, but to continue in it carries conditions. Even though this man belongs to the new group of invitees, he is one who produces no fruit, and so is no less liable to forfeit his new-found privilege than those who were excluded before him. As the parable of the sower has reminded us, there is many a slip between initial response to the word of God and ultimate fruitfulness.

"Tie him hand and foot, and throw him into the darkness" is similar to the language of *1 En.* 10:4 on the fate of Azazel, the leader of the fallen angels.[24] For the full formula, "the darkness outside . . . weeping and gnashing of teeth," cf. 8:12; 25:30. The weeping and gnashing of teeth also appears in 13:42, 50; 24:51, in each case to draw out the significance of a parable of ultimate rejection.[25] See on 8:12 for the conventional use of this phrase for the fate of the ungodly.

14 This epigram[26] sums up the message of this parable, and indeed also of the two which precede it. It picks up the language of the parable: the first group of guests had all been "invited" (vv. 3, 4, 8), but that did not mean that they would enjoy the feast. So in their place others have been "invited" (v. 9), but now even one of them has failed to make the grade. Who then are the "chosen"? The term will recur in 24:22, 24 to designate God's true people, threatened but protected through the time of trial, and in 24:31 for those summoned from all over the world to make up the new people of God after the failure of the old regime. It is a term with strongly ideological overtones deriving from the OT concept of Israel as God's chosen people.[27] But its use here and in 24:31 introduces a radically new element to that ideological concept: the true "chosen people" is not automatically identified with those who

23. See R. J. Bauckham, *JBL* 115 (1996) 485-86, for the narrative plausibility of this scene.

24. D. C. Sim, *JSNT* 47 (1992) 3-19, argues that Matthew composed these words directly from the text of *1 Enoch*. But direct dependence is not the only, or perhaps the most likely, explanation of the use of common apocalyptic imagery. Sim's consequent interpretation of vv. 11-13 as drawing on the imagery in the *Apocalypse of Abraham* of a heavenly garment forfeited by Azazel in favor of Abraham is therefore not compelling.

25. "Attendants" (διάκονοι) here stands out as a different word from the "slaves" who issued the invitations. Gundry, 440, suggests that it represents the angels who carry out the judgment in 13:41, 49.

26. The same saying is also inappropriately added to 20:16 in many MSS.

27. It is this linguistic background which determines the connotations of the term here rather than the Pauline language of "election" (still less later Reformed theology). Those who turn out not to be "chosen" have made their own choice in vv. 3-6.

belong to the Israelite community, not even those who are its official leaders: these are the invited, but not necessarily the chosen. The "many" and the "few"[28] speak of a weeding process, whereby many of those invited will not make it to the feast.[29] The chosen are the new tenants who will produce the fruit, who, as we have seen in the last parable, may be Jewish or Gentile; their chosenness does not depend on their racial origin but on their response to God's summons and their readiness to give God his due. The principle applies both to the old Israel (vv. 3-7) and to those who have taken their place (vv. 8-13).

C. THREE CHALLENGES AND A COUNTERCHALLENGE (22:15-46)

After Jesus' long parabolic monologue, the dialogue which began in 21:23-27 is resumed. The grouping in threes which we have noted since the beginning of ch. 21 continues now with a series of three questions addressed to Jesus by representative groups of religious leaders in Jerusalem (Pharisees with Herodians, Sadducees, and a Pharisee), each of which concerns a genuine issue in theology or ethics, but each of which also requires diplomacy to avoid causing offense to at least one influential group. Matthew therefore says that the first question was designed as a trap, and that the third was a "test," while the derisory tone of the second speaks for itself. Jesus' reply to the first question leaves his opponents "amazed," and his response to the second "silences" the Sadducees; no mention is made of any reaction after the third encounter, but Jesus' reply has left no obvious grounds for objection.

The series is concluded by a searching counterquestion from Jesus to the Pharisees, to which they attempt no answer, and as a result the sequence comes to an end since "no one dared ask him any more questions." Jesus is left in possession of the field, and immediately takes advantage of his dominant position to utter a long and devastating monologue against the scribes and Pharisees in ch. 23.

The scene throughout remains in the temple courtyard, and we are reminded of the listening crowd (for which see on 21:45-46 above) by a single notice in v. 33 that they were astonished at Jesus' teaching. Their favorable

28. Cf. 7:13-14 and the comments there on the idea of the saved as a minority. Hagner, 2:632, following B. F. Meyer, *NTS* 36 (1990) 89-97, argues, however, that the terms are a Semitic idiom for "all" and "not all" rather than focusing on the fewness of the chosen. On the other hand, B. Charette, *Recompense,* 150, n. 3, asserts that "'few' is a *heilsgeschichtlich* category" and speaks of the chosen as "merely a remnant."

29. Davies and Allison, 3:206, are reminded of "Judas, who was 'called' (10:1-4) but not 'chosen.'"

reaction will be presupposed in the way Jesus takes them to be on his side against the scribes and Pharisees in 23:1-12.

1. The Question about the Poll Tax (22:15-22)

> 15 *Then the Pharisees went and consulted together on how they could trap him in what he said.*[1] 16 *So they sent their disciples to him together with the Herodians, with the question, "Teacher, we know that you are a truthful person and that you teach the way of God in truth and take no notice of anyone, since you are not impressed by people's status.*[2] 17 *So tell us what you think: Is it right to pay the poll tax to the emperor or not?"* 18 *Jesus recognized their malicious intention and replied, "Why are you trying to trap me, you hypocrites?* 19 *Show me the coin which is used for paying the poll tax." They brought him a denarius,* 20 *and he asked them, "Whose image and inscription is this?"* 21 *"The emperor's," they replied. Then he said to them, "So give back to the emperor what is the emperor's, and to God what is God's."* 22 *They were amazed when they heard this, and they left him and went away.*

The first question is the one with the most obvious political implications. The poll tax had been among the taxes imposed on Judea following the imposition of direct Roman rule in A.D. 6, not long before, and had been fiercely resented by patriotic Jews, resulting in a serious revolt led by Judas (Josephus, *War* 2.117-18; *Ant.* 18.4-10). That revolt was the inspiration for the later Zealot movement which led to the war of independence beginning in A.D. 66 and so to the fall of Jerusalem and the destruction of its temple in A.D. 70. Judas, the leader of that first revolt, had been a Galilean, and now here was another Galilean who claimed to be a leader of his people; so what was his view on this political hot potato? The question had a superficial innocence about it since Jesus, as a Galilean under Herod's jurisdiction, was not subject to this particular tax, and so was in a position to give an "objective" opinion without his personal political status being affected. But there is little doubt that a negative answer would have been used to denounce him to the Roman authorities (as Luke 20:20 says explicitly) as another Galilean

---

1. The metaphor of a verbal "snare" is not just about getting the better of him in argument, but inducing him to say something which might prove incriminating.

2. Literally, "you do not look at people's face." Cf. προσωπολημψία, "face-taking," as a term for partiality or concern with status in Acts 10:34; Rom 2:11; Jas 2:1, 9 and our phrase "loss of face." λαμβάνω πρόσωπον is an LXX term for partiality (Ps 82:2; cf. θαυμάζω πρόσωπον, Lev 19:15; Deut 10:17; Prov 18:5). Cf. also 1 Sam 16:7 for "looking at the outward appearance."

inciting the Judeans to rebellion as Judas had before him. On the other hand, a positive answer would not have endeared Jesus to the Jerusalem crowd, whose patriotism and resentment of Roman rule made them naturally sympathetic to "Zealot" ideology.

Jesus' answer famously avoids either of those dangerous alternatives. Is it then simply a clever evasion? As with his non-answer to the authorities in 21:23-27, there is more to it than that. In two ways it undercuts his questioners' position, and in so doing provides an answer in principle which has much wider application than simply to their trick question.

In the first place, Jesus' request for a denarius was more than just the provision of a visual aid. Pious Jews objected to the "idolatrous" coin, which carried not only a human portrait (in contravention of the second commandment, Exod 20:4) but also an inscription which described the Roman emperor as *Divi Filius,* son of a god (in contravention of the first commandment, Exod 20:3). Roman imperial policy, aware of this sensitivity, allowed the Jews to coin their own nonidolatrous copper money, which sufficed for normal everyday business;[3] there was therefore no need for them to carry the silver denarius, a coin of higher value.[4] And Jesus apparently did not have one — but they did, and in the holy precincts of the temple at that! Well then, if they were using the emperor's (idolatrous) coinage, they could hardly object to paying his tax. The verb in v. 21, "give *back* to the emperor," neatly presses the point, and underlines Jesus' description of them as "hypocrites" (v. 18).[5]

In the second place, Jesus' answer in v. 21 calls into question the basic presupposition behind their question, that there is an essential incompatibility between loyalty to the governing authority and loyalty to God. This was precisely Judas's position as explained by Josephus in *War* 2.118 (cf. *Ant.* 18.23): to pay the tax was to tolerate a mortal sovereign in place of God. Jesus asserts that this is not necessarily so: it is possible to pay one's dues *both* to the emperor *and* to God, to be both a dutiful citizen and a loyal servant of God. This principle, more fully expounded in Rom 13:1-7 and 1 Pet 2:13-17, has now been so widely recognized for so long that it causes no surprise to many of us in many parts of the world, but in first-century Palestine under Roman rule it was not at all so obvious. The theocratic basis of OT Israel, even if it had not been able to prevent periods of tyranny under unscrupulous

3. For the coinage of first-century Palestine see Schürer, 2:62-66, and for the issue of nonidolatrous coins Schürer, 1:379-81.
4. It represented a normal full day's wage (see 20:2). The silver coins themselves were not necessarily used to pay the "denarii" to the workmen in 20:1-10; the story is concerned with the total amount of their wage, not with the currency used.
5. This paragraph follows the argument of J. D. M. Derrett, *Law,* 313-37, which provides much interesting background information.

rulers, had at least in theory held its rulers accountable to God. But the Roman emperor was not under Israel's God, or indeed under any god — according to imperial propaganda he *was* a god. But Jesus' response here puts him in his place: it is possible to be subject to the emperor as ruler, but at the same time to honor God as God.[6]

In practice it is not always so straightforward, as Christians soon discovered, and in the book of Revelation we have an early Christian subversive tract against the "beast" which is Rome and which is in fundamental opposition to the rule of God. When the governing authority takes it upon itself to ignore and to oppose the will of God, loyalty to God may mean that it is no longer possible to accept the authority of the government, and many Christians today find themselves in such a situation, though it is often a matter of controversial judgment as to when the line has been crossed. But Jesus' teaching here is that, contrary to his questioners' assumption, that situation is not the norm. His answer assumes that the Roman government under Tiberius was not yet, as it would become later, in opposition to God. Matthew, in recording this exchange, may well have reflected that in a very short time the local representative of that government would be pronouncing the death sentence on Jesus himself, but his account of that event in ch. 27 will make it clear that Pilate was not acting on his own initiative. In John 19:11 we hear Jesus himself acknowledging Pilate's legitimate authority.[7]

15-16a The Pharisees, already mentioned in 21:45 as among those opposing Jesus in the temple, now take the initiative; it will be one of their number who also asks the third question (vv. 34-35), and it will be to them that Jesus' counterquestion is addressed in v. 41. As those who specialized in matters of the law, embracing both theology and ethics, they would be the natural leaders in controversy with a visiting teacher whose interpretation of the law was a matter of concern. The present question is an ethical one with theological overtones. Its political dimension falls well within the Pharisaic area of interest: it was a Pharisee called Zadok who had been Judas's chief partner in leading the tax revolt (Josephus, *Ant.* 18.4, 9-10). But it is not a dispassionate inquiry. It is designed as a "trap"; see above for the dilemma it was intended to create.

The mention of "Herodians" as associates of the Pharisees is unex-

---

6. *Gos. Thom.* 100 complicates the issue by adding a third clause, "and give to me what is mine." In the absence of any explanation in the text we can only speculate as to how what is due to Jesus might differ from what is due to God. A more expansive version in P. Egerton 2 contains in the preamble elements which parallel John 3:2 and Matt 15:7-9, but unfortunately breaks off before Jesus' answer is given.

7. Keener, 524, n. 201, rightly draws a parallel between Jesus' antirevolutionary answer and the stance of prophets such as Jeremiah who also provoked the hostility of revolutionary nationalists.

pected, since this incident takes place in Judea, which, unlike Galilee, was no longer under Herodian rule. Mark also mentions Herodians in Galilee (Mark 3:6, again in association with Pharisees) as well as here, but the term is not familiar from other first-century sources. The name suggests supporters of the Herodian dynasty, hence perhaps the appropriateness of their involvement in this politically angled approach. Herodians in Jerusalem,[8] where the last Herodian ruler had been deposed in A.D. 6, may still have hankered for the former regime, and so resented the direct Roman government; we may therefore suppose that they were at least uneasy over the poll tax. Most interpreters, however, take them to be pro-Roman establishment figures since the Herodian dynasty owed its power to Rome. We simply do not know.[9]

16b-17 Each of the three questions in vv. 16, 24, and 36 is addressed to Jesus as "Teacher," a title used in Matthew by outsiders rather than by disciples, and appropriate here to one who has set himself up to teach the crowds in the temple courtyard. But the following lengthy, flattering introduction to the question underlines the insincerity of the questioners, already signaled by Matthew's statement of their motive in v. 15. Their estimate of Jesus does, however, correspond well with what we have seen of his style of teaching, unafraid to speak his mind and to challenge accepted traditions. They therefore assume that Jesus prides himself on his independence, and so plan to use it to lead him into a politically sensitive pronouncement.

There were many types of tax under Roman rule, some indirectly levied on trade and movement of goods (see on 9:9). But the poll tax[10] was a direct tax levied on every adult Jew (including women and slaves),[11] and so was a potent symbol of political subjection. See above on 17:25 for the principle that such taxes are levied only on "strangers," in this case subject peoples rather than Roman citizens. The question whether it is "right" (or lawful) to pay it is clearly not concerned with Roman law (which allowed no such question), but with what is right for the people of God under the Torah.

8. These might, however, be Galileans who had accompanied Antipas to Jerusalem for his Passover visit (see Luke 23:7).

9. For discussion of their identity see H. Hoehner, *Herod*, 331-42; N. Hillyer, *NIDNTT* 3:441-43. J. P. Meier, *Marginal Jew*, 3:560-65 (and *JBL* 119 [2000] 740-46), surveys theories of who the "Herodians" were, and, having eliminated the "silliest explanations," offers a further fourteen proposals. His own view is that the term refers to "the servants, courtiers or officials of Herod Antipas" (562).

10. Matthew's term κῆνσος is a Greek transliteration of the Latin *census*, which properly refers to the registration on which the tax was based.

11. See Schürer, 1:401-4, for the quite complicated systems of taxation in the Roman Empire. There was considerable local variation, but it seems likely that the census of A.D. 6 was the basis both for a property tax and for a flat-rate capitation tax (poll tax) proper.

It thus already presupposes the Zealot assumption that what Rome demands God may forbid. It is a question appropriately directed to a religious teacher.

18 In saying that Jesus "recognized" their intention Matthew perhaps intends us to think of his supernatural knowledge of people's thoughts, but the sycophantic nature of their question was in itself enough to betray their insincerity. "Trying to trap me" translates *peirazō,* for which see the introductory comments on 4:1-11; it has been used of Pharisaic approaches to Jesus already in 16:1; 19:3. There is certainly an element of "testing" here, but the malicious intent of the questioners makes this more akin to the devil's "tempting," trying to get Jesus to do or say something which he should not. For "hypocrites" see on 6:2; here its use is closer to our modern sense: they are acting a part, concealing their true motives under a cloak of respectful religious inquiry.

19-21a For the purpose of Jesus' request for a denarius, as a part of his exposure of their hypocrisy, see the introductory comments above. In the light of the itinerant and dependent lifestyle of Jesus and his disciples, it is hardly surprising that they did not have so large a coin available, even if they had been willing to use one. A denarius of Tiberius would carry his garlanded portrait surrounded by the inscription "Ti[berius] Caesar Divi Aug[usti] F[ilius] Augustus"; on the reverse would be "Pontif[ex] Maxim[us]."[12] He is thus proclaimed to be not only son of the divine Augustus, but also a high priest; the two titles together could hardly be more calculated to offend Jewish piety.

The use of "image" to describe the official portrait has been explained by some interpreters as an allusion to the OT concept of the "image of God" in humanity. The implication would then be that if what is due to the emperor is the coin which bears his image, what is due to God is oneself as a person bearing the image of God.[13] It is true that *eikōn* is the LXX term for the "image" of God in Genesis and is used to echo and develop that idea several times in the NT (1 Cor 11:7; 2 Cor 4:4; Col 1:15; 3:10), but it is also used more generally for a visual representation of something, especially in connection with idolatry (Rom 1:23; Rev 13:14-15, etc.), and Josephus uses it specifically of portraits or statues of the emperor (*War* 2.169, 194; *Ant.* 19.185) without any obvious echo of its OT usage. In the absence of any contextual indication of such an echo here, the suggested theological nuance, even though not in itself objectionable, should probably not be assumed.

21b "So" indicates that Jesus' pronouncement is a direct inference from what has been said about the coin. It is the emperor's and so should be returned to him. The verb "give back" (pointedly differing from the ordinary verb to "give" or "pay" which they had used in their question, v. 17) indicates

---

12. See H. StJ. Hart, in E. Bammel and C. F. D. Moule (eds.), *Jesus,* 241-48.
13. So C. H. Giblin, *CBQ* 33 (1971) 510-27; D. T. Owen-Ball, *NovT* 35 (1993) 8-12. The idea is suggested as early as Tertullian.

either the return of something borrowed or the payment of what is due (cf. its use in 5:26, 33; 6:4, 6, 18; 18:25-34; 20:8, etc.).[14] The tax is thus presented not as an arbitrary imposition but as a due payment for the benefits received from the imperial government, which they have acknowledged by using the imperial currency. To Jews smarting under Roman occupation this must have seemed an extraordinary idea; it is certainly not one which a Zealot could have voiced.[15] But see the introductory comments above on the far-reaching ideology of "church and state" which results when this clause is combined with giving to God what is his due — which is just what the Zealots thought they were doing by *opposing* Rome. That ideology needs to be worked out practically for any given situation, and there will be circumstances in which the complementary claims of God and the emperor are not so easily compatible, but Jesus does not allow us to assume that the two are inevitably in conflict. His pronouncement provides a basic principle which, if taken seriously, might have averted many a catastrophe in the relations between religion and politics throughout Christian history.

For giving back to God what is God's cf. the parable of the vineyard, which focuses on the importance of "giving back" (21:41, using the same verb as here) to God the fruits which are his due (21:34, 41, 43); is there the implication that in their concern over what is demanded by the emperor they have forgotten their more important obligation?

22 Their amazement is perhaps initially over Jesus' ability to escape the trap they have set, but it may also include their awareness that he has also expressed a profoundly significant ethical/theological principle. Whether or not his answer earned the grudging respect of those who had raised the question, it is likely that this pronouncement contributed to the (admiring?) astonishment of the listening crowd which will be mentioned in v. 33. The final clause indicates the defeat of this first challenge, leaving Jesus victorious and ready to face a challenge from a different theological direction.

---

14. N. T. Wright, *Victory,* 502-7, sees in the use of this term a deliberate echo of 1 Macc 2:68, where Mattathias calls on his sons to "Pay back the Gentiles in full, and obey the commands of the law" (the Greek is not the same, using ἀνταποδίδωμι rather than simply ἀποδίδωμι and with the addition of the cognate noun ἀνταπόδομα as object, whereas the implied object here is the denarius, but the echo might still be heard by those aware of the text). The sense there is of "paying back" in revenge, not in submission, and Wright develops an argument that Jesus' reply was deliberately coded so that it could be heard either as a call to rebellion or as a call to pay the tax. Such an interpretation, which is not supported by any other aspect of the wording of this pericope, must depend on the familiarity of his audience with 1 Maccabees.

15. On the attempt of S. G. F. Brandon, *Zealots,* 345ff., to interpret Jesus' answer as compatible with Zealot ideology see F. F. Bruce, in E. Bammel and C. F. D. Moule (eds.), *Jesus,* 259-60. Bruce's article contains much useful background on this pericope as a whole.

2. The Question about Resurrection and Marriage (22:23-33)

23 *That same day Jesus was approached by Sadducees, who say*[1] *there is no resurrection. They asked him,* 24 *"Teacher, Moses said, 'If anyone dies without having children, his brother is to marry*[2] *his wife and raise up offspring for his brother.'* 25 *Now there were seven broth- ers among us. The first married and then died, and since he had no offspring, he left his wife to his brother.* 26 *The same thing happened with the second and the third, and so on for all seven.* 27 *Last of all, the woman died.* 28 *So in the resurrection which of the seven will she be the wife of, since they all had her?"*

29 *Jesus replied to them, "You are wide of the mark, because you know neither the Scriptures nor the power of God.* 30 *For in the resur- rection people do not marry and are not married, but they are like angels*[3] *in heaven.* 31 *But about the resurrection of the dead: Haven't you read what was declared to you by God when he said,* 32 *'I am the God of Abraham, and the God of Isaac, and the God of Jacob'? He is not the God*[4] *of the dead but of the living."*

33 *And as the crowd listened, they were astonished at his teaching.*

---

1. Many MSS make the nature of this clause clear by reading οἱ λέγοντες rather than simply λέγοντες, but even the latter reading (which, as the rougher syntax, is probably the original) is surely intended here to have a relative sense rather than introducing direct speech, since their question is introduced by a second λέγοντες at the beginning of v. 24. I find it most unlikely (*pace* GNB, NRSV) that Matthew would portray them as first explicitly stating that there is no resurrection and then going straight on to ask a question which presupposes that belief. Still less compelling is the argument of J. P. Meier, *Law,* 18-19, that Matthew's λέγοντες reveals his ignorance of the general Sadducean position by suggesting that this was merely their approach on this particular occasion; see my *Matthew: Evangelist,* 106.

2. This is not the normal verb for "marry," but ἐπιγαμβρεύω, which occurs no- where else in the NT and is a term used in the LXX for "to become related to by mar- riage." It is derived from a term which in LXX means "father-in-law" or "son-in-law," but in classical Greek also "brother-in-law"; so here it means "be an in-law to," i.e., do what is the duty of a (brother-)in-law. The OT law makes it clear that that duty was marriage, not merely providing an heir. The uncompounded form γάμβρευσαι occurs in LXX Gen 38:8, which Matthew is here echoing.

3. Some MSS add an article, "the angels," and many go further and say "God's angels." Most critics think it more likely that an originally simpler text was expanded, but the meaning is not significantly affected.

4. MSS and critics are divided as to whether there was originally an article before θεός. The question affects the syntax (with an article "God" is the subject; without it the predicate) but not the meaning, since "He [God, understood from the previous sentence] is not God of the dead but of the living" and "God is not of the dead but of the living" come to the same thing, so that it is impossible to tell which reading the versions followed. Some later MSS, aware of the syntactical problem, made sure by adding a further θεός.

With the spotlight now moving to the Sadducees,[5] we meet the other main theological viewpoint within the Sanhedrin (Acts 23:6-10), which most of the priests, and probably the elders, would have supported. Jesus has disposed of his Pharisaic questioners, so now the attack comes from the other wing. This time, however, it is not a politically loaded question, but one which asks Jesus to declare his stance on one of the main theological issues which divided Jewish opinion. The question presupposes (and ridicules) the Pharisaic belief in resurrection, presumably with the expectation that Jesus would declare his position in favor of the Pharisaic view[6] and thus alienate a large (and probably at this time the more influential) part of the Sanhedrin. Josephus (*Ant.* 18.15-17) tells us that the Pharisees enjoyed greater popular support, but their "progressive" theology was rejected by the more conservative ruling classes. But the aim is not simply to get Jesus to align himself publicly with one faction, but also to discredit him as a teacher by making him appear foolish in public: the scenario which the Sadducees propose is designed to expose the whole resurrection idea, which Jesus is assumed to support, as ridiculous.

Belief in life after death seems to emerge late in the development of OT thought. Many of the expressions of future hope especially in the Psalms (Pss 16:9-11; 49:15; 73:23-26; cf. Job 19:25-27), which are naturally taken to refer to life after death once that belief is established, need not have been so understood originally. The resuscitation of dead bodies in Ezek 37:1-14 was only a symbolic expression of the hope of the restoration of Israel; even Isa 26:19 *could* be interpreted in the same way. The explicit prediction in Dan 12:2 that the dead will rise stands out as exceptional (and late) within the OT canon. From the second century B.C. onward belief in life after death is expressed increasingly clearly in Jewish literature, particularly in connection with the martyrs of the Maccabean period.[7] But it was easy for the Sadducees, for whom the five books of Moses were the supreme authority (Josephus, *Ant.* 18.16), to dismiss this as an aberration from the this-worldly focus of the true Mosaic religion. For them Sheol was the final resting place, and any futurity was to be looked for in terms of reputation and posterity, not personal survival or resurrection.

5. For a recent discussion of the historical evidence for the Sadducees see G. G. Porton, *ABD* 5:892-95. More fully, Schürer, 2:404-14.

6. A belief in life after death is presupposed in some of Jesus' sayings: see Luke 14:14; 16:19-31; 23:43, and more generally his teaching on judgment and eternal life or eternal punishment (25:31-46 etc.). His prediction of his own resurrection (16:21; 17:9, 23; 20:19), while it relates only to his own unique situation, presupposes that resurrection is possible.

7. OT and later Jewish beliefs about resurrection are fully surveyed by G. W. E. Nickelsburg, *Resurrection;* H. C. C. Cavallin, *Life after Death: Part 1.* See also a brief summary in Keener, 710-11.

Jesus' response is on two fronts. First he takes up the specific issue they have raised and explains how they have misunderstood the nature of resurrection life by assuming that it must be analogous to the present life (v. 30). But then he turns to the basic issue underlying their question, whether there are scriptural grounds for believing in resurrection at all. Aware of the Sadducees' disregard for the later parts of the OT, he draws his argument from a central text within the books of Moses themselves (vv. 31-32). As with all the places in this gospel where Jesus asks "Haven't you read?" the text is one with which they are very familiar, but the inference Jesus draws from it is one which they would not have thought of. In this case one must feel some sympathy for them, since Jesus' argument is so briefly and cryptically expressed that even the Christian reader with a belief in resurrection needs to read between the lines to see how this text supports it. But the narrative gives the impression that it was an unanswerable argument, leaving the crowd favorably impressed and the Sadducees silenced (vv. 33-34).

23 "That same day" is an editorial connection (cf. 13:1 for the same phrase), which serves to hold together the series of disparate debating topics as part of a single complex; an equally clear connective in v. 34 will lead into the third. We have met Sadducees in 3:7 and in 16:1-12, in each case associated with Pharisees. But here Matthew makes it clear that he is well aware of the fundamental difference between these two groups despite the "coalition" which they operated within the Sanhedrin. For the beliefs of the Sadducees see Josephus, *War* 2.164-65; *Ant.* 13.278-79; 18.16-17 (N.B., "souls disappear along with bodies"); Acts 23:8. Josephus speaks of them as a minority movement, finding their support among the wealthy and powerful but with little popular appeal. They included some of the leading priestly families[8] and so controlled the temple establishment.[9] After the destruction of the temple their power quickly waned. Their disbelief in life after death was not necessarily their most important tenet, but it is mentioned here, as in Acts 23:8, as the key to understanding the question they raise. It also exposes the cynical nature of their question, which presupposes a belief they themselves reject.

24 For "Teacher" see on v. 16b; its politeness here is ironical, since they are going on to embarrass him on the basis of what he teaches. Their starting point is the Mosaic institution of levirate marriage, which was designed to provide a continuing family line for a man who died childless and so preserve both his name and his material inheritance.[10] As a policy it was

---

8. Including apparently that of the current high priest, Caiaphas; see Acts 5:17 with 4:6.

9. See J. Jeremias, *Jerusalem,* 228-32.

10. Josephus, *Ant.* 4.254, also points out its value as a provision for an otherwise destitute widow.

perhaps more honored in theory than in actual practice. There are only two instances of a similar principle being invoked in the OT, in both of which the surviving relative proves reluctant (Gen 38:6-11; Ruth 4:5-10), though the existence of a large body of rabbinic regulation for levirate marriage (*m. Yebamot*) shows that it continued to be valid, at least in theory. The Sadducees give a summary of the essence of the law rather than an actual quotation. It outlines the provision of Deut 25:5-6, but the clause "marry her and raise up offspring [literally, "seed"] for his brother" echoes the LXX of the prototype example in Gen 38:8 (including the LXX special term for such marriage; see p. 835, n. 2). "Raise up" is *anistēmi*, the cognate verb of *anastasis*, "resurrection," which is the underlying issue (vv. 23, 28, 30, 31), and the echo is surely deliberate: the production of an heir is the only sort of "resurrection" of the dead brother that their theology allows.

25-28   The story they tell is not necessarily factual, despite "among us," though it is theoretically possible.[11] It is intended as a *reductio ad absurdum* of the idea of resurrection since the woman is destined to spend eternity as the wife of seven men at once, and polyandry is not acceptable in Jewish culture. But even though the question is intended to be facetious, it does in fact raise a significant pastoral issue for those who believe in life after death, since even without levirate marriage there are and always have been many people who have been married more than once; if what were successive marriages on earth become "contemporaneous" in heaven, what does that do to the nature of the marriage relationship? For many people the prospect of encountering more than one former spouse in the afterlife is a real one. The question, even if not the questioners, deserves a serious answer.

29   Jesus traces their error to two related causes, with which he will deal in reverse order in vv. 30-32: their ignorance of what is written in Scripture (in response to which he will mount a scriptural argument in vv. 31-32) and their basically secular viewpoint, "not knowing the power of God"[12] (a viewpoint which results from not being sufficiently open to scriptural truth). The accusation of not knowing the Scriptures would be particularly provocative when addressed to a group whose beliefs were proudly founded on the books of Moses rather than on later (unscriptural) developments. Josephus's description of Sadducean ideas focuses on their contempt for supernatural explanations: they do not believe in fate and "place God beyond doing any-

11. The seven successive unconsummated marriages of Sarah in Tob 3:7-9 are not strictly comparable, since her husbands are not said to be brothers. The recurrence of the number "seven" in the two stories is probably a folklore motif (so Davies and Allison, 3:225, n. 27, citing "Seven Brides for Seven Brothers").

12. D. Instone-Brewer, *Traditions,* 1:115-16, suggests that Jesus' words may allude to the well-known (Pharisaic) prayer, the Eighteen Benedictions, which included the declaration, "You are powerful . . . raising the dead."

thing evil or even seeing it," and as a result attribute everything to human free will, and will have nothing to do with judgment and rewards or penalties after death (*War* 2.164-68). They sound rather like what later became known as Deists. Because they see everything in terms of this world, and do not reckon on any real divine dimension, of course they are not going to be able to understand about life after death.

30 "In the resurrection" speaks not of the *event* of being raised from death, but of the state of life which follows from it, so that in effect it means "in heaven."[13] Since the question raised has been about marriage, it is on that aspect of heavenly life that Jesus' answer focuses, but the principle could be stated more broadly: it is a mistake to picture life in heaven as being simply an extrapolation of life on earth (cf. the argument of 1 Cor 15:35-50). "The power of God" (v. 29) creates something different, fitted to a life which is not temporary but eternal. Sexual life is obviously affected by this, since procreation belongs to earthly not to heavenly life where there is no birth, growth, or death. Marriage, as the institution within which earthly procreation is set, is therefore out of place. And that means that the exclusiveness which links one man with one woman in a jealously guarded relationship will no longer apply. People in heaven will be like the angels, who do not marry or procreate because they are eternal.[14]

That seems to be the logic of Jesus' response as it relates to the problem of multiple earthly marriages. It solves the problem by declaring the marriage relationship to be a temporary, earthly thing. But is this too high a price to pay? Those who have found some of the deepest joys of earthly life in the special bond of a married relationship may be dismayed to hear that that must be left behind. But note that what Jesus declares to be inappropriate in heaven is marriage,[15] not love. So perhaps heavenly relationships are not something *less* than marriage, but something *more*. He does not say that the love between those who have been married on earth will vanish, but rather implies that it will be broadened so that no one is excluded. Our problem is that we, like the Sadducees, have only this life's experience by which to measure what is to come. We do not know what it is like to be like angels in heaven.

13. *Pace* Hagner, 2:638, who speaks of the resurrection as "a future event" and so translates all the present tenses here as futures.
14. Cf. *1 En.* 15:7: God did not make wives for the angels because they are "the spiritual beings of heaven." Angels are always described as male in biblical and related literature; female angels are a later idea. Davies and Allison, 3:229-30, provide much interesting information on the sexuality of angels.
15. The process of "marrying and being married." The two verbs γαμέω and γαμίζω normally refer respectively to the role of the bridegroom and of the bride's father ("give in marriage"), so that the combined expression describes the initial joining of bridegroom and bride.

31-32 *Peri de,* "But about . . . ," signals a change of subject (see below on 24:36). Jesus has answered the specific question asked, but now turns to the basic theology which prompted it. Since the Sadducees accepted only the five books of Moses (which they have quoted as "Moses" in v. 24) as their basic scriptural authority, he draws his argument from within those books,[16] even though it could have been more obviously derived from Dan 12:2 or other prophetic and wisdom texts (see above). The text is God's address[17] to Moses at the burning bush (Exod 3:6), slightly abbreviated from the LXX.[18] While addressed to Moses in the narrative setting, as part of Holy Scripture it is also God's declaration "to you." This description of Yahweh as the God of the patriarchs is very familiar from all over the OT; what is not familiar is the inference Jesus draws from it. By identifying himself with these famous men, whose earthly life was finished centuries before he spoke to Moses, God implies that that relationship still holds good. It is sometimes suggested that Jesus' argument depends on the tense of the verb, "I am" rather than "I was," and that this argument must therefore depend on the LXX since no verb is expressed in the Hebrew.[19] But that is too superficial an account of Jesus' reasoning. The argument is not linguistic: "I am the God of Abraham" would be a perfectly intelligible way for God to identify himself as the God whom Abraham worshiped long ago. The argument is based rather on the nature of God's relationship with his human followers: the covenant by which he binds himself to them is too strong to be terminated by their death. To be associated with the living God is to be taken beyond the temporary life of earth into a relationship which lasts as long as God lasts. Those with whom the living God identifies himself cannot be truly dead, and therefore they must be alive with

16. Cf. *b. Sanh.* 90b, which lists a number of rabbinic (and therefore Pharisaic) attempts to prove the resurrection from the Torah. One of them (R. Simai, c. A.D. 210) is quite similar to Jesus' argument here: Exod 6:4 says that God had made a covenant with "them" (Abraham, Isaac, and Jacob) to give them the land of Canaan; "it does not say 'to give you' but 'to give them'; thus the resurrection is proved from the Torah." There is also a similar argument based on Deut 11:9 attributed to R. Gamaliel. *M. Sanh.* 10:1 includes among those who have no share in the world to come "anyone who says that resurrection of the dead is not stated in the Torah" (presumably the Sadducees, who would hardly be worried by this threat!).

17. For the participle τὸ ῥηθέν as the mark of a divine pronouncement see p. 55, n. 54.

18. Matthew's inclusion of the article before each occurrence of θεός probably derives from this abbreviation; in the LXX the article of the summary clause which he has omitted, ὁ θεὸς τοῦ πατρός σου, does duty for the following subsidiary phrases, but in Matthew's abbreviated form they must stand alone and therefore need their own article.

19. R. H. Gundry, *Use,* 21, speculates that the verb may have been absent from the LXX too, and added later as a stylistic improvement. He nonetheless argues that "the present tense, whether expressed or understood, is necessary to [Jesus'] argument."

him after their earthly life is finished. It is an argument of faith rather than of strict logic,[20] and Sadducean theology, with its distant God and human autonomy, would probably not find it convincing. But for those who give more weight to "the power of God" (v. 29) it provides an assurance that life after death was not just an innovative theology of the intertestamental period, but finds its root in the essential nature of the living, covenant-making God himself. "God of the dead" is not a title appropriate to the God revealed in the Pentateuch.[21]

33 These words are closely similar to 7:28, the reaction of the Galilean crowd after Jesus' first extended teaching. It was clear there that the "astonishment" was in a positive sense: they are strongly and favorably impressed. In relation to the pericope just concluded this fits Josephus's description of Sadducean theology as an unpopular minority position, whereas the majority supported the Pharisees with their more "spiritual" beliefs, including life after death; the crowd gratefully judges that Jesus has won that theological argument. But the "listening" on which their favorable verdict is based is probably intended to be wider than just this pericope.[22] What is expressed here is the cumulative impact of Jesus' teaching in Jerusalem up to this point. He has the crowd on his side.

3. The Question about the Greatest Commandment (22:34-40)

34 *But when the Pharisees heard that he had silenced the Sadducees, they came together,*[1] 35 *and one of them, a lawyer,*[2] *asked him a*

20. An interesting article by D. Cohn-Sherbok, *JSNT* 11 (1981) 64-73, also argues that Jesus' argument here does not follow the rules of rabbinic hermeneutics; see, however, some cautionary comments by Davies and Allison, 3:232-33.

21. J. G. Janzen, *JSNT* 23 (1985) 43-58, suggests a further nuance in that a prominent element in the stories of the patriarchs referred to (and in the story of Judah to which the Gen 38:8 allusion in v. 24 refers) was sterility and the lack of an heir, which was overcome by the power of God. In that way, he suggests, Jesus' answer here deals not merely with the underlying issue of life after death but also with the test case in vv. 25-28 of a failure to provide an heir through levirate marriage.

22. There is no expressed object after the verb "listened," despite the "this" or "it" found in most English versions.

1. The phrase ἐπὶ τὸ αὐτό ("together," "in the same place") seems redundant after συνάγομαι (literally, "be brought together"). It serves not to add to the sense but to convey an allusion to the LXX (see below). I have therefore left it untranslated.

2. A few MSS agree with Luke 10:25 in reading here νομικός τις rather than simply νομικός, while a few omit the term altogether (perhaps influenced by Mark, where the same question is asked not by a "lawyer" but by a scribe). The vast majority, including most of the oldest MSS, read νομικός. The indefinite τις would be inappropriate here when he has already been identified as one of the Pharisees.

test question: 36 *"Teacher, which is the great commandment in the law?"* 37 *Jesus replied, " 'You are to love the Lord your God with all your heart and with all your soul and with all your thinking.'* 38 *This is the great and first commandment.* 39 *But there is a second which is like it: 'You are to love your neighbor as yourself.'* 40 *The whole law and the prophets hang on these two commandments."*

With the third question we return to the original questioners, the Pharisees. There is a marked sequence between this and the last pericope, which can be obscured by the paragraph division: the Sadducees have been routed and the crowd are on Jesus' side, so the Pharisees decide it is time to regain the initiative. The question is posed by a single Pharisee, but Matthew's depiction of the purposeful gathering of the group suggests that this single lawyer is a spokesman for them all, and the repetition of the term *peirazō,* "test" (see on v. 18 and cf. its use also in 16:1; 19:3, and the even stronger "trap" in v. 15), makes it clear that this is not simply academic debate.

But the question is not political like the previous Pharisaic question. Like the Sadducees' question it is essentially theological, but this time with a focus on the law which gives it a more strongly ethical slant. As an issue going to the heart of the Mosaic law it is appropriately raised by a Pharisaic lawyer. It would not be an unfamiliar question, since rabbis did discuss which of the commandments were "heavy" and which "light,"[3] and sometimes tried to summarize the main thrust of the Mosaic law in terms of a key OT text (see below on v. 36). Since the five books of Moses contained, by rabbinic calculation, 613 commandments,[4] some means of assessing their relative importance would be widely appreciated.[5] But to provide this must involve choosing one legal principle over others, and this carried the risk that other teachers, who might have made a different choice, could accuse their colleague of belittling the importance of some other equally scriptural principle. Any answer must risk pleasing some at the expense of alienating others, and therein perhaps is the element of "test" from an unsympathetic dialogue partner, particularly in view of the suspicion already noted in 5:17 that Jesus had come to "abolish" the law. If he differed radically from mainstream Jewish orthodoxy, this question ought to reveal it.

---

3. See on 23:23 below. "Light" did not mean dispensable; all commandments remained in force, but priority could nonetheless be discussed. The Jesus who here singles out two commandments as fundamental nevertheless insists in 5:18-19 that none are to be discarded.

4. So R. Simlai (c. A.D. 250) in *b. Mak.* 23b.

5. Cf. the famous request to Shammai and Hillel to "teach me the whole law while I am standing on one leg," to which Hillel offers a response similar to Jesus' summary of "the law and the prophets" in 7:12 (*b. Šabb.* 31a); see the comments on 7:12.

In Mark's version this questioner is both himself a man of spiritual discernment and impressed by Jesus' response, but Matthew's briefer account gives no such positive slant, and the participle *peirazōn* indicates a much less complimentary motive. In the absence of any comment on his or the crowd's reaction to Jesus' pronouncement, the reader is left to assume, by analogy with the previous questions, that Jesus has escaped the trap.

Jesus' choice of Deut 6:5 and Lev 19:18 is notable for two reasons. In the first place, by focusing on "love" rather than on more tangible regulations to be obeyed it lifts the discussion above merely adjudicating between competing rules, and gives the priority to a principle which has potential application to virtually every aspect of religious and communal life. When Jesus declares that "the whole law and the prophets" depend on this principle, he is repeating the point he made in 7:12, "this *is* the law and the prophets." The ethical principle he there laid down did not use the word "love," but that is what it was all about.[6] The priority of love in the life of a disciple will be a frequently repeated NT principle (see on 7:12), and one which it would be very hard to object to.

In the second place, by bringing these two texts together Jesus asserts that the one principle of love applies equally to the two main aspects of religious duty, one's attitude to God and one's attitude to other people. It is these two foci which provide the framework of the Decalogue, with its two "tables" covering these two aspects in turn. If the Decalogue is itself a sort of epitome of the law, these two quotations in turn sum up the Decalogue. Commentators discuss whether Jesus was the first Jewish teacher to bring the two texts together in this paradigmatic way. Given the paucity of evidence for Jewish teaching in the second temple period any such assertion would be rash, and there is certainly evidence that others had combined love for God and for neighbor in a summary of religious duty (see *Jub.* 36:7-8; *T. Dan* 5:3; *T. Iss.* 5:2; 7:6;[7] Philo, *Spec. leg.* 2.63;[8] *Abr.* 208). But as far as our sources

---

6. The natural connection between these two texts is shown by the fact that the *Didache* begins with a summary of Jesus' double love-commandment as given here together with a paraphrase of Matt 7:12, the whole being described as "the way of life" (*Did.* 1:2).

7. In view of the clear presence of Christian additions in some parts of the *Testaments of the Twelve Patriarchs* it is possible that these references reflect knowledge of Jesus' teaching rather than independent Jewish thought.

8. Philo's discussion in *Spec. leg.* 2.63 is interesting in that he refers to piety toward God and justice toward other people as the two ἀνωτάτω κεφάλαια, by which it has been suggested that he means the superscriptions over the two tables of the Decalogue; cf. *Decal.* 108–10 where Philo describes those who keep the first table as φιλόθεοι and those who keep the second as φιλάνθρωποι.

go, there is no actual parallel to Jesus' use of this double quotation to make the point.[9]

34-35 The rivalry between the Sadducean and Pharisaic viewpoints within the Sanhedrin (Acts 23:6-10) underlies this introduction: where one "party" has failed to put Jesus on the spot, the other will try in its turn. In picturing the Pharisees acting together as a coherent group in opposition to Jesus Matthew provocatively uses a stylistically redundant expression (see p. 841, n. 1) which echoes LXX Ps 2:2, where it is the (non-Jewish) rulers of the nations who come together in opposition to the Lord and his anointed.[10]

This is the only time Matthew mentions a "lawyer" (and some critics therefore doubt the reading here; see p. 841, n. 2). Luke uses the term several times, perhaps because it was more familiar than "scribe" to someone of a non-Jewish background. Since the scribes were the professional students and exponents of the law within Judaism, it seems likely that "lawyer" refers to the same people.[11] Its use here may be intended to alert the reader that the issue raised is central to understanding Mosaic law.

36 The issue brought up by the "lawyer" is one which was familiar in rabbinic debate (see above). "The great" commandment in the law means in effect the greatest,[12] the one of central importance. *Poios,* which I have translated "which," means strictly "what kind of," so that the question might be understood to be about categories of law rather than asking for a specific text, but by NT times *poios* had come to be used often simply for "which" (as in 19:18), and Jesus' reply will suggest that he so understood the question. A rabbinic discussion of this issue in *b. Mak.* 24a suggests that the law may be found summarized in eleven principles in Ps 15, in six in Isa 33:15-16, in three in Mic 6:8, in two in Isa 56:1, and in one in Amos 5:4b and in Hab 2:4b; cf. *b. Ber.* 63a, where Prov 3:6 is said to be a "short

9. J. Piper, *Love,* 92-94, criticizes the attempt of C. Burchard to show that this two-part summary of the law was neither original nor derived from Jesus. It should be noted, however, that Luke's version of this pericope has the double commandment expressed by the lawyer and accepted by Jesus (Luke 10:27-28), so that Luke clearly did not regard it as Jesus' exclusive property. Davies and Allison, 3:237-38, helpfully summarize the debate.

10. Cf. the similar use of the same psalm in Acts 4:25-26, again with reference to the Jewish leaders, though there the Gentile authorities are linked with them.

11. Schürer, 2:324, speaks of "special" νομικοί within the "general designation" scribe, but does not suggest in what way they were "special." For H.-H. Esser, *NIDNTT* 2:443, they are "the theological leaders of the Pharisees." Most commentators agree with the view of W. Gutbrod, *TDNT* 4:1088, that the term is synonymous with "scribe," νομικός being used "only in contexts which deal with the administration or understanding of the law."

12. BDF 245(2); N. Turner, *Grammar,* 31, §6. Cf. 5:19, where μέγας, "great," is used as the counterpart to ἐλάχιστος, "smallest."

text on which all the essential principles of the Torah depend."[13] It is interesting that none of these suggested summaries are taken from the Pentateuch itself; by contrast Jesus' two key texts are both drawn from within the books of Moses.

37 Jesus could hardly have chosen a more familiar text for his reply. As part of the *Š*[e]*ma*ʿ Deut 6:5 was recited twice daily by all pious Jews[14] and written on their doorposts and phylacteries (see on 23:5) as instructed in Deut 6:8-9. It was therefore already marked out in its original context as having central importance as a summary of the duty of God's people. It draws out the implications of the first commandment in Exod 20:2-3. The quotation here follows the LXX version for the first two clauses,[15] but the use of *dianoia*, "thinking," in place of LXX *dynamis*, "strength," is surprising.[16] The LXX rendering is the normal understanding of Hebrew *m*[e]*ʾōd*, though it can also mean "abundance," and the targums translate it by *māmôn*, "possessions" (see on 6:24). In Mark 12:30 both *dianoia* and *ischys*, "strength," are used, resulting in four clauses instead of the three of Deut 6:5. The existence of variant versions of a text in constant liturgical use[17] is not surprising (cf. versions of the Lord's Prayer today), but "thinking" looks more like a variant of either "heart" or "soul" than of "strength."[18] It is therefore possible that Matthew took Mark's expanded version (the *four* clauses of which have no parallel in contemporary literature except here in Luke) and, realizing that the original had only three clauses, removed the last rather than one of the more nearly synonymous first three. The resultant list has a rather more "internal" feel as compared with the more practical implications of loving God

---

13. For further examples see Str-B 1:900-908.

14. This widespread assumption is questioned by P. Foster, *JBL* 122 (2003) 321-31, who argues that the evidence for its regular liturgical use cannot safely be traced before the mishnaic period.

15. There is a minor variation in the prepositions used: Matthew (unlike Mark) uses ἐν, which is a more literal rendering of the Hebrew than LXX ἐξ, but the sense is not affected.

16. Gundry, 449, speculates that διανοία represents a misreading of the third Hebrew term as *maddāʿkā* (a rare term for "knowledge, thought" which occurs only in later books of the OT) instead of *m*[e]*ʾōdekā*, but the words are quite dissimilar, and it is unlikely that Matthew would have been unaware of the standard Hebrew form of such a well-known text. There is no other evidence for such a reading of the Hebrew.

17. See R. H. Gundry, *Use*, 22-24, and the table of variations in K. Stendahl, *School*, 73-74. More simply, Davies and Allison, 3:242. The data are fully set out by P. Foster, *JBL* 122 (2003) 313-21.

18. διανοία occurs in the corrected B text of LXX (the original is undecipherable), but as an alternative to καρδία, not for the final clause. In a parallel text, Josh 22:5, LXX B again has διανοία for "heart."

with one's strength or possessions. But the main point remains clear, that one is to love God with all that one is and has.[19]

38-39 Even though the love of God as expressed in Deut 6:5 rightly takes first place, Jesus goes beyond the scope of the original question to assert that "a second" must be placed alongside it. It is "like" Deut 6:5 not only in that it is equally important, but also in the formal sense that it uses the same verbal form, "you are to love,"[20] and more fundamentally in that it equally insists that one's religious duty is focused outside oneself. It might be possible to think even of love for God as a self-centered spiritual experience, but love for one's neighbor is inescapably practical and altruistic. Love for God is "first," so that R. Mohrlang is justified in insisting that "the second great commandment is properly understood only when viewed within the context of the more fundamental demand of the first,"[21] but the first without the second leaves the demand of love insufficiently specified.

Lev 19:18 is a text with which Matthew's reader is already familiar, from 5:43-47 where Jesus rescued the love of "neighbor" from a limited concern only for one's immediate circle, and from 19:19 where it was used to sum up the ethical implications of the second table of the Decalogue. Its appropriateness as an ethical summary was recognized by R. Akiba, who called it "a great principle in the Torah" (*Sifra* Lev 19:18), and Paul (Rom 13:10; Gal 5:14) and James (Jas 2:8) similarly give it pride of place as summing up the demands of the Decalogue and as itself "the royal law."[22] While there was a clearly limited sense to "neighbor" both in the original text and in later Jewish understanding of it (see on 5:43), Jesus makes it clear in 5:43-47 and in the parable of the Good Samaritan (Luke 10:25-37) that for his disciples no such limitation is acceptable.[23] The neighbor is everyone, and the nature of the "love" which God expects is equally unlimited: "as (you love) yourself." The text assumes, surely realistically, that it is normal to love (i.e., to be concerned for the interests of) oneself, and that such love generally takes precedence over the interests of others.

---

19. "With every globule of one's being" (Davies and Allison, 3:241)!

20. In the Hebrew OT this particular jussive form, $w^{e^2}\bar{a}habt\bar{a}$, occurs only in these two texts and in the derivative texts Deut 11:1 and Lev 19:34. Such a linkage on the basis of verbal similarity follows the rabbinic principle of $g^{e}z\bar{e}r\hat{a}$ $\check{s}\bar{a}w\hat{a}$.

21. R. Mohrlang, *Matthew*, 99; cf. also ibid., 95. Contrast the assertion of Davies and Allison, 3:243, following BAGD, that δεύτερος here is "purely numerical"; in the revised edition (BDAG), however, that phrase has been eliminated.

22. Davies and Allison, 3:44-45, list several other similar uses of Lev 19:18 in Jewish and Christian sources.

23. *Gos. Thom.* 25 appears to reinstate a similar limitation when it quotes Jesus as saying, "Love your *brother* as your own soul; keep him as the apple of your eye." This is presented as an independent saying, not as an OT quotation.

40 The comprehensive nature of the love which these two texts demand makes them eminently suitable for the role of summarizing the law, as the Pharisaic lawyer has asked. Together they cover the two main foci of human responsibility under God. They summarize not only the law (which was the question asked) but also the prophets, since the whole scriptural revelation is understood to witness to the same divine will. For the graphic use of "hang" as a term for dependence[24] cf. the famous rabbinic comment that the sabbath laws "are as mountains hanging by a hair, for Scripture is scanty but the rules are many" (*m. Ḥag.* 1:8). By contrast, the two texts chosen by Jesus are together sufficiently strong to bear the weight of the whole OT. This does not mean, as some modern ethicists have argued, that "all you need is love," so that one can dispense with the ethical rules set out in the Torah. It is rather to say that those rules find their true role in working out the practical implications of the love for God and neighbor on which they are based. Far from making the law irrelevant, therefore, love thus becomes "the primary hermeneutical principle for interpreting and applying the law."[25]

4. Jesus' Question about the Messiah (22:41-46)

> 41 *While the Pharisees were gathered together, Jesus asked them,* 42 *"What do you think about the Messiah? Whose son is he?" "David's," they replied.* 43 *He said to them, "Then how is it that David, inspired by the Spirit, calls him 'lord' when he says,*
>
> 44 *'The Lord said to my lord,*
>> *"Sit at my right hand*
>> *until I put your enemies under your feet"'?*
>
> 45 *So if David calls him 'lord', how can he be his son?"*
> 46 *And no one could give him an answer, nor did anyone from that time on dare to ask him any more questions.*

---

24. It is used by the rabbis especially for laws which are derivable from others. See G. Bertram, *TDNT* 3:919-21, for the background and for some interesting comments on the interpretation of this verse. See also D. J. Moo, *JSNT* 20 (1984) 6-7, with references to further discussion.

25. R. Mohrlang, *Matthew*, 95. See further D. C. Sim, *Gospel*, 127-28, pointing out that other Jewish teachers who produced summaries of the law never saw them as *replacing* the law. T. L. Donaldson, *CBQ* 57 (1995) 689-709, explores the tension involved in Matthew's use of this rabbinic terminology despite holding a more radical view of the "fulfillment" of the law than the rabbis would have approved.

Three hostile questions (four, if we go back to 21:23) have failed to defeat Jesus. His answers have impressed the crowd and left his questioners with nothing to say in return. So the sequence of direct dialogue between Jesus and the Jerusalem leaders ends with Jesus himself taking the initiative and asking a question which they in their turn are unable to answer. Verse 46 then underlines Jesus' total victory in the debate.

This question, too, is posed as an academic discussion topic; Jesus invites the Pharisees to clarify their understanding of the expected Messiah.[1] But their conventional response to his opening inquiry is met in good rabbinic fashion by a counterquotation which suggests a different answer. Normally rabbinic discussion would go on to propose a resolution of the discrepancy, but this question is left hanging in the air. From an academic point of view it is hardly a satisfactory dialogue. But in the highly charged context of the rival authority-claims of Jesus and the Jerusalem authorities it is most unlikely that it would be taken, or indeed intended, as a purely objective puzzle. The implications are not spelled out, but they seem to be twofold: first, the traditional understanding of Messiahship is inadequate; and secondly, in the light of Jesus' "messianic" arrival and self-presentation in Jerusalem (21:1-16), both the leaders and the people must have realized that it was his own status that he was talking about, even if they had not picked up the messianic implications of the figure of the son in his vineyard parable (21:37). Consistently with his approach so far, Jesus implies his messianic role without making an open statement that could be used against him.

The title "Son of David" has been prominent throughout the gospel story (9:27; 12:23; 15:22; 20:30-31), and on his arrival at Jerusalem it has been openly attributed to Jesus in 21:9, 15, when he has not only accepted it without rebuke but even defended its use against the objections of the chief priests and scribes. Moreover, the reader knows from the repeated emphasis in ch. 1 that Matthew sets great store by this as a title to explain the role of Jesus as Messiah. It therefore seems incongruous that here we find Jesus questioning its appropriateness as a title for the Messiah, and therefore also by implication for himself. But the argument seems to be not that the title is wrong, but that it is inadequate: the Messiah is *more than* David's son; he is his lord. Cf. the "greater than" formula in 12:6, 41, 42, and the comments on 12:3-4 for its application also to David. It would make no sense for Jesus, after all that has happened in the preceding chapter, to dismiss the title "Son of

---

1. See D. L. Bock, *Blasphemy*, 220-22, against the suggestion that this pericope represents a debate in the early church rather than during Jesus' ministry. It is unlikely that a church which honored Jesus as the Son of David would have invented a dialogue which appears to question that belief.

David" altogether. And if he had done so, his followers could hardly have continued to declare his Davidic descent as a matter of faith (Rom 1:3; cf. 2 Tim 2:8).[2]

Matthew's way of setting up the question perhaps gives a clue to what he understood to be at stake. Whereas in Mark and Luke the pericope is a monologue by Jesus, who himself introduces the title "Son of David" and then questions its validity, in Matthew Jesus poses the open question "Whose son is the Messiah?" and only when the Pharisees volunteer the traditional answer does he go on to question it. When the debate is framed in that way, the question "Whose son?" remains after the first suggested answer has been put aside, inviting the reader to provide an alternative answer. And in the light of the preceding pericopes that answer is not difficult to find: in 21:37 Jesus has implicitly laid claim to the status of Son of God. It is that implication which he now invites his hearers to draw out, for surely one who is the lord of David, the most distinguished of all historical Israelites, must be himself more than just another human king. If David calls him "lord," he is clearly the son of someone far superior to David. For the uninstructed reader the question remains tantalizingly open as the pericope ends, but Matthew's Christian reader is not going to find it difficult to answer the question, "Whose son is he?" Indeed, even the high priest himself will put before Jesus the combined title "Messiah, Son of God," and Jesus will affirm that that is how he understands his position (26:63-64), and thus "in effect answers the question left unanswered in 22:45."[3]

After this point the title "Son of David" will not be heard again. It is likely that one of Jesus' reasons for putting a question mark against it here was the danger that it could foster too political and nationalistic a view of his mission — as perhaps it already had among the Galilean crowd in 21:8-9. Like the title "Messiah" in 16:16-23, "Son of David" is not incorrect, but its public use is open to misunderstanding.[4] What lies ahead of him now is not a triumphant reign over God's people but rejection by them, not a royal throne but a humiliating execution. It is only after that mission is accomplished that he can look forward to sitting at the right hand of his Father in a heavenly, not an earthly, kingship, as his further allusion to this same psalm in 26:64 will make clear.

2. For Jesus' Davidic descent both in Christian belief and historically see R. E. Brown, *Birth,* 505-12.

3. Davies and Allison, 3:528. For an early interpretation along these lines see *Barn.* 12:10-11, where a précis of this pericope follows the assertion that Jesus is "not the son of a human being but the Son of God." See further D. J. Verseput, *NTS* 33 (1987) 545-46, drawing on his more general demonstration of the close link between "Son of David" and "Son of God" in Matthew (ibid., 541-48).

4. See J. Marcus, *Way,* 146-49.

41-42 Whereas in Mark the dialogue is now finished, and Jesus addresses this question to the crowd inviting them to question what "the scribes say," in Matthew the direct confrontation is maintained. The repetition of the same verb as in v. 34 indicates that Jesus takes advantage of the deliberate (and hostile) "gathering" of the Pharisees to respond with his own question to what has become the leading group of his opponents.

See on 1:1 for the titles "Messiah" and "Son of David." For many Jews at the time they would have been synonymous,[5] so that the Pharisees' answer to Jesus' question would be automatic. *Ps. Sol.* 17 gives eloquent expression to the hope of a coming Son of David held by at least one leading Pharisee before Jesus' time.[6] But while Messiah, "the anointed one," was properly a royal title, it was apparently already being used in a broader sense for other models of a God-sent deliverer expected within various Jewish circles,[7] so that the question was not an empty one, even though the Pharisaic answer could be confidently predicted.

43-45 Jesus' argument is based on a well-known psalm, which, as a "psalm of David," was obviously relevant to the question. But it is not merely David's psalm. "In the Spirit" presupposes that this psalm owes its origin to the Spirit of God rather than merely to human initiative; cf. the idea that David was a prophet in Acts 2:30.[8] For a similar understanding of Scripture more generally cf. Acts 1:16; 4:25; 28:25; Heb 3:7; 9:8; 10:15; 2 Pet 1:21. Apart from this underlying presupposition that the scriptural text is divinely inspired and therefore authoritative, this introductory formula makes three hermeneutical assumptions which will be crucial to Jesus' argument:[9] (a) that the speaker in Ps 110 is David; (b) that David is speaking about the Messiah; (c) that someone described as "my lord" is superior to the one speaking. Of these the third is the most obvious: superiority is inherent in the meaning of the word "lord," in all the various social relationships to which it may be applied, whether in Hebrew *('ādôn)*,[10] Aramaic *(mar)*, or Greek *(kyrios)*. You

---

5. *Pace* B. D. Chilton, *JSNT* 14 (1982) 88-112, who offers the novel proposal that Jesus here asserts that he is the Son of David but not the Messiah. In response see J. Marcus, *Way*, 151-52.

6. Cf. the earlier title "Branch of David" in Jer 23:5; 33:15; also Isa 11:1-10.

7. Note especially the two "Messiahs" of Qumran, one priestly and one royal.

8. ἐν πνεύματι could of course mean "in his (human) spirit," but it is hard to imagine what that could mean when what is being quoted is not an unspoken musing but a written text. For God's Spirit as the source of inspired human utterance cf. 10:20; Mark 13:11; Luke 1:41, 67, etc. Mark 12:36 specifies that David spoke by "the Holy Spirit," and there is no reason to believe that Matthew's abbreviated version has any other meaning.

9. I discuss these three premises in my *Jesus and the OT*, 163-69. See that study for more detail on what follows.

10. In English versions of Ps 110:1 the word "lord" occurs twice, first as the tradi-

would not speak of your son as your "lord."[11] The other two are more controversial in the light of modern scholarship.

Psalm 110 is one of the seventy-two psalms with the heading "to David," traditionally understood as an ascription of authorship. These headings are part of the traditional Hebrew and LXX text and were almost certainly familiar in Jesus' day, so that it would have been taken for granted by both Jesus and his hearers that the speaker in Ps 110 was David, inspired by the Spirit. On that point, then, Jesus' argument holds good both for his immediate audience and for Matthew's original readers.

And if David spoke of someone else as his "lord," it might seem a reasonable assumption that he was speaking of the Messiah. Who else, under God, was above David? That assumption underlies the very frequent use of Ps 110 in the NT. Yet in rabbinic references from the earliest datable one in the early second century until the middle of the third it is usually understood to be speaking of Abraham. P. Billerbeck (Str-B 4:452-58) attributes this difference to a deliberate reinterpretation by the fanatically anti-Christian R. Ishmael, replacing a traditional messianic interpretation in order to counter Christian claims based on this psalm; but after about A.D. 250, when the immediate polemical situation had receded, the messianic interpretation returns and soon becomes commonplace.[12]

Modern scholars are sceptical as to an originally messianic intention in the psalm, since it is seen as a typical royal psalm in which a courtier speaks in exaggerated terms about the dignity of the current king, not of a future Messiah.[13] But if David is himself the speaker, he is presumably not

----

tional rendering of the divine name "Yahweh," and then as the psalmist's description of the person whom God is addressing; only in the latter case does ʾādôn occur in the Hebrew text. The LXX rendering, like the English, has only the one word κύριος to render the two Hebrew terms, resulting in a pleasing wordplay; a similar wordplay would also occur in *spoken* Hebrew, in which ʾᵃdōnay would be said in place of the name "Yahweh." It has sometimes been suggested that Jesus' argument depends on this LXX wordplay and could not have been made from the Hebrew text, but that is a strange argument: even in Greek there is no possibility of confusion between κύριος (God) as the speaker and τῷ κυρίῳ μου for the addressee, and "my lord" implies superiority in any language.

11. It is this social nuance that is the basis of the argument, rather than the title κύριος as it has been applied to Jesus throughout the gospel without reference to David, though Matthew's readers might well also make the connection.

12. A messianic understanding of the psalm at the time of Jesus has been more recently argued by, e.g., D. M. Hay, *Glory,* 26-33; D. Juel, *Exegesis,* 137-39; J. Marcus, *Way,* 133-34. L. Novakovic, *Messiah,* 55-57, argues, however, that a messianic interpretation at the time is not well evidenced: it was "only one among several interpretative possibilities, so that it could not have been unambiguously used for apologetic purposes."

13. L. C. Allen, *Psalms 101–150,* 83-85, conveniently sets out modern views of this psalm. If, like other royal psalms, it is addressed *to* the king (whether David or a suc-

speaking about himself as "my lord." So the messianic understanding of the psalm depends on its authorship. For those who, like Jesus and his audience, accepted it as a psalm of David, Jesus' argument holds.[14]

The first verse of Ps 110 is quoted almost exactly according to the LXX version.[15] Jesus will allude to the same text in 26:64 when he pictures himself in his future glory seated at God's right hand; there too its messianic reference is taken for granted. It becomes a favorite messianic proof-text (Acts 2:34-35; Heb 1:13, and the frequent references to sitting at God's right hand in Acts, Paul, and Hebrews), while the writer of Hebrews goes on to explore the implications of the fourth verse of the same psalm for Jesus' priestly role (Heb 5:6, 10; 6:20; ch. 7 passim).[16] This is not, then, a purely academic argument: it will become clear to Matthew's reader that it is about Jesus' own messianic role. And in the heated atmosphere in the temple courtyard it is likely that at least some of those present would have seen where the question was tending.

46 This verse partly parallels Mark 12:34, which came *before* the current pericope; by retaining it until now Matthew has ensured that the question about the Messiah is seen as the final item in the debate, not as subsequent to it (see on v. 41). Now the dialogue is finished, and while Jesus will continue to speak to and about the Pharisees, they will not respond or raise further questions. At this point there is no mention (as there is in Mark) of the reaction of the crowd to the brief and allusive argument just recorded, but Jesus will immediately go on to address the crowds in a way which assumes

---

cessor) rather than spoken *by* him, it could be considered messianic not in its original intention but only insofar as the historical monarchy which it celebrates subsequently served as a model for messianic hope.

14. In my *Jesus and the OT,* 164-68, I argued that Davidic authorship of Ps 110 (and therefore also its messianic reference) is not only consonant with first-century understanding but can also be defended from the perspective of modern scholarship; so also R. H. Gundry, *Use,* 228-29. I still think the case is less closed than many scholars suggest, particularly with regard to the classification of Ps 110 (with its priestly element in v. 4) as a typical *royal* psalm, but would now be less confident in my conclusions. But, in any case, the exegesis of Matthew does not require this issue to be resolved, since Jesus' argument depends on the agreed understanding of his day. See further my *Mark,* 486-87.

15. Matthew differs from the LXX only in omitting the article before the first κύριος (according to the earliest MSS; most MSS include the article) and in substituting the more prosaic "under your feet" (perhaps influenced by Ps 8:6) for LXX's reproduction of the vivid Hebrew metaphor "your footstool."

16. N. T. Wright, *Victory,* 507-9, argues that in this pericope, set within the wider "Messiah-and-temple theme" of chs. 21–22, Jesus refers to Ps 110 with an eye not only to the quoted v. 1 but also to v. 4, and so is asserting his role as the ultimate priest-king who "will supersede the present high-priestly regime." While this fits well with the christology of Hebrews, it is not explicit in the present context, and it is cast in doubt by Matthew's characterization of the opponents here as Pharisees rather than priests.

their sympathy with him rather than with the scribes and Pharisees, so that we must assume their continuing approval of his teaching.

D. JESUS' VERDICT ON JERUSALEM AND ITS LEADERSHIP (23:1–24:2)

After the question about the Messiah as the Son of David, Mark and Luke include a brief warning against the hypocrisy of the scribes and the exemplary tale of the widow's offering before going on to record Jesus' prediction of the destruction of the temple and the discourse which follows from it. In Matthew this sequence has been strikingly developed into a wide-ranging denunciation of the "scribes and Pharisees, hypocrites." Jesus, the unquestioned victor in the debate with the Jerusalem authorities, now uses his dominant position to spell out in painful detail some of the failings of the current religious leadership, both in their personal obedience to the will of God and in their responsibility as the leaders of God's people.

As the monologue progresses, it predicts the consequences of the corporate failure of Israel's leadership: Israel's rejection of God's messengers through the ages has now reached the point of no return, and it is time for judgment to fall on "this generation." Thus when we come in Matthew to Jesus' prediction of the destruction of the temple, the ground has been well prepared; Jerusalem's rejection of its last chance to repent means that "your house is left to you deserted" (23:36-38). After that there is a melancholy significance in Jesus' going out for the last time from the temple (see on 24:1), and his explicit prediction of its physical destruction follows appropriately. The fate of the building is bound up with the judgment on the religious leaders of the nation. It is time for a change. The climactic discourse of chs. 24–25 will then spell out what that change will mean.

Jesus' target throughout this section is "the scribes and Pharisees" (for the combination see on 5:20),[1] not just the scribes as in the brief denunciations in Mark and Luke. Pharisees have been increasingly prominent in Matthew's account of the Jerusalem confrontation so far (21:45; 22:15, 34, 41), and scribes have been linked with the chief priests as those determined to silence Jesus (16:21; 20:18; 21:15), but it is surprising that the chief priests (and the elders?), who have been and will continue to be the prime movers in the plot against Jesus, do not feature in this section, particularly in view of their dominant role in the affairs of the temple, whose fate is the climax of Jesus' diatribe. But it seems that for Matthew the Pharisees particularly exem-

---

1. Keener, 537-40, usefully surveys the data with special reference to this chapter. See also D. E. Garland, *Intention,* 41-46; K. G. C. Newport, *Sources,* 111-16.

plify all that is wrong with Jerusalem's current leadership.[2] While it is probably true that historically it was the Sadducees rather than the Pharisees who at this time dominated the internal politics of Israel, the degeneration in Israel's religious condition which Jesus depicts is now too general to be linked with the priestly leadership alone, and the scribes and the Pharisees, as the self-appointed arbiters of all matters of religious law and practice, must bear the blame for a nation which has spiritually lost its way.

In such a section it is probably not exegetically profitable to try to distinguish the polemic of Jesus against the scribes and Pharisees of his day from Matthew's attitude to the Judaism of his own period, in which Pharisaism was increasingly becoming the dominant strand.[3] It is generally agreed that the sharpness of the polemic reflects the painful period of separation of church from synagogue within which Matthew's gospel was written.[4] But it is also clear that historically Jesus did find himself in sharp disagreement with the Jewish leadership, especially in Jerusalem, and there is no reason to suppose that this antagonism was kept within the confines of gentlemanly debate, on Jesus' side any more than on theirs.

The tone of Jesus' accusations is harsh,[5] and prompts the question

2. For Matthew's characterization of the Pharisees see my *Matthew: Evangelist*, 219-22; also R. Mohrlang, *Matthew*, 20-21.

3. S. H. Brooks, *Community*, 116-17, suggests that the whole chapter is designed to reflect the historical development of Jewish-Christian relations with which Matthew's readers would be familiar: he finds four stages, from vv. 2-3a where "religious life is circumscribed by the authority of the Jewish synagogue leaders" to the final break with Judaism reflected in vv. 37-39. It must surely be questioned whether any of Matthew's readers would possess the literary sophistication to trace this progressive development in what purports to be a speech delivered by Jesus all at one time.

4. See G. N. Stanton, *Gospel*, 156-57, for an effective brief summary of the sort of scenario envisaged, though I doubt whether the process of separation from official Judaism was as clearly defined or as precisely datable as Stanton's phrase "recently parted company" implies (see above, p. 16). D. C. Sim, *Gospel*, 120-23, effectively dismisses earlier theories that Matthew's polemic reveals that he was already far distant from Judaism, and argues rather that the very sharpness of the language indicates a close contact which made it the more important to emphasize the lines of difference.

5. It is of course right to note that ancient rhetoric tended to be more colorful than most modern standards allow, and that this diatribe should be read in that context; so especially L. T. Johnson, *JBL* 108 (1989) 419-41. Davies and Allison, 3:258-61, developing Johnson's argument, give an intriguing list of roughly contemporary Jewish polemical parallels to almost all the charges leveled by Jesus in ch. 23, from which they conclude that "Matthew 23 is full of conventional accusations." They therefore speak of the language as "stereotyped." See also J. A. Overman, *Gospel*, 19-23, for the prevalence of hostile attacks on "the Jewish leadership" among sectarian Jewish groups of the period. But the sense of unfairness which the critique of scribal/Pharisaic religion in Matt 23 evokes in many readers applies to its material content as well as to the rhetoric used.

whether all scribes and Pharisees were really so bad and "hypocritical" as this chapter alleges. Is Matthew unfair to the historical scribes and Pharisees?[6] Josephus speaks of the high respect in which the Pharisees were held, and Mark 12:28-34 portrays one scribe in a much more favorable light. But Matthew's recasting of that pericope in 22:34-40 suggests that he found such a characterization inappropriate; the only good scribe he knows is the one who has become a disciple (see on 13:52 and cf. 23:34). But the focus of this chapter is not so much on individual scribes and Pharisees as on the nature of the movement they represented. Personal inconsistency will of course be mentioned, notably in vv. 3-4, but the main thrust of the chapter relates rather to their fundamental approach to religious life. The "hypocrisy" which is alleged is not so much conscious insincerity as a distorted perspective which makes them think that they are doing the will of God when they are missing the main point (see on 6:2 for Matthew's use of "hypocrite"). The attitude attacked in this chapter is a religion of externals, a matter of ever more detailed attention to rules and regulations while failing to discern God's priorities. Many, perhaps most, scribes and Pharisees did indeed, as Josephus indicates, admirably fulfill their religious duties as they understood them. But Jesus' charge is that that understanding was fundamentally flawed, and that the resultant religious zeal could do more harm than good. The attack on this group of "hypocrites" is probably intended by Matthew to apply also to people in his own church context who have similarly missed the point, and in vv. 8-12 this secondary target becomes clearly visible.[7] The failings here ascribed to scribal/Pharisaic religion have their parallels in most religious traditions when the form comes to matter more than the substance.

In the last two chapters we have noted a tension between a specific focus on the failings of the current leadership and repeated hints that the coming judgment will have a broader effect than merely a change of leadership (see especially pp. 800-801). The same tension continues in this section, in that initially the crowds are set apart from the scribes and Pharisees in 23:1-12, but by the end of the chapter a more universal catastrophe is predicted, with judgment falling on the temple itself (and by implication on the city of which it is the focus) rather than simply on its controlling authorities. It is

6. See D. E. Garland, *Intention,* 1-2, for a brief survey of Jewish reactions to Matt 23, including that of B. J. Bamberger that its "picture of Pharisaism is biased, unfair and even libellous." U. Luz, *Theology,* 121-25, emphasizes the contrast between this chapter and Jesus' teaching on love even of enemies in the rest of the gospel, and concludes that "In view of Jesus' own preaching . . . Matthew should never have allowed him to speak so unfeelingly as he does in chapter 23."

7. D. E. Garland, *Intention,* 117-23, argues that the primary aim of the woes, which are ostensibly directed at the Jewish leaders, is in fact to warn Christian leaders against similar "hypocrisy."

"this generation" as a whole which will suffer (v. 36) and the unresponsive-ness of "Jerusalem" which is lamented (v. 37). The following discourse will make it clear that all of "Judea" (24:16) is caught up in the disaster, and the cosmic language of 24:29-31 will depict a far more radical upheaval than merely a change of Israel's leadership.

Within ch. 23 there is an obvious division between vv. 1-12 in which Jesus speaks to the crowd about the scribes and Pharisees, and vv. 13-36 in which he speaks directly to the scribes and Pharisees.[8] The latter section is marked by a series of seven "Woe" pronouncements, of which the last is ex-tended into a more general charge of religious rebellion. This in turn pro-vides the basis for the lament over Jerusalem in vv. 37-39, which stands as a coda to the rest of the chapter, and provides the bridge to the temple-prediction which follows at the beginning of ch. 24. The whole complex sug-gests a deliberate Matthean compilation[9] along lines similar to those of the five discourses,[10] but lacking a concluding discourse formula (see next para-graph). It has parallels at this point in the other Synoptic Gospels only in the brief denunciation of the scribes in Mark 12:38-40; Luke 20:45-47 and in the temple saying. But a good part of its material finds parallels in Luke 11:37-52 in Jesus' comments at a Pharisee's dinner party, including six "woes," three pronounced against Pharisees and three against lawyers;[11] most of Luke 11:37-52 is roughly paralleled in Matt 23, but not in the same order. The final lament over Jerusalem is quite closely parallel to Luke 13:34-35.

Because of its similar compositional style, and because it leads di-rectly into the discourse on the Mount of Olives in 24:3–25:46, this section is sometimes treated as part of the same discourse, so that the concluding for-mula in 26:1 covers the whole of chs. 23–25, making this the longest of all

---

8. D. E. Garland, *Intention,* 118-20, however, points out that no change of audi-ence is signaled at v. 13, and concludes that the second-person address is a literary device, the real target audience being still the crowds and the disciples.

9. This generally accepted view is challenged by K. G. C. Newport, *Sources,* es-pecially 68-79, who argues that vv. 2-31 derive from a pre-Matthean Jewish-Christian source (cf. the proposal of H. D. Betz concerning the origin of the Sermon on the Mount, above, p. 154, n. 6, on which Newport comments, ibid., 158, n. 1). Newport argues that this source took a higher view of the authority of the traditional Jewish leadership, and particularly of the validity of their teaching of the law, than Matthew himself does. The ar-gument depends on Matthew's willingness to incorporate in his gospel material with which he himself did not agree, a surprising scenario for which Newport does not offer a convincing explanation.

10. See D. E. Garland, *Intention,* 20-23, for evidence that the discourse is a Matthean compilation. Hagner, 2:653, points out, however, that the consistently negative tone of this chapter distinguishes it from the other discourses.

11. See D. E. Garland, *Intention,* 9-12, for comparison and contrast between Luke's woes and Matthew's.

the Matthean discourses. Many commentators, however, note that Matthew seems to have deliberately separated the two complexes of teaching, by a change of location (temple; Mount of Olives) and of audience (crowd/scribes and Pharisees; disciples). More significantly, the subject matter, while not unrelated, changes radically with the new double question which the disciples ask in 24:3 and which determines the content of the discourse which follows. It may also be noted that chs. 24–25 follow the classic discourse pattern in developing and expanding a shorter Synoptic discourse, in this case Mark 13:3-37; Luke 21:7-36, whereas ch. 23 finds its parallels elsewhere (mainly in Luke 11; see above). Chapter 23 will therefore be treated here as a separate section from the following Mount of Olives discourse.[12]

Matthew's omission of the story of the widow (Mark 12:41-44; Luke 21:1-4) is not easily explained on the basis that the story was uncongenial to him; as an attack on ostentatious religious donation (and as a eulogy on a "little one") it would surely have appealed to the Matthew who includes 23:5-7 and has already dealt with the same issue in 6:1-4. It is better explained by Matthew's literary plan. The hugely expanded attack on the scribes and Pharisees hardly leaves room for this homely story, and it would have interrupted the deliberate sequence from the diatribe and the lament over Jerusalem to the prediction of the end of the temple. It drops out under the pressure of other, more weighty material. Matthew has more important fish to fry.

1. Warning against the Scribes and Pharisees (23:1-12)

1 *Then Jesus addressed the crowds and his own disciples:* 2 *"The scribes and the Pharisees have taken their seat on Moses' chair.* 3 *So practice and keep whatever they say to you — but do not act as they do: they talk but do not practice.* 4 *They tie up heavy, cumbersome*[13] *loads and put them on other people's shoulders, but they themselves are not willing to move them with their finger.* 5 *They do all that they do with a view to being noticed by other people; they make their phylacteries broad and their fringes long,* 6 *and they love the most prominent couch*[14] *at dinner and the front seats in the synagogues* 7 *and re-*

12. See also J. A. Gibbs, *Jerusalem,* 168-69.

13. δυσβάστακτα, "hard to carry," is missing from a few later Greek MSS and several early versions, prompting the suspicion that it has been introduced into the Matthean tradition from Luke 11:46 (where it stands alone, without "heavy"). But the thrust of the saying is not affected.

14. The scene is a Roman-style *triclinium* arrangement in which the guests recline on couches around the table. An idiomatic British equivalent might be "the top table," though the fact that the term is singular may indicate more specifically the individual place of honor next to the host.

spectful greetings in the marketplaces, with people calling them 'Rabbi.' **8** *But you must not be called 'Rabbi,' because for you there is just one teacher, and you are all brothers and sisters.*[15] **9** *And do not call anyone your father*[16] *on earth because for you there is just one heavenly Father.* **10** *And you must not be called instructors because you have just one instructor, the Messiah.* **11** *The greatest*[17] *among you is to be your servant;* **12** *anyone who lifts himself up will be brought low,*[18] *and anyone who lowers himself will be lifted high."*

The setting is still in the temple courtyard (see 24:1), so that the same crowd is envisaged surrounding Jesus. Among them are Jesus' disciples, and so Matthew mentions both groups as the audience. The content of this section suggests that it begins with the crowd as the primary audience, warning them against those they have been taught to regard as their teachers and leaders; but from v. 8 onward, and unmistakably in v. 10, the disciples are more directly in view, with the last two verses returning to what have already been familiar themes in Jesus' teaching of his disciples (see 18:1-5; 20:25-28). Those earlier instructions and their Synoptic parallels (and cf. also John 13:13-16) indicate that already among the pre-Easter disciple group the issue of status and ambition was a real one, but the wording of vv. 8-10, especially the unparalleled (in Matthew) reference by Jesus to "the Messiah" in the third person with apparent reference to himself, suggests that the teaching has been adapted to address an inappropriate concern for status and respect in the church of Matthew's own day.

The immediate target, however, is the scribes and the Pharisees, two groups who belong naturally together and probably in fact overlapped to a large extent, most scribes being Pharisaically inclined (see on 5:20). They enjoyed popular respect and authority as the recognized experts in understanding and applying the OT law and its subsequent elaborations, and Jesus' opening words note the authority of their office, though in the light of what follows there is surely an element of irony in his endorsement. His criticism focuses, however, not on the role they purport to fulfill but on the way they fulfill it. The charge of inconsistency in their behavior (v. 3b) is not devel-

15. There seems to be no gender-specific element in the term ἀδελφοί here, where Jesus is speaking about relations between disciples in general (and in the hearing of a larger crowd); see 27:55 for women among the disciple group at this stage.

16. Some MS variations over whether to read ὑμῶν, "your father," or ὑμῖν, "a father to you," or in a few cases to omit the pronoun altogether, make no significant difference to the sense.

17. See p. 675, n. 10, for the superlative sense of μείζων.

18. See on 18:4 for the meaning of the ταπεινός word-group. Here, as there, a reference to social standing, not to a mental quality, is required.

oped at this point, but much of what follows in vv. 13-36 will fill it out. But two more specific charges are developed, their lack of consideration for the problems their teaching generates for ordinary people (v. 4), and their concern for appearances and reputation (vv. 5-7). It is the latter which triggers Jesus' return to his disciples' preoccupation with status, which takes up the rest of the paragraph.

1-2   Teachers normally sat to teach (see on 5:1; and cf. 13:1-2; 24:3), and 26:55 will tell us that Jesus followed this custom during this period in the temple courtyard. Given that cultural norm, it is likely that to "sit on Moses' chair" is simply a figurative expression (cf. our professorial "chair") for teaching[19] with an authority derived from Moses.[20] Moses himself gave Israel the basic law, but ever since then it had been necessary for other teachers to expound and apply it, and those who did so with due authority "sat on Moses' chair." There is evidence of special front seats for synagogue leaders at the time of Jesus (see v. 6), but the suggestion that such a chair was literally described as the "chair of Moses" lacks clear evidence.[21] Not all Pharisees occupied a formal teaching role, but they no less than the scribes saw themselves as the true successors to the Mosaic tradition. On the face of it this statement acknowledges the legitimate teaching authority of the scribes, but in what follows Jesus will dispute their right to that authoritative role, so that it is probably right to read this verse, like the exhortation which follows in v. 3a, as ironical.[22]

---

19. Carter, 452 (following M. A. Powell, *JBL* 114 [1995] 419-35), argues that the focus is not on teaching as such but on "their powerful political, religious and social position." This is undoubtedly a factor in what this chapter deals with, but the name "Moses" surely speaks primarily of teaching and law, and the immediately following reference to doing what they "say" reinforces that impression.

20. B. T. Viviano, *JSNT* 39 (1990) 10-11, suggests that the reference is more specifically to the rabbinic assembly at Jamnia, regarded corporately as "the seat of Moses."

21. D. E. Garland, *Intention,* 42-43, n. 27; Davies and Allison, 3:268; more fully K. G. C. Newport, *Sources,* 81-85. The earliest known use of "chair of Moses," apparently to describe a literal seat, is in the later rabbinic work *Pesiq. Rab Kah.* 7b, but the context does not make it clear that a synagogue seat is being referred to. For the archeological evidence see L. Y. Rahmani, *IEJ* 40 (1990) 192-214; Rahmani argues (following C. Roth) that in some synagogues a "chair of Moses" was used to support the Torah scroll, but finds no evidence that the term was used for a teacher's chair. The survey of archeological and literary data by L. I. Levine, *Synagogue,* 323-27, also claims no specific evidence, and Newport (see above), while arguing that a literal teacher's chair is intended, offers no evidence for the term being so used.

22. K. G. C. Newport, *Sources,* 119-24, acknowledges the tension between these verses taken at face value and the general attitude of Matthew (and, I would add, of Jesus), and explains it by his theory that Matthew has in 23:2-31 incorporated an earlier Jewish-Christian tract which took a more conservative line than he himself approved (see p. 856, n. 9).

3 Jesus' injunction to the crowds to follow the scribes' teaching[23] is often cited along with v. 23 of this chapter ("not neglecting the others") as evidence both that Jesus himself conformed to the scribal tradition and that Matthew's church still operated within the confines of rabbinic law and was not yet in conflict with the Jewish establishment.[24] But the words must be read in their context. In the first place, the whole thrust of this passage is against such a view: the scribes and Pharisees will be declared quite unfit to guide God's people. Secondly, this (like "while not neglecting the others" in v. 23) is one clause of a two-part sentence which must be interpreted as a whole. Here the positive instruction acts as a foil to a following negative instruction, not to copy the scribes' example. The rhetorical effect might be paraphrased: "Follow their teaching if you must, *but be sure not to follow their example.*" In view of the rest of the chapter, even that is probably too generous a reading of the first clause, which is better seen as heavily ironical.[25] Their behavior in effect annuls their "Mosaic" authority.[26] The clause can hardly be meant to be taken at face value, since Jesus has in fact already clashed with scribal/Pharisaic teaching on the sabbath (12:1-14), purity (15:1-20), and divorce (19:3-9) and in more general terms in 16:6-12. The very next verse further underlines his disagreement with their whole approach to lawkeeping.[27]

23. Note, however, the argument of M. A. Powell, *JBL* 114 (1995) 431-35, that what the scribes "say" (Matthew does not say "teach") is not their teaching but simply the law of Moses which they are authorized to read (to a largely illiterate populace). In that case, there is no endorsement of scribal *teaching* here at all. Powell fails to carry conviction, however, in including scribal *teaching* within their ἔργα, "deeds." Despite his protestation that a dichotomy between words and deeds is foreign to ancient Jewish culture, the terms used here surely demand such a distinction between "saying" and "deeds."

24. Several commentators try to avoid this conclusion by claiming that the clause refers to "whatever they teach *as long is it what Moses taught*" (but not their interpretation of Moses), but this suggestion depends on reading a lot between the lines, and seems to empty "sitting on Moses' chair" of any real meaning.

25. J. Jeremias, *Theology,* 210. Carson, 471-74, makes this point particularly strongly. He argues that not only v. 3a but also v. 2 is ironical: they have "seated themselves" on Moses' seat, claiming an authority to which their behavior shows they are not entitled. His ironical interpretation of the two verses does not depend, however, on that reading of ἐκάθισαν, "have taken their seat," which is not in itself necessarily pejorative.

26. R. E. Menninger, *Israel,* 31-32, makes a distinction between the "desire" of the scribes and Pharisees and their conduct which in effect undermines their (genuine) wish to understand and practice God's will. But the wording focuses on what they "say" rather than their desire.

27. R. J. Banks, *Jesus,* 175-77, argues effectively against the view that this verse gives a blanket endorsement to scribal teaching. See also D. E. Garland, *Intention,* 46-55, who reaches a similar conclusion without explicitly calling the saying "ironical" by argu-

4   By saying and not doing (v. 3) they imposed rules on other people but gave them no help in coping with them.[28] So in contrast to experiencing the "kind yoke" and "light burden" of following Jesus (11:30), those who follow the scribes and Pharisees find themselves "toiling and heavily loaded" (11:28), struggling under the weight of a hugely expanded legal code which enslaves rather than liberates those who follow it.[29] The imagery of the scribes "tying up" these loads before placing them on people's shoulders is perhaps intended to allude to the extensive hermeneutical study and debate which have gone into formulating the scribal rules;[30] see, for example, the introductory comments on 12:1-14 concerning the sabbath regulations. Yet they are not willing to help those whose troubles they have themselves caused; far from reaching out to the *'am-hā'āreṣ,* the Pharisees kept them at a distance (see on 9:10-11). Contrast Jesus himself, who offers rest to the burdened (11:28-30).

5-7   A second charge against the scribes and Pharisees is that their religious practices were designed to win the approval of other people rather than that of God. These verses strongly recall 6:1-6, 16-18, where Jesus has already spoken of the preoccupation of "the hypocrites" with gaining human applause for piety rather than pleasing God. To the examples given there, he now adds others which focus on clothing and on social status.

Phylacteries were the small leather boxes *(tefillîn)* containing key texts from the law which were (and are) worn on the forehead and arm in literal fulfillment of Deut 6:8; 11:18.[31] They were presumably intended as a spiritual aid for the wearer, but they provided an opportunity for religious ostentation: either the boxes themselves or the straps by which they were

---

ing that "what appears to be a concession to the ordained authority of the scribes and Pharisees" is in fact "a stratagem which sets the scene for an impeachment."

28. K. G. C. Newport, *Sources,* 124-27, draws attention to "the parallelism between 'they say but they do not do' [vv. 2-3] and 'they load . . . but they do not lift a finger,'" and argues that in each case the first element is positive and only the second negative; here then, as in vv. 2-3 (on Newport's view see above), the teaching authority of the scribes is approved. This can be maintained only by proposing that βαρύς here be understood, as in v. 23, to mean "important" (positive) rather than "heavy" (negative). But when combined with φορτία, "loads," it is hard to read "heavy" as a commendation, especially if the reader remembers 11:28-30.

29. For similar imagery applied to ritual requirements see Acts 15:10, 28.

30. See on 16:19 for the metaphor of "tying up" applied to legal prohibitions, though the Greek word is not the same here.

31. The use of the same formula in Exod 13:9, 16, where there is no obvious text to be written and physically worn, suggests that the original sense was metaphorical. For the development in use of both the *tefillîn* and the *ṣîṣît* see Schürer, 2:479-81. For details about *tefillîn* and the use of the Greek term φυλακτήριον see also Davies and Allison, 1:17-19; K. G. C. Newport, *Sources,* 85-88.

fastened could be made more conspicuous by making them "broad."[32] The "fringes" are the tassels *(ṣîṣît)* on the corners of Jewish cloaks which were required by Num 15:38-39; Deut 22:12. In biblical times they were worn on the ordinary outer garment, as Jesus himself did (9:20; 14:36); it is only in subsequent Judaism that the *ṭallît,* the fringed shawl worn especially for prayer, has developed. The fringes, too, were intended as spiritual visual aids (Num 15:39), but to increase their length was an obvious way to draw people's attention to one's piety. Their length was discussed in Jesus' day, the school of Shammai favoring longer tassels than that of Hillel *(Sifre* on Num 15:37-41).

The social opportunities for enjoying people's adulation are found both in secular life (dinners and marketplaces) and in worship. For the best couch at dinner cf. Luke 14:7-11; Josephus, *Ant.* 15.21. Remains of early Jewish synagogue buildings include some individual stone seats[33] which presumably stood in front of the benches where other worshipers sat and were for the leading members, among whom the scribes and Pharisees would expect to be. For a graphic example of preferential seating in a Christian *synagōgē* see Jas 2:2-4. By the second century the title "Rabbi" (etymologically "my great one") was properly used of those who had been trained and formally recognized as scribes (like our "Reverend"), but this technical use probably came in after the time of Jesus: as applied to Jesus (26:25, 49; Mark 9:5; 10:51; 11:21; John 1:49; 3:2, etc.)[34] it was apparently an honorary title, based on his reputation rather than his official status.[35]

8 In contrast with the scribes' love of human approbation, Jesus calls on those who follow him to avoid honorific titles. For "But you" cf. the repeated "but as for you" of 6:3, 6, 17. Verses 8-10, while taking up the theme of the scribes' craving for public respect, are clearly aimed primarily at Jesus' own disciples (the "scribes" of the kingdom of heaven, 13:52),[36] those for whom he ("the Messiah," v. 10) is the one true teacher and leader.

32. *M. Meg.* 4:8 condemns "sectaries" for ostentatious use of phylacteries (decorating them with gold or putting them on top of the sleeve). See further S. T. Lachs, *Rabbinic Commentary,* 366-67. D. E. Garland, *Intention,* 56, n. 84, suggests that the reference is to wearing the *ṭᵉfillîn* for longer than the required period of time.

33. For details see Schürer, 2:442 (part of n. 67).

34. This is probably also the term used when the evangelists report people addressing Jesus as διδάσκαλε, "Teacher." John 1:38 equates the two.

35. For the development of the title see A. J. Overman, *Gospel,* 44-48; K. G. C. Newport, *Sources,* 90-95. Overman describes its use in the gospels as "general, honorific and non-technical," and suggests that Matthew dislikes the term because he "equates 'rabbi' with the Jewish leadership in his setting."

36. D. E. Garland, *Intention,* 61-63, draws out how these verses apply to the "scribal" status and responsibilities of Christian leaders.

They highlight a concern for status which, while taken for granted in secular society (20:25), ought not to characterize those who follow Jesus (20:26). Matthew's inclusion of this warning in his gospel testifies to the fact that the problem had not gone away, as indeed it still has not among Christians today. The three titles singled out were probably all being used in Matthew's church. It is not difficult for a modern reader to think of similar honorifics in use today, and to discern behind the titles an excessive deference to academic or ecclesiastical qualifications.

In Matthew's gospel Jesus himself is addressed as "Teacher" only by outsiders, never by his disciples, and the actual Hebrew term "Rabbi" is heard only from the lips of Judas after his apostasy (26:25, 49). But the title is not in itself objectionable, since it is here forbidden not for Jesus himself but for his disciples, and the reason for the ban is to avoid confusion with the only true "teacher" they have, Jesus himself.[37] To recognize him as such is not false adulation but sober fact, but not even the most prominent of his followers is to be placed alongside him in this position of authority. Cf. the comment in 7:28-29 on the unique authority of Jesus the teacher in contrast with "their scribes" who are here under the spotlight. If anyone is entitled to "sit on Moses' chair," it is Jesus.

The statement that "you are all brothers and sisters" might seem more appropriate after the next verse; here we might have expected "fellow disciples" as the correlative to "teacher." But "brothers and sisters" is apparently for Jesus a way of expressing *equality;* it is not for one brother to be set above the others. This usage deserves to be noticed by those who value the biblical view of disciples as brothers and sisters: the term rules out differences of status, for the discourse of ch. 18 (which also made prominent use of the term "brother") has cast us all together in the role of "little ones."

9   The introduction of familial terminology in "you are all brothers" now leads into another family title which is open to abuse: "father." It is found in the OT as a term of respect, usually applied to someone older and/or socially superior to the speaker (e.g., 1 Sam 24:11; 2 Kgs 2:12; 5:13; 6:21).[38] Its use in Judaism for an authoritative teacher is illustrated by the title of the mishnaic tractate *'Abot,* "The Fathers," a collection of sayings of revered teachers past and present.[39] But Jesus' special emphasis on the disciple's re-

---

37. Does the elimination of human "teachers" allude to the ideal situation which Jeremiah foresaw under the new covenant when "they will no longer teach one another . . . for they will all know me" (Jer 31:34; cf. Isa 54:13)? So M. Knowles, *Jeremiah,* 209-12.

38. Cf. Luke 16:24, 27, 30 and the plural use in Acts 7:2; 22:1. Also Josephus, *Ant.* 15.21.

39. See D. E. Garland, *Intention,* 59-60, n. 98; K. G. C. Newport, *Sources,* 95-96.

lationship with God as the one "heavenly Father" (especially prominent in the Sermon on the Mount) means that it should no longer be thoughtlessly used of other people — except of course in its literal sense. Paul will speak of his evangelistic role as that of a "father" to those whom he has brought to faith (1 Cor 4:15; cf. Phlm 10), but there is no NT record of him or any other Christian leader being *addressed* as "father."

10   The third title, "instructor," occurs only here in the NT, nor is it found in the LXX. Its original sense was "leader" or "guide," one who shows the way, but it came to be more commonly used for teachers, those who show the way intellectually or spiritually. It may therefore be a virtual synonym of "teacher" in v. 8; perhaps our term "mentor" might convey the same sense. As in v. 8, Jesus is the only person who truly fulfills that role for his followers.[40]

It is surprising that Matthew here portrays Jesus as using "the Messiah" as a third-person title (Mark 9:41 is the only other Synoptic example), especially as he has forbidden his disciples to use that term to describe him (16:20) and has hitherto carefully avoided doing so himself. His disciples were, of course, well aware by now that Jesus did see his mission in messianic terms, and would have understood him here to be speaking of himself, as in v. 8. But the audience is still, according to v. 1, the general public as well as his disciples. We noted above, however, that from v. 8 the primary audience is clearly Jesus' disciples, and in such a context Matthew has not found the title inappropriate, perhaps because the wording does not actually say that "the Messiah" is Jesus, however obvious this must have been to his disciples at the time, as it would also be to Matthew's Christian readers.

11-12   Further sayings about status, already familiar from Jesus' teaching in 18:1-5 and 20:26-27, complete the paragraph. Cf. Prov 29:23 for an aphorism similar to v. 12 (and for other parallels Davies and Allison, 3:279). Such sayings occur at several places in the Synoptic tradition, v. 12 being closely paralleled twice in Luke in different contexts (Luke 14:11; 18:14). Like "The first will be last, and the last first" (19:30; 20:16), these sayings encapsulate Jesus' repeated assault on pomp and self-importance, and reinforce the portrait of Jesus' disciples as a community of "little ones" which is important to Matthew (see above, p. 674).

---

40. S. Byrskog, *Jesus,* 287-90, sets out the evidence from nonbiblical usage, and concludes that for Matthew καθηγητής signifies "a teacher of a higher dignity than the ordinary διδάσκαλος." B. W. Winter, *TynBul* 42 (1991) 152-57, argues from a papyrus usage for the meaning (personal) "tutor." MM 312a mention that in Modern Greek καθηγητής means "Professor."

2. Seven Woes on the Scribes and Pharisees (23:13-36)

13 "But woe to you, scribes and Pharisees, hypocrites, because you shut the kingdom of heaven in other people's faces: you yourselves do not go in, and you won't let others go in who want to.[1]

15 "Woe to you, scribes and Pharisees, hypocrites, because you travel all over the sea and the dry land to recruit one proselyte, and when you have gained him, you make him twice as much a child of hell as yourselves.

16 "Woe to you, blind guides, who say, 'If anyone swears by the sanctuary,[2] that is nothing; but anyone who swears by the gold in the sanctuary is bound by the oath.' 17 You blind fools, which is greater: the gold, or the sanctuary which gives the gold its sanctity? 18 You say too, 'If anyone swears by the altar, that is nothing; but anyone who swears by the sacrifice on the altar is bound by the oath.' 19 You blind men,[3] which is greater: the sacrifice, or the altar which gives it its sanctity? 20 So anyone who swears by the altar swears both by it and by everything placed on it, 21 and anyone who swears by the sanctuary swears both by it and by the one[4] who lives in it. 22 And anyone who swears by heaven swears by the throne of God and by the one who sits on it.

23 "Woe to you, scribes and Pharisees, hypocrites, because you tithe your mint and dill and cummin but you have neglected the weightier matters of the law — justice, mercy, and faithfulness.[5] These

---

1. Many later MSS and some early versions add an eighth woe (traditionally numbered v. 14) which reproduces the accusation against the scribes in Mark 12:40 (= Luke 11:47) but with an introduction to fit the pattern of this discourse: "Woe to you, scribes and Pharisees, hypocrites, because you eat up widows' houses and for a pretext utter long prayers; therefore you will receive a greater condemnation." This woe is more commonly added before v. 13, but sometimes after it. Its absence from all the earliest MSS and some of the earliest versions convinces most critics that it was not part of Matthew's scheme, with its distinctive group of seven woes.

2. The term used throughout this paragraph (and in v. 35) is ναός, the temple building itself in which the priests carried out their duties, rather than the broader term ἱερόν, denoting the whole temple complex, which was used for the area of Jesus' activity in 21:12-15, 23.

3. Many MSS repeat the formula "blind fools" from v. 17, but the absence of the term "fools" here from a significant group of early MSS and versions probably indicates that it was not in the original text, since there is no obvious reason to omit it the second time, and it would be natural to repeat the previous formula.

4. Analogy with the preceding clause leads us to expect a reference to the gold of vv. 16-17, and the dative case could be either masculine or neuter, but the verb κατοικέω, "to dwell in," strongly suggests a personal subject, and the sequel in v. 22 confirms this reading.

5. Or "faith"; see the comments below.

865

are the things you ought to have done, while not neglecting the others. 24 *You blind guides: you strain out the gnat but swallow the camel!*

25 *"Woe to you, scribes and Pharisees, hypocrites, because you clean the outside of the cup and the dish while inside they are full of violence and greed.*[6] 26 *You blind Pharisee, first clean the inside*[7] *of the cup, so that its outside*[8] *may be clean as well.*

27 *"Woe to you, scribes and Pharisees, hypocrites, because you are like white-washed burial places, which look lovely from the outside while inside they are full of the bones of the dead and all sorts of uncleanness.* 28 *You are like that: from the outside you give people the impression that you are righteous, but inside you are full of hypocrisy and lawlessness.*

29 *"Woe to you, scribes and Pharisees, hypocrites, because you build the burial places of the prophets and decorate the tombs of the righteous,* 30 *and say, 'If we had lived in the time of our ancestors, we wouldn't have taken part with them in killing the prophets.'* 31 *So you identify yourselves as*[9] *the descendants of those who murdered the prophets;* 32 *well then, complete your ancestors' task*[10] *yourselves!* 33 *You snakes, you brood of vipers, how can you escape being condemned to hell?* 34 *Look, that is why I am sending to you prophets, wise men, and scribes; some of them you will kill and crucify, and some of them you will flog in your assemblies*[11] *and persecute in one town after another,* 35 *so that you may bear responsibility for*[12] *all the righteous blood which is being shed on the earth, from the blood of righteous Abel to the blood of Zechariah son of Berechiah, whom you*

6. Literally, "plunder and lack of self-control." For the former see on 11:12, where a cognate term describes the action of the "violent people"; the latter term, ἀκρασία, is a philosophical term for people's inability to control their baser instincts (its unfamiliarity as a "Christian" word probably accounts for the later MSS which substitute "unrighteousness," "uncleanness," or "wickedness," the latter being the reading of Luke 11:39). The two terms together function as a hendiadys denoting an unrestrained selfishness which rides roughshod over the rights and interests of others.

7. Or "contents": so J. D. M. Derrett, *ZNW* 77 (1986) 261.

8. There is a wide variation in readings of this verse, caused partly by the inclusion of dish as well as cup in many MSS and the consequent pluralizing of the pronoun in some, but not all, of those MSS; but there are many other minor variations. The reading given above is perhaps the one which best explains the origin of the others, but the overall effect of the saying is not affected.

9. Literally, "testify about yourselves that you are."

10. Literally, "fill up your ancestors' measure."

11. For the meaning of συναγωγή see on 4:23 (and p. 149, n. 6); also p. 388, n. 3.

12. Literally "upon you may come." For this way of expressing responsibility for an innocent death see the comments below.

murdered between the sanctuary and the altar. 36 *I tell you truly: all these things will come upon this generation."*

The language of Jesus' third-person comments on the scribes and Pharisees in vv. 2-7, while robust, was still relatively objective, even if not polite. But now when he turns to address them directly,[13] the tone is radically sharpened. In addition to the sevenfold "Woe" with its accompanying description "hypocrites" there are further insulting epithets ("child of hell," "blind guides" twice, "blind fools,"[14] "blind men," "blind Pharisee," "snakes, brood of vipers"),[15] and the accusations made about them are phrased in ways which would be especially offensive to scribes and Pharisees ("violence and greed," "bones of the dead and all uncleanness," "hypocrisy and lawlessness," "murdering the prophets and the righteous"). See above, pp. 853-56, for the significance of this denunciation in the development of Matthew's story, and p. 854, n. 5 for the prevalence of such polemical rhetoric in the ancient world. There are many places in the gospels where Jesus' language is far from "meek and mild," but nothing else at this level of invective except perhaps in the dialogue with "the Jews" in John 8.[16]

The polemic is structured around seven "woes"; for other Matthean woes see 11:21-24 (unrepentant towns), 18:7b (those who cause others to stumble), 26:24 (Judas),[17] and for the "woe" formula see on 11:21.[18] The id-

---

13. But see p. 856, n. 8, for the possibility that the second-person address is not to be taken at face value.

14. See on 5:22 for Jesus' objection to the thoughtless use of the term "fool." The difference here is perhaps that this is not a thoughtless insult but a considered verdict on their lack of understanding. See p. 201, n. 85, for a less satisfactory explanation of the apparent inconsistency.

15. The metaphorical use of blindness to represent spiritual failure has become so familiar that its use as a term of abuse does not shock us as it should. For a salutary corrective see the comments of a blind exegete, J. M. Hull, *Darkness,* especially pp. 157-59: "Unfortunately, my Lord Jesus, my gentle master, does not, in this matter, provide us with a satisfactory model."

16. The question of how the invective of this chapter can be squared with Jesus' preaching of love for enemies exercises commentators. Particularly interesting is R. Mohrlang, *Matthew,* 99-100: Mohrlang is palpably eager to minimize the contradiction, but nonetheless must conclude that "at this point Matthew's Jesus himself could perhaps be viewed as guilty of the charge he levels at those who 'preach but do not practice' (23.3). And to the extent such invective betrays the attitude of Matthew himself, he fails to measure up to his own convictions of Jesus' ideals."

17. The "woes" in 18:7a and 24:19 are different in character, as they simply speak of misfortune without the clear attribution of blame.

18. The background and meaning of the "woe" formula as used in Matt 23 is discussed at length by D. E. Garland, *Intention,* 64-90.

iom is particularly characteristic of Isaiah, and the series of six woes against the ungodly in Isa 5:8-23 may have influenced this passage.[19] "Seven" is not elsewhere in Matthew a structurally significant number:[20] even the six "sevens" which make up the list of Jesus' ancestors are expressed as three "fourteens" (1:17). It is possible that the sense of completeness often associated with the number "seven" in Jewish thought is intended to underline the message of the final culmination of Israel's guilt in "this generation," but that thought is clearly expressed in its own right in vv. 29-36, and needs no numerical symbolism to support it. The first six woes may be seen as three pairs with matching themes: the first pair (vv. 13-15) speak of keeping people out of the kingdom of heaven; the second pair (vv. 16-24) focus on the distorted perspective which puts concern with details before the basic principles of religion and ethics; the third pair (vv. 25-28) contrast outward and inward purity. The seventh woe then brings the denunciation to its climax with the charge of complicity in the murder of God's messengers.

Those who regard ch. 23 as part of Matthew's final discourse sometimes suggest that these woes balance the beatitudes with which the first discourse began in 5:3-10, but see above, pp. 856-57, for reasons for doubting that view of ch. 23. The beatitudes of 5:3-10 are eight, not seven, in number[21] and are very brief by comparison. Nor are the contents of these woes parallel to the set of woes which Luke 6:24-26 provides as a counterbalance to his shorter set of beatitudes.[22]

The seventh woe is expanded to express the cumulative force of the whole denunciation in the final judgment now about to fall on "this generation." Some interpreters therefore prefer to set off vv. 33-36 (or vv. 34-36) as a general conclusion to the whole sequence, but the subject matter in these verses remains closely linked specifically to the seventh woe concerning the treatment of the prophets. It is because the current generation is continuing in the same tradition of hostility to God's messengers that it now faces judgment, and that judgment results not only from their own failings but from the whole tradition from Abel to Zechariah to which they are the willing heirs.

---

19. M. D. Goulder, *Midrash,* 420, argues this in the light of the clear allusion to the first part of the same chapter of Isaiah as recently as 21:33. But the formula occurs frequently in the prophets, and there is another sequence of (five) woes in Hab 2:6-20. Cf. the repeated series of woes (thirty in all) throughout *1 En.* 94–100. There are two series of three woes each in Rev 8:13 with 9:12 and 11:14 and in Rev 18:9-20.

20. A parallel is sometimes claimed in the parables of ch. 13, but see the discussion there for my understanding of that collection as comprising eight, not seven, parables.

21. Was the insertion of an eighth woe (see above, p. 865, n. 1) partly due to the desire for a closer beatitude/woe parallel?

22. The attempt by M. D. Goulder, *Midrash,* 421-22, to draw a parallel between the contents of the beatitudes of 5:3-10 and the woes of this chapter seems to me very contrived.

The direct address to the scribes and Pharisees continues throughout these verses. It will be in vv. 37-39, with their change of address, that the true conclusion to the diatribe will come.

13 For "scribes and Pharisees, hypocrites"[23] see above, pp. 854-55, and for "hypocrisy" in Matthew generally see on 6:2. The nature of the "hypocrisy" exposed in this sequence varies with the different items, but its essential nature is not deliberate deception but rather self-deceit, in that they are accused of having missed the point of true religion especially by focusing on minutiae and externals instead of on the essentials of the sort of life God really desires.[24] This tragically distorted perspective has become so firmly entrenched that it has made them enemies of God's true messengers (vv. 29-36).

In this *first woe,* then, the charge is not of insincerity or double standards: they treat other people as they treat themselves, allowing neither to enter the kingdom of heaven. To "enter the kingdom of heaven" has been used in 5:20; 7:21; 8:11; 18:3; 19:23-24; 21:31 as a term for ultimate salvation (cf. "enter [eternal] life" in 7:13-14; 18:8-9; 19:17), for belonging to the true people of God, those who are under his kingship. The same metaphor is now graphically developed in the idea of a door to the kingdom of heaven (cf. 7:13-14)[25] which can be shut against those who wish to enter; the same imagery will be used in an eschatological context in 25:10, "the door was shut." As the official guardians of God's will revealed in the law the scribes and Pharisees had the responsibility for helping others to live by the will of God, but instead their teaching and example has kept people out, and they themselves have failed to find the right way in.[26] This first woe does not spell out how this has happened,[27] but v. 4 has already given the charge some content,

23. The phrase is delightfully translated by Albright and Mann, 276-79, as "You pettifogging Pharisee lawyers"!

24. D. E. Garland, *Intention,* 96-117, discusses the background and use of the term "hypocrite" at length, and concludes that in this chapter its emphasis falls not so much on a discrepancy between profession and practice as on "the Pharisees' false interpretation of the law, and . . . their failure as God's appointed leaders"; cf. also ibid., 159-62.

25. Cf. also the "keys of the kingdom of heaven" in 16:19, but see the comments there, and especially p. 625, n. 40: the primary reference there is to stewardship rather than controlling admission.

26. Luke 11:52 sharpens this complaint (addressed to "lawyers"): "you have taken away the key of knowledge; you yourselves have not gone in, and you have stopped those who tried to go in." *Gos. Thom.* 39 develops the imagery further: the Pharisees and scribes "have received the keys of knowledge and have hidden them." Another saying in *Gos. Thom.* 102 makes the same charge against the Pharisees by drawing on Aesop's fable of the dog in the manger instead of the imagery of the closed door

27. K. G. C. Newport, *Sources,* 133-34, is right to point out that the widespread assumption that this charge relates to their teaching of the law (which would conflict with

and the woes that follow will give it more substance. The reader may recall that the "righteousness of the scribes and the Pharisees" does not even begin to meet the requirements of the kingdom of heaven (5:20).

15 The *second woe* shows that their problem is not lack of enthusiasm. Their zeal extends even beyond their primary charge, the people of Israel, to the gaining of proselytes from among other nations. In the book of Acts we are introduced to proselytes (Acts 2:11; 6:5; 13:43), non-Jewish adherents to the religion and ethics of Judaism, and to a wider circle of "worshipers" who apparently respected and learned from Judaism without themselves becoming formally enrolled as proselytes (Acts 13:50; 16:14; 17:4, 17; 18:7). For the baptism of proselytes see on 3:6. There is considerable disagreement about how extensive and how successful Jewish attempts to gain proselytes were at this period, and the generally negative impression of Judaism gained from extant Greek and Latin literature suggests that it may have been an uphill task. But Jews in the diaspora made serious efforts to combat Gentile prejudice and to commend the religion of Yahweh: the works of Philo and Josephus are clear evidence of this, notably Josephus's apologetic work, *Against Apion.* For evidence of successful proselytism in the diaspora see Schürer, 3:160-64; rabbinic discussions of the admission of proselytes (Schürer, 3:173-76) indicate at least openness to their reception, if not active recruitment.[28] There is, however, less evidence that Palestinian rabbis of the first century were as zealous in proselytizing as Jesus here describes.[29] It is possible that Jesus refers here not so much to the initial conversion of pagans as to the Pharisaic desire to persuade less fully committed Gentile "worshipers" to accept the full responsibilities of proselytism.[30]

The convert sometimes outdoes the zeal of the converter, with more fanaticism than discernment. "Child of hell" is Semitic idiom for one who

---

his reading of vv. 2-31 as a whole) is not explicit in the text. It is generally argued from the surrounding context. Newport's alternative proposal is that they kept people out of the kingdom of heaven by "their failure to recognize Jesus for who he was, and, more specifically, their policy of attempting to turn away would-be adherents to the Jewish sect which had grown up in allegiance to him."

28. There is a useful general coverage of the topic of proselytes by K. G. Kuhn, *TDNT* 6:730-42.

29. See the full discussion by S. McKnight, *Light,* in response to the more positive earlier accounts of, e.g., J. Jeremias, *Promise,* 11-19.

30. So McKnight, ibid., 106-8, citing the "judaizers" of Galatia as a parallel. A possible example is found in the celebrated conversion of the royal family of Adiabene (in northern Mesopotamia) during the first century A.D. as recounted by Josephus, *Ant.* 20.34-48. The original "missionary" was "a certain Jewish merchant" who advised the young king to stop short of circumcision for prudential reasons; it was another Galilean Jew who was "reputed to be very strict about the ancestral laws" (a Pharisee?) who later persuaded him to become a full proselyte.

belongs to and is destined for hell (*geēnna,* for which see on 5:22); cf. "children of the Evil One" (13:38) and "children of the kingdom" (8:12; 13:38). On the principle set out in 12:30, those who offer and follow a different concept of religious commitment, however well intentioned, are enemies of the kingdom of heaven.

16-22 In 5:33-37 Jesus has warned his disciples against taking oaths at all. But this *third woe*[31] operates at the lower level of scribal/Pharisaic religion, in which the principle of oath-taking remained unquestioned.[32] Even if that principle is granted, however, their rulings about the relative validity of different oaths (which were also at issue in 5:33-37) reveal a casuistry which is against even common sense. The sanctity of the items presented in worship (the gold[33] and the sacrifices) derives from the sanctity of the place where they are offered (the temple and the altar; for the principle see Exod 29:37) and not vice versa. There is no profound theology involved here, just an almost jocular exposé of how silly such legal casuistry can become. We have no clear evidence from the time of Jesus of these specific oaths being used or evaluated in the way that is here described, but given the ingenuity of the mishnaic debates about oath formulae (tractate *Šᵉbûʿōt*), there is nothing surprising in the allegation; for a comparable example see *b. Ned.* 14b, where a vow by the Torah is not binding, but one by the Torah's contents is. The basis of Jesus' criticism here is that the scribal approach is superficial, and fails to think through the principles underlying the details on which their debate is focused. For the epithet "blind guides" (here and in v. 24) see on 15:14; cf. the impaired vision of the would-be helper in 7:3-5. The use of "blind" three times in this pericope draws attention to their lack of spiritual perception.

In the further comments in vv. 20-22, which underline the same charge, the principle of swearing oaths remains formally unquestioned, but in vv. 21 and 22 there is a reminder of 5:34-35 in that oaths which may be

---

31. This woe is differently constructed in that the address "scribes and Pharisees, hypocrites" is replaced by "blind guides," and is followed not by "because" but by "who say. . . ." Presumably to add "scribes and Pharisees, hypocrites" to "blind guides" (which will stand alone again in v. 24) would have been too cumbersome, and would have been redundant in that "blind guides" makes the same point. S. H. Brooks, *Community,* 68-69, argues that therefore vv. 16-22 were originally an independent woe-saying which resisted assimilation to the pattern of the other six.

32. There is, however, evidence of considerable diversity of teaching and practice concerning oaths and vows among rabbis; some, it seems, would have shared Jesus' dislike of casuistry in this area. See D. E. Garland, *Intention,* 133-35, drawing on the work of S. Lieberman.

33. The gold referred to could be either that presented to and kept in the temple treasury or that used in the decoration of the building. There is no obvious way of deciding which is intended, and the sense is hardly affected.

thought less serious are shown to involve the invocation of God himself; v. 22 in effect repeats what was said in 5:34. The reader who remembers that earlier discussion should therefore be reminded of its conclusion, that such oaths are better avoided. There is a significant escalation within these three statements. Verse 20 simply draws out the logic of the rhetorical question in v. 19. Verse 21 looks as if it is going to do the same for v. 17, but instead of focusing on the "gold" which was the subject of v. 17, it raises the stakes by asserting that the real object of the oath is the God whose temple it is (see p. 865, n. 4). Verse 22 then extends the same notion by introducing an oath-formula not previously mentioned in this pericope ("by heaven") and drawing the same conclusion: heaven derives its sanctity from the God who is enthroned there. See above on 5:34b-35 for this specific oath, and on 5:37 for the relevance of such considerations to oath-taking today.

We should note in passing that the preoccupation with temple rituals here (as in 5:23-24; see p. 203, n. 89) presupposes a period when the temple was still standing. While it is possible that Matthew simply preserved Jesus' pre-70 sayings in a changed situation, his retention of this material is one of the incidental pointers to an earlier date for the gospel than many critics will allow.

23-24   The *fourth woe,* too, focuses on a meticulous concern for detail which leaves the essential principles of religion untouched.[34] Tithing, like the swearing of oaths, is a matter covered by the OT law; it was the means by which the priesthood was maintained.[35] The principle of setting aside a tenth of all vegetable produce (Lev 27:30; Deut 14:22), while not specifically applied in the OT to garden herbs, was reasonably assumed to cover them,[36] and Jesus has no objection to the practice as such: "while not neglecting the others."[37] What he objects to is the unbalanced piety which sets great

---

34. G. B. Caird, *Language,* 92, explains the pragmatic appeal of such an approach: "They concentrated on the minor and practicable pieties, to the neglect of the broad and inexhaustible principles."

35. This point is emphasized especially by A. J. Saldarini, *Community,* 142-43.

36. The tractate *m. Ma'aś.* discusses the specific application of the tithing law in detail, covering some herbs and condiments as well as fruit and vegetables. In 4:5 dill is specifically mentioned along with coriander and other herbs, and there is some rabbinic dispute as to whether the plant should be tithed as well as its seeds. Cummin is also mentioned as tithable in *m. Dem.* 2:1, but some herbs, including rue, which Luke substitutes here, were treated as wild and so not tithable (*m. Šebu.* 9:1). Mint is not mentioned in the mishnaic discussions. See further K. G. C. Newport, *Sources,* 102-3.

37. The wording does not support the suggestion of D. Instone-Brewer, *Traditions,* 1:315-17, that Jesus' objection was to the practical problems faced by a small farmer in handling such small tithes: "This kind of ruling made sense for commercial growers, but Jesus complained on behalf of the common people that they were being oppressed by such rules."

store by these relatively insignificant rules but misses the things that really matter. *Tauta,* "these things," normally refers to the nearer of two antecedents, *ekeina,* "those things," to the further; so the things which ought to have been done are judgment, mercy, and faithfulness, without neglecting tithing herbs. The double use of "neglect" is thus rhetorically effective: at the moment you are neglecting the things that matter; those are the things you ought to be concentrating on, but that does not mean therefore neglecting the others. In this way emphasis is placed on the "weightier matters" as the primary obligation, leaving the acceptance of the tithing rules as the minor element, perhaps to be read more as a concession than as enthusiastic endorsement.[38] In the light of the comments above on v. 3a, there may be an ironical element here too: "I can't object to your tithing herbs, but what matters is that you focus on justice, mercy, and faithfulness."

For other summaries of the essential principles of the law cf. 7:12 and 22:37-40, and the comments especially on the latter. The "weightier matters" listed here are strongly reminiscent of the famous summary in Mic 6:8, "to act justly, to love mercy, and to walk humbly with God." These are, of course, positive principles which no one could object to. There is no suggestion that the scribes and Pharisees were opposed in principle to justice, mercy, and faithfulness. The problem was that they did not devote the same care to working out the practical implications of these basic principles as they did to the minutiae of tithing herbs. *Krisis,* which I have translated "justice," could also mean "judgment" or "condemnation" (as in 5:21, 22), meaning that they had failed to reckon with God's judgment, but that would be an incongruous reading when the other two items in the list are matters of ethical principle; *krisis* has the positive sense of "justice" in the LXX quotation in 12:18, 20 (see p. 467, n. 5). For "mercy" as an essential principle in doing God's will see 5:7, and cf. the words of Hos 6:6, "I desire mercy and not sacrifice," which Jesus has already quoted in 9:13 and 12:7 to justify his own less rigid but more loving practice over against Pharisaic objections. The same text could well sum up the contrast in this chapter between the religion of the "hypocrites," with its focus on externals, and what it means for Jesus to do the will of God. *Pistis,* which I have translated "faithfulness," elsewhere in Matthew means "faith" (in God or Jesus), and that could be the sense here too: they have neglected their relationship with God (cf. the "walking with God" of Mic 6:8). But when Jesus speaks of things to be "done," that meaning seems less likely here than

---

38. D. C. Sim, *Gospel,* 131-32, argues that since in rabbinic thought "less important" does not mean unimportant, we must assume that "Matthew's group strictly kept the dietary and purity laws of Judaism," so that the approval of tithing here is more than a concession. This conclusion depends, of course, on a broader theory of Matthew's relation to rabbinic Judaism than this saying alone can justify.

the ethical sense, "faithfulness,"[39] which fits more appropriately with justice and mercy as outlining the lifestyle God's law requires.

The grotesque imagery of straining out the gnat (from wine or water before drinking)[40] and swallowing the camel belongs to the same class of burlesque as the splinter and the plank in 7:3-5 or the camel going through the eye of a needle in 19:24. It depends on the relative size of the smallest and largest creatures in Palestine. The gnat, as an insect, was unclean (Lev 11:20-23; cf. also the "swarming creatures" of Lev 11:41-44) and therefore must not be ingested; but then the camel was no less unclean (Lev 11:4), and a lot bigger! The joke may have been helped by an Aramaic wordplay between *qalmâ* (gnat) and *gamlâ* (camel).[41]

25-26 The saying about the gnat and the camel has introduced the subject of purity laws, and purity is the subject of this *fifth woe*.[42] Again Jesus is returning to old ground, since in 15:11, 17-20 he has expressed his disapproval of a concept of purity which is purely external. The concern of scribes and Pharisees with the ritual cleanness of vessels used for food and drink was well recognized, if we may judge from Mark's comment on the eating habits of "the Pharisees and all the Jews" in Mark 7:3-4; much of the long mishnaic tractate *Kelim* is devoted to the subject. But, as with the tithing, this is to put the emphasis in the wrong place. The contrast here between "outside" and "inside" is clearly concerned with more than the two physical surfaces of the vessel,[43] for what Jesus says is on the "inside" is not the sort of ritual uncleanness which washing was designed to remove but moral uncleanness[44] — cf. the things which "come out of the heart," which

---

39. BDAG 818b give as the first meaning of πίστις "faithfulness, reliability, fidelity, commitment," though by far the majority of NT uses have the meaning "faith," "trust." In many cases the sense is debatable, but it clearly means "faithfulness" in Rom 3:3 and Tit 2:10, and most take it in that sense in Gal 5:22.

40. The practice is illustrated in *t. Ter.* 7:11: see D. Instone-Brewer, *Traditions*, 1:290-93. See also K. G. C. Newport, *Sources*, 103-5, for likely practice in this regard.

41. Justin, *Dial.* 112.4, conflates vv. 23 and 24 with the amusing result, "You tithe the mint but swallow the camel"!

42. H. Maccoby, *JSNT* 14 (1982) 7-8, may be right to argue that all that Jesus' argument requires is a simple concern with hygiene, but the elements of ritual purity both in the following woe and in Jesus' other discussion of purity in 15:11-20 suggest that that dimension was also in view here, even though it forms the basis for a metaphor rather than for a ritual ruling.

43. The relative significance of the inner and outer surfaces of a vessel is discussed in *m. Kelim* 25 (see J. Neusner, *NTS* 22 [1975/6] 486-95), but Jesus' argument, though using the language of that debate, moves immediately to the less literal sense of the words "outside" and "inside."

44. The construction γέμω ἐκ is probably to be understood in a partitive sense (BDF 172), "be full of"; cf. the cognate γεμίζω ἐκ, "fill with," in Rev 8:5. But the unusual

"make a person unclean" (15:18-19). So the inside (= contents) and outside of the vessel is being used as a metaphor for the inside and outside of the person, just as the inside and outside of the tomb will be in vv. 27-28.[45] Ritual purity without moral cleanness is a sham.[46] "Violence and greed" (see p. 866, n. 6, for the translation) are not the sort of vices people would naturally have associated with scribes and Pharisees, but as in 15:19 Jesus seems to regard the heart as capable of much that other people will never see (cf. murder and adultery in the heart, 5:22, 28). The "eating up of widows' houses" of which the scribes are accused in Mark 12:40; Luke 20:47 may illustrate Jesus' charge here; it is an example of the lack of "justice, mercy, and faithfulness."

The address to a singular Pharisee in v. 26 is surprising, when the rest of the diatribe is addressed to the scribes and Pharisees in the plural. It seems to be intended to sharpen the focus by envisaging the actions of one representative Pharisee dealing with a single cup. The priority of "inside" over "outside" is clear, but the purposive form of the second clause, "so that," might seem to bring us back to the issue of the literal cleaning of vessels. It is, however, more likely to maintain the metaphorical sense of the previous accusation: when the inside (of the person) is clean, the outside will automatically be clean as well, so that the issue of ritual purity becomes irrelevant. This is, then, a reaffirmation of what Jesus has taught in 15:11, 17-20.[47]

27-28 The themes of cleanness and of outside/inside continue in this *sixth woe.* The uncleanness contracted by touching a dead body or a human bone or grave was the most serious in the Mosaic law (Num 19:11-22; cf. Lev 21:1-11; Num 6:6-7; for the comparative scale of seriousness see *m. Kelim* 1:4). The marking of graves[48] with lime-plaster was intended not so

---

syntax has led some to suggest that the ἐκ denotes the source rather than the nature of the contents ("full of the proceeds of violence and greed"); so D. E. Garland, *Intention,* 148-49. Even if that sense be granted, however, the emphasis falls not on the physical nature of the contents but on moral disapproval of how they were acquired.

45. This is rightly argued by H. Maccoby, *JSNT* 14 (1982) 3-7, against Neusner (see n. 43), who thinks Jesus is trying to contribute to the debate on ritual cleanness. D. E. Garland, *Intention,* 142-50, following Neusner, insists that the "inside" and "outside" are to be understood literally, but because he nonetheless recognizes the centrality of the moral issue of violence and greed, his interpretation does not in the end differ substantially from that which regards the language as metaphorical throughout.

46. For a similar theme cf. the early apocryphal story in P. Oxy. 840, where Jesus dismisses the ritual washing of the temple authorities as like the self-beautification of "prostitutes and flute girls" who "inwardly are filled with scorpions and all unrighteousness."

47. *Gos. Thom.* 22 reflects the idea, though not directly the wording, of this saying when it includes in a long list of qualifications for "entering the kingdom" the clause "when you make the inside like the outside and the outside like the inside."

48. S. T. Lachs, *HTR* 68 (1975) 385-88, suggests that the reference may be to os-

much for cosmetic purposes[49] as to warn people against touching them and so contracting uncleanness (*m. Šeqal.* 1:1; *m. Ma'aś. Š.* 5:1).[50] The contrast between the bright outside and the uncleanness inside makes an apt illustration for Jesus' charge of hypocrisy; cf. the similar use of "white-washed wall" in Acts 23:3, drawing on the imagery of Ezek 13:10-16, where the whitewash is an attempt to cover up structural defects. Here we are closer to our modern sense of "hypocrisy," giving a fine impression which is belied by the reality behind the facade. The outward impression is of "righteousness," probably especially in the sense we noted at 1:19, scrupulous observance of the law. In that case the charge that they are really "lawless" inside is particularly wounding, but we have seen in 5:17-48 that for Jesus keeping the law does not mean the exact observance of regulations but a sensitive awareness of and obedience to the essential will of God which underlies the minutiae, being "perfect as your heavenly Father is perfect." In that sense, for all their lawkeeping, they do not live according to the law.[51]

29-32   The extended *seventh woe* begins like the others, and the mention of decorated tombs links it verbally with the sixth, but now the tombs are literal and the charge is more serious: despite their pious protestations, they are responsible for the deaths which the tombs mark. The veneration of the tombs of holy people[52] and martyrs is a feature of Jewish as of

---

suaries, which contained the bones of a dead person, and were often decorated with a marble and lime plaster. But τάφος means a burial place for a whole body rather than the ossuary into which the bones were subsequently collected; the only supportive evidence Lachs cites is the use of the cognate ταφή for a funerary urn once in Sophocles. See further D. E. Garland, *Intention,* 152-53, for Jewish practice: (rock-cut) tombs with stones over the entrance would be obvious enough; what is in view here is less conspicuous graves which might otherwise not be noticed.

49. Indeed, many have argued that it was not cosmetic at all, and that the white plaster would not be regarded as beautiful but as a mark of uncleanness. Matthew's positive term "lovely," which is required to make the imagery work, is then attributed to the building of fine monuments rather than to the perfunctory marking of graves as a warning (see Davies and Allison, 3:300-302, for the discussion; also D. E. Garland, *Intention,* 154-57). But all that the imagery requires is the contrast between the white outside and the dark and dirty inside, and the regular whitewashing of burial places supplies that contrast.

50. The whitewashing took place annually shortly before Passover (*m. Šeqal.* 1:1), making this a topical illustration.

51. An interesting discussion by W. D. Davies, *Setting,* 202-6, of the meaning of ἀνομία in Matthew concludes that it is not concerned primarily with the Jewish law as such, but with "failure to recognize and obey the true will of God." See contra D. C. Sim, *Gospel,* 204-6, who, however, states that Davies' view is held by "the majority of scholars."

52. Note the careful marking of the burial sites of the patriarchs in Gen 23; 25:9-10; 35:19-20; 50:4-14, and the exception of Moses which proves the rule, Deut 34:6.

many other cultures.[53] *Lives of the Prophets* (probably written in the first century A.D.) makes a point of mentioning where each of the prophets was buried (except, of course, Elijah), and indulges in detailed description of some of their tombs (*Liv. Pro.* 1:9-12; 3:3-4). See above, p. 813, n. 24, for the martyrdom of prophets in the OT and in later Jewish tradition; for the association of "prophets" and "the righteous" cf. 13:17; 10:41. Those who killed the prophets were usually kings and ruling officials, but Neh 9:26 lists the killing of the prophets among the causes of the troubles which have come upon the whole people, and that sense of corporate responsibility underlies Jesus' words here; the theme will be picked up again in Acts 7:52.[54] We may assume that the scribes and Pharisees have not themselves killed prophets and righteous people, but their rejection of God's true messengers, notably John the Baptist and now Jesus himself, puts them in the same camp. For "sons of" as an idiom of identification see the comments above on v. 15. The ironic command[55] of v. 32 looks forward to the part they are soon to play in what has been predicted in 21:35-39 as the culminating act of rebellion, the execution of Jesus the Messiah. For the idea of a "measure" (see p. 866, n. 10) of rebellion against God which remains to be completed cf. Gen 15:16; Dan 8:23; 9:24; 2 Macc 6:14, and for a similar thought applied to Jewish persecution of Christians cf. 1 Thess 2:14-16.[56]

33 The continuity between the missions of John and of Jesus, and the consequent link between their deaths as martyrs (see 17:12), is underlined not only by Jesus' use of John's uncomplimentary epithet, "brood of vipers" (3:7), but also by a very similar rhetorical question to John's about escaping the coming judgment. This time, however, the threat is more explicit: the addition of "hell" both makes clear the ultimate nature of the judgment and indicates that as far as they are concerned the verdict is already clear.

---

53. Josephus, *War* 4.532, speaks of the visiting of the tombs of the patriarchs in Hebron, and of their magnificence. In *Ant.* 16.182, he speaks of a very expensive white marble monument erected by Herod at the entrance to David's tomb (mentioned also in Acts 2:29), though in this case the motive was guilt rather than piety. See also *Ant.* 20.95, and for earlier Jewish practice 1 Macc 13:27-30. J. Jeremias, *Theology*, 146, n. 2, summarizing his study *Heiligengräber*, speaks of a "'tomb-renaissance' which flourished at the time of Jesus." See also K. G. C. Newport, *Sources*, 107-10.

54. D. E. Garland, *Intention*, 179-81, traces the background to the theme of the martyrdom of prophets.

55. For similar ironic commands to sin issued by OT prophets see Isa 6:9; 29:9; Jer 44:25; Amos 4:4-5.

56. For the prevalence of this idea in OT and Jewish thought see D. E. Garland, *Intention*, 168, n. 25. Garland goes on, ibid., 169-70, to examine the parallel with 1 Thess 2:15-16. Cf. K. G. C. Newport, *Sources*, 171.

34   The exposé of the failings of God's people now moves from the past into the present, and indeed into the future, as Jesus speaks of his own mission and that of his disciples. "That is why I am sending . . ." may link directly with v. 33: the "prophets, wise men, and scribes" are sent to warn people of the coming judgment before it is too late. But perhaps more likely the connection is with v. 32: they are being sent so that the measure of guilt may be filled up when they are rejected and killed. At any rate, this verse envisages a succession of people sent "to you": in the light of v. 37 "you" refers probably not to the scribes and Pharisees specifically so much as to the people of Jerusalem more generally. But whereas vv. 29-31 have spoken of prophets and righteous people sent to them before the coming of Jesus, and 21:34-36 has spoken of God's sending the prophets before sending his Son, the reference now is to the present ("I am sending") and future ("you *will* kill, crucify, flog, persecute"), and the sender is not God but Jesus himself.[57] We have heard in ch. 10 of Jesus sending out his disciples, but nothing more has been made of their mission since then, and Matthew has depicted them acting only in association with Jesus himself, not as "sent" by him. Moreover, the future tenses which describe their fate in this saying indicate that this is not about the pre-Easter mission of the Twelve, but about what is to happen after Jesus' own death. Those who take his message to Israel will meet the same fate as he has himself, and as he predicted for the Twelve in 10:16-23; note the clear echo of that passage in the phrases "flog in your assemblies" (see on 10:17) and "persecute in one town after another" (cf. 10:23).[58] Cf. again 1 Thess 2:14-16 (see already above on v. 32) for the continuity between "killing the Lord Jesus and the prophets" and the continuing Jewish persecution of Christians.

The words used to denote these future missionaries are interesting. They are described not as evangelists or apostles (though the verb used is *apostellō,* "send out") but as "prophets, wise men, and scribes." The least surprising term is "prophet," since Jesus' warning against false prophets (7:15-20) indicates that real prophets were to be expected among his own followers, and in 10:41 Jesus has spoken of prophets in parallel with righteous people and disciples; Acts and the Pauline letters provide ample evidence of the hon-

---

57. D. E. Orton, *Scribe,* 154-55, emphasizes this "accentuation" of the authority of Jesus, comparing the wording of v. 34a with LXX Jer 8:17. A more relevant comparison, though not verbally so close, is Jer 7:25.

58. The inclusion of crucifixion in the list is more surprising, since there is no historical record of any of Jesus' disciples being crucified (though later tradition asserted this), and this seems unlikely in a Jewish context, nor is there any record of the Jewish authorities handing over followers of Jesus for Roman execution. It seems that at this point Jesus' own fate has become identified with that of his followers. D. C. Sim, *Gospel,* 160, therefore argues that this is not a reflection of past experience on the part of Matthew and his church, but a fear for the future based on Jesus' demand that his followers "take up the cross."

ored activity of prophets within the early Christian communities. "Wise men" is less familiar as a Christian term,[59] though one honored in the OT through the teaching of the wise from whom the books of Proverbs, Job, Ecclesiastes, and several of the psalms derive, and in the Wisdom tradition perpetuated especially in the apocryphal book of Ben Sira.[60] Most surprising in view of its use elsewhere in Matthew is "scribes," but 13:52 has envisaged a scribe who is also a disciple (see comments there), and the reference here is presumably to such people, the Christian counterpart to the failed "scribes and Pharisees" who are here under attack. All three categories represent significant groups through whom God has taught his people during the OT and subsequent periods, and this saying looks forward to a continuation of that teaching tradition but now among those specifically sent by Jesus. As such they will find themselves in opposition to the teaching establishment which has rejected him; they will represent an alternative and persecuted religious tradition. The words chosen here may have been familiar in Matthew's own church, but all three already have a strong background in non-Christian Judaism.[61]

In the parallel in Luke 11:49 an abbreviated form of the same declaration is attributed not directly to Jesus but to what, according to Jesus, "the Wisdom of God said." Commentators on Luke are not agreed on where and when "God's Wisdom" is supposed to have made this statement; in extant Jewish traditions Wisdom does not send messengers, but rather acts herself as God's emissary. But it has been claimed that in transferring Wisdom's words directly to the mouth of Jesus Matthew has deliberately equated Jesus with Wisdom: what Wisdom said, Jesus says. We have noted in 11:28-30 the clear use of Wisdom language in Jesus' invitation to the burdened, so that the suggestion that he here speaks as Wisdom is not out of keeping with Matthean theology, but here there is no verbal echo of a known wisdom passage, and the alleged Wisdom christology depends entirely on the silence of Matthew as compared with Luke. Quite apart from the source-critical as-

59. Indeed, Paul will view the "wise" with suspicion, 1 Cor 1:18–2:16; cf. in this gospel 11:25.

60. M. D. Goulder, *Midrash,* 428, speaks of the "wise" (Hebrew *ḥᵃkāmîm*) as a "higher grade" of rabbinic teacher than the scribes. See further S. Byrskog, *Jesus,* 242, who, however, thinks that for Matthew "the mention of wise men and scribes probably serves as one comprehensive reference to teachers." D. E. Orton, *Scribe,* 155, regards "wise man" and "scribe" as "practically identical," especially in Ben Sira.

61. S. Byrskog, *Jesus,* 241-43, discusses the background to the terms, and favors the view that the three terms together were already in Jewish usage a stylized expression for teachers, so that "the triad he now sends out represents the continuation of the former mission by the prophets and righteous men." For a full and sensitive discussion of the possible nuances intended in the three terms chosen, and especially "scribe," see D. E. Orton, *Scribe,* 155-59.

sumptions underlying that inference, it is not easy to see how a reader of Matthew alone could be expected to make the connection, and there is no reason to think that Matthew expected his readers to be familiar with Luke or any common source.[62] As far as Matthew is concerned, this is a declaration by Jesus in his own right, not an echo of an unknown wisdom saying.[63]

35 For the phrase "righteous blood"[64] compare Judas's words, "I have betrayed innocent blood" (27:4), though the adjective is not the same. The death of Jesus will be the culmination of the pattern of martyrdom here described; the present participle "which is being shed" shows that the process is not yet complete. And the idea of that blood "coming upon" (an OT idiom for responsibility for death; cf. 2 Sam 1:16; Jonah 1:14) the people of Jerusalem will be terribly confirmed in the cry of "all the people," "His blood on us and on our children" (27:25). The tradition of the murder of the righteous is traced from the first to the last such deaths recorded in the OT, that of Abel in Gen 4:8[65] and that of Zechariah in 2 Chr 24:20-22. The death of Zechariah in the late ninth century B.C. was of course not the last martyrdom in historical sequence, but because it is recorded toward the end of 2 Chronicles, the last book of the Hebrew canon, it suitably rounds off the biblical record of God's servants killed for their loyalty.[66] Moreover, as he died, Zechariah called out for God to see and avenge; taken with the statement that Abel's blood cries out from the ground (Gen 4:10),[67] this marks out these two deaths as not merely martyrdoms, but martyrdoms requiring retribution. Their blood remains to be accounted for.

The Zechariah killed in the temple was the son of Jehoiada;[68] Berechiah was the father of the canonical prophet Zechariah, who lived some three hundred years later and whom Jewish tradition declared to have died peacefully at a great age (*Liv. Pro.* 15:6). The identity of the Zechariah here in view is confirmed by the statement of his death "between the sanctuary

62. Cf. D. E. Orton, *Scribe,* 154.

63. The proposals for finding Wisdom themes throughout vv. 34-39 are well summarized by C. Deutsch, *Lady Wisdom,* 68-75. They depend fairly heavily on discovering a deliberate identification of Jesus as Wisdom in what v. 34 does *not* say!

64. Possibly an echo of LXX Lam 4:13; so R. H. Gundry, *Use,* 86.

65. For the characterization of Abel as "righteous" cf. Heb 11:4; 1 John 3:12.

66. The coincidence that their initials in English are A and Z is of course irrelevant: Z is not the last letter in either the Hebrew or the Greek alphabet.

67. The phrase here, "shed on the earth," perhaps echoes Gen 4:10. It would be possible to translate here "shed upon the land" (of Israel; cf. Num 35:33), which would fit the focus in this pericope on the guilt of Israel, but the echo of Gen 4:10 probably requires the more usual translation.

68. In order to avoid the problem Carson, 486, speculates that he may have been Jehoiada's grandson, with an otherwise unknown Berechiah intervening as his father. The same conjecture was more fully argued by J. W. Wenham, *Christ and the Bible,* 77-81.

and the altar," since 2 Chr 24:21 says he was killed "in the court of the LORD's house"; he was the son of the high priest and presumably himself a priest.[69] Various Zechariahs (there are thirty of them in the OT) were confused in Jewish writings,[70] and Christian legends concerning Zechariah the father of John the Baptist[71] add to the complexity; see R. H. Gundry, *Use,* 86-88, n. 1. Matthew apparently shares, or exploits,[72] that confusion.[73]

36 The "Amen" formula (see on 5:18) marks the solemn climax of this recitation of Israel's historical rejection of God's messengers. The repetition of "coming upon" language from v. 35 indicates that "all these things" must mean the consequences of their responsibility for the death of the prophets and the righteous. What those consequences are will be spelled out in v. 38 and in 24:2, and the first part of the following discourse in 24:4-35 will insist again that all the disaster which Jesus predicts will fall on "this generation" (24:34). There the disaster will be linked with the "coming of the Son of Man" (24:30), and Jesus has already said that that "coming" will take place while some of those around him are still alive (10:23; 16:28); in 26:64 he will tell the members of the Sanhedrin that they themselves are soon to witness it (26:64). For the meaning of such language see on 10:23. The

---

69. *Liv. Pro.* 23 concludes with the murder of Zechariah son of Jehoiada, after which portents occurred in the temple and the priests were unable to receive divine revelation. His murder is located "near the altar," and his blood was poured out in front of the vestibule of the sanctuary; this corresponds closely to the tradition recorded here in Jesus' saying.

70. Note especially Zechariah son of Jeberechiah (LXX Berechiah) in Isa 8:2, though he, while a "witness" (μάρτυς), was not a martyr. The confusion is further increased by the LXX, which calls the son of Jehoiada Azariah, not Zechariah (so that *neither* of Matthew's names Ζαχαρίας τοῦ Βαραχίου corresponds to the LXX of 2 Chr 24:20!). A further Zechariah, son of Baris, was killed "in the middle of the temple" by the Zealots in A.D. 67/8, according to Josephus, *War* 4.334-44. If Matthew's gospel is dated late enough, this might be thought to be a further element in the confusion of names, but the OT data are alone sufficient to account for it. This later Zechariah would be quite irrelevant to Jesus' attribution of responsibility for *past* murders. D. E. Garland, *Intention,* 182-83, n. 69, is attracted by the theory, but eventually dismisses it in favor of "a simple confusion between Zechariah the prophet and Zechariah the priest."

71. *Prot. Jas.* 23:3 (second century A.D.) has this Zechariah killed by Herod's men "at the threshold of the Lord's temple."

72. Gundry, 471, suggests that Matthew's conflation of the two Zechariahs is influenced by the fact that he will use a prophecy of Zechariah son of Berechiah to explain the betrayal of Jesus' "innocent blood" (27:4) in 27:9-10. M. Knowles, *Jeremiah,* 138-39, also argues, on different grounds, that this is deliberate conflation rather than confusion.

73. Luke 11:51 wisely does not mention Zechariah's parentage. It is surprising that the only MS of Matthew which omits the embarrassing "son of Berechiah" is א, and even there the phrase is restored by a corrector. Jerome mentions that the *Gospel of the Nazarenes* substituted Jehoiada for Berechiah here.

"coming of the Son of Man" is in itself a concept which may be applied to different periods in the development of God's plan, but the clear time-scale expressed in this complex of texts indicates that "this generation" is to be taken literally: "all these things" will happen to those who are alive when Jesus is speaking. The same phrase "all these things" will be used again in 24:34 to make the same point. "This generation," which Jesus has already condemned repeatedly in 11:16; 12:39, 41-42, 45; 16:7; 17:17, is the generation which is about to reject the Messiah, God's final messenger. God's judgment on his rebellious people can no longer be delayed.

3. Judgment on Jerusalem (23:37-39)

37 *"Jerusalem, Jerusalem, who kills the prophets and stones those who are sent to her; how often have I wanted to gather your children together as a bird gathers her chicks under her wings, and you[1] were not willing. 38 Look, your house is left to you deserted.[2] 39 For I tell you, from now on you will never see me until[3] you say, 'Blessed is he who comes in the Lord's name.'"*

In the last of the seven woes the focus has begun to move away from the specific failings of the scribes and Pharisees to the more general hostility of Jerusalem to God's messengers, and to the consequent judgment which is to fall not just on the religious leaders but on "this generation." This coda to the denunciation now turns away from the scribes and Pharisees altogether to address Jerusalem as a whole and to speak of the judgment which will fall not just upon the people but upon "your house." It thus prepares the way for the more explicit prediction of the destruction of the temple which will be given privately to the disciples in 24:2 after Jesus has, for the last time, left the temple behind. This is, then, the end of his public appeal to the people of Jerusalem, and Jesus vigorously asserts that there will be no future resumption of relations between himself and the Jewish capital unless they take the initia-

1. In the first part of v. 37 Jerusalem has been addressed in the singular, but this "you" is plural, referring to the people corporately. The plural continues through vv. 38-39.

2. ἔρημος, "deserted," is missing from some early witnesses. This may be due to assimilation to Luke 13:35, where ἔρημος was probably not in the original text. ἔρημος, probably an allusion to LXX Jer 22:5, may also have been dropped to produce a more elegant Greek sentence. M. Knowles, *Jeremiah*, 185-86, concludes that ἔρημος was in Matthew's original text. See also D. E. Garland, *Intention*, 200-201, n. 120.

3. English idiom has no easy equivalent to the indefinite sense of ἕως ἄν with the subjunctive. The ἄν indicates that this condition may or may not be fulfilled: "until (as you might not) you were to say." The sense here might better be represented by "unless." See the comments below.

tive by responding to the enigmatic demand in v. 39, on which see the comments below.

37 The same charge of killing the prophets which Jesus has directed to the scribes and Pharisees in vv. 29-32 (and by implication to the chief priests and elders in 21:34-36) is now applied to the city as a whole; the specific mention of stoning (cf. 21:35) reflects what happened to the Zechariah of v. 35, according to 2 Chr 24:21 (and to Jeremiah according to later legend, *Liv. Pro.* 2:1). But it will soon be the fate of Stephen as well, also in Jerusalem (Acts 7:58-59), and since Jesus has just spoken in v. 34 of how his own emissaries will soon be treated, there may be a future as well as a past dimension to this charge.

Jesus' words suggest a more frequent and extended appeal to Jerusalem than has been recorded just in chs. 21–22; this is one of the hints which occur in the Synoptic Gospels that the writers were aware of Jesus' previous visits to Jerusalem (as the Fourth Gospel records them) even though they have chosen to record only the one climactic arrival. His appeal to them as Messiah should have been unifying and protective, like the instinctive action of a mother bird,[4] but it has instead been counterproductive, and will result not in safety but in destruction. The blame is placed firmly on their choice, like the Jerusalem of Isaiah's day who refused God's offer of security through trusting him (Isa 30:15-16).

The almost wistful note of this lament over Jerusalem provides an important counterbalance to the sharpness of the preceding polemic. As Jesus contemplates what lies ahead of the people he came to save, it gives him no pleasure. He had "wanted" to gather them, not to condemn them.[5]

38 Jerusalem's failure to respond is to have drastic consequences. "Your house," especially when spoken in the temple courtyard, naturally refers to the temple building[6] which would be visible from there, and the more explicit prediction of 24:2 confirms this reference.[7] In that case there is a sad

---

4. This is familiar OT imagery; see, e.g., Pss 17:8; 91:4; Isa 31:5; cf. Deut 32:11.

5. The theme of repeated appeal to God's people has sometimes been attributed to an underlying tradition of Wisdom issuing her appeal in vain; so R. Bultmann, *History,* 114-15, developed by M. J. Suggs, *Wisdom,* 66-67; C. Deutsch, *NovT* 32 (1990) 39-45. But there are no clear echoes of known wisdom texts, and the interpretation depends rather on the association of this passage with the supposed wisdom theme of v. 34 (on which see above). See further my *Matthew: Evangelist,* 305.

6. For suggestions that it means either the city as a whole or the whole "house of Israel" meaning the people (as in 10:6; 15:24), see D. E. Garland, *Intention,* 198-200. Garland himself prefers to allow all three meanings "since the city, Temple and the national life of the people were all bound together."

7. See on 24:2 for the question of Jesus' foreknowledge of the historical event of A.D. 70.

irony in that what was described in 21:13 as God's house is now "*your* house," and it has been left "to you" because God has abandoned it, as Jesus himself is about to do in 24:1; see the comments there on the echo of Ezekiel's vision of God leaving the temple.[8] There is a special poignancy in the juxtaposition of "house" (a place meant to be lived in) and *erēmos*, "uninhabited," which describes not so much its physical dissolution as its being deserted; its consequent destruction will merely complete the process. The desolation of God's house was predicted in similar terms by Jeremiah (Jer 12:7; cf. 26:6), and *erēmos* here perhaps echoes the LXX *erēmōsis* in Jer 22:5[9] (cf. Matt 24:15 with its echo of similar *erēmōsis* language from Daniel). See the comments on 16:14 for Jesus' echoing of Jeremiah's prophecies of disaster on Jerusalem. For the theological background to this theme see 1 Kgs 9:6-9: when God's people forsake God's way, the "house" will be "cast out of my sight" and ruined.

39 The *gar*, "for," which links this saying with v. 38 suggests that Jesus here speaks of the only condition on which the desertion of the house can be reversed or averted. It is significant that he speaks of seeing "me" (not God, whose house it was) again. As we have noted before (see on 3:3, 11; 11:10, 14; 21:16, 44, and pp. 784-85), for Matthew the presence of Jesus *is* the presence of God. Once Jesus has physically left the temple (24:1), "from now on" his only connection with it will be to announce and explain its coming destruction (24:2, 4ff.), but he himself will have abandoned it. This act of judgment can be averted only if the people of Jerusalem are prepared to follow the lead given by the Galilean pilgrims in 21:9 (the acclamation from Ps 118:26 is here given in the same words) and welcome Jesus as their Messiah.[10] As a matter of fact, some of them will probably "see" him within the next few days, when they stand outside the governor's palace shouting "Crucify him," and "His blood on us and on our children." The contrast with the welcoming words from Ps 118 could hardly be greater, and the one they welcome then will be Jesus Barabbas, not Jesus the Messiah. It is not that sort of "seeing" that Jesus is speaking of here.

There is no prediction here, only a condition. Or, rather, the only pre-

8. D. E. Garland, *Intention,* 201-2, n. 121, traces in Jewish thought the idea of the removal of God's presence (the *Shekinah*) from the temple.

9. The immediate reference in Jer 22:5 is apparently to the king's house rather than the temple, but the similarity of the language probably meant that the oracles were interpreted together. M. Knowles, *Jeremiah,* 186-88, concludes that the primary reference is to Jer 12:7, and that the addition of ἔρημος reflects "stereotyped OT language of desolation," of which Jer 22:5 is just one example.

10. That is the natural reading of "Blessed is he who comes in the Lord's name" in the light of the recent use of the same text in 21:9. The positive tone of the wording does not support the view that Jesus is here talking of Jerusalem, still hostile, acknowledging his authority when he comes as judge (so D. E. Garland, *Intention,* 206-8).

diction is an emphatic negative, "from now on you will certainly not see me," to which the following "until" clause provides the only possible exception. They will not see him again *until* they welcome him, but the indefinite phrasing of the second clause[11] gives no assurance that such a welcome will ever be forthcoming.[12] Jesus will tell the Sanhedrin that "from now on" they will "see" the Son of Man vindicated and enthroned (26:64), but there is no suggestion there that they will welcome him even then as the one who comes in the Lord's name. The discussion as to whether Matthew, like Paul in Rom 11:1-32, holds out any hope for the future repentance and return of Israel thus finds no material in this saying.[13] Its spells out the condition on which Jerusalem may be restored to a relationship with its Messiah, but it gives no indication as to whether or not that condition will ever be met.[14] For the present, the dissociation is final.[15]

4. Jesus Leaves the Temple and Predicts Its Destruction (24:1-2)

1 *And Jesus went out from the temple and was going away when his disciples came to him to draw his attention to the temple build-*

---

11. ἕως ἄν with the subjunctive makes this in effect what grammarians call an unreal condition: if you were to do this, you would see me, but whether you will do so remains unknown. For the grammatical point see D. C. Allison, *JSNT* 18 (1983) 78-79. It is remarkable that so many interpreters can find a positive prediction in what is in fact an emphatically negative prediction (οὐ μή with subjunctive) with only an indefinite possibility (ἕως ἄν) set against it.

12. This point seems to have been missed by G. R. Beasley-Murray, *Kingdom,* 305-7, and by many other commentators, who argue rightly that the acclamation indicates a real welcome but assume wrongly that the saying predicts that such an acclamation will in fact be forthcoming. Cf. G. N. Stanton, *Gospel,* 248-50, who finds here, following the OT prophetic pattern of sin–exile–return, "a declaration of a 'return' and salvation." Sadly, it "declares" nothing of the sort.

13. So D. E. Garland, *Intention,* 204-9. I would take issue, however, with his assumptions (1) that the saying refers to the *parousia* (see n. 15) and (2) that the acclamation (which Garland, like those mentioned in the previous note, apparently takes to be firmly predicted) is of Jesus as judge by an unrepentant Israel, not as saving Messiah (see n. 10).

14. See my *Matthew: Evangelist,* 237-38, in agreement with D. C. Allison, *JSNT* 18 (1983) 75-84. Similarly J. A. Gibbs, *Jerusalem,* 124-25.

15. Interpreters sometimes take this saying as referring to Jesus' *parousia,* when, it is supposed, Israel will repent and welcome him as Lord when they see him returning. But there is nothing in either the wording or the context to suggest a *parousia* reference. Some would connect this saying with the prediction in 24:30 that Israel will mourn when they "see the Son of Man coming," but I shall argue there that that prediction relates not to the *parousia* but to the destruction of the temple. The messianic welcome (not mourning) spoken of here is the *condition* for "seeing" him, not the result of it.

ings. 2 But he said in reply, "Don't you see all these things? I tell you truly: not one stone will be left here on top of another; it will all be demolished."[1]

The traditional chapter division leads most commentators to treat these verses as the start of the long discourse which follows in 24:3–25:46, and it is true that they form the basis for the question which will launch that discourse in v. 3. But they are also in an important sense the climax to the whole section 21:23–23:39, which has depicted Jesus in the temple. Now, having entered the temple dramatically and controversially in 21:12-16, he leaves it with an equally emphatic and more far-reaching statement about its future. He is abandoning it, never to return, and after that it has no future except to be destroyed. What has been hitherto the earthly focus of the presence of God among his people is so no longer.[2] There is a direct sequence from 23:38: the "house" which is now being left deserted (by God and by Jesus) is ripe for demolition, to make way for "something greater than the temple" (12:6); cf. Mark's language, surprisingly not taken up by Matthew, of a temple not made by hands to replace the one made by hands (Mark 14:58).

This little pericope links the two locations of teaching, the temple for chs. 21–23 and the Mount of Olives for the discourse to follow. Like other bridge passages in the gospel, it has links both with what precedes and with what follows,[3] but it does more justice to its theological impact to see it as the climax of the standoff between Jesus and official Judaism than to treat the prediction of the temple's destruction as if it introduced a new subject.[4] Both Jesus' going out from the temple and his statement about its destruction form the culmination of the whole confrontation in chs. 21–22, and especially of

1. Literally, "There will certainly not be left here stone on stone which will not be destroyed," but the sense is clearly the demolition of the buildings, not the destruction of the individual stones. The verb is καταλύω, "to dissolve, break up," which was used in 5:17 for "abolishing" the law and the prophets.
2. D. D. Kupp, *Emmanuel,* 93-94, for the significance of these verses for the theme of "presence."
3. I appreciate the reasons which lead J. A. Gibbs, *Jerusalem,* 168-70, to insist (against F. W. Burnett) that there is no "major structural break between 24:2 and 24:3," especially if such a break is used to argue that the following discourse is not concerned with the destruction of the temple. But it seems to me that, while there is a clear literary distinction between the diatribe of ch. 23 and the discourse of chs. 24–25 (see above, pp. 856-57), there is a continuity of theme precisely in the focus on the fate of the temple, and to mark a new section as beginning at 24:1 is perhaps more destructive of this continuity than to put a break after 24:2. All such structural divisions are for the convenience of the commentator, and there is no suggestion that Matthew divided his text into separable sections. 24:1-2 is thus a typical bridge-passage.
4. So especially D. E. Garland, *Intention,* 26-30.

the denunciation of ch. 23 with its climax in judgment on "this generation." Later we shall hear of the authorities repudiating Jesus, but here Jesus, the unquestioned winner in the "contest" in the Court of the Gentiles, himself takes the initiaitive and severs the connection.

1 Matthew's two verbs where one would do, "went out" and "was going away," draw attention to the significance of this departure. The "house" is abandoned (23:38), and those in it will not see Jesus again unless they change their minds (23:39). The place which he had hoped to preserve as a house of prayer (21:13) has proved as fruitless as the fig tree which he has symbolically destroyed (21:18-20). While there is little direct verbal link with Ezekiel's vision of the glory of God leaving the temple (Ezek 10:18-19; 11:22-23), the reader might be expected to remember that powerful imagery,[5] especially when Jesus immediately goes and sits on the Mount of Olives, the "mountain east of the city" where the Lord's glory also stopped after going out over the east gate of the temple (Ezek 11:23).[6]

To reach the Mount of Olives Jesus and his disciples would leave the temple precincts through the east gate and take the steep path down into the Kidron valley. This brief exchange is set somewhere on the way out. Mark 13:1 puts the disciples' touristic enthusiasm into words: "What big stones and what big buildings!" Josephus (*War* 5.184-226; *Ant.* 15.392-402, 410-20) and the rabbis[7] agree that Herod's temple and its associated structures (at this time still in process of completion) were awesome both in size and in magnificence, well calculated to impress a Galilean visitor.[8] The disciples have been in a position to admire them for a few days already, of course, but perhaps we are meant to understand this latest approach as a response to what Jesus has just said in 23:38: can he really mean that such a splendid complex is to be abandoned? At any rate, their superficial admiration for the buildings forms a powerful foil to Jesus' negative verdict on them.

2 For "not one stone on top of another" cf. Luke 19:44, where the reference is to Jerusalem as a whole rather than simply to the temple. But the phrase has particular relevance to the temple, the size of whose stones was

---

5. Keener, 563, n. 92, gives numerous references to the Jewish tradition that "God's presence departs from Israel or the sanctuary when their sin becomes unbearable."

6. In Ezek 43:1-5 the glory returns by the same route to the restored temple, though the Mount of Olives is not mentioned in that passage.

7. "It used to be said: He who has not seen the temple in its full splendor has never seen a beautiful building" (*h. Suk.* 51b; *b. B. Bat.* 4a). Cf. Josephus, *War* 6.267: "the most amazing structure of all we have seen or heard of, both in its construction and scale and also in the lavishness of every part and the splendor of its holy places."

8. Note the description in Josephus, *War* 5.222-23, of the stunning visual impact of the whole complex.

and still is a matter of amazement.[9] Was it really possible for such massive masonry to be demolished?

Jesus' prediction of the physical destruction of the temple plays a significant role in the story of his trial and death: it will be used against him in 26:61 and as a taunt when he is on the cross (27:40). It remained a central charge against Jesus and his movement (Acts 6:13-14). In making this prediction Jesus stood in a prophetic tradition: the possibility of the destruction of the temple is already envisaged in 1 Kgs 9:6-9, and Micah (Mic 3:12), Jeremiah (Jer 7:11-14; 26:1-19), and Uriah (Jer 26:20-23) all warned that Solomon's temple would be destroyed, as indeed it was in 586 B.C.[10] After Jesus' death his prediction concerning Herod's temple was repeated not only by his own follower Stephen (Acts 6:13-14; cf. 7:48-50) but by the quite unrelated prophetic figure of Jesus ben Hananiah a generation later (Josephus, *War* 6.300-309),[11] and it, too, proved literally true: the Roman destruction of Herod's temple in A.D. 70 was so complete[12] that all that now remains is part of the substructure of the temple precincts, not of the temple buildings themselves. This is the most explicit prediction of the temple's fate which Matthew records (cf. 22:7; 23:38), and his placing of it still in the public arena as Jesus and his disciples go out of the temple courtyard, rather than as part of the private discourse which begins with v. 3, allows the reader to assume that it was people's memory of this saying which formed the basis for the accusation brought against Jesus at his trial.

The Synoptic account of this saying does not include the "rebuilding in three days" motif which is part of the charge at Jesus' trial (see on 26:61).[13] But however that particular motif found its way into the charge, the

---

9. The huge Herodian blocks which visitors admire today (the largest in the Western Wall is over five meters long) are part of the temple's substructure, not of the buildings themselves. Josephus, *Ant.* 15.392, says (probably with some exaggeration) that the stones used in the temple buildings were twelve meters long (in *War* 5.224 he speaks of some measuring more than twenty meters!).

10. Josephus (or a Christian editor of his work) declares that the prophecies of Jeremiah and of Daniel concerning the destruction/desecration of the temple were also to be understood of what happened in A.D. 70 (*Ant.* 10.79, 276).

11. *B. Yoma* 39b also attributes a prediction of the destruction of the temple to Jesus' younger contemporary, Johanan ben Zakkai. Cf. *T. Levi* 15:1, though this may be Christian. More positively, Ezekiel's vision of a new temple (Ezek 40–48) and other eschatological hopes based on it (e.g., Tob 14:5; 11QTemple 29:8-10; 4Q174 [*Florilegium*] 1:1-3; *Sib. Or.* 5:422-423) must envisage any existing temple being demolished in order to make room for the new one; this is explicit in *1 En.* 90:28-29. For non-Christian predictions of the destruction of the temple see M. Bockmuehl, *Crux* 25/3 (1989) 12-15.

12. Josephus, *War* 7.1-3, speaks of it being deliberately leveled to the ground; it had previously been gutted by fire (*War* 6.249-66).

13. The Fourth Gospel does include the rebuilding in Jesus' words, but goes on to

---

Synoptic accounts indicate that by the time of his trial and death Jesus was widely understood to have threatened the destruction of the temple. Nor does there seem to be any reason historically to doubt that Jesus, like others before and after him, did make some such prophetic declaration and that this was one of the major causes of his rejection not only by the Jewish leadership but also by the people of Jerusalem, to whom such a notion was not only sacrilegious but also deeply unpatriotic (as Jeremiah's message had been perceived).[14] Even those who are not prepared to credit Jesus with supernatural foreknowledge are often prepared to concede that a reasonably intelligent observer of Jewish politics in the first half of the first century might have foreseen what was coming. And Jesus was not just a political observer, but had been engaged since his arrival in Jerusalem in a sustained theological critique of the temple and of its leadership. Unless all of this material is to be explained as an extensive rewriting of Jesus by his earliest followers, there seems little reason, other than a dogmatic refusal to accept that Jesus could predict, to suggest that the particular prediction recorded here (and less explicitly in 22:7 and 23:38) is a *vaticinium ex eventu,* composed by Mark or some other early Christian teacher.[15] A historical prediction of the destruction of the temple by Jesus is a more economical explanation of all the data.[16]

E. THE END OF THE OLD ORDER AND THE REIGN OF THE SON OF MAN: *THE DISCOURSE ON THE FUTURE* (24:3–25:46)

This final discourse[1] is about the future, with emphasis especially on the theme of judgment (see above, pp. 856-57, for reasons for not including ch.

---

interpret it allegorically of the resurrection (John 2:19-22). In *Gos. Thom.* 71 rebuilding is mentioned only as an impossibility: "I shall destroy this house, and no one will be able to rebuild it."

14. E. P. Sanders, *Jesus,* especially pp. 61-90, 301-5, argues that it was this above all which united all segments of Jewish society in rejecting and eliminating Jesus.

15. One might have expected such a *vaticinium ex eventu* to mention the burning of the temple (see n. 12) as well as its leveling. Nowhere in the NT is this mentioned, unless it is understood to be included in burning "their city" in 22:7 (see comments there).

16. Cf. E. P. Sanders, *Jesus,* 71-76; Keener, 560-63. For the wider setting of this prediction in Jesus' attitude to Jerusalem and the temple see N. T. Wright, *Victory,* 333-36, and also Wright's analysis of the significance of the temple in contemporary Judaism (ibid., 405-12) and his interpretation of Jesus' demonstration in the temple in that context (ibid., 413-28).

1. Many of the issues raised by the study of this discourse are given full treatment, with a painstaking survey of scholarly views, in G. R. Beasley-Murray, *Jesus and the Last Days,* a revised and updated conflation of his earlier works, *Jesus and the Future* and *A Commentary on Mark 13.* But since Beasley-Murray's work, like most study of the so-

23 in the discourse). It takes its cue from the disciples' question in 24:3, which combines two aspects of the future, the predicted destruction of the temple and Jesus' "*parousia* and the end of the age." With regard to the former the question is "When?" with regard to the latter "What will be the sign?" The former question is in focus in the first part of the discourse, the latter in its later sections.

So far most interpreters are agreed.[2] But there is disagreement about where the subject of the destruction of the temple gives way to that of the more ultimate future, and about how far, if at all, the latter subject is also in view while the former is being dealt with. My understanding of the discourse, which is enshrined in the way I have divided the text for comment, is that 24:4-35 is concerned with the destruction of the temple, answering the question "When?" with a clear time-scale summed up in v. 34, and that the second question about the *parousia* comes into the frame only with the new beginning in 24:36[3] ("but concerning . . ."), which, in contrast with what has gone before, speaks of a "day and hour" which no one can predict, not even Jesus himself (who has just predicted quite specifically the time within which the temple will be destroyed). This second issue will be addressed, as the disciples' question requires, not in terms of a specific time-scale but in terms of "being ready" for an unspecified time which may be expected to catch people unawares. The only mention of Jesus' *parousia* within the first section of the discourse (24:27) is precisely to state that when it happens it will be universally clear, and so quite unlike the confusion which will characterize the days leading up to Jerusalem's fall. Any other reference to the end of the age within 24:4-35 can be claimed only by interpreting Jesus' colorful language about coming events in a way which ignores the clear progression of the discourse as it has been determined by the dual form of the disciples' question.

---

called Synoptic Apocalypse, focuses entirely on Mark 13, it is not easily applied to the much longer and differently structured Matthean discourse.

2. An important exception is N. T. Wright, *Victory;* see below, p. 892, n. 6.

3. The same division is recognized by D. E. Garland, *Reading Matthew* (New York: Crossroad, 1993), 234-45; Garland's reading of the passage follows very much the same lines as those of the present commentary. So also J. A. Gibbs, *Jerusalem,* ch. 6, especially pp. 170-74, 207-8; A. I. Wilson, *When,* 133-35 and passim. Davies and Allison also place the major literary division after v. 35, declaring v. 36 to be "the introduction" to the following long section (which they conclude at 25:30 rather than 25:46). They do not, however, accept that the *subject matter* changes at that point, since they regard the whole discourse as combining past, present, and future in "a depiction of the entire post-Easter period, interpreted in terms of the messianic woes" (3:331). Blomberg, 338, similarly proposes the same major division, even though he takes 24:29-31 as referring to "Christ's Second Coming" and the preceding verses to "The Great Tribulation."

The point at which this interpretation most obviously conflicts with that of many readers of the passage is with regard to 24:29-31, which are traditionally understood to relate to the end of the world and the *parousia* (even though that word is conspicuously absent from them). I shall argue in the commentary below that this "natural" understanding of the terms used is in fact natural only to those who have been conditioned to it by a long tradition of Christian exegesis, and that in the context of first-century Jewish thought it is far from obvious. The "cosmic" language of 24:29 is drawn directly from OT prophetic passages where it functions not to predict the physical dissolution of the universe but as a symbolic representation of catastrophic political changes within history. The language of 24:30 is closely modeled on that of Dan 7:13-14, where (as we have seen above in relation to 10:23) the "coming [not *parousia*] of the Son of Man" into the presence of God (not to the earth) speaks of vindication and enthronement. We shall see very similar language used by Jesus in 26:64 with reference to what his judges will be able to see "from now on" (not in the indefinite future), and the close linking of such language with a specific time-scale within the living generation (which we have noted already at 10:23 and 16:28) is also confirmed in this context by the explicit "this generation" prediction in 24:34. The gathering of God's people in 24:31, which is modeled on OT promises of the regathering of Israel within history, follows naturally from the enthronement of the Son of Man as the new focus of authority after the temple, the traditional power base of the people of God, has been removed. In other words, Jesus' predictive words in 24:29-31 not only allow but, when understood against their OT background, *need* to be interpreted as part of the answer to the first part of the disciples' question about the coming destruction of the temple. It will mark the end of the old order, to be superseded by the sovereignty of the vindicated Son of Man.

I argued for this interpretation in my 1985 commentary on Matthew. This was based on a parallel study of Mark 13 in my *Jesus and the OT* (1971), 227-39, to which I have subsequently added (in the light of some reactions to that earlier study)[4] in my *Divine Government* (1990) and more

---

4. I am aware of only four published responses directly to my arguments on this point, though of course several commentators and others refer to (and dismiss!) my interpretation in passing, without directly engaging with the arguments. M. Casey, *Son of Man*, 172-76, bases his counterargument on the assertion that Dan 7:13 describes an earthward coming, and that all NT allusions to it must therefore be *parousia* references, both of which exegetical options would be widely disputed in biblical scholarship, the latter particularly with reference to Mark 14:62 (see below on Matt 26:64). D. Wenham, in H. H. Rowdon (ed.), *Christ the Lord,* 138-42, similarly asserts that this is the "natural" understanding of language about "coming on the clouds of heaven." Both simply assume the traditional Christian understanding of such language, and seem to me to have been unable

fully in my commentary on *Mark* (2002).[5] The essential elements in the exegesis of the discourse in Mark and Matthew are the same, but while I originally developed this interpretation in relation to Mark 13, it seems to me that this approach is even more compelling in Matthew in that (1) Matthew, unlike Mark, introduces the discourse with a double question in v. 3 which defines the dual subject-matter of what is to follow; (2) Matthew actually uses the word *parousia* four times, in such a way as to differentiate that event not only from the experiences of the siege of Jerusalem but also from the "coming of the Son of Man" in v. 30; and (3) Matthew's much fuller collection of material relating to the *parousia* and the final judgment in 24:36–25:46 draws attention more clearly to the dual focus of the discourse and to the marked change of subject in v. 36, in comparison with the relatively brief appendix in Mark 13:32-37. Indeed, some interpreters who agree that Mark 13:5-31 relates to the destruction of the temple doubt whether the relatively brief and enigmatic sequel in Mark 13:32-37 really does introduce the subject of the *parousia* at all, and argue that the whole discourse responds to the (single) Marcan introductory question, "When will these things be, and what is the sign when all these things are about to be accomplished?"[6] I have given my reasons in my *Mark,* 501-2, for dis-

---

to achieve that detachment from Christian tradition which my argument requires in order to understand the terminology in its first-century Jewish context. A brief section in G. R. Beasley-Murray, *Last Days,* 247-49 (subsequent to my 1990 discussion), simply says that my interpretation "will not do." He accepts the political reference of cosmic language in the OT prophets but nonetheless argues that such judgments are also to be read as "the pattern for the Lord's anticipated action in the future." I agree, but the issue remains what is the intended reference in this context following the disciples' question and in the overall development of the discourse. The fourth and most recent response is that of E. Adams in *TynBul* 56 (2005) 39-61, for which see below, n. 7. Among commentators Carson, 492-94, is unusually generous in the space he devotes to reviewing this interpretation, but unfortunately wrote before I had published my interpretation of Matthew's version of the discourse. The recent dissertations of J. A. Gibbs, *Jerusalem;* and of A. I. Wilson, *When,* agree essentially with my understanding of the structure and exegesis of the passage. T. Hatina, *BBR* 6 (1996) 43-66, supports my exegesis of Mark 13:24-27, but, like Wright, disputes any *parousia* reference in the latter part of Mark 13; his study does not deal with the Matthew parallel. Hatina has taken this approach further in his Ph.D. dissertation (Bristol, 1999).

5. *Divine Government,* ch. 4, especially pp. 73-80; *Mark,* 497-505 and the commentary that follows.

6. This position is argued most notably and attractively by N. T. Wright, *Victory,* 339-67, who believes that not only Mark 13 but also Matt 24–25 does not envisage anything beyond the period of the destruction of the temple. His argument focuses mainly on Mark 13 (pp. 339-67), but references to the longer Matthean discourse (e.g., pp. 345-46, 632-39, 640) show that he does not find a *parousia* reference there either. This commentary will, however, be in basic agreement with Wright's exegesis as far as v. 35.

agreeing with this view, and for finding a *parousia* reference in Mark 13:32-37 as well as in Matt 24:36ff., but the case is undoubtedly stronger in relation to Matthew's fuller discourse with its more explicit differentiation of the two issues.

It would be tedious to go through all those earlier arguments again at this point; their exegetical basis will be explored in the commentary as it progresses. Suffice it to say that in the forty years since I first argued for this interpretation I have become more convinced that it best meets the exegetical demands of this controversial passage, and have been pleased to find it increasingly being shared, in whole or in part, by other scholars. At this point I would simply urge the reader to refrain from prejudging the issue simply because this exegesis conflicts with the traditional interpretation, and to try to hear Jesus' words as they would have been heard by his Jewish disciples as they listened to this answer to their double question, as yet uninfluenced by a tradition which conditions Christian readers now to assume that "the stars falling from heaven" and "the Son of Man coming on the clouds of heaven" *can only* refer to the end of the world and the *parousia.* If in the process it emerges that the equally traditional embarrassment of a Jesus who mistakenly claimed that the *parousia* would take place within the current generation was all the time the result of false exegesis, I hope this will be accepted as a bonus rather than as a sign that the interpretation here offered must have been motivated by special pleading.[7]

In order to make clear the essential structure of the discourse I have divided it into only three sections: the disciples' double question (24:3), Jesus' answer to the first part of that question (24:4-35), and his answer to the second

---

7. E. Adams, *TynBul* 56 (2005) 39-61, has recently responded to my *Mark* commentary (and to N. T. Wright; see previous note). He restates the traditional exegesis of the three Marcan "coming of the Son of Man" passages (unfortunately he does not also look at the extensions of this imagery in Matthew, nor the implications of the structure of the Matthean eschatological discourse). His argument is that the traditional view better suits the OT imagery employed, which he sees as focusing on the hope of the eschatological coming of *God,* seen as fulfilled in the *parousia* of the Son of Man; in Mark 8:38 he gives Zech 14:5 precedence over Dan 7:13 in determining the meaning of "coming." His discussion is somewhat uneven, devoting little attention to Mark 14:62, the point at which the traditional view is now most widely questioned, and mentioning only in brief footnotes the problems of the "coming" being predicted within "this generation" in 9:1 and 13:30; in the former case he in effect detaches 9:1 from 8:38 (the old chapter division strikes again!) in a way which he could not have done with the parallel in Matt 16:27-28. A commentary on Matthew is not the place to respond to Adams' argument in detail; suffice it to say that he sets out a more traditional view (with regard to the Mark parallels) in a way which suitably allows it to be set alongside and compared with the view which I restate here. The reader must judge which does more justice both to the bearing of the OT imagery and to the integrity of Matthew's report of Jesus' teaching.

part of that question (24:36–25:46). This results in two sections which are too long for convenient exegetical comment, and so the two parts of the discourse will each be subdivided; but the reader is urged to keep in view the continuity and the coherence of subject area within each main section.

1. The Disciples' Double Question (24:3)

> 3 *Now as Jesus was sitting on the Mount of Olives, his disciples came to him and asked him privately, "Tell us, when will these things happen, and what will be the sign of your visitation[8] and the end of the age?"*

The prediction of the destruction of the temple now needs to be clarified. Here again a public pronouncement is followed by a request for elucidation by the disciples in private — the same phrase *kat' idian,* "privately," has been used to mark this pattern previously in 17:19 (and cf. 13:10, 36; 15:15; 19:10). The Mount of Olives, besides being symbolically significant in the light of Ezek 11:23 (see on v. 1),[9] gave a panoramic view over the temple whose destruction has just been pronounced.[10] Mark 13:3 restricts the questioning group (and therefore the audience for the discourse) to the four fishermen, but Matthew remains consistent with his pattern, which makes the disciple group as a whole the audience of each of the major discourses. For the question about when predicted events will take place cf. Dan 12:6-7 (cf. Dan 8:13); the noun *synteleia* in the disciples' question echoes the repeated use of that word in LXX Dan 12:6-7.

The twofold focus of the question[11] is indicated by the two interrogative markers, "When?" and "What sign?" as well as by the terms used, "these things" (which in context refers to the destruction of the temple just predicted) and "your *parousia* and the end of the age."[12] Note the difference

---

8. See below, n. 14, for this translation of παρουσία.

9. It is sometimes suggested that Matthew also has in mind the role of the Mount of Olives in the eschatological events according to Zech 14:4, though Jesus' sitting there teaching is very different from Yahweh's warlike stance and the splitting of the mountain. The attempt of T. L. Donaldson, *Jesus,* 75, to show the eschatological significance of the Mount of Olives in first-century Judaism produces no evidence beyond Zech 14:4 and its use as the location from which "the Egyptian" guerilla leader invited his followers to watch the walls of Jerusalem collapse (Josephus, *Ant.* 20.169-72).

10. D. C. Allison, *Moses,* 254-56, toys with the idea that Jesus sitting on the mountain is meant to "summon the specter of Moses," but finds himself unable to "pass beyond the interrogative mode."

11. Its double form and content is well argued by J. A. Gibbs, *Jerusalem,* 170-74.

12. These two terms are linked together as a single subject by the lack of a

894

from the wording of the question in Mark, which also has two parts ("When will these things be, and what will be the sign when all these things are about to be accomplished") but in which the same subject, "these things," makes the two parts parallel rather than distinct. In Mark the disciples ask only about the fulfillment of Jesus' prediction about the temple, not about the *parousia* and the end of the age. It appears therefore that Matthew has deliberately expanded the question (using some of the same terms[13] but now in a new way) to make it clear that the discourse that follows is not concerned only with the destruction of the temple. In so doing he has introduced the term *parousia,* which he alone uses among the gospel writers but which was already established in Christian usage by the time he wrote (note its repeated use in Paul's two letters to Thessalonica), and which he will repeat three times in this chapter (24:27, 37, 39) to highlight the climactic event which will be the theme of the second part of the discourse.[14] From what Matthew has told us so far we have no indication that Jesus has yet talked in such terms about his future coming (see comments on 10:23; 16:28; 19:28), so that it is hard to say why the disciples should have raised the issue in this form, or why they should have thought it appropriate to link this separate question with that about the temple. Perhaps we may assume an undefined sense that so cataclysmic an event as the destruction of the temple must usher in the end of the present world order. If so, Jesus' answer will cause them to rethink their assumption: whatever the ideological linkage, the two events are not to be chronologically connected.[15] Matthew's wording of the question allows this distinction to be made.

For "the end of the age" see above on 13:39 and p. 531, n. 3. This term, unlike "your *parousia,*" conveys a sense already familiar within this

---

resumptive article before "end of the age" which English idiom does not allow the translation to reproduce. An article is inserted in D W f[13] and many later MSS, but it is not easy to see why it should have disappeared from the earlier MSS if it was in the original text; it looks like a stylistic "improvement."

13. "Accomplished" is the verb συντελεῖσθαι, an obvious cognate of the noun συντέλεια, "end."

14. παρουσία is not a purely Christian term. Outside the NT παρουσία (which by etymology means "presence," hence "arrival") is used for a formal visit by a dignitary (king, governor, etc.), or for the manifestation of a divine figure; for many examples see A. Oepke, *TDNT* 5:859-65. Its use in the NT as a technical designation for Jesus' eventual return is traditionally translated "coming," but in this context that translation would invite confusion with the different term ἐρχόμενος in v. 30. I have therefore translated it with "visitation" in an attempt to capture its wider connotation, but in the commentary I shall use the transliterated term *parousia* for clarity.

15. Cf. the argument of J. A. Gibbs, *Jerusalem,* 179-81, that Matthew intends us to regard the disciples' point of view as mistaken, and that Jesus' answer will be designed to correct their inappropriate linkage of the two subjects.

gospel (13:39, 40, 49; and cf. 28:20) and one which reflects a conventional Jewish "two-age" eschatology.

2. Jesus Answers the Question about the Destruction of the Temple (24:4-35)

4 Jesus replied to them: "Be careful that no one deceives you; 5 for many will come in my name, saying, 'I am the Messiah,' and they will deceive many people. 6 You are sure[1] to hear of wars and talk about wars;[2] do not let yourselves become alarmed, because such things[3] must happen, but it is not yet the end. 7 For one nation will fight against another, and one kingdom against another, and there will be famines and earthquakes[4] in various places. 8 All this is just the beginning of the labor pains.

9 "Then they will hand you over to be ill-treated and will kill you, and you will be hated by all the nations because of my name. 10 And then many will be caused to stumble, and will betray[5] one another and hate one another; 11 and many false prophets will arise and deceive many people. 12 And because of the increasing lawlessness the love of most people[6] will become cold. 13 But it is the person who remains faithful[7] to the end who will be saved. 14 And this good news of the kingdom will be proclaimed all over the world as a witness to all the nations; and then the end will come.

15 "So when you see the devastating pollution[8] which Daniel the

---

1. For the translation of μέλλω see p. 663, n. 2.

2. Literally, "hearings of wars," but what is heard may include not only reports of actual wars but also rumors of impending warfare.

3. The subject of "must happen" is not expressed in the earliest MSS. Many later MSS and versions add "these things" (in agreement with Luke) or "everything" or "all these things," probably as a stylistic improvement to the rather curt expression which Matthew shares with Mark.

4. Many MSS also include "plagues," probably under the influence of Luke 21:11. It is also likely that the similarity of λιμός, "famine," and λοιμός, "plague," influenced the insertion. The variation in the order of λιμοί and λοιμοί in those MSS and versions that include both, and the lack of an obvious reason for dropping λοιμοί (unless accidentally because of the similarity) suggest that the shorter reading of B D etc. is the original.

5. See p. 374, n. 3, for this sense of παραδίδωμι.

6. The use of the article here with πολλοί (in contrast with the other three uses of πολλοί in vv. 10-11) is probably intended to indicate not just "many" but "the majority."

7. For this translation see p. 388, n. 4, on the identical clause in 10:22.

8. This phrase represents τὸ βδέλυγμα τῆς ἐρημώσεως, the LXX and Thdt rendering of the phrase used in Dan 11:31; 12:11 (cf. Dan 9:27; 8:13), which combines the ideas

prophet spoke[9] about set up[10] in the holy place (let the reader under-
stand this), 16 *then let those who are in Judea escape into the hills,* 17 *let*
the person who is on the roof not come down to take things out of their
house, 18 *and the person who is out on the farm not go back to get their*
cloak. 19 *Woe to those who are pregnant or nursing babies in those days.*
20 *But pray that you may not have to escape in the winter or on the sab-*
bath. 21 *For then there will be great distress such as has not happened*
from the beginning of the world until now, nor ever will be again. 22 *And*
if those days had not been cut short, nobody at all[11] would have been
saved; but because of the chosen people those days will be cut short.

23 *"Then if anyone says to you, 'Look, here is the Messiah' or*
'Here,' don't believe them. 24 *For false Messiahs and false prophets*
will appear, who will perform great signs and wonders so as to de-
ceive, if possible, even the chosen people. 25 *Look, I have forewarned*
you. 26 *So if they say to you, 'Look, he is in the wilderness,' don't go*
out there, or if they say, 'Look, he is in the storerooms,' don't believe
it. 27 *For as lightning flashes across the sky from east to west,[12] so will*
the visitation[13] of the Son of Man be. 28 *Wherever the carcass is, there*
the vultures[14] will congregate.

29 *"But immediately after the distress of those days*

> *'the sun will be darkened,*
>   *and the moon will not give its light;*
> *and the stars will fall from heaven,[15]*
>   *and the powers of the heavens will be shaken.'*

---

of disgust or pollution (a concept generally associated with idolatry) and of destruction or
leaving deserted (the same root as for ἔρημος, "deserted," in 23:38).

9. See p. 55, n. 54, for Matthew's use of τὸ ῥηθέν to mark biblical quotations.

10. Literally, "standing," but the participle is neuter (in agreement with
βδέλυγμα), which indicates an (idolatrous) object "set up" rather than a person "standing."

11. Literally, "not all flesh." In biblical usage the phrase normally refers to human
beings rather than to the whole animate creation.

12. Literally, "comes out from the east and shines to the west."

13. See p. 895, n. 14, for this translation of παρουσία.

14. The Greek word properly means "eagles," but the "carcass" suggests that vultures are intended (eagles normally eat live prey rather than carrion, and they are not communal feeders). The term probably reflects popular usage, which does not distinguish
large birds of prey (γύψ, "vulture," does not occur in the NT; the LXX uses both terms for
the bird of Job 39:27-30, to which the present saying probably alludes). See contra, however, W. Carter, *JBL* 122 (2003) 469-72, for whom the "eagles" are symbolically important (see comments below).

15. The term [ὁ] οὐρανός occurs three times in vv. 29-31, and the plural [οἱ]
οὐρανοί twice (there is no clear difference in usage between the singular and plural); ei-

30 And then will appear the sign of the Son of Man in heaven, and then all the tribes of the land[16] will mourn as they see the Son of Man coming on the clouds of heaven with great power and glory.[17] 31 And he will send out his angels with a great trumpet blast,[18] and they will gather together his chosen people from the four winds, from one end of heaven to the other.

32 "Learn a lesson[19] from the fig tree: when its shoots become tender and it produces leaves, you know that summer is near; 33 in the same way you too, when you see all these things, can know[20] that it[21] is near, on the threshold.[22] 34 I tell you truly that this generation will certainly not pass away before all these things happen. 35 Heaven and earth may[23] pass away, but my words will never pass away."

Throughout this part of the discourse there is variation between second-person exhortation (vv. 4, 6b, 20, 23, 25-26, 32-33), second-person warnings about what the disciples are to expect (vv. 9, 15), and third-person description of future events (most of the rest); in vv. 16-18 the imperatives are expressed in the third person, as if Jesus is issuing instructions to a wider group

---

ther "the sky" or "heaven" is a possible rendering, and the former may be thought to fit better in this first occurrence, but I prefer to keep the same English term in translation so as not to obscure the verbal links; see the comments below on v. 30 for the exegetical issues raised by the choice.

16. See the comments below for the justification for translating "the land" (of Israel) here rather than "the earth."

17. The adjective πολλῆς could be read only with δόξης, "with power and much glory," but it more probably governs both the preceding nouns taken together as a hendiadys: "with much power-and-glory."

18. The original reading was probably literally "with a great trumpet" (derived from LXX Isa 27:13), to which several MSS add φωνῆς, "sound" (perhaps influenced by LXX Exod 19:16), presumably because a single trumpet, taken literally, did not fit well with plural angels. A few MSS and most of the Latin versions then also divided the two nouns with an "and," producing both a trumpet and a loud "shout."

19. The Greek term is παραβολή, reflecting the character of the following saying as a simile.

20. The verb could be read either as indicative, "you know," or as imperative, "know." The same verb in v. 32 *could* also be read either way, but the indicative seems there to be clearly the more natural reading.

21. The subject of the verb is not expressed, and the adverb ἐγγύς gives no clue as to whether a thing, person, or event is meant. For the most likely meaning in context see the comments below.

22. Literally, "at the doors."

23. The verb is a simple future indicative, "will pass away." See the comments below for how this clause functions in relation to the sentence as a whole, and the consequent translation "may."

than only the disciples. This variation, which is equally noticeable in Mark 13, perhaps derives from the composite origin of this discourse as a collection of distinct sayings of Jesus, but, if so, the variation has been deliberately maintained in the finished text. It leaves room for uncertainty at several points as to how wide the perspective is intended to be, particularly in the section concerning the siege of Jerusalem, where warning to the disciples shades into concern for the population at large.[24] Jesus answers the disciples' question primarily by focusing on what they are to experience in the troubled times before the temple is destroyed, but he does so against the backdrop of a more wide-ranging description of coming events, so that they can set their own experiences within a fuller understanding of how God's purpose for his people is to be played out.

The first part of the question posed by the disciples was "*When* will these things happen?" and the answer is accordingly structured around a series of time indicators which lead up to the climax of the destruction of the temple within the current generation. This is in sharp contrast to the new section which will begin in 24:36, and which will answer the second half of the disciples' question: in that section there are no specific time indicators, and indeed the starting point for the whole section is that the day and hour of the *parousia* cannot be predicted, and that it will come without any "sign" or prior warning, so that one must always be ready for it. Thus one event (the destruction of the temple) falls within defined and predictable history, and those who know what to look for can see it coming, while the other (the *parousia*) cannot be tied down to a time frame, and even Jesus does not know when it will be and so will offer no "sign."

The time indicators of this section may be set out on p. 900.[25] There is, then, a clear sequence running through this whole section from the initial question to its answer in vv. 29-31, followed by a summary of the main points of the whole prediction; and that summary makes explicit what is already clearly implied by the temporal markers throughout the section, that there are no long periods of history dividing these events from one another, but all form part of a coherent historical development which will reach its climax within the living generation. Note in particular that the climactic events of vv. 29-31 are to follow "immediately after" the siege described in vv. 15-28; there is no room here for an indefinite period of delay such as must be assumed by those who take vv. 29-31 to refer to the *parousia* (unless of course

24. Since the disciples were Galileans, it is in any case not to be taken for granted that any or all of them would be in Jerusalem or even in Judea at the time of the siege. This consideration may have influenced the third-person form of the imperatives in vv. 16-18.

25. This chart follows the wording of Matthew's version of the discourse; for a similar chart based on Mark 13 see my *Divine Government,* 128 and my *Mark,* 504.

Vv. 4-8   **Preliminary events, not to be taken as signs of the end:**
v. 6   It is not yet the end
v. 8   This is only the beginning of labor pains

Vv. 9-14   **Persecution and discouragement during that period,[26] but stand firm until . . .**
v. 14   Then the end will come

Vv. 15-28 **Description of the beginning of the end (the siege of Jerusalem)**
v. 15   But when you see . . .
v. 16   Then . . .
v. 19   . . . in those days
v. 21   Then . . .
v. 22   . . . those days; those days
v. 23   Then . . .
           [vv. 27-28   Do not confuse "those days" with the *parousia*]

Vv. 29-31 **The climax of the sequence which began at v. 15**
v. 29   *Immediately after* the distress of "those days" (echoing vv. 19, 22)
v. 30   And then . . . ; and then . . .

Vv. 32-35 **Summary of the answer to the question, "When?"**
vv. 32-33 When you see (echoing v. 15) . . . it is near (a parable about temporal sequence)
v. 34   All these things (echoing v. 3) will happen within *this genera-tion*
v. 35   You can trust my prediction.

---

they argue that Jesus, or Matthew, mistakenly predicted that the *parousia* would take place at the time of the destruction of the temple).

The main, perhaps the only, reason why this simple chronological structure has not been generally recognized is the unquestioned assumption that the language used in vv. 29-31 must refer not to the destruction of the temple but to the *parousia* and related events. When we come to the com-

---

26. In common with most interpreters, I take the τότε which introduces v. 9 not as marking a *following* period but rather as introducing another aspect of the period already described in vv. 5-8. The τότε which introduces v. 10 then continues with that same period, though there is probably a causal rather than temporal sequence in that the stumbling of the many *results from* the persecution and universal hatred of v. 9. See p. 916, n. 71, for the similar use of τότε in vv. 16, 21, and 23 resumptively for the period already under discussion rather than as the marker of a new phase.

mentary on that section, I shall explain why the words should not be taken in that traditional sense. Once that exegesis is granted, the whole section falls into a clear and carefully marked chronological sequence.

Interspersed with the answer to the question "When?" is a series of warnings against misreading the significance of historical events and so succumbing to premature eschatological excitement. This part of the discourse, therefore, does not simply answer the disciples' chronological question, but also gives pastoral guidance for puzzled disciples in unsettling times: they are to keep their heads when all around them are panicking or falling prey to opportunists. Verses 6-8 focus on this theme: catastrophic world events are not in themselves signs of "the end." The preceding warning in vv. 4-5 suggests that this "end" was in some way linked with the messianic claimants, and the same theme will emerge more fully in vv. 22-26 with specific reference to the period of the siege of Jerusalem. When events begin to look threatening, there will be a tendency to imagine that this is the beginning of the eschatological climax, the "messianic" age, and people will take advantage of that notion to press their own claims. For Christian readers, of course, the Messiah has already come, but in these future years there will remain the prospect of Jesus' own messianic return in his *parousia,* and the association of this theme with that of the destruction of the temple in the disciples' question indicates how easily that connection could be made. But the message of this first part of the discourse (and indeed in a different way of the second part) is that it is a false connection. The temple will fall, but that does not mean that the *parousia* must follow. That is why the *parousia* will be explicitly mentioned in v. 27, not to associate it with the fall of the temple but precisely to differentiate it from the chaotic events of the siege of Jerusalem which these impostors will use as the basis for their messianic claims. When the *parousia* occurs, it will not be a matter of such dubious claims and speculation, but will be obvious to everyone (vv. 27-28). The disciples are therefore specifically warned against associating the *parousia* with the events predicted in vv. 15-31, and in vv. 36ff. that theme will be resumed as Jesus speaks of a *parousia* which will come when no one expects it and which, like the lightning, will catch people unawares; then there will be no mistaking it, and no need for speculation.

Against the background of this general understanding of vv. 4-35, we shall proceed to see how its component parts contribute to the whole, and to do so we shall, for convenience, divide the text into the subsections noted in the outline on pp. 899-900 above.

a. The End Is Not Yet (24:4-8)

It is remarkable how often occurrences such as those mentioned in these verses are appealed to by those who are trying to work out a pattern for eschatological events, whereas in fact they are mentioned here precisely in order to *discourage* such speculation and to assert that the events described are *not* part of an eschatological scenario, but rather routine events within world history which must not be given more weight than they deserve. Each generation has its share of political and natural disasters, and each is tempted to think that its own experiences are somehow worse and of more ultimate significance than the sufferings of other generations, but "it is not yet the end"; at the most, such events can be seen as "the beginning of labor pains," but the period from the first labor pains to childbirth may be short or long.

4-5 The first "false alarm" is in the form of messianic claimants. A Christian reader, prompted by the specific mention of the *parousia* in v. 3, might think that those who will come "in Jesus' name" claiming to be Messiah are claiming actually to *be* Jesus, returning at the end of the age. But the declaration "I am the Messiah" would not be the most natural way to make that claim; it sounds more like a would-be liberator presenting himself to the Jewish people for the first time. He would be coming "in Jesus' name" not because he is impersonating Jesus but because he is claiming the role and title which properly belong to Jesus. And there were plenty of such claimants in the unsettled years leading up to the Jewish revolt and the eventual destruction of the temple. See, for instance, Josephus, *Ant.* 18.85-87 (a Samaritan); 20.97-99 (Theudas), 102 (the sons of Judas of Galilee), 169-72 ("the Egyptian"), 160-61, 167-68, 188 (various unnamed "impostors"). Josephus does not say that any of these people actually claimed the title "Messiah" (though Bar Kochba certainly did in the early second century), but that some presented themselves as "prophets" (*Ant.* 20.97, 169; *War* 6.285-87)[27] or "kings" (*Ant.* 17.274, 278, 285; *War* 2.433-34) and claimed to be divinely sent and empowered (*War* 2.258-59), which suggests messianic aspirations.[28] If Jesus spoke these words before his arrest in Jerusalem, they would most naturally have been understood to predict such future Jewish pretenders. The subject will be resumed in vv. 23-28, where the setting is explicitly at the time of the Jewish revolt and the siege of Jerusalem.

For the ability of such claimants to "deceive many people" cf. Acts

---

27. D. C. Allison, *Moses,* 78-83, argues convincingly that these "sign-prophets" were claiming to be the "prophet like Moses" (Deut 18:15-19), who was for many in the first century a quasi-messianic figure.

28. Note that χριστός, "anointed," is a royal title. Josephus's failure to use the word Χριστός in connection with these figures should be seen in the light of the fact that in all his voluminous works the word occurs only in the two passages relating to Jesus of Nazareth (*Ant.* 18.63; 20.200), the first of which is almost certainly a Christian revision while the second is qualified by λεγόμενος in order to dissociate Josephus himself from its use. It seems that, probably for political reasons in the light of his Roman patronage, Josephus preferred not to use this subversive Jewish title.

5:36 for the four hundred followers of Theudas (Josephus, *Ant.* 20.97, speaks of "the majority of the crowd" or "the huge crowd") and Acts 21:38 for the four thousand *sicarii* who followed the Egyptian (Josephus, *War* 2.261, says they were thirty thousand). Given the "zealot" ideology which derived from the revolt of Judas (see on 22:15-22) and which eventually resulted in the revolt of A.D. 66, the popularity of such "messianic" figures is not surprising.

6 "Wars and talk about wars"[29] are naturally linked with messianic pretenders in the Jewish context. The period from the 30s to the 60s was relatively peaceful in the Roman Empire as a whole, but in the east there were wars with Parthia in and after A.D. 36, and a more local war between Antipas and the Nabatean king Aretas in which the Romans became involved in A.D. 36-37. Later the Roman Empire itself would be torn by civil war in the "year of the four emperors," A.D. 68/9. In Judea the stirrings of revolt mentioned in the comments on vv. 4-5 made war an increasingly likely prospect even before the crucial revolt actually erupted in A.D. 66, and the suppression of nationalist leaders like Theudas and the Egyptian involved serious military operations. For an inhabitant of Palestine they were unsettling times.

But history is full of such troubled periods; the disciples must not get things out of perspective, or be panicked into imagining that "the end" is imminent. It is not spelled out here what that "end" *(telos)* is,[30] but the same term will occur in v. 14, where it leads into a description of the coming siege of Jerusalem. It seems probable therefore that the word has the same reference here, and that v. 14 is a deliberate pickup from this pronouncement: "it is *not yet* the end . . . but *then* the end will come." The question which Jesus is here answering was about when the temple would be destroyed, and that is the "end" most naturally understood here.[31] It is coming soon, and v. 34 will spell out how soon, but that does not mean that it is imminent as soon as war is on the horizon.

7-8 The basis of the "wars and talk about wars" in v. 6 is spelled out in terms of political rivalry, using language reminiscent of Isa 19:2 (and thus reinforcing the point that such events tend to recur throughout history). But in addition to these human disturbances natural disasters will continue to occur through this interim period just as they do in all periods of history. Such

29. The apparently redundant second phrase may be intended to allude to Dan 11:44, where the "king of the north" will be alarmed by "reports" from the east and north; so R. H. Gundry, *Use,* 46. See also the call not to be disturbed by "rumors" in Jer 51:46. Cf. also p. 896, n. 2; the reference may be to wars present and future.

30. *Pace* Davies and Allison, 3:340, who assert with no supporting evidence that "'The end' means 'the end of the age' (cf. v. 3)," even though the Greek word used in v. 3 is not the same as here.

31. Note that the word used is τέλος, not συντέλεια, which in v. 3b denotes the "end" of the age.

historical records as we have for the first century mention earthquakes in Asia Minor in A.D. 61and in Italy in A.D. 62, in Jerusalem in A.D. 67, and another serious earthquake at an unspecified earlier date in Palestine.[32] A widespread famine around A.D. 46 is mentioned in Acts 11:28 and Josephus, *Ant.* 3.320; 20.51-53, 101. Other more localized occurrences which did not get into historical records may also be assumed (note the mention of local earthquakes in 27:51 and Acts 16:26).

Such natural occurrences, like wars, are part of normal experience, not signs of the end. As part of the world's woes they are no more than the "beginning of labor pains": there is worse to come, and it may be protracted. "Labor pains" in itself implies "not yet" (the pains precede the birth, sometimes for a long period), and with the addition of "the beginning" the phrase clearly echoes the message of v. 6, that "it is not yet the end." In the OT labor pains are a metaphor for the suffering of nations and cities (Isa 13:8; Jer 6:24; 22:23; Mic 4:9-10) apparently within history rather than eschatologically, while in Isa 26:17-18 the context seems more eschatological. In later rabbinic literature the phrase "the labor pain [always singular] of the Messiah" comes to be used almost as a technical term for the period of suffering preceding the Messiah's coming, but this usage is not attested as early as the NT period. The wide range of metaphorical senses for such birth imagery in the NT (see John 16:21; Acts 2:24; Rom 8:22; Gal 4:19; 1 Thess 5:3) indicates a live metaphor which had as yet no recognized specific reference.[33] It gains its sense from the context, and the context here is of the suffering of Jerusalem which will be more fully described in vv. 15-22.

b. Standing Firm in Difficult Times (24:9-14)

The "then" at the beginning of vv. 9 and 10 links the contents of these verses with the same interim period which has been the subject of vv. 4-8, but the spotlight now moves away from world affairs and their impact on the morale of Jesus' disciples to the more specific experience of the disciple community in those troubled times.

The relationship of these verses to those which occupy the parallel position in Mark 13:9-13 (and in a modified form in Luke 21:12-19) is interesting. The most direct parallel to those verses of Mark has already appeared in Matt 10:17-22. Here, rather than simply repeat that material, Matthew has apparently inserted further traditional sayings of Jesus about persecution and

---

32. See, respectively, Pliny, *Hist. nat.* 2.84; Josephus, *War* 4.286-87; 1.370.

33. See further my *Mark*, 509, 512-13, and for a fuller account of Jewish usage see G. Bertram, *TDNT* 9:668-72. See also C. Gempf, *TynBul* 45 (1994) 119-35, for an overview of the background and use of this metaphor in the NT.

its effects, including two key clauses from that earlier collection (24:9b, 13, echoing the two clauses of 10:22); this new collection better suits the climactic note of this discourse as it looks beyond the temporary mission of the Twelve in Palestine during Jesus' lifetime to a time when his disciples will have gone among "all the nations."[34] Perhaps Matthew agreed with those modern commentators who feel that the more personal focus of Mark 13:9-13 as a whole seems out of place in a so-called "eschatological discourse."

The warning of unpopularity for Jesus' sake remains essentially the same, but the persecution which in ch. 10 was predicted for Jesus' disciples in their regular mission is now focused more particularly in the testing days ahead. The basis of their unpopularity is still the "name" of Jesus (10:18, 22; 24:9), a concept which is now the more readily understood since Jesus has declared himself (and therefore also his followers) against the temple and thus has set up what will become one of the main causes of popular resentment against Christians. We find here the same exhortation as in 10:22, "it is the person who remains faithful to the end who will be saved" (v. 13), but this time the issue underlying that clause is more fully developed: the persecution will be such as to threaten the faith of many even within the disciple community. Some will apostatize completely and will betray their fellow disciples (v. 10); some will succumb to false teaching which destroys their faith (v. 11); and some will simply "cool off" and so become useless for the kingdom of God (v. 12). All these outcomes mark the end of effective discipleship. In the spelling out of these dangers we can probably hear the echo of the experiences of Matthew's own Christian community as it has faced up to persecution in the years since Jesus first issued the warning.[35] Against all these threats, the only safeguard is to stand firm against all opposition. That is the only way of ultimate salvation (v. 13), but it is also the way in which the message of God's kingship will continue to be proclaimed against all odds, so that the pericope ends on an unexpectedly upbeat note (v. 14). This last saying takes up the one aspect of Mark 13:9-13 which Matthew did not see fit to include in 10:17-22, the preaching of the good news to all nations (Mark 13:10), since it points to a time more clearly in the future than the exclusive mission to Israel which was the subject of ch. 10.

9   For the connotations of "hand over" see on 17:22. The word is used

---

34. Note that in contrast with the second-person focus of Mark 13:9-13, where Jesus is addressing the Twelve, this section in Matthew is entirely in the third person after v. 9. J. Taylor, *RB* 96 (1989) 352-57, argues that this section has particular reference to the experience of Christians in Rome under the persecution by Nero in A.D. 64.

35. There are several close parallels with vv. 9-13 (and v. 4) in *Did.* 16:1-5, but in a form which does not suggest direct literary dependence on this passage alone. There are similar but less extensive echoes in Justin, *Dial.* 35:3; 82:1-2. It seems that these sayings entered into the general parenetical language of the early church.

for the fates of John the Baptist, of Jesus himself, and of his followers, as 10:17-22 has already explained. That passage has also spelled out something of the "suffering" to be expected, including judicial processes and flogging as well as martyrdom. The universal hatred there predicted was primarily in a Jewish context, though 10:18 did speak also of being brought before governors and kings and of a consequent witness to the Gentiles. Here the persecutors ("they") are not identified in the first clause, and one naturally links it with the Jewish persecution of 10:17, but in the second clause "all the nations" are also involved in the hatred and persecution of the followers of Jesus, just as "the whole world" is to hear their message (v. 14). The stakes are becoming higher as the Jesus movement begins to be influential beyond its native territory.[36]

10 For Matthew's use of the metaphor of "stumbling" see on 5:29-30. This saying is one of those where it seems to have its most serious sense, of a fall which is not just a temporary setback but involves the abandonment of God's way and the loss of salvation (as in 5:29-30; 13:21; 18:6-9), since a disciple who betrays fellow disciples has turned decisively away from the community of faith. The mutual love and concern which should be the distinguishing mark of true disciples (as the discourse of ch. 18 has made clear) has turned to hatred and repudiation.

11 See above on 7:15 for the problem of false prophets in the early church.[37] The unsettled times ahead will provide them with an opportunity to play on people's fears and hopes, as may be seen from Josephus's record of the enthusiastic response to those nationalist leaders who claimed prophetic status (see above on vv. 4-5). Here, as in 7:15, the focus appears to be on impostors within the disciple community rather than the messianic claimants predicted in vv. 4-5. The result of their teaching is described here (as with the false Messiahs of v. 5) as deceit or leading people astray (ironically the same charge which later rabbinic polemic made against Jesus himself; cf. already 27:63-64), but the language about "savage wolves" in 7:15 (cf. Acts 20:29-30) suggests something more far-reaching than simply intellectual error.

12 Lawlessness in Matthew refers not only to criminal activity, but to a lifestyle which is outside the law of God;[38] even the morally scrupulous

---

36. D. C. Sim, *Apocalyptic,* 204-8, argues that the reference is to the persecution of Jews by Gentiles during and after the Jewish War, in which Matthew's community, as Jewish Christians, were caught up.

37. D. C. Sim, *Apocalyptic,* 165-67, argues that the same prophets are in view. Since he believes that the discourse at this point is describing the end of the age, he concludes that Matthew's church believed itself to be already living in the eschaton. On the understanding of the discourse I have argued, however, no such conclusion follows: these are false prophets of the time when "it is not yet the end."

38. See the discussion by W. D. Davies, *Setting,* 202-6, especially the long note on p. 206 concerning the usage of ἀνομία in the NT as a whole.

906

scribes and Pharisees have been accused of lawlessness (23:28). The growth of such an attitude and lifestyle both within and outside the disciple community will have a devastating effect. If "love" (for God and for other people) is the key principle of living as the people of God (22:37-40), and so the opposite to "lawlessness," the "cooling" of love marks the end of effective discipleship. A love which is cold is like a fire which has gone out; cf. the devastating effects of the loss of the first love in Rev 2:4-5. Note the fourfold repetition of "many" in vv. 10-12; these verses describe a time of general decline, when it will be a minority of disciples who remain faithful (see p. 896, n. 6).[39] Cf. 7:13-14 for the "few" who find the way of life.[40]

13 In response to both the outward threats of vv. 4-8 and the destabilizing tendencies within the disciple community (vv. 9-12) the only remedy is deliberate, sustained faithfulness to the values and demands of God's kingdom. This verse repeats the exhortation of 10:22b; see the comments there. We noted there that "the phrase *eis telos,* 'to the end,' can hardly have . . . a specific reference, but simply means persevering for as long as may be necessary" and that "the thought loosely echoes Dan 12:12-13, a beatitude on those who remain faithful and will receive their reward 'at the end of the days.'" Here, however, it comes between two references to "the end" in vv. 6 and 14 which clearly have a more specific reference. If, as the context here suggests, that "end" is the destruction of the temple which is the subject of the disciples' question (see on v. 6), it would be possible to read *eis telos* here in the same sense: whoever stands firm throughout the historical process which will culminate in the destruction of the temple will be saved. But it is not easy to see what sort of "salvation" fits that scenario, and it is more likely that the adverbial phrase *eis telos* (not *eis to telos*) functions independently of the articular noun *to telos,* and has the same sense here that it had in 10:22b;[41] in that case the call is for faithfulness "for as long as it takes," and the promise is of the ultimate spiritual security (see on 10:22) of those who have stood firm in their discipleship. It is that promise, rather than physical safety at the time of the fall of Jerusalem, which best matches the dangers to faith spelled out in vv. 9-12.

14 This saying comes unexpectedly here, not only because it pro-

39. S. Brown, *JSNT* 4 (1979) 9, unusually argues that τῶν πολλῶν here is an objective genitive, "love *for* the many," and identifies "the many" as "all the nations" (vv. 9 and 14), so that the Christian community is forgetting its call to mission to the nations.

40. D. Wenham, *TynBul* 31 (1980) 155-62, argues that vv. 10-12 (like much else in this chapter) reflect the language of Daniel, v. 12 being an echo of Dan 12:4.

41. For similar usage of εἰς τέλος without reference to any specific "end," see Luke 18:5; John 13:1; in the LXX it often translates the poetical term *lānesah,* "forever." Even τὸ τέλος does not in itself have a specifically eschatological reference, as may be seen in 26:58.

vides a note of hope and triumph in an otherwise threatening context, but also because, like 26:13, it already envisages a worldwide proclamation of the good news[42] (in contrast with the restrictions of 10:5-6 and 15:24) which will not be formally launched until after Jesus' resurrection in 28:19. But Jesus has already spoken in 8:11-12 of an influx of Gentiles into the kingdom of heaven, and Matthew has prepared for the idea by the story of the magi, the healing of the centurion's servant, and the ministry outside Israel which was recounted in 15:21-39. The previous sayings about persecution also included the concept of testimony to "governors and kings" and to "the nations" in 10:18. But now those sporadic hints are taken up into what appears to be a deliberate program of worldwide evangelization (for the phrase "good news of the kingdom" see on 4:23).[43] The church's response to persecution and spiritual apathy must be to declare Jesus' message as a witness to all the nations.[44]

But this universal proclamation is not only an end in itself, but is also a sign of the coming of "the end"; the implication seems to be that the "end" will not come until the proclamation has already reached "all over the world." Those who interpret the "end" here as the *parousia* and the final judgment have sometimes taken this saying as a spur to evangelism in our day: in the early twentieth century there was an influential missionary slogan, "Evangelize to a finish to bring back the King!" The phrase "all the nations" has also been pressed into a program to bring the gospel to every known nation and tribe in the modern world (including those unknown to the Eurasian world of Jesus' day) so as to hasten the *parousia.* But that is to take this text quite out of context. In particular, this passage does not speak of

42. G. N. Stanton, *Gospel,* 15-18, argues that Matthew's phrase "*this* gospel of the kingdom" (and cf. "*this* gospel" in 26:13) is intended to refer specifically to his written document as a "gospel" (and thus that it was Matthew who initiated this literary usage). He thus goes further than J. D. Kingsbury, *Matthew: Structure,* 130-31, 163, whom he quotes. Kingsbury suggests that this is Matthew's "capsule-summary" for the *content* of his book (so also Gundry, 480 and n. 180), Stanton that "his writing *is* 'a gospel'" (my italics). This could not, however, be the meaning if these words were spoken by Jesus, and since the phrase "the good news of the kingdom" has already been used in 4:23 and 9:35 for Jesus' own message, it does not seem impossible that he could himself refer to the continuation of his message as "this good news of the kingdom."

43. D. C. Sim, *Gospel,* 242-47, argues that Matthew recognized the legitimacy and importance of the mission to Gentiles but that his own church did not regard it as their responsibility, and envisaged it only as an eschatological event. This seems to most interpreters to be an unnecessarily abstruse reading between the lines of passages like this and 26:13 and 28:19, and one which would not have been attempted if it were not for the overall thesis Sim is proposing. It does not, in any case, affect the exegesis of what the text actually says.

44. "All the nations" of course still includes the Jews, even though it draws attention to the new dimension of Gentile evangelism; see on 28:19.

worldwide evangelization as the cause of the "end," but as a necessary preliminary. And we have argued at v. 6 that the "end" *(telos)* in view here is not the "end *(synteleia)* of the age" but the destruction of the temple, which happened long ago.

In what sense, then, would the good news of God's kingdom be heard "all over the world" before that event occurred? The "world" here is *hē oikoumenē*,[45] the "inhabited world," the world of people, which at that time meant primarily the area surrounding the Mediterranean and the lesser known areas to the east, around which stretched mysterious regions (comprising much of our "old world") beyond the fringes of civilization. More narrowly it was sometimes used for the area covered by the Roman Empire (as in Luke 2:1). The same phrase *holē hē oikoumenē* is used to describe the extent of the famine in Acts 11:28 and the extent of Artemis worship in Acts 19:27. Such uses suggest caution in interpreting it too literally, even in terms of the then known world. The point is that the gospel will go far outside Judea, as indeed it certainly did in the decades following Jesus' resurrection, so that Col 1:6 can speak of the gospel already "bearing fruit in the whole world" (cf. also Col 1:23) and Rom 16:26 of the gospel having already been "made known to all the nations" (cf. Rom 10:18); Paul can speak of the area from Jerusalem to the Adriatic as already fully evangelized in the mid-fifties, with the result that he has no more scope for mission there and is already planning to go on to Spain (Rom 15:18-24). Unless one insists on a woodenly literal meaning for the phrase, the good news of God's kingdom was indeed being proclaimed "all over the world" before the temple was destroyed. The additional phrase "to all the nations (Gentiles)" draws attention here as in Mark 13:10 to the extension of the Christian mission outside Judaism, but does not demand a literal reading so that, for instance, the British must be included, let alone Americans and Australians!

If the "end" referred to is the destruction of the temple, the connection between that "end" and the universal proclamation of the gospel may be more than merely temporal. The physical temple in Jerusalem is to be replaced by "something greater than the temple"; see the comments at 12:6 on what that "something greater" may be. If, as we there considered, Matthew shares the NT concept of the "new temple" consisting of the community of those who follow Jesus, it is appropriate that the proclamation to all nations, and thus the gathering of the members of that new and more extensive community, should take place before the old temple is removed. The "new temple" that will replace it will already be under construction through the universal mission of the church. It will then follow appropriately that after the Jerusalem temple is destroyed God's chosen people will be gathered in from

---

45. The usage of the word is helpfully outlined by O. Flender, *NIDNTT* 1:518-19.

all over the world (which has already received the good news) to become the people of this new temple (v. 31).

c. The Beginning of the End for Jerusalem (24:15-28)

The "So" *(oun)* which begins this paragraph ties it closely to the preceding statement, "Then the end will come." After the various preliminary events and experiences of vv. 4-14, which are "not yet the end," here we begin the sequence of events which do in fact bring the "end" (the destruction of the temple; see on v. 6), and thus the answer to the first part of the disciples' question. The "end" itself will not be announced until vv. 29-31, but since those verses describe what will happen "immediately after" the events of vv. 15-28, the latter may appropriately be described as the beginning of the end. These verses thus speak of the unparalleled period of distress leading up to and during the siege of Jerusalem which will culminate in the destruction of the temple. The focus is now clearly limited to Judea.

The Jewish revolt began in A.D. 66, and during 67-68 the Roman commander Vespasian conquered most of Palestine. The Roman civil war in 68-69 led to a suspension of military operations in the East, but during that period Jerusalem was torn apart by its own civil war, as different Jewish parties battled for control, with the temple (the inner courts controlled by the Zealots under Eleazar and the outer court by John of Gischala) at the center of the fighting. When eventually the Roman attack was resumed in 69, Jerusalem was already in a weakened and demoralized state. The rest of Judea was quickly reduced (apart from the strongholds of Herodium and Masada), and when Vespasian returned to Rome to take up his new office as emperor, his son Titus put Jerusalem under siege for five terrible months until the temple and much of the city were destroyed in the fall of A.D. 70.

The depiction of these events in vv. 15-28 is in the allusive language of OT prophecy and apocalyptic, so that it is not necessary, and probably not possible, to identify specific aspects of the final events, as we know them from Josephus's account, with the terms used. This is, after all, presented to us as prediction, not as historical narration.[46] The sequence begins with a predicted horror (the "devastating pollution"; see comments below) which will be clear enough to provide the cue for "those in Judea" to escape, but thereafter the language about flight and distress is too general to invite specific iden-

---

46. Hagner, 2:701, 703, rightly points out that this lack of precision makes it improbable that this is the *vaticinium ex eventu* which some interpreters suppose it to be, and that it best suits the view that Matthew was writing before A.D. 70. In addition, as Davies and Allison, 3:349, point out, it would be particularly odd to instruct people to pray about the timing of an event already in the past (v. 20).

tification, and the claims of "false Messiahs and false prophets" could be made at any time during this troubled period.

All this, says Jesus, will be so terrible for those involved that it may look like the end of everything. But it is not. "Those days" will be cut short, so that God's people can survive. By contrast, the *parousia* of the Son of Man, when it comes, will be on a different scale altogether, as universal and unmistakable as a flash of lightning (vv. 27-28). The siege will mark "the end *(telos)*" for Jerusalem, but it will not be the time of the *parousia* and the "end *(synteleia)* of the age." For, as vv. 29-31 will go on to explain, the end of the old order will be the cue for the establishment of the universal reign of the Son of Man and the gathering of a new people of God from the ends of the earth. The Son of Man will reign in heaven, but his future return to earth will be at a time no one can predict; only when it happens will they know.

15 The most obvious sign that "the end" is near in Jerusalem is cryptically described in familiar scriptural language. The "devastating pollution"[47] is explicitly identified as a motif from Daniel, though the phrase is sufficiently distinctive to be recognized even without explicit attribution, as Mark clearly believed. In Daniel the phrase stands for the horrifying sacrilege which was to be perpetrated by the "king of the north" when he abolished the regular sacrificial ritual of the Jerusalem temple (Dan 8:13; 9:27; 11:31; 12:11). The reference is clearly to the events of 167 B.C., when Antiochus Epiphanes conquered Jerusalem and prohibited Jewish sacrificial worship, setting up an altar for pagan sacrifices (including the slaughter of pigs) on top of the altar of burnt offering (Josephus, *Ant.* 12.253); it stood in the temple for three years until Judas Maccabeus regained control of Jerusalem, purified the temple, and restored its true worship. 1 Macc 1:54 describes this pagan altar by the same phrase *bdelygma erēmōseōs;*[48] for the reconsecration of the temple see 1 Macc 4:41-58.

The specific desecration referred to in Daniel was now long in the past,[49] and Jesus is speaking of something still to come. That is why discernment is needed: hence the editorial aside,[50] "let the reader understand this" —

---

47. See p. 896, n. 8, for this rendering of what is traditionally "the abomination of desolation."

48. Josephus, *Ant.* 12.320, also uses the cognate verb ἐρημόω to describe the effect of Antiochus's actions on the temple.

49. See, however, Keener, 575-76, for the view that even within the book of Daniel itself the Antiochus event was only one manifestation of the desecration motif; he regards Dan 9:27 as applying it also to a different time "close to the time of Jesus." This is not the same as the (valid) observation that Jesus and others "freely reapplied such images."

50. Since Matthew, unlike Mark, has mentioned a written text (Daniel), these words can be taken as part of the original saying: Jesus is calling on the reader of Daniel to understand what is found written there. But it seems more likely that it is an editorial com-

which itself recalls the comment in Dan 12:10 that only the wise will understand the secrets revealed to Daniel.[51] The reader[52] is presumably to identify
something which is in recognizable continuity with the devastating pollution
set up by Antiochus, but just what form it will take is left to the imagination.
The wording suggests some sort of offensive pollution "set up in the holy
place," which should mean the temple,[53] and the context requires that it be of
such a nature and at such a time as to allow those who see it to escape before it
is too late. The neuter participle "set up" (see p. 897, n. 10) is apparently a deliberate change from Mark's masculine,[54] and so denotes an object or occurrence rather than a person.[55] Those who believe that this whole section is a
"prediction" written up in the light of what actually happened have attempted
without much agreement to suggest a suitable identification (see below); those
who regard it as genuine prediction may feel that any such specific identification is neither possible nor necessary, and that all that the text asserts is that
some act of sacrilege will alert Judeans that disaster is about to fall.

Our limited knowledge of events in first-century Palestine has

---

ment in Matthew, as it certainly is in Mark. In that case the reference might be either to the
reader of Daniel or to the reader of Matthew's gospel.

51. R. H. Gundry, *Use,* 49, argues for a deliberate echo of Dan 12:10 here.

52. In normal NT usage ὁ ἀναγινώσκων would probably mean the person reading
the text aloud to the congregation rather than a solitary, silent reader. Is this an invitation to
the public reader of Matthew to attempt a topical interpretation for the sake of the audience?

53. Cf. Acts 6:13; 21:28. It would not naturally be understood of Jerusalem more
generally, which Matthew refers to as "the holy city" (4:5; 27:52). All the references to
the "devastating pollution" in Daniel relate it to the cessation of sacrifices and thus specifically to the temple.

54. Mark's masculine has been taken to refer to the setting up in the temple of a
statue of Zeus (to whom Antiochus rededicated the building, 2 Macc 6:2), which was also
believed by some to have been part of Antiochus's desecration (but was not the specific referent of the phrase βδέλυγμα ἐρημώσεως, at least according to 1 Macc 1:54); see G. R.
Beasley-Murray, *Last Days,* 409-10. L. Gaston, *No Stone,* 24, argues that there was in fact no
such statue, but that it nevertheless became a fixed element in Jewish and Christian tradition.

55. A personal identification of this figure has often been proposed on the basis of
2 Thess 2:3-10, which speaks of the παρουσία of the "man of lawlessness" who takes his
seat in the temple and uses false signs and wonders to deceive the people; the association
is perhaps already made in *Did.* 16:4, where a personal "deceiver of the world" is linked
with the spiritual declension of Matt 24:9-12. Keener, 573-75, has a useful survey of the
development of the idea of a personal "antichrist." But whatever may be the case for
Mark, it is most unlikely that if Matthew had such a scenario in mind he would have used
the neuter participle here (against Mark), and the signs and wonders that he speaks of in
v. 24 are not attributed to the "devastating pollution" but to (plural) messianic pretenders.
It is perhaps significant that D. C. Sim, *Apocalyptic,* 101-2, argues that Matthew envisages
a personal antichrist not on the basis of what Matthew actually says but on the assumption
that he knew the antichrist tradition of 2 Thess 2.

prompted three main proposals of historical events which might have been recognized as the "devastating pollution" by those who had heard of Jesus' prediction.[56] (a) In A.D. 40 the emperor Gaius gave orders for a statue of himself to be set up in the temple at Jerusalem; fortunately the order had still not been carried out when Gaius was assassinated in A.D. 41, thus averting what would have been a bloody uprising. (b) Probably during the winter of A.D. 67/8 the Zealots took over the temple as their headquarters, and Josephus speaks with horror of the way they "invaded the sanctuary with polluted feet" and mocked the temple ritual, while the sanctuary was defiled with blood as factional fighting broke out (Josephus, *War* 4.150-57, 196-207).[57] (c) When the Roman troops eventually broke into the temple, the presence of their (idolatrous) standards in the sacred precincts would inevitably remind Jews of Antiochus; Josephus even mentions Roman soldiers offering sacrifices to their standards in the temple courts (*War* 6.316). Luke's parallel to this verse (Luke 21:20, "Jerusalem surrounded by armies") apparently understands the "devastating pollution" in this sense. None of these three events quite fits what this verse says: the Gaius event was too early (and in fact never happened) and the Roman presence in the sanctuary too late to provide a signal for escape before the end came, while the Zealot occupation, which took place at the right time, was perhaps not quite the type of pagan defilement envisaged by Daniel. It seems wiser not to claim a specific tie-up with recorded history, but to recognize that desecration of the temple was an ever-present threat once the Roman invasion had been provoked.

It may be remarked in passing that if, as many claim, Matthew was writing after the event, it is strange that he could not produce a clearer and more convincing account of this preliminary sign. What had he to gain by writing so cryptically, and by failing to achieve a satisfying tie-up with what would then have been quite recent history? It makes better sense of the enigmatic nature of the sign to believe that Matthew was not only recording what Jesus said some decades before the event, but was also himself writing at a time when events were yet to unfold to the climax of the war with Rome.[58]

16-18   Verse 15 has spoken of what "you" will see, but now Jesus is-

56. The famous incident in which Pilate introduced (idolatrous) Roman standards into the temple (Josephus, *War* 2.169-71; *Ant.* 18.55-59) probably occurred in A.D. 26, well before Jesus' public ministry, though the memory of it might perhaps have provided a model for the sort of "pollution" he predicted.

57. Keener, 576-77, takes Matt 24:15 to be referring to "the sanctuary's desecration in A.D. 66." The references he gives in Josephus indicate that he has the Zealot incursion in mind; the dates and sequence of Zealot outrages in the temple during the period of the revolt are not always clear.

58. I have developed this argument more fully with regard to the date of Mark in my *Mark,* 521.

sues instructions not to the disciples directly, but in the third person "to whom it may concern." The scope is broad, addressing not merely those associated with the temple, nor even the whole population of Jerusalem, but more generally "those in Judea."[59] No towns or villages will be safe as the Roman forces restore control, and people must seek the time-honored refuge of "the hills,"[60] just as the Maccabees had done when the first "devastating pollution" was set up (1 Macc 2:28, using the same phrase *eis ta orē*) to be joined by other patriots in "the wilderness" (1 Macc 2:29-31). The reference to "Judea" suggests that the period envisaged is before the final siege of Jerusalem, when the wider province was being brought under Roman control, but when escape was still possible (as it would not be for those in Jerusalem itself after the siege began). The urgency of flight is underlined by the vivid images of the person who hears the news while resting on the roof of the house and dare not go inside (the roof was reached by an outside staircase) to pack a travel bag, and the field worker whose outer garment, removed for work, must be left behind. Luke 17:31 uses the same imagery with regard to the *parousia;* it is perhaps standard language for an emergency.[61]

19-20 The plight of refugees is always wretched, but for some of those caught up in the Judean emergency it will be even worse. This "woe" is not, like those of 11:21; 18:7b; 26:24, and those against the scribes and Pharisees in ch. 23, one of condemnation, but of sympathy for those who will suffer (see 18:7a for another noncondemnatory "woe"; and cf. the "woes" of Rev 8:13; 12:12). The problems of pregnant women and nursing mothers in such a situation are easily envisaged. Bad weather will only make things worse: it can be very cold in the Judean hills in winter, and heavy rain and flooding can make traveling conditions difficult or even impossible.[62] But

---

59. This third-person exhortation is apparently not specifically addressed to Christians; it is the whole population which is at risk. This makes it unlikely that it was these words which constituted the "oracle" which, according to Eusebius, *Hist. eccl.* 3.5.3, caused the Christian community in Jerusalem to flee to Pella before the war began. Nor is it likely that Eusebius would have referred to reported words of Jesus as "an oracle given by revelation to the approved people there," though it is possible that the "oracle" was a later adaptation of this saying of Jesus. Pella is, in any case, not in "the hills," but in the lowlands of the Jordan valley, and the flight described by Eusebius is dated before any likely historical candidate for "seeing the devastating pollution." There has been debate as to whether Eusebius's Pella tradition is historically founded; see, briefly, G. R. Beasley-Murray, *Last Days,* 412-13; also S. Sowers, *TZ* 26 (1970) 305-20; J. J. Gunther, *TZ* 29 (1973) 81-84; C. Koester, *CBQ* 51 (1989) 90-106.

60. For refuge in the hills cf. Gen 14:10; Ps 11:1; Jer 16:16; Ezek 7:16.

61. Cf. Gen 19:17, 26 for the danger of "looking back"; that passage provides the background for Luke's saying.

62. See Keener, 580-81, for details on the problems of winter travel in the ancient world.

what is the problem about escaping on the sabbath (a problem which only Matthew notices)? Was Jesus thinking of the faithful Jew (and more conservative Jewish Christian) who would not want to break the developed scribal rules which by now allowed only a "sabbath day's journey" of less than one mile?[63] Or has Matthew himself added this comment for the benefit of his own Christian community which, following the "lax" attitude which Jesus himself displayed in 12:1-14, has ceased to observe the sabbath strictly, but by escaping on that day would draw the hostile attention of non-Christian Jews who still observed it?[64] Or is all that too subtly ideological, and is the point simply that the lack of facilities to buy food and other practical difficulties arising from the stricter observance of the sabbath by other Jews could be expected to be a problem for the refugees?[65]

21-22   Josephus's lurid description of the horrors of the siege (*War* 5.424-38, 512-18, 567-72; 6.193-213) shows that, while v. 21 uses the hyperbolic language of apocalyptic (cf. Dan 12:1; Joel 2:2; 1QM 1:11-12; *T. Mos.* 8:1; Rev 16:18), it is an assessment which those involved in the events would have been agreed on.[66] In passing, we should note that "nor ever will be again" confirms that this passage is about a historical event, not about the end of the world! The horror was in fact "cut short" by the Roman capture of the city after five months, bringing physical relief to those who had survived the famine in the city. But even this "natural" process of conquest is attributed to the purpose of God (the passive verb without expressed agent often indicates divine agency; in Mark 13:20 it is explicit) to enable his "chosen people" to survive.[67] These same "chosen people" will reappear in vv. 24 and 31, where

---

63. Though they might have remembered how the Maccabean heroes, faced with the threat of annihilation, had agreed that sabbath regulations could give way in an emergency (1 Macc 2:32-41).

64. So G. N. Stanton, *Gospel,* 192-206 (= *JSNT* 37 [1989] 17-30), drawing attention to the fact that the words "your escape" are in Matthew but not in Mark; this shows, he argues, that Matthew has angled this saying specifically to the concerns of his own Christian community. In response, E. K.-C. Wong, *JSNT* 44 (1991) 3-18, suggests that there may have been differing attitudes to the sabbath within Matthew's community, and that his concern is to maintain its unity, which might be strained if some hesitated to escape on the sabbath while others were happy to do so.

65. This explanation is preferred by R. J. Banks, *Jesus,* 102-3 and Gundry, 483, and is argued more fully by Y.-E. Yang, *Jesus,* 230-41: "not that flight on the sabbath was wrong in itself, but that it would be practically difficult." Yang rightly points out that this understanding of μηδὲ σαββάτῳ makes it unnecessary to suppose that it originated as an addition by Matthew.

66. Josephus himself, who was involved in the events, claims that none of the disasters since the world began can compare to the fate of Jerusalem (*War* 1.12).

67. This is the more probable meaning of "because of" in this context, though it is also possible that the presence of the chosen people among the population, like that of

they are the people who belong to the Son of Man; the boast of Israel to be God's chosen people (Exod 19:5-6; Lev 20:26, etc.) is now being applied not to the nation as a whole but to those from among Israel and from the ends of the earth (v. 31) who constitute the new messianic community (cf. 8:11-12). See further above on 22:14. These true people of God will not be spared the experience of the siege[68] but will be enabled to survive through it both physically (v. 22) and spiritually (v. 24).[69] And it is because of their presence among the people of Jerusalem that the siege will not be more protracted and disastrous.[70]

23-26 The catastrophic situation in Jerusalem during those last days[71] before its capture will provide a fertile breeding-ground for the sort of messianic claimants already predicted in vv. 5 and 11 as part of the more general upheaval of the period before the siege.[72] Anyone who offered new hope of divine intervention would be eagerly listened to, and the more so if they were able to offer "signs and wonders" to support their claim. And such miraculous proofs were, according to Josephus, offered by several of the na-

---

"righteous people" in Sodom (Gen 18:22-32), is seen as alleviating the punishment the city deserves.

68. *Pace* Eusebius; see p. 914, n. 59.

69. Dan 12:1, which is probably echoed in v. 21, may also lie behind v. 22b, in that it speaks of "your people, everyone whose name is found written in the book," being delivered from the unparalleled time of distress. Cf. also Isa 59:8, where judgment is held back "for my servants' sake." G. R. Beasley-Murray, *Last Days,* 419, n. 124, argues, however, that there is no real parallel in Jewish apocalyptic to the idea of the days being "cut short."

70. Carson, 502, wishes to separate v. 22 from v. 21 (and even places a paragraph break between them), seeing v. 21 as referring specifically to the siege of Jerusalem but v. 22 as more generally about "the entire period of which vv. 15-21 are only a part"; this requires, improbably, that "those days" in v. 22 must have a different meaning from the same phrase in v. 19 (and the resumptive "then" of v. 21). By this unusual exegesis Carson aims to separate "those days" in v. 29 (where it picks up the language of this verse) from the period of the siege, and thus to argue that vv. 29-31 describe a distant event unconnected with A.D. 70 (504-505). The proposal seems to be determined by a prior assumption as to the scope of the passage as a whole rather than a natural understanding of what this verse says in context. See further below on v. 29.

71. As in vv. 9-10 (see p. 899, n. 26) the τότε which introduces v. 23 (like those in vv. 16, 21) indicates a further feature of the period being described, not a subsequent phase of the story. It is equivalent to "in those days."

72. Such "false Messiahs and false prophets" active during the siege might include Simon bar-Giora (Josephus, *War* 4.503-44 etc.), who was regarded as a "king" (510) and eventually paraded and executed in the Roman triumph as "the enemy's general" (*War* 7.153-54), and also "many" false prophets noted anonymously in *War* 6.285-88; that last passage goes on to relate (6.289-300) a series of signs and wonders occurring in the period before the city was destroyed, which some took (wrongly) to be omens of deliverance.

tionalist leaders he mentions: he cites specifically the parting the Jordan (*Ant.* 20.97), the collapse of the city walls (*Ant.* 20.170), the uncovering of Moses' sacred vessels (*Ant.* 18.85), as well as more generally "conspicuous wonders and signs" (*Ant.* 20.168) and God-given "signs of freedom" (*War* 2.259). These "sign prophets"[73] drew on the biblical tradition of authenticating signs (see above on 12:38), and NT writers do in fact expect such "signs and wonders" to accompany the true work of God (Acts 2:43; 4:16, 30; 5:12; etc.), even though it is also recognized that divine miracles can be counterfeited (Acts 8:9-11; 2 Thess 2:9; Rev 13:13-14; 16:14; cf. Deut 13:1-3).[74] Even the "chosen people" may not be immune to such deceit, though the addition of "if possible" suggests that they, unlike the rest of the people in the city, have the spiritual resources to resist it. They have been forewarned (v. 25), and their memory of Jesus' miracles ought to enable them to see the difference. For the wilderness as a plausible place to look for a God-sent deliverer see above on 3:1, and cf. 11:7-9 for going out into the wilderness to find a prophet.[75] The storerooms[76] are a less obvious place to look, but as the most secret part of the building (see on 6:6) they might suit the ideology of a "hidden Messiah" (John 7:27).[77]

27 This verse is a sort of "aside" which draws a sharp distinction between the events during the siege and the still future *parousia*. The real *parousia*, when it comes, will not be like the claims of impostors during the siege. The "for" which introduces this saying indicates how it fits into this context: "don't believe them, because. . . ." In contrast with a so-called Messiah who has to be sought out in an obscure place and who needs authenticating signs to convince people of his claim, the *parousia* of the Son of Man will be as unmissable as a flash of lightning which blazes across the whole sky. This warning was perhaps prompted by the disciples' question in v. 3, which,

---

73. The term is used in a study covering the period A.D. 40-70 by P. W. Barnett, *NTS* 27 (1981) 679-97.

74. R. H. Gundry, *Use*, 50-51, suggests that the wording here is based on Deut 13:1-3.

75. The fact that the Qumran community was set up in "the wilderness" is further testimony to the ideological appeal of the idea, but the concept of salvation coming from the wilderness is much wider and older than Qumran, and there is no reason to see a specific reference to Qumran here, any more than there is to connect wilderness-based nationalist leaders such as Theudas and the Egyptian with Qumran.

76. See G. R. Beasley-Murray, *Kingdom*, 315, for the suggestion that the wilderness and the storerooms come from "an overliteral rendering of the poetical Hebrew antithesis *miḥus umeḥodarim*, 'in the open country and in the inner rooms' (Deut. 32:25)," an idiom for "inside and outside" and so meaning "anywhere" rather than singling out specific locations.

77. For the Jewish concept of a "hidden Messiah" underlying the Gospel of John see M. de Jonge, *NTS* 19 (1972/3) 254-57.

while differentiating the *parousia* and the end of the age from "these things" (the destruction of the temple), has nevertheless suggested some association between the two events, probably supposing that the one cannot occur without the other. Not so, says Jesus. The time of the siege and capture of the city will be characterized by the claims and counterclaims of those who pretend to a messianic role, but the *parousia* of the Son of Man will need no such claims or proofs: everyone will see and recognize it (as he will go on to spell out in vv. 36-44). He is thus setting the *parousia* and the end of the age decisively apart from the coming destruction of the temple. The one may be seen coming and prepared for (that is what vv. 15ff. have been about), but the other will carry no prior warning. So the disciples' request for a "sign" for his *parousia* was misguided;[78] unlike the messianic pretenders, with their offer of "signs," the Son of Man will give no warning sign of his *parousia*. There is no sign that lightning is coming, but when it comes, no one can escape the sudden illumination.[79]

So the mention of the *parousia* in this context is intended precisely to distinguish it from the events currently being considered; it will be only after a marked change of subject in v. 36 that the *parousia* will itself become the focus of the discourse.

28 This proverbial saying[80] about vultures (see p. 897, n. 14) recalls Job 39:30: "Where the dead are, there it [the vulture] is." It may be understood either (a) from the point of view of the vultures or (b) from that of the observer. (a) Vultures are able to discover a carcass from far away because of their keen sight (Job 39:29), and once they have seen it they take action. This could be a parable of the keen-eyed disciple who reads the significance of events and acts on it, perhaps reflecting the "when you see . . . then escape" of vv. 15-16. (b) Anyone who sees a gathering of vultures knows that there must be a carcass. This could be applied in two quite different ways, depending on whether it is a reflection on the whole preceding paragraph (when you see all the horrors of the siege you may be sure that Jerusalem is doomed)[81] or merely on the preceding verse (the *parousia* of the Son of Man will be as obvious as the presence of the carcass). The placing of the saying after v. 27

78. The request will not be granted when that subject is addressed in vv. 36ff.; see below, p. 936.

79. Carter, 476, finds a political nuance here in that lightning was associated with Jupiter and with the imperial power of Rome as his deputy; Jesus' visitation will "signify the end of Rome's, or any, empire and the establishment of God's empire." But it is doubtful whether so obvious and universal a symbol as lightning would be understood to carry this specific connotation.

80. For some nonbiblical parallels see Davies and Allison, 3:355.

81. Morris, 608, suggests a more specific reference to the false prophets, gathering to "feed on" those they have deceived.

supports the last option, as does the fact that Luke uses it in a context referring to the *parousia* (Luke 17:37), but the saying remains enigmatic. Its gruesome subject-matter suits this ominous context, but to allegorize it as depicting the "corpse" of Jerusalem surrounded by the "eagles" (military
standards) of the Roman army[82] is to look for too literal a reference in proverbial language.[83]

d. The End of the Temple and the Triumph of the Son of Man (24:29-31)

It is with v. 29 that the traditional interpretation becomes most uncomfortable. If it is agreed that vv. 15-28 relate to the siege of Jerusalem (apart from
the aside about its difference from the *parousia* in v. 27), and if it is assumed
that vv. 29-31 describe the "*parousia* and the end of the age" (even though
they use none of those terms), the opening phrase "But immediately after the
distress of those days" constitutes a formidable problem unless one is prepared to argue that Jesus (and Matthew) really did expect the *parousia* to take
place in the late first century A.D., and that he was mistaken. As a result many
interpreters resort to imprecise talk about "prophetic perspective" which
merges far distant events into a single time-frame, while others argue that either "immediately after" or "those days" does not mean what it appears to
mean; for such proposals see below on v. 29.[84]

This commentary takes the temporal connection at its face value. In
response to the disciples' question when the temple would be destroyed, Jesus has first mentioned intervening events which do not constitute reliable
"signs" (vv. 4-14) and has then spoken of the real sign that the "end" is near,

---

82. Even more imaginatively Carter, 476-77, supposes that it is Rome's own empire that is to be destroyed (cf. n. 79 above), the corpses (why plural?) representing Rome's
fallen soldiers and the eagles their military standards "cast about on the ground in defeat."
Carter's interpretation is enthusiastically presented in *JBL* 122 (2003) 467-87. Given the
rather obvious symbolism of the gathering of vultures to feast on a corpse (and the background in Job 39:30), it is surely a step too far to make the "eagles" themselves the victims.

83. For this and other even more unlikely allegorizations see Davies and Allison,
3:355-56. Those who hear "Too many cooks spoil the broth" do not need to identify what
the broth represents.

84. Hagner, 2:711-13, discusses the issue as helpfully as can be done if one assumes that vv. 29-31 are describing the *parousia*. His suggestion is that Matthew has
added the εὐθέως because he, writing before A.D. 70, really believed that the *parousia*
would immediately follow the destruction of the temple, but that Jesus did not intend his
predictions to be so closely coupled. This setting of Matthew against Jesus is clearly uncomfortable to Hagner as a conservative scholar, but he concludes that "no hypothesis is
able to dissolve completely the tensions that lie in the material of the discourse." Unfortunately he declines to consider the exegesis followed in this commentary, which shows the
supposed "tensions" to be illusory.

the appearance of the devastating pollution. This has led into a description of the horrors of the Roman war and the siege of Jerusalem, repeatedly characterized as "those days" (vv. 19, 22, 22), but apparently without as yet reaching the actual climax of the destruction of the temple. That climax is still awaited at the end of v. 28, and the words which follow provide it: "immediately after the distress of 'those days' . . . ." The specific time-scale provided in v. 34 will confirm that all this is to happen before the present generation has passed away. Thus by the time we get to v. 35 the disciples' first question "When will these things happen?" has been carefully and specifically answered, and it will be time to move on to their second question, "What will be the sign of your *parousia* and the end of the age?" of which a parenthetical preview has already been given in v. 27.

If this analysis is right, vv. 29-31 are to be understood as Jesus' way of speaking, in the colorful language of OT prophecy, of the climactic event of the destruction of the temple and of his own authority as the vindicated Son of Man, which provides the necessary counterpart to the loss of what has been hitherto the earthly focus of God's rule among his people. Most of the wording of vv. 29-31 is made up of OT allusions, and I shall argue in what follows that if these are understood against the background of their meaning in their OT contexts, they provide a striking and (for those who are at home in OT imagery) a theologically rich account of the far-reaching developments in the divine economy which are to be focused in the historical event of the destruction of the temple. The problem is that modern Christian readers are generally not very comfortably at home in OT prophetic imagery, and are instead heirs to a long tradition of Christian exegesis which takes it for granted that such cosmic language and in particular the imagery of Dan 7:13-14 can only be understood of the *parousia* and the end of the world.[85] But Jesus was speaking before that tradition developed, and his words must be understood within their own context, where it was the OT that provided the natural template for interpreting such imagery.[86]

29 Two verbal echoes tie the opening phrase closely with vv. 15-28: "distress" echoes the term used for the experience of God's people during the siege in v. 21, and "those days" picks up the language of vv. 19 and

85. I have discussed the development of the *parousia* understanding especially of Dan 7:13-14 within and beyond the NT in my *Jesus and the OT,* 202-4, 210-11, 214-17, 220-23. I argue there that the book of Revelation marks the most significant shift away from Jesus' own use of Daniel's imagery toward a *parousia* interpretation which quickly became standardized in subsequent Christian thought.

86. A. I. Wilson, *When,* 108-32, usefully surveys the debate on the appropriate interpretation of such "apocalyptic" language as used by Jesus, and strongly supports the exegetical approach here followed. Cf. ibid., 144-52, with special reference to language about "the Son of Man coming."

22 (twice). "Immediately after" makes the link even tighter. Matthew does not share Mark's famously frequent use of "immediately" as a storytelling device, but when he does use it to link events or stages in a story, it always carries its normal sense; here it is deliberately introduced, and, when combined with "after," it can only mean that there is no delay separating the two events. Attempts to evade the force of Matthew's language have usually therefore focused on "those days," notably Carson's proposal (see p. 916, n. 70) that while v. 21 refers to the siege of Jerusalem, the phrase "those days" which follows in v. 22 (and which has just been used to refer to the siege in v. 19) refers instead to a much longer period, the whole "inter-advent" age, of which the siege is only one limited example ("one particularly violent display of judgment," Carson, 495), and that v. 29 is then picking up "those days" in its v. 22 sense rather than its v. 19 sense. Others, while not wishing to introduce a gratuitous break between vv. 21 and 22, are still drawn to the suggestion that somehow a larger perspective has now been introduced and that "those days" here means something other than the days of the Roman war. Such an evasion of the natural meaning of Matthew's words is surely a counsel of despair: it is supposed that "immediately after the distress of those days" simply cannot be allowed to mean what it says, since the sun and moon do still shine, heaven has not collapsed, and the Son of Man has not come on the clouds of heaven. In view of this instinctive reaction, it is important that we consider what such "cosmic" language might originally have been understood to mean in such a context[87] and whether the quasiliteral sense which is so commonly assumed would really have been the natural way to read it.

The words of v. 29 which follow the opening temporal phrase, while not a simple verbatim quotation, are so closely modeled on two OT passages that they are appropriately set out in the translation above as a poetic allusion. The first two lines are taken from Isa 13:10: the words are almost all the same as those of the LXX, though the first clause has been recast ("it will be darkened as the sun rises" becomes "the sun will be darkened"). That same text also speaks of the "stars of heaven" not giving their light, which links up with the thought of the second allusion, but the latter is in fact verbally closer to Isa 34:4. In this case the echo is less exact, but the LXX Isaiah text speaks

---

87. "Original understanding" will of course depend on who the hearers are. B. Van Iersel, *Bib* 77 (1996) 84-92, commenting on the parallel in Mark, argues that readers in Rome would be likely to take the sun, moon, and stars as representing pagan gods, so that this language refers to "the dethronement of the pagan idols." Whatever may have been the case in Rome, it is unlikely that Matthew's readers would take it that way; still less should Greco-Roman usage be used to determine what Jesus may have meant by it. But at least Van Iersel is willing to accept that the language need not be understood of actual cosmic events.

both of the stars falling from heaven[88] and of heaven itself "rolled up like a scroll," while the probable Hebrew text also adds the idea of the host of heaven "rotting away."[89] These two Isaiah texts are the most obvious sources for Jesus' words here, but there are other examples in the OT prophets of similar imagery drawn from cosmic disorder and darkness; see Ezek 32:7-8; Amos 8:9; Joel 2:10, 30-31; 3:15. In most of these passages the immediate context is of God's threatened judgment on cities and nations, both pagan and Israelite; in the case of Joel the judgment is already actual in the form of the locust swarms which cut off the light of the sun, though this experience is also used as a model for a more universal judgment to come. In Isa 13:10 the reference is to the coming destruction of Babylon, and in Isa 34:4 to a threatened judgment on "all nations," which is then narrowed down specifically to Edom. Language about cosmic collapse, then, is used by the OT prophets to symbolize God's acts of judgment within history, with the emphasis on catastrophic political reversals.[90]

When Jesus borrows Isaiah's imagery, it is reasonable to understand it in a similar sense.[91] If such language was appropriate to describe the end of Babylon or Edom under the judgment of God, why should it not equally describe God's judgment on Jerusalem's temple and the power structure which it symbolized? It is certainly shocking that Isaiah's patriotic denunciation of Babylon and Edom could be turned against Jerusalem, and God's own city reduced to the level of a pagan power, but we shall see that this reversal of roles is at the heart of the message of these verses, as it has been already of such key pronouncements as 8:11-12. It should also be noted that the same sort of cosmic language is used of judgments not on pagan nations but on the northern and southern kingdoms of Israel in Amos 8:9 and Joel 2:10 respectively. The language is extravagant and vivid, but that does not mean that its use by Jesus must be divorced from historical events any more than it was in

88. N. T. Wright, *Victory,* 354-55, suggests a further allusion to the taunt against the king of Babylon as the "day star, fallen from heaven" in Isa 14:12, an equally clearly political image.

89. For details of how the words relate to both Hebrew and LXX texts of Isa 34:4 see my *Jesus and the OT,* 255-56; the imagery is of the "host of heaven" (the stars) falling like withered leaves off a tree. The verb "shake" here may reflect the OT image of the dead leaves shaken off the tree, or it may be influenced by the similar passage, Joel 2:10 (LXX σεισθήσεται ὁ οὐρανός).

90. N. T. Wright, *Victory* 362, compares our use of the term "earth-shattering" to describe major turning points within history.

91. The political nature of the imagery is recognized by Carter, 477-78, who, however, consistently with his interpretation of vv. 27-28 (see pp. 918-19, nn. 79, 82), understands it of the Roman emperors who used the sun and moon to symbolize their power: "It is 'lights out' time for all tyrants."

Isaiah. It is natural that such language should also be able to be extended (as it is already especially in Joel) to speak of more eschatological judgment, but that is no reason to deny its primary reference to historical events where the context requires.[92] On that understanding, therefore, v. 29 is now at last providing in symbolic language the answer to the disciples' first question. This is the act of historic judgment which Jesus has already predicted in more prosaic terms in v. 2. But the use of this prophetic imagery enables the reader to understand that what is to be destroyed is not just a magnificent building, but a center of power comparable to ancient Babylon. And when such a power structure collapses, another is needed to take its place; this will be supplied in vv. 30-31 with its vision of the enthronement of the Son of Man and the gathering of his chosen people from all over the world.

30   The concluding clause of this verse, with its clear echo of Dan 7:13, is parallel to the prediction which follows the cosmic imagery at this point in both Mark and Luke. But before that Matthew adds two further clauses, concerning the visibility of "the sign of the Son of Man in heaven" and the mourning of the tribes (the latter introducing a further OT allusion, to Zech 12:10-14). We shall return to these Matthean additions when we have considered the meaning of the allusion to Daniel.

See the comments on 10:23 for the importance of allusions to Dan 7:13-14 in Matthew and the range of application of such language. This saying belongs to the group of three Matthean allusions (16:28; 24:30; 26:64) which are shared with Mark (Mark 8:38; 13:26; 14:62), and which have certain significant features in common: all of them speak of a "coming of the Son of Man" which is visible, which is associated with power, and which is to take place within the lifetime of those to whom he is speaking (in this case, "this generation" in v. 34).[93] We have seen at 10:23 how the imagery of Daniel's vision requires that these passages be interpreted not of a "coming" to earth at the *parousia* but of a "coming" to God in heaven to be given the universal dominion declared in Dan 7:14. These are enthronement texts. In 26:64 that exegesis is now widely recognized (see comments there), not least because that pronouncement speaks explicitly of what is to be true "from now on," not at some separate time in the future. And yet the present passage, which uses very similar language to allude to the same OT text, is persistently given a different reference by commentators, even though v. 34 will

92. J. A. Gibbs, *Jerusalem,* 188-95, demonstrates at length the OT use of such figurative language in "theophanic or eschatological" contexts which in fact relate to events within history, and argues cogently (ibid., 195-97) for a similar reference here in Matt 24: "the cosmos and its powers will be shaken as divine judgment comes down upon the temple and city."

93. I have discussed these three Marcan texts as a group in ch. 4 of my *Divine Government.*

make its contemporary application quite as explicit as that of 26:64. The basis for this inconsistency of approach seems to be the influence of the term *parousia* occurring in this context, though it must be stressed that it is not used in this verse, which speaks of "coming" *(erchomenos), not parousia.*[94] But we have seen that in v. 27 the point of mentioning the *parousia* is actually to dissociate it from the events surrounding the destruction of the temple, and we shall see that the recurrence of *parousia* in vv. 37 and 39 is with reference not to the "coming" described here but to a different "day and hour" introduced in v. 36, whose timing, unlike that of the destruction of the temple, cannot be known. If then this verse is interpreted in terms of what it actually says, rather than by merging it into a *parousia* context from which the text in fact explicitly differentiates it, there is no reason why we should not understand the "coming of the Son of Man" here in the same way as in the related texts in 16:28 and 26:64 (and, as we have suggested earlier, in 10:23, to which there is no Marcan parallel), and in the imagery of Daniel's vision, of a "coming" to God to receive sovereign power. The time of the temple's destruction will also be the time when it will become clear that the Son of Man, rejected by the leaders of his people, has been vindicated and enthroned at the right hand of God, and that it is he who is now to exercise the universal kingship which is his destiny. That is how Daniel's vision is to be fulfilled.[95]

As in v. 29, this is a shocking reversal of roles. The "one like a son of man" who is the subject of Daniel's vision is a symbol for Israel, the people of God, in their eventual vindication and triumph over the pagan empires who have hitherto oppressed them. But in Jesus' use of the phrase "the Son of Man" that corporate symbolism has become focused in an individual to whom the kingship is now to be given. He, too, will be vindicated over his enemies, but those enemies have now become the leaders of the very people he has come to represent. When Israel's leaders reject and execute Jesus the Son of Man, they put themselves outside the ongoing purpose of God, and the true people of God will be found not in them but in the individual "Son of Man" they have repudiated, and derivatively in the community of those who have accepted the good news of God's kingship as it has come to them in the rejected and vindicated Messiah. It is this reconstituted people of God whose ingathering will be described in v. 31.

The witnesses of the "Son of Man coming on the clouds of heaven" will be "all the tribes of the land," who will greet his vindication not with acclamation but with mourning. The allusion is to Zech 12:10-14: "they will look on the one they have pierced, and they will mourn for him." There the

94. It is ironic that Keener, 585, chooses v. 30, where the word παρουσία does *not* occur, to discuss the implications of that term!
95. Cf. J. A. Gibbs, *Jerusalem,* 200-201.

mourners are identified as "the house of David and the inhabitants of Jerusalem" (v. 10), who are then listed by families (the families of David, Nathan, Levi, Shimei, and others, vv. 12-14). That is why the phrase *pasai hai phylae tēs gēs* must here refer to all the tribes of the land (i.e., as in Zech 12, a specifically Jewish mourning), not "of the earth."[96] This is also required by the use of *phylē*, which in the NT (as normally in the LXX)[97] is used specifically of the OT tribes (Matt 19:28; Luke 2:36; Acts 13:21; Rom 11:1; Heb 7:13-14; etc.).[98] There are problems in both the text and the interpretation of the Zechariah passage, but it appears to speak of the Israelite families mourning over one of their own whom "they have pierced," suggesting a blend of genuine sorrow and remorse. And in the overall pattern of Zech 9–14 this "one they have pierced" is usually interpreted as a rejected messianic figure, who appears also as the rejected shepherd in Zech 11:4-14 and the shepherd killed by the sword in Zech 13:7-9. In this gospel both of those latter passages will be applied to Jesus' death in Jerusalem (see on 26:31; 27:9-10), and the present allusion should therefore probably be taken in the same way. Jesus' words here suggest then, in the light of their OT background, that the people of Jerusalem will recognize what they have done to their Messiah, but their mourning will be prompted by seeing his eventual vindication and triumph, when it will be too late to avert the consequences of having rejected him.[99]

Matthew's other addition to the Son of Man saying of Mark 13:26 is the puzzling introductory clause "And then will appear the sign of the Son of Man in heaven," which, because of its obscurity, I have left to the end for comment in the hope that the sense of the rest of the saying may cast light on it. Some interpreters take the "of" to be epexegetic: "the sign *which is* the Son of Man in heaven";[100] in that case there is no separate "sign" in view, but the Son of Man himself. But if it is taken to speak of an actual sign *belonging to* or *about* the Son of Man, the sense will depend on whether "in heaven" is

---

96. Matthew's clause κόψονται πᾶσαι αἱ φυλαὶ τῆς γῆς echoes, though it does not directly quote, LXX Zech 12:12's κόψεται ἡ γῆ κατὰ φυλὰς φυλάς, "the land will mourn tribe by tribe," where the context, with its listing of Israelite families, requires that ἡ γῆ be understood here, as often in the LXX, as "the land (of Israel)," not "the earth."

97. For LXX usage see C. Maurer, *TDNT* 9:246-48.

98. The only NT use where it is applied to non-Israelite tribes is in the set phrase "every tribe and language and people and nation" (Rev 5:9; 7:9; 11:9; 13:7; 14:6); elsewhere in Revelation it refers specifically to Israelite tribes, except perhaps in Rev 1:7, but since that verse is apparently based on the present text, it cannot be used to determine the usage here.

99. See further my *Jesus and the OT*, 236-38, for the meaning of the Zechariah allusion here. I am baffled by Carson's statement (505) that "those who follow Kik and France" do not want to keep the OT idea of mourning; that is the central point of the allusion.

100. See, e.g., S. Brown, *JSNT* 4 (1979) 13 and n. 47; Gundry, 488.

taken to specify the location in which the "sign" will be seen or as linked more closely with the immediately preceding words — "the sign of the-Son-of-Man-in-heaven," that is, the sign of the heavenly authority of the Son of Man. Some take it in the former sense and speak of a symbol visible in the sky, but there is little in the context to indicate what sort of "sign" might be expected.[101] Some patristic writers supposed that the prediction was of a vision of a cross in the sky such as Constantine is reputed to have seen (Eusebius, *Vit. Const.* 1.28), but nothing in the context suggests that, and surely it would require some indication of what sort of "sign" to look for. If, however, "in heaven" is taken with "the Son of Man,"[102] the following clauses perhaps suggest an answer. The tribes are to *see* the vindication and enthronement of the Son of Man in heaven, but *how* are they to "see" it, that is, to know that it is true? Not perhaps by a celestial phenomenon, but by what is happening on earth as the temple is destroyed and the reign of the "Son-of-Man-in-heaven" begins to take effect in the gathering of his chosen people. In that case the "sign" is not a preliminary warning of an event still to come, but the visible manifestation of a heavenly reality already established, that the Son of Man is in heaven sitting at the right hand of Power (26:64).[103]

The disciples had asked for a "sign" of the *parousia* and the end of the age, but Jesus will give no such sign because the *parousia* will be sudden and unexpected (vv. 27, 36-44). He has urged them, too, not to interpret current events as signs of the end for Jerusalem (vv. 4-14), and while he has himself

---

101. What looks like an early attempt to interpret this "sign" is in *Did.* 16:6, where, in a passage largely modeled on this part of Matthew 24, the author specifies three "signs of truth" which will appear: an "opening" (?; literally "spreading out") in heaven, the sound of a trumpet, and the raising of the dead. (Davies and Allison, 3:359, oddly render σημεῖον ἐκπετάσεως, "a sign of spreading out," as "the sign spread out"; parallelism with the following clause rules out that rendering even if the syntax could be stretched that far.)

102. This exegesis is defended by J. A. Gibbs, *Jerusalem*, 198-99. He translates "At that time, that which shows this man who is in heaven will appear."

103. The LXX uses σημεῖον for the "standard" or "signal" *(nēs)* which is a summons for the gathering of God's people in Isa 11:12 (cf. Isa 49:22, though LXX there uses σύσσημον), and so it has been suggested (e.g., by T. F. Glasson, *JTS* 15 [1964] 299-300) that this motif anticipates v. 31, where the Son of Man will gather his people from the ends of the earth. The association of the *nēs* with a trumpet call in other passages (Isa 18:3; Jer 4:21; 51:27) might support this idea. Schweizer, 455-56, develops this suggestion at some length from these passages without even mentioning Isa 11:12! Cf. also Davies and Allison, 3:359-60, following J. A. Draper, *NTS* 39 (1993) 1-21; D. C. Sim, *Apocalyptic*, 104-5. But, despite the grateful welcome given by some commentators to Glasson's suggested resolution of a long-standing puzzle, it is doubtful whether this different sense of σημεῖον would be the first to come to mind in a context where the term has already been used twice in its more normal sense (vv. 3, 24).

given them one cryptic sign of when that event is to be expected (v. 15), he has warned them that visible "signs and wonders" are rather the province of false prophets (v. 24). It would be consonant with that generally negative approach to the sort of "signs" the disciples (and earlier the Jewish leaders, 12:38; 16:1) wanted that the "sign" here offered is not a prior notification but simply the visible evidence of what has already been achieved.

31 The sequel to the enthronement of the Son of Man as king is the gathering together of the subjects of his kingdom, his "chosen people" (see on 22:14 and cf. 24:22, 24). They will come not only from Judea but from all over the world. As in vv. 29-30, the language continues to be drawn from OT prophecy. The gathering of God's people from the ends of the earth is a recurrent OT theme (see on 8:11-12), but the passages most closely echoed here are Deut 30:4, which speaks of God "gathering"[104] his people who were scattered "from the end of heaven to the end of heaven,"[105] and LXX Zech 2:10 (EVV 2:6), where God says to his scattered people, "I will gather you from the four winds of heaven."[106] The "great trumpet blast" echoes another such regathering prophecy in Isa 27:13.[107] These were, of course, in their original context, prophecies of the regathering of scattered *Israel*, but again Jesus' discourse takes passages about the OT people of God and applies them to the "chosen people" of the Son of Man. We saw the same pattern in the OT allusions in 8:11-12, where those who would come "from east and west" would no longer be the scattered tribes of Israel but those whose faith in Jesus enabled them, like the Gentile centurion, to become members of God's international kingdom.[108]

The agents of this gathering will be "his angels"; see on 13:41 and 16:27 for the idea that God's angels also serve the Son of Man in his heavenly glory (and cf. 26:53). In human terms the ingathering of the chosen people may be expected to be through the work of human "messengers," and it would be possible to take *angeloi* here in that sense,[109] which it carries in 11:10. But in all other uses in Matthew (including 16:28, which is also based on the vision of Dan 7) it denotes heavenly beings, and in this context of the

---

104. LXX uses συνάγω in both Deut 30:4 and Zech 2:10; the double compound ἐπισυνάγω used here by Matthew (and Mark) perhaps echoes the LXX of Ps 147:2, which also speaks of the gathering of dispersed Israel.

105. So LXX; Hebrew has simply "to the end of heaven."

106. LXX differs from the Hebrew here; the latter reads "for I have scattered you as [or in some MSS 'in'] the four winds of heaven," though the context is a call to return from that dispersion.

107. For these allusions see my *Jesus and the OT*, 63-64, 256-57.

108. For "gathering" as denoting in Matthew "the period of mission that precedes the last day" see J. A. Gibbs, *Jerusalem*, 202-3.

109. As I did in my *Jesus and the OT*, 238. So still J. A. Gibbs, *Jerusalem*, 202.

heavenly authority of the Son of Man it probably refers to the spiritual power underlying human evangelization. The "great trumpet blast" which Matthew alone includes at this point also suits a more supernatural dimension to this ingathering.

Verses 29-31, as interpreted here on the basis of the OT imagery from which they are composed, thus speak of the predicted destruction of the temple from a dual perspective. On the one hand it is a climactic act of judgment, comparable to God's earlier judgment on pagan cities and nations, but now incurred by the failure of his own people Israel.[110] But on the other hand it is also the symbol of a new beginning, the heavenly enthronement of the Son of Man, on whom, as Daniel 7:14 had declared, will be conferred universal and everlasting sovereignty. These verses thus look forward to the new situation which will already have become reality when the risen Jesus meets his disciples in Galilee: "All authority in heaven and earth has been given to me" (28:18). It is on the basis of that authority that he will then send his disciples to gather a new community out of all nations (28:19), and it is as a result of that ingathering that a new and far more inclusive "chosen people" will be formed to take on the mission of God's people which had hitherto been focused in Jerusalem and its temple. As in Daniel's vision, the loss of one power structure opens the way for another, greater one, and one which has a universality which a temple-focused system could never have achieved.

e. Summary of the Answer to the Disciples' First Question (24:32-35)

Jesus' answer to the question "When will these things happen?" is rounded off with three final comments:

> (i) As surely as summer follows spring, you may be sure that the preliminary events I have mentioned will lead directly to the "end" (vv. 32-33);
>
> (ii) It will all be over before this generation is finished (v. 34);
>
> (iii) You can rely on my prediction (v. 35).

None of these sayings add further substance to the answer; they simply draw out more clearly the implications of the sometimes cryptic language of the

110. We have noted that the OT allusions in these verses consistently take prophetic language concerning Israel's triumph and restoration and reverse its application so that it is now Jesus and his people who are the beneficiaries of God's climactic acts of judgment and salvation, while the existing Jerusalem establishment centered on the temple takes over the role of Israel's pagan enemies in the OT. The consistency of this bold reinterpretive strategy throughout the passage speaks in favor of the exegesis here adopted.

preceding sayings, and in particular the tight time-scale within which they are contained. They thus rule out decisively any suggestion that the preceding verses (apart from the anticipatory comment in v. 27) are concerned with some more ultimate "end" than the destruction of the temple which the disciples had asked about.

32-33   When a fig tree featured in the story at 21:18-20, I argued that in that context it was meant to evoke OT symbolism concerning the people of God. But there is no need to find any similar symbolism here.[111] This is simply a proverb-type saying which draws a simile from observation of the natural world; the fig tree is used because it is the most prominent deciduous tree in Palestine, and one whose summer fruiting was eagerly awaited.[112] The appearance of its new shoots is a clear harbinger of summer, and once they appear the observer may know for sure how long it will be before the fruit is ready.[113] In the same way the occurrence of the preliminary events (the "devastating pollution" and the Roman advance and siege) will inform Jesus' disciples clearly that the process which will end in the temple's destruction is under way and the end is "near, on the threshold"; note the verbal echo of v. 15 in the phrase "when you see." Some versions (e.g., NRSV, NJB) and commentators translate "*he* is near," but nothing in the Greek suggests a personal subject;[114] such a translation is suggested not by the wording of this passage but by the prior assumption that its subject is the *parousia*. In context it is surely more likely that "it" here is "the end" spoken of in vv. 6 and 14 (as indeed REB explicitly translates it here), whose imminence will be further underlined in v. 34.[115]

34   Jesus' answer to the disciples' question "When?" does not offer a specific date, but it does conclude with a definite time within which "these things" (v. 3)[116] will take place, and that time-scale is introduced with all the

---

111. *Pace* W. R. Telford, *Temple,* 216-17.

112. I take it, with the majority of interpreters, that "the fig tree" is generic, not a reference to a particular tree; the romantic idea that Jesus is talking about the same fig tree which he had cursed in 21:18-20 returning to life as a sign of the end is set out and rightly criticized by W. R. Telford, *Temple,* 214-15.

113. Except, of course, in the case of a fig tree which flouts the natural order, as in 21:18-20 (see comments there).

114. Gundry, 490, argues that "'at the door' favors a reference to the Son of Man rather than to 'the end,'" and explains further in his commentary on Mark that "events do not come through doors, persons do." But this is to treat the "doors" too literally; ἐπὶ θύραις is a "fixed idiom" (N. Turner, *A Grammar of NT Greek,* vol. 3: *Syntax,* 27; cf. J. Jeremias, *TDNT* 3:173-74); cf. the use of πρὸ τῶν θύρων in Jas 5:9 as a synonym for "near."

115. Luke's version, "know that the kingdom of God is near," while it shifts the focus, also supplies an impersonal subject for "is near."

116. J. A. Gibbs, *Jerusalem,* 205-6, notes and defends a shift in the sense of "these things" between vv. 33 and 34: in v. 33 it refers to the preliminary events of the

solemnity of an *amen* saying (see on 5:18), compounded by the emphatic negative construction which I have rather woodenly represented by "certainly not." "Generation," as elsewhere in Matthew, is a temporal term (note especially its use in 1:17). "This generation" has been used frequently in this gospel for Jesus' contemporaries, especially in a context of God's impending judgment; see 11:16; 12:39, 41-42, 45; 16:4; 17:17, and especially 23:36, where God's judgment on "this generation" leads up to Jesus' first prediction of the devastation of the temple in 23:38. It may safely be concluded that if it had not been for the embarrassment caused by supposing that Jesus was here talking about his *parousia,* no one would have thought of suggesting any other meaning for "this generation," such as "the Jewish race" or "human beings in general" or "all the generations of Judaism that reject him"[117] or even "this kind" (meaning scribes, Pharisees, and Sadducees).[118] Such broad senses, even if they were lexically possible, would offer no help in response to the disciples' question "When?" Now that we have seen that the reference is to the destruction of the temple, which did as a matter of fact take place some forty years later while many of Jesus' contemporaries must have been still alive, all such contrived renderings may be laid to rest. This verse refers to the same time-scale as 16:28 (which was also concerned with the fulfillment of Dan 7:13-14): "some of those standing here will certainly not taste death before . . ." (cf. also 10:23, with the same Daniel reference: "you will not go through all the towns of Israel before . . .").[119]

35 The first section of the discourse concludes with a ringing formula of assurance, reminiscent of OT language about the reliability of the word of God. For the formula "until heaven and earth pass away" see above on 5:18: such language is used to affirm the permanence of God's covenant faithfulness (Isa 51:6; 54:10; Jer 31:35-36; 33:20-21, 25-26), while the impermanence of vegetation is contrasted with the permanence of God's word (Isa 40:8). Here an even stronger formula asserts the permanent validity of the word of Jesus himself. To suggest, as some have done, that Jesus here (and presumably also in 5:18?) predicts an actual dissolution of heaven and earth as part of his vision of eschatological events is to read this proverbial language too literalistically; as in the prophetic passages just listed, the first

---

siege, in v. 34 the whole complex of events including the actual destruction of the temple (as in the disciples' question in v. 3).

117. So Schweizer, 458.

118. So Gundry, 491.

119. E. Lövestam, in J. Lambrecht (ed.), *L'Apocalypse johannique,* 412-13, suggests that a recognition of the OT background to "this generation" in Jesus' teaching (see p. 433, n. 47) enables its use here to be extended as far as the unknown time of the *parousia;* but this is to ignore both the clearly temporal nature of the disciples' question and the clear temporal limitations expressed in other words in the parallel passages noted above.

clause functions rhetorically as a foil to the positive declaration in the second, which, with a further emphatic negative as in v. 34, underlines the total reliability of what Jesus has just said about the destruction of the temple.[120] Even if (unthinkably) heaven and earth were to pass away, Jesus' words will remain secure. Note the rhetorical effect of the threefold repetition in vv. 34-35 of the verb "pass away."[121]

3. Jesus Answers the Question about the Parousia and the End of the Age (24:36–25:46)

> 36 *"But about that day and hour no one knows, not the angels of heaven, nor the Son,[1] but only the Father. 37 For just like the days of Noah, so will the visitation[2] of the Son of Man be. 38 For as in the[3] days before the flood people were feeding[4] and drinking, marrying and giving in marriage, until the day when Noah got into the ark,*

---

120. C. Fletcher-Louis, in K. E. Brower and M. W. Elliott (eds.), *"The Reader Must Understand,"* 145-69, suggests that the passing away of heaven and earth both here and in 5:18 (see p. 185, n. 22) is itself symbolic language for the destruction of the temple, which was viewed within second-temple Judaism as "the cosmos in miniature," so that the referent here is the same as in v. 29: the temple will fall, but Jesus' words will not. This verse, therefore, rather than vv. 29-31, is *"the* definitive statement that the expected destruction . . . has now arrived" (162). While this is certainly more appropriate to the context than talk of a literal cosmic collapse, it is questionable whether the rhetorical function of the clause requires such a specific referent.

121. See G. R. Beasley-Murray, *Last Days,* 445, for some comments on the biblical usage of παρέρχομαι.

1. The phrase "nor the Son" is missing in a wide variety of MSS and versions, but its presence in the early witnesses ℵ* B D Θ f¹³, most OL MSS, and most early patristic citations makes it more likely that it was increasingly dropped for dogmatic reasons (Jesus could not be allowed to confess his own ignorance) than that it was inserted under the influence of the Marcan parallel, especially as textual influence is normally of Matthew on Mark rather than vice versa. The references by Jerome and Ambrose to Greek MSS which omit the phrase indicate that it was then in the generally received text, but that by that time some were finding it uncomfortable (for some patristic attempts to explain it see Davies and Allison, 3:379). In ℵ a corrector deleted the phrase, only to have it restored by a second corrector. Without the phrase the preceding οὐδέ would lack its correlative.

2. For this translation of παρουσία here and in v. 37 see p. 895, n. 14.

3. Some MSS have "those days," but this is probably an unthinking assimilation to the phrase "those days" in vv. 19, 22, and 29 on the part of scribes who (like some modern commentators!) did not recognize the change of subject with the introduction of "that day and hour" in v. 36. See the comments below.

4. The verb τρώγω occurs only here in Matthew, who usually uses ἐσθίω for "eat." It is a coarser term (like German *fressen* as opposed to *essen*), perhaps used here to portray the crudeness of life before the Flood.

39 *and they knew nothing until the flood came and swept them all away, so will the visitation of the Son of Man be.* 40 *Then there will be two men on the farm: one is taken and one left;* 41 *there will be two women grinding grain with a hand mill: one is taken and one left.* 42 *So keep awake, since you don't know on what[5] day[6] your lord[7] is coming.* 43 *But know[8] this: if the master of the house had known at what time of night the burglar was coming, he would have kept awake and not allowed his house to be broken into.[9]* 44 *So you, too, must be ready, because the Son of Man is coming at a time you don't expect.*

45 *"Well then, who is the trustworthy, sensible slave who is appointed by his master to take charge of his household[10] and give them their rations at the proper time?* 46 *Happy is that slave if his master on his return finds him doing his job.* 47 *I tell you truly that he will put him in charge of all that he possesses.* 48 *But if that wicked slave says to himself, 'My master is away a long time,'* 49 *and begins to hit his fellow slaves and to eat and drink with drunkards,* 50 *that slave's master will come on a day when he doesn't expect him and at an hour he doesn't know about,* 51 *and he will cut him in two and will consign him to the fate of[11] the hypocrites, where there will be weeping and gnashing of teeth.*

25:1 *"Then the kingdom of heaven will be like[12] ten girls[13] who*

---

5. ποῖος, used here and in v. 43 ("at what watch [of the night]"), originally meant "what sort of," but it was increasingly being used as a synonym for τίς. There is here a sense of an *unexpected* day or watch, but to translate it "what sort of day/watch" would be pedantic.

6. Some later MSS have "hour" instead of "day," and the presence of this reading in most OL MSS shows that it arose early. But the weight of the earlier MSS is against it. And since the "day" and the "hour" are closely associated throughout this passage (see vv. 36, 44, 50; 25:13), the meaning is hardly affected.

7. In vv. 45-50 κύριος will be used repeatedly for the (human) "master" of the slave in the parable — who is, however, a symbol for the returning "Lord." Here the term may be used in that fuller sense, the "Lord" being the "Son of Man" of vv. 37 and 39, but it may also be used in anticipation of the following parable. My rendering, "lord" without a capital L, is intended to preserve this ambiguity.

8. Or "you know"; the verb could be read as either imperative or indicative.

9. Literally, "dug through," the same word as in 6:19-20; see p. 256, n. 3.

10. οἰκετεία occurs only here in the NT. It refers to the other slaves of the household, over whom this one slave is given a supervisory role.

11. Literally, "will appoint his part with."

12. See p. 522, n. 1, where the Greek formula is the same except that the tense here is future.

13. Literally, "virgins," presumably unmarried friends of the bride and/or bridegroom. See below for their possible role in the wedding procedure.

took their torches and went out to meet the bridegroom.[14] *2 Five of
them were silly and five were sensible: 3 the silly ones took their
torches but didn't take any oil with them, 4 while the sensible ones
took oil in jars along with their torches. 5 As the bridegroom was a
long time coming, the girls all nodded off and were soon fast asleep.
6 But in the middle of the night there was a shout, 'Here comes the
bridegroom; go out to meet him.' 7 Then all those girls woke up and
got their torches ready. 8 But the silly ones said to the sensible ones,
'Give us some of your oil; our torches are going out.' 9 The sensible
ones replied, 'No way; there would never be enough for us and you.
Instead, go to the oil sellers and buy some for yourselves.' 10 But while
they were going off to buy oil, the bridegroom arrived. Then those who
were ready went in with him to the wedding feast,*[15] *and the door was
closed. 11 Later the other girls arrived, and said, 'Lord, Lord, open
the door for us.' 12 But he replied, 'I tell you truly, I don't know you.'
13 So keep awake, because you don't know the day or the hour.*[16]

14 "It's like when[17] *a man who was going away from home called
his own slaves and entrusted his possessions to them. 15 To one of
them he gave five talents,*[18] *to another two, and to another just one,
depending on each one's ability; then he went away. 16 The slave who
had been given five talents went straight*[19] *off and traded with them;*

14. Some MSS add "and the bride," perhaps because this read more naturally in
non-Jewish cultures and may indeed have been presupposed even in the original scenario
(see comments below, especially p. 946, nn. 45, 47). Since the bride plays no part in the
story, however, her mention here is probably an explanatory addition, which in fact dis-
tracts from the imagery of the bridegroom who represents the returning Son of Man.

15. The term is τοὺς γάμους; see above, p. 820, n. 4, and comments below.

16. Several later MSS add "in which the Son of Man comes," an obviously explanatory addition based on v. 44.

17. Literally, "For just as a man who. . . ." The sentence is never completed by an
explicit comparison, but the language indicates another parable, which will in fact be left
to the reader to interpret.

18. The Greek "talent" is of course a (very large) sum of money (as in 18:24). Our
English use of the word to mean an aptitude or ability (first attested c. 1430, according to
the *OED*) derives from the assumed interpretation of this parable, but the Greek τάλαντον
has no such meaning. Hence the decision of some English versions to use a phrase like
"bags of gold" (NEB, TNIV), so as to prevent the English reader from supposing that "talent" here carries our metaphorical sense.

19. This represents εὐθέως, which in the Greek word order comes first in the sentence. Since Greek MSS had no punctuation, it is therefore possible to read it with "went
away" in the previous sentence instead of with the description of the first slave's action,
and on that basis it is traditionally included in v. 15. But the unnatural position after the
verb "went away" (Matthew does not elsewhere place εὐθέως after the verb it modifies),

and he made another five. 17 *In the same way the slave who was given two made another two.* 18 *But the one who was given only one went off and dug a hole in the ground and buried his master's money.* 19 *A long time later the master of those slaves came back and settled accounts with them.* 20 *And the slave who was given the five talents came to him and presented him with five talents more; 'Master,' he said, 'you left me with five talents; look, I've made another five talents.'* 21 *'Well done, you good, trustworthy slave,' said his master. 'You've been trustworthy over a few things; I'll put you in charge of many things. Come in and share*[20] *your master's happiness.'* 22 *The slave who was given the two talents also came to him and said, 'Master, you left me with two talents; look, I've made another two talents.'* 23 *'Well done, you good, trustworthy slave,' said his master. 'You've been trustworthy over a few things; I'll put you in charge of many things. Come in and share your master's happiness.'* 24 *But then the slave who had received one talent also came to him and said, 'Master, I knew that you are a hard man, harvesting where you didn't sow and collecting from places where you didn't scatter.* 25 *So I was afraid and went and buried your talent in the ground; here, you have your own back.'* 26 *But his master replied, 'You wicked, cowardly*[21] *slave! So you knew that I harvest where I didn't sow and collect from places where I didn't scatter?*[22] 27 *Well then, you should have deposited my money with the bankers, and then I would have received my own back with interest when I came back.* 28 *So take the talent from him and give it to the one who has the ten talents.* 29 *(For to everyone who has, more will be given, and they will have more than enough; but whoever does not have, even what they have will be taken away from them.)*[23] 30 *And*

and the probable lack of any other connective word in v. 16, convinces most readers that εὐθέως belongs to the following clause rather than to the preceding. Many MSS attempted to resolve the ambiguity by inserting a δέ which, by its fixed position as the second word in a clause, would determine where the new sentence began, but unfortunately both options are strongly represented among those MSS which use this expedient!

20. Literally, "Come into your master's happiness," here and in v. 23. The phrasing is not commercial, but imports something of the application into the story.

21. ὀκνηρός essentially means one who hesitates or holds back, from fear or uncertainty. Here it is usually translated "lazy," but the sense is not that the slave couldn't be bothered, but that he was too timid to take a risk with his master's money.

22. The decision whether to punctuate this sentence as a statement or a rhetorical question does not depend on the Greek syntax but is simply a matter of choosing the best idiom to convey the rhetoric of a repetition of the slave's claim in order to turn it against him.

23. While it is possible that this verse is meant to be read as part of the master's speech, it interrupts his sequence of instructions and is therefore more likely an editorial comment, closely echoing 13:12, which is why I have put it in parentheses.

934

take the useless slave and throw him out into the darkness outside, where there will be weeping and gnashing of teeth.'

31 *"But when the Son of Man comes in his glory, and all the angels with him, then he will take his seat on his glorious throne,* 32 *and all the nations will be gathered in front of him, and he will separate them*[24] *from one another as a shepherd separates the sheep from the goats;* 33 *he will place the sheep on his right side and the goats on his left.* 34 *Then the king will say to those on his right, 'Come, you whom my Father has blessed; inherit the kingship which has been prepared for you since the foundation of the world.* 35 *For I was hungry and you gave me food, I was thirsty and you gave me a drink, I was a foreigner and you made me your guest,*[25] 36 *naked and you gave me clothes, I was ill and you visited me, I was in prison and you came to me.'* 37 *Then the righteous ones will answer, 'Lord, when did we see you hungry and feed you, or thirsty and give you a drink?* 38 *When did we see you as a foreigner and make you our guest, or naked and give you clothes?* 39 *When did we see you ill or in prison and come to you?'* 40 *And the king will respond, 'I tell you truly, insofar as you did these things for one of these my smallest brothers and sisters,*[26] *you did them for me.'* 41 *Then he will say to those on his left, 'Go away from me, you who have been cursed, into the eternal fire which has been prepared for the devil and his angels.* 42 *For I was hungry and you gave me nothing to eat, I was thirsty and you gave me nothing to drink,* 43 *I was a foreigner and you did not make me your guest, naked and you gave me no clothes, I was ill and in prison and you did not visit me.'* 44 *Then they, too, will answer, 'Lord, when did we see you hungry or thirsty or a foreigner or naked or ill or in prison and not look after you?'* 45 *Then he will reply, 'I tell you truly, insofar as you did not do these things for one of these smallest ones, you did not do them for me.'* 46 *Then these people will go away into eternal punishment, but the righteous ones to eternal life."*

24. This "them" is masculine plural rather than the neuter which would be required if it were a separation of nation from nation. The focus is now, and remains, on the individuals who make up "all the nations."

25. Literally, "gathered me," probably an idiom for welcoming someone and taking them home.

26. I hope that by this stage it is no longer necessary to argue that ἀδελφῶν (which because of its genitive case here could be either masculine or feminine) is used generically rather than for a specific gender, as the English "brothers" alone would inevitably suggest.

In the introductory comments on 24:3–25:46 (see above, pp. 890-94) I have explained why I think it important to keep this very long second part of the discourse together as a single section. After Jesus has answered the first part of the disciples' question, "When will these things [the destruction of the temple] happen?" he now turns to the second part of the question, "What will be the sign of your *parousia* and the end of the age?" and that question provides the agenda for the whole of the rest of the discourse, which culminates in a majestic depiction of the final judgment in 25:31-46. The unexpected and unpredictable arrival of the *parousia* is described in a collection of shorter sayings in 24:36-44, and this programmatic section is then underlined by a series of three parables (24:45-51; 25:1-13; 25:14-30) which all focus on the theme of awaiting the imminent arrival of an authority figure, and the need to have made appropriate provision so as not to be caught unprepared and punished. The final pericope of the discourse (25:31-46) takes up the same theme, not now in the form of a parable (see below, p. 960) but in a judgment scene which explains the basis of the final verdict, when the division between the saved and the lost will be irrevocable. Here, too, the element of surprise dominates. Throughout this whole long section Jesus deliberately refuses to give the disciples the "sign" they have asked for. The timing of the *parousia* and the final judgment cannot be calculated and foreseen. Readiness for those climactic events can be achieved only by living all the time in such a way that their unannounced arrival need not be a disaster but rather a time of praise and reward for a life well lived and opportunities well taken. Each parable in turn adds further substance to the reader's understanding of what it means to be ready.

The first part of the disciples' question has received a specific answer in vv. 1-35; we now know, in broad terms, "when" that event is to take place — before this generation is over. But no such answer can be offered to the second part, because the events of which it speaks are not part of predictable history. And so there can be no "sign" of Jesus' *parousia* and the end of the age. That would be the easy way out, but what God requires of his people is not a last-minute turning over of a new leaf prompted by a warning "sign," but a life of constant readiness.

Several features in the wording of v. 36, and of the following passage, make it clear that a new subject is taken up at this point:

1. "But about . . ." *(peri de)* occurred similarly in 22:31 to mark a change of subject, when Jesus turned from the specific question which had been asked to deal with the basic theology which prompted it. Paul uses the same phrase several times in 1 Corinthians (7:1, 25; 8:1; 12:1; 16:1, 12) to move from one of the issues raised by his correspondents to another (cf. also Acts 21:25; 1 Thess 4:9; 5:1). In each case *peri de* is the rhetorical formula for a new beginning. The analogy with 1 Corinthians indicates that here the

phrase marks the transition from the first of the two questions asked in v. 3 to the second.[27]

2. "That day and hour" is the first mention in this discourse of a *singular* "day" or "hour," in clear contrast to the plural "those days" which has been used in vv. 19, 22, and 29 for the period of the Roman war. The singular "day" (or, in some MSS, "hour"; see p. 932, n. 6) will recur in 24:42, the "hour" in 24:44, and both "day" and "hour" in 24:50 and 25:13; in each case the term is now singular. This shift in terminology marks the change of subject. The demonstrative "*that* day" serves to remind the reader of the "day" of the *parousia* which was the subject of the second part of the disciples' question. See also below on v. 36 for the idiom "that day" as a recognized term for the day of judgment.

3. Whereas vv. 4-35 have spoken of an event whose time can be predicted (v. 34) and for whose coming signs can be given (so especially v. 15), from here on Jesus speaks of an event whose time is both unknown and unknowable, and which will therefore come without prior warning. If even Jesus himself, who has just given a solemn and confident prediction of the time when "all these things" are going to happen, confesses himself ignorant of "that day and hour," it is surely obvious that the subject has changed.[28]

4. The event predicted in vv. 4-35 has been described as the "coming of the Son of Man," using the participle *erchomenos,* which echoes the vision of Dan 7:13-14. The only mention of the *parousia* in that section was to say that it will *not* be like the events of those days (v. 27). But now the term *parousia* (which does not occur in the Greek translations of Dan 7:13-14) comes into play in vv. 37 and 39. Since this was the term used in the second part of the disciples' question, it is clear that that second issue is now being addressed.[29]

27. Cf. also the use of περὶ δέ to introduce a new subject in *Did.* 6:3; 7:1; 9:1; 11:3 (A. J. P. Garrow, *Gospel,* 93ff. and passim uses this distinctive idiom as a marker for a compositional layer of the *Didache,* the "*peri* layer"). J. A. Gibbs, *Jerusalem,* 172-74, spells out the literary function of the phrase within the NT.

28. The suggestion sometimes offered that Jesus was prepared to speak in broad terms of the "generation" of the *parousia* but now admits that he cannot specify the precise time for it within that generation is robustly dismissed as "beyond the bounds of credibility" by A. I. Wilson, *When,* 225. Those who have nonetheless adopted this "incredible" interpretation have been governed more by their assumption that vv. 29-31 are about the *parousia* than by the wording of the discourse as a whole, which clearly now introduces a new and different "day and hour" and contrasts the knowability of the one with the unknowability of the other. Wilson goes on, "It surely places unbearable strain on Matthew's credibility as a redactor and/or on Jesus' credibility as a teacher to claim that Jesus is referring to the same event in vv. 33-4 and in v. 36."

29. A. I. Wilson, *When,* 227, also notes that in this section where the *parousia* is explicitly in view "there is no mention of any of the attendant circumstances related to the 'coming Son of Man' found in Dan. 7 and in other texts in Matthew (clouds, glory, etc.)."

5. Negatively it should be noted that whereas vv. 4-35 were linked by repeated uses of temporal connections ("then," "in those days," "immediately after," "it is near"), there is no such temporal introduction to this paragraph. Its contents stand apart from the historical sequence hitherto described.

This long second section of the discourse is then in the proper sense of the word "eschatological," unlike the first part which dealt with events within history. Apart from the opening declaration in v. 36 it is almost entirely independent of Mark. Matthew, following the same anthological principle as in the other discourses, has collected here a range of material, some of which has parallels in Luke's eschatological sections in Luke 17:26-35 and 12:39-46, which speaks not now of striking events within history, but of the future and final visitation of the Son of Man, and of the fate of those who are and are not ready for his appearance. And it concludes, appropriately, with a judgment scene which relates not specifically to Jerusalem or to the Jewish people but to "all the nations," gathered before the enthroned Son of Man in his heavenly glory.

Included within this sequence of parables are a number of references to the long time which may elapse before the *parousia* takes place; see on 24:48; 25:5; 25:19. Probably already by the time Matthew wrote there were those who were surprised and disappointed that it had not yet happened (cf. 2 Thess 2:1-3; 2 Pet 3:3-10), and the wording of these three parables (and indeed the element of extended absence which is built into their story lines) recognizes that problem. But alongside the recognition of delay is the warning of imminence: an unknown time may be near as well as distant. To reckon on an assumption of delay and so to postpone readiness is to court disaster. It is how God's people are living *now* that will be the key to their fate at the end. This message is as relevant to readers two millennia on as it was to Matthew's readers a generation or two after Jesus spoke these words. Delay and imminence are not in conflict: they are the two sides of the same coin, which is a time which no one knows or can know.

The comments on this long section will be subdivided, using the very obvious subsections (general statement, three parables, and concluding judgment scene) noted in the first paragraph above.

a. The Unknown Time of the Parousia (24:36-44)

This short section sets out three connected aspects of the *parousia:* (a) the time of the *parousia* is unknown (v. 36); (b) therefore it will catch people unawares (vv. 37-41); (c) therefore disciples must always be ready (vv. 42-44). Vivid illustrations from history and from ordinary life underline the second and third points: point (b) is illustrated by the sudden irruption of the Genesis Flood into normal life and by the banal occupations of people who will suddenly find themselves divided; point (c) is illustrated by the householder who is unprepared for the coming of the burglar. All three points rule out the sort of warning "sign" which the disciples had asked for, and their request is thus firmly refused.

But this section does not spell out in what way a disciple should aim to "be ready" (v. 44), and the call to "keep awake" (v. 42) may seem to suggest that life must be lived in a constant state of red alert which probably already for readers in Matthew's day, and certainly for those two thousand years later, seems hardly realistic: normal life must surely go on. It will be the function of the following parables to explore this question, and their cumulative effect will be to suggest that "being ready" is to be understood more ethically than intellectually. It demands a continuously acceptable lifestyle, not an attempt to calculate the timing of the *parousia* so as to "prepare" specifically for that event. The final scene in 25:31-46 will reveal that the criteria of judgment relate not to conscious alertness but to a life lived, even unknowingly, as Jesus would have it lived. This suggests that we should be cautious of reading too much into the picture language of "keeping awake," which depends on the following illustration of the householder and the burglar, but which is in striking contrast to the fact that all ten girls, not just the silly ones, will go to sleep while waiting in 25:5. When the passage is taken as a whole, it becomes clear that parable and metaphor should not be interpreted too prosaically.

36   The preceding pages have explained what is the subject matter of this surprising declaration. "That day" refers back to the day of Jesus' *parousia* which was the subject of the second half of the disciples' question (v. 3). The phrase is also appropriate in that it reflects the frequent OT references to the "day" of Yahweh. This gospel has already spoken of "the day of judgment" in 10:15; 11:22, 24; 12:36, and the phrase "that day" clearly has the same reference in 7:22, without the identity of the "day" needing to be spelled out (see comments there).[30] In 7:22 it is Jesus himself (not God, as in the OT) who appears as the judge "on that day," and that theme will also be developed in the rest of this discourse until it reaches its climax in 25:31-34, where it is the Son of Man who sits on "his" glorious throne as "the king" and judges all the nations (cf. also 13:41; 16:27-28; 19:28).

But for now that role of the Son of Man remains unspoken, and instead we have the remarkable paradox that "the Son," who is to play the central role in that "day," is himself ignorant of when it will be. That God should keep his angels in ignorance of so crucial an event is remarkable enough (see also 1 Pet 1:12 for divine secrets apparently hidden from angels), but "the Son" is uniquely close to his Father, as we have seen in 11:27, and the same

---

30. "That day" is used similarly without a clear antecedent in Luke 10:12, where the following v. 14 confirms that the reference is to the day of judgment. Cf. also 2 Tim 1:12, 18; 4:8.

title will appear in 28:19 as part of the trinitarian formula for the God to whom disciples' allegiance is pledged. In view of that usage, and especially of the way it is developed in 11:27, it is clear that "the Son" (an abbreviation which appears only alongside "the Father") is short for "the Son of God"; the fixed phrase "the Son of Man" is never so abbreviated.

The structure of this saying places "the Son" on a level above the angels, second only to the Father. But this high christology (for which see further on 11:27) is combined with a frank admission of ignorance. This saying has accordingly been one of the main evidences used for a "kenotic" christology, which accepts the full divinity of the Son but argues that for the period of his incarnation certain divine attributes (in this case omniscience) were voluntarily put aside. Such arguments, however, belong to a much later period of Christian dogmatic development. For Matthew perhaps the paradox was not so much a matter of doctrinal embarrassment (as it became for later copyists; see p. 931, n. 1) as of wonder at the relationship between Father and Son which is implied here and in 11:27, one which combines a uniquely close relationship with a recognition of priority or subordination, a paradox neatly summed up in the Johannine declarations "I and the Father are one" (John 10:30) and "The Father is greater than I" (John 14:28). For a similar recognition of the priority of the Father cf. 20:23.

For the idea that only God knows the time of the eschatological consummation cf. *Ps. Sol.* 17:21; *2 Bar.* 21:8 (and probably Zech 14:7). It is also picked up in Acts 1:7.

37-39 If the time of the *parousia* is unknown, it follows that people will be caught unawares. The previous mention of the *parousia* in v. 27 has used the image of lightning to portray both its unmistakable nature and its suddenness. It is a universal event, not a hole-and-corner occurrence (in the wilderness or the storerooms, v. 26) which most of the world would be able to ignore. Everyone will be affected by it. In all these ways the sudden and universal onset of the Flood as described in Gen 7:6-24 provides a powerful analogy; people were caught unawares, no one could evade it, and only those who had made advance preparation escaped — a point which will be picked up especially in the parables of 25:1-30. The description of normal life in v. 38 underlines the lack of any prior warning: things were being done just as they had always been (as the "scoffers" observe in 2 Pet 3:4). But the time of normal banality is potentially also the time of danger.

40-41 The sense of everyday banality continues. What could be more normal and unthreatening than working on the farm or grinding grain?[31]

31. Is the mention of the hand mill a subtle allusion to Exod 11:5, another situation of sudden division between those killed and those preserved? So M. D. Goulder, *Midrash*, 435.

Yet in those routine situations there will be a sudden crisis which will result in one being "taken" while the other is left behind. But where are the unlucky (or lucky?) ones "taken," and for what purpose? The verb is *paralambanō* rather than a simple *lambanō,* and if the compound is more than just a stylistic variation, it might be understood to mean "take to oneself" (as in 1:20; 17:1; 18:16; 20:17). If the passive verbs are understood as "divine passives," that would mean that God has taken selected people to himself, leaving the rest to continue their life on earth. Some have therefore suggested that this passage speaks of a "rapture" of the faithful to heaven before judgment falls on the earth. This is not the place to investigate the complex dispensational scheme which underlies this nineteenth-century theory, but it should be noted that insofar as this passage forms a basis for that theology, it rests on an uncertain foundation. We are not told where or why they are "taken," and the similar sayings in vv. 17-18 about people caught out in the course of daily life by the Roman advance presupposed a situation of threat rather than of rescue; to be "taken" in such circumstances would be a negative experience, and Matthew will use *paralambanō* in a similarly threatening context in 27:27. The verb in itself does not determine the purpose of the "taking," and it could as well be for judgment (as in Jer 6:11) as for refuge. In the light of the preceding verses, when the Flood "swept away" the unprepared, that is probably the more likely sense here.[32]

The different fates of two apparently similar people (as also the different fates of Noah and his contemporaries) raise the issue of "readiness": what is it that will determine who is and is not "taken"? The example of Noah suggests that it is not purely arbitrary, and the rest of the discourse will explore the basis of the division between the saved and the lost, which reaches its climax in the separation of good and bad in the judgment scene in 25:31-46. For the moment saved and lost live and work together (as in the parable of the weeds, 13:30), but when "that day" comes, the separation will be made and will be final.

42 This is the only call to "keep awake" in Matthew's version of the discourse (except for its inappropriate insertion at 25:13; see comments there), as compared with its insistent repetition in Mark 13:33-37 (together with the related charge to avoid sleep in the verb *agrypneō*). The following parables, with their message about being prepared in advance and living a continuously good life, suggest that Matthew had a less frenetic approach to "readiness" than Mark (and Paul; see 1 Thess 5:1-7), and the acceptance in 25:5 that it is alright to sleep suggests a different perspective. But the call to

---

32. The saying in *Gos. Thom.* 61, "Two will be resting on a bed; one will die and the other will live," appears to be based on the related text Luke 17:34; it also suggests a negative reading of παραλαμβάνω, which is used in Luke as in Matthew. See further A. I. Wilson, *When,* 227-29, in dialogue with N. T. Wright, *Victory,* 366.

be ready at any time is nonetheless appropriately symbolized by staying awake,[33] as the simile in the next verse will show.

The event for which they must be ready is described as the day when "your lord comes." The language anticipates the following parable (vv. 46, 50), where the *kyrios* is the returning master of the slaves; so also in 25:19. Indeed, in the parallel at Mark 13:35 this *kyrios* is explicitly the "master of the house" (referring back to a different mini-parable in Mark 13:34 which Matthew does not include). But the Christian reader will naturally identify the "Lord" as Jesus, and so will think of the "day" (cf. v. 36) of the *parousia* of the Son of Man, even though the term *parousia* will not be used again. In its place here is the ordinary verb *erchomai,* "come," but not now with the accompanying terms "the Son of Man" and "on the clouds of heaven" which in v. 30 indicated a primary allusion to the enthronement scene in Dan 7:13-14. In v. 44 the same verb will be used with the Son of Man as subject and clearly with reference to the *parousia* as here, and it may be that in these uses of *erchomai* we have an allusive hint that the *parousia* may be viewed as a further and final fulfillment of that enthronement vision. That would tally with the use of Dan 7:13-14 language in 19:28 and 25:31-34 with reference to the "new age" and the final judgment (see comments on 10:23): the heavenly authority of the Son of Man which is to be demonstrated through the events of the Roman war according to v. 30 will finally be consummated in his *parousia* at the end of the age. But that may be to read too much into so everyday a word as *erchomai* here, especially when the following parable gives it a sense quite appropriate to the story line without demanding an OT allusion.

43 Jesus' metaphor of the coming of a burglar as a model for the unexpected time of the *parousia* made a strong impression on the early church: cf. Luke 12:39; 1 Thess 5:2, 4; 2 Pet 3:10; Rev 3:3; 16:15; *Gos. Thom.* 21, 103. Here it takes the form of a miniparable about a householder and his loss.[34] Surprise is the essence of burglary, and he was caught napping. That is how it is bound to be at the *parousia,* because everyone, like the householder, is ignorant of "the day and the hour." In this imagery, as in the "keep awake" of v. 42, the call seems to be for a constant alert, since no amount of calcula-

33. I. H. Jones, *Parables,* 430-31, suggests four components to Matthew's idea of "keeping awake": avoiding "unthinking security"; avoiding "sleep" (as in Gethsemane); avoiding "being caught unready"; and acknowledgment of the Son of Man.

34. There is no need, however, to endorse the romantic speculation of J. Jeremias, *Parables,* 49, that "Jesus draws the parable from an actual happening, some recently effected burglary, about which the whole village is talking." Burglary was a common experience which everyone would understand; see C. D. Stanley, *NTS* 48 (2002) 472-81, for details about the activities of burglars in the ancient world, and the fear they inspired especially among the more vulnerable members of society.

tion can anticipate the surprise; but the following parables will suggest a different perspective on how one may be ready.

44 The message of vv. 36-43 is now summed up in a clear call to be ready for the *parousia*[35] at any time. The burglar illustrates not only that the time of the *parousia* is unknown, but more specifically that it will be "a time you don't expect." So the moral of v. 43 is directly applied to the disciples ("you too," like the householder), but not now in terms of staying awake as in v. 42 but of "being ready." The following parables will begin to unpack what "readiness" for the *parousia* and the judgment means, but perhaps the preceding verses already give the reader a clue. Noah and his family may not have been able to predict the exact date of the Flood (and are unlikely to have lain awake waiting for it), but when it came they were ready, while the rest of the world was caught out. In the same way disciples can have no more idea than anyone else just when the *parousia* will occur, but they have been forewarned *that* it will come, and so they, unlike others, can be prepared to survive the crisis. Jesus will now go on to spell out how.

b. The Parable of the Slaves Left in Charge (24:45-51)

After the miniparable of v. 43, here is a fuller story-parable about being ready. It is closely parallel to Luke 12:42-46, where the context is similarly eschatological, following the sayings about the burglar and about being ready because the Son of Man will come when he is not expected. Matthew does not, however, follow Luke in the concluding comments (Luke 12:47-48) about the different degrees of culpability depending on whether the slave knew what his master expected of him.

Like the parable of 11:16-19, this one begins with a rhetorical question, but the question form is quickly abandoned and the pericope develops as, apparently, the parallel stories of two slaves placed in identical situations of responsibility but who respond very differently to that responsibility. A different pattern, however, seems to be indicated by the reference in v. 48 to *"that* wicked slave," where only the one (good) slave has been mentioned so far. Is what follows then not the story of a separate slave but of that same slave, now hypothetically responding in the opposite way to his master's charge? But the slave introduced in v. 45 is unequivocally good, and his story is not told hypothetically — unless that is somehow the effect of the rhetorical question? It seems that two different ways of setting up the contrast, one with two separate slaves and one with the same slave under two opposite aspects, are rather awkwardly merged. But the moral is clear even if the style is not smooth.

35. See on v. 42 for how the possible echo of Dan 7:13 in the phrase "the Son of Man comes" may relate to the *parousia*.

As with each of the parables in this discourse, what begins as a plausible real-life situation is invaded by elements drawn from the intended application of the story. The language about the master's unexpected return (v. 50) echoes that of vv. 36 and 44, and the description of the slave's punishment in v. 51 is both unnaturally lurid (cutting him in two) and theologically weighted ("the fate of the hypocrites"), and concludes with a favorite Matthean formula for final judgment ("weeping and gnashing of teeth"; cf. 8:12; 13:42, 50; 22:13; 25:30). These elements, together with the context in which the parable is set, ensure that the reader interprets it as a warning about the serious consequences of not being ready for the *parousia*. But the readiness of the good slave consists not in sitting by the window watching for his master, but in getting on with the job he has been given, while the fault of the bad slave is in his assumption that the master will not be back soon and that therefore he will not be held to account. The eschatological themes of delay and imminence (see above, p. 938) are thus interwoven, and applied to the question of the disciple's responsibility during the time of waiting.

45 For the role of the steward in a large household see above on 16:19. In his master's absence this slave has unsupervised control over both his fellow slaves and the material resources of the household.[36] "Trustworthy" is a natural term in such a context (cf. its similar use in 25:21, 23); "sensible" is also a good, down-to-earth, practical word (cf. its use in 7:24 and in the parable which follows in 25:1-13) and as such fits the story situation well, but it has also been used in 10:16 for the enlightened self-interest of the disciple, so that here also it may have a connotation of spiritual perception (as in 1 Cor 10:15).

46-47 These two verses together form a beatitude of the same type as in 5:3-10, though less concise: v. 46 congratulates[37] the person who has made the right choice, and v. 47 provides the "payoff" which justifies that congratulation. In place of a temporary commission in his master's absence he will be promoted to a permanent and very responsible role as steward. As in the third parable of the series, the reward for responsible service is greater responsibility, not an easing of the master's demands (cf. 25:21, 23). The "I tell you truly" formula draws the hearer's attention to this outcome, which makes the challenging assumption that faithful disciples will welcome this further and heavier commitment rather than feeling that they have earned a rest.

48-49 The verb I have translated "is away a long time" *(chronizō)* will recur in 25:5 for the delay in the bridegroom's arrival (and the idea, not

---

36. R. H. Gundry, *Use,* 89, suggests that the phrase "to give them their rations at the proper time" is drawn from Ps 104:27, where the LXX uses similar words. But it is hard to see what such an allusion might have been meant to convey here, where the slave does not represent God (*pace* Schweizer, 463).

37. For this sense of μακάριος see above, pp. 160-61.

using the same verb, in 25:19 for the long absence of the master). The repetition of this verb probably indicates Matthew's recognition of the problem of the delay of the *parousia* (see above, p. 938), but in all these three parables the motif of an extended period of absence is essential to the story, so that its possible apologetic role should not be stressed.[38] The point within the story is that the period of absence provides the second slave with an opportunity to indulge his selfish irresponsibility at the expense of his fellow slaves.[39] He can think only of the present, not of the inevitable end of that opportunity when his master returns.

50-51   Neither slave knew when the master would return, but for the first slave that did not matter because he was ready at any time. It is only the irresponsible who need worry about the *parousia,* and yet it is precisely they who do not worry about it, and will suffer as a result. The repetition of the terms "day" and "hour" reminds us again of v. 36 and so further underlines the message of the unpredictability of the parousia.

The term used for the slave's punishment, "cut in two," occurs elsewhere in biblical literature only for the dismemberment of sacrifical animals.[40] There is no evidence for its use elsewhere as merely a metaphor for severe punishment, and it is probably to be taken here literally as a particularly brutal execution (cf. 1 Sam 15:33; Jer 34:18; Dan 3:29; Heb 11:37),[41] which goes far beyond the parameters of the story and is meant (like the "torturers" of 18:34) to shock the reader into a response.[42] "Hypocrites" is surprising in this context, since the slave's action was blatant rather than

---

38. See I. H. Jones, *Parables,* 436-38.

39. Gundry, 495-97, finds the primary focus of this parable in the mistreatment of the fellow slaves. This is "a special warning to ecclesiastical leaders, who are supposed to show love to the little people in the church." This reading, shared by some other commentators, seems to me to give too much weight to a detail in the story. The focus in context is on the two slaves and their readiness, not on the specific role they were called to fulfill; the parable is better interpreted like those that follow, as an exhortation to *all* disciples (all of whom have responsibilities to their master, even if not in the form of church leadership), not just to church leaders.

40. This practice is, however, taken as a model for human punishment in Jer 34:18. The appearance of διχοτομέω with reference to the punishment of human beings in the Greek text of *3 Bar.* 16:3 is probably due to the influence of this passage in Matthew. MM 165 quote a later inscription which apparently uses the term for the shortening of life. It is employed metaphorically in Greek philosophical writings, hence our derivative "dichotomy."

41. M. A. Beavis, *JBL* 111 (1992) 42-43, illustrates the sadistic punishments to which slaves were liable in the ancient world.

42. See Davies and Allison, 3:389-91, for the interesting suggestion that this is part of a sequence of motifs in this parable which derive from the popular story of Ahiqar, relating to the behavior and subsequent fate of the wicked Nathan.

hypocritical, but after the repeated use of the word in ch. 23 we may perhaps understand it here as a general term for those who place themselves outside the will of God[43] (the Lucan parallel is "the unbelievers"). If the same term can be used for the unfaithful disciple as for the failed Jewish leadership, the Christian reader is warned that merely belonging to the disciple community is not in itself a guarantee of ultimate salvation. See above on 8:12 for "weeping and gnashing of teeth" as the ultimate fate of the wicked; as in 22:13 the imagery of the parable indicates that it is here the fate of someone who was ostensibly an insider but has failed to fulfill his master's expectations.

c. The Parable of the Girls Waiting for the Bridegroom (25:1-13)

The second parable about being ready adopts a more social setting for its story. Weddings provided one of the high points in village life, and the question of who was and was not included affected one's social standing. Our knowledge of Jewish wedding customs[44] at the time is limited, leaving scholars to suggest analogies from other cultures; but it is probably wiser to admit our ignorance. This story mentions only two parties, the bridegroom and the ten girls. The precise role of the latter in the ceremonies is not clear (which is why it is perhaps better to avoid so culture-specific a term as "bridesmaids"),[45] but the Greek term (literally, "virgins") indicates unmarried[46] friends or relatives of either the bride or the bridegroom.[47] The story tells us that their role

43. See I. H. Jones, *Parables,* 440-41. This seems better in context than to look for a more specific manifestation of "hypocrisy" in the parable, e.g., in his use of "my master" (v. 48) while disobeying his instructions.

44. A. W. Argyle, *ExpT* 86 (1974/5) 214-15, provides data to show how this parable fits in with what we know of wedding customs at the time.

45. I. H. Jones, *Parables,* 446 etc., more appropriately identifies them as the "bridegroom's maids of honour." R. Zimmermann, *NTS* 48 (2002) 48-70, gives a detailed account of Hellenistic-Roman marriage customs, which he argues would also apply in Jewish circles at the time, and proposes that the girls are servants from the bridegroom's house, awaiting the return of the bridegroom with his bride after the wedding feast at her house (see, however, n. 49 below: the γάμοι which take place after the arrival at the bridegroom's house more naturally refers to the wedding feast — or did they have two feasts?!).

46. And therefore at most in their early teens; see on 1:18.

47. Albright and Mann, 302, declare confidently that "they would always have been attendant on the bride, never the bridegroom" (and for that reason support the minority reading "and the bride" in v. 1; see p. 933, n. 14). It may indeed have been their duties to the bride that required them to greet the bridegroom, but since the bride plays no part in the story, this need not be mentioned. See J. Jeremias, *Parables,* 172-73, for possible cultural parallels which may throw doubt on the confident assertion of Albright and Mann.

included escorting the bridegroom in a torchlight procession (and dance?) to his house, but that they were not present at whatever part of the ceremonies immediately preceded this procession. The unexpected delay at that point in the proceedings may have been caused by extended bargaining over the financial settlement,[48] or by any number of other causes, deliberate or accidental. It does not matter; all that matters is the delay, and the effect it had on the readiness of the girls when the time for their part in the ceremonies eventually arrived. The sequel to the procession is the wedding feast[49] in the bridegroom's house, the high point of the celebration. To miss that is to miss everything, and the ending of the story again shades off into the language of eschatological judgment, with the emphatic closure of the door and the unavailing appeal by the excluded girls. Their address to the bridegroom as "Lord, Lord" and his response, "I don't know you," read oddly in the narrative situation — of course the bridegroom knew his own wedding party! — but clearly recall the fate of the pseudodisciples of 7:21-23.

Why then did the five silly girls miss the feast? It was not that five slept and five stayed awake: v. 5 says explicitly that they all slept and all had to be awakened by the midnight shout. The problem goes back to the preparations they had made before going to sleep. We are offered no allegorical identification for the oil, and the best efforts of commentators and preachers to supply one are no more than speculation. The preceding and following parables both indicate an ethical understanding of what it means to be ready, and this will be further underlined in vv. 31-46, but within this parable that is not spelled out.[50] If there is any hint here as to what was lacking, it is in the bridegroom's verdict "I don't know you," which, as in 7:21-23, indicates a criterion deeper than merely ethical correctness. But the point is simply that readiness, whatever form it takes, is not something that can be achieved by a last-minute adjustment. It depends on long-term provision, and if that has been made, the wise disciple can sleep secure in the knowledge that everything is ready.[51]

---

48. So J. Jeremias, *Parables,* 172-74, though it may be questioned how far the features of modern Arab weddings which he describes reflect Jewish practice two millennia ago.

49. The term used in v. 10 is simply τοὺς γάμους, but we have seen in 22:1-10 that the plural can be used specifically for the wedding *feast;* see p. 820, n. 4.

50. It may, however, be plausibly suggested on the basis that Jesus has used lamplight as a symbol for effective discipleship expressed in "good deeds" in 5:15-16 (so Gundry, 499).

51. In *b. Šabb.* 153a we find a similar first-century rabbinic parable, where the wise guests invited to the king's banquet got ready and waited at the door, while the foolish went about their business and left preparation to the last minute — when it was too late, and they had to watch while the wise went into the banquet without them. The context applies it to the danger of leaving repentance until one's deathbed.

If that is what the parable means, the addition of v. 13 seems quite inappropriate to the story on which it comments: "keeping awake" is precisely what *none* of the ten girls did, and the sensible ones did not suffer because of their dozing. The verse looks like an editorial comment, virtually repeating 24:42, where it preceded a parable which *was* about staying awake. But the metaphor of keeping awake was more concerned with readiness than with disrupting the normal routine of life (see comments on 24:42), and that sense is indeed appropriate here, even though the metaphor used to express it is literally incompatible with the different imagery of the parable just concluded.

Luke 12:35-38 has a comparable section about being ready to greet the "master" in a wedding context, but the details are all different[52] and the story less developed. They are best understood as independent traditions.[53]

1-4 The opening formula is similar to that which introduced parables in 13:24; 18:23; 22:2 (see p. 522, n. 1), but whereas in those cases the verb was in the aorist tense, here it is in the future (*"will* be compared to"), as in 7:24, 26, probably because of the eschatological situation to which this parable will be applied: it speaks not of how things are now, but of how they will be at the *parousia* of the Son of Man. This future perspective is underlined by the opening "Then," which refers back to the "day" and "hour" which have been the focus of this discourse since 24:36. This, then, is a parable about how the kingdom of heaven will be (i.e., how God's purpose will be worked out) when the *parousia* takes place. The girls' role in meeting and escorting "the bridegroom" reminds the reader of Jesus' image of himself as the bridegroom in 9:15.

The words I have translated "sensible" and "silly" (traditionally "wise" and "foolish") have been used for the two protagonists in the parable of the two house builders in 7:24-27, and "sensible" for the first slave in the parable of 24:45-51; practical common sense stands for spiritual wisdom. The portable torches for outdoor use (the word is not the same as that used for a standing domestic lamp in 5:15 and 6:22) would be bundles of cloth mounted on a carrying stick and soaked with oil.[54] The jars held the oil into

---

52. Indoor lamps, not outdoor torches; male slaves; the master returning from a wedding feast and himself knocking at the door; the slaves remaining awake to let him in.

53. Some of the same motifs occur in *Did.* 16:1, including the command to stay awake and not to let your lamps go out, but the wording is generally closer to Luke 12:35-38 than to Matthew, including Luke's word "lamps" rather than Matthew's "torches."

54. The same word is used in John 18:3 for the torches carried by the arresting party in Gethsemane. For further detail see J. Jeremias, in J. M. Richards (ed.), *Soli Deo Gloria,* 83-87. The word also came to be used for lamps (so probably in Acts 20:8; in Jdt 10:22 they are made of silver), and this meaning is sometimes found in the papyri, but the context here is decisively against it. See Keener, 596, for further references. Davies and Allison, 3:395-96, discuss the data, but are surprisingly reluctant to accept the normal

which the torch was dipped before lighting. A torch without a jar of oil was as useless as a modern flashlight without a battery.

5-6 The story gives the impression that the girls thought they knew when the bridegroom would arrive, and had not reckoned on the delay. A torchlight procession would of course be after dark, but might be expected to be before the middle of the night. The parable thus illustrates both the fact that the time of the *parousia* is unknown and may not be as soon as people might expect, and also its sudden, unexpected nature when it does come, the middle of the night being the time when people are least alert.[55] By the time Matthew wrote his gospel both of these factors might be expected to be in play, with some Christians anxious over the delay of the "imminent" *parousia,* and others complacent after years of unfulfilled prediction. But the story does not develop as the call to vigilance in 24:36-51 might have led us to expect: the sensible girls did not stay awake while their companions slept. All were equally disappointed by the delay, all fell asleep, and all were equally taken by surprise by the eventual shout.

7-9 We do not know whether the torches had been lighted when the girls first set out, but, if so, they would not have stayed burning while they slept; even a well-soaked torch would not burn for much more than a quarter of an hour (Schweizer, 466). So the sensible girls now had to resoak and light their torches, while the attempts of the silly girls to light theirs were of course futile: "our torches are going out" suggests that as they lighted the cloths they immediately went out again, having no more oil to keep them burning. The response of the sensible girls to their natural request for a share of the oil may sound selfish, and perhaps in a real-life situation they might have been willing to share — though if their supply, too, was limited, to keep it for themselves ensured that at least *some* torches would stay alight. But in a parable things do not always happen according to real life, and the hard-nosed realism of the sensible girls invites the reader to reflect that spiritual preparedness is not something that others can provide for you: each needs their own oil.

10-12 When the bridegroom arrives, the feast begins, and the reader is likely to remember those other feasts which have depicted the blessings of the kingdom of heaven in 8:11-12 and 22:1-13. It is only those who are ready who will enjoy it. The closing of the door is another element in the story

---

meaning here, because they "wonder whether people carried oil in vessels to replenish torches." The short burning period of a torch as compared with a lamp seems to me to make it much more likely that extra oil would be needed for torches than it would be for lamps.

55. M. D. Goulder, *Midrash,* 438, suggests an allusion to Exod 12:29-30, the great cry at midnight at the time of the Passover, but that was a cry of mourning, not of summons.

which seems out of place in the open hospitality and conviviality of a village wedding; late arrival is not normally an issue in oriental society, certainly not penalized in such a dramatic fashion. But this has become, like so many of the other parables, a story of insiders and outsiders, of the saved and the lost, and the closing of the door symbolizes that final division at the last judgment, as we have seen it in 13:30, 48; 21:31, 41; 22:8-10, 13.[56] If Matthew this time refrains from speaking of "the darkness outside" and "weeping and gnashing of teeth" (as he did in connection with the other feasts in 8:12; 22:13), he has made the same point unmistakably clear in the pathetic picture of the silly girls futilely calling outside a closed door.

The bridegroom's dismissive words ("I don't know you" is perhaps more a formula of dissociation than a literal statement of nonacquaintance) are, as we noted above, based on 7:23, another account of the exclusion of those who thought they ought to be included. With the emphatic formula, "I tell you truly," they have the force of a judicial verdict. The comparatively trivial lapse of a failure to be provided with oil has come to symbolize an ultimately false relationship; they are not part of Jesus' true family (12:50).

13 These words can hardly be part of the original parable, and as an editorial comment they seem to miss its point (see p. 948 above). They reflect the background theme of this part of the discourse as a whole — the call to be alert for the unexpected *parousia* of the Son of Man — rather than the specific story of the sleeping girls, who were not literally "awake" when the bridegroom was announced. A more appropriate reflection on this particular story might have been the slogan of 22:14, "Many are invited, but few are chosen."

d. The Parable of the Slaves Entrusted with a Lot of Money (25:14-30)

The third in the series of parables about being ready returns to a setting similar to that of the first, a master dealing with his slaves. But this time there is a more specific focus on their commercial responsibility in their master's absence.[57] Each is left with a very large sum of money, with no instructions on

56. For a similar image, using much of the same language as v. 10, cf. Luke 13:25.

57. Carter, 487-88, criticizes the parable for taking "the perspective of the wealthy elite" and "punishing the one who subverts the system": "On the basis of Jesus' teaching in 19:16-22, the master and the first two slaves could rightly be rebuked for their greedy and acquisitive actions. The third slave should be commended for not adding to the master's wealth by not depriving others!" (Cf. B. A. Reid, *CBQ* 66 [2004] 251: "The third slave is the honorable one because he unmasks the wickedness of the master" — though Reid herself mentions this exegesis only as a "possibility" which she does not in fact adopt.) Carter thus feels it necessary to apologize for the parable's presuppositions, which

what to do with it, and the story turns on their different ways of exercising this responsibility. There is again a division between good and bad, between success and failure. Yet the "failure" of the bad slave consists not in any loss of money, but in returning it without increase. It was not that he did something wrong — he simply did nothing. This is, then, apparently, a parable about maximizing opportunities, not wasting them. To be "ready" for the master's return means to use the intervening time to maximum profit; it is again about continuing life and work rather than about calculating the date and being alert for his actual arrival. This third parable is thus essentially making the same point about readiness for the *parousia* as the two preceding ones.

But does it give any further clue as to what *sort* of lifestyle will render a person "ready"? There is no explicit identification of what the money represents. This fact has been obscured for most English readers by the ambiguity of the English word "talent," an ambiguity which is not in the Greek term *talanton* (see p. 933, n. 18). The Greek term means simply a large sum of money (or, strictly, weight of precious metal; see on 18:24) and has no metaphorical sense. But readers of this parable have traditionally interpreted the money as representing natural aptitudes or abilities, and so "talent" has come to be used in English in that transferred sense, which has completely eclipsed the original literal meaning in common usage. It is thus hard for the English reader to set aside the covert interpretation embodied in the very word "talent."

But this traditional reading of the parable is not the most likely either in terms of the way the story is told or in the light of the context in which it is set. If the Lucan form of the story (see below) may be taken as a guide, the money was given to the slaves specifically so that it should be used in trade (Luke 19:13), and in Matthew's version this is also indicated by the master's immediate settling of accounts on his return, his delight in the achievement of the first two slaves, and his rejection of the third slave's "prudent" policy of no return. It is then more about responsibility than about natural endowment, though the degree of responsibility given to each depends on their individual ability (v. 15). The "talents," however, do not *represent* that individual ability but are allocated on the basis of it. They represent not the natural gifts and aptitudes which everyone has, but the specific privileges and opportunities of the kingdom of heaven and the responsibilities they entail.[58] The para-

---

he attributes to Matthew as "a creature of his cultural context." But did Jesus really teach that trade is exploitation? This is not the only parable which assumes the validity of acquiring wealth and of private ownership.

58. B. Chenoweth, *TynBul* 56 (2005) 61-72, argues for a more specific identification of the talents as "the knowledge of the secrets of the kingdom of heaven" (13:11); his argument depends partly on noting that the following verse (13:12) is taken up again in this parable at v. 29.

ble thus teaches that each disciple has God-given gifts and opportunities to be of service to their Lord, and that these are not the same for everyone, but it is left to the reader to discern just what those gifts and opportunities are. This is appropriate to the open-ended nature of parables, and different readers may rightly place the emphasis on different aspects of their discipleship.[59] What matters is that, however precisely the "talents" are interpreted, each disciple should live and work in such a boldly enterprising way that the returning master will say, "Well done, you good, trustworthy slave." That is what it means to "be ready" for the *parousia,* just as in the earlier parable it was the slave who was found hard at work who was rewarded (24:46-47).

As in the previous parables, the eschatological application of the story affects the way it is told. The repeated invitation, "Come in and share your master's happiness" (vv. 21, 23), sounds more like the language of heaven than of commerce; and the ultimate fate of the unsuccessful slave is described in v. 30 in the eschatological terms which have become familiar from other judgment sayings and parables (8:12; 22:13; cf. 13:42, 50; 24:51). The "reward" in the form of additional responsibility (vv. 21, 23) recalls that of the sensible slave in 24:47, and goes beyond what the story requires. Another curious feature is that the first slave appears in v. 28 to have been given his ten talents back after he had returned them to the master in v. 20, and is even given the single talent in addition; see the comments below on what this surprising feature of the story may be intended to symbolize.

This parable has a rudimentary "parallel" (to the basic story situation, but with none of the detail) in Mark 13:34, and a much fuller one in Luke 19:11-27.[60] Luke's parable has a different setting, an explicit explanatory introduction (Luke 19:11), and the added motif of the journey "to receive kingship" and the rebellious subjects and their punishment[61] (Luke 19:14, 27).

---

59. Blomberg, 375, unusually takes the monetary imagery of the parable as the basis for applying it specifically to the Christian's use of money, though he recognizes that this is only one possible application.

60. Eusebius's reference (text in Elliott, *The Apocryphal NT,* 11) to a different version found in "the gospel that came to us in Hebrew characters" is too brief to provide a meaningful "parallel." It had three slaves, one who traded successfully, one who hid the talent, and one who squandered his master's money with prostitutes and flute girls; the first was commended, the second rebuked, and the third imprisoned. Eusebius gives us no further details of the story or its wording, but C. A. Evans, *Ancient Texts,* 330-33, uses Eusebius's speculative comments to argue for an original version of the parable which condemned the slave who made the exorbitant profit (and thus also his master who commended him); cf. Carter's reading, n. 57 above. As with other attempts to discover the "originals" behind the gospel parables, this results in a tension between what Jesus is alleged to have said and what Matthew has made of it which does not offer much help with the exegesis of the gospel text as it stands.

61. Normally taken to be a reference to the unsuccessful attempt of Archelaus in 4

Moreover, the details of the story in Luke differ significantly: ten slaves, each given the same amount; much smaller sums of money (one mina = a hundred denarii); authority over cities as the reward for good trading. But the essential pattern of the story of trading in the master's absence is the same, with three slaves singled out, similar commendation of the successful slaves, the same excuses by the third slave and the same response from the master, the one talent/mina given to the slave with ten, and even the same apparently editorial comment in Luke 19:26 as in Matt 25:29. Yet the wording, while similar, is seldom quite the same. All this suggests a memorable story line reused for different occasions and purposes; but whether the reuse was by Jesus himself,[62] or by one or other evangelist adapting the material for his own purposes, is not easily determined. As far as Matthew's version is concerned, it is clearly well adapted to its present setting, in which the extraneous elements of the Lucan bestowal of kingship and rebellion by the new king's subjects would have been an unhelpful distraction.[63]

14-15   The previous parable was introduced, like most parables in Matthew, explicitly as a comparison with the kingdom of heaven (v. 1). Its sequel lacks that specific identification, but the opening phrase, *hōsper gar,* literally "for just as" (see p. 933, n. 17), indicates that the same subject is under discussion. The setting is similar to that of 24:45-51, focusing on the responsibility of slaves in their master's absence, but now the stakes are higher. This is not about domestic management, but about high-level commercial responsibility.[64] For the monetary value of a talent see on 18:24, where I reckon that it represents "what a laborer might hope to earn in half a lifetime." Even one talent is thus a small fortune; five is an extraordinarily large sum of capital to trade with.

The principle of different levels of responsibility depending on the slaves' individual ability hints at the parable's intended application. The king-

---

B.C. to gain the title "king," and his savage revenge on those of his subjects who had opposed his claim.

62. I have commented on this possibility in R. N. Longenecker (ed.), *Challenge,* 184: "It is remarkable how resistant some NT scholars are to the possibility that Jesus, in the course of several months or even years of public ministry, may have used and reused similar material a number of times with different audiences and for different purposes. Any preacher could have told them that this is the most natural scenario in the world!" Cf. N. T. Wright, *Victory,* 632-33.

63. N. T. Wright, *Victory,* 632-39, argues that the parable is not about Jesus' *parousia* but about the OT hope of "YHWH's return to Zion," symbolized and embodied in Jesus' own coming to Jerusalem. This proposal fits much better with the introduction in Luke 19:11 than with the Matthean context, unless one is prepared to argue, as Wright does, that there is no idea of Jesus' *parousia* anywhere in this discourse (or, indeed, anywhere in the gospels).

64. For the responsible positions sometimes held by slaves see on 18:23.

dom of heaven is not a "one-size-fits-all" economy. Cf. the different yields produced by the good seed in 13:8. God's people are different, and he treats them differently; "much will be expected of those to whom much has been given" (Luke 12:48). In the Lucan version of this parable the point is made by the different trading results of slaves who are given the same initial capital; here the principle of individuality is built into the initial distribution. It will be the slaves' responsibility not to look with envy at the different hand which has been dealt to their colleagues, but to make the most of what they have, and it will be important to note that the first two slaves will receive identical commendations in vv. 21 and 23 even though the sums they have gained differ, since each has succeeded in proportion to his initial endowment.

16-18 The first slave's eagerness — he "went straight off and . . ." (see p. 933, n. 19) — is a model for enthusiastic discipleship. He and his first colleague achieve spectacular results (100% profit), but clearly there was a risk involved, which their other colleague was unwilling to face. No doubt he would have justified his action as prudent rather than cowardly (his master's term for it, v. 26), but his prudence results in no benefit to his master. See on 13:44 for the practice of burying treasure for safety.[65]

19 The "long time" in this parable corresponds to the delay in 24:48 and 25:5. This parable simply assumes that the "imminent" *parousia* will not be *immediate*. There is time for life (and trade) to take its normal course, and on the use of that interim period the readiness of the disciple at the *parousia* will depend. The settling of accounts immediately on the master's return indicates what the opening scene has not made explicit, that the master was expecting his money to have been put to good use in the interval.

20-23 The achievement and reward of the first two slaves are presented in almost identical words. Their initial endowment was different, but each has achieved the same rate of return, and the master's commendation is as warm for the less fully endowed as for the more favored.[66] Cf. 20:1-16, where some did not have the opportunity to work as long as others, but all were equally rewarded. These slaves are commended, like the slave of 24:45, as "trustworthy": they have done what was expected of them. In other contexts *pistos* might be understood as "believing," but that would be inappropriate to these story situations (which are Matthew's only uses of the term), and its normal sense of reliability is clearly needed here. But the reward for reliability, as for the slave in 24:47, is not to be set free from slavery or released from responsibility but to be given more of it. You don't "retire" from being a

---

65. Cf. the rabbinic comment on the untrustworthiness of bankers, that "Money can only be kept safe by placing it in the earth" (*b. B. Meṣi'a* 42a).

66. Contrast Luke, where different rates of return from the same endowment result in differential rewards.

disciple. If so large a sum as five talents is "a few things," the "many things" which follow will be a huge responsibility indeed. But along with the added responsibility goes a significant change of status, the new relationship of sharing the master's happiness.[67] Cf. 19:28 for the idea that in the "new age" the reward for faithfulness will be to share the authority of the enthroned Son of Man. Is it reading too much into the parable to envisage heaven as a state not of indolent pleasure but of active cooperation with the purpose of God as well as enjoyment of his favor?

24-27 The third slave's inaction is perhaps to be attributed to simple self-interest: he could not expect to get any significant personal benefit from whatever his trading might achieve,[68] so why bother? He may also have been afraid of how such a master might react if his commercial venture failed, but, if so, he has chosen his words badly: his description of his master's "hardness" explicitly recognizes the desire for profit[69] which makes his own safety-first policy so unacceptable to his master. So his own words are rightly turned against him; even the minimal profit available from "the bankers" would have been better than nothing. Banking as we know it had hardly begun in the Roman world of the first century;[70] lending of money at interest by individuals had long been common (though disapproved within Jewish society), but the practice of depositing money with the expectation of regular growth was not widespread.[71] The "bankers" who might have accepted such a loan would not be a regulated commercial firm, but individual entrepreneurs, moneylenders or money changers, whose honesty and competence might be questionable.[72] In the circumstances, to bury money in the ground was probably the better way to keep it safe; the course of action demanded by

---

67. For "joy" as a term for the situation of the righteous in the world to come see Keener, 600, n. 220.

68. J. D. M. Derrett, *Law,* 18-26, sets out a possible understanding of the commercial arrangements.

69. The two clauses, "harvesting where you didn't sow and collecting from places where you didn't scatter," appear to be synonymous, though the fact that in the Lucan parallel one of the clauses uses banking language (so J. Jeremias, *Parables,* 59, n. 40) may suggest a more commercial sense for διασκορπίζω, "scatter," perhaps in the sense of distributing goods or money in commercial ventures.

70. See S. E. Sidebotham, *ABD* 6:629-33.

71. See B. W. Frier, *ABD* 3:423-24.

72. For possible means of depositing money by the end of the second century see *m. B. Meṣiʿa* 3:11. One of the options mentioned is to leave it with a money changer or a shopkeeper (which is the closest approach to the idea of "bankers" here); it is stated that if money deposited with a money changer is sealed up, the depositor is not liable if it is lost, but loss of the capital is clearly understood to be a real possibility. According to Keener, 601 (evidence in n. 221), temples, including the Jerusalem temple, also functioned as banks, but that possibility would not be open to a Palestinian who did not live in Jerusalem.

the master may have been no less risky than the commercial ventures attempted by the other two slaves. But risk is at the heart of discipleship (10:39; 16:25-26); by playing safe the cautious slave has achieved nothing, and it is his timidity and lack of enterprise (see p. 934, n. 21) which is condemned. Schweizer, 473, pertinently describes his attitude as representing "a religion concerned only with not doing anything wrong."

The slave's pen-portrait of an unreasonable, grasping despot is not of course meant to be taken as a sober assessment of God's expectations of his people.[73] Parables often use surprising characters to illustrate aspects of God's activity,[74] and the parable reader must learn to distinguish between the message conveyed and the vehicle. But even if God is not unreasonable and exploitative, the parable as a whole emphasizes that he makes exacting demands on his people. He is not to be fobbed off with a lame excuse.

28-30   The surprising twist to the story in v. 28 moves the spotlight away from the master (who according to the slave's portrayal in v. 24 should have been determined to hang on to the proceeds of his slaves' trading as well as the talent just returned) to the successful slave who represents effective discipleship. But why is he now in possession of the ten talents which he had previously surrendered to his master (v. 20)? Should we suppose that the money has been returned to him for further trading (perhaps this is what the "many things" of v. 21 referred to)? Otherwise eleven talents seems a ridiculously large sum for a slave to be given. But probably we should not expect the parable to mirror real life, and this is a way of underlining the theme of the disproportionate rewards which God gives to his faithful people; cf. 19:27-29 and the comments there. So this slave's success attracts further reward, on top of what has already been declared in v. 21, and the same proverbial saying which was used of the progressive enlightenment of the disciples in 13:12[75] (see comments there) now underlines the theme that success breeds further success, while failure is further compounded. It would, however, be pressing the imagery too far to infer that the blessing of the good disciple is *at the expense of* the forfeiture of the bad.

There is thus a fundamental division between good and bad disciples, between the saved and the lost, and the language of ultimate judgment is deployed again to warn the reader to take the parable's message seriously. What ultimately condemned this disciple, and made him unready to meet his Lord

---

73. See, however, I. H. Jones, *Parables,* 478, for the view that God's "harshness" was a problem for Christians.

74. The burglar, 24:43; the eccentric employer, 20:1-16; the grudging neighbor, Luke 11:5-8; the lazy judge, Luke 18:1-8; the man who commends his steward's dishonest practice, Luke 16:8.

75. See p. 951, n. 58, for a possible significance in this echo for the interpretation of the parable.

at the *parousia*, was the fact that he had proved to be "useless" for the kingdom of heaven. Like the man ejected from the wedding feast in 22:13, his performance had not matched his profession, and it is only those who "do the will of my Father who is in heaven" (12:50) who ultimately belong to his kingdom.

e. The Final Judgment by the Son of Man (25:31-46)

Since 24:36 the theme of being ready to face the Son of Man at his *parousia* has dominated the latter part of the discourse. Now that theme comes to its majestic climax in a vision of the judgment that will then take place, when in fulfillment of the vision of Dan 7:13-14 the Son of Man is enthroned as judge over all the nations, and the great division will take place between those who are ready and those who are not ready. In the preceding parables we have seen indications of what "readiness" may be understood to mean, in terms of the lifestyle which the master will commend at his coming. Now we find a more explicit statement of the criterion of judgment, in the way people have treated "one of these my smallest brothers and sisters."

This passage has traditionally been an embarrassment especially to Protestant readers because it appears to say that one's final destiny — and nothing could be much more final than "eternal punishment" or "eternal life," v. 46 — depends on acts of philanthropy, a most un-Pauline theology and one which sounds uncomfortably like Pelagianism. Some interpreters are happy to take it that way, pointing out that this is Matthew and not Paul, and that Matthew regularly calls for "righteousness" and for "doing the will of God" as the characteristic of God's people. Just as the preceding parables have told us that the master on his return will praise the slave who has been getting on with the job (24:46) and who has achieved good results (25:21, 23), this, too, is a call to good works which will be rewarded. The "For" which begins vv. 35 and 42 at least states that these acts of kindness are the evidence that the reward or punishment is deserved; but it may equally be read as stating the actual basis, or at least part of the basis, for the judgment given.

But there is one feature of this scene which has led probably the majority of recent interpreters[76] to a different conclusion. The recipients of the

---

76. So, e.g., R. H. Stein, *Parables,* 135-40, and among recent commentators Gundry, Carson, Hagner, Keener, and Carter. For a contrary opinion from an evangelical scholar see D. Wenham, *Parables,* 90-92; cf. Davies and Allison, 3:428-29. For a survey of the debate at an earlier stage see G. E. Ladd, in R. N. Longenecker and M. C. Tenney (eds.), *New Dimensions,* 191-99; more recently see I. H. Jones, *Parables,* 246-49. The discussion of this and other exegetical issues in the pericope by G. N. Stanton, *Gospel,* 207-31, concludes firmly for the "particularist" view, that the "smallest brothers" are disciples

acts of kindness are Jesus' "smallest brothers and sisters," and what is done to them is done to him (v. 40). So is the final judgment concerned not with response to human need in general, but to the need of disciples in particular, and thus indirectly with how people have responded to Jesus himself in the person of his earthly representatives? Has their response to disciples in need been their way of "acknowledging Jesus," which was presented as the basis of judgment in 10:32-33? That interpretation has a firm foundation in the earlier language of this gospel, which has spoken of true disciples as Jesus' brothers and sisters (12:46-50; cf. 28:10) and has used the phrase "these little ones" to denote members of the disciple community (10:42; 18:6, 10, 14 — note in particular 18:6, "these little ones who believe in me"). In 18:5 we have been told that to welcome one such child in Jesus' name is to welcome him (cf. also 10:40 for the same idea), and that child becomes the basis for the phrase "these little ones" in the following verses. Several go further and argue that these "smallest brothers and sisters" of Jesus are not just any disciples, but those sent out as missionaries of the good news;[77] in that case people's response to them would be a measure of their response to the gospel, as in 10:11-15, 40. But this more specific identification, while clearly consonant with the theme of the mission discourse in ch. 10, is not required by the wording of this passage: "one of these my smallest brothers and sisters" sounds like an inclusive term for any disciple, however insignificant, and we shall note below that the hardships they suffer are not peculiar to missionaries.

It is probably right to read "these my smallest brothers and sisters" as a description of disciples. But to draw that conclusion does not establish that the "sheep" are commended because their treatment of disciples reveals their

---

(especially pp. 214-21). P. Luomanen, *Entering,* 184-90, recognizes the force of the arguments for a "particularist" reading within the pericope itself, but argues that in its wider Matthean context a "universalistic interpretation" is needed; so he suggests that Matthew took an originally particularist tradition and gave it a broader application. S. W. Gray, *The Least,* gives a full catalogue of twentieth-century interpretations of this pericope up to the mid-eighties (pp. 255-72) and finds that among the majority who take this to be a universal judgment, 305 regard the "least" as denoting people in general, while eighty-six take it to mean Christians in general, and thirteen to mean a more restricted group of Christians (missionaries or, in one case, Jewish Christians); among the minority who think this is a more restricted judgment the proportion who take "the least" to be specifically Christian is substantially higher. For a more accessible survey of the competing schools of interpretation see U. Luz, in D. R. Bauer and M. A. Powell (eds.), *Treasures,* 273-86.

77. So, e.g., J. R. Michaels, *JBL* 84 (1965) 27-37; U. Luz, *Theology,* 129-31; idem, in D. R. Bauer and M. A. Powell (eds.), *Treasures,* 302-5 ("wandering charismatics"); J. A. Gibbs, *Jerusalem,* 217-20. Gundry, 511, calls them "the persecuted messengers of Jesus" (though he also denies that they are "an elite corps of Christian preachers in the church," 514). Keener, 605-6, appears to incline this way.

positive attitude to Jesus himself. For the striking feature of this judgment scene is that both sheep and goats claim that they *did not know* that their actions were directed toward Jesus. Each is as surprised as the other to find their actions interpreted in that light. They have helped, or failed to help, not a Jesus recognized in his representatives, but a Jesus *incognito*. As far as they were concerned, it was simply an act of kindness to a fellow human being in need, not an expression of their attitude to Jesus. They seem closer to what some modern theologians call "anonymous Christians" than to openly declared supporters of Jesus himself.

So it does not seem to be possible to read this passage as expressing a "Pauline" doctrine of salvation through explicit faith in Jesus.[78] A systematic theologian can devise a scheme whereby justification by grace through faith and judgment according to works are together parts of a greater whole, but Matthew is not writing systematic theology, and the present passage brings to its fullest expression his conviction that when the Son of Man comes he will "repay every person according to what they have done" (16:27). This is the ultimate outworking of the Matthean motif of reward for those who have lived according to the will of God (see on 5:12). And that will is here spelled out in terms of the way people have responded to the human needs of "these my smallest brothers and sisters."

The debate about the criterion of judgment, however, theologically important as it is, should not be allowed to distract the reader from what is surely the main thrust of this passage as the climax of the discourse on judgment, its portrayal of the ultimate sovereignty of the Son of Man as the universal judge. This theme has been developed in Matthew especially through the imagery of Dan 7:13-14, and that passage provides the language in which the scene is set in v. 31. We have considered at 10:23 the range of situations to which this Danielic imagery is applied in Matthew, from the immediate postresurrection sovereignty of the Son of Man in 28:18 through a more universally visible vindication and authority which will be seen within the contemporary generation (10:23; 16:28; 24:30; 26:64), to its ultimate fulfillment in the final judgment (19:28; 25:31-34). The sovereign authority displayed in the judgment on the temple (24:30) now finds its eschatological counterpart in the judgment of all nations (v. 32). The focus on Jesus' *parousia* in the preceding part of the discourse from 24:36 to 25:30 encourages the reader to associate this final judgment also with the *parousia,* as part of the same complex of eschatological motifs, but the scene itself is apparently set, like that of Dan 7:9-14, in the heavenly throne room, to which all people are summoned. There is no indication within this passage of the Son of Man coming

---

78. For some thoughtful comments on the comparison between Matthew and Paul in their presentation of rewards and judgment see R. Mohrlang, *Matthew,* 67-71.

to earth, unless that is assumed to be the meaning of the language of Dan 7:13, and we have already seen repeatedly that that is not how the Daniel vision is framed. The word *parousia* is not used here. The "coming" of v. 31 is no more specifically *parousia* language than it was in 24:30 and in all the other allusions to Dan 7:13-14; it is the context rather than the wording of this passage which allows the reader to associate this judgment scene with the time of the *parousia.*

This pericope is often referred to as "the parable of the sheep and the goats." It should be noted, however, that the imagery of a shepherd dividing his flock occurs only in vv. 32-33, where it occurs in v. 32 as a simile within the judgment scene rather than as a story-parable in its own right. The terms "sheep" and "goats" are taken from the simile in v. 33 and applied to the two contrasted groups of people, but thereafter the image is dropped, and they are referred to as people, not as animals. The pericope as a whole is not therefore a "parable" like those of 24:45-51; 25:1-13, and 25:14-30.[79] Its genre is closer to the majestic visions of divine judgment in the book of Revelation than to the Synoptic parables.[80]

31 The judgment scene is set in language largely drawn from Dan 7:13-14 and its wider setting. For similar imagery cf. 19:28.[81] "The Son of Man," "comes," "glory" all directly echo those verses, as does the idea of enthronement. The specific term "throne," the accompanying angels, and the theme of judgment are all derived from the setting of the vision in Dan 7:9-10, but whereas the one who there sat on the heavenly throne among the angels was God himself, now it is the Son of Man whose enthronement, depicted in Dan 7:14, has been achieved. When in v. 34 the Son of Man is described simply as "the king," this is the culmination of the process throughout this gospel whereby the kingdom of God/heaven becomes embodied in the kingship of the Son of Man (13:41; 16:28; 19:28; cf. 20:21). In a passage so loaded with OT echoes it is also likely that the phrase "all the angels with him" echoes not only the imagery of Dan 7:10 but also the last clause of Zech 14:5, where very similar words depict the eschatological coming of

79. J. Jeremias, *Parables,* 206, justifies calling it a parable by classing it as "a *māšāl*" or "an apocalyptic revelation" like those of *1 Enoch.* It is questionable, however, whether this sense of "parable" is either recognizable or helpful to most English readers.

80. See G. N. Stanton, *Gospel,* 221-30, for an extensive defense of the description of this pericope as "an apocalyptic discourse." Stanton finds significant similarities between its theme and language and that of some passages from roughly contemporary Jewish apocalyptic writings *(4 Ezra, 2 Baruch, 1 Enoch).* Davies and Allison, 3:419, set out in tabular form the structural similarities between several such visions.

81. Note, however, the different scale of the judgment in these two passages: in 19:28 Jesus is accompanied by his twelve disciples and judges the tribes of Israel; here he is accompanied by all the angels and judges all the nations.

God.[82] In this climactic vision, then, the OT expectation of the eschatologi-cal visitation of God in judgment and salvation finds its fulfillment in Jesus the Son of Man, who sits on *his* glorious throne and pronounces judgment.

32-33 The OT imagery continues with the gathering[83] of all nations for judgment, as in Joel 3:1-12 (Hebrew; LXX 4:1-12), with a likely verbal echo of Joel 3:2, "I will gather all the nations . . . into judgment." Again, a passage which depicts God himself as judge is echoed in a description of judgment by the Son of Man. In Joel the judgment is specifically of the Gentiles in relation to their mistreatment of Israel, but there is no such re-striction here, and in the light of the judgment on Jerusalem in ch. 24 it seems likely that Jews and Gentiles together are called to this final assize (see on 28:19 for "all the nations," and cf. 24:9, 14).[84] The eschatological tone of the whole pericope indicates that this judgment is universal, including both pro-fessing disciples and other people without distinction.[85]

The motif of an ultimate division between the saved and the lost has recurred in many different contexts in this gospel; see especially 7:13-27; 8:11-12; 10:32-33; 13:40-43, 49-50; 16:25-26, and the whole of 24:36–25:30. Now it is underlined by an image perhaps based on Ezek 34:17, where God, the shepherd, judges between different members of his flock.[86] In the Middle East sheep and goats were (and are) often pastured in mixed flocks. The sheep, though generally lighter colored than goats, are not as predomi-nantly white as the flocks familiar to us; some are brown, and some have sub-stantial dark patches (even when clean!), so that it can take a practiced eye to distinguish the two species.[87] The purpose of separating the two is not clear,[88]

---

82. For the allusion see my *Jesus and the OT,* 157-58; it is closer to the LXX, which has μετ᾽ αὐτοῦ, "with him," instead of the MT second-person *'immāk,* though the latter is so awkward in context that it may well be a corruption of an original *'immô,* "with him."

83. Or, in the light of the following simile, perhaps the "herding together"; so Schweizer, 476.

84. See I. H. Jones, *Parables,* 245-51, for the debate about who are judged.

85. Cf. G. N. Stanton, *Gospel,* 212-14; U. Luz, in D. R. Bauer and M. A. Powell (eds.), *Treasures,* 292-95.

86. See p. 935, n. 24; the separation is between individuals who make up "all the nations," not between nation and nation.

87. The close link between the two species is shown by the fact that some lan-guages, such as Tamil, use the same word for both.

88. J. Jeremias, *Parables,* 206, following G. Dalman, stated that at the end of the day the mixed flock must be separated, perhaps for milking, but also because the less hardy goats need to be taken indoors while the sheep prefer to stay in the open; this expla-nation has been repeated by subsequent commentators without further evidence. But see the cautionary comments of U. Luz, in D. R. Bauer and M. A. Powell (eds.), *Treasures,* 296-97. Luz rightly points out that ἔριφος normally means a "kid" as opposed to a full-grown goat, and suggests that the young he-goats are being separated off for slaughter.

but it is the process, not its purpose, which is the point of the simile. The imagery provides a memorable illustration of the final division of people who have up to that point lived together indistinguishably — cf. the imagery of the wheat and the weeds (13:29-30) or of the silly and sensible girls (25:1-12). To other people (and even to themselves, vv. 37-39, 44?) the saved and the lost may look very similar; it takes the expertise of the "king" to know which is which.[89] The righthand side often signifies the place of favor, so that the left is comparatively that of disfavor.[90]

34 For "the king" see on v. 31. The fact that that "king" who sits in the place of God now nonetheless refers to God as "my Father" further enriches the christological nuances of this pericope; one is reminded of John 5:27, where the Father "has given authority to the Son to execute judgment, because he is the Son of Man." In this scene the promise of 10:32 is fulfilled: Jesus acknowledges his true followers before his Father. "Blessed" here is the same word as in the quotations of Ps 118:26 in 21:9; 23:39. It denotes someone who enjoys God's good favor; it is a more theologically loaded word than *makarios*, "happy" (traditionally translated "blessed"), as used in the Beatitudes (see pp. 160-61).

The blessedness of those on the right hand is spelled out as "inheriting a kingship," which is sometimes taken to mean, as in the first and last beati-

89. The point of the imagery is the separation of two superficially similar species, and does not require any inherent difference in value between sheep and goats. Jeremias's statement (*Parables,* 206) that sheep were more valuable than goats is supported by reference only to G. Dalman, *Arbeite und Sitte VI,* 99, 217, whose bald statement to that effect is not clearly supported by his following biblical references; in any case, lower economic value would not be a basis for total rejection: "one does not throw away ten-dollar bills because twenty-dollar bills are more valuable" (K. Weber, *CBQ* 59 [1997] 669). In ancient society both species were highly valued both for their meat and milk and for their wool/hair and skins, and both were equally acceptable as sacrifices (see G. S. Cansdale, *Animals,* 44-56, especially the section on the use of goats, 45-48). The choice of goats for the negative side of the division is not because goats are in themselves inferior or undesirable (nor, I hope, on the basis of their color, though in Song 4:1-2; 6:5-6 sheep and goats are used to represent white and black respectively; K. Weber, *CBQ* 59 [1997] 668, points out, however, that while in biblical literature light and darkness symbolize good and evil, white and black are not so used), but because the simile requires two groups to be symbolized; so one or the other had to represent the "baddies," and the sheep naturally took the favored side since the imagery of God's people as his sheep was familiar from the OT (whereas they are never his goats, except in Ezek 34:17 and perhaps Jer 50:8). The survey of OT material by K. Weber, *CBQ* 59 (1997) 669-73, provides no negative imagery associated with goats with the one specific exception of the scapegoat. The use of the imagery here therefore does not predispose the reader to expect the condemnation of the "goats" (ibid., 673-75).

90. J. M. Court, *NTS* 31 (1985) 223-29, analyzes the imagery of right and left in biblical and Jewish literature.

tudes in 5:3, 10, that they are confirmed as members of God's kingdom, as his accepted subjects, who will therefore share its eternal blessings (summed up in v. 46 as "eternal life"). But this "kingship" is not here said to be "the kingdom of God/heaven." Rather, it is a kingship prepared "for you": they themselves will become kings, sharing in the kingly authority of their Lord. This is what Jesus has promised to the Twelve in 19:28, and the same idea is found in Luke 12:32, where the kingship is given to the "little flock" of Jesus' disciples. The theme of disciples sharing Jesus' kingship will recur elsewhere in the NT: see 1 Cor 4:8; Eph 2:6; Rev 1:6; 5:10; 20:6; 22:5. Thus the "righteous" will receive the status of "kings," an even stronger statement of the principle we have seen in 24:47; 25:21, 23, that faithfulness is rewarded by additional authority.

This new status is not an afterthought but the culmination of God's purpose for them "since the foundation of the world." We have noted in 20:23 that God has already "prepared" who is to sit at Jesus' right and left in his kingship; here the idea is extended beyond those specific places of honor to all who will "inherit" that kingship, and that decision predates the creation of the world. As with other such apparently deterministic language in the NT, it is possible to read "for you" here in either a more general or a more personal sense. Traditional Calvinism has favored the more rigorous, personal interpretation which concludes that the identity of the individuals who will enjoy these blessings is already decreed before they are born. Others have understood the "you" to refer to the class of the saved as a whole: God has prepared this kingship for those who will prove to be worthy of it, but who those people will be remains to be discovered on the basis of their response to the gospel and to the will of God. On that reading what is determined in advance is that those who prove at the time of judgment to be "sheep" will inherit the kingship, rather than that certain individuals have been "pre-selected" before their birth to be "sheep." See on 13:10-17 for the related issue of the secrets of the kingdom of heaven being "given" to some and not to others.

35-39 The list of hardships and their relief, repeated with little variation in the response of the "righteous ones," covers many of the most basic human needs (cf. the similar but shorter list in Isa 58:7,10).[91] They are not specific to any one group, and in a society less materially favored than the modern Western world they represent common experience.[92] The only items in the list which might be thought to indicate a particularly Christian element

---

91. R. H. Gundry, *Use,* 142-143, regards vv. 35-36 as "a targumic adaptation of Is 58:7."

92. I. H. Jones, *Parables,* 257-59, drawing on the work of D. R. Catchpole, *BJRL* 61 (1979) 389ff., demonstrates that these are "six typical acts of kindness" found in a wide range of both Jewish and pagan literature.

to these experiences (see introductory comments above) are being a foreigner and being in prison, if these are understood as some of the occupational hazards faced by those who traveled and incurred opposition as preachers of the gospel. But Christians have no monopoly on such experiences, and in the mobile and politically volatile world of the Roman Empire there would be many others who shared them. The acts of kindness listed ought perhaps to have been expected on the basis of the duty of hospitality as it was and still is honored in Middle Eastern society, but no doubt performance did not always match up to expectation. The only act which might seem to go beyond the normal call of duty is the visiting of a prisoner, particularly if they were not a member of the family, and in Heb 10:34 this is mentioned as a mark of Christian love shown toward persecuted fellow Christians (cf. Heb 13:3). But it is questionable whether that particular scenario is the only one to explain these words. Prisons, for whatever reason one was put in them, were places of misery, where survival might depend on a well-wisher prepared to take one's part.

The "sheep" are now described as "righteous" in anticipation of the final verdict in v. 46. If "righteousness" in Matthew is doing the will of God (see p. 119, n. 15),[93] the term is well applied to these people who have given practical expression to Jesus' basic summary of the law, by treating others as they would wish to be treated themselves (7:12; cf. also 22:39-40). Their surprise when the Son of Man himself claims to have been the object of their loving action must throw doubt on the suggestion that their actions were specifically directed toward those they knew to be disciples (see introductory comments above). They thought they were merely meeting human need.

40 The formula "I tell you truly" here and in v. 45 emphasizes the principle of solidarity. Whether they knew it or not, the people they helped were associated with Jesus, to such an extent that they could be said to *be* Jesus. The more general principle of Prov 19:17 that "the person who is kind to the poor lends to the LORD" is thus here more specifically applied to Jesus and his people. As we have noted in the introductory comments above, the terms used in this verse strongly reflect language used earlier in this gospel to describe Jesus' disciples as "these little ones" (10:42; 18:6, 10, 14) and as Jesus' "brothers and sisters" (12:50; cf. also 28:10). Jesus has spoken in 18:20 of being present where his people have come together in his name. Here his identification with his people goes further: their experiences are his experiences, and what is done to them is done to him. Cf. 10:40, "Anyone who wel-

93. The more forensic sense of the δίκαιος word group which is familiar from Pauline usage would also be appropriate here, since these are people on whom a favorable judicial verdict has just been pronounced, but in the light of Matthew's use of the terms elsewhere this seems less likely to be the intended sense.

comes you welcomes me," and 18:5, "Anyone who welcomes one such child in my name welcomes me." This passage thus expands on the message of 10:40-42: how people respond to Jesus' representatives is both a sign of their attitude to him and the basis for their reward. This sense of solidarity between Jesus and his people will be creatively developed by the author of Hebrews when he explains how it was necessary for the Savior to share the experiences of those he saves, so that he rightly calls them his brothers and sisters (Heb 2:10-18).

It is possible that this sense of identification is helped here (as in Heb 2) by the use of the title "the Son of Man," since that title originated from a passage where the "one like a son of man" was a visionary representation of the holy people of God corporately (Dan 7:13-14, 22, 27); Jesus "*the* Son of Man" sums up in himself the people represented by the "one like a son of man." But this is probably to read too much later christological sophistication into a title which in its many other occurrences in the gospels is used clearly with reference to the individual mission and achievement of Jesus himself. See, however, above on 19:28 for another Son of Man saying which has a corporate dimension.

41 The words spoken to those on the left are the mirror image of those spoken in v. 34 to the "righteous": "go away" instead of "come," "cursed" instead of "blessed," "eternal fire" instead of kingship, and a fate prepared in advance, though in this case not specifically for "you" but for the devil and his angels, whose lot the unrighteous are to share. The blessing in v. 34 was specifically attributed to "my Father," but this verse stops short of saying explicitly that these people are cursed *by God.* This is, however, often the implication of an unattributed passive, and here the reference must be to the displeasure of God which results in their punishment. For the "eternal fire" see further on v. 46. Fire has been a repeated image for ultimate judgment; see 3:10, 12; 5:22; 7:19; 13:40, 42, 50; 18:8, 9. The parallelism with v. 34 would lead us to expect "prepared for you since the foundation of the world," but that is not said here. There is thus a difference between God's eternal purpose of blessing and the regrettable need for a "plan B" to deal with spiritual rebellion when it emerged to spoil God's perfect creation.

The devil's angels represent all the forces of spiritual evil, probably including the demons or "unclean spirits" we have met throughout the gospel as Jesus' opponents in cases of exorcism. In much Jewish thought by this time Satan was pictured as the leader of a spritual host in opposition to God and his angels, and it is the ultimate elimination of all that spiritual opposition which is here envisaged. The theme will be graphically developed in the book of Revelation, where the devil and all his followers are thrown at last into the lake of fire (Rev 19:20; 20:10, 14-15; 21:8). There, as here, the same punishment is awarded to human beings who have followed Satan as to his spiritual forces. And there, as here, the offenses listed seem hardly to fit so melodramatic an end: they include the "cowardly" and "liars" as well as murderers and idolaters (Rev 21:8), just as here the failure to provide humanitarian aid may seem to us relatively low on the scale of spiritual evil. But the imagery of this pericope, as of the book of Revelation, allows for only two categories, the saved and the lost; there is no allowance for grades of good or evil.

42-45 The exchange between the judge and the unrighteous mirrors that with the righteous, though suitably abbreviated to avoid tedious repetition. The verb which as a result is used in v. 44 to summarize the whole range of acts of kindness is the very mundane word *diakoneō,* "look after"; see on 4:11; 8:15; 27:55, and cf. the cognate noun *diakonos* used for the unselfish care for others which marks true discipleship in 20:26; 23:11. This verb further underlines the down-to-earth character of the criterion of judgment in this whole scene. The omission of "brothers and sisters" with reference to the "smallest" in v. 45 is to be attributed to literary abbreviation rather than to any change in the identity of the people concerned, as the reader will naturally understand the phrase in the light of the fuller expression in v. 40. The fault of the "cursed" is not so much that they have done wrong but that they have failed to do right (cf. the silly girls in vv. 1-12 and the failing slave in vv. 24-27).

46 There are only two possible outcomes to the judgment; for the sharp polarization of these two destinies cf. Dan 12:2. The phrase "eternal life" is already familiar to us from 19:16, 29 (cf. also 7:14; 18:8, 9), where it has been seen to be synonymous with being saved or with entering the kingdom of heaven. This is, however, the only time we meet the phrase "eternal punishment" in Matthew, or indeed in the whole NT. It appears to be synonymous with the "eternal fire" of v. 41 and of 18:8, and cf. the "hellfire" of 5:22 and 18:9. All these passages raise the question whether this fire is regarded as destroying and thus annihilating those consigned to it, or as a continuing agony of conscious punishment such as is explicitly attributed to the devil, the beast, and the false prophet in the lake of fire in Rev 20:10 (see above on v. 41). In the debate among evangelical theologians on the issue of annihilation as against continuing punishment,[94] the phrase "eternal punishment" here in Matt 25:46 is commonly cited as a proof-text for the latter position. But this is usually on the assumption that "eternal" is a synonym for "everlasting." That assumption depends more on modern English usage than on the meaning of *aiōnios,* which we have seen to be related to the concept of the two ages.[95] "Eternal punishment," so understood, is punishment which

---

94. For the relevance of this text to that debate cf. C. Brown, *NIDNTT* 3:98-99.
95. See on 18:8, and for the two ages more fully on 12:32.

relates to the age to come rather than punishment which continues forever, so that the term does not in itself favor one side or the other in the annihilationist debate. Insofar as the metaphor of fire may be pressed, however, it suggests destruction rather than punishment, especially if the imagery of the incineration of rubbish is understood to underlie the idea of hell (see on 5:22); the fire of Gehenna goes on burning not because the rubbish is not destroyed by it, but because more is continually added. The imagery of incineration in relation to the final destiny of the wicked also occurs more explicitly in 13:42: the weeds are destroyed, not kept burning forever. We have also noted the use of the verb "destroy" in relation to hell in 10:28. These pointers suggest that an annihilationist theology (sometimes described as "conditional immortality") does more justice to Matthew's language in general, and if so the sense of "eternal punishment" here will not be "punishment which goes on forever"[96] but "punishment which has eternal consequences," the loss of eternal life through being destroyed by fire.[97]

V. JERUSALEM: THE MESSIAH REJECTED, KILLED, AND VINDICATED (26:1–28:15)

See above, pp. 767-68, for my reasons for dividing the Jerusalem section of Matthew's narrative into two main parts. There is no change of location between the end of the discourse in chs. 24–25 and the following passion narrative. Indeed, the latter begins with the concluding formula for the former. But the long-running confrontation between Jesus and the Jerusalem authorities, which ended with his leaving the temple and declaring its impending fate in 23:37–24:2, now reaches its inevitable outcome as their rejection of Jesus turns from words to deeds, and the paradoxical climax of Jesus' messianic mission, as he has predicted it since Caesarea Philippi (16:21), now unfolds. Throughout ch. 26 we shall be concerned only with Jesus' Jewish opponents, and by the end of that chapter his fate will have been decided. The necessary

---

96. Tasker, 240, comments on the KJV translation of αἰώνιος by "everlasting" here and in v. 41: "It would certainly be difficult to exaggerate the harmful effect of this unfortunate mistranslation."

97. D. C. Sim, *Apocalyptic,* 130-39, argues that Matthew envisages (and "fervently and constantly promotes") the idea of "eternal torture by flames which would burn but not consume." His argument recognizes that other NT accounts of the fate of the wicked (except in Revelation) are better understood of annihilation than of continuing torture, but he strangely fails to consider whether this sense may also underlie Matthew's references to "eternal" fire and punishment, and he uses the phrases "forever" and "everlasting" as if they meant the same as Matthew's word "eternal."

involvement of the Roman occupying power in ch. 27 adds a further dimension to the apparently universal rejection of the "king of the Jews," but even then it will be the Jewish crowd and their leaders who mock Jesus on the cross, while a dissenting opinion is expressed by at least some of the Romans involved (27:54). Matthew leaves us in no doubt where the primary responsibility for the rejection of the Messiah lies (27:24-25).

Throughout this climactic narrative section of the gospel Matthew's account runs closely parallel with that of Mark, whereas Luke and especially John incorporate substantial independent traditions. Matthew will include a number of short but significant additions of material not found in the other gospels, of which 27:3-10 is the longest, but from this point on there will be no "Q material." The story is told in a natural sequence which breaks down into a number of clearly distinguishable phases: after an elaborate setting of the scene (26:1-16) we hear first of Jesus' final hours with his disciples at the last supper and in Gethsemane (26:17-46), after which the disciples will play no further part in the story (apart from the accounts of Peter's collapse and of Judas's remorse); Jesus will face his enemies alone. The arrest and trials of Jesus are narrated in 26:47–27:26, with a natural progression from the substantive Jewish trial to the Roman endorsement of their verdict. Then follow the execution and burial of Jesus in 27:27-66, only to be overturned by the evidence of his resurrection which will be set out in 28:1-15.

But all this is not just a chronicle of events, as Matthew will give the reader repeated opportunities to reflect on the significance of what is happening, and in particular on the underlying truth about Jesus. A sustained irony contrasts his apparent helplessness in the hands of his enemies with his ultimate sovereignty. The one who has just been portrayed in 25:31-46 as the king on his glorious throne will undergo this rejection and suffering not because he has no choice but because it is his Father's paradoxical purpose which he has freely chosen to fulfill (26:39, 42, 52-54). Even as the court condemns him, he is entering into his sovereignty (26:64). When the Roman soldiers mock him as King of the Jews (27:27-31) and the Jewish crowds mock him as temple builder, savior, king of Israel, and Son of God (27:39-43), they speak more truly than they know. The supernatural events accompanying his death on the cross (27:51-54) reveal in vivid symbolism that this is not the end but the beginning, and the supreme title "Son of God" is declared even by neutral observers. The resurrection reverses the human verdict of Jerusalem (28:1-15), and in the concluding scene of the gospel the resultant sovereignty of the enthroned Son of Man will be triumphantly declared (28:18-20).

Jesus' death, then, is not a defeat for the divine purpose. It is the basis of his eternal sovereignty. But why was it necessary? There are hints in the titles hurled at Jesus on the cross and in the tearing of the temple curtain and the resurrection of the people of God at the time of Jesus' death, but the most direct explanation has already been given by Jesus himself at the last supper, where in the redemptive context of the Passover festival, and using the OT language of covenant, he speaks of his blood shed for many for the forgiveness of sins (26:28). This echo of Isaiah's servant prophecy, picking up that already heard in 20:28, provides a suggestive theological context in which to think about Jesus' death as the source of life for others, and the "forgiveness of sins" recalls the initial declaration of Jesus' mission in 1:21. The last supper, then, is much more than a farewell meal. It provides the theological template within which the events which follow are to be understood.

A. SETTING THE SCENE (26:1-16)

The beginning of the passion narrative in Matthew, as in Mark, consists of a "concentric" drawing out of three aspects of the setting. The outer layer, in vv. 1-2 and 17-19, is the approach of the Passover festival, which provides both the historical and the theological context for what is to follow. Within that broader context we hear of the plotting of the priestly authorities against Jesus, and their recruiting of Judas (vv. 3-5 and 14-16). And set within that framework is the symbolic incident of the anointing of Jesus by a woman at Bethany (vv. 6-13). The devotion of this unnamed woman contrasts with the hostility of the priests and the treachery of Judas, while Jesus' interpretation of her act (v. 12) prepares the reader for the success of their plot. But all this is to be understood in the context of the Passover, the festival of God's redemption of his people and the occasion of the covenant which constituted Israel as the people of God.

1. The Passover (26:1-2)

1 *And then,*[1] *when Jesus had come to the end of all these sayings, he said to his disciples,* 2 *"You know*[2] *that in two days' time it will be*[3] *the Passover, and the Son of Man will be handed over*[4] *to be crucified."*

1. For this rendering of the Semitic idiom καὶ ἐγένετο, "and it happened," see p. 297, n. 1.
2. The verb could also be read as an imperative, "Know," making this an announcement rather than a reminder. But they would hardly need to be informed about the calendar, and Jesus has already repeatedly told them about his approaching death.
3. Both verbs which I have translated as futures in this verse are present in Greek; such a "prophetic present" does not communicate so well in English.
4. For the translation of παραδίδωμι see p. 374, n. 3, and p. 752, n. 2. Here, as in

The formula which concludes the discourse follows the pattern familiar from 7:28; 11:1; 13:53; 19:1 except for the addition of "all," perhaps to suggest to the reader that it is not just the discourse of chs. 24–25 which is over, but all the discourses.[5] After this there will not be any extended teaching by Jesus.

Before we hear of the priests' plot against Jesus, we hear Jesus himself foretelling what is to come. The order of these verses thus tells us that Jesus will not be taken by surprise, but willingly accepts his fate. The apparently free initiative of the priests (vv. 3-5) is to be understood within the context of an already determined divine plan.

Jesus' statement to the disciples seems curiously unfinished; its implications will in fact be drawn out for the disciples in vv. 17-18, when the event has moved a day closer, but the preliminary warning at this point serves to alert the reader to the significant context in which the story is now set. See p. 771 for the importance of Passover, and for its historical background and redemptive significance see Exod 12:1-27. An early targumic tradition based on Exod 12:42 identifies four nights which Israel must remember, of which the third is the night of redemption from Egypt at the Passover, and the fourth that of the messianic redemption at the end of the age.[6] The original setting of the Passover and the ritual which had developed for its observance were a perpetual reminder to Israel of what it meant to be the chosen people of God. This is the first time Jesus' death has been directly linked with the Passover, but the significance of the date will become an important part of the meaning of the last supper and of the explanation Jesus then gives of the purpose of his death.

"After two days" probably means "the day after tomorrow," but it remains unclear on which day these words are understood to have been spoken, depending on whether "the Passover" here refers to Nisan 14, when the lambs were killed in the afternoon ready for that evening's Passover meal, or to Nisan 15, the "day" on which that meal was held (after sunset when the new day had begun). The properly "Passover" observances thus spanned those two (Jewish) days; see further on v. 17.

20:19, the immediate reference is apparently less directly to the action of Judas than to the handing over of Jesus by the Jewish authorities to the Romans for execution.

5. Cf. the formula in Deut 31:1; 32:45 for the end of Moses' teaching; also Deut 31:24.

6. The material, drawn from the Palestinian targums, is usefully set out by B. D. Chilton, *GP* 1:28-30.

2. The Priests Plot to Kill Jesus (26:3-5)

> 3 Then the chief priests and the elders of the people were gathered together in the courtyard[1] of the high priest, who was called Caiaphas, 4 and discussed how they might arrest Jesus by stealth and kill him. 5 "Not during the festival," they said, "or there might be a riot among the people."

"Were gathered" probably means no more than that they met together (as it does in 13:2; 22:34, 41), but the passive verb may suggest (as it does in 25:32) that they were deliberately summoned to a meeting by the high priest.[2] Only two of the three main component groups of the Sanhedrin (see on 16:21) are mentioned. The chief priests and elders perhaps represent the more "political" grouping. Only when Jesus has been safely secured will Matthew mention the presence of the scribes once the more legal and theological procedures begin (26:57). A meeting in the high priest's courtyard (see n. 1 below) would not be a formal meeting of the Sanhedrin; this is rather an ad hoc planning group.

Joseph Caiaphas, named here and in 26:57 as the president at Jesus' trial, is more generally referred to in the NT simply by his office, "the high priest." The term *archiereus* has hitherto been used only in the plural, to denote those leading priestly figures who belonged to the Sanhedrin, but the singular designates its president. The office traditionally stemmed from Aaron, but in Maccabean times it had become as much political as religious, and in Herodian and Roman times the high priest was appointed by the ruling power and acted as chief representative of the nation.[3] Caiaphas's political skill and his acceptability to the Roman prefects are indicated by the fact that he held office for eighteen years, A.D. 18-36, by far the longest tenure of any high priest in the period.[4]

The need for "stealth" (more literally, "deceit") is explained by v. 5. The manner of Jesus' arrival at the city in 21:1-11 had been enough to alert them to his potential as a popular leader, and his robust performance in de-

---

1. This is the meaning of αὐλή in vv. 58 and 69. The word can also mean the whole house or palace complex, but it is unlikely to be used in different senses so close together and with reference to the same place.

2. It is probably overexegesis to take the verb as a "divine passive" indicating that their plotting fulfilled God's purpose. But the verb may be intended to recall the plotting by the enemies of God and of his servant in Ps 2:2 and/or Ps 31:13, the former of which uses exactly the same verb form in the LXX, the latter a related compound. For the Ps 31 allusion see R. H. Gundry, *Use*, 56; D. J. Moo, *The OT*, 234-35.

3. For first-century high priests see Schürer, 2:227-36, and for their role as president of the Sanhedrin, ibid., 215-18.

4. See J. Blinzler, *Trial*, 91-93.

bate with Pharisaic and other leaders during the following days in the temple courtyard would be likely to have won further support. Note his popular reputation as a prophet (21:11, 46) like John (21:26). Given the volatile mood of the crowded city during the festival,[5] a public arrest of Jesus would be very risky; the reaction of the Galileans among the pilgrims would be particularly likely to erupt into violence. Yet they could hardly have intended to wait until after the full eight-day festival period, as Jesus would be likely to have left Jerusalem by then. J. Jeremias[6] has therefore argued that the Greek phrase here means "not in the presence of the festival *crowd*," and perhaps that represents the gist of their thinking, even though it is not a natural sense of *en tē heortē*. It certainly represents what in fact happened, a secret arrest at night away from the crowds, especially Jesus' Galilean supporters; vv. 14-16 will explain how this proved to be possible, more quickly than they may have expected. According to the chronology for which I shall argue in the comments on v. 17, it was not strictly *during* the festival but before it began, on Passover Eve, though of course the city was already by then crowded with pilgrims.

3. A Woman Anoints Jesus (26:6-13)

6 *While Jesus was in Bethany, in the house of Simon the leper,* 7 *a woman came up to him carrying a vase[1] of very expensive anointing oil and poured it over his head as he was sitting at table.[2]* 8 *When the disciples saw this, they were indignant and said, "Why this waste?* 9 *That could have been sold for a high price and the money given to the poor."* 10 *But Jesus noticed, and said to them, "Why are you giving the woman a hard time? She has done a lovely thing to me.* 11 *For you always have the poor with you, but you won't[3] always have me.* 12 *When this woman poured this oil on my body, she did it to prepare me for burial.* 13 *I tell you truly: wherever this good news is proclaimed in the whole world, what this woman did will also be told as a memorial for her."[4]*

5. For the extra precautions taken by the Roman prefects in Jerusalem at festival times see Josephus, *War* 2.223-27 (cf. *Ant.* 20.107).

6. J. Jeremias, *Words,* 71-73, followed by Gundry, 519.

1. ἀλάβαστρος (-ov; see BDF 49[1] for the form) means a perfume vase, commonly but not necessarily made of what we now call alabaster.

2. For this meaning of ἀνακείμαι, "recline," see J. Jeremias, *Words,* 48-49; R. T. France, *NIDNTT* 3:587-89. In John 12:2 the incident is explicitly set at a dinner.

3. The Greek verb is present, but the sense is that Jesus, now present, will soon not be there.

4. This translation assumes that αὐτῆς is an objective genitive. The alternative that it is subjective, proposed by J. H. Greenlee, *ExpT* 71 (1959-60) 245, would produce the less likely meaning "as her memorial [to me]."

Matthew, Mark, and John (12:1-8) tell this story at the beginning of their passion narratives, all three locating it in Bethany. Luke (7:36-50) tells a very different story of a prostitute anointing Jesus' feet at a Pharisee's house in Galilee; the fact that in both cases the host is called Simon is as likely to be due to coincidence[5] as to literary dependence. John's account, however, shares with Luke's the anointing of Jesus' feet rather than his head and the use of the woman's hair as a towel, while he is independent of Matthew and Mark in naming the woman as Mary (and underlining the identification in John 11:2), in locating the incident in her house[6] rather than that of Simon the leper, and in placing it before Jesus' ride to Jerusalem. The complex literary phenomena are probably best accounted for by two originally separate stories of a woman anointing Jesus, John being aware of elements of both but linking this story with the Bethany family in whom he had a special interest (John 11:1-45; 12:9-11).

The focus on an unnamed woman to the discomfiture of the disciples gives further expression to the gospel principle that the last will be first and the first last, and prepares us for the final act of the story, when it will be Jesus' women followers rather than the men who stay with him (27:55-56, 61; 28:1). The anonymity of this woman in Matthew and Mark is the more remarkable in that her deed is to be a perpetual memorial to her (v. 13). She is to be remembered, but she has no name! Jesus refers to her simply as "the woman" in v. 10 and twice as "this woman" in vv. 12 and 13. It seems that what she did, and its significance in that setting, is more important than her personal identity.[7]

And it was indeed a memorable act, an act of spontaneous extravagance which horrified the pragmatic disciples, but which Jesus defended as "lovely." Not for the first time, the disciples' conventional attitudes are found to be out of step with Jesus' thinking. Yet most readers feel some sympathy with them, and are equally taken aback by the apparently self-centered response of Jesus when he dismisses the prior claim of the poor. How can he call on one rich man to sell all he has in favor of the poor (19:21) and yet allow this woman to waste a year's wages on a personal cosmetic? But Jesus is not concerned with personal gratification, but with the symbolism of the act. To anoint him may have been intended merely as an act of social acceptance and gratification, but in this context the reader is likely to think of its symbol-

5. Simon was one of the commonest names in first-century Palestine (see on 4:18).

6. John's account is usually read in this sense, but Carson, 526, suggests that ἐποίησαν in John 12:2 could be a general reference to people in Bethany rather than specifically designating Lazarus's family as the hosts.

7. The popular speculation that she was Mary of Magdala is first found in Ephraem in the fourth century.

ism as marking him out as the Messiah, and that may well also have been in the woman's mind. That, however, is not the aspect which Jesus comments on. Whatever the woman's intention, she has in fact done for him what his executioners will not do, given him the wherewithal for a decent burial. So Jesus' interest is not in his present physical comfort, or even in his messianic status, but in his impending dishonorable death. The woman's extravagant loyalty offsets the shameful horror of crucifixion. That is why it must always be remembered, not simply as a model for uncalculating devotion (though it is certainly that) but as an affirmation of the value of his death from the point of view of faith.

It is a matter of priorities (cf. the rather different lesson on the priority of the spiritual over the mundane, also set in Bethany, in Luke 10:38-42). A definitive moment is upon them, and even the duty of helping the poor must take second place. Once this unique drama has been played out, the claims of the poor will rightly reassert themselves. It is because this unnamed woman has seized on that sense of special occasion that her act is to be remembered. Probably without realizing it, she has provided a pointer to the theology of the cross.

6-7 The scene is set at a meal in a supporter's house. For Bethany as the base for Jesus and his group during this week see on 21:17. Simon "the leper" is otherwise unknown. Presumably his nickname derived either from some family connection or from his having been previously cured of a skin infection (see p. 305, n. 17); someone with active "leprosy" could hardly have hosted a dinner. See above on the identity of the woman; her naming as Mary in John 12:3 depends on his different location for the meal, though Mary was also of course a resident of Bethany. Mark gives a fuller description of the unguent and its value (over three hundred denarii, a year's wages; so also John 12:5). The *myron* is perhaps oil of myrrh (see on 2:11), or a compound of it,[8] but the term was also used more generally for fragrant anointing oils. For perfumed oil as a cosmetic especially in contexts of celebration see Pss 23:5; 45:7-8; 104:15; Isa 61:3; Amos 6:6. Luke 7:46 indicates that oil for the head was an expected part of hospitality at a meal. But the most prominent use of oil in the OT, especially when poured over the head, was for the anointing of kings and priests to mark them out for their divinely approved office,[9] and the woman's act may have included a "messianic" connotation; at least the reader is likely to understand it so.

8-9 Again the disciples' instinctive reaction puts them at odds with Jesus; cf. their disapproval of those who brought the children in 19:13-14. That Jesus "noticed" (rather than "heard") their comment (v. 10) may suggest

---

8. Mark and John mention "nard," an expensive perfume imported from India.
9. For the liberal application of oil to the head of a priest cf. Ps 133:2.

that it was muttered rather than openly voiced; cf. Matthew's use of the same participle in 12:15; 16:8; 22:18, in each case with reference to thoughts or intentions not openly expressed. See above on 19:21 for the Jewish tradition of giving alms to the poor. It would be especially on the disciples' mind at this time since such charitable giving was an obligation particularly associated with pilgrimage to Jerusalem at the festivals[10] (cf. John 13:29). Perhaps they also recall Jesus' recent statement about the importance of acts of kindness to those in need (25:35-40).

10 What for the disciples was "waste" is for Jesus a "lovely" gesture. It may be overtranslation to render *kalos* here as "lovely," since Matthew seems to use *kalos* equally with *agathos* in the general sense of "good" (see p. 285, n. 5), and *kalos* was used for "good deeds" in 5:16. But the original sense of *kalos* as "beautiful," "fine" is still sometimes discernible in the NT period, and offers a powerful "aesthetic" contrast here to the disciples' pragmatic accusation of waste.

11 The thought (though not the wording) echoes the recognition of Deut 15:11 that "the poor will never disappear from the land." That comment is made in the context of the principal provision for poor relief in the law (Deut 15:1-11): even though ideally poverty should be eliminated among God's people (Deut 15:4), in practice the need will never go away. Nothing in Jesus' words detracts from that ethical and social demand, which in our global economy is even more pressing now than it was then. But in contrast with this permanent obligation, the opportunity to care for Jesus in his time of need will be very brief. His expectation of being "taken away" was expressed as early as 9:15, but now in v. 2 it has been given much more specific focus and a clear date has been set. This immediate and short-lived opportunity thus takes priority.

12 Anyone who had heard Jesus' announcement in v. 2 and who knew the reality of Roman crucifixion should have realized that he must expect to be denied the proper burial rituals which were so important among Jewish people (see below, p. 1088). It is possible that the woman had been there to hear those words and so had consciously planned to make good the lack of due respect to his body, but it is more likely that this is Jesus' own interpretation of what had been in her intention simply a spontaneous act of love and loyalty. John tells us that Jesus' body was in fact expensively prepared for burial in the traditional manner (John 19:39-40), while Mark, unaware of that tradition, speaks of the women's desire to make good the omission after he was buried (Mark 16:1-2). Matthew, perhaps aware of the tension between either of those traditions and this saying of Jesus, will say nothing on the subject.

10. J. Jeremias, *Jerusalem*, 129-30.

13 This saying stands alongside 24:14 as envisaging a world-wide[11] proclamation of the good news in the period after Jesus' death and resurrection, and so anticipating the instruction he will give to his disciples in 28:19-20.[12] See on 24:14 for this theme, and for what "this good news" may be understood to mean in the context of Jesus' own time. If the woman's anticipation of Jesus' burial is to be part of what is proclaimed, the significance of Jesus' death must itself be integral to the good news. Furthermore, for Jesus to speak of a continuing proclamation of "this good news" immediately after reflecting on his own impending death must indicate that his death is not the end: if Jesus were to remain dead and buried, where would the "good news" be? The resurrection, which has been an insistent element in Jesus' passion predictions (16:21; 17:9, 23; 20:19), is surely assumed here also. In this saying, unlike the one in 24:14, the proclamation of "this good news" is not linked with the coming of "the end"; it is simply an unlimited future prospect.

Current preaching of the Christian gospel seldom gives to the woman's act the place which Jesus says it deserves. In her anonymity she is not much remembered.

4. Judas Offers to Help the Priests (26:14-16)

14 *Then one of the Twelve, the one called Judas Iscariot, went to the chief priests* 15 *and said, "What will you give me, and I will hand him over to you?" And they agreed with him on*[1] *thirty silver coins.*

11. There is no obvious reason why the world should be κόσμος here and οἰκουμένη in 24:14; they seem to be effectively synonyms. See on 24:14 for the usage of ἡ οἰκουμένη; it might be argued that its potentially more limited sense better fits the pre-70 situation envisaged there, whereas here a wider scope for the gospel is suggested, but general usage does not support so clear a difference of meaning.

12. P. Foster, *Community,* 237-39, is right to point out that this saying does not specifically mention preaching to *Gentiles.* It might then be suggested that the good news is here envisaged as going to Jews of the diaspora. But as Foster recognizes, the balance of the rest of the gospel, and especially the explicit mention of "all nations" in 24:14 and 28:19, make such a reading improbable; here as in 24:14 Jesus looks beyond the temporary restriction to Israel (10:5-6; 15:24) to the period of universal proclamation which will follow his death and resurrection.

1. The verb ἵστημι includes within its wide range of meanings both "come to an agreement" and "weigh," and both meanings have been proposed here. The latter is probably the meaning in LXX Zech 11:12, the passage from which the thirty coins derive, where it translates Hebrew *šql,* "weigh," but BDAG 482a-b rightly point out that by NT times the use of coinage rather than weights of metal made this term literally inappropriate (it may have also been used nonliterally in the LXX of Zechariah), so that here the intended sense is probably "agree on," "strike a bargain."

16 *And from then on he was looking for a good opportunity to hand Jesus over.*

The devotion of the unnamed woman is sharply contrasted with the treachery of one of Jesus' inner circle, and her uncalculating generosity with his sordid bargaining. The reader has been prepared for this development not only by the repeated use of the verb *paradidōmi* ("hand over," "betray") in Jesus' predictions of what is to come (17:22; 20:18; 26:2) but also by the specific identification of Judas Iscariot in 10:4 as the one "who also betrayed him." For the translation of the verb see p. 374, n. 3. Here, as used by Judas himself in v. 15, it can hardly be meant to be self-condemnatory, but the reader knows well that in effect what is being talked about is betrayal. Indeed, when a follower of Jesus "hands him over" to his avowed enemies who are known to be plotting his death, it is hard to see what else it could mean. This has not, however, prevented some scholars from noting that there is a more specific term for betrayal, *prodidōmi,* and that with the single exception of Luke 6:16 the gospels do not use this term or its derivatives for what Judas did. So it has been suggested that while later Christian orthodoxy inevitably saw Judas as simply a traitor, and increasingly demonized him, the original reality may have been more nuanced. One of the more daring of these revisionist interpretations[2] argues that Judas saw himself as the honest broker, arranging a meeting between Jesus and his opponents with the hope that this might result in constructive dialogue; when this did not in fact happen, Judas was horrified at the result of his well-intentioned mediation, and this was the basis for his bitter remorse in 27:3-5. Whatever may be the merits of this as a historical reconstruction — and I have not yet seen evidence that it has been given much credence — it cannot stand as an exegesis of any of the gospel texts as we have them; even Mark, who is allegedly the least biased against Judas, gives no basis for such a positive view of his motives, and the role of Judas in the accounts of Jesus' arrest does not sound like the arrangement of an innocuous conference. What made Judas act as he did remains a fascinating area for speculation, and one which has been well exploited, but that he had decisively turned against Jesus and was now determined to help in his elimination seems beyond doubt as the consistent testimony of the gospels.

Among the proposed reasons for Judas's change of sides, it may be worth noting that Judas *may* have been the only non-Galilean member of this provincial movement (see on 10:4), and thus, in addition to perhaps resenting the leading role of Galilean fishermen, would have found himself in an awkward position when they came south and found themselves in confrontation with the Judean authorities. At any rate, it seems that his close association

2. W. Klassen, *Judas.*

with Jesus and his paradoxical values had led Judas to the conclusion that this was not the sort of movement he thought he had signed up to, and that far from being the national deliverer he had hoped for, Jesus now seemed determined to pursue a course inevitably destined to end in failure and defeat (as v. 12 has just powerfully underlined). His volte-face might then be seen as the logical conclusion to the way Peter instinctively responded to Jesus' original announcement of his mission in 16:21-23. Judas may even have come genuinely to believe (like Saul of Tarsus) that Jesus was a threat to Israel's national interests and religious tradition, in line with the later rabbinic polemic against Jesus as the one who "led Israel astray." For whatever reason (and it can only ever be guesswork), Judas had concluded that it was in his own best interest, and perhaps in the best interest of Israel, to dissociate himself from Jesus before it was too late. Few have been able to believe that so small a sum as thirty denarii (see below) would in itself have been sufficient to buy the loyalty of a man who had invested so much of his own life into the Jesus movement if he was not already disillusioned, and Matthew significantly describes the offer as preceding the agreement of the price.

The importance to the priests of an inside informer has already been indicated in vv. 4-5, and is underlined by the phrase "looking for *a good opportunity* to hand him over." It was a matter of letting the authorities know of Jesus' likely movements so that he could be arrested away from the crowds. The secluded hillside of Gethsemane would offer the ideal answer. There Judas will act as guide to the arresting party, as well as identifying Jesus to them in the dark. We shall note, too, that at the trial the high priest seems remarkably well informed about Jesus' alleged claims, more so than Jesus' recorded public statements would easily explain, and it may be that Judas's role as informer included passing on aspects of Jesus' private teaching as well.

The sum paid to Judas is mentioned only by Matthew, who will use it in 27:9-10 as the basis for a formula-quotation which consists of Zech 11:12-13 (where the same phrase occurs) and related texts. The same text is presumably alluded to here, inviting the reader to compare the "price" of Jesus with that of the rejected shepherd in Zech 11:4-14, who is a paradoxical messianic figure. See further the comments on 27:9-10. The insulting sum is ironically described in Zech 11:13 as a "noble price." Those with a close knowledge of the OT might also recall that thirty silver shekels was the compensation set for the loss of a slave in Exod 21:32,[3] but Matthew does nothing to draw attention to that further background, still less to the "twenty silver coins" for which Joseph was sold as a slave (Gen 37:28). The silver coins of

---

3. Cf. the same sum given as the "value" of an adult woman in Lev 27:4 (a man is worth fifty!).

Zech 11:12 were probably shekels, but in Roman Palestine "silver coins" would normally denote denarii;[4] if a denarius was a fair day's pay (see on 20:2), this is something like a month's wages, not a negligible sum (enough to buy a burial plot, 27:7) but surely not enough by itself to alter the direction of a person's whole life (see above). Whatever his motives, however, Judas will go down in history in the inglorious role of a paid informer.[5]

B. JESUS' LAST HOURS WITH HIS DISCIPLES (26:17-46)

Ever since the account of the calling of the four fishermen in 4:18-22 this has been the story not of Jesus alone but of Jesus and his disciples. Even where the focus has been firmly on the actions and teaching of Jesus himself, the disciples have been there as companions and audience, and increasingly, especially during the journey narrative in 16:21–20:34, Jesus has concentrated his attention on them as he prepares them for what lies ahead. Now that close association is about to be broken. In 26:56 the disciples will abandon him, and thereafter they will have no contact with him until after the resurrection in 28:16-20. Jesus will be left alone in the hands of his enemies to go through the experience of rejection, suffering, and death. But before he does so, there is one last opportunity to prepare the disciples for what is to come, both to help them to understand what his own sacrifice is all about and to alert them to the dangers they themselves will face and the pathetic role they are soon to play as deserters.

The context for this final instruction is the Passover meal (see below on v. 17 for its timing), for which this close-knit group of traveling companions forms the "family" group who share the ceremonial meal. It is the group's last meal together, but already the presence of the traitor casts a cloud over the Passover celebration, and when Jesus goes on to explain the meaning of his own approaching death, by means of a creative reinterpretation of the traditional Passover ceremonial, the atmosphere of foreboding is deepened. By the time the bewildered disciples reach Gethsemane they are already present with Jesus only in body, as they sleep while he struggles. They will be of no help when the crisis comes, and their physical desertion will inevitably follow.

But in the borrowed guestroom they have been given, through Jesus'

---

4. The Tyrian silver shekel (reckoned at the value of four denarii) was used for payment of the temple tax (see on 17:24), but the fact that money changers were needed (21:12) shows that this special currency was not in normal circulation. Even the denarius was not used by everyone (see introductory comments on 22:15-22), but a "silver" coin would normally be a denarius unless it was specifically destined for the temple treasury.

5. For an overview of scholarly discussion about all aspects of Judas see R. E. Brown, *Death,* 1394-1418.

demonstration that the coming events will not take him by surprise, and through his profound theological interpretation of the meaning of his coming death and of its benefits for them and "for many," the resources they will need to enable them to survive the crisis and eventually to rise above their own demoralizing failure. His last words at the supper in v. 29 will leave them with a vision of a brighter future in "the kingdom of my Father," and in v. 32 he will prepare them for a postresurrection reunion in Galilee.

1. Preparing the Passover Meal (26:17-19)

> 17 On the first day of Unleavened Bread the disciples came to Jesus and asked, "Where do you want us to prepare for you to eat the Passover meal?"[1] 18 He replied, "Go into the city to so-and-so's house[2] and say to him, 'The teacher says, "My time is near; I plan to hold[3] the Passover meal with my disciples at your house."'" 19 And the disciples did as Jesus had instructed them, and they prepared the Passover meal.

The commemorative meal, prescribed in Exod 12:1-27 as a "perpetual ordinance" for Israel in memory of the events of the exodus from Egypt, and developed in Jewish tradition into a carefully prescribed ritual (see p. 987, n. 12) with explanatory questions and answers accompanying the meal, was the high point of the annual celebration for Jewish families. The meal was normally eaten by a family or "household" group together (Exod 12:3-4), but any appropriate group could form such a "household" for the occasion; Jesus and the Twelve (his "true family," 12:46-50) would meet the requirement, the average group being about ten to twelve.[4] This was the purpose of their visit to Jerusalem, and it is clear from these verses that Jesus has already made his plans for how it is to be celebrated. This particular group would not differ outwardly from many other groups of pilgrims who had made arrangements

---

1. The three expressions φαγεῖν τὸ πάσχα (v. 17), ποιεῖν τὸ πάσχα (v. 18), and ἑτοιμάζειν τὸ πάσχα all clearly refer to the Passover meal, even though τὸ πάσχα can also be used for the whole Passover festival (as in v. 2) or for the Passover lamb (Mark 14:12a).

2. "So-and-so" translates ὁ δεῖνα, an idiomatic Greek expression for someone who was clearly identified but whose name the author does not wish to record or does not know, "Mr. X" (or sometimes when the name has been forgotten, "What's-his-name"). This is the only time it is used in the NT. It indicates that Jesus told them which house to go to; they were not to apply at random.

3. The Greek verb is present, literally "I do the Passover"; the event is still future, but Jesus has already made his plans.

4. J. Jeremias, *Jerusalem*, 83. *B. Pesaḥ.* 64b indicates that at a later stage ten was regarded as the minimum.

to eat the meal together in Jerusalem at that time, except for one striking difference: according to the chronology for which I shall argue in the comments on v. 17, they held it one day before the official date. Set within the Passover festival season, it was deliberately planned by Jesus as a Passover meal, but he knew that when the official time came the following evening, he would no longer be there to share it with them, and so he held it a day in advance. This in itself would give a special poignancy to the occasion, and what Jesus said once the meal began would lift it far out of the ordinary run of Passover celebrations.

17 Originally there was probably a one-day festival of Passover (Nisan 14) immediately followed by a seven-day festival of Unleavened Bread (Nisan 15-21). But by the first century the two had effectively merged into a single festival, which might be referred to as a whole either as "Passover" or as "Unleavened Bread" (since the bread used at the Passover meal was unleavened). The expression Matthew uses, "the first day of Unleavened Bread," should strictly mean Nisan 15, but in view of the looser popular usage just mentioned this cannot be pressed, and Mark 14:12 makes clear what the term means in this context by adding "when they used to sacrifice the Passover lamb," which identifies the day clearly as Nisan 14 (Exod 12:6).[5]

The Fourth Gospel states that at the time of Jesus' trial the Passover meal had not yet been eaten (John 18:28), and specifically describes the day of Jesus' trial and crucifixion as "the preparation of the Passover" (John 19:14); cf. John 13:1, where the last supper is dated "before the Passover festival." It is therefore generally agreed that John presents Jesus' last supper as taking place on the evening which began Nisan 14 (remember that the Jewish day ran from sunset to sunset), so that by the time the lambs were killed the following afternoon (in preparation for the Passover meal on the evening which began Nisan 15) Jesus was already on the cross. It has therefore been traditionally supposed that there is a chronological disagreement between John and the Synoptic Gospels as to the date of the last supper and therefore also of Jesus' trial and death, John dating it one day earlier than the Synoptic writers, who are understood to place the last supper at the official time for the

---

5. Josephus, *War* 5.99, speaks of "the fourteenth of the month Xanthicus" (the Macedonian term for what the Jews called Nisan) as "the day of Unleavened Bread." This usage corresponds to the fact that the removal of leaven from the houses began on the evening which *began* Nisan 14, i.e., the evening before the killing of the lambs, a day ahead of the official beginning of "Unleavened Bread" on Nisan 15 (*m. Pesah.* 1:1-3). See further Gundry, 524. A. G. Arnott, *BT* 35 (1984) 235-38, points out that the word "bread" is not in the Greek, and suggests that the confusion over dating might be eased by translating "the first day of unleavened (things)," but since "unleavened" is normally applied only to bread, this would not help very much; it is better to recognize the fluidity of terminology in ordinary usage.

Passover meal, the evening which began Nisan 15.[6] Scholars then take opposing sides as to whether the "Johannine" or the "Synoptic" chronology is more likely to represent the historical situation, and discuss why either John or the Synoptics should have wished to alter it.

It may seem foolhardy to question the validity of this complex and time-honored debate, but I believe that it is based on a Western cultural misunderstanding: in the Jewish day, which begins at sunset, the evening is the *beginning* of the day, not its ending as it is for us. So the Synoptic statement that the meal (which was eaten at night; see below) was prepared on Nisan 14 may be understood to mean that it was prepared and eaten during the evening and night which *began* Nisan 14, rather than that it was prepared late on Nisan 14 (before sunset) and eaten the next (Jewish) day, at the official time for the Passover meal on Nisan 15. This would be an equally natural way for a Jewish reader to understand their words; it is our unfamiliarity with the Jewish method of reckoning days which prevents Western readers from recognizing that the evening *preceding* the killing of the lambs is already the same day, Nisan 14. In that case they are describing the same day as the Fourth Gospel.[7] The last supper and the subsequent trial and death of Jesus all take place on the same (Jewish) day as the killing of the lambs in the afternoon which *concludes* Nisan 14 and thus on the (Jewish) day before the date for the official Passover meal. The last supper is, then, an *anticipated* Passover meal, in the Synoptics no less than in John.[8]

The debate is far too complicated to enter fully here.[9] I have surveyed

6. Some have attempted to reinterpret John's statements in order to make his account conform to a supposedly "Synoptic" chronology; for a good example see Carson, 528-32. Most interpreters regard such reinterpretations as a harmonizing device rather than as giving the natural sense of John's words. It will be seen from what follows that I believe that if harmonization is to be attempted it is more plausibly done by asking whether the Synoptic wording does in fact conflict with the Johannine chronology.

7. L. C. Boughton, *TynBul* 48 (1997) 257-59, argues similarly that the apparent difference in dating between John and the Synoptics is the result of difference in terminology, not of historical disagreement.

8. This conclusion is reached by C. J. Humphreys and W. G. Waddington, *TynBul* 43 (1992) 334-40, though without discussing the exegesis of this verse, on which the issue hangs. They confidently date the crucifixion on Friday, 3 April 33!

9. In particular I have omitted the various suggestions based on the assertion that different calendars were in operation at the time (Qumran v. Jerusalem; Sadducees v. Pharisees; Galilee v. Judea; Palestine v. the Diaspore) and that the Synoptics represent one calendrical scheme and the Fourth Gospel another. I have surveyed and commented on the proposals in *Vox Evangelica* 16 (1986) 44-47. I have also left out of account the earlier suggestions, now not so often heard, that this was not meant to be a Passover meal but some other sort of "fellowship meal" (the terms *haburah* and *qiddush* were often used in this connection, but without clearly agreed meanings).

the scholarly discussion and spelled out my view in an article in *Vox Evangelica* 16 (1986) 43-54, and more briefly but with reference to more recent discussion in my *Mark,* 559-62. Since there is no significant difference between Matthew and Mark with regard to this issue, I hope readers who wish to pursue the matter more fully may be willing to look at that discussion. In a nutshell, it seems to me that all the relevant external evidence[10] speaks consistently in favor of the "Johannine" dating, and that if due allowance is made for the fact that Nisan 14 began with the sunset which *preceded* the killing of the lambs, the Synoptic writers do not disagree with it.[11] Two objections have, however, been urged against this view, first that the preparations for so special a meal could hardly have been begun and concluded between sunset and the time when the meal was eaten, and second that the emphasis on this as a *Passover* meal is not compatible with its being held a day before the official date. Both objections may be briefly considered.

Many English versions foreclose the discussion by translating *opsias genomenēs* at the beginning of v. 20 by something like "when evening came." That rendering suggests that the meal must have been prepared before the "evening," that is, during the afternoon. But we have seen above, p. 565, n. 1, that *opsias genomenēs,* literally "when it had become late," is not so limited in meaning, and that at least in 14:23 it indicates a time long after dark, which in that case I translated "well into the night." The Passover meal was traditionally held at night (Exod 12:8; cf. *m. Pesaḥ.* 10:1), not in the early evening. If Jesus followed that tradition (as 1 Cor 11:23 says he did), there would be time to make preparations for the meal during the eve-

---

10. The following points are relevant: (a) Astronomical evidence strongly suggests that whereas Nisan 14 probably fell on a Friday (which all the gospels agree to be the day on which Jesus was executed) in either or both of A.D. 30 and 33, there is no date between A.D. 27 and 34 when it is likely that Nisan 15 fell on a Friday (for the data see C. J. Humphreys and W. G. Waddington, *TynBul* 43 [1992] 334-40); (b) there is a rabbinic tradition that Jesus was executed on "the eve of the Passover" (*b. Sanh.* 43a; cf. 67a); (c) *Gos. Pet.* 2(5) says that Pilate "delivered him to the people before the first day of unleavened bread, their festival"; (d) Paul's view of Jesus as "our Passover sacrificed" (1 Cor 5:7), while it does not demand that Jesus died on the same day as the lambs were killed, points strongly to that understanding. See further J. Finegan, *Chronology,* 292-96; G. Ogg, *Chronology,* 237-42; idem, in D. E. Nineham et al., *History and Chronology,* 92-96. For features within the Synoptic accounts themselves which suggest that Jesus died *before* Nisan 15 see J. Jeremias, *Words,* 62-84; Jeremias proposes arguments to neutralize all these pointers, but the fact that so much special pleading is required to support his case speaks for itself. J. Blinzler, *Trial,* 76-77, adds a further argument that the Passover amnesty (27:15) took place before the Passover meal, but this depends on an interpretation of *m. Pesaḥ.* 8:6 which is debatable (see below, p. 1056, n. 26).

11. Indeed, certain details in the Synoptic narratives also suggest this chronology; see below, p. 1089, n. 26, and comments on 27:62.

ning in order to eat it that night.[12] We need not suppose that Jesus' specially arranged meal, in advance of the official Passover celebration, would demand the detailed preparations required by the later mishnaic regulations as set out in *m. Pesaḥim* (see p. 987, n. 12), so that it would not take many hours to set it up. Mark 14:15 says that the room was already prepared for the meal before the disciples came, so that all they had to prepare was the food. If the meal was held a day early, it presumably had to be held without the Passover lamb (see below), which would normally be the centerpiece of the meal but which could not be officially slaughtered in the temple until the next day;[13] having no lamb to roast would also considerably reduce the time needed for preparation.

But was a meal held a day early a "Passover," especially if it therefore had no lamb? It should be noted that Jews who were not in Jerusalem could not slaughter lambs in the temple, and so for them presumably "there was no slaughter of a paschal lamb and a meal of unleavened bread had to suffice."[14] That does not seem to have prevented them from regarding the meal as the Passover. There is no need to invoke the later Christian symbolism of Jesus himself as the Passover lamb (so that no animal was needed) in order to understand how a meal deliberately held a day early could be in all other aspects a "Passover" but without the lamb. If there was a lamb, it is surprising that there is no mention of it[15] in any of the gospel accounts of the last supper.[16] Nor is it

12. It is therefore unnecessary to adopt the unnatural translation suggested by Albright and Mann, 319: "'*With reference to* the first day of Unleavened Bread' — i.e., the disciples were asking Jesus for guidance as to the procedures to be followed *for the next day*" (my italics).

13. M. Casey, *Sources,* 224, argues from *m. Zebaḥ.* 1:3 that early slaughter of lambs may have been allowed because the numbers were too great to cope with on a single afternoon. Cf. M. Casey, *TynBul* 48 (1997) 245-47; D. Instone-Brewer, *TynBul* 50 (1999) 295-97. But the considerations raised in the next paragraph tell against this possibility in the case of Jesus' "Passover" meal.

14. I. H. Marshall, *Last Supper,* 68. After the destruction of the temple the ritual slaughter of lambs became impossible, and a "Passover" meal without the lamb became the norm; so G. F. Moore, *Judaism,* 2:40-41; J. Jeremias, *Words,* 67; Schürer, 1:522-23. *M. Pesaḥ.* 10:3 indicates that the lamb was not part of the post-70 celebration.

15. M. Casey, *Sources,* 222-24, takes it for granted that φαγεῖν τὸ πάσχα actually means "to eat the passover *lamb.*" The usage of the gospels suggests, however, that τὸ πάσχα was used for the festival as a whole and more specifically for the meal, without necessarily singling out the lamb, even though of course in normal circumstances the lamb would have been its main component.

16. This fact is clearly an embarrassment to J. Jeremias in his argument that the last supper was a full Passover meal held on the official date; J. Jeremias, *Words,* 66-67. His argument from *m. Pesaḥ.* 5ff. seems to me to point the opposite way to what he intends: in the Mishnah there is nothing about the lamb (except in the historical reminis-

unlikely that Jesus, whom we have seen to be willing to challenge current scribal rules on other issues, should feel free to diverge from the official date for observing the festival.[17] Perhaps if circumstances had allowed, he would have followed the traditional pattern, but his words at the last supper make it clear that he knew that by the next night he would not be there to eat with his disciples, and, as Luke tells us, he was very keen to eat this last Passover with them (Luke 22:15). To describe this as a Passover meal correctly conveys Jesus' intention and the context within which his disciples would have understood it, even if it was unavoidably a day in advance.[18]

The disciples,[19] aware of Jesus' intention, and fulfilling their proper "disciple" role in looking after their teacher's practical arrangements, want to know where the meal is to be held. This was not a silly question. It was expected that the Passover meal would be eaten within "greater Jerusalem,"[20] and Jesus and his disciples are from a distant province and have no local property. Their temporary accommodation in Bethany is outside the city. So where can they eat together?

18-19 But, as with the earlier provision of the donkey (see on 21:2-3), Jesus has already made his plans.[21] Matthew's evasive formula (see p. 980, n. 2) does not disclose who this sympathetic householder was, but here is another incidental indication that Jesus already has contacts in the area, despite the impression conveyed by the (artificial?) Synoptic outline of the story that Jesus has never been to Jerusalem before (see also on 23:37). This unnamed householder is one who will recognize "the teacher" as a title of Jesus,[22] and who has agreed to make available to him a valuable meeting room at a time of maximum pressure on accommodation. The formula, "My time is near," sug-

---

cence mentioned in n. 14) because, as Jeremias himself points out, after A.D. 70 the meal was eaten without a lamb. The silence of the gospels about the lamb is best explained by the same cause.

17. This point is powerfully argued by N. T. Wright, *Victory,* 556. On pp. 557-59 he goes on to argue that Jesus' view of the significance of what was happening actually made it *necessary* that his Passover should be differentiated from the routine celebration; it was a deliberate alternative.

18. If I may quote my own analogy (*Vox Evangelica* 16 [1986] 54): "We find no difficulty in describing as a 'birthday party' a ceremony held for practical reasons a day or more in advance of the 'official' date, even if it necessarily lacks some of the presents etc. which will follow at the proper time."

19. All of them, apparently, in Matthew's version, though Mark 14:13 says only two were sent to make preparations.

20. See p. 771 and the comments on 21:17

21. Mark 14:13-15 gives a fuller picture of the prearrangement.

22. Because in Matthew disciples address Jesus as κύριε rather than διδάσκαλε, Hagner, 2:765, suggests that this man "may not have been a follower of Jesus"; in that case he was presumably a less closely associated well-wisher.

gests that he may also have been privy to Jesus' announcements to his disciples of his coming passion. Is it also a covert explanation of why Jesus plans to hold his Passover meal before others (see comments on v. 17)? For "my time" (*kairos*, usually a climactic or special time, as in 8:29; 13:30; 21:34) cf. "the hour has arrived" in v. 45, and the frequent Johannine references to Jesus' "hour": this is the time for the fulfillment of a predetermined plan.[23]

2. Jesus' Last Meal with His Disciples (26:20-30)

20 *Later on*[1] *he sat at table with the twelve disciples.*[2]

21 *And as they were eating, he said, "I tell you truly that one of you will betray*[3] *me." 22 And they were horrified,*[4] *and every one of them began saying to him, "You don't mean me, do you, Lord?" 23 He replied, "The one who has dipped his hand in the bowl together with me is the one who will betray me. 24 The Son of Man is indeed*[5] *going away as it is written about him, but woe to that man by whom the Son of Man is betrayed; it would be good for that man if he had not been born." 25 Judas, who was betraying him,*[6] *spoke up*[7] *and asked, "You don't mean me, do you, Rabbi?" Jesus replied, "You have said it."*

26 *As they were eating, Jesus took bread, and when he had said a blessing,*[8] *he broke it and gave it to the disciples, and said, "Take this*

---

23. See D. P. Senior, *Passion,* 57-63, for the sense of eschatological fulfillment inherent in Matthew's distinctive use of καιρός here (and of ὥρα in v. 45).

1. See on v. 17 for the likely time of beginning the meal, and p. 565, n. 1, for the meaning of ὀψίας γενομένης. Here it refers to a time after they have made the preparations, and presumably conforms to the normal practice of eating the Passover meal at night, not early in the evening.

2. As in 20:17, many MSS and versions have simply "the Twelve" here, in agreement with the parallel in Mark 14:17. As noted there, Matthew tends not to use "the Twelve" as a title as much as Mark and Luke, so perhaps here, too, the distinctive longer reading is original.

3. For this meaning of παραδίδωμι see p. 374, n. 3.

4. The same phrase as in 18:31, and as "utterly dismayed" in 17:23.

5. The μὲν . . . δέ . . . construction emphasizes the equal validity of two contrasting thoughts, that while the event is foreordained, the responsibility of the one who perpetrates it is no less real.

6. The present tense of the participle reminds the reader that Judas's act of betrayal has already begun in vv. 14-16.

7. See p. 439, n. 1; p. 574, n. 9; p. 642, n. 4. The "answer" here is not to what Jesus has just said but to the pronouncement of v. 21, but the wording highlights Judas's individual response over against the general response in v. 22.

8. For the meaning of εὐλογέω in connection with the host's role at a meal see on 14:19 and p. 562, n. 18.

and eat it. This is my body." 27 And he took a⁹ cup, and when he had given thanks, he gave it to them, saying, "Drink from it, all of you. 28 For this is my blood of the covenant¹⁰ which is being poured out for many, for the forgiveness of sins. 29 But I tell you, from now on I will never drink from this fruit of the vine until that day when I drink it new with you in the kingdom of my Father."

30 And when they had sung [the psalms],¹¹ they went out onto the Mount of Olives.

The framing verses 20 and 30 mark the beginning and end of the meal; between them two paragraphs (vv. 21-25 and 26-29) tell of two significant pronouncements, each made by Jesus "as they were eating." The Passover meal was marked by explanatory dialogue (Exod 12:26-27) which probably already by the first century had developed into a set question from the son followed by an expository response from the father (the Passover haggadah), at the time of the second of the four cups of wine prescribed for the meal.¹² Jesus' second pronouncement in vv. 26-29 fits that setting, as it explains the significance of elements of the meal (bread and wine) in a context of redemptive sacrifice, though in a way quite different from what the father would normally be expected to say at Passover. But Jesus' first pronouncement, concerning his imminent betrayal, is not directly linked with the symbolism of the meal. It is a matter which Jesus wishes to bring into the open to prepare his disciples for what is to come. Insofar as it focuses on the necessary preliminary to his death, it provides the background for the following pronouncement in which that death is the central theme.

The symbolism of bread and wine is directly linked to Jesus' ap-

---

9. The MSS are divided over whether the reference is to "a cup" or "the cup," but it is more likely that the latter would be inserted under the influence of liturgical familiarity than that the article would be dropped.

10. Many MSS and patristic citations add "new" to "covenant," under the influence of the liturgical tradition represented by Luke 22:20 and 1 Cor 11:25; again it is most unlikely that the adjective would be dropped.

11. The verb ὑμνέω, used here without an object, does not specify what was sung, though the verb tends to be used in more formal settings. For the likely content of their "singing" see the comments below.

12. *M. Pesah.* 10:4. It is of course uncertain whether the form of Passover observance set out in the Mishnah (*Pesah.* 10) represents the accepted practice at the time of Jesus, but most commentators assume that it would have been the same in essence, even if not always in detail. See the discussion by J. Jeremias, *Words,* 84-88, and by G. J. Bahr, *NovT* 12 (1970) 181-202. See also R. Routledge, *TynBul* 53 (2002) 210-20, for an account of what were "probably" the elements in a first-century Passover meal (drawn from the Mishnah, but with reference also to some later material), with suggestions as to how details of the gospel accounts might fit into them.

proaching death, which is "for many, for the forgiveness of sins," language which clearly recalls the earlier pronouncement in 20:28 with its echo of the vicarious death of God's servant "for many" in Isa 53, but which now makes more explicit that it is deliverance from "sins" which is at the heart of that redemption. As the disciples are instructed to eat the bread and drink the wine which are Jesus' body and blood, it is clear that they are among the "many" who are to benefit from his death, but the use of "for many" rather than "for you" deliberately extends the benefit more widely than to the immediately present disciple group. All this is said in the context of the Passover meal, when the father would normally have expounded the story of the redemption from Egypt which marked the original formation of Israel as the people of God. The implication is startling, and is underlined by the phrase "my blood of the covenant," echoing the original covenant ceremony at Sinai (Exod 24:8): Jesus' death is the redemptive sacrifice which is now to inaugurate a new covenant community. While Matthew does not directly echo Jeremiah's new covenant prophecy with its promise of the forgiveness of sins (Jer 31:31-34), its thought cannot be far from his mind when he writes of Jesus' "blood of the covenant." Here, too, is the fulfillment of the new exodus typology which we have noted in Matthew's application to Jesus of exodus-related texts especially in 2:15 and 4:1-11, but now with the addition of a shocking new dimension: Jesus is not only the new Israel, the focus of the restored people of God, but himself also the sacrifice by which it is to be achieved.

But Jesus' vision is not confined to his coming death, central as that is. He looks beyond it in v. 29 to renewed fellowship with his disciples in "my Father's kingdom." As the earlier passion predictions have consistently insisted, death is to be followed by new life (16:21; 17:9, 23; 20:19). Jesus will himself still be at the heart of the new people of God which his death has created.

Matthew includes no words to indicate that the eating and drinking is to continue as a Christian ritual (that is made explicit probably in Luke 22:19 and certainly in 1 Cor 11:24-25), but by the time this gospel was written there would have been no need to spell that out within the Christian community, whose worship had from the earliest days centered on the reenactment of these symbolic acts and words of Jesus. The four verbs concerning the bread ("took," "blessed," "broke," "gave") which we have seen repeated carefully in the accounts of the feeding miracles in 14:19 and 15:36 (see comments there) represent a familiar liturgical sequence, and the further verb "gave thanks" (as in 15:36) associated with "took" and "gave" in relation to the wine completes the range of eucharistic language.

20 For the time when the meal began see above on v. 17. It would be sometime after dark, as was normal for a Passover meal, but in time to allow it to be completed before midnight (*m. Pesah.* 10:9). There was to be no sleep that night, as the story takes us straight from the meal to Gethsemane and to the arrest of Jesus and the hearing before the Sanhedrin, which will be concluded in time for Jesus to be taken before Pilate early on the morning of Nisan 14, the day when the Passover lambs would be slaughtered in the temple.

The verb *anakeimai* ("sat at table") is used especially for more formal or festive meals, when the diners reclined in the Roman style on couches around a central table.[13] Matthew's words suggest that, as Western art has generally assumed, only thirteen people were at the table, which would be a typical size for a Passover meal. But other people, including women (27:55), had followed Jesus from Galilee, and Passover meals were normally family occasions including women and children, so it has been suggested that this, too, might have been a larger group of Jesus' supporters.[14] But Matthew gives no hint of the presence of others,[15] and it is apparently to the Twelve specifically that the next words are addressed.

21-23 Jesus has spoken of being "handed over" or "betrayed"[16] to his opponents in 17:22; 20:18-19; 26:2, but has so far given no indication of who is to be the agent, even though Matthew has left his readers in no doubt (10:4; 26:14-16). Given the close-knit nature of the group of the Twelve, especially during the period of traveling from Galilee to Jerusalem in chs. 16–20, it is a deeply disturbing revelation, especially when given "as they were eating" together, an act which especially symbolized close association. The incredulous form of the question[17] perhaps indicates an outraged sense of loyalty, though the disciples' constant failure to match up to Jesus' high expectations may also have engendered an element of self-doubt, which Jesus will shortly fuel with his pronouncement in v. 31. Jesus' reply in v. 23 simply repeats more graphically (and possibly with an echo of Ps 41:9, more clearly alluded to in Mark 14:18)[18] the prediction of betrayal from within the inner

---

13. The synonymous verbs ἀνακεῖμαι and ἀνακλίνομαι have appeared in 8:11; 9:10; 22:10-11; 26:7, all of which refer to special meals; see also on 14:19 for the suggestive use of this terminology when Jesus fed the five thousand. For the usage see J. Jeremias, *Words,* 48-49; R. T. France, *NIDNTT* 3:587-89. The description in John 13:23, 25; 21:20 of the Beloved Disciple as reclining against Jesus' chest at the last supper confirms a *triclinium*-type arrangement (*pace* Leonardo da Vinci and most Western art!).

14. So M. Casey, *Sources,* 227-28; Casey estimates that about thirty may have been present.

15. *Pace* Gundry, 525, πρὸς σέ in v. 18 does not necessarily imply that the unnamed host would be present at the meal.

16. For the meaning of παραδίδωμι see p. 374, n. 3, and the comments on 17:22; 20:18-19.

17. A question introduced by μή expects the answer No, and the emphatic form μήτι used here (as in 7:16; 12:23) makes the idea sound even more far-fetched: "Surely not!"

18. See D. J. Moo, *The OT,* 235-40, for the influence of Ps 41:9 on the gospel passion narratives.

circle; they have been in the habit of sharing meals together, where each dipped his bread into a common dish to scoop up the sauce and herbs. "The one who" is thus general rather than specific; it could be any one of them. Even in the Fourth Gospel, which speaks of a piece of food handed to Judas apparently as a specific identification, the disciples are said to remain unaware of his purpose (John 13:21-30). In the Synoptics there is no such identification, and we may reasonably assume that if Judas had been clearly identified, the others would have tried to prevent him.

24 This carefully balanced statement (see p. 986, n. 5) provides a classic expression of the paradox which runs throughout biblical thinking, that what happens according to the declared will of God is nonetheless also a free and responsible human act; neither truth invalidates the other (cf. 18:7 for a similar balance). Jesus has predicted his betrayal and death not as the natural outcome of a political process but as the fulfillment of a scriptural pattern. The earlier passion predictions in Matthew have not been specifically attributed to what "is written" (contrast Mark 9:12; Luke 18:31), but such statements have increasingly been colored by the thought of Isa 53 (see on 16:21 and 20:28), and in 21:42 the pattern of Jesus' rejection and vindication has been traced to "the scriptures." His conviction that his suffering and death will fulfill a scriptural mandate is now made explicit and will be further underlined in vv. 31, 54, and 56. But that does not mean that the person who initiates the process is merely a pawn in the divine game. He has made a free decision and must take the consequences, as 27:3-10 will demonstrate. See on 11:21-22 for the "woe" formula, and compare 18:6 for another comparison of a worse and a better fate where, as here, the worse is left unspecified (contrast 18:8-9, where the two fates are explicit). That it was better not to have been born was a conventional way of describing the worst possible fate; see Keener, 626, for examples.

25 Judas's question exactly matches that of the other disciples in v. 22, except that in place of the normal disciple address "Lord" he uses "Rabbi," the Jewish form of "Teacher," a title which in Matthew (unlike Mark) is never used by Jesus' other disciples (in Greek or Hebrew), but is used of Jesus by people outside the group. Judas's language, here and in v. 49,[19] thus befits his status as no longer a true part of the disciple group. We know from vv. 14-16 that Judas's question is insincere, since he is already contracted to betray Jesus; he merely echoes the other disciples so as not to appear out of line. Perhaps he hopes that while Jesus is aware that he has a traitor in his inner circle, he has not yet worked out who it is.

19. These are the only uses of the Hebrew form "Rabbi" in Matthew as an address to Jesus. S. Byrskog, *Jesus,* 284-87, discusses ῥαββί as "a negative titular label in Matthew."

We are probably intended to understand Jesus' reply as spoken privately (see above on vv. 21-23). "You have said it" is an affirmative response in Greek as it is in English, though on the other occasions when Jesus will use this or a closely similar formula we shall note that it is a *qualified* affirmative, not in the sense that the truth of the preceding proposal is in doubt, but that what the questioner understands by the words is not the way Jesus himself sees it (see comments on 26:64; 27:11). Here the affirmation does not need to be qualified, but the use of this formula rather than a simple "It is you" may be a way of conveying that Judas's question, though insincere, has in fact expressed the truth about his intentions. Like Jesus' opponents in 21:31 and 21:41, he has unintentionally pronounced his own condemnation.

Matthew does not tell us at what point Judas left the group. John 13:30 says that it was during the meal, but in Matthew the immediate sequence from this question and answer to the account of Jesus' words over the bread and wine (which do not feature in John's account) more naturally suggests that Judas was still there then. Since Judas's role was to lead the arresting party to Jesus, we would naturally suppose that he left the group after they arrived at Gethsemane, so that he knew exactly where to take the posse. But the phrase "as was his custom" in Luke 22:39 may suggest that Judas would have known in advance where they would be, and John 18:2 asserts that Gethsemane was their regular rendezvous. The old question whether Judas shared in the "eucharistic" bread and wine[20] thus remains open, but Matthew is most naturally read as indicating that he did.

26 In this ominous setting of betrayal and "going away," Jesus introduces a creative new element to the traditional Passover ritual; his memorable words and actions have become the basis for Christian worship ever since. For the sequence of four "eucharistic" verbs see the introductory comments on 14:13-21, and also p. 562, n. 18, for the meaning of the "blessing." The form of words traditionally used was "Blessed are you, Lord our God, king of the world, who bring forth bread from the earth." At a Passover meal the bread Jesus took would be unleavened, unlike the leavened loaves presumably used at the feeding miracles in 14:17-20 and 15:34-37. The traditional Passover ritual included an explanation of the meaning of the unleavened bread and herbs (*m. Pesaḥ.* 10:3-5), and Jesus takes that opportunity to introduce a new level of symbolism. The Passover bread did not directly symbolize the killing of the lamb, but when Jesus identifies it as his body,[21] the symbolism of death is clearly intended,[22] and the shedding of

---

20. See R. E. Brown, *Death,* 1398-99.

21. Cf. the reference in v. 12 to his "body" (the same word) prepared for burial.

22. This is disputed by D. B. Carmichael, *JSNT* 42 (1991) 45-67, who takes up the controversial argument of D. Daube that the bread Jesus took was the *afikoman* (men-

blood in v. 28 will confirm this. In breaking the bread he symbolizes his own death, and makes it unmistakably clear that his predictions of death in Jerusalem are to be literally fulfilled. The vicarious words "given for you" are not found here in Matthew and Mark (see Luke 22:19; 1 Cor 11:24),[23] but in telling his disciples to take the bread and eat it (see below on vv. 27-28 for the shocking nature of the symbolism) Jesus implies that his death is in some sense for their benefit. Just as eating the Passover lamb identified the participant with the redemption from Egypt, eating the bread and drinking the wine convey the benefits of Jesus' redemptive death to those who share his table. Only Matthew includes the explicit commands to "eat" and "drink" (though these are of course implied by the giving of the bread and the cup in the other accounts), perhaps reflecting the words used by the eucharistic minister in his own church context, as in subsequent eucharistic liturgies.

Subsequent Christian debate about the sense in which the bread "is" Jesus' body and the wine "is" his blood (v. 28) cannot be settled by the choice of the verb, since "is" can have a range of meaning from complete identity (surely impossible when Jesus is physically *holding* the bread) to symbolic equivalence; for a suggestive example of the latter sense from within this gospel cf. the statements "the sower is the Son of Man," "the field is the world," and the like in 13:36-39 (similarly in 13:19-23).[24] It is also relevant that the most vivid NT language about eating and drinking Jesus' flesh and blood is found in John 6:48-58, where the context makes no reference to literal bread and wine.

---

tioned but variously translated in *m. Pesaḥ.* 10:8), which Daube, following a proposal of R. Eisler, takes to be a piece of unleavened bread reserved until the end of the meal and eaten as a symbol of the Messiah, the "coming one" (Greek ἀφικόμενος). Daube therefore argues that the bread was Jesus' self-revelation as the Messiah, and that the idea that it represented his death arose later through association with the originally unconnected interpretation of the wine. The thesis is intriguing, but offers many areas for debate, not least over the original nature and meaning of the *afikoman.* It is also questionable whether "my *body*" would be an appropriate way to express this symbolism.

23. There are several verbal variations between the four NT accounts of Jesus' "words of institution" (not to mention an array of textual variations within each account, often aiming to assimilate the different wordings), perhaps representing developments in liturgical usage in the period before they were compiled. For a discussion of their relative originality see I. H. Marshall, *Last Supper,* 43-51; Davies and Allison, 3:465-69; B. D. Smith, *ZNW* 83 (1992) 166-86. The variations do not, however, affect the essential symbolism of the bread and wine as Jesus' body and blood and the assertion that to eat and drink them symbolizes participation in the benefits of his death.

24. Since Jesus' Aramaic words would probably have had no expressed verb, any theological deductions drawn from the Greek wording must, in any case, be treated with care.

27-28 The wording indicates a single cup from which they all drank; rabbinic evidence indicates the use of individual cups at Passover, but it is not clear what practice was normally followed in the first century.[25] The traditional formula of benediction for wine was "Blessed are you, Lord our God, king of the world, who create the fruit of the vine." The tradition (see p. 987, n. 12) was that four cups of wine were drunk at the Passover meal. According to *m. Pesaḥ.* 10:4 it was when the second cup was mixed that the explanatory dialogue took place. Jesus' words about the cup of wine may have been an extension of or a substitute for that traditional dialogue, or he may have given his own interpretive statement at the time of the third cup, when a benediction was traditionally given (*m. Pesaḥ.* 10:7). Matthew, Mark, and Paul mention only one cup; Luke (if we accept the longer text of Luke 22:17-20) mentions two, the eucharistic words being spoken over the second and Luke's equivalent to Matt 26:29 over the first. All the NT accounts are thus presumably selective descriptions, focusing only on the words of specifically Christian interest within the traditional Passover context.

By identifying the cup of wine as "my blood poured out" Jesus adds to the symbolism of the broken bread in v. 26: it is his own imminent death that is the basis of his new interpretation of the Passover. The blood of the Passover lamb featured prominently in the original Passover ritual (Exod 12:7, 13, 22-23), but now it will be Jesus' blood which is his people's salvation. But the lamb's blood was smeared on the doorposts, certainly not drunk; the idea would have been unthinkable to a Jew, for whom the consumption of *any* blood was strictly forbidden. Yet now the disciples, who have just been invited to "eat Jesus' body," are also invited to "drink Jesus' blood." Long familiarity with eucharistic language has blunted the profoundly shocking nature of this imagery, which conjures up ideas of both human sacrifice and cannibalism, as well as overriding the Mosaic taboo on consuming blood. It can be a salutary experience to hear the reactions of those outside the Christian tradition when they first encounter such language.[26] The effect on these Jewish disciples when it was first presented to them in that already highly charged atmosphere can only be imagined. But within a few decades the imagery had become familiar and acceptable enough to be expressed in quite starkly "cannibalistic" terms in John 6:48-58, though with due acknowledgment of its inevitable offensiveness to non-Christian Judaism.

The words by which Jesus explains this extraordinary idea combine three phrases which together draw out the redemptive significance of his

25. See I. H. Marshall, *Last Supper,* 63.
26. For a graphic example see J. Fenton, *Theology* 94 (1991) 414-23; one need not buy into Fenton's eccentric explanation in order to sense the reality of the problem.

death.[27] (a) "Blood of the covenant" directly echoes Exod 24:8[28] (and cf. Exod 24:6 for the "pouring out" of that blood) and so recalls the original basis of Israel's life as the special people of God;[29] mention of "the covenant" also recalls Jeremiah's prophecy (Jer 31:31-34) that at the heart of God's restoration of his people there would be a "new covenant," grounded in a new relationship of "knowing God" and in the forgiving and forgetting of their sins.[30] (b) "Poured out for many" recalls the "many" who are repeatedly referred to in Isa 53:11-12 as the beneficiaries of the suffering and death of the servant of God, an allusion already familiar to us from 20:28 (see comments there), where again it was specifically linked to the purpose of Jesus' death; here the Isa 53 allusion is further suggested by the verb "poured out," which is used in Isa 53:12 of the servant "pouring out[31] his life to death."[32] (c) The final phrase, "for the forgiveness of sins," not only recalls the servant's death for the sins of his people (Isa 53:5-6, 8, 10, 11, 12) but also further reinforces the allusion to Jeremiah's new covenant prophecy, where the basis of this new relationship is that "I will forgive their wickedness, and will remember their sins no more"; it also recalls to the reader the original statement of Jesus' mission in 1:21, to "save his people from their sins."[33]

There is thus a rich mixture of allusive elements in these words. The result is the most comprehensive statement in Matthew's gospel of the redemptive purpose and achievement of Jesus' death. And by expressing it in terms of a "covenant," a relationship between God and his people, Jesus has directed attention to the new community which is to result from his redemp-

---

27. See D. J. Moo, *The OT,* 301-11, for an analysis of the OT sacrificial language underlying this saying.

28. See my *Jesus and the OT,* 66-67. An additional echo of Zech 9:11 is quite possible; in that case a link is established with a further messianic prophecy, the one Jesus has already enacted by his ride to Jerusalem (21:4-5). But the allusion to Exod 24:8 is generally agreed to be primary.

29. D. C. Allison, *Moses,* 260-61, argues that the interpretation in Heb 9:15-22 of Exod 24:6-8 as a model for the sacrifice of Jesus derives from meditation on Jesus' words at the last supper.

30. M. Knowles, *Jeremiah,* 207-9. See above, p. 987, n. 10, for the probability that Matthew's text did not originally contain here the word "new," which would have made this allusion even more obvious, as in Luke 22:20; 1 Cor 11:25.

31. The LXX verb παραδίδωμι, a more prosaic rendering of the graphic Hebrew image of "pouring out" or "laying bare" (*'ārâ*). See my *Jesus and the OT,* 244, n. 18, for the meaning of the verb. The pouring out of blood, which represented the giving of life, was a prominent element in OT sacrificial ritual.

32. For the influence of Isa 53 on the wording here see my *Jesus and the OT,* 121-23; D. J. Moo, *The OT,* 127-32.

33. D. C. Allison, *Moses,* 258-59, adds that while Exod 24:8 does not itself speak of the forgiveness of sins, this aspect is added to Moses' Sinai sacrifice in the targums.

tive death. Here then is the essential theological basis for that new community of the restored people of God which this gospel has increasingly set before us as the result of Jesus' ministry. It is as people are associated with him and the benefits of his saving death that they are confirmed as members of the newly reconstituted people of God.

29 There is a striking contrast between vv. 26-28, with their focus on imminent death, and this final pronouncement which, while it recognizes the end of Jesus' earthly life (no more drinking of wine), looks forward to a triumphant future for Jesus and his disciples together in "the kingdom of my Father." Their companionship, which will so soon be broken by death, is to be restored. The wine[34] which is a symbol of death will also be the focus of future rejoicing. New wine is a powerful OT symbol of joyful well-being (e.g., Gen 27:28; Deut 33:28; Prov 3:10; Amos 9:13). Jesus has used it in 9:17 as a symbol of the new life his disciples enjoy in contrast with the old wine-skins of religious tradition. Here it speaks of the life of the kingdom of God, understood perhaps (as in 8:11-12; see comments there) as the messianic banquet. This saying does not specify when this future drinking of wine will take place, but "new" is a word often used in connection with the messianic fulfillment and ultimate salvation.[35] It is therefore unlikely that Jesus is looking forward only to the forty days during which he will be with them again on earth before his ascension (Acts 1:3; 10:41).[36] "The kingdom of my Father" refers rather to the heavenly fulfillment of God's purpose of blessing for his people. But the phrase "from now on" (for which see on 26:64, and cf. 23:39) indicates that this new situation is now imminent; the life of heaven is already breaking in. The strong negative *ou mē*, "I will never," is used to underline the certainty of Jesus' vision of what is to come; it is overexegesis to find in it a vow of abstinence to account for Jesus' refusal of wine on the cross (27:34).[37]

---

34. "Fruit of the vine" is a traditional term used in the formal thanksgiving for wine (*m. Ber.* 6:1).

35. J. Behm, *TDNT* 3:449; A. M. Ambrozic, *Kingdom,* 189-91. The wine at the messianic banquet will be well aged according to Isa 25:6, but this formal discrepancy falls well within the tolerance of metaphorical language. 1QSa (1Q28a) 2:17-20 looks forward to drinking new wine with the Messiah.

36. This view, which has some patristic support, was held by Karl Barth, according to C. E. B. Cranfield, *Mark,* 428.

37. So J. Jeremias, *Words,* 207-18; M. Bockmuehl, *JTS* 49 (1998) 571-72, speaks of it specifically as a "Nazirite vow." Contra J. A. Ziesler, *Colloquium* 5/1 (1972) 12-14; 6/1 (1973) 49-50. See further A. M. Ambrozic, *Kingdom,* 191-95. D. Daube, *Rabbinic Judaism,* 330-31, suggests another nuance: Jesus is declining the normal fourth, celebratory cup of the Passover meal, which must wait until the fulfillment of God's kingship; so also D. Instone-Brewer, *Traditions,* 1:83.

30 The Passover meal traditionally ended with the chanting[38] of the latter part of the Hallel (Pss 113–118), and that is the probable reference of "singing" (*hymneō;* see p. 987, n. 11) here. According to *m. Pesah.* 10:6-7, Pss 113–114 (or just Ps 113 in the school of Shammai) were chanted after the second cup of wine, the remainder over the fourth. "The Mount of Olives" covers a wide area east of the city, but v. 36 will narrow the reference to a place on its western slope which, unlike Bethany on the other side of the hill, fell within the extended boundaries of Jerusalem recognized for the observance of Passover. It is possible that this is the place where, according to Luke 21:37, Jesus and his disciples had regularly camped "on the Mount of Olives" during the week, but see on 21:17, where I suggest that Luke's phrase may rather refer to Bethany, which Matthew understands to be their regular campsite.

3. Jesus Predicts the Disciples' Failure (26:31-35)

31 *Then Jesus said to them, "All of you will be caused to stumble[1] because of[2] me tonight, for it is written,*

'I will strike the shepherd, and the sheep of the flock will be scattered.'

32 *But after I have been raised, I will go ahead of[3] you into Galilee."*

33 *Peter replied, "If they are all caused to stumble because of you, I will never stumble."* 34 *Jesus said to him, "I tell you truly that to-*

---

38. M. Casey, *Sources,* 222, reminds us that this was not like our hymn singing: "This did not sound like Handel's *Messiah.* To our ears, it would be a strange, loud and raucous noise."

1. Here and in v. 33 I have translated σκανδαλίζομαι literally, in order to draw attention to this frequently repeated metaphor (cf. especially 11:6; 13:21, 57; 15:12; 18:6-9; 24:10). See the comments below for the nature of the "stumbling."

2. The Greek preposition, here and in v. 33, is ἐν, and it has been suggested that its sense is instrumental, "by me" (so K. Stendahl, *School,* 82); but "by me" would suggest that Jesus has deliberately caused them to stumble, which is most unlikely to be Matthew's meaning. The same preposition follows σκανδαλίζομαι in 11:6 and 13:57; in each case Jesus is the potential object of misunderstanding but does not actively promote it.

3. As in 2:9 (see note there), it would be possible to translate προάγω as "lead," a sense which would fit well with the preceding metaphor of the shepherd and the flock. But Matthew's other uses of προάγω (14:22; 21:9, 31) do not support the sense "lead," and the narrative in 28:16-17 will indicate that the disciples have made their own way to Galilee and see Jesus for the first time when they get there (as indeed the instructions at 28:10 also envisage), rather than having been led there by him. In 28:7 the present tense of the verb cannot refer to Jesus "leading" the disciples, who at that point have not yet even been informed of his resurrection.

*night, before the cock crows, you will deny me three times." 35 Peter
replied, "Even if I have to die with you, I will never deny you." All the
disciples also said the same thing.*

The sense of foreboding which has resulted from Jesus' words at the supper
about betrayal and death is now underlined as the group makes its way out of
the city. But the focus is now not so much on what is to happen to Jesus but
on the effect it will have on his disciples. The scriptural pattern which is to be
fulfilled includes not only his own death but also their failure, and the imagery of shepherd and flock shows how closely the two are related. Their inability to grasp the seriousness of the situation shows up by contrast Jesus'
own awareness and acceptance of his messianic destiny.

This discouraging scene contains three predictions of Jesus whose literal fulfillment the reader will later be invited to notice, and thus to reflect on
how Jesus, apparently the victim of circumstances, is in fact in full control of
what is happening. The prediction of the scattering of the disciples will be
fulfilled very soon in v. 56. The prediction of a postresurrection meeting in
Galilee will be twice repeated in 28:7, 10 and fulfilled in the gospel's closing
scene in 28:16-20. It serves to remind the reader that the hostility and apparent triumph of Jerusalem is not the end of the story. But alongside that hopeful note for the future stands Jesus' detailed prediction of how Peter will first
succumb to pressure, and again we shall be invited in 26:69-75 to reflect on
how precisely that, too, is to be fulfilled. Jesus, informed by the prophetic
model, will not be taken by surprise. Here, by alerting his disciples to what is
to come, he aims to prepare them for the shock not only of his own arrest and
execution but also of their own inability to stand with him when the test
comes.

At the supper Jesus spoke of betrayal by one disciple (vv. 21-25); now
he speaks of desertion by all of them, and of denial by Peter. There is thus a
sequence of predictions of the failure of disciples (Judas, vv. 21-25; the
Twelve, v. 31; Peter, v. 34), which will all be fulfilled in the same sequence in
the following narrative (Judas, vv. 47-50; the Twelve, v. 56; Peter, vv. 69-75).
And the failure of the disciples, no less than that of Judas (v. 24), has already
been foretold in Scripture. The effect is to underline Jesus' knowledge of the
future and of the weakness of his disciples, but also to emphasize that from
now on he will be left alone to face his enemies.

31 The metaphor of "stumbling" has been used with varying degrees of seriousness or finality. Sometimes the context indicates a final loss
of salvation, as in 5:29-30; 13:21; 18:8-9; 24:10, whereas elsewhere it represents a setback which is not necessarily ultimately fatal (11:6; 13:57; 17:27).
Here it falls somewhere between merely "taking offense" and ultimate spiritual disaster. The failure which is predicted for the disciples is as serious as it

could be short of final apostasy, but they will eventually be restored to effective discipleship; they will fall to rise again (except Judas, whose presence among the group at this point is possible but not certain; see on v. 25).

The text of Zech 13:7 is quoted in a form which is quite unlike the probable text[4] of the LXX, and closer to the Hebrew, but which differs from it in the addition of "of the flock"[5] and, more noticeably, in making the opening verb a future indicative, "I will strike," rather than the imperative, "Strike," which occurs in all known versions of the OT text.[6] This difference, however, is not as significant as it appears, since the imperative is addressed by God to his sword, so that in effect it is God who is striking; the clause which follows the words quoted here reverts to an indicative statement with God as the subject. So when these two clauses are quoted without the opening address to the sword, the change to the indicative is a simple and obvious way to preserve the meaning of the graphic Hebrew idiom.[7] Zech 13:7-9 is one of a sequence of passages in Zech 9–14 which appear to present a messianic figure who is nonetheless rejected, wounded, and killed, a model which seems to have been important for Jesus in understanding his own messianic suffering, and which Matthew draws on several times in his account of Jesus in Jerusalem (cf. 21:4-5 [Zech 9:9-10]; 24:30 [Zech 12:10-14]; 27:3-10 [Zech 11:12-13]).[8] The shepherd in Zech 13:7 is described as *God's* shepherd, the man who is God's "associate" ("who is close to me," NJB, TNIV). That so exalted a figure should nonetheless be struck down, and indeed by the sword of God himself, expresses in a remarkable way the paradox of a Messiah who is to be killed in accordance with the will of God declared in the scriptures. The sheep in the prophecy are the people of God (as in Ezek 34), scattered when they lose their leader, but destined to be refined and restored, even if only one third of them (Zech 13:8-9). So for Jesus his disciples form the nucleus of the new people of God under the leadership of the Messiah.[9] The fact that the

4. There are many LXX textual variants; see my *Jesus and the OT,* 246.
5. This additional phrase is found in LXX A of Zech 13:7, but it is debated whether Matthew derived it from that source or whether LXX A has been conformed to Matthew. The addition possibly reflects the wording of Ezek 34:31. M. J. J. Menken, *Matthew's Bible,* 221-22, suggests that Matthew added τῆς ποίμνης to indicate that the disciples constitute Jesus' flock as opposed to the rest of Israel, who remain "lost sheep."
6. Except one late MS of the LXX, probably influenced by the NT text.
7. On the text form see further R. H. Gundry, *Use,* 25-28; D. J. Moo, *The OT,* 183-85.
8. On this complex of passages in relation to the gospel passion narratives see my *Jesus and the OT,* 103-10, 205-10; also B. Lindars, *Apologetic,* 110-34; F. F. Bruce, *This Is That,* 100-114; D. J. Moo, *The OT,* 173-224; J. Marcus, *Way,* 154-64; I. Duguid in P. E. Satterthwaite et al. (eds.), *The Lord's Anointed,* 265-80.
9. R. E. Menninger, *Israel,* 142-48, studies the use of the imagery of shepherd and flock in Matthew as a pointer to Matthew's underlying "remnant" theology.

following clause in Zech 13:7 refers to them as "the little ones" may have appealed especially to Matthew (cf. 10:42; 18:6-14).

32 Just as Jesus' words about his death at the supper had been followed by a vision of future restoration (v. 29), so again he looks beyond his death, which has just been so starkly portrayed. The three passion predictions of 16:21; 17:22-23; 20:18-19 all concluded with a bald statement that he would "be raised on the third day" (cf. also 17:9), but now the picture is filled out a little. His resurrection will be the preface to a reunion with his disciples. The dire prediction from Zech 13:7 is not the end of their story any more than it was of his; their stumbling will not be terminal. Just as the striking of the shepherd will lead to the scattering of the flock, so his restoration will lead to their regrouping.[10] And the fact that the reunion is set in Galilee gives new hope to the reader who has followed Matthew's careful distinction between the northern and southern provinces: Galilee is the place of light (4:15-16). The promise, like the preceding quotation, is shared with Mark, but in Matthew it will be given added emphasis by its double repetition in 28:7, 10 (cf. Mark 16:7) and by its literal fulfillment in 28:16-20.[11] Galilee, the place of Jesus' first preaching (4:17), is also to be the place for a new beginning which will spread out to "all the nations." And in that process the disciples, restored after their imminent disgrace, are to have the leading role.

33-35 Peter's outspoken objection (with the other disciples as a mere echo, v. 35) is typical of his role in this gospel as leader and representative of the Twelve (cf. 10:2; 14:28-32; 16:16-19, 22-23; 17:24-27; 19:27-30). But in this case his role is more distinctive. His boast of loyalty will be more nearly fulfilled in that he alone of the Twelve will stay close to Jesus after his arrest (v. 58), but that very boldness will set him up for a more spectacular fall than the rest of them. Peter is a man of extremes, an example and warning written large for the instruction of subsequent disciples. But Jesus' response raises the stakes: Peter will not merely desert Jesus, like the rest of them, but will even actively "deny" him. This possibility has already been raised in 10:33, where it was envisaged as a potential response to persecution, but one which would have disastrous consequences in that the denier would in turn be denied by Jesus before his Father. We noted there, however, that Peter's subsequent rehabilitation suggests that the mutual denial spoken of in 10:33 refers to a settled course of dissociation rather than a temporary lapse under pressure; Peter's bitter remorse in v. 75 shows that he had not permanently

---

10. So D. J. Moo, *The OT*, 215-17.

11. I have argued in my *Mark*, 670-74, that Mark originally intended a similar ending to his gospel, and that perhaps he wrote a pericope, subsequently lost, which became the model for Matt 28:16-20.

turned his back on Jesus and so did not ultimately come under the threat of 10:33. That Peter now squarely faces the possibility of having to die with Jesus shows how much he has learned since 16:22, when he objected so forcefully to Jesus' prediction of his own death, only to be faced with the subsequent unwelcome demand to "take up one's cross and follow" Jesus and to lose one's life in order to preserve it (16:24-26). He is now, he thinks, prepared to do what he then could not face up to.

The crowing of the cock has occasioned an inordinate amount of interest, largely because Mark, unlike the other three evangelists, has a double crowing. This discrepancy has resulted in significant textual variations in Mark,[12] but is probably best accounted for by a natural desire on the part of the other three evangelists to simplify their narrative by omitting an unnecessary detail. Attempts to explain why Mark should have wanted to insert an extra cockcrow into an tradition which originally had only one have not been compelling.[13] The crowing of the cock, whether once or twice, is not in itself important. It is simply a marker of time: before the night is over, you will have denied me three times.[14]

4. Jesus Prays in Gethsemane While the Disciples Sleep (26:36-46)

36 *Then Jesus came with them to an estate[1] called Gethsemane, and he said to his disciples, "Sit here while I go away over there and pray." 37 He took Peter and the two sons of Zebedee with him, and he began to be overcome with distress.[2] 38 Then he said to them, "My soul is deeply distressed to the point of death.[3] Stay here and keep awake with me." 39 And he went on a little way and fell on his face in prayer, saying, "My Father, if it is possible, let this cup pass away from me; and yet not as I wish but as you wish." 40 And he came to the disciples and found them asleep, and he said to Peter, "So you*

12. See the textual note in my *Mark,* 573, and n. 68 there.

13. E.g., D. Brady, *JSNT* 4 (1979) 54-55.

14. For a fascinating study of the habits of cocks in modern Jerusalem see H. Kosmala, *ASTI* 2 (1963) 118-20; 6 (1968) 132-34. Kosmala's and other findings are discussed by D. Brady, *JSNT* 4 (1979) 46-52, who concludes sensibly that Mark's "twice" refers to the repeated crowing, which could normally be expected before dawn rather than to two distinct periods of the night.

1. χωρίον is not just a "place," but a specific plot of land, such as a field or orchard. John 18:1 calls it a κῆπος, a garden or other cultivated area.

2. Matthew uses two verbs which are roughly synonymous, "to be distressed and sorely troubled," which together depict a state of extreme agitation.

3. See the comments below on the significance of ἕως θανάτου, literally "until death," in this context.

couldn't keep awake with me for a single hour![4] 41 *Keep awake and pray that you may not be put to the test.*[5] *For the spirit is eager, but the flesh is weak."* 42 *Again he went away a second time and prayed, "My Father, if this cannot pass away without my drinking it, let your will be done."* 43 *And he came and again found them asleep, because their eyes were weighed down.* 44 *And he left them and went away again and prayed a third time, saying the same thing.*[6] 45 *Then he came to the disciples and said to them, "Sleep on and rest!*[7] *Look, the time*[8] *has come,*[9] *and the Son of Man is being betrayed into the hands of sinners.* 46 *Get up, and let's go. Look, my betrayer has arrived."*

The last scene in which we find Jesus alone with his disciples (until after the resurrection in 28:16-20) has a dual focus. Its primary subject is Jesus' own prayer as he faces up to the reality of his approaching death, and the reader witnesses the extraordinary emotional turmoil which this situation now evokes in one who up to this point has spoken of it with a sense of purpose and settled resolve. But the spotlight also falls on his disciples, or more particularly on the inner circle of Peter, James, and John, in their human weakness and their inability to play even a supporting role when Jesus most needs them. The contrast is profound, and the reader is thus prepared for the different responses of Jesus and his disciples when the crisis comes: his prayer will have restored his sense of purpose and his authority, while the disciples, after an initial futile attempt at resistance, will simply give up and abandon him.

Matthew sets out the succession of three prayers and three return visits to the sleeping disciples more clearly than Mark, who gives no direct speech for the second prayer and says nothing about the third (though his narrative presupposes it). This scheme allows the reader to make an interesting comparison with the threefold testing and threefold failure of Peter in vv.

4. Jesus' comment could be read as a question: "So couldn't you keep awake with me for a single hour?" Either way it is an ironical reproach. The "you" is plural, here and in v. 41 (including the imperatives).

5. Literally, "come into testing (or temptation)"; for the range of meaning of πειρασμός see the introductory comments on 4:1-13, and on 6:13 where the phrase "bring into testing" is similar to "come into testing" here.

6. Matthew's use of the singular λόγος rather than the plural probably refers to the same content rather than the same actual words.

7. See the comments below on whether these words should be understood as an instruction, an ironical comment, or an exasperated question.

8. The use of ὥρα here should not be taken as indicating a Johannine idea of the passion as Jesus' "hour"; Matthew shows no sign of such usage elsewhere, but regularly uses ὥρα to mean "time," here the time predicted by Jesus at the last supper.

9. For this meaning of ἤγγικεν, literally "has come near," here and in v. 46 ("has arrived") see on 3:2 (and cf. 4:17; 10:7). Here it corresponds to Mark's ἦλθεν, "has come."

69-75. It also gives a fuller account of the nature of Jesus' prayer, with a sequence from the request for removal of the cup if possible in the first prayer to the acceptance that it may not be possible in the second, with the clear conclusion, "Let your will be done."

Matthew, unlike Mark, has shown us little of Jesus' emotion up to this point. Jesus' recorded words have sometimes expressed anger, disappointment, joy, or determination, but Matthew has not drawn attention to these emotions in his editorial comments. Jesus has appeared throughout as totally in control of the situation and of himself. The scene in Gethsemane, with its extravagantly expressed emotions in vv. 37-38, thus offers a powerful new insight into what it meant for Jesus to face up in practice to the fate that he had so long predicted as his divinely appointed calling. His agonized plea for some other way reveals a deep inner revulsion at what was to come,[10] but even now he looks only for what is "possible" within his Father's will, and the ultimate "Let your will be done" assures the reader that there was no other way. Only as we are allowed to share Jesus' deep distress are we enabled to grasp the seriousness of the settled purpose of God which calls for his Son to be rejected and killed in Jerusalem. But even so, the will of God is not imposed on an unwitting victim, but is deliberately faced and shared by the Son himself.[11] The relationship of trust and loyalty between Father and Son which was put under scrutiny at the outset of Jesus' ministry (4:1-11) proves able to survive even this ultimate test. Only in the terrible cry from the cross in 27:46 will we be given a similar insight into Jesus' emotional turmoil, when for a moment even the hard-won harmony of will achieved in Gethsemane will appear to be disrupted. For profound comment on what this episode reveals about Jesus' role in salvation see Heb 5:7-9.[12]

The three fishermen-disciples have already been chosen to share a specially privileged moment with Jesus on the mountain in 17:1-13; see on 17:1. In this case, however, the story is told from the perspective of Jesus, not from that of the three disciples. This time their role is apparently not so much to be witnesses of this intimate moment but to offer human companionship for Jesus when he felt the need for support. These were the three disciples

---

10. It has often been noted that Jesus' apparent fear of death contrasts with the noble, even serene, martyrdom accounts of, e.g., Socrates or the Maccabean martyrs, a point which early Christian apologists found it necessary to defend (e.g., Origen, *Cels.* 2.24). Christian theology has therefore concluded that it was not simply a painful death that Jesus wished to escape, but one which would involve the bearing of sin (2 Cor 5:21; Gal 3:13; 1 Pet 2:24; 3:18, etc.), and which would disrupt even his relationship with his Father (27:46). At the same time, Jesus' emotional turmoil speaks strongly of his fully human nature.

11. J. H. Neyrey, *Honor,* 149, explores how an ancient reader might have read this pericope as an example of Jesus' courage, freely accepting the noble choice.

12. R. E. Brown, *Death,* 227-34, surveys discussions linking the two passages.

who had declared their willingness to share Jesus' fate (26:35; 20:22 with the same metaphor of the "cup" as will be used in v. 39), yet now, even before the crisis comes, their inability to stay awake makes them ineffective even in the role of providing moral support. The repeated emphasis on their sleepiness provides a basis for Jesus' exhortation and warning in v. 41, which has a wider application to the demands of discipleship than just to that particular situation. It also emphasizes the isolation of Jesus, as the one person who remains alert to face up to the challenge.

The motif of the disciples' sleepiness has also of course given rise to the problem of historical veracity (the "'village atheist' objection," as R. E. Brown, *Death,* 174, delightfully calls it): if all the potential witnesses were asleep, who was responsible for recording how Jesus prayed? It is possible that the prayer was protracted, so that the disciples may have heard the gist of it before they went to sleep; in the crowded state of the Jerusalem area at Passover it is also quite possible that Gethsemane was not as private as the narratives suggest, and that others heard what was happening;[13] it is also not unlikely that Jesus himself after the resurrection shared with them some of his memories of this momentous night. At any rate, it soon became clear from Jesus' demeanor in the face of the arresting party that his earlier emotional turmoil had been resolved as he had faced and overcome it through his prayer.

36 The location of this scene is on the Mount of Olives (v. 30). The specific place-name Gethsemane (probably meaning "oil press") is not otherwise known, but Matthew describes it as an "estate," probably a walled plot, and its name suggests that it was an olive orchard.[14] This would tally with John's description of it as a "garden." Its exact location on the Mount of Olives is not stated, but the traditional site on the western slope opposite the city would be suitable. Unlike Bethany, it was within the bounds of "greater Jerusalem" approved for Passover night (see p. 771), was easily accessible for Jesus and his group after a late Passover meal, and allowed Judas to bring the arresting party there quickly from the city.

Matthew has previously mentioned Jesus going off on his own to pray (14:23), in accordance with his own precept in 6:6, though 11:25-26 has recorded what appears to be a public address to his Father. The intriguing blend here of secrecy (leaving the majority of the disciples behind) and yet his taking of Peter, James, and John with him suggests a strong need for human companionship. But even they will be kept at a distance (v. 39); this is a private transaction between Father and Son.

13. So B. Saunderson, *Bib* 70 (1989) 224-33, with special reference to the anonymous young man of Mark 14:51-52.
14. See J. Jeremias, *Jerusalem,* 6-7, for the growing of olives in the area east of Jerusalem.

37-38 It is to Peter, James, and John, rather than to the whole group of the Twelve, that Jesus now reveals his emotional stress, just as only they had seen his divine glory in 17:1-8. The statement that he "*began* to be overcome with distress" perhaps alerts the reader that here is a new note to Jesus' self-disclosure. Matthew's descriptive terms reveal the depth of the emotion rather than its cause, but the recorded words of Jesus go further. They echo the refrain of Pss 42:5-6, 11; 43:5,[15] using the same uncommon adjective *perilypos,* "deeply distressed," which occurs there in the LXX to describe the state of the psalmist's "soul."[16] For the range of meanings of *psychē* see on 10:39; 16:25-26, and p. 399, n. 4; here, as in Pss 42–43, it refers to the "inner self" and its use emphasizes that this is real, deeply felt emotion, not an outward show. The additional phrase, which literally means "until death," should probably be taken, as in Jonah 4:9 ("angry to death," using the same phrase in LXX), as expressing the vehemence of the emotion;[17] it might be paraphrased "so very sorrowful that I could die" or even "so very sorrowful that it is killing me."[18] In this context where Jesus' literal death is imminent and is the cause of his distress, it might be supposed that the phrase means "at the approach of death" or "in the face of death," but that would not be a natural reading of the Greek preposition. The specific instruction to "stay awake with me" prepares the reader for the disciples' total failure to do so, thus leaving Jesus unsupported in his distress.

39 The "little way" (Luke 22:41 says it was about a stone's throw) suggests that Jesus was still within earshot of Peter, James, and John (prayer was normally aloud, even when praying alone). Falling with one's face to the ground was a posture of supplication (Luke 5:12; 17:16) and a response to a supernatural experience (Matt 17:6; Luke 24:5; cf. Gen 17:3; Dan 8:17), but as an attitude for prayer it underlines the depth of Jesus' emotion.

Jesus often referred to God as "my Father," but the vocative "My Father" in prayer here and in v. 42, rather than the simple "Father" as in 11:25-26, further emphasizes that it is the relationship between Father and Son which is here being tested and reaffirmed. "My Father" is Jesus' personal

---

15. For the allusion see my *Jesus and the OT,* 57-58; R. E. Brown, *Death,* 154-55; D. J. Moo, *The OT,* 240-42.

16. Cf. also Mark 6:26, where it described Antipas's revulsion at the request for John's head.

17. Cf. our phrases "scared to death," "worried to death."

18. These paraphrases are suggested by R. E. Brown, *Death,* 155-56. Brown rightly questions the suggestion of J. Héring, in W. C. Van Unnik (ed.), *Neotestamentica et Patristica,* 64-69 (adopted also by J. W. Holleran, *Gethsemane,* 14-16), that it means "so sad that I want to die," since Jesus' following prayer is not to die but to be spared death. Héring avoids this problem by supposing that it was the cross that Jesus wished to avoid; a peaceful death in Gethsemane would have been preferable.

equivalent of the "Our Father" which he taught his disciples to use corporately in 6:9. This is the first of three echoes of the Lord's Prayer in this pericope; cf. vv. 41 and 42. For the "cup" as a metaphor for suffering see on 20:22-23;[19] we noted there that in the OT the metaphor also carried the connotation of God's anger and thus of punishment, and in the light of Jesus' words over the "cup" in v. 28 the metaphor may be used here to focus especially on the element of vicarious punishment in Jesus' death (though of course the "cup" offered to the disciples was not that of Jesus' vicarious suffering in itself, but of their participation in its benefits). It was that aspect of his suffering, not merely the physical pain and death in themselves, that most distressed him; perhaps we should understand that in speaking of the cup (of God's anger) he was already aware of the coming separation from his Father which 27:46 will so graphically describe. That is something he simply does not want to have to go through, but the clause "if it is possible" already recognizes the conflict between his natural revulsion and the purpose of his Father, and the concluding clause, "not as I wish but as you wish," makes it plain where his ultimate loyalty lies. There is no question of his refusing the will of God once it is clear that there is no "Plan B." Jesus' repeated predictions of his death, and his statement in vv. 24 and 31 that this is to happen "as it is written," show that he was already well aware of his Father's will; what is happening in Gethsemane is not the discovery of this as a new fact, but the need to come to terms in emotion and will with what he has already known in theory.

40-41   Jesus' earnest prayer contrasts with the failure of even his closest supporters to stay awake in his support. "The disciples" here must mean only Peter, James, and John, who are now separate from the rest of the group, since Peter is directly addressed (though the verbs are plural, including the other two disciples as well). Jesus discovers them already failing in their duty; note the dramatic effect of the historic present tenses of v. 40 ("comes," "finds," "says" in the Greek), and the colloquial "So" which introduces Jesus' ironical comment adds to their discomfiture. To his earlier instruction to "keep awake" Jesus now adds "pray." Their prayer is not to be for him but for themselves, who have been shown to need it even more than he does. It is the same prayer[20] which Jesus had told them to use back in 6:13: "Do not bring us into testing, but rescue us from the Evil One." See on 6:13 for the nature of the "testing/temptation" which may be in view; here it most

---

19. R. E. Brown, *Death,* 168-70, surveys views about the significance of the metaphor here.

20. I take the ἵνα here as closely linked with προσεύχεσθε, specifying the *content* of the prayer, "pray that you may . . ." (BDAG 476, §2aγ) rather than as introducing a separate final clause, "keep awake and pray, in order that you may . . ."; but the sense is not very different.

immediately refers to the test of their loyalty which will come with the arrival of the arresting party (a "test" which also brings the "temptation" to run away), a test which, because of their failure to keep awake and pray, they will fail miserably.

The aphorism[21] about the spirit and the flesh can be applied much more widely than just to the specific situation of the three disciples; it expresses in a nutshell one of the main problems of Christian discipleship (and indeed of human nature in general), and Matthew no doubt expected his readers to apply it to themselves, not only to Peter, James, and John. The spirit/flesh contrast does not occur elsewhere in Matthew, and is more typical of Paul (cf. also John 3:6; 6:63); here (in contrast to the letters of Paul) the "flesh" is not so much evil or in itself opposed to the will of God, but represents human weakness over against the desire of the "inner self" to do the will of God (for a comparable use of "spirit" see 5:3). Initial enthusiasm and professions of loyalty too often succumb to human lethargy or fear of the consequences. *Prothymos* sounds a more positive note than the traditional translation "willing": it portrays zeal and commitment, perhaps with special reference to Peter's unconditional promise of loyalty in vv. 33 and 35. Peter's problem is not lack of enthusiasm for Jesus, but lack of the moral stamina to face up to what it will mean in practice.

42   The second prayer is not simply a repeat of the first.[22] It suggests that Jesus now knows the answer to the request of v. 39, and has accepted that no alternative is possible. In that case there can be only one course for Jesus to take: "Let your will be done." This is the third echo in this pericope of the wording of the Lord's Prayer (6:10), and shows that Jesus not only instructs his disciples in how to pray but himself follows the same principle. When we realize the profound consequences of such a prayer for Jesus in Gethsemane, it gives added solemnity to our own use of the words he taught his disciples. From this point on there will be no further indication of reluctance on Jesus' part to fulfill his God-given role until the cry of 27:46 when Jesus has already accepted and implemented his Father's will. He will not resist arrest (even though he could easily have done so, vv. 53-54), and at his trials he will offer no defense (26:62-63; 27:13-14) but rather a defiant declaration which will hasten his condemnation (26:64). In Gethsemane the die has been cast.

43-44   The repetition of the same sequence of return to the sleeping

---

21. The classical μὲν . . . δέ construction, together with the general nature of the language, suggests a proverbial expression — as it has indeed become in modern usage.

22. *Pace* Davies and Allison, 3:500. The difference lies not, as they say, in that Jesus is "now more resigned than he was then." There was never any suggestion that Jesus would refuse to do God's will; but his previous prayer explored what that will was, while in this one the question has been resolved.

disciples and renewed prayer provides no new elements to the story except the brief comment that the disciples' eyes were weighed down. Despite the opening "because" this does not in itself explain but rather restates the problem of their sleepiness. Any explanation of why they seem to have been exceptionally tired can only be conjectural. It was by now well into the night,[23] and they had been through a series of stressful experiences since the meal began. The sense of impending catastrophe may have sapped their energy (cf. Luke 22:45, "sleeping from grief").

45-46 Jesus' words on his final return to the sleeping disciples are hard to interpret as a whole; they seem to pull in opposite directions. The opening words, taken at their face value, give permission to the disciples to go on sleeping, while v. 46 tells them to wake up. Two kinds of solution have been pursued: either there is a significant time lag incorporated within what appears to be a continuous speech, with something occurring in the middle which changes Jesus' attitude, or the opening words are not to be taken at their face value. The first type of solution may be supported by v. 45b, the announcement of Judas's imminent arrival. So perhaps after saying "Sleep on and rest" Jesus heard or saw the approach of the arresting party and so concluded that after all there was no more time for sleep. But if that is what Matthew intended, the lack of any narrative indication of an interruption between vv. 45a and 45b is at best clumsy.[24] Most interpreters therefore look for an alternative way of understanding Jesus' opening words. They have been taken as an ironical question ("Are you still sleeping and resting?"), an indignant observation ("You are still sleeping and resting!"), or an ironical command ("Sleep on[25] and rest!") intending that they should in fact do just the oppo-

---

23. See above on vv. 17 and 20 for the timing of the Passover meal.

24. Hagner, 2:784, tries to make the transition less abrupt by extending their sleep backward: pointing out rightly that "he left them" in v. 44 may be understood to mean that he allowed them to go on sleeping (in contrast with Mark's comment that on this second occasion "they did not know what answer to give him"); he suggests that this reading is "in agreement with the command of v. 45 that they go on with their sleeping." On this understanding the disciples have so far been awakened only once, in v. 40, and thus have been able to enjoy a relatively long period of sleep. But this still leaves no explanation as to why the permission to go on sleeping in v. 45 is immediately countermanded.

25. Those who take this as either an ironical question or an indignant comment usually include "still" in their translation. But that is not a natural sense of Matthew's word or phrase [τὸ] λοιπόν (MSS are divided on whether the article is present, but the sense is not affected), literally "the remainder," often used to mean "from now on." That is why I have opted rather for the ironical command, which could then be paraphrased, "Go ahead and enjoy the rest of your sleep!"; that seems a more probable sense for τὸ λοιπόν. The suggestions of BDAG 602 §3aα, "Do you intend to sleep on and on?" or "A fine time you've chosen to sleep!" pursue similar ideas, but with a freer approach to the meaning of the Greek phrase. See further my *Mark,* 588 and n. 34 there.

site. All these suggestions come to much the same conclusion, that Jesus did not in fact want the disciples to go on sleeping at this point any more than he did before, and in that case vv. 45b-46 follow more naturally. Appeals to a supposed ironic intention are of course always suspect as an easy way to avoid an exegetical embarrassment, but in this case, by giving no indication of a time lag or change of situation between v. 45a and v. 45b, Matthew seems to have left us little choice.

The "time" which has now arrived is the time of his betrayal as he has just predicted it in v. 21, together with the time of the scattering of the disciples which he has said will take place "tonight" (v. 31). When Jesus has said previously to whom he would be betrayed, he has called them simply "people" (17:22) or, more specifically, "the chief priests and the scribes" (20:18). This time the more weighted term "sinners"[26] prepares the reader for the clear division between the forces of good and evil which will dominate the following narrative. With the arrival of the betrayer the long-awaited drama has begun. The following narrative will make it clear that Jesus' command "Let's go" is not an invitation to try to escape, but a call to be ready to meet the arresting party.

C. THE ARREST AND TRIALS OF JESUS (26:47–27:26)

Events now move steadily forward to the long-predicted climax of the story. The disciples quickly leave the stage, and Jesus is left in the hands of his enemies. It is they who will take the initiative throughout the remainder of chs. 26–27, and Jesus will offer no resistance; even the pathetic attempt at resistance by one disciple is quickly scotched (vv. 51-52). Jesus' following words (vv. 53-54) make it clear that it is not that he *cannot* resist but that he *will not*. In Gethsemane he has accepted his Father's will.

After the arrest the story of Jesus' trial goes through two main phases, one before the Jewish authorities, the other before the Roman prefect. We shall consider the formal and legal characteristics of these hearings as we come to them. Formally speaking, it had to be the Roman authorization of the death penalty which ultimately decided Jesus' fate, but it is clear that for Matthew the Jewish hearing is the one that really matters. It is there that Jesus finally confronts the assembled dignitaries of Jerusalem and his defiant declaration of his messianic authority brings about the predicted condemnation to death. The subsequent transfer to Roman jurisdiction is presented as a formality required to effect the execution the Jewish leaders have already de-

---

26. Previously in this gospel "sinners" has referred to those who were the objects of Jesus' concern (9:10-13; 11:19), but here its negative tone is unrelieved.

cided on, a process which does not go as smoothly as they might have wished but which they are able to manipulate to achieve the desired outcome. Pontius Pilate appears almost as a stooge rather than as the ultimately responsible authority. Even though Jesus will ultimately die by Roman execution under a Roman charge as "the king of the Jews," we are left in no doubt as to whose initiative has brought this about. In a striking (and much abused) cameo in 27:24-25 Matthew will set out clearly his understanding of who was responsible for Jesus' death.

Set within this continuous narrative are two interludes in which the spotlight shifts briefly from Jesus himself to one of his disciples. Both involve a disciple repudiating Jesus and then regretting his decision. In the first case, that of Peter (26:69-75), subsequent history will tell us that the lapse was only temporary, though the story as we read it in this pericope does not spell that out. The second story, that of Judas (27:3-10), by contrast ends in despair and suicide. The reader is thus invited to learn from the stories of these two failing disciples both by discerning how their experiences differed and by noting their very different ultimate fates. And both stand out by contrast with Jesus, within the story of whose trial they are set: Peter buckles under pressure, Judas has deliberately changed sides, but Jesus remains true to his calling and to his Father's will.

1. The Arrest of Jesus (26:47-56)

> 47 And while Jesus was still speaking, Judas, one of the Twelve, did indeed[1] arrive, bringing a large crowd armed with swords and sticks, sent by the chief priests and the elders of the people. 48 Jesus' betrayer had given[2] them a signal: "The person I kiss is the one; arrest him." 49 So he went straight up to Jesus and said, "Hello, Rabbi," and kissed[3] him. 50 Jesus said to him, "My friend,[4] [do] what

---

1. An attempt to represent the force of Matthew's graphic ἰδού, which here takes up the ἰδού of Jesus' announcement in v. 46b. That which Jesus there drew to their attention now comes onto the stage.

2. The tense is aorist, whereas Mark has a pluperfect, but it is surely overexegesis to insist that whereas Mark describes a signal arranged in advance, in Matthew it is arranged only on arrival.

3. This verb is the compound καταφιλέω, as opposed to the simple φιλέω in v. 48, but attempts to find a significant difference in meaning (to kiss warmly, repeatedly, or on the hand or foot) are straining at a stylistic variation. The more emphatic verb form serves to draw attention to the act.

4. This form of address is peculiar to Matthew in the NT; cf. 20:13; 22:12. In each case there is an element of reproach and of distance, which is hard to reproduce in any accepted English idiom. "My friend," taken in its lexical sense, is too warm and welcoming,

you've come for."[5] *Then they came up and laid hands on Jesus and arrested him.*

51 *Just then*[6] *one of those who were with Jesus stretched out his hand and drew his sword and struck the high priest's slave, cutting off his ear.* 52 *Then Jesus said to him, "Put your sword back where it belongs; for all those who take up the sword will die by the sword.* 53 *Or do you imagine that I am not able to call on my Father, and he would provide*[7] *me here and now with more than twelve*[8] *legions of angels?* 54 *How then would the Scriptures be fulfilled which say that this is how it must be?"*

55 *At that time Jesus said to the crowds, "You have come out with swords and sticks to overpower*[9] *me as if I were a bandit.*[10] *Each day*[11] *I have been sitting teaching in the temple, and you did not arrest me.* 56 *But all this has happened so that the scriptures of the prophets may be fulfilled."*[12]

Then all the disciples left him and ran away.

---

but we do sometimes use it in this rather formal way to address someone who is not in fact a friend at all. In all three Matthean uses it "denotes a mutually binding relation between the speaker and the hearer which the latter has disregarded and scorned" (K. H. Rengstorf, *TDNT* 2:701). The comment of Davies and Allison, 3:509, that "Jesus remains friendly to his betrayer" depends more on the lexical meaning of ἑταῖρος than on the idiom as it is used in Matthew. R. E. Brown, *Death,* 256-57, stresses the ironic function of the term here and in its other Matthean uses.

5. See the comments below for suggestions as to what the elliptical expression, literally "for which you are present," a relative clause with no main verb, might mean in context.

6. Another attempt to represent καὶ ἰδού.

7. The verb παρίστημι (by etymology "place beside") probably here conveys to put at my disposal, i.e., send to my defense.

8. There are several textual variations relating to the grammatical way "more than twelve" is expressed, but all seem to agree that that is what the phrase means. For the omission of ἤ, "than," see BDF 185(4).

9. συλλαμβάνω here functions as a synonym for κρατέω, which I have translated "arrest" in vv. 48, 50, 55b, and 57, but Jesus' protest about the inappropriate use of force perhaps justifies this stronger rendering for the alternative verb.

10. This sentence may equally be read as an indignant question. Either way it is a protest.

11. Or perhaps "during the day" (so A. W. Argyle, *ExpT* 63 [1952] 354), so that Jesus would be highlighting their stealthy approach at night in contrast with an open arrest in the daytime.

12. This last sentence might be taken as an editorial aside rather than as part of Jesus' speech, but in that case it would more appropriately follow v. 56b, which would otherwise be left separated from the occasion for the disciples' running away. The wording is of course similar to that of Matthew's regular quotation-formula (especially in the form

While I am treating 26:47–27:26 as a new section of the narrative, in which the predictions of the preceding pericopes begin to come true and Jesus is seen no longer with his disciples but in the hands of his enemies, there is nonetheless no break in the continuity of the story. The scene is still Gethsemane, and the action follows immediately from Jesus' warning in vv. 45-46. Judas's arrival has been signaled, and now he appears and fulfills his bargain with the priests.

For Judas's role and motivation see above on vv. 14-16. His betrayal of Jesus has been well signaled in advance (10:4; 26:14-16, 21-25, 46) and is now carried out with a degree of armed support which leaves nothing to chance. But while Jesus now has no chance of escape, the narrative nonetheless reads as if he is in charge of the situation. The contrast with his emotional prayer in the preceding pericope is striking. The Jesus whom Judas and his posse meet is now resolute, calm, and authoritative. He himself makes no attempt to resist arrest, and when one of his disciples tries to defend him, it is Jesus himself, not the arresting party, who puts an end to the attempt. He speaks of the supernatural resources available to him, and declares that it is his choice not to call on them, because his purpose is that the Scriptures should be fulfilled. He even reprimands those who have come to arrest him for supposing that he would need to be overcome by armed force, and his challenge remains unanswered. While Matthew does not go so far as John in depicting the arresting party as recoiling in fear from Jesus' supernatural authority (John 18:5-6), his Jesus seems able to lecture them from a superior height even while he is being led away. Jesus is taken into the power of the Jerusalem authorities not because he had no choice but because this is the will of his Father, declared in the Scriptures, which he has accepted as his messianic calling.

47   To describe Judas as "one of the Twelve" is hardly necessary after 10:4 and 26:14, but underlines the shocking fulfillment of Jesus' prediction in v. 21. See on v. 25 for Judas's movements since the Passover meal. Matthew's silence on when he left the group allows for the possibility that he went with them as far as Gethsemane so that he knew exactly where Jesus would be, and then went and collected his troops to bring them there while Jesus prayed and the rest of the disciples slept. But if, as John 18:2 says (cf. Luke 22:39), Gethsemane was a regular rendezvous for the group, he may have known in advance where to take the arresting party that night. A force sent out by the "chief priests and the elders of the people" sounds like an official posse recruited by or on behalf of the Sanhedrin (and including, perhaps led by, "the high priest's slave"), and so would probably have consisted of some of the temple guards,[13] perhaps augmented by less formal recruits or

found in 1:22), but that is no reason why he should not have used this expression in expanding the direct speech of Mark 14:49b.

13. For the temple guards see Schürer, 2:284-87.

volunteers; v. 55 appears to be addressed to temple guards. There is no suggestion here of Roman troops being involved,[14] and their fairly basic arma-
ments suggest something less strictly military — the word translated "sticks"
means pieces of wood, perhaps clubs or staves, or possibly something more
makeshift (think of baseball bats?). The armed group was "a large crowd" in
comparison with the unprepared disciples, but this remained an undercover
operation, as had been planned in vv. 3-5.

48-49 It was dark, and to the Jerusalem guards one Galilean visitor
would look much like another. Hence Judas's notorious kiss, which in a culture less restrained in physical contact than ours may not have stood out as an
unusual greeting;[15] the point of the "signal" lies in whom Judas greets rather
than how. His verbal greeting is also not out of the ordinary (see on 28:9), but
again, as in v. 25, he addresses Jesus by the occupational title "Rabbi" rather
than the more theologically weighted "Lord" which the other disciples habit-
ually use. Here, as already in v. 25, the title betrays his alienation from Jesus
and what he stands for.

50 Unlike the clear reproach of Luke 22:48, "Judas, do you betray
the Son of Man with a kiss?" Jesus' response in Matthew is so concise as to
be quite obscure.[16] The literal meaning, "My friend,[17] for which you are present," requires that one supply a main verb, which could be indicative, interrogative, imperative, or exclamatory. Most versions opt for an imperative,
"Do what you have come to do" (i.e., "Get on with it!"; cf. John 13:27), but
other suggestions include "So this is why you are here," or "What an errand
you have come on!" A question, "What have you come for?" (KJV, RSV,
NIV mg.) is less likely, as it would naturally be expressed with an interrogative rather than a relative pronoun;[18] moreover, Jesus is already well aware of
Judas's purpose, though of course a sarcastic question might be possible. The

---

14. John's use of the term σπεῖρα and mention of a χιλίαρχος (John 18:3, 12) has
been taken to indicate Roman troops, but J. Blinzler, *Trial*, 61-70, argues that even in John
the troops are all Jewish.

15. For kissing as a standard greeting see Luke 7:45; Acts 20:37; Rom 16:16, etc.
For further evidence see Keener, 642, especially n. 98; W. Klassen, *NTS* 39 (1993) 122-
28. See, however, Albright and Mann, 329, for the suggestion (following M. Aberbach)
that etiquette did not allow a disciple to take the initiative in greeting his master, so that
Judas's act was a "studied insult."

16. R. E. Brown, *Death*, 1385-88, surveys proposed renderings.

17. For this form of address see above, p. 1009, n. 4.

18. N. Turner, *A Grammar of NT Greek*, vol. 3: *Syntax*, 49, asserts boldly that
"confusion of relative and interrogative pronouns is usual in Hellenistic Greek," but even
he will say only that the interrogative reading here "may not be too bold." Davies and
Allison, 3:509, n. 26, even though they admit that "there seems to be no clear example in
Koine of ὅ used as an interrogative in a direct question," nonetheless prefer this reading on
the basis of patristic interpretation.

account of the actual arrest emphasizes its physical nature; the Hebraic expression "to lay hands on" is perhaps intended to echo Jesus' words about the "hands" of people/sinners (17:22; 26:45). We are thus prepared for Jesus' protest about the unnecessary use of force (v. 55).

51-52 The expression "one of those who were with Jesus" avoids specifically mentioning the disciples, perhaps in order to suggest that others were there in the orchard with Jesus and the Twelve.[19] It is only John who names the attacker as Peter (and also names the high priest's slave as Malchus). Luke 22:38 tells us, however, that, surprisingly, there were at least two swords among the group who ate the Passover meal, so the attacker may have been a disciple,[20] and such impulsive action would suit the character of Peter, especially after his declaration of loyalty even to death (v. 35). The reference to "the [rather than "a"] slave of the high priest" may indicate a person of some consequence, perhaps the leader of the arresting party; as such he would be an obvious object of attack.[21] The redundant Hebraic expression "stretched out his hand and" (cf. 8:3; 14:31; the idiom is frequent in the OT, e.g., in Gen 22:10; Exod 3:20; Judg 3:21, etc.) perhaps echoes the "hands" laid on Jesus in v. 50.

Jesus' indignant repudiation of this natural show of loyalty stems from his earlier acceptance that his Father's will was not to be averted. But while it is his particular situation which makes the use of force inappropriate here, his words about "those who take up the sword" are quite general and provide *prima facie* support for the belief that physical violence, and particularly retaliatory violence, is incompatible with following Jesus (see 5:39 for the principle of nonresistance). Whether these words (reported only by Matthew) can be taken as the basis for a thoroughgoing pacifism will depend on a wider assessment of the relevant biblical material. But as a proverbial observation (cf. Rev 13:10) on the tendency of violence to recoil on those who perpetrate it[22] Jesus' aphorism reflects common experience, even though not every historical example conforms to this pattern.

19. As Mark 14:51-52 indicates; indeed, Mark here speaks of "one of the bystanders."

20. R. E. Brown, *Death*, 268-71, discusses the likelihood of a disciple carrying a sword at this time.

21. The fact that he is described simply as a slave, not himself a priest, makes unlikely the suggestion of D. Daube, *JTS* 11 (1960) 59-62; G. W. H. Lampe, in E. Bammel and C. F. D. Moule (eds.), *Jesus*, 343-45; B. Viviano, *RB* 96 (1989) 71-80, that the cutting off of the ear is intended either actually or symbolically to disqualify from priestly duty.

22. Cf. the principle of Gen 9:6, and for a comparable motif see Isa 50:11. The targum of Isa 50:11 adds sword to fire as a source of self-destruction, thus providing a closer analogy to Jesus' words here (see B. D. Chilton, *Rabbi*, 99-100, 108-9, following R. H. Gundry, *Use*, 144; H. Kosmala, *NovT* 4 [1960/1] 3-5).

53-54 Physical resistance was not only wrong in principle but also unnecessary, since Jesus had far more force at his disposal, if he chose to summon it, than a few human supporters could offer. Angels are available to help God's people in need (see 4:6, quoting Ps 91:11-12; also 4:11), and are envisaged in military terms in the OT phrase "the host [army] of heaven" (1 Kgs 22:19), and especially in the angelic armies led by Michael in Dan 10:13, 20-21; 12:1; Rev 12:7. The idea of angels fighting for the cause of God and his people is prominent in the Qumran literature. While "legions" here might be understood primarily as a term for vast numbers (there were six thousand men in a Roman legion),[23] the choice of such a military term in connection with defense against an armed posse is surely deliberate. If there is to be fighting, it is to be done by supernatural forces, not by human volunteers. But Jesus will not ask his Father for such help because he now knows what is his Father's will. Indeed, he had known it already, even before the struggle in Gethsemane (see on v. 39), because his fate was already prescribed in "the Scriptures." The reference may be especially to Zech 13:7-9, just quoted in v. 31, but the plural term suggests the wider scriptural motif to which he has referred in v. 24, and which we considered above in relation to the statement in 16:21 (see comments there), that his suffering was "necessary." Verse 54 is rather awkwardly connected with what precedes by a "therefore" where we might have expected "but in that case": the two preceding scenarios of human or angelic resistance would equally have prevented the working out of God's declared purpose.

55-56 Jesus' protest over the manner of his arrest serves to underline the contrast between the Jerusalem establishment, which depends on stealth and physical force, and Jesus' open and nonviolent presentation of his claims in the temple courtyard. They have failed to silence him in public debate, so instead they have resorted to coercion, avoiding a public arrest because of their fear of crowd reaction (26:5). So they are treating him like a "bandit," probably meaning simply a common thief (cf. its use in 21:13), though this is the term Josephus would regularly use for the violent supporters of Jewish nationalism, more generally known as the Zealots. If Matthew has the latter usage in view, its modern equivalent might be "terrorist." In view of Jesus' clear repudiation of the bandit image here, it is ironical that he would eventually end up crucified along with two such bandits (27:38, 44).

"All this has happened so that . . . may be fulfilled" closely echoes the

---

23. The use of the name Λεγιών in Mark 5:9 (again for a large number of supernatural beings) focuses on their number rather than any military role. "More than twelve" may be intended to recall either the tribes of Israel or the twelve disciples, with whose ineffective resistance the angelic force is compared; the "more than" makes it unlikely that Jesus is thinking of one legion each for himself and the remaining eleven disciples.

quotation-formula in 1:22; 21:4;[24] here as there it refers to the specific details of the immediately preceding narrative, which are understood within the wider context of the fulfillment of God's purpose, even though in this case no particular text is cited to indicate in what way the manner of Jesus' arrest "fulfills the scriptures of the prophets."[25] Matthew may be thinking, as Luke did (Luke 22:37), of the statement that God's servant would be "counted among the lawbreakers" (Isa 53:12), but perhaps the logic is not meant to be as tight as that. A further repetition of the general theme of scriptural fulfillment (in this chapter already in vv. 24, 31, and 54) reinforces the conviction that nothing is happening by chance, so that even underhand human schemes serve only to advance the declared purpose of God.

After what Jesus has said, there is clearly no point in further resistance, nor is there anything to be gained from staying with Jesus; the disciples all run away, though one of them, we shall find out in v. 58, does not go very far.

2. The Hearing before the Sanhedrin (26:57-68)

57 *Those who had arrested Jesus took him to Caiaphas the high priest, where the scribes and the elders were gathered together.*

58 *But Peter was following Jesus at a distance as far as the high priest's courtyard, where he went in and sat inside among the servants to see the end.*

59 *The chief priests and the whole Sanhedrin were looking for false testimony against Jesus so that they could have him executed,* 60 *and they did not find any even though many false witnesses came forward. But in the end two came forward* 61 *and said, "This man said, 'I can destroy God's sanctuary and rebuild it*[1] *in three days.'"* 62 *Then the high priest stood up and said to him, "Have you no answer to these men's testimony against you?"*[2] 63 *But Jesus said nothing. And*

---

24. See D. P. Senior, *Passion,* 152-54, for the significance of this echo.

25. See p. 1010, n. 12, for these words as part of Jesus' speech rather than an editorial comment.

1. The verb is simply οἰκοδομέω, "build" (with no object expressed), but the sequence of thought requires that here it means "rebuild it" or "build another one" (Mark 14:58 specifies that it would be "another").

2. The syntax of this sentence is awkward, with τί ("what?") apparently functioning as the object of ἀποκρίνομαι, "answer"; some have therefore suggested that it be read as two sentences: "Do you not answer? What are these men testifying against you?" But the high priest's question is not about the content of the accusation, but about Jesus' response to it, so that a single colloquially expressed sentence is preferable; see BDF 298(4); 299(1). The sense is not significantly different.

the high priest said to him, "I put you under oath by the living God to tell us whether you are the Messiah, the Son of God." 64 Jesus replied, "You have said it. And yet I tell you,[3] from now on you will see the Son of Man seated at the right hand of power and coming on the clouds of heaven."

65 Then the high priest tore his robes and said, "He has blasphemed. Why do we need any more witnesses? Look, now you have heard his blasphemy; 66 what do you think?" And they replied, "He deserves to die." 67 Then they spat in his face and beat him, and some slapped him, 68 saying, "Prophesy to us, Messiah, who was it that hit you?"

This is the point at which Jesus' death is sealed; all that follows involving the Roman prefect is only the formal implementation of a verdict already decided by the Jewish authorities. And the final basis of the Jewish verdict is Jesus' own words in v. 64, in which far from retracting his supposed messianic claims he defiantly escalates them to a level which his judges cannot pass over — even if they had wished to do so, and Matthew has made it clear in v. 59 that they were only too willing to convict. Here then is the climax of the tussle over authority which has been developing ever since Jesus arrived in Jerusalem, and it ends in a remarkable paradox, with Jesus asserting his superior, God-given authority in ringing tones, but the Jerusalem leaders in fact having the upper hand in terms of the legal process and its outcome. The reader is left feeling that this is not a proper resolution of the conflict, and Jesus' words themselves direct our attention beyond the earthly judgment scene to one of heavenly authority, where those who are now his judges "will see" him as the heavenly judge. Nor is this a vision for the distant future. It will be true "from now on." So the reader is prepared for the climax when, only a few days later, the vindicated Messiah can declare that he now has "all power in heaven and on earth" (28:18); his reign at the right hand of power has begun.

But for now he is in their power, "so that the Scriptures may be fulfilled" (vv. 54, 56). The scene will end with Jesus as the apparently helpless butt of the rough justice of his outraged captors. Except for his defiant declaration in v. 64 Jesus remains resolutely silent throughout in the face of false accusation, ill-treatment, and insult. Apart from a two-word response to Pilate's formal charge he will say nothing more until his terrible cry from the cross in 27:46. He seems aloof from what is going on around him. After the protest in Gethsemane about the way his arrest has been set up (v. 55) there is no more to be said. They know where they are going, and Jesus lets events

---

3. This and the following "you" are plural; "you have said it" is singular.

take their course, and even helps them on their way by the undiplomatic language he uses in v. 64.

Yet it is, paradoxically, in this setting of the apparent helplessness and defeat of Jesus that we reach the climactic statement of who he is. The setting could not be more dramatically effective. Jesus has spoken frequently of his coming confrontation with the chief priests, the elders, and the scribes, those who represent the official leadership of the people of God. Now he stands before them, not in the relatively neutral territory of a crowded Court of the Gentiles but on their own ground, with no one to take his side. And here, in response to the high priest's challenge, the element of secrecy concerning Jesus' messianic claim is finally discarded, and the three titles "Messiah," "Son of God," and "Son of Man" are brought together in an open self-disclosure, which then goes beyond any mere title to assert Jesus' unique place at the right hand of God. The gauntlet is openly thrown down, and they are not slow to take it up.

In contrast to this high drama in front of the high priest, a brief insert in v. 58 turns the spotlight onto the very different figure of Peter as he sits outside in the courtyard "to see the end." The spotlight will return to him in the next pericope, but for now the mention of his presence outside alerts the reader to a secondary story-line which is developing alongside the central drama. Peter is to face his "trial" among the servants, just as Jesus does among the Sanhedrin, and the contrast between the response of the two Galileans gives a dramatic tension to the whole scene.[4] The reader is invited to choose between two models of how the man of God behaves under pressure, the one who escapes death but with his spiritual reputation in tatters and the one who will be killed only to live again in triumph; so the reader is reminded that "anyone who finds their life will lose it, and anyone who loses their life will find it" (10:39; 16:25).

The "Sanhedrin trial" has been the subject of immense historical debate, which has focused on three main areas of disagreement. (a) What was the nature of the hearing which led up to Jesus' transfer to the Roman prefect? (b) How does the gospel record relate to such evidence as we have for legal process at the time? (c) On what charge was Jesus condemned? Fortunately the debate has recently been well surveyed and judiciously assessed by Darrell Bock,[5] so that only a few summary remarks need be given here.

4. For this reading of the narrative see especially B. Gerhardsson, *JSNT* 13 (1981) 46-66.

5. D. L. Bock, *Blasphemy and Exaltation in Judaism and the Final Examination of Jesus.* As the title indicates, Bock's primary focus is on the meaning of the term "blasphemy," but his account of the nature of the examination (184-95) gives a good overview of recent debate, particularly on the question of its legality. See further K. Schubert in E. Bammel and C. F. D. Moule (eds.), *Jesus,* 385-402, for a defense of the essential histo-

(a) *The nature of the hearing.* Only the Synoptic Gospels relate the hearing in Caiaphas's house.[6] Apart from one significant nuance (see below on v. 60b) Matthew follows Mark's account closely. Luke 22:66-71 has a similar, though differently structured, account of the Sanhedrin hearing, but places it in the early morning rather than when Jesus was first brought to the high priest's house at night, whereas Mark and Matthew apparently have the hearing at night followed by what is sometimes taken to be a second session early in the morning (Mark 15:1; Matt 27:1). If, however, the phrase *symboulion poiēsantes / symboulion elabon* is understood not to refer to convening a separate meeting but to the conclusion of a judicial process which has continued through the night, and in particular to forming a plan as to how their previously agreed decision could best be presented to the prefect to obtain his official sanction for the execution, there is no need to think in terms of two separate hearings in Mark and Matthew either.[7] This commentary will therefore read Matthew's account as of a single, all-night hearing.

There is now widespread agreement[8] with John's statement that at this time the Jews did not have the right to carry out a death sentence (John 18:31), as indeed was the general policy with regard to subject nations in the Roman Empire. The Synoptic accounts all assume that even after agreeing on the death penalty the Sanhedrin had no option but to go to the Roman prefect to have it implemented. The well-known exceptions of the lynching of Stephen (Acts 7:54-60) and the execution of James the Just and his associates (Josephus, *Ant.* 20.200) are probably to be understood as unauthorized exceptions, the latter being explicitly attributed to the high priest's seizing his opportunity when there was no procurator in place (he was deposed as a result). The right to execute Gentiles who crossed the barrier into the restricted

---

ricity of the trial account in the light of earlier scepticism. Both studies focus on the account in Mark, but on almost all relevant points Matthew's differs little. On the historicity of the Synoptic accounts see also D. R. Catchpole, in E. Bammel (ed.), *Trial,* 47-65.

6. The Fourth Gospel tells of Jesus being taken to Caiaphas's house and from there to the Roman prefect, but says nothing of what happened at Caiaphas's house. Instead it has a quite different and apparently informal hearing before Annas (John 18:19-24) prior to Jesus' transfer to Caiaphas's house; Peter's denial is set in Annas's courtyard (John 18:15-18, 25-27).

7. I have argued for this view, following D. L. Bock, *Blasphemy,* 189-95, in my *Mark,* 602, 627. For the meaning of συμβούλιον λαμβάνω see p. 1034, n. 1.

8. This is based especially on the study by A. N. Sherwin-White, *Roman Society,* 32-47. In response to earlier denials, especially by H. Lietzmann and P. Winter, Sherwin-White points out that capital jurisdiction was delegated by Rome only in the case of a select number of *civitates liberae,* of which Jerusalem was certainly not one. The Jerusalem Talmud includes a statement that the Jews lost the right to execute "forty years before the temple was destroyed." The issue is surveyed by R. E. Brown, *Death,* 363-72; Keener, 664-65; cf. also J. Blinzler, *Trial,* 157-63; D. R. Catchpole, in E. Bammel (ed.), *Trial,* 58-63.

area of the temple is specifically noted as an officially sanctioned exception to the general rule (Josephus, *War* 6.126). So a hearing by the Sanhedrin, however clear its verdict, could not be formally a capital trial. It was, legally speaking, Pilate's verdict which sentenced Jesus to death. From the Jewish point of view, no doubt, what happened in Caiaphas's house was the "real" trial, but, formally speaking, it was more in the nature of a preliminary hearing to determine first that Jesus deserved to be brought before Pilate on a capital charge, and secondly to agree on the nature of that charge so as to ensure its success.[9] This dual role then accounts for the two phases of the hearing as they are described by Mark and Matthew. The first phase (26:59-68) determined that Jesus was guilty and must be put to death; the second (27:1-2) formulated an appropriate charge to bring to the prefect. But the two phases are closely connected, and there seems no reason to suppose that they were separated, or that anyone went to bed between 26:68 and 27:1.

(b) *The legality of the proceedings.* It has often been noted that the details of the Sanhedrin hearing do not conform at several points to the rules laid down for capital trials in *m. Sanhedrin.* In particular such trials must be held during the daytime, must take place in one of three specified courtrooms (which do not include the high priest's house), must begin by hearing the case for the defense, must not reach a conviction on the same day as the trial began, and therefore must not be held on the eve of a festival or of the sabbath (*m. Sanh.* 4:1; 11:2); at all these points the hearing as described in the gospels is defective. But it is questionable what currency these rules formulated at the end of the second century A.D. might have had in the period before the destruction of the temple; indeed, it is hard to see how they could have been practically applied since the Roman occupation prevented a Jewish court from carrying out the kind of capital sentences the Mishnah prescribes.

In any case, however, if, as has been argued above, this was not a formally constituted capital court but a less formal preliminary hearing, the issue does not arise.[10] It is unlikely that the whole membership of the Sanhedrin was present at least for the earlier stages of this hastily convened hearing, and it is probably more realistic to suppose that members continued to arrive to join the assembly during the night. Indeed, Mark's listing of "the chief priests with the elders and scribes and all the Sanhedrin" as present at the final stage of the hearing early in the morning (Mark 15:1) may be taken to imply that not all of

---

9. D. L. Bock, *Blasphemy,* 191, concludes that "this gathering was never seen or intended as a formal Jewish capital case, but as a kind of preliminary hearing to determine if Jesus was as dangerous as the leadership sensed and whether he could be credibly sent to Rome." In line with this finding Bock has conspicuously avoided using the term "trial" in the title of his book, preferring "examination."

10. The exceptional nature of the occasion is well brought out by Hagner, 2:797.

them had been there for the earlier phase, despite his phrase "the whole San-hedrin" in 14:55. This does not mean, however, that even in its earlier stages this gathering could dispense with all concern for correct procedure. Mat-thew's account does not suggest an impartial search for justice (see especially 26:59), but the dismissal of false testimony suggests that at least the form of a proper judicial hearing was observed, and the high priest's ritual tearing of his robes conforms to the mishnaic convention for a trial on the charge of blas-phemy (*m. Sanh.* 7:5). The hearing thus carried legitimacy as an official ex-pression of Jewish repudiation of Jesus as a blasphemer, but it did not need to observe the formal procedure of a capital court since it was at the Roman trial that the legal verdict would be given.

(c) *The charge against Jesus.* This is of course quite specifically stated twice in v. 65 as "blasphemy." There has nevertheless been consider-able disagreement as to how this relates to what actually happened at the hearing. Part of the problem has been the assumption that the mishnaic "defi-nition" of blasphemy would already have been current and accepted at the time of Jesus: *m. Sanh.* 7:5 says that "the blasphemer is not culpable unless he pronounces the Name itself." Since Jesus' reply to the high priest has con-spicuously avoided pronouncing the name of God by referring to him as "the power" (v. 64), whereas the high priest's question, in its Matthean form, *has* used the name of God,[11] this is clearly too restrictive to make sense of the present scene, and it is unlikely that at this time any such precise usage was established. Darrell Bock's detailed study[12] has concluded that "blasphemy" was at this time more widely understood, and therefore argues convincingly that Jesus' "blasphemy" consisted not in a formal misuse of God's name but in claiming for himself a unique association with God, sitting at his right hand. While a claim to be the Messiah was not in itself blasphemous,[13] what Jesus said in response to the high priest went far beyond that claim: he was

---

11. In Mark he, too, uses a periphrasis, "the Blessed."

12. D. L. Bock, *Blasphemy,* 30-183. Bock first analyzes Jewish understandings of blasphemy, showing that the term could be used more broadly than the mishnaic "defini-tion" suggests, to cover arrogant speech or action against God and his people (and the temple). He then goes on to consider the background to Jesus' claim to be seated at God's right hand and concludes that only a few very special figures (such as Enoch and Moses) were envisaged as allowed to sit (rather than stand) in the presence of God; for anyone else to claim such a right for himself would thus also be regarded as blasphemous. See also D. R. Catchpole, *Trial,* 126-48.

13. Note, however, the interesting suggestion of J. Marcus, *NovT* 31 (1989) 125-41, that the high priest's question is not simply about Messiahship in general but about a particular view of Messiahship, that of a "Messiah–Son-of-God" as opposed to the "Messiah–Son-of-David," and that the former "introduces an idea of quasi-divinity that is the basis of Jesus' condemnation."

not only Messiah and Son of God but also, as the Son of Man predicted in Dan 7:13-14, he was now to share God's throne. Such outrageous claims must either be accepted, which was unthinkable, or repudiated as blasphemous and their author eliminated as a threat to orthodox religious belief. That he had also, as part of this radically subversive agenda, threatened the destruction and replacement of the temple was also not a side issue; that alone came dangerously close to "blasphemy." (See further below on vv. 65-66.)

57 For Caiaphas see above on v. 3. Matthew says that Jesus was taken to him, rather than to his house, but it becomes clear in the next verse that this episode is set at his house, the same place where we have seen the members of the Sanhedrin plotting together in vv. 3-5. This is not, therefore, a formal meeting of the Sanhedrin, which would take place in the "chamber of hewn stone" on the western side of the temple mount,[14] not at the high priest's house (the location of which is debated). Matthew mentions two of the three component groups of the Sanhedrin (see on 16:21), perhaps because the mention of the high priest renders a further mention of the "chief priests" unnecessary here (but they will reappear in v. 59). The scribes would, of course, be an important element in any legal decisions reached. See the introductory comments above on the nature of this gathering; if Judas had been able to give only short notice of when the arrest might be possible, the number present may have been limited, probably augmented as the night went on.

58 A brief mention of Peter outside in the courtyard sets the scene for vv. 69-75 when his informal "trial" will follow that of Jesus. So far his boasted loyalty (vv. 33, 35) has persisted at least to the extent of not wishing to lose touch with Jesus altogether, though the imperfect tense "was following" perhaps conveys a note of tentativeness, as does the phrase "at a distance." The courtyard was probably a semipublic unroofed area[15] where those not involved in the hearing, slaves and lesser members of the household, would gather. The assertion by two of the women that Peter had been "with Jesus" (vv. 69, 71) probably indicates (as John 18:26 makes explicit) that they had been with the arresting party who had now returned successfully and were waiting outside, like Peter, to see what happened to their prisoner in the house.

59-60a The spotlight moves back from Peter in the courtyard to Jesus on trial in the house. For a useful brief overview of what is known about the Jerusalem Sanhedrin (to which this is the only reference by name in Matthew) see Keener, 614-16.[16] If the above discussion of the nature of this gath-

---

14. See Schürer, 2:223-25.
15. John 18:15 suggests, however, that there was restricted access.
16. See also J. Blinzler, *Trial,* 93-97, for its constituent groups. For a wide-

ering is correct, "the whole Sanhedrin" here and in Mark 14:55 must be a broad generalization rather than claiming that all seventy-one members of the Sanhedrin were present, which would be unlikely for a meeting convened at night at short notice. The point is that it was not just the priests, who had taken the initiative, who were present but representatives of all the constituent parts of the Sanhedrin; a third of the membership was recognized as the quorum for a capital case (*m. Sanh.* 1:1). This is thus a body competent to represent official Jewish opinion.

There is as yet no charge against Jesus; it is the purpose of this gathering to formulate one. Matthew's phrase "looking for false testimony against Jesus" sounds loaded, but is perhaps a compressed way of saying that they wanted to find evidence against Jesus but what they found proved to be false; it was not in their interest that it should prove inadmissible. If two or more witnesses failed to agree under cross-examination,[17] that charge could not be admitted and must be declared false (Deut 19:15 etc.; see above on 18:16). What they failed to find was not false witnesses, of which there were "many,"[18] but two witnesses whose testimony, whether strictly true or not, could at least be admitted as valid because they agreed. But the final clause "so that they could have him executed" indicates that this was not to be an impartial hearing: the verdict has already been decided (see v. 4), and the only problem is how it may be justified. When the verdict precedes the charge, a proper "trial" is not to be expected.

60b-61 After the fiasco of inconsistent false testimonies, a more serious charge is now put forward. Whereas Mark presents the temple charge also as "false witness," specifically saying that this, too, was not in agreement (Mark 14:57-59), Matthew sees it differently. Those who brought this charge are distinguished from the earlier "false witnesses" by the phrase "but in the end" *(hysteron de),* and two of them are presented as speaking together. This then was legally valid evidence,[19] as the high priest's challenge in v. 62 makes clear: unlike the previous attempts, this charge requires an answer. And it is a charge which goes to the heart of Jesus' mission and of the radical ideology with regard to the temple which was one of the main reasons why Jerusalem had repudiated his message. The phrasing, "I *can* destroy," clearly focuses the charge on Jesus' claim to personal authority over the temple.

Formally speaking, of course, this charge, too, is false, as far as our

---

ranging discussion of the nature and procedures of the Sanhedrin see R. E. Brown, *Death,* 339-57.

17. See *m. Sanh.* 4:5–5:4 for the later rules on questioning witnesses.

18. The imperfect tense "were looking" may indicate a protracted search.

19. D. P. Senior, *Passion,* 166-68.

records go: Jesus had not said that he himself would or could destroy the temple,[20] only that it would be destroyed,[21] nor had he spoken of rebuilding it. And the only thing which he has predicted as happening within three days is his own resurrection (12:40; 16:21; 17:23; 20:19). John 2:19 does indeed record Jesus as speaking of the restoration of "this temple" in three days with reference, John says, to his own body (John 2:21), and since that prediction is set in the context of Jesus' demonstration against the temple regime it is not surprising that it was taken literally; but it attributes the destruction not to Jesus but to "you." That is John, however, and Matthew has given no such basis for this charge.[22] But it is not impossible that Jesus had used the sort of imagery John 2:19-21 presupposes, speaking of his own resurrection in connection with the replacement of the temple.[23] Something of the sort may well be implied in his reference to "something greater than the temple" in 12:6. Such language, together with his clear prediction that the temple would be destroyed, and his "antitemple" demonstration in 21:12-13, would give a basis for this charge in the minds of those who did not, or would not, follow through the logic of Jesus' imagery. The crowd at the cross will show that this is the sort of thing people were saying about Jesus (27:40), and the same popular understanding of Jesus' antitemple agenda will reemerge in the charge against Stephen in Acts 6:13-14, which shows how central this motif was to early opposition to the Jesus movement.

---

20. *Gos. Thom.* 71 gives as a saying of Jesus, "I shall destroy this house, and no one will be able to rebuild it." If the "house" here is the temple (the saying occurs without context), this quite distinctive text is, however, more likely a reflection of the charge at Jesus' trial (in the light of the subsequent destruction of the temple) than an independent record of an earlier saying of Jesus.

21. There is also a difference in wording, which is, however, probably not significant. The charge is that Jesus plans to destroy τὸν ναὸν τοῦ θεοῦ (so also, without τοῦ θεοῦ, in 27:40), whereas Jesus' predictions have focused on "your house" (23:38) and on "here" (24:2), which refers back to the phrase "the buildings of the temple (ἱερόν)" in 24:1. If ναός is used here (as Matthew uses it elsewhere: 23:16-21, 35; 27:5, 51) in its proper sense of the sanctuary building itself rather than the whole temple complex (τὸ ἱερόν), it does of course refer to a more limited area, but one which is necessarily included in the destruction of τὸ ἱερόν, and focuses on the most sensitive part of it.

22. *Pace* Gundry, 542-43, who believes that Matthew "is identifying the Temple of God with the Son of God."

23. "In three days" might just be an idiom for "in a short time" (J. Jeremias, *Theology*, 285), but it is a remarkably vivid idiom to use for the replacement of a huge building, and the fact that the phrase "on the third day" has occurred repeatedly in Jesus' resurrection predictions suggests some more specific link. The point is suggestively developed by E. E. Ellis in J. B. Green and M. Turner (eds.), *Jesus of Nazareth,* 197-202. Ellis argues that the alleged saying was a prediction of Jesus' self-resurrection and thus an implicit claim to divinity.

This is the only substantive charge brought against Jesus in this hearing other than his "blasphemy" in v. 64, and it will remain in the public consciousness as the (or at least a) reason for his execution (27:40). That is why Matthew cannot simply dismiss it as just another "false testimony." Jesus, like Jeremiah before him, is on trial for his unpatriotic and sacrilegious threats to the temple. And since to purify and restore the temple was a prerogative of the Messiah,[24] the question of the high priest in v. 63 is not a *non sequitur*, but rather a follow-up to the theological implications of Jesus' alleged intention to replace the existing Jerusalem temple. The two charges will both be recalled in the mockery of Jesus on the cross, the temple charge by the passersby and the Messiah and Son of God charge by the Sanhedrin members (27:39-43).

62-63 By emphasizing Jesus' silence both here and in 27:14 Matthew portrays Jesus as allowing events to take their course; had he wished he could no doubt have disputed the accuracy of the wording attributed to him, and explained that his polemic against the temple did not involve a personal demolition project. Matthew probably also expects his readers to catch the echo of Isa 53:7, which speaks of God's servant, oppressed and afflicted and about to be "led to the slaughter," remaining silent and not opening his mouth.[25] But Jesus' apparent aloofness, even in the face of a legally admissible charge, only exasperates the high priest. He stands up to signal that he is taking personal control of the investigation, and demands a response under oath,[26] not now to the temple charge alone but to an even more fundamental question about the nature of Jesus' claim. The oath "by the living God" uses none of the evasive formulae which Jesus has dismissed in 5:34-36 and 23:16-22, but imposes the strongest possible sanction, echoing God's own oath formula in the OT: "As I live, says the LORD."[27]

Jesus' own public teaching and actions have perhaps given sufficient basis for the high priest to press him on the two alleged claims, to be "Messiah" and "Son of God." His approach to the city as the messianic king of Zech 9:9, and the resultant Hosannas which he refused to repudiate (21:9,

---

24. For the Messiah as temple builder see especially 2 Sam 7:12-14 and Zech 6:12. See the introductory comments on 21:12-17. At that point we focused on Jewish hopes that the Messiah would *purify* the temple rather than that he would *rebuild* it. For the latter idea in targums and at Qumran see D. Juel, *Messiah,* 172-96; more briefly R. E. Brown, *Death,* 441-43. D. L. Bock, *Blasphemy,* 213, n. 69, surveys the discussion on the issue of the Messiah and the temple.

25. For the allusion see D. J. Moo, *The OT,* 148-51.

26. Cf. 1 Kgs 22:16 for the similar use of an oath to force a true answer; for rabbinic custom see *m. Šebu.* 4:13.

27. For the wording of the oath formula, to "add solemnity and dramatic force," see D. P. Senior, *Passion,* 174-75.

15-16), would alone have been enough, but his demonstration in the temple and his subsequent teaching have increased the impression that he is putting himself in a unique category of authority, even though there has been no overt verbal claim to be the Messiah. His one reference to the title in 22:42-45 has teasingly avoided applying the question about the Messiah as Son of David directly to his own status, but in context it was clearly not just an academic argument (see introductory comments on 22:41-46). As for "Son of God," Jesus' one direct reference to himself under this title since coming to Jerusalem was in private with the disciples (24:36), but the figure of the landowner's son in the parable of the vineyard (21:37-39) was a transparent reference to his own status and his coming rejection and execution by the Jerusalem authorities. And Jesus' argument about the status of the Messiah in 22:42-45 has given a broad hint that he regards himself as "Messiah, Son of God." So even in Jesus' public words and deeds since coming to Jerusalem there was probably enough to justify the high priest's question. It may reflect what ordinary people in Jerusalem were already beginning to say about the claims of the Galilean preacher (see on 27:40). But we have noted above that Judas's role may also have included the provision of inside information to the priests, and Jesus' language in private with his disciples has been less guarded, in particular his frequent references to God as "my Father" in a way which implied a unique relationship (notably 11:25-27).

In Luke 22:67, 70 the questions "Are you the Messiah?" and "Are you the Son of God?" are asked separately, though the second is provoked by the answer to the first. It has sometimes been suggested that this must have been so, since there was no Jewish belief in the Messiah as the Son of God. In the light of evidence from Qumran[28] this objection has now been generally abandoned, but it was always insecurely based in that the Qumran usage is based on two OT passages which already spoke of the anointed king as God's son (2 Sam 7:14; Ps 2:7). In any case, the high priest is not asking a general theological question, but is probing Jesus' alleged claims, and the parable of the vineyard alone would have been enough to suggest that he saw himself as "the Messiah, the Son of God." Judas may also have informed him that it was with this same combination of titles that Peter had hailed Jesus in 16:16,[29] and that Jesus has accepted the declaration with pleasure.[30]

64   In the light of his own teaching in 5:34, 37 we might expect Jesus

28. 4Q174 *(Florilegium);* 4Q246 *(Aramaic Apocalypse)* 2:1; perhaps 1QSa(28a) 2:11-12. See, e.g., D. Juel, *Messiah,* 108-14; M. Hengel, *Son of God,* 43-45.

29. Note the recurrence of the phrase "the living God" here, though not now as part of the title "Son of God," as it was in 16:16.

30. See p. 1020, n. 13, for Marcus's suggestion that "Messiah–Son-of-God" is intended to separate one type of messianic role from another.

to repudiate the high priest's oath formula and to maintain his silence. But the question goes to the heart of his mission, and the time has come to bring his claim into the open before the highest court of Israel. True to 5:34, 37, however, he himself, unlike the high priest, uses no oath formula, but simply states his position.[31] In Mark 14:62 his reply begins with a clear "I am," conforming to the simple "yes" or "no" which Jesus has demanded of his disciples (5:37); why then does his reply in Matthew sound more evasive? The formula "You have said it" has already appeared at v. 25, where it is Jesus' reply to Judas's question, "You don't mean me, do you?" and it will appear again (with a change of tense which does not affect the meaning) in 27:11 in response to Pilate's "Are you the king of the Jews?" In the former case it is clearly affirmative, but the affirmation is expressed by turning the questioner's words back on himself. Here and in 27:11 it has the same effect, but it is a qualified affirmative[32] in that by drawing attention to the questioner's own words Jesus probably indicates that the proposition, while correct, is not phrased as he would have phrased it, or that he does not accept the connotations which he assumes to be in the questioner's mind. It might be paraphrased "Yes, but that's not how I would have put it" or "Yes, but I don't mean by that what you mean."[33] In this case the element of reluctance probably stems especially from the term "Messiah," which in popular Jewish thought would have had nationalistic connotations which did not correspond to Jesus' understanding of his messianic mission (see above on 16:16, 20, 22-23), and which could easily be construed, as indeed it will be in 27:11ff., as a mark of political ambition. Caiaphas's question arises not from a search for understanding but from a search for ammunition to use against Jesus.

But the words he has used nonetheless express the truth, and Jesus now goes on to build on it. The opening "And yet" places a clear distinction between what "you have said" and what "I tell you": Jesus is now going to explain his messianic mission in his own preferred terms. He is not disagreeing with what the high priest has said, but is reformulating it in a way which goes far beyond it. In place of the title "Messiah" he uses his own preferred

31. J. A. Brant, *JSNT* 63 (1996) 15-17, analyzes the intention of Caiaphas in using the oath formula and the significance of Jesus' response.

32. This interpretation of the phrase is now widely agreed on, especially in the light of the study by D. R. Catchpole, *NTS* 17 (1970/1) 213-26, which finds such a formula in Jewish usage to be "affirmative in content, and reluctant or circumlocutory in formulation" (226); "an affirmation modified only by a preference for not stating the matter *expressis verbis*" (217).

33. "Jesus may well be implying that the High Priest has no idea what he is actually saying" (Schweizer, 499). At the other end of the scale, Gundry, 544-45, thinks that here Jesus "stoutly affirms that the questioner himself knows the affirmative answer as obvious" (as in v. 25).

title "the Son of Man" (see on 8:20), and in place of the sort of earthly power the high priest's question probably implied he speaks of a heavenly glory and authority. Two OT texts provide the language for this bold assertion: sitting at God's right hand derives from Ps 110:1, which Jesus has already referred to in connection with the status of the Messiah in 22:42-45; coming with the clouds of heaven takes up the allusion to Dan 7:13-14 already implicit in the title "the Son of Man," a vision to which Jesus has already referred several times (10:23; 16:27-28; 19:28; 24:30; 25:31). See the comments on 10:23 and 22:43-45 for the OT context and meaning of these two texts. Uniquely in the OT,[34] they share the motif of the heavenly enthronement of someone in-vited by God to share his authority,[35] so that by bringing them together Jesus is making a remarkable claim. He, who appears now to be the helpless victim of a biased human court, is soon to be seen as the highest authority next to God himself. The implication in the phrase "you [plural] will see" is that the tables will be turned, and that he who is now being judged by the Sanhedrin will soon be recognized as himself their judge. This is the same reversal of roles which was the message of the first part of Jesus' discourse on the Mount of Olives (24:4-35): the imminent collapse of the existing regime will be the prelude to the universal sovereignty of the Son of Man.

On this understanding of the imagery the "coming on the clouds of heaven" cannot be read as a reference to the *parousia,* as has been the tradi-tional exegesis until relatively recently.[36] See on 24:30 for a parallel issue, where exactly the same words are used (without the intervening reference to Ps 110:1) with reference, as I argued there, to the enthronement of the Son of Man in contrast to the destruction of the temple. There the event predicted

---

34. N. T. Wright, *Victory,* 642-43, argues, following M. Hengel, *Studies,* 185-89, that these are the two texts in the OT which "pointed towards an enthronement in which the Messiah, or the 'son of man,' would share the very throne of Israel's god," and which together also inspired the enthronement of the "son of man" figure in *1 Enoch.*

35. To recognize this is to dissolve the difficulty some interpreters have felt with the order of clauses, with the sitting preceding the coming. I remember G. M. Styler at a Cambridge seminar explaining this apparently unchronological order by the analogy of the notice outside the fellows' car park of St. Catherine's College: "These gates may be closed at any time and unauthorised cars will be removed." The problem arose from the then dominant view that "coming with the clouds of heaven" depicted the *parousia.* But once it is recognized that there is no temporal sequence between the two clauses, but that each describes in different imagery the state of sharing God's authority, there is no "chro-nological" problem to apologize for.

36. G. R. Beasley-Murray, *Kingdom,* 300, while himself still favoring the older view, recognizes a "considerable shift of opinion" toward an exaltation rather than *parousia* interpretation, which he traces especially to the work of T. F. Glasson and J. A. T. Robinson. He even, perhaps with a little exaggeration, calls the non-*parousia* in-terpretation now "a major consensus."

was to take place within "this generation," and here, too, Matthew's wording demands a fulfillment which is imminent rather than set in the indefinite future:[37] it is something which "you" (the current Sanhedrin members) "will see," and it will come true "from now on."[38] It is fully consonant with this prediction that in 28:18, only a few days later, the risen and vindicated Jesus will declare the fulfillment of Dan 7:14 in his assertion that "all authority in heaven and on earth has been given to me" (28:18). In the vindication of the repudiated Messiah and in the powerful growth of the movement which they have attempted to suppress,[39] they "will see" that it is he who is now seated on the heavenly throne. There may also be an echo here of the mourning of the tribes of the land when they "see" the triumph of the one they have pierced (24:30).

Jesus' use of "power"[40] to refer to God may reflect the reticence of a pious Jew in uttering the actual name of God,[41] and as such may have made the high priest's charge of "blasphemy" less easy to establish (see introductory comments above). But Jesus has hitherto shown no diffidence about using God's name, in public as well as in private (see 22:21, 29, 31-32, 37; 23:22; and "kingdom of God" [not "heaven"] in 21:31, 43), so that the substitution here may be for the more positive purpose of emphasizing that the seat at God's right hand places him in a position to exercise power and authority (the "dominion" and "kingship" predicted in Dan 7:14). Note how "power" is associated elsewhere with the fulfillment of the Daniel vision (24:30; 28:18 ["authority"]; Mark 8:38–9:1).

---

37. *Pace* NIV, which unjustifiably translated ἀπ' ἄρτι here by "in the future" (so also Hagner, 2:794; though on p. 800 he distances himself from NIV), presumably to make space for a delayed *parousia*. That apologetic mistranslation has rightly been corrected in TNIV. Cf. RSV, "hereafter," similarly corrected in NRSV.

38. The objection of M. Casey, *Son of Man,* 189, that "'from now on you will see' must be followed by a continuous state, not a single event, as the object of the vision" begs the question by assuming that this saying refers to the event of the *parousia* rather than to the state of authority which Jesus will enjoy continuously at the right hand of God. For Matthew's use of ἀπ' ἄρτι, "from now on," as "a strong divider between the immediate past and an entirely new future" see D. P. Senior, *Passion,* 178-83.

39. For the range of possible historical referents for the visible "coming of the Son of Man" see above on 10:23 and 16:28. J. A. Gibbs, *Jerusalem,* 142-48, agrees substantially with the exegesis given here, but lays stress especially on the coming destruction of Jerusalem as the "evidence that this man, Jesus, whom they rejected as the Son of God, is seated at the right hand of power."

40. Or "the Power"? — the definite article allows either reading.

41. Several rabbinic texts refer to God as *haggebûrâ,* "the power," though this usage is after the NT period: see D. L. Bock, *Blasphemy,* 217-19, and more fully A. M. Goldberg, *BZ* 8 (1964) 284-93. For the basis of such language in the OT see O. F. J. Seitz, *SE* 6 (1973) 494.

65-66   The high priest at last has enough evidence to justify a guilty verdict. See the introductory comments above for the nature of the "blasphemy" contained in Jesus' words. By placing himself at God's right hand he had overstepped the boundary of what might properly be claimed by any human being, however exalted, let alone a Galilean village preacher of questionable orthodoxy.

Darrell Bock, in applying his massive study of blasphemy to the condemnation of Jesus, concludes that this was the main focus of the charge, but he also goes on to suggest a secondary element of "cultural blasphemy" which added to the offense. Blasphemy included speaking and acting not only against God but also against his temple and his appointed leaders in Israel (note Exod 22:28).[42] The record of Jesus' teaching and actions in Jerusalem has provided ample evidence of both these offenses, and his climactic declaration in v. 64 has been directed against the members of the Sanhedrin ("you"), over whom he now claims the ultimate sovereignty. This was at least undiplomatic, but according to Bock it also contributed to the overall charge of blasphemy.[43]

According to *m. Sanh.* 7:5, when blasphemy is uttered "the judges stand up and tear their robes, and they may not mend them again." Tearing one's clothes was a traditional gesture of mourning (Gen 37:29, 34; Josh 7:6; 2 Sam 1:11, etc.), which was also a way of dissociating oneself from what one has heard (Num 14:6; 2 Kgs 18:37; 19:1; cf. Acts 14:14), but its use by the high priest is a mark of how seriously blasphemy was taken, since the law forbade the high priest to tear his robes in mourning even for a close personal relative (Lev 21:10-11).[44] Despite the later mishnaic regulation we are not told here that the rest of the Sanhedrin followed the high priest's lead in this. But they are required to express their response verbally, and it is not just that Jesus is guilty but that the crime carries the death penalty,[45] as indeed the law demanded (Lev 24:11-16). They do not specify how Jesus should be executed, and indeed this was out of their jurisdiction; the method of execution laid down in Leviticus was stoning (so also *m. Sanh.* 7:4), but this was not a Roman procedure. It is in-

42. For a summary of the detailed discussion of Jewish evidence see D. L. Bock, *Blasphemy,* 111-12, and for the relevance of this to Jesus' examination before the Sanhedrin, ibid., 206-9.

43. For a stimulating discussion of Jesus' claim and the basis of his condemnation see also N. T. Wright, *Victory,* 524-28.

44. The reference here is not, however, to the formal vestments of the high priest, which were locked away for use only on special occasions (Josephus, *Ant.* 18.91-94; cf. 15.403-5). On the tearing of clothes see further R. E. Brown, *Death,* 517-19.

45. ἔνοχος means both "guilty" and "liable," so that the phrase ἔνοχος θανάτου conveys both Jesus' guilt ("guilty" of blasphemy) and the punishment due to that crime ("liable" to death).

teresting to note, however, that at Qumran the penalty for one who "slanders his people" was to be hung on a tree to die (11Q19[Temple] 64:7-9), "the first-century cultural equivalent of which was crucifixion."[46] If this principle was known outside the closed community of Qumran, it may suggest that the demand of the Jewish crowd, inspired by the priests, that Jesus be crucified (27:20-23) was not as culturally alien as it has often been thought.[47] This hearing, however, does not have the legal competence to pronounce the sentence; that will be for the Roman prefect. "He deserves to die" simply expresses their agreement that Jesus is guilty on a capital charge.

67-68 The quasiofficial proceedings of the preceding verses now descend into undignified physical abuse. This seems such inappropriate behavior for the members of the Sanhedrin that Mark has softened the impact by saying it was done by "some people" (unspecified) with the participation also of "servants," while Luke attributes it to "the men who were holding Jesus." Matthew allows no such latitude: the subject of these verbs is the same as for the declaration of Jesus' guilt. Perhaps we expect too great a sense of decorum in this gathering of influential people of Jerusalem, particularly as this was probably not a formal trial (see above). But perhaps also there is a closer connection between the judicial verdict and the physical abuse than we would expect in our culture. An interesting case is made by J. D. M. Derrett[48] that the spitting[49] and physical ill-treatment were, like the tearing of the clothes, an accepted symbol of dissociation from the blasphemer. He also suggests that the striking of Jesus with a demand to "prophesy"[50] by saying who had struck him derives from the popular belief, based on Isa 11:3, that a true Messiah should be able to identify his assailant by smell without seeing him (Mark mentions that they blindfolded him, Mark 14:65).[51] Jesus, we are left to assume, did not rise to the bait, but the reader is left with the irony that the Messiah whose "prophetic" abilities they are mocking has in fact predicted the very rejection and condemnation that he is now undergoing (16:21; 20:19). The spitting in the face and the blows recall Isaiah's prophecy of the physical abuse of God's servant (Isa 50:6),[52] and

---

46. D. L. Bock, *Blasphemy,* 208.

47. This was argued even before the discovery of 11Q19 by E. Bammel in E. Bammel (ed.), *Trial,* 162-65. Cf. M. Hengel, *Crucifixion,* 84-85.

48. J. D. M. Derrett, *Law,* 407-8; cf. J. Jeremias, *Theology,* 77-78.

49. For spitting in the face of someone judged guilty see Deut 25:9, and cf. also Num 12:14.

50. The use of this verb may also suggest an allusion to the law of Deut 18:20 condemning a false prophet to death.

51. For ancient "games," sometimes quite violent, involving blindfolding the victim see D. L. Miller, *JBL* 90 (1971) 309-13; R. E. Brown, *Death,* 574-76.

52. See D. J. Moo, *The OT,* 139-44, for this as a deliberate allusion.

the use of the verb "slap" not only echoes the LXX of Isa 50:6 but also invites the reader to reflect on how Jesus here exemplifies his own teaching in 5:39 (the only other use of the verb in the NT). The mocking of Jesus' claimed title "Messiah"[53] by the Jewish leaders here parallels the mocking of his alleged claim to be "king of the Jews" by the Roman soldiers in 27:27-31.

3. Peter's Failure (26:69-75)

> 69 Meanwhile Peter was sitting outside in the courtyard. One servant girl came up to him and said, "You, too, were with Jesus the Galilean." 70 But he denied it in front of them all, saying, "I don't know what you are talking about." 71 He went out into the gateway, where another girl saw him and said to the people there, "This man[1] was with Jesus the Nazorean."[2] 72 He denied it again, with an oath: "I don't know the man." 73 But a bit later the people standing there came up to Peter and said, "Yes, you really are one of them: your accent[3] gives you away." 74 Then he began to curse,[4] and to swear, "I don't know the man." And just then the cock crowed. 75 Peter remembered Jesus' prediction,[5] "Before the cock crows, you will deny me three times"; and he went outside and wept bitterly.

Here is the culmination of the parallel "trial" of Peter for which we were prepared in v. 58 (see above, p. 1017), and which was signaled by Jesus' prediction in v. 34. The detailed fulfillment of Jesus' prediction shows him to be a true prophet, despite the jibe of v. 68. Despite Peter's earlier bravado,

53. This is the only use of the vocative Χριστέ in the NT (in contrast with later liturgical use); to address someone by the unadorned title in this way is clearly as sarcastic as the vocative βασιλεῦ τῶν Ἰουδαίων used by the Roman soldiers in 27:29.
1. Many MSS have a καί, "this man too," but this is probably an assimilation to the form of the first and third challenges in vv. 69, 73, perhaps influenced also by the καί which introduces all three challenges in Luke.
2. For the form of the name see above, p. 89, n. 4. This and 2:23 are the only two uses of the adjective in Matthew; the name "Nazareth" occurs in 2:23; 4:13; 21:11.
3. The Greek term means simply "speech," but see the comments below for the likely reference.
4. The verb requires an object, which is, however, left unexpressed. See the comments below.
5. Literally, "the utterance of Jesus having declared that. . . ." Matthew's infrequent uses of ῥῆμα rather than λόγος sometimes denote a marked pronouncement (cf. 4:4; 12:36), and here, combined with the verb form εἴρηκα (see p. 55, n. 54), it draws attention to a particularly significant utterance of Jesus. For a similar phrase see LXX Josh 1:13.

and his willingness to stay closer to Jesus than any of the other disciples
have done, he will collapse under pressure. His name will not appear again
in this gospel (contrast Mark 16:7), and his bitter weeping is left
uninterpreted for the moment. But the Christian reader already knows that
this is not the end of the story of Peter, and so is prepared to read a more
positive repentance into Peter's weeping than into the unavailing remorse of
Judas (27:3-5), and the careful specification that it was *eleven* disciples who
met Jesus in Galilee (28:16) ensures that Peter is included in the "disciples"
of 28:7 and the "brothers" of 28:10. The careful reader may remember that a
word spoken against the Son of Man is forgivable (12:32), and may even
find in 14:28-32 a parable of Peter's restoration after nearly sinking.[6] For
the contrast between the apparently parallel failures of Peter and of Judas
see below on 27:3-10.

The story is told with a vivid simplicity, in three escalating scenes.
The pressure builds as the first challenge comes from a single servant girl,
the second from another girl now appealing to the bystanders, and the third
from a group of those bystanders coming at him together. And Peter's response escalates accordingly: first comes an evasive denial, then a direct
denial on oath, and finally a much stronger response which (see below) is
probably to be understood as actually uttering a curse against Jesus. There
is also physical movement "further and further away from Jesus" (Davies
and Allison, 3:542), in that Peter is at first in the courtyard, then moves out
to its gateway, and finally (v. 75) escapes right outside. So Peter has comprehensively failed the test of loyalty, and Jesus' prediction has been exactly fulfilled.

69-70 For Peter's situation in the courtyard see on v. 58. The phrasing of the first two challenges, "You were [this man was] with Jesus," suggests that the speakers were present at Jesus' arrest and had seen Peter there,
though the reference might be to the earlier period when they were seen together in the temple courtyard. The *kai* which introduces the first challenge
links Peter directly with the man now on trial: "you, too." But the first chal-
lenger does not seem to be a significant threat: the Greek might be translated
"one little servant girl." "One" serves to differentiate her from "another" in
v. 71, but perhaps also emphasizes that so far she stands alone. Matthew often uses "one" to stress that it is "*only* one" that is in view; cf. 5:18, 19; 6:27;
10:29, etc., and see p. 323, n. 3. And *paidiskē,* while it is the regular term for

6. D. J. Weaver, *Discourse,* 149, offers an unusually positive perspective on this
incident. She finds "the one visible sign of hope with regard to the disciples" in two details of this story: Peter has "followed" Jesus as far as the high priest's house, and he "remembered Jesus' prediction"; in these two aspects, therefore, "Peter is still active as a
disciple."

a female servant, is diminutive in form, and probably carries a dismissive connotation — *only* a servant girl.

The three challenges all in different ways point out the "foreignness" of Jesus and his group in Jerusalem. The two epithets for Jesus, "the Galilean" and "the Nazorean," mark him as a visitor from the north, and pick up the terms used by the pilgrim crowd when they introduced Jesus to the sceptical people of Jerusalem in 21:11, and Peter himself is marked out as a foreigner by the way he speaks (see on v. 73): he must be "one of them," not one of us. There is, probably, an element of xenophobia in the way these Jerusalem servants react to the presence of this provincial group of troublemakers.

"Denied in front of them all" echoes 10:33.[7] In the narrative context it indicates a group of people listening, though not yet directly involved in the exchange. Peter's response is not an explicit repudiation of his relationship with Jesus (as it is in Luke and John), but rather a pretense of ignorance, but in reply to a challenge which explicitly linked him with Jesus it is in effect a denial.

71-72 Verbal evasion is followed by physical evasion: Peter is trying to avoid being noticed. But the gateway is no less crowded, and another girl recognizes him and appeals to the bystanders for confirmation. This time Peter feels obliged to utter a direct denial, and underlines it with an oath. Matthew's readers will note the irony of Jesus' leading disciple failing to follow his master's teaching about oaths (5:34, 37), particularly in view of Jesus' own response in v. 64 to the high priest's attempt to put him on oath.

For the description *Nazōraios* see above on 2:23, where we noted the likely derogatory connotations of a person being so described. Now we see the predicted fulfillment of "what had been declared through the prophets, that he should be called a Nazorean" (2:23).

73-74a The two previous exchanges have drawn in the listening crowd of servants as a whole, and they now present a united challenge. Peter is the odd man out. As soon as he opens his mouth, it is clear that he does not belong in Jerusalem. A different dialect of Aramaic was spoken in Galilee, and Judeans made fun of the slovenly pronunciation of consonants by Galileans (*b. 'Erub.* 53b).[8] Peter's northern accent, especially in the high priest's courtyard, marked him out as "one of them."

Again Peter denies, and again he uses an oath. But this time Matthew's wording goes further, and the verb "began" indicates a new element in

---

7. G. W. H. Lampe, *BJRL* 55 (1972/3) 353, speaks of "deny" in such a context as "already in the NT a technical term in the vocabulary of persecution, martyrdom, apostasy and infidelity." See further ibid., 355-68, for the way the story of Peter's denial was drawn on in the debates about apostasy during the early patristic period.

8. See G. Vermes, *Jesus*, 52-54.

this third denial. The verb "swear" alone would have indicated merely another oath as in v. 72, but it is preceded by *katathematizō*, a verb which occurs only here but is generally agreed to be synonymous with the verb used in the Marcan parallel, *anathematizō*, "to curse, anathematize" (and in the LXX "to devote," especially to destruction). *Anathematizō* elsewhere is always a transitive verb[9] requiring a direct object to denote the person cursed; cf. Paul's use of *anathema* as a curse formula in 1 Cor 12:3; 16:22; Gal 1:8, 9, in each case applied to a person other than the speaker. If the verb here meant, as some versions have suggested, that Peter is putting *himself* under a curse if he is lying, it would require "himself" as object, as it has in Acts 21:12, 14, 21. Here, where the object is not expressed, it means that Peter is cursing someone other than himself, and the most natural sense in this context would be that he now began to curse *Jesus,* as a way of dissociating himself from him; this was precisely what Pliny later required those accused of being Christians to do, in order to prove their innocence (Pliny, *Ep.* 10.96.5; cf. also Justin, *1 Apol.* 31.6). Matthew and Mark, by leaving the object unexpressed, refrain from stating in so many words that Peter cursed Jesus, but it is hard to see what else the choice of these transitive verbs could be meant to convey.[10]

74b-75   Under the pressure of the moment Peter has allowed his loyalty to be compromised. The crowing of the cock reminds him of his earlier boast (vv. 33, 35), and he realizes how far he has fallen short. His bitter weeping, once he has gotten safely away from the place of danger ("he went outside," following his already "going out" to the gateway, v. 71, marks the final stage of withdrawal), arises perhaps from a mixture of self-disgust and true sorrow for what he has done. See 2 Cor 7:10 for the "godly sorrow" of repentance which leads to salvation contrasted with the "worldly sorrow" which ends in death; Peter and Judas may be seen as examples of the two.

4. Jesus Brought to the Roman Prefect for Trial (27:1-2)

> 1 *Early in the morning all the chief priests and the elders of the people consulted together*[1] *against Jesus to have him executed;* 2 *they*

---

9. BDAG 63b single out this one use of the verb as intransitive, but give no justification for this (and the two articles they cite in fact argue against it!); their suggestion owes more to traditional exegesis than to any linguistic evidence.

10. This exegesis is argued by H. Merkel, in E. Bammel (ed.), *Trial,* 66-71; cf. G. W. H. Lampe, *BJRL* 55 (1972/3) 354; B. Gerhardsson, *JSNT* 13 (1981) 54-55.

1. συμβούλιον can mean either a council (a gathering of people) or a plan, but in all Matthew's other uses of the phrase συμβούλιον λαμβάνω (12:14; 22:15; 27:7; 28:12; the phrase is used only by Matthew in the NT) it clearly means to consult together to form a (generally hostile) plan. Cf. A. N. Sherwin-White, *Roman Society,* 44-45. Mark here has

tied him up and took him off to hand him over to Pontius Pilate,[2] the governor.

I have argued above (pp. 1018-19) that this is not a new hearing but the culmination of an all-night session which has already agreed that Jesus deserves to be executed but must now formulate a plan to get the Roman prefect, who alone had the power to order his execution, to endorse and implement their verdict. A charge of blasphemy, which was the basis of their verdict, would carry no weight in Roman law; they needed a charge which was sufficiently political and sufficiently alarming to the occupying power to ensure a capital sentence, and in v. 11 we shall see how they have gone about formulating it. It was the formulation of this charge, and perhaps also agreeing on a tactic for making sure that Pilate took it seriously (see below on v. 20), which took up the final part of their gathering in the high priest's house before the prefect would be prepared to receive them the first thing in the morning.

Matthew's phrase is literally "when it had become early," probably meaning at first light;[3] this follows appropriately from the cockcrow of 26:74. This is the first time we hear of Jesus being tied up, though the verb *krateō* used for his arrest in 26:48, 50, 57 indicates that they took no chances. Now, as they have to take him through the crowded streets, they make sure that he cannot escape or be rescued. Besides, a firmly secured prisoner will lend credibility to their charge that he is a political danger. The Roman prefects probably used Herod's former palace, on the west side of the city, as their headquarters when in Jerusalem.[4] There Jesus is "handed over" to Pilate in fulfillment of his own prediction in 20:19.

συμβούλιον ποιέω, which even more clearly means "make a plan." See also D. P. Senior, *Passion,* 213-15, though Senior unnecessarily drives a wedge between Mark and Matthew in their understanding of the judicial procedure.

2. Most MSS and versions have the name Ποντίῳ before Πιλάτῳ, and as this is the first mention of Pilate in this gospel, it is likely that Matthew gave his fuller name here. Its omission from several significant MSS and versions might be due to assimilation to Mark and Luke, neither of which includes the gentilic Pontius at this point. Generally in the NT Pilate is referred to by his cognomen alone, as are the later procurators Felix and Festus, but in Acts 24:27 Festus's gentilic Porcius is similarly given when he is first mentioned. Luke (3:1) and Josephus (*Ant.* 18.35) also include Pontius the first time they mention Pilate but not thereafter.

3. The same phrase is used in John 21:4 for Jesus seen beside the lake in the light of early dawn after a night of unsuccessful fishing. A. N. Sherwin-White, *Roman Society,* 45-46, illustrates how early a Roman official's day began. Roman trials generally began at daybreak.

4. The traditional *Via Dolorosa* is based on the supposition that Jesus was tried at the Antonia fortress on the north side of the temple area, but such information as we have points strongly to Herod's Palace (on the site of what is now known as the Citadel, south

Pontius Pilatus was prefect[5] of Judea A.D. 26-36, directly appointed from Rome but under the supervision of the legate of the imperial province of Syria. He is better known to us than most minor Roman governors of the period not only from the NT accounts of Jesus' trial but also because Josephus and Philo record several examples of his insensitive style of government which led to brutal clashes with his Jewish and Samaritan subjects (Josephus, *Ant.* 18.55-59, 60-62, 85-87; Philo, *Legat.* 299–305; cf. what appears to be a separate such incident in Luke 13:1). He was eventually deposed following a complaint against his heavy-handed suppression of a supposed Samaritan insurrection. His aim was, of course, to keep the peace while maintaining the Roman occupation, but he seems to have had little understanding of or sympathy for his oriental subjects and their religious differences.[6] It was not likely to be easy for the Sanhedrin delegation to get him to rubber-stamp their decision, especially if he suspected, like a later Roman governor placed in a similar position, that their complaint concerned merely "questions about words and names and your own law" (Acts 18:14; cf. Acts 25:19-20).

5. The Remorse and Suicide of Judas (27:3-10)

> 3 Then Judas, his betrayer, when he saw that Jesus had been condemned, regretted what he had done and returned the thirty silver coins to the chief priests and elders, 4 saying, "I was wrong; I have betrayed innocent[1] blood." "What has that to do with us?" they re-

---

of the Jaffa Gate), described by Philo, *Legat.* 299, as "the residence of the prefects." See J. Blinzler, *Trial,* 173-76; J. Wilkinson, *Jerusalem,* 137-40; R. E. Brown, *Death,* 705-10; Schürer, 1:361, especially n. 38. A further possibility is Herod's "Lower Palace," on the west side of the Tyropoeon valley, championed by B. Pixner, *ABD* 5:447-49; cf. R. Riesner, *BK* 41 (1986) 34-37.

5. This title, rather than the traditional "procurator" (a term used for the governors of Judea after A.D. 44), is confirmed by an inscription found at Caesarea on which Pilate is specifically named as "prefect." The Greek term Matthew uses, ἡγεμών, is a general term for a ruler (cf. 2:6), appropriate to provincial governors whatever their precise status, and used in Acts for the later procurators.

6. J. Blinzler, *Trial,* 177-84, represents this traditionally negative view of Pilate. For a rather less uncomplimentary assessment of his quality as a governor, and general information on his prefecture, see R. E. Brown, *Death,* 693-705. For a full account of all that is known of Pilate in relation to his portrayal in the NT see H. K. Bond, *Pontius Pilate.*

1. The minority reading αἷμα δίκαιον, "righteous blood," is probably the deliberate substitution (perhaps under the influence of the phrase αἷμα δίκαιον in 23:35) of a more common adjective for the more technical ἀθῷος, "innocent," which occurs in the NT only here and in v. 24. "Righteous" occurs mainly in the versions, but in few Greek MSS, probably because Greek copyists were more aware of the LXX phrase αἷμα ἀθῷον (see below on v. 4), which is here echoed.

plied; "that's your problem."[2] 5 *So he threw the money into the sanctuary and left them, and he went off and hanged himself.*

6 *The chief priests took the money and said, "It would not be right to add this to the treasury,*[3] *since it is the price of blood." 7 They consulted together, and bought the potter's field with the money, as a place to bury strangers. 8 That is why that field is*[4] *still known as Blood Field even today.*

9 *Then was fulfilled what had been declared through Jeremiah*[5] *the prophet, who said,*

"And I took[6] *the thirty silver coins, the price of the one whose price was set, on whom they had set a price from*[7] *the sons of Israel, 10 and I paid*[8] *them for the potter's field, as the Lord had instructed me."*

This digression, the only substantial addition by Matthew to the structure of Mark's passion narrative, delays the action between Jesus' transferal to the

2. Literally, "*you* will see" (with emphasis on the "you"), i.e., "you see to it yourself." The same formula will be used in the plural in v. 24.

3. The word refers to the accumulated offerings in the temple rather than to the place they were kept; see the comments below.

4. The Greek verb is aorist, "was called," but the following "until today" puts the emphasis on the fact that the name then given is still current.

5. The omission of the name, or the substitution of that of Zechariah (or, in one OL MS, Isaiah!), in a few versions and patristic citations is a natural correction of what appears to be an erroneous attribution; see the comments below.

6. The verb form ἔλαβον could be either "I took" or "they took." See the comments below for the reason for preferring the first-person sense, which is clearly that of the LXX text alluded to.

7. Matthew's ἀπό, corresponding to the Hebrew *mē'al* (see p. 1044, n. 32), is obscure. Following a middle verb with an active sense, "they valued," it cannot be instrumental as the Hebrew preposition (which follows "I was valued") probably is. The most probable sense here is "from among" (i.e., as a matter of comparison with; see p. 1044, n. 32). Some interpreters (e.g., D. J. Moo, *The OT*, 193; M. J. J. Menken, *Matthew's Bible,* 186) take it as meaning "some of" and identifying the subject of the verb, "on whom some of the sons of Israel had set a price," but there is no clear parallel to such a syntactically harsh use of ἀπό, despite the appeal to some similar uses of ἐκ noted by BDF 164(2). The use of ἐξ αὐτῶν twice in Matt 23:34 to differentiate two groups as *objects* of the verb is not a true parallel (*pace* K. Stendahl, *School,* 126, n. 1), nor is τίνα ἀπὸ τῶν δύο in v. 21 (*pace* Davies and Allison, 3:570).

8. The majority of MSS and versions read ἔδωκαν, "they paid." But the first-person form ἔδωκα appears in ℵ B² W and syrˢ, where it might be explained by the influence of μοι in the next clause, but may equally represent an original first-person reading of the whole "quotation," subsequently altered under the influence of a third-person reading of ἔλαβον (itself inflenced by λάβοντες in v. 6); see n. 6. See further comments below.

prefect's palace and the beginning of his trial there. Matthew may have intended to create dramatic suspense, though that would be more typical of Mark's style than of Matthew's. At any rate, the incident described is chronologically out of place. Formally speaking, Jesus will not be condemned to death until v. 26, though perhaps for Judas, whose agreement was with the priests rather than with the Romans, it is the verdict of the Sanhedrin that counts. However, this incident cannot have taken place between the Sanhedrin hearing and the Roman trial since it locates the chief priests in the temple rather than on the way between Caiaphas's house and the prefect's palace, involving them in a commercial transaction just at the time they are supposed to be presenting their case before the prefect. It would more likely have followed Jesus' official condemnation and death, but for Matthew to have reported it there would have interrupted the flow of the narrative from Jesus' trial and execution to his burial and resurrection. So Matthew's plan here is certainly not simple chronological sequence. There are perhaps three main purposes in inserting this strange pericope here.[9] (a) It sets the treachery of Judas alongside the failure of Peter, and allows the reader to compare and contrast their faults and their different fates. (b) It narrates the fulfillment of Jesus' dire prediction about the fate of his betrayer (26:24), just as his prediction of Peter's failure (26:34) has been precisely fulfilled. (c) It allows Matthew to introduce the most complex and creative of his formula-quotations, to show that even in the betrayal of the Messiah and in the fate of his betrayer Scripture continues to provide the pattern, even to the most incidental details.

This pericope introduces a theme which will be picked up again in vv. 24-25, the question of who is responsible for the shedding of Jesus' "innocent blood." Judas tries, and fails, to rid himself of the responsibility. The priests refuse to accept it, but by using the blood money become themselves complicit.[10] Later Pilate will wash his hands to disclaim responsibility and will explicitly transfer it to the people, who will formally accept it. R. E. Brown appropriately compares this "haunting . . . scene of blood that cannot be easily eradicated" with the famously guilty conscience of Lady Macbeth.[11]

The whole pericope appears only in Matthew; Luke's account of Judas's death (Acts 1:18-19) is quite different in detail, though it also involves the buying of ground (by Judas himself) and the explanation of the name Blood Field. Clearly there was a tradition linking Judas (and his death) with the field called Akeldama, but the link was differently explained, and there seems to be

---

9. See further D. P. Senior, *Passion,* 346-52.

10. L. Nortjé, *Neot* 28 (1994) 41-51, argues that the guilt of the priests is the primary focus of the whole pericope.

11. R. E. Brown, *Death,* 637; on p. 641 Brown explores further the motif of blood-guilt in Jewish and Christian literature.

no way of deciding which of the two versions (if either) is the more factual. Attempts to interpret them as literally compatible (involving a suicide attempt complicated by the breaking of the rope or the tree branch) do not inspire confidence, nor do they account for Matthew's involvement of the priests.[12]

But to explain Matthew's story as simply spun out of the OT text is no more convincing here than it was in the case of the infancy narratives which culminated in formula-quotations. In each case Matthew's story is indeed told in the light of the following quotation in such a way as to maximize the claim of fulfillment. Yet the "quotation" itself is so creatively compiled, from a variety of scriptural texts, that it is hard to see how it could have come about if the narrative tradition were not already in place to supply the data for the claim to fulfillment.[13] See above, pp. 40-45, for the nature of the formula-quotations of 1:18–2:23; the same dialectic between narrative tradition and scriptural text seems to be even more creatively at work in this final formula-quotation.[14]

As we have noted, Matthew's placing of this pericope invites the reader to compare Judas with Peter, and to reflect why the one story ends in despair and suicide and the other eventually in the full rehabilitation of the future leader of the church. In both stories there is failure, followed by regret. Peter's bitter weeping does not in itself sound more heartfelt than Judas's "regret," followed by his confession of guilt ("I have done wrong"), his acceptance that he is responsible for the death of the innocent, and his restitution of the proceeds of his treachery. But all this is, it seems, "the worldly sorrow that leads to death" rather than "the godly sorrow which leads to repentance for salvation" (2 Cor 7:10).[15] Peter has sinned by words, under the pressure of the moment, and for him there can be a new start; Judas has sinned in deed, in a premedi-

---

12. R. E. Brown, *Death,* 1404-6, surveys and comments on proposed harmonizations. He concludes, "These two accounts cannot be harmonized." He goes on (1408-10) to reproduce and discuss the more detailed and lurid story of the fate of Judas attributed to Papias, which he judges to be independent of either.

13. For a full study of this issue see D. J. Moo, *GP* 3 (1983), 157-75 (cf. also his *The OT,* 189-210, covering similar ground); Moo concludes that "there is reason to doubt whether any important part of the narrative in Matt 27:3-8 has been created under the influence of OT passages" (165).

14. See further my *Matthew: Evangelist,* 178-81. M. J. J. Menken, *Matthew's Bible,* 192-97, argues for the traditional origin of the bulk of this narrative, finding the influence of the Zechariah quotation only in the number "thirty" and in the throwing of the money into the temple.

15. Davies and Allison, 3:561-63, are unusual in entertaining the possibility that Judas is meant to be seen as truly repentant, and even that his suicide could be understood as making atonement for his sin. But see Keener, 658-60, to the contrary. Keener presents a wide range of evidence for ancient attitudes to suicide, and concludes that even by Roman standards Judas's suicide was a dishonorable one.

tated, settled course of action which has now borne fruit which, too late, he wishes he could have undone. Alongside the constant scriptural testimony to the extraordinary mercy of God, there is also, as the Letter to the Hebrews insists so memorably, a point of no return, a time when it is too late to repent.

3-4a For the relation of this scene to Jesus' official "condemnation" see the introductory comments above. The verb for "regret" is *metamelomai* (not *metanoeō,* the normal term for "repent"), which need mean no more than a change of mind (as in 21:29; Heb 7:21), but here, as in 2 Cor 7:8, it surely denotes sorrow or remorse, or, as BDAG 639b put it, "to have regrets about something, in the sense that one wishes it could be undone." His attempt to return the money is presumably a tangible way of trying to abdicate responsibility (like Pilate's washing in v. 24).[16] For the suggestion that Judas had been trying to arrange a constructive meeting and never intended Jesus to be executed see above on 26:14-16; more likely the actual occurrence of what he had willingly set in motion has at last brought home to him the enormity of what he has done. It is possible that he has heard from his priestly contacts about Jesus' behavior and declaration before the Sanhedrin, and that that has at last convinced him of Jesus' truly messianic character. The phrase "shed innocent blood" (LXX uses the same adjective *athōos*) is a standard OT expression (Deut 27:25; 1 Sam 25:31; 2 Kgs 21:16; Ps 106:38, etc.), which occurs several times in Jeremiah to condemn the sins of Israel (Jer 2:34; 7:6; 19:4; 22:3, 17; 26:15); see below on vv. 9-10 for this as an element in the scriptural mosaic Matthew has created. Both words will recur in 27:24, again with reference to responsibility for Jesus' death, though there the "innocence" is claimed by Pilate, not attributed to Jesus.

4b-5 The priests have achieved their end, and have no further interest in the man whose disloyalty they had profited from. For "that's your problem" cf. v. 24, where Pilate will use the same formula in the plural to transfer responsibility for Jesus' death to the people. The priests conveniently forget that it was they who had initiated the deal. Their refusal to accept Judas's gesture seals his despair. Not being himself a priest, he was allowed to go only as far as the Court of Israel, not into the sanctuary[17] itself, but Matthew (or Judas) may not be concerned about exact protocol, or we may be intended to visualize Judas throwing the money across the Court of the Priests toward the sanctuary entrance. The location in the temple (which fits awkwardly at

---

16. J. Jeremias, *Jerusalem,* 139-40, explains it on the analogy of a procedure for revoking a sale which involved the purchase money being deposited in the temple (*m. 'Arak.* 9:4); but the nature of the mishnaic procedure is far from clear, and Judas's transaction had been very different from a sale of property.

17. Matthew's uses of ναός in 23:35 and 27:51 show that for him it referred specifically to the building containing the Holy Place and the Holy of Holies, rather than the whole temple complex (which he calls τὸ ἱερόν). See p. 1023, n. 21.

this point in the narrative; see above) is important for the following "quotation" because the scene of Zech 11:13 is "in the house of the LORD,"[18] even though Matthew's "quotation" does not include that phrase.[19] The two words "he went off and hanged himself" echo the LXX of 2 Sam 17:23, where that was the fate of Ahithophel, who had betrayed King David by siding with his rebellious son Absalom. Judas, by turning against the Son of David, has thus joined the ranks of the great traitors.[20]

6-8   The priests receive and use the blood money (which had come from them in the first place), thus also implicating themselves in the responsibility for Jesus' death. Their concern to maintain ritual purity in the use of the blood money provides an ironical counterpoint to their willingness to allow the innocent blood to be shed. Their decision to use the money for a burial ground is in itself quite plausible; when visitors, who had no family to look after them, died in Jerusalem (as must have happened especially among the huge crowds at festival times), Jewish piety demanded that they be given a proper burial, and since most burials would be in family tombs or plots, a designated area for the burial of outsiders would be needed. But as Matthew tells this part of the story, the wordplay becomes more intense. The "treasury"[21] perhaps prepares for the citation of Zech 11:13, where the repeated word "potter" is rendered "treasury" in the Syriac version (the two words differ by only one letter in Hebrew), and this seems to have been a recognized interpretation of what the surprising term "potter" referred to, possibly even a known variant of the Hebrew text.[22] If so, both variant readings ("treasury" in v. 6 and "pot-

18. In the Hebrew of Zech 11:13 the phrase "house of the LORD" (with no preposition) stands awkwardly before "to the potter" at the end of the verse; it is usually taken as a statement of location, as in LXX εἰς τὸν οἶκον κυρίου.

19. The location in the temple is one of the features of this pericope which lead J. A. Gibbs, *Jerusalem,* 149, to understand it as pointing forward to the coming destruction of the temple, as a result of the shedding of "innocent blood."

20. For an unusually full list of suggested parallels between Judas and Ahithophel, going far beyond the specific verbal allusion noted above, see Davies and Allison, 3:565-66. See also T. F. Glasson, *ExpT* 85 (1973/4) 118-19.

21. Matthew uses the transliterated Aramaic word *korbanas,* used also in Josephus, *War* 2.175, for the accumulated temple funds; see on 15:5 for the term *qorbān* to designate temple offerings.

22. The targum renders the potter here by the title of a temple official (defined in Jastrow's lexicon as a "trustee superintending the cashiers"), which might reflect an understanding of the text as referring to the treasury, but the rendering may be a free attempt to clarify an obscure text rather than testimony to a different reading. Many interpreters have been attracted by the theory of C. C. Torrey, *JBL* 55 (1936) 247-60, that the "potter" (the word means essentially one who forms or molds) was the name of a temple official whose job it was to melt down and mold metal offerings made to the temple, so that what was given to the treasury was in fact given to the "molder." The proposal remains purely

ter" in vv. 7 and 10) may be involved in Matthew's wordplay.[23] The phrase "price of blood" picks up both the "innocent blood" of v. 4 and name "Blood Field" in v. 8, while the Greek word for "price" will be thrice repeated in cognate forms in Matthew's version of the quotation in v. 9. The buying of the potter's field will be picked up in v. 10. By the time we get to v. 9 therefore the ground has been well prepared for the formula-quotation.

In view of the other echoes of Jer 19:1-13 in this passage, v. 8 recalls another such naming in Jer 19:6: "Therefore . . . this place shall . . . be called . . . 'the Valley of Slaughter.'" "Blood Field" (Akeldama, Acts 1:19) has traditionally been located near the foot of the valley of Hinnom, just outside Jerusalem on the south. See above on 5:22 for the unsavory reputation of this valley as a place of blood, death, and destruction. This, too, will feed into Matthew's creative scriptural mosaic in vv. 9-10, particularly as a place already scripturally associated with potters, and lying just outside the Potsherd Gate (Jer 19:1-2). The valley was apparently a source of potters' clay, hence perhaps the previous name "potter's field." Jews would not want to live in such a site, so that the land would be readily available to buy for the burial of strangers, even if it might not have been acceptable for a Jewish cemetery.[24] Unclean money[25] is thus used for what would become, by its use as a cemetery, an unclean site.

9-10 The story of Judas's unavailing remorse has been told in such a way as to provide the cue for a creatively compiled formula-quotation. The introductory formula is identical with that of 2:17 (see comments there), but whereas there a recognizable quotation from Jeremiah followed, here the words that follow are primarily based on Zech 11:13. This is, however, not a simple quotation of a single text, but a mosaic of scriptural motifs,[26] some of which do in fact come from Jeremiah (see below). Like the combined quotation of Mark 1:2-3, it is attributed to the better known of the prophets concerned, even though its opening words are from the minor prophet. As a "quotation" about a potter's field it was naturally associated with Jeremiah as the prophet most memorably associated with potters and with the buying of a

---

conjectural, though it fits well with the LXX's use here of χωνευτήριον, a foundry or smelting furnace.

23. This widely favored suggestion is roundly dismissed by R. H. Gundry, *Use,* 122-23; similarly and more fully D. J. Moo, *The OT,* 202-4. But Gundry's argument presupposes a more exegetically precise use of the text by Matthew than is evident in this passage as a whole.

24. For the site and its significance see R. W. Smith, *ABD* 1:134-35.

25. For the principle of money being unclean on account of its origin cf. Deut 23:18, where it is forbidden to bring the earnings of prostitution into the house of the Lord.

26. For other composite quotations in Matthew see on 2:6; 11:10; 21:5.

field. Note that Matthew's attributed quotations name only the major prophets Isaiah and Jeremiah (2:17; 3:3; 4:14; 8:17; 12:17; 13:14; 15:7; 27:9), together with one specific allusion to Daniel (24:15), while formal quotations
drawn from the minor prophets are elsewhere left anonymous (2:5, 15;
11:10; 21:4; 26:31); see above on 2:17.[27]

The most obvious scriptural motif is the thirty silver coins, already
noted in 26:15, and a prominent feature of Zech 11:12-13. From that text,
too, come the motifs of a valuation ("this noble price at which I was valued
by them"), the "taking" of the coins and throwing them into the treasury in
the house of the Lord (see above, vv. 5-6), and the payment made to a mysterious potter. That is sufficient to form the basis of the "quotation," though
Matthew's wording is seldom identical with that of LXX Zech 11:13.[28] But
woven into this base text are a number of other elements reflecting well-
known Jeremiah motifs. In Jer 18:1-11 Jeremiah went to the house of the potter (the same Greek word as Matthew uses) and based a sermon on the potter's work. In Jer 19:1-13 he used a potter's jug as a visual aid for a sermon
delivered in the valley of Hinnom (near the Potsherd Gate) denouncing the
people of Jerusalem for shedding "innocent blood" (v. 4, the same phrase as
in Matt 27:4); and there in Topheth, in the valley of Hinnom, "they shall bury
until there is no more room to bury."[29] Finally, in Jer 32 Jeremiah famously
bought a field (a narrative in which another earthenware jar features, Jer
32:14, though with no explicit reference to a potter).[30] Echoes of all these
Jeremiah passages, especially Jer 19:1-13, would no doubt be heard by readers well versed in the OT, so that they would recognize Matthew's adapted
version of Zech 11:13 not as a quotation of that text alone but as a mosaic of
familiar and related prophetic motifs. This is not simple proof-texting, but
the product of long and creative engagement with Scripture which delights to
draw connections between passages and to trace in the details as well as in

27. For several less probable explanations of the attribution to Jeremiah see D. J.
Moo, *GP* 3:168-69, n. 2; R. H. Gundry, *Use,* 125-26, n. 3; Davies and Allison, 3:568-69.
M. Knowles, *Jeremiah,* 60-67, lists and discusses eight other proposals, before concluding
in favor of a "mixed quotation" as outlined above.

28. Even the word for "potter" is different, LXX referring to a "foundry." For a
detailed study of the textual links between these verses and Zech 11:13 see D. P. Senior,
Passion, 353-62.

29. The links between the present passage and Jer 19:1-13 are well set out by
R. H. Gundry, *Use,* 124-25. He denies any influence from Jer 18 and 32; D. J. Moo, *The
OT,* 194-95, also finds such influences "tenuous at best." M. Knowles, *Jeremiah,* 67-76,
surveys the verbal and conceptual links at greater length, concluding that Jer 19:1-13 provides the primary basis for the attribution to Jeremiah.

30. M. J. J. Menken, *Matthew's Bible,* 188-89, 191, surprisingly sees Jer 32 as the
only influence from Jeremiah on the wording of Matthew's quotation.

the basic meaning of the text the pattern of God's fulfillment of his prophetically declared agenda.

But two parts of Matthew's "quotation" do not derive from these Jeremiah passages and do not correspond closely to either the Hebrew or the LXX of Zech 11:13. The concluding clause, "as the Lord had instructed me," probably picks up, though in a different position, the opening clause of Zech 11:13, "And the LORD said to me."[31] More striking is the cumbersome phrase which describes the thirty silver coins as "the price of the one whose price was set, on whom they had set a price from the sons of Israel," which I have translated in this rather wooden way in order to bring out the threefold repetition of the word "price" *(time)* in either noun or verb form. This long description corresponds to a simpler phrase in the Hebrew, literally meaning probably "the splendor of the value which I was valued by[32] them"; this is normally understood to be an ironic aside[33] commenting on the derisory wages paid to the messianic shepherd. Matthew's version has expanded and thus emphasized the phrase, in particular by providing a triple repetition of the root *time* against the double occurrence of the *yqr* root in the Hebrew; it owes nothing to LXX, which uses the root *dokimos* (twice) rather than *time,* so that Matthew's clumsy phrase looks like an independent rendering.[34] It is apparently designed to draw attention to the fact that Jesus, like the rejected shepherd of Zech 11, was despised and undervalued by or among[35] "the sons of Israel."[36]

The Zechariah text is expressed throughout in the first person, the speaker being the rejected shepherd. In Matthew it can be so understood as well, as in my translation above, but the ambiguity of the verb form *elabon* (see p. 1037, n. 6) and the textual variant "they paid" for "I paid" (see p. 1037, n. 8) allow it to be read as a description of the action of the priests, which more

31. The actual formulation, including the unusual form καθά (only here in the NT) instead of the normal καθώς, derives from a regular LXX formula found, e.g., in Exod 36:8, 12, 14, 28, 33, etc. for Moses' obedience to Yahweh's commands.

32. The Hebrew preposition *mē'al* is used in many different ways, but an instrumental sense seems required by the context here; Matthew's ἀπό, "from," looks like a more literal rendering, and might suggest that he understood it as meaning "from among" (i.e., the shepherd's valuation is in relation to the other sons of Israel).

33. TNIV is a typical rendering in this sense: "the handsome price at which they valued me!"

34. M. J. J. Menken, *Matthew's Bible,* 185-86, explains the insertion of τοῦ τετιμημένου as Matthew's need to make it clear that in his application of the text, in contrast to Zechariah's, the one for whom the money was paid (Jesus) is not the same person as its recipient(s).

35. See p. 1037, n. 7.

36. M. D. Goulder, *Midrash,* 447, suggests that this phrase is added to allude to "the pricing of Joseph by the sons of Israel" at twenty silver shekels in Gen 37:26-28.

naturally fits the narrative which introduces the quotation. Most interpreters take it that way. That reading is hampered, however, by the "me" in the concluding clause, which is present in all textual witnesses. That seems to me to swing the balance in favor of a first-person reading throughout, corresponding to the meaning of the OT text. In that case Matthew has left it for his readers to work out how the first-person (messianic) subject of the OT text can be related to the actions of Judas (throwing down the money) and the priests (buying the field). Like everything in this extraordinary scriptural argument, the correspondence is not straightforward!

While it was the thirty silver coins which presumably first drew Matthew's attention to Zech 11:12-13, his reference to that passage also makes a more substantial contribution to his theme of the fulfillment of Scripture in the life and passion of Jesus. We have noted already three references to apparently messianic figures in Zech 9–14 as fulfilled in Jesus' coming to Jerusalem and what is happening to him there. See above on 21:4-5 (Zech 9:9-10); 24:30 (Zech 12:10-14); 26:31 (Zech 13:7). Many interpreters of Zechariah take these three passages together with 11:4-14 as parts of a unified concept of a shepherd-king whose coming will lead paradoxically to his rejection and death; that all four passages should have been taken up into Matthew's Jerusalem narrative strongly indicates that he, too, saw them in that light, and found in this mysterious rejected and suffering Messiah a powerful scriptural model which could stand alongside the suffering servant of Isaiah and the suffering righteous figures of some of the psalms as a model for understanding why Jesus, the Messiah of Israel, must suffer and die in Jerusalem.[37] How much of that underlying theology his readers might be expected to discern through this altered "quotation" with its associated reminiscences of Jeremiah, and in relation to a relatively minor element in the passion story, would presumably depend on how familiar they were with the scriptural material Matthew is working on, and with the creative tradition of interpretation which he has employed to produce this complex interweaving of biblical motifs with the story of Judas and the priests.

6. The Roman Trial (27:11-26)

> 11 *Jesus stood before the governor, and the governor questioned him, "Are you the king of the Jews?" "You say it,"[1] Jesus replied.*

---

37. For the significance of Zech 9–14 in the gospel passion narratives see p. 777, n. 26, and for literature on the subject p. 998, n. 8.

1. This is the same formula as in 26:25, 64, but now in the present tense. See the comments below.

12 *And as he was being accused by the chief priests and the elders, he made no reply.* 13 *Then Pilate said to him, "Don't you hear how much testimony they are giving against you?"* 14 *Jesus made no reply to him, not even to a single charge,*[2] *so that the governor was very surprised.*

15 *At festival time it was the governor's custom to release to the crowd one prisoner, chosen by them.* 16 *At that time they had a well-known prisoner called Jesus*[3] *Barabbas.* 17 *So when they were gathered together, Pilate asked them, "Which do you want me to release for you, Jesus Barabbas or Jesus who is known as Messiah?"* 18 *For he was aware that it was out of rivalry*[4] *that they had handed him over. (*19 *While he was hearing the case,*[5] *his wife sent him a message: "Don't get involved with*[6] *that righteous man; I've had a really bad dream about him today."*)[7] 20 *But the chief priests and the elders per-*

2. Matthew uses ῥῆμα sparingly, and with reference to the *content* of an utterance rather than meaning simply a "word" (see p. 1031, n. 5); here, as in 18:16, the context supplies the nature of the "utterances" referred to.

3. Matthew is the only gospel to tell us that Barabbas's first name was Jesus. And here and in v. 17 Ἰησοῦν is not found in most of our extant MSS; the only significant Greek MSS which include the name are Θ and f[1], which are supported by the Sinaitic Syriac and a few later versions. But the situation is explained by Origen, who comments that "in many copies it is not stated that Barabbas was also called Jesus," and goes on to approve the omission of the name since "Jesus" is not an appropriate name for a sinner. This statement, predating our earliest Greek MSS, shows that in the third century "Jesus Barabbas" was the received reading (a later scribal note [see B. M. Metzger, *Textual Commentary,* 67] also mentions that "some very ancient copies" said that Barabbas was called Jesus), but that it was found objectionable by some, and no doubt for that reason the Ἰησοῦν had already begun to be deleted in "many copies." In the light of this sensitivity it is inconceivable that the name could have been added if it were not originally in the text; the remarkable thing is that it survived at all. Origen and his Greek-speaking colleagues seem to have been unaware that Jesus (Joshua) was one of the commonest Jewish names in the first century, and was carried by many who were no doubt as much "sinners" as Barabbas (see p. 34, n. 27). See further D. P. Senior, *Passion,* 238-39.

4. φθόνος is normally translated "envy" or "jealousy," but that seems a weak rendering here where the sense is clearly political. The Jewish leaders saw Jesus as a threat to their position and authority; it was a matter of competing claims and of self-interest rather than "envy" in the more normal psychological sense. See, however, Keener, 662, n. 160, for a defense of the translation "envy" here; cf. J. H. Neyrey, *Honor,* 19, and more fully A. C. Hagedorn and J. H. Neyrey, *JSNT* 69 (1998) 15-56, whose anthropological study makes it clear that "envy" in the ancient world had a more powerful and sociopolitical ring than in most modern usage.

5. Literally, "sitting on the tribunal," the official platform (βῆμα) on which the governor sat to hear judicial cases (cf. Acts 18:12-17).

6. Literally, "Nothing to you and to. . . ." For similar formulae of dissociation see 8:29 (and p. 322, n. 8); Mark 1:24; John 2:4.

7. Literally, "for I have suffered many things in a dream today because of him."

suaded the crowds to ask for Barabbas and have Jesus executed.[8]
21 *So when*[9] *the governor asked them, "Which of the two do you want
me to release for you?" they replied, "Barabbas." 22 Pilate asked
them, "So what shall I do with Jesus who is known as Messiah?" They
all said, "Let him be crucified!" 23 "Why?*[10] *What has he done
wrong?" asked Pilate. But they just shouted the more loudly, "Let him
be crucified!"*

24 *When Pilate saw that he was getting nowhere, but that instead
a riot was beginning, he took water and washed his hands in front of
the crowd, saying, "I am innocent of this*[11] *man's blood; it's your responsibility."*[12] 25 *And all the people replied, "His blood is*[13] *on us and
on our children."*

26 *Then he released Barabbas for them, but he had Jesus flogged,
and then handed him over to be crucified.*

While the hearing before the Sanhedrin established Jesus' guilt in Jewish
eyes and called for the death penalty, it is the Roman prefect who must actually implement that verdict, and this scene relates the formal trial and pronouncement of sentence. Yet that formal business takes up only a small part
of the pericope, an apparently perfunctory examination by Pilate in vv. 11-14
and the sentencing in v. 26.[14] The intervening verses focus not on the trial of

8. Matthew's phrasing, "that they should ask for Barabbas but destroy Jesus," expresses the outcome as their deliberate intention rather than the inevitable consequence of
their choice of Barabbas.

9. The phrase ἀποκριθεὶς δέ often marks a new contribution to the conversation
(see notes on the translation of 11:25; 15:15; 17:4). Here its function is rather resumptive,
returning to and repeating Pilate's question which has been left aside during the explanatory comments of vv. 18-20. My translation attempts to indicate that the question is now
repeated as a basis for the crowd's answer, itself in response to the persuasion of v. 20.

10. "Why?" is added to bring out the force of the γάρ in Pilate's question, which
challenges them to give a reason for their demand (cf. BDF 452[1]).

11. Many MSS and versions have τοῦ δικαίου in addition to τούτου, but it is more
likely that "righteous" would have been added to emphasize Jesus' innocence (and in echo
of v. 19) than that it would be deliberately omitted, resulting in the curt description of Jesus as simply "this man." The fact that those MSS which include τοῦ δικαίου differ on its
position in the word order also suggests that it is an insertion.

12. The same formula (in the plural) as in v. 4; see p. 1037, n. 2.

13. There is no verb in the Greek. In such cases the normal default position is the
indicative of the verb "to be" (as, e.g., in Luke 22:20, where the Synoptic parallels have
ἐστιν). There is no syntactical justification for making it into a wish, "*Let* his blood *be* on
us . . . ," as some versions do, resulting in the traditional but erroneous understanding that
this is "a self-curse, a prophecy, or a blood-thirsty wish" (R. E. Brown, *Death,* 837).

14. For attempts to reconstruct the actual proceedings in the light of Roman judi-

Jesus as such but on Pilate's abortive attempt to find a convenient way to avoid pronouncing the sentence demanded on a man he has apparently concluded is not guilty from a Roman point of view but who is clearly anathema to the Jewish establishment. The narrative will focus on the primary responsibility of the Jewish leaders and people for Jesus' death, but Pilate does not come out of it well; first he tries to evade his official responsibility, then, despite his wife's warning, he cynically gives orders for an admittedly guiltless man to be executed. His theatrical abdication of responsibility (v. 24) is not likely to convince anyone but himself.[15]

The charge which the Sanhedrin members have agreed to present to Pilate is phrased in political language: Jesus has claimed to be "the king of the Jews." This term, which we have so far met only in 2:2 as the title used by the magi for the newborn ruler, now becomes central to the story, as the basis of Jesus' condemnation, of his mockery by the Roman soldiers (v. 29), and of his public humiliation on the cross (v. 37), while the Jewish leaders will use their own more Jewish version of it to mock Jesus (v. 42). "King of the Jews" is used only by non-Jews — the magi, Pilate, and Roman soldiers; the Jewish leaders use their preferred self-designation "Israel." But it is the term "king" which is deliberately sensitive:[16] a Roman governor dare not ignore a claim to political leadership among the Jews, whose last official "king" was Herod,[17] now replaced by the direct rule of the Roman prefect of Judea. And Jesus has given the Jewish leaders a sound basis for this charge by his acceptance of the title "Messiah," underlined by his ride up to the city proclaimed as the "son of David" (21:9), the "king" predicted in Zech 9:9-10. "King of the Jews" is thus an appropriate translation of Jesus' messianic claim into language a Roman governor could understand and must take seriously. Pilate will, however, show in vv. 17 and 22 that he is also aware of the Jewish term: "Jesus who is known as Messiah." We have noted earlier the ambivalence of Jesus toward messianic language (see on 16:16, 20); now we see in practice how it can be used against him.[18]

---

cial practice see R. E. Brown, *Death,* 710-22. E. Bammel, in E. Bammel and C. F. D. Moule (eds.), *Jesus,* 415-51, subjects the trial before Pilate, as recorded in all four gospels, to minute examination in the light of known Jewish and Roman legal procedures.

15. For Matthew's ironical portrayal of the powerlessness of the man who allegedly held all power see D. J. Weaver, in D. R. Bauer and M. A. Powell (eds.), *Treasures,* 191-95.

16. For the title "king" claimed by would-be Jewish leaders in the early first century see Josephus, *Ant.* 17.271-72, 273-74, 278-81; cf. *Ant.* 17.285 for a more general statement about how insurrectionist leaders claimed the title.

17. For Herod's title "King of the Jews" see Josephus, *Ant.* 16.311; cf. 15.373. For the use of the title in an earlier Hasmonean inscription see *Ant.* 14.36.

18. R. E. Brown, *Death,* 679-93, provides an overview of the various types of prophetic and/or nationalist leaders known in first-century Jewish history.

Yet it seems that for Pilate the charge does not ring true. His attempt to free Jesus under the amnesty, and his subsequent disclaiming of responsibility, indicate that he does not regard Jesus as guilty on a capital charge. Matthew notes three reasons for this reluctance to convict. First, Pilate is apparently impressed by Jesus' silence under interrogation: his "surprise" probably indicates a favorable impression (see below). Second, he has correctly assessed that the Jewish leaders' desire to eliminate Jesus stems not from concern for Roman law and order but from their own religio-political self-interest (v. 18). And third, his wife's dream provides a supposedly supernatural attestation to Jesus' innocence (v. 19).

It is often alleged that Pilate's favorable attitude to Jesus (which in different ways appears in all four gospel accounts) owes more to Christian apologetic than to historical reality. Certainly there was a growing Christian tendency to absolve Pilate of any blame,[19] which reached its absurd culmination in his actually being made a saint and martyr of the Coptic church. But there is nothing historically improbable in his reluctance to allow the Jewish leadership, with whom he was never on the best of terms, to dictate to him in his own court. If he concluded that the issue was one of internal Jewish dispute rather than of threat to the Roman power, he is not likely to have had an interest in taking the side of the Sanhedrin. There is a partial parallel in the attitude of Gallio to the Jewish accusers of Paul in Acts 18:12-17, though it was easier for Gallio to dismiss the Jews as a minority group in Corinth than it was for Pilate to thwart the dominant community in Jerusalem. More relevant is Albinus, procurator of Judea some thirty years later, in his treatment of the prophet Jesus ben Hananiah, whose polemic against Jerusalem and its temple so incensed the leading citizens that they brought him before the procurator: Albinus had him flogged, but, having failed to get him to utter a word in self-defense, "pronounced him a maniac and released him" (Josephus, *War* 6.300-305). Pilate would apparently have been happy to do the same, but the pressure put on him by both Sanhedrin members and the Jerusalem crowd did not allow him that option. His eventual "capitulation," even if not in accordance with justice, was probably the most prudent course he could take — wiser than most of his other recorded responses to confrontation with Jewish and Samaritan interests (see above on vv. 1-2). The fuller account of the Roman trial in John 18:28–19:16 provides further insights into

19. But Gundry, 561-65, goes too far in suggesting that Matthew has deliberately "Christianized" Pilate. To emphasize that Pilate believed Jesus to be innocent of the charge is not at all the same thing as to make him a Christian. H. K. Bond, *Pontius Pilate*, 124-37, is nearer the mark in arguing that Pilate is simply a less important actor for Matthew even than he is for Mark, used primarily to direct the reader's attention to the culpability of the Jewish people under the influence of their leaders.

the pressures Pilate was under, and the reasons for his ambivalent attitude to Jesus.[20] He was in a no-win situation.

Pilate's attempt to have Jesus "Messiah" substituted for Jesus Barabbas was not well judged. See the comments below for the likely nature of Barabbas's crime and the basis of his popularity. If Pilate had heard about the enthusiastic crowds who had welcomed Jesus as king outside the city walls, he may have supposed that the Galilean Jesus would be a popular choice for the amnesty. As an outsider he was perhaps unaware (like some modern preachers!) of the difference in outlook between the pilgrim group arriving at the city and the local population with whom he was now confronted. The choice between Jesus of Nazareth and Jesus Barabbas would not be difficult for a Jerusalem crowd to make, both because a Galilean would not be their natural choice, and because the type of "Messiahship" represented by this Galilean, with his talk of loving enemies, had far less popular appeal than the direct action represented by Barabbas's "insurrection" (Mark 15:7).[21] Set within this narrative is a short but immensely influential passage found only in Matthew (vv. 24-25), in which the issue of responsibility for the death of Jesus, already broached in vv. 4-5, is taken further. That this is not just a passing element in Pilate's bargaining with the Jerusalem crowd is indicated by Matthew's use, uniquely here, of the LXX phrase *pas ho laos,* "all the people," and by the people's inclusion of their children in the acceptance of responsibility. See the comments below for the nature and the results of the responsibility they accept. It cannot be denied that these words have been the basis, however inappropriately, of much of the terrible history of Christian persecution of Jews as the "Christ killers." Perhaps the best way to combat such misuse is to discern how these words fit into Matthew's overall understanding of the status of both the city and the Jewish people, and so to try to read this scene in the wider context of the theology of fulfillment developed by Matthew the Jew.

Following on the uniquely Matthean account of Judas's remorse for shedding innocent blood, the two further elements in this pericope, which occur only in Matthew (v. 19, Pilate's wife's dream; vv. 24-25, the transference of guilt), further underline the innocence of Jesus. Even Judas the traitor, the

---

20. Keener, 665-67, provides a useful overview of Pilate's situation, and his vulnerability, in the wider Roman political context at the time, particularly in view of the waning fortunes of his patron Sejanus. An interesting article by B. C. McGing, *CBQ* 53 (1991) 416-38, argues that the apparently incompatible portraits of Pilate given by Philo and Josephus on the one hand and the NT gospels on the other are in fact compatible given the different circumstances with which Pilate was faced.

21. The contrast is imaginatively brought out by G. Theissen, *Shadow,* who portrays his fictional hero Andreas as required to choose between the contrasting ideologies of the two Jesuses; note especially the letter of Barabbas to Andreas (ibid., 177).

Gentile woman, and the hard-bitten Roman governor can see what the Jewish leaders and crowd refuse to acknowledge.

11 From the involvement of the crowd in most of this scene, it seems that the hearing took place in public; the *bēma* (see p. 1046, n. 5) was probably a raised platform in front of the governor's residence.[22] There Jesus stands before the seated governor (v. 19), an ironic reversal of the destined position of Jesus as the seated judge of the world (25:31). For the title "the king of the Jews" see the introductory comments above. The question "Are you the king of the Jews?" (which takes the same form in all four gospels) is clearly ironical when posed by the man who in fact held political authority over Judea. We shall note at 28:15 that *Ioudaioi* in the NT sometimes has a more restricted reference to Judeans rather than to ethnic Jews generally, and a provincial reference would be especially relevant to Pilate, whose jurisdiction covered Judea and Samaria, but not Galilee and Perea with their substantial Jewish populations. But Romans were probably not very sensitive to the tribal distinctions of Palestine: for Pilate, as for most non-Jews, probably *Ioudaioi* covered all the various subgroups in much the same way that for many Americans anyone who lives in Britain is "English." His concern was with his own province of Judea and Samaria, but the fact that Jesus was not a Judean but a Galilean probably made little difference to his view of the charge.[23] For the Sanhedrin to have put the title "king of the Judeans" into the mouth of the Galilean Jesus would have been sarcastic in the extreme. Perhaps Matthew wants us to read it as such, but it is probably more likely that the term is being used here in the wider ethnic sense (as in 2:2), even though the trial is taking place in the Judean capital. The Jewish substitution of "king of Israel" for "king of the *Ioudaioi*" in v. 42 suggests as much.

Jesus' reply (which, like the question, is the same in all four gospels, though John 18:37 adds "that I am a king") is affirmative but qualified, as in 26:64.[24] Jesus would not wish to deny his kingly role as Messiah of Israel; his arrival at the city had been designed to assert it. But what Pilate would naturally construe as a political claim is for Jesus a truth at a different level. When he used the same formula, "You have said it," in response to Caiaphas, he went on to explain how his messianic vision differed from that of the Sanhedrin (26:64). This time, however, "You say it" is not followed by any ex-

---

22. Josephus, *War* 2.301, describes a similar *bēma* set up by the later procurator Florus.

23. See, however, Luke 23:6-7 for an abortive attempt to take the provincial difference seriously.

24. See the comments there and on 26:25; the change to the present tense here does not significantly change the force of the expression.

planation of why his "kingship" is no threat to Rome (for this see John 18:33-38). To try to explain the finer points of messianic theology to a pagan administrator would no doubt have been futile (as Paul found later with Festus, Acts 25:17-20; 26:24). At any rate, Jesus has clearly decided to let matters take their course; his enigmatic "You say it" is the last word Pilate will hear him utter.

12-14 Matthew does not tell us what accusations the Jewish leaders made. Presumably they amplified his alleged claim to be "the king of the Jews" with appropriate accounts of what Jesus had said and done. But the emphasis falls not on their speech but on Jesus' silence, now more pronounced even than it had been before the Sanhedrin (26:62-63; see comments there). Pilate could have read this silence as an acceptance of the truth of the allegations,[25] but Matthew's statement that he was "very surprised" suggests otherwise, especially in view of the later comment on Pilate's assessment of the motivation of the Sanhedrin (v. 18). All earlier uses of *thaumazō,* "be surprised," have denoted being favorably impressed, whether the subject was Jesus himself (8:10) or the people who have witnessed his miracles (8:27; 9:33; 15:31; 21:20) or his words (22:22). Jesus was not like other defendants, and Pilate was impressed.

15 There is no evidence outside the gospels for this custom of an individual amnesty at festival time.[26] The phrase used by Matthew and Mark, with no article, might be read as applying to *all* festivals, but John 18:39 says that it was specifically a Passover custom, and the phrase used by Matthew and Mark is better read with the same sense as referring to Passover as the greatest of the pilgrimage festivals. There are known examples of the release of prisoners, as a means of gaining popular support, elsewhere in the ancient world, some of which are associated with festivals,[27] and in Palestine we hear of one-off amnesties by Archelaus (Josephus, *War* 2.4, 28) and twice later by Albinus (Josephus, *Ant.* 20.208-10, 215).[28] Such a policy on the part of Pilate is historically conceivable, especially given his unpopularity with his subjects, but an annual Passover amnesty goes beyond any parallels known to us.

---

25. A. N. Sherwin-White, *Roman Society,* 25-26, mentions a Roman principle of allowing a silent defendant three opportunities before convicting by default, since "Roman judges disliked sentencing an undefended man" (cf. Acts 25:16).

26. The provision for Passover sacrifice on behalf of "one whom they have promised to bring out of prison" in *m. Pesaḥ.* 8:6 is too unspecific to provide confirmation, and too late to be used as evidence specifically for the custom followed by Pilate, nearly two hundred years before the compilation of the Mishnah.

27. J. Blinzler, *Trial,* 205-8, 218-21; R. E. Brown, *Death,* 814-19; R. L. Merritt, *JBL* 104 (1985) 57-68. Brown is sceptical about the historicity of Pilate's amnesty.

28. In *Ant.* 20.208-10, however, the release was under duress, in exchange for hostages.

Its effectiveness would depend on the people having the right to select their candidate for release.[29]

16-17 Matthew's impersonal "they had" might be understood as referring to the Romans ("they were holding"), but since Matthew when speaking of the Roman authority normally refers only to Pilate in the singular, it is more likely that this plural verb refers not to the Romans but to the Jerusalem crowd: knowing that the amnesty was due, "they had" their own candidate already selected, and presumably Pilate had been informed of this. So the only name under consideration is that of Jesus[30] Barabbas until Pilate, under the impression that Jesus of Nazareth was also a popular leader (see introductory comments above), decides to try offering them a different Jesus. It is even possible that he had heard shouts in favor of Jesus (Barabbas) and assumed it was the other Jesus they were shouting for. At any rate, the coincidence of names gives sharper point to Pilate's question: "Which Jesus do you want, the son of Abba or the one who is known as Messiah?" The phrase *ton legomenon Christon,* which will be repeated in v. 22, is Pilate's way of identifying the alleged claim of Jesus of Nazareth (which he assumes the crowd will accept) without himself endorsing it;[31] it is the same phrase which Josephus uses, equally noncommittally, to identify Jesus of Nazareth in *Ant.* 20.200. Pilate's use of this phrase rather than repeating "the king of the Jews" shows that he has been well briefed on the language Jesus is understood to have used among Jews. Cf. 26:68 for the title "Messiah" used by Jesus' opponents to mock his alleged claim.

Jesus Barabbas[32] is known to us only from the gospel passion narratives.[33] Mark 15:7 identifies him as a leader in a recent (otherwise unknown) violent insurrection. Mark says that others were imprisoned with him awaiting sentence for the same offense, and the fact that Matthew describes Jesus

29. E. Bammel, in E. Bammel and C. F. D. Moule (eds.), *Jesus,* 427-28, argues for the historical plausibility of the annual Passover amnesty as a Jewish custom (in John 18:39 Pilate says, "*you* have a custom") taken over by the Roman governors from the Hasmoneans.

30. See p. 1046, n. 3, for Barabbas's personal name, Jesus.

31. *Pace* Gundry, 561-62, who argues that Matthew has "Christianized" Pilate, and that here "Pilate *confesses* Jesus as the Christ."

32. Barabbas ("a common name," BDAG 166a) is an Aramaic patronymic, probably meaning "son of Abba" (Abba is found in rabbinic literature both as a name and as a title, "Father") or perhaps "son of a teacher (Rabban)"; see Schürer, 1:385, n. 138; R. E. Brown, *Death,* 799-800. Jerome reports that a Jewish-Christian gospel interpreted the name as "son of their teacher."

33. Against the "novelistic reconstruction" of a few scholars that there was originally only one Jesus (of Nazareth), whom some referred to as *bar abba,* "son of the Father," and that Mark either mistakenly or deliberately made a separate figure out of the patronymic, see R. E. Brown, *Death,* 811-12.

as crucified between two "bandits" (vv. 38, 44), using the term *lēstēs* which Josephus regularly uses for those who fought against the Roman occupation,[34] leads many to conclude that they, too, were members of Barabbas's group. John 18:40 directly describes Barabbas as a *lēstēs*. These data, together with the fact that the crowd wanted Barabbas released, strongly suggest that he was not a common criminal[35] but a freedom fighter — to the Romans an insurrectionist, but to the Jews a patriot. Matthew's adjective "well-known" will thus have different connotations depending on who is speaking: "notorious" (so NIV, NRSV, NJB) represents the official view, but GNB and TNIV are surely right to translate it "well-known,"[36] especially if the subject of "they had" is the people (see above). To them he was not "notorious" but "notable" and so the popular choice, perhaps a folk hero in the mold of Robin Hood. The presence of such insurrectionists in prison at that time would lend further color to the accusation that Jesus of Nazareth was claiming to be "the king of the Jews."

18 Pilate's assessment of the situation shows a shrewd awareness of the domestic politics of his subjects. See p. 1046, n. 4, for the term I have translated "rivalry." Pilate's perception is valid: the purpose of Jesus' trial was not to punish a breach of the law but to get rid of a man whose claims threatened the status and authority of the current Jewish leaders. This perception did not depend on any esoteric knowledge; it would be obvious from the way the charge had been presented and pressed by the authorities, and from Pilate's own observation of Jesus under questioning.

19 This unexpected interruption of the trial narrative further explains Pilate's reluctance to convict Jesus. We need not assume that the message arrived at this precise moment in the trial. Matthew locates it more generally "while Pilate was hearing the case," and it may be that the message had reached him earlier and therefore explains his attempt to avoid having to make a judicial decision by invoking the amnesty. His wife is otherwise unknown, though of course Christian legend has developed her role and even made her a Christian saint, called Claudia Procula.[37] We know of a number of Gentile women at the period who were attracted to Judaism,[38] and this might

34. See p. 787, n. 21, and the comments on 26:55.

35. With regard to the men crucified alongside Jesus, who have traditionally been described as "thieves" or "robbers," Davies and Allison, 3:616, n. 42, point out that theft was not a capital offense under Roman law.

36. ἐπίσημος has this positive sense in its only other NT use, Rom 16:7, and in the LXX.

37. The traditions are usefully summarized by R. E. Brown, *Death,* 803-4.

38. For examples see Josephus, *War* 2.560; *Ant.* 20.195. Josephus was not an unbiased witness, but the trend is confirmed by stories such as that of Helena of Adiabene; for her and for other examples drawn from Latin literature see Schürer, 3:162-64.

explain her interest in the case. She seems to have been aware of it even before Jesus was formally brought before Pilate, which perhaps indicates that Pilate had prior warning of the Jewish leaders' intention. Dreams were commonly regarded as a means of divine guidance in the ancient world (see on 1:20). In Matthew the only other people said to be guided by dreams are the magi and Joseph (1:20; 2:12, 13, 19, 22). The intervention of Pilate's wife serves only to deepen the guilt of the Jewish leaders: even a Gentile woman can see that Jesus is innocent.[39] But of course she knew this only because God had told her, in the dream. It is God, rather than just Pilate's wife, who thus testifies to Jesus' righteousness, over against the accusations of the Jewish leaders.

20 The crowd who heard Jesus' teaching and debates in the temple seem to have been favorably impressed (21:15, 46; 22:33, 46), so that in ch. 23 Jesus has been able to appeal to the crowd against the scribes and Pharisees. But now the crowd is on the side of the Jewish leaders. This is of course a different crowd: those gathered around the governor's palace early in the morning would more likely be local people, whereas the majority of Passover pilgrims would be in the temple area, where Jesus had previously enjoyed their support. And the leaders mentioned here are not scribes and Pharisees but the chief priests and elders, the leading representatives of local authority in Jerusalem. It is possible, too, that the preparations made by the Sanhedrin members for the presentation before Pilate had included making sure that a sympathetic crowd was in attendance — the aorist verb "persuaded" could be read in a pluperfect sense: they "had persuaded" the crowd, which was therefore now in place and ready to respond vociferously. If it was known that this was the time for Pilate to announce the Passover amnesty, supporters of Barabbas may have made up much of the crowd. At any rate, the final demand for Jesus' execution will come not just from the Sanhedrin but from a representative group of the people of Jerusalem. At the narrative level this will contribute to Pilate's decision that it would be unwise to continue to oppose the move against Jesus; at another level it will be the basis for Matthew's reflection in vv. 24-25 on who was responsible for Jesus' death.

21-23 Pilate's question is repeated from v. 17, and receives the answer which anyone but he could have predicted. But the crowd is not just pro-Barabbas but now equally definitely anti-Jesus. Probably those who had earlier been willing to back Jesus in his disputes with the authorities have now been swung by the fact that he has been officially judged a blasphemer by their recognized leaders; he is no longer an interesting novelty but a dangerous heretic. The repeated demand for crucifixion reads unpleasantly as

39. For similar truths perceived by Gentiles in contrast with Jews cf. 2:1-11; 8:10; 27:54.

the proposal of a *Jewish* crowd, for whom crucifixion, though by now only too familiar as a Roman penalty, was still probably culturally alien and barbaric (see above on 10:38, but also pp. 1029-30). But they would be aware that if Pilate was to order Jesus' execution, it would necessarily be by the means preferred by the Romans for political rebels; this was already the fate awaiting Barabbas and his associates. Pilate's question as to what Jesus' crime was receives no answer, simply a renewed call for execution. The outcome will be based not on justice but on political expediency.

24-25   On other occasions Pilate seems not to have worried about provoking a riot (Josephus, *Ant.* 18.55-59, 60-62; Philo, *Legat.* 299–305), but this time the issue is not important enough to him to warrant such a threat to public order (and thus to his reputation as governor). His attempt to resolve the issue by amnesty has failed, and he is now prepared to let events take their course. But before passing sentence he will make it clear that it is against his better judgment, and he does not wish to be held responsible.[40] The symbolism of washing away bloodguilt is obvious enough (Deut 21:6-9; Pss 26:6; 73:13; and for pagan examples Sophocles, *Ajax* 654–56; Virgil, *Aeneid* 2.718-20), and Pilate's words spell it out, using the same almost technical term for "innocent" (in relation to bloodguilt)[41] as Judas had used about Jesus in v. 4.[42] But if he will not bear the responsibility, someone else must, and he passes it on to the crowd whose shouts for Jesus' death have forced his hand.

The response of the crowd is a direct acceptance of responsibility rather than a wish, as it is often tendentiously translated (see p. 1047, n. 13). They are saying yes to Pilate's statement: he is not responsible, they are. Jesus has been duly convicted under Jewish law, and they are willing to be answerable for his death, which they, unlike Pilate, believe to be deserved. For the formula "x's blood on y" as a statement of responsibility for death cf. Lev 20:9; Deut 19:10; Josh 2:19; 2 Sam 1:16; Ezek 18:13; 33:4-6; Acts 5:28; 18:6. Note, too, the formula in 23:35-36 about the blood of the righteous "coming upon" this generation.

40. *Gos. Pet.* 1 has an interesting variation on Matthew's account, where it appears that Pilate invited the Jewish leaders to join him in washing their hands, but "neither Herod nor any of his judges" were willing to do so. Later (11[46]), when the Jewish elders report back to Pilate on Jesus' resurrection, he responds, "I am clean from the blood of the Son of God; it was you who desired it."

41. Cf. Thdt Sus 46 (B text) for the same formula, ἀθῷός εἰμι ἀπὸ τοῦ αἵματος ταύτης. In LXX Ps 73:13 the same term is used together with the imagery of washing hands. Cf. a similar formula in Acts 20:26, but with καθαρός instead of ἀθῷος.

42. Note, however, the comment of H. K. Bond, *Pontius Pilate*, 134: "Whilst Judas in 27.4 uses 'innocent' to describe Jesus, Pilate uses the adjective to describe himself. This is significant: Pilate is not proclaiming Jesus' innocence . . . but affirming that he is not responsible for Jesus' execution."

But there are two features of v. 25 which add further weight to this declaration. First, Matthew's attribution of these words to "all the people" indicates that for him this is more than the thoughtless words of a few hooligans who happened to be present. The words are spoken by the same crowd as in vv. 20-23, but now Matthew does not refer to them as "the crowd," as is his normal habit when talking about the people of Jerusalem, but he uses the term *laos*,[43] which in the LXX and later Jewish use is especially associated with the community of Israel as God's chosen people.[44] A declaration by "all the *laos*" is made by a representative group of Israel;[45] cf. Acts 2:36, where Peter will declare to "the whole house of Israel" that God has vindicated Jesus, "whom you crucified." And secondly, the responsibility rests not only on those speaking but also "on our children."[46] Pilate's challenge did not require this addition, but by including it Matthew extends the principle to the next generation.

The fact that this text (especially when translated as a wish rather than a statement) has been misused as an excuse for Christian persecution of Jews through the centuries[47] creates a natural embarrassment which makes it difficult for us to hear what Matthew intended us to hear from it.[48] We may assume that Matthew, as a Jew, was not condemning all Jews for all time. But

43. For the negative connotations of Matthew's uses of λαός as opposed to ὄχλος see P. Luomanen, *Entering,* 125-26. Contrast the attempt by A. J. Saldarini, *Community,* 32-34, to reduce it to a mere synonym of ὄχλος, "not a term burdened with salvation-historical weight."

44. For the usage of λαός see, e.g., D. P. Senior, *Passion,* 258-59. The phrase πᾶς ὁ λαός in, e.g., LXX Exod 19:8 and in the refrain of Deut 27:15-26 draws attention to significant declarations by the whole covenant community.

45. Cf. the OT principle that capital punishment should be endorsed by the whole Israelite community (Lev 24:13-16; Num 35:12). M. Knowles, *Jeremiah,* 202, notes (following H. Kosmala) that the same phrase is used in Jer 26:9-12 of the people who threatened Jeremiah with death because of his prophecy against the temple; the same passage goes on to speak of them "bringing innocent blood upon yourselves and upon this city" (v. 15); see the next note.

46. For the idea of hereditary bloodguilt see 2 Sam 3:29; 1 Kgs 2:33; in Jer 26:15 it can spread to a whole city. But the concept of hereditary guilt is famously repudiated in Ezek 18 (cf. Jer 31:29-30).

47. Against this see especially H. Kosmala, *ASTI* 7 (1968/9) 94-126; also J. A. Fitzmyer, *TS* 26 (1965) 667-71; R. E. Brown, *Death,* 831-39. I have considered more generally the charge that Matthew fosters anti-Jewish prejudice in my *Matthew: Evangelist,* 238-41.

48. Modern Christian embarrassment over these words may be slightly mitigated by the recognition that "by the measure of Hellenistic conventions, and certainly by the measure of contemporary Jewish polemic, the NT's slander against fellow-Jews is remarkably mild" (L. T. Johnson, *JBL* 108 [1989] 441; see above, p. 854, n. 5; Johnson does not apply his findings specifically to this passage).

his choice of the phrase "all the *laos*" and his inclusion of "our children" show that he was thinking of more than the particular group who happened to be in front of the governor's palace that morning. The reference to "our children" was probably prompted by Matthew's reflection that it would be a new generation who bore the brunt of the Roman onslaught on Jerusalem in A.D. 70.[49] In the discourse of chs. 24–25 we have been alerted to the fundamental shift in the divine economy which would come about with Jerusalem's rejection of Jesus and which is symbolized in the coming destruction of the temple. The kingdom of heaven is no longer to be focused in the *laos,* the city and the temple, but in the vindicated and enthroned Son of Man who, after the temple is destroyed, will gather his chosen people from all the corners of the earth. All this will happen within this generation (cf. "us and our children"). Jerusalem's rejection of the Son of Man has set the seal on the expulsion of the former tenants from the vineyard, and a new "nation" is to take over the tenancy (21:43), a nation made up of those who belong to the Son of Man and who are therefore the continuing members of the kingdom of heaven. As early as 8:11-12 Matthew has given notice of this impending change when he talked of many coming from east and west to share in the banquet of the kingdom of heaven with Abraham, Isaac, and Jacob while those who seemed the natural "sons of the kingdom" would be thrown out.

The terrible words of all the *laos* in 27:25 are, I believe, best understood as reflecting that overall theology of a new people of God rather than as pronouncing the permanent culpability of Jews as Jews. The people of Jerusalem, like their leaders, have rejected the Son sent to them by the owner of the vineyard, and the status of ethnic Israel as the chosen people of God can never be the same again. Together with the city and the temple the people of Jerusalem represent the *ancien régime,* which is soon to be swept away in the events of A.D. 70. It will be a new sort of "nation" (made up of Jews as well as non-Jews) which will henceforth be the community of the people of God, and to which he will look to produce the fruits of his kingdom. And this new situation will be the result of the choice made by "this generation" (23:35-36).[50]

26 Pilate fulfills both parts of the crowd's demand, the release of Jesus Barabbas and the sentencing of Jesus "Messiah" to crucifixion. This brief clause is the nearest Matthew gets to recording the official judicial condemnation of Jesus which resulted in his execution. The preliminary flogging

49. Cf. Luke 23:28, also with reference to the coming destruction of Jerusalem.
50. T. B. Cargal, *NTS* 37 (1991) 101-12, suggests (following Bonnard) that Matthew intended his text to be read at two levels, *both* as a statement of responsibility for Jesus' death (in which he believes Matthew wishes to implicate Pilate as much as Judas and the priests) *and* as a pointer to the future redemption of Israel through Jesus' (saving) blood being "on them." Most interpreters find little in this context to support this inference from the use of "blood" in 26:28.

was an accepted part of the process leading to crucifixion;[51] it was done with leather whips sometimes weighted with pieces of metal or bone, and was a brutal process which inflicted serious injury and could itself sometimes prove fatal.[52] The gospel narratives, both at this point and at the point of crucifixion, make no attempt to draw out the sheer physical horror of the procedure, though Matthew's first readers would have known, as modern readers do not, that Roman "flogging" was something far more serious and obscene than a few strokes with a whip.

Of the four verbs in Jesus' prediction in 20:19, three appear in this verse ("hand over," "flog," "crucify"); the fourth ("mock") will be fulfilled in the verses that follow.

D. THE DEATH AND BURIAL OF JESUS (27:27-66)

The judicial process, such as it was, is over, and now the sentence is to be carried out. Jesus is now in the hands not of the judicial authorities, Jewish or Roman, but of the Roman execution squad. The grim process will run its course, but as it does it will become apparent that this execution, superficially just like any other crucifixion, is unique on account of the person who is being crucified. This will be most obvious in the verses which speak of Jesus' death and the events which accompanied it (vv. 45-54). But even before that, in the mock homage to the "king of the Jews" by the non-Jewish soldiers and the laconic charge written above Jesus' head, and in the more theologically nuanced mockery by Jewish bystanders and opponents, Matthew expects his readers to catch the ironical truth of the honors heaped upon Jesus in jest and mockery: even in a setting of public humiliation and torture, this really *is* the king of the Jews, the temple builder, the Savior, the Son of God. And while the uncomprehending bystanders mock, Jesus' chilling cry of abandonment, followed by the drama of the earthquake, the tearing of the temple curtain, and the restoration to life of the pious dead, will tell all who are willing to hear that something of profound and world-changing significance is taking place there in the darkness, so that eventually even the hard-bitten soldiers who so recently had knelt in derision before the disgraced "king of the Jews" can now see that "This man really was God's son."

But, nonetheless, Jesus really does die on the cross, and the hurried arrangements made for his burial attest to the reality of that death. So all the pieces are put in place which will contribute to the dramatic climax of the Je-

---

51. Josephus, *War* 2.306-8; 5.449; 7.200-202. See M. Hengel, *Crucifixion,* 25-29; A. N. Sherwin-White, *Roman Society,* 26-28.

52. See C. Schneider, *TDNT* 4:517-19; J. Blinzler, *Trial,* 222-23.

rusalem story: the watching women to ensure that no mistake is made, the solid rock of Joseph's tomb and the huge stone which sealed it, and an official guard at the tomb to ensure that Jesus stays dead and buried.

In all this climactic sequence of events Matthew will add no further fulfillment formulae. The only verbatim quotation of an OT text will be in the opening words of Ps 22 which supply Jesus' brief shout from the cross. But the conviction that Jesus' death takes place in accordance with the Scriptures (26:31, 54, 56) will find expression in a series of less formal allusions, especially to Pss 22 (see on vv. 35-36, 39, 43, 46, 50) and 69 (see on vv. 34, 48), psalms which depict the suffering righteous servant of God.[1] The ultimate explanation of the cross is neither Jewish hostility nor Roman injustice, but the declared purpose of God.

1. Jesus Mocked by the Roman Soldiers (27:27-31)

27 *Then the governor's soldiers took Jesus with them into the guard room*[2] *and gathered the whole cohort around him.* 28 *They took off his clothes*[3] *and put a red cloak around him;* 29 *and they wove a crown*[4] *out of thorns and put it on his head and a stick*[5] *in his right*

---

1. For the influence of Ps 22 on the gospel passion narratives see R. E. Brown, *Death,* 1455-65. It is remarkable that there is no NT allusion to Ps 22:16c, which refers to the hands and feet of the sufferer, but there was probably as much uncertainty then as now as to what the obscure Hebrew text meant. The received MT has, apparently, *"like a lion my hands and my feet,"* with no verb. The verb supplied in the LXX, ὤρυξαν, "they dug" (usually understood to mean "pierced"), might suggest crucifixion, but the later Greek versions of the OT prefer "they bound"; the Syriac "they tore" perhaps draws on the lion image of the Hebrew text, as the targum does explicitly, "biting like a lion."

2. πραιτώριον here probably designates the governor's official residence, outside which the trial has been held, but presumably the soldiers had their own area within the palace. Mark 15:16 describes it as an αὐλή, probably in the sense of courtyard rather than palace (cf. p. 971, n. 1).

3. Several MSS have ἐνδύσαντες αὐτόν instead of ἐκδύσαντες αὐτόν, probably under the influence of Mark 15:17 (D and some Latin and Syriac versions have also introduced the purple cloak from John 19:2, thus apparently envisaging two cloaks!). But in Matthew this would make the following περιέθηκαν redundant, whereas in Mark περιτίθημι is used for the crown, not the cloak. Matthew's first verb must therefore describe the initial removal of Jesus' clothes (which will be presupposed in v. 31); some later MSS and versions make this explicit by adding "his clothes" (as English idiom also requires; see the translation above).

4. The term στέφανος does not in itself necessarily mean a royal crown. It is a wreath such as was worn by successful athletes, or as a mark of honor. But the context requires that we think here of a parody of a royal crown.

5. κάλαμος was used for a "reed" in 11:7 and 12:20. It can also denote a measuring rod (Rev 11:1; 21:15). The use of this term suggests something less substantial than a

hand, and kneeling in front of him they made fun of him, saying, "Hail, King of the Jews!" 30 *They spat on him, and took the stick and kept striking[6] him on the head.* 31 *Then, when they had made fun of him,[7] they took the cloak off him and put his own clothes on him, and took him off to crucify him.*

After Jesus was condemned by the Jewish leaders, they abused and mocked him (26:67-68). Now that the Roman trial is finished,[8] the governor's soldiers do the same, but in a suitably cruder and more violent way.[9] To have a sup-posedly self-proclaimed king in their power offered unusually good sport, and for non-Jewish soldiers to have such an opportunity of abusing a Jewish dignitary with impunity was a chance not to be missed.[10] The whole scene is a mock enthronement, with improvised cheap substitutes doing duty for the royal robe, crown, and scepter, and physical abuse substituted for loyal hom-age. After the brutal torture of the Roman flogging Jesus would be in no state to resist even if he had wished, and his already battered physical condition would only add to the pathetic appearance of this Jewish "king." All this takes place out of the public domain, where there are no Jewish onlookers to take racial offense. By the time Jesus emerges into the open on the way to the cross, the instruments of mockery have been removed and Jesus is back in his normal clothes.

It may seem surprising that Matthew is willing to give so detailed a description of what is to the Christian reader an extremely distasteful epi-sode, but within the scheme of his passion narrative it serves (a) to provide a

---

"staff," ῥαβδός. A piece of cane (probably bamboo or similar) was used as a mocking sub-stitute for a royal scepter.

6. The imperfect tense suggests that the striking was repeated.

7. Many MSS have the imperfect rather than the aorist tense, which would mean "while they were making fun of him," which reads less appropriately in context. It may have been influenced by the imperfect tense of the previous verb, ἔτυπτον (see last note).

8. John 19:1-5, however, places this incident, and the preceding flogging, during the trial.

9. In *Gos. Pet.* 3 (6-9) the mockers are not identified as soldiers, and the sequence suggests that they are some of "the people." They are made to refer to Jesus as "the Son of God" as they mock and ill-treat him. His enthronement is "on the judgment seat," where they call on him to "Judge justly, King of Israel." All this fits the generally anti-Jewish tenor of the *Gospel of Peter.*

10. Philo, *Flacc.* 36–39, records a similar display of anti-Jewish prejudice in Al-exandria a few years later, with the mock enthronement of a Jewish imbecile. A less close parallel is the mock installation of a peasant as high priest by Jewish insurrectionists in the temple (Josephus, *War* 4.155-57). For other suggested parallels from the Greco-Roman world see R. E. Brown, *Death,* 874-77.

Gentile counterpart to the Jewish mocking (26:67-68), (b) to show the detailed fulfillment of Jesus' own prediction in 20:19, (c) to depict Jesus once more as the suffering servant of Isaiah (Isa 50:6), and (d) to allow the reader to reflect on the reality of Jesus' kingship which the soldiers can see only as a joke. In 28:18 we shall read of the *real* enthronement.

The soldiers detailed to carry out the crucifixion must presumably have been among this mocking crowd. It will therefore be the more remarkable when we hear them declare in v. 54 that, after all, Jesus was the Son of God. Matthew's readers know, of course, that the kingship the soldiers made fun of was in fact real; but the way Jesus dies will cause even some of those same soldiers to change their mind about him.

27 Pilate's soldiers would be auxiliaries rather than Roman legionaries (there was no legion stationed in Palestine at this time);[11] they are likely to have been drawn from the non-Jewish population of surrounding areas, who would have had little sympathy with a supposed Jewish king. The gathering in the praetorium (see p. 1060, n. 2) would thus be large and rowdy;[12] "the whole cohort" would strictly mean some six hundred men, but Matthew may not be using the term in its technical sense.

28-30 A prisoner would normally have been stripped for the flogging; it is not clear whether some clothing had been replaced after the flogging or whether some basic clothing had been left on until now. The royal regalia for this mock enthronement are improvised from what was ready to hand. The word for "cloak" here is specifically used for a military cloak, shorter than a standard *himation* and colored with a cheap red dye; this did duty for the much more expensive purple robes worn by the Roman nobility and especially by royalty. The "thorns" from which they wove the "crown" may have been from any common spiny plant;[13] even if the intention was primarily mockery rather than physical torture,[14] such a wreath would inevitably be painful. For the "stick" (or cane) see p. 1060, n. 5. On an already bleeding, naked man these parodies of a king's robe and symbols of power would produce a ludicrous effect, which is then exploited by the soldiers'

---

11. For Roman forces in Palestine at this period see Schürer, 1:362-67.

12. In view of the other echoes of Ps 22 in this chapter, it is possible that this hostile gathering around Jesus reflects Ps 22:16a-b, but there are no verbal echoes of the LXX.

13. R. E. Brown, *Death,* 866-67, lists some suggestions.

14. See H. StJ. Hart, *JTS* 3 (1952) 66-75, for the proposal that the "thorns" (perhaps the spikes at the base of palm leaves) were intended to represent the form of the crown found on several coins of oriental rulers, which have rays (as of the sun) projecting outward from the crown (not inward toward the head of the person wearing it). For this and other speculation concerning the crown of thorns see W. Grundmann, *TDNT* 7:632-33.

mock homage. "Hail, King of the Jews!" perhaps parodies the formal imperial greeting, *Ave, Caesar!* When spitting and repeated blows are added, the scene combines cruelty with extreme dishonor (with an echo again of Isa 50:6, as in 26:67-68).[15]

31 The replacement of Jesus' own clothes for the walk to Golgotha was probably a concession to Jewish scruples about public nakedness (*Jub.* 3:30-31; cf. Gen 9:20-27). Crucifixion was normally naked, and in v. 35 Jesus' clothes will again have been removed; *m. Sanh.* 6:3 specifies that the clothes should be removed only at the place of execution, not on the way there. None of the gospels tells us whether the crown of thorns was left on Jesus' head after the mockery, as later Christian art has traditionally assumed,[16] but perhaps the fact that the removal of the military cloak is specifically mentioned allows us to assume that the crown stayed in place.[17]

2. The Crucifixion (27:32-38)

> 32 *As they went out, they found a man from Cyrene called Simon, and they dragooned him to carry Jesus' cross.* 33 *And when they reached a place called Golgotha, which means "Skull Place,"* 34 *they gave him a drink of drugged[1] wine, and after tasting it, he refused to drink it.* 35 *When they had crucified him, they divided up his clothes by drawing lots,[2]* 36 *and they sat and kept watch over him there.* 37 *They had put above his head a written statement of the charge against him:* *"This is Jesus, the king of the Jews."* 38 *Then two bandits were crucified along with him, one on his right and one on his left.*

15. See D. J. Moo, *The OT*, 139-44, for the influence of this servant passage on the gospel accounts of Jesus' ill-treatment.

16. R. E. Brown, *Death*, 870, notes, however, that "in most early art of the crucifixion Jesus is depicted without a crown."

17. *Pace* J. Blinzler, *Trial*, 244-45, who argues that public mockery of a Jewish "king" would not have been allowed. In view of the public reaction to Jesus at his trial it is unlikely that a crown of thorns on his head would have been construed as mocking the Jews as a people.

1. Literally, "wine mixed with bile"; see the comments below for the nature and purpose of the added ingredient.

2. Some later MSS and versions add here, "This was to fulfill what had been declared through the prophet: 'They divided up my garments among themselves and cast lots for my clothes.'" It is easy to understand the addition of such an extra formula-quotation to help readers spot the allusion to Ps 22:18, especially since John 19:24 does so explicitly, but hard to imagine why it should be missing from all the earlier MSS if it was original. The omission of the participle λέγοντος which occurs in all other formula-quotations of a specific text (see on 2:23) betrays a non-Matthean origin, though the attribution of a psalm quotation to "the prophet" would have been in character (see 13:35).

The account of the crucifixion runs as a continuous narrative through to the death of Jesus and its immediate sequel in vv. 50-54, but a concentrated depiction of Jewish mockery of the crucified Messiah (more developed than the parallel in Mark) forms a distinct unit within this narrative. It bridges the time interval between Jesus' being fastened on the cross, probably still quite early in the morning,[3] and the final events which followed some six hours later, at the ninth hour. We shall therefore consider this narrative in three sections, covering respectively the crucifixion (vv. 32-38), the mockery (vv. 39-44), and the death of Jesus (vv. 45-54).

The account of the actual fastening to the cross is remarkably restrained — simply a participle stating the fact, with no descriptive content.[4] Even the means of fastening are not specified — it is only in John 20:25, after the event, that we hear of nails (they are probably also implied in Luke 24:39). The overenthusiastic attempts to draw out the physical horror of crucifixion which disfigure some Christian preaching (and at least one recent movie) find no echo in the gospels.[5] Perhaps the original readers were too familiar with both the torture and the shame of crucifixion to need any help in envisaging what it really meant. At any rate, the narrative focus in these verses is rather on the surrounding events and the people involved (Simon, the soldiers, the bandits), together with the ironical placard over Jesus' head which sums up the Roman dismissal of his claims.

32 The condemned man would normally be made to carry his own crossbeam (which was to be attached to an upright already erected at the site of execution); see on 10:38. We are not told why Jesus was not made to do so, but it is a reasonable assumption that after the flogging he was not physically capable of it, or at least that he managed it only as far as the city gate ("as they went out" probably refers to leaving the city; see below). Using their right to commandeer local labor,[6] the soldiers forced a bystander to carry it

---

3. Matthew does not specify the time of the crucifixion. For the problem of harmonizing Mark's statement (Mark 15:25) that Jesus was crucified at "the third hour" (9 A.M.) with the statement of John 19:14 that Pilate pronounced sentence "about the sixth hour" (noon) see my *Mark,* 644-45; J. V. Miller, *JETS* 26 (1983) 158-66; R. E. Brown, *Death,* 958-60. J. Blinzler, *Trial,* 265-70, finds Mark's statement so uncomfortable that he resorts to eliminating it from the text without any evidence! But in fact Mark's timing better suits the sequence of the Synoptic narrative from a trial at daybreak to the coming of darkness at noon (v. 45) when Jesus has apparently already been on the cross for some time.

4. For details of how it was done see M. Hengel, *Crucifixion,* 24-32; D. G. Burke, *ISBE* 1:825-30; J. A. Fitzmyer, *CBQ* 40 (1978) 493-513; R. E. Brown, *Death,* 945-52.

5. Still less, however, do the gospels reflect the docetism of *Gos. Pet.* 4 (10), which depicts Jesus as keeping silent during the crucifixion "as if he felt no pain."

6. See above on 5:41 for the practice of *angareia.* The same technical term is used

instead. The preservation of Simon's name and country of origin suggests that he may subsequently have been involved with the Christian community, but there is nothing to suggest that he had hitherto had anything to do with Jesus.[7] Jesus' known disciples, whom he had earlier told to be ready to carry their own cross after him (10:38; 16:24), were nowhere to be seen now that the moment for literal obedience to that demand had come; the reader might especially notice the need for a new Simon to take the place of the Simon who had so loudly protested his loyalty in 26:33, 35.

33   *Golgotha* is a Greek transliteration of the Aramaic *gulgultā'* (Hebrew *gulgōlet*), "skull"; Luke gives the name in Greek as simply "Skull," without "Place." The origin of the name is unknown, but it perhaps derives from the use of the site as a place of execution. By offering a translation Matthew ensures that his readers do not miss its sinister implications. The traditional identification of Golgotha as a rocky mound just outside the then city wall[8] and now enclosed within the Church of the Holy Sepulchre is unlikely to be provable, but it matches adequately with the biblical data for the place of Jesus' death and burial.[9] If the Roman trial took place at Herod's palace

---

here. This prompts D. C. Allison, *CBQ* 56 (1994) 703-5, to argue that Matthew intended his readers to notice this and other verbal links with 5:38-42, and so to view Jesus (in the light of the servant of Isa 50:4-9) as fulfilling his own injunctions to his disciples.

7. Mark's mention of his sons' names (Mark 15:21) adds to the probability that the family was known in the early church. Simon may well have been Jewish (though Simon was also a Greek name), since Cyrene had a significant Jewish community, from which presumably many came to Jerusalem for the Passover. But Simon's family may already have been resident in Jerusalem, as were many Cyrenian Jews (Acts 6:9; 11:20). For a first-century Cyrenian Jewish cemetery outside Jerusalem, where an ossuary of a certain "Alexander son of Simon" was found, see N. Avigad, *IEJ* 12 (1962) 9-12.

8. Hence Matthew's verb "went *out*" in v. 32; cf. also 21:39. John 19:20 says the site was "near the city."

9. The traditional site is supported by the presence of a number of Jewish rock-tombs of the period (a burial ground was necessarily outside the city). The alternative site promoted by some Protestants and known as "Gordon's Calvary" was identified by General Charles Gordon not on the basis of archeology but of his own idiosyncratic typological conclusions from Lev 1:11 (together with other reasons which he himself described as "fanciful"). His arguments are reprinted in J. Wilkinson, *Jerusalem,* 198-200; they do not inspire confidence in his identification! Equally "fanciful" is the common suggestion that the hill Gordon identified looks like a skull and was so named as a result. The NT never describes Golgotha as a "hill" (*pace* Mrs. Alexander's "green hill far away"). The bare top of the rocky mound of the traditional Golgotha might have been thought to resemble the top of a skull, but the reason given above for the name is at least as likely as any physical feature. For data supporting the traditional site see R. E. Brown, *Death,* 912-23; cf. ibid., 937-40. For a more nuanced view, supporting the traditional site of Jesus' burial, but suggesting that the crucifixion took place some two hundred meters further south, see J. E. Taylor, *NTS* 44 (1998) 180-203.

(see p. 1035, n. 4), the route to this site would be a short one, less than half a mile out through the city gate beside the palace and north along the western wall, rather than the longer *Via Dolorosa* which tradition has based on the assumption that the trial took place at the Antonia fortress.

34 The purpose of the offered drink of "wine mixed with bile" (see p. 1063, n. 1) is not explained. The basic meaning of the Greek word *cholē* [10] is "bile," the product of the gall bladder, but the bitter taste of bile led to the term also being used for bitter vegetable substances such as wormwood. Matthew no doubt chooses this term to echo LXX Ps 68:22 (EVV 69:21), where it stands in parallel with *oxos,* "vinegar" (see on v. 48).[11] Mark's parallel here has *esmyrnismenon,* treated with myrrh; myrrh was sometimes added to wine both as a flavoring spice (like our mulled wine) and possibly to produce a narcotic effect. It is impossible to be sure just what drug the soldiers put in the wine, though it is unlikely to have been the literal animal-product bile. The intention of the "bile" in Ps 69 was apparently to make the food unpalatable,[12] but in the context of preparing a man for crucifixion the addition to the wine is more likely to have been a narcotic to ease the pain of crucifixion, such as the women of Jerusalem, inspired by Prov 31:6-7, used to provide, according to *b. Sanh.* 43a.[13] Such a considerate act on the part of the soldiers (unless it was a routine part of the crucifixion process, for which we have no other evidence) seems out of character after the brutality of vv. 27-31,[14] and it is possible that the original tradition referred to women or left the subject unspecified, but Matthew's syntax seems to require that the soldiers are the subject. A similar problem arises in vv. 47-49; see the comments there.

10. The noun occurs elsewhere in the NT only in Acts 8:23, metaphorically for "bitterness."

11. The continued influence of the psalm text is seen in *Gos. Pet.* 5 (16) and in *Barn.* 7:3, 5, where the two separate drinks of Matthew ("bile" here and "vinegar" in v. 48) are combined into a single drink of bile and vinegar mixed together.

12. The Hebrew *rô'š,* which the LXX translates by χολή, is often understood to refer to a poison, but its usage elsewhere in the OT is closely linked with wormwood, which is bitter but not poisonous, and in Ps 69 it is paralleled with vinegar, again not a poison. The focus appears to be on taste, not toxicity. It is therefore precarious to argue from a supposed meaning of the Hebrew word (not the Greek) in the psalm that the χολή here in Matthew is a poison, making this drink "an invitation to commit suicide" (Davies and Allison, 3:613).

13. The drug specified there is frankincense. For further references and discussion see my *Mark,* 642-43; Keener, 678; R. E. Brown, *Death,* 940-42.

14. Many commentators therefore take the offer of the drink in Matthew (both here and in v. 48) as a hostile act, as it is in the psalm. Some even regard this drink in Mark as similarly hostile in intent; so Gundry, *Use,* 202-3; D. J. Moo, *The OT,* 250-51; Carson, 575. More commonly Matthew is regarded as differing from Mark on this point; so R. E. Brown, *Death,* 942-44; Hagner, 2:835; Davies and Allison, 3:612-13.

The allusion to Ps 69 identifies Jesus as the righteous sufferer who, in that psalm, is ill-treated because of his loyalty to God. The psalm's description of his sufferings, both physical and mental, quickly established itself alongside that of Ps 22 as a scriptural model for the suffering of Jesus on the cross. All four gospels (Matthew and Mark twice each) mention drinks given to Jesus at his crucifixion, picking up v. 21 of the psalm, and other parts of the psalm are quoted or alluded to in this connection in John 15:25; Acts 1:20; Rom 15:3 (cf. also John 2:17; Rom 11:9-10).

Jesus' refusal of the laced wine might be simply because it was, as in the psalm, an unpleasant drink offered in spite. But if, as is more likely, it was intended to dull the pain, Matthew may have mentioned Jesus' refusal in order to show his determination to go through the ordeal in full consciousness. He has chosen to drink the cup which his Father has given him (26:39-42), and will not be deflected by any human potion, however well meaning. This seems a more likely explanation of the comment than that Jesus is constrained by literal adherence to a "vow of abstinence" supposedly uttered in 26:29 (see comments there).

35-36 The actual fastening to the cross is passed over almost in silence (see above). It was done sometimes with ropes but sometimes, more cruelly, with nails; John 20:25 tells us that the latter method was used for Jesus. Men were crucified naked, so the clothes which were restored to Jesus in v. 31 are now again removed and become the perquisite of the execution squad. In the soldiers' method of dividing up this meager bonus Matthew expects his readers to note (see p. 1063, n. 2) the first of several allusions to Ps 22, in this case to Ps 22:18, clearly echoing the LXX wording, and it is possible that in the further comment that they "kept watch over him there" he intends a further allusion to the preceding clause in the psalm, "they eyed and looked at me" (though here without direct echo of the LXX). For other allusions to Ps 22 in the passion narrative see above, p. 1060; the most prominent, and the one which no doubt drew Christian attention to the psalm in the first place, will be Jesus' shout in v. 46. Like Ps 69 (see on v. 34), this psalm spells out the sufferings of God's righteous servant at the hands of the ungodly, and Christian devotion quickly noted its remarkably literal fulfillment in what happened to Jesus.

The soldiers' keeping watch near the cross (to guard against a rescue attempt?), as well as possibly enhancing the allusion to Ps 22, serves in the narrative context to provide the actor required for the second offer of a drink in v. 48, but more importantly prepares the reader for the response of the soldiers when Jesus dies, where their "keeping watch" is again noted. As witnesses to all that will happen up to that point they will be well qualified to draw their remarkable conclusion in v. 54.

37 One purpose of public crucifixion was as a deterrent to other would-be rebels; a written charge displayed on the cross meant that onlookers, whether they knew of Jesus' trial or not, would see the folly of challenging Roman power. The board was probably hung around Jesus' neck or carried in front of him on the way to the cross,[15] and then fastened to it. If it was, as Matthew says, "above his head," we should perhaps envisage a cross of the traditional shape with an upward projection rather than the T-shape which was probably more commonly used, though the latter is possible if the head hung below the level of the fastened hands. The wording is given most fully by John, "Jesus of Nazareth, the king of the Jews," while Mark and Luke have only "The king of the Jews"; by adding the name Jesus Matthew perhaps intends to carry forward the contrast of the two men called Jesus which he has set up in vv. 16-23; see the following comments.[16]

38 We have noted the possibility that these two "bandits" were involved in the same patriotic uprising which had put Jesus Barabbas in prison.[17] If that is so, it is possible that the third, central cross, had originally been intended for Barabbas (the leader of the group?) and that the other Jesus literally took his place. That would seem an appropriate end for a declared "king of the Jews." There is thus a harsh irony in the fact that Jesus dies associated with a movement from which he has attempted to distance himself in the face of the unthinking enthusiasm of his followers (see on 16:22-23; 21:1-11; 22:15-22). This is just what the Sanhedrin had planned in the charge they framed to bring before Pilate. Another ironic note, for those who remember the request of James and John through their mother in 20:20-21, is to see who it is who in fact occupy the places at Jesus' right and left in his "kingship," while James and John themselves are nowhere to be seen.[18]

3. Jesus Mocked by Fellow Jews (27:39-44)

39 *People who were going by abused[1] him, shaking their heads*
40 *and saying, "You who can destroy the temple and rebuild it in three*

---

15. E. Bammel, in E. Bammel and C. F. D. Moule (eds.), *Jesus,* 353-54, provides evidence of this custom; the subsequent fixing of the placard to the cross is not otherwise attested, but it is not improbable.

16. The further addition of "this is" is probably simply a pedantic spelling out of the obvious. Gundry's suggestion (570) that this addition "changes the accusation from an insulting joke to a Christian confession" puts too much weight on a stylistic variation.

17. See on vv. 16-17; also for the meaning of ληστής, "bandit."

18. Many commentators think that the evangelists mention Jesus' position between two criminals in order to claim the fulfillment of Isa 53:12 ("numbered among the transgressors"), but see D. J. Moo, *The OT,* 154-55, for some cautionary comments on the lack of verbal similarity.

1. βλασφημέω here primarily carries its more "secular" sense (see on 12:31) of

days, save yourself; if you are God's son,[2] come down from the cross."
41 In the same way also the chief priests, with the scribes and elders,
made fun of him, saying, 42 "He saved others, but he cannot save him-
self. He is[3] the king of Israel! Let him come down now from the cross,
and we will believe in him. 43 He put his trust in God. Let God rescue
him now, if he wants him, because he said that he was God's son." 44 In
the same way even the bandits crucified along with him taunted him.

We have already seen Jesus mocked by the Sanhedrin members immediately
after they have convicted him of blasphemy (26:67-68). Now, with Jesus duly
secured on the cross, they return to the attack, but this time supported by
other Jews, the general public (v. 39), and the men on the other crosses. This
is then a Jewish counterpart to the mockery by the Gentile soldiers in vv. 27-
31; each ethnic group makes fun of Jesus' alleged claims, focusing on the
terms to which they more naturally relate, the soldiers on the political claim
to kingship, the Jews on the religious issues of temple building and of being
God's son. This combination of representatives of the Jewish people at several different levels (Sanhedrin members, ordinary passersby, and failed insurrectionists)[4] provides a poignant picture of the rejection of Jesus by his
own people.

---

slander against a fellow human, though Matthew may well have intended his readers also
to reflect that in this abuse of a dying man they were in fact speaking against God.

2. Some MSS and versions have an "and" here, which would mean reading "if
you are God's son" as dependent on "save yourself," and "come down from the cross" on
its own as a further challenge. The better-supported reading without "and," however, is
best construed as making "come down from the cross" dependent on "if you are God's
son"; it then parallels the call to "save yourself" which similarly depends on the alleged
temple claim. The variant could have arisen accidentally in that KAI could easily have
been either omitted or added under the influence of the following letters KAT.

3. Most MSS and versions have "If he is"; this looks like a rather prosaic spelling
out of the logic of how the bolder ironical declaration leads into the following challenge
(echoing the similar construction in v. 40). The less "obvious" wording found in some of
the earliest MSS is more likely to be original, as its unqualified "declaration" parallels
that of the preceding clause, "he saved others."

4. The three groups are linked by two phrases meaning "in the same way" which
introduce vv. 41 and 44; cf. T. L. Donaldson, *JSNT* 41 (1991) 7-12. This deliberate linking
makes it unlikely, as Hagner, 2:839, surprisingly suggests, that we need not envisage the
Sanhedrin members as being present at the cross but rather "mocking . . . behind closed
doors"; nothing in the narrative indicates such a distinction, and after the authorities' open
role in Jesus' condemnation it is hard to see why they should not publicly enjoy their triumph. The verb ἐμπαίζω, "make fun of," more naturally indicates that they, like the other
mockers, were there in front of him (cf. its use for the mockery by the soldiers gathered
around Jesus in vv. 29, 31). Cf. Keener, 681, n. 225.

But, as with the Roman mocking, Matthew expects his readers to recognize that what is being thrown at Jesus in jest is in fact true. His messianic
authority *does* mean the end of the temple and its replacement by "something
greater" (12:6), "my *ekklēsia*" (16:18); he *is* the Son of God; he *is* the king of
Israel, though not in the political sense his mockers imagine; he *has* saved
others and will continue to do so — and, indeed, that is the very reason why
he cannot come down from the cross before his Father's purpose is achieved.
If he had saved himself, he would not have been able to save others (cf. the
theme of losing one's life in order to save it, 16:25; cf. 10:39).

To this weight of theological reflection, even if ironically expressed,
this section of the narrative adds a further two allusions to Ps 22, in vv. 39
and 43 (on which see below). The second of these allusions is to a section of
the psalm which had been further developed by the author of the Wisdom of
Solomon, and that more developed tradition is also echoed here. The portrait
of Jesus as the righteous sufferer thus continues to develop alongside the reminder of his positive role as Messiah and Savior, and the way is prepared for
the dynamic climax of this dual role in v. 46.

39-40 The place of execution was deliberately in a well-frequented
area so as to maximize the deterrent effect. The mocking bystanders, who
represent ordinary Jews,[5] are described by a phrase, "shaking their heads,"[6]
which in Ps 22:7 describes those who see the righteous sufferer and mock
him; their words of mockery (Ps 22:8) will be taken up in v. 43. These bystanders know two things about Jesus' alleged claims, the threat against the
temple (as in 26:61) and the claim to be God's son (as in 26:63); perhaps the
news of the charges at the Sanhedrin hearing has already leaked out, but
more likely these two charges against Jesus at the hearing had been based on
what was already the common gossip about the Galilean prophet (see on
26:61, 63). In either capacity, as one with miraculous power to destroy and
rebuild or as one with a special claim on the power of God, he ought not to be
dying on the cross. His present helpless situation is the proof of the falsity of
his claims.

"If you are the Son of God" echoes the preamble to two of the devil's
temptations in 4:3, 6; here again Jesus must have felt the force of the temptation to exploit his special relationship with God in order to escape physical
suffering. But that temptation had already been faced and overcome in Geth-

---

5. R. E. Brown, *Death,* 986-87, points out that these are not, like the hostile crowd
at the trial, directly influenced by the authorities; they represent the average reaction of local people.

6. See 2 Kgs 19:2; Job 16:4; Jer 18:16; Lam 2:15; Sir 12:18; 13:7 for the same
motion as an expression of scorn. Lam 2:15 is also echoed in the description of these
mockers as "those who were going by"; LXX Lam 2:15 uses the same phrase, οἱ
παραπορευόμενοι. See D. J. Moo, *The OT,* 258; M. Knowles, *Jeremiah,* 203-4.

semane (and cf. 26:53-54). Indeed, it is that very relationship as "Son of God" which paradoxically requires Jesus to go through with his Father's purpose on the cross. In some sense even the Gentile soldiers will see the truth of this in v. 54.[7]

41-43   The second group of mockers are already very familiar to us, and for only the second time (see on 16:21) Matthew gives the full list of the three main component groups of the Sanhedrin, so as to underline the comprehensive rejection of Jesus by the whole Jewish establishment. Their mockery is more theologically sophisticated than that of the general public. They, too, challenge Jesus to "save himself" and "come down from the cross," but the first invitation is linked with his alleged claim to be able to "save" other people, and the second with his royal claim as Messiah. "Save" has not been used in the theological sense to describe Jesus' mission since 1:21, where it was in a statement by the angel, not in Jesus' own words, and it is possible that it is here used in the more normal Matthean sense of physical healing and rescue. But "salvation" in some sense was a term many would have associated with a claim to be the Messiah. It is also possible that the shouts of "Hosanna" on Jesus' arrival in Jerusalem (21:9, 15) had been construed by some as claiming that Jesus was to save his people.[8] To contrast this alleged claim with Jesus' palpable inability to "save" himself from death and suffering (the more common sense of "save" in Matthew) was a clever witticism. "King of Israel," again perhaps taking up the royal tone of Jesus' arrival at the city, was in Jewish mouths an even more clearly messianic title, whatever the Romans may have made of "King of the Jews" (see above, p. 1048). The added jibe, "and we will believe in him," perhaps pokes fun at the credulous Galileans who had followed Jesus as a miracle worker; here in Jerusalem he has been more sparing with miracles — surely now if ever is the time for one (note the repeated "now" in vv. 42 and 43; it is now or never). A miracle worker who cannot even keep himself alive deserves no belief.

Verse 43 clearly echoes Ps 22:8, both in content and to some extent in the LXX wording ("let him rescue" and "he wants him" use the same words). The righteous sufferer is mocked for his trust in a God who, it seems, will not respond to his devotion with practical help. That alone would be a telling scriptural echo, but the following words, "because he said that he was God's son," extend the allusion. In Wis 2:12-20 the wicked plot against the righteous man, and are particularly incensed by his claim to be "a child of the Lord" (2:13); the claim is repeated in 2:16, "he boasts that God is his Father,"

7. For the importance of "Son of God" in the whole gospel and its relevance to the present pericope see T. L. Donaldson, *JSNT* 41 (1991) 7-12.
8. See on 21:9 for the derivation and meaning of "Hosanna."

and in 2:18, "if the righteous man is God's son." It is because of this claim that they take up the theme of Ps 22:8:

> Let us see if his words are true,
>   and let us test how he comes to the end of his life;
> for if the righteous man is God's son, he will help him
>   and rescue him from the hand of his enemies.
>
> (Wis 2:17-18; cf. also v. 20)

A reader of Matthew who knew the Wisdom of Solomon would naturally recognize in the words of the Jewish authorities Wisdom's portrait of the cynicism of the wicked and of their persecution of the godly,[9] which in its turn was derived from motifs found in the OT psalms of the righteous sufferer.[10]

44 The taunts of the third group, the bandits crucified with Jesus, are not spelled out (contrast Luke 23:39). They were no doubt more earthy and less sophisticated than those of the Sanhedrin members. If they were associates of Jesus Barabbas (see on vv. 16-17, 38), their hostility to this Jesus underlines further the contrast between two programs of "liberation" which Matthew has already set up by having the two Jesuses offered as rival candidates for the Passover amnesty in vv. 15-23.

4. The Death of Jesus (27:45-54)

> 45 But from the sixth hour darkness came over the whole land until the ninth hour. 46 And about the ninth hour Jesus shouted out with a loud voice, "Ēli, ēli, lema sabachthani?"[1] which means "My God, my God, why have you abandoned me?" 47 When they heard this, some of those who stood there said, "This man is calling for Elijah." 48 Immediately one of them ran and took a sponge, soaked it in vinegar, put it

9. Davies and Allison, 3:609, set out a series of suggested verbal links with Wis 2:12-20 not only in Matt 27:43 but in the wider context. See also D. P. Senior, *Passion*, 288-89.

10. D. J. Moo, *The OT*, 260-61, however, argues that Matthew's allusion is only to Ps 22, which both Wisdom and Matthew use independently.

1. The form of the transliterated words given above (which appears to be part Hebrew, part Aramaic, but see p. 1075, n. 15) is that of most MSS, but several assimilate to Mark's probable form ἐλωΐ instead of ἠλί, so that the whole utterance becomes a clearly Aramaic quotation, while others have λαμά (Hebrew) instead of λεμά (Aramaic). D and a few OL MSS give the fourth word as ζαφθάνι (Hebrew) instead of σαβαχθάνι (Aramaic). There was probably considerable speculation in the early church over the exact form of Jesus' words, which was complicated by uncertainty over which language he had used and by the unfamiliarity of these foreign words to Greek-speaking Christians.

on a stick, and offered him a drink.[2] *49 But the others were saying, "Stop,[3] let's see whether Elijah comes to save him."[4] 50 But Jesus cried out again with a loud voice, and breathed his last.*[5]

51 And look! The curtain of the sanctuary was torn in two from the top to the bottom; and the earth was shaken and the rocks were split, 52 and the tombs were opened and many bodies of God's people[6] who had died[7] were raised; 53 and coming out of the tombs after Jesus' resurrection[8] they came into the holy city and were seen by many people.

54 But the centurion and those who were keeping watch with him over Jesus, when they saw the earthquake and what had happened, were terrified and said, "This man really was God's son!"

In Matthew's narrative sequence the mockery of vv. 39-44 took place in the early stages of Jesus' time on the cross, during the morning. Now a new phase begins about noon, reaching its climax in Jesus' death soon after the ninth hour (3 P.M.). The focus is not now on the wider circle of bystanders,

---

2. The imperfect tense following all the aorist participles in the rest of this verse may suggest that the attempt to "give him a drink" (the basic meaning of ποτίζω) was unsuccessful, and/or that it was repeated.

3. Ἄφες, literally "Leave," is probably a call to the man offering the drink to stop doing so and to leave Jesus alone to see whether his supposed appeal is successful. It is sometimes taken to be merely part of the deliberative phrase, ἄφες ἴδωμεν, "let us see," in which case the ἄφες would have no force of its own but simply underline the deliberative effect of the following subjunctive (so Gundry, 574; cf. BDF 364; BDAG 157a, §5b). There is a partial parallel to that usage in 7:4, though there the ἄφες has the effect of requesting permission, which is not the case here. Generally when Matthew uses the imperative of ἀφίημι, it has its own imperatival force and does not function as an auxiliary to a deliberative subjunctive.

4. Several early MSS include here, "but another took a spear and stabbed his side, and out came water and blood." This, while not verbally identical with John 19:34, closely parallels it, and is probably an early addition to Matthew's account of what had become, from its prominence in John, a standard part of the passion story. If it was originally in Matthew, it is hard to explain why the vast majority of MSS and versions should omit it. S. Pennells, *JSNT* 19 (1983) 99-115, argues that it represents a tradition found in some patristic writings that a spear thrust was the cause of Jesus' death, rather than, as in the Fourth Gospel, happening after he had died.

5. Literally, "let go his spirit/breath"; see the comments below.

6. Literally, "the holy ones"; see the comments below for who they may have been.

7. Literally, "slept," but using the term κοιμάομαι, which is regularly used as a euphemism for death, not καθεύδω, which denotes literal sleep (see on 9:24).

8. The Greek word order allows "after Jesus' resurrection" to be read either with "coming out of their tombs," as above, or with "they came into the holy city"; see the comments below. Gundry, 576, regards the latter as more in keeping with Matthean idiom.

but on Jesus himself, whose only words on the cross (in Matthew, as in Mark) provide a startling insight into the meaning of what is happening, and on those immediately around the cross, the centurion and soldiers. But alongside the human drama at the cross Matthew records a series of physical events, the darkness, the tearing of the temple curtain, the earthquake, and the resurrection of dead people, which add a powerful sense of the far-reaching significance of the death of Jesus, and contribute to the climactic exclamation of the soldiers in v. 54. The last of these events, the raising of the dead, is described at some length; the problems which arise in understanding its status as literal history must not be allowed to distract attention from its clear symbolic significance for Matthew, who is the only evangelist to record this particular phenomenon. J. P. Meier summarizes the impact of these verses as follows: "Here, with the full panoply of apocalyptic imagery, Mt portrays the death of Christ as the end of the Old Testament cult, as the earth-shaking beginning of the new aeon (bringing about the resurrection of the dead), and as the moment when the Gentiles first come to full faith in the Son of God."[9]

Within this dramatic setting, the actual death of Jesus (like his being fastened to the cross in v. 35) is recorded in one brief phrase which, however, seems carefully chosen to avoid the impression that he simply faded away (see below on v. 50). The loud cry which precedes Jesus' death, and his equally loud shout in v. 46, indicate that, unlike most crucified men, Jesus died in full control of his faculties, perhaps even that he died when he himself chose.

Among all the powerful motifs which crowd these verses, two seem to be of particular theological significance for understanding Jesus' death, his sense of abandonment by God (v. 46) and the tearing of the temple curtain (v. 51). Each of these will be discussed in the comments below. Together they provide a suggestive basis for thinking through what Jesus may have meant when he spoke of "giving his life as a ransom for many" (20:28) and of his "blood of the covenant poured out for many for the forgiveness of sins" (26:28; cf. 1:21, "save his people from their sins"), and for reflecting on the consequences of that blood-shedding for the future relationship between God and his people.

45 Matthew has not noted the time of Jesus' crucifixion, but his narrative makes coherent sense if we follow the statement of Mark 15:25 that it was at the third hour (9 A.M.),[10] which allows some three hours from day-

---

9. J. P. Meier, *Law,* 31; on pp. 31-35 Meier argues that in these verses Matthew portrays Jesus' death-resurrection as the eschatological turning point.

10. See p. 1063, n. 3, for the problem of reconciling this explicit timing with John 19:14.

break for the Roman trial and the preparations for crucifixion. Jesus' death soon after the ninth hour (3 P.M.)[11] then allows time for the arrangements to be made for burial before sunset and the beginning of the sabbath (see on 27:62 and 28:1). While none of the time indications need be taken as precise, Matthew clearly describes an unnatural darkness in the early afternoon, lasting for some three hours. He cannot be describing a solar eclipse, since the Passover festival was at full moon.[12] The phrase "over the whole land"[13] is in any case more likely to describe a local phenomenon, which in physical terms might be ascribed to a dust storm or to unusually heavy cloud cover, but which Matthew surely intends us to see as a visible expression of God's displeasure, as in Amos 8:9-10 (cf. Deut 28:29; Jer 15:9); cf. the thick darkness over "the whole land of Egypt" at the first Passover in Exod 10:22, which was also only in a limited area (Exod 10:23). This darkness is localized because it is in Jerusalem that the event is taking place; cf. the symbolism of cosmic phenomena, including the loss of the light of sun and moon, which Jesus has used in connection with the fate of Jerusalem in 24:29.[14]

46 The "loud voice," here and in v. 50, perhaps marks a difference between Jesus and other crucified men who, at least in the later stages of their crucifixion, gradually lost strength (and eventually consciousness). This is not just a cry of pain, but an anguished appeal to God which reveals for a moment something of the mental and spiritual torment of the "cup" Jesus had accepted in Gethsemane. The words are taken directly from the opening of Ps 22,[15] to which we have already seen allusions in vv. 35-36,

---

11. On the chronology I have argued in the comments on 26:17, this would place Jesus' death about the time the official slaughter of the Passover lambs began on Nisan 14 "between the two evenings" (Exod 12:6), which was interpreted, according to Josephus, *War* 6.423, as meaning from the ninth to the eleventh hours (cf. *m. Pesaḥ.* 5:1, 3). Matthew, however, does not draw attention to this aspect of the timing.

12. This point was made as early as the third century by Julius Africanus in response to an earlier work by one Thallus (otherwise unknown) who had attributed this darkness to an eclipse. See F. F. Bruce, *Jesus and Christian Origins,* 29-30.

13. For this translation rather than "over the whole earth" compare 24:30, and p. 925, n. 96; cf. also the phrase ὅλη ἡ γῆ in 9:26, 31, with a similarly localized sense. *Gos. Pet.* 5 (15) takes it as localized: "darkness came down on all of Judea."

14. D. C. Allison, *End,* 26-30, surveys many symbolic darknesses in ancient literature, particularly associated with the death of great men, but concludes that this tradition in the gospels is particularly influenced by the eschatological vision of Amos 8:9-10. See also D. J. Moo, *The OT,* 342-44. For the symbolism of darkness more generally see H. C. Hahn, *NIDNTT* 1:421-25.

15. The transliterated words as printed above are commonly understood to represent a version in which the address to God, ἠλὶ ἠλί, is in Hebrew while the remainder is in Aramaic, whereas in Mark the whole utterance is Aramaic — though the considerable textual variations (see p. 1072, n. 1) do not allow certainty on the text form in either gospel. But the

39, 43; the psalm expresses the spiritual desolation of a man who continues to trust and to appeal to God in spite of the fact that his ungodly opponents mock and persecute him with impunity. In the end, the psalm turns to joyful thanksgiving for deliverance in vv. 22-31, and some interpreters have suggested that it is the latter part of the psalm that Jesus has in mind as well as its traumatic beginning, so that this is in effect a shout of defiant trust in the God whom he fully expects to rescue him. But that is to read a lot between the lines, especially after Gethsemane where Jesus has accepted that he must drink the cup to the full: he did not expect to be rescued. The words Jesus chose to utter are those of unqualified desolation, and Matthew and Mark (who alone record this utterance)[16] give no hint that he did not mean exactly what he said.[17]

The expression "my God," while of course it is already provided by the psalm, nonetheless draws attention as a unique utterance by Jesus, who elsewhere in Matthew frequently refers to God as his Father but never as "my God," and who in prayer has used "Father" to address God (11:25, 26; 26:39, 42; cf. 6:9). It thus marks a change of mood from Gethsemane, where, even though the cross was in view, Jesus could still address and trust God as his "Father." Now that relationship appears to be broken, and Jesus feels himself "abandoned." This "God-forsakenness" rather than the physical suffering is, perhaps, what he had most dreaded in Gethsemane, so that he begged for the cup to be taken away. In giving his life as a ransom for many for the forgiveness of sins he must, for the moment, be separated from his Father. But it is surely also significant that Jesus, like the abandoned psalmist, still addresses

---

targum of Ps 22:1 has the form ἠλί ("an accepted Hebraism"; K. Stendahl, *School,* 84), so that it seems that the "Hebrew" form could also be used in Aramaic. If both forms were available in Aramaic, the form ἠλί would have an obvious advantage here, as it offers a more plausible basis for the following suggestion that Jesus is calling for Elijah (see below). Both λεμά and σαβαχθάνι approximate more closely to the Aramaic *lᵉmā'* and *šᵉbaqtanî* than to the Hebrew *lāmâ* and *ʿazabtānî*. It is likely, then, that Matthew, like Mark, understood Jesus to have used his vernacular Aramaic at this moment of supreme personal crisis. See further D. J. Moo, *The OT,* 264-68, who concludes that the words are Aramaic in both Mark and Matthew; also R. E. Brown, *Death,* 1051-53. The Greek translation that Matthew adds is literal rather than following the LXX.

16. *Gos. Pet.* 5 (19) has a derivative form, "My power, my power, you have left me" (or "have you left me?"). This looks like an attempt to avoid the christological problem of Jesus' separation from God. (The suggestion that it derives from an independent reading of *'ēlî* as *ḥêlî*, Hebrew for "my strength," is unlikely in that the *Gospel of Peter* is a Greek document which shows no obvious sign of Semitic knowledge.) The "power" referred to may be either Jesus' physical strength, now draining away, or his miraculous power (to escape the cross). See further R. E. Brown, *Death,* 1056-58.

17. See further D. J. Moo, *The OT,* 271-74; R. E. Brown, *Death,* 1047-51, on this and other attempts to evade the force of the cry.

God as *"my* God"; this shout expresses not a loss of faith, but a (temporary) loss of contact. Matthew does not give us any further guidance in discerning the theology of atonement which lies behind this terrible shout, still less in exploring the psychology of the Son of God in this unique moment of separation from his Father. Nor does he tell us how long this separation was felt, but we note with relief in Luke's account that when Jesus died he again addressed God as "Father" (Luke 23:46).[18]

47-49 If Jesus used the form *Ēli* in his shout from the cross (see p. 1075, n. 15), it might have been heard as the name of Elijah, *Ēlias* in Greek, and a Jewish listener might naturally construe this as a call for Elijah's help in view of the expectation of Elijah's eschatological return (see on 17:10).[19] There is some later Jewish evidence for the belief that Elijah would come from heaven to help God's people in danger.[20] But those standing by the cross were Gentile soldiers, and it is they who would have access to a suitable drink and be authorized to approach the cross; it is unlikely that they would allow any Jewish interference. Luke 23:36 says explicitly that it was soldiers who gave Jesus the "vinegar." Should we then assume that Gentile soldiers knew of this Jewish belief in Elijah, and, being unfamiliar with the Aramaic form of the divine name, took it as Elijah's? Or that Jewish bystanders somehow got the soldiers' permission to interfere? Matthew does not resolve this question for us.

At this moment of high drama the apparently inconsequential little scene about Elijah reads almost like light relief. But it is the setting for an aspect of the crucifixion story which features in all four gospels, the offer of "vinegar" to Jesus to drink. In Matthew, Mark, and John this immediately precedes Jesus' death, while Luke records it earlier as part of the mockery. In John it happens in response to Jesus' statement that he is thirsty, which is itself said to fulfill Scripture (perhaps Ps 22:15). The mention of "vinegar" in all four gospels, however, indicates that they were also thinking of Ps 69:21, already clearly alluded to by Matthew in v. 34. Matthew and Mark both mention two offers of drink, in the first case in Mark without allusion to Ps 69:21, but Matthew, by including "bile" in the previous offer and "vinegar" here, has spread the fulfillment of Ps 69:21 over both incidents. "Vinegar" sounds to us like an unpleasant thing to drink, and that is clearly its purpose in the

18. J. H. Neyrey, *Honor,* 152-61, presents a stimulating argument that this cry is a true prayer, which demonstrates Jesus' piety. The mockeries of vv. 39-44 evoke a sense of shame which Jesus expresses in the time-honored idiom of the psalms of lament, a "complaint-protest" that God has not upheld his honor. The events of vv. 51-54 then follow as God's response to this call for vindication.

19. See S. C. Layton, *ZAW* 108 (1996) 611-12, who argues that ἠλί was current as a shortened form of the name Ἠλίας, making it indistinguishable from "my God."

20. J. Jeremias, *TDNT* 2:930; Str-B 4/2:769-79.

psalm. But what might be available at the cross (cf. John 19:29) would be cheap wine for the soldiers to drink,²¹ and most commentators assume that that is what was offered. In that case it was, as it certainly seems to be in John, an act of kindness by one person (and as such was disapproved of by the rest), though Luke presents it as part of the soldiers' cruelty. Matthew and Mark do not say whether it was meant kindly or cruelly, though the echo of the psalm would suggest the latter. But see on v. 34 for the comparable issue that arises there. The need to use a sponge on a stick suggests that the cross on which Jesus was crucified was higher than some which barely lifted the feet above the ground.²²

50 The verb used here for "cry" is not the same as the "shout" of v. 46; it is used three times in the LXX of Ps 22 (vv. 2, 5, 24) for the sufferer's appeals to God, and its use here might be a further echo of that psalm. Matthew does not tell us the nature of this second loud cry. It is tempting to identify it as the triumphant "It is finished" which Jesus utters at this point in John 19:30, or with Luke's "Father, into your hands I entrust my spirit," and thus to find here the reversal of the sense of desolation in v. 46; the conviction of the watching soldiers that Jesus really was God's son (v. 54) would also follow more naturally from a noble or peaceful death than from one of despair. But Matthew does not tell us its content, and he links this cry with that of v. 46 by using the same phrase, "with a loud voice." The loudness of the cry at the time of death again indicates that Jesus is not just fading away, but dying while in full possession of his senses.

"He let go his spirit/breath" *(aphēken to pneuma)* is an unusual way to describe death.²³ The ambiguity of the Greek *pneuma,* "breath" or "spirit," leaves some uncertainty as to why Matthew chose this phrase. At least it means, like the verb *exepneusen* used by Mark and Luke, that he "stopped breathing" (so Hagner here), and perhaps that is all it means, but the unexpected phrase with its active verb may suggest a sense of Jesus voluntarily relinquishing his life (for the idea cf. John 10:17-18). Cf. John's phrase *paredōken to pneuma,* which perhaps means he handed his spirit over to God (and cf. Acts 7:59); this would agree with the last words of Jesus in Luke, "Father, into your hands I entrust my spirit," quoting Ps 31:6. "Spirit" here

21. BDAG 715a, define ὄξος as "sour wine, wine vinegar, it relieved thirst more effectively than water and, being cheaper than regular wine, it was a favorite beverage of the lower ranks of society and of those in moderate circumstances, esp. of soldiers." R. E. Brown, *Death,* 1059-66, refers to the ὄξος throughout as "vinegary wine."

22. For the height of crosses see J. Blinzler, *Trial,* 249-50; R. E. Brown, *Death,* 948-49.

23. There is a partial parallel in LXX Gen 35:18, the death of Rachel, but there the noun is ψυχή ("life/soul"), not πνεῦμα, and the phrase is immediately followed by the explanation, "for she was dying."

means "that which animates or gives life to the body";[24] there is no reason to see any reference to the Holy Spirit.[25]

51 The dramatic *kai idou,* "And look!" indicates that the extraordinary events which follow in vv. 51-53 were the immediate effect of Jesus' death. The earthquake, which will be followed by another in 28:2, is a well-known symbol of God's mighty intervention in the affairs of his world (e.g., Judg 5:4-5; Ps 114:4-7), especially in judgment (e.g., Jer 10:10; Joel 3:16; Nah 1:5-6),[26] and, following on the unnatural darkness of v. 45 (note that earthquake and darkness occur together in Amos 8:8-10), tells the reader that supernatural events of great significance are taking place. It also provides the context for the opening of the tombs which follows in v. 52, and perhaps explains how the temple curtain was torn — note that Matthew uses the same verb twice in v. 51 for the "tearing" of the curtain and the "splitting" of the rocks. But the tearing of the temple curtain does not belong to the conventional language of theophany, and is apparently a more specific symbol of what Jesus' death signifies or accomplishes.[27]

None of the Synoptic evangelists specify whether this is the great outer curtain which covered the entrance to the sanctuary as a whole,[28] or the inner curtain which separated the Holy of Holies from the sanctuary's outer chamber.[29] The former would be the only one whose destruction would be

24. So BDAG 832b, §2. See examples there of the Greek idea of the spirit leaving the body at death. D. P. Senior, *Passion,* 306, rightly links Matthew's phrase with the OT concept of "the breath (or spirit) of life" given to humans in creation (Gen 2:7) and returned to God at death (Ps 104:29; Eccl 12:7).

25. *Pace* Albright and Mann, 350-51, who find here Matthew's equivalent to the Lucan Pentecost, "the gift of the Spirit." S. Motyer, *NTS* 33 (1987) 155-57, finds a similar implication in Mark's verb ἐξέπνευσεν, which does not even offer the noun πνεῦμα as a clue. R. E. Brown, *Death,* 1080-83, interestingly is prepared to support this "pentecostal" interpretation for John's wording, but not for Matthew's.

26. For the symbolism of earthquakes in biblical literature see G. Bornkamm, *TDNT* 7:197-200.

27. There is no independent record of this damage to the curtain, though it has been thought to lie behind the rabbinic tradition that "during the last forty years before the destruction of the temple the doors of the sanctuary would open by themselves" (*b. Yoma* 39b). The fact that materials for repairing the temple curtain were among the spoils taken by the Romans in A.D. 70 (Josephus, *War* 6.390) is hardly relevant to an event forty years earlier.

28. Josephus, *War* 5.211-12, says this curtain in Herod's temple was fifty-five cubits high (about twenty-five meters, the height of a seven-story house); it hung in front of gold-plated wooden doors of the same height.

29. R. E. Brown, *Death,* 1109-13, usefully collects the data about curtains in the temple and surveys the discussion. He himself regards the debate as of no value, since he assumes that none of the evangelists would have known, or expected their readers to know, the details of temple structure and symbolism.

visible to anyone but the priests, and since Mark, and perhaps Matthew, may have intended their readers to think of a sign visible to observers,[30] this is more likely the one they meant. The inner curtain, however, would offer a more potent symbol of cultic exclusion.[31]

The fact that such a tall curtain is torn from the top rather than from below indicates that this is God's work. After the mockery of Jesus' enemies, this is the "divine riposte" which vindicates Jesus' honor especially over against the "wickedness of the temple personnel."[32] Interpreters suggest various more specific symbolic meanings,[33] including especially: (1) a sign that God no longer needs the temple and its rituals; (2) a sign of its coming destruction[34] as predicted by Jesus (and so a divine riposte to the mockery of Jesus' threat to the temple in v. 40); (3) a symbol of mourning (as in 2 Kgs 2:12) either for the death of Jesus or for the approaching end of the temple;[35] (4) a sign of the opening of the way into God's presence, hitherto closed by the cultic exclusion symbolized by the curtain (the symbolism developed by Hebrews);[36] (5) an apocalyptic sign of "divine revelation triggered by the death of Jesus."[37] These levels of symbolism are not mutually exclusive: 1, 2, and 3 naturally go together; 4 offers the positive counterpart to 2; and the revelation proposed in 5 is in fact of a new "accessibility to God not seen since the Garden of Eden," as in 4. Where the emphasis

30. This has been argued especially for Mark; see H. M. Jackson, *NTS* 33 (1987) 16-37, and the comments of R. E. Brown, *Death,* 1144-45. Note, however, that Brown, ibid., 939, does not believe that Matthew intended to say that the centurion and soldiers saw the tearing of the curtain, and see further the comments on v. 54 below.

31. The inner curtain is apparently the one envisaged in the development of this theme in Heb 6:19; 10:19-20 (Heb 9:3 calls it "the second curtain"). The Day of Atonement imagery developed by Hebrews makes it virtually certain that it is through this curtain, not the outer one, that the writer pictures Jesus going as the high priest did in the Day of Atonement ritual.

32. So J. H. Neyrey, *Honor,* 141-44.

33. T. J. Geddert, *Watchwords,* 140-45, lists thirty-five different suggestions! See M. de Jonge, *HTR* 79 (1986) 72-79, for a similar variety of exegesis in early patristic writers.

34. Cf. the reports of the temple doors opening by themselves shortly before the temple was destroyed in A.D. 70: Josephus, *War* 6.293-96; Tacitus, *Hist.* 5.13. For this and other reported portents of destruction see R. E. Brown, *Death,* 1113-18.

35. D. Daube, *Rabbinic Judaism,* 23-25.

36. Hagner, 2:849, emphasizes this aspect of the symbolism, concluding with the sweeping statement that "the death of Jesus establishes the priesthood of all believers."

37. This interpretation, based on a Jewish view that the temple curtain represented the heavenly firmament of Gen 1:6 (so that its tearing conveys the apocalyptic symbol of the opening of heaven), is developed by D. M. Gurtner in a dissertation (Ph.D., St. Andrews, 2005) summarized in *TynBul* 56 (2005) 147-50. Similarly T. E. Schmidt, *NovT* 34 (1992) 229-46. For the curtain as a cosmic symbol see especially the lyrical description of the embroidery of the Herodian curtain in Josephus, *War* 5.212-14.

is placed depends on the interpreter's more general understanding of Matthew's theology of the temple and its replacement. In the light of the understanding of the Mount of Olives discourse outlined above, the tearing of the curtain suggests that as Jesus dies the transfer of authority from the old temple-focused regime (which has been responsible for his death) to the shortly-to-be-vindicated Son of Man is already taking place. The result will be that access to God will no longer be through the old, discredited cultic system but through Jesus himself, and more specifically through his death as a ransom for many.

52-53 This resurrection of dead people has no parallel in the other gospel accounts, and leaves plenty of unanswered questions for the historically minded interpreter.[38] Matthew gives us no explanation of the delay between the opening of the tombs and the appearance of the dead people in Jerusalem[39] two days later, nor of what happened to them afterward. We can only speculate on what a cinecamera might have recorded, and on why the appearance of "many" dead worthies to "many" people left no other trace in historical sources. As with many of Jesus' scientifically unexplainable miracles, Matthew is not interested in satisfying our natural curiosity or answering empirical scepticism. He tells the story for its symbolic significance.[40]

The "holy people who had died" are presumably to be understood as pious Jews,[41] but we do not know whether Matthew is thinking of recent contemporaries or of well-known people from the OT period buried around Jerusalem.[42] Several OT texts talk of resurrection for God's people in some sense,

---

38. Most interpreters simply dismiss it as fiction. For more nuanced discussion see D. Wenham, *TynBul* 24 (1973) 42-46; N. T. Wright, *Resurrection*, 632-36. Wright concludes: "Some stories are so odd that they may just have happened. This may be one of them, but in historical terms there is no way of finding out." Hagner, 2:850-52, helpfully discusses the historical status of the report, concluding that it is "a piece of realized and historicized apocalyptic." Much more radical is the bold proposal of K. L. Waters, *JBL* 122 (2003) 489-515, that Matthew does not even intend the scene to be read as past history but, despite the "historical" form of the narrative, saw this as "an event of the apocalyptic future," set in the "new Jerusalem" at the end of time.

39. For the traditional designation of Jerusalem as "the holy city" see on 4:5. R. E. Brown, *Death*, 1131, notes and rightly dismisses the suggestion that the reference is not to Jerusalem but to heaven.

40. R. E. Brown, *Death*, 1126, comments laconically of this narrative, "Its forte is atmosphere, not details."

41. οἱ ἅγιοι, used as a noun, occurs only here in Matthew. Normally in the NT it refers to members of the Christian community, but that is inappropriate here, and the background to the phrase is perhaps to be found in the usage of Dan 7:18, 21-22, etc., where the "holy ones" are God's faithful people of Israel. The other significant use of the phrase in the LXX, to denote angels, is clearly not relevant here since these people had died.

42. Is Matthew here expressing in narrative form the theology of fulfillment

the most explicit being Dan 12:2 and, probably, Isa 26:19.[43] Matthew's wording here especially calls to mind Ezek 37:13, "when I open your graves and bring you up out of your graves, my people" (note also the earthquake-like imagery in Ezek 37:7), though there resurrection is a metaphor for national restoration rather than a promise of personal life after death.[44] Matthew explicitly links the resurrection of these unidentified people with that of Jesus, even though the earthquake which releases them occurs at the time of his death.[45] His word order allows us to understand either that they did not come out of the opened tombs until after Jesus' resurrection, or (rather less naturally) that they emerged immediately but remained outside the city until then (see p. 1073, n. 8). Either way there is some narrative awkwardness, but this makes it the more likely that we are meant to notice the sequence, "*after* Jesus' resurrection."[46] His resurrection is the first, theirs the consequence (cf. 1 Cor 15:20-23; 1 Thess 4:14). In order to make this point, however, Matthew might more appropriately have linked this occurrence with the second earthquake which will reveal Jesus' empty tomb in 28:2. That he nonetheless records it here, despite the difficulty of postponing their resurrection and/or appearance for two days after the earthquake, suggests that he sees Jesus' death, not just his resurrection, as the key to the new life which is now made available to God's people.

---

which is expressed in Heb 11:39-40, that the people of faith in Israel's history still awaited their "completion" when Jesus came to bring the history of salvation to its climax?

43. See above, p. 836, for the development of belief in life after death in the OT and later Judaism.

44. The linking of Ezek 37:1-14 in Jewish thought with the idea of an eschatological resurrection (apparently drawing also on Zech 14:4-5) is illustrated by a third-century wall painting in the synagogue of Dura Europos; it is described by R. E. Brown, *Death,* 1123. On the OT background, and especially the influence of Ezek 37, see D. P. Senior, *Passion,* 319-22: the resurrection is part of "an ensemble of traditional eschatological signs of the last day, the moment of the completion of God's salvific activity."

45. The suggestion of J. W. Wenham, *JTS* 32 (1981) 150-52, that a period be placed after "were opened," thus separating the earthquake and its effects from the raising of the saints, involves breaking up Matthew's breathless series of paratactic clauses with aorist passive verbs (on which see R. E. Brown, *Death,* 1118-19, 1129). Even if accepted, it still leaves the tombs being opened when Jesus died, not after his resurrection, so that the awkward time lag between the opening of the tombs and the appearance of the resurrected saints remains, unless one argues with Wenham that their resurrection was independent of the opening of the tombs.

46. D. C. Allison, *End,* 45-46, uses Matthew's awkward insertion of "after his resurrection" as evidence that he is modifying an existing tradition, not composing the scene himself. But see contra R. E. Brown, *Death,* 1139-40. Davies and Allison, 3:634, "(in a change of mind) suspect it [the phrase 'after his resurrection'] is an early gloss," though without MS or versional evidence.

Cf. John 5:25-29 for the idea of an eschatological resurrection of the dead to be judged by the Son of Man, when "those in the tombs will hear his voice and will come out, those who have done good to the resurrection of life." That eschatological event, says Jesus in John 5:25, "is coming and is now." Albright and Mann, 351, regard Matthew's scene as a "dramatization" of the Johannine saying.[47]

54 The soldiers whom Matthew has already described as "keeping watch" over Jesus on the cross (v. 36; the centurion in charge of the squad is here mentioned for the first time) can now be called on as witnesses to what it all means. Matthew's inclusion of the other soldiers with the centurion provides a witness by "two or three" which is therefore valid (see on 18:16). They have seen and heard all that has gone on since then, including the mockery of Jesus as one who had claimed to be God's son. The only event Matthew specifies here is the earthquake, which was presumably the primary reason for their terror — Matthew uses here the same strong expression as he used for the disciples, overwhelmed by the supernatural manifestation on the mountain (17:6). His further expression, "what had happened," might be taken to mean specifically the events linked with the earthquake, namely, the tearing of the curtain and the resurrection of the dead, but, historically speaking, soldiers at Golgotha could not see the tearing of the temple curtain[48] (as Matthew would presumably have known), and the resurrected dead will not be seen until after Jesus' resurrection. Matthew's phrase therefore more likely refers to the whole sequence of events at the cross, notably Jesus' loud shout and the manner of his death (note Mark's wording, "when the centurion . . . saw that he died in this way"). The earthquake explains their terror, but it was the whole scenario of Jesus' crucifixion and death which triggered their "confession of faith."[49]

---

47. A further eschatological element in the present scene has been proposed by D. C. Allison, *End*, 43-44 (cf. Davies and Allison, 3:628-29); he understands the splitting of the rocks as an echo of the splitting (same verb in LXX) of the Mount of Olives in Zech 14:4-5. But while Allison can show that some later Jewish interpretation took Zech 14:4-5 as speaking of future resurrection (see n. 44), this is not the most obvious interpretation of its wording, and the ἅγιοι who appear with Yahweh in 14:5 are normally understood to be angels, not resurrected humans. Nor is the Mount of Olives mentioned in the present passage. An alternative "source" for the symbolism (along with Ezek 37) is suggested by R. L. Troxel, *NTS* 48 (2002) 43-47, in the eschatological vision of *1 En.* 93:6, read in the light of the emptying of Sheol in *1 En.* 51:1-2; Troxel argues that this allusion more suitably provokes the declaration of Jesus as the "Son of God" in v. 54.

48. H. M. Jackson, *NTS* 33 (1987) 24-25, thinks that Mark supposed Golgotha to be on the Mount of Olives, from which the east side of the sanctuary, where the curtain hung, was visible. E. L. Martin, *Secrets,* even proposes that this was the historical site of Jesus' crucifixion.

49. Most interpreters take it for granted that Matthew intends his readers to read

The phrase "God's son"[50] would come more easily to a Gentile than to a Jew: in Greek and Roman religion gods often got involved in human affairs, and male gods had many children by human women. Divine or semidivine properties could be credited to prominent men, and the Roman emperors were officially entitled "son of God."[51] So to these soldiers[52] the phrase need mean no more than that Jesus was someone special — though even that, spoken about a condemned man who has just been shamefully executed, is remarkable enough. But as they stood on guard, they have heard Jewish people, and even their religious leaders, mocking Jesus for having claimed to be God's son (vv. 40, 43), and while they may have had little understanding of how momentous a claim this would be in a Jewish context, they have seen enough now to conclude that the truth is on the side of Jesus rather than on that of his mockers. This declaration thus represents a sharp volte-face: they recognize now that their own earlier mocking of the "king of the Jews" (vv. 27-31) was out of place.

Whatever the soldiers themselves meant by it, for Matthew's readers this declaration is a climactic theological moment. God has twice declared that Jesus is his son (3:17; 17:5); demons have recognized him as such (4:3, 6; 8:29); Jesus has said so himself (11:25-27; cf. 24:36), has frequently referred to God as his "Father," and has even on two occasions hinted publicly

---

this as a positive response to Jesus and thus a foreshadowing of Gentile Christianity. For an alternative view see D. C. Sim, *HeyJ* 34 (1993) 401-24; Sim sees it as a cry of defeat in the face of divine power, so that these soldiers "represent the wicked on the day of judgment" (Sim, *Gospel,* 226). Cf. a similar argument by J. Pobee in reference to the Mark parallel in E. Bammel (ed.), *Trial,* 91-102.

50. The Greek phrase, without articles, is sometimes taken to mean "*a* son of God" (or even "a son of a god") rather than "*the* Son of God." For arguments (both grammatical and contextual) against this proposal see R. E. Brown, *Death,* 1146-51; and cf. my *Mark,* 660, especially n. 75. Whatever the phrase may have meant to the soldiers, it is clear that for Matthew (as for Mark) it conveys nothing less than the full christological sense. Note that the wording of 14:33 is very similar (with the same lack of articles); there it is a christological affirmation by Jewish disciples.

51. *Divi filius,* usually with the name of their predecessor added: "son of the divine Augustus" and the like.

52. E. S. Johnson, *JSNT* 31 (1987) 12-13, gives interesting information on religious beliefs in the Roman army (though he focuses more on the Roman legions than on the auxiliary troops who would be in Jerusalem at this period). He questions whether a direct confrontation with the emperor cult is intended here; in *Bib* 81 (2000) 407-10 he takes this argument further, though in both cases his argument is focused on the wording of Mark rather than that of Matthew. By contrast T. H. Kim, *Bib* 79 (1998) 221-41, argues that Mark (and presumably Matthew?) intended his readers to find here a challenge to the emperor's official title, and R. L. Mowery, *Bib* 83 (2002) 100-10, points out that Matthew's actual phrase θεοῦ υἱός (without articles), used in the NT only here and in Matt 14:33; 27:43, corresponds closely to Roman imperial usage.

that he is God's "Son" (21:37-39; 22:42-45); the disciples have hailed him as "God's son" in a moment of crisis (14:33, a declaration very similar to this one), and Peter has included this title in his considered estimate of Jesus (16:16). But right up to the time of Jesus' trial no human observer outside the disciple group has used such language of Jesus, and at the Sanhedrin hearing it has formed part of the basis of his condemnation (26:63), subsequently providing the ammunition for Jewish mockery of this preposterous claim (27:40, 43). Now, however, people outside the community of faith have recognized and declared the truth, and so reversed that mockery, and the fact that they are not even Jews reinforces Matthew's message that the new *ekklēsia* is not to be restricted to the children of Abraham. Like the other centurion we met earlier in the gospel, this officer and his men have displayed faith beyond that of "anyone in Israel" (8:10), and so they, too, represent the many who will come from east and west to join the Jewish patriarchs in the kingdom of heaven (8:11-12).[53]

5. Women Who Witnessed Jesus' Death and Burial (27:55-56)

> 55 *Watching from a distance were many women who had followed Jesus from Galilee and looked after[1] him.* 56 *Among them were[2] Mary the Magdalene and Mary the mother of James and Joseph, and the mother of the sons of Zebedee.*

This brief paragraph forms a bridge between the accounts of the death of Jesus and his burial, in that the women were witnesses of both. "Mary the Magdalene and the other Mary" will reappear in v. 61 and in 28:1, so that they form an important line of continuity through the whole process from death to burial to resurrection. They are therefore the guarantee that when the tomb is found to be empty there has been no mistake: these same women saw him die and saw where he was buried; they would not have gone to the wrong tomb. It will also be they who are the first to meet the risen Jesus in 28:8-10. So this short notice, introducing the focal characters of this latter part of the story of Jesus, deserves to be treated on its own rather than either as an appendage to the account of Jesus' death or as the introduction to the burial.

---

53. Davies and Allison, 3:636, point out the close association of the title "Son of God" with the theme of the destruction of the temple, in three successive passages: 26:61-64; 27:40; 27:51-54.

1. For the various uses of διακονέω in Matthew see 4:11 ("take care of"), 8:15 ("wait on"), 20:28 ("serve"), 25:44 ("look after"). Here the sense of practical, domestic service seems most prominent.

2. The verb is singular, applying initially only to Mary the Magdalene, with the other two women added as secondary subjects. See p. 1088, n. 3.

This paragraph is also important in that it supplies information which we have not hitherto been given about the makeup of Jesus' entourage during the earlier part of the gospel. While a number of women have entered the story as the recipients of Jesus' ministry, and one unnamed woman has shown her appreciation by anointing him in 26:6-13, the reader of Matthew (and Mark) up to this point could have imagined (apart from a hint at 12:50; see comments there) that the twelve male disciples who accompanied Jesus around Galilee and on his journey to Jerusalem were the only people closely associated with him. But now we find that there have also been "many women." Luke 8:2-3 is the only account in the earlier Synoptic narratives of such a group, but now we find that they have been there all along.[3] And now that the male disciples have deserted Jesus (26:56), it is these women who have stayed to watch even when they are no longer able to help. In contrast with the soldiers who have direct access to the cross, the women must necessarily watch "from a distance"; the term here does not connote a lack of courage or identification (as in 26:58), merely the practical reality.

These women are not part of the Twelve, but they are described as having "followed" Jesus, a term which we have earlier seen to denote discipleship in the broader sense (see on 8:18-23).[4] And as disciples they have literally "followed" Jesus all the way south from Galilee to Jerusalem; they must have been part of the traveling group in chs. 16–20 and of the noisy crowd of supporters in 21:1-9, even though the only one of them whom Matthew has mentioned so far has been the mother of the sons of Zebedee (20:20). Now we find that she was not alone as a female fellow traveler. The description of these women as "looking after" him (and the Twelve?) suggests a sort of practical support group. Luke 8:3 uses the same verb of the women who were with Jesus in Galilee (again including Mary the Magdalene); Luke also adds that their practical support came out of their own possessions, and since at least one of them had influential connections (the wife of Herod's steward), they may have included some quite wealthy supporters. Clearly any impression we have gained from the story so far of an all-male movement needs serious modification.

The names given for the women at the cross and the tomb vary among the four gospels. The one constant feature is Mary the Magdalene, who is also mentioned in Luke 8:2-3. Christian tradition has woven increasingly col-

---

3. Strictly speaking, Matthew says only that they had followed Jesus "from Galilee," i.e., on the journey south, but there is no reason to suppose that he intends to correct Mark's statement that they had already been following and looking after Jesus "while he was in Galilee" (Mark 15:41).

4. It is regularly noted that for a Jewish teacher to have female followers was unconventional to the point of scandal. The point is emphasized especially by Keener, 689-90, who supplies many references for attitudes to women in ancient society.

orful legends around her, but all we know of her from the gospels is that Jesus had expelled seven demons from her (Luke 8:2), and that she came presumably from Magdala, on the northwest shore of the Lake of Galilee. "Mary the mother of James and Joseph" *could* be an oblique way of referring to Jesus' mother (see 13:55 for her sons' names),[5] but few interpreters believe that Matthew would deliberately obscure her relationship to Jesus in that way, or would refer to Jesus' mother simply as "the other Mary" in v. 61 and 28:1. Nor does the earlier mention of Jesus' mother in 12:46-50 suggest that she was among those who followed Jesus in Galilee. James and Joseph were common names, and there were two Jameses among the Twelve (10:2-3). Mark's phrase here, "the lesser James," is usually taken to refer to that second James in distinction from the "greater" son of Zebedee; his brother Joseph[6] is not mentioned elsewhere. Luke 24:10 refers simply to "Mary of James." "The mother of the sons of Zebedee" is familiar to us from 20:20, but she is not named by Matthew and will not be included in the further mentions of the women in v. 61 and 28:1; she is probably to be identified with the Salome mentioned here by Mark; Salome, like Mary, was a very common name at the time.[7]

6. The Burial of Jesus (27:57-61)

> 57 *As evening came on,*[1] *there came a rich man from Arimathea, called Joseph, who also himself had become a disciple of Jesus —* 58 *this man came to Pilate and asked him for the body of Jesus. Then Pilate gave orders for it to be given*[2] *to him.* 59 *Joseph took the body, wrapped it in a clean cloth,* 60 *and put it in his own new tomb which he had cut in the rock; then he rolled a great stone against the entrance*

---

5. So Gundry, 579.

6. Or, according to Mark, Joses: Ἰωσῆς is a more Greek form of the same Jewish name. Here and in 13:55 (par. Mark 6:3) and Mark 15:47 the MSS of both gospels include support for both forms of the name, but in Mark the evidence for the more Greek form of the name is stronger, whereas in Matthew the more clearly Hebrew form predominates.

7. T. Ilan, *JJS* 40 (1989) 186-200, has shown that roughly half of all Jewish women whose names are recorded in Palestine at this time were called Mary or Salome. See R. J. Bauckham, *NovT* 33 (1991) 245-75, for the development of Christian traditions about this Salome and a sister of Jesus of the same name. For further discussion of the women mentioned in the gospel passion narratives see R. J. Bauckham, *Jude*, 9-19.

1. For the flexible time-reference of this phrase ὀψίας γενομένης see p. 565, n. 1 and pp. 983-84. Here the context requires that it refer to a period before sunset, so that the body could be buried before the sabbath.

2. Matthew's verb often means "give *back*"; is the idea that in some sense Jesus' body *belonged* to Joseph as a disciple? So Gundry, 581; R. E. Brown, *Death,* 1226.

of the tomb, and went away. 61 *But Mary the Magdalene and the other Mary were*[3] *there, sitting opposite the burial place.*

The bodies of those who had died by crucifixion were often not given a proper burial, but left on the crosses to disintegrate or thrown on the ground to be disposed of by scavengers and natural decay. But Jewish piety objected to any body being left unburied (Deut 21:22-23), and so there was provision there for the burial of those executed (Josephus, *War* 4.317) in a common burial plot rather than in a family tomb.[4] To provide proper burial for someone otherwise unprovided for was a valued act of charity (Tob 1:16-18); cf. the provision for the burial of "strangers" in 27:7. But the provision of a new, rock-cut tomb for Jesus was quite exceptional, and indicates that Joseph was motivated by more than conventional piety.[5] It is, like the act of the woman who anointed Jesus in 26:6-13, a quite extravagant act of devotion.

Joseph is described throughout as acting alone. In his approach to Pilate, with the political risk involved, he may well have been alone, but he would need help for the practical process of taking down the body and preparing it for burial, and especially for the placing of the "great stone." The singular verbs describe what Joseph caused to be done rather than his own agency (note that even the quarrying of the tomb is described as what Joseph did, in the singular). John 19:39-42 mentions Nicodemus as his collaborator, but as a rich man Joseph no doubt also had workers to do the manual work.

57 Matthew has not yet mentioned the day of the week, but will do so obliquely in v. 62 and again in 28:1. The other gospels confirm that the crucifixion took place on a Friday (Mark 15:42; Luke 23:54; John 19:31, 42), so that the sabbath would begin at sunset. The considerable work involved in

---

3. As in v. 56, Matthew again uses a singular verb at the beginning of the sentence, but this time it is followed by a plural participle for "sitting." The sentence thus begins by focusing on Mary the Magdalene, but "the other Mary" is added to make up the plural subject of "sitting." Cf. 28:1, where again a singular verb describes the coming of Mary the Magdalene, but "the other Mary" is then added. Some have taken this repeated pattern of an initial singular verb to suggest that the tradition originally spoke only of Mary the Magdalene (as in John 20:1-18), but Matthew's careful designation of three women in v. 56 makes this improbable; it is more likely a stylistic trait, focusing on the best-known person first.

4. *M. Sanh.* 6:5. R. E. Brown, *Death*, 1207-11, surveys the evidence for Roman and Jewish practice in this regard; see also his article in *CBQ* 50 (1988) 234-38. See also the full and informative treatment, including a wide range of ancient references, by Keener, 691-94.

5. For the official view cf. Josephus, *Ant.* 4.202, where the Pentateuchal law on blasphemy (Lev 24:16) is expanded by the provision that the body of the one executed by stoning must be hung up during the day and then buried ἀτίμως καὶ ἀφανῶς, "without honor and in obscurity."

removing and burying the body (and the purchase of the cloth and other ne-
cessities for burial) would be against conventional sabbath practice,[6] and
John 19:31 also mentions Jewish objections to having the bodies on display
on the sabbath.[7] So Joseph's action would need to be completed by sunset
(see p. 1087, n. 1). If Jesus died soon after the ninth hour, that leaves nearly
three hours before the sabbath officially began — and indeed Joseph might
have made his approach to Pilate before Jesus was actually dead.

In vv. 55-56 we have been introduced to a group of hitherto unmentioned disciples of Jesus. Now we meet another, from a more surprising
background. Arimathea was a Judean town, probably some twenty miles
north-west of Jerusalem, but Joseph himself had apparently settled in Jerusalem, where he had prepared a new family tomb. Only Matthew mentions that
Joseph was "rich,"[8] perhaps to echo Isa 53:9 (Hebrew, not LXX), "they made
his grave . . . with a rich man."[9] As a wealthy man he was a prominent member of Jerusalem society; in fact, according to Mark 15:43 and Luke 23:50,
he was a member of the Sanhedrin. Matthew does not mention that last fact,
and so has no need to explain how a "disciple" could be a member of the
group who condemned Jesus (see Luke 23:51). He is accordingly more
explicit[10] in calling Joseph a "disciple" than is Mark ("expecting the kingdom of God") or John ("a disciple of Jesus, but secretly for fear of the
Jews"); his unusual use of the verb rather than the noun (literally, "who had
been discipled to Jesus"; cf. 28:19) reminds us of the "discipled scribe" in
13:52, one who has come into the Jesus movement from an unusual background. How did a prominent member of Jerusalem society come to be a disciple of the Galilean Jesus? It is possible that his "conversion" has taken
place in the course of the last week, but perhaps more likely that this is another indication of the artificiality of the Synoptic narrative outline, which
brings Jesus to Jerusalem only in his final week; on the Johannine historical

6. All this would also be forbidden on the Passover (Nisan 15), whatever day of
the week it fell (*m. Beṣah* 5:2; *m. Meg.* 1:5). Here is another incidental confirmation of the
chronology I argued for at 26:17, whereby the crucifixion took place on Nisan 14, when it
was an ordinary Friday, not yet the Passover. On the more commonly supposed "Synoptic
chronology" Joseph's actions, even though completed before sabbath began, would have
violated the sanctity of the Passover festival.

7. Indeed, bodies were not allowed to be left exposed on any day after sunset
(Deut 21:23).

8. The new family tomb in a prime location, sealed with "a great stone," underlines his affluence.

9. See D. J. Moo, *The OT,* 144-45.

10. *Pace* R. E. Brown, *Death,* 1223-25, who argues that Joseph was not yet a disciple either in Mark's view or in reality, and that Matthew here unhistorically "anticipates
his post Easter career as a Christian." Similarly Davies and Allison, 3:649.

scheme Joseph could have been recruited on a previous visit to the south. At any rate, here is a rich man who has apparently surmounted the obstacle which his possessions place in the way of entry to the kingdom of heaven (19:22-26).

58 Matthew mentions neither the audacity involved in such an approach nor Pilate's surprise at the speed of Jesus' death (both points are included in Mark 15:43-45). It may have been an unusual request,[11] and if Pilate really believed Jesus to be an insurrectionist, it would presumably be dangerous to be publicly associated with him. But Matthew has made it clear that Pilate did not regard Jesus as guilty, and so does not mention the problem. Any objection to Joseph's initiative was more likely to come from his Sanhedrin colleagues, but it is not they who must give permission to bury the body (though they will soon hear of it; see vv. 62-64). Matthew's concern at this point is not with the "politics" of the situation but with the fact and the manner of Jesus' burial.

59-60 To take down the body from the cross would probably require several people;[12] if Joseph used his workers to do it (see introductory comments), this would not necessitate his personally touching the body and so contracting defilement for seven days (Num 19:11) just before the sabbath and the Passover festival. The burial, even if done hurriedly, is properly and respectfully carried out. Perhaps because he has already mentioned the anointing of Jesus "for burial" in 26:6-13, Matthew says nothing about the use of oils or spices either before the burial (John 19:39-40) or after (Mark 16:1; Luke 23:56–24:1). The "clean cloth" sounds more like a single shroud[13] than the closely wound bandages probably envisaged in John 19:40; 20:6 (cf. John 11:44), but the term is not very specific.[14]

There are many rock-cut tombs of the period in and around Jerusalem.[15] Many are large family vaults with spaces for a considerable number of

---

11. See the introductory comments above. *Gos. Pet.* 2 (3) explains it by making Joseph a "friend of Pilate" (as well as of Jesus), who had already made arrangements for the body before the crucifixion took place. In the *Gospel of Peter* the whole scene has been significantly expanded and altered in ways which reflect later anti-Jewish polemic and the beginning of the developing Joseph legend rather than the historical situation (see R. E. Brown, *Death,* 1232-34).

12. R. E. Brown, *Death,* 1252, suggests, however, that Matthew understood the body to have been taken down by the soldiers and then given to Joseph.

13. Hence the appeal of the so-called "Turin shroud," once claimed to be Jesus' burial cloth but now demonstrated to be of medieval origin.

14. The same term is used for the loose garment worn by the young man in Mark 14:51-52. For discussion of the nature of the σινδών, "cloth," see R. E. Brown, *Death,* 1244-45.

15. Tombs were made outside the city, but as the city expanded, many were later incorporated within it.

bodies,[16] and Joseph, as a rich man, is likely to have had such a tomb quarried out for his own family.[17] That he should be prepared to use it for Jesus is a mark of considerable loyalty, especially when it was "new," which both Luke and John explain as meaning that no one had yet been buried there. The point is significant for apologetics, in that it makes it more difficult to explain the women's discovery as due to mistaken identity: there was only one body in the tomb. A large stone was the normal way of sealing a tomb against robbers or animals; the door stones which survive are usually shaped so as to roll against the low entrance[18] and are large and heavy enough to require several men to move them. The apparently unnecessary comment that Joseph "went away" when he had done what was necessary both provides a contrast with the women who remained at the site and prepares for the sending of the guard to seal the tomb in v. 66.

61   The aorist verb which described Joseph's departure in v. 60 contrasts with the imperfect which now describes the women as still there, watching;[19] it might be paraphrased, "but the women stayed on there after he had gone." See on vv. 55-56 for the identities of Mary the Magdalene and "the other Mary," and for their role as witnesses providing continuity through the story of Jesus' death, burial, and resurrection. Presumably they left before the guard was posted the next morning; they will return in 28:1 once the sabbath is over.

7. The Guard at the Tomb (27:62-66)

62 The next day, that is, the day after the Preparation,[1] the chief priests and the Pharisees made a joint approach to Pilate. 63 "Sir," they said, "we remember that while that impostor was still alive he

16. The so-called Sanhedrin Tombs in the northern part of Jerusalem give the present-day visitor a good impression of what Joseph's tomb may have been like. The larger of them contain several chambers (each with spaces for a number of bodies), sometimes on two levels; the largest I have been in had spaces for more than sixty bodies. For details of tombs see J. Wilkinson, *Jerusalem,* 155-59; more fully J. Finegan, *Archeology,* 181-202; M. Avi-Yonah (ed.), *Encyclopedia,* 2:627-41.

17. Cf. Isa 22:16 for such a tomb as a status symbol.

18. Good examples can be seen at the so-called Tombs of the Kings north of the Old City (the burial place of Queen Helena of Adiabene) and at the Herodian tomb behind the King David Hotel. Later Jewish tombs substituted huge hinged doors of rock, as in the Sanhedrin Tombs and in the rabbinic cemetery at Bet She'arim.

19. Carter, 539, drawing on his article in *ExpT* 107 (1996) 201-5, argues that they were watching because they, unlike the male disciples, were expecting Jesus' resurrection.

1. ἡ παρασκευή, "the Preparation," in Greek-speaking Judaism designated what we call Friday, the sixth day of the week, the day of preparation for the sabbath; cf. Mark 15:42, where it is also described as προσάββατον, and John 19:31, 42; also Josephus, *Ant.* 16.163. See BDAG 771a. See the comments below for Matthew's surprising use of the term here.

said, 'After three days I will be² raised.' 64 *So give an order that the burial place be made secure until the third day, so that his disciples cannot come and steal him and then say to the people, 'He has been raised from the dead'; that last fraud would be worse than the first."* 65 *Pilate replied, "You have³ a guard; off you go and make it as secure as you can."* 66 *They went away and made the burial place secure by putting a seal on the stone and placing the guard.*⁴

The sealing of the tomb and the placing of an armed guard, mentioned only by Matthew,⁵ add to the dramatic triumph of Jesus' resurrection despite every human precaution. This pericope, with its corresponding scene of reporting back in 28:11-15, also provides Matthew with a suitable final scene depicting the discomfiture of Jesus' opponents in Jerusalem. They held all the cards of earthly power, including access to the Roman governor, but despite all their efforts they could not contain the Son of God. They will be last seen arranging a lying cover-up story, but by then Jerusalem will have become irrelevant to Matthew's story, and the risen Jesus will be back in Galilee, commissioning his restored followers to begin a triumphant mission to all nations which will last to the end of time.

It is likely that Matthew included this story to counter rumors, still current in his day (28:15), that Jesus had not risen from the dead but that his body had been stolen by the disciples.⁶ This charge is spelled out both in the

---

2. The Greek verb is in the present tense, but the sense is clearly future.

3. The verb could be either indicative or imperative, and some versions take it as imperative, "Have a guard," meaning "Take a guard," though ἔχω more naturally means "have" than "take." See the comments below.

4. Literally, "sealing the stone with the guard"; "sealing" is to be understood literally of some sort of physical security attached to the stone, so that two actions are combined in this one phrase.

5. The story of the guard is more fully developed by the *Gospel of Peter* (see p. 1095, n. 18). W. J. C. Weren, in R. Bieringer et al. (eds.), *Resurrection,* 156-62, argues that the *Gospel of Peter* version, which is more integrally woven into the resurrection narrative, is not simply an imaginative expansion from Matthew, but represents an independent development from a common tradition. In that case "Matthew's story is not a *creatio ex nihilo.* The evangelist went back to an old tradition" (162).

6. The prevalence of grave robbing is illustrated by an imperial decree now in Paris, said to have come from Nazareth and dated perhaps in the reign of Claudius (A.D. 41-54), which prohibits on pain of death any disturbance of tombs including removing bodies from them "with malicious intent." For the text and discussion see F. F. Bruce, *NT History,* 284-86; more fully B. M. Metzger, in E. E. Ellis and E. Grässer (eds.), *Jesus und Paulus,* 221-38. Its association with Nazareth prompts the speculation that the decree was issued in response to garbled reports of "Nazarenes" who had allegedly removed a body from a tomb and were now causing trouble, but the provenance and background of the in-

initial request of the Jewish authorities (vv. 63-64) and in their cover-up story after the event (28:13-15). Justin, *Dial.* 108, tells us that this charge was still being actively propagated in the middle of the second century;[7] it was an obvious countermove to Christian claims of Jesus' resurrection. It is hardly likely that Christians would have invented such a convenient weapon for their critics if the story were not already in circulation.[8]

62 "The Preparation" means what we call Friday, so the day following it is of course the sabbath (as 28:1 will also confirm). Why then does Matthew use the cumbersome phrase "the day after the Preparation" when he could have said simply "the sabbath"? This would seem the more appropriate in that this pericope will depict the highest authorities of Judaism as acting or causing others to act in a way incompatible with their sabbath regulations (unlike Joseph, who has been careful to complete the burial before sunset). Matthew surprisingly does not draw attention to that embarrassing fact by mentioning the sabbath by name. He may have used this more oblique phrase because, on the chronological scheme I am following (see on 26:17), this was not an ordinary sabbath but also the day of the Passover meal, Nisan 15. In this year, therefore, the Friday was the day of preparation not only for the sabbath but also for the chief day of the festival, so that the phrase "the Preparation" does double duty.

The Pharisees have not been mentioned during the account of Jesus' trial and death (though the "scribes" mentioned in 26:57; 27:41 represent the same ideological grouping, as ch. 23 has shown), but they reappear here (as in 3:7 and 16:1) in "coalition" with the largely Sadducean chief priests.[9] It is in the interest of all the different factions of the Sanhedrin to prevent any spread of the Galilean heresy.

63-64 Jesus and his followers represent a dangerous deviation from Jewish orthodoxy. The terms "impostor" and "fraud"[10] were to become im-

---

scription are uncertain. The inscription does show, however, that the allegation of body stealing would have sounded plausible.

7. Justin's comments clearly reflect knowledge of this material in Matthew, notably his use of the term πλάνος, "impostor," for Jesus and πλανάω for the disciples' report of the resurrection (cf. the repeated language of vv. 63, 64), but his account of this report as a deliberate propaganda campaign by "picked men sent into all the world" seems to derive from more recent experience.

8. For this apologetic background, and for other factors suggesting the historical basis of Matthew's story of the guard, see N. T. Wright, *Resurrection,* 636-40. Cf. also W. L. Craig, *NTS* 30 (1984) 273-81.

9. For the historical context of Matthew's combination (here and in 21:45) of chief priests and Pharisees see U. C. Von Wahlde, *NTS* 42 (1996) 506-22, especially pp. 518-20.

10. These are cognate terms in Greek, and come from the same route as "deceive" in 24:4, 5, 11, 24; also "wander" in 18:12-13 and "wide of the mark" in 22:29.

portant in later Jewish polemic against Jesus as one who "led Israel astray."[11] Here the "deceit" is not only in Jesus' allegedly deviant teaching and false messianic claims,[12] but also in the possibility of a faked "resurrection." What made the authorities think of this? The only reference to "three days" at Jesus' trial has been in reference to his alleged designs on the temple (26:61; cf. 27:40), and Jesus' predictions of his resurrection "on the third day" have been spoken only in private to his disciples (16:21; 17:23; 20:19). Matthew may suppose that Judas had briefed the authorities on this claim, or perhaps that some version of Jesus' more public statement (to scribes and Pharisees) about the sign of Jonah, with its "three days and three nights in the heart of the earth" (12:40), had found its way down from Galilee.[13] But the form of the phrase here is closer to (though not identical with) those in 26:61 and 27:40; see the comments on 26:61, where we considered the possibility that Jesus had used similar words about the future temple and his own resurrection, though, if so, Matthew (unlike John 2:19-22) has not told us of this.

The authorities' fears focus (explicitly at least) not on the possibility that Jesus might actually rise from death, but on the opportunity for his disciples to cash in on such language to stage a fake resurrection (an explanation which they will continue to uphold even after the event, 28:13-15). A Messiah allegedly returned to life after being officially executed for blasphemy will, they rightly perceive, be far more dangerous to their religious authority than Jesus had been while alive.

65-66 True to form, Pilate is not willing to accommodate their request — if the translation given above is correct. The Jewish leaders want Pilate to deploy his own troops,[14] but he prefers to leave the responsibility to them; "you have a guard" refers to the Jewish temple guards (see on 26:47).[15] It is their problem; let them take care of it with their own resources.[16] The

---

11. See G. N. Stanton, *Gospel,* 237-43; also ibid., 171-80; M. Hengel, *Leader,* 41, n. 14; N. T. Wright, *Victory,* 439-42.

12. "His life is summed up as 'deception'"; G. N. Stanton, *Gospel,* 179.

13. So Gundry, 583; Davies and Allison, 3:654; U. Luz, *Theology,* 115; G. N. Stanton, *Gospel,* 82. More fully C. H. Giblin, *NTS* 21 (1974/5) 414-19. The phrase "after three days," used only here in Matthew, more closely echoes 12:40 than the other sayings which use "the third day" or "in three days."

14. The Sanhedrin would not need Pilate's permission to deploy their own guards in the normal way (as they had in 26:47). But now that a Roman execution was involved, they needed an official Roman guard, and, besides, they were looking for maximum security.

15. Matthew's use of the Latin loanword κουστωδία, which is not used elsewhere in the NT, does not necessarily indicate that the troops were Roman.

16. ὑπάγετε, "off you go," sounds more like dismissal than compliance, as in several of Matthew's uses of the imperative of ὑπάγω elsewhere; cf. 4:10; 5:24; 16:23; 19:21; 20:14.

less natural alternative translation, "Take a guard" (see p. 1092, n. 3),[17] would probably indicate that Pilate made a detachment of his own soldiers available,[18] and the fear of punishment by the governor (v. 14) has led some to assume that this was so (but see comments there and on 28:11). But the fact that the guard will subsequently report back not to Pilate but to the priests (28:11), and that the governor's hearing of their failure is mentioned only as a possibility (28:14), makes it more probable that it was the temple guards that were used.[19] The sealing of the tomb[20] is an additional precaution along with the presence of a guard who were supposed to maintain constant watch.

E. THE EMPTY TOMB AND THE RISEN JESUS (28:1-10)

1 *At the end of the sabbath,*[1] *as it was becoming light on the first day of the week, Mary the Magdalene and the other Mary came*[2] *to look at the burial place.* 2 *And suddenly*[3] *there was a great earthquake, for an angel of the Lord came down from heaven and, coming to the tomb, rolled away the stone and sat on top of it.* 3 *His appear-*

17. Some interpreters suggest that the indicative might be understood as granting rather than refusing the request: "You have [i.e., I now grant you] the guard you asked for." This is, however, hardly the natural reading of the sentence.

18. *Gos. Pet.* 8 (28-33) takes the guard to be Roman, and even names the centurion in charge as (probably) Petronius. Further elaborations to the Matthean story follow in the *Gospel of Peter:* the stone is set in place not by Joseph but by "elders and scribes" together with the Roman soldiers, and is sealed with seven seals, while the soldiers set up a tent for themselves.

19. That, together with the more natural reading of Pilate's words (and the fact that noncooperation would be more in character), is why I have changed my mind since my earlier commentary, *Matthew,* 404-5, even though the majority of recent commentators suppose the troops to be Roman. See further below on 28:11-15, where several features of the story are found to make better sense on this understanding.

20. *Sphragizō* denotes some sort of physical closure, probably with an authenticating wax seal, to ensure that any attempt to open the tomb would be detectable. Cf. the sealing of the lions' den in Dan 6:17. N. T. Wright, *Resurrection,* 640, thinks this is deliberately echoed in Matthew's story. Cf. M. D. Goulder, *Midrash,* 447-48; Goulder suggests that the story of the guard also echoes Josh 10:18, where stones are placed over the mouth of a cave and a guard is set.

1. ὀψὲ σαββάτων should mean literally something like "late on the sabbath," but the following phrase apparently fixes the time as dawn rather than sunset. See the comments below.

2. As in 27:56, 61, the verb is singular. See p. 1088, n. 3.

3. Here and in v. 9 this is another attempt to capture the dramatic force of καὶ ἰδού, "and behold."

ance was like lightning, and his clothing white as snow. 4 The guards[4] were shaken with fear of him and became like corpses. 5 But the angel spoke to[5] the women and said, "You[6] need not be afraid, for I know that you are looking for Jesus, who was crucified. 6 He is not here; he has been raised, as he said. Come here and see the place where he[7] was laid. 7 Then go quickly and tell his disciples, 'He has been raised from the dead, and look, he is going ahead of[8] you into Galilee; that is where you will see him.' That is my message to you."[9]

8 The women quickly left[10] the tomb, with fear and great joy,[11] and ran to report to his disciples. 9 Suddenly[12] Jesus met them and said, "Hello!" But they came up to him and took hold of his feet and bowed before[13] him. 10 Then Jesus said to them, "Don't be afraid. Off

4. οἱ τηροῦντες, "those who were keeping watch," is not as specific as Matthew's other terms for the guard (κουστωδία, στρατιῶται), but following vv. 62-66 they are the obvious referent, especially as the women, the only other witnesses mentioned, are specifically differentiated from them in v. 5.

5. Another example of Matthew's use of ἀποκριθείς, "answering," to indicate speech which responds to the situation rather than to a preceding verbal communication (cf. 17:4, in a similarly numinous situation). The angel is responding to the unspoken fear of the women.

6. The emphatic inclusion of the pronoun sets the women in contrast to the terrified guards.

7. Most MSS and versions have the explicit subject "the Lord." But the absence of ὁ κύριος from several of the earliest witnesses suggests that this was an early explanatory addition. This would be the only use in Matthew of ὁ κύριος as a narrative title for Jesus (see on 21:3), but would come naturally to a church in which that (Lucan) idiom had later become established.

8. For this sense rather than "lead" see p. 996, n. 3.

9. Literally, "Behold, I have told you." Some interpreters take this as still part of the message the women are to give to the disciples, but the first-person singular verb reads awkwardly on that understanding as the preceding words have made no mention of the angel.

10. The alternative reading "came out from" in many MSS probably derives from memory of Mark's account, which, unlike Matthew, mentions the women both entering and leaving the tomb (and running away from it in fear).

11. The phrase "with fear and great joy" can be construed either with "left the tomb" or with "ran to report." The sense is not significantly affected. The single preposition prevents us from separating the "fear" (at the tomb) from the "great joy" (of their report to the disciples).

12. For "suddenly" see n. 3 above. Many MSS begin the sentence with "But as they were going to report to his disciples," a clarification (basically repeating the previous verse) which leads very uncomfortably into the καὶ ἰδού that follows; the καί would not naturally follow a subordinate clause, and this suggests that the opening clause is a secondary addition.

13. See the comments below on how far προσκυνέω here should be understood in its religious sense, "worship."

you go and tell my brothers to go away to Galilee; that is where they will see me."

The accounts of the finding of the empty tomb in all four gospels display an intriguing mixture of agreement and independence.[14] Negatively, all agree in refraining from giving any account of Jesus actually leaving the tomb (contrast *Gos. Pet.* 9–10 [34-42]), and simply report how the women found it already empty. Positively, all agree on an early morning visit to the tomb by one or more women (one of whom is Mary the Magdalene), on the tomb being empty, and on an encounter with an angel or angels,[15] but each develops the narrative around these elements in different ways. Matthew's account, as usual, follows a similar pattern to Mark's, including the important instruction to the disciples to go to Galilee, but adds four distinctive features: the earthquake, the angel rolling away the stone, the effect on the guards, and the women's meeting with Jesus himself on their way from the tomb. The first three of these are peculiar to Matthew; the last may be compared with the account of Mary the Magdalene meeting Jesus outside the tomb in John 20:14-17.[16] Matthew's account of the empty tomb is thus, like his account of the death of Jesus, more dramatic than Mark's, and supplies the surprisingly missing element in Mark 16:1-8, an actual encounter with the risen Jesus.[17]

The action of the angel in removing the stone from the entrance to the tomb draws attention even more clearly than in the other gospels to the fact

14. D. Wenham, *TynBul* 24 (1973) 21-54, gives a full study of the distinctive features of Matthew's account, and discusses the issues of historicity which it raises. The historicity of the gospel resurrection narratives as a whole is doughtily defended by W. L. Craig, *Assessing,* 163-305.

15. Luke's "two men in dazzling clothes" are later identified as angels in Luke 24:23; Mark's "young man in a white robe" is not said to be an angel, but most commentators agree that this was what Mark meant by mentioning the white robe.

16. A common tradition underlying these accounts in Matthew and John may be indicated by the fact that both speak of touching Jesus and both include a message to "my brothers."

17. This is not the place to discuss the famous conundrum of Mark's anticlimactic ending. For my views, and for an overview of the discussion, see my *Mark,* 670-74, and for the textual evidence concerning the additions after Mark 16:8, ibid., 685-88. I think it most likely that Mark 16:8, though the conclusion of our extant text, was not the intended ending of the gospel, and that Mark also intended to speak of one or more encounters with the risen Jesus, and in particular one in Galilee, though it is impossible to know whether that additional material was lost or never written. It is, however, at least arguable that Matthew's additional material in 28:16-20 (and perhaps also 28:9-10) corresponds to an original final section of Mark, clearly anticipated in Mark 14:28; 16:7, but now lost. Similarly Gundry, 590-91; N. T. Wright, *Resurrection,* 617-24.

that Jesus has already left the tomb, while the stone was still in place.[18] This is not an account of the resurrection of Jesus (as some editors still unaccountably describe it in their section headings), but a demonstration that Jesus *has* risen. We are not told at what point between the burial on Friday evening and the opening of the tomb on Sunday morning Jesus actually left the tomb, though the repeated "third day/three days" language (and even more the "three days and three nights" of 12:40) presupposes that he was in the tomb for most of that period. What matters to the narrators is not when or how he left, but the simple fact that now, early on Sunday morning, "he is not here" (v. 6).

All the gospels stress the significance of the women[19] as the first witnesses of the empty tomb. This is hardly likely to be a fictional invention, in a society where women were not generally regarded as credible witnesses,[20] especially as the singling out of the women for this honor detracts from the prestige of the male disciples. We have seen how 27:55-56 and 27:61 have prepared the ground for the women's role as guarantors of the reality of the resurrection. It is now through them that the male disciples are to hear the news and to receive the instructions of their risen Lord. But in Matthew (and in John with regard to Mary the Magdalene alone) their privilege is even more pronounced, in that it is they who are chosen to be the first to meet with the risen Jesus himself. The male disciples must wait until they get to Galilee (and even then some will "doubt," v. 17), but he reveals himself to the women even in Jerusalem. It is Luke rather than Matthew who is generally regarded as placing special emphasis on the contribution of women to the origins of Christianity, but here Matthew gives them a place of honor which not even Luke can envisage (Luke 24:22-24).[21]

1 As in 27:62, Matthew's note of time is awkwardly expressed. The two expressions, which literally mean something like "late on the sabbath"[22]

---

18. The suggestion that the angel in Matthew rolls away the stone in order to allow Jesus to leave the tomb (Gundry, 587; Schweizer, 524) must assume that Jesus left invisibly. In view of the accounts in John 20:19, 26 of the risen Jesus not being limited by physical obstacles (cf. his sudden appearance and disappearance in Luke 24:31, 36), this seems an unnecessary subtlety, especially as Jesus will be plainly visible in v. 9.

19. John mentions only Mary the Magdalene, but her use of a plural verb in John 20:2 hints at the presence of one or more others.

20. For evidence of this see Davies and Allison, 3:662, n. 5; Keener, 698-99, especially n. 282.

21. Cf. Luke 24:34, which names Peter as the first to see the risen Lord; so also 1 Cor 15:5.

22. For the suggestion that ὀψὲ σαββάτων could mean "*after* the sabbath" see BDAG 746b; BDF 164(4); E. Lohse, *TDNT* 7:20, n. 158. Some commentators opt for that convenient rendering here on the basis of what Matthew *must* have meant rather than be-

and "as it was dawning into the first day of the week," seem to point in opposite directions, the first to the sabbath evening around sunset, the second to the following sunrise. They would be more coherent if the "day" were understood to begin at sunrise rather than, as on normal Jewish reckoning, at sunset, but such a use would be unique in Matthew. It seems most likely, however, that, oddly as he has expressed it, Matthew refers, as the other three evangelists clearly do in different ways (Mark 16:2; Luke 24:1; John 20:1), to early on Sunday morning, as it was getting light.[23] The purpose of the women's visit, "to look at the burial place," sounds rather colorless,[24] but Matthew has chosen not to mention their intention to anoint Jesus' body (Mark 16:1; Luke 23:56–24:1), perhaps because the anointing has already been done in advance (26:12; see comments on 27:59-60) but also because access to the tomb, already barred by the stone, has in his account also been precluded by the sealing and the guard.

2-4   The earthquake, like that of 27:51, adds to the drama of the scene, and to the sense of divine intervention (see on 27:51). But whereas in 27:51 it was apparently the earthquake that opened the tombs, here the removal of the stone from Jesus' tomb is attributed not to the earthquake but to the direct action of an angel. Indeed, Matthew's connective "for" suggests that the quake is itself the result, or at least the context, of the angel's coming, so that emphasis falls on the angel rather than the earthquake. The same phrase "an angel of the Lord" is used here as in 1:20, 24; 2:13, 19, and here,

---

cause it is the natural sense of ὀψέ, which with its cognates is used elsewhere in the NT of lateness, not to refer to something now over. There is no parallel to the proposed sense in early Christian or Jewish literature (J. M. Winger, *NTS* 40 [1994] 285).

23. So, e.g., M. D. Goulder, *NTS* 24 (1977/8) 237-38. Contra Schweizer, 523, who believes that Matthew has deliberately "transferred the women's visit to the evening of the sabbath." Gundry, 585-86, argues more fully for this reading, pointing out that Matthew's verb ἐπιφώσκω, which would normally speak of the coming of daylight, apparently refers in Luke 23:54 to the beginning of the sabbath in the evening. See also J. M. Winger, *NTS* 40 (1994) 285-88; D. Boyarin, *JTS* 52 (2001) 678-88, who explain Matthew's phrase as a wooden translation of a Semitic idiom. But see the response of Davies and Allison, 3:663-64.

24. The suggestion of T. R. W. Longstaff, *NTS* 27 (1981) 277-82, that they were following a Jewish custom of visiting graves "until the third day" to ensure that no one had been inadvertently buried alive hardly fits Matthew's account of the sealed tomb and the large stone: how could they expect to tell? In any case, they had seen Jesus die and be buried. W. Carter, *ExpT* 107 (1996) 201-5, argues that they came because they were expecting his resurrection, and wanted to see it happen; but "to look at *the burial place*" seems an odd way to express this. The verb θεωρέω, which Matthew uses only here and in 27:55 of the same women watching Jesus' death, simply denotes observation. Carter's argument from Matthew's use of "seeing" language to speak of "insightful comprehension of and commitment to God's purposes" is based on his use of verbs *other than* θεωρέω.

as there, the angel is not identified as either *"the* angel of the Lord" or a particular named angel such as Gabriel (see p. 52, n. 43). In chs. 1 and 2, the only other place where an angel plays a narrative role in Matthew (though plural "angels" appear in 4:11), the angel is seen or heard in dreams. Here, however, the angel is presented as robustly physical, rolling a huge stone, sitting on it, and visible not just to the women but also to the guards. The visual description in v. 3 recalls that of other supernatural beings as seen by humans, for example, in Dan 10:5-6 (and cf. the description of God in Dan 7:9); Rev 1:13-16; *1 En.* 62:15-16; 71:1; 87:2; see further above on 17:2.[25] A being of such awesome power and authority is not to be obstructed either by the size and weight of the stone or by the official seal, still less by a detachment of terrified guards. The repetition of the verb "were shaken" which described the earthquake of 27:51 (and its cognate noun is used in v. 2) vividly depicts their terror; for the simile "like corpses" to depict human reaction to a supernatural appearance cf. Dan 10:8-9; Rev 1:17; *4 Ezra* 10:30. Note the irony that those assigned to guard the corpse themselves become "corpses," while the one they guarded is already alive. The attempt at human security has been neutralized, and the guards play no further part in the scene until they have to report back in vv. 11-15.[26]

5-6 The angel ignores the guards, and speaks directly to the women, for whose sake he has apparently come, so that they can see inside the already empty tomb and carry the message to Jesus' disciples. They, unlike the guards, have no need to be afraid. We have not been told of their reaction, but presumably they, too, were in awe of the supernatural visitor ("fear" will be mentioned again in v. 8); but the angel reassures them as Jesus had reassured the disciples at the equally numinous experience of the Transfiguration (17:7) and will himself reassure the women in v. 10. The poignant description of Jesus as "the one who has been crucified" leaves no room for doubt of the real death of the one who is now alive again. But the absence of his body from the place where it had been (as the women knew, 27:61) shows that his resurrection is no less real and physical than his death. It is explained simply by the fulfillment of Jesus' repeated predictions that he would "be raised," using the same verb as in 16:21; 17:9, 23; 20:19; 26:32 (cf. also 27:63, 64). Note that it is as-

---

25. Davies and Allison, 3:660-61, set out in tabular form the parallels between this angelophany and others in Dan 10, Matt 1, *Apoc. Abr.* 10, and *2 En.* 1, and conclude that this is "a stereotyped narrative."

26. Contrast *Gos. Pet.* 9-11 (35-45), where the story of the resurrection is told mainly from the point of view of the guard (who in the *Gospel of Peter* include Jewish elders as well as soldiers), while "a crowd from Jerusalem and the country round about" also witness the events. The account of the discovery of the empty tomb by the women then follows as a separate element in the story; their role as witnesses is thus played down, and they are given no message for the disciples.

sumed that the women, no less than the male disciples, have been privy to Jesus' predictions about his own destiny; for their membership in the "disciple" group on the journey to Jerusalem see on 27:55-56. However little they may have understood what he meant at the time[27] (see on 16:21), now that the event has given substance to his words, they have them in their memory as a frame of reference for understanding this unprecedented occurrence.

7 The women are not only themselves the witnesses of the empty tomb, but also the chosen messengers to convey the amazing news to Jesus' male disciples.[28] Note the assumption that, despite their "scattering" (26:31) in Gethsemane, the disciples will still be found together as a group. The same verb for "being raised" is now supplemented with the phrase "from the dead"[29] to indicate that this is not just a metaphor. Jesus is no longer a corpse; he does not belong among "the dead." The women are to remind the disciples of Jesus' bold promise in 26:32, the words of which are here closely echoed: "he is going ahead of you into Galilee." But now the corollary of his "going ahead" is spelled out: when they get to Galilee, they will see him — not just an empty tomb but a living Jesus. But, unlike the women (v. 9), the male disciples must wait until Galilee before they can see him.

The angel's final words to the women (see p. 1069, n. 9), literally "Look, I have told you," are reminiscent of the frequent OT formula, "The LORD has spoken" (Isa 1:2; 25:8; Joel 3:8 etc.) or "I, the LORD, have spoken" (Num 14:35; Ezek 5:15, 17, etc.). The formula marks an authoritative pronouncement (perhaps even that the angel speaks for God),[30] and functions now as a call to action. The message has been delivered, and now it is up to the women to act on it.

8 The combination of fear (in the face of supernatural reality) and joy (at the message of Jesus' triumph over death) is typical of the resurrection stories. The contrast with Mark's enigmatic final verse[31] is striking. In each case the women run away from the tomb in fear, but whereas in Mark the fear is unrelieved and the message remains undelivered, in Matthew there is also

---

27. According to W. Carter (see above, p. 1099, n. 24), they have understood him very well, and are not surprised by what they are now witnessing. If so, the angel appears to be unaware of their prior expectation (vv. 5-6).

28. In view of the prominence of Peter in Matthew's gospel, it is surprising that he does not here include a specific message to Peter, as in Mark 16:7, thus underlining the rehabilitation of Peter after his spectacular failure in 26:69-75. But the specification that it was "eleven" disciples who met Jesus in Galilee (v. 16) will make it clear that Peter, unlike Judas, is again part of the group, though there, too, he will not be singled out by name.

29. Literally, "from the corpses"; the phrase has been used similarly in 14:2; 17:9, and 27:64.

30. So E. L. Bode, *Easter,* 53-54.

31. If it was the final verse, see above, p. 1097, n. 17.

"great joy," and the women run to pass on the angel's message to the disciples. Perhaps, as I suggested in n. 17, Mark's original plan (or his lost original text) was to counterbalance the fear and silence with joy and an obedient report. At any rate, Matthew has realized that the matter cannot be left where it is at Mark 16:8. Even without the further instruction from Jesus in v. 10, the women are already on their way to deliver their message.

9 The first of Matthew's two accounts of appearances of the risen Jesus (the other will be in vv. 16-20) is surprisingly low-key, though another dramatic *kai idou* prepares us for something remarkable. To say simply that "Jesus met them," when the last we saw of him was as a corpse sealed in a tomb, is a masterly understatement, and his greeting, *Chairete,* "Hello," is almost banal in its everyday familiarity.[32] Jesus is with his friends again. The women's response, of course, is less matter-of-fact. To take hold of the feet is a recognized act of supplication and homage (Mark 5:22; 7:25; Luke 17:16). Such an act requires a low posture, and it is possible that *proskyneō,* which we have seen elsewhere to denote homage or obeisance to someone of superior social status or authority (see p. 59, n. 3 and p. 303, n. 6; for obvious examples of this social usage see 18:26; 20:20), means only that they bowed down in order to touch Jesus' feet. But the element of "worship" which is also strongly built into the usage of this verb in Matthew (see especially 4:9, 10; 14:33) is surely also prominent here, as it will be in the meeting of the male disciples with the risen Jesus in 28:17. You do not simply offer conventional politeness to someone just raised from the dead. There is an interesting contrast between the women's taking hold of Jesus' feet, apparently without being repulsed, and his instruction to Mary not to touch him (or to let go of him?) in John 20:17. The Johannine prohibition is explained by speaking of Jesus' future ascension to heaven, but that is not a theme which Matthew will take up. The women's touch, like the invitation to touch him and the eating of food in Luke 24:39-43, demonstrates to the reader the physical reality of Jesus' risen body: he is not a ghost.

10 Jesus' words largely repeat the reassurance and the message given to the women by the angel in vv. 5-7. The result of this repetition is that the importance of the coming meeting in Galilee is further underlined, so that the reader is well prepared for the climactic scene of the gospel in vv. 16-20. But, in addition to the fact that this time the message comes directly from Jesus himself, rather than through an intermediary, there is one significant new

---

32. Cf. 26:49; in 27:29 it is the context rather than the word which gives it a more formal tone. BDAG 1075a suggest here simply, "Good morning"! It is true that the root meaning of χαίρω is to be happy, and that the cognate χαρά, "joy," has appeared in v. 8, but in view of the regular use of χαίρε(τε) as a conventional greeting, it is unlikely that the root meaning is intended here. In any case, the women are already very happy (v. 8).

element, the description of the male disciples as "my brothers" (as in John 20:17). The concept itself is not new; cf. 12:46-50; 25:40.[33] This time, however, it follows the abject failure of the Twelve to stand with Jesus when the pressure was on, a failure which was hardly less shameful because Jesus had predicted it in 26:31. But now it is time for the second half of that prediction to be fulfilled (26:32), and that Galilean meeting will eventually restore the family relationship which they must surely have thought had come to an end in Gethsemane.

F. LAST GLIMPSE OF JERUSALEM:
THE PRIESTS COVER UP (28:11-15)

11 *As the women were going away,*[1] *some of the guard went into the city and reported to the chief priests all that had happened.* 12 *The chief priests got together with the elders and formed a plan:*[2] *they gave a good sum of money*[3] *to the soldiers* 13 *and said, "Say, 'His disciples came in the night and stole him while we were asleep.'* 14 *And if this comes to the governor's ears, we will make it alright with him, so that you will not need to worry."*[4] 15 *So they took the money and did as they had been taught. And this story has been spread around among people in Judea*[5] *to this very day.*

This little pericope rounds off the story of the guard which Matthew introduced in 27:62-66.[6] Having been no more than passive spectators when the

33. In view of this already established usage it seems unnecessary to explain the phrase "my brothers" as an allusion to Ps 22:22, even though that psalm has been echoed several times in the preceding chapter.

1. Matthew has yet another ἰδού, "behold," after this clause, to draw attention to a new turn in the story which the reader is invited to envisage alongside and in contrast with the triumphant mission and report of the women. To insert "look!" in English would be more intrusive than Matthew's ἰδού, which I have therefore here left untranslated.

2. This is the same phrase, συμβούλιον λαμβάνω, which I have translated "consult together" in 12:14; 22:15; 27:1, 7; here, where their getting together has already been mentioned, the focus is apparently on the plan formed rather than the process. See above, p. 1034, n. 1.

3. ἀργύρια ἱκανά means "enough money" (to persuade them?), but Matthew's phrase probably reflects the idiomatic use of ἱκανός for a substantial quantity, as in Mark 10:46; Luke 7:12; 8:32; 23:8, etc.

4. Literally, "We will persuade him and will make you unworried."

5. See the comments below on this unique editorial use of Ἰουδαῖοι by Matthew.

6. *Gos. Pet.* 11 (43-49) has a corresponding account, but in detail it is quite different. The report is made directly to Pilate, and the Jewish elders, who were part of the guard

angel appeared and the tomb was opened (vv. 2-4), they must now account for the failure of their watch. The very thing they were posted there to prevent (27:64) has happened. The cover-up story which the priests and elders concoct as a result then enables Matthew to explain the current charge of grave robbing which we noted (in the introductory comments to 27:62-66) as the likely reason for Matthew including the guard in his account at all. It was because this story was still current in Jewish circles, as a countermeasure to Christian preaching of Jesus' resurrection, that it was important for Christians to set the record straight. But at the same time the fact that the priests must resort to this lie underlines that the tomb really was empty; even the priests cannot deny that fact.

But the overall structure of Matthew's narrative gives a further significance to this short cameo. It is in Jerusalem that Jesus has been rejected and killed, as he had predicted, but with his resurrection that part of his story is now over. It will be far to the north in Galilee that the final phase of the story will begin in v. 16. But before the scene transfers to Galilee, we are given a last glimpse of the discredited Jerusalem regime, as the guards report back in "the city." The chief priests and elders who have seemed to hold all the cards and who have so smugly celebrated their triumph over the northern prophet (27:41-43) are now in total disarray. Their careful plans to get rid of the new Galilean movement have unraveled, and they are left with an embarrassing failure to explain. The best thing they can do is to concoct a cover-up story, backed by bribes to the guards and, if necessary, also to the governor. So the last view we have of Jerusalem is of its leaders engaged in a sordid face-saving exercise, while the women are summoning Jesus' disciples to meet their risen Lord back in the home territory of Galilee. Jerusalem, which has throughout the gospel been a symbol of opposition to God's purpose and of judgment to come, can be left to wallow in its own discomfiture, while the reader turns with relief to Galilee, the place where once again light is dawning (4:14-16).

11 The opening clause invites the reader to compare two groups hurrying away from the tomb with a message to deliver (the same verb for bringing news, *apangellō,* is used in vv. 8, 10, and 11): the women have a message of hope and victory for the disciples, the guards one of confusion and failure for the priests. That the guards report back not to the governor but to the priests strongly suggests that they were Jewish temple guards, not a Roman platoon (see above on 27:65-66). It is only a possibility that the governor will get to hear of what has happened (v. 14), whereas if they had been troops responsible to him, there was no way this could be avoided, and indeed they

---

in the *Gospel of Peter* (see above, p. 1095, n. 18), are present and beg Pilate (who again asserts his innocence and their guilt) to order the soldiers to keep quiet, which he accordingly does. Nothing is said about a cover-up story of either Jewish or Roman origin.

would have been obliged to report to him themselves. The willingness of the guards to take orders from the priests about what they are to say, and to accept their money as a bribe, also suggests Jewish rather than Roman soldiers.

12-13 The cover-up story is devised by the chief priests together with the elders, who have been mentioned frequently in Matthew as the natural allies of the priests in planning the elimination of Jesus (26:3, 47; 27:1, 12, 20); they have been mentioned as "plotting together" (see p. 1103, n. 2) in 26:4; 27:1, 7. The two groups together represented the power structure focused on the temple to which Jesus had been so obvious a threat, so that it is in their interests to collaborate in a damage-limitation exercise now that their plan has backfired. The story invented is what they had already envisaged, and tried to prevent, in 27:64. Now that something much worse has happened, it is better to pretend that their plan to thwart Jesus' disciples had failed than to admit the reality of the resurrection they knew his disciples would now claim as fact.[7] But, quite apart from the implausibility of the guards being able to know what happened while they were asleep, for soldiers to admit to sleeping on duty would be at least a serious loss of face, and would normally have been a basis for disciplinary proceedings against them. In this case, however, it was their own employers who required them to make the admission, knowing it to be untrue, so that an adequate bribe would suffice to offset the damage to their reputation as guards.[8] This is the second time the priests and elders together have been prepared to pay money to protect their interests (cf. 26:15).

14 But the guard had been set up with the governor's knowledge, if not his direct approval, so that if he heard about it he might be expected to treat such failure, even by Jewish guards, as a matter for discipline. Since they were not Pilate's troops, the priests hope that it may be possible for him to be kept in the dark, but they know their man well enough to be confident that, if necessary, he can be kept happy with a further bribe.[9] If these had been his own soldiers, it is not likely that he could have been bribed to ignore

---

7. *Gos. Pet.* 11 (48) polemically attributes to them the calculation that "it is better for us to incur the greatest sin before God than to fall into the hands of the people of the Jews and be stoned."

8. It is often asserted that sleeping on duty would have been a capital offense, but the evidence cited (e.g., Keener, 714, nn. 333, 334) relates to Roman and other non-Jewish soldiers (in Acts 12:19 the guards are those of King Agrippa I, who ruled under Roman auspices). The only evidence Keener cites relating to Jewish temple guards is from the Mishnah: a temple guard found asleep was beaten and had his cloak burned (it does not say that the guard himself was "set aflame," *pace* Keener) but was apparently not executed (*m. Mid.* 1:2); if this was the situation in the first century, it would be less risky for Jewish guards than for Romans to spread this story against themselves, given sufficient incentive.

9. See Philo, *Legat.* 302, for Pilate's known venality; cf. Acts 24:26 for an equally greedy successor.

a capital offense (see p. 1105, n. 8), but a failure by local troops not directly under his command need not concern him overmuch.

15 Note the ironical use of the verb *didaskō,* "teach" — the guards' story has been put into their mouths; what the priests and elders "teach" is only a self-serving lie (contrast the "teaching" of Jesus and his disciples, v. 20). The fact that the story is spread among Jewish people is further indication that it was Jewish temple guards who were spreading it, not Roman soldiers. Matthew has used *Ioudaioi* only in the phrase "king of the *Ioudaioi*" (2:2; 27:11, 29, 37), where in each case it is spoken or written by non-Jews. See above on 27:11 for the question whether it means Jewish people in general or more specifically Judeans. I have suggested there and in 2:2 that non-Jewish speakers are less likely to have been aware of the significance of regional differences. But here the term is used editorially, by an author who has shown throughout that the distinction between Galilee and Judea is not only very familiar to him but also a matter of some importance. In this context, where the falsehood being spread in Jerusalem contrasts with the proclamation of truth which is about to be launched in Galilee in vv. 16-20, it is likely that Matthew uses the term in its stricter geographical sense: this was a southern propaganda campaign, based in Jerusalem.[10] For Justin's assertion that this story was still in circulation in the second century see above, p. 1093.

VI. GALILEE:
THE MESSIANIC MISSION IS LAUNCHED (28:16-20)

16 *The eleven disciples went to Galilee, into the hills*[1] *where Jesus had told them to go.*[2] 17 *And when they saw him, they worshiped him;*

---

10. There is nothing to connect this single editorial usage (as commentators have persistently done) with the pervasive use of οἱ Ἰουδαῖοι in the Fourth Gospel as a term for the opponents of Jesus. Note that Matthew here uses Ἰουδαῖοι without the article ("among Judean people"), whereas in John it always has the article to denote a specific group (though one whose identity remains controversial); its one anarthrous use in John is in 4:9, where, like here, it carries a broader ethnic sense. This is insecure ground on which to base the conclusion that "Matthew's church is distinct from Judaism" (so R. E. Menninger, *Israel,* 34-35). A. J. Saldarini, *Community,* 35-37, interestingly compares this Matthean use with Josephus's occasional use of "Jews" to describe those members of his own people to whom he was opposed.

1. For this sense rather than a specific "mountain" see on 5:1-2.

2. "To go" is added for the sake of English idiom; literally, just "where Jesus had arranged for them" or "instructed them." See the comments below for the nature of the rendezvous.

but some were hesitant. 18 Jesus came to them and spoke to them: "All authority in heaven and on earth has been given to me. 19 So go and make disciples of all the nations, baptizing them into the name of the Father and of the Son and of the Holy Spirit, 20 teaching them to keep all that I have commanded you; and look, I am with you all the time until the end of the age."[3]

In the geographical scheme which we have seen to be central to Matthew's planning of his book (see above, pp. 2-5) this final short paragraph plays a crucial role, which justifies its being set apart as a final main section of the narrative structure. The movement from north to south which has formed the underlying plot of the gospel since 4:12 is now suddenly reversed, so that the story is concluded where it began, in the hills of Galilee. The geographical shift has been well signaled in advance (26:32; 28:7, 10), and brings the narrative to the satisfying conclusion which is so conspicuously absent from Mark's otherwise comparable narrative structure.[4] The extended period of confrontation and rejection in Jerusalem, which ended in the apparent triumph of the opposition, is now relegated to the past. Jesus the Galilean has triumphed against all the odds, and back in his home territory (and that of his disciples) where the mission was originally launched, the good news of the kingdom of heaven is sent out in a proclamation which will continue until the "end of the age." There is about this Galilean ending something of the triumphant and hope-filled *akōlytōs,* "without hindrance," with which Luke concluded his account of Christian origins (Acts 28:31).[5]

But it is not only the geographical setting that enables Matthew's final paragraph to give his story such a sense of completeness. In these few words many of the most central themes of the gospel reach their resolution and culmination. The preparation of the Twelve as Jesus' task force, which had apparently ended in irreversible disaster in 26:56, is now resumed as they (or rather eleven of them) are restored to their position of trust and responsibility

3. Many MSS and versions add "Amen" here.

4. See p. 1095, n. 17, for the possibility that Mark, too, originally had, or planned, a similar ending.

5. Matthew makes no attempt to explain how this Galilean scene relates to the first phases of the church's corporate life and witness *in Jerusalem,* as we know of them from Acts. We can only assume that after this commissioning in Galilee the disciples returned to Jerusalem, hostile territory though it was, so that it was from there rather than from Galilee that the mission to all the nations was actually launched. But to have made reference to any such subsequent geographical movement would have detracted from the symbolic significance of Galilee in Matthew's gospel scheme, and would have destroyed the satisfyingly rounded tale of a movement which, despite all that the Jerusalem establishment could do to thwart it, is now boldly and definitively relaunched in its place of origin.

and given the final instructions for fulfilling the mission for which they were originally called in 10:1-15. Jesus himself, risen from the dead, is now revealed in all his glory as the vindicated and enthroned Son of Man, a status which he has hitherto spoken of only as a future expectation, but which has now become a reality. The proclamation of good news with which the narrative began (3:2; 4:17), but which has been in abeyance during the last few chapters as Jesus has been locked in conflict with his enemies in Jerusalem, can now be resumed. But now its scope is far wider: it is no longer a mission simply to the "lost sheep of Israel" (10:6; 15:24) but to all the nations, as Jesus had already predicted in 24:14 (cf. 26:13). The almost imperceptible mustard seed is now about to grow into a mighty tree; the kingdom of heaven is to be established over all the earth. The baptism which John had originally instituted as a symbol of a new beginning for repentant Israel (3:1-12) is now to be extended to people from all nations. And at the heart of this new community of faith is the risen Jesus himself, as he had said he would be (18:20): they are to be *his* disciples, obeying *his* commandments, and sustained by *his* unending presence among them. This new international community will be *his ekklēsia* (16:18) because it is *he* who now holds all authority in heaven and on earth (an authority greater than that which he was initially offered by Satan and refused, 4:8-10); see below on v. 18 for the culmination of the theme of kingship. And, perhaps most remarkably of all, the human Jesus of the hills of Galilee is now to be understood not as the preacher and promoter of faith, but as himself its object. The unprecedented formula for the baptism of new disciples links the Son with the Father and the Holy Spirit in a single "name." Throughout the gospel there have been hints, and more than hints, that Jesus is more than just a human preacher, or even a Messiah. He is related to God as Son to Father, and in different ways Matthew has allowed us to see him acting with divine authority; in his coming, God has come to visit his people.[6] Now the inclusion of the title "the Son" (cf. 11:27; 24:36; 26:63-64) in the "name" of the God to whom disciples owe allegiance brings this paradoxical trajectory to its most explicit point. It is thus entirely appropriate that the last words of Jesus in this gospel, "I am with you all the time until the end of the age" echo the title with which he was first introduced in 1:23, "Immanuel — God with us."[7]

I hope this brief attempt to survey some of the threads which are woven together into Matthew's concluding paragraph gives some idea of why so many interpreters have spoken of these last five verses as the key to under-

6. For this theme in Matthew see my *Matthew: Evangelist,* 308-11.
7. For other parallels with the opening two chapters of the gospel not only here but throughout 27:51–28:20, see D. D. Kupp, *Emmanuel,* 101. Most of his suggested parallels are less impressive than the clear link between 1:23 and 28:20.

standing Matthew's whole gospel.[8] Theologically one may read back from this final scene to illuminate the significance of much that has been said and done in earlier chapters. But from a literary and aesthetic point of view it is far more satisfying to read the story as Matthew has presented it to us, to follow the unfolding revelation of the Son of God and to share with the crowds and with his disciples the growing awareness that something of much greater significance is taking place than they had at first imagined, and so to arrive at last at this final pericope in which all the strands have come together, and the triumph of the Son of Man who is also the Son of God can at last be openly and fearlessly proclaimed.[9] Note the word "all" repeated four times in vv. 18-20; here all the partial glimpses of Jesus' universal authority are brought together in a final comprehensive declaration. For the reader who has carefully followed the journey this far the only appropriate response is to join the eleven disciples in worship and obedience to the Lord of heaven and earth, to play one's own part in the proclamation of the good news of the kingdom of God to all the nations, and to revel in the assurance that despite the worst that a hostile world can offer, "I am with you all the time until the end of the age."

Jesus' final words in this gospel are often referred to as "the Great Commission," and scholars have pointed out how closely this scene resembles, in its overall sense and content if not in detail, the commissioning narratives which occur throughout the OT where God's often reluctant and inadequate servants are sent out to fulfill his purpose with the assurance of his empowering and his presence to go with them; such stories are told notably of Abraham, Moses, Joshua, Gideon, Samuel, Isaiah, and Jeremiah.[10] Such stories mark the begin-

---

8. For some representative expressions of this view see O. Michel in G. N. Stanton (ed.), *Interpretation,* 39-51; A. Vögtle, *SE* 2 (1964) 266-94; W. Trilling, *Israel,* 21-51; G. Bornkamm in J. M. Robinson (ed.), *The Future of Our Religious Past,* 203-29; J. P. Meier, *JBL* 96 (1977) 407-24; O. S. Brooks, *JSNT* 10 (1981) 2-18; T. L. Donaldson, *Jesus,* 170-90; D. R. Bauer, *Structure,* 115-27.

9. This seems to me a more suitable way of describing the literary function of this final pericope than the suggestion (perhaps tongue-in-cheek?) of G. N. Stanton, *Gospel* 230, that it is "in a sense an anticlimax since so many of its themes have been anticipated earlier"!

10. This background to Matt 28:16-20 has been explored especially by B. J. Hubbard, *Commissioning,* who draws attention to twenty-seven such commissioning stories in the OT (not all of which are as clearly relevant as those listed above). D. C. Allison, *Moses,* 263-65 (the argument is also summarized in Davies and Allison, 3:679-80), drawing on Hubbard's thesis, argues that the most relevant background to the present pericope is Moses' commissioning of Joshua to be his successor, and so concludes that the theme of Jesus as the new Moses is dominant here. Against this it should be noted that such commissioning scenes (including that of Josh 1:1-9, which takes place after Moses is dead) speak of *God,* not any human intermediary, as the commissioner, and it is the presence of God, not of Moses or any other human guide, that is promised to those commissioned.

ning, not the end, of that person's service, and that is how it is here for the disciples. I have always enjoyed the fact that the ceremony which marks the end of seminary training, and which we in Britain call "Graduation," is in America often known as "Commencement." For the disciples, and for Matthew's readers, this conclusion is in fact a beginning, a commencement.

16 For "the eleven disciples" at this period between the last supper and the election of Matthias cf. Luke 24:9, 33; Acts 1:26. The Twelve, minus Judas, have apparently remained together despite their earlier "scattering" (26:31, 56). They have remained in Jerusalem long enough to receive the women's message (vv. 7, 10), but then have set off back home to Galilee (as they would in any case have done after the festival). But as a result of the women's message, this is not the dejected return of a defeated group but an expectant journey to fulfill a rendezvous. The phrase "where Jesus had told them [to go]"[11] is sometimes taken to mean that he had prearranged a specific place, but 26:32; 28:7, 10 have spoken only in general terms of "Galilee," and the place is described now only by the broad term "into the hills."[12] They are returning to the general scene of their earlier Galilean activity, perhaps to a favorite and familiar place, but probably more likely waiting for the risen Jesus to take the initiative and meet with them, as he had with the women, once they are in the area indicated. There is no more reason here than in 5:1; 14:23, and 15:29 to suppose that *eis to oros* denotes a specific mountain. If that had been Matthew's intention, the following clause would have been better expressed by a relative pronoun ("the mountain which . . .") rather than by the adverb "where."

17 Even though they have come here to meet the risen Jesus, the meeting, when it happens, brings a divided reaction from the disciples. While *proskyneō* here may well include its less specifically religious sense of bowing before a person (see above on v. 9), there is little doubt that here Matthew intends the full sense of "worship," implying that Jesus is now recognized as more than human — cf. the same verb used of the disciples with the exclamation "You are the Son of God" in 14:33. The disciples have had several days to get used to the idea of Jesus' resurrection and are expecting to meet him, so that their reaction should not be one of bewilderment: they know what they are seeing. It is therefore the more surprising to read that "some were hesitant." The

11. Davies and Allison, 3:681, suggest that τάσσομαι here might refer not to Jesus' instructions for this postresurrection rendezvous but to his earlier Galilean teaching (in particular, the Sermon on the Mount); this would, however, be a unique and misleading way to refer to Jesus' teaching (τάσσομαι means to make arrangements or give instructions); if that were the sense, we would rather have expected διδάσκω, and probably also some indication that the reference is to the more distant past.

12. The same nonspecific phrase was used for the scene of Jesus' teaching, prayer, and healing in 5:1; 14:23; 15:29. See above on 5:1-2; see also p. 134, n. 30, and my *Matthew: Evangelist,* 313, n. 82.

suggestion that these are people outside the group of the Twelve[13] is improbable in the context. Matthew has very specifically limited the number of people present to eleven, and has mentioned no additional group whose reaction may be contrasted with that of the eleven. Moreover, if the conjunction *hoi de,* "but some," were intended to denote a separate group, it would naturally be preceded by *hoi men;* coming as it does after a clause describing the reaction of the eleven as a group but without *men,* it is best understood as introducing a countercurrent within that group, affecting some but not all of them.[14]

So what sort of "hesitation" was this?[15] The verb *distazō* occurs only once elsewhere in the NT,[16] where it describes Peter's loss of confidence in the face of the elements in 14:31; interestingly, there, too, the "hesitation" is linked with "worship" (14:33). It denotes not intellectual doubt so much as practical uncertainty, being in two minds.[17] In this context it could indicate that some were not sure whether it was Jesus they were seeing[18] (cf. the rec-

13. So M. D. Goulder, *Midrash,* 343-44 (see above, p. 381, n. 8). N. B. Stonehouse, *Witness,* 168-82, argued that this incident should be identified with the appearance to over five hundred mentioned by Paul in 1 Cor 15:6. Carson, 593-94, also favors the view that others beside the eleven are meant.

14. Cf. 26:67, where οἱ δέ probably marks out among the mocking members of the Sanhedrin a group of them who actually hit Jesus; see BDF 250 for these two uses of οἱ δέ as indicating that "what was said first did not apply to all." For fuller discussion of Matthew's use of οἱ δέ see K. Grayston, *JSNT* 21 (1984) 105-6, though Grayston concludes (contrary to natural Greek idiom) that here it denotes *all* the eleven, "they worshipped, though they doubted." K. L. McKay, *JSNT* 24 (1985) 71-72, shows in response to Grayston that οἱ δέ requires a distinction of subject from the preceding clause; see further P. W. Van der Horst, *JSNT* 27 (1986) 27-30. Hagner, 2:884, supports Grayston on the grounds of "Matthean usage," but his list of eighteen uses of οἱ δέ in Matthew in fact undermines his argument, since in all of them except 26:67 (see above) the phrase designates a group *other than* the subject of the preceding clause, which is how οἱ δέ normally functions. There is no case where it is used for a second reference to the *same* subject, nor is it easy to see how the phrase could be used to mean that. The proposal of C. H. Giblin, *CBQ* 37 (1975) 68-75, to put a period after προσεκύνησαν, thus making οἱ δὲ ἐδίστασαν (which he takes to refer to all the eleven) the beginning of a new sentence explaining Jesus' following reassurance, has not been widely accepted, and still falls outside the pattern of Matthew's uses of οἱ δέ elsewhere.

15. See Hagner, 2:884-85, for an intriguing list of proposals, mostly evincing some embarrassment with the idea of combining "worship" with "doubt."

16. It is a relatively rare verb, not found at all in the LXX. In classical Greek it conveys the idea of uncertainty, puzzlement, being at a loss.

17. In my *Matthew: Evangelist,* 314, n. 83, I defined its use in Matthew as "the disorientation produced by an unfamiliar and overwhelming situation."

18. This might be suggested by the following statement that Jesus "came to" them — so did they first see him at a distance, as in John 21:4, so that they could not at first tell who it was?

ognition problem in Luke 24:16, 31-32, 37; John 20:15; 21:4-7), but there is no such uncertainty in the other resurrection appearance Matthew records (vv. 9-10), and they are expecting to meet Jesus (see above). More likely it indicates that they did not know how to respond to Jesus[19] in this new situation, where he was familiar and yet now different;[20] cf. the bewilderment and fear of the three disciples who witnessed the Transfiguration (17:1-7). Luke similarly refers to uncertainty and disbelief when the disciples met the risen Jesus (Luke 24:38, 41), as does John most famously with regard to Thomas (John 20:24-29). But a further factor may be relevant here: the last time these eleven disciples had seen Jesus was as they ran away from him in Gethsemane; so what sort of reception could they now expect from the master they had deserted? The conflicting instincts to worship the risen Jesus and to avoid a potentially embarrassing encounter make very human sense in this context.[21]

18 Jesus' declaration and commission which will conclude the gospel are introduced not by a simple "Jesus said" but by a combination of three verbs: he "came to" them, "spoke to" them, and "said." This rather fulsome introductory clause not only emphasizes the climactic role of this speech but also responds to the disciples' hesitation: Jesus' "coming to" his frightened disciples is an act of reassurance (as in 17:7; see comments there for the use of this verb in Matthew), he "speaks to" them to restore the broken relationship (as his words via the women have already indicated, v. 10), and the words he will now utter will leave their failure far behind, swallowed up in the much greater reality of the mission to which they are now called. The disciples themselves speak no words in this final scene, where the focus falls fully on Jesus himself; their role is to listen, to understand, and to obey.

"All authority in heaven and on earth has been given to me" echoes Dan 7:14, "To him was given dominion and glory and kingship, that all peoples, nations, and languages should serve him," a kingship which is to be everlasting and indestructible; there will be further echoes of Dan 7:14 in the mission to "all the nations" (v. 19), and in Jesus' powerful presence until "the end of the age" (v. 20).[22] Jesus has spoken several times, using the language of Dan 7:13-

---

19. L. G. Parkhurst, *ExpT* 90 (1978/9) 179-80, suggests that they were uncertain whether it was right to *worship* Jesus, and that his words in v. 18 give his approval to such worship.

20. So N. T. Wright, *Resurrection,* 643-44: "The risen Jesus both was and was not 'the same' as he had been before. . . . there was a mystery about him which even those who knew him best were now unable to penetrate."

21. K. Grayston, *JSNT* 21 (1984) 105-9, emphasizes this uncertainty about how Jesus would receive them, and paraphrases rather boldly, "When they saw him, they threw themselves down in submission, though they doubted its effect."

22. The echo of Dan 7:14 here, classically argued by W. D. Davies, *Setting,* 197-98, is widely recognized. See my *Jesus and the OT,* 142-43. For a full study see J. Scha-

14, of the future sovereignty of the Son of Man (16:28; 19:28; 24:30-31; 25:31-34; 26:64);[23] three of those passages have indicated that that sovereignty would be achieved in the near future, to be seen by those then alive (16:28; 24:30-34; 26:64; cf. also 10:23). But now what had been a vision for the future, albeit the imminent future, has become present reality. The risen Jesus, vindicated over those who tried to destroy him, is now established as the universal sovereign, and his realm embraces not only the whole earth, which was to be the dominion of the "one like a son of man" in Daniel's vision, but heaven as well. At the beginning of the gospel Satan offered Jesus sovereignty over the whole earth, but his offer was refused (4:8-10); now Jesus, going the way of obedience to his Father's will even to the cross, has received far more than Satan could offer. He has spoken already in 11:27 of "everything entrusted to me by my Father"; now that authority is fully spelled out — indeed, Jesus himself now possesses the authority that he attributed to his Father as "Lord of heaven and earth" in 11:25. It is this universal sovereignty that is the essential basis of the commission which is to follow in vv. 19-20, and thus of the continuing life of the disciple community until the end of the age.[24]

Here at the end of the gospel, then, we find the culmination of the theme of kingship which was introduced by the Davidic royal genealogy (1:1-17), developed in the magi's search for the "king of the Jews" and the political threat to Herod in ch. 2, adumbrated in the developing language of Messiahship, and dramatically enacted in Jesus' royal ride to Jerusalem (21:1-11); since then Jesus' alleged claim to kingship has been a matter of accusation and mockery (27:11, 29, 37, 42), but now the true nature of that kingship is revealed. It stands far above local politics and extends far beyond the people of Israel. It is the universal kingship of the Son of Man which has emerged as a distinctive feature of Matthew's presentation of Jesus: 13:41; 16:28; 19:28; 20:21; 25:31-34.[25]

---

berg, *The Father*, 111-41. The allusion is disputed by D. R. Bauer, *Structure*, 111-12, but his arguments concern ways in which the Matthew text *transcends* the limits of the Daniel text. That Matthew's vision goes far beyond the Danielic model does not in the least conflict with Dan 7:14 being the source (or at least *a* source) of its language and imagery; it is what Matthew's concept of fulfillment would lead one to expect. Gundry, having acknowledged an allusion to Dan 7:14 in his *Use*, 147, doubts it in his commentary, 595, on the curious grounds that "in the present passage we do not discover a forward reference to the parousia"; that is to beg a large question about the use of Dan 7:13-14 in Matthew generally (see on 10:23 above).

23. See the comments on 10:23 for the use of Dan 7:13-14 in Matthew as a whole.

24. Carter, 549-50, helpfully sets out the challenge which Jesus' claim and mission constitute to the worldwide authority and mission of the Roman Empire.

25. N. T. Wright, *Resurrection*, 643, also points out that the theme of kingship in heaven and earth echoes the opening of the Lord's Prayer: "This, it seems, is how the prayer is being answered."

19 Jesus' vision of the future heavenly enthronement of the Son of Man in 24:30 led naturally into a mission to gather his chosen people from all over the earth (24:31). The first part of that vision is now achieved (v. 18), and so the second part can begin. But the agents of this ingathering are not now to be the angels (though their unseen presence may be presumed to be part of the divine strategy) but those who are already Jesus' disciples. In the first instance that means the eleven men there in the Galilean hills, but as their numbers are increased (and already we have been given hints of a larger number of committed disciples; see on 27:55, 57) the mission will be extended more widely until "all the nations" are included in its scope.

The phrase *panta ta ethnē*, "all the nations," has occurred already in 24:9, 14; 25:32 to denote the area of the disciples' future activity, the scope of the proclamation of the "good news of the kingdom," and the extent of the jurisdiction of the enthroned Son of Man. In each case we have seen that the emphasis falls positively on the universal scope of Jesus' mission rather than negatively on "Gentiles" as opposed to Jews. Some have argued for such a restrictive sense here, and have suggested that Matthew has reached the point of giving up on the Jewish mission and urging the church to go *instead* to "all the Gentiles."[26] But nothing in the text indicates that;[27] the suggestion depends on the fact that *ta ethnē* can mean Gentiles as opposed to Jews (as in 6:32; 10:5, 18; 20:19), but that is a specialized use which does not apply to all Matthew's uses of *ethnos*,[28] and is most unlikely when *ta ethnē* is qualified by *panta*, "all."[29] The commission is of course to go far *beyond* Israel, but that does not require that Israel be excluded.[30] If the Jewish writer Mat-

---

26. So D. R. A. Hare and D. J. Harrington, *CBQ* 37 (1975) 359-69 (and for the fuller proposed scenario see D. R. A. Hare, *Theme*). For some responses to their thesis see my *Matthew: Evangelist*, 235-37; R. E. Menninger, *Israel*, 43-45. J. P. Meier responded directly to Hare and Harrington in *CBQ* 39 (1977) 94-102. S. Hre Kio, *BT* 41 (1990) 230-238, argues for the meaning "Gentiles" here on the basis of a study of the usage of (τὰ) ἔθνη which fails to give weight to Matthew's usage of the full phrase πάντα τὰ ἔθνη.

27. The introductory πορευθέντες, "going," is too common and general a verb to be pressed into an indication that Jesus speaks here of moving to a new area or field of mission; indeed, it has been used of the mission specifically to Israel in 10:6, 7. In due course a mission to "all the nations" will no doubt involve disciples moving outside their home territory, but there were plenty of non-Jewish people to be reached, along with Jews, even without going outside "Galilee of the nations" (4:15).

28. In several cases the Gentile connotation may well be present but the context does not require that Jews be excluded; see 4:15; 12:18, 21; 20:25.

29. Carson, 596, helpfully notes the echo of the promise to Abraham in Gen 12:3 etc., that in him all the nations would be blessed. That blessing in no way excluded Israel itself.

30. The view that this commission was to take the gospel *only* to Gentiles finds a curious converse in the proposal of D. C. Sim, *Gospel*, 243-47, that, while Matthew ac-

thew had intended to say that to his probably largely Jewish-Christian readers, he would surely have made it explicit. "The Gentile mission extends the
Jewish mission — not replaces it; Jesus nowhere revokes the mission to Israel (10:6), but merely adds a new mission revoking a previous prohibition
(10:5)."[31]

The commission is expressed not in terms of the means, to proclaim
the good news, but of the end, to "make disciples."[32] It is not enough that the
nations hear the message; they must also respond with the same wholehearted commitment which was required of those who became disciples of
Jesus during his ministry (see, e.g., 8:19-22; 19:21-22, 27-29).[33] The sentence structure is of a main verb in the imperative, "make disciples," followed by two uncoordinated participles, "baptizing" and "teaching," which
spell out the process of making disciples.[34]

The order in which these two participles occur differs from what has

---

cepted a mission to Gentiles in principle, he and his church were not engaged in it, but
took their message *only* to Jews! According to Sim, the evangelization of the Gentiles
was, for Matthew, in any case only to be expected at the eschaton, not within history. He
argues that Matthew's church was opposed to the Pauline, "law-free" mission to Gentiles,
and would have recognized only a "law-observant" mission which Sim believes to have
originated from Jerusalem under the auspices of James, but in which Matthew's own
church was not involved. This reading is demanded by Sim's overall thesis, but would not
occur to most readers of this text without some further elaboration; most interpreters find
it hard to imagine that Matthew would have concluded his gospel with an emphatic command to Jesus' representative disciples which he did not regard as relevant to himself and
his church. P. Foster, *Community,* 242-46, responds to Sim's interpretation.

31. Keener, 719.

32. The wording might suggest that the nations are to be "discipled" as corporate
entities, but while such a wholesale response would no doubt be welcomed, the practical
reality is presumably to be understood as the recruitment of individuals or groups from
among the nations, as has been the case within Israel during Jesus' ministry. Hagner,
2:887 (similarly Keener, 719), finds in the use of the masculine αὐτούς (rather than the
neuter αὐτά), evidence that this instruction "of course, cannot be understood as the collective conversion of national groups," though that is perhaps to put too much weight on the
natural use of a masculine after a collective antecedent referring to groups of people.

33. See my *Matthew: Evangelist,* 261-62, for Matthew's language of discipleship.
Against the attempt to find a conceptual distinction between the noun μαθητής and the
verb μαθητεύω see B. Przybylski, *Righteousness,* 109-10; M. J. Wilkins, *Disciple,* 160-62.
On the concept of disciple-making in Greek and Jewish culture see Keener, 719, and much
more fully Wilkins, *Disciple,* 11-125.

34. The third subordinate participle, "going," which precedes the main verb, is
sometimes treated as in itself also a key element in the commission (even as the primary
basis of the church's mandate for foreign missions), but Matthew's use of this participle
elsewhere to lead into an imperative (2:8; 9:13; 11:4; 17:24; cf. 10:7) suggests caution in
making too much of it here; see above n. 27.

become common practice in subsequent Christian history, in that baptism is, in many Christian circles, administered only after a period of "teaching," to those who have already learned. It can become in such circles more a graduation ceremony than an initiation. If the order of Matthew's participles is meant to be noticed, he is here presenting a different model whereby baptism is the point of enrollment into a process of learning which is never complete; the Christian community is a school of learners at various stages of development rather than divided into the baptized (who have "arrived") and those who are "not yet ready."[35]

This is the first mention of baptism in Matthew since John's baptism (and Jesus' acceptance of it) in ch. 3. There has been no indication that those who followed Jesus were baptized (unless they had already been baptized by John), and Jesus has spoken of John's baptism as if it were a distinctive rite, not one which he and his disciples had continued (21:25). Moreover, the baptism which John predicted Jesus would bring was not with water but with the Holy Spirit and fire (3:11). Yet now the full-blown rite of Christian baptism is introduced without any indication that this is something new. For Matthew's readers it was presumably so familiar as to need no explanation, but its sudden appearance right at the end of the gospel is surprising in the narrative context. We know from Acts and the letters of Paul that baptism in the name of Jesus was the unquestioned initiation rite of the post-Easter church (Acts 2:38, 41; 8:12, 36-38; Rom 6:3-4; 1 Cor 1:13-17, etc.), but it is hard to suppose that the practice emerged fully formed at the first Christian Pentecost. Was it then this instruction by Jesus that first launched Christian baptism, or should we take note of the assumption in John 3:22-26; 4:1-2 that from the beginning the Jesus movement adopted John's practice of water baptism, even though after that point it receives no further mention in the gospel narratives? I have argued elsewhere that the latter is the more likely scenario.[36] In that case the lack of explanation of baptism here (and of how water baptism relates to baptism with the Holy Spirit and fire) is to be explained by the fact that, despite Matthew's earlier silence on the subject, the practice was already familiar to the disciples.

Baptisms in Acts are said to be in (or into)[37] the name of Jesus (Acts

35. A sustained attempt to apply this Matthean perspective to modern church life was attempted in an interesting but little noticed book by Robert Brow, *"Go Make Learners."* I have commented further on Brow's book in the article mentioned in the next note, pp. 109-10.

36. R. T. France, "Jesus the Baptist?" in J. B. Green and M. M. B. Turner (eds.), *Jesus,* 94-111. See also above, p. 99, and comments on 3:11.

37. The εἰς which introduces the baptismal formula in Matt 28:19 and in most of the other NT baptism texts is perhaps to be understood as drawing attention to the new relationship and allegiance *into* which the one baptized is thus introduced, though

2:38; 8:16; 10:48; 19:5; 22:16; cf. Rom 6:3; Gal 3:27), and there is no other reference in the NT to a trinitarian baptismal formula, though this was well established by the time of *Did.* 7:1, 3[38] (cf. Justin, *1 Apol.* 61:3, 11, 13). In view of the gradual movement within the NT toward trinitarian (or at least triadic) forms of expression, with the three persons mentioned in a variety of orders, the wording here in Matthew draws attention as more formally corresponding to later patristic formulations than might be expected within the NT period, let alone in the words of Jesus himself. If Jesus had put the matter as explicitly as this, it is surprising that it took his followers so long to catch up with his formulation. There is, however, no evidence that this is not an original part of the Gospel of Matthew,[39] so that at least the formula must correspond to what Matthew knew of Christian baptism, and therefore presumably to the accepted practice of his church (which may be related to that reflected in the *Didache*). What process led from baptism simply in the name of Jesus to the acceptance of this fuller formula, and how widely it was followed by the time Matthew wrote, can only be a matter of speculation.[40] It is not impossible that Jesus did mention Father, Son, and Holy Spirit together, perhaps originally not to lay down a liturgical formula so much as to spell out the threefold nature of disciples' allegiance.[41] But such a memorable phrase prescribed by Jesus himself, in direct connection with baptism, would so nat-

---

L. Hartman, *NTS* 20 (1974) 432-40, argues on the basis of Jewish usage that "into the name of" need mean no more than "with reference to," defining Christian baptism as against any other baptism. The debate is surveyed (without a clear conclusion) by J. Schaberg, *The Father,* 16-23. A study of the contexts in which εἰς, ἐν, and ἐπί are used with the "name" in relation to baptism does not suggest any clear distinction in their use.

38. Note, however, that the *Didache* also speaks of baptism "into the name of the Lord" (which in context appears to mean Jesus), *Did.* 9:5.

39. Eusebius in his earlier writings regularly quotes the text "Go and make disciples of all nations in my name" (without specific mention of baptism), but since in his later writings he several times quotes the full text as we know it, it must be assumed that the earlier references were abbreviated allusions rather than evidence that Eusebius knew the text without the trinitarian formula. H. Kosmala, *ASTI* 4 (1965) 132-47, argued that the shorter Eusebius version represents the original text of Matthew (Hagner, 2:887-88, favors his view), but this has found little support; see contra B. J. Hubbard, *Commissioning,* 151-75; J. Schaberg, *The Father,* 27-29.

40. J. Schaberg, *The Father* (especially 143-221, 319-49), offers an intriguing suggestion that NT triadic language, and Matt 28:19b in particular, derives from an apocalyptic tradition, which she finds most strongly exemplified in Dan 7, of a "triad" consisting of the Ancient of Days, the one like a son of man, and the angels, which she finds echoed elsewhere in the NT (263-317).

41. The reader of Matthew will probably remember that when Jesus himself was baptized, God, the Holy Spirit, and God's Son were all involved (3:16-17). They will also remember that Jesus has been introduced as the one who will baptize with the Holy Spirit (3:11).

urally lend itself to liturgical use that it is surprising that the "in the name of Jesus" form prevailed for so long. It is more likely that Matthew here expresses Jesus' instructions in terms which would be taken for granted in his own church but which, while consonant with the teaching of Jesus, would not yet have crystallized into their later formulation at the time he initially sent his disciples out to baptize.[42]

The debate about the origin of the formula must not distract the reader from recognizing what a profoundly important theological step has been taken here. It is one thing for Jesus to speak about his relationship with God as Son with Father (notably 11:27; 24:36; 26:63-64) and to draw attention to the close links between himself and the Holy Spirit (12:28, 31-32), but for "the Son" to take his place as the middle member, between the Father and the Holy Spirit, in a threefold depiction of the object of the disciple's allegiance is extraordinary. The human leader of the disciple group has become the rightful object of their worship. And the fact that the three divine persons are spoken of as having a single "name" is a significant pointer toward the trinitarian doctrine of three persons in one God.

20 Hitherto in Matthew's narrative it has been Jesus who has been the "teacher." But now the verb "teach" is used with the disciples as subject, marking the decisive change which follows Jesus' death and resurrection.[43] But even so their duty of teaching derives from the authority of the risen Lord (v. 18).[44] So they are to teach not their own ideas, but what Jesus has "commanded," *entellomai,* a term which hitherto has been especially associated with the "commandments" (the cognate noun *entolē;* cf. 5:19; 15:3; 19:17; 22:36-40) given by God through Moses.[45] The basis of living as the people of God will henceforth be the new "commandments" given by Jesus.[46] Not that

42. Keener, 717, especially n. 343, is unusually open to the possibility that the formula goes back to Jesus' own words, arguing on the basis of early "trinitarian" language in Paul and elsewhere in the NT. But to say that "the trinitarian formula is established by the period of our first extant Christian documents" is to overstate the evidence. The three persons are indeed mentioned together, sometimes clearly intentionally, but in such a variety of orders and literary forms that to speak of a "formula" is anachronistic.

43. See S. Byrskog, *Jesus,* 258-61.

44. For the close link between "authority" and "teaching" both in this final pericope and in the gospel as a whole see O. S. Brooks, *JSNT* 10 (1981) 2-18.

45. ἐντέλλομαι is so used in 15:4; 19:7, but also for instructions given by Jesus to his disciples in 17:9. For LXX parallels to the phrase πάντα ὅσα ἐνετειλάμην ὑμῖν, "all that I have commanded you," cf., e.g., Exod 7:2; 25:22; 29:35; Deut 1:3; Jer 1:7. These references are, of course, to *God's* commands, though similar language is used in Josh 22:2 for the commands of Moses and Joshua; cf. also Deut 4:39-40, where the commands are God's but given by Moses, and where the LXX has also the phrases "in heaven and on earth" (cf. v. 18) and "all the time" (cf. v. 20).

46. The vocabulary here recalls 5:19, where the true disciple was one who

these are necessarily opposed to the commandments of the OT, but as we have seen in 5:17-48, Jesus' teaching has given a new interpretation to the old law, and it is by obedience to *his* words that salvation is henceforth to be found (7:24-27). To be a disciple is to obey Jesus' teaching.[47]

But the presence of Jesus himself among his people (cf. 18:20) ensures that it is not simply a relationship of formal obedience. In context this assurance is focused not on the personal comfort of the individual disciple but on the successful completion of the mission entrusted to the community as a whole. In OT commissioning scenes the assurance of God's presence was to empower his often inadequate servants to fulfill the task he had called them to (Exod 3:12; 4:12; Josh 1:5, 9; Judg 6:16; Jer 1:8; cf. also the angel sent with the Israelites in Exod 23:20-23). So here it is to the commissioned disciples as they set about their daunting task that the divine presence is promised, without which they cannot be expected to succeed. But the difference now is that it is not God himself who promises to be "with" them,[48] still less an angel sent by him, but the risen Jesus, who has just been declared to stand alongside the Father and the Holy Spirit in heavenly sovereignty. In the Fourth Gospel Jesus promises the continuing presence of the Spirit with his disciples after he has left them (John 14:16-17, 25-26; 16:7), but in Matthew the presence is that of Jesus himself. And this is not simply for a short-term objective, for the mission they have been given will keep them (and their successors) busy to "the end of the age." Jesus' physical presence with his disciples was limited to the period of his earthly life span, but the spiritual presence of the risen Jesus has no such limitation: it is as an eternal, divine being that Jesus will be among his obedient people, "God with us."

"teaches" others to live according to the "commandments" of the law; here Jesus' commandments stand in the same place of authority. See the comments on 5:19 for how the two may be related. This conclusion to the gospel strongly supports our interpretation of 5:17-20 as placing the emphasis on Jesus' interpretation of the law rather than on the continuing validity of the OT law as regulations to be implemented by the Christian church.

47. D. C. Sim, *Gospel*, 251-55, believing (see p. 1114, n. 30) that Matthew's church restricted salvation to Jews (whether by birth or by proselytism), argues that the "commandments" of Jesus included a demand to keep the whole law, and thus assumed that Gentile converts would be circumcised as well as baptized. Those (like me, *Matthew: Evangelist*, 234-35) who argue that, because this final pericope mentions baptism and the commands of Jesus but not circumcision and the commands of the law, it represents a mission to Gentiles without the full requirements of the Jewish law are thus accused by Sim of reading Matthew in the light of Paul.

48. For the extensive OT tradition of "I am with you" sayings see D. D. Kupp, *Emmanuel*, 138-56.

INDEX OF MODERN AUTHORS

References to the commentaries on Matthew listed on pp. xxix-xxx (which are cited in the footnotes by author's name alone) are too numerous to list here. Where the names of those authors appear in this list, the reference is to works other than those commentaries.

INDEX OF SUBJECTS

This is a selective index, both in the choice of subjects to be listed and in the references collected under each heading. It does not aim to record every occurrence of a given word or theme, but only those which are likely to be of most interest to the reader, and which together provide a guide to how that subject is treated in this commentary.

INDEX OF BIBLICAL AND
OTHER ANCIENT REFERENCES

Where the verse and/or chapter numbering of the Hebrew or LXX differs from that of the English versions, the latter is followed here.